Mac OS X Core
Dump Analysis
Accelerated

Version 2.0

Dmitry Vostokov
Software Diagnostics Services

Published by OpenTask, Republic of Ireland

OpenTask books and magazines are available through booksellers and distributors worldwide. For further information or comments send requests to press@opentask.com.

A CIP catalogue record for this book is available from the British Library.

ISBN-l3: 978-1-908043-71-9 (Paperback)

1st printing, 2014

Contents

Presentation Slides and Transcript

Mac OS X
Core Dump Analysis
Accelerated

Version 2.0

Dmitry Vostokov
Software Diagnostics Services

Hello everyone, my name is Dmitry Vostokov and I teach this training course. The second version or edition of this course covers LLDB debugger that replaced GDB in Mac OS X Mavericks. Since the previous Mac OS X versions use GDB we decided to keep old exercises too because you might need to maintain and debug older versions.

Prerequisites

Basic Mac OS X troubleshooting

The prerequisites are hard to define. Some of you have software development experience and some not. However, one thing is certain that to get most of this training you are expected to have basic troubleshooting experience. Another thing I expect you to be familiar with is hexadecimal notation and that you have seen or can read programming source code in some language. The ability to read assembly language has some advantages but not necessary for this training. Windows memory dump analysis experience may really help here and ease transition but not absolutely necessary. If you have attended a training or read a book **Accelerated Windows Memory Dump Analysis** you would find the similar approach here.

Training Goals

- ◉ Review fundamentals

- ◉ Learn how to collect core dumps

- ◉ Learn how to analyze core dumps

Our primary goal is to learn core dump analysis in accelerated fashion. So first we review absolutely essential fundamentals necessary for core dump analysis. Also this training is about user process core dump analysis and not about kernel core dump analysis. Additional goal is to leverage Windows debugging and memory dump analysis experience you may have.

Training Principles

⊙ Talk only about what I can show

⊙ Lots of pictures

⊙ Lots of examples

⊙ Original content

© 2014 Software Diagnostics Services

For me there were many training formats to consider and I decided that the best way is to concentrate on hands-on exercises. Specifically for this training I developed 12 of them and they utilize the same pattern-driven approach I used in **Accelerated Windows Memory Dump Analysis** training.

Schedule Summary

Day 1

- Analysis Fundamentals (30 minutes)

- Core dump collection methods (10 minutes)

- Basic Core Memory Dumps (1 hour 20 minutes)

Day 2

- Core Memory Dumps (2 hours)

This is a rough planned schedule.

Part 1: Fundamentals

Now I present you some pictures. We use 64-bit examples because all recent Macs are 64-bit. Most of the time fundamentals do not change when we move to older 32-bit Mac OS X and the analysis process most of the time is the same.

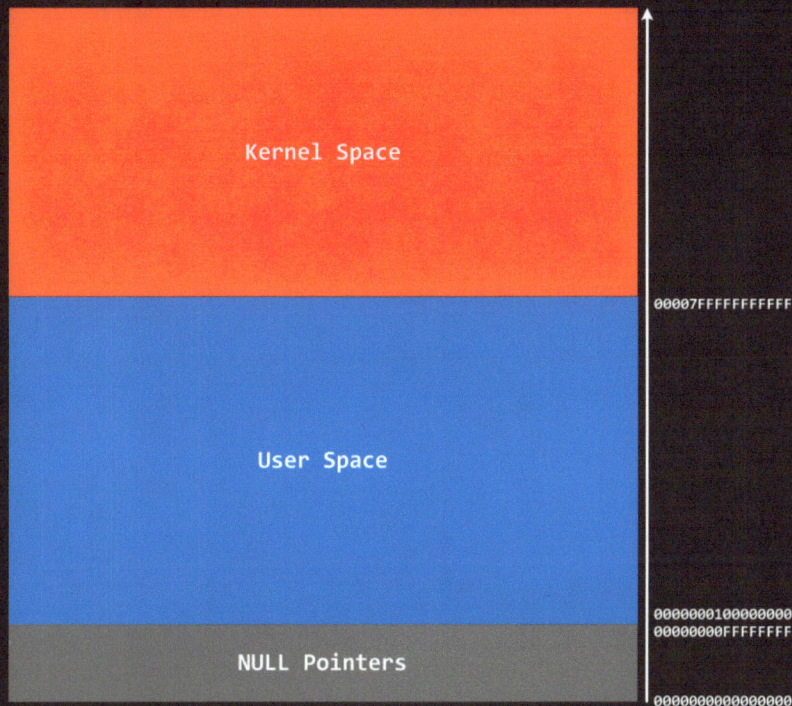

Memory/Kernel/User Space

Kernel Space

User Space

NULL Pointers

00007FFFFFFFFFFF

0000000100000000
00000000FFFFFFFF

0000000000000000

© 2014 Software Diagnostics Services

If you are coming from Windows background you find fundamentals almost the same. For every process Mac OS X memory range is divided into kernel space part, user space part and 4GB non accessible part to catch null pointers. This non-accessible region is different from Windows where it is only a few Kb. I follow the long tradition to use red color for kernel and blue color for user part. Please note that there is a difference between space and mode. Mode is execution privilege attribute, for example, code running in kernel space has higher execution privilege than code running in user space, however, kernel code can access user space and access data there. We say that such code is running in kernel mode. On the contrary the application code from user space is running in user mode and because of its lower privilege it cannot access kernel space. This prevents accidental kernel modifications. Otherwise you could easily crash your system. I put addresses on the right. This uniform memory space is called process virtual space because it is an abstraction that allows us to analyze core dumps without thinking about how it is all organized in physical memory. When we look at process dumps we are concerned with virtual space only. In this training we would only see user space.

13

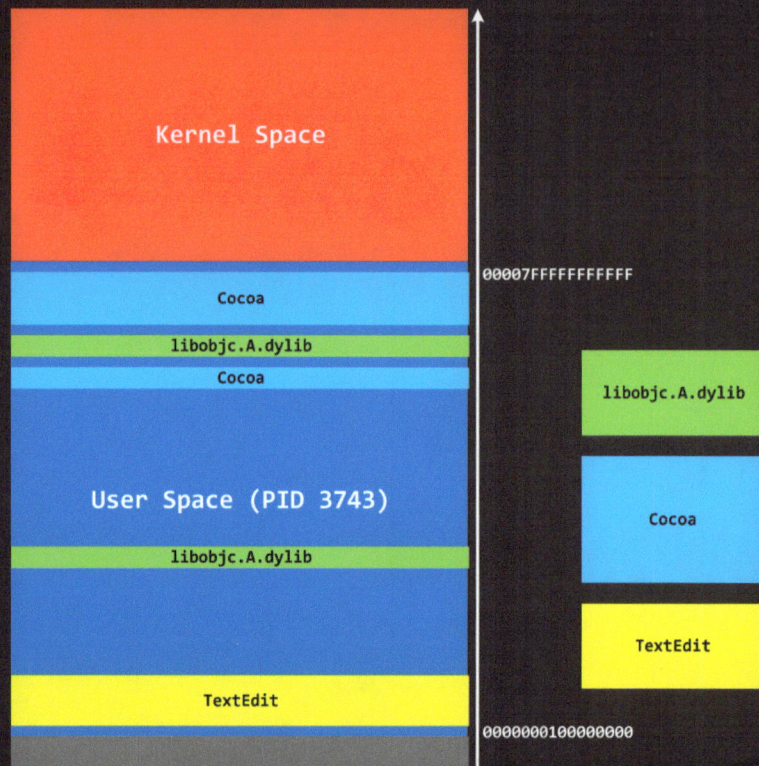

When an app is loaded all its referenced frameworks and dynamic libraries are mapped to virtual memory space. Different sections of the same file (like code and data) may be mapped into different portion of memory. In contrast, modules in Windows are organized sequentially in virtual memory space. A process then is setup for running and a process ID is assigned to it. If you run another such app it will have the different virtual memory space.

Process Memory Dump

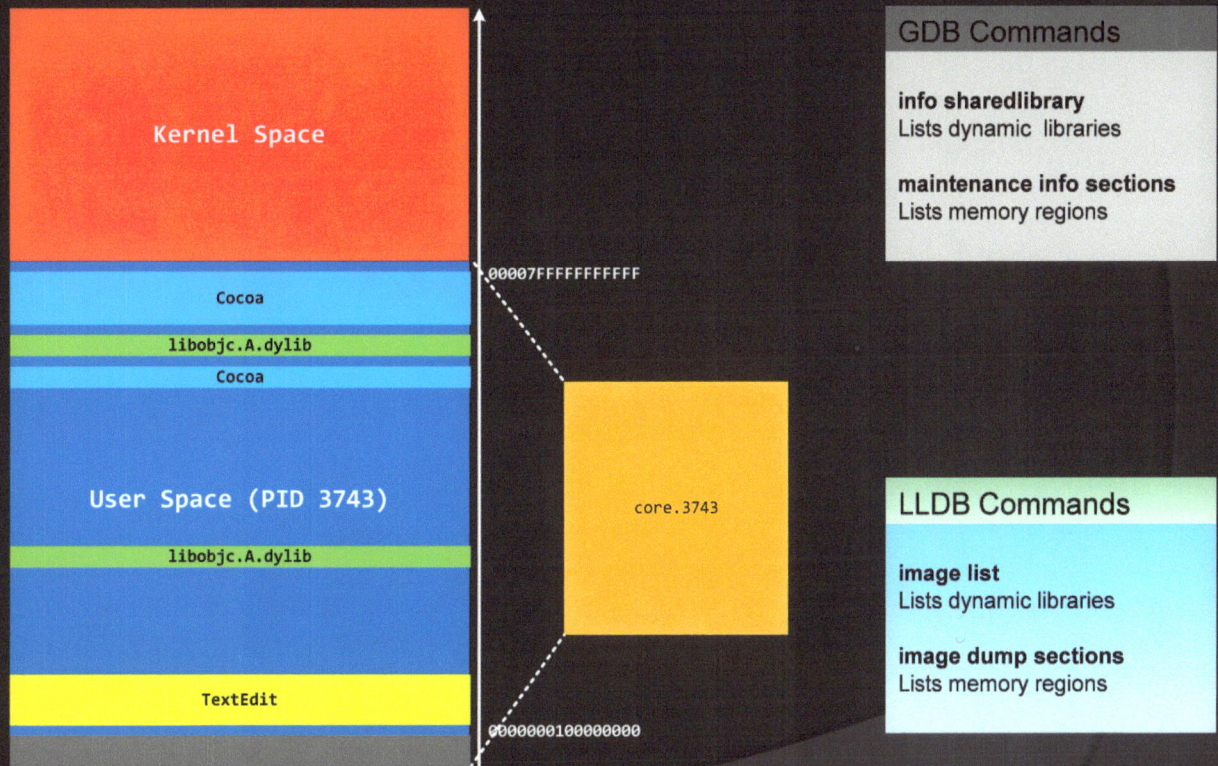

When we save a process core memory dump a user space portion of the process space is saved without any kernel space stuff. However, we never see such large core dumps unless we have memory leaks. This is because process space has gaps unfilled with code and data. These unallocated parts are not saved in a core dump. However, if some parts were paged out and reside in a page file they are usually brought back before saving a core dump.

Process Threads

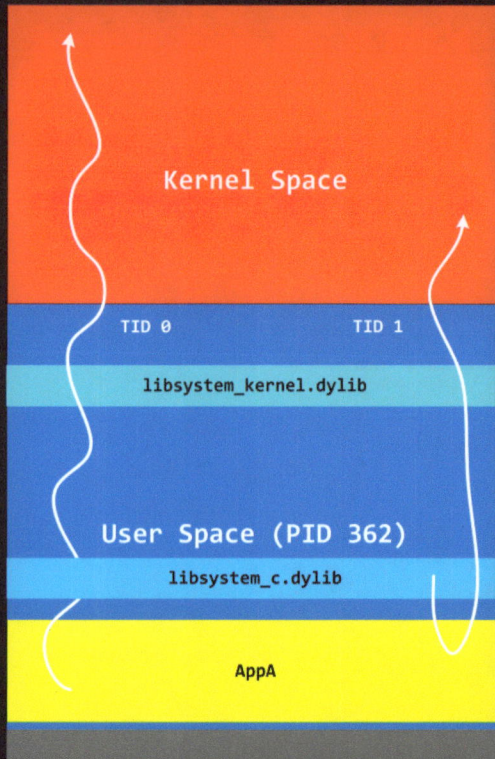

GDB Commands

info threads
Lists threads

thread <n>
Switches between threads

thread apply all bt
Lists stack traces from all threads

LLDB Commands

thread list
Lists threads

thread select <n>
Switches between threads

thread backtrace all
Lists stack traces from all threads

Kernel Space

TID 0   TID 1

libsystem_kernel.dylib

User Space (PID 362)

libsystem_c.dylib

AppA

Now we come to another important fundamental concept in Mac OS X core dump analysis: a thread. It is basically a unit of execution and there can be many threads in a given process. Every thread just executes some code and performs various tasks. Every thread has its ID. In this training we also learn how to navigate between process threads. Note that threads transition to kernel space via libsystem_kernel dynamic library similar to ntdll on Windows. Threads additional to the main thread (Posix Threads) originate from libsystem_c dynamic library.

Thread Stack Raw Data

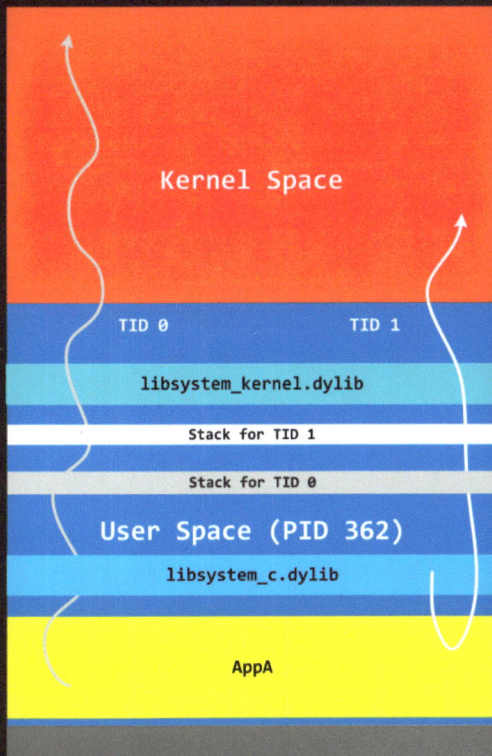

Every thread needs a temporary memory region to store its execution history and temporary data. This region is called a thread stack. Please note that the stack region is just any other memory region and you can use any GDB or LLDB data dumping commands there. We will also learn how to get thread stack region address range. Examining raw stack data can give some hints to the past app behavior: the so called **Execution Residue** pattern.

Thread Stack Trace

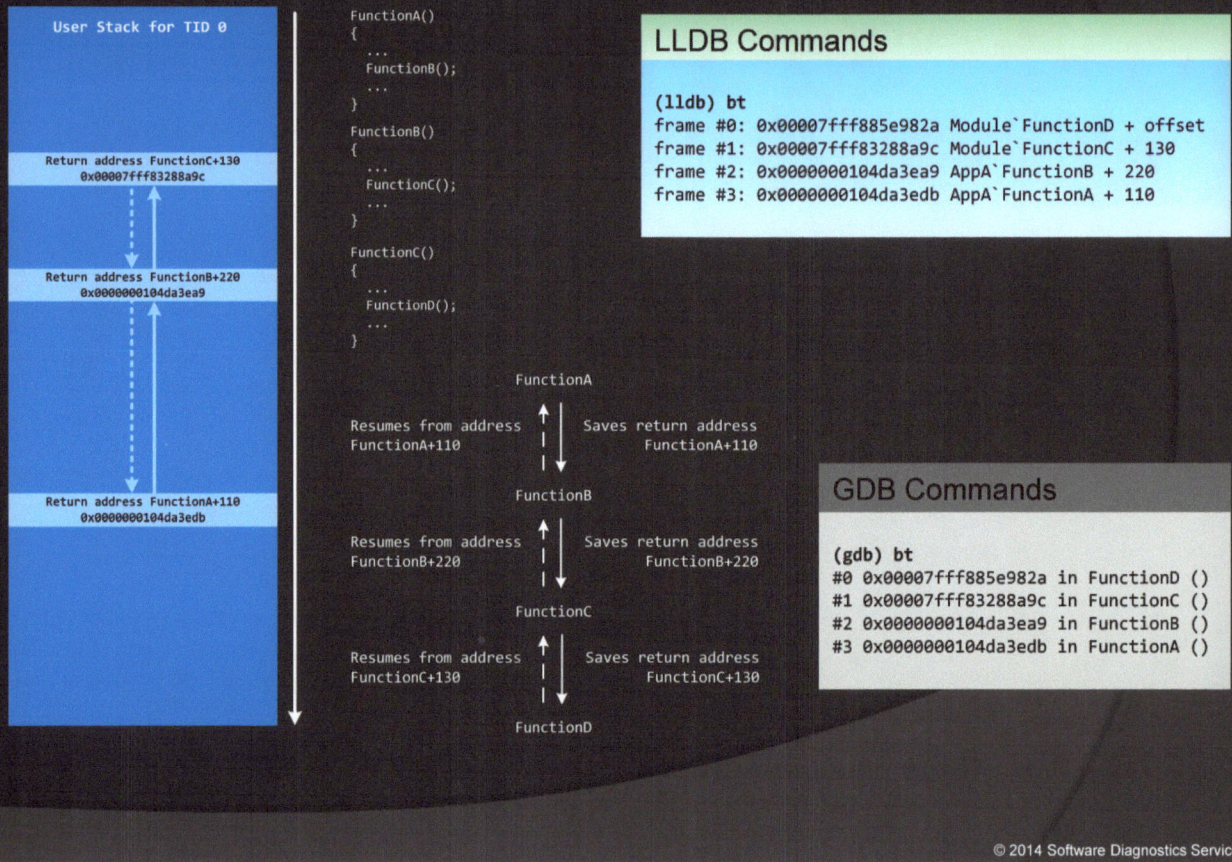

Now we explain thread stack traces. Suppose we have source code where FunctionA calls FunctionB at some point and FunctionB calls FunctionC and so on. This is a thread of execution. If FunctionA calls FunctionB you expect the execution thread to return to the same place where it left and resume from there. This is achived by saving a return address on the thread stack region. So every return address is saved and then restored during the course of a thread execution. Although the memory addresses grow from top to bottom on this picture return addresses are saved from bottom to top.This might seem counter-intuitive to all previous pictures but this is how you would see the output from GDB or LLDB commands. What GDB or LLDB does when you instruct it to dump a back trace from a given thread is to analyze the thread raw stack data and figure out return addresses, map them to a symbolic form according to symbol files and show them from top to bottom. Note that FunctionD is not present on the raw stack data on the left because it is a currently executing function called from FunctionC. However, FunctionC called FunctionD and the return address of FunctionC was saved. In the boxes on the right we see the results of GDB and LLDB commands.

GDB and LLDB vs. WinDbg

GDB Commands

```
(gdb) bt
#0 0x00007fff885e982a in FunctionD ()
#1 0x00007fff83288a9c in FunctionC ()
#2 0x0000000104da3ea9 in FunctionB ()
#3 0x0000000104da3edb in FunctionA ()
```

LLDB Commands

```
(lldb) bt
frame #0: 0x00007fff885e982a Module`FunctionD + offset
frame #1: 0x00007fff83288a9c Module`FunctionC + 130
frame #2: 0x0000000104da3ea9 AppA`FunctionB + 220
frame #3: 0x0000000104da3edb AppA`FunctionA + 110
```

WinDbg Commands

```
0:000> kn
00 00007fff83288a9c Module!FunctionD+offset
01 0000000104da3ea9 Module!FunctionC+130
02 0000000104da3edb AppA!FunctionB+220
03 0000000000000000 AppA!FunctionA+110
```

The difference from WinDbg here is that the return address is on the same line for the function to return (except for FunctionD, where the address is the next instruction to execute) whereas in WinDbg it is for the function on the next line.

19

Thread Stack Trace (no dSYM)

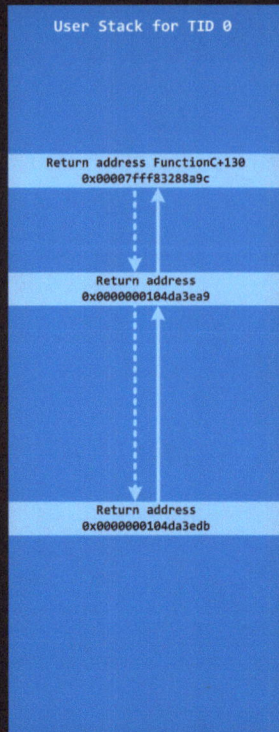

```
User Stack for TID 0




Return address FunctionC+130
      0x00007fff83288a9c



     Return address
     0x0000000104da3ea9




     Return address
     0x0000000104da3edb
```

```
Symbol file AppA.dSYM

FunctionA 22000 - 23000
FunctionB 32000 - 33000
```

GDB Commands

```
(gdb) bt
#0 0x00007fff885e982a in FunctionD ()
#1 0x00007fff83288a9c in FunctionC ()
#2 0x0000000104da3ea9 in ?? ()
#3 0x0000000104da3edb in ?? ()
```

LLDB Commands

```
(lldb) bt
frame #0: 0x00007fff885e982a Module`FunctionD + offset
frame #1: 0x00007fff83288a9c Module`FunctionC + 130
frame #2: 0x0000000104da3ea9 AppA`___lldb_unnamed_function1$$AppA + 220
frame #3: 0x0000000104da3edb AppA`___lldb_unnamed_function2$$AppA + 110
```

Here I'd like to show you why symbol files are important and what stack traces you get without them. Symbol files just provide mappings between memory address ranges and associated symbols like the table of contents in a book. So in the absence of symbols we are left with bare addresses that are saved in a dump. For example, without AppA symbols we have the output shown in boxes on the right.

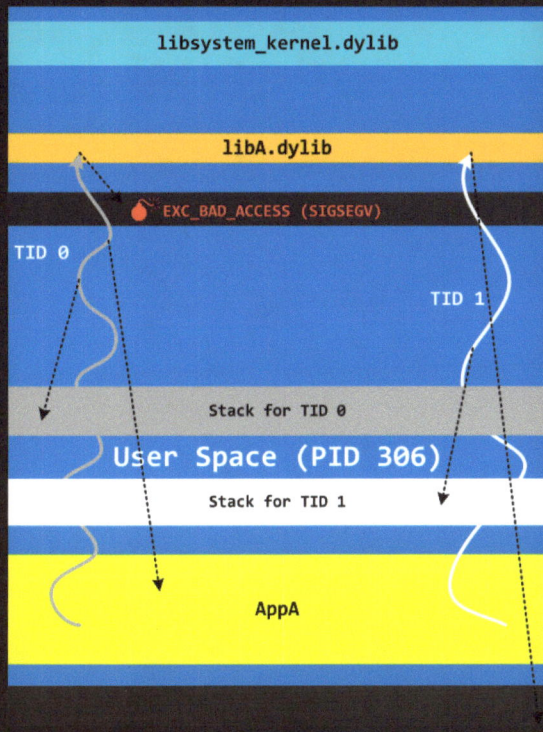

Exceptions (Access Violation)

libsystem_kernel.dylib

libA.dylib

EXC_BAD_ACCESS (SIGSEGV)

TID 0

TID 1

Stack for TID 0

User Space (PID 306)

Stack for TID 1

AppA

NULL pointer 0x0

GDB Commands

```
(gdb) x <address>
0x<address>: Cannot access
memory at address 0x<address>
```

LLDB Commands

```
(lldb) x <address>
error: core file does not contain 0x<address>
```

Now we talk about access violation exceptions. During the thread execution it accesses various memory addresses doing reads and writes. Sometimes memory is not present due to gaps in virtual address space or different protection levels like read-only or no-execute memory regions. If a thread tries to violate that we get an exception that is also translated to a traditional UNIX signal. Certain regions are forbidden to read and write such as the first 4GB. If we have such an access violation there then it is called a NULL pointer access. Note that every thread can have an exception (a victim thread) and it often happens that there are multiple exceptions. It is also sometimes the case that code can catch these exceptions preventing a user from seeing error messages. Such exceptions can contribute to corruption and we call then hidden.

Exceptions (Runtime)

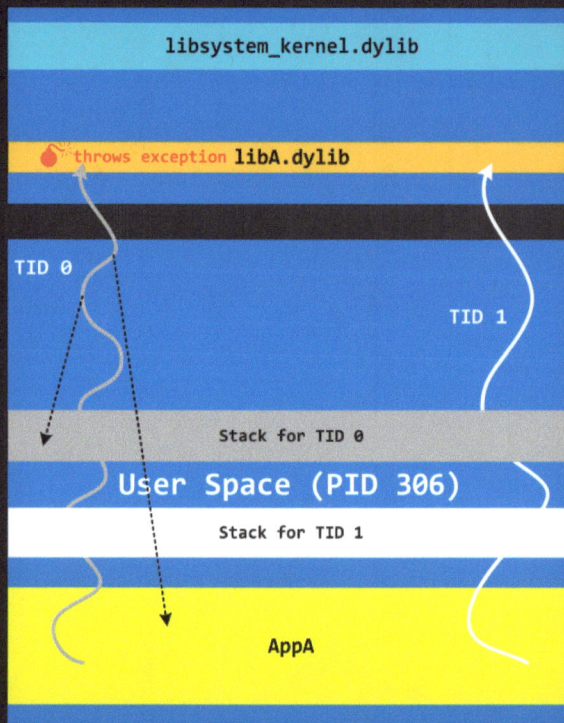

However, not all exceptions happen from invalid access. Many exceptions are generated by code itself when it checks for some condition and it is not satisfied, for example, when code checks a buffer or an array to verify whether it is full before trying to add more data. If it finds it is already full the code throws an exception translated to SIGABRT. We would see that in one of our practice examples when C++ code throws a C++ exception. Such exceptions are usually called runtime exceptions.

Pattern-Driven Analysis

Pattern: a common recurrent identifiable problem together with a set of recommendations and possible solutions to apply in a specific context

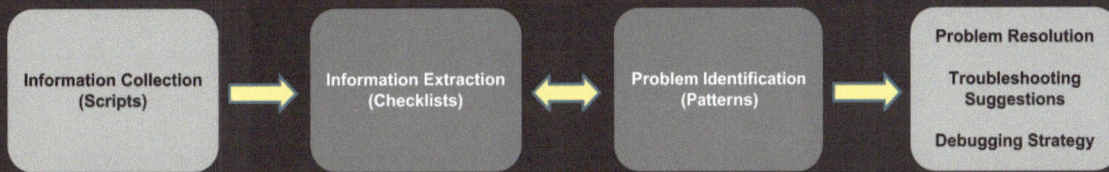

| Information Collection (Scripts) | → | Information Extraction (Checklists) | ↔ | Problem Identification (Patterns) | → | Problem Resolution, Troubleshooting Suggestions, Debugging Strategy |

A few words about logs, checklists, and patterns. Core memory dump analysis is usually an analysis of a text for the presence of patterns. We run commands, they output text and then we look at that textual output and when we find something suspicious we execute more commands. Here checklists can be very useful.

Core Dump Collection

Part 2: Core Dump Collection

Here I'd like to show you how to collect core dumps because by default this option is switched off on Mac OS X.

Enabling Collection

- Temporary for the current terminal session:

```
$ ulimit -c unlimited
```

- Permanent for every user:

```
$ sudo vi /etc/launchd.conf
```

Add the line: `limit core unlimited`

You should also have a directory **/cores** where all process core dumps are stored.

Generation Methods

- Command line:

```
$ kill -s SIGQUIT PID
$ kill -s SIGABRT PID
```

- GUI:

Utilities \ Activity Monitor

View \ Send Signal to Process

Practice Exercises

© 2014 Software Diagnostics Services

Now we come to practice. The goal is to show you important commands and how their output helps in recognizing patterns of abnormal software behaviour.

Links

⊙ **Memory Dumps:**

Links are below on this page

⊙ **Exercise Transcripts:**

Included in this book

http://www.patterndiagnostics.com/Training/AMCDA/AMCDA-Dumps.zip
http://www.patterndiagnostics.com/Training/AMCDA/AMCDA-Dumps-Part2.zip
http://www.patterndiagnostics.com/Training/AMCDA/AMCDA-Dumps-Part3.zip

Exercise 0 (GDB)

- **Goal:** Install Xcode and check if GDB loads a core dump correctly

- **Patterns:** Incorrect Stack Trace

- \AMCDA-Dumps\Exercise-A0-GDB.pdf

Exercise 0 (GDB)

Goal: Install Xcode and check if GDB loads a core dump correctly.

1.   Download and install the latest version of Xcode from App Store

2.   Open a terminal window

3.   Add the location of Xcode GDB to your path variable by executing this command:

```
echo 'export PATH=/Applications/Xcode.app/Contents/Developer/usr/bin/:$PATH' >> ~/.profile
```

4.   Exit the terminal window and then reopen it.

5.   Verify that GDB is accessible and then exit it (**q** command):

```
$ gdb
GNU gdb 6.3.50-20050815 (Apple version gdb-1820) (Sat Jun 16 02:40:11 UTC 2012)
Copyright 2004 Free Software Foundation, Inc.
GDB is free software, covered by the GNU General Public License, and you are
welcome to change it and/or distribute copies of it under certain conditions.
Type "show copying" to see the conditions.
There is absolutely no warranty for GDB.  Type "show warranty" for details.
This GDB was configured as "x86_64-apple-darwin".

(gdb) q
$
```

6.   Load a core dump core.339 and App0 executable:

```
$ gdb -c ~/Documents/AMCDA-Dumps/core.339 -e ~/Documents/AMCDA-
Dumps/Apps/App0/Build/Products/Release/App0

GNU gdb 6.3.50-20050815 (Apple version gdb-1820) (Sat Jun 16 02:40:11 UTC 2012)
Copyright 2004 Free Software Foundation, Inc.
GDB is free software, covered by the GNU General Public License, and you are
welcome to change it and/or distribute copies of it under certain conditions.
Type "show copying" to see the conditions.
There is absolutely no warranty for GDB.  Type "show warranty" for details.
This GDB was configured as "x86_64-apple-darwin".
Reading symbols for shared libraries . done
Reading symbols for shared libraries ........................ done
#0  0x00007fff8a10c82a in __kill ()
```

7.   Verify that the stack trace (back trace) is shown correctly with symbols:

```
(gdb) bt
#0  0x00007fff8a10c82a in __kill ()
#1  0x00007fff84daba9c in abort ()
#2  0x00000001071bcea9 in bar ()
#3  0x00000001071bceb9 in foo ()
#4  0x00000001071bcedb in main ()
```

8.   To avoid possible confusion and glitches we recommend to exit GDB after each exercise.

Exercise 0 (LLDB)

- **Goal:** Install Xcode and check if LLDB loads a core dump correctly

- **Patterns:** Incorrect Stack Trace

- \AMCDA-Dumps\Exercise-A0-LLDB.pdf

Exercise 0 (LLDB)

Goal: Install Xcode and check if LLDB loads a core dump correctly.

1.   Download and install the latest version of Xcode from App Store

2.   Open a terminal window

3.   Load a core dump core.339 and App0 executable:

```
$ lldb -c ~/Documents/AMCDA-Dumps/core.339 -f ~/Documents/AMCDA-
Dumps/Apps/App0/Build/Products/Release/App0
error: core.339 is a corrupt mach-o file: load command 35 LC_SEGMENT_64 has a fileoff +
filesize (0x15e27000) that extends beyond the end of the file (0x15e25000), the segment will be
truncated
Core file '/Users/DumpAnalysis/Documents/AMCDA-Dumps/core.339' (x86_64) was loaded.
Process 0 stopped
* thread #1: tid = 0x0000, 0x00007fff8a10c82a libsystem_kernel.dylib`__kill + 10, stop reason =
signal SIGSTOP
    frame #0: 0x00007fff8a10c82a libsystem_kernel.dylib`__kill + 10
libsystem_kernel.dylib`__kill + 10:
-> 0x7fff8a10c82a:  jae    0x7fff8a10c831            ; __kill + 17
   0x7fff8a10c82c:  jmpq   0x7fff8a10dffc            ; cerror
   0x7fff8a10c831:  ret
   0x7fff8a10c832:  nop
(lldb)
```

Note: There is an error about possible corruption. This appears only in LLDB output and can be ignored for all exercises.

4.   Verify that the stack trace (back trace) is shown correctly with symbols:

```
(lldb) bt
* thread #1: tid = 0x0000, 0x00007fff8a10c82a libsystem_kernel.dylib`__kill + 10, stop reason =
signal SIGSTOP
    frame #0: 0x00007fff8a10c82a libsystem_kernel.dylib`__kill + 10
    frame #1: 0x00007fff84daba9c libsystem_c.dylib`abort + 177
    frame #2: 0x00000001071bcea9 App0`bar + 9
    frame #3: 0x00000001071bceb9 App0`foo + 9
    frame #4: 0x00000001071bcedb App0`main + 27
    frame #5: 0x00000001071bce94 App0`start + 52
(lldb)
```

5.   To avoid possible confusion and glitches we recommend to exit LLDB after each exercise:

```
(lldb) q
$
```

Process Core Dumps

Exercises A1-A12

All exercises were modelled on real-life examples using specially constructed applications. We will learn how to recognize more than 30 patterns.

Exercise A1 (GDB)

- **Goal:** Learn how to list stack traces, disassemble functions, check their correctness, dump data, compare core dumps with diagnostic reports, get environment

- **Patterns:** Manual Dump, Stack Trace, Stack Trace Collection, Annotated Disassembly, Paratext, Not My Version, Environment Hint

- \AMCDA-Dumps\Exercise-A1-GDB.pdf

Exercise A1 (GDB)

Goal: Learn how to list stack traces, disassemble functions, check their correctness, dump data, compare core dumps with diagnostic reports, get environment

Patterns: Manual Dump, Stack Trace, Stack Trace Collection, Annotated Disassembly, Paratext, Not My Version, Environment Hint

1.   Load a core dump core.1394 and App1 executable:

```
$ gdb -c ~/Documents/AMCDA-Dumps/core.1394 -e ~/Documents/AMCDA-
Dumps/Apps/App1/Build/Products/Release/App1
GNU gdb 6.3.50-20050815 (Apple version gdb-1820) (Sat Jun 16 02:40:11 UTC 2012)
Copyright 2004 Free Software Foundation, Inc.
GDB is free software, covered by the GNU General Public License, and you are
welcome to change it and/or distribute copies of it under certain conditions.
Type "show copying" to see the conditions.
There is absolutely no warranty for GDB.  Type "show warranty" for details.
This GDB was configured as "x86_64-apple-darwin".
Reading symbols for shared libraries . done
Reading symbols for shared libraries ........................ done
#0  0x00007fff8a10ce42 in __semwait_signal ()
```

2.   List all threads:

```
(gdb) info threads
  6 0x00007fff8a10ce42 in __semwait_signal ()
  5 0x00007fff8a10ce42 in __semwait_signal ()
  4 0x00007fff8a10ce42 in __semwait_signal ()
  3 0x00007fff8a10ce42 in __semwait_signal ()
  2 0x00007fff8a10ce42 in __semwait_signal ()
* 1 0x00007fff8a10ce42 in __semwait_signal ()
```

3.   Get all thread stack traces:

```
(gdb) thread apply all bt

Thread 6 (core thread 5):
#0  0x00007fff8a10ce42 in __semwait_signal ()
#1  0x00007fff84d6edea in nanosleep ()
#2  0x00007fff84d6ec2c in sleep ()
#3  0x00007fff84d6ec08 in sleep ()
#4  0x000000010390bbb2 in bar_five ()
#5  0x000000010390bbc9 in foo_five ()
#6  0x000000010390bbe1 in thread_five ()
#7  0x00007fff84db88bf in _pthread_start ()
#8  0x00007fff84dbbb75 in thread_start ()
```

```
Thread 5 (core thread 4):
#0  0x00007fff8a10ce42 in __semwait_signal ()
#1  0x00007fff84d6edea in nanosleep ()
#2  0x00007fff84d6ec2c in sleep ()
#3  0x00007fff84d6ec08 in sleep ()
#4  0x000000010390bb52 in bar_four ()
#5  0x000000010390bb69 in foo_four ()
#6  0x000000010390bb81 in thread_four ()
#7  0x00007fff84db88bf in _pthread_start ()
#8  0x00007fff84dbbb75 in thread_start ()

Thread 4 (core thread 3):
#0  0x00007fff8a10ce42 in __semwait_signal ()
#1  0x00007fff84d6edea in nanosleep ()
#2  0x00007fff84d6ec2c in sleep ()
#3  0x00007fff84d6ec08 in sleep ()
#4  0x000000010390baf2 in bar_three ()
#5  0x000000010390bb09 in foo_three ()
#6  0x000000010390bb21 in thread_three ()
#7  0x00007fff84db88bf in _pthread_start ()
#8  0x00007fff84dbbb75 in thread_start ()

Thread 3 (core thread 2):
#0  0x00007fff8a10ce42 in __semwait_signal ()
#1  0x00007fff84d6edea in nanosleep ()
#2  0x00007fff84d6ec2c in sleep ()
#3  0x00007fff84d6ec08 in sleep ()
#4  0x000000010390ba92 in bar_two ()
#5  0x000000010390baa9 in foo_two ()
#6  0x000000010390bac1 in thread_two ()
---Type <return> to continue, or q <return> to quit---
#7  0x00007fff84db88bf in _pthread_start ()
#8  0x00007fff84dbbb75 in thread_start ()

Thread 2 (core thread 1):
#0  0x00007fff8a10ce42 in __semwait_signal ()
#1  0x00007fff84d6edea in nanosleep ()
#2  0x00007fff84d6ec2c in sleep ()
#3  0x00007fff84d6ec08 in sleep ()
#4  0x000000010390ba32 in bar_one ()
#5  0x000000010390ba49 in foo_one ()
#6  0x000000010390ba61 in thread_one ()
#7  0x00007fff84db88bf in _pthread_start ()
#8  0x00007fff84dbbb75 in thread_start ()

Thread 1 (core thread 0):
#0  0x00007fff8a10ce42 in __semwait_signal ()
#1  0x00007fff84d6edea in nanosleep ()
#2  0x00007fff84d6ec2c in sleep ()
#3  0x00007fff84d6ec08 in sleep ()
#4  0x000000010390bcc3 in main ()
```

4.   Switch to the thread #3 and get its stack trace:

```
(gdb) thread 3
[Switching to thread 3 (core thread 2)]
0x00007fff8a10ce42 in __semwait_signal ()
```

```
(gdb) bt
#0  0x00007fff8a10ce42 in __semwait_signal ()
#1  0x00007fff84d6edea in nanosleep ()
#2  0x00007fff84d6ec2c in sleep ()
#3  0x00007fff84d6ec08 in sleep ()
#4  0x000000010390ba92 in bar_two ()
#5  0x000000010390baa9 in foo_two ()
#6  0x000000010390bac1 in thread_two ()
#7  0x00007fff84db88bf in _pthread_start ()
#8  0x00007fff84dbbb75 in thread_start ()
```

5.   Check that bar_two called sleep function:

```
(gdb) disassemble bar_two
Dump of assembler code for function bar_two:
0x000000010390ba80 <bar_two+0>:   push   %rbp
0x000000010390ba81 <bar_two+1>:   mov    %rsp,%rbp
0x000000010390ba84 <bar_two+4>:   sub    $0x10,%rsp
0x000000010390ba88 <bar_two+8>:   mov    $0xffffffff,%edi
0x000000010390ba8d <bar_two+13>:  callq  0x10390bce0 <dyld_stub_sleep>
0x000000010390ba92 <bar_two+18>:  mov    %eax,-0x4(%rbp)
0x000000010390ba95 <bar_two+21>:  add    $0x10,%rsp
0x000000010390ba99 <bar_two+25>:  pop    %rbp
0x000000010390ba9a <bar_two+26>:  retq
0x000000010390ba9b <bar_two+27>:  nopl   0x0(%rax,%rax,1)
End of assembler dump.
```

6.   Compare with intel disassembly flavor:

```
(gdb) set disassembly-flavor intel
```

```
(gdb) disassemble bar_two
Dump of assembler code for function bar_two:
0x000000010390ba80 <bar_two+0>:   push   rbp
0x000000010390ba81 <bar_two+1>:   mov    rbp,rsp
0x000000010390ba84 <bar_two+4>:   sub    rsp,0x10
0x000000010390ba88 <bar_two+8>:   mov    edi,0xffffffff
0x000000010390ba8d <bar_two+13>:  call   0x10390bce0 <dyld_stub_sleep>
0x000000010390ba92 <bar_two+18>:  mov    DWORD PTR [rbp-0x4],eax
0x000000010390ba95 <bar_two+21>:  add    rsp,0x10
0x000000010390ba99 <bar_two+25>:  pop    rbp
0x000000010390ba9a <bar_two+26>:  ret
0x000000010390ba9b <bar_two+27>:  nop    DWORD PTR [rax+rax+0x0]
End of assembler dump.
```

```
(gdb) set disassembly-flavor att
```

7.   Follow bar_two to sleep function code:

```
(gdb) disassemble bar_two
Dump of assembler code for function bar_two:
0x000000010390ba80 <bar_two+0>:   push    %rbp
0x000000010390ba81 <bar_two+1>:   mov     %rsp,%rbp
0x000000010390ba84 <bar_two+4>:   sub     $0x10,%rsp
0x000000010390ba88 <bar_two+8>:   mov     $0xffffffff,%edi
0x000000010390ba8d <bar_two+13>:  callq   0x10390bce0 <dyld_stub_sleep>
0x000000010390ba92 <bar_two+18>:  mov     %eax,-0x4(%rbp)
0x000000010390ba95 <bar_two+21>:  add     $0x10,%rsp
0x000000010390ba99 <bar_two+25>:  pop     %rbp
0x000000010390ba9a <bar_two+26>:  retq
0x000000010390ba9b <bar_two+27>:  nopl    0x0(%rax,%rax,1)
End of assembler dump.

(gdb) disassemble dyld_stub_sleep
Dump of assembler code for function dyld_stub_sleep:
0x000000010390bce0 <dyld_stub_sleep+0>:jmpq    *0x362(%rip)        # 0x10390c048
End of assembler dump.
```

8.   Dump the annotated value as a memory address interpreting its contents as a symbol and then disassemble it:

```
(gdb) x/a 0x10390c048
0x10390c048: 0x7fff84d6ebef <sleep>


(gdb) disassemble 0x7fff84d6ebef
Dump of assembler code for function sleep:
0x00007fff84d6ebef <sleep+0>:    push    %rbp
0x00007fff84d6ebf0 <sleep+1>:    mov     %rsp,%rbp
0x00007fff84d6ebf3 <sleep+4>:    push    %rbx
0x00007fff84d6ebf4 <sleep+5>:    sub     $0x28,%rsp
0x00007fff84d6ebf8 <sleep+9>:    test    %edi,%edi
0x00007fff84d6ebfa <sleep+11>:   mov     %edi,%ebx
0x00007fff84d6ebfc <sleep+13>:   jns     0x7fff84d6ec11 <sleep+34>
0x00007fff84d6ebfe <sleep+15>:   mov     $0x7fffffff,%edi
0x00007fff84d6ec03 <sleep+20>:   callq   0x7fff84d6ebef <sleep>
0x00007fff84d6ec08 <sleep+25>:   lea     -0x7fffffff(%rbx,%rax,1),%eax
0x00007fff84d6ec0f <sleep+32>:   jmp     0x7fff84d6ec4f <sleep+96>
0x00007fff84d6ec11 <sleep+34>:   mov     %ebx,%eax
0x00007fff84d6ec13 <sleep+36>:   mov     %rax,-0x18(%rbp)
0x00007fff84d6ec17 <sleep+40>:   movq    $0x0,-0x10(%rbp)
0x00007fff84d6ec1f <sleep+48>:   lea     -0x18(%rbp),%rdi
0x00007fff84d6ec23 <sleep+52>:   lea     -0x28(%rbp),%rsi
0x00007fff84d6ec27 <sleep+56>:   callq   0x7fff84d6ed46 <nanosleep>
0x00007fff84d6ec2c <sleep+61>:   cmp     $0xffffffffffffffff,%eax
0x00007fff84d6ec2f <sleep+64>:   je      0x7fff84d6ec37 <sleep+72>
0x00007fff84d6ec31 <sleep+66>:   xor     %ebx,%ebx
0x00007fff84d6ec33 <sleep+68>:   mov     %ebx,%eax
0x00007fff84d6ec35 <sleep+70>:   jmp     0x7fff84d6ec4f <sleep+96>
0x00007fff84d6ec37 <sleep+72>:   callq   0x7fff84e0cc88 <__error>
0x00007fff84d6ec3c <sleep+77>:   cmpl    $0x4,(%rax)
0x00007fff84d6ec3f <sleep+80>:   jne     0x7fff84d6ec33 <sleep+68>
0x00007fff84d6ec41 <sleep+82>:   cmpq    $0x0,-0x20(%rbp)
0x00007fff84d6ec46 <sleep+87>:   setne   %al
0x00007fff84d6ec49 <sleep+90>:   movzbl  %al,%eax
0x00007fff84d6ec4c <sleep+93>:   add     -0x28(%rbp),%eax
0x00007fff84d6ec4f <sleep+96>:   add     $0x28,%rsp
```

```
0x00007fff84d6ec53 <sleep+100>:  pop    %rbx
0x00007fff84d6ec54 <sleep+101>:  pop    %rbp
0x00007fff84d6ec55 <sleep+102>:  retq
End of assembler dump.
```

9.   Repeat the same with resolving DYLD trampoline stub command:

```
(gdb) disassemble bar_two
Dump of assembler code for function bar_two:
0x000000010390ba80 <bar_two+0>:   push   %rbp
0x000000010390ba81 <bar_two+1>:   mov    %rsp,%rbp
0x000000010390ba84 <bar_two+4>:   sub    $0x10,%rsp
0x000000010390ba88 <bar_two+8>:   mov    $0xffffffff,%edi
0x000000010390ba8d <bar_two+13>:  callq  0x10390bce0 <dyld_stub_sleep>
0x000000010390ba92 <bar_two+18>:  mov    %eax,-0x4(%rbp)
0x000000010390ba95 <bar_two+21>:  add    $0x10,%rsp
0x000000010390ba99 <bar_two+25>:  pop    %rbp
0x000000010390ba9a <bar_two+26>:  retq
0x000000010390ba9b <bar_two+27>:  nopl   0x0(%rax,%rax,1)
End of assembler dump.
```

```
(gdb) info trampoline 0x10390bce0
Function at 0x10390bce0 becomes 0x7fff84d6ebef becomes 0x0
```

10.   Compare stack trace for thread #3 (core thread 2) and its module info with the diagnostic report
App1_1394.crash:

```
Process:         App1 [1394]
Path:            /Users/USER/Documents/*/App1
Identifier:      App1
Version:         ??? (???)
Code Type:       X86-64 (Native)
Parent Process:  bash [661]

Date/Time:       2012-07-24 00:20:26.078 +0100
OS Version:      Mac OS X 10.7.4 (11E53)
Report Version:  9

Crashed Thread:  0  Dispatch queue: com.apple.main-thread

Exception Type:  EXC_CRASH (SIGABRT)
Exception Codes: 0x0000000000000000, 0x0000000000000000

Thread 0 Crashed:: Dispatch queue: com.apple.main-thread
0   libsystem_kernel.dylib        0x00007fff8a10ce42 __semwait_signal + 10
1   libsystem_c.dylib             0x00007fff84d6edea nanosleep + 164
2   libsystem_c.dylib             0x00007fff84d6ec2c sleep + 61
3   libsystem_c.dylib             0x00007fff84d6ec08 sleep + 25
4   App1                          0x000000010390bcc3 main + 195
5   App1                          0x000000010390ba14 start + 52

Thread 1:
0   libsystem_kernel.dylib        0x00007fff8a10ce42 __semwait_signal + 10
1   libsystem_c.dylib             0x00007fff84d6edea nanosleep + 164
2   libsystem_c.dylib             0x00007fff84d6ec2c sleep + 61
3   libsystem_c.dylib             0x00007fff84d6ec08 sleep + 25
4   App1                          0x000000010390ba32 bar_one + 18
5   App1                          0x000000010390ba49 foo_one + 9
6   App1                          0x000000010390ba61 thread_one + 17
7   libsystem_c.dylib             0x00007fff84db88bf _pthread_start + 335
8   libsystem_c.dylib             0x00007fff84dbbb75 thread_start + 13
```

```
Thread 2:
0   libsystem_kernel.dylib          0x00007fff8a10ce42 __semwait_signal + 10
1   libsystem_c.dylib               0x00007fff84d6edea nanosleep + 164
2   libsystem_c.dylib               0x00007fff84d6ec2c sleep + 61
3   libsystem_c.dylib               0x00007fff84d6ec08 sleep + 25
4   App1                            0x000000010390ba92 bar_two + 18
5   App1                            0x000000010390baa9 foo_two + 9
6   App1                            0x000000010390bac1 thread_two + 17
7   libsystem_c.dylib               0x00007fff84db88bf _pthread_start + 335
8   libsystem_c.dylib               0x00007fff84dbbb75 thread_start + 13

Thread 3:
0   libsystem_kernel.dylib          0x00007fff8a10ce42 __semwait_signal + 10
1   libsystem_c.dylib               0x00007fff84d6edea nanosleep + 164
2   libsystem_c.dylib               0x00007fff84d6ec2c sleep + 61
3   libsystem_c.dylib               0x00007fff84d6ec08 sleep + 25
4   App1                            0x000000010390baf2 bar_three + 18
5   App1                            0x000000010390bb09 foo_three + 9
6   App1                            0x000000010390bb21 thread_three + 17
7   libsystem_c.dylib               0x00007fff84db88bf _pthread_start + 335
8   libsystem_c.dylib               0x00007fff84dbbb75 thread_start + 13

Thread 4:
0   libsystem_kernel.dylib          0x00007fff8a10ce42 __semwait_signal + 10
1   libsystem_c.dylib               0x00007fff84d6edea nanosleep + 164
2   libsystem_c.dylib               0x00007fff84d6ec2c sleep + 61
3   libsystem_c.dylib               0x00007fff84d6ec08 sleep + 25
4   App1                            0x000000010390bb52 bar_four + 18
5   App1                            0x000000010390bb69 foo_four + 9
6   App1                            0x000000010390bb81 thread_four + 17
7   libsystem_c.dylib               0x00007fff84db88bf _pthread_start + 335
8   libsystem_c.dylib               0x00007fff84dbbb75 thread_start + 13

Thread 5:
0   libsystem_kernel.dylib          0x00007fff8a10ce42 __semwait_signal + 10
1   libsystem_c.dylib               0x00007fff84d6edea nanosleep + 164
2   libsystem_c.dylib               0x00007fff84d6ec2c sleep + 61
3   libsystem_c.dylib               0x00007fff84d6ec08 sleep + 25
4   App1                            0x000000010390bbb2 bar_five + 18
5   App1                            0x000000010390bbc9 foo_five + 9
6   App1                            0x000000010390bbe1 thread_five + 17
7   libsystem_c.dylib               0x00007fff84db88bf _pthread_start + 335
8   libsystem_c.dylib               0x00007fff84dbbb75 thread_start + 13

Thread 0 crashed with X86 Thread State (64-bit):
  rax: 0x0000000000000004  rbx: 0x00007fff6350aa08  rcx: 0x00007fff6350a9c8  rdx: 0x0000000000000001
  rdi: 0x0000000000000c03  rsi: 0x0000000000000000  rbp: 0x00007fff6350a9f0  rsp: 0x00007fff6350a9c8
   r8: 0x000000007fffffff   r9: 0x0000000000000000  r10: 0x0000000000000001  r11: 0xffffff80002da8d0
  r12: 0x0000000000000000  r13: 0x0000000000000000  r14: 0x00007fff6350aa18  r15: 0x0000000000000000
  rip: 0x00007fff8a10ce42  rfl: 0x0000000000000247  cr2: 0x0000000103d0b880
Logical CPU: 0

Binary Images:
       0x10390b000 -        0x10390bfff +App1 (??? - ???) <5BC0342F-7E97-3A7D-8EA6-75A0468021EA>
/Users/USER/Documents/*/App1
    0x7fff6350b000 -     0x7fff6353fbaf  dyld (195.6 - ???) <0CD1B35B-A28F-32DA-B72E-452EAD609613> /usr/lib/dyld
    0x7fff849f2000 -     0x7fff84a0ffff  libxpc.dylib (77.19.0 - compatibility 1.0.0) <9F57891B-D7EF-3050-BEDD-
21E7C6668248> /usr/lib/system/libxpc.dylib
    0x7fff84d68000 -     0x7fff84d69ff7  libsystem_blocks.dylib (53.0.0 - compatibility 1.0.0) <8BCA214A-8992-34B2-
A8B9-B74DEACA1869> /usr/lib/system/libsystem_blocks.dylib
    0x7fff84d6a000 -     0x7fff84e47fef  libsystem_c.dylib (763.13.0 - compatibility 1.0.0) <41B43515-2806-3FBC-ACF1-
A16F35B7E290> /usr/lib/system/libsystem_c.dylib
    0x7fff85022000 -     0x7fff85030fff  libdispatch.dylib (187.9.0 - compatibility 1.0.0) <1D5BE322-A9B9-3BCE-8FAC-
076FB07CF54A> /usr/lib/system/libdispatch.dylib
    0x7fff855f0000 -     0x7fff855f1fff  libunc.dylib (24.0.0 - compatibility 1.0.0) <337960EE-0A85-3DD0-A760-
7134CF4C0AFF> /usr/lib/system/libunc.dylib
    0x7fff85ae3000 -     0x7fff85ae4ff7  libremovefile.dylib (21.1.0 - compatibility 1.0.0) <739E6C83-AA52-3C6C-A680-
B37FE2888A04> /usr/lib/system/libremovefile.dylib
    0x7fff89114000 -     0x7fff89118fff  libmathCommon.A.dylib (2026.0.0 - compatibility 1.0.0) <FF83AFF7-42B2-306E-
90AF-D539C51A4542> /usr/lib/system/libmathCommon.A.dylib
    0x7fff89119000 -     0x7fff8911dfff  libdyld.dylib (195.5.0 - compatibility 1.0.0) <380C3F44-0CA7-3514-8080-
46D1C9DF4FCD> /usr/lib/system/libdyld.dylib
    0x7fff89740000 -     0x7fff89741ff7  libsystem_sandbox.dylib (??? - ???) <96D38E74-F18F-3CCB-A20B-E8E3ADC4E166>
/usr/lib/system/libsystem_sandbox.dylib
    0x7fff8a0ef000 -     0x7fff8a0f5fff  libmacho.dylib (800.0.0 - compatibility 1.0.0) <165514D7-1BFA-38EF-A151-
676DCD21FB64> /usr/lib/system/libmacho.dylib
```

```
    0x7fff8a0f6000 -     0x7fff8a116fff  libsystem_kernel.dylib (1699.26.8 - compatibility 1.0.0) <1DDC0B0F-DB2A-34D6-
895D-E5B2B5618946> /usr/lib/system/libsystem_kernel.dylib
    0x7fff8a2ac000 -     0x7fff8a2b4fff  libsystem_dnssd.dylib (??? - ???) <D9BB1F87-A42B-3CBC-9DC2-FC07FCEF0016>
/usr/lib/system/libsystem_dnssd.dylib
    0x7fff8ae26000 -     0x7fff8ae61fff  libsystem_info.dylib (??? - ???) <35F90252-2AE1-32C5-8D34-782C614D9639>
/usr/lib/system/libsystem_info.dylib
    0x7fff8b248000 -     0x7fff8b24afff  libquarantine.dylib (36.6.0 - compatibility 1.0.0) <0EBF714B-4B69-3E1F-9A7D-
6BBC2AACB310> /usr/lib/system/libquarantine.dylib
    0x7fff8b3b4000 -     0x7fff8b3b4fff  libkeymgr.dylib (23.0.0 - compatibility 1.0.0) <61EFED6A-A407-301E-B454-
CD18314F0075> /usr/lib/system/libkeymgr.dylib
    0x7fff8b3dd000 -     0x7fff8b3e2fff  libcompiler_rt.dylib (6.0.0 - compatibility 1.0.0) <98ECD5F6-E85C-32A5-98CD-
8911230CB66A> /usr/lib/system/libcompiler_rt.dylib
    0x7fff8bd1a000 -     0x7fff8bd1bfff  libdnsinfo.dylib (395.11.0 - compatibility 1.0.0) <853BAAA5-270F-3FDC-B025-
D448DB72E1C3> /usr/lib/system/libdnsinfo.dylib
    0x7fff8c528000 -     0x7fff8c52dff7  libsystem_network.dylib (??? - ???) <5DE7024E-1D2D-34A2-80F4-08326331A75B>
/usr/lib/system/libsystem_network.dylib
    0x7fff8cfa3000 -     0x7fff8cfadff7  liblaunch.dylib (392.38.0 - compatibility 1.0.0) <6ECB7F19-B384-32C1-8652-
2463C1CF4815> /usr/lib/system/liblaunch.dylib
    0x7fff8fe02000 -     0x7fff8fe09fff  libcopyfile.dylib (85.1.0 - compatibility 1.0.0) <0AB51EE2-E914-358C-AC19-
47BC024BDAE7> /usr/lib/system/libcopyfile.dylib
    0x7fff8fe4b000 -     0x7fff8fe8dff7  libcommonCrypto.dylib (55010.0.0 - compatibility 1.0.0) <BB770C22-8C57-365A-
8716-4A3C36AE7BFB> /usr/lib/system/libcommonCrypto.dylib
    0x7fff90c0f000 -     0x7fff90c18ff7  libsystem_notify.dylib (80.1.0 - compatibility 1.0.0) <A4D651E3-D1C6-3934-
AD49-7A104FD14596> /usr/lib/system/libsystem_notify.dylib
    0x7fff91376000 -     0x7fff913a3fe7  libSystem.B.dylib (159.1.0 - compatibility 1.0.0) <7BEBB139-50BB-3112-947A-
F4AA168F991C> /usr/lib/libSystem.B.dylib
    0x7fff91489000 -     0x7fff9148fff7  libunwind.dylib (30.0.0 - compatibility 1.0.0) <1E9C6C8C-CBE8-3F4B-A5B5-
E03E3AB53231> /usr/lib/system/libunwind.dylib
    0x7fff91a22000 -     0x7fff91a27fff  libcache.dylib (47.0.0 - compatibility 1.0.0) <1571C3AB-BCB2-38CD-B3B2-
C5FC3F927C6A> /usr/lib/system/libcache.dylib

External Modification Summary:
  Calls made by other processes targeting this process:
    task_for_pid: 2
    thread_create: 0
    thread_set_state: 0
  Calls made by this process:
    task_for_pid: 0
    thread_create: 0
    thread_set_state: 0
  Calls made by all processes on this machine:
    task_for_pid: 2696
    thread_create: 0
    thread_set_state: 0

VM Region Summary:
ReadOnly portion of Libraries: Total=50.2M resident=50.2M(100%) swapped_out_or_unallocated=0K(0%)
Writable regions: Total=38.9M written=10.8M(28%) resident=42.6M(110%) swapped_out=0K(0%)
unallocated=16777216.0T(45221404475392%)

REGION TYPE                VIRTUAL
===========                =======
MALLOC                      1220K
Stack                       66.6M
__DATA                       464K
__LINKEDIT                  47.7M
__TEXT                      2484K
shared memory                 12K
===========                =======
TOTAL                      118.4M
```

11.   Get App1 data section from the output of vmmap_1394.log:

```
Virtual Memory Map of process 1394 (App1)
Output report format:  2.2  -- 64-bit process


==== Non-writable regions for process 1394
__TEXT                 000000010390b000-000000010390c000 [    4K] r-x/rwx SM=COW  /Users/DumpAnalysis/Documents/AMCDA-
Dumps/Apps/App1/Build/Products/Release/App1


[...]


==== Writable regions for process 1394
__DATA                 000000010390c000-000000010390d000 [    4K] rw-/rwx SM=PRV  /Users/DumpAnalysis/Documents/AMCDA-
Dumps/Apps/App1/Build/Products/Release/App1


[...]
```

12.   Compare with the section information in the core dump:

```
(gdb) maintenance info sections
Exec file:
    `/Users/DumpAnalysis/Documents/AMCDA-Dumps/Apps/App1/Build/Products/Release/App1', file type mach-o-le.
    0x0000000000000000->0x0000000000000000 at 0x00000000: LC_SEGMENT.__PAGEZERO ALLOC LOAD CODE HAS_CONTENTS
    0x0000000100000000->0x0000000100001000 at 0x00000000: LC_SEGMENT.__TEXT ALLOC LOAD CODE HAS_CONTENTS
    0x00000001000009e0->0x0000000100000cd3 at 0x000009e0: LC_SEGMENT.__TEXT.__text ALLOC LOAD READONLY CODE
HAS_CONTENTS
    0x0000000100000cd4->0x0000000100000ce6 at 0x00000cd4: LC_SEGMENT.__TEXT.__stubs ALLOC LOAD CODE HAS_CONTENTS
    0x0000000100000ce8->0x0000000100000d16 at 0x00000ce8: LC_SEGMENT.__TEXT.__stub_helper ALLOC LOAD CODE HAS_CONTENTS
    0x0000000100000d16->0x0000000100000d66 at 0x00000d16: LC_SEGMENT.__TEXT.__unwind_info ALLOC LOAD CODE HAS_CONTENTS
    0x0000000100000d68->0x0000000100001000 at 0x00000d68: LC_SEGMENT.__TEXT.__eh_frame ALLOC LOAD CODE HAS_CONTENTS
    0x0000000100001000->0x0000000100002000 at 0x00001000: LC_SEGMENT.__DATA ALLOC LOAD CODE HAS_CONTENTS
    0x0000000100001000->0x0000000100001028 at 0x00001000: LC_SEGMENT.__DATA.__program_vars ALLOC LOAD CODE
HAS_CONTENTS
    0x0000000100001028->0x0000000100001038 at 0x00001028: LC_SEGMENT.__DATA.__nl_symbol_ptr ALLOC LOAD CODE
HAS_CONTENTS
    0x0000000100001038->0x0000000100001050 at 0x00001038: LC_SEGMENT.__DATA.__la_symbol_ptr ALLOC LOAD CODE
HAS_CONTENTS
    0x0000000100001050->0x0000000100001070 at 0x00000000: LC_SEGMENT.__DATA.__common ALLOC
    0x0000000100002000->0x00000001000023b0 at 0x00002000: LC_SEGMENT.__LINKEDIT ALLOC LOAD CODE HAS_CONTENTS
    0x0000000000000000->0x00000000000001a0 at 0x000020d0: LC_SYMTAB.stabs HAS_CONTENTS
    0x0000000000000000->0x0000000000000120 at 0x00002290: LC_SYMTAB.stabstr HAS_CONTENTS
    0x0000000000000000->0x0000000000000100 at 0x000020d0: LC_DYSYMTAB.localstabs HAS_CONTENTS
    0x0000000000000000->0x00000000000000a0 at 0x000021d0: LC_DYSYMTAB.nonlocalstabs HAS_CONTENTS
    0x0000000000000000->0x0000000000000018 at 0x000004b0: LC_LOAD_DYLINKER HAS_CONTENTS
    0x0000000000000000->0x00000000000000a8 at 0x00000500: LC_THREAD.x86_THREAD_STATE64.0 HAS_CONTENTS
    0x0000000000000000->0x0000000000000030 at 0x000005b0: LC_LOAD_DYLIB HAS_CONTENTS
Core file:
    `/Users/DumpAnalysis/Documents/AMCDA-Dumps/core.1394', file type mach-o-le.
    0x000000010390b000->0x000000010390c000 at 0x00002000: LC_SEGMENT. ALLOC LOAD CODE HAS_CONTENTS
    0x000000010390c000->0x000000010390d000 at 0x00003000: LC_SEGMENT. ALLOC LOAD CODE HAS_CONTENTS
    0x000000010390d000->0x000000010390e000 at 0x00004000: LC_SEGMENT. ALLOC LOAD CODE HAS_CONTENTS
    0x000000010390e000->0x000000010390f000 at 0x00005000: LC_SEGMENT. ALLOC LOAD CODE HAS_CONTENTS
    0x000000010390f000->0x0000000103910000 at 0x00006000: LC_SEGMENT. ALLOC LOAD CODE HAS_CONTENTS
    0x0000000103910000->0x0000000103911000 at 0x00007000: LC_SEGMENT. ALLOC LOAD CODE HAS_CONTENTS
    0x0000000103911000->0x0000000103926000 at 0x00008000: LC_SEGMENT. ALLOC LOAD CODE HAS_CONTENTS
    0x0000000103926000->0x0000000103927000 at 0x0001d000: LC_SEGMENT. ALLOC LOAD CODE HAS_CONTENTS
    0x0000000103927000->0x0000000103928000 at 0x0001e000: LC_SEGMENT. ALLOC LOAD CODE HAS_CONTENTS
    0x0000000103928000->0x000000010393d000 at 0x0001f000: LC_SEGMENT. ALLOC LOAD CODE HAS_CONTENTS
    0x000000010393d000->0x000000010393e000 at 0x00034000: LC_SEGMENT. ALLOC LOAD CODE HAS_CONTENTS
    0x000000010393e000->0x000000010393f000 at 0x00035000: LC_SEGMENT. ALLOC LOAD CODE HAS_CONTENTS
    0x000000010393f000->0x0000000103940000 at 0x00036000: LC_SEGMENT. ALLOC LOAD CODE HAS_CONTENTS
    0x0000000103940000->0x00000001039c2000 at 0x00037000: LC_SEGMENT. ALLOC LOAD CODE HAS_CONTENTS
    0x0000000103a00000->0x0000000103b00000 at 0x000b9000: LC_SEGMENT. ALLOC LOAD CODE HAS_CONTENTS
    0x0000000103b00000->0x0000000103b01000 at 0x001b9000: LC_SEGMENT. ALLOC LOAD CODE HAS_CONTENTS
    0x0000000103b01000->0x0000000103b83000 at 0x001ba000: LC_SEGMENT. ALLOC LOAD CODE HAS_CONTENTS
    0x0000000103b83000->0x0000000103b84000 at 0x0023c000: LC_SEGMENT. ALLOC LOAD CODE HAS_CONTENTS
    0x0000000103b84000->0x0000000103c06000 at 0x0023d000: LC_SEGMENT. ALLOC LOAD CODE HAS_CONTENTS
    0x0000000103c06000->0x0000000103c07000 at 0x002bf000: LC_SEGMENT. ALLOC LOAD CODE HAS_CONTENTS
    0x0000000103c07000->0x0000000103c89000 at 0x002c0000: LC_SEGMENT. ALLOC LOAD CODE HAS_CONTENTS
    0x0000000103c89000->0x0000000103c8a000 at 0x00342000: LC_SEGMENT. ALLOC LOAD CODE HAS_CONTENTS
    0x0000000103c8a000->0x0000000103d0c000 at 0x00343000: LC_SEGMENT. ALLOC LOAD CODE HAS_CONTENTS
```

```
0x00007fff5f50b000->0x00007fff62d0b000 at 0x003c5000: LC_SEGMENT. ALLOC LOAD CODE HAS_CONTENTS
0x00007fff62d0b000->0x00007fff6350a000 at 0x03bc5000: LC_SEGMENT. ALLOC LOAD CODE HAS_CONTENTS
0x00007fff6350a000->0x00007fff6350b000 at 0x043c4000: LC_SEGMENT. ALLOC LOAD CODE HAS_CONTENTS
0x00007fff6350b000->0x00007fff63540000 at 0x043c5000: LC_SEGMENT. ALLOC LOAD CODE HAS_CONTENTS
0x00007fff63540000->0x00007fff63542000 at 0x043fa000: LC_SEGMENT. ALLOC LOAD CODE HAS_CONTENTS
0x00007fff63542000->0x00007fff6357c000 at 0x043fc000: LC_SEGMENT. ALLOC LOAD CODE HAS_CONTENTS
0x00007fff6357c000->0x00007fff6358f000 at 0x04436000: LC_SEGMENT. ALLOC LOAD CODE HAS_CONTENTS
0x00007fff749b8000->0x00007fff74a00000 at 0x04449000: LC_SEGMENT. ALLOC LOAD CODE HAS_CONTENTS
0x00007fff74a00000->0x00007fff74c00000 at 0x04491000: LC_SEGMENT. ALLOC LOAD CODE HAS_CONTENTS
0x00007fff74c00000->0x00007fff74e00000 at 0x04691000: LC_SEGMENT. ALLOC LOAD CODE HAS_CONTENTS
0x00007fff74e00000->0x00007fff75000000 at 0x04891000: LC_SEGMENT. ALLOC LOAD CODE HAS_CONTENTS
0x00007fff75000000->0x00007fff75200000 at 0x04a91000: LC_SEGMENT. ALLOC LOAD CODE HAS_CONTENTS
0x00007fff75200000->0x00007fff75400000 at 0x04c91000: LC_SEGMENT. ALLOC LOAD CODE HAS_CONTENTS
0x00007fff75400000->0x00007fff75600000 at 0x04e91000: LC_SEGMENT. ALLOC LOAD CODE HAS_CONTENTS
0x00007fff75600000->0x00007fff75800000 at 0x05091000: LC_SEGMENT. ALLOC LOAD CODE HAS_CONTENTS
0x00007fff75800000->0x00007fff75a00000 at 0x05291000: LC_SEGMENT. ALLOC LOAD CODE HAS_CONTENTS
0x00007fff75a00000->0x00007fff75c00000 at 0x05491000: LC_SEGMENT. ALLOC LOAD CODE HAS_CONTENTS
0x00007fff75c00000->0x00007fff75e00000 at 0x05691000: LC_SEGMENT. ALLOC LOAD CODE HAS_CONTENTS
0x00007fff75e00000->0x00007fff76200000 at 0x05891000: LC_SEGMENT. ALLOC LOAD CODE HAS_CONTENTS
0x00007fff76200000->0x00007fff76400000 at 0x05c91000: LC_SEGMENT. ALLOC LOAD CODE HAS_CONTENTS
0x00007fff76400000->0x00007fff764ac000 at 0x05e91000: LC_SEGMENT. ALLOC LOAD CODE HAS_CONTENTS
0x00007fff849b8000->0x00007fff91a28000 at 0x05f3d000: LC_SEGMENT. ALLOC LOAD CODE HAS_CONTENTS
0x00007fff91a28000->0x00007fff94b30000 at 0x12fad000: LC_SEGMENT. ALLOC LOAD CODE HAS_CONTENTS
0x00007ffffffe00000->0x00007fffffffe02000 at 0x160b5000: LC_SEGMENT. ALLOC LOAD CODE HAS_CONTENTS
0x0000000000000000->0x00000000000000b0 at 0x00000d68: LC_THREAD.x86_THREAD_STATE.0 HAS_CONTENTS
0x0000000000000000->0x0000000000000214 at 0x00000e20: LC_THREAD.x86_FLOAT_STATE.0 HAS_CONTENTS
0x0000000000000000->0x0000000000000018 at 0x0000103c: LC_THREAD.x86_EXCEPTION_STATE.0 HAS_CONTENTS
0x0000000000000000->0x00000000000000b0 at 0x00001064: LC_THREAD.x86_THREAD_STATE.1 HAS_CONTENTS
0x0000000000000000->0x0000000000000214 at 0x0000111c: LC_THREAD.x86_FLOAT_STATE.1 HAS_CONTENTS
0x0000000000000000->0x0000000000000018 at 0x00001338: LC_THREAD.x86_EXCEPTION_STATE.1 HAS_CONTENTS
0x0000000000000000->0x00000000000000b0 at 0x00001360: LC_THREAD.x86_THREAD_STATE.2 HAS_CONTENTS
0x0000000000000000->0x0000000000000214 at 0x00001418: LC_THREAD.x86_FLOAT_STATE.2 HAS_CONTENTS
0x0000000000000000->0x0000000000000018 at 0x00001634: LC_THREAD.x86_EXCEPTION_STATE.2 HAS_CONTENTS
0x0000000000000000->0x00000000000000b0 at 0x0000165c: LC_THREAD.x86_THREAD_STATE.3 HAS_CONTENTS
0x0000000000000000->0x0000000000000214 at 0x00001714: LC_THREAD.x86_FLOAT_STATE.3 HAS_CONTENTS
0x0000000000000000->0x0000000000000018 at 0x00001930: LC_THREAD.x86_EXCEPTION_STATE.3 HAS_CONTENTS
0x0000000000000000->0x00000000000000b0 at 0x00001958: LC_THREAD.x86_THREAD_STATE.4 HAS_CONTENTS
0x0000000000000000->0x0000000000000214 at 0x00001a10: LC_THREAD.x86_FLOAT_STATE.4 HAS_CONTENTS
0x0000000000000000->0x0000000000000018 at 0x00001c2c: LC_THREAD.x86_EXCEPTION_STATE.4 HAS_CONTENTS
0x0000000000000000->0x00000000000000b0 at 0x00001c54: LC_THREAD.x86_THREAD_STATE.5 HAS_CONTENTS
0x0000000000000000->0x0000000000000214 at 0x00001d0c: LC_THREAD.x86_FLOAT_STATE.5 HAS_CONTENTS
0x0000000000000000->0x0000000000000018 at 0x00001f28: LC_THREAD.x86_EXCEPTION_STATE.5 HAS_CONTENTS
```

13.   Dump data with possible symbolic information:

```
(gdb) x/512a 0x000000010390c000
0x10390c000: 0x10390b000   0x10390c050 <NXArgc>
0x10390c010: 0x10390c058 <NXArgv>       0x10390c060 <environ>
0x10390c020: 0x10390c068 <__progname>   0x7fff8911a6a0 <dyld_stub_binder>
0x10390c030: 0x7fff63546d80       0x10390bcf8
0x10390c040: 0x7fff84dbab01 <pthread_create>  0x7fff84d6ebef <sleep>
0x10390c050 <NXArgc>:       0x1    0x7fff6350aaf0
0x10390c060 <environ>:      0x7fff6350ab00      0x7fff6350ac73
0x10390c070: 0x0       0x0
0x10390c080: 0x0       0x0
0x10390c090: 0x0       0x0
0x10390c0a0: 0x0       0x0
0x10390c0b0: 0x0       0x0
0x10390c0c0: 0x0       0x0
0x10390c0d0: 0x0       0x0
0x10390c0e0: 0x0       0x0
0x10390c0f0: 0x0       0x0
0x10390c100: 0x0       0x0
0x10390c110: 0x0       0x0
0x10390c120: 0x0       0x0
0x10390c130: 0x0       0x0
0x10390c140: 0x0       0x0
```

```
0x10390c150:  0x0     0x0
0x10390c160:  0x0     0x0
0x10390c170:  0x0     0x0
0x10390c180:  0x0     0x0
0x10390c190:  0x0     0x0
0x10390c1a0:  0x0     0x0
0x10390c1b0:  0x0     0x0
0x10390c1c0:  0x0     0x0
0x10390c1d0:  0x0     0x0
0x10390c1e0:  0x0     0x0
0x10390c1f0:  0x0     0x0
0x10390c200:  0x0     0x0
0x10390c210:  0x0     0x0
0x10390c220:  0x0     0x0
0x10390c230:  0x0     0x0
0x10390c240:  0x0     0x0
0x10390c250:  0x0     0x0
0x10390c260:  0x0     0x0
0x10390c270:  0x0     0x0
0x10390c280:  0x0     0x0
0x10390c290:  0x0     0x0
---Type <return> to continue, or q <return> to quit---q
Quit
```

14.   Dump the contents of memory pointed to by environ variable in null-terminated string format:

```
(gdb) x/100s 0x7fff6350ab00
[...]
0x7fff6350abd5:        ""
0x7fff6350abd6:        ""
0x7fff6350abd7:        ""
0x7fff6350abd8:        "/Users/DumpAnalysis/Documents/AMCDA-
Dumps/Apps/App1/Build/Products/Release/App1"
0x7fff6350ac28:        "/Users/DumpAnalysis/Documents/AMCDA-
Dumps/Apps/App1/Build/Products/Release/App1"
0x7fff6350ac78:        "TERM_PROGRAM=Apple_Terminal"
0x7fff6350ac94:        "TERM=xterm-256color"
0x7fff6350aca8:        "SHELL=/bin/bash"
0x7fff6350acb8:        "TMPDIR=/var/folders/ww/rmtqfhl93yj4213dnl2rqy6w0000gn/T/"
0x7fff6350acf1:        "Apple_PubSub_Socket_Render=/tmp/launch-mYEvtN/Render"
0x7fff6350ad26:        "TERM_PROGRAM_VERSION=303.2"
0x7fff6350ad41:        "TERM_SESSION_ID=2B039506-8384-4620-B354-120BE31AEA84"
0x7fff6350ad76:        "USER=DumpAnalysis"
0x7fff6350ad88:        "COMMAND_MODE=unix2003"
0x7fff6350ad9e:        "SSH_AUTH_SOCK=/tmp/launch-9sm7dH/Listeners"
0x7fff6350adc9:        "__CF_USER_TEXT_ENCODING=0x1F5:0:0"
0x7fff6350adeb:        "Apple_Ubiquity_Message=/tmp/launch-tWsFs8/Apple_Ubiquity_Message"
0x7fff6350ae2c:
"PATH=/Applications/Xcode.app/Contents/Developer/usr/bin/:/usr/bin:/bin:/usr/sbin:/sbin:/usr/lo
cal/bin:/usr/X11/bin"
0x7fff6350ae9f:        "PWD=/Users/DumpAnalysis"
0x7fff6350aeb7:        "LANG=en_IE.UTF-8"
---Type <return> to continue, or q <return> to quit---
0x7fff6350aec8:        "SHLVL=1"
0x7fff6350aed0:        "HOME=/Users/DumpAnalysis"
0x7fff6350aee9:        "LOGNAME=DumpAnalysis"
0x7fff6350aefe:        "DISPLAY=/tmp/launch-M8cgb1/org.x:0"
0x7fff6350af21:        "SECURITYSESSIONID=186af"
```

```
0x7fff6350af39:          "_=/Users/DumpAnalysis/Documents/AMCDA-
Dumps/Apps/App1/Build/Products/Release/App1"
0x7fff6350af8b:          "OLDPWD=/usr/share/man/man1"
0x7fff6350afa6:          ""
0x7fff6350afa7:          ""
0x7fff6350afa8:          "stack_guard=0x74843dc6068699c3"
0x7fff6350afc7:          "malloc_entropy=0x7406669509034332,0x71e4e2253a6d22b0"
0x7fff6350affc:          ""
0x7fff6350affd:          ""
```

15.   Get the list of loaded modules:

```
(gdb) info sharedlibrary
The DYLD shared library state has been initialized from the executable's shared library information.  All symbols should be present, but the addresses of some
symbols may move when the program is executed, as DYLD may relocate library load addresses if necessary.
                                    Requested State Current State
Num Basename                 Type Address      Reason | | Source
 | |                           | |             | | | |
 1 App1                       - 0x10390b000    exec Y Y /Users/DumpAnalysis/Documents/AMCDA-Dumps/Apps/App1/Build/Products/Release/App1 at 0x10390b000
(offset 0x390b000)
                                             (objfile is) [memory object "/Users/DumpAnalysis/Documents/AMCDA-Dumps/Apps/App1/Build/Products/Release/App1" at
0x10390b000]
 2 dyld                       - 0x7fff6350b000    dyld Y Y /usr/lib/dyld at 0x7fff6350b000 (offset 0x7fff6350b001) with prefix "__dyld_"
                                             (objfile is) [memory object "/usr/lib/dyld" at 0x7fff6350b000]
 3 libSystem.B.dylib          - 0x7fff91376000    dyld Y Y /usr/lib/libSystem.B.dylib at 0x7fff91376000 (offset 0x49b8000)
                                             (objfile is) [memory object "/usr/lib/libSystem.B.dylib" at 0x7fff91376000]
 4 libcache.dylib             - 0x7fff91a22000    dyld Y Y /usr/lib/system/libcache.dylib at 0x7fff91a22000 (offset 0x49b8000)
                                             (objfile is) [memory object "/usr/lib/system/libcache.dylib" at 0x7fff91a22000]
 5 libcommonCrypto.dylib      - 0x7fff8fe4b000    dyld Y Y /usr/lib/system/libcommonCrypto.dylib at 0x7fff8fe4b000 (offset 0x49b8000)
                                             (objfile is) [memory object "/usr/lib/system/libcommonCrypto.dylib" at 0x7fff8fe4b000]
 6 libcompiler_rt.dylib       - 0x7fff8b3dd000    dyld Y Y /usr/lib/system/libcompiler_rt.dylib at 0x7fff8b3dd000 (offset 0x49b8000)
                                             (objfile is) [memory object "/usr/lib/system/libcompiler_rt.dylib" at 0x7fff8b3dd000]
 7 libcopyfile.dylib          - 0x7fff8fe02000    dyld Y Y /usr/lib/system/libcopyfile.dylib at 0x7fff8fe02000 (offset 0x49b8000)
                                             (objfile is) [memory object "/usr/lib/system/libcopyfile.dylib" at 0x7fff8fe02000]
 8 libdispatch.dylib          - 0x7fff85022000    dyld Y Y /usr/lib/system/libdispatch.dylib at 0x7fff85022000 (offset 0x49b8000)
                                             (objfile is) [memory object "/usr/lib/system/libdispatch.dylib" at 0x7fff85022000]
 9 libdnsinfo.dylib           - 0x7fff8bd1a000    dyld Y Y /usr/lib/system/libdnsinfo.dylib at 0x7fff8bd1a000 (offset 0x49b8000)
                                             (objfile is) [memory object "/usr/lib/system/libdnsinfo.dylib" at 0x7fff8bd1a000]
10 libdyld.dylib              - 0x7fff89119000    dyld Y Y /usr/lib/system/libdyld.dylib at 0x7fff89119000 (offset 0x49b8000)
                                             (objfile is) [memory object "/usr/lib/system/libdyld.dylib" at 0x7fff89119000]
11 libkeymgr.dylib            - 0x7fff8b3b4000    dyld Y Y /usr/lib/system/libkeymgr.dylib at 0x7fff8b3b4000 (offset 0x49b8000)
                                             (objfile is) [memory object "/usr/lib/system/libkeymgr.dylib" at 0x7fff8b3b4000]
12 liblaunch.dylib            - 0x7fff8cfa3000    dyld Y Y /usr/lib/system/liblaunch.dylib at 0x7fff8cfa3000 (offset 0x49b800---Type <return> to continue,
or q <return> to quit---
0)
                                             (objfile is) [memory object "/usr/lib/system/liblaunch.dylib" at 0x7fff8cfa3000]
13 libmacho.dylib             - 0x7fff8a0ef000    dyld Y Y /usr/lib/system/libmacho.dylib at 0x7fff8a0ef000 (offset 0x49b8000)
                                             (objfile is) [memory object "/usr/lib/system/libmacho.dylib" at 0x7fff8a0ef000]
14 libmathCommon.A.dylib      - 0x7fff89114000    dyld Y Y /usr/lib/system/libmathCommon.A.dylib at 0x7fff89114000 (offset 0x49b8000)
                                             (objfile is) [memory object "/usr/lib/system/libmathCommon.A.dylib" at 0x7fff89114000]
15 libquarantine.dylib        - 0x7fff8b248000    dyld Y Y /usr/lib/system/libquarantine.dylib at 0x7fff8b248000 (offset 0x49b8000)
                                             (objfile is) [memory object "/usr/lib/system/libquarantine.dylib" at 0x7fff8b248000]
16 libremovefile.dylib        - 0x7fff85ae3000    dyld Y Y /usr/lib/system/libremovefile.dylib at 0x7fff85ae3000 (offset 0x49b8000)
                                             (objfile is) [memory object "/usr/lib/system/libremovefile.dylib" at 0x7fff85ae3000]
17 libsystem_blocks.dylib     - 0x7fff84d68000    dyld Y Y /usr/lib/system/libsystem_blocks.dylib at 0x7fff84d68000 (offset 0x49b8000)
                                             (objfile is) [memory object "/usr/lib/system/libsystem_blocks.dylib" at 0x7fff84d68000]
18 libsystem_c.dylib          - 0x7fff84d6a000    dyld Y Y /usr/lib/system/libsystem_c.dylib at 0x7fff84d6a000 (offset 0x49b8000)
                                             (objfile is) [memory object "/usr/lib/system/libsystem_c.dylib" at 0x7fff84d6a000]
19 libsystem_dnssd.dylib      - 0x7fff8a2ac000    dyld Y Y /usr/lib/system/libsystem_dnssd.dylib at 0x7fff8a2ac000 (offset 0x49b8000)
                                             (objfile is) [memory object "/usr/lib/system/libsystem_dnssd.dylib" at 0x7fff8a2ac000]
20 libsystem_info.dylib       - 0x7fff8ae26000    dyld Y Y /usr/lib/system/libsystem_info.dylib at 0x7fff8ae26000 (offset 0x49b8000)
                                             (objfile is) [memory object "/usr/lib/system/libsystem_info.dylib" at 0x7fff8ae26000]
21 libsystem_kernel.dylib     - 0x7fff8a0f6000    dyld Y Y /usr/lib/system/libsystem_kernel.dylib at 0x7fff8a0f6000 (offset 0x49b8000)
                                             (objfile is) [memory object "/usr/lib/system/libsystem_kernel.dylib" at 0x7fff8a0f6000]
22 libsystem_network.dylib    - 0x7fff8c528000    dyld Y Y /usr/lib/system/libsystem_network.dylib at 0x7fff8c528000 (offset 0x49b8000)
                                             (objfile is) [memory object "/usr/lib/system/libsystem_network.dylib" at 0x7fff8c528000]
23 libsystem_notify.dylib     - 0x7fff90c0f000    dyld Y Y /usr/lib/system/libsystem_notify.dylib at 0x7fff90c0f000 (offset 0x49b8000)
---Type <return> to continue, or q <return> to quit---
                                             (objfile is) [memory object "/usr/lib/system/libsystem_notify.dylib" at 0x7fff90c0f000]
24 libsystem_sandbox.dylib    - 0x7fff89740000    dyld Y Y /usr/lib/system/libsystem_sandbox.dylib at 0x7fff89740000 (offset 0x49b8000)
                                             (objfile is) [memory object "/usr/lib/system/libsystem_sandbox.dylib" at 0x7fff89740000]
25 libunc.dylib               - 0x7fff855f0000    dyld Y Y /usr/lib/system/libunc.dylib at 0x7fff855f0000 (offset 0x49b8000)
                                             (objfile is) [memory object "/usr/lib/system/libunc.dylib" at 0x7fff855f0000]
26 libunwind.dylib            - 0x7fff91489000    dyld Y Y /usr/lib/system/libunwind.dylib at 0x7fff91489000 (offset 0x49b8000)
                                             (objfile is) [memory object "/usr/lib/system/libunwind.dylib" at 0x7fff91489000]
27 libxpc.dylib               - 0x7fff849f2000    dyld Y Y /usr/lib/system/libxpc.dylib at 0x7fff849f2000 (offset 0x49b8000)
                                             (objfile is) [memory object "/usr/lib/system/libxpc.dylib" at 0x7fff849f2000]
```

Exercise A1 (LLDB)

- **Goal:** Learn how to list stack traces, disassemble functions, check their correctness, dump data, compare core dumps with diagnostic reports, get environment

- **Patterns:** Manual Dump, Stack Trace, Stack Trace Collection, Annotated Disassembly, Paratext, Not My Version, Environment Hint

- \AMCDA-Dumps\Exercise-A1-LLDB.pdf

Exercise A1 (LLDB)

Goal: Learn how to list stack traces, disassemble functions, check their correctness, dump data, compare core dumps with diagnostic reports, get environment

Patterns: Manual Dump, Stack Trace, Stack Trace Collection, Annotated Disassembly, Paratext, Not My Version, Environment Hint

1.   Load a core dump core.1394 and App1 executable:

```
$ lldb -c ~/Documents/AMCDA-Dumps/core.1394 -f ~/Documents/AMCDA-
Dumps/Apps/App1/Build/Products/Release/App1
error: core.1394 is a corrupt mach-o file: load command 46 LC_SEGMENT_64 has a fileoff +
filesize (0x160b7000) that extends beyond the end of the file (0x160b5000), the segment will
be truncated
Core file '/Users/DumpAnalysis/Documents/AMCDA-Dumps/core.1394' (x86_64) was loaded.
Process 0 stopped
* thread #1: tid = 0x0000, 0x00007fff8a10ce42 libsystem_kernel.dylib`__semwait_signal + 10,
stop reason = signal SIGSTOP
    frame #0: 0x00007fff8a10ce42 libsystem_kernel.dylib`__semwait_signal + 10
libsystem_kernel.dylib`__semwait_signal + 10:
-> 0x7fff8a10ce42:  jae    0x7fff8a10ce49           ; __semwait_signal + 17
   0x7fff8a10ce44:  jmpq   0x7fff8a10dffc           ; cerror
   0x7fff8a10ce49:  ret
   0x7fff8a10ce4a:  nop
  thread #2: tid = 0x0001, 0x00007fff8a10ce42 libsystem_kernel.dylib`__semwait_signal + 10,
stop reason = signal SIGSTOP
    frame #0: 0x00007fff8a10ce42 libsystem_kernel.dylib`__semwait_signal + 10
libsystem_kernel.dylib`__semwait_signal + 10:
-> 0x7fff8a10ce42:  jae    0x7fff8a10ce49           ; __semwait_signal + 17
   0x7fff8a10ce44:  jmpq   0x7fff8a10dffc           ; cerror
   0x7fff8a10ce49:  ret
   0x7fff8a10ce4a:  nop
  thread #3: tid = 0x0002, 0x00007fff8a10ce42 libsystem_kernel.dylib`__semwait_signal + 10,
stop reason = signal SIGSTOP
    frame #0: 0x00007fff8a10ce42 libsystem_kernel.dylib`__semwait_signal + 10
libsystem_kernel.dylib`__semwait_signal + 10:
-> 0x7fff8a10ce42:  jae    0x7fff8a10ce49           ; __semwait_signal + 17
   0x7fff8a10ce44:  jmpq   0x7fff8a10dffc           ; cerror
   0x7fff8a10ce49:  ret
   0x7fff8a10ce4a:  nop
  thread #4: tid = 0x0003, 0x00007fff8a10ce42 libsystem_kernel.dylib`__semwait_signal + 10,
stop reason = signal SIGSTOP
    frame #0: 0x00007fff8a10ce42 libsystem_kernel.dylib`__semwait_signal + 10
libsystem_kernel.dylib`__semwait_signal + 10:
-> 0x7fff8a10ce42:  jae    0x7fff8a10ce49           ; __semwait_signal + 17
   0x7fff8a10ce44:  jmpq   0x7fff8a10dffc           ; cerror
   0x7fff8a10ce49:  ret
   0x7fff8a10ce4a:  nop
```

```
   thread #5: tid = 0x0004, 0x00007fff8a10ce42 libsystem_kernel.dylib`__semwait_signal + 10,
stop reason = signal SIGSTOP
    frame #0: 0x00007fff8a10ce42 libsystem_kernel.dylib`__semwait_signal + 10
libsystem_kernel.dylib`__semwait_signal + 10:
-> 0x7fff8a10ce42:  jae    0x7fff8a10ce49            ; __semwait_signal + 17
   0x7fff8a10ce44:  jmpq   0x7fff8a10dffc            ; cerror
   0x7fff8a10ce49:  ret
   0x7fff8a10ce4a:  nop
   thread #6: tid = 0x0005, 0x00007fff8a10ce42 libsystem_kernel.dylib`__semwait_signal + 10,
stop reason = signal SIGSTOP
    frame #0: 0x00007fff8a10ce42 libsystem_kernel.dylib`__semwait_signal + 10
libsystem_kernel.dylib`__semwait_signal + 10:
-> 0x7fff8a10ce42:  jae    0x7fff8a10ce49            ; __semwait_signal + 17
   0x7fff8a10ce44:  jmpq   0x7fff8a10dffc            ; cerror
   0x7fff8a10ce49:  ret
   0x7fff8a10ce4a:  nop
(lldb)
```

Note: We see LLDB listed 6 threads with their TIDs numbered from 0. Also we have code disassembly starting from the next instruction that was to be executed if dump wasn't saved. The nice feature is annotated disassembly that shows symbolic names for jump and call destinations.

2.   List all threads:

```
(lldb) thread list
Process 0 stopped
* thread #1: tid = 0x0000, 0x00007fff8a10ce42 libsystem_kernel.dylib`__semwait_signal + 10,
stop reason = signal SIGSTOP
  thread #2: tid = 0x0001, 0x00007fff8a10ce42 libsystem_kernel.dylib`__semwait_signal + 10,
stop reason = signal SIGSTOP
  thread #3: tid = 0x0002, 0x00007fff8a10ce42 libsystem_kernel.dylib`__semwait_signal + 10,
stop reason = signal SIGSTOP
  thread #4: tid = 0x0003, 0x00007fff8a10ce42 libsystem_kernel.dylib`__semwait_signal + 10,
stop reason = signal SIGSTOP
  thread #5: tid = 0x0004, 0x00007fff8a10ce42 libsystem_kernel.dylib`__semwait_signal + 10,
stop reason = signal SIGSTOP
  thread #6: tid = 0x0005, 0x00007fff8a10ce42 libsystem_kernel.dylib`__semwait_signal + 10,
stop reason = signal SIGSTOP
```

Note: Compared to GDB here threads are listed according to increasing thread number order.

3.   Get all thread stack traces:

```
(lldb) thread backtrace all
```

```
* thread #1: tid = 0x0000, 0x00007fff8a10ce42 libsystem_kernel.dylib`__semwait_signal + 10,
stop reason = signal SIGSTOP
    frame #0: 0x00007fff8a10ce42 libsystem_kernel.dylib`__semwait_signal + 10
    frame #1: 0x00007fff84d6edea libsystem_c.dylib`nanosleep + 164
    frame #2: 0x00007fff84d6ec2c libsystem_c.dylib`sleep + 61
    frame #3: 0x00007fff84d6ec08 libsystem_c.dylib`sleep + 25
    frame #4: 0x000000010390bcc3 App1`main + 195
    frame #5: 0x000000010390ba14 App1`start + 52
```

```
  thread #2: tid = 0x0001, 0x00007fff8a10ce42 libsystem_kernel.dylib`__semwait_signal + 10,
stop reason = signal SIGSTOP
    frame #0: 0x00007fff8a10ce42 libsystem_kernel.dylib`__semwait_signal + 10
    frame #1: 0x00007fff84d6edea libsystem_c.dylib`nanosleep + 164
    frame #2: 0x00007fff84d6ec2c libsystem_c.dylib`sleep + 61
    frame #3: 0x00007fff84d6ec08 libsystem_c.dylib`sleep + 25
    frame #4: 0x000000010390ba32 App1`bar_one + 18
    frame #5: 0x000000010390ba49 App1`foo_one + 9
    frame #6: 0x000000010390ba61 App1`thread_one + 17
    frame #7: 0x00007fff84db88bf libsystem_c.dylib`_pthread_start + 335
    frame #8: 0x00007fff84dbbb75 libsystem_c.dylib`thread_start + 13

  thread #3: tid = 0x0002, 0x00007fff8a10ce42 libsystem_kernel.dylib`__semwait_signal + 10,
stop reason = signal SIGSTOP
    frame #0: 0x00007fff8a10ce42 libsystem_kernel.dylib`__semwait_signal + 10
    frame #1: 0x00007fff84d6edea libsystem_c.dylib`nanosleep + 164
    frame #2: 0x00007fff84d6ec2c libsystem_c.dylib`sleep + 61
    frame #3: 0x00007fff84d6ec08 libsystem_c.dylib`sleep + 25
    frame #4: 0x000000010390ba92 App1`bar_two + 18
    frame #5: 0x000000010390baa9 App1`foo_two + 9
    frame #6: 0x000000010390bac1 App1`thread_two + 17
    frame #7: 0x00007fff84db88bf libsystem_c.dylib`_pthread_start + 335
    frame #8: 0x00007fff84dbbb75 libsystem_c.dylib`thread_start + 13

  thread #4: tid = 0x0003, 0x00007fff8a10ce42 libsystem_kernel.dylib`__semwait_signal + 10,
stop reason = signal SIGSTOP
    frame #0: 0x00007fff8a10ce42 libsystem_kernel.dylib`__semwait_signal + 10
    frame #1: 0x00007fff84d6edea libsystem_c.dylib`nanosleep + 164
    frame #2: 0x00007fff84d6ec2c libsystem_c.dylib`sleep + 61
    frame #3: 0x00007fff84d6ec08 libsystem_c.dylib`sleep + 25
    frame #4: 0x000000010390baf2 App1`bar_three + 18
    frame #5: 0x000000010390bb09 App1`foo_three + 9
    frame #6: 0x000000010390bb21 App1`thread_three + 17
    frame #7: 0x00007fff84db88bf libsystem_c.dylib`_pthread_start + 335
    frame #8: 0x00007fff84dbbb75 libsystem_c.dylib`thread_start + 13

  thread #5: tid = 0x0004, 0x00007fff8a10ce42 libsystem_kernel.dylib`__semwait_signal + 10,
stop reason = signal SIGSTOP
    frame #0: 0x00007fff8a10ce42 libsystem_kernel.dylib`__semwait_signal + 10
    frame #1: 0x00007fff84d6edea libsystem_c.dylib`nanosleep + 164
    frame #2: 0x00007fff84d6ec2c libsystem_c.dylib`sleep + 61
    frame #3: 0x00007fff84d6ec08 libsystem_c.dylib`sleep + 25
    frame #4: 0x000000010390bb52 App1`bar_four + 18
    frame #5: 0x000000010390bb69 App1`foo_four + 9
    frame #6: 0x000000010390bb81 App1`thread_four + 17
    frame #7: 0x00007fff84db88bf libsystem_c.dylib`_pthread_start + 335
    frame #8: 0x00007fff84dbbb75 libsystem_c.dylib`thread_start + 13

  thread #6: tid = 0x0005, 0x00007fff8a10ce42 libsystem_kernel.dylib`__semwait_signal + 10,
stop reason = signal SIGSTOP
    frame #0: 0x00007fff8a10ce42 libsystem_kernel.dylib`__semwait_signal + 10
    frame #1: 0x00007fff84d6edea libsystem_c.dylib`nanosleep + 164
    frame #2: 0x00007fff84d6ec2c libsystem_c.dylib`sleep + 61
    frame #3: 0x00007fff84d6ec08 libsystem_c.dylib`sleep + 25
    frame #4: 0x000000010390bbb2 App1`bar_five + 18
    frame #5: 0x000000010390bbc9 App1`foo_five + 9
    frame #6: 0x000000010390bbe1 App1`thread_five + 17
    frame #7: 0x00007fff84db88bf libsystem_c.dylib`_pthread_start + 335
    frame #8: 0x00007fff84dbbb75 libsystem_c.dylib`thread_start + 13
```

4.   Switch to the thread #3 and get its stack trace:

```
(lldb) thread select 3
* thread #3: tid = 0x0002, 0x00007fff8a10ce42 libsystem_kernel.dylib`__semwait_signal + 10,
stop reason = signal SIGSTOP
    frame #0: 0x00007fff8a10ce42 libsystem_kernel.dylib`__semwait_signal + 10
libsystem_kernel.dylib`__semwait_signal + 10:
-> 0x7fff8a10ce42:  jae     0x7fff8a10ce49                ; __semwait_signal + 17
   0x7fff8a10ce44:  jmpq    0x7fff8a10dffc                ; cerror
   0x7fff8a10ce49:  ret
   0x7fff8a10ce4a:  nop
```

```
(lldb) bt
* thread #3: tid = 0x0002, 0x00007fff8a10ce42 libsystem_kernel.dylib`__semwait_signal + 10,
stop reason = signal SIGSTOP
    frame #0: 0x00007fff8a10ce42 libsystem_kernel.dylib`__semwait_signal + 10
    frame #1: 0x00007fff84d6edea libsystem_c.dylib`nanosleep + 164
    frame #2: 0x00007fff84d6ec2c libsystem_c.dylib`sleep + 61
    frame #3: 0x00007fff84d6ec08 libsystem_c.dylib`sleep + 25
    frame #4: 0x000000010390ba92 App1`bar_two + 18
    frame #5: 0x000000010390baa9 App1`foo_two + 9
    frame #6: 0x000000010390bac1 App1`thread_two + 17
    frame #7: 0x00007fff84db88bf libsystem_c.dylib`_pthread_start + 335
    frame #8: 0x00007fff84dbbb75 libsystem_c.dylib`thread_start + 13
```

Note: We can also list any thread stack trace without switching to it:

```
(lldb) thread backtrace 4
  thread #4: tid = 0x0003, 0x00007fff8a10ce42 libsystem_kernel.dylib`__semwait_signal + 10,
stop reason = signal SIGSTOP
    frame #0: 0x00007fff8a10ce42 libsystem_kernel.dylib`__semwait_signal + 10
    frame #1: 0x00007fff84d6edea libsystem_c.dylib`nanosleep + 164
    frame #2: 0x00007fff84d6ec2c libsystem_c.dylib`sleep + 61
    frame #3: 0x00007fff84d6ec08 libsystem_c.dylib`sleep + 25
    frame #4: 0x000000010390baf2 App1`bar_three + 18
    frame #5: 0x000000010390bb09 App1`foo_three + 9
    frame #6: 0x000000010390bb21 App1`thread_three + 17
    frame #7: 0x00007fff84db88bf libsystem_c.dylib`_pthread_start + 335
    frame #8: 0x00007fff84dbbb75 libsystem_c.dylib`thread_start + 13
```

5.   Check that *bar_two* called *sleep* function:

```
(lldb) di -n bar_two
App1`bar_two:
   0x10390ba80:  pushq  %rbp
   0x10390ba81:  movq   %rsp, %rbp
   0x10390ba84:  subq   $16, %rsp
   0x10390ba88:  movl   $4294967295, %edi
   0x10390ba8d:  callq  0x10390bce0                    ; symbol stub for: sleep
   0x10390ba92:  movl   %eax, -4(%rbp)
   0x10390ba95:  addq   $16, %rsp
   0x10390ba99:  popq   %rbp
   0x10390ba9a:  ret
   0x10390ba9b:  nopl   (%rax,%rax)
```

```
(lldb) bt
* thread #3: tid = 0x0002, 0x00007fff8a10ce42 libsystem_kernel.dylib`__semwait_signal + 10,
stop reason = signal SIGSTOP
    frame #0: 0x00007fff8a10ce42 libsystem_kernel.dylib`__semwait_signal + 10
    frame #1: 0x00007fff84d6edea libsystem_c.dylib`nanosleep + 164
    frame #2: 0x00007fff84d6ec2c libsystem_c.dylib`sleep + 61
    frame #3: 0x00007fff84d6ec08 libsystem_c.dylib`sleep + 25
    frame #4: 0x000000010390ba92 App1`bar_two + 18
    frame #5: 0x000000010390baa9 App1`foo_two + 9
    frame #6: 0x000000010390bac1 App1`thread_two + 17
    frame #7: 0x00007fff84db88bf libsystem_c.dylib`_pthread_start + 335
    frame #8: 0x00007fff84dbbb75 libsystem_c.dylib`thread_start + 13
```

6.   Compare with Intel disassembly flavor:

```
(lldb) settings set target.x86-disassembly-flavor intel
```

```
(lldb) di -n bar_two
App1`bar_two:
    0x10390ba80:  push    RBP
    0x10390ba81:  mov     RBP, RSP
    0x10390ba84:  sub     RSP, 16
    0x10390ba88:  mov     EDI, 4294967295
    0x10390ba8d:  call    0x10390bce0              ; symbol stub for: sleep
    0x10390ba92:  mov     DWORD PTR [RBP - 4], EAX
    0x10390ba95:  add     RSP, 16
    0x10390ba99:  pop     RBP
    0x10390ba9a:  ret
    0x10390ba9b:  nop     DWORD PTR [RAX + RAX]
```

```
(lldb) set disassembly-flavor att
(lldb)
```

7.   Follow *bar_two* function to *sleep* function code:

```
(lldb) di -n bar_two
App1`bar_two:
    0x10390ba80:  pushq   %rbp
    0x10390ba81:  movq    %rsp, %rbp
    0x10390ba84:  subq    $16, %rsp
    0x10390ba88:  movl    $4294967295, %edi
    0x10390ba8d:  callq   0x10390bce0             ; symbol stub for: sleep
    0x10390ba92:  movl    %eax, -4(%rbp)
    0x10390ba95:  addq    $16, %rsp
    0x10390ba99:  popq    %rbp
    0x10390ba9a:  ret
    0x10390ba9b:  nopl    (%rax,%rax)
```

```
(lldb) di -a 0x10390bce0
App1`symbol stub for: sleep:
    0x10390bce0:  jmpq    *866(%rip)             ; (void *)0x00007fff84d6ebef: sleep
```

8.   Disassemble the annotated value:

```
(lldb) di -a 0x00007fff84d6ebef
libsystem_c.dylib`sleep:
    0x7fff84d6ebef:  pushq   %rbp
    0x7fff84d6ebf0:  movq    %rsp, %rbp
    0x7fff84d6ebf3:  pushq   %rbx
    0x7fff84d6ebf4:  subq    $40, %rsp
    0x7fff84d6ebf8:  testl   %edi, %edi
    0x7fff84d6ebfa:  movl    %edi, %ebx
    0x7fff84d6ebfc:  jns     0x7fff84d6ec11             ; sleep + 34
    0x7fff84d6ebfe:  movl    $2147483647, %edi
    0x7fff84d6ec03:  callq   0x7fff84d6ebef             ; sleep
    0x7fff84d6ec08:  leal    -2147483647(%rbx,%rax), %eax
    0x7fff84d6ec0f:  jmp     0x7fff84d6ec4f             ; sleep + 96
    0x7fff84d6ec11:  movl    %ebx, %eax
    0x7fff84d6ec13:  movq    %rax, -24(%rbp)
    0x7fff84d6ec17:  movq    $0, -16(%rbp)
    0x7fff84d6ec1f:  leaq    -24(%rbp), %rdi
    0x7fff84d6ec23:  leaq    -40(%rbp), %rsi
    0x7fff84d6ec27:  callq   0x7fff84d6ed46             ; nanosleep
    0x7fff84d6ec2c:  cmpl    $-1, %eax
    0x7fff84d6ec2f:  je      0x7fff84d6ec37             ; sleep + 72
    0x7fff84d6ec31:  xorl    %ebx, %ebx
    0x7fff84d6ec33:  movl    %ebx, %eax
    0x7fff84d6ec35:  jmp     0x7fff84d6ec4f             ; sleep + 96
    0x7fff84d6ec37:  callq   0x7fff84e0cc88             ; __error
    0x7fff84d6ec3c:  cmpl    $4, (%rax)
    0x7fff84d6ec3f:  jne     0x7fff84d6ec33             ; sleep + 68
    0x7fff84d6ec41:  cmpq    $0, -32(%rbp)
    0x7fff84d6ec46:  setne   %al
    0x7fff84d6ec49:  movzbl  %al, %eax
    0x7fff84d6ec4c:  addl    -40(%rbp), %eax
    0x7fff84d6ec4f:  addq    $40, %rsp
    0x7fff84d6ec53:  popq    %rbx
    0x7fff84d6ec54:  popq    %rbp
```

9.   Compare stack trace for thread #3 (core thread 2) and its module info with the diagnostic report App1_1394.crash:

```
Process:         App1 [1394]
Path:            /Users/USER/Documents/*/App1
Identifier:      App1
Version:         ??? (???)
Code Type:       X86-64 (Native)
Parent Process:  bash [661]

Date/Time:       2012-07-24 00:20:26.078 +0100
OS Version:      Mac OS X 10.7.4 (11E53)
Report Version:  9

Crashed Thread:  0  Dispatch queue: com.apple.main-thread

Exception Type:  EXC_CRASH (SIGABRT)
Exception Codes: 0x0000000000000000, 0x0000000000000000

Thread 0 Crashed:: Dispatch queue: com.apple.main-thread
0   libsystem_kernel.dylib          0x00007fff8a10ce42 __semwait_signal + 10
1   libsystem_c.dylib               0x00007fff84d6edea nanosleep + 164
2   libsystem_c.dylib               0x00007fff84d6ec2c sleep + 61
3   libsystem_c.dylib               0x00007fff84d6ec08 sleep + 25
4   App1                            0x000000010390bcc3 main + 195
5   App1                            0x000000010390ba14 start + 52
```

```
Thread 1:
0   libsystem_kernel.dylib          0x00007fff8a10ce42 __semwait_signal + 10
1   libsystem_c.dylib               0x00007fff84d6edea nanosleep + 164
2   libsystem_c.dylib               0x00007fff84d6ec2c sleep + 61
3   libsystem_c.dylib               0x00007fff84d6ec08 sleep + 25
4   App1                            0x000000010390ba32 bar_one + 18
5   App1                            0x000000010390ba49 foo_one + 9
6   App1                            0x000000010390ba61 thread_one + 17
7   libsystem_c.dylib               0x00007fff84db88bf _pthread_start + 335
8   libsystem_c.dylib               0x00007fff84dbbb75 thread_start + 13

Thread 2:
0   libsystem_kernel.dylib          0x00007fff8a10ce42 __semwait_signal + 10
1   libsystem_c.dylib               0x00007fff84d6edea nanosleep + 164
2   libsystem_c.dylib               0x00007fff84d6ec2c sleep + 61
3   libsystem_c.dylib               0x00007fff84d6ec08 sleep + 25
4   App1                            0x000000010390ba92 bar_two + 18
5   App1                            0x000000010390baa9 foo_two + 9
6   App1                            0x000000010390bac1 thread_two + 17
7   libsystem_c.dylib               0x00007fff84db88bf _pthread_start + 335
8   libsystem_c.dylib               0x00007fff84dbbb75 thread_start + 13

Thread 3:
0   libsystem_kernel.dylib          0x00007fff8a10ce42 __semwait_signal + 10
1   libsystem_c.dylib               0x00007fff84d6edea nanosleep + 164
2   libsystem_c.dylib               0x00007fff84d6ec2c sleep + 61
3   libsystem_c.dylib               0x00007fff84d6ec08 sleep + 25
4   App1                            0x000000010390baf2 bar_three + 18
5   App1                            0x000000010390bb09 foo_three + 9
6   App1                            0x000000010390bb21 thread_three + 17
7   libsystem_c.dylib               0x00007fff84db88bf _pthread_start + 335
8   libsystem_c.dylib               0x00007fff84dbbb75 thread_start + 13

Thread 4:
0   libsystem_kernel.dylib          0x00007fff8a10ce42 __semwait_signal + 10
1   libsystem_c.dylib               0x00007fff84d6edea nanosleep + 164
2   libsystem_c.dylib               0x00007fff84d6ec2c sleep + 61
3   libsystem_c.dylib               0x00007fff84d6ec08 sleep + 25
4   App1                            0x000000010390bb52 bar_four + 18
5   App1                            0x000000010390bb69 foo_four + 9
6   App1                            0x000000010390bb81 thread_four + 17
7   libsystem_c.dylib               0x00007fff84db88bf _pthread_start + 335
8   libsystem_c.dylib               0x00007fff84dbbb75 thread_start + 13

Thread 5:
0   libsystem_kernel.dylib          0x00007fff8a10ce42 __semwait_signal + 10
1   libsystem_c.dylib               0x00007fff84d6edea nanosleep + 164
2   libsystem_c.dylib               0x00007fff84d6ec2c sleep + 61
3   libsystem_c.dylib               0x00007fff84d6ec08 sleep + 25
4   App1                            0x000000010390bbb2 bar_five + 18
5   App1                            0x000000010390bbc9 foo_five + 9
6   App1                            0x000000010390bbe1 thread_five + 17
7   libsystem_c.dylib               0x00007fff84db88bf _pthread_start + 335
8   libsystem_c.dylib               0x00007fff84dbbb75 thread_start + 13

Thread 0 crashed with X86 Thread State (64-bit):
  rax: 0x0000000000000004  rbx: 0x00007fff6350aa08  rcx: 0x00007fff6350a9c8  rdx: 0x0000000000000001
  rdi: 0x0000000000000c03  rsi: 0x0000000000000000  rbp: 0x00007fff6350a9f0  rsp: 0x00007fff6350a9c8
   r8: 0x000000007fffffff   r9: 0x0000000000000000  r10: 0x0000000000000001  r11: 0xffffff80002da8d0
  r12: 0x0000000000000000  r13: 0x0000000000000000  r14: 0x00007fff6350aa18  r15: 0x0000000000000000
  rip: 0x00007fff8a10ce42  rfl: 0x0000000000000247  cr2: 0x0000000103d0b880
Logical CPU: 0
```

```
Binary Images:
       0x10390b000 -        0x10390bfff +App1 (??? - ???) <5BC0342F-7E97-3A7D-8EA6-75A0468021EA>
/Users/USER/Documents/*/App1
    0x7fff6350b000 -        0x7fff6353fbaf  dyld (195.6 - ???) <0CD1B35B-A28F-32DA-B72E-452EAD609613> /usr/lib/dyld
    0x7fff849f2000 -        0x7fff84a0ffff  libxpc.dylib (77.19.0 - compatibility 1.0.0) <9F57891B-D7EF-3050-BEDD-
21E7C6668248> /usr/lib/system/libxpc.dylib
    0x7fff84d68000 -        0x7fff84d69ff7  libsystem_blocks.dylib (53.0.0 - compatibility 1.0.0) <8BCA214A-8992-34B2-
A8B9-B74DEACA1869> /usr/lib/system/libsystem_blocks.dylib
    0x7fff84d6a000 -        0x7fff84e47fef  libsystem_c.dylib (763.13.0 - compatibility 1.0.0) <41B43515-2806-3FBC-ACF1-
A16F35B7E290> /usr/lib/system/libsystem_c.dylib
    0x7fff85022000 -        0x7fff85030fff  libdispatch.dylib (187.9.0 - compatibility 1.0.0) <1D5BE322-A9B9-3BCE-8FAC-
076FB07CF54A> /usr/lib/system/libdispatch.dylib
    0x7fff855f0000 -        0x7fff855f1fff  libunc.dylib (24.0.0 - compatibility 1.0.0) <337960EE-0A85-3DD0-A760-
7134CF4C0AFF> /usr/lib/system/libunc.dylib
    0x7fff85ae3000 -        0x7fff85ae4ff7  libremovefile.dylib (21.1.0 - compatibility 1.0.0) <739E6C83-AA52-3C6C-A680-
B37FE2888A04> /usr/lib/system/libremovefile.dylib
    0x7fff89114000 -        0x7fff89118fff  libmathCommon.A.dylib (2026.0.0 - compatibility 1.0.0) <FF83AFF7-42B2-306E-
90AF-D539C51A4542> /usr/lib/system/libmathCommon.A.dylib
    0x7fff89119000 -        0x7fff8911dfff  libdyld.dylib (195.5.0 - compatibility 1.0.0) <380C3F44-0CA7-3514-8080-
46D1C9DF4FCD> /usr/lib/system/libdyld.dylib
    0x7fff89740000 -        0x7fff89741ff7  libsystem_sandbox.dylib (??? - ???) <96D38E74-F18F-3CCB-A20B-E8E3ADC4E166>
/usr/lib/system/libsystem_sandbox.dylib
    0x7fff8a0ef000 -        0x7fff8a0f5fff  libmacho.dylib (800.0.0 - compatibility 1.0.0) <165514D7-1BFA-38EF-A151-
676DCD21FB64> /usr/lib/system/libmacho.dylib
    0x7fff8a0f6000 -        0x7fff8a116fff  libsystem_kernel.dylib (1699.26.8 - compatibility 1.0.0) <1DDC0B0F-DB2A-34D6-
895D-E5B2B5618946> /usr/lib/system/libsystem_kernel.dylib
    0x7fff8a2ac000 -        0x7fff8a2b4fff  libsystem_dnssd.dylib (??? - ???) <D9BB1F87-A42B-3CBC-9DC2-FC07FCEF0016>
/usr/lib/system/libsystem_dnssd.dylib
    0x7fff8ae26000 -        0x7fff8ae61fff  libsystem_info.dylib (??? - ???) <35F90252-2AE1-32C5-8D34-782C614D9639>
/usr/lib/system/libsystem_info.dylib
    0x7fff8b248000 -        0x7fff8b24afff  libquarantine.dylib (36.6.0 - compatibility 1.0.0) <0EBF714B-4B69-3E1F-9A7D-
6BBC2AACB310> /usr/lib/system/libquarantine.dylib
    0x7fff8b3b4000 -        0x7fff8b3b4fff  libkeymgr.dylib (23.0.0 - compatibility 1.0.0) <61EFED6A-A407-301E-B454-
CD18314F0075> /usr/lib/system/libkeymgr.dylib
    0x7fff8b3dd000 -        0x7fff8b3e2fff  libcompiler_rt.dylib (6.0.0 - compatibility 1.0.0) <98ECD5F6-E85C-32A5-98CD-
8911230CB66A> /usr/lib/system/libcompiler_rt.dylib
    0x7fff8bd1a000 -        0x7fff8bd1bfff  libdnsinfo.dylib (395.11.0 - compatibility 1.0.0) <853BAAA5-270F-3FDC-B025-
D448DB72E1C3> /usr/lib/system/libdnsinfo.dylib
    0x7fff8c528000 -        0x7fff8c52dff7  libsystem_network.dylib (??? - ???) <5DE7024E-1D2D-34A2-80F4-08326331A75B>
/usr/lib/system/libsystem_network.dylib
    0x7fff8cfa3000 -        0x7fff8cfadff7  liblaunch.dylib (392.38.0 - compatibility 1.0.0) <6ECB7F19-B384-32C1-8652-
2463C1CF4815> /usr/lib/system/liblaunch.dylib
    0x7fff8fe02000 -        0x7fff8fe09fff  libcopyfile.dylib (85.1.0 - compatibility 1.0.0) <0AB51EE2-E914-358C-AC19-
47BC024BDAE7> /usr/lib/system/libcopyfile.dylib
    0x7fff8fe4b000 -        0x7fff8fe8dff7  libcommonCrypto.dylib (55010.0.0 - compatibility 1.0.0) <BB770C22-8C57-365A-
8716-4A3C36AE7BFB> /usr/lib/system/libcommonCrypto.dylib
    0x7fff90c0f000 -        0x7fff90c18ff7  libsystem_notify.dylib (80.1.0 - compatibility 1.0.0) <A4D651E3-D1C6-3934-
AD49-7A104FD14596> /usr/lib/system/libsystem_notify.dylib
    0x7fff91376000 -        0x7fff913a3fe7  libSystem.B.dylib (159.1.0 - compatibility 1.0.0) <7BEBB139-50BB-3112-947A-
F4AA168F991C> /usr/lib/libSystem.B.dylib
    0x7fff91489000 -        0x7fff9148fff7  libunwind.dylib (30.0.0 - compatibility 1.0.0) <1E9C6C8C-CBE8-3F4B-A5B5-
E03E3AB53231> /usr/lib/system/libunwind.dylib
    0x7fff91a22000 -        0x7fff91a27fff  libcache.dylib (47.0.0 - compatibility 1.0.0) <1571C3AB-BCB2-38CD-B3B2-
C5FC3F927C6A> /usr/lib/system/libcache.dylib

External Modification Summary:
  Calls made by other processes targeting this process:
    task_for_pid: 2
    thread_create: 0
    thread_set_state: 0
  Calls made by this process:
    task_for_pid: 0
    thread_create: 0
    thread_set_state: 0
  Calls made by all processes on this machine:
    task_for_pid: 2696
    thread_create: 0
    thread_set_state: 0
```

```
VM Region Summary:
ReadOnly portion of Libraries: Total=50.2M resident=50.2M(100%) swapped_out_or_unallocated=0K(0%)
Writable regions: Total=38.9M written=10.8M(28%) resident=42.6M(110%) swapped_out=0K(0%)
unallocated=16777216.0T(45221404475392%)

REGION TYPE                    VIRTUAL
===========                    =======
MALLOC                          1220K
Stack                           66.6M
__DATA                           464K
__LINKEDIT                      47.7M
__TEXT                          2484K
shared memory                     12K
===========                    =======
TOTAL                          118.4M
```

10.   Get App1 data section from the output of vmmap_1394.log:

```
Virtual Memory Map of process 1394 (App1)
Output report format:  2.2  -- 64-bit process

==== Non-writable regions for process 1394
__TEXT                 000000010390b000-000000010390c000 [    4K] r-x/rwx SM=COW   /Users/DumpAnalysis/Documents/AMCDA-
Dumps/Apps/App1/Build/Products/Release/App1

[...]

==== Writable regions for process 1394
__DATA                 000000010390c000-000000010390d000 [    4K] rw-/rwx SM=PRV   /Users/DumpAnalysis/Documents/AMCDA-
Dumps/Apps/App1/Build/Products/Release/App1

[...]
```

11.   Compare with the section information in the core dump:

```
(lldb) image dump sections App1
Sections for '/Users/DumpAnalysis/Documents/AMCDA-Dumps/Apps/App1/Build/Products/Release/App1' (x86_64):
  SectID     Type            Load Address                             File Off.  File Size  Flags       Section Name
  ---------- --------------- ---------------------------------------- ---------- ---------- ----------  -------------------------
  0x00000100 container       [0x0000000000000000-0x0000000100000000)* 0x00000000 0x00000000 0x00000000  App1.__PAGEZERO
  0x00000200 container       [0x000000010390b000-0x000000010390c000)  0x00000000 0x00001000 0x00000000  App1.__TEXT
  0x00000001 code            [0x000000010390b9e0-0x000000010390bcd3)  0x000009e0 0x000002f3 0x80000400  App1.__TEXT.__text
  0x00000002 code            [0x000000010390bcd4-0x000000010390bce6)  0x00000cd4 0x00000012 0x80000408  App1.__TEXT.__stubs
  0x00000003 code            [0x000000010390bce8-0x000000010390bd16)  0x00000ce8 0x0000002e 0x80000400  App1.__TEXT.__stub_helper
  0x00000004 code            [0x000000010390bd16-0x000000010390bd66)  0x00000d16 0x00000050 0x00000000  App1.__TEXT.__unwind_info
  0x00000005 eh-frame        [0x000000010390bd68-0x000000010390c000)  0x00000d68 0x00000298 0x00000000  App1.__TEXT.__eh_frame
  0x00000300 container       [0x000000010390c000-0x000000010390d000)  0x00001000 0x00001000 0x00000000  App1.__DATA
  0x00000006 data            [0x000000010390c000-0x000000010390c028)  0x00001000 0x00000028 0x00000000  App1.__DATA.__program_vars
  0x00000007 data-ptrs       [0x000000010390c028-0x000000010390c038)  0x00001028 0x00000010 0x00000006  App1.__DATA.__nl_symbol_ptr
  0x00000008 data-ptrs       [0x000000010390c038-0x000000010390c050)  0x00001038 0x00000018 0x00000007  App1.__DATA.__la_symbol_ptr
  0x00000009 zero-fill       [0x000000010390c050-0x000000010390c070)  0x00000000 0x00000020 0x00000001  App1.__DATA.__common
  0x00000400 container       [0x000000010390d000-0x000000010390d3b0)  0x00002000 0x000003b0 0x00000000  App1.__LINKEDIT
```

12.   Dump data with possible symbolic information:

```
(lldb) x/512a 0x000000010390c000
error: Normally, 'memory read' will not read over 1024 bytes of data.
error: Please use --force to override this restriction just once.
error: or set target.max-memory-read-size if you will often need a larger limit.
```

```
(lldb) x/512a 0x000000010390c000 --force
0x10390c000: 0x000000010390b000
0x10390c008: 0x000000010390c050 App1`NXArgc
0x10390c010: 0x000000010390c058 App1`NXArgv
0x10390c018: 0x000000010390c060 App1`environ
0x10390c020: 0x000000010390c068
0x10390c028: 0x00007fff8911a6a0 libdyld.dylib`dyld_stub_binder
0x10390c030: 0x00007fff63546d80 dyld`initialPoolContent + 2128
0x10390c038: 0x000000010390bcf8
0x10390c040: 0x00007fff84dbab01 libsystem_c.dylib`pthread_create
0x10390c048: 0x00007fff84d6ebef libsystem_c.dylib`sleep
0x10390c050: 0x0000000000000001
0x10390c058: 0x00007fff6350aaf0
0x10390c060: 0x00007fff6350ab00
0x10390c068: 0x00007fff6350ac73
0x10390c070: 0x0000000000000000
0x10390c078: 0x0000000000000000
0x10390c080: 0x0000000000000000
0x10390c088: 0x0000000000000000
0x10390c090: 0x0000000000000000
[...]
```

13.   Dump the contents of memory pointed to by *environ* variable in null-terminated string format:

```
(lldb) x/100s 0x00007fff6350ab00
[...]
0x7fff6350abd5:  ""
0x7fff6350abd6:  ""
0x7fff6350abd7:  ""
0x7fff6350abd8:  "/Users/DumpAnalysis/Documents/AMCDA-Dumps/Apps/App1/Build/Products/Release/App1"
0x7fff6350ac28:  "/Users/DumpAnalysis/Documents/AMCDA-Dumps/Apps/App1/Build/Products/Release/App1"
0x7fff6350ac78:  "TERM_PROGRAM=Apple_Terminal"
0x7fff6350ac94:  "TERM=xterm-256color"
0x7fff6350aca8:  "SHELL=/bin/bash"
0x7fff6350acb8:  "TMPDIR=/var/folders/ww/rmtqfhl93yj4213dnl2rqy6w0000gn/T/"
0x7fff6350acf1:  "Apple_PubSub_Socket_Render=/tmp/launch-mYEvtN/Render"
0x7fff6350ad26:  "TERM_PROGRAM_VERSION=303.2"
0x7fff6350ad41:  "TERM_SESSION_ID=2B039506-8384-4620-B354-120BE31AEA84"
0x7fff6350ad76:  "USER=DumpAnalysis"
0x7fff6350ad88:  "COMMAND_MODE=unix2003"
0x7fff6350ad9e:  "SSH_AUTH_SOCK=/tmp/launch-9sm7dH/Listeners"
0x7fff6350adc9:  "__CF_USER_TEXT_ENCODING=0x1F5:0:0"
0x7fff6350adeb:  "Apple_Ubiquity_Message=/tmp/launch-tWsFs8/Apple_Ubiquity_Message"
0x7fff6350ae2c:
"PATH=/Applications/Xcode.app/Contents/Developer/usr/bin/:/usr/bin:/bin:/usr/sbin:/sbin:/usr/local/bin:/usr/X11/bin"
0x7fff6350ae9f:  "PWD=/Users/DumpAnalysis"
0x7fff6350aeb7:  "LANG=en_IE.UTF-8"
---Type <return> to continue, or q <return> to quit---
0x7fff6350aec8:  "SHLVL=1"
0x7fff6350aed0:  "HOME=/Users/DumpAnalysis"
0x7fff6350aee9:  "LOGNAME=DumpAnalysis"
0x7fff6350aefe:  "DISPLAY=/tmp/launch-M8cgb1/org.x:0"
0x7fff6350af21:  "SECURITYSESSIONID=186af"
0x7fff6350af39:  "_=/Users/DumpAnalysis/Documents/AMCDA-Dumps/Apps/App1/Build/Products/Release/App1"
0x7fff6350af8b:  "OLDPWD=/usr/share/man/man1"
0x7fff6350afa6:  ""
0x7fff6350afa7:  ""
0x7fff6350afa8:  "stack_guard=0x74843dc6068699c3"
0x7fff6350afc7:  "malloc_entropy=0x7406669509034332,0x71e4e2253a6d22b0"
0x7fff6350affc:  ""
0x7fff6350affd:  ""
```

14.   Get the list of loaded modules:

```
(lldb) image list
[  0] 5BC0342F-7E97-3A7D-8EA6-75A0468021EA 0x000000010390b000 /Users/DumpAnalysis/Documents/AMCDA-
Dumps/Apps/App1/Build/Products/Release/App1
[  1] 7BEBB139-50BB-3112-947A-F4AA168F991C 0x00007fff91376000 /usr/lib/libSystem.B.dylib (0x00007fff91376000)
[  2] 1571C3AB-BCB2-38CD-B3B2-C5FC3F927C6A 0x00007fff91a22000 /usr/lib/system/libcache.dylib (0x00007fff91a22000)
[  3] BB770C22-8C57-365A-8716-4A3C36AE7BFB 0x00007fff8fe4b000 /usr/lib/system/libcommonCrypto.dylib (0x00007fff8fe4b000)
[  4] 98ECD5F6-E85C-32A5-98CD-8911230CB66A 0x00007fff8b3dd000 /usr/lib/system/libcompiler_rt.dylib (0x00007fff8b3dd000)
[  5] 0AB51EE2-E914-358C-AC19-47BC024BDAE7 0x00007fff8fe02000 /usr/lib/system/libcopyfile.dylib (0x00007fff8fe02000)
[  6] 1D5BE322-A9B9-3BCE-8FAC-076FB07CF54A 0x00007fff85022000 /usr/lib/system/libdispatch.dylib (0x00007fff85022000)
[  7] 853BAAA5-270F-3FDC-B025-D448DB72E1C3 0x00007fff8bd1a000 /usr/lib/system/libdnsinfo.dylib (0x00007fff8bd1a000)
[  8] 380C3F44-0CA7-3514-8080-46D1C9DF4FCD 0x00007fff89119000 /usr/lib/system/libdyld.dylib (0x00007fff89119000)
[  9] 61EFED6A-A407-301E-B454-CD18314F0075 0x00007fff8b3b4000 /usr/lib/system/libkeymgr.dylib (0x00007fff8b3b4000)
[ 10] 6ECB7F19-B384-32C1-8652-2463C1CF4815 0x00007fff8cfa3000 /usr/lib/system/liblaunch.dylib (0x00007fff8cfa3000)
[ 11] 165514D7-1BFA-38EF-A151-676DCD21FB64 0x00007fff8a0ef000 /usr/lib/system/libmacho.dylib (0x00007fff8a0ef000)
[ 12] FF83AFF7-42B2-306E-90AF-D539C51A4542 0x00007fff89114000 /usr/lib/system/libmathCommon.A.dylib (0x00007fff89114000)
[ 13] 0EBF714B-4B69-3E1F-9A7D-6BBC2AACB310 0x00007fff8b248000 /usr/lib/system/libquarantine.dylib (0x00007fff8b248000)
[ 14] 739E6C83-AA52-3C6C-A680-B37FE2888A04 0x00007fff85ae3000 /usr/lib/system/libremovefile.dylib (0x00007fff85ae3000)
[ 15] 8BCA214A-8992-34B2-A8B9-B74DEACA1869 0x00007fff84d68000 /usr/lib/system/libsystem_blocks.dylib (0x00007fff84d68000)
[ 16] 41B43515-2806-3FBC-ACF1-A16F35B7E290 0x00007fff84d6a000 /usr/lib/system/libsystem_c.dylib (0x00007fff84d6a000)
[ 17] D9BB1F87-A42B-3CBC-9DC2-FC07FCEF0016 0x00007fff8a2ac000 /usr/lib/system/libsystem_dnssd.dylib (0x00007fff8a2ac000)
[ 18] 35F90252-2AE1-32C5-8D34-782C614D9639 0x00007fff8ae26000 /usr/lib/system/libsystem_info.dylib (0x00007fff8ae26000)
[ 19] 1DDC0B0F-DB2A-34D6-895D-E5B2B5618946 0x00007fff8a0f6000 /usr/lib/system/libsystem_kernel.dylib (0x00007fff8a0f6000)
[ 20] 5DE7024E-1D2D-34A2-80F4-08326331A75B 0x00007fff8c528000 /usr/lib/system/libsystem_network.dylib (0x00007fff8c528000)
[ 21] A4D651E3-D1C6-3934-AD49-7A104FD14596 0x00007fff90c0f000 /usr/lib/system/libsystem_notify.dylib (0x00007fff90c0f000)
[ 22] 96D38E74-F18F-3CCB-A20B-E8E3ADC4E166 0x00007fff89740000 /usr/lib/system/libsystem_sandbox.dylib (0x00007fff89740000)
[ 23] 337960EE-0A85-3DD0-A760-7134CF4C0AFF 0x00007fff855f0000 /usr/lib/system/libunc.dylib (0x00007fff855f0000)
[ 24] 1E9C6C8C-CBE8-3F4B-A5B5-E03E3AB53231 0x00007fff91489000 /usr/lib/system/libunwind.dylib (0x00007fff91489000)
[ 25] 9F57891B-D7EF-3050-BEDD-21E7C6668248 0x00007fff849f2000 /usr/lib/system/libxpc.dylib (0x00007fff849f2000)
[ 26] 0CD1B35B-A28F-32DA-B72E-452EAD609613 0x00007fff6350b000 /usr/lib/dyld (0x00007fff6350b000)
(lldb)
```

Exercise A2 (GDB)

- **Goal:** Learn how to identify multiple exceptions, find problem CPU instructions

- **Patterns:** Multiple Exceptions, NULL Pointer (data), NULL Pointer (code)

- \AMCDA-Dumps\Exercise-A2-GDB.pdf

Exercise A2 (GDB)

Goal: Learn how to identify multiple exceptions, find problem CPU instructions

Patterns: Multiple Exceptions, NULL Pointer (data), NULL Pointer (code)

1.   Identify a crash in diagnostic report App2_1995.crash (thread, module, function name):

```
Process:        App2 [1995]
Path:           /Users/USER/Documents/*/App2
Identifier:     App2
Version:        ??? (???)
Code Type:      X86-64 (Native)
Parent Process: bash [1549]

Date/Time:      2012-07-24 13:41:10.529 +0100
OS Version:     Mac OS X 10.7.4 (11E53)
Report Version: 9

Crashed Thread: 2

Exception Type:  EXC_BAD_ACCESS (SIGSEGV)
Exception Codes: KERN_INVALID_ADDRESS at 0x0000000000000000

VM Regions Near 0:
-->
    __TEXT                 000000010fe0a000-000000010fe0b000 [    4K] r-x/rwx SM=COW  /Users/USER/Documents/*

Thread 0:: Dispatch queue: com.apple.main-thread
0   libsystem_kernel.dylib          0x00007fff8a10c4de __bsdthread_create + 10
1   libsystem_c.dylib               0x00007fff84dbae9d pthread_create + 924
2   App2                            0x000000010fe0ac66 main + 182
3   App2                            0x000000010fe0a9a4 start + 52

Thread 1:
0   libsystem_kernel.dylib          0x00007fff8a10ce42 __semwait_signal + 10
1   libsystem_c.dylib               0x00007fff84d6edea nanosleep + 164
2   libsystem_c.dylib               0x00007fff84d6ec2c sleep + 61
3   libsystem_c.dylib               0x00007fff84d6ec08 sleep + 25
4   App2                            0x000000010fe0aa02 bar_one + 18
5   App2                            0x000000010fe0aa19 foo_one + 9
6   App2                            0x000000010fe0aa31 thread_one + 17
7   libsystem_c.dylib               0x00007fff84db88bf _pthread_start + 335
8   libsystem_c.dylib               0x00007fff84dbbb75 thread_start + 13

Thread 2 Crashed:
0   App2                            0x000000010fe0a9c0 procA + 16
1   App2                            0x000000010fe0aa59 bar_two + 9
2   App2                            0x000000010fe0aa69 foo_two + 9
3   App2                            0x000000010fe0aa81 thread_two + 17
4   libsystem_c.dylib               0x00007fff84db88bf _pthread_start + 335
5   libsystem_c.dylib               0x00007fff84dbbb75 thread_start + 13

Thread 3:
0   libsystem_kernel.dylib          0x00007fff8a10ce42 __semwait_signal + 10
1   libsystem_c.dylib               0x00007fff84d6edea nanosleep + 164
2   libsystem_c.dylib               0x00007fff84d6ec2c sleep + 61
3   libsystem_c.dylib               0x00007fff84d6ec08 sleep + 25
4   App2                            0x000000010fe0aab2 bar_three + 18
5   App2                            0x000000010fe0aac9 foo_three + 9
6   App2                            0x000000010fe0aae1 thread_three + 17
7   libsystem_c.dylib               0x00007fff84db88bf _pthread_start + 335
8   libsystem_c.dylib               0x00007fff84dbbb75 thread_start + 13
```

```
Thread 4:
0   ???                               000000000000000000 0 + 0
1   App2                              0x000000010fe0a9e5 procB + 21
2   App2                              0x000000010fe0ab09 bar_four + 9
3   App2                              0x000000010fe0ab19 foo_four + 9
4   App2                              0x000000010fe0ab31 thread_four + 17
5   libsystem_c.dylib                 0x00007fff84db88bf _pthread_start + 335
6   libsystem_c.dylib                 0x00007fff84dbbb75 thread_start + 13

Thread 5:
0   libsystem_c.dylib                 0x00007fff84dbbb68 thread_start + 0

Thread 2 crashed with X86 Thread State (64-bit):
  rax: 0x0000000000000000  rbx: 0x0000000000000000  rcx: 0x00007fff8a10d0c2  rdx: 0x0000000000000000
  rdi: 0x0000000000000000  rsi: 0x0000000000000000  rbp: 0x0000000110080ed0  rsp: 0x0000000110080ed0
   r8: 0x00007fff74a67fb8   r9: 0x0000000000000001  r10: 0x00007fff84dbbb94  r11: 0x0000000000000202
  r12: 0x0000000000001303  r13: 0x0000000110081000  r14: 0x0000000000000000  r15: 0x000000010fe0aa70
  rip: 0x000000010fe0a9c0  rfl: 0x0000000000010206  cr2: 0x0000000000000000
Logical CPU: 3

Binary Images:
       0x10fe0a000 -        0x10fe0afff +App2 (??? - ???) <198471D0-89AB-3F3A-9AD9-962662E8C412>
/Users/USER/Documents/*/App2
    0x7fff6fa0a000 -     0x7fff6fa3ebaf  dyld (195.6 - ???) <0CD1B35B-A28F-32DA-B72E-452EAD609613> /usr/lib/dyld
    0x7fff849f2000 -     0x7fff84a0ffff  libxpc.dylib (77.19.0 - compatibility 1.0.0) <9F57891B-D7EF-3050-BEDD-
21E7C6668248> /usr/lib/system/libxpc.dylib
    0x7fff84d68000 -     0x7fff84d69ff7  libsystem_blocks.dylib (53.0.0 - compatibility 1.0.0) <8BCA214A-8992-34B2-
A8B9-B74DEACA1869> /usr/lib/system/libsystem_blocks.dylib
    0x7fff84d6a000 -     0x7fff84e47fef  libsystem_c.dylib (763.13.0 - compatibility 1.0.0) <41B43515-2806-3FBC-ACF1-
A16F35B7E290> /usr/lib/system/libsystem_c.dylib
    0x7fff85022000 -     0x7fff85030fff  libdispatch.dylib (187.9.0 - compatibility 1.0.0) <1D5BE322-A9B9-3BCE-8FAC-
076FB07CF54A> /usr/lib/system/libdispatch.dylib
    0x7fff855f0000 -     0x7fff855f1fff  libunc.dylib (24.0.0 - compatibility 1.0.0) <337960EE-0A85-3DD0-A760-
7134CF4C0AFF> /usr/lib/system/libunc.dylib
    0x7fff85ae3000 -     0x7fff85ae4ff7  libremovefile.dylib (21.1.0 - compatibility 1.0.0) <739E6C83-AA52-3C6C-A680-
B37FE2888A04> /usr/lib/system/libremovefile.dylib
    0x7fff89114000 -     0x7fff89118fff  libmathCommon.A.dylib (2026.0.0 - compatibility 1.0.0) <FF83AFF7-42B2-306E-
90AF-D539C51A4542> /usr/lib/system/libmathCommon.A.dylib
    0x7fff89119000 -     0x7fff8911dfff  libdyld.dylib (195.5.0 - compatibility 1.0.0) <380C3F44-0CA7-3514-8080-
46D1C9DF4FCD> /usr/lib/system/libdyld.dylib
    0x7fff89740000 -     0x7fff89741ff7  libsystem_sandbox.dylib (??? - ???) <96D38E74-F18F-3CCB-A20B-E8E3ADC4E166>
/usr/lib/system/libsystem_sandbox.dylib
    0x7fff8a0ef000 -     0x7fff8a0f5fff  libmacho.dylib (800.0.0 - compatibility 1.0.0) <165514D7-1BFA-38EF-A151-
676DCD21FB64> /usr/lib/system/libmacho.dylib
    0x7fff8a0f6000 -     0x7fff8a116fff  libsystem_kernel.dylib (1699.26.8 - compatibility 1.0.0) <1DDC0B0F-DB2A-34D6-
895D-E5B2B5618946> /usr/lib/system/libsystem_kernel.dylib
    0x7fff8a2ac000 -     0x7fff8a2b4fff  libsystem_dnssd.dylib (??? - ???) <D9BB1F87-A42B-3CBC-9DC2-FC07FCEF0016>
/usr/lib/system/libsystem_dnssd.dylib
    0x7fff8ae26000 -     0x7fff8ae61fff  libsystem_info.dylib (??? - ???) <35F90252-2AE1-32C5-8D34-782C614D9639>
/usr/lib/system/libsystem_info.dylib
    0x7fff8b248000 -     0x7fff8b24afff  libquarantine.dylib (36.6.0 - compatibility 1.0.0) <0EBF714B-4B69-3E1F-9A7D-
6BBC2AACB310> /usr/lib/system/libquarantine.dylib
    0x7fff8b3b4000 -     0x7fff8b3b4fff  libkeymgr.dylib (23.0.0 - compatibility 1.0.0) <61EFED6A-A407-301E-B454-
CD18314F0075> /usr/lib/system/libkeymgr.dylib
    0x7fff8b3dd000 -     0x7fff8b3e2fff  libcompiler_rt.dylib (6.0.0 - compatibility 1.0.0) <98ECD5F6-E85C-32A5-98CD-
8911230CB66A> /usr/lib/system/libcompiler_rt.dylib
    0x7fff8bd1a000 -     0x7fff8bd1bfff  libdnsinfo.dylib (395.11.0 - compatibility 1.0.0) <853BAAA5-270F-3FDC-B025-
D448DB72E1C3> /usr/lib/system/libdnsinfo.dylib
    0x7fff8c528000 -     0x7fff8c52dff7  libsystem_network.dylib (??? - ???) <5DE7024E-1D2D-34A2-80F4-08326331A75B>
/usr/lib/system/libsystem_network.dylib
    0x7fff8cfa3000 -     0x7fff8cfadff7  liblaunch.dylib (392.38.0 - compatibility 1.0.0) <6ECB7F19-B384-32C1-8652-
2463C1CF4815> /usr/lib/system/liblaunch.dylib
    0x7fff8fe02000 -     0x7fff8fe09fff  libcopyfile.dylib (85.1.0 - compatibility 1.0.0) <0AB51EE2-E914-358C-AC19-
47BC024BDAE7> /usr/lib/system/libcopyfile.dylib
    0x7fff8fe4b000 -     0x7fff8fe8dff7  libcommonCrypto.dylib (55010.0.0 - compatibility 1.0.0) <BB770C22-8C57-365A-
8716-4A3C36AE7BFB> /usr/lib/system/libcommonCrypto.dylib
    0x7fff90c0f000 -     0x7fff90c18ff7  libsystem_notify.dylib (80.1.0 - compatibility 1.0.0) <A4D651E3-D1C6-3934-
AD49-7A104FD14596> /usr/lib/system/libsystem_notify.dylib
    0x7fff91376000 -     0x7fff913a3fe7  libSystem.B.dylib (159.1.0 - compatibility 1.0.0) <7BEBB139-50BB-3112-947A-
F4AA168F991C> /usr/lib/libSystem.B.dylib
    0x7fff91489000 -     0x7fff9148fff7  libunwind.dylib (30.0.0 - compatibility 1.0.0) <1E9C6C8C-CBE8-3F4B-A5B5-
E03E3AB53231> /usr/lib/system/libunwind.dylib
    0x7fff91a22000 -     0x7fff91a27fff  libcache.dylib (47.0.0 - compatibility 1.0.0) <1571C3AB-BCB2-38CD-B3B2-
C5FC3F927C6A> /usr/lib/system/libcache.dylib
```

```
External Modification Summary:
  Calls made by other processes targeting this process:
    task_for_pid: 0
    thread_create: 0
    thread_set_state: 0
  Calls made by this process:
    task_for_pid: 0
    thread_create: 0
    thread_set_state: 0
  Calls made by all processes on this machine:
    task_for_pid: 3632
    thread_create: 0
    thread_set_state: 0

VM Region Summary:
ReadOnly portion of Libraries: Total=50.2M resident=50.2M(100%) swapped_out_or_unallocated=8K(0%)
Writable regions: Total=38.9M written=22.2M(57%) resident=42.5M(109%) swapped_out=196K(0%)
unallocated=16777216.0T(45221404475392%)

REGION TYPE                VIRTUAL
===========                =======
MALLOC                       1220K
Stack                        66.6M
__DATA                        464K
__LINKEDIT                   47.7M
__TEXT                       2484K
shared memory                  12K
===========                =======
TOTAL                       118.4M
```

2.   Load a core dump core.1995 and App2 executable:

$ gdb -c ~/Documents/AMCDA-Dumps/core.1995 -e ~/Documents/AMCDA-Dumps/Apps/App2/Build/Products/Release/App2
```
GNU gdb 6.3.50-20050815 (Apple version gdb-1820) (Sat Jun 16 02:40:11 UTC 2012)
Copyright 2004 Free Software Foundation, Inc.
GDB is free software, covered by the GNU General Public License, and you are
welcome to change it and/or distribute copies of it under certain conditions.
Type "show copying" to see the conditions.
There is absolutely no warranty for GDB.  Type "show warranty" for details.
This GDB was configured as "x86_64-apple-darwin".
Reading symbols for shared libraries . done
Reading symbols for shared libraries ......................... done
#0  0x00007fff8a10c4de in __bsdthread_create ()
```

3.   List all threads:

```
(gdb) info threads
  6 0x00007fff84dbbb68 in thread_start ()
  5 0x0000000000000000 in ?? ()
  4 0x00007fff8a10ce42 in __semwait_signal ()
  3 0x000000010fe0a9c0 in procA ()
  2 0x00007fff8a10ce42 in __semwait_signal ()
* 1 0x00007fff8a10c4de in __bsdthread_create ()
```

3.   Switch to the problem thread identified in the diagnostic report (core thread 2, thread #3):

```
(gdb) thread 3
[Switching to thread 3 (core thread 2)]
0x000000010fe0a9c0 in procA ()

(gdb) bt
#0  0x000000010fe0a9c0 in procA ()
#1  0x000000010fe0aa59 in bar_two ()
#2  0x000000010fe0aa69 in foo_two ()
#3  0x000000010fe0aa81 in thread_two ()
#4  0x00007fff84db88bf in _pthread_start ()
#5  0x00007fff84dbbb75 in thread_start ()
```

4.   Disassemble the problem instruction and check CPU register(s) details (NULL Data Pointer):

```
(gdb) x/i 0x000000010fe0a9c0
0x10fe0a9c0 <procA+16>:    movl    $0x1,(%rax)

(gdb) info r $rax
rax            0x0  0

(gdb) x $rax
0x0:   Cannot access memory at address 0x0
```

5.   List all thread stack traces and identify other anomalies:

```
(gdb) thread apply all bt

Thread 6 (core thread 5):
#0  0x00007fff84dbbb68 in thread_start ()
#1  0x0000000000000000 in ?? ()

Thread 5 (core thread 4):
#0  0x0000000000000000 in ?? ()
#1  0x000000010fe0a9e5 in procB ()
#2  0x000000010fe0ab09 in bar_four ()
#3  0x000000010fe0ab19 in foo_four ()
#4  0x000000010fe0ab31 in thread_four ()
#5  0x00007fff84db88bf in _pthread_start ()
#6  0x00007fff84dbbb75 in thread_start ()

Thread 4 (core thread 3):
#0  0x00007fff8a10ce42 in __semwait_signal ()
#1  0x00007fff84d6edea in nanosleep ()
#2  0x00007fff84d6ec2c in sleep ()
#3  0x00007fff84d6ec08 in sleep ()
#4  0x000000010fe0aab2 in bar_three ()
#5  0x000000010fe0aac9 in foo_three ()
#6  0x000000010fe0aae1 in thread_three ()
#7  0x00007fff84db88bf in _pthread_start ()
#8  0x00007fff84dbbb75 in thread_start ()
```

```
Thread 3 (core thread 2):
#0  0x000000010fe0a9c0 in procA ()
#1  0x000000010fe0aa59 in bar_two ()
#2  0x000000010fe0aa69 in foo_two ()
#3  0x000000010fe0aa81 in thread_two ()
#4  0x00007fff84db88bf in _pthread_start ()
#5  0x00007fff84dbbb75 in thread_start ()

Thread 2 (core thread 1):
#0  0x00007fff8a10ce42 in __semwait_signal ()
#1  0x00007fff84d6edea in nanosleep ()
#2  0x00007fff84d6ec2c in sleep ()
#3  0x00007fff84d6ec08 in sleep ()
#4  0x000000010fe0aa02 in bar_one ()
#5  0x000000010fe0aa19 in foo_one ()
#6  0x000000010fe0aa31 in thread_one ()
#7  0x00007fff84db88bf in _pthread_start ()
---Type <return> to continue, or q <return> to quit---
#8  0x00007fff84dbbb75 in thread_start ()

Thread 1 (core thread 0):
#0  0x00007fff8a10c4de in __bsdthread_create ()
#1  0x00007fff84dbae9d in pthread_create ()
#2  0x000000010fe0ac66 in main ()
```

6.   Check the CPU instruction and the stack trace pointer for thread #6 (core thread 5) for any signs of stack overflow:

```
(gdb) thread 6
[Switching to thread 6 (core thread 5)]
0x00007fff84dbbb68 in thread_start ()

(gdb) bt
#0  0x00007fff84dbbb68 in thread_start ()
#1  0x0000000000000000 in ?? ()

(gdb) x/i 0x00007fff84dbbb68
0x7fff84dbbb68 <thread_start>:   push   %rbp

(gdb) x/xg $rsp
0x110209f80: 0x0000000000000000

(gdb) x/xg $rsp-8
0x110209f78: 0x0000000000000000

(gdb) x/xg $rsp-0x10
0x110209f70: 0x0000000000000000
```

7.   Check the CPU instruction and a dereferenced pointer for thread #5 (core thread 5) for any signs of NULL pointers:

```
(gdb) thread 5
[Switching to thread 5 (core thread 4)]
0x0000000000000000 in ?? ()
```

```
(gdb) bt
#0  0x0000000000000000 in ?? ()
#1  0x000000010fe0a9e5 in procB ()
#2  0x000000010fe0ab09 in bar_four ()
#3  0x000000010fe0ab19 in foo_four ()
#4  0x000000010fe0ab31 in thread_four ()
#5  0x00007fff84db88bf in _pthread_start ()
#6  0x00007fff84dbbb75 in thread_start ()

 (gdb) disassemble 0x000000010fe0a9e5
Dump of assembler code for function procB:
0x000000010fe0a9d0 <procB+0>:    push   %rbp
0x000000010fe0a9d1 <procB+1>:    mov    %rsp,%rbp
0x000000010fe0a9d4 <procB+4>:    sub    $0x10,%rsp
0x000000010fe0a9d8 <procB+8>:    movq   $0x0,-0x8(%rbp)
0x000000010fe0a9e0 <procB+16>:   mov    $0x0,%al
0x000000010fe0a9e2 <procB+18>:   callq  *-0x8(%rbp)
0x000000010fe0a9e5 <procB+21>:   add    $0x10,%rsp
0x000000010fe0a9e9 <procB+25>:   pop    %rbp
0x000000010fe0a9ea <procB+26>:   retq
0x000000010fe0a9eb <procB+27>:   nopl   0x0(%rax,%rax,1)
End of assembler dump.

(gdb) x/xg $rbp-8
0x110186ec8: 0x0000000000000000
```

8.   Switch to the thread #1 (core thread 0) and verify that main function was engaged in thread creation (this should correlate with thread #6 caught in being created):

```
(gdb) thread 1
[Switching to thread 1 (core thread 0)]
0x00007fff8a10c4de in __bsdthread_create ()

(gdb) bt
#0  0x00007fff8a10c4de in __bsdthread_create ()
#1  0x00007fff84dbae9d in pthread_create ()
#2  0x000000010fe0ac66 in main ()
```

```
(gdb) disassemble main
Dump of assembler code for function main:
0x000000010fe0abb0 <main+0>:      push    %rbp
0x000000010fe0abb1 <main+1>:      mov     %rsp,%rbp
0x000000010fe0abb4 <main+4>:      sub     $0x50,%rsp
0x000000010fe0abb8 <main+8>:      lea     -0x18(%rbp),%rax
0x000000010fe0abbc <main+12>:     mov     $0x0,%rcx
0x000000010fe0abc6 <main+22>:     lea     -0x1ad(%rip),%rdx        # 0x10fe0aa20 <thread_one>
0x000000010fe0abcd <main+29>:     movl    $0x0,-0x4(%rbp)
0x000000010fe0abd4 <main+36>:     mov     %edi,-0x8(%rbp)
0x000000010fe0abd7 <main+39>:     mov     %rsi,-0x10(%rbp)
0x000000010fe0abdb <main+43>:     mov     %rax,%rdi
0x000000010fe0abde <main+46>:     mov     %rcx,%rsi
0x000000010fe0abe1 <main+49>:     callq   0x10fe0ac8a <dyld_stub_pthread_create>
0x000000010fe0abe6 <main+54>:     lea     -0x20(%rbp),%rdi
0x000000010fe0abea <main+58>:     mov     $0x0,%rcx
0x000000010fe0abf4 <main+68>:     lea     -0x18b(%rip),%rdx        # 0x10fe0aa70 <thread_two>
0x000000010fe0abfb <main+75>:     mov     %rcx,%rsi
0x000000010fe0abfe <main+78>:     mov     %eax,-0x3c(%rbp)
0x000000010fe0ac01 <main+81>:     callq   0x10fe0ac8a <dyld_stub_pthread_create>
0x000000010fe0ac06 <main+86>:     lea     -0x28(%rbp),%rdi
0x000000010fe0ac0a <main+90>:     mov     $0x0,%rcx
0x000000010fe0ac14 <main+100>:    lea     -0x14b(%rip),%rdx        # 0x10fe0aad0 <thread_three>
0x000000010fe0ac1b <main+107>:    mov     %rcx,%rsi
0x000000010fe0ac1e <main+110>:    mov     %eax,-0x40(%rbp)
0x000000010fe0ac21 <main+113>:    callq   0x10fe0ac8a <dyld_stub_pthread_create>
0x000000010fe0ac26 <main+118>:    lea     -0x30(%rbp),%rdi
0x000000010fe0ac2a <main+122>:    mov     $0x0,%rcx
0x000000010fe0ac34 <main+132>:    lea     -0x11b(%rip),%rdx        # 0x10fe0ab20 <thread_four>
0x000000010fe0ac3b <main+139>:    mov     %rcx,%rsi
0x000000010fe0ac3e <main+142>:    mov     %eax,-0x44(%rbp)
0x000000010fe0ac41 <main+145>:    callq   0x10fe0ac8a <dyld_stub_pthread_create>
0x000000010fe0ac46 <main+150>:    lea     -0x38(%rbp),%rdi
0x000000010fe0ac4a <main+154>:    mov     $0x0,%rcx
0x000000010fe0ac54 <main+164>:    lea     -0xdb(%rip),%rdx         # 0x10fe0ab80 <thread_five>
0x000000010fe0ac5b <main+171>:    mov     %rcx,%rsi
0x000000010fe0ac5e <main+174>:    mov     %eax,-0x48(%rbp)
0x000000010fe0ac61 <main+177>:    callq   0x10fe0ac8a <dyld_stub_pthread_create>
0x000000010fe0ac66 <main+182>:    mov     $0x3,%edi
0x000000010fe0ac6b <main+187>:    mov     %eax,-0x4c(%rbp)
0x000000010fe0ac6e <main+190>:    callq   0x10fe0ac90 <dyld_stub_sleep>
0x000000010fe0ac73 <main+195>:    mov     $0x0,%edi
0x000000010fe0ac78 <main+200>:    mov     %eax,-0x50(%rbp)
---Type <return> to continue, or q <return> to quit---
0x000000010fe0ac7b <main+203>:    mov     %edi,%eax
0x000000010fe0ac7d <main+205>:    add     $0x50,%rsp
0x000000010fe0ac81 <main+209>:    pop     %rbp
0x000000010fe0ac82 <main+210>:    retq
End of assembler dump.
```

Exercise A2 (LLDB)

- **Goal:** Learn how to identify multiple exceptions, find problem CPU instructions

- **Patterns:** Multiple Exceptions, NULL Pointer (data), NULL Pointer (code)

- \AMCDA-Dumps\Exercise-A2-LLDB.pdf

Exercise A2 (LLDB)

Goal: Learn how to identify multiple exceptions, find problem CPU instructions

Patterns: Multiple Exceptions, NULL Pointer (data), NULL Pointer (code)

1.   Identify a crash in diagnostic report App2_1995.crash (thread, module, function name):

```
Process:        App2 [1995]
Path:           /Users/USER/Documents/*/App2
Identifier:     App2
Version:        ??? (???)
Code Type:      X86-64 (Native)
Parent Process: bash [1549]

Date/Time:      2012-07-24 13:41:10.529 +0100
OS Version:     Mac OS X 10.7.4 (11E53)
Report Version: 9

Crashed Thread: 2

Exception Type:  EXC_BAD_ACCESS (SIGSEGV)
Exception Codes: KERN_INVALID_ADDRESS at 0x0000000000000000

VM Regions Near 0:
-->
    __TEXT                 000000010fe0a000-000000010fe0b000 [    4K] r-x/rwx SM=COW  /Users/USER/Documents/*

Thread 0:: Dispatch queue: com.apple.main-thread
0   libsystem_kernel.dylib          0x00007fff8a10c4de __bsdthread_create + 10
1   libsystem_c.dylib               0x00007fff84dbae9d pthread_create + 924
2   App2                            0x000000010fe0ac66 main + 182
3   App2                            0x000000010fe0a9a4 start + 52

Thread 1:
0   libsystem_kernel.dylib          0x00007fff8a10ce42 __semwait_signal + 10
1   libsystem_c.dylib               0x00007fff84d6edea nanosleep + 164
2   libsystem_c.dylib               0x00007fff84d6ec2c sleep + 61
3   libsystem_c.dylib               0x00007fff84d6ec08 sleep + 25
4   App2                            0x000000010fe0aa02 bar_one + 18
5   App2                            0x000000010fe0aa19 foo_one + 9
6   App2                            0x000000010fe0aa31 thread_one + 17
7   libsystem_c.dylib               0x00007fff84db88bf _pthread_start + 335
8   libsystem_c.dylib               0x00007fff84dbbb75 thread_start + 13

Thread 2 Crashed:
0   App2                            0x000000010fe0a9c0 procA + 16
1   App2                            0x000000010fe0aa59 bar_two + 9
2   App2                            0x000000010fe0aa69 foo_two + 9
3   App2                            0x000000010fe0aa81 thread_two + 17
4   libsystem_c.dylib               0x00007fff84db88bf _pthread_start + 335
5   libsystem_c.dylib               0x00007fff84dbbb75 thread_start + 13

Thread 3:
0   libsystem_kernel.dylib          0x00007fff8a10ce42 __semwait_signal + 10
1   libsystem_c.dylib               0x00007fff84d6edea nanosleep + 164
2   libsystem_c.dylib               0x00007fff84d6ec2c sleep + 61
3   libsystem_c.dylib               0x00007fff84d6ec08 sleep + 25
4   App2                            0x000000010fe0aab2 bar_three + 18
5   App2                            0x000000010fe0aac9 foo_three + 9
6   App2                            0x000000010fe0aae1 thread_three + 17
7   libsystem_c.dylib               0x00007fff84db88bf _pthread_start + 335
8   libsystem_c.dylib               0x00007fff84dbbb75 thread_start + 13
```

```
Thread 4:
0    ???                              000000000000000000 0 + 0
1    App2                             0x000000010fe0a9e5 procB + 21
2    App2                             0x000000010fe0ab09 bar_four + 9
3    App2                             0x000000010fe0ab19 foo_four + 9
4    App2                             0x000000010fe0ab31 thread_four + 17
5    libsystem_c.dylib                0x00007fff84db88bf _pthread_start + 335
6    libsystem_c.dylib                0x00007fff84dbbb75 thread_start + 13

Thread 5:
0    libsystem_c.dylib                0x00007fff84dbbb68 thread_start + 0

Thread 2 crashed with X86 Thread State (64-bit):
  rax: 0x0000000000000000  rbx: 0x0000000000000000  rcx: 0x00007fff8a10d0c2  rdx: 0x0000000000000000
  rdi: 0x0000000000000000  rsi: 0x0000000000000000  rbp: 0x0000000110080ed0  rsp: 0x0000000110080ed0
   r8: 0x00007fff74a67fb8   r9: 0x0000000000000001  r10: 0x00007fff84dbbb94  r11: 0x0000000000000202
  r12: 0x0000000000001303  r13: 0x0000000110081000  r14: 0x0000000000000000  r15: 0x000000010fe0aa70
  rip: 0x000000010fe0a9c0  rfl: 0x0000000000010206  cr2: 0x0000000000000000
Logical CPU: 3

Binary Images:
       0x10fe0a000 -        0x10fe0afff +App2 (??? - ???) <198471D0-89AB-3F3A-9AD9-962662E8C412>
/Users/USER/Documents/*/App2
    0x7fff6fa0a000 -     0x7fff6fa3ebaf  dyld (195.6 - ???) <0CD1B35B-A28F-32DA-B72E-452EAD609613> /usr/lib/dyld
    0x7fff849f2000 -     0x7fff84a0ffff  libxpc.dylib (77.19.0 - compatibility 1.0.0) <9F57891B-D7EF-3050-BEDD-
21E7C6668248> /usr/lib/system/libxpc.dylib
    0x7fff84d68000 -     0x7fff84d69ff7  libsystem_blocks.dylib (53.0.0 - compatibility 1.0.0) <8BCA214A-8992-34B2-
A8B9-B74DEACA1869> /usr/lib/system/libsystem_blocks.dylib
    0x7fff84d6a000 -     0x7fff84e47fef  libsystem_c.dylib (763.13.0 - compatibility 1.0.0) <41B43515-2806-3FBC-ACF1-
A16F35B7E290> /usr/lib/system/libsystem_c.dylib
    0x7fff85022000 -     0x7fff85030fff  libdispatch.dylib (187.9.0 - compatibility 1.0.0) <1D5BE322-A9B9-3BCE-8FAC-
076FB07CF54A> /usr/lib/system/libdispatch.dylib
    0x7fff855f0000 -     0x7fff855f1fff  libunc.dylib (24.0.0 - compatibility 1.0.0) <337960EE-0A85-3DD0-A760-
7134CF4C0AFF> /usr/lib/system/libunc.dylib
    0x7fff85ae3000 -     0x7fff85ae4ff7  libremovefile.dylib (21.1.0 - compatibility 1.0.0) <739E6C83-AA52-3C6C-A680-
B37FE2888A04> /usr/lib/system/libremovefile.dylib
    0x7fff89114000 -     0x7fff89118fff  libmathCommon.A.dylib (2026.0.0 - compatibility 1.0.0) <FF83AFF7-42B2-306E-
90AF-D539C51A4542> /usr/lib/system/libmathCommon.A.dylib
    0x7fff89119000 -     0x7fff8911dfff  libdyld.dylib (195.5.0 - compatibility 1.0.0) <380C3F44-0CA7-3514-8080-
46D1C9DF4FCD> /usr/lib/system/libdyld.dylib
    0x7fff89740000 -     0x7fff89741ff7  libsystem_sandbox.dylib (??? - ???) <96D38E74-F18F-3CCB-A20B-E8E3ADC4E166>
/usr/lib/system/libsystem_sandbox.dylib
    0x7fff8a0ef000 -     0x7fff8a0f5fff  libmacho.dylib (800.0.0 - compatibility 1.0.0) <165514D7-1BFA-38EF-A151-
676DCD21FB64> /usr/lib/system/libmacho.dylib
    0x7fff8a0f6000 -     0x7fff8a116fff  libsystem_kernel.dylib (1699.26.8 - compatibility 1.0.0) <1DDC0B0F-DB2A-34D6-
895D-E5B2B5618946> /usr/lib/system/libsystem_kernel.dylib
    0x7fff8a2ac000 -     0x7fff8a2b4fff  libsystem_dnssd.dylib (??? - ???) <D9BB1F87-A42B-3CBC-9DC2-FC07FCEF0016>
/usr/lib/system/libsystem_dnssd.dylib
    0x7fff8ae26000 -     0x7fff8ae61fff  libsystem_info.dylib (??? - ???) <35F90252-2AE1-32C5-8D34-782C614D9639>
/usr/lib/system/libsystem_info.dylib
    0x7fff8b248000 -     0x7fff8b24afff  libquarantine.dylib (36.6.0 - compatibility 1.0.0) <0EBF714B-4B69-3E1F-9A7D-
6BBC2AACB310> /usr/lib/system/libquarantine.dylib
    0x7fff8b3b4000 -     0x7fff8b3b4ff7  libkeymgr.dylib (23.0.0 - compatibility 1.0.0) <61EFED6A-A407-301E-B454-
CD18314F0075> /usr/lib/system/libkeymgr.dylib
    0x7fff8b3dd000 -     0x7fff8b3e2fff  libcompiler_rt.dylib (6.0.0 - compatibility 1.0.0) <98ECD5F6-E85C-32A5-98CD-
8911230CB66A> /usr/lib/system/libcompiler_rt.dylib
    0x7fff8bd1a000 -     0x7fff8bd1bfff  libdnsinfo.dylib (395.11.0 - compatibility 1.0.0) <853BAAA5-270F-3FDC-B025-
D448DB72E1C3> /usr/lib/system/libdnsinfo.dylib
    0x7fff8c528000 -     0x7fff8c52dff7  libsystem_network.dylib (??? - ???) <5DE7024E-1D2D-34A2-80F4-08326331A75B>
/usr/lib/system/libsystem_network.dylib
    0x7fff8cfa3000 -     0x7fff8cfadff7  liblaunch.dylib (392.38.0 - compatibility 1.0.0) <6ECB7F19-B384-32C1-8652-
2463C1CF4815> /usr/lib/system/liblaunch.dylib
    0x7fff8fe02000 -     0x7fff8fe09fff  libcopyfile.dylib (85.1.0 - compatibility 1.0.0) <0AB51EE2-E914-358C-AC19-
47BC024BDAE7> /usr/lib/system/libcopyfile.dylib
    0x7fff8fe4b000 -     0x7fff8fe8dff7  libcommonCrypto.dylib (55010.0.0 - compatibility 1.0.0) <BB770C22-8C57-365A-
8716-4A3C36AE7BFB> /usr/lib/system/libcommonCrypto.dylib
    0x7fff90c0f000 -     0x7fff90c18fff  libsystem_notify.dylib (80.1.0 - compatibility 1.0.0) <A4D651E3-D1C6-3934-
AD49-7A104FD14596> /usr/lib/system/libsystem_notify.dylib
    0x7fff91376000 -     0x7fff913a3fe7  libSystem.B.dylib (159.1.0 - compatibility 1.0.0) <7BEBB139-50BB-3112-947A-
F4AA168F991C> /usr/lib/libSystem.B.dylib
    0x7fff91489000 -     0x7fff9148fff7  libunwind.dylib (30.0.0 - compatibility 1.0.0) <1E9C6C8C-CBE8-3F4B-A5B5-
E03E3AB53231> /usr/lib/system/libunwind.dylib
    0x7fff91a22000 -     0x7fff91a27fff  libcache.dylib (47.0.0 - compatibility 1.0.0) <1571C3AB-BCB2-38CD-B3B2-
C5FC3F927C6A> /usr/lib/system/libcache.dylib
```

```
External Modification Summary:
  Calls made by other processes targeting this process:
    task_for_pid: 0
    thread_create: 0
    thread_set_state: 0
  Calls made by this process:
    task_for_pid: 0
    thread_create: 0
    thread_set_state: 0
  Calls made by all processes on this machine:
    task_for_pid: 3632
    thread_create: 0
    thread_set_state: 0

VM Region Summary:
ReadOnly portion of Libraries: Total=50.2M resident=50.2M(100%) swapped_out_or_unallocated=8K(0%)
Writable regions: Total=38.9M written=22.2M(57%) resident=42.5M(109%) swapped_out=196K(0%)
unallocated=16777216.0T(45221404475392%)

REGION TYPE                 VIRTUAL
===========                 =======
MALLOC                       1220K
Stack                        66.6M
__DATA                        464K
__LINKEDIT                   47.7M
__TEXT                       2484K
shared memory                  12K
===========                 =======
TOTAL                       118.4M
```

2.   Load a core dump core.1995 and App2 executable:

$ lldb -c ~/Documents/AMCDA-Dumps/core.1995 -f ~/Documents/AMCDA-Dumps/Apps/App2/Build/Products/Release/App2

error: core.1995 is a corrupt mach-o file: load command 45 LC_SEGMENT_64 has a fileoff + filesize (0x160b7000) that extends beyond the end of the file (0x160b5000), the segment will be truncated
Core file '/Users/DumpAnalysis/Documents/AMCDA-Dumps/core.1995' (x86_64) was loaded.
Process 0 stopped
* thread #1: tid = 0x0000, 0x00007fff8a10c4de libsystem_kernel.dylib`__bsdthread_create + 10,
stop reason = signal SIGSTOP
    frame #0: 0x00007fff8a10c4de libsystem_kernel.dylib`__bsdthread_create + 10
libsystem_kernel.dylib`__bsdthread_create + 10:
-> 0x7fff8a10c4de: jae   0x7fff8a10c4e5   ; __bsdthread_create + 17
   0x7fff8a10c4e0: jmpq   0x7fff8a10dffc   ; cerror
   0x7fff8a10c4e5: ret
   0x7fff8a10c4e6: nop
  thread #2: tid = 0x0001, 0x00007fff8a10ce42 libsystem_kernel.dylib`__semwait_signal + 10,
stop reason = signal SIGSTOP
    frame #0: 0x00007fff8a10ce42 libsystem_kernel.dylib`__semwait_signal + 10
libsystem_kernel.dylib`__semwait_signal + 10:
-> 0x7fff8a10ce42: jae   0x7fff8a10ce49   ; __semwait_signal + 17
   0x7fff8a10ce44: jmpq   0x7fff8a10dffc   ; cerror
   0x7fff8a10ce49: ret
   0x7fff8a10ce4a: nop
```
```

```
  thread #3: tid = 0x0002, 0x000000010fe0a9c0 App2`procA + 16, stop reason = signal SIGSTOP
    frame #0: 0x000000010fe0a9c0 App2`procA + 16
App2`procA + 16:
-> 0x10fe0a9c0:  movl    $1, (%rax)
   0x10fe0a9c6:  popq    %rbp
   0x10fe0a9c7:  ret
   0x10fe0a9c8:  nopl    (%rax,%rax)
  thread #4: tid = 0x0003, 0x00007fff8a10ce42 libsystem_kernel.dylib`__semwait_signal + 10,
stop reason = signal SIGSTOP
    frame #0: 0x00007fff8a10ce42 libsystem_kernel.dylib`__semwait_signal + 10
libsystem_kernel.dylib`__semwait_signal + 10:
-> 0x7fff8a10ce42:  jae     0x7fff8a10ce49               ; __semwait_signal + 17
   0x7fff8a10ce44:  jmpq    0x7fff8a10dffc               ; cerror
   0x7fff8a10ce49:  ret
   0x7fff8a10ce4a:  nop
  thread #5: tid = 0x0004, 0x0000000000000000, stop reason = signal SIGSTOP
    frame #0: 0x0000000000000000
error: core file does not contain 0x0
  thread #6: tid = 0x0005, 0x00007fff84dbbb68 libsystem_c.dylib`thread_start, stop reason =
signal SIGSTOP
    frame #0: 0x00007fff84dbbb68 libsystem_c.dylib`thread_start
libsystem_c.dylib`thread_start:
-> 0x7fff84dbbb68:  pushq   %rbp
   0x7fff84dbbb69:  movq    %rsp, %rbp
   0x7fff84dbbb6c:  subq    $24, %rsp
   0x7fff84dbbb70:  callq   0x7fff84db8770               ; _pthread_start
```

2.   Switch to the problem thread identified in the diagnostic report (core thread 2, thread #3):

```
(lldb) thread select 3
* thread #3: tid = 0x0002, 0x000000010fe0a9c0 App2`procA + 16, stop reason = signal SIGSTOP
    frame #0: 0x000000010fe0a9c0 App2`procA + 16
App2`procA + 16:
-> 0x10fe0a9c0:  movl    $1, (%rax)
   0x10fe0a9c6:  popq    %rbp
   0x10fe0a9c7:  ret
   0x10fe0a9c8:  nopl    (%rax,%rax)

(lldb) bt
* thread #3: tid = 0x0002, 0x000000010fe0a9c0 App2`procA + 16, stop reason = signal SIGSTOP
    frame #0: 0x000000010fe0a9c0 App2`procA + 16
    frame #1: 0x000000010fe0aa59 App2`bar_two + 9
    frame #2: 0x000000010fe0aa69 App2`foo_two + 9
    frame #3: 0x000000010fe0aa81 App2`thread_two + 17
    frame #4: 0x00007fff84db88bf libsystem_c.dylib`_pthread_start + 335
    frame #5: 0x00007fff84dbbb75 libsystem_c.dylib`thread_start + 13
```

3.   Disassemble the problem instruction and check CPU register(s) details (NULL Data Pointer):

```
(lldb) x/i 0x000000010fe0a9c0
0x10fe0a9c0:  c7 00 01 00 00 00  movl    $1, (%rax)

(lldb) re r rax
     rax = 0x0000000000000000
```

```
(lldb) x $rax
error: core file does not contain 0x0
```

4.   List all thread stack traces and identify other anomalies:

```
(lldb) thread backtrace all
  thread #1: tid = 0x0000, 0x00007fff8a10c4de libsystem_kernel.dylib`__bsdthread_create + 10,
stop reason = signal SIGSTOP
    frame #0: 0x00007fff8a10c4de libsystem_kernel.dylib`__bsdthread_create + 10
    frame #1: 0x00007fff84dbae9d libsystem_c.dylib`pthread_create + 924
    frame #2: 0x000000010fe0ac66 App2`main + 182
    frame #3: 0x000000010fe0a9a4 App2`start + 52

  thread #2: tid = 0x0001, 0x00007fff8a10ce42 libsystem_kernel.dylib`__semwait_signal + 10,
stop reason = signal SIGSTOP
    frame #0: 0x00007fff8a10ce42 libsystem_kernel.dylib`__semwait_signal + 10
    frame #1: 0x00007fff84d6edea libsystem_c.dylib`nanosleep + 164
    frame #2: 0x00007fff84d6ec2c libsystem_c.dylib`sleep + 61
    frame #3: 0x00007fff84d6ec08 libsystem_c.dylib`sleep + 25
    frame #4: 0x000000010fe0aa02 App2`bar_one + 18
    frame #5: 0x000000010fe0aa19 App2`foo_one + 9
    frame #6: 0x000000010fe0aa31 App2`thread_one + 17
    frame #7: 0x00007fff84db88bf libsystem_c.dylib`_pthread_start + 335
    frame #8: 0x00007fff84dbbb75 libsystem_c.dylib`thread_start + 13

* thread #3: tid = 0x0002, 0x000000010fe0a9c0 App2`procA + 16, stop reason = signal SIGSTOP
    frame #0: 0x000000010fe0a9c0 App2`procA + 16
    frame #1: 0x000000010fe0aa59 App2`bar_two + 9
    frame #2: 0x000000010fe0aa69 App2`foo_two + 9
    frame #3: 0x000000010fe0aa81 App2`thread_two + 17
    frame #4: 0x00007fff84db88bf libsystem_c.dylib`_pthread_start + 335
    frame #5: 0x00007fff84dbbb75 libsystem_c.dylib`thread_start + 13

  thread #4: tid = 0x0003, 0x00007fff8a10ce42 libsystem_kernel.dylib`__semwait_signal + 10,
stop reason = signal SIGSTOP
    frame #0: 0x00007fff8a10ce42 libsystem_kernel.dylib`__semwait_signal + 10
    frame #1: 0x00007fff84d6edea libsystem_c.dylib`nanosleep + 164
    frame #2: 0x00007fff84d6ec2c libsystem_c.dylib`sleep + 61
    frame #3: 0x00007fff84d6ec08 libsystem_c.dylib`sleep + 25
    frame #4: 0x000000010fe0aab2 App2`bar_three + 18
    frame #5: 0x000000010fe0aac9 App2`foo_three + 9
    frame #6: 0x000000010fe0aae1 App2`thread_three + 17
    frame #7: 0x00007fff84db88bf libsystem_c.dylib`_pthread_start + 335
    frame #8: 0x00007fff84dbbb75 libsystem_c.dylib`thread_start + 13

  thread #5: tid = 0x0004, 0x0000000000000000, stop reason = signal SIGSTOP
    frame #0: 0x0000000000000000
    frame #1: 0x000000010fe0ab09 App2`bar_four + 9
    frame #2: 0x000000010fe0ab19 App2`foo_four + 9
    frame #3: 0x000000010fe0ab31 App2`thread_four + 17
    frame #4: 0x00007fff84db88bf libsystem_c.dylib`_pthread_start + 335
    frame #5: 0x00007fff84dbbb75 libsystem_c.dylib`thread_start + 13

  thread #6: tid = 0x0005, 0x00007fff84dbbb68 libsystem_c.dylib`thread_start, stop reason =
signal SIGSTOP
    frame #0: 0x00007fff84dbbb68 libsystem_c.dylib`thread_start
```

5.   Check the CPU instruction and the stack trace pointer for thread #6 (core thread 5) for any signs of stack overflow:

```
(lldb) thread select 6
* thread #6: tid = 0x0005, 0x00007fff84dbbb68 libsystem_c.dylib`thread_start, stop reason =
signal SIGSTOP
    frame #0: 0x00007fff84dbbb68 libsystem_c.dylib`thread_start
libsystem_c.dylib`thread_start:
-> 0x7fff84dbbb68:  pushq  %rbp
   0x7fff84dbbb69:  movq   %rsp, %rbp
   0x7fff84dbbb6c:  subq   $24, %rsp
   0x7fff84dbbb70:  callq  0x7fff84db8770             ; _pthread_start

(lldb) x/xg $rsp
0x110209f80: 0x0000000000000000

(lldb) x/xg $rsp-8
0x110209f78: 0x0000000000000000

(lldb) x/xg $rsp-0x10
0x110209f70: 0x0000000000000000
```

Note: Memory is readable so we don't expect a stack overflow here. Perhaps the thread was just caught during its start.

6.   Check the CPU instruction and a dereferenced pointer for thread #5 (core thread 5) for any signs of NULL pointers:

```
(lldb) thread select 5
* thread #5: tid = 0x0004, 0x0000000000000000, stop reason = signal SIGSTOP
    frame #0: 0x0000000000000000
error: core file does not contain 0x0

(lldb) bt
* thread #5: tid = 0x0004, 0x0000000000000000, stop reason = signal SIGSTOP
    frame #0: 0x0000000000000000
    frame #1: 0x000000010fe0ab09 App2`bar_four + 9
    frame #2: 0x000000010fe0ab19 App2`foo_four + 9
    frame #3: 0x000000010fe0ab31 App2`thread_four + 17
    frame #4: 0x00007fff84db88bf libsystem_c.dylib`_pthread_start + 335
    frame #5: 0x00007fff84dbbb75 libsystem_c.dylib`thread_start + 13

(lldb) di -a 0x000000010fe0a9e5
App2`procB:
    0x10fe0a9d0:  pushq  %rbp
    0x10fe0a9d1:  movq   %rsp, %rbp
    0x10fe0a9d4:  subq   $16, %rsp
    0x10fe0a9d8:  movq   $0, -8(%rbp)
    0x10fe0a9e0:  movb   $0, %al
    0x10fe0a9e2:  callq  *-8(%rbp)
    0x10fe0a9e5:  addq   $16, %rsp
    0x10fe0a9e9:  popq   %rbp
    0x10fe0a9ea:  ret
    0x10fe0a9eb:  nopl   (%rax,%rax)

(lldb) x/xg $rbp-8
0x110186ec8: 0x0000000000000000
```

7.   Switch to the thread #1 (core thread 0) and verify that main function was engaged in thread creation (this should correlate with thread #6 caught in being created):

```
(lldb) thread select 1
* thread #1: tid = 0x0000, 0x00007fff8a10c4de libsystem_kernel.dylib`__bsdthread_create + 10,
stop reason = signal SIGSTOP
    frame #0: 0x00007fff8a10c4de libsystem_kernel.dylib`__bsdthread_create + 10
libsystem_kernel.dylib`__bsdthread_create + 10:
-> 0x7fff8a10c4de:  jae     0x7fff8a10c4e5              ; __bsdthread_create + 17
   0x7fff8a10c4e0:  jmpq    0x7fff8a10dffc             ; cerror
   0x7fff8a10c4e5:  ret
   0x7fff8a10c4e6:  nop


(lldb) bt
* thread #1: tid = 0x0000, 0x00007fff8a10c4de libsystem_kernel.dylib`__bsdthread_create + 10,
stop reason = signal SIGSTOP
    frame #0: 0x00007fff8a10c4de libsystem_kernel.dylib`__bsdthread_create + 10
    frame #1: 0x00007fff84dbae9d libsystem_c.dylib`pthread_create + 924
    frame #2: 0x000000010fe0ac66 App2`main + 182
    frame #3: 0x000000010fe0a9a4 App2`start + 52


(lldb) di -n main
App2`main:
   0x10fe0abb0:  pushq    %rbp
   0x10fe0abb1:  movq     %rsp, %rbp
   0x10fe0abb4:  subq     $80, %rsp
   0x10fe0abb8:  leaq     -24(%rbp), %rax
   0x10fe0abbc:  movabsq  $0, %rcx
   0x10fe0abc6:  leaq     -429(%rip), %rdx           ; thread_one
   0x10fe0abcd:  movl     $0, -4(%rbp)
   0x10fe0abd4:  movl     %edi, -8(%rbp)
   0x10fe0abd7:  movq     %rsi, -16(%rbp)
   0x10fe0abdb:  movq     %rax, %rdi
   0x10fe0abde:  movq     %rcx, %rsi
   0x10fe0abe1:  callq    0x10fe0ac8a                ; symbol stub for: pthread_create
   0x10fe0abe6:  leaq     -32(%rbp), %rdi
   0x10fe0abea:  movabsq  $0, %rcx
   0x10fe0abf4:  leaq     -395(%rip), %rdx           ; thread_two
   0x10fe0abfb:  movq     %rcx, %rsi
   0x10fe0abfe:  movl     %eax, -60(%rbp)
   0x10fe0ac01:  callq    0x10fe0ac8a                ; symbol stub for: pthread_create
   0x10fe0ac06:  leaq     -40(%rbp), %rdi
   0x10fe0ac0a:  movabsq  $0, %rcx
   0x10fe0ac14:  leaq     -331(%rip), %rdx           ; thread_three
   0x10fe0ac1b:  movq     %rcx, %rsi
   0x10fe0ac1e:  movl     %eax, -64(%rbp)
   0x10fe0ac21:  callq    0x10fe0ac8a                ; symbol stub for: pthread_create
   0x10fe0ac26:  leaq     -48(%rbp), %rdi
   0x10fe0ac2a:  movabsq  $0, %rcx
   0x10fe0ac34:  leaq     -283(%rip), %rdx           ; thread_four
   0x10fe0ac3b:  movq     %rcx, %rsi
   0x10fe0ac3e:  movl     %eax, -68(%rbp)
   0x10fe0ac41:  callq    0x10fe0ac8a                ; symbol stub for: pthread_create
   0x10fe0ac46:  leaq     -56(%rbp), %rdi
   0x10fe0ac4a:  movabsq  $0, %rcx
   0x10fe0ac54:  leaq     -219(%rip), %rdx           ; thread_five
   0x10fe0ac5b:  movq     %rcx, %rsi
   0x10fe0ac5e:  movl     %eax, -72(%rbp)
   0x10fe0ac61:  callq    0x10fe0ac8a                ; symbol stub for: pthread_create
   0x10fe0ac66:  movl     $3, %edi
```

```
0x10fe0ac6b:  movl   %eax, -76(%rbp)
0x10fe0ac6e:  callq  0x10fe0ac90                    ; symbol stub for: sleep
0x10fe0ac73:  movl   $0, %edi
0x10fe0ac78:  movl   %eax, -80(%rbp)
0x10fe0ac7b:  movl   %edi, %eax
0x10fe0ac7d:  addq   $80, %rsp
0x10fe0ac81:  popq   %rbp
0x10fe0ac82:  ret
```

Exercise A3 (GDB)

- **Goal:** Learn how to identify spiking threads

- **Patterns:** Spiking Thread

- \AMCDA-Dumps\Exercise-A3-GDB.pdf

Exercise A3 (GDB)

Goal: Learn how to identify spiking threads

Patterns: Spiking Thread

1.   Load a core dump core.2374 and App3 executable:

```
$ gdb -c ~/Documents/AMCDA-Dumps/core.2374 -e ~/Documents/AMCDA-
Dumps/Apps/App3/Build/Products/Release/App3
GNU gdb 6.3.50-20050815 (Apple version gdb-1820) (Sat Jun 16 02:40:11 UTC 2012)
Copyright 2004 Free Software Foundation, Inc.
GDB is free software, covered by the GNU General Public License, and you are
welcome to change it and/or distribute copies of it under certain conditions.
Type "show copying" to see the conditions.
There is absolutely no warranty for GDB.  Type "show warranty" for details.
This GDB was configured as "x86_64-apple-darwin".
Reading symbols for shared libraries . done
Reading symbols for shared libraries ........................ done
#0  0x00007fff8a10ce42 in __semwait_signal ()
```

2.   List all threads:

```
(gdb) info threads
  6 0x00007fff913842df in sqrt$fenv_access_off ()
  5 0x00007fff8a10ce42 in __semwait_signal ()
  4 0x00007fff8a10ce42 in __semwait_signal ()
  3 0x00007fff8a10ce42 in __semwait_signal ()
  2 0x00007fff8a10ce42 in __semwait_signal ()
* 1 0x00007fff8a10ce42 in __semwait_signal ()
```

3.   Switch to the problem thread #6:

```
(gdb) thread 6
[Switching to thread 6 (core thread 5)]
0x00007fff913842df in sqrt$fenv_access_off ()

(gdb) bt
#0  0x00007fff913842df in sqrt$fenv_access_off ()
#1  0x000000010a66f9bf in procB ()
#2  0x000000010a66fb49 in bar_five ()
#3  0x000000010a66fb59 in foo_five ()
#4  0x000000010a66fb71 in thread_five ()
#5  0x00007fff84db88bf in _pthread_start ()
#6  0x00007fff84dbbb75 in thread_start ()
```

4.   Disassemble the problem instruction and check if it is normal:

(gdb) **x/i 0x00007fff913842df**
0x7fff913842df <sqrt$fenv_access_off+15>:   pop   %rbp

5.   Identify exception type and problem thread in diagnostic report App3_2374.crash:


```
Process:         App3 [2374]
Path:            /Users/USER/Documents/*/App3
Identifier:      App3
Version:         ??? (???)
Code Type:       X86-64 (Native)
Parent Process:  bash [1549]

Date/Time:       2012-07-24 20:16:21.424 +0100
OS Version:      Mac OS X 10.7.4 (11E53)
Report Version:  9

Crashed Thread:  0  Dispatch queue: com.apple.main-thread

Exception Type:  EXC_CRASH (SIGABRT)
Exception Codes: 0x0000000000000000, 0x0000000000000000

Thread 0 Crashed:: Dispatch queue: com.apple.main-thread
0   libsystem_kernel.dylib          0x00007fff8a10ce42 __semwait_signal + 10
1   libsystem_c.dylib               0x00007fff84d6edea nanosleep + 164
2   libsystem_c.dylib               0x00007fff84d6ec2c sleep + 61
3   libsystem_c.dylib               0x00007fff84d6ec08 sleep + 25
4   App3                            0x000000010a66fc53 main + 195
5   App3                            0x000000010a66f974 start + 52

Thread 1:
0   libsystem_kernel.dylib          0x00007fff8a10ce42 __semwait_signal + 10
1   libsystem_c.dylib               0x00007fff84d6edea nanosleep + 164
2   libsystem_c.dylib               0x00007fff84d6ec2c sleep + 61
3   libsystem_c.dylib               0x00007fff84d6ec08 sleep + 25
4   App3                            0x000000010a66f9e2 bar_one + 18
5   App3                            0x000000010a66f9f9 foo_one + 9
6   App3                            0x000000010a66fa11 thread_one + 17
7   libsystem_c.dylib               0x00007fff84db88bf _pthread_start + 335
8   libsystem_c.dylib               0x00007fff84dbbb75 thread_start + 13

Thread 2:
0   libsystem_kernel.dylib          0x00007fff8a10ce42 __semwait_signal + 10
1   libsystem_c.dylib               0x00007fff84d6edea nanosleep + 164
2   libsystem_c.dylib               0x00007fff84d6ec2c sleep + 61
3   libsystem_c.dylib               0x00007fff84d6ec08 sleep + 25
4   App3                            0x000000010a66fa42 bar_two + 18
5   App3                            0x000000010a66fa59 foo_two + 9
6   App3                            0x000000010a66fa71 thread_two + 17
7   libsystem_c.dylib               0x00007fff84db88bf _pthread_start + 335
8   libsystem_c.dylib               0x00007fff84dbbb75 thread_start + 13

Thread 3:
0   libsystem_kernel.dylib          0x00007fff8a10ce42 __semwait_signal + 10
1   libsystem_c.dylib               0x00007fff84d6edea nanosleep + 164
2   libsystem_c.dylib               0x00007fff84d6ec2c sleep + 61
3   App3                            0x000000010a66f992 procA + 18
4   App3                            0x000000010a66fa99 bar_three + 9
5   App3                            0x000000010a66faa9 foo_three + 9
6   App3                            0x000000010a66fac1 thread_three + 17
7   libsystem_c.dylib               0x00007fff84db88bf _pthread_start + 335
8   libsystem_c.dylib               0x00007fff84dbbb75 thread_start + 13
```

```
Thread 4:
0    libsystem_kernel.dylib           0x00007fff8a10ce42 __semwait_signal + 10
1    libsystem_c.dylib                0x00007fff84d6edea nanosleep + 164
2    libsystem_c.dylib                0x00007fff84d6ec2c sleep + 61
3    libsystem_c.dylib                0x00007fff84d6ec08 sleep + 25
4    App3                             0x000000010a66faf2 bar_four + 18
5    App3                             0x000000010a66fb09 foo_four + 9
6    App3                             0x000000010a66fb21 thread_four + 17
7    libsystem_c.dylib                0x00007fff84db88bf _pthread_start + 335
8    libsystem_c.dylib                0x00007fff84dbbb75 thread_start + 13

Thread 5:
0    libSystem.B.dylib                0x00007fff913842df sqrt + 15
1    App3                             0x000000010a66f9bf procB + 31
2    App3                             0x000000010a66fb49 bar_five + 9
3    App3                             0x000000010a66fb59 foo_five + 9
4    App3                             0x000000010a66fb71 thread_five + 17
5    libsystem_c.dylib                0x00007fff84db88bf _pthread_start + 335
6    libsystem_c.dylib                0x00007fff84dbbb75 thread_start + 13

Thread 0 crashed with X86 Thread State (64-bit):
  rax: 0x0000000000000004  rbx: 0x00007fff6a26ea48  rcx: 0x00007fff6a26ea08  rdx: 0x0000000000000001
  rdi: 0x0000000000000c03  rsi: 0x0000000000000000  rbp: 0x00007fff6a26ea30  rsp: 0x00007fff6a26ea08
   r8: 0x000000007fffffff   r9: 0x0000000000000000  r10: 0x0000000000000001  r11: 0xffffff80002da8d0
  r12: 0x0000000000000000  r13: 0x0000000000000000  r14: 0x00007fff6a26ea58  r15: 0x0000000000000000
  rip: 0x00007fff8a10ce42  rfl: 0x0000000000000247  cr2: 0x000000010aa8e880
Logical CPU: 0

Binary Images:
       0x10a66f000 -        0x10a66fff7 +App3 (??? - ???) <D5B8B74D-BE02-3529-BE03-A2E4AFD43E57>
/Users/USER/Documents/*/App3
    0x7fff6a26f000 -     0x7fff6a2a3baf  dyld (195.6 - ???) <0CD1B35B-A28F-32DA-B72E-452EAD609613> /usr/lib/dyld
    0x7fff849f2000 -     0x7fff84a0ffff  libxpc.dylib (77.19.0 - compatibility 1.0.0) <9F57891B-D7EF-3050-BEDD-
21E7C6668248> /usr/lib/system/libxpc.dylib
    0x7fff84d68000 -     0x7fff84d69ff7  libsystem_blocks.dylib (53.0.0 - compatibility 1.0.0) <8BCA214A-8992-34B2-
A8B9-B74DEACA1869> /usr/lib/system/libsystem_blocks.dylib
    0x7fff84d6a000 -     0x7fff84e47fef  libsystem_c.dylib (763.13.0 - compatibility 1.0.0) <41B43515-2806-3FBC-ACF1-
A16F35B7E290> /usr/lib/system/libsystem_c.dylib
    0x7fff85022000 -     0x7fff85030fff  libdispatch.dylib (187.9.0 - compatibility 1.0.0) <1D5BE322-A9B9-3BCE-8FAC-
076FB07CF54A> /usr/lib/system/libdispatch.dylib
    0x7fff855f0000 -     0x7fff855f1fff  libunc.dylib (24.0.0 - compatibility 1.0.0) <337960EE-0A85-3DD0-A760-
7134CF4C0AFF> /usr/lib/system/libunc.dylib
    0x7fff85ae3000 -     0x7fff85ae4ff7  libremovefile.dylib (21.1.0 - compatibility 1.0.0) <739E6C83-AA52-3C6C-A680-
B37FE2888A04> /usr/lib/system/libremovefile.dylib
    0x7fff89114000 -     0x7fff89118fff  libmathCommon.A.dylib (2026.0.0 - compatibility 1.0.0) <FF83AFF7-42B2-306E-
90AF-D539C51A4542> /usr/lib/system/libmathCommon.A.dylib
    0x7fff89119000 -     0x7fff8911dfff  libdyld.dylib (195.5.0 - compatibility 1.0.0) <380C3F44-0CA7-3514-8080-
46D1C9DF4FCD> /usr/lib/system/libdyld.dylib
    0x7fff89740000 -     0x7fff89741ff7  libsystem_sandbox.dylib (??? - ???) <96D38E74-F18F-3CCB-A20B-E8E3ADC4E166>
/usr/lib/system/libsystem_sandbox.dylib
    0x7fff8a0ef000 -     0x7fff8a0f5fff  libmacho.dylib (800.0.0 - compatibility 1.0.0) <165514D7-1BFA-38EF-A151-
676DCD21FB64> /usr/lib/system/libmacho.dylib
    0x7fff8a0f6000 -     0x7fff8a116fff  libsystem_kernel.dylib (1699.26.8 - compatibility 1.0.0) <1DDC0B0F-DB2A-34D6-
895D-E5B2B5618946> /usr/lib/system/libsystem_kernel.dylib
    0x7fff8a2ac000 -     0x7fff8a2b4fff  libsystem_dnssd.dylib (??? - ???) <D9BB1F87-A42B-3CBC-9DC2-FC07FCEF0016>
/usr/lib/system/libsystem_dnssd.dylib
    0x7fff8ae26000 -     0x7fff8ae61fff  libsystem_info.dylib (??? - ???) <35F90252-2AE1-32C5-8D34-782C614D9639>
/usr/lib/system/libsystem_info.dylib
    0x7fff8b248000 -     0x7fff8b24afff  libquarantine.dylib (36.6.0 - compatibility 1.0.0) <0EBF714B-4B69-3E1F-9A7D-
6BBC2AACB310> /usr/lib/system/libquarantine.dylib
    0x7fff8b3b4000 -     0x7fff8b3b4fff  libkeymgr.dylib (23.0.0 - compatibility 1.0.0) <61EFED6A-A407-301E-B454-
CD18314F0075> /usr/lib/system/libkeymgr.dylib
    0x7fff8b3dd000 -     0x7fff8b3e2fff  libcompiler_rt.dylib (6.0.0 - compatibility 1.0.0) <98ECD5F6-E85C-32A5-98CD-
8911230CB66A> /usr/lib/system/libcompiler_rt.dylib
    0x7fff8bd1a000 -     0x7fff8bd1bfff  libdnsinfo.dylib (395.11.0 - compatibility 1.0.0) <853BAAA5-270F-3FDC-B025-
D448DB72E1C3> /usr/lib/system/libdnsinfo.dylib
    0x7fff8c528000 -     0x7fff8c52dff7  libsystem_network.dylib (??? - ???) <5DE7024E-1D2D-34A2-80F4-08326331A75B>
/usr/lib/system/libsystem_network.dylib
    0x7fff8cfa3000 -     0x7fff8cfadff7  liblaunch.dylib (392.38.0 - compatibility 1.0.0) <6ECB7F19-B384-32C1-8652-
2463C1CF4815> /usr/lib/system/liblaunch.dylib
    0x7fff8fe02000 -     0x7fff8fe09fff  libcopyfile.dylib (85.1.0 - compatibility 1.0.0) <0AB51EE2-E914-358C-AC19-
47BC024BDAE7> /usr/lib/system/libcopyfile.dylib
    0x7fff8fe4b000 -     0x7fff8fe8dff7  libcommonCrypto.dylib (55010.0.0 - compatibility 1.0.0) <BB770C22-8C57-365A-
8716-4A3C36AE7BFB> /usr/lib/system/libcommonCrypto.dylib
    0x7fff90c0f000 -     0x7fff90c18ff7  libsystem_notify.dylib (80.1.0 - compatibility 1.0.0) <A4D651E3-D1C6-3934-
AD49-7A104FD14596> /usr/lib/system/libsystem_notify.dylib
```

```
    0x7fff91376000 -     0x7fff913a3fe7  libSystem.B.dylib (159.1.0 - compatibility 1.0.0) <7BEBB139-50BB-3112-947A-
F4AA168F991C> /usr/lib/libSystem.B.dylib
    0x7fff91489000 -     0x7fff9148fff7  libunwind.dylib (30.0.0 - compatibility 1.0.0) <1E9C6C8C-CBE8-3F4B-A5B5-
E03E3AB53231> /usr/lib/system/libunwind.dylib
    0x7fff91a22000 -     0x7fff91a27fff  libcache.dylib (47.0.0 - compatibility 1.0.0) <1571C3AB-BCB2-38CD-B3B2-
C5FC3F927C6A> /usr/lib/system/libcache.dylib

External Modification Summary:
  Calls made by other processes targeting this process:
    task_for_pid: 2
    thread_create: 0
    thread_set_state: 0
  Calls made by this process:
    task_for_pid: 0
    thread_create: 0
    thread_set_state: 0
  Calls made by all processes on this machine:
    task_for_pid: 4321
    thread_create: 0
    thread_set_state: 0

VM Region Summary:
ReadOnly portion of Libraries: Total=50.2M resident=50.2M(100%) swapped_out_or_unallocated=0K(0%)
Writable regions: Total=38.9M written=10.8M(28%) resident=42.6M(110%) swapped_out=0K(0%)
unallocated=16777216.0T(45221404475392%)

REGION TYPE                 VIRTUAL
===========                 =======
MALLOC                      1220K
Stack                       66.6M
__DATA                      464K
__LINKEDIT                  47.7M
__TEXT                      2484K
shared memory               12K
===========                 =======
TOTAL                       118.4M
```

Exercise A3 (LLDB)

- **Goal:** Learn how to identify spiking threads

- **Patterns:** Spiking Thread

- \AMCDA-Dumps\Exercise-A3-LLDB.pdf

Exercise A3 (LLDB)

Goal: Learn how to identify spiking threads

Patterns: Spiking Thread

1.   Load a core dump core.2374 and App3 executable:

```
$ lldb -c ~/Documents/AMCDA-Dumps/core.2374 -f ~/Documents/AMCDA-
Dumps/Apps/App3/Build/Products/Release/App3
error: core.2374 is a corrupt mach-o file: load command 46 LC_SEGMENT_64 has a fileoff +
filesize (0x160b7000) that extends beyond the end of the file (0x160b5000), the segment will be
truncated
Core file '/Users/DumpAnalysis/Documents/AMCDA-Dumps/core.2374' (x86_64) was loaded.
Process 0 stopped
* thread #1: tid = 0x0000, 0x00007fff8a10ce42 libsystem_kernel.dylib`__semwait_signal + 10,
stop reason = signal SIGSTOP
    frame #0: 0x00007fff8a10ce42 libsystem_kernel.dylib`__semwait_signal + 10
libsystem_kernel.dylib`__semwait_signal + 10:
-> 0x7fff8a10ce42:  jae    0x7fff8a10ce49            ; __semwait_signal + 17
   0x7fff8a10ce44:  jmpq   0x7fff8a10dffc            ; cerror
   0x7fff8a10ce49:  ret
   0x7fff8a10ce4a:  nop
  thread #2: tid = 0x0001, 0x00007fff8a10ce42 libsystem_kernel.dylib`__semwait_signal + 10,
stop reason = signal SIGSTOP
    frame #0: 0x00007fff8a10ce42 libsystem_kernel.dylib`__semwait_signal + 10
libsystem_kernel.dylib`__semwait_signal + 10:
-> 0x7fff8a10ce42:  jae    0x7fff8a10ce49            ; __semwait_signal + 17
   0x7fff8a10ce44:  jmpq   0x7fff8a10dffc            ; cerror
   0x7fff8a10ce49:  ret
   0x7fff8a10ce4a:  nop
  thread #3: tid = 0x0002, 0x00007fff8a10ce42 libsystem_kernel.dylib`__semwait_signal + 10,
stop reason = signal SIGSTOP
    frame #0: 0x00007fff8a10ce42 libsystem_kernel.dylib`__semwait_signal + 10
libsystem_kernel.dylib`__semwait_signal + 10:
-> 0x7fff8a10ce42:  jae    0x7fff8a10ce49            ; __semwait_signal + 17
   0x7fff8a10ce44:  jmpq   0x7fff8a10dffc            ; cerror
   0x7fff8a10ce49:  ret
   0x7fff8a10ce4a:  nop
  thread #4: tid = 0x0003, 0x00007fff8a10ce42 libsystem_kernel.dylib`__semwait_signal + 10,
stop reason = signal SIGSTOP
    frame #0: 0x00007fff8a10ce42 libsystem_kernel.dylib`__semwait_signal + 10
libsystem_kernel.dylib`__semwait_signal + 10:
-> 0x7fff8a10ce42:  jae    0x7fff8a10ce49            ; __semwait_signal + 17
   0x7fff8a10ce44:  jmpq   0x7fff8a10dffc            ; cerror
   0x7fff8a10ce49:  ret
   0x7fff8a10ce4a:  nop
```

```
  thread #5: tid = 0x0004, 0x00007fff8a10ce42 libsystem_kernel.dylib`__semwait_signal + 10,
stop reason = signal SIGSTOP
    frame #0: 0x00007fff8a10ce42 libsystem_kernel.dylib`__semwait_signal + 10
libsystem_kernel.dylib`__semwait_signal + 10:
-> 0x7fff8a10ce42:  jae     0x7fff8a10ce49            ; __semwait_signal + 17
   0x7fff8a10ce44:  jmpq    0x7fff8a10dffc            ; cerror
   0x7fff8a10ce49:  ret
   0x7fff8a10ce4a:  nop
  thread #6: tid = 0x0005, 0x00007fff913842df libSystem.B.dylib`sqrt$fenv_access_off + 15, stop
reason = signal SIGSTOP
    frame #0: 0x00007fff913842df libSystem.B.dylib`sqrt$fenv_access_off + 15
libSystem.B.dylib`sqrt$fenv_access_off + 15:
-> 0x7fff913842df:  popq    %rbp
   0x7fff913842e0:  ret
   0x7fff913842e1:  nopl    (%rax)
   0x7fff913842e8:  nopl    (%rax,%rax)
```

2.   Switch to the problem thread #6:

```
(lldb) thread select 6
* thread #6: tid = 0x0005, 0x00007fff913842df libSystem.B.dylib`sqrt$fenv_access_off + 15, stop
reason = signal SIGSTOP
    frame #0: 0x00007fff913842df libSystem.B.dylib`sqrt$fenv_access_off + 15
libSystem.B.dylib`sqrt$fenv_access_off + 15:
-> 0x7fff913842df:  popq    %rbp
   0x7fff913842e0:  ret
   0x7fff913842e1:  nopl    (%rax)
   0x7fff913842e8:  nopl    (%rax,%rax)
```

```
(lldb) bt
* thread #6: tid = 0x0005, 0x00007fff913842df libSystem.B.dylib`sqrt$fenv_access_off + 15, stop
reason = signal SIGSTOP
    frame #0: 0x00007fff913842df libSystem.B.dylib`sqrt$fenv_access_off + 15
    frame #1: 0x000000010a66f9bf App3`procB + 31
    frame #2: 0x000000010a66fb49 App3`bar_five + 9
    frame #3: 0x000000010a66fb59 App3`foo_five + 9
    frame #4: 0x000000010a66fb71 App3`thread_five + 17
    frame #5: 0x00007fff84db88bf libsystem_c.dylib`_pthread_start + 335
    frame #6: 0x00007fff84dbbb75 libsystem_c.dylib`thread_start + 13
```

Note: We see that the thread was caught inside *sqrt* function. It is not in some waiting state like other threads in the same process (*__semwait_signal*). Most likely this was a running thread.

3.   Disassemble the problem instruction and check if it is normal:

```
(lldb) x/i 0x00007fff913842df
0x7fff913842df:  5d   popq   %rbp
```

Note: We see that the instuction is normal, it pops RBP register from the thread stack and doesn't involve memory reads and writes such as PUSH or MOV where we need to check for possible access violations.

4.   Identify exception type and problem thread in diagnostic report App3_2374.crash:

```
Process:        App3 [2374]
Path:           /Users/USER/Documents/*/App3
Identifier:     App3
Version:        ??? (???)
Code Type:      X86-64 (Native)
Parent Process: bash [1549]

Date/Time:      2012-07-24 20:16:21.424 +0100
OS Version:     Mac OS X 10.7.4 (11E53)
Report Version: 9

Crashed Thread:  0  Dispatch queue: com.apple.main-thread

Exception Type:  EXC_CRASH (SIGABRT)
Exception Codes: 0x0000000000000000, 0x0000000000000000

Thread 0 Crashed:: Dispatch queue: com.apple.main-thread
0   libsystem_kernel.dylib          0x00007fff8a10ce42 __semwait_signal + 10
1   libsystem_c.dylib               0x00007fff84d6edea nanosleep + 164
2   libsystem_c.dylib               0x00007fff84d6ec2c sleep + 61
3   libsystem_c.dylib               0x00007fff84d6ec08 sleep + 25
4   App3                            0x000000010a66fc53 main + 195
5   App3                            0x000000010a66f974 start + 52

Thread 1:
0   libsystem_kernel.dylib          0x00007fff8a10ce42 __semwait_signal + 10
1   libsystem_c.dylib               0x00007fff84d6edea nanosleep + 164
2   libsystem_c.dylib               0x00007fff84d6ec2c sleep + 61
3   libsystem_c.dylib               0x00007fff84d6ec08 sleep + 25
4   App3                            0x000000010a66f9e2 bar_one + 18
5   App3                            0x000000010a66f9f9 foo_one + 9
6   App3                            0x000000010a66fa11 thread_one + 17
7   libsystem_c.dylib               0x00007fff84db88bf _pthread_start + 335
8   libsystem_c.dylib               0x00007fff84dbbb75 thread_start + 13

Thread 2:
0   libsystem_kernel.dylib          0x00007fff8a10ce42 __semwait_signal + 10
1   libsystem_c.dylib               0x00007fff84d6edea nanosleep + 164
2   libsystem_c.dylib               0x00007fff84d6ec2c sleep + 61
3   libsystem_c.dylib               0x00007fff84d6ec08 sleep + 25
4   App3                            0x000000010a66fa42 bar_two + 18
5   App3                            0x000000010a66fa59 foo_two + 9
6   App3                            0x000000010a66fa71 thread_two + 17
7   libsystem_c.dylib               0x00007fff84db88bf _pthread_start + 335
8   libsystem_c.dylib               0x00007fff84dbbb75 thread_start + 13

Thread 3:
0   libsystem_kernel.dylib          0x00007fff8a10ce42 __semwait_signal + 10
1   libsystem_c.dylib               0x00007fff84d6edea nanosleep + 164
2   libsystem_c.dylib               0x00007fff84d6ec2c sleep + 61
3   App3                            0x000000010a66f992 procA + 18
4   App3                            0x000000010a66fa99 bar_three + 9
5   App3                            0x000000010a66faa9 foo_three + 9
6   App3                            0x000000010a66fac1 thread_three + 17
7   libsystem_c.dylib               0x00007fff84db88bf _pthread_start + 335
8   libsystem_c.dylib               0x00007fff84dbbb75 thread_start + 13

Thread 4:
0   libsystem_kernel.dylib          0x00007fff8a10ce42 __semwait_signal + 10
1   libsystem_c.dylib               0x00007fff84d6edea nanosleep + 164
2   libsystem_c.dylib               0x00007fff84d6ec2c sleep + 61
3   libsystem_c.dylib               0x00007fff84d6ec08 sleep + 25
4   App3                            0x000000010a66faf2 bar_four + 18
5   App3                            0x000000010a66fb09 foo_four + 9
6   App3                            0x000000010a66fb21 thread_four + 17
7   libsystem_c.dylib               0x00007fff84db88bf _pthread_start + 335
8   libsystem_c.dylib               0x00007fff84dbbb75 thread_start + 13
```

```
Thread 5:
0   libSystem.B.dylib                    0x00007fff913842df sqrt + 15
1   App3                                 0x000000010a66f9bf procB + 31
2   App3                                 0x000000010a66fb49 bar_five + 9
3   App3                                 0x000000010a66fb59 foo_five + 9
4   App3                                 0x000000010a66fb71 thread_five + 17
5   libsystem_c.dylib                    0x00007fff84db88bf _pthread_start + 335
6   libsystem_c.dylib                    0x00007fff84dbbb75 thread_start + 13

Thread 0 crashed with X86 Thread State (64-bit):
  rax: 0x0000000000000004  rbx: 0x00007fff6a26ea48  rcx: 0x00007fff6a26ea08  rdx: 0x0000000000000001
  rdi: 0x0000000000000c03  rsi: 0x0000000000000000  rbp: 0x00007fff6a26ea30  rsp: 0x00007fff6a26ea08
   r8: 0x000000007fffffff   r9: 0x0000000000000000  r10: 0x0000000000000001  r11: 0xffffff80002da8d0
  r12: 0x0000000000000000  r13: 0x0000000000000000  r14: 0x00007fff6a26ea58  r15: 0x0000000000000000
  rip: 0x00007fff8a10ce42  rfl: 0x0000000000000247  cr2: 0x000000010aa8e880
Logical CPU: 0

Binary Images:
       0x10a66f000 -        0x10a66fff7 +App3 (??? - ???) <D5B8B74D-BE02-3529-BE03-A2E4AFD43E57>
/Users/USER/Documents/*/App3
    0x7fff6a26f000 -     0x7fff6a2a3baf  dyld (195.6 - ???) <0CD1B35B-A28F-32DA-B72E-452EAD609613> /usr/lib/dyld
    0x7fff849f2000 -     0x7fff84a0ffff  libxpc.dylib (77.19.0 - compatibility 1.0.0) <9F57891B-D7EF-3050-BEDD-
21E7C6668248> /usr/lib/system/libxpc.dylib
    0x7fff84d68000 -     0x7fff84d69ff7  libsystem_blocks.dylib (53.0.0 - compatibility 1.0.0) <8BCA214A-8992-34B2-
A8B9-B74DEACA1869> /usr/lib/system/libsystem_blocks.dylib
    0x7fff84d6a000 -     0x7fff84e47fef  libsystem_c.dylib (763.13.0 - compatibility 1.0.0) <41B43515-2806-3FBC-ACF1-
A16F35B7E290> /usr/lib/system/libsystem_c.dylib
    0x7fff85022000 -     0x7fff85030fff  libdispatch.dylib (187.9.0 - compatibility 1.0.0) <1D5BE322-A9B9-3BCE-8FAC-
076FB07CF54A> /usr/lib/system/libdispatch.dylib
    0x7fff855f0000 -     0x7fff855f1fff  libunc.dylib (24.0.0 - compatibility 1.0.0) <337960EE-0A85-3DD0-A760-
7134CF4C0AFF> /usr/lib/system/libunc.dylib
    0x7fff85ae3000 -     0x7fff85ae4ff7  libremovefile.dylib (21.1.0 - compatibility 1.0.0) <739E6C83-AA52-3C6C-A680-
B37FE2888A04> /usr/lib/system/libremovefile.dylib
    0x7fff89114000 -     0x7fff89118fff  libmathCommon.A.dylib (2026.0.0 - compatibility 1.0.0) <FF83AFF7-42B2-306E-
90AF-D539C51A4542> /usr/lib/system/libmathCommon.A.dylib
    0x7fff89119000 -     0x7fff8911dfff  libdyld.dylib (195.5.0 - compatibility 1.0.0) <380C3F44-0CA7-3514-8080-
46D1C9DF4FCD> /usr/lib/system/libdyld.dylib
    0x7fff89740000 -     0x7fff89741ff7  libsystem_sandbox.dylib (??? - ???) <96D38E74-F18F-3CCB-A20B-E8E3ADC4E166>
/usr/lib/system/libsystem_sandbox.dylib
    0x7fff8a0ef000 -     0x7fff8a0f5fff  libmacho.dylib (800.0.0 - compatibility 1.0.0) <165514D7-1BFA-38EF-A151-
676DCD21FB64> /usr/lib/system/libmacho.dylib
    0x7fff8a0f6000 -     0x7fff8a116fff  libsystem_kernel.dylib (1699.26.8 - compatibility 1.0.0) <1DDC0B0F-DB2A-34D6-
895D-E5B2B5618946> /usr/lib/system/libsystem_kernel.dylib
    0x7fff8a2ac000 -     0x7fff8a2b4fff  libsystem_dnssd.dylib (??? - ???) <D9BB1F87-A42B-3CBC-9DC2-FC07FCEF0016>
/usr/lib/system/libsystem_dnssd.dylib
    0x7fff8ae26000 -     0x7fff8ae61fff  libsystem_info.dylib (??? - ???) <35F90252-2AE1-32C5-8D34-782C614D9639>
/usr/lib/system/libsystem_info.dylib
    0x7fff8b248000 -     0x7fff8b24afff  libquarantine.dylib (36.6.0 - compatibility 1.0.0) <0EBF714B-4B69-3E1F-9A7D-
6BBC2AACB310> /usr/lib/system/libquarantine.dylib
    0x7fff8b3b4000 -     0x7fff8b3b4fff  libkeymgr.dylib (23.0.0 - compatibility 1.0.0) <61EFED6A-A407-301E-B454-
CD18314F0075> /usr/lib/system/libkeymgr.dylib
    0x7fff8b3dd000 -     0x7fff8b3e2fff  libcompiler_rt.dylib (6.0.0 - compatibility 1.0.0) <98ECD5F6-E85C-32A5-98CD-
8911230CB66A> /usr/lib/system/libcompiler_rt.dylib
    0x7fff8bd1a000 -     0x7fff8bd1bfff  libdnsinfo.dylib (395.11.0 - compatibility 1.0.0) <853BAAA5-270F-3FDC-B025-
D448DB72E1C3> /usr/lib/system/libdnsinfo.dylib
    0x7fff8c528000 -     0x7fff8c52dff7  libsystem_network.dylib (??? - ???) <5DE7024E-1D2D-34A2-80F4-08326331A75B>
/usr/lib/system/libsystem_network.dylib
    0x7fff8cfa3000 -     0x7fff8cfadff7  liblaunch.dylib (392.38.0 - compatibility 1.0.0) <6ECB7F19-B384-32C1-8652-
2463C1CF4815> /usr/lib/system/liblaunch.dylib
    0x7fff8fe02000 -     0x7fff8fe09fff  libcopyfile.dylib (85.1.0 - compatibility 1.0.0) <0AB51EE2-E914-358C-AC19-
47BC024BDAE7> /usr/lib/system/libcopyfile.dylib
    0x7fff8fe4b000 -     0x7fff8fe8dff7  libcommonCrypto.dylib (55010.0.0 - compatibility 1.0.0) <BB770C22-8C57-365A-
8716-4A3C36AE7BFB> /usr/lib/system/libcommonCrypto.dylib
    0x7fff90c0f000 -     0x7fff90c18ff7  libsystem_notify.dylib (80.1.0 - compatibility 1.0.0) <A4D651E3-D1C6-3934-
AD49-7A104FD14596> /usr/lib/system/libsystem_notify.dylib
    0x7fff91376000 -     0x7fff913a3fe7  libSystem.B.dylib (159.1.0 - compatibility 1.0.0) <7BEBB139-50BB-3112-947A-
F4AA168F991C> /usr/lib/libSystem.B.dylib
    0x7fff91489000 -     0x7fff9148fff7  libunwind.dylib (30.0.0 - compatibility 1.0.0) <1E9C6C8C-CBE8-3F4B-A5B5-
E03E3AB53231> /usr/lib/system/libunwind.dylib
    0x7fff91a22000 -     0x7fff91a27fff  libcache.dylib (47.0.0 - compatibility 1.0.0) <1571C3AB-BCB2-38CD-B3B2-
C5FC3F927C6A> /usr/lib/system/libcache.dylib
```

```
External Modification Summary:
  Calls made by other processes targeting this process:
    task_for_pid: 2
    thread_create: 0
    thread_set_state: 0
  Calls made by this process:
    task_for_pid: 0
    thread_create: 0
    thread_set_state: 0
  Calls made by all processes on this machine:
    task_for_pid: 4321
    thread_create: 0
    thread_set_state: 0

VM Region Summary:
ReadOnly portion of Libraries: Total=50.2M resident=50.2M(100%) swapped_out_or_unallocated=0K(0%)
Writable regions: Total=38.9M written=10.8M(28%) resident=42.6M(110%) swapped_out=0K(0%)
unallocated=16777216.0T(45221404475392%)

REGION TYPE                 VIRTUAL
===========                 =======
MALLOC                       1220K
Stack                        66.6M
__DATA                        464K
__LINKEDIT                   47.7M
__TEXT                       2484K
shared memory                  12K
===========                 =======
TOTAL                       118.4M
```

Exercise A4 (GDB)

- **Goal:** Learn how to identify heap regions and heap corruption

- **Patterns:** Heap Corruption

- \AMCDA-Dumps\Exercise-A4-GDB.pdf

Exercise A4 (GDB)

Goal: Learn how to identify heap regions and heap corruption

Patterns: Heap Corruption

1.   Identify the problem thread and application specific diagnostic from the diagnostic report App4_2636.crash:

```
Process:        App4 [2636]
Path:           /Users/USER/Documents/*/App4
Identifier:     App4
Version:        ??? (???)
Code Type:      X86-64 (Native)
Parent Process: bash [1549]

Date/Time:      2012-07-24 21:19:38.344 +0100
OS Version:     Mac OS X 10.7.4 (11E53)
Report Version: 9

Crashed Thread: 3

Exception Type:  EXC_CRASH (SIGABRT)
Exception Codes: 0x0000000000000000, 0x0000000000000000

Application Specific Information:
*** error for object 0x7f88dc001408: incorrect checksum for freed object - object was probably modified after being
freed.


Thread 0:: Dispatch queue: com.apple.main-thread
0   libsystem_kernel.dylib          0x00007fff8a10ce42 __semwait_signal + 10
1   libsystem_c.dylib               0x00007fff84d6edea nanosleep + 164
2   libsystem_c.dylib               0x00007fff84d6ec2c sleep + 61
3   libsystem_c.dylib               0x00007fff84d6ec08 sleep + 25
4   App4                            0x000000010bf55c33 main + 195
5   App4                            0x000000010bf55724 start + 52

Thread 1:
0   libsystem_kernel.dylib          0x00007fff8a10ce42 __semwait_signal + 10
1   libsystem_c.dylib               0x00007fff84d6edea nanosleep + 164
2   libsystem_c.dylib               0x00007fff84d6ec2c sleep + 61
3   libsystem_c.dylib               0x00007fff84d6ec08 sleep + 25
4   App4                            0x000000010bf559b2 bar_one + 18
5   App4                            0x000000010bf559c9 foo_one + 9
6   App4                            0x000000010bf559e1 thread_one + 17
7   libsystem_c.dylib               0x00007fff84db88bf _pthread_start + 335
8   libsystem_c.dylib               0x00007fff84dbbb75 thread_start + 13

Thread 2:
0   libsystem_kernel.dylib          0x00007fff8a10ce42 __semwait_signal + 10
1   libsystem_c.dylib               0x00007fff84d6edea nanosleep + 164
2   libsystem_c.dylib               0x00007fff84d6ec2c sleep + 61
3   libsystem_c.dylib               0x00007fff84d6ec08 sleep + 25
4   App4                            0x000000010bf55a12 bar_two + 18
5   App4                            0x000000010bf55a29 foo_two + 9
6   App4                            0x000000010bf55a41 thread_two + 17
7   libsystem_c.dylib               0x00007fff84db88bf _pthread_start + 335
8   libsystem_c.dylib               0x00007fff84dbbb75 thread_start + 13
```

```
Thread 3 Crashed:
0   libsystem_kernel.dylib              0x00007fff8a10cce2 __pthread_kill + 10
1   libsystem_c.dylib                   0x00007fff84dba7d2 pthread_kill + 95
2   libsystem_c.dylib                   0x00007fff84daba7a abort + 143
3   libsystem_c.dylib                   0x00007fff84dcd4ac szone_error + 459
4   libsystem_c.dylib                   0x00007fff84dcd4e8 free_list_checksum_botch + 29
5   libsystem_c.dylib                   0x00007fff84dcda7b small_free_list_remove_ptr + 163
6   libsystem_c.dylib                   0x00007fff84dd1bf7 szone_free_definite_size + 3403
7   libsystem_c.dylib                   0x00007fff84e0a789 free + 194
8   App4                                0x000000010bf55933 proc + 515
9   App4                                0x000000010bf55a69 bar_three + 9
10  App4                                0x000000010bf55a79 foo_three + 9
11  App4                                0x000000010bf55a91 thread_three + 17
12  libsystem_c.dylib                   0x00007fff84db88bf _pthread_start + 335
13  libsystem_c.dylib                   0x00007fff84dbbb75 thread_start + 13

Thread 4:
0   libsystem_kernel.dylib              0x00007fff8a10ce42 __semwait_signal + 10
1   libsystem_c.dylib                   0x00007fff84d6edea nanosleep + 164
2   libsystem_c.dylib                   0x00007fff84d6ec2c sleep + 61
3   libsystem_c.dylib                   0x00007fff84d6ec08 sleep + 25
4   App4                                0x000000010bf55ac2 bar_four + 18
5   App4                                0x000000010bf55ad9 foo_four + 9
6   App4                                0x000000010bf55af1 thread_four + 17
7   libsystem_c.dylib                   0x00007fff84db88bf _pthread_start + 335
8   libsystem_c.dylib                   0x00007fff84dbbb75 thread_start + 13

Thread 5:
0   libsystem_kernel.dylib              0x00007fff8a10ce42 __semwait_signal + 10
1   libsystem_c.dylib                   0x00007fff84d6edea nanosleep + 164
2   libsystem_c.dylib                   0x00007fff84d6ec2c sleep + 61
3   libsystem_c.dylib                   0x00007fff84d6ec08 sleep + 25
4   App4                                0x000000010bf55b22 bar_five + 18
5   App4                                0x000000010bf55b39 foo_five + 9
6   App4                                0x000000010bf55b51 thread_five + 17
7   libsystem_c.dylib                   0x00007fff84db88bf _pthread_start + 335
8   libsystem_c.dylib                   0x00007fff84dbbb75 thread_start + 13

Thread 3 crashed with X86 Thread State (64-bit):
  rax: 0x0000000000000000  rbx: 0x0000000000000006  rcx: 0x000000010c286ba8  rdx: 0x0000000000000000
  rdi: 0x0000000000001403  rsi: 0x0000000000000006  rbp: 0x000000010c286bd0  rsp: 0x000000010c286ba8
   r8: 0x00007fff74a67fb8   r9: 0x0000000000000000  r10: 0x00007fff8a10cd0a  r11: 0xffffff80002da8d0
  r12: 0x000000010bf58000  r13: 0x000000010bf89000  r14: 0x000000010c287000  r15: 0x000000010bf890c0
  rip: 0x00007fff8a10cce2  rfl: 0x0000000000000246  cr2: 0x00007fff74a67fb8
Logical CPU: 0

Binary Images:
       0x10bf55000 -        0x10bf55fff +App4 (??? - ???) <EAEF8835-E281-36D8-B291-81804730D297>
/Users/USER/Documents/*/App4
    0x7fff6bb55000 -     0x7fff6bb89baf  dyld (195.6 - ???) <0CD1B35B-A28F-32DA-B72E-452EAD609613> /usr/lib/dyld
    0x7fff849f2000 -     0x7fff84a0ffff  libxpc.dylib (77.19.0 - compatibility 1.0.0) <9F57891B-D7EF-3050-BEDD-
21E7C6668248> /usr/lib/system/libxpc.dylib
    0x7fff84d68000 -     0x7fff84d69ff7  libsystem_blocks.dylib (53.0.0 - compatibility 1.0.0) <8BCA214A-8992-34B2-
A8B9-B74DEACA1869> /usr/lib/system/libsystem_blocks.dylib
    0x7fff84d6a000 -     0x7fff84e47fef  libsystem_c.dylib (763.13.0 - compatibility 1.0.0) <41B43515-2806-3FBC-ACF1-
A16F35B7E290> /usr/lib/system/libsystem_c.dylib
    0x7fff85022000 -     0x7fff85030fff  libdispatch.dylib (187.9.0 - compatibility 1.0.0) <1D5BE322-A9B9-3BCE-8FAC-
076FB07CF54A> /usr/lib/system/libdispatch.dylib
    0x7fff855f0000 -     0x7fff855f1fff  libunc.dylib (24.0.0 - compatibility 1.0.0) <337960EE-0A85-3DD0-A760-
7134CF4C0AFF> /usr/lib/system/libunc.dylib
    0x7fff85ae3000 -     0x7fff85ae4ff7  libremovefile.dylib (21.1.0 - compatibility 1.0.0) <739E6C83-AA52-3C6C-A680-
B37FE2888A04> /usr/lib/system/libremovefile.dylib
    0x7fff89114000 -     0x7fff89118fff  libmathCommon.A.dylib (2026.0.0 - compatibility 1.0.0) <FF83AFF7-42B2-306E-
90AF-D539C51A4542> /usr/lib/system/libmathCommon.A.dylib
    0x7fff89119000 -     0x7fff8911dfff  libdyld.dylib (195.5.0 - compatibility 1.0.0) <380C3F44-0CA7-3514-8080-
46D1C9DF4FCD> /usr/lib/system/libdyld.dylib
    0x7fff89740000 -     0x7fff89741ff7  libsystem_sandbox.dylib (??? - ???) <96D38E74-F18F-3CCB-A20B-E8E3ADC4E166>
/usr/lib/system/libsystem_sandbox.dylib
    0x7fff8a0ef000 -     0x7fff8a0f5fff  libmacho.dylib (800.0.0 - compatibility 1.0.0) <165514D7-1BFA-38EF-A151-
676DCD21FB64> /usr/lib/system/libmacho.dylib
    0x7fff8a0f6000 -     0x7fff8a116fff  libsystem_kernel.dylib (1699.26.8 - compatibility 1.0.0) <1DDC0B0F-DB2A-34D6-
895D-E5B2B5618946> /usr/lib/system/libsystem_kernel.dylib
    0x7fff8a2ac000 -     0x7fff8a2b4fff  libsystem_dnssd.dylib (??? - ???) <D9BB1F87-A42B-3CBC-9DC2-FC07FCEF0016>
/usr/lib/system/libsystem_dnssd.dylib
    0x7fff8ae26000 -     0x7fff8ae61fff  libsystem_info.dylib (??? - ???) <35F90252-2AE1-32C5-8D34-782C614D9639>
/usr/lib/system/libsystem_info.dylib
```

```
    0x7fff8b248000 -     0x7fff8b24afff  libquarantine.dylib (36.6.0 - compatibility 1.0.0) <0EBF714B-4B69-3E1F-9A7D-
6BBC2AACB310> /usr/lib/system/libquarantine.dylib
    0x7fff8b3b4000 -     0x7fff8b3b4fff  libkeymgr.dylib (23.0.0 - compatibility 1.0.0) <61EFED6A-A407-301E-B454-
CD18314F0075> /usr/lib/system/libkeymgr.dylib
    0x7fff8b3dd000 -     0x7fff8b3e2fff  libcompiler_rt.dylib (6.0.0 - compatibility 1.0.0) <98ECD5F6-E85C-32A5-98CD-
8911230CB66A> /usr/lib/system/libcompiler_rt.dylib
    0x7fff8bd1a000 -     0x7fff8bd1bfff  libdnsinfo.dylib (395.11.0 - compatibility 1.0.0) <853BAAA5-270F-3FDC-B025-
D448DB72E1C3> /usr/lib/system/libdnsinfo.dylib
    0x7fff8c528000 -     0x7fff8c52dff7  libsystem_network.dylib (??? - ???) <5DE7024E-1D2D-34A2-80F4-08326331A75B>
/usr/lib/system/libsystem_network.dylib
    0x7fff8cfa3000 -     0x7fff8cfadff7  liblaunch.dylib (392.38.0 - compatibility 1.0.0) <6ECB7F19-B384-32C1-8652-
2463C1CF4815> /usr/lib/system/liblaunch.dylib
    0x7fff8fe02000 -     0x7fff8fe09fff  libcopyfile.dylib (85.1.0 - compatibility 1.0.0) <0AB51EE2-E914-358C-AC19-
47BC024BDAE7> /usr/lib/system/libcopyfile.dylib
    0x7fff8fe4b000 -     0x7fff8fe8dff7  libcommonCrypto.dylib (55010.0.0 - compatibility 1.0.0) <BB770C22-8C57-365A-
8716-4A3C36AE7BFB> /usr/lib/system/libcommonCrypto.dylib
    0x7fff90c0f000 -     0x7fff90c18ff7  libsystem_notify.dylib (80.1.0 - compatibility 1.0.0) <A4D651E3-D1C6-3934-
AD49-7A104FD14596> /usr/lib/system/libsystem_notify.dylib
    0x7fff91376000 -     0x7fff913a3fe7  libSystem.B.dylib (159.1.0 - compatibility 1.0.0) <7BEBB139-50BB-3112-947A-
F4AA168F991C> /usr/lib/libSystem.B.dylib
    0x7fff91489000 -     0x7fff9148fff7  libunwind.dylib (30.0.0 - compatibility 1.0.0) <1E9C6C8C-CBE8-3F4B-A5B5-
E03E3AB53231> /usr/lib/system/libunwind.dylib
    0x7fff91a22000 -     0x7fff91a27fff  libcache.dylib (47.0.0 - compatibility 1.0.0) <1571C3AB-BCB2-38CD-B3B2-
C5FC3F927C6A> /usr/lib/system/libcache.dylib

External Modification Summary:
  Calls made by other processes targeting this process:
    task_for_pid: 2
    thread_create: 0
    thread_set_state: 0
  Calls made by this process:
    task_for_pid: 0
    thread_create: 0
    thread_set_state: 0
  Calls made by all processes on this machine:
    task_for_pid: 4660
    thread_create: 0
    thread_set_state: 0

VM Region Summary:
ReadOnly portion of Libraries: Total=50.2M resident=50.2M(100%) swapped_out_or_unallocated=0K(0%)
Writable regions: Total=46.9M written=14.0M(30%) resident=50.7M(108%) swapped_out=0K(0%)
unallocated=16777216.0T(37504992411648%)

REGION TYPE              VIRTUAL
===========              =======
MALLOC                     9412K
Stack                      66.6M
VM_ALLOCATE                   4K
__DATA                      464K
__LINKEDIT                 47.7M
__TEXT                     2484K
shared memory                12K
===========              =======
TOTAL                     126.4M
```

2.   Load a core dump core.2636 and App4 executable:

```
$ gdb -c ~/Documents/AMCDA-Dumps/core.2636 -e ~/Documents/AMCDA-
Dumps/Apps/App4/Build/Products/Release/App4
GNU gdb 6.3.50-20050815 (Apple version gdb-1820) (Sat Jun 16 02:40:11 UTC 2012)
Copyright 2004 Free Software Foundation, Inc.
GDB is free software, covered by the GNU General Public License, and you are
welcome to change it and/or distribute copies of it under certain conditions.
Type "show copying" to see the conditions.
There is absolutely no warranty for GDB.  Type "show warranty" for details.
This GDB was configured as "x86_64-apple-darwin".
Reading symbols for shared libraries . done
Reading symbols for shared libraries ......................... done
#0  0x00007fff8a10ce42 in __semwait_signal ()
```

3.   Go to the identifed problem core thread 3 (thread #4):

```
(gdb) thread 4
[Switching to thread 4 (core thread 3)]
0x00007fff8a10cce2 in __pthread_kill ()

(gdb) bt
#0  0x00007fff8a10cce2 in __pthread_kill ()
#1  0x00007fff84dba7d2 in pthread_kill ()
#2  0x00007fff84daba7a in abort ()
#3  0x00007fff84dcd4ac in szone_error ()
#4  0x00007fff84dcd4e8 in free_list_checksum_botch ()
#5  0x00007fff84dcda7b in small_free_list_remove_ptr ()
#6  0x00007fff84dd1bf7 in szone_free_definite_size ()
#7  0x00007fff84e0a789 in free ()
#8  0x000000010bf55933 in proc ()
#9  0x000000010bf55a69 in bar_three ()
#10 0x000000010bf55a79 in foo_three ()
#11 0x000000010bf55a91 in thread_three ()
#12 0x00007fff84db88bf in _pthread_start ()
#13 0x00007fff84dbbb75 in thread_start ()
```

4.   Check the corrupt heap entry address specified in the diagnostic report:

```
(gdb) x/s 0x7f88dc001408
0x7f88dc001408:      "ash!"

(gdb) x/s 0x7f88dc001400
0x7f88dc001400:      "Hello Crash!"
```

5.   Switch to the stack frame 8 to check heap free functions and blocks they free:

```
(gdb) frame 8
#8  0x000000010bf55933 in proc ()
```

```
(gdb) disass proc
Dump of assembler code for function proc:
0x000000010bf55730 <proc+0>:      push   %rbp
0x000000010bf55731 <proc+1>:      mov    %rsp,%rbp
0x000000010bf55734 <proc+4>:      sub    $0x80,%rsp
0x000000010bf5573b <proc+11>:     mov    $0x400,%rdi
0x000000010bf55745 <proc+21>:     callq  0x10bf55c56 <dyld_stub_malloc>
0x000000010bf5574a <proc+26>:     mov    $0x400,%rdi
0x000000010bf55754 <proc+36>:     mov    %rax,-0x8(%rbp)
0x000000010bf55758 <proc+40>:     callq  0x10bf55c56 <dyld_stub_malloc>
0x000000010bf5575d <proc+45>:     mov    $0x400,%rdi
0x000000010bf55767 <proc+55>:     mov    %rax,-0x10(%rbp)
0x000000010bf5576b <proc+59>:     callq  0x10bf55c56 <dyld_stub_malloc>
0x000000010bf55770 <proc+64>:     mov    $0x400,%rdi
0x000000010bf5577a <proc+74>:     mov    %rax,-0x18(%rbp)
0x000000010bf5577e <proc+78>:     callq  0x10bf55c56 <dyld_stub_malloc>
0x000000010bf55783 <proc+83>:     mov    $0x400,%rdi
0x000000010bf5578d <proc+93>:     mov    %rax,-0x20(%rbp)
0x000000010bf55791 <proc+97>:     callq  0x10bf55c56 <dyld_stub_malloc>
0x000000010bf55796 <proc+102>:    mov    $0x400,%rdi
0x000000010bf557a0 <proc+112>:    mov    %rax,-0x28(%rbp)
0x000000010bf557a4 <proc+116>:    callq  0x10bf55c56 <dyld_stub_malloc>
0x000000010bf557a9 <proc+121>:    mov    $0x400,%rdi
0x000000010bf557b3 <proc+131>:    mov    %rax,-0x30(%rbp)
0x000000010bf557b7 <proc+135>:    callq  0x10bf55c56 <dyld_stub_malloc>
0x000000010bf557bc <proc+140>:    mov    %rax,-0x38(%rbp)
0x000000010bf557c0 <proc+144>:    mov    -0x30(%rbp),%rdi
0x000000010bf557c4 <proc+148>:    callq  0x10bf55c50 <dyld_stub_free>
0x000000010bf557c9 <proc+153>:    mov    -0x20(%rbp),%rdi
0x000000010bf557cd <proc+157>:    callq  0x10bf55c50 <dyld_stub_free>
0x000000010bf557d2 <proc+162>:    mov    -0x10(%rbp),%rdi
0x000000010bf557d6 <proc+166>:    callq  0x10bf55c50 <dyld_stub_free>
0x000000010bf557db <proc+171>:    mov    $0xffffffffffffffff,%rax
0x000000010bf557e5 <proc+181>:    cmp    $0xffffffffffffffff,%rax
0x000000010bf557eb <proc+187>:    je     0x10bf55814 <proc+228>
0x000000010bf557f1 <proc+193>:    lea    0x4bc(%rip),%rsi        # 0x10bf55cb4
0x000000010bf557f8 <proc+200>:    mov    $0xffffffffffffffff,%rdx
0x000000010bf55802 <proc+210>:    mov    -0x10(%rbp),%rdi
0x000000010bf55806 <proc+214>:    callq  0x10bf55c44 <dyld_stub___strcpy_chk>
0x000000010bf5580b <proc+219>:    mov    %rax,-0x40(%rbp)
0x000000010bf5580f <proc+223>:    jmpq   0x10bf55828 <proc+248>
0x000000010bf55814 <proc+228>:    lea    0x499(%rip),%rsi        # 0x10bf55cb4
0x000000010bf5581b <proc+235>:    mov    -0x10(%rbp),%rdi
---Type <return> to continue, or q <return> to quit---
0x000000010bf5581f <proc+239>:    callq  0x10bf55970 <__inline_strcpy_chk>
0x000000010bf55824 <proc+244>:    mov    %rax,-0x48(%rbp)
0x000000010bf55828 <proc+248>:    mov    $0xffffffffffffffff,%rax
0x000000010bf55832 <proc+258>:    mov    -0x20(%rbp),%rcx
0x000000010bf55836 <proc+262>:    cmp    $0xffffffffffffffff,%rax
0x000000010bf5583c <proc+268>:    mov    %rcx,-0x50(%rbp)
0x000000010bf55840 <proc+272>:    je     0x10bf55869 <proc+313>
0x000000010bf55846 <proc+278>:    lea    0x467(%rip),%rsi        # 0x10bf55cb4
0x000000010bf5584d <proc+285>:    mov    $0xffffffffffffffff,%rdx
0x000000010bf55857 <proc+295>:    mov    -0x20(%rbp),%rdi
0x000000010bf5585b <proc+299>:    callq  0x10bf55c44 <dyld_stub___strcpy_chk>
0x000000010bf55860 <proc+304>:    mov    %rax,-0x58(%rbp)
0x000000010bf55864 <proc+308>:    jmpq   0x10bf5587d <proc+333>
0x000000010bf55869 <proc+313>:    lea    0x444(%rip),%rsi        # 0x10bf55cb4
0x000000010bf55870 <proc+320>:    mov    -0x20(%rbp),%rdi
0x000000010bf55874 <proc+324>:    callq  0x10bf55970 <__inline_strcpy_chk>
```

```
0x000000010bf55879 <proc+329>:    mov     %rax,-0x60(%rbp)
0x000000010bf5587d <proc+333>:    mov     $0xffffffffffffffff,%rax
0x000000010bf55887 <proc+343>:    mov     -0x30(%rbp),%rcx
0x000000010bf5588b <proc+347>:    cmp     $0xffffffffffffffff,%rax
0x000000010bf55891 <proc+353>:    mov     %rcx,-0x68(%rbp)
0x000000010bf55895 <proc+357>:    je      0x10bf558be <proc+398>
0x000000010bf5589b <proc+363>:    lea     0x412(%rip),%rsi        # 0x10bf55cb4
0x000000010bf558a2 <proc+370>:    mov     $0xffffffffffffffff,%rdx
0x000000010bf558ac <proc+380>:    mov     -0x30(%rbp),%rdi
0x000000010bf558b0 <proc+384>:    callq   0x10bf55c44 <dyld_stub___strcpy_chk>
0x000000010bf558b5 <proc+389>:    mov     %rax,-0x70(%rbp)
0x000000010bf558b9 <proc+393>:    jmpq    0x10bf558d2 <proc+418>
0x000000010bf558be <proc+398>:    lea     0x3ef(%rip),%rsi        # 0x10bf55cb4
0x000000010bf558c5 <proc+405>:    mov     -0x30(%rbp),%rdi
0x000000010bf558c9 <proc+409>:    callq   0x10bf55970 <__inline_strcpy_chk>
0x000000010bf558ce <proc+414>:    mov     %rax,-0x78(%rbp)
0x000000010bf558d2 <proc+418>:    mov     $0x200,%rdi
0x000000010bf558dc <proc+428>:    callq   0x10bf55c56 <dyld_stub_malloc>
0x000000010bf558e1 <proc+433>:    mov     $0x400,%rdi
0x000000010bf558eb <proc+443>:    mov     %rax,-0x10(%rbp)
0x000000010bf558ef <proc+447>:    callq   0x10bf55c56 <dyld_stub_malloc>
0x000000010bf558f4 <proc+452>:    mov     $0x200,%rdi
0x000000010bf558fe <proc+462>:    mov     %rax,-0x20(%rbp)
0x000000010bf55902 <proc+466>:    callq   0x10bf55c56 <dyld_stub_malloc>
0x000000010bf55907 <proc+471>:    mov     $0x12c,%edi
0x000000010bf5590c <proc+476>:    mov     %rax,-0x30(%rbp)
---Type <return> to continue, or q <return> to quit---
0x000000010bf55910 <proc+480>:    callq   0x10bf55c62 <dyld_stub_sleep>
0x000000010bf55915 <proc+485>:    mov     -0x38(%rbp),%rdi
0x000000010bf55919 <proc+489>:    mov     %eax,-0x7c(%rbp)
0x000000010bf5591c <proc+492>:    callq   0x10bf55c50 <dyld_stub_free>
0x000000010bf55921 <proc+497>:    mov     -0x30(%rbp),%rdi
0x000000010bf55925 <proc+501>:    callq   0x10bf55c50 <dyld_stub_free>
0x000000010bf5592a <proc+506>:    mov     -0x28(%rbp),%rdi
0x000000010bf5592e <proc+510>:    callq   0x10bf55c50 <dyld_stub_free>
0x000000010bf55933 <proc+515>:    mov     -0x20(%rbp),%rdi
0x000000010bf55937 <proc+519>:    callq   0x10bf55c50 <dyld_stub_free>
0x000000010bf5593c <proc+524>:    mov     -0x18(%rbp),%rdi
0x000000010bf55940 <proc+528>:    callq   0x10bf55c50 <dyld_stub_free>
0x000000010bf55945 <proc+533>:    mov     -0x10(%rbp),%rdi
0x000000010bf55949 <proc+537>:    callq   0x10bf55c50 <dyld_stub_free>
0x000000010bf5594e <proc+542>:    mov     -0x8(%rbp),%rdi
0x000000010bf55952 <proc+546>:    callq   0x10bf55c50 <dyld_stub_free>
0x000000010bf55957 <proc+551>:    mov     $0xffffffff,%edi
0x000000010bf5595c <proc+556>:    callq   0x10bf55c62 <dyld_stub_sleep>
0x000000010bf55961 <proc+561>:    mov     %eax,-0x80(%rbp)
0x000000010bf55964 <proc+564>:    add     $0x80,%rsp
0x000000010bf5596b <proc+571>:    pop     %rbp
0x000000010bf5596c <proc+572>:    retq
0x000000010bf5596d <proc+573>:    nopl    (%rax)
End of assembler dump.

(gdb) x/xg $rbp-0x28
0x10c286ea8: 0x00007f88dc001000

(gdb) x/s 0x7f88dc001000
0x7f88dc001000:        ""

(gdb) x/xg $rbp-0x20
0x10c286eb0: 0x00007f88dc000400
```

```
(gdb) x/s 0x7f88dc000400
0x7f88dc000400:         "Hello Crash!"

(gdb) x/xg $rbp-0x30
0x10c286ea0: 0x000000010c000ac0

(gdb) x/xg $rbp-0x38
0x10c286e98: 0x00007f88dc001800

(gdb) x/xg $rbp-0x18
0x10c286eb8: 0x00007f88dc000800

(gdb) x/xg $rbp-0x10
0x10c286ec0: 0x000000010c0008c0

(gdb) x/xg $rbp-0x8
0x10c286ec8: 0x00007f88dc000000
```

6.   Notice different sections for heap metadata and heap block base addresses 0x7f88dc000000 and
0x000000010c000000 and find them on vmmap report vmmap_2636.log:

```
(gdb) maintenance info sections
Exec file:
    `/Users/DumpAnalysis/Documents/AMCDA-Dumps/Apps/App4/Build/Products/Release/App4', file type mach-o-le.
    0x0000000000000000->0x0000000000000000 at 0x00000000: LC_SEGMENT.__PAGEZERO ALLOC LOAD CODE HAS_CONTENTS
    0x0000000100000000->0x0000000100001000 at 0x00000000: LC_SEGMENT.__TEXT ALLOC LOAD CODE HAS_CONTENTS
    0x00000001000006f0->0x0000000100000c43 at 0x000006f0: LC_SEGMENT.__TEXT.__text ALLOC LOAD READONLY CODE
HAS_CONTENTS
    0x0000000100000c44->0x0000000100000c68 at 0x00000c44: LC_SEGMENT.__TEXT.__stubs ALLOC LOAD CODE HAS_CONTENTS
    0x0000000100000c68->0x0000000100000cb4 at 0x00000c68: LC_SEGMENT.__TEXT.__stub_helper ALLOC LOAD CODE HAS_CONTENTS
    0x0000000100000cb4->0x0000000100000cc1 at 0x00000cb4: LC_SEGMENT.__TEXT.__cstring ALLOC LOAD CODE HAS_CONTENTS
    0x0000000100000cc1->0x0000000100000d11 at 0x00000cc1: LC_SEGMENT.__TEXT.__unwind_info ALLOC LOAD CODE HAS_CONTENTS
    0x0000000100000d18->0x0000000100001000 at 0x00000d18: LC_SEGMENT.__TEXT.__eh_frame ALLOC LOAD CODE HAS_CONTENTS
    0x0000000100001000->0x0000000100002000 at 0x00001000: LC_SEGMENT.__DATA ALLOC LOAD CODE HAS_CONTENTS
    0x0000000100001000->0x0000000100001028 at 0x00001000: LC_SEGMENT.__DATA.__program_vars ALLOC LOAD CODE
HAS_CONTENTS
    0x0000000100001028->0x0000000100001038 at 0x00001028: LC_SEGMENT.__DATA.__nl_symbol_ptr ALLOC LOAD CODE
HAS_CONTENTS
    0x0000000100001038->0x0000000100001068 at 0x00001038: LC_SEGMENT.__DATA.__la_symbol_ptr ALLOC LOAD CODE
HAS_CONTENTS
    0x0000000100001068->0x0000000100001088 at 0x00000000: LC_SEGMENT.__DATA.__common ALLOC
    0x0000000100002000->0x0000000100002480 at 0x00002000: LC_SEGMENT.__LINKEDIT ALLOC LOAD CODE HAS_CONTENTS
    0x0000000000000000->0x00000000000001f0 at 0x00002100: LC_SYMTAB.stabs HAS_CONTENTS
    0x0000000000000000->0x0000000000000158 at 0x00002328: LC_SYMTAB.stabstr HAS_CONTENTS
    0x0000000000000000->0x0000000000000120 at 0x00002100: LC_DYSYMTAB.localstabs HAS_CONTENTS
    0x0000000000000000->0x00000000000000d0 at 0x00002220: LC_DYSYMTAB.nonlocalstabs HAS_CONTENTS
    0x0000000000000000->0x0000000000000018 at 0x00000500: LC_LOAD_DYLINKER HAS_CONTENTS
    0x0000000000000000->0x00000000000000a8 at 0x00000550: LC_THREAD.x86_THREAD_STATE64.0 HAS_CONTENTS
    0x0000000000000000->0x0000000000000030 at 0x00000600: LC_LOAD_DYLIB HAS_CONTENTS
Core file:
    `/Users/DumpAnalysis/Documents/AMCDA-Dumps/core.2636', file type mach-o-le.
    0x000000010bf55000->0x000000010bf56000 at 0x00002000: LC_SEGMENT. ALLOC LOAD CODE HAS_CONTENTS
    0x000000010bf56000->0x000000010bf57000 at 0x00003000: LC_SEGMENT. ALLOC LOAD CODE HAS_CONTENTS
    0x000000010bf57000->0x000000010bf58000 at 0x00004000: LC_SEGMENT. ALLOC LOAD CODE HAS_CONTENTS
    0x000000010bf58000->0x000000010bf59000 at 0x00005000: LC_SEGMENT. ALLOC LOAD CODE HAS_CONTENTS
    0x000000010bf59000->0x000000010bf5a000 at 0x00006000: LC_SEGMENT. ALLOC LOAD CODE HAS_CONTENTS
    0x000000010bf5a000->0x000000010bf5b000 at 0x00007000: LC_SEGMENT. ALLOC LOAD CODE HAS_CONTENTS
    0x000000010bf5b000->0x000000010bf70000 at 0x00008000: LC_SEGMENT. ALLOC LOAD CODE HAS_CONTENTS
    0x000000010bf70000->0x000000010bf71000 at 0x0001d000: LC_SEGMENT. ALLOC LOAD CODE HAS_CONTENTS
    0x000000010bf71000->0x000000010bf72000 at 0x0001e000: LC_SEGMENT. ALLOC LOAD CODE HAS_CONTENTS
    0x000000010bf72000->0x000000010bf87000 at 0x0001f000: LC_SEGMENT. ALLOC LOAD CODE HAS_CONTENTS
    0x000000010bf87000->0x000000010bf88000 at 0x00034000: LC_SEGMENT. ALLOC LOAD CODE HAS_CONTENTS
    0x000000010bf88000->0x000000010bf89000 at 0x00035000: LC_SEGMENT. ALLOC LOAD CODE HAS_CONTENTS
    0x000000010bf89000->0x000000010bf8a000 at 0x00036000: LC_SEGMENT. ALLOC LOAD CODE HAS_CONTENTS
    0x000000010c000000->0x000000010c100000 at 0x00037000: LC_SEGMENT. ALLOC LOAD CODE HAS_CONTENTS
    0x000000010c100000->0x000000010c101000 at 0x00137000: LC_SEGMENT. ALLOC LOAD CODE HAS_CONTENTS
    0x000000010c101000->0x000000010c183000 at 0x00138000: LC_SEGMENT. ALLOC LOAD CODE HAS_CONTENTS
    0x000000010c183000->0x000000010c184000 at 0x001ba000: LC_SEGMENT. ALLOC LOAD CODE HAS_CONTENTS
```

```
0x000000010c184000->0x000000010c206000 at 0x001bb000: LC_SEGMENT. ALLOC LOAD CODE HAS_CONTENTS
0x000000010c206000->0x000000010c207000 at 0x0023d000: LC_SEGMENT. ALLOC LOAD CODE HAS_CONTENTS
0x000000010c207000->0x000000010c289000 at 0x0023e000: LC_SEGMENT. ALLOC LOAD CODE HAS_CONTENTS
0x000000010c289000->0x000000010c28a000 at 0x002c0000: LC_SEGMENT. ALLOC LOAD CODE HAS_CONTENTS
0x000000010c28a000->0x000000010c30c000 at 0x002c1000: LC_SEGMENT. ALLOC LOAD CODE HAS_CONTENTS
0x000000010c30c000->0x000000010c30d000 at 0x00343000: LC_SEGMENT. ALLOC LOAD CODE HAS_CONTENTS
0x000000010c30d000->0x000000010c38f000 at 0x00344000: LC_SEGMENT. ALLOC LOAD CODE HAS_CONTENTS
0x00007f88dc000000->0x00007f88dc800000 at 0x003c6000: LC_SEGMENT. ALLOC LOAD CODE HAS_CONTENTS
0x00007fff67b55000->0x00007fff6b355000 at 0x00bc6000: LC_SEGMENT. ALLOC LOAD CODE HAS_CONTENTS
0x00007fff6b355000->0x00007fff6bb54000 at 0x043c6000: LC_SEGMENT. ALLOC LOAD CODE HAS_CONTENTS
0x00007fff6bb54000->0x00007fff6bb55000 at 0x04bc5000: LC_SEGMENT. ALLOC LOAD CODE HAS_CONTENTS
0x00007fff6bb55000->0x00007fff6bb8a000 at 0x04bc6000: LC_SEGMENT. ALLOC LOAD CODE HAS_CONTENTS
0x00007fff6bb8a000->0x00007fff6bb8c000 at 0x04bfb000: LC_SEGMENT. ALLOC LOAD CODE HAS_CONTENTS
0x00007fff6bb8c000->0x00007fff6bbc6000 at 0x04bfd000: LC_SEGMENT. ALLOC LOAD CODE HAS_CONTENTS
0x00007fff6bbc6000->0x00007fff6bbd9000 at 0x04c37000: LC_SEGMENT. ALLOC LOAD CODE HAS_CONTENTS
0x00007fff749b8000->0x00007fff74a00000 at 0x04c4a000: LC_SEGMENT. ALLOC LOAD CODE HAS_CONTENTS
0x00007fff74a00000->0x00007fff74c00000 at 0x04c92000: LC_SEGMENT. ALLOC LOAD CODE HAS_CONTENTS
0x00007fff74c00000->0x00007fff74e00000 at 0x04e92000: LC_SEGMENT. ALLOC LOAD CODE HAS_CONTENTS
0x00007fff74e00000->0x00007fff75000000 at 0x05092000: LC_SEGMENT. ALLOC LOAD CODE HAS_CONTENTS
0x00007fff75000000->0x00007fff75200000 at 0x05292000: LC_SEGMENT. ALLOC LOAD CODE HAS_CONTENTS
0x00007fff75200000->0x00007fff75400000 at 0x05492000: LC_SEGMENT. ALLOC LOAD CODE HAS_CONTENTS
0x00007fff75400000->0x00007fff75600000 at 0x05692000: LC_SEGMENT. ALLOC LOAD CODE HAS_CONTENTS
0x00007fff75600000->0x00007fff75800000 at 0x05892000: LC_SEGMENT. ALLOC LOAD CODE HAS_CONTENTS
0x00007fff75800000->0x00007fff75a00000 at 0x05a92000: LC_SEGMENT. ALLOC LOAD CODE HAS_CONTENTS
0x00007fff75a00000->0x00007fff75c00000 at 0x05c92000: LC_SEGMENT. ALLOC LOAD CODE HAS_CONTENTS
0x00007fff75c00000->0x00007fff75e00000 at 0x05e92000: LC_SEGMENT. ALLOC LOAD CODE HAS_CONTENTS
0x00007fff75e00000->0x00007fff76200000 at 0x06092000: LC_SEGMENT. ALLOC LOAD CODE HAS_CONTENTS
0x00007fff76200000->0x00007fff76400000 at 0x06492000: LC_SEGMENT. ALLOC LOAD CODE HAS_CONTENTS
0x00007fff76400000->0x00007fff764ac000 at 0x06692000: LC_SEGMENT. ALLOC LOAD CODE HAS_CONTENTS
0x00007fff849b8000->0x00007fff91a28000 at 0x0673e000: LC_SEGMENT. ALLOC LOAD CODE HAS_CONTENTS
0x00007fff91a28000->0x00007fff94b30000 at 0x137ae000: LC_SEGMENT. ALLOC LOAD CODE HAS_CONTENTS
0x00007ffffffe00000->0x00007ffffffe02000 at 0x168b6000: LC_SEGMENT. ALLOC LOAD CODE HAS_CONTENTS
0x0000000000000000->0x00000000000000b0 at 0x00000df8: LC_THREAD.x86_THREAD_STATE.0 HAS_CONTENTS
0x0000000000000000->0x0000000000000214 at 0x00000eb0: LC_THREAD.x86_FLOAT_STATE.0 HAS_CONTENTS
0x0000000000000000->0x0000000000000018 at 0x000010cc: LC_THREAD.x86_EXCEPTION_STATE.0 HAS_CONTENTS
0x0000000000000000->0x00000000000000b0 at 0x000010f4: LC_THREAD.x86_THREAD_STATE.1 HAS_CONTENTS
0x0000000000000000->0x0000000000000214 at 0x000011ac: LC_THREAD.x86_FLOAT_STATE.1 HAS_CONTENTS
0x0000000000000000->0x0000000000000018 at 0x000013c8: LC_THREAD.x86_EXCEPTION_STATE.1 HAS_CONTENTS
0x0000000000000000->0x00000000000000b0 at 0x000013f0: LC_THREAD.x86_THREAD_STATE.2 HAS_CONTENTS
0x0000000000000000->0x0000000000000214 at 0x000014a8: LC_THREAD.x86_FLOAT_STATE.2 HAS_CONTENTS
0x0000000000000000->0x0000000000000018 at 0x000016c4: LC_THREAD.x86_EXCEPTION_STATE.2 HAS_CONTENTS
0x0000000000000000->0x00000000000000b0 at 0x000016ec: LC_THREAD.x86_THREAD_STATE.3 HAS_CONTENTS
0x0000000000000000->0x0000000000000214 at 0x000017a4: LC_THREAD.x86_FLOAT_STATE.3 HAS_CONTENTS
0x0000000000000000->0x0000000000000018 at 0x000019c0: LC_THREAD.x86_EXCEPTION_STATE.3 HAS_CONTENTS
0x0000000000000000->0x00000000000000b0 at 0x000019e8: LC_THREAD.x86_THREAD_STATE.4 HAS_CONTENTS
0x0000000000000000->0x0000000000000214 at 0x00001aa0: LC_THREAD.x86_FLOAT_STATE.4 HAS_CONTENTS
0x0000000000000000->0x0000000000000018 at 0x00001cbc: LC_THREAD.x86_EXCEPTION_STATE.4 HAS_CONTENTS
0x0000000000000000->0x00000000000000b0 at 0x00001ce4: LC_THREAD.x86_THREAD_STATE.5 HAS_CONTENTS
0x0000000000000000->0x0000000000000214 at 0x00001d9c: LC_THREAD.x86_FLOAT_STATE.5 HAS_CONTENTS
0x0000000000000000->0x0000000000000018 at 0x00001fb8: LC_THREAD.x86_EXCEPTION_STATE.5 HAS_CONTENTS
```

```
Virtual Memory Map of process 2636 (App4)
Output report format:  2.2  -- 64-bit process


==== Non-writable regions for process 2636
  __TEXT               000000010bf55000-000000010bf56000 [    4K] r-x/rwx SM=COW  /Users/DumpAnalysis/Documents/AMCDA-
Dumps/Apps/App4/Build/Products/Release/App4
  __LINKEDIT           000000010bf57000-000000010bf58000 [    4K] r--/rwx SM=COW  /Users/DumpAnalysis/Documents/AMCDA-
Dumps/Apps/App4/Build/Products/Release/App4
  MALLOC metadata      000000010bf58000-000000010bf59000 [    4K] r--/rwx SM=ZER
  MALLOC guard page    000000010bf5a000-000000010bf5b000 [    4K] ---/rwx SM=NUL
  MALLOC guard page    000000010bf70000-000000010bf72000 [    8K] ---/rwx SM=NUL
  MALLOC guard page    000000010bf87000-000000010bf88000 [    4K] ---/rwx SM=NUL
  MALLOC metadata      000000010bf88000-000000010bf89000 [    4K] r--/rwx SM=PRV
  STACK GUARD          000000010c100000-000000010c101000 [    4K] ---/rwx SM=NUL  stack guard for thread 1
  STACK GUARD          000000010c183000-000000010c184000 [    4K] ---/rwx SM=NUL  stack guard for thread 2
  STACK GUARD          000000010c206000-000000010c207000 [    4K] ---/rwx SM=NUL  stack guard for thread 3
  STACK GUARD          000000010c289000-000000010c28a000 [    4K] ---/rwx SM=NUL  stack guard for thread 4
  STACK GUARD          000000010c30c000-000000010c30d000 [    4K] ---/rwx SM=NUL  stack guard for thread 5
  STACK GUARD          00007fff67b55000-00007fff6b355000 [  56.0M] ---/rwx SM=NUL  stack guard for thread 0
  __TEXT               00007fff6bb55000-00007fff6bb8a000 [  212K] r-x/rwx SM=COW  /usr/lib/dyld
  __LINKEDIT           00007fff6bbc6000-00007fff6bbd9000 [   76K] r--/rwx SM=COW  /usr/lib/dyld
  __TEXT               00007fff849f2000-00007fff84a10000 [  120K] r-x/r-x SM=COW  /usr/lib/system/libxpc.dylib
  __TEXT               00007fff84d68000-00007fff84d6a000 [    8K] r-x/r-x SM=COW
/usr/lib/system/libsystem_blocks.dylib
  __TEXT               00007fff84d6a000-00007fff84e48000 [  888K] r-x/r-x SM=COW  /usr/lib/system/libsystem_c.dylib
  __TEXT               00007fff85022000-00007fff85031000 [   60K] r-x/r-x SM=COW  /usr/lib/system/libdispatch.dylib
  __TEXT               00007fff855f0000-00007fff855f2000 [    8K] r-x/r-x SM=COW  /usr/lib/system/libunc.dylib
  __TEXT               00007fff85ae3000-00007fff85ae5000 [    8K] r-x/r-x SM=COW  /usr/lib/system/libremovefile.dylib
  __TEXT               00007fff89114000-00007fff89119000 [   20K] r-x/r-x SM=COW
/usr/lib/system/libmathCommon.A.dylib
  __TEXT               00007fff89119000-00007fff8911e000 [   20K] r-x/r-x SM=COW  /usr/lib/system/libdyld.dylib
  __TEXT               00007fff89740000-00007fff89742000 [    8K] r-x/r-x SM=COW
/usr/lib/system/libsystem_sandbox.dylib
  __TEXT               00007fff8a0ef000-00007fff8a0f6000 [   28K] r-x/r-x SM=COW  /usr/lib/system/libmacho.dylib
  __TEXT               00007fff8a0f6000-00007fff8a117000 [  132K] r-x/r-x SM=COW
/usr/lib/system/libsystem_kernel.dylib
  __TEXT               00007fff8a2ac000-00007fff8a2b5000 [   36K] r-x/r-x SM=COW
/usr/lib/system/libsystem_dnssd.dylib
  __TEXT               00007fff8ae26000-00007fff8ae62000 [  240K] r-x/r-x SM=COW  /usr/lib/system/libsystem_info.dylib
  __TEXT               00007fff8b248000-00007fff8b24b000 [   12K] r-x/r-x SM=COW  /usr/lib/system/libquarantine.dylib
  __TEXT               00007fff8b3b4000-00007fff8b3b5000 [    4K] r-x/r-x SM=COW  /usr/lib/system/libkeymgr.dylib
  __TEXT               00007fff8b3dd000-00007fff8b3e3000 [   24K] r-x/r-x SM=COW  /usr/lib/system/libcompiler_rt.dylib
  __TEXT               00007fff8bd1a000-00007fff8bd1c000 [    8K] r-x/r-x SM=COW  /usr/lib/system/libdnsinfo.dylib
  __TEXT               00007fff8c528000-00007fff8c52e000 [   24K] r-x/r-x SM=COW
/usr/lib/system/libsystem_network.dylib
  __TEXT               00007fff8cfa3000-00007fff8cfae000 [   44K] r-x/r-x SM=COW  /usr/lib/system/liblaunch.dylib
  __TEXT               00007fff8fe02000-00007fff8fe0a000 [   32K] r-x/r-x SM=COW  /usr/lib/system/libcopyfile.dylib
  __TEXT               00007fff8fe4b000-00007fff8fe8e000 [  268K] r-x/r-x SM=COW
/usr/lib/system/libcommonCrypto.dylib
  __TEXT               00007fff90c0f000-00007fff90c19000 [   40K] r-x/r-x SM=COW
/usr/lib/system/libsystem_notify.dylib
  __TEXT               00007fff91376000-00007fff913a4000 [  184K] r-x/r-x SM=COW  /usr/lib/libSystem.B.dylib
  __TEXT               00007fff91489000-00007fff91490000 [   28K] r-x/r-x SM=COW  /usr/lib/system/libunwind.dylib
  __TEXT               00007fff91a22000-00007fff91a28000 [   24K] r-x/r-x SM=COW  /usr/lib/system/libcache.dylib
  __LINKEDIT           00007fff91b86000-00007fff94b30000 [  47.7M] r--/r-- SM=COW  /usr/lib/system/libxpc.dylib
  shared memory        00007ffffffe00000-00007ffffffe02000 [    8K] r-x/r-x SM=SHM


==== Writable regions for process 2636
  __DATA               000000010bf56000-000000010bf57000 [    4K] rw-/rwx SM=PRV  /Users/DumpAnalysis/Documents/AMCDA-
Dumps/Apps/App4/Build/Products/Release/App4
  MALLOC metadata      000000010bf59000-000000010bf5a000 [    4K] rw-/rwx SM=ZER
  MALLOC metadata      000000010bf5b000-000000010bf70000 [   84K] rw-/rwx SM=PRV
  MALLOC metadata      000000010bf72000-000000010bf87000 [   84K] rw-/rwx SM=PRV
  MALLOC_TINY          000000010c000000-000000010c100000 [ 1024K] rw-/rwx SM=PRV  DefaultMallocZone_0x10bf58000
  Stack                000000010c101000-000000010c183000 [  520K] rw-/rwx SM=PRV  thread 1
  Stack                000000010c184000-000000010c206000 [  520K] rw-/rwx SM=PRV  thread 2
  Stack                000000010c207000-000000010c289000 [  520K] rw-/rwx SM=PRV  thread 3
  Stack                000000010c28a000-000000010c30c000 [  520K] rw-/rwx SM=PRV  thread 4
  Stack                000000010c30d000-000000010c38f000 [  520K] rw-/rwx SM=PRV  thread 5
  MALLOC_SMALL         00007f88dc000000-00007f88dc800000 [ 8192K] rw-/rwx SM=PRV  DefaultMallocZone_0x10bf58000
  Stack                00007fff6b355000-00007fff6bb54000 [ 8188K] rw-/rwx SM=ZER  thread 0
  Stack                00007fff6bb54000-00007fff6bb55000 [    4K] rw-/rwx SM=COW  thread 0
  __DATA               00007fff6bb8a000-00007fff6bbc6000 [  240K] rw-/rwx SM=COW  /usr/lib/dyld
  __DATA               00007fff749c0000-00007fff749c3000 [   12K] rw-/rwx SM=COW  /usr/lib/system/libxpc.dylib
  __DATA               00007fff74a60000-00007fff74a61000 [    4K] rw-/rwx SM=COW
/usr/lib/system/libsystem_blocks.dylib
```

```
__DATA                    00007fff74a61000-00007fff74a71000 [   64K] rw-/rwx SM=COW  /usr/lib/system/libsystem_c.dylib
__DATA                    00007fff74ac4000-00007fff74aca000 [   24K] rw-/rwx SM=COW  /usr/lib/system/libdispatch.dylib
__DATA                    00007fff74b90000-00007fff74b91000 [    4K] rw-/rwx SM=COW  /usr/lib/system/libunc.dylib
__DATA                    00007fff74c11000-00007fff74c12000 [    4K] rw-/rw- SM=COW  /usr/lib/system/libremovefile.dylib
__DATA                    00007fff75141000-00007fff75142000 [    4K] rw-/rwx SM=COW  /usr/lib/system/libdyld.dylib
__DATA                    00007fff751a3000-00007fff751a4000 [    4K] rw-/rwx SM=COW
/usr/lib/system/libsystem_sandbox.dylib
__DATA                    00007fff75281000-00007fff75282000 [    4K] rw-/rwx SM=COW  /usr/lib/system/libmacho.dylib
__DATA                    00007fff75282000-00007fff75285000 [   12K] rw-/rwx SM=COW
/usr/lib/system/libsystem_kernel.dylib
__DATA                    00007fff752d8000-00007fff752d9000 [    4K] rw-/rwx SM=COW
/usr/lib/system/libsystem_dnssd.dylib
__DATA                    00007fff75453000-00007fff75456000 [   12K] rw-/rwx SM=COW  /usr/lib/system/libsystem_info.dylib
__DATA                    00007fff7551f000-00007fff75520000 [    4K] rw-/rwx SM=COW  /usr/lib/system/libquarantine.dylib
__DATA                    00007fff75559000-00007fff7555a000 [    4K] rw-/rwx SM=COW  /usr/lib/system/libkeymgr.dylib
__DATA                    00007fff75563000-00007fff75564000 [    4K] rw-/rwx SM=COW  /usr/lib/system/libcompiler_rt.dylib
__DATA                    00007fff75633000-00007fff75634000 [    4K] rw-/rw- SM=COW  /usr/lib/system/libdnsinfo.dylib
__DATA                    00007fff756d6000-00007fff756d7000 [    4K] rw-/rw- SM=COW
/usr/lib/system/libsystem_network.dylib
__DATA                    00007fff75813000-00007fff75814000 [    4K] rw-/rwx SM=COW  /usr/lib/system/liblaunch.dylib
__DATA                    00007fff75e41000-00007fff75e42000 [    4K] rw-/rw- SM=COW  /usr/lib/system/libcopyfile.dylib
__DATA                    00007fff75e4a000-00007fff75e50000 [   24K] rw-/rw- SM=COW
/usr/lib/system/libcommonCrypto.dylib
__DATA                    00007fff76342000-00007fff76343000 [    4K] rw-/rw- SM=COW
/usr/lib/system/libsystem_notify.dylib
__DATA                    00007fff763fd000-00007fff763fe000 [    4K] rw-/rw- SM=COW  /usr/lib/libSystem.B.dylib
__DATA                    00007fff76401000-00007fff76402000 [    4K] rw-/rw- SM=COW  /usr/lib/system/libunwind.dylib
__DATA                    00007fff764ab000-00007fff764ac000 [    4K] rw-/rw- SM=COW  /usr/lib/system/libcache.dylib

==== Legend
SM=sharing mode:
        COW=copy_on_write PRV=private NUL=empty ALI=aliased
        SHM=shared ZER=zero_filled S/A=shared_alias
==== Summary for process 2636
ReadOnly portion of Libraries: Total=50.2M resident=50.2M(100%) swapped_out_or_unallocated=0K(0%)
Writable regions: Total=36.6M written=120K(0%) resident=20.6M(56%) swapped_out=0K(0%) unallocated=16.0M(44%)


REGION TYPE                     VIRTUAL
===========                     =======
MALLOC                           9216K      see MALLOC ZONE table below
MALLOC guard page                  16K
MALLOC metadata                   180K
STACK GUARD                      56.0M
Stack                            10.5M
__DATA                            464K
__LINKEDIT                       47.7M
__TEXT                           2484K
shared memory                       8K
===========                     =======
TOTAL                           126.4M


                            VIRTUAL ALLOCATION     BYTES
MALLOC ZONE                    SIZE      COUNT  ALLOCATED  % FULL
===========                 ======= ==========  ========= ======
DefaultMallocZone_0x10bf58000  9216K         40         8K     0%
```

Exercise A4 (LLDB)

- **Goal:** Learn how to identify heap regions and heap corruption

- **Patterns:** Heap Corruption

- \AMCDA-Dumps\Exercise-A4-LLDB.pdf

Exercise A4 (LLDB)

Goal: Learn how to identify heap regions and heap corruption

Patterns: Heap Corruption

1.   Identify the problem thread and application specific diagnostic from the diagnostic report App4_2636.crash:

```
Process:         App4 [2636]
Path:            /Users/USER/Documents/*/App4
Identifier:      App4
Version:         ??? (???)
Code Type:       X86-64 (Native)
Parent Process:  bash [1549]

Date/Time:       2012-07-24 21:19:38.344 +0100
OS Version:      Mac OS X 10.7.4 (11E53)
Report Version:  9

Crashed Thread:  3

Exception Type:  EXC_CRASH (SIGABRT)
Exception Codes: 0x0000000000000000, 0x0000000000000000

Application Specific Information:
*** error for object 0x7f88dc001408: incorrect checksum for freed object - object was probably modified after being
freed.


Thread 0:: Dispatch queue: com.apple.main-thread
0   libsystem_kernel.dylib          0x00007fff8a10ce42 __semwait_signal + 10
1   libsystem_c.dylib               0x00007fff84d6edea nanosleep + 164
2   libsystem_c.dylib               0x00007fff84d6ec2c sleep + 61
3   libsystem_c.dylib               0x00007fff84d6ec08 sleep + 25
4   App4                            0x000000010bf55c33 main + 195
5   App4                            0x000000010bf55724 start + 52

Thread 1:
0   libsystem_kernel.dylib          0x00007fff8a10ce42 __semwait_signal + 10
1   libsystem_c.dylib               0x00007fff84d6edea nanosleep + 164
2   libsystem_c.dylib               0x00007fff84d6ec2c sleep + 61
3   libsystem_c.dylib               0x00007fff84d6ec08 sleep + 25
4   App4                            0x000000010bf559b2 bar_one + 18
5   App4                            0x000000010bf559c9 foo_one + 9
6   App4                            0x000000010bf559e1 thread_one + 17
7   libsystem_c.dylib               0x00007fff84db88bf _pthread_start + 335
8   libsystem_c.dylib               0x00007fff84dbbb75 thread_start + 13

Thread 2:
0   libsystem_kernel.dylib          0x00007fff8a10ce42 __semwait_signal + 10
1   libsystem_c.dylib               0x00007fff84d6edea nanosleep + 164
2   libsystem_c.dylib               0x00007fff84d6ec2c sleep + 61
3   libsystem_c.dylib               0x00007fff84d6ec08 sleep + 25
4   App4                            0x000000010bf55a12 bar_two + 18
5   App4                            0x000000010bf55a29 foo_two + 9
6   App4                            0x000000010bf55a41 thread_two + 17
7   libsystem_c.dylib               0x00007fff84db88bf _pthread_start + 335
8   libsystem_c.dylib               0x00007fff84dbbb75 thread_start + 13
```

```
Thread 3 Crashed:
0    libsystem_kernel.dylib          0x00007fff8a10cce2 __pthread_kill + 10
1    libsystem_c.dylib               0x00007fff84dba7d2 pthread_kill + 95
2    libsystem_c.dylib               0x00007fff84daba7a abort + 143
3    libsystem_c.dylib               0x00007fff84dcd4ac szone_error + 459
4    libsystem_c.dylib               0x00007fff84dcd4e8 free_list_checksum_botch + 29
5    libsystem_c.dylib               0x00007fff84dcda7b small_free_list_remove_ptr + 163
6    libsystem_c.dylib               0x00007fff84dd1bf7 szone_free_definite_size + 3403
7    libsystem_c.dylib               0x00007fff84e0a789 free + 194
8    App4                            0x000000010bf55933 proc + 515
9    App4                            0x000000010bf55a69 bar_three + 9
10   App4                            0x000000010bf55a79 foo_three + 9
11   App4                            0x000000010bf55a91 thread_three + 17
12   libsystem_c.dylib               0x00007fff84db88bf _pthread_start + 335
13   libsystem_c.dylib               0x00007fff84dbbb75 thread_start + 13

Thread 4:
0    libsystem_kernel.dylib          0x00007fff8a10ce42 __semwait_signal + 10
1    libsystem_c.dylib               0x00007fff84d6edea nanosleep + 164
2    libsystem_c.dylib               0x00007fff84d6ec2c sleep + 61
3    libsystem_c.dylib               0x00007fff84d6ec08 sleep + 25
4    App4                            0x000000010bf55ac2 bar_four + 18
5    App4                            0x000000010bf55ad9 foo_four + 9
6    App4                            0x000000010bf55af1 thread_four + 17
7    libsystem_c.dylib               0x00007fff84db88bf _pthread_start + 335
8    libsystem_c.dylib               0x00007fff84dbbb75 thread_start + 13

Thread 5:
0    libsystem_kernel.dylib          0x00007fff8a10ce42 __semwait_signal + 10
1    libsystem_c.dylib               0x00007fff84d6edea nanosleep + 164
2    libsystem_c.dylib               0x00007fff84d6ec2c sleep + 61
3    libsystem_c.dylib               0x00007fff84d6ec08 sleep + 25
4    App4                            0x000000010bf55b22 bar_five + 18
5    App4                            0x000000010bf55b39 foo_five + 9
6    App4                            0x000000010bf55b51 thread_five + 17
7    libsystem_c.dylib               0x00007fff84db88bf _pthread_start + 335
8    libsystem_c.dylib               0x00007fff84dbbb75 thread_start + 13

Thread 3 crashed with X86 Thread State (64-bit):
  rax: 0x0000000000000000  rbx: 0x0000000000000006  rcx: 0x000000010c286ba8  rdx: 0x0000000000000000
  rdi: 0x0000000000001403  rsi: 0x0000000000000006  rbp: 0x000000010c286bd0  rsp: 0x000000010c286ba8
   r8: 0x00007fff74a67fb8   r9: 0x0000000000000000  r10: 0x00007fff8a10cd0a  r11: 0xffffff80002da8d0
  r12: 0x000000010bf58000  r13: 0x000000010bf89000  r14: 0x000000010c287000  r15: 0x000000010bf890c0
  rip: 0x00007fff8a10cce2  rfl: 0x0000000000000246  cr2: 0x00007fff74a67fb8
Logical CPU: 0

Binary Images:
       0x10bf55000 -        0x10bf55fff +App4 (??? - ???) <EAEF8835-E281-36D8-B291-81804730D297>
/Users/USER/Documents/*/App4
    0x7fff6bb55000 -     0x7fff6bb89baf  dyld (195.6 - ???) <0CD1B35B-A28F-32DA-B72E-452EAD609613> /usr/lib/dyld
    0x7fff849f2000 -     0x7fff84a0ffff  libxpc.dylib (77.19.0 - compatibility 1.0.0) <9F57891B-D7EF-3050-BEDD-
21E7C6668248> /usr/lib/system/libxpc.dylib
    0x7fff84d68000 -     0x7fff84d69ff7  libsystem_blocks.dylib (53.0.0 - compatibility 1.0.0) <8BCA214A-8992-34B2-
A8B9-B74DEACA1869> /usr/lib/system/libsystem_blocks.dylib
    0x7fff84d6a000 -     0x7fff84e47fef  libsystem_c.dylib (763.13.0 - compatibility 1.0.0) <41B43515-2806-3FBC-ACF1-
A16F35B7E290> /usr/lib/system/libsystem_c.dylib
    0x7fff85022000 -     0x7fff85030fff  libdispatch.dylib (187.9.0 - compatibility 1.0.0) <1D5BE322-A9B9-3BCE-8FAC-
076FB07CF54A> /usr/lib/system/libdispatch.dylib
    0x7fff855f0000 -     0x7fff855f1fff  libunc.dylib (24.0.0 - compatibility 1.0.0) <337960EE-0A85-3DD0-A760-
7134CF4C0AFF> /usr/lib/system/libunc.dylib
    0x7fff85ae3000 -     0x7fff85ae4ff7  libremovefile.dylib (21.1.0 - compatibility 1.0.0) <739E6C83-AA52-3C6C-A680-
B37FE2888A04> /usr/lib/system/libremovefile.dylib
    0x7fff89114000 -     0x7fff89118fff  libmathCommon.A.dylib (2026.0.0 - compatibility 1.0.0) <FF83AFF7-42B2-306E-
90AF-D539C51A4542> /usr/lib/system/libmathCommon.A.dylib
    0x7fff89119000 -     0x7fff8911dfff  libdyld.dylib (195.5.0 - compatibility 1.0.0) <380C3F44-0CA7-3514-8080-
46D1C9DF4FCD> /usr/lib/system/libdyld.dylib
    0x7fff89740000 -     0x7fff89741ff7  libsystem_sandbox.dylib (??? - ???) <96D38E74-F18F-3CCB-A20B-E8E3ADC4E166>
/usr/lib/system/libsystem_sandbox.dylib
    0x7fff8a0ef000 -     0x7fff8a0f5fff  libmacho.dylib (800.0.0 - compatibility 1.0.0) <165514D7-1BFA-38EF-A151-
676DCD21FB64> /usr/lib/system/libmacho.dylib
    0x7fff8a0f6000 -     0x7fff8a116fff  libsystem_kernel.dylib (1699.26.8 - compatibility 1.0.0) <1DDC0B0F-DB2A-34D6-
895D-E5B2B5618946> /usr/lib/system/libsystem_kernel.dylib
    0x7fff8a2ac000 -     0x7fff8a2b4fff  libsystem_dnssd.dylib (??? - ???) <D9BB1F87-A42B-3CBC-9DC2-FC07FCEF0016>
/usr/lib/system/libsystem_dnssd.dylib
    0x7fff8ae26000 -     0x7fff8ae61fff  libsystem_info.dylib (??? - ???) <35F90252-2AE1-32C5-8D34-782C614D9639>
/usr/lib/system/libsystem_info.dylib
```

```
   0x7fff8b248000 -     0x7fff8b24afff  libquarantine.dylib (36.6.0 - compatibility 1.0.0) <0EBF714B-4B69-3E1F-9A7D-
6BBC2AACB310> /usr/lib/system/libquarantine.dylib
   0x7fff8b3b4000 -     0x7fff8b3b4fff  libkeymgr.dylib (23.0.0 - compatibility 1.0.0) <61EFED6A-A407-301E-B454-
CD18314F0075> /usr/lib/system/libkeymgr.dylib
   0x7fff8b3dd000 -     0x7fff8b3e2fff  libcompiler_rt.dylib (6.0.0 - compatibility 1.0.0) <98ECD5F6-E85C-32A5-98CD-
8911230CB66A> /usr/lib/system/libcompiler_rt.dylib
   0x7fff8bd1a000 -     0x7fff8bd1bfff  libdnsinfo.dylib (395.11.0 - compatibility 1.0.0) <853BAAA5-270F-3FDC-B025-
D448DB72E1C3> /usr/lib/system/libdnsinfo.dylib
   0x7fff8c528000 -     0x7fff8c52dff7  libsystem_network.dylib (??? - ???) <5DE7024E-1D2D-34A2-80F4-08326331A75B>
/usr/lib/system/libsystem_network.dylib
   0x7fff8cfa3000 -     0x7fff8cfadff7  liblaunch.dylib (392.38.0 - compatibility 1.0.0) <6ECB7F19-B384-32C1-8652-
2463C1CF4815> /usr/lib/system/liblaunch.dylib
   0x7fff8fe02000 -     0x7fff8fe09fff  libcopyfile.dylib (85.1.0 - compatibility 1.0.0) <0AB51EE2-E914-358C-AC19-
47BC024BDAE7> /usr/lib/system/libcopyfile.dylib
   0x7fff8fe4b000 -     0x7fff8fe8dff7  libcommonCrypto.dylib (55010.0.0 - compatibility 1.0.0) <BB770C22-8C57-365A-
8716-4A3C36AE7BFB> /usr/lib/system/libcommonCrypto.dylib
   0x7fff90c0f000 -     0x7fff90c18ff7  libsystem_notify.dylib (80.1.0 - compatibility 1.0.0) <A4D651E3-D1C6-3934-
AD49-7A104FD14596> /usr/lib/system/libsystem_notify.dylib
   0x7fff91376000 -     0x7fff913a3fe7  libSystem.B.dylib (159.1.0 - compatibility 1.0.0) <7BEBB139-50BB-3112-947A-
F4AA168F991C> /usr/lib/libSystem.B.dylib
   0x7fff91489000 -     0x7fff9148fff7  libunwind.dylib (30.0.0 - compatibility 1.0.0) <1E9C6C8C-CBE8-3F4B-A5B5-
E03E3AB53231> /usr/lib/system/libunwind.dylib
   0x7fff91a22000 -     0x7fff91a27fff  libcache.dylib (47.0.0 - compatibility 1.0.0) <1571C3AB-BCB2-38CD-B3B2-
C5FC3F927C6A> /usr/lib/system/libcache.dylib

External Modification Summary:
  Calls made by other processes targeting this process:
    task_for_pid: 2
    thread_create: 0
    thread_set_state: 0
  Calls made by this process:
    task_for_pid: 0
    thread_create: 0
    thread_set_state: 0
  Calls made by all processes on this machine:
    task_for_pid: 4660
    thread_create: 0
    thread_set_state: 0

VM Region Summary:
ReadOnly portion of Libraries: Total=50.2M resident=50.2M(100%) swapped_out_or_unallocated=0K(0%)
Writable regions: Total=46.9M written=14.0M(30%) resident=50.7M(108%) swapped_out=0K(0%)
unallocated=16777216.0T(37504992411648%)

REGION TYPE                 VIRTUAL
===========                 =======
MALLOC                         9412K
Stack                          66.6M
VM_ALLOCATE                       4K
__DATA                          464K
__LINKEDIT                     47.7M
__TEXT                         2484K
shared memory                    12K
===========                 =======
TOTAL                         126.4M
```

2.   Load a core dump core.2636 and App4 executable:

$ lldb -c ~/Documents/AMCDA-Dumps/core.2636 -f ~/Documents/AMCDA-Dumps/Apps/App4/Build/Products/Release/App4

```
error: core.2636 is a corrupt mach-o file: load command 48 LC_SEGMENT_64 has a fileoff +
filesize (0x168b8000) that extends beyond the end of the file (0x168b6000), the segment will be
truncated
Core file '/Users/DumpAnalysis/Documents/AMCDA-Dumps/core.2636' (x86_64) was loaded.
Process 0 stopped
* thread #1: tid = 0x0000, 0x00007fff8a10ce42 libsystem_kernel.dylib`__semwait_signal + 10,
stop reason = signal SIGSTOP
```

```
     frame #0: 0x00007fff8a10ce42 libsystem_kernel.dylib`__semwait_signal + 10
libsystem_kernel.dylib`__semwait_signal + 10:
-> 0x7fff8a10ce42:  jae    0x7fff8a10ce49              ; __semwait_signal + 17
   0x7fff8a10ce44:  jmpq   0x7fff8a10dffc              ; cerror
   0x7fff8a10ce49:  ret
   0x7fff8a10ce4a:  nop
  thread #2: tid = 0x0001, 0x00007fff8a10ce42 libsystem_kernel.dylib`__semwait_signal + 10,
stop reason = signal SIGSTOP
     frame #0: 0x00007fff8a10ce42 libsystem_kernel.dylib`__semwait_signal + 10
libsystem_kernel.dylib`__semwait_signal + 10:
-> 0x7fff8a10ce42:  jae    0x7fff8a10ce49              ; __semwait_signal + 17
   0x7fff8a10ce44:  jmpq   0x7fff8a10dffc              ; cerror
   0x7fff8a10ce49:  ret
   0x7fff8a10ce4a:  nop
  thread #3: tid = 0x0002, 0x00007fff8a10ce42 libsystem_kernel.dylib`__semwait_signal + 10,
stop reason = signal SIGSTOP
     frame #0: 0x00007fff8a10ce42 libsystem_kernel.dylib`__semwait_signal + 10
libsystem_kernel.dylib`__semwait_signal + 10:
-> 0x7fff8a10ce42:  jae    0x7fff8a10ce49              ; __semwait_signal + 17
   0x7fff8a10ce44:  jmpq   0x7fff8a10dffc              ; cerror
   0x7fff8a10ce49:  ret
   0x7fff8a10ce4a:  nop
  thread #4: tid = 0x0003, 0x00007fff8a10cce2 libsystem_kernel.dylib`__pthread_kill + 10, stop
reason = signal SIGSTOP
     frame #0: 0x00007fff8a10cce2 libsystem_kernel.dylib`__pthread_kill + 10
libsystem_kernel.dylib`__pthread_kill + 10:
-> 0x7fff8a10cce2:  jae    0x7fff8a10cce9              ; __pthread_kill + 17
   0x7fff8a10cce4:  jmpq   0x7fff8a10dffc              ; cerror
   0x7fff8a10cce9:  ret
   0x7fff8a10ccea:  nop
  thread #5: tid = 0x0004, 0x00007fff8a10ce42 libsystem_kernel.dylib`__semwait_signal + 10,
stop reason = signal SIGSTOP
     frame #0: 0x00007fff8a10ce42 libsystem_kernel.dylib`__semwait_signal + 10
libsystem_kernel.dylib`__semwait_signal + 10:
-> 0x7fff8a10ce42:  jae    0x7fff8a10ce49              ; __semwait_signal + 17
   0x7fff8a10ce44:  jmpq   0x7fff8a10dffc              ; cerror
   0x7fff8a10ce49:  ret
   0x7fff8a10ce4a:  nop
  thread #6: tid = 0x0005, 0x00007fff8a10ce42 libsystem_kernel.dylib`__semwait_signal + 10,
stop reason = signal SIGSTOP
     frame #0: 0x00007fff8a10ce42 libsystem_kernel.dylib`__semwait_signal + 10
libsystem_kernel.dylib`__semwait_signal + 10:
-> 0x7fff8a10ce42:  jae    0x7fff8a10ce49              ; __semwait_signal + 17
   0x7fff8a10ce44:  jmpq   0x7fff8a10dffc              ; cerror
   0x7fff8a10ce49:  ret
   0x7fff8a10ce4a:  nop
```

3.   Go to the identifed problem core thread 3 (thread #4):

```
(lldb) thread select 4
* thread #4: tid = 0x0003, 0x00007fff8a10cce2 libsystem_kernel.dylib`__pthread_kill + 10, stop
reason = signal SIGSTOP
    frame #0: 0x00007fff8a10cce2 libsystem_kernel.dylib`__pthread_kill + 10
libsystem_kernel.dylib`__pthread_kill + 10:
-> 0x7fff8a10cce2:  jae     0x7fff8a10cce9            ; __pthread_kill + 17
   0x7fff8a10cce4:  jmpq    0x7fff8a10dffc            ; cerror
   0x7fff8a10cce9:  ret
   0x7fff8a10ccea:  nop

(lldb) bt
* thread #4: tid = 0x0003, 0x00007fff8a10cce2 libsystem_kernel.dylib`__pthread_kill + 10, stop
reason = signal SIGSTOP
    frame #0: 0x00007fff8a10cce2 libsystem_kernel.dylib`__pthread_kill + 10
    frame #1: 0x00007fff84dba7d2 libsystem_c.dylib`pthread_kill + 95
    frame #2: 0x00007fff84daba7a libsystem_c.dylib`abort + 143
    frame #3: 0x00007fff84dcd4ac libsystem_c.dylib`szone_error + 459
    frame #4: 0x00007fff84dcd4e8 libsystem_c.dylib`free_list_checksum_botch + 29
    frame #5: 0x00007fff84dcda7b libsystem_c.dylib`small_free_list_remove_ptr + 163
    frame #6: 0x00007fff84dd1bf7 libsystem_c.dylib`szone_free_definite_size + 3403
    frame #7: 0x00007fff84e0a789 libsystem_c.dylib`free + 194
    frame #8: 0x000000010bf55933 App4`proc + 515
    frame #9: 0x000000010bf55a69 App4`bar_three + 9
    frame #10: 0x000000010bf55a79 App4`foo_three + 9
    frame #11: 0x000000010bf55a91 App4`thread_three + 17
    frame #12: 0x00007fff84db88bf libsystem_c.dylib`_pthread_start + 335
    frame #13: 0x00007fff84dbbb75 libsystem_c.dylib`thread_start + 13
```

4.   Check the corrupt heap entry address specified in the diagnostic report:

```
(lldb) x/s 0x7f88dc001408
0x7f88dc001408:        "ash!"

(lldb) x/s 0x7f88dc001408-8
0x7f88dc001400:        "Hello Crash!"
```

5.   Switch to the stack frame 8 to check heap free functions and blocks they free:

```
(lldb) f 8
frame #8: 0x000000010bf55933 App4`proc + 515
App4`proc + 515:
-> 0x10bf55933:  movq    -32(%rbp), %rdi
   0x10bf55937:  callq   0x10bf55c50               ; symbol stub for: free
   0x10bf5593c:  movq    -24(%rbp), %rdi
   0x10bf55940:  callq   0x10bf55c50               ; symbol stub for: free

(lldb) di -n proc
App4`proc:
   0x10bf55730:  pushq   %rbp
   0x10bf55731:  movq    %rsp, %rbp
   0x10bf55734:  subq    $128, %rsp
   0x10bf5573b:  movabsq $1024, %rdi
   0x10bf55745:  callq   0x10bf55c56               ; symbol stub for: malloc
   0x10bf5574a:  movabsq $1024, %rdi
   0x10bf55754:  movq    %rax, -8(%rbp)
   0x10bf55758:  callq   0x10bf55c56               ; symbol stub for: malloc
   0x10bf5575d:  movabsq $1024, %rdi
```

```
0x10bf55767:    movq    %rax, -16(%rbp)
0x10bf5576b:    callq   0x10bf55c56              ; symbol stub for: malloc
0x10bf55770:    movabsq $1024, %rdi
0x10bf5577a:    movq    %rax, -24(%rbp)
0x10bf5577e:    callq   0x10bf55c56              ; symbol stub for: malloc
0x10bf55783:    movabsq $1024, %rdi
0x10bf5578d:    movq    %rax, -32(%rbp)
0x10bf55791:    callq   0x10bf55c56              ; symbol stub for: malloc
0x10bf55796:    movabsq $1024, %rdi
0x10bf557a0:    movq    %rax, -40(%rbp)
0x10bf557a4:    callq   0x10bf55c56              ; symbol stub for: malloc
0x10bf557a9:    movabsq $1024, %rdi
0x10bf557b3:    movq    %rax, -48(%rbp)
0x10bf557b7:    callq   0x10bf55c56              ; symbol stub for: malloc
0x10bf557bc:    movq    %rax, -56(%rbp)
0x10bf557c0:    movq    -48(%rbp), %rdi
0x10bf557c4:    callq   0x10bf55c50              ; symbol stub for: free
0x10bf557c9:    movq    -32(%rbp), %rdi
0x10bf557cd:    callq   0x10bf55c50              ; symbol stub for: free
0x10bf557d2:    movq    -16(%rbp), %rdi
0x10bf557d6:    callq   0x10bf55c50              ; symbol stub for: free
0x10bf557db:    movabsq $-1, %rax
0x10bf557e5:    cmpq    $-1, %rax
0x10bf557eb:    je      0x10bf55814             ; proc + 228
0x10bf557f1:    leaq    1212(%rip), %rsi        ; "Hello Crash!"
0x10bf557f8:    movabsq $-1, %rdx
0x10bf55802:    movq    -16(%rbp), %rdi
0x10bf55806:    callq   0x10bf55c44             ; symbol stub for: __strcpy_chk
0x10bf5580b:    movq    %rax, -64(%rbp)
0x10bf5580f:    jmpq    0x10bf55828             ; proc + 248
0x10bf55814:    leaq    1177(%rip), %rsi        ; "Hello Crash!"
0x10bf5581b:    movq    -16(%rbp), %rdi
0x10bf5581f:    callq   0x10bf55970             ; __inline_strcpy_chk
0x10bf55824:    movq    %rax, -72(%rbp)
0x10bf55828:    movabsq $-1, %rax
0x10bf55832:    movq    -32(%rbp), %rcx
0x10bf55836:    cmpq    $-1, %rax
0x10bf5583c:    movq    %rcx, -80(%rbp)
0x10bf55840:    je      0x10bf55869             ; proc + 313
0x10bf55846:    leaq    1127(%rip), %rsi        ; "Hello Crash!"
0x10bf5584d:    movabsq $-1, %rdx
0x10bf55857:    movq    -32(%rbp), %rdi
0x10bf5585b:    callq   0x10bf55c44             ; symbol stub for: __strcpy_chk
0x10bf55860:    movq    %rax, -88(%rbp)
0x10bf55864:    jmpq    0x10bf5587d             ; proc + 333
0x10bf55869:    leaq    1092(%rip), %rsi        ; "Hello Crash!"
0x10bf55870:    movq    -32(%rbp), %rdi
0x10bf55874:    callq   0x10bf55970             ; __inline_strcpy_chk
0x10bf55879:    movq    %rax, -96(%rbp)
0x10bf5587d:    movabsq $-1, %rax
0x10bf55887:    movq    -48(%rbp), %rcx
0x10bf5588b:    cmpq    $-1, %rax
0x10bf55891:    movq    %rcx, -104(%rbp)
0x10bf55895:    je      0x10bf558be             ; proc + 398
0x10bf5589b:    leaq    1042(%rip), %rsi        ; "Hello Crash!"
0x10bf558a2:    movabsq $-1, %rdx
0x10bf558ac:    movq    -48(%rbp), %rdi
0x10bf558b0:    callq   0x10bf55c44             ; symbol stub for: __strcpy_chk
0x10bf558b5:    movq    %rax, -112(%rbp)
0x10bf558b9:    jmpq    0x10bf558d2             ; proc + 418
```

```
0x10bf558be:  leaq    1007(%rip), %rsi          ; "Hello Crash!"
0x10bf558c5:  movq    -48(%rbp), %rdi
0x10bf558c9:  callq   0x10bf55970              ; __inline_strcpy_chk
0x10bf558ce:  movq    %rax, -120(%rbp)
0x10bf558d2:  movabsq $512, %rdi
0x10bf558dc:  callq   0x10bf55c56             ; symbol stub for: malloc
0x10bf558e1:  movabsq $1024, %rdi
0x10bf558eb:  movq    %rax, -16(%rbp)
0x10bf558ef:  callq   0x10bf55c56             ; symbol stub for: malloc
0x10bf558f4:  movabsq $512, %rdi
0x10bf558fe:  movq    %rax, -32(%rbp)
0x10bf55902:  callq   0x10bf55c56             ; symbol stub for: malloc
0x10bf55907:  movl    $300, %edi
0x10bf5590c:  movq    %rax, -48(%rbp)
0x10bf55910:  callq   0x10bf55c62             ; symbol stub for: sleep
0x10bf55915:  movq    -56(%rbp), %rdi
0x10bf55919:  movl    %eax, -124(%rbp)
0x10bf5591c:  callq   0x10bf55c50             ; symbol stub for: free
0x10bf55921:  movq    -48(%rbp), %rdi
0x10bf55925:  callq   0x10bf55c50             ; symbol stub for: free
0x10bf5592a:  movq    -40(%rbp), %rdi
0x10bf5592e:  callq   0x10bf55c50             ; symbol stub for: free
-> 0x10bf55933:  movq    -32(%rbp), %rdi
0x10bf55937:  callq   0x10bf55c50             ; symbol stub for: free
0x10bf5593c:  movq    -24(%rbp), %rdi
0x10bf55940:  callq   0x10bf55c50             ; symbol stub for: free
0x10bf55945:  movq    -16(%rbp), %rdi
0x10bf55949:  callq   0x10bf55c50             ; symbol stub for: free
0x10bf5594e:  movq    -8(%rbp), %rdi
0x10bf55952:  callq   0x10bf55c50             ; symbol stub for: free
0x10bf55957:  movl    $4294967295, %edi
0x10bf5595c:  callq   0x10bf55c62             ; symbol stub for: sleep
0x10bf55961:  movl    %eax, -128(%rbp)
0x10bf55964:  addq    $128, %rsp
0x10bf5596b:  popq    %rbp
0x10bf5596c:  ret
0x10bf5596d:  nopl    (%rax)
```

```
(lldb) re r rbp
    rbp = 0x000000010c286ed0

(lldb) x/xg 0x000000010c286ed0-40
0x10c286ea8: 0x00007f88dc001000

(lldb) x/s 0x00007f88dc001000
0x7f88dc001000:        ""

(lldb) x/xg 0x000000010c286ed0-32
0x10c286eb0: 0x00007f88dc000400

(lldb) x/s 0x00007f88dc000400
0x7f88dc000400:        "Hello Crash!"

(lldb) x/xg 0x000000010c286ed0-48
0x10c286ea0: 0x000000010c000ac0

(lldb) x/xg 0x000000010c286ed0-56
0x10c286e98: 0x00007f88dc001800
```

```
(lldb) x/xg 0x000000010c286ed0-24
0x10c286eb8: 0x00007f88dc000800

(lldb) x/xg 0x000000010c286ed0-16
0x10c286ec0: 0x000000010c0008c0

(lldb) x/xg 0x000000010c286ed0-8
0x10c286ec8: 0x00007f88dc000000
```

6.   Notice different sections for heap metadata and heap block base addresses 0x7f88dc000000 and 0x000000010c000000 and find them on vmmap report vmmap_2636.log:

```
Virtual Memory Map of process 2636 (App4)
Output report format:  2.2  -- 64-bit process

==== Non-writable regions for process 2636
__TEXT                 000000010bf55000-000000010bf56000 [    4K] r-x/rwx SM=COW  /Users/DumpAnalysis/Documents/AMCDA-
Dumps/Apps/App4/Build/Products/Release/App4
__LINKEDIT             000000010bf57000-000000010bf58000 [    4K] r--/rwx SM=COW  /Users/DumpAnalysis/Documents/AMCDA-
Dumps/Apps/App4/Build/Products/Release/App4
MALLOC metadata        000000010bf58000-000000010bf59000 [    4K] r--/rwx SM=ZER
MALLOC guard page      000000010bf5a000-000000010bf5b000 [    4K] ---/rwx SM=NUL
MALLOC guard page      000000010bf70000-000000010bf72000 [    8K] ---/rwx SM=NUL
MALLOC guard page      000000010bf87000-000000010bf88000 [    4K] ---/rwx SM=NUL
MALLOC metadata        000000010bf88000-000000010bf89000 [    4K] r--/rwx SM=PRV
STACK GUARD            000000010c100000-000000010c101000 [    4K] ---/rwx SM=NUL  stack guard for thread 1
STACK GUARD            000000010c183000-000000010c184000 [    4K] ---/rwx SM=NUL  stack guard for thread 2
STACK GUARD            000000010c206000-000000010c207000 [    4K] ---/rwx SM=NUL  stack guard for thread 3
STACK GUARD            000000010c289000-000000010c28a000 [    4K] ---/rwx SM=NUL  stack guard for thread 4
STACK GUARD            000000010c30c000-000000010c30d000 [    4K] ---/rwx SM=NUL  stack guard for thread 5
STACK GUARD            00007fff67b55000-00007fff6b355000 [ 56.0M] ---/rwx SM=NUL  stack guard for thread 0
__TEXT                 00007fff6bb55000-00007fff6bb8a000 [  212K] r-x/rwx SM=COW  /usr/lib/dyld
__LINKEDIT             00007fff6bbc6000-00007fff6bbd9000 [   76K] r--/rwx SM=COW  /usr/lib/dyld
__TEXT                 00007fff849f2000-00007fff84a10000 [  120K] r-x/r-x SM=COW  /usr/lib/system/libxpc.dylib
__TEXT                 00007fff84d68000-00007fff84d6a000 [    8K] r-x/r-x SM=COW
/usr/lib/system/libsystem_blocks.dylib
__TEXT                 00007fff84d6a000-00007fff84e48000 [  888K] r-x/r-x SM=COW  /usr/lib/system/libsystem_c.dylib
__TEXT                 00007fff85022000-00007fff85031000 [   60K] r-x/r-x SM=COW  /usr/lib/system/libdispatch.dylib
__TEXT                 00007fff855f0000-00007fff855f2000 [    8K] r-x/r-x SM=COW  /usr/lib/system/libunc.dylib
__TEXT                 00007fff85ae3000-00007fff85ae5000 [    8K] r-x/r-x SM=COW  /usr/lib/system/libremovefile.dylib
__TEXT                 00007fff89114000-00007fff89119000 [   20K] r-x/r-x SM=COW
/usr/lib/system/libmathCommon.A.dylib
__TEXT                 00007fff89119000-00007fff8911e000 [   20K] r-x/r-x SM=COW  /usr/lib/system/libdyld.dylib
__TEXT                 00007fff89740000-00007fff89742000 [    8K] r-x/r-x SM=COW
/usr/lib/system/libsystem_sandbox.dylib
__TEXT                 00007fff8a0ef000-00007fff8a0f6000 [   28K] r-x/r-x SM=COW  /usr/lib/system/libmacho.dylib
__TEXT                 00007fff8a0f6000-00007fff8a117000 [  132K] r-x/r-x SM=COW
/usr/lib/system/libsystem_kernel.dylib
__TEXT                 00007fff8a2ac000-00007fff8a2b5000 [   36K] r-x/r-x SM=COW
/usr/lib/system/libsystem_dnssd.dylib
__TEXT                 00007fff8ae26000-00007fff8ae62000 [  240K] r-x/r-x SM=COW  /usr/lib/system/libsystem_info.dylib
__TEXT                 00007fff8b248000-00007fff8b24b000 [   12K] r-x/r-x SM=COW  /usr/lib/system/libquarantine.dylib
__TEXT                 00007fff8b3b4000-00007fff8b3b5000 [    4K] r-x/r-x SM=COW  /usr/lib/system/libkeymgr.dylib
__TEXT                 00007fff8b3dd000-00007fff8b3e3000 [   24K] r-x/r-x SM=COW  /usr/lib/system/libcompiler_rt.dylib
__TEXT                 00007fff8bd1a000-00007fff8bd1c000 [    8K] r-x/r-x SM=COW  /usr/lib/system/libdnsinfo.dylib
__TEXT                 00007fff8c528000-00007fff8c52e000 [   24K] r-x/r-x SM=COW
/usr/lib/system/libsystem_network.dylib
__TEXT                 00007fff8cfa3000-00007fff8cfae000 [   44K] r-x/r-x SM=COW  /usr/lib/system/liblaunch.dylib
__TEXT                 00007fff8fe02000-00007fff8fe0a000 [   32K] r-x/r-x SM=COW  /usr/lib/system/libcopyfile.dylib
__TEXT                 00007fff8fe4b000-00007fff8fe8e000 [  268K] r-x/r-x SM=COW
/usr/lib/system/libcommonCrypto.dylib
__TEXT                 00007fff90c0f000-00007fff90c19000 [   40K] r-x/r-x SM=COW
/usr/lib/system/libsystem_notify.dylib
__TEXT                 00007fff91376000-00007fff913a4000 [  184K] r-x/r-x SM=COW  /usr/lib/libSystem.B.dylib
__TEXT                 00007fff91489000-00007fff91490000 [   28K] r-x/r-x SM=COW  /usr/lib/system/libunwind.dylib
__TEXT                 00007fff91a22000-00007fff91a28000 [   24K] r-x/r-x SM=COW  /usr/lib/system/libcache.dylib
__LINKEDIT             00007fff91b86000-00007fff94b30000 [ 47.7M] r--/r-- SM=COW  /usr/lib/system/libxpc.dylib
shared memory          00007ffffe00000-00007ffffe02000 [    8K] r-x/r-x SM=SHM
```

```
==== Writable regions for process 2636
__DATA                000000010bf56000-000000010bf57000 [    4K] rw-/rwx SM=PRV  /Users/DumpAnalysis/Documents/AMCDA-
Dumps/Apps/App4/Build/Products/Release/App4
MALLOC metadata       000000010bf59000-000000010bf5a000 [    4K] rw-/rwx SM=ZER
MALLOC metadata       000000010bf5b000-000000010bf70000 [   84K] rw-/rwx SM=PRV
MALLOC metadata       000000010bf72000-000000010bf87000 [   84K] rw-/rwx SM=PRV
MALLOC_TINY           000000010c000000-000000010c100000 [ 1024K] rw-/rwx SM=PRV  DefaultMallocZone_0x10bf58000
Stack                 000000010c101000-000000010c183000 [  520K] rw-/rwx SM=PRV  thread 1
Stack                 000000010c184000-000000010c206000 [  520K] rw-/rwx SM=PRV  thread 2
Stack                 000000010c207000-000000010c289000 [  520K] rw-/rwx SM=PRV  thread 3
Stack                 000000010c28a000-000000010c30c000 [  520K] rw-/rwx SM=PRV  thread 4
Stack                 000000010c30d000-000000010c38f000 [  520K] rw-/rwx SM=PRV  thread 5
MALLOC_SMALL          00007f88dc000000-00007f88dc800000 [ 8192K] rw-/rwx SM=PRV  DefaultMallocZone_0x10bf58000
Stack                 00007fff6b355000-00007fff6bb54000 [ 8188K] rw-/rwx SM=ZER  thread 0
Stack                 00007fff6bb54000-00007fff6bb55000 [    4K] rw-/rwx SM=COW  thread 0
__DATA                00007fff6bb8a000-00007fff6bbc6000 [  240K] rw-/rwx SM=COW  /usr/lib/dyld
__DATA                00007fff749c0000-00007fff749c3000 [   12K] rw-/rwx SM=COW  /usr/lib/system/libxpc.dylib
__DATA                00007fff74a60000-00007fff74a61000 [    4K] rw-/rwx SM=COW
/usr/lib/system/libsystem_blocks.dylib
__DATA                00007fff74a61000-00007fff74a71000 [   64K] rw-/rwx SM=COW  /usr/lib/system/libsystem_c.dylib
__DATA                00007fff74ac4000-00007fff74aca000 [   24K] rw-/rwx SM=COW  /usr/lib/system/libdispatch.dylib
__DATA                00007fff74b90000-00007fff74b91000 [    4K] rw-/rwx SM=COW  /usr/lib/system/libunc.dylib
__DATA                00007fff74c11000-00007fff74c12000 [    4K] rw-/rw- SM=COW  /usr/lib/system/libremovefile.dylib
__DATA                00007fff75141000-00007fff75142000 [    4K] rw-/rwx SM=COW  /usr/lib/system/libdyld.dylib
__DATA                00007fff751a3000-00007fff751a4000 [    4K] rw-/rwx SM=COW
/usr/lib/system/libsystem_sandbox.dylib
__DATA                00007fff75281000-00007fff75282000 [    4K] rw-/rwx SM=COW  /usr/lib/system/libmacho.dylib
__DATA                00007fff75282000-00007fff75285000 [   12K] rw-/rwx SM=COW
/usr/lib/system/libsystem_kernel.dylib
__DATA                00007fff752d8000-00007fff752d9000 [    4K] rw-/rwx SM=COW
/usr/lib/system/libsystem_dnssd.dylib
__DATA                00007fff75453000-00007fff75456000 [   12K] rw-/rwx SM=COW  /usr/lib/system/libsystem_info.dylib
__DATA                00007fff7551f000-00007fff75520000 [    4K] rw-/rwx SM=COW  /usr/lib/system/libquarantine.dylib
__DATA                00007fff75559000-00007fff7555a000 [    4K] rw-/rwx SM=COW  /usr/lib/system/libkeymgr.dylib
__DATA                00007fff75563000-00007fff75564000 [    4K] rw-/rwx SM=COW  /usr/lib/system/libcompiler_rt.dylib
__DATA                00007fff75633000-00007fff75634000 [    4K] rw-/rw- SM=COW  /usr/lib/system/libdnsinfo.dylib
__DATA                00007fff756d6000-00007fff756d7000 [    4K] rw-/rw- SM=COW
/usr/lib/system/libsystem_network.dylib
__DATA                00007fff75813000-00007fff75814000 [    4K] rw-/rwx SM=COW  /usr/lib/system/liblaunch.dylib
__DATA                00007fff75e41000-00007fff75e42000 [    4K] rw-/rw- SM=COW  /usr/lib/system/libcopyfile.dylib
__DATA                00007fff75e4a000-00007fff75e50000 [   24K] rw-/rw- SM=COW
/usr/lib/system/libcommonCrypto.dylib
__DATA                00007fff76342000-00007fff76343000 [    4K] rw-/rw- SM=COW
/usr/lib/system/libsystem_notify.dylib
__DATA                00007fff763fd000-00007fff763fe000 [    4K] rw-/rw- SM=COW  /usr/lib/libSystem.B.dylib
__DATA                00007fff76401000-00007fff76402000 [    4K] rw-/rw- SM=COW  /usr/lib/system/libunwind.dylib
__DATA                00007fff764ab000-00007fff764ac000 [    4K] rw-/rw- SM=COW  /usr/lib/system/libcache.dylib

==== Legend
SM=sharing mode:
        COW=copy_on_write PRV=private NUL=empty ALI=aliased
        SHM=shared ZER=zero_filled S/A=shared_alias
==== Summary for process 2636
ReadOnly portion of Libraries: Total=50.2M resident=50.2M(100%) swapped_out_or_unallocated=0K(0%)
Writable regions: Total=36.6M written=120K(0%) resident=20.6M(56%) swapped_out=0K(0%) unallocated=16.0M(44%)
```

REGION TYPE	VIRTUAL	
===========	=======	
MALLOC	9216K	see MALLOC ZONE table below
MALLOC guard page	16K	
MALLOC metadata	180K	
STACK GUARD	56.0M	
Stack	10.5M	
__DATA	464K	
__LINKEDIT	47.7M	
__TEXT	2484K	
shared memory	8K	
===========	=======	
TOTAL	126.4M	

MALLOC ZONE	VIRTUAL SIZE	ALLOCATION COUNT	BYTES ALLOCATED	% FULL
===========	=======	=========	=========	======
DefaultMallocZone_0x10bf58000	9216K	40	8K	0%

Exercise A5 (GDB)

- **Goal:** Learn how to identify stack corruption

- **Patterns:** Local Buffer Overflow, Execution Residue

- \AMCDA-Dumps\Exercise-A5-GDB.pdf

Exercise A5 (GDB)

Goal: Learn how to identify stack corruption

Patterns: Local Buffer Overflow, Execution Residue

1.   Identify the problem thread and application specific diagnostic from the diagnostic report App5_3365.crash (the problem was wrongly classified as stack overflow):

```
Process:         App5 [3365]
Path:            /Users/USER/Documents/*/App5
Identifier:      App5
Version:         ??? (???)
Code Type:       X86-64 (Native)
Parent Process:  bash [1549]

Date/Time:       2012-07-25 15:19:05.112 +0100
OS Version:      Mac OS X 10.7.4 (11E53)
Report Version:  9
Sleep/Wake UUID: 4C0A9B6D-7E93-4764-8BC3-971D136863D8

Crashed Thread:  1

Exception Type:  EXC_CRASH (SIGABRT)
Exception Codes: 0x0000000000000000, 0x0000000000000000

Application Specific Information:
[3365] stack overflow

Thread 0:: Dispatch queue: com.apple.main-thread
0   libsystem_kernel.dylib          0x00007fff8a10ce42 __semwait_signal + 10
1   libsystem_c.dylib               0x00007fff84d6edea nanosleep + 164
2   libsystem_c.dylib               0x00007fff84d6ec2c sleep + 61
3   libsystem_c.dylib               0x00007fff84d6ec08 sleep + 25
4   App5                            0x00000001090b6ba3 main + 195
5   App5                            0x00000001090b67a4 start + 52

Thread 1 Crashed:
0   libsystem_kernel.dylib          0x00007fff8a10cce2 __pthread_kill + 10
1   libsystem_c.dylib               0x00007fff84dba7d2 pthread_kill + 95
2   libsystem_c.dylib               0x00007fff84dabb4a __abort + 159
3   libsystem_c.dylib               0x00007fff84da8070 __stack_chk_fail + 223
4   App5                            0x00000001090b6907 procA + 87

Thread 2:
0   libsystem_kernel.dylib          0x00007fff8a10ce42 __semwait_signal + 10
1   libsystem_c.dylib               0x00007fff84d6edea nanosleep + 164
2   libsystem_c.dylib               0x00007fff84d6ec2c sleep + 61
3   libsystem_c.dylib               0x00007fff84d6ec08 sleep + 25
4   App5                            0x00000001090b6972 bar_two + 18
5   App5                            0x00000001090b6989 foo_two + 9
6   App5                            0x00000001090b69a1 thread_two + 17
7   libsystem_c.dylib               0x00007fff84db88bf _pthread_start + 335
8   libsystem_c.dylib               0x00007fff84dbbb75 thread_start + 13

Thread 3:
0   libsystem_kernel.dylib          0x00007fff8a10ce42 __semwait_signal + 10
1   libsystem_c.dylib               0x00007fff84d6edea nanosleep + 164
2   libsystem_c.dylib               0x00007fff84d6ec2c sleep + 61
3   libsystem_c.dylib               0x00007fff84d6ec08 sleep + 25
4   App5                            0x00000001090b69d2 bar_three + 18
5   App5                            0x00000001090b69e9 foo_three + 9
6   App5                            0x00000001090b6a01 thread_three + 17
7   libsystem_c.dylib               0x00007fff84db88bf _pthread_start + 335
8   libsystem_c.dylib               0x00007fff84dbbb75 thread_start + 13
```

```
Thread 4:
0   libsystem_kernel.dylib          0x00007fff8a10ce42 __semwait_signal + 10
1   libsystem_c.dylib               0x00007fff84d6edea nanosleep + 164
2   libsystem_c.dylib               0x00007fff84d6ec2c sleep + 61
3   libsystem_c.dylib               0x00007fff84d6ec08 sleep + 25
4   App5                            0x00000001090b6a32 bar_four + 18
5   App5                            0x00000001090b6a49 foo_four + 9
6   App5                            0x00000001090b6a61 thread_four + 17
7   libsystem_c.dylib               0x00007fff84db88bf _pthread_start + 335
8   libsystem_c.dylib               0x00007fff84dbbb75 thread_start + 13

Thread 5:
0   libsystem_kernel.dylib          0x00007fff8a10ce42 __semwait_signal + 10
1   libsystem_c.dylib               0x00007fff84d6edea nanosleep + 164
2   libsystem_c.dylib               0x00007fff84d6ec2c sleep + 61
3   libsystem_c.dylib               0x00007fff84d6ec08 sleep + 25
4   App5                            0x00000001090b6a92 bar_five + 18
5   App5                            0x00000001090b6aa9 foo_five + 9
6   App5                            0x00000001090b6ac1 thread_five + 17
7   libsystem_c.dylib               0x00007fff84db88bf _pthread_start + 335
8   libsystem_c.dylib               0x00007fff84dbbb75 thread_start + 13

Thread 1 crashed with X86 Thread State (64-bit):
  rax: 0x0000000000000000  rbx: 0x0000000000000006  rcx: 0x0000000109280dc8  rdx: 0x0000000000000000
  rdi: 0x0000000000001203  rsi: 0x0000000000000006  rbp: 0x0000000109280df0  rsp: 0x0000000109280dc8
   r8: 0x00007fff74a67fb8   r9: 0x0000000000000000  r10: 0x00007fff8a10cd0a  r11: 0xffffff80002da8d0
  r12: 0x0000000000001203  r13: 0x0000000109281000  r14: 0x0000000109281000  r15: 0x00000001090b6930
  rip: 0x00007fff8a10cce2  rfl: 0x0000000000000246  cr2: 0x000000001090eb000
Logical CPU: 0

Binary Images:
       0x1090b6000 -        0x1090b6fff +App5 (??? - ???) <A70EF751-A40B-34B8-BC98-3F5409E81658>
/Users/USER/Documents/*/App5
    0x7fff68cb6000 -     0x7fff68ceabaf  dyld (195.6 - ???) <0CD1B35B-A28F-32DA-B72E-452EAD609613> /usr/lib/dyld
    0x7fff849f2000 -     0x7fff84a0ffff  libxpc.dylib (77.19.0 - compatibility 1.0.0) <9F57891B-D7EF-3050-BEDD-
21E7C6668248> /usr/lib/system/libxpc.dylib
    0x7fff84d68000 -     0x7fff84d69ff7  libsystem_blocks.dylib (53.0.0 - compatibility 1.0.0) <8BCA214A-8992-34B2-
A8B9-B74DEACA1869> /usr/lib/system/libsystem_blocks.dylib
    0x7fff84d6a000 -     0x7fff84e47fef  libsystem_c.dylib (763.13.0 - compatibility 1.0.0) <41B43515-2806-3FBC-ACF1-
A16F35B7E290> /usr/lib/system/libsystem_c.dylib
    0x7fff85022000 -     0x7fff85030fff  libdispatch.dylib (187.9.0 - compatibility 1.0.0) <1D5BE322-A9B9-3BCE-8FAC-
076FB007CF54A> /usr/lib/system/libdispatch.dylib
    0x7fff855f0000 -     0x7fff855f1fff  libunc.dylib (24.0.0 - compatibility 1.0.0) <337960EE-0A85-3DD0-A760-
7134CF4C0AFF> /usr/lib/system/libunc.dylib
    0x7fff85ae3000 -     0x7fff85ae4ff7  libremovefile.dylib (21.1.0 - compatibility 1.0.0) <739E6C83-AA52-3C6C-A680-
B37FE2888A04> /usr/lib/system/libremovefile.dylib
    0x7fff89114000 -     0x7fff89118fff  libmathCommon.A.dylib (2026.0.0 - compatibility 1.0.0) <FF83AFF7-42B2-306E-
90AF-D539C51A4542> /usr/lib/system/libmathCommon.A.dylib
    0x7fff89119000 -     0x7fff8911dfff  libdyld.dylib (195.5.0 - compatibility 1.0.0) <380C3F44-0CA7-3514-8080-
46D1C9DF4FCD> /usr/lib/system/libdyld.dylib
    0x7fff89740000 -     0x7fff89741ff7  libsystem_sandbox.dylib (??? - ???) <96D38E74-F18F-3CCB-A20B-E8E3ADC4E166>
/usr/lib/system/libsystem_sandbox.dylib
    0x7fff8a0ef000 -     0x7fff8a0f5fff  libmacho.dylib (800.0.0 - compatibility 1.0.0) <165514D7-1BFA-38EF-A151-
676DCD21FB64> /usr/lib/system/libmacho.dylib
    0x7fff8a0f6000 -     0x7fff8a116fff  libsystem_kernel.dylib (1699.26.8 - compatibility 1.0.0) <1DDC0B0F-DB2A-34D6-
895D-E5B2B5618946> /usr/lib/system/libsystem_kernel.dylib
    0x7fff8a2ac000 -     0x7fff8a2b4fff  libsystem_dnssd.dylib (??? - ???) <D9BB1F87-A42B-3CBC-9DC2-FC07FCEF0016>
/usr/lib/system/libsystem_dnssd.dylib
    0x7fff8ae26000 -     0x7fff8ae61fff  libsystem_info.dylib (??? - ???) <35F90252-2AE1-32C5-8D34-782C614D9639>
/usr/lib/system/libsystem_info.dylib
    0x7fff8b248000 -     0x7fff8b24afff  libquarantine.dylib (36.6.0 - compatibility 1.0.0) <0EBF714B-4B69-3E1F-9A7D-
6BBC2AACB310> /usr/lib/system/libquarantine.dylib
    0x7fff8b3b4000 -     0x7fff8b3b4fff  libkeymgr.dylib (23.0.0 - compatibility 1.0.0) <61EFED6A-A407-301E-B454-
CD18314F0075> /usr/lib/system/libkeymgr.dylib
    0x7fff8b3dd000 -     0x7fff8b3e2fff  libcompiler_rt.dylib (6.0.0 - compatibility 1.0.0) <98ECD5F6-E85C-32A5-98CD-
8911230CB66A> /usr/lib/system/libcompiler_rt.dylib
    0x7fff8bd1a000 -     0x7fff8bd1bfff  libdnsinfo.dylib (395.11.0 - compatibility 1.0.0) <853BAAA5-270F-3FDC-B025-
D448DB72E1C3> /usr/lib/system/libdnsinfo.dylib
    0x7fff8c528000 -     0x7fff8c52dff7  libsystem_network.dylib (??? - ???) <5DE7024E-1D2D-34A2-80F4-08326331A75B>
/usr/lib/system/libsystem_network.dylib
    0x7fff8cfa3000 -     0x7fff8cfadff7  liblaunch.dylib (392.38.0 - compatibility 1.0.0) <6ECB7F19-B384-32C1-8652-
2463C1CF4815> /usr/lib/system/liblaunch.dylib
    0x7fff8fe02000 -     0x7fff8fe09fff  libcopyfile.dylib (85.1.0 - compatibility 1.0.0) <0AB51EE2-E914-358C-AC19-
47BC024BDAE7> /usr/lib/system/libcopyfile.dylib
    0x7fff8fe4b000 -     0x7fff8fe8dff7  libcommonCrypto.dylib (55010.0.0 - compatibility 1.0.0) <BB770C22-8C57-365A-
8716-4A3C36AE7BFB> /usr/lib/system/libcommonCrypto.dylib
```

116

```
    0x7fff90c0f000 -    0x7fff90c18ff7  libsystem_notify.dylib (80.1.0 - compatibility 1.0.0) <A4D651E3-D1C6-3934-
AD49-7A104FD14596> /usr/lib/system/libsystem_notify.dylib
    0x7fff91376000 -    0x7fff913a3fe7  libSystem.B.dylib (159.1.0 - compatibility 1.0.0) <7BEBB139-50BB-3112-947A-
F4AA168F991C> /usr/lib/libSystem.B.dylib
    0x7fff91489000 -    0x7fff9148fff7  libunwind.dylib (30.0.0 - compatibility 1.0.0) <1E9C6C8C-CBE8-3F4B-A5B5-
E03E3AB53231> /usr/lib/system/libunwind.dylib
    0x7fff91a22000 -    0x7fff91a27fff  libcache.dylib (47.0.0 - compatibility 1.0.0) <1571C3AB-BCB2-38CD-B3B2-
C5FC3F927C6A> /usr/lib/system/libcache.dylib

External Modification Summary:
  Calls made by other processes targeting this process:
    task_for_pid: 0
    thread_create: 0
    thread_set_state: 0
  Calls made by this process:
    task_for_pid: 0
    thread_create: 0
    thread_set_state: 0
  Calls made by all processes on this machine:
    task_for_pid: 5654
    thread_create: 0
    thread_set_state: 0

VM Region Summary:
ReadOnly portion of Libraries: Total=50.2M resident=50.2M(100%) swapped_out_or_unallocated=0K(0%)
Writable regions: Total=38.9M written=22.2M(57%) resident=42.6M(110%) swapped_out=36K(0%)
unallocated=16777216.0T(45221404475392%)

REGION TYPE                 VIRTUAL
===========                 =======
MALLOC                       1220K
Stack                        66.6M
__DATA                        464K
__LINKEDIT                   47.7M
__TEXT                       2484K
shared memory                 12K
===========                 =======
TOTAL                       118.4M
```

2.   Load a core dump core.3365 and App5 executable:


```
$ gdb -c ~/Documents/AMCDA-Dumps/core.3365 -e ~/Documents/AMCDA-
Dumps/Apps/App5/Build/Products/Release/App5
GNU gdb 6.3.50-20050815 (Apple version gdb-1820) (Sat Jun 16 02:40:11 UTC 2012)
Copyright 2004 Free Software Foundation, Inc.
GDB is free software, covered by the GNU General Public License, and you are
welcome to change it and/or distribute copies of it under certain conditions.
Type "show copying" to see the conditions.
There is absolutely no warranty for GDB.  Type "show warranty" for details.
This GDB was configured as "x86_64-apple-darwin".
Reading symbols for shared libraries . done
Reading symbols for shared libraries ........................ done
#0  0x00007fff8a10ce42 in __semwait_signal ()
```


3.   Go to the identifed problem core thread 1 (thread #2):

```
(gdb) thread 2
[Switching to thread 2 (core thread 1)]
0x00007fff8a10cce2 in __pthread_kill ()
```

```
(gdb) bt
#0  0x00007fff8a10cce2 in __pthread_kill ()
#1  0x00007fff84dba7d2 in pthread_kill ()
#2  0x00007fff84dabb4a in __abort ()
#3  0x00007fff84da8070 in __stack_chk_fail ()
#4  0x00000001090b6907 in procA ()
```

4.   We don't see expected beginning stack trace frames as on a normal thread:

```
(gdb) thread apply 3 bt

Thread 3 (core thread 2):
#0  0x00007fff8a10ce42 in __semwait_signal ()
#1  0x00007fff84d6edea in nanosleep ()
#2  0x00007fff84d6ec2c in sleep ()
#3  0x00007fff84d6ec08 in sleep ()
#4  0x00000001090b6972 in bar_two ()
#5  0x00000001090b6989 in foo_two ()
#6  0x00000001090b69a1 in thread_two ()
#7  0x00007fff84db88bf in _pthread_start ()
#8  0x00007fff84dbbb75 in thread_start ()
```

5.   Dump raw stack data from the current stack pointer and find ASCII buffers around return addresses:

```
(gdb) x/100a $rsp
0x109280dc8:  0x7fff84dba7d2 <pthread_kill+95> 0x109280e20
0x109280dd8:  0x120384db7e8e        0x109280e10
0x109280de8:  0x0     0x109280e20
0x109280df8:  0x7fff84dabb4a <__abort+159>     0xffffffff00001203
0x109280e08:  0x0     0xffffffdf
0x109280e18:  0x109280e60   0x109280ea0
0x109280e28:  0x7fff84da8070 <__guard_setup>   0x6c61000035707041
0x109280e38:  0x6b7300        0x0
0x109280e48:  0x0     0x0
0x109280e58:  0x0     0x73205d353633335b
0x109280e68:  0x65766f206b636174  0x776f6c6672
0x109280e78:  0x0     0x0
0x109280e88:  0x0     0x35363333280ed0
0x109280e98:  0x0     0x109280ed0
0x109280ea8:  0x1090b6907 <procA+87>     0x0
0x109280eb8:  0x794d000000000000  0x6769422077654e20
0x109280ec8:  0x6666754220726567  0x7265
0x109280ed8:  0x0     0x0
0x109280ee8:  0x0     0x0
0x109280ef8:  0x0     0x0
0x109280f08:  0x0     0x0
0x109280f18:  0x0     0x0
0x109280f28:  0x0     0x0
0x109280f38:  0x0     0x0
0x109280f48:  0x0     0x109280f78
0x109280f58:  0x7fff84dbbb75 <thread_start+13> 0x0
0x109280f68:  0x0     0x0
0x109280f78:  0x0     0x0
0x109280f88:  0x0     0x0
0x109280f98:  0x0     0x0
0x109280fa8:  0x0     0x0
0x109280fb8:  0x0     0x0
0x109280fc8:  0x0     0x0
```

```
0x109280fd8: 0x0      0x0
0x109280fe8: 0x0      0x0
0x109280ff8: 0x0      0x54485244
0x109281008: 0x0      0x2701010100000000
0x109281018: 0x1000 0xa0000001f
0x109281028: 0x0      0x0
0x109281038: 0x0      0x120300000000
0x109281048: 0x1090b6930 <thread_one>   0x0
0x109281058: 0x3      0x109281000
---Type <return> to continue, or q <return> to quit---
0x109281068: 0x0      0x0
0x109281078: 0x0      0x0
0x109281088: 0x0      0x0
0x109281098: 0x0      0x0
0x1092810a8: 0x0      0x0
0x1092810b8: 0x0      0x0
0x1092810c8: 0x0      0x0
0x1092810d8: 0x0      0x0

(gdb) x/s 0x109280e58+8
0x109280e60:  "[3365] stack overflow"

(gdb) x/s 0x109280eb8+8
0x109280ec0:  " New Bigger Buffer"
```

Exercise A5 (LLDB)

- **Goal:** Learn how to identify stack corruption

- **Patterns:** Local Buffer Overflow, Execution Residue

- \AMCDA-Dumps\Exercise-A5-LLDB.pdf

Exercise A5 (LLDB)

Goal: Learn how to identify stack corruption

Patterns: Local Buffer Overflow, Execution Residue

1.   Identify the problem thread and application specific diagnostic from the diagnostic report App5_3365.crash (the problem was wrongly classified as stack overflow):

```
Process:         App5 [3365]
Path:            /Users/USER/Documents/*/App5
Identifier:      App5
Version:         ??? (???)
Code Type:       X86-64 (Native)
Parent Process:  bash [1549]

Date/Time:       2012-07-25 15:19:05.112 +0100
OS Version:      Mac OS X 10.7.4 (11E53)
Report Version:  9
Sleep/Wake UUID: 4C0A9B6D-7E93-4764-8BC3-971D136863D8

Crashed Thread:  1

Exception Type:  EXC_CRASH (SIGABRT)
Exception Codes: 0x0000000000000000, 0x0000000000000000

Application Specific Information:
[3365] stack overflow

Thread 0:: Dispatch queue: com.apple.main-thread
0   libsystem_kernel.dylib          0x00007fff8a10ce42 __semwait_signal + 10
1   libsystem_c.dylib               0x00007fff84d6edea nanosleep + 164
2   libsystem_c.dylib               0x00007fff84d6ec2c sleep + 61
3   libsystem_c.dylib               0x00007fff84d6ec08 sleep + 25
4   App5                            0x00000001090b6ba3 main + 195
5   App5                            0x00000001090b67a4 start + 52

Thread 1 Crashed:
0   libsystem_kernel.dylib          0x00007fff8a10cce2 __pthread_kill + 10
1   libsystem_c.dylib               0x00007fff84dba7d2 pthread_kill + 95
2   libsystem_c.dylib               0x00007fff84dabb4a __abort + 159
3   libsystem_c.dylib               0x00007fff84da8070 __stack_chk_fail + 223
4   App5                            0x00000001090b6907 procA + 87

Thread 2:
0   libsystem_kernel.dylib          0x00007fff8a10ce42 __semwait_signal + 10
1   libsystem_c.dylib               0x00007fff84d6edea nanosleep + 164
2   libsystem_c.dylib               0x00007fff84d6ec2c sleep + 61
3   libsystem_c.dylib               0x00007fff84d6ec08 sleep + 25
4   App5                            0x00000001090b6972 bar_two + 18
5   App5                            0x00000001090b6989 foo_two + 9
6   App5                            0x00000001090b69a1 thread_two + 17
7   libsystem_c.dylib               0x00007fff84db88bf _pthread_start + 335
8   libsystem_c.dylib               0x00007fff84dbbb75 thread_start + 13

Thread 3:
0   libsystem_kernel.dylib          0x00007fff8a10ce42 __semwait_signal + 10
1   libsystem_c.dylib               0x00007fff84d6edea nanosleep + 164
2   libsystem_c.dylib               0x00007fff84d6ec2c sleep + 61
3   libsystem_c.dylib               0x00007fff84d6ec08 sleep + 25
4   App5                            0x00000001090b69d2 bar_three + 18
5   App5                            0x00000001090b69e9 foo_three + 9
6   App5                            0x00000001090b6a01 thread_three + 17
7   libsystem_c.dylib               0x00007fff84db88bf _pthread_start + 335
8   libsystem_c.dylib               0x00007fff84dbbb75 thread_start + 13
```

```
Thread 4:
0   libsystem_kernel.dylib            0x00007fff8a10ce42 __semwait_signal + 10
1   libsystem_c.dylib                 0x00007fff84d6edea nanosleep + 164
2   libsystem_c.dylib                 0x00007fff84d6ec2c sleep + 61
3   libsystem_c.dylib                 0x00007fff84d6ec08 sleep + 25
4   App5                              0x00000001090b6a32 bar_four + 18
5   App5                              0x00000001090b6a49 foo_four + 9
6   App5                              0x00000001090b6a61 thread_four + 17
7   libsystem_c.dylib                 0x00007fff84db88bf _pthread_start + 335
8   libsystem_c.dylib                 0x00007fff84dbbb75 thread_start + 13

Thread 5:
0   libsystem_kernel.dylib            0x00007fff8a10ce42 __semwait_signal + 10
1   libsystem_c.dylib                 0x00007fff84d6edea nanosleep + 164
2   libsystem_c.dylib                 0x00007fff84d6ec2c sleep + 61
3   libsystem_c.dylib                 0x00007fff84d6ec08 sleep + 25
4   App5                              0x00000001090b6a92 bar_five + 18
5   App5                              0x00000001090b6aa9 foo_five + 9
6   App5                              0x00000001090b6ac1 thread_five + 17
7   libsystem_c.dylib                 0x00007fff84db88bf _pthread_start + 335
8   libsystem_c.dylib                 0x00007fff84dbbb75 thread_start + 13

Thread 1 crashed with X86 Thread State (64-bit):
  rax: 0x0000000000000000  rbx: 0x0000000000000006  rcx: 0x0000000109280dc8  rdx: 0x0000000000000000
  rdi: 0x0000000000001203  rsi: 0x0000000000000006  rbp: 0x0000000109280df0  rsp: 0x0000000109280dc8
   r8: 0x00007fff74a67fb8   r9: 0x0000000000000000  r10: 0x00007fff8a10cd0a  r11: 0xffffff80002da8d0
  r12: 0x0000000000001203  r13: 0x0000000109281000  r14: 0x0000000109281000  r15: 0x00000001090b6930
  rip: 0x00007fff8a10cce2  rfl: 0x0000000000000246  cr2: 0x00000001090eb000
Logical CPU: 0

Binary Images:
       0x1090b6000 -        0x1090b6fff +App5 (??? - ???) <A70EF751-A40B-34B8-BC98-3F5409E81658>
/Users/USER/Documents/*/App5
    0x7fff68cb6000 -     0x7fff68ceabaf  dyld (195.6 - ???) <0CD1B35B-A28F-32DA-B72E-452EAD609613> /usr/lib/dyld
    0x7fff849f2000 -     0x7fff84a0ffff  libxpc.dylib (77.19.0 - compatibility 1.0.0) <9F57891B-D7EF-3050-BEDD-
21E7C6668248> /usr/lib/system/libxpc.dylib
    0x7fff84d68000 -     0x7fff84d69ff7  libsystem_blocks.dylib (53.0.0 - compatibility 1.0.0) <8BCA214A-8992-34B2-
A8B9-B74DEACA1869> /usr/lib/system/libsystem_blocks.dylib
    0x7fff84d6a000 -     0x7fff84e47fef  libsystem_c.dylib (763.13.0 - compatibility 1.0.0) <41B43515-2806-3FBC-ACF1-
A16F35B7E290> /usr/lib/system/libsystem_c.dylib
    0x7fff85022000 -     0x7fff85030fff  libdispatch.dylib (187.9.0 - compatibility 1.0.0) <1D5BE322-A9B9-3BCE-8FAC-
076FB07CF54A> /usr/lib/system/libdispatch.dylib
    0x7fff855f0000 -     0x7fff855f1fff  libunc.dylib (24.0.0 - compatibility 1.0.0) <337960EE-0A85-3DD0-A760-
7134CF4C0AFF> /usr/lib/system/libunc.dylib
    0x7fff85ae3000 -     0x7fff85ae4ff7  libremovefile.dylib (21.1.0 - compatibility 1.0.0) <739E6C83-AA52-3C6C-A680-
B37FE2888A04> /usr/lib/system/libremovefile.dylib
    0x7fff89114000 -     0x7fff89118fff  libmathCommon.A.dylib (2026.0.0 - compatibility 1.0.0) <FF83AFF7-42B2-306E-
90AF-D539C51A4542> /usr/lib/system/libmathCommon.A.dylib
    0x7fff89119000 -     0x7fff8911dfff  libdyld.dylib (195.5.0 - compatibility 1.0.0) <380C3F44-0CA7-3514-8080-
46D1C9DF4FCD> /usr/lib/system/libdyld.dylib
    0x7fff89740000 -     0x7fff89741ff7  libsystem_sandbox.dylib (??? - ???) <96D38E74-F18F-3CCB-A20B-E8E3ADC4E166>
/usr/lib/system/libsystem_sandbox.dylib
    0x7fff8a0ef000 -     0x7fff8a0f5fff  libmacho.dylib (800.0.0 - compatibility 1.0.0) <165514D7-1BFA-38EF-A151-
676DCD21FB64> /usr/lib/system/libmacho.dylib
    0x7fff8a0f6000 -     0x7fff8a116fff  libsystem_kernel.dylib (1699.26.8 - compatibility 1.0.0) <1DDC0B0F-DB2A-34D6-
895D-E5B2B5618946> /usr/lib/system/libsystem_kernel.dylib
    0x7fff8a2ac000 -     0x7fff8a2b4fff  libsystem_dnssd.dylib (??? - ???) <D9BB1F87-A42B-3CBC-9DC2-FC07FCEF0016>
/usr/lib/system/libsystem_dnssd.dylib
    0x7fff8ae26000 -     0x7fff8ae61fff  libsystem_info.dylib (??? - ???) <35F90252-2AE1-32C5-8D34-782C614D9639>
/usr/lib/system/libsystem_info.dylib
    0x7fff8b248000 -     0x7fff8b24afff  libquarantine.dylib (36.6.0 - compatibility 1.0.0) <0EBF714B-4B69-3E1F-9A7D-
6BBC2AACB310> /usr/lib/system/libquarantine.dylib
    0x7fff8b3b4000 -     0x7fff8b3b4fff  libkeymgr.dylib (23.0.0 - compatibility 1.0.0) <61EFED6A-A407-301E-B454-
CD18314F0075> /usr/lib/system/libkeymgr.dylib
    0x7fff8b3dd000 -     0x7fff8b3e2fff  libcompiler_rt.dylib (6.0.0 - compatibility 1.0.0) <98ECD5F6-E85C-32A5-98CD-
8911230CB66A> /usr/lib/system/libcompiler_rt.dylib
    0x7fff8bd1a000 -     0x7fff8bd1bfff  libdnsinfo.dylib (395.11.0 - compatibility 1.0.0) <853BAAA5-270F-3FDC-B025-
D448DB72E1C3> /usr/lib/system/libdnsinfo.dylib
    0x7fff8c528000 -     0x7fff8c52dff7  libsystem_network.dylib (??? - ???) <5DE7024E-1D2D-34A2-80F4-08326331A75B>
/usr/lib/system/libsystem_network.dylib
    0x7fff8cfa3000 -     0x7fff8cfadff7  liblaunch.dylib (392.38.0 - compatibility 1.0.0) <6ECB7F19-B384-32C1-8652-
2463C1CF4815> /usr/lib/system/liblaunch.dylib
    0x7fff8fe02000 -     0x7fff8fe09fff  libcopyfile.dylib (85.1.0 - compatibility 1.0.0) <0AB51EE2-E914-358C-AC19-
47BC024BDAE7> /usr/lib/system/libcopyfile.dylib
    0x7fff8fe4b000 -     0x7fff8fe8dff7  libcommonCrypto.dylib (55010.0.0 - compatibility 1.0.0) <BB770C22-8C57-365A-
8716-4A3C36AE7BFB> /usr/lib/system/libcommonCrypto.dylib
```

```
    0x7fff90c0f000 -     0x7fff90c18ff7  libsystem_notify.dylib (80.1.0 - compatibility 1.0.0) <A4D651E3-D1C6-3934-
AD49-7A104FD14596> /usr/lib/system/libsystem_notify.dylib
    0x7fff91376000 -     0x7fff913a3fe7  libSystem.B.dylib (159.1.0 - compatibility 1.0.0) <7BEBB139-50BB-3112-947A-
F4AA168F991C> /usr/lib/libSystem.B.dylib
    0x7fff91489000 -     0x7fff9148fff7  libunwind.dylib (30.0.0 - compatibility 1.0.0) <1E9C6C8C-CBE8-3F4B-A5B5-
E03E3AB53231> /usr/lib/system/libunwind.dylib
    0x7fff91a22000 -     0x7fff91a27fff  libcache.dylib (47.0.0 - compatibility 1.0.0) <1571C3AB-BCB2-38CD-B3B2-
C5FC3F927C6A> /usr/lib/system/libcache.dylib

External Modification Summary:
  Calls made by other processes targeting this process:
    task_for_pid: 0
    thread_create: 0
    thread_set_state: 0
  Calls made by this process:
    task_for_pid: 0
    thread_create: 0
    thread_set_state: 0
  Calls made by all processes on this machine:
    task_for_pid: 5654
    thread_create: 0
    thread_set_state: 0

VM Region Summary:
ReadOnly portion of Libraries: Total=50.2M resident=50.2M(100%) swapped_out_or_unallocated=0K(0%)
Writable regions: Total=38.9M written=22.2M(57%) resident=42.6M(110%) swapped_out=36K(0%)
unallocated=16777216.0T(45221404475392%)

REGION TYPE                 VIRTUAL
===========                 =======
MALLOC                       1220K
Stack                        66.6M
__DATA                        464K
__LINKEDIT                   47.7M
__TEXT                       2484K
shared memory                  12K
===========                 =======
TOTAL                       118.4M
```

2.   Load a core dump core.3365 and App5 executable:

$ lldb -c ~/Documents/AMCDA-Dumps/core.3365 -f ~/Documents/AMCDA-Dumps/Apps/App5/Build/Products/Release/App5

```
error: core.3365 is a corrupt mach-o file: load command 45 LC_SEGMENT_64 has a fileoff +
filesize (0x160b7000) that extends beyond the end of the file (0x160b5000), the segment will be
truncated
Core file '/Users/DumpAnalysis/Documents/AMCDA-Dumps/core.3365' (x86_64) was loaded.
Process 0 stopped
* thread #1: tid = 0x0000, 0x00007fff8a10ce42 libsystem_kernel.dylib`__semwait_signal + 10,
stop reason = signal SIGSTOP
    frame #0: 0x00007fff8a10ce42 libsystem_kernel.dylib`__semwait_signal + 10
libsystem_kernel.dylib`__semwait_signal + 10:
-> 0x7fff8a10ce42:  jae    0x7fff8a10ce49            ; __semwait_signal + 17
   0x7fff8a10ce44:  jmpq   0x7fff8a10dffc            ; cerror
   0x7fff8a10ce49:  ret
   0x7fff8a10ce4a:  nop
```

```
   thread #2: tid = 0x0001, 0x00007fff8a10cce2 libsystem_kernel.dylib`__pthread_kill + 10, stop
reason = signal SIGSTOP
    frame #0: 0x00007fff8a10cce2 libsystem_kernel.dylib`__pthread_kill + 10
libsystem_kernel.dylib`__pthread_kill + 10:
-> 0x7fff8a10cce2:  jae    0x7fff8a10cce9            ; __pthread_kill + 17
   0x7fff8a10cce4:  jmpq   0x7fff8a10dffc            ; cerror
   0x7fff8a10cce9:  ret
   0x7fff8a10ccea:  nop
   thread #3: tid = 0x0002, 0x00007fff8a10ce42 libsystem_kernel.dylib`__semwait_signal + 10,
stop reason = signal SIGSTOP
    frame #0: 0x00007fff8a10ce42 libsystem_kernel.dylib`__semwait_signal + 10
libsystem_kernel.dylib`__semwait_signal + 10:
-> 0x7fff8a10ce42:  jae    0x7fff8a10ce49            ; __semwait_signal + 17
   0x7fff8a10ce44:  jmpq   0x7fff8a10dffc            ; cerror
   0x7fff8a10ce49:  ret
   0x7fff8a10ce4a:  nop
   thread #4: tid = 0x0003, 0x00007fff8a10ce42 libsystem_kernel.dylib`__semwait_signal + 10,
stop reason = signal SIGSTOP
    frame #0: 0x00007fff8a10ce42 libsystem_kernel.dylib`__semwait_signal + 10
libsystem_kernel.dylib`__semwait_signal + 10:
-> 0x7fff8a10ce42:  jae    0x7fff8a10ce49            ; __semwait_signal + 17
   0x7fff8a10ce44:  jmpq   0x7fff8a10dffc            ; cerror
   0x7fff8a10ce49:  ret
   0x7fff8a10ce4a:  nop
   thread #5: tid = 0x0004, 0x00007fff8a10ce42 libsystem_kernel.dylib`__semwait_signal + 10,
stop reason = signal SIGSTOP
    frame #0: 0x00007fff8a10ce42 libsystem_kernel.dylib`__semwait_signal + 10
libsystem_kernel.dylib`__semwait_signal + 10:
-> 0x7fff8a10ce42:  jae    0x7fff8a10ce49            ; __semwait_signal + 17
   0x7fff8a10ce44:  jmpq   0x7fff8a10dffc            ; cerror
   0x7fff8a10ce49:  ret
   0x7fff8a10ce4a:  nop
   thread #6: tid = 0x0005, 0x00007fff8a10ce42 libsystem_kernel.dylib`__semwait_signal + 10,
stop reason = signal SIGSTOP
    frame #0: 0x00007fff8a10ce42 libsystem_kernel.dylib`__semwait_signal + 10
libsystem_kernel.dylib`__semwait_signal + 10:
-> 0x7fff8a10ce42:  jae    0x7fff8a10ce49            ; __semwait_signal + 17
   0x7fff8a10ce44:  jmpq   0x7fff8a10dffc            ; cerror
   0x7fff8a10ce49:  ret
   0x7fff8a10ce4a:  nop
```

3.   Go to the identifed problem core thread 1 (thread #2):

```
(lldb) thread select 2
* thread #2: tid = 0x0001, 0x00007fff8a10cce2 libsystem_kernel.dylib`__pthread_kill + 10, stop
reason = signal SIGSTOP
    frame #0: 0x00007fff8a10cce2 libsystem_kernel.dylib`__pthread_kill + 10
libsystem_kernel.dylib`__pthread_kill + 10:
-> 0x7fff8a10cce2:  jae    0x7fff8a10cce9            ; __pthread_kill + 17
   0x7fff8a10cce4:  jmpq   0x7fff8a10dffc            ; cerror
   0x7fff8a10cce9:  ret
   0x7fff8a10ccea:  nop
```

```
(lldb) bt
* thread #2: tid = 0x0001, 0x00007fff8a10cce2 libsystem_kernel.dylib`__pthread_kill + 10, stop
reason = signal SIGSTOP
    frame #0: 0x00007fff8a10cce2 libsystem_kernel.dylib`__pthread_kill + 10
    frame #1: 0x00007fff84dba7d2 libsystem_c.dylib`pthread_kill + 95
    frame #2: 0x00007fff84dabb4a libsystem_c.dylib`__abort + 159
    frame #3: 0x00007fff84da8070 libsystem_c.dylib`__stack_chk_fail + 223
    frame #4: 0x00000001090b6907 App5`procA + 87
```

4.   We don't see expected beginning stack trace frames as on a normal thread:

```
(lldb) thread backtrace 3
  thread #3: tid = 0x0002, 0x00007fff8a10ce42 libsystem_kernel.dylib`__semwait_signal + 10,
stop reason = signal SIGSTOP
    frame #0: 0x00007fff8a10ce42 libsystem_kernel.dylib`__semwait_signal + 10
    frame #1: 0x00007fff84d6edea libsystem_c.dylib`nanosleep + 164
    frame #2: 0x00007fff84d6ec2c libsystem_c.dylib`sleep + 61
    frame #3: 0x00007fff84d6ec08 libsystem_c.dylib`sleep + 25
    frame #4: 0x00000001090b6972 App5`bar_two + 18
    frame #5: 0x00000001090b6989 App5`foo_two + 9
    frame #6: 0x00000001090b69a1 App5`thread_two + 17
    frame #7: 0x00007fff84db88bf libsystem_c.dylib`_pthread_start + 335
    frame #8: 0x00007fff84dbbb75 libsystem_c.dylib`thread_start + 13
```

5.   Dump raw stack data from the current stack pointer and find ASCII buffers around return addresses:

```
(lldb) x/100a $rsp
0x109280dc8: 0x00007fff84dba7d2 libsystem_c.dylib`pthread_kill + 95
0x109280dd0: 0x0000000109280e20
0x109280dd8: 0x0000120384db7e8e
0x109280de0: 0x0000000109280e10
0x109280de8: 0x0000000000000000
0x109280df0: 0x0000000109280e20
0x109280df8: 0x00007fff84dabb4a libsystem_c.dylib`__abort + 159
0x109280e00: 0xffffffff00001203
0x109280e08: 0x0000000000000000
0x109280e10: 0x00000000ffffffdf
0x109280e18: 0x0000000109280e60
0x109280e20: 0x0000000109280ea0
0x109280e28: 0x00007fff84da8070 libsystem_c.dylib`__guard_setup
0x109280e30: 0x6c61000035707041
0x109280e38: 0x00000000006b7300
0x109280e40: 0x0000000000000000
0x109280e48: 0x0000000000000000
0x109280e50: 0x0000000000000000
0x109280e58: 0x0000000000000000
0x109280e60: 0x73205d353633335b
0x109280e68: 0x65766f206b636174
0x109280e70: 0x000000776f6c6672
0x109280e78: 0x0000000000000000
0x109280e80: 0x0000000000000000
0x109280e88: 0x0000000000000000
0x109280e90: 0x003536333328ed0
0x109280e98: 0x0000000000000000
0x109280ea0: 0x0000000109280ed0
0x109280ea8: 0x00000001090b6907 App5`procA + 87
0x109280eb0: 0x0000000000000000
0x109280eb8: 0x794d000000000000
0x109280ec0: 0x6769422077654e20
0x109280ec8: 0x6666754220726567
```

```
0x109280ed0: 0x0000000000007265
0x109280ed8: 0x0000000000000000
0x109280ee0: 0x0000000000000000
0x109280ee8: 0x0000000000000000
0x109280ef0: 0x0000000000000000
0x109280ef8: 0x0000000000000000
0x109280f00: 0x0000000000000000
0x109280f08: 0x0000000000000000
0x109280f10: 0x0000000000000000
0x109280f18: 0x0000000000000000
0x109280f20: 0x0000000000000000
0x109280f28: 0x0000000000000000
0x109280f30: 0x0000000000000000
0x109280f38: 0x0000000000000000
0x109280f40: 0x0000000000000000
0x109280f48: 0x0000000000000000
0x109280f50: 0x0000000109280f78
0x109280f58: 0x00007fff84dbbb75 libsystem_c.dylib`thread_start + 13
0x109280f60: 0x0000000000000000
0x109280f68: 0x0000000000000000
0x109280f70: 0x0000000000000000
0x109280f78: 0x0000000000000000
0x109280f80: 0x0000000000000000
0x109280f88: 0x0000000000000000
0x109280f90: 0x0000000000000000
0x109280f98: 0x0000000000000000
0x109280fa0: 0x0000000000000000
0x109280fa8: 0x0000000000000000
0x109280fb0: 0x0000000000000000
0x109280fb8: 0x0000000000000000
0x109280fc0: 0x0000000000000000
0x109280fc8: 0x0000000000000000
0x109280fd0: 0x0000000000000000
0x109280fd8: 0x0000000000000000
0x109280fe0: 0x0000000000000000
0x109280fe8: 0x0000000000000000
0x109280ff0: 0x0000000000000000
0x109280ff8: 0x0000000000000000
0x109281000: 0x0000000054485244
0x109281008: 0x0000000000000000
0x109281010: 0x2701010100000000
0x109281018: 0x0000000000001000
0x109281020: 0x0000000a0000001f
0x109281028: 0x0000000000000000
0x109281030: 0x0000000000000000
0x109281038: 0x0000000000000000
0x109281040: 0x0000120300000000
0x109281048: 0x00000001090b6930 App5`thread_one
0x109281050: 0x0000000000000000
0x109281058: 0x0000000000000003
0x109281060: 0x0000000109281000
0x109281068: 0x0000000000000000
0x109281070: 0x0000000000000000
0x109281078: 0x0000000000000000
0x109281080: 0x0000000000000000
0x109281088: 0x0000000000000000
0x109281090: 0x0000000000000000
0x109281098: 0x0000000000000000
0x1092810a0: 0x0000000000000000
0x1092810a8: 0x0000000000000000
```

```
0x1092810b0: 0x0000000000000000
0x1092810b8: 0x0000000000000000
0x1092810c0: 0x0000000000000000
0x1092810c8: 0x0000000000000000
0x1092810d0: 0x0000000000000000
0x1092810d8: 0x0000000000000000
0x1092810e0: 0x0000000000000000

(lldb) x/s 0x109280e60
0x109280e60:  "[3365] stack overflow"

(lldb) x/s 0x109280ec0
0x109280ec0:  " New Bigger Buffer"
```

Note: We see the expected *thread_start* function on the raw stack so it could be the case of a local buffer overflow.

Exercise A6 (GDB)

- **Goal:** Learn how to identify stack overflow, stack boundaries, reconstruct stack trace

- **Patterns:** Stack Overflow, Execution Residue

- \AMCDA-Dumps\Exercise-A6-GDB.pdf

Exercise A6 (GDB)

Goal: Learn how to identify stack overflow, stack boundaries, reconstruct stack trace

Patterns: Stack Overflow, Execution Residue

1.   Identify the problem thread and application specific diagnostic from the diagnostic report App6_3769.crash:

```
Process:         App6 [3769]
Path:            /Users/USER/Documents/*/App6
Identifier:      App6
Version:         ??? (???)
Code Type:       X86-64 (Native)
Parent Process:  bash [1549]

Date/Time:       2012-07-25 17:27:15.333 +0100
OS Version:      Mac OS X 10.7.4 (11E53)
Report Version:  9
Sleep/Wake UUID: 4C0A9B6D-7E93-4764-8BC3-971D136863D8

Crashed Thread:  1

Exception Type:  EXC_BAD_ACCESS (SIGBUS)
Exception Codes: KERN_PROTECTION_FAILURE at 0x0000000102820e38

VM Regions Near 0x102820e38:
    MALLOC metadata        000000010281f000-0000000102820000 [    4K] r--/rwx SM=COW
--> Stack                  0000000102820000-0000000102821000 [    4K] r--/rwx SM=PRV  thread 1
    Stack                  0000000102821000-00000001028a3000 [  520K] rw-/rwx SM=PRV

Thread 0:: Dispatch queue: com.apple.main-thread
0   libsystem_kernel.dylib           0x00007fff8a10ce42 __semwait_signal + 10
1   libsystem_c.dylib                0x00007fff84d6edea nanosleep + 164
2   libsystem_c.dylib                0x00007fff84d6ec2c sleep + 61
3   libsystem_c.dylib                0x00007fff84d6ec08 sleep + 25
4   App6                             0x00000001027ecc53 main + 195
5   App6                             0x00000001027ec8c4 start + 52

Thread 1 Crashed:
0   App6                             0x00000001027ec905 procF + 53
1   App6                             0x00000001027ec938 procF + 104
2   App6                             0x00000001027ec938 procF + 104
3   App6                             0x00000001027ec938 procF + 104
4   App6                             0x00000001027ec938 procF + 104
5   App6                             0x00000001027ec938 procF + 104
6   App6                             0x00000001027ec938 procF + 104
7   App6                             0x00000001027ec938 procF + 104
8   App6                             0x00000001027ec938 procF + 104
9   App6                             0x00000001027ec938 procF + 104
10  App6                             0x00000001027ec938 procF + 104
11  App6                             0x00000001027ec938 procF + 104
12  App6                             0x00000001027ec938 procF + 104
13  App6                             0x00000001027ec938 procF + 104
14  App6                             0x00000001027ec938 procF + 104
15  App6                             0x00000001027ec938 procF + 104
16  App6                             0x00000001027ec938 procF + 104
17  App6                             0x00000001027ec938 procF + 104
18  App6                             0x00000001027ec938 procF + 104
19  App6                             0x00000001027ec938 procF + 104
20  App6                             0x00000001027ec938 procF + 104
21  App6                             0x00000001027ec938 procF + 104
22  App6                             0x00000001027ec938 procF + 104
23  App6                             0x00000001027ec938 procF + 104
24  App6                             0x00000001027ec938 procF + 104
25  App6                             0x00000001027ec938 procF + 104
26  App6                             0x00000001027ec938 procF + 104
27  App6                             0x00000001027ec938 procF + 104
28  App6                             0x00000001027ec938 procF + 104
```

```
29  App6                          0x00000001027ec938 procF + 104
30  App6                          0x00000001027ec938 procF + 104
31  App6                          0x00000001027ec938 procF + 104
32  App6                          0x00000001027ec938 procF + 104
33  App6                          0x00000001027ec938 procF + 104
34  App6                          0x00000001027ec938 procF + 104
35  App6                          0x00000001027ec938 procF + 104
36  App6                          0x00000001027ec938 procF + 104
37  App6                          0x00000001027ec938 procF + 104
38  App6                          0x00000001027ec938 procF + 104
39  App6                          0x00000001027ec938 procF + 104
40  App6                          0x00000001027ec938 procF + 104
41  App6                          0x00000001027ec938 procF + 104
42  App6                          0x00000001027ec938 procF + 104
43  App6                          0x00000001027ec938 procF + 104
44  App6                          0x00000001027ec938 procF + 104
45  App6                          0x00000001027ec938 procF + 104
46  App6                          0x00000001027ec938 procF + 104
47  App6                          0x00000001027ec938 procF + 104
48  App6                          0x00000001027ec938 procF + 104
49  App6                          0x00000001027ec938 procF + 104
50  App6                          0x00000001027ec938 procF + 104
51  App6                          0x00000001027ec938 procF + 104
52  App6                          0x00000001027ec938 procF + 104
53  App6                          0x00000001027ec938 procF + 104
54  App6                          0x00000001027ec938 procF + 104
55  App6                          0x00000001027ec938 procF + 104
56  App6                          0x00000001027ec938 procF + 104
57  App6                          0x00000001027ec938 procF + 104
58  App6                          0x00000001027ec938 procF + 104
59  App6                          0x00000001027ec938 procF + 104
60  App6                          0x00000001027ec938 procF + 104
61  App6                          0x00000001027ec938 procF + 104
62  App6                          0x00000001027ec938 procF + 104
63  App6                          0x00000001027ec938 procF + 104
64  App6                          0x00000001027ec938 procF + 104
65  App6                          0x00000001027ec938 procF + 104
66  App6                          0x00000001027ec938 procF + 104
67  App6                          0x00000001027ec938 procF + 104
68  App6                          0x00000001027ec938 procF + 104
69  App6                          0x00000001027ec938 procF + 104
70  App6                          0x00000001027ec938 procF + 104
71  App6                          0x00000001027ec938 procF + 104
72  App6                          0x00000001027ec938 procF + 104
73  App6                          0x00000001027ec938 procF + 104
74  App6                          0x00000001027ec938 procF + 104
75  App6                          0x00000001027ec938 procF + 104
76  App6                          0x00000001027ec938 procF + 104
77  App6                          0x00000001027ec938 procF + 104
78  App6                          0x00000001027ec938 procF + 104
79  App6                          0x00000001027ec938 procF + 104
80  App6                          0x00000001027ec938 procF + 104
81  App6                          0x00000001027ec938 procF + 104
82  App6                          0x00000001027ec938 procF + 104
83  App6                          0x00000001027ec938 procF + 104
84  App6                          0x00000001027ec938 procF + 104
85  App6                          0x00000001027ec938 procF + 104
86  App6                          0x00000001027ec938 procF + 104
87  App6                          0x00000001027ec938 procF + 104
88  App6                          0x00000001027ec938 procF + 104
89  App6                          0x00000001027ec938 procF + 104
90  App6                          0x00000001027ec938 procF + 104
91  App6                          0x00000001027ec938 procF + 104
92  App6                          0x00000001027ec938 procF + 104
93  App6                          0x00000001027ec938 procF + 104
94  App6                          0x00000001027ec938 procF + 104
95  App6                          0x00000001027ec938 procF + 104
96  App6                          0x00000001027ec938 procF + 104
97  App6                          0x00000001027ec938 procF + 104
98  App6                          0x00000001027ec938 procF + 104
99  App6                          0x00000001027ec938 procF + 104
100 App6                          0x00000001027ec938 procF + 104
101 App6                          0x00000001027ec938 procF + 104
102 App6                          0x00000001027ec938 procF + 104
103 App6                          0x00000001027ec938 procF + 104
104 App6                          0x00000001027ec938 procF + 104
```

```
105 App6                              0x00000001027ec938 procF + 104
106 App6                              0x00000001027ec938 procF + 104
107 App6                              0x00000001027ec938 procF + 104
108 App6                              0x00000001027ec938 procF + 104
109 App6                              0x00000001027ec938 procF + 104
110 App6                              0x00000001027ec938 procF + 104
111 App6                              0x00000001027ec938 procF + 104
112 App6                              0x00000001027ec938 procF + 104
113 App6                              0x00000001027ec938 procF + 104
114 App6                              0x00000001027ec938 procF + 104
115 App6                              0x00000001027ec938 procF + 104
116 App6                              0x00000001027ec938 procF + 104
117 App6                              0x00000001027ec938 procF + 104
118 App6                              0x00000001027ec938 procF + 104
119 App6                              0x00000001027ec938 procF + 104
120 App6                              0x00000001027ec938 procF + 104
121 App6                              0x00000001027ec938 procF + 104
122 App6                              0x00000001027ec938 procF + 104
123 App6                              0x00000001027ec938 procF + 104
124 App6                              0x00000001027ec938 procF + 104
125 App6                              0x00000001027ec938 procF + 104
126 App6                              0x00000001027ec938 procF + 104
127 App6                              0x00000001027ec938 procF + 104
128 App6                              0x00000001027ec938 procF + 104
129 App6                              0x00000001027ec938 procF + 104
130 App6                              0x00000001027ec938 procF + 104
131 App6                              0x00000001027ec938 procF + 104
132 App6                              0x00000001027ec938 procF + 104
133 App6                              0x00000001027ec938 procF + 104
134 App6                              0x00000001027ec938 procF + 104
135 App6                              0x00000001027ec938 procF + 104
136 App6                              0x00000001027ec938 procF + 104
137 App6                              0x00000001027ec938 procF + 104
138 App6                              0x00000001027ec938 procF + 104
139 App6                              0x00000001027ec938 procF + 104
140 App6                              0x00000001027ec938 procF + 104
141 App6                              0x00000001027ec938 procF + 104
142 App6                              0x00000001027ec938 procF + 104
143 App6                              0x00000001027ec938 procF + 104
144 App6                              0x00000001027ec938 procF + 104
145 App6                              0x00000001027ec938 procF + 104
146 App6                              0x00000001027ec938 procF + 104
147 App6                              0x00000001027ec938 procF + 104
148 App6                              0x00000001027ec938 procF + 104
149 App6                              0x00000001027ec938 procF + 104
150 App6                              0x00000001027ec938 procF + 104
151 App6                              0x00000001027ec938 procF + 104
152 App6                              0x00000001027ec938 procF + 104
153 App6                              0x00000001027ec938 procF + 104
154 App6                              0x00000001027ec938 procF + 104
155 App6                              0x00000001027ec938 procF + 104
156 App6                              0x00000001027ec938 procF + 104
157 App6                              0x00000001027ec938 procF + 104
158 App6                              0x00000001027ec938 procF + 104
159 App6                              0x00000001027ec938 procF + 104
160 App6                              0x00000001027ec938 procF + 104
161 App6                              0x00000001027ec938 procF + 104
162 App6                              0x00000001027ec938 procF + 104
163 App6                              0x00000001027ec938 procF + 104
164 App6                              0x00000001027ec938 procF + 104
165 App6                              0x00000001027ec938 procF + 104
166 App6                              0x00000001027ec938 procF + 104
167 App6                              0x00000001027ec938 procF + 104
168 App6                              0x00000001027ec938 procF + 104
169 App6                              0x00000001027ec938 procF + 104
170 App6                              0x00000001027ec938 procF + 104
171 App6                              0x00000001027ec938 procF + 104
172 App6                              0x00000001027ec938 procF + 104
173 App6                              0x00000001027ec938 procF + 104
174 App6                              0x00000001027ec938 procF + 104
175 App6                              0x00000001027ec938 procF + 104
176 App6                              0x00000001027ec938 procF + 104
177 App6                              0x00000001027ec938 procF + 104
178 App6                              0x00000001027ec938 procF + 104
179 App6                              0x00000001027ec938 procF + 104
180 App6                              0x00000001027ec938 procF + 104
```

```
181 App6                      0x00000001027ec938 procF + 104
182 App6                      0x00000001027ec938 procF + 104
183 App6                      0x00000001027ec938 procF + 104
184 App6                      0x00000001027ec938 procF + 104
185 App6                      0x00000001027ec938 procF + 104
186 App6                      0x00000001027ec938 procF + 104
187 App6                      0x00000001027ec938 procF + 104
188 App6                      0x00000001027ec938 procF + 104
189 App6                      0x00000001027ec938 procF + 104
190 App6                      0x00000001027ec938 procF + 104
191 App6                      0x00000001027ec938 procF + 104
192 App6                      0x00000001027ec938 procF + 104
193 App6                      0x00000001027ec938 procF + 104
194 App6                      0x00000001027ec938 procF + 104
195 App6                      0x00000001027ec938 procF + 104
196 App6                      0x00000001027ec938 procF + 104
197 App6                      0x00000001027ec938 procF + 104
198 App6                      0x00000001027ec938 procF + 104
199 App6                      0x00000001027ec938 procF + 104
200 App6                      0x00000001027ec938 procF + 104
201 App6                      0x00000001027ec938 procF + 104
202 App6                      0x00000001027ec938 procF + 104
203 App6                      0x00000001027ec938 procF + 104
204 App6                      0x00000001027ec938 procF + 104
205 App6                      0x00000001027ec938 procF + 104
206 App6                      0x00000001027ec938 procF + 104
207 App6                      0x00000001027ec938 procF + 104
208 App6                      0x00000001027ec938 procF + 104
209 App6                      0x00000001027ec938 procF + 104
210 App6                      0x00000001027ec938 procF + 104
211 App6                      0x00000001027ec938 procF + 104
212 App6                      0x00000001027ec938 procF + 104
213 App6                      0x00000001027ec938 procF + 104
214 App6                      0x00000001027ec938 procF + 104
215 App6                      0x00000001027ec938 procF + 104
216 App6                      0x00000001027ec938 procF + 104
217 App6                      0x00000001027ec938 procF + 104
218 App6                      0x00000001027ec938 procF + 104
219 App6                      0x00000001027ec938 procF + 104
220 App6                      0x00000001027ec938 procF + 104
221 App6                      0x00000001027ec938 procF + 104
222 App6                      0x00000001027ec938 procF + 104
223 App6                      0x00000001027ec938 procF + 104
224 App6                      0x00000001027ec938 procF + 104
225 App6                      0x00000001027ec938 procF + 104
226 App6                      0x00000001027ec938 procF + 104
227 App6                      0x00000001027ec938 procF + 104
228 App6                      0x00000001027ec938 procF + 104
229 App6                      0x00000001027ec938 procF + 104
230 App6                      0x00000001027ec938 procF + 104
231 App6                      0x00000001027ec938 procF + 104
232 App6                      0x00000001027ec938 procF + 104
233 App6                      0x00000001027ec938 procF + 104
234 App6                      0x00000001027ec938 procF + 104
235 App6                      0x00000001027ec938 procF + 104
236 App6                      0x00000001027ec938 procF + 104
237 App6                      0x00000001027ec938 procF + 104
238 App6                      0x00000001027ec938 procF + 104
239 App6                      0x00000001027ec938 procF + 104
240 App6                      0x00000001027ec938 procF + 104
241 App6                      0x00000001027ec938 procF + 104
242 App6                      0x00000001027ec938 procF + 104
243 App6                      0x00000001027ec938 procF + 104
244 App6                      0x00000001027ec938 procF + 104
245 App6                      0x00000001027ec938 procF + 104
246 App6                      0x00000001027ec938 procF + 104
247 App6                      0x00000001027ec938 procF + 104
248 App6                      0x00000001027ec938 procF + 104
249 App6                      0x00000001027ec938 procF + 104
250 App6                      0x00000001027ec938 procF + 104
251 App6                      0x00000001027ec938 procF + 104
252 App6                      0x00000001027ec938 procF + 104
253 App6                      0x00000001027ec938 procF + 104
254 App6                      0x00000001027ec938 procF + 104
255 App6                      0x00000001027ec938 procF + 104
256 App6                      0x00000001027ec938 procF + 104
```

```
257 App6                              0x00000001027ec938 procF + 104
258 App6                              0x00000001027ec938 procF + 104
259 App6                              0x00000001027ec938 procF + 104
260 App6                              0x00000001027ec938 procF + 104
261 App6                              0x00000001027ec938 procF + 104
262 App6                              0x00000001027ec938 procF + 104
263 App6                              0x00000001027ec938 procF + 104
264 App6                              0x00000001027ec938 procF + 104
265 App6                              0x00000001027ec938 procF + 104
266 App6                              0x00000001027ec938 procF + 104
267 App6                              0x00000001027ec938 procF + 104
268 App6                              0x00000001027ec938 procF + 104
269 App6                              0x00000001027ec938 procF + 104
270 App6                              0x00000001027ec938 procF + 104
271 App6                              0x00000001027ec938 procF + 104
272 App6                              0x00000001027ec938 procF + 104
273 App6                              0x00000001027ec938 procF + 104
274 App6                              0x00000001027ec938 procF + 104
275 App6                              0x00000001027ec938 procF + 104
276 App6                              0x00000001027ec938 procF + 104
277 App6                              0x00000001027ec938 procF + 104
278 App6                              0x00000001027ec938 procF + 104
279 App6                              0x00000001027ec938 procF + 104
280 App6                              0x00000001027ec938 procF + 104
281 App6                              0x00000001027ec938 procF + 104
282 App6                              0x00000001027ec938 procF + 104
283 App6                              0x00000001027ec938 procF + 104
284 App6                              0x00000001027ec938 procF + 104
285 App6                              0x00000001027ec938 procF + 104
286 App6                              0x00000001027ec938 procF + 104
287 App6                              0x00000001027ec938 procF + 104
288 App6                              0x00000001027ec938 procF + 104
289 App6                              0x00000001027ec938 procF + 104
290 App6                              0x00000001027ec938 procF + 104
291 App6                              0x00000001027ec938 procF + 104
292 App6                              0x00000001027ec938 procF + 104
293 App6                              0x00000001027ec938 procF + 104
294 App6                              0x00000001027ec938 procF + 104
295 App6                              0x00000001027ec938 procF + 104
296 App6                              0x00000001027ec938 procF + 104
297 App6                              0x00000001027ec938 procF + 104
298 App6                              0x00000001027ec938 procF + 104
299 App6                              0x00000001027ec938 procF + 104
300 App6                              0x00000001027ec938 procF + 104
301 App6                              0x00000001027ec938 procF + 104
302 App6                              0x00000001027ec938 procF + 104
303 App6                              0x00000001027ec938 procF + 104
304 App6                              0x00000001027ec938 procF + 104
305 App6                              0x00000001027ec938 procF + 104
306 App6                              0x00000001027ec938 procF + 104
307 App6                              0x00000001027ec938 procF + 104
308 App6                              0x00000001027ec938 procF + 104
309 App6                              0x00000001027ec938 procF + 104
310 App6                              0x00000001027ec938 procF + 104
311 App6                              0x00000001027ec938 procF + 104
312 App6                              0x00000001027ec938 procF + 104
313 App6                              0x00000001027ec938 procF + 104
314 App6                              0x00000001027ec938 procF + 104
315 App6                              0x00000001027ec938 procF + 104
316 App6                              0x00000001027ec938 procF + 104
317 App6                              0x00000001027ec938 procF + 104
318 App6                              0x00000001027ec938 procF + 104
319 App6                              0x00000001027ec938 procF + 104
320 App6                              0x00000001027ec938 procF + 104
321 App6                              0x00000001027ec938 procF + 104
322 App6                              0x00000001027ec938 procF + 104
323 App6                              0x00000001027ec938 procF + 104
324 App6                              0x00000001027ec938 procF + 104
325 App6                              0x00000001027ec938 procF + 104
326 App6                              0x00000001027ec938 procF + 104
327 App6                              0x00000001027ec938 procF + 104
328 App6                              0x00000001027ec938 procF + 104
329 App6                              0x00000001027ec938 procF + 104
330 App6                              0x00000001027ec938 procF + 104
331 App6                              0x00000001027ec938 procF + 104
332 App6                              0x00000001027ec938 procF + 104
```

```
333 App6                        0x00000001027ec938 procF + 104
334 App6                        0x00000001027ec938 procF + 104
335 App6                        0x00000001027ec938 procF + 104
336 App6                        0x00000001027ec938 procF + 104
337 App6                        0x00000001027ec938 procF + 104
338 App6                        0x00000001027ec938 procF + 104
339 App6                        0x00000001027ec938 procF + 104
340 App6                        0x00000001027ec938 procF + 104
341 App6                        0x00000001027ec938 procF + 104
342 App6                        0x00000001027ec938 procF + 104
343 App6                        0x00000001027ec938 procF + 104
344 App6                        0x00000001027ec938 procF + 104
345 App6                        0x00000001027ec938 procF + 104
346 App6                        0x00000001027ec938 procF + 104
347 App6                        0x00000001027ec938 procF + 104
348 App6                        0x00000001027ec938 procF + 104
349 App6                        0x00000001027ec938 procF + 104
350 App6                        0x00000001027ec938 procF + 104
351 App6                        0x00000001027ec938 procF + 104
352 App6                        0x00000001027ec938 procF + 104
353 App6                        0x00000001027ec938 procF + 104
354 App6                        0x00000001027ec938 procF + 104
355 App6                        0x00000001027ec938 procF + 104
356 App6                        0x00000001027ec938 procF + 104
357 App6                        0x00000001027ec938 procF + 104
358 App6                        0x00000001027ec938 procF + 104
359 App6                        0x00000001027ec938 procF + 104
360 App6                        0x00000001027ec938 procF + 104
361 App6                        0x00000001027ec938 procF + 104
362 App6                        0x00000001027ec938 procF + 104
363 App6                        0x00000001027ec938 procF + 104
364 App6                        0x00000001027ec938 procF + 104
365 App6                        0x00000001027ec938 procF + 104
366 App6                        0x00000001027ec938 procF + 104
367 App6                        0x00000001027ec938 procF + 104
368 App6                        0x00000001027ec938 procF + 104
369 App6                        0x00000001027ec938 procF + 104
370 App6                        0x00000001027ec938 procF + 104
371 App6                        0x00000001027ec938 procF + 104
372 App6                        0x00000001027ec938 procF + 104
373 App6                        0x00000001027ec938 procF + 104
374 App6                        0x00000001027ec938 procF + 104
375 App6                        0x00000001027ec938 procF + 104
376 App6                        0x00000001027ec938 procF + 104
377 App6                        0x00000001027ec938 procF + 104
378 App6                        0x00000001027ec938 procF + 104
379 App6                        0x00000001027ec938 procF + 104
380 App6                        0x00000001027ec938 procF + 104
381 App6                        0x00000001027ec938 procF + 104
382 App6                        0x00000001027ec938 procF + 104
383 App6                        0x00000001027ec938 procF + 104
384 App6                        0x00000001027ec938 procF + 104
385 App6                        0x00000001027ec938 procF + 104
386 App6                        0x00000001027ec938 procF + 104
387 App6                        0x00000001027ec938 procF + 104
388 App6                        0x00000001027ec938 procF + 104
389 App6                        0x00000001027ec938 procF + 104
390 App6                        0x00000001027ec938 procF + 104
391 App6                        0x00000001027ec938 procF + 104
392 App6                        0x00000001027ec938 procF + 104
393 App6                        0x00000001027ec938 procF + 104
394 App6                        0x00000001027ec938 procF + 104
395 App6                        0x00000001027ec938 procF + 104
396 App6                        0x00000001027ec938 procF + 104
397 App6                        0x00000001027ec938 procF + 104
398 App6                        0x00000001027ec938 procF + 104
399 App6                        0x00000001027ec938 procF + 104
400 App6                        0x00000001027ec938 procF + 104
401 App6                        0x00000001027ec938 procF + 104
402 App6                        0x00000001027ec938 procF + 104
403 App6                        0x00000001027ec938 procF + 104
404 App6                        0x00000001027ec938 procF + 104
405 App6                        0x00000001027ec938 procF + 104
406 App6                        0x00000001027ec938 procF + 104
407 App6                        0x00000001027ec938 procF + 104
408 App6                        0x00000001027ec938 procF + 104
```

```
409 App6                          0x00000001027ec938 procF + 104
410 App6                          0x00000001027ec938 procF + 104
411 App6                          0x00000001027ec938 procF + 104
412 App6                          0x00000001027ec938 procF + 104
413 App6                          0x00000001027ec938 procF + 104
414 App6                          0x00000001027ec938 procF + 104
415 App6                          0x00000001027ec938 procF + 104
416 App6                          0x00000001027ec938 procF + 104
417 App6                          0x00000001027ec938 procF + 104
418 App6                          0x00000001027ec938 procF + 104
419 App6                          0x00000001027ec938 procF + 104
420 App6                          0x00000001027ec938 procF + 104
421 App6                          0x00000001027ec938 procF + 104
422 App6                          0x00000001027ec938 procF + 104
423 App6                          0x00000001027ec938 procF + 104
424 App6                          0x00000001027ec938 procF + 104
425 App6                          0x00000001027ec938 procF + 104
426 App6                          0x00000001027ec938 procF + 104
427 App6                          0x00000001027ec938 procF + 104
428 App6                          0x00000001027ec938 procF + 104
429 App6                          0x00000001027ec938 procF + 104
430 App6                          0x00000001027ec938 procF + 104
431 App6                          0x00000001027ec938 procF + 104
432 App6                          0x00000001027ec938 procF + 104
433 App6                          0x00000001027ec938 procF + 104
434 App6                          0x00000001027ec938 procF + 104
435 App6                          0x00000001027ec938 procF + 104
436 App6                          0x00000001027ec938 procF + 104
437 App6                          0x00000001027ec938 procF + 104
438 App6                          0x00000001027ec938 procF + 104
439 App6                          0x00000001027ec938 procF + 104
440 App6                          0x00000001027ec938 procF + 104
441 App6                          0x00000001027ec938 procF + 104
442 App6                          0x00000001027ec938 procF + 104
443 App6                          0x00000001027ec938 procF + 104
444 App6                          0x00000001027ec938 procF + 104
445 App6                          0x00000001027ec938 procF + 104
446 App6                          0x00000001027ec938 procF + 104
447 App6                          0x00000001027ec938 procF + 104
448 App6                          0x00000001027ec938 procF + 104
449 App6                          0x00000001027ec938 procF + 104
450 App6                          0x00000001027ec938 procF + 104
451 App6                          0x00000001027ec938 procF + 104
452 App6                          0x00000001027ec938 procF + 104
453 App6                          0x00000001027ec938 procF + 104
454 App6                          0x00000001027ec938 procF + 104
455 App6                          0x00000001027ec938 procF + 104
456 App6                          0x00000001027ec938 procF + 104
457 App6                          0x00000001027ec938 procF + 104
458 App6                          0x00000001027ec938 procF + 104
459 App6                          0x00000001027ec938 procF + 104
460 App6                          0x00000001027ec938 procF + 104
461 App6                          0x00000001027ec938 procF + 104
462 App6                          0x00000001027ec938 procF + 104
463 App6                          0x00000001027ec938 procF + 104
464 App6                          0x00000001027ec938 procF + 104
465 App6                          0x00000001027ec938 procF + 104
466 App6                          0x00000001027ec938 procF + 104
467 App6                          0x00000001027ec938 procF + 104
468 App6                          0x00000001027ec938 procF + 104
469 App6                          0x00000001027ec938 procF + 104
470 App6                          0x00000001027ec938 procF + 104
471 App6                          0x00000001027ec938 procF + 104
472 App6                          0x00000001027ec938 procF + 104
473 App6                          0x00000001027ec938 procF + 104
474 App6                          0x00000001027ec938 procF + 104
475 App6                          0x00000001027ec938 procF + 104
476 App6                          0x00000001027ec938 procF + 104
477 App6                          0x00000001027ec938 procF + 104
478 App6                          0x00000001027ec938 procF + 104
479 App6                          0x00000001027ec938 procF + 104
480 App6                          0x00000001027ec938 procF + 104
481 App6                          0x00000001027ec938 procF + 104
482 App6                          0x00000001027ec938 procF + 104
483 App6                          0x00000001027ec938 procF + 104
484 App6                          0x00000001027ec938 procF + 104
```

```
485 App6                          0x00000001027ec938 procF + 104
486 App6                          0x00000001027ec938 procF + 104
487 App6                          0x00000001027ec938 procF + 104
488 App6                          0x00000001027ec938 procF + 104
489 App6                          0x00000001027ec938 procF + 104
490 App6                          0x00000001027ec938 procF + 104
491 App6                          0x00000001027ec938 procF + 104
492 App6                          0x00000001027ec938 procF + 104
493 App6                          0x00000001027ec938 procF + 104
494 App6                          0x00000001027ec938 procF + 104
495 App6                          0x00000001027ec938 procF + 104
496 App6                          0x00000001027ec938 procF + 104
497 App6                          0x00000001027ec938 procF + 104
498 App6                          0x00000001027ec938 procF + 104
499 App6                          0x00000001027ec938 procF + 104
500 App6                          0x00000001027ec938 procF + 104
501 App6                          0x00000001027ec938 procF + 104
502 App6                          0x00000001027ec938 procF + 104
503 App6                          0x00000001027ec938 procF + 104
504 App6                          0x00000001027ec938 procF + 104
505 App6                          0x00000001027ec938 procF + 104
506 App6                          0x00000001027ec938 procF + 104
507 App6                          0x00000001027ec938 procF + 104
508 App6                          0x00000001027ec938 procF + 104
509 App6                          0x00000001027ec938 procF + 104
510 App6                          0x00000001027ec938 procF + 104
511 App6                          0x00000001027ec938 procF + 104

Thread 2:
0   libsystem_kernel.dylib        0x00007fff8a10ce42 __semwait_signal + 10
1   libsystem_c.dylib             0x00007fff84d6edea nanosleep + 164
2   libsystem_c.dylib             0x00007fff84d6ec2c sleep + 61
3   libsystem_c.dylib             0x00007fff84d6ec08 sleep + 25
4   App6                          0x00000001027ec9ef bar_two + 31
5   App6                          0x00000001027eca09 foo_two + 9
6   App6                          0x00000001027eca21 thread_two + 17
7   libsystem_c.dylib             0x00007fff84db88bf _pthread_start + 335
8   libsystem_c.dylib             0x00007fff84dbbb75 thread_start + 13

Thread 3:
0   libsystem_kernel.dylib        0x00007fff8a10ce42 __semwait_signal + 10
1   libsystem_c.dylib             0x00007fff84d6edea nanosleep + 164
2   libsystem_c.dylib             0x00007fff84d6ec2c sleep + 61
3   libsystem_c.dylib             0x00007fff84d6ec08 sleep + 25
4   App6                          0x00000001027eca5f bar_three + 31
5   App6                          0x00000001027eca79 foo_three + 9
6   App6                          0x00000001027eca91 thread_three + 17
7   libsystem_c.dylib             0x00007fff84db88bf _pthread_start + 335
8   libsystem_c.dylib             0x00007fff84dbbb75 thread_start + 13

Thread 4:
0   libsystem_kernel.dylib        0x00007fff8a10ce42 __semwait_signal + 10
1   libsystem_c.dylib             0x00007fff84d6edea nanosleep + 164
2   libsystem_c.dylib             0x00007fff84d6ec2c sleep + 61
3   libsystem_c.dylib             0x00007fff84d6ec08 sleep + 25
4   App6                          0x00000001027ecacf bar_four + 31
5   App6                          0x00000001027ecae9 foo_four + 9
6   App6                          0x00000001027ecb01 thread_four + 17
7   libsystem_c.dylib             0x00007fff84db88bf _pthread_start + 335
8   libsystem_c.dylib             0x00007fff84dbbb75 thread_start + 13

Thread 5:
0   libsystem_kernel.dylib        0x00007fff8a10ce42 __semwait_signal + 10
1   libsystem_c.dylib             0x00007fff84d6edea nanosleep + 164
2   libsystem_c.dylib             0x00007fff84d6ec2c sleep + 61
3   libsystem_c.dylib             0x00007fff84d6ec08 sleep + 25
4   App6                          0x00000001027ecb3f bar_five + 31
5   App6                          0x00000001027ecb59 foo_five + 9
6   App6                          0x00000001027ecb71 thread_five + 17
7   libsystem_c.dylib             0x00007fff84db88bf _pthread_start + 335
8   libsystem_c.dylib             0x00007fff84dbbb75 thread_start + 13
```

```
Thread 1 crashed with X86 Thread State (64-bit):
  rax: 0x0000000102820e40  rbx: 0x0000000000000000  rcx: 0x0000000000000000  rdx: 0x0000000000000200
  rdi: 0x0000000102820e40  rsi: 0x0000000000000000  rbp: 0x0000000102821050  rsp: 0x0000000102820e40
   r8: 0x000000000000012c   r9: 0x0000000000000000  r10: 0x00000000000a0000  r11: 0x0000000102821060
  r12: 0x0000000000001203  r13: 0x00000001028a1000  r14: 0x0000000000000000  r15: 0x00000001027ec9a0
  rip: 0x00000001027ec905  rfl: 0x0000000000010202  cr2: 0x0000000102820e38
Logical CPU: 2

Binary Images:
       0x1027ec000 -        0x1027ecfff +App6 (??? - ???) <6ABD6ECF-CF97-3178-8C66-8DDAA2A029E1>
/Users/USER/Documents/*/App6
    0x7fff623ec000 -     0x7fff62420baf  dyld (195.6 - ???) <0CD1B35B-A28F-32DA-B72E-452EAD609613> /usr/lib/dyld
    0x7fff849f2000 -     0x7fff84a0ffff  libxpc.dylib (77.19.0 - compatibility 1.0.0) <9F57891B-D7EF-3050-BEDD-
21E7C6668248> /usr/lib/system/libxpc.dylib
    0x7fff84d68000 -     0x7fff84d69ff7  libsystem_blocks.dylib (53.0.0 - compatibility 1.0.0) <8BCA214A-8992-34B2-
A8B9-B74DEACA1869> /usr/lib/system/libsystem_blocks.dylib
    0x7fff84d6a000 -     0x7fff84e47fef  libsystem_c.dylib (763.13.0 - compatibility 1.0.0) <41B43515-2806-3FBC-ACF1-
A16F35B7E290> /usr/lib/system/libsystem_c.dylib
    0x7fff85022000 -     0x7fff85030fff  libdispatch.dylib (187.9.0 - compatibility 1.0.0) <1D5BE322-A9B9-3BCE-8FAC-
076FB07CF54A> /usr/lib/system/libdispatch.dylib
    0x7fff855f0000 -     0x7fff855f1fff  libunc.dylib (24.0.0 - compatibility 1.0.0) <337960EE-0A85-3DD0-A760-
7134CF4C0AFF> /usr/lib/system/libunc.dylib
    0x7fff85ae3000 -     0x7fff85ae4ff7  libremovefile.dylib (21.1.0 - compatibility 1.0.0) <739E6C83-AA52-3C6C-A680-
B37FE2888A04> /usr/lib/system/libremovefile.dylib
    0x7fff89114000 -     0x7fff89118fff  libmathCommon.A.dylib (2026.0.0 - compatibility 1.0.0) <FF83AFF7-42B2-306E-
90AF-D539C51A4542> /usr/lib/system/libmathCommon.A.dylib
    0x7fff89119000 -     0x7fff8911dfff  libdyld.dylib (195.5.0 - compatibility 1.0.0) <380C3F44-0CA7-3514-8080-
46D1C9DF4FCD> /usr/lib/system/libdyld.dylib
    0x7fff89740000 -     0x7fff89741ff7  libsystem_sandbox.dylib (??? - ???) <96D38E74-F18F-3CCB-A20B-E8E3ADC4E166>
/usr/lib/system/libsystem_sandbox.dylib
    0x7fff8a0ef000 -     0x7fff8a0f5fff  libmacho.dylib (800.0.0 - compatibility 1.0.0) <165514D7-1BFA-38EF-A151-
676DCD21FB64> /usr/lib/system/libmacho.dylib
    0x7fff8a0f6000 -     0x7fff8a116fff  libsystem_kernel.dylib (1699.26.8 - compatibility 1.0.0) <1DDC0B0F-DB2A-34D6-
895D-E5B2B5618946> /usr/lib/system/libsystem_kernel.dylib
    0x7fff8a2ac000 -     0x7fff8a2b4fff  libsystem_dnssd.dylib (??? - ???) <D9BB1F87-A42B-3CBC-9DC2-FC07FCEF0016>
/usr/lib/system/libsystem_dnssd.dylib
    0x7fff8ae26000 -     0x7fff8ae61fff  libsystem_info.dylib (??? - ???) <35F90252-2AE1-32C5-8D34-782C614D9639>
/usr/lib/system/libsystem_info.dylib
    0x7fff8b248000 -     0x7fff8b24afff  libquarantine.dylib (36.6.0 - compatibility 1.0.0) <0EBF714B-4B69-3E1F-9A7D-
6BBC2AACB310> /usr/lib/system/libquarantine.dylib
    0x7fff8b3b4000 -     0x7fff8b3b4fff  libkeymgr.dylib (23.0.0 - compatibility 1.0.0) <61EFED6A-A407-301E-B454-
CD18314F0075> /usr/lib/system/libkeymgr.dylib
    0x7fff8b3dd000 -     0x7fff8b3e2fff  libcompiler_rt.dylib (6.0.0 - compatibility 1.0.0) <98ECD5F6-E85C-32A5-98CD-
8911230CB66A> /usr/lib/system/libcompiler_rt.dylib
    0x7fff8bd1a000 -     0x7fff8bd1bfff  libdnsinfo.dylib (395.11.0 - compatibility 1.0.0) <853BAAA5-270F-3FDC-B025-
D448DB72E1C3> /usr/lib/system/libdnsinfo.dylib
    0x7fff8c528000 -     0x7fff8c52dff7  libsystem_network.dylib (??? - ???) <5DE7024E-1D2D-34A2-80F4-08326331A75B>
/usr/lib/system/libsystem_network.dylib
    0x7fff8cfa3000 -     0x7fff8cfadff7  liblaunch.dylib (392.38.0 - compatibility 1.0.0) <6ECB7F19-B384-32C1-8652-
2463C1CF4815> /usr/lib/system/liblaunch.dylib
    0x7fff8fe02000 -     0x7fff8fe09fff  libcopyfile.dylib (85.1.0 - compatibility 1.0.0) <0AB51EE2-E914-358C-AC19-
47BC024BDAE7> /usr/lib/system/libcopyfile.dylib
    0x7fff8fe4b000 -     0x7fff8fe8dff7  libcommonCrypto.dylib (55010.0.0 - compatibility 1.0.0) <BB770C22-8C57-365A-
8716-4A3C36AE7BFB> /usr/lib/system/libcommonCrypto.dylib
    0x7fff90c0f000 -     0x7fff90c18ff7  libsystem_notify.dylib (80.1.0 - compatibility 1.0.0) <A4D651E3-D1C6-3934-
AD49-7A104FD14596> /usr/lib/system/libsystem_notify.dylib
    0x7fff91376000 -     0x7fff913a3fe7  libSystem.B.dylib (159.1.0 - compatibility 1.0.0) <7BEBB139-50BB-3112-947A-
F4AA168F991C> /usr/lib/libSystem.B.dylib
    0x7fff91489000 -     0x7fff9148fff7  libunwind.dylib (30.0.0 - compatibility 1.0.0) <1E9C6C8C-CBE8-3F4B-A5B5-
E03E3AB53231> /usr/lib/system/libunwind.dylib
    0x7fff91a22000 -     0x7fff91a27fff  libcache.dylib (47.0.0 - compatibility 1.0.0) <1571C3AB-BCB2-38CD-B3B2-
C5FC3F927C6A> /usr/lib/system/libcache.dylib

External Modification Summary:
  Calls made by other processes targeting this process:
    task_for_pid: 2
    thread_create: 0
    thread_set_state: 0
  Calls made by this process:
    task_for_pid: 0
    thread_create: 0
    thread_set_state: 0
  Calls made by all processes on this machine:
    task_for_pid: 6134
    thread_create: 0
    thread_set_state: 0
```

137

```
VM Region Summary:
ReadOnly portion of Libraries: Total=50.2M resident=50.2M(100%) swapped_out_or_unallocated=0K(0%)
Writable regions: Total=38.9M written=10.8M(28%) resident=42.6M(110%) swapped_out=0K(0%)
unallocated=16777216.0T(45221404475392%)

REGION TYPE                 VIRTUAL
===========                 =======
MALLOC                       1220K
Stack                        66.6M
__DATA                        464K
__LINKEDIT                   47.7M
__TEXT                       2484K
shared memory                  12K
===========                 =======
TOTAL                       118.4M
```

2.   Load a core dump core.3769 and App6 executable:

$ gdb -c ~/Documents/AMCDA-Dumps/core.3769 -e ~/Documents/AMCDA-Dumps/Apps/App6/Build/Products/Release/App6

```
GNU gdb 6.3.50-20050815 (Apple version gdb-1820) (Sat Jun 16 02:40:11 UTC 2012)
Copyright 2004 Free Software Foundation, Inc.
GDB is free software, covered by the GNU General Public License, and you are
welcome to change it and/or distribute copies of it under certain conditions.
Type "show copying" to see the conditions.
There is absolutely no warranty for GDB.  Type "show warranty" for details.
This GDB was configured as "x86_64-apple-darwin".
Reading symbols for shared libraries . done
Reading symbols for shared libraries ........................ done
#0  0x00007fff8a10ce42 in __semwait_signal ()
```

3.   Go to the identifed problem core thread 1 (thread #2) ('q' doesn't work here):

```
(gdb) thread 2
[Switching to thread 2 (core thread 1)]
0x00000001027ec905 in procF ()

(gdb) bt
#0  0x00000001027ec905 in procF ()
#1  0x00000001027ec938 in procF ()
#2  0x00000001027ec938 in procF ()
#3  0x00000001027ec938 in procF ()
#4  0x00000001027ec938 in procF ()
#5  0x00000001027ec938 in procF ()
#6  0x00000001027ec938 in procF ()
#7  0x00000001027ec938 in procF ()
#8  0x00000001027ec938 in procF ()
#9  0x00000001027ec938 in procF ()
#10 0x00000001027ec938 in procF ()
#11 0x00000001027ec938 in procF ()
#12 0x00000001027ec938 in procF ()
#13 0x00000001027ec938 in procF ()
#14 0x00000001027ec938 in procF ()
#15 0x00000001027ec938 in procF ()
#16 0x00000001027ec938 in procF ()
#17 0x00000001027ec938 in procF ()
#18 0x00000001027ec938 in procF ()
#19 0x00000001027ec938 in procF ()
#20 0x00000001027ec938 in procF ()
#21 0x00000001027ec938 in procF ()
```

```
#22 0x00000001027ec938 in procF ()
#23 0x00000001027ec938 in procF ()
#24 0x00000001027ec938 in procF ()
#25 0x00000001027ec938 in procF ()
#26 0x00000001027ec938 in procF ()
#27 0x00000001027ec938 in procF ()
#28 0x00000001027ec938 in procF ()
#29 0x00000001027ec938 in procF ()
#30 0x00000001027ec938 in procF ()
#31 0x00000001027ec938 in procF ()
#32 0x00000001027ec938 in procF ()
#33 0x00000001027ec938 in procF ()
#34 0x00000001027ec938 in procF ()
#35 0x00000001027ec938 in procF ()
#36 0x00000001027ec938 in procF ()
#37 0x00000001027ec938 in procF ()
#38 0x00000001027ec938 in procF ()
#39 0x00000001027ec938 in procF ()
#40 0x00000001027ec938 in procF ()
#41 0x00000001027ec938 in procF ()
---Type <return> to continue, or q <return> to quit---q
#43 0x00000001027ec938 in procF ()
#44 0x00000001027ec938 in procF ()
#45 0x00000001027ec938 in procF ()
#46 0x00000001027ec938 in procF ()
#47 0x00000001027ec938 in procF ()
#48 0x00000001027ec938 in procF ()
#49 0x00000001027ec938 in procF ()
#50 0x00000001027ec938 in procF ()
#51 0x00000001027ec938 in procF ()
#52 0x00000001027ec938 in procF ()
#53 0x00000001027ec938 in procF ()
#54 0x00000001027ec938 in procF ()
[...]
#950 0x00000001027ec938 in procF ()
#951 0x00000001027ec938 in procF ()
#952 0x00000001027ec938 in procF ()
#953 0x00000001027ec938 in procF ()
#954 0x00000001027ec938 in procF ()
#955 0x00000001027ec938 in procF ()
#956 0x00000001027ec938 in procF ()
#957 0x00000001027ec938 in procF ()
#958 0x00000001027ec938 in procF ()
#959 0x00000001027ec938 in procF ()
#960 0x00000001027ec938 in procF ()
#961 0x00000001027ec938 in procF ()
#962 0x00000001027ec938 in procF ()
#963 0x00000001027ec938 in procF ()
#964 0x00000001027ec96e in procE ()
#965 0x00000001027ec98a in bar_one ()
#966 0x00000001027ec999 in foo_one ()
#967 0x00000001027ec9b1 in thread_one ()
#968 0x00007fff84db88bf in _pthread_start ()
---Type <return> to continue, or q <return> to quit---
#969 0x00007fff84dbbb75 in thread_start ()
```

4.   Check if this is a stack overflow indeed. Stack region can be identified from the diagnostic report or vmmap_3769.log based on thread number.

```
Virtual Memory Map of process 3769 (App6)
Output report format:  2.2  -- 64-bit process

==== Non-writable regions for process 3769
__TEXT          00000001027ec000-00000001027ed000 [    4K] r-x/rwx SM=COW  /Users/DumpAnalysis/Documents/AMCDA-
Dumps/Apps/App6/Build/Products/Release/App6
__LINKEDIT      00000001027ee000-00000001027ef000 [    4K] r--/rwx SM=COW  /Users/DumpAnalysis/Documents/AMCDA-
Dumps/Apps/App6/Build/Products/Release/App6
MALLOC metadata 00000001027ef000-00000001027f0000 [    4K] r--/rwx SM=ZER
MALLOC guard page 00000001027f1000-00000001027f2000 [    4K] ---/rwx SM=NUL
MALLOC guard page 0000000102807000-0000000102809000 [    8K] ---/rwx SM=NUL
MALLOC guard page 000000010281e000-000000010281f000 [    4K] ---/rwx SM=NUL
MALLOC metadata 000000010281f000-0000000102820000 [    4K] r--/rwx SM=PRV
STACK GUARD     0000000102820000-0000000102821000 [    4K] ---/rwx SM=NUL  stack guard for thread 1
STACK GUARD     0000000102a00000-0000000102a01000 [    4K] ---/rwx SM=NUL  stack guard for thread 2
STACK GUARD     0000000102a83000-0000000102a84000 [    4K] ---/rwx SM=NUL  stack guard for thread 3
STACK GUARD     0000000102b06000-0000000102b07000 [    4K] ---/rwx SM=NUL  stack guard for thread 4
STACK GUARD     0000000102b89000-0000000102b8a000 [    4K] ---/rwx SM=NUL  stack guard for thread 5
STACK GUARD     00007fff5e3ec000-00007fff61bec000 [ 56.0M] ---/rwx SM=NUL  stack guard for thread 0
__TEXT          00007fff623ec000-00007fff62421000 [  212K] r-x/rwx SM=COW  /usr/lib/dyld
__LINKEDIT      00007fff6245d000-00007fff62470000 [   76K] r--/rwx SM=COW  /usr/lib/dyld
__TEXT          00007fff849f2000-00007fff84a10000 [  120K] r-x/r-x SM=COW  /usr/lib/system/libxpc.dylib
__TEXT          00007fff84d68000-00007fff84d6a000 [    8K] r-x/r-x SM=COW
/usr/lib/system/libsystem_blocks.dylib
__TEXT          00007fff84d6a000-00007fff84e48000 [  888K] r-x/r-x SM=COW  /usr/lib/system/libsystem_c.dylib
__TEXT          00007fff85022000-00007fff85031000 [   60K] r-x/r-x SM=COW  /usr/lib/system/libdispatch.dylib
__TEXT          00007fff855f0000-00007fff855f2000 [    8K] r-x/r-x SM=COW  /usr/lib/system/libunc.dylib
__TEXT          00007fff85ae3000-00007fff85ae5000 [    8K] r-x/r-x SM=COW  /usr/lib/system/libremovefile.dylib
__TEXT          00007fff89114000-00007fff89119000 [   20K] r-x/r-x SM=COW
/usr/lib/system/libmathCommon.A.dylib
__TEXT          00007fff89119000-00007fff8911e000 [   20K] r-x/r-x SM=COW  /usr/lib/system/libdyld.dylib
__TEXT          00007fff89740000-00007fff89742000 [    8K] r-x/r-x SM=COW
/usr/lib/system/libsystem_sandbox.dylib
__TEXT          00007fff8a0ef000-00007fff8a0f6000 [   28K] r-x/r-x SM=COW  /usr/lib/system/libmacho.dylib
__TEXT          00007fff8a0f6000-00007fff8a117000 [  132K] r-x/r-x SM=COW
/usr/lib/system/libsystem_kernel.dylib
__TEXT          00007fff8a2ac000-00007fff8a2b5000 [   36K] r-x/r-x SM=COW
/usr/lib/system/libsystem_dnssd.dylib
__TEXT          00007fff8ae26000-00007fff8ae62000 [  240K] r-x/r-x SM=COW  /usr/lib/system/libsystem_info.dylib
__TEXT          00007fff8b248000-00007fff8b24b000 [   12K] r-x/r-x SM=COW  /usr/lib/system/libquarantine.dylib
__TEXT          00007fff8b3b4000-00007fff8b3b5000 [    4K] r-x/r-x SM=COW  /usr/lib/system/libkeymgr.dylib
__TEXT          00007fff8b3dd000-00007fff8b3e3000 [   24K] r-x/r-x SM=COW  /usr/lib/system/libcompiler_rt.dylib
__TEXT          00007fff8bd1a000-00007fff8bd1c000 [    8K] r-x/r-x SM=COW  /usr/lib/system/libdnsinfo.dylib
__TEXT          00007fff8c528000-00007fff8c52e000 [   24K] r-x/r-x SM=COW
/usr/lib/system/libsystem_network.dylib
__TEXT          00007fff8cfa3000-00007fff8cfae000 [   44K] r-x/r-x SM=COW  /usr/lib/system/liblaunch.dylib
__TEXT          00007fff8fe02000-00007fff8fe0a000 [   32K] r-x/r-x SM=COW  /usr/lib/system/libcopyfile.dylib
__TEXT          00007fff8fe4b000-00007fff8fe8e000 [  268K] r-x/r-x SM=COW
/usr/lib/system/libcommonCrypto.dylib
__TEXT          00007fff90c0f000-00007fff90c19000 [   40K] r-x/r-x SM=COW
/usr/lib/system/libsystem_notify.dylib
__TEXT          00007fff91376000-00007fff913a4000 [  184K] r-x/r-x SM=COW  /usr/lib/libSystem.B.dylib
__TEXT          00007fff91489000-00007fff91490000 [   28K] r-x/r-x SM=COW  /usr/lib/system/libunwind.dylib
__TEXT          00007fff91a22000-00007fff91a28000 [   24K] r-x/r-x SM=COW  /usr/lib/system/libcache.dylib
__LINKEDIT      00007fff91b86000-00007fff94b30000 [ 47.7M] r--/r-- SM=COW  /usr/lib/system/libxpc.dylib
shared memory   00007ffffe00000-00007ffffe02000 [    8K] r-x/r-x SM=SHM

==== Writable regions for process 3769
__DATA          00000001027ed000-00000001027ee000 [    4K] rw-/rwx SM=PRV  /Users/DumpAnalysis/Documents/AMCDA-
Dumps/Apps/App6/Build/Products/Release/App6
MALLOC metadata 00000001027f0000-00000001027f1000 [    4K] rw-/rwx SM=ZER
MALLOC metadata 00000001027f2000-0000000102807000 [   84K] rw-/rwx SM=PRV
MALLOC metadata 0000000102809000-000000010281e000 [   84K] rw-/rwx SM=PRV
Stack           0000000102821000-00000001028a3000 [  520K] rw-/rwx SM=PRV  thread 1
MALLOC_TINY     0000000102900000-0000000102a00000 [ 1024K] rw-/rwx SM=PRV  DefaultMallocZone_0x1027ef000
Stack           0000000102a01000-0000000102a83000 [  520K] rw-/rwx SM=PRV  thread 2
Stack           0000000102a84000-0000000102b06000 [  520K] rw-/rwx SM=PRV  thread 3
Stack           0000000102b07000-0000000102b89000 [  520K] rw-/rwx SM=PRV  thread 4
Stack           0000000102b8a000-0000000102c0c000 [  520K] rw-/rwx SM=PRV  thread 5
Stack           00007fff61bec000-00007fff623eb000 [ 8188K] rw-/rwx SM=ZER  thread 0
```

140

```
Stack                  00007fff623eb000-00007fff623ec000 [    4K] rw-/rwx SM=COW  thread 0
__DATA                 00007fff62421000-00007fff6245d000 [  240K] rw-/rwx SM=COW  /usr/lib/dyld
__DATA                 00007fff749c0000-00007fff749c3000 [   12K] rw-/rwx SM=COW  /usr/lib/system/libxpc.dylib
__DATA                 00007fff74a60000-00007fff74a61000 [    4K] rw-/rwx SM=COW
/usr/lib/system/libsystem_blocks.dylib
__DATA                 00007fff74a61000-00007fff74a71000 [   64K] rw-/rwx SM=COW  /usr/lib/system/libsystem_c.dylib
__DATA                 00007fff74ac4000-00007fff74aca000 [   24K] rw-/rwx SM=COW  /usr/lib/system/libdispatch.dylib
__DATA                 00007fff74b90000-00007fff74b91000 [    4K] rw-/rwx SM=COW  /usr/lib/system/libunc.dylib
__DATA                 00007fff74c11000-00007fff74c12000 [    4K] rw-/rw- SM=COW  /usr/lib/system/libremovefile.dylib
__DATA                 00007fff75141000-00007fff75142000 [    4K] rw-/rwx SM=COW  /usr/lib/system/libdyld.dylib
__DATA                 00007fff751a3000-00007fff751a4000 [    4K] rw-/rwx SM=COW
/usr/lib/system/libsystem_sandbox.dylib
__DATA                 00007fff75281000-00007fff75282000 [    4K] rw-/rwx SM=COW  /usr/lib/system/libmacho.dylib
__DATA                 00007fff75282000-00007fff75285000 [   12K] rw-/rwx SM=COW
/usr/lib/system/libsystem_kernel.dylib
__DATA                 00007fff752d8000-00007fff752d9000 [    4K] rw-/rwx SM=COW
/usr/lib/system/libsystem_dnssd.dylib
__DATA                 00007fff75453000-00007fff75456000 [   12K] rw-/rwx SM=COW  /usr/lib/system/libsystem_info.dylib
__DATA                 00007fff7551f000-00007fff75520000 [    4K] rw-/rwx SM=COW  /usr/lib/system/libquarantine.dylib
__DATA                 00007fff75559000-00007fff7555a000 [    4K] rw-/rwx SM=COW  /usr/lib/system/libkeymgr.dylib
__DATA                 00007fff75563000-00007fff75564000 [    4K] rw-/rwx SM=COW  /usr/lib/system/libcompiler_rt.dylib
__DATA                 00007fff75633000-00007fff75634000 [    4K] rw-/rw- SM=COW  /usr/lib/system/libdnsinfo.dylib
__DATA                 00007fff756d6000-00007fff756d7000 [    4K] rw-/rw- SM=COW
/usr/lib/system/libsystem_network.dylib
__DATA                 00007fff75813000-00007fff75814000 [    4K] rw-/rwx SM=COW  /usr/lib/system/liblaunch.dylib
__DATA                 00007fff75e41000-00007fff75e42000 [    4K] rw-/rw- SM=COW  /usr/lib/system/libcopyfile.dylib
__DATA                 00007fff75e4a000-00007fff75e50000 [   24K] rw-/rw- SM=COW
/usr/lib/system/libcommonCrypto.dylib
__DATA                 00007fff76342000-00007fff76343000 [    4K] rw-/rw- SM=COW
/usr/lib/system/libsystem_notify.dylib
__DATA                 00007fff763fd000-00007fff763fe000 [    4K] rw-/rw- SM=COW  /usr/lib/libSystem.B.dylib
__DATA                 00007fff76401000-00007fff76402000 [    4K] rw-/rw- SM=COW  /usr/lib/system/libunwind.dylib
__DATA                 00007fff764ab000-00007fff764ac000 [    4K] rw-/rw- SM=COW  /usr/lib/system/libcache.dylib

==== Legend
SM=sharing mode:
        COW=copy_on_write PRV=private NUL=empty ALI=aliased
        SHM=shared ZER=zero_filled S/A=shared_alias

==== Summary for process 3769
ReadOnly portion of Libraries: Total=50.2M resident=50.2M(100%) swapped_out_or_unallocated=0K(0%)
Writable regions: Total=28.6M written=108K(0%) resident=20.6M(72%) swapped_out=0K(0%) unallocated=8244K(28%)

REGION TYPE                VIRTUAL
===========                =======
MALLOC                      1024K        see MALLOC ZONE table below
MALLOC guard page             16K
MALLOC metadata              180K
STACK GUARD                 56.0M
Stack                       10.5M
__DATA                       464K
__LINKEDIT                  47.7M
__TEXT                      2484K
shared memory                 8K
===========                =======
TOTAL                      118.4M
```

MALLOC ZONE	VIRTUAL SIZE	ALLOCATION COUNT	BYTES ALLOCATED	% FULL
===========	=======	=========	=========	======
DefaultMallocZone_0x1027ef000	1024K	33	2240	0%

5.   We check that manually based on the stack pointer value:

```
(gdb) x $rsp
0x102820e40: 0x00000000

(gdb) frame 1
#1  0x00000001027ec938 in procF ()
```

141

```
(gdb) x $rsp
0x102821060: 0xffffffff


(gdb) frame 2
#2  0x00000001027ec938 in procF ()


(gdb) x $rsp
0x102821280: 0xffffffff


(gdb) maintenance info sections
Exec file:
    `/Users/DumpAnalysis/Documents/AMCDA-Dumps/Apps/App6/Build/Products/Release/App6', file type mach-o-le.
    0x0000000000000000->0x0000000000000000 at 0x00000000: LC_SEGMENT.__PAGEZERO ALLOC LOAD CODE HAS_CONTENTS
    0x0000000100000000->0x0000000100001000 at 0x00000000: LC_SEGMENT.__TEXT ALLOC LOAD CODE HAS_CONTENTS
    0x0000000100000890->0x0000000100000c63 at 0x00000890: LC_SEGMENT.__TEXT.__text ALLOC LOAD READONLY CODE
HAS_CONTENTS
    0x0000000100000c64->0x0000000100000c82 at 0x00000c64: LC_SEGMENT.__TEXT.__stubs ALLOC LOAD CODE HAS_CONTENTS
    0x0000000100000c84->0x0000000100000cc6 at 0x00000c84: LC_SEGMENT.__TEXT.__stub_helper ALLOC LOAD CODE HAS_CONTENTS
    0x0000000100000cc6->0x0000000100000d16 at 0x00000cc6: LC_SEGMENT.__TEXT.__unwind_info ALLOC LOAD CODE HAS_CONTENTS
    0x0000000100000d18->0x0000000100001000 at 0x00000d18: LC_SEGMENT.__TEXT.__eh_frame ALLOC LOAD CODE HAS_CONTENTS
    0x0000000100001000->0x0000000100002000 at 0x00001000: LC_SEGMENT.__DATA ALLOC LOAD CODE HAS_CONTENTS
    0x0000000100001000->0x0000000100001028 at 0x00001000: LC_SEGMENT.__DATA.__program_vars ALLOC LOAD CODE
HAS_CONTENTS
    0x0000000100001028->0x0000000100001038 at 0x00001028: LC_SEGMENT.__DATA.__nl_symbol_ptr ALLOC LOAD CODE
HAS_CONTENTS
    0x0000000100001038->0x0000000100001040 at 0x00001038: LC_SEGMENT.__DATA.__got ALLOC LOAD CODE HAS_CONTENTS
    0x0000000100001040->0x0000000100001068 at 0x00001040: LC_SEGMENT.__DATA.__la_symbol_ptr ALLOC LOAD CODE
HAS_CONTENTS
    0x0000000100001068->0x0000000100001088 at 0x00000000: LC_SEGMENT.__DATA.__common ALLOC
    0x0000000100002000->0x0000000100002494 at 0x00002000: LC_SEGMENT.__LINKEDIT ALLOC LOAD CODE HAS_CONTENTS
    0x0000000000000000->0x00000000000001f0 at 0x00002118: LC_SYMTAB.stabs HAS_CONTENTS
    0x0000000000000000->0x0000000000000158 at 0x0000233c: LC_SYMTAB.stabstr HAS_CONTENTS
    0x0000000000000000->0x0000000000000120 at 0x00002118: LC_DYSYMTAB.localstabs HAS_CONTENTS
    0x0000000000000000->0x00000000000000d0 at 0x00002238: LC_DYSYMTAB.nonlocalstabs HAS_CONTENTS
    0x0000000000000000->0x0000000000000018 at 0x00000500: LC_LOAD_DYLINKER HAS_CONTENTS
    0x0000000000000000->0x00000000000000a8 at 0x00000550: LC_THREAD.x86_THREAD_STATE64.0 HAS_CONTENTS
    0x0000000000000000->0x0000000000000030 at 0x00000600: LC_LOAD_DYLIB HAS_CONTENTS
Core file:
    `/Users/DumpAnalysis/Documents/AMCDA-Dumps/core.3769', file type mach-o-le.
    0x00000001027ec000->0x00000001027ed000 at 0x00002000: LC_SEGMENT. ALLOC LOAD CODE HAS_CONTENTS
    0x00000001027ed000->0x00000001027ee000 at 0x00003000: LC_SEGMENT. ALLOC LOAD CODE HAS_CONTENTS
    0x00000001027ee000->0x00000001027ef000 at 0x00004000: LC_SEGMENT. ALLOC LOAD CODE HAS_CONTENTS
    0x00000001027ef000->0x00000001027f0000 at 0x00005000: LC_SEGMENT. ALLOC LOAD CODE HAS_CONTENTS
    0x00000001027f0000->0x00000001027f1000 at 0x00006000: LC_SEGMENT. ALLOC LOAD CODE HAS_CONTENTS
    0x00000001027f1000->0x00000001027f2000 at 0x00007000: LC_SEGMENT. ALLOC LOAD CODE HAS_CONTENTS
    0x00000001027f2000->0x0000000102807000 at 0x00008000: LC_SEGMENT. ALLOC LOAD CODE HAS_CONTENTS
    0x0000000102807000->0x0000000102808000 at 0x0001d000: LC_SEGMENT. ALLOC LOAD CODE HAS_CONTENTS
    0x0000000102808000->0x0000000102809000 at 0x0001e000: LC_SEGMENT. ALLOC LOAD CODE HAS_CONTENTS
    0x0000000102809000->0x000000010281e000 at 0x0001f000: LC_SEGMENT. ALLOC LOAD CODE HAS_CONTENTS
    0x000000010281e000->0x000000010281f000 at 0x00034000: LC_SEGMENT. ALLOC LOAD CODE HAS_CONTENTS
    0x000000010281f000->0x0000000102820000 at 0x00035000: LC_SEGMENT. ALLOC LOAD CODE HAS_CONTENTS
    0x0000000102820000->0x0000000102821000 at 0x00036000: LC_SEGMENT. ALLOC LOAD CODE HAS_CONTENTS
    0x0000000102821000->0x00000001028a3000 at 0x00037000: LC_SEGMENT. ALLOC LOAD CODE HAS_CONTENTS
    0x0000000102900000->0x0000000102a00000 at 0x000b9000: LC_SEGMENT. ALLOC LOAD CODE HAS_CONTENTS
    0x0000000102a00000->0x0000000102a01000 at 0x001b9000: LC_SEGMENT. ALLOC LOAD CODE HAS_CONTENTS
    0x0000000102a01000->0x0000000102a83000 at 0x001ba000: LC_SEGMENT. ALLOC LOAD CODE HAS_CONTENTS
    0x0000000102a83000->0x0000000102a84000 at 0x0023c000: LC_SEGMENT. ALLOC LOAD CODE HAS_CONTENTS
    0x0000000102a84000->0x0000000102b06000 at 0x0023d000: LC_SEGMENT. ALLOC LOAD CODE HAS_CONTENTS
    0x0000000102b06000->0x0000000102b07000 at 0x002bf000: LC_SEGMENT. ALLOC LOAD CODE HAS_CONTENTS
    0x0000000102b07000->0x0000000102b89000 at 0x002c0000: LC_SEGMENT. ALLOC LOAD CODE HAS_CONTENTS
    0x0000000102b89000->0x0000000102b8a000 at 0x00342000: LC_SEGMENT. ALLOC LOAD CODE HAS_CONTENTS
    0x0000000102b8a000->0x0000000102c0c000 at 0x00343000: LC_SEGMENT. ALLOC LOAD CODE HAS_CONTENTS
    0x00007fff5e3ec000->0x00007fff61bec000 at 0x003c5000: LC_SEGMENT. ALLOC LOAD CODE HAS_CONTENTS
    0x00007fff61bec000->0x00007fff623eb000 at 0x03bc5000: LC_SEGMENT. ALLOC LOAD CODE HAS_CONTENTS
    0x00007fff623eb000->0x00007fff623ec000 at 0x043c4000: LC_SEGMENT. ALLOC LOAD CODE HAS_CONTENTS
    0x00007fff623ec000->0x00007fff62421000 at 0x043c5000: LC_SEGMENT. ALLOC LOAD CODE HAS_CONTENTS
    0x00007fff62421000->0x00007fff62423000 at 0x043fa000: LC_SEGMENT. ALLOC LOAD CODE HAS_CONTENTS
    0x00007fff62423000->0x00007fff6245d000 at 0x043fc000: LC_SEGMENT. ALLOC LOAD CODE HAS_CONTENTS
    0x00007fff6245d000->0x00007fff62470000 at 0x04436000: LC_SEGMENT. ALLOC LOAD CODE HAS_CONTENTS
    0x00007fff749b8000->0x00007fff74a00000 at 0x04449000: LC_SEGMENT. ALLOC LOAD CODE HAS_CONTENTS
    0x00007fff74a00000->0x00007fff74c00000 at 0x04491000: LC_SEGMENT. ALLOC LOAD CODE HAS_CONTENTS
    0x00007fff74c00000->0x00007fff74e00000 at 0x04691000: LC_SEGMENT. ALLOC LOAD CODE HAS_CONTENTS
    0x00007fff74e00000->0x00007fff75000000 at 0x04891000: LC_SEGMENT. ALLOC LOAD CODE HAS_CONTENTS
```

```
0x00007fff75000000->0x00007fff75200000 at 0x04a91000: LC_SEGMENT. ALLOC LOAD CODE HAS_CONTENTS
0x00007fff75200000->0x00007fff75400000 at 0x04c91000: LC_SEGMENT. ALLOC LOAD CODE HAS_CONTENTS
0x00007fff75400000->0x00007fff75600000 at 0x04e91000: LC_SEGMENT. ALLOC LOAD CODE HAS_CONTENTS
0x00007fff75600000->0x00007fff75800000 at 0x05091000: LC_SEGMENT. ALLOC LOAD CODE HAS_CONTENTS
0x00007fff75800000->0x00007fff75a00000 at 0x05291000: LC_SEGMENT. ALLOC LOAD CODE HAS_CONTENTS
0x00007fff75a00000->0x00007fff75c00000 at 0x05491000: LC_SEGMENT. ALLOC LOAD CODE HAS_CONTENTS
---Type <return> to continue, or q <return> to quit---
0x00007fff75c00000->0x00007fff75e00000 at 0x05691000: LC_SEGMENT. ALLOC LOAD CODE HAS_CONTENTS
0x00007fff75e00000->0x00007fff76200000 at 0x05891000: LC_SEGMENT. ALLOC LOAD CODE HAS_CONTENTS
0x00007fff76200000->0x00007fff76400000 at 0x05c91000: LC_SEGMENT. ALLOC LOAD CODE HAS_CONTENTS
0x00007fff76400000->0x00007fff764ac000 at 0x05e91000: LC_SEGMENT. ALLOC LOAD CODE HAS_CONTENTS
0x00007fff849b8000->0x00007fff91a28000 at 0x05f3d000: LC_SEGMENT. ALLOC LOAD CODE HAS_CONTENTS
0x00007fff91a28000->0x00007fff94b30000 at 0x12fad000: LC_SEGMENT. ALLOC LOAD CODE HAS_CONTENTS
0x00007fffffffe00000->0x00007fffffffe02000 at 0x160b5000: LC_SEGMENT. ALLOC LOAD CODE HAS_CONTENTS
0x0000000000000000->0x00000000000000b0 at 0x00000d68: LC_THREAD.x86_THREAD_STATE.0 HAS_CONTENTS
0x0000000000000000->0x0000000000000214 at 0x00000e20: LC_THREAD.x86_FLOAT_STATE.0 HAS_CONTENTS
0x0000000000000000->0x0000000000000018 at 0x0000103c: LC_THREAD.x86_EXCEPTION_STATE.0 HAS_CONTENTS
0x0000000000000000->0x00000000000000b0 at 0x00001064: LC_THREAD.x86_THREAD_STATE.1 HAS_CONTENTS
0x0000000000000000->0x0000000000000214 at 0x0000111c: LC_THREAD.x86_FLOAT_STATE.1 HAS_CONTENTS
0x0000000000000000->0x0000000000000018 at 0x00001338: LC_THREAD.x86_EXCEPTION_STATE.1 HAS_CONTENTS
0x0000000000000000->0x00000000000000b0 at 0x00001360: LC_THREAD.x86_THREAD_STATE.2 HAS_CONTENTS
0x0000000000000000->0x0000000000000214 at 0x00001418: LC_THREAD.x86_FLOAT_STATE.2 HAS_CONTENTS
0x0000000000000000->0x0000000000000018 at 0x00001634: LC_THREAD.x86_EXCEPTION_STATE.2 HAS_CONTENTS
0x0000000000000000->0x00000000000000b0 at 0x0000165c: LC_THREAD.x86_THREAD_STATE.3 HAS_CONTENTS
0x0000000000000000->0x0000000000000214 at 0x00001714: LC_THREAD.x86_FLOAT_STATE.3 HAS_CONTENTS
0x0000000000000000->0x0000000000000018 at 0x00001930: LC_THREAD.x86_EXCEPTION_STATE.3 HAS_CONTENTS
0x0000000000000000->0x00000000000000b0 at 0x00001958: LC_THREAD.x86_THREAD_STATE.4 HAS_CONTENTS
0x0000000000000000->0x0000000000000214 at 0x00001a10: LC_THREAD.x86_FLOAT_STATE.4 HAS_CONTENTS
0x0000000000000000->0x0000000000000018 at 0x00001c2c: LC_THREAD.x86_EXCEPTION_STATE.4 HAS_CONTENTS
0x0000000000000000->0x00000000000000b0 at 0x00001c54: LC_THREAD.x86_THREAD_STATE.5 HAS_CONTENTS
0x0000000000000000->0x0000000000000214 at 0x00001d0c: LC_THREAD.x86_FLOAT_STATE.5 HAS_CONTENTS
0x0000000000000000->0x0000000000000018 at 0x00001f28: LC_THREAD.x86_EXCEPTION_STATE.5 HAS_CONTENTS
```

6.   Dump the bottom of the raw stack to see execution residue such as thread startup:

```
(gdb) x/1024a 0x00000001028a3000-0x4000
0x10289f000: 0x0       0x0
0x10289f010: 0x0       0x0
0x10289f020: 0x0       0x0
0x10289f030: 0x0       0x0
0x10289f040: 0x0       0x0
0x10289f050: 0x0       0x0
0x10289f060: 0x0       0x0
0x10289f070: 0x0       0x0
0x10289f080: 0x0       0x0
0x10289f090: 0x0       0x0
0x10289f0a0: 0x0       0x0
0x10289f0b0: 0x0       0x0
0x10289f0c0: 0x0       0x0
0x10289f0d0: 0x0       0x0
0x10289f0e0: 0xf00000000    0x74e4ebf24818a8b6
0x10289f0f0: 0x10289f310    0x1027ec938 <procF+104>
0x10289f100: 0xffffffff   0xf
0x10289f110: 0xffffffff   0x0
0x10289f120: 0x0       0x0
0x10289f130: 0x0       0x0
0x10289f140: 0x0       0x0
0x10289f150: 0x0       0x0
0x10289f160: 0x0       0x0
0x10289f170: 0x0       0x0
0x10289f180: 0x0       0x0
0x10289f190: 0x0       0x0
0x10289f1a0: 0x0       0x0
0x10289f1b0: 0x0       0x0
0x10289f1c0: 0x0       0x0
```

```
0x10289f1d0:  0x0        0x0
0x10289f1e0:  0x0        0x0
0x10289f1f0:  0x0        0x0
0x10289f200:  0x0        0x0
0x10289f210:  0x0        0x0
0x10289f220:  0x0        0x0
0x10289f230:  0x0        0x0
0x10289f240:  0x0        0x0
0x10289f250:  0x0        0x0
0x10289f260:  0x0        0x0
0x10289f270:  0x0        0x0
0x10289f280:  0x0        0x0
0x10289f290:  0x0        0x0
---Type <return> to continue, or q <return> to quit---
0x10289f2a0:  0x0        0x0
0x10289f2b0:  0x0        0x0
0x10289f2c0:  0x0        0x0
0x10289f2d0:  0x0        0x0
0x10289f2e0:  0x0        0x0
0x10289f2f0:  0x0        0x0
0x10289f300:  0xe00000000    0x74e4ebf24818a8b6
0x10289f310:  0x10289f530    0x1027ec938 <procF+104>
0x10289f320:  0xffffffff     0xe
0x10289f330:  0xffffffff     0x0
0x10289f340:  0x0        0x0
0x10289f350:  0x0        0x0
0x10289f360:  0x0        0x0
0x10289f370:  0x0        0x0
0x10289f380:  0x0        0x0
0x10289f390:  0x0        0x0
0x10289f3a0:  0x0        0x0
0x10289f3b0:  0x0        0x0
0x10289f3c0:  0x0        0x0
0x10289f3d0:  0x0        0x0
0x10289f3e0:  0x0        0x0
0x10289f3f0:  0x0        0x0
0x10289f400:  0x0        0x0
0x10289f410:  0x0        0x0
0x10289f420:  0x0        0x0
0x10289f430:  0x0        0x0
0x10289f440:  0x0        0x0
0x10289f450:  0x0        0x0
0x10289f460:  0x0        0x0
0x10289f470:  0x0        0x0
0x10289f480:  0x0        0x0
0x10289f490:  0x0        0x0
0x10289f4a0:  0x0        0x0
0x10289f4b0:  0x0        0x0
0x10289f4c0:  0x0        0x0
0x10289f4d0:  0x0        0x0
0x10289f4e0:  0x0        0x0
0x10289f4f0:  0x0        0x0
0x10289f500:  0x0        0x0
0x10289f510:  0x0        0x0
0x10289f520:  0xd00000000    0x74e4ebf24818a8b6
0x10289f530:  0x10289f750    0x1027ec938 <procF+104>
---Type <return> to continue, or q <return> to quit---
0x10289f540:  0xffffffff     0xd
0x10289f550:  0xffffffff     0x0
0x10289f560:  0x0        0x0
```

144

```
0x10289f570:  0x0         0x0
0x10289f580:  0x0         0x0
0x10289f590:  0x0         0x0
0x10289f5a0:  0x0         0x0
0x10289f5b0:  0x0         0x0
0x10289f5c0:  0x0         0x0
0x10289f5d0:  0x0         0x0
0x10289f5e0:  0x0         0x0
0x10289f5f0:  0x0         0x0
0x10289f600:  0x0         0x0
0x10289f610:  0x0         0x0
0x10289f620:  0x0         0x0
0x10289f630:  0x0         0x0
0x10289f640:  0x0         0x0
0x10289f650:  0x0         0x0
0x10289f660:  0x0         0x0
0x10289f670:  0x0         0x0
0x10289f680:  0x0         0x0
0x10289f690:  0x0         0x0
0x10289f6a0:  0x0         0x0
0x10289f6b0:  0x0         0x0
0x10289f6c0:  0x0         0x0
0x10289f6d0:  0x0         0x0
0x10289f6e0:  0x0         0x0
0x10289f6f0:  0x0         0x0
0x10289f700:  0x0         0x0
0x10289f710:  0x0         0x0
0x10289f720:  0x0         0x0
0x10289f730:  0x0         0x0
0x10289f740:  0xc00000000  0x74e4ebf24818a8b6
0x10289f750:  0x10289f970  0x1027ec938 <procF+104>
0x10289f760:  0xffffffff   0xc
0x10289f770:  0xffffffff   0x0
0x10289f780:  0x0         0x0
0x10289f790:  0x0         0x0
0x10289f7a0:  0x0         0x0
0x10289f7b0:  0x0         0x0
0x10289f7c0:  0x0         0x0
0x10289f7d0:  0x0         0x0
---Type <return> to continue, or q <return> to quit---
0x10289f7e0:  0x0         0x0
0x10289f7f0:  0x0         0x0
0x10289f800:  0x0         0x0
0x10289f810:  0x0         0x0
0x10289f820:  0x0         0x0
0x10289f830:  0x0         0x0
0x10289f840:  0x0         0x0
0x10289f850:  0x0         0x0
0x10289f860:  0x0         0x0
0x10289f870:  0x0         0x0
0x10289f880:  0x0         0x0
0x10289f890:  0x0         0x0
0x10289f8a0:  0x0         0x0
0x10289f8b0:  0x0         0x0
0x10289f8c0:  0x0         0x0
0x10289f8d0:  0x0         0x0
0x10289f8e0:  0x0         0x0
0x10289f8f0:  0x0         0x0
0x10289f900:  0x0         0x0
0x10289f910:  0x0         0x0
```

```
0x10289f920: 0x0      0x0
0x10289f930: 0x0      0x0
0x10289f940: 0x0      0x0
0x10289f950: 0x0      0x0
0x10289f960: 0xb00000000    0x74e4ebf24818a8b6
0x10289f970: 0x10289fb90    0x1027ec938 <procF+104>
0x10289f980: 0xffffffff     0xb
0x10289f990: 0xffffffff     0x0
0x10289f9a0: 0x0      0x0
0x10289f9b0: 0x0      0x0
0x10289f9c0: 0x0      0x0
0x10289f9d0: 0x0      0x0
0x10289f9e0: 0x0      0x0
0x10289f9f0: 0x0      0x0
0x10289fa00: 0x0      0x0
0x10289fa10: 0x0      0x0
0x10289fa20: 0x0      0x0
0x10289fa30: 0x0      0x0
0x10289fa40: 0x0      0x0
0x10289fa50: 0x0      0x0
0x10289fa60: 0x0      0x0
0x10289fa70: 0x0      0x0
---Type <return> to continue, or q <return> to quit---
0x10289fa80: 0x0      0x0
0x10289fa90: 0x0      0x0
0x10289faa0: 0x0      0x0
0x10289fab0: 0x0      0x0
0x10289fac0: 0x0      0x0
0x10289fad0: 0x0      0x0
0x10289fae0: 0x0      0x0
0x10289faf0: 0x0      0x0
0x10289fb00: 0x0      0x0
0x10289fb10: 0x0      0x0
0x10289fb20: 0x0      0x0
0x10289fb30: 0x0      0x0
0x10289fb40: 0x0      0x0
0x10289fb50: 0x0      0x0
0x10289fb60: 0x0      0x0
0x10289fb70: 0x0      0x0
0x10289fb80: 0xa00000000    0x74e4ebf24818a8b6
0x10289fb90: 0x10289fdb0    0x1027ec938 <procF+104>
0x10289fba0: 0xffffffff     0xa
0x10289fbb0: 0xffffffff     0x0
0x10289fbc0: 0x0      0x0
0x10289fbd0: 0x0      0x0
0x10289fbe0: 0x0      0x0
0x10289fbf0: 0x0      0x0
0x10289fc00: 0x0      0x0
0x10289fc10: 0x0      0x0
0x10289fc20: 0x0      0x0
0x10289fc30: 0x0      0x0
0x10289fc40: 0x0      0x0
0x10289fc50: 0x0      0x0
0x10289fc60: 0x0      0x0
0x10289fc70: 0x0      0x0
0x10289fc80: 0x0      0x0
0x10289fc90: 0x0      0x0
0x10289fca0: 0x0      0x0
0x10289fcb0: 0x0      0x0
0x10289fcc0: 0x0      0x0
```

```
0x10289fcd0: 0x0      0x0
0x10289fce0: 0x0      0x0
0x10289fcf0: 0x0      0x0
0x10289fd00: 0x0      0x0
0x10289fd10: 0x0      0x0
---Type <return> to continue, or q <return> to quit---
0x10289fd20: 0x0      0x0
0x10289fd30: 0x0      0x0
0x10289fd40: 0x0      0x0
0x10289fd50: 0x0      0x0
0x10289fd60: 0x0      0x0
0x10289fd70: 0x0      0x0
0x10289fd80: 0x0      0x0
0x10289fd90: 0x0      0x0
0x10289fda0: 0x900000000   0x74e4ebf24818a8b6
0x10289fdb0: 0x10289ffd0   0x1027ec938 <procF+104>
0x10289fdc0: 0xffffffff    0x9
0x10289fdd0: 0xffffffff    0x0
0x10289fde0: 0x0      0x0
0x10289fdf0: 0x0      0x0
0x10289fe00: 0x0      0x0
0x10289fe10: 0x0      0x0
0x10289fe20: 0x0      0x0
0x10289fe30: 0x0      0x0
0x10289fe40: 0x0      0x0
0x10289fe50: 0x0      0x0
0x10289fe60: 0x0      0x0
0x10289fe70: 0x0      0x0
0x10289fe80: 0x0      0x0
0x10289fe90: 0x0      0x0
0x10289fea0: 0x0      0x0
0x10289feb0: 0x0      0x0
0x10289fec0: 0x0      0x0
0x10289fed0: 0x0      0x0
0x10289fee0: 0x0      0x0
0x10289fef0: 0x0      0x0
0x10289ff00: 0x0      0x0
0x10289ff10: 0x0      0x0
0x10289ff20: 0x0      0x0
0x10289ff30: 0x0      0x0
0x10289ff40: 0x0      0x0
0x10289ff50: 0x0      0x0
0x10289ff60: 0x0      0x0
0x10289ff70: 0x0      0x0
0x10289ff80: 0x0      0x0
0x10289ff90: 0x0      0x0
0x10289ffa0: 0x0      0x0
0x10289ffb0: 0x0      0x0
---Type <return> to continue, or q <return> to quit---
0x10289ffc0: 0x800000000   0x74e4ebf24818a8b6
0x10289ffd0: 0x1028a01f0   0x1027ec938 <procF+104>
0x10289ffe0: 0xffffffff    0x8
0x10289fff0: 0xffffffff    0x0
0x1028a0000: 0x0      0x0
0x1028a0010: 0x0      0x0
0x1028a0020: 0x0      0x0
0x1028a0030: 0x0      0x0
0x1028a0040: 0x0      0x0
0x1028a0050: 0x0      0x0
0x1028a0060: 0x0      0x0
```

147

```
0x1028a0070:  0x0      0x0
0x1028a0080:  0x0      0x0
0x1028a0090:  0x0      0x0
0x1028a00a0:  0x0      0x0
0x1028a00b0:  0x0      0x0
0x1028a00c0:  0x0      0x0
0x1028a00d0:  0x0      0x0
0x1028a00e0:  0x0      0x0
0x1028a00f0:  0x0      0x0
0x1028a0100:  0x0      0x0
0x1028a0110:  0x0      0x0
0x1028a0120:  0x0      0x0
0x1028a0130:  0x0      0x0
0x1028a0140:  0x0      0x0
0x1028a0150:  0x0      0x0
0x1028a0160:  0x0      0x0
0x1028a0170:  0x0      0x0
0x1028a0180:  0x0      0x0
0x1028a0190:  0x0      0x0
0x1028a01a0:  0x0      0x0
0x1028a01b0:  0x0      0x0
0x1028a01c0:  0x0      0x0
0x1028a01d0:  0x0      0x0
0x1028a01e0:  0x700000000   0x74e4ebf24818a8b6
0x1028a01f0:  0x1028a0410   0x1027ec938 <procF+104>
0x1028a0200:  0xffffffff    0x7
0x1028a0210:  0xffffffff    0x0
0x1028a0220:  0x0      0x0
0x1028a0230:  0x0      0x0
0x1028a0240:  0x0      0x0
0x1028a0250:  0x0      0x0
---Type <return> to continue, or q <return> to quit---
0x1028a0260:  0x0      0x0
0x1028a0270:  0x0      0x0
0x1028a0280:  0x0      0x0
0x1028a0290:  0x0      0x0
0x1028a02a0:  0x0      0x0
0x1028a02b0:  0x0      0x0
0x1028a02c0:  0x0      0x0
0x1028a02d0:  0x0      0x0
0x1028a02e0:  0x0      0x0
0x1028a02f0:  0x0      0x0
0x1028a0300:  0x0      0x0
0x1028a0310:  0x0      0x0
0x1028a0320:  0x0      0x0
0x1028a0330:  0x0      0x0
0x1028a0340:  0x0      0x0
0x1028a0350:  0x0      0x0
0x1028a0360:  0x0      0x0
0x1028a0370:  0x0      0x0
0x1028a0380:  0x0      0x0
0x1028a0390:  0x0      0x0
0x1028a03a0:  0x0      0x0
0x1028a03b0:  0x0      0x0
0x1028a03c0:  0x0      0x0
0x1028a03d0:  0x0      0x0
0x1028a03e0:  0x0      0x0
0x1028a03f0:  0x0      0x0
0x1028a0400:  0x600000000   0x74e4ebf24818a8b6
0x1028a0410:  0x1028a0630   0x1027ec938 <procF+104>
```

```
0x1028a0420: 0xffffffff     0x6
0x1028a0430: 0xffffffff     0x0
0x1028a0440: 0x0     0x0
0x1028a0450: 0x0     0x0
0x1028a0460: 0x0     0x0
0x1028a0470: 0x0     0x0
0x1028a0480: 0x0     0x0
0x1028a0490: 0x0     0x0
0x1028a04a0: 0x0     0x0
0x1028a04b0: 0x0     0x0
0x1028a04c0: 0x0     0x0
0x1028a04d0: 0x0     0x0
0x1028a04e0: 0x0     0x0
0x1028a04f0: 0x0     0x0
---Type <return> to continue, or q <return> to quit---
0x1028a0500: 0x0     0x0
0x1028a0510: 0x0     0x0
0x1028a0520: 0x0     0x0
0x1028a0530: 0x0     0x0
0x1028a0540: 0x0     0x0
0x1028a0550: 0x0     0x0
0x1028a0560: 0x0     0x0
0x1028a0570: 0x0     0x0
0x1028a0580: 0x0     0x0
0x1028a0590: 0x0     0x0
0x1028a05a0: 0x0     0x0
0x1028a05b0: 0x0     0x0
0x1028a05c0: 0x0     0x0
0x1028a05d0: 0x0     0x0
0x1028a05e0: 0x0     0x0
0x1028a05f0: 0x0     0x0
0x1028a0600: 0x0     0x0
0x1028a0610: 0x0     0x0
0x1028a0620: 0x500000000    0x74e4ebf24818a8b6
0x1028a0630: 0x1028a0850    0x1027ec938 <procF+104>
0x1028a0640: 0xffffffff     0x5
0x1028a0650: 0xffffffff     0x0
0x1028a0660: 0x0     0x0
0x1028a0670: 0x0     0x0
0x1028a0680: 0x0     0x0
0x1028a0690: 0x0     0x0
0x1028a06a0: 0x0     0x0
0x1028a06b0: 0x0     0x0
0x1028a06c0: 0x0     0x0
0x1028a06d0: 0x0     0x0
0x1028a06e0: 0x0     0x0
0x1028a06f0: 0x0     0x0
0x1028a0700: 0x0     0x0
0x1028a0710: 0x0     0x0
0x1028a0720: 0x0     0x0
0x1028a0730: 0x0     0x0
0x1028a0740: 0x0     0x0
0x1028a0750: 0x0     0x0
0x1028a0760: 0x0     0x0
0x1028a0770: 0x0     0x0
0x1028a0780: 0x0     0x0
0x1028a0790: 0x0     0x0
---Type <return> to continue, or q <return> to quit---
0x1028a07a0: 0x0     0x0
0x1028a07b0: 0x0     0x0
```

```
0x1028a07c0:  0x0        0x0
0x1028a07d0:  0x0        0x0
0x1028a07e0:  0x0        0x0
0x1028a07f0:  0x0        0x0
0x1028a0800:  0x0        0x0
0x1028a0810:  0x0        0x0
0x1028a0820:  0x0        0x0
0x1028a0830:  0x0        0x0
0x1028a0840:  0x400000000    0x74e4ebf24818a8b6
0x1028a0850:  0x1028a0a70    0x1027ec938 <procF+104>
0x1028a0860:  0xffffffff    0x4
0x1028a0870:  0xffffffff    0x0
0x1028a0880:  0x0        0x0
0x1028a0890:  0x0        0x0
0x1028a08a0:  0x0        0x0
0x1028a08b0:  0x0        0x0
0x1028a08c0:  0x0        0x0
0x1028a08d0:  0x0        0x0
0x1028a08e0:  0x0        0x0
0x1028a08f0:  0x0        0x0
0x1028a0900:  0x0        0x0
0x1028a0910:  0x0        0x0
0x1028a0920:  0x0        0x0
0x1028a0930:  0x0        0x0
0x1028a0940:  0x0        0x0
0x1028a0950:  0x0        0x0
0x1028a0960:  0x0        0x0
0x1028a0970:  0x0        0x0
0x1028a0980:  0x0        0x0
0x1028a0990:  0x0        0x0
0x1028a09a0:  0x0        0x0
0x1028a09b0:  0x0        0x0
0x1028a09c0:  0x0        0x0
0x1028a09d0:  0x0        0x0
0x1028a09e0:  0x0        0x0
0x1028a09f0:  0x0        0x0
0x1028a0a00:  0x0        0x0
0x1028a0a10:  0x0        0x0
0x1028a0a20:  0x0        0x0
0x1028a0a30:  0x0        0x0
---Type <return> to continue, or q <return> to quit---
0x1028a0a40:  0x0        0x0
0x1028a0a50:  0x0        0x0
0x1028a0a60:  0x362427d80    0x74e4ebf24818a8b6
0x1028a0a70:  0x1028a0c90    0x1027ec938 <procF+104>
0x1028a0a80:  0xffffffff    0x3
0x1028a0a90:  0xffffffff    0x0
0x1028a0aa0:  0x0        0x0
0x1028a0ab0:  0x0        0x0
0x1028a0ac0:  0x0        0x0
0x1028a0ad0:  0x0        0x0
0x1028a0ae0:  0x0        0x0
0x1028a0af0:  0x0        0x0
0x1028a0b00:  0x0        0x0
0x1028a0b10:  0x0        0x0
0x1028a0b20:  0x0        0x0
0x1028a0b30:  0x0        0x0
0x1028a0b40:  0x0        0x0
0x1028a0b50:  0x0        0x0
0x1028a0b60:  0x0        0x0
```

```
0x1028a0b70: 0x0      0x0
0x1028a0b80: 0x0      0x0
0x1028a0b90: 0x0      0x0
0x1028a0ba0: 0x0      0x0
0x1028a0bb0: 0x0      0x0
0x1028a0bc0: 0x0      0x0
0x1028a0bd0: 0x0      0x0
0x1028a0be0: 0x0      0x0
0x1028a0bf0: 0x0      0x0
0x1028a0c00: 0x0      0x0
0x1028a0c10: 0x0      0x0
0x1028a0c20: 0x0      0x0
0x1028a0c30: 0x0      0x0
0x1028a0c40: 0x0      0x0
0x1028a0c50: 0x0      0x0
0x1028a0c60: 0x0      0x0
0x1028a0c70: 0x0      0x0
0x1028a0c80: 0x2028a0eb0   0x74e4ebf24818a8b6
0x1028a0c90: 0x1028a0eb0   0x1027ec938 <procF+104>
0x1028a0ca0: 0xffffffff    0x2
0x1028a0cb0: 0xffffffff    0x0
0x1028a0cc0: 0x0      0x0
0x1028a0cd0: 0x0      0x0
---Type <return> to continue, or q <return> to quit---
0x1028a0ce0: 0x0      0x0
0x1028a0cf0: 0x0      0x0
0x1028a0d00: 0x0      0x0
0x1028a0d10: 0x0      0x0
0x1028a0d20: 0x0      0x0
0x1028a0d30: 0x0      0x0
0x1028a0d40: 0x0      0x0
0x1028a0d50: 0x0      0x0
0x1028a0d60: 0x0      0x0
0x1028a0d70: 0x0      0x0
0x1028a0d80: 0x0      0x0
0x1028a0d90: 0x0      0x0
0x1028a0da0: 0x0      0x0
0x1028a0db0: 0x0      0x0
0x1028a0dc0: 0x0      0x0
0x1028a0dd0: 0x0      0x0
0x1028a0de0: 0x0      0x0
0x1028a0df0: 0x0      0x0
0x1028a0e00: 0x0      0x0
0x1028a0e10: 0x0      0x0
0x1028a0e20: 0x0      0x0
0x1028a0e30: 0x0      0x0
0x1028a0e40: 0x0      0x0
0x1028a0e50: 0x0      0x0
0x1028a0e60: 0x0      0x0
0x1028a0e70: 0x0      0x0
0x1028a0e80: 0x0      0x0
0x1028a0e90: 0x0      0x0
0x1028a0ea0: 0x100000000   0x74e4ebf24818a8b6
0x1028a0eb0: 0x1028a0ec0   0x1027ec96e <procE+14>
0x1028a0ec0: 0x1028a0ee0   0x1027ec98a <bar_one+26>
0x1028a0ed0: 0x0      0x0
0x1028a0ee0: 0x1028a0ef0   0x1027ec999 <foo_one+9>
0x1028a0ef0: 0x1028a0f10   0x1027ec9b1 <thread_one+17>
0x1028a0f00: 0x0      0x0
0x1028a0f10: 0x1028a0f50   0x7fff84db88bf <_pthread_start+335>
```

151

```
0x1028a0f20: 0x0     0x0
0x1028a0f30: 0x0     0x0
0x1028a0f40: 0x0     0x0
0x1028a0f50: 0x1028a0f78  0x7fff84dbbb75 <thread_start+13>
0x1028a0f60: 0x0     0x0
0x1028a0f70: 0x0     0x0
---Type <return> to continue, or q <return> to quit---q
Quit
```

7.   See that the reconstruction of the stack trace is possible because of standard function prologue and epilogue:

```
[...]
0x10289f0f0: 0x10289f310  0x1027ec938 <procF+104>
0x10289f310: 0x10289f530  0x1027ec938 <procF+104>
0x10289f530: 0x10289f750  0x1027ec938 <procF+104>
0x10289f750: 0x10289f970  0x1027ec938 <procF+104>
0x10289f970: 0x10289fb90  0x1027ec938 <procF+104>
0x10289fb90: 0x10289fdb0  0x1027ec938 <procF+104>
0x10289fdb0: 0x10289ffd0  0x1027ec938 <procF+104>
0x10289ffd0: 0x1028a01f0  0x1027ec938 <procF+104>
0x1028a01f0: 0x1028a0410  0x1027ec938 <procF+104>
0x1028a0410: 0x1028a0630  0x1027ec938 <procF+104>
0x1028a0630: 0x1028a0850  0x1027ec938 <procF+104>
0x1028a0850: 0x1028a0a70  0x1027ec938 <procF+104>
0x1028a0a70: 0x1028a0c90  0x1027ec938 <procF+104>
0x1028a0c90: 0x1028a0eb0  0x1027ec938 <procF+104>
0x1028a0eb0: 0x1028a0ec0  0x1027ec96e <procE+14>
0x1028a0ec0: 0x1028a0ee0  0x1027ec98a <bar_one+26>
0x1028a0ee0: 0x1028a0ef0  0x1027ec999 <foo_one+9>
0x1028a0ef0: 0x1028a0f10  0x1027ec9b1 <thread_one+17>
0x1028a0f10: 0x1028a0f50  0x7fff84db88bf <_pthread_start+335>
0x1028a0f50: 0x1028a0f78  0x7fff84dbbb75 <thread_start+13>
```

```
(gdb) disass procF
Dump of assembler code for function procF:
0x00000001027ec8d0 <procF+0>:    push   %rbp
0x00000001027ec8d1 <procF+1>:    mov    %rsp,%rbp
0x00000001027ec8d4 <procF+4>:    sub    $0x210,%rsp
0x00000001027ec8db <procF+11>:   mov    0x756(%rip),%rax        # 0x1027ed038
0x00000001027ec8e2 <procF+18>:   mov    (%rax),%rax
0x00000001027ec8e5 <procF+21>:   mov    %rax,-0x8(%rbp)
0x00000001027ec8e9 <procF+25>:   mov    $0x0,%esi
0x00000001027ec8ee <procF+30>:   mov    $0x200,%rdx
0x00000001027ec8f8 <procF+40>:   lea    -0x210(%rbp),%rax
0x00000001027ec8ff <procF+47>:   mov    %edi,-0xc(%rbp)
0x00000001027ec902 <procF+50>:   mov    %rax,%rdi
0x00000001027ec905 <procF+53>:   callq  0x1027ecc70 <dyld_stub_memset>
0x00000001027ec90a <procF+58>:   movl   $0xffffffff,-0x210(%rbp)
0x00000001027ec914 <procF+68>:   mov    -0xc(%rbp),%esi
0x00000001027ec917 <procF+71>:   add    $0x1,%esi
0x00000001027ec91d <procF+77>:   mov    %esi,-0x208(%rbp)
0x00000001027ec923 <procF+83>:   movl   $0xffffffff,-0x200(%rbp)
0x00000001027ec92d <procF+93>:   mov    -0x208(%rbp),%edi
0x00000001027ec933 <procF+99>:   callq  0x1027ec8d0 <procF>
0x00000001027ec938 <procF+104>:  mov    0x6f9(%rip),%rax        # 0x1027ed038
```

```
0x00000001027ec93f <procF+111>:   mov     (%rax),%rax
0x00000001027ec942 <procF+114>:   mov     -0x8(%rbp),%rdx
0x00000001027ec946 <procF+118>:   cmp     %rdx,%rax
0x00000001027ec949 <procF+121>:   jne     0x1027ec958 <procF+136>
0x00000001027ec94f <procF+127>:   add     $0x210,%rsp
0x00000001027ec956 <procF+134>:   pop     %rbp
0x00000001027ec957 <procF+135>:   retq
0x00000001027ec958 <procF+136>:   callq   0x1027ecc64 <dyld_stub___stack_chk_fail>
0x00000001027ec95d <procF+141>:   nopl    (%rax)
End of assembler dump.
```

8.   Now use back trace command variant to get to the bottom of the stack trace:

```
(gdb) bt -20
#950 0x00000001027ec938 in procF ()
#951 0x00000001027ec938 in procF ()
#952 0x00000001027ec938 in procF ()
#953 0x00000001027ec938 in procF ()
#954 0x00000001027ec938 in procF ()
#955 0x00000001027ec938 in procF ()
#956 0x00000001027ec938 in procF ()
#957 0x00000001027ec938 in procF ()
#958 0x00000001027ec938 in procF ()
#959 0x00000001027ec938 in procF ()
#960 0x00000001027ec938 in procF ()
#961 0x00000001027ec938 in procF ()
#962 0x00000001027ec938 in procF ()
#963 0x00000001027ec938 in procF ()
#964 0x00000001027ec96e in procE ()
#965 0x00000001027ec98a in bar_one ()
#966 0x00000001027ec999 in foo_one ()
#967 0x00000001027ec9b1 in thread_one ()
#968 0x00007fff84db88bf in _pthread_start ()
#969 0x00007fff84dbbb75 in thread_start ()
```

Exercise A6 (LLDB)

- **Goal:** Learn how to identify stack overflow, stack boundaries, reconstruct stack trace

- **Patterns:** Stack Overflow, Execution Residue

- \AMCDA-Dumps\Exercise-A6-LLDB.pdf

Exercise A6 (LLDB)

Goal: Learn how to identify stack overflow, stack boundaries, reconstruct stack trace

Patterns: Stack Overflow, Execution Residue

1.   Identify the problem thread and application specific diagnostic from the diagnostic report App6_3769.crash:

```
Process:         App6 [3769]
Path:            /Users/USER/Documents/*/App6
Identifier:      App6
Version:         ??? (???)
Code Type:       X86-64 (Native)
Parent Process:  bash [1549]

Date/Time:       2012-07-25 17:27:15.333 +0100
OS Version:      Mac OS X 10.7.4 (11E53)
Report Version:  9
Sleep/Wake UUID: 4C0A9B6D-7E93-4764-8BC3-971D136863D8

Crashed Thread:  1

Exception Type:  EXC_BAD_ACCESS (SIGBUS)
Exception Codes: KERN_PROTECTION_FAILURE at 0x0000000102820e38

VM Regions Near 0x102820e38:
    MALLOC metadata        000000010281f000-0000000102820000 [    4K] r--/rwx SM=COW
--> Stack                  0000000102820000-0000000102821000 [    4K] r--/rwx SM=PRV  thread 1
    Stack                  0000000102821000-00000001028a3000 [  520K] rw-/rwx SM=PRV

Thread 0:: Dispatch queue: com.apple.main-thread
0   libsystem_kernel.dylib          0x00007fff8a10ce42 __semwait_signal + 10
1   libsystem_c.dylib               0x00007fff84d6edea nanosleep + 164
2   libsystem_c.dylib               0x00007fff84d6ec2c sleep + 61
3   libsystem_c.dylib               0x00007fff84d6ec08 sleep + 25
4   App6                            0x00000001027ecc53 main + 195
5   App6                            0x00000001027ec8c4 start + 52

Thread 1 Crashed:
0   App6                            0x00000001027ec905 procF + 53
1   App6                            0x00000001027ec938 procF + 104
2   App6                            0x00000001027ec938 procF + 104
3   App6                            0x00000001027ec938 procF + 104
4   App6                            0x00000001027ec938 procF + 104
5   App6                            0x00000001027ec938 procF + 104
6   App6                            0x00000001027ec938 procF + 104
7   App6                            0x00000001027ec938 procF + 104
8   App6                            0x00000001027ec938 procF + 104
9   App6                            0x00000001027ec938 procF + 104
10  App6                            0x00000001027ec938 procF + 104
11  App6                            0x00000001027ec938 procF + 104
12  App6                            0x00000001027ec938 procF + 104
13  App6                            0x00000001027ec938 procF + 104
14  App6                            0x00000001027ec938 procF + 104
15  App6                            0x00000001027ec938 procF + 104
16  App6                            0x00000001027ec938 procF + 104
17  App6                            0x00000001027ec938 procF + 104
18  App6                            0x00000001027ec938 procF + 104
19  App6                            0x00000001027ec938 procF + 104
20  App6                            0x00000001027ec938 procF + 104
21  App6                            0x00000001027ec938 procF + 104
22  App6                            0x00000001027ec938 procF + 104
23  App6                            0x00000001027ec938 procF + 104
24  App6                            0x00000001027ec938 procF + 104
25  App6                            0x00000001027ec938 procF + 104
26  App6                            0x00000001027ec938 procF + 104
27  App6                            0x00000001027ec938 procF + 104
28  App6                            0x00000001027ec938 procF + 104
```

```
29  App6                    0x00000001027ec938 procF + 104
30  App6                    0x00000001027ec938 procF + 104
31  App6                    0x00000001027ec938 procF + 104
32  App6                    0x00000001027ec938 procF + 104
33  App6                    0x00000001027ec938 procF + 104
34  App6                    0x00000001027ec938 procF + 104
35  App6                    0x00000001027ec938 procF + 104
36  App6                    0x00000001027ec938 procF + 104
37  App6                    0x00000001027ec938 procF + 104
38  App6                    0x00000001027ec938 procF + 104
39  App6                    0x00000001027ec938 procF + 104
40  App6                    0x00000001027ec938 procF + 104
41  App6                    0x00000001027ec938 procF + 104
42  App6                    0x00000001027ec938 procF + 104
43  App6                    0x00000001027ec938 procF + 104
44  App6                    0x00000001027ec938 procF + 104
45  App6                    0x00000001027ec938 procF + 104
46  App6                    0x00000001027ec938 procF + 104
47  App6                    0x00000001027ec938 procF + 104
48  App6                    0x00000001027ec938 procF + 104
49  App6                    0x00000001027ec938 procF + 104
50  App6                    0x00000001027ec938 procF + 104
51  App6                    0x00000001027ec938 procF + 104
52  App6                    0x00000001027ec938 procF + 104
53  App6                    0x00000001027ec938 procF + 104
54  App6                    0x00000001027ec938 procF + 104
55  App6                    0x00000001027ec938 procF + 104
56  App6                    0x00000001027ec938 procF + 104
57  App6                    0x00000001027ec938 procF + 104
58  App6                    0x00000001027ec938 procF + 104
59  App6                    0x00000001027ec938 procF + 104
60  App6                    0x00000001027ec938 procF + 104
61  App6                    0x00000001027ec938 procF + 104
62  App6                    0x00000001027ec938 procF + 104
63  App6                    0x00000001027ec938 procF + 104
64  App6                    0x00000001027ec938 procF + 104
65  App6                    0x00000001027ec938 procF + 104
66  App6                    0x00000001027ec938 procF + 104
67  App6                    0x00000001027ec938 procF + 104
68  App6                    0x00000001027ec938 procF + 104
69  App6                    0x00000001027ec938 procF + 104
70  App6                    0x00000001027ec938 procF + 104
71  App6                    0x00000001027ec938 procF + 104
72  App6                    0x00000001027ec938 procF + 104
73  App6                    0x00000001027ec938 procF + 104
74  App6                    0x00000001027ec938 procF + 104
75  App6                    0x00000001027ec938 procF + 104
76  App6                    0x00000001027ec938 procF + 104
77  App6                    0x00000001027ec938 procF + 104
78  App6                    0x00000001027ec938 procF + 104
79  App6                    0x00000001027ec938 procF + 104
80  App6                    0x00000001027ec938 procF + 104
81  App6                    0x00000001027ec938 procF + 104
82  App6                    0x00000001027ec938 procF + 104
83  App6                    0x00000001027ec938 procF + 104
84  App6                    0x00000001027ec938 procF + 104
85  App6                    0x00000001027ec938 procF + 104
86  App6                    0x00000001027ec938 procF + 104
87  App6                    0x00000001027ec938 procF + 104
88  App6                    0x00000001027ec938 procF + 104
89  App6                    0x00000001027ec938 procF + 104
90  App6                    0x00000001027ec938 procF + 104
91  App6                    0x00000001027ec938 procF + 104
92  App6                    0x00000001027ec938 procF + 104
93  App6                    0x00000001027ec938 procF + 104
94  App6                    0x00000001027ec938 procF + 104
95  App6                    0x00000001027ec938 procF + 104
96  App6                    0x00000001027ec938 procF + 104
97  App6                    0x00000001027ec938 procF + 104
98  App6                    0x00000001027ec938 procF + 104
99  App6                    0x00000001027ec938 procF + 104
100 App6                    0x00000001027ec938 procF + 104
101 App6                    0x00000001027ec938 procF + 104
102 App6                    0x00000001027ec938 procF + 104
103 App6                    0x00000001027ec938 procF + 104
104 App6                    0x00000001027ec938 procF + 104
```

```
105 App6                          0x00000001027ec938 procF + 104
106 App6                          0x00000001027ec938 procF + 104
107 App6                          0x00000001027ec938 procF + 104
108 App6                          0x00000001027ec938 procF + 104
109 App6                          0x00000001027ec938 procF + 104
110 App6                          0x00000001027ec938 procF + 104
111 App6                          0x00000001027ec938 procF + 104
112 App6                          0x00000001027ec938 procF + 104
113 App6                          0x00000001027ec938 procF + 104
114 App6                          0x00000001027ec938 procF + 104
115 App6                          0x00000001027ec938 procF + 104
116 App6                          0x00000001027ec938 procF + 104
117 App6                          0x00000001027ec938 procF + 104
118 App6                          0x00000001027ec938 procF + 104
119 App6                          0x00000001027ec938 procF + 104
120 App6                          0x00000001027ec938 procF + 104
121 App6                          0x00000001027ec938 procF + 104
122 App6                          0x00000001027ec938 procF + 104
123 App6                          0x00000001027ec938 procF + 104
124 App6                          0x00000001027ec938 procF + 104
125 App6                          0x00000001027ec938 procF + 104
126 App6                          0x00000001027ec938 procF + 104
127 App6                          0x00000001027ec938 procF + 104
128 App6                          0x00000001027ec938 procF + 104
129 App6                          0x00000001027ec938 procF + 104
130 App6                          0x00000001027ec938 procF + 104
131 App6                          0x00000001027ec938 procF + 104
132 App6                          0x00000001027ec938 procF + 104
133 App6                          0x00000001027ec938 procF + 104
134 App6                          0x00000001027ec938 procF + 104
135 App6                          0x00000001027ec938 procF + 104
136 App6                          0x00000001027ec938 procF + 104
137 App6                          0x00000001027ec938 procF + 104
138 App6                          0x00000001027ec938 procF + 104
139 App6                          0x00000001027ec938 procF + 104
140 App6                          0x00000001027ec938 procF + 104
141 App6                          0x00000001027ec938 procF + 104
142 App6                          0x00000001027ec938 procF + 104
143 App6                          0x00000001027ec938 procF + 104
144 App6                          0x00000001027ec938 procF + 104
145 App6                          0x00000001027ec938 procF + 104
146 App6                          0x00000001027ec938 procF + 104
147 App6                          0x00000001027ec938 procF + 104
148 App6                          0x00000001027ec938 procF + 104
149 App6                          0x00000001027ec938 procF + 104
150 App6                          0x00000001027ec938 procF + 104
151 App6                          0x00000001027ec938 procF + 104
152 App6                          0x00000001027ec938 procF + 104
153 App6                          0x00000001027ec938 procF + 104
154 App6                          0x00000001027ec938 procF + 104
155 App6                          0x00000001027ec938 procF + 104
156 App6                          0x00000001027ec938 procF + 104
157 App6                          0x00000001027ec938 procF + 104
158 App6                          0x00000001027ec938 procF + 104
159 App6                          0x00000001027ec938 procF + 104
160 App6                          0x00000001027ec938 procF + 104
161 App6                          0x00000001027ec938 procF + 104
162 App6                          0x00000001027ec938 procF + 104
163 App6                          0x00000001027ec938 procF + 104
164 App6                          0x00000001027ec938 procF + 104
165 App6                          0x00000001027ec938 procF + 104
166 App6                          0x00000001027ec938 procF + 104
167 App6                          0x00000001027ec938 procF + 104
168 App6                          0x00000001027ec938 procF + 104
169 App6                          0x00000001027ec938 procF + 104
170 App6                          0x00000001027ec938 procF + 104
171 App6                          0x00000001027ec938 procF + 104
172 App6                          0x00000001027ec938 procF + 104
173 App6                          0x00000001027ec938 procF + 104
174 App6                          0x00000001027ec938 procF + 104
175 App6                          0x00000001027ec938 procF + 104
176 App6                          0x00000001027ec938 procF + 104
177 App6                          0x00000001027ec938 procF + 104
178 App6                          0x00000001027ec938 procF + 104
179 App6                          0x00000001027ec938 procF + 104
180 App6                          0x00000001027ec938 procF + 104
```

```
181 App6                      0x00000001027ec938 procF + 104
182 App6                      0x00000001027ec938 procF + 104
183 App6                      0x00000001027ec938 procF + 104
184 App6                      0x00000001027ec938 procF + 104
185 App6                      0x00000001027ec938 procF + 104
186 App6                      0x00000001027ec938 procF + 104
187 App6                      0x00000001027ec938 procF + 104
188 App6                      0x00000001027ec938 procF + 104
189 App6                      0x00000001027ec938 procF + 104
190 App6                      0x00000001027ec938 procF + 104
191 App6                      0x00000001027ec938 procF + 104
192 App6                      0x00000001027ec938 procF + 104
193 App6                      0x00000001027ec938 procF + 104
194 App6                      0x00000001027ec938 procF + 104
195 App6                      0x00000001027ec938 procF + 104
196 App6                      0x00000001027ec938 procF + 104
197 App6                      0x00000001027ec938 procF + 104
198 App6                      0x00000001027ec938 procF + 104
199 App6                      0x00000001027ec938 procF + 104
200 App6                      0x00000001027ec938 procF + 104
201 App6                      0x00000001027ec938 procF + 104
202 App6                      0x00000001027ec938 procF + 104
203 App6                      0x00000001027ec938 procF + 104
204 App6                      0x00000001027ec938 procF + 104
205 App6                      0x00000001027ec938 procF + 104
206 App6                      0x00000001027ec938 procF + 104
207 App6                      0x00000001027ec938 procF + 104
208 App6                      0x00000001027ec938 procF + 104
209 App6                      0x00000001027ec938 procF + 104
210 App6                      0x00000001027ec938 procF + 104
211 App6                      0x00000001027ec938 procF + 104
212 App6                      0x00000001027ec938 procF + 104
213 App6                      0x00000001027ec938 procF + 104
214 App6                      0x00000001027ec938 procF + 104
215 App6                      0x00000001027ec938 procF + 104
216 App6                      0x00000001027ec938 procF + 104
217 App6                      0x00000001027ec938 procF + 104
218 App6                      0x00000001027ec938 procF + 104
219 App6                      0x00000001027ec938 procF + 104
220 App6                      0x00000001027ec938 procF + 104
221 App6                      0x00000001027ec938 procF + 104
222 App6                      0x00000001027ec938 procF + 104
223 App6                      0x00000001027ec938 procF + 104
224 App6                      0x00000001027ec938 procF + 104
225 App6                      0x00000001027ec938 procF + 104
226 App6                      0x00000001027ec938 procF + 104
227 App6                      0x00000001027ec938 procF + 104
228 App6                      0x00000001027ec938 procF + 104
229 App6                      0x00000001027ec938 procF + 104
230 App6                      0x00000001027ec938 procF + 104
231 App6                      0x00000001027ec938 procF + 104
232 App6                      0x00000001027ec938 procF + 104
233 App6                      0x00000001027ec938 procF + 104
234 App6                      0x00000001027ec938 procF + 104
235 App6                      0x00000001027ec938 procF + 104
236 App6                      0x00000001027ec938 procF + 104
237 App6                      0x00000001027ec938 procF + 104
238 App6                      0x00000001027ec938 procF + 104
239 App6                      0x00000001027ec938 procF + 104
240 App6                      0x00000001027ec938 procF + 104
241 App6                      0x00000001027ec938 procF + 104
242 App6                      0x00000001027ec938 procF + 104
243 App6                      0x00000001027ec938 procF + 104
244 App6                      0x00000001027ec938 procF + 104
245 App6                      0x00000001027ec938 procF + 104
246 App6                      0x00000001027ec938 procF + 104
247 App6                      0x00000001027ec938 procF + 104
248 App6                      0x00000001027ec938 procF + 104
249 App6                      0x00000001027ec938 procF + 104
250 App6                      0x00000001027ec938 procF + 104
251 App6                      0x00000001027ec938 procF + 104
252 App6                      0x00000001027ec938 procF + 104
253 App6                      0x00000001027ec938 procF + 104
254 App6                      0x00000001027ec938 procF + 104
255 App6                      0x00000001027ec938 procF + 104
256 App6                      0x00000001027ec938 procF + 104
```

```
257 App6                          0x00000001027ec938 procF + 104
258 App6                          0x00000001027ec938 procF + 104
259 App6                          0x00000001027ec938 procF + 104
260 App6                          0x00000001027ec938 procF + 104
261 App6                          0x00000001027ec938 procF + 104
262 App6                          0x00000001027ec938 procF + 104
263 App6                          0x00000001027ec938 procF + 104
264 App6                          0x00000001027ec938 procF + 104
265 App6                          0x00000001027ec938 procF + 104
266 App6                          0x00000001027ec938 procF + 104
267 App6                          0x00000001027ec938 procF + 104
268 App6                          0x00000001027ec938 procF + 104
269 App6                          0x00000001027ec938 procF + 104
270 App6                          0x00000001027ec938 procF + 104
271 App6                          0x00000001027ec938 procF + 104
272 App6                          0x00000001027ec938 procF + 104
273 App6                          0x00000001027ec938 procF + 104
274 App6                          0x00000001027ec938 procF + 104
275 App6                          0x00000001027ec938 procF + 104
276 App6                          0x00000001027ec938 procF + 104
277 App6                          0x00000001027ec938 procF + 104
278 App6                          0x00000001027ec938 procF + 104
279 App6                          0x00000001027ec938 procF + 104
280 App6                          0x00000001027ec938 procF + 104
281 App6                          0x00000001027ec938 procF + 104
282 App6                          0x00000001027ec938 procF + 104
283 App6                          0x00000001027ec938 procF + 104
284 App6                          0x00000001027ec938 procF + 104
285 App6                          0x00000001027ec938 procF + 104
286 App6                          0x00000001027ec938 procF + 104
287 App6                          0x00000001027ec938 procF + 104
288 App6                          0x00000001027ec938 procF + 104
289 App6                          0x00000001027ec938 procF + 104
290 App6                          0x00000001027ec938 procF + 104
291 App6                          0x00000001027ec938 procF + 104
292 App6                          0x00000001027ec938 procF + 104
293 App6                          0x00000001027ec938 procF + 104
294 App6                          0x00000001027ec938 procF + 104
295 App6                          0x00000001027ec938 procF + 104
296 App6                          0x00000001027ec938 procF + 104
297 App6                          0x00000001027ec938 procF + 104
298 App6                          0x00000001027ec938 procF + 104
299 App6                          0x00000001027ec938 procF + 104
300 App6                          0x00000001027ec938 procF + 104
301 App6                          0x00000001027ec938 procF + 104
302 App6                          0x00000001027ec938 procF + 104
303 App6                          0x00000001027ec938 procF + 104
304 App6                          0x00000001027ec938 procF + 104
305 App6                          0x00000001027ec938 procF + 104
306 App6                          0x00000001027ec938 procF + 104
307 App6                          0x00000001027ec938 procF + 104
308 App6                          0x00000001027ec938 procF + 104
309 App6                          0x00000001027ec938 procF + 104
310 App6                          0x00000001027ec938 procF + 104
311 App6                          0x00000001027ec938 procF + 104
312 App6                          0x00000001027ec938 procF + 104
313 App6                          0x00000001027ec938 procF + 104
314 App6                          0x00000001027ec938 procF + 104
315 App6                          0x00000001027ec938 procF + 104
316 App6                          0x00000001027ec938 procF + 104
317 App6                          0x00000001027ec938 procF + 104
318 App6                          0x00000001027ec938 procF + 104
319 App6                          0x00000001027ec938 procF + 104
320 App6                          0x00000001027ec938 procF + 104
321 App6                          0x00000001027ec938 procF + 104
322 App6                          0x00000001027ec938 procF + 104
323 App6                          0x00000001027ec938 procF + 104
324 App6                          0x00000001027ec938 procF + 104
325 App6                          0x00000001027ec938 procF + 104
326 App6                          0x00000001027ec938 procF + 104
327 App6                          0x00000001027ec938 procF + 104
328 App6                          0x00000001027ec938 procF + 104
329 App6                          0x00000001027ec938 procF + 104
330 App6                          0x00000001027ec938 procF + 104
331 App6                          0x00000001027ec938 procF + 104
332 App6                          0x00000001027ec938 procF + 104
```

```
333 App6                    0x00000001027ec938 procF + 104
334 App6                    0x00000001027ec938 procF + 104
335 App6                    0x00000001027ec938 procF + 104
336 App6                    0x00000001027ec938 procF + 104
337 App6                    0x00000001027ec938 procF + 104
338 App6                    0x00000001027ec938 procF + 104
339 App6                    0x00000001027ec938 procF + 104
340 App6                    0x00000001027ec938 procF + 104
341 App6                    0x00000001027ec938 procF + 104
342 App6                    0x00000001027ec938 procF + 104
343 App6                    0x00000001027ec938 procF + 104
344 App6                    0x00000001027ec938 procF + 104
345 App6                    0x00000001027ec938 procF + 104
346 App6                    0x00000001027ec938 procF + 104
347 App6                    0x00000001027ec938 procF + 104
348 App6                    0x00000001027ec938 procF + 104
349 App6                    0x00000001027ec938 procF + 104
350 App6                    0x00000001027ec938 procF + 104
351 App6                    0x00000001027ec938 procF + 104
352 App6                    0x00000001027ec938 procF + 104
353 App6                    0x00000001027ec938 procF + 104
354 App6                    0x00000001027ec938 procF + 104
355 App6                    0x00000001027ec938 procF + 104
356 App6                    0x00000001027ec938 procF + 104
357 App6                    0x00000001027ec938 procF + 104
358 App6                    0x00000001027ec938 procF + 104
359 App6                    0x00000001027ec938 procF + 104
360 App6                    0x00000001027ec938 procF + 104
361 App6                    0x00000001027ec938 procF + 104
362 App6                    0x00000001027ec938 procF + 104
363 App6                    0x00000001027ec938 procF + 104
364 App6                    0x00000001027ec938 procF + 104
365 App6                    0x00000001027ec938 procF + 104
366 App6                    0x00000001027ec938 procF + 104
367 App6                    0x00000001027ec938 procF + 104
368 App6                    0x00000001027ec938 procF + 104
369 App6                    0x00000001027ec938 procF + 104
370 App6                    0x00000001027ec938 procF + 104
371 App6                    0x00000001027ec938 procF + 104
372 App6                    0x00000001027ec938 procF + 104
373 App6                    0x00000001027ec938 procF + 104
374 App6                    0x00000001027ec938 procF + 104
375 App6                    0x00000001027ec938 procF + 104
376 App6                    0x00000001027ec938 procF + 104
377 App6                    0x00000001027ec938 procF + 104
378 App6                    0x00000001027ec938 procF + 104
379 App6                    0x00000001027ec938 procF + 104
380 App6                    0x00000001027ec938 procF + 104
381 App6                    0x00000001027ec938 procF + 104
382 App6                    0x00000001027ec938 procF + 104
383 App6                    0x00000001027ec938 procF + 104
384 App6                    0x00000001027ec938 procF + 104
385 App6                    0x00000001027ec938 procF + 104
386 App6                    0x00000001027ec938 procF + 104
387 App6                    0x00000001027ec938 procF + 104
388 App6                    0x00000001027ec938 procF + 104
389 App6                    0x00000001027ec938 procF + 104
390 App6                    0x00000001027ec938 procF + 104
391 App6                    0x00000001027ec938 procF + 104
392 App6                    0x00000001027ec938 procF + 104
393 App6                    0x00000001027ec938 procF + 104
394 App6                    0x00000001027ec938 procF + 104
395 App6                    0x00000001027ec938 procF + 104
396 App6                    0x00000001027ec938 procF + 104
397 App6                    0x00000001027ec938 procF + 104
398 App6                    0x00000001027ec938 procF + 104
399 App6                    0x00000001027ec938 procF + 104
400 App6                    0x00000001027ec938 procF + 104
401 App6                    0x00000001027ec938 procF + 104
402 App6                    0x00000001027ec938 procF + 104
403 App6                    0x00000001027ec938 procF + 104
404 App6                    0x00000001027ec938 procF + 104
405 App6                    0x00000001027ec938 procF + 104
406 App6                    0x00000001027ec938 procF + 104
407 App6                    0x00000001027ec938 procF + 104
408 App6                    0x00000001027ec938 procF + 104
```

```
409 App6                    0x00000001027ec938 procF + 104
410 App6                    0x00000001027ec938 procF + 104
411 App6                    0x00000001027ec938 procF + 104
412 App6                    0x00000001027ec938 procF + 104
413 App6                    0x00000001027ec938 procF + 104
414 App6                    0x00000001027ec938 procF + 104
415 App6                    0x00000001027ec938 procF + 104
416 App6                    0x00000001027ec938 procF + 104
417 App6                    0x00000001027ec938 procF + 104
418 App6                    0x00000001027ec938 procF + 104
419 App6                    0x00000001027ec938 procF + 104
420 App6                    0x00000001027ec938 procF + 104
421 App6                    0x00000001027ec938 procF + 104
422 App6                    0x00000001027ec938 procF + 104
423 App6                    0x00000001027ec938 procF + 104
424 App6                    0x00000001027ec938 procF + 104
425 App6                    0x00000001027ec938 procF + 104
426 App6                    0x00000001027ec938 procF + 104
427 App6                    0x00000001027ec938 procF + 104
428 App6                    0x00000001027ec938 procF + 104
429 App6                    0x00000001027ec938 procF + 104
430 App6                    0x00000001027ec938 procF + 104
431 App6                    0x00000001027ec938 procF + 104
432 App6                    0x00000001027ec938 procF + 104
433 App6                    0x00000001027ec938 procF + 104
434 App6                    0x00000001027ec938 procF + 104
435 App6                    0x00000001027ec938 procF + 104
436 App6                    0x00000001027ec938 procF + 104
437 App6                    0x00000001027ec938 procF + 104
438 App6                    0x00000001027ec938 procF + 104
439 App6                    0x00000001027ec938 procF + 104
440 App6                    0x00000001027ec938 procF + 104
441 App6                    0x00000001027ec938 procF + 104
442 App6                    0x00000001027ec938 procF + 104
443 App6                    0x00000001027ec938 procF + 104
444 App6                    0x00000001027ec938 procF + 104
445 App6                    0x00000001027ec938 procF + 104
446 App6                    0x00000001027ec938 procF + 104
447 App6                    0x00000001027ec938 procF + 104
448 App6                    0x00000001027ec938 procF + 104
449 App6                    0x00000001027ec938 procF + 104
450 App6                    0x00000001027ec938 procF + 104
451 App6                    0x00000001027ec938 procF + 104
452 App6                    0x00000001027ec938 procF + 104
453 App6                    0x00000001027ec938 procF + 104
454 App6                    0x00000001027ec938 procF + 104
455 App6                    0x00000001027ec938 procF + 104
456 App6                    0x00000001027ec938 procF + 104
457 App6                    0x00000001027ec938 procF + 104
458 App6                    0x00000001027ec938 procF + 104
459 App6                    0x00000001027ec938 procF + 104
460 App6                    0x00000001027ec938 procF + 104
461 App6                    0x00000001027ec938 procF + 104
462 App6                    0x00000001027ec938 procF + 104
463 App6                    0x00000001027ec938 procF + 104
464 App6                    0x00000001027ec938 procF + 104
465 App6                    0x00000001027ec938 procF + 104
466 App6                    0x00000001027ec938 procF + 104
467 App6                    0x00000001027ec938 procF + 104
468 App6                    0x00000001027ec938 procF + 104
469 App6                    0x00000001027ec938 procF + 104
470 App6                    0x00000001027ec938 procF + 104
471 App6                    0x00000001027ec938 procF + 104
472 App6                    0x00000001027ec938 procF + 104
473 App6                    0x00000001027ec938 procF + 104
474 App6                    0x00000001027ec938 procF + 104
475 App6                    0x00000001027ec938 procF + 104
476 App6                    0x00000001027ec938 procF + 104
477 App6                    0x00000001027ec938 procF + 104
478 App6                    0x00000001027ec938 procF + 104
479 App6                    0x00000001027ec938 procF + 104
480 App6                    0x00000001027ec938 procF + 104
481 App6                    0x00000001027ec938 procF + 104
482 App6                    0x00000001027ec938 procF + 104
483 App6                    0x00000001027ec938 procF + 104
484 App6                    0x00000001027ec938 procF + 104
```

```
485 App6                          0x00000001027ec938 procF + 104
486 App6                          0x00000001027ec938 procF + 104
487 App6                          0x00000001027ec938 procF + 104
488 App6                          0x00000001027ec938 procF + 104
489 App6                          0x00000001027ec938 procF + 104
490 App6                          0x00000001027ec938 procF + 104
491 App6                          0x00000001027ec938 procF + 104
492 App6                          0x00000001027ec938 procF + 104
493 App6                          0x00000001027ec938 procF + 104
494 App6                          0x00000001027ec938 procF + 104
495 App6                          0x00000001027ec938 procF + 104
496 App6                          0x00000001027ec938 procF + 104
497 App6                          0x00000001027ec938 procF + 104
498 App6                          0x00000001027ec938 procF + 104
499 App6                          0x00000001027ec938 procF + 104
500 App6                          0x00000001027ec938 procF + 104
501 App6                          0x00000001027ec938 procF + 104
502 App6                          0x00000001027ec938 procF + 104
503 App6                          0x00000001027ec938 procF + 104
504 App6                          0x00000001027ec938 procF + 104
505 App6                          0x00000001027ec938 procF + 104
506 App6                          0x00000001027ec938 procF + 104
507 App6                          0x00000001027ec938 procF + 104
508 App6                          0x00000001027ec938 procF + 104
509 App6                          0x00000001027ec938 procF + 104
510 App6                          0x00000001027ec938 procF + 104
511 App6                          0x00000001027ec938 procF + 104

Thread 2:
0   libsystem_kernel.dylib        0x00007fff8a10ce42 __semwait_signal + 10
1   libsystem_c.dylib             0x00007fff84d6edea nanosleep + 164
2   libsystem_c.dylib             0x00007fff84d6ec2c sleep + 61
3   libsystem_c.dylib             0x00007fff84d6ec08 sleep + 25
4   App6                          0x00000001027ec9ef bar_two + 31
5   App6                          0x00000001027eca09 foo_two + 9
6   App6                          0x00000001027eca21 thread_two + 17
7   libsystem_c.dylib             0x00007fff84db88bf _pthread_start + 335
8   libsystem_c.dylib             0x00007fff84dbbb75 thread_start + 13

Thread 3:
0   libsystem_kernel.dylib        0x00007fff8a10ce42 __semwait_signal + 10
1   libsystem_c.dylib             0x00007fff84d6edea nanosleep + 164
2   libsystem_c.dylib             0x00007fff84d6ec2c sleep + 61
3   libsystem_c.dylib             0x00007fff84d6ec08 sleep + 25
4   App6                          0x00000001027eca5f bar_three + 31
5   App6                          0x00000001027eca79 foo_three + 9
6   App6                          0x00000001027eca91 thread_three + 17
7   libsystem_c.dylib             0x00007fff84db88bf _pthread_start + 335
8   libsystem_c.dylib             0x00007fff84dbbb75 thread_start + 13

Thread 4:
0   libsystem_kernel.dylib        0x00007fff8a10ce42 __semwait_signal + 10
1   libsystem_c.dylib             0x00007fff84d6edea nanosleep + 164
2   libsystem_c.dylib             0x00007fff84d6ec2c sleep + 61
3   libsystem_c.dylib             0x00007fff84d6ec08 sleep + 25
4   App6                          0x00000001027ecacf bar_four + 31
5   App6                          0x00000001027ecae9 foo_four + 9
6   App6                          0x00000001027ecb01 thread_four + 17
7   libsystem_c.dylib             0x00007fff84db88bf _pthread_start + 335
8   libsystem_c.dylib             0x00007fff84dbbb75 thread_start + 13

Thread 5:
0   libsystem_kernel.dylib        0x00007fff8a10ce42 __semwait_signal + 10
1   libsystem_c.dylib             0x00007fff84d6edea nanosleep + 164
2   libsystem_c.dylib             0x00007fff84d6ec2c sleep + 61
3   libsystem_c.dylib             0x00007fff84d6ec08 sleep + 25
4   App6                          0x00000001027ecb3f bar_five + 31
5   App6                          0x00000001027ecb59 foo_five + 9
6   App6                          0x00000001027ecb71 thread_five + 17
7   libsystem_c.dylib             0x00007fff84db88bf _pthread_start + 335
8   libsystem_c.dylib             0x00007fff84dbbb75 thread_start + 13
```

```
Thread 1 crashed with X86 Thread State (64-bit):
  rax: 0x0000000102820e40  rbx: 0x0000000000000000  rcx: 0x0000000000000000  rdx: 0x0000000000000200
  rdi: 0x0000000102820e40  rsi: 0x0000000000000000  rbp: 0x0000000102821050  rsp: 0x0000000102820e40
   r8: 0x000000000000012c   r9: 0x0000000000000000  r10: 0x00000000000a0000  r11: 0x0000000102821060
  r12: 0x0000000000001203  r13: 0x00000001028a1000  r14: 0x0000000000000000  r15: 0x00000001027ec9a0
  rip: 0x00000001027ec905  rfl: 0x0000000000010202  cr2: 0x0000000102820e38
Logical CPU: 2

Binary Images:
       0x1027ec000 -        0x1027ecfff +App6 (??? - ???) <6ABD6ECF-CF97-3178-8C66-8DDAA2A029E1>
/Users/USER/Documents/*/App6
    0x7fff623ec000 -     0x7fff62420baf  dyld (195.6 - ???) <0CD1B35B-A28F-32DA-B72E-452EAD609613> /usr/lib/dyld
    0x7fff849f2000 -     0x7fff84a0ffff  libxpc.dylib (77.19.0 - compatibility 1.0.0) <9F57891B-D7EF-3050-BEDD-
21E7C6668248> /usr/lib/system/libxpc.dylib
    0x7fff84d68000 -     0x7fff84d69ff7  libsystem_blocks.dylib (53.0.0 - compatibility 1.0.0) <8BCA214A-8992-34B2-
A8B9-B74DEACA1869> /usr/lib/system/libsystem_blocks.dylib
    0x7fff84d6a000 -     0x7fff84e47fef  libsystem_c.dylib (763.13.0 - compatibility 1.0.0) <41B43515-2806-3FBC-ACF1-
A16F35B7E290> /usr/lib/system/libsystem_c.dylib
    0x7fff85022000 -     0x7fff85030fff  libdispatch.dylib (187.9.0 - compatibility 1.0.0) <1D5BE322-A9B9-3BCE-8FAC-
076FB07CF54A> /usr/lib/system/libdispatch.dylib
    0x7fff855f0000 -     0x7fff855f1fff  libunc.dylib (24.0.0 - compatibility 1.0.0) <337960EE-0A85-3DD0-A760-
7134CF4C0AFF> /usr/lib/system/libunc.dylib
    0x7fff85ae3000 -     0x7fff85ae4ff7  libremovefile.dylib (21.1.0 - compatibility 1.0.0) <739E6C83-AA52-3C6C-A680-
B37FE2888A04> /usr/lib/system/libremovefile.dylib
    0x7fff89114000 -     0x7fff89118fff  libmathCommon.A.dylib (2026.0.0 - compatibility 1.0.0) <FF83AFF7-42B2-306E-
90AF-D539C51A4542> /usr/lib/system/libmathCommon.A.dylib
    0x7fff89119000 -     0x7fff8911dfff  libdyld.dylib (195.5.0 - compatibility 1.0.0) <380C3F44-0CA7-3514-8080-
46D1C9DF4FCD> /usr/lib/system/libdyld.dylib
    0x7fff89740000 -     0x7fff89741ff7  libsystem_sandbox.dylib (??? - ???) <96D38E74-F18F-3CCB-A20B-E8E3ADC4E166>
/usr/lib/system/libsystem_sandbox.dylib
    0x7fff8a0ef000 -     0x7fff8a0f5fff  libmacho.dylib (800.0.0 - compatibility 1.0.0) <165514D7-1BFA-38EF-A151-
676DCD21FB64> /usr/lib/system/libmacho.dylib
    0x7fff8a0f6000 -     0x7fff8a116fff  libsystem_kernel.dylib (1699.26.8 - compatibility 1.0.0) <1DDC0B0F-DB2A-34D6-
895D-E5B2B5618946> /usr/lib/system/libsystem_kernel.dylib
    0x7fff8a2ac000 -     0x7fff8a2b4fff  libsystem_dnssd.dylib (??? - ???) <D9BB1F87-A42B-3CBC-9DC2-FC07FCEF0016>
/usr/lib/system/libsystem_dnssd.dylib
    0x7fff8ae26000 -     0x7fff8ae61fff  libsystem_info.dylib (??? - ???) <35F90252-2AE1-32C5-8D34-782C614D9639>
/usr/lib/system/libsystem_info.dylib
    0x7fff8b248000 -     0x7fff8b24afff  libquarantine.dylib (36.6.0 - compatibility 1.0.0) <0EBF714B-4B69-3E1F-9A7D-
6BBC2AACB310> /usr/lib/system/libquarantine.dylib
    0x7fff8b3b4000 -     0x7fff8b3b4fff  libkeymgr.dylib (23.0.0 - compatibility 1.0.0) <61EFED6A-A407-301E-B454-
CD18314F0075> /usr/lib/system/libkeymgr.dylib
    0x7fff8b3dd000 -     0x7fff8b3e2fff  libcompiler_rt.dylib (6.0.0 - compatibility 1.0.0) <98ECD5F6-E85C-32A5-98CD-
8911230CB66A> /usr/lib/system/libcompiler_rt.dylib
    0x7fff8bd1a000 -     0x7fff8bd1bfff  libdnsinfo.dylib (395.11.0 - compatibility 1.0.0) <853BAAA5-270F-3FDC-B025-
D448DB72E1C3> /usr/lib/system/libdnsinfo.dylib
    0x7fff8c528000 -     0x7fff8c52dff7  libsystem_network.dylib (??? - ???) <5DE7024E-1D2D-34A2-80F4-08326331A75B>
/usr/lib/system/libsystem_network.dylib
    0x7fff8cfa3000 -     0x7fff8cfadff7  liblaunch.dylib (392.38.0 - compatibility 1.0.0) <6ECB7F19-B384-32C1-8652-
2463C1CF4815> /usr/lib/system/liblaunch.dylib
    0x7fff8fe02000 -     0x7fff8fe09fff  libcopyfile.dylib (85.1.0 - compatibility 1.0.0) <0AB51EE2-E914-358C-AC19-
47BC024BDAE7> /usr/lib/system/libcopyfile.dylib
    0x7fff8fe4b000 -     0x7fff8fe8dff7  libcommonCrypto.dylib (55010.0.0 - compatibility 1.0.0) <BB770C22-8C57-365A-
8716-4A3C36AE7BFB> /usr/lib/system/libcommonCrypto.dylib
    0x7fff90c0f000 -     0x7fff90c18ff7  libsystem_notify.dylib (80.1.0 - compatibility 1.0.0) <A4D651E3-D1C6-3934-
AD49-7A104FD14596> /usr/lib/system/libsystem_notify.dylib
    0x7fff91376000 -     0x7fff913a3fe7  libSystem.B.dylib (159.1.0 - compatibility 1.0.0) <7BEBB139-50BB-3112-947A-
F4AA168F991C> /usr/lib/libSystem.B.dylib
    0x7fff91489000 -     0x7fff9148fff7  libunwind.dylib (30.0.0 - compatibility 1.0.0) <1E9C6C8C-CBE8-3F4B-A5B5-
E03E3AB53231> /usr/lib/system/libunwind.dylib
    0x7fff91a22000 -     0x7fff91a27fff  libcache.dylib (47.0.0 - compatibility 1.0.0) <1571C3AB-BCB2-38CD-B3B2-
C5FC3F927C6A> /usr/lib/system/libcache.dylib

External Modification Summary:
  Calls made by other processes targeting this process:
    task_for_pid: 2
    thread_create: 0
    thread_set_state: 0
  Calls made by this process:
    task_for_pid: 0
    thread_create: 0
    thread_set_state: 0
  Calls made by all processes on this machine:
    task_for_pid: 6134
    thread_create: 0
    thread_set_state: 0
```

```
VM Region Summary:
ReadOnly portion of Libraries: Total=50.2M resident=50.2M(100%) swapped_out_or_unallocated=0K(0%)
Writable regions: Total=38.9M written=10.8M(28%) resident=42.6M(110%) swapped_out=0K(0%)
unallocated=16777216.0T(45221404475392%)

REGION TYPE                     VIRTUAL
===========                     =======
MALLOC                           1220K
Stack                            66.6M
__DATA                            464K
__LINKEDIT                       47.7M
__TEXT                           2484K
shared memory                      12K
===========                     =======
TOTAL                           118.4M
```

2.   Load a core dump core.3769 and App6 executable:

$ lldb -c ~/Documents/AMCDA-Dumps/core.3769 -f ~/Documents/AMCDA-Dumps/Apps/App6/Build/Products/Release/App6

error: core.3769 is a corrupt mach-o file: load command 46 LC_SEGMENT_64 has a fileoff + filesize (0x160b7000) that extends beyond the end of the file (0x160b5000), the segment will be truncated

Core file '/Users/DumpAnalysis/Documents/AMCDA-Dumps/core.3769' (x86_64) was loaded.
Process 0 stopped
* thread #1: tid = 0x0000, 0x00007fff8a10ce42 libsystem_kernel.dylib`__semwait_signal + 10,
stop reason = signal SIGSTOP
    frame #0: 0x00007fff8a10ce42 libsystem_kernel.dylib`__semwait_signal + 10
libsystem_kernel.dylib`__semwait_signal + 10:
-> 0x7fff8a10ce42: jae   0x7fff8a10ce49   ; __semwait_signal + 17
   0x7fff8a10ce44: jmpq   0x7fff8a10dffc   ; cerror
   0x7fff8a10ce49: ret
   0x7fff8a10ce4a: nop
  thread #2: tid = 0x0001, 0x00000001027ec905 App6`procF + 53, stop reason = signal SIGSTOP
    frame #0: 0x00000001027ec905 App6`procF + 53
App6`procF + 53:
-> 0x1027ec905: callq 0x1027ecc70   ; symbol stub for: memset
   0x1027ec90a: movl $4294967295, -528(%rbp)
   0x1027ec914: movl   -12(%rbp), %esi
   0x1027ec917: addl $1, %esi
  thread #3: tid = 0x0002, 0x00007fff8a10ce42 libsystem_kernel.dylib`__semwait_signal + 10,
stop reason = signal SIGSTOP
    frame #0: 0x00007fff8a10ce42 libsystem_kernel.dylib`__semwait_signal + 10
libsystem_kernel.dylib`__semwait_signal + 10:
-> 0x7fff8a10ce42: jae   0x7fff8a10ce49   ; __semwait_signal + 17
   0x7fff8a10ce44: jmpq   0x7fff8a10dffc   ; cerror
   0x7fff8a10ce49: ret
   0x7fff8a10ce4a: nop
  thread #4: tid = 0x0003, 0x00007fff8a10ce42 libsystem_kernel.dylib`__semwait_signal + 10,
stop reason = signal SIGSTOP
    frame #0: 0x00007fff8a10ce42 libsystem_kernel.dylib`__semwait_signal + 10
libsystem_kernel.dylib`__semwait_signal + 10:
-> 0x7fff8a10ce42: jae   0x7fff8a10ce49   ; __semwait_signal + 17
   0x7fff8a10ce44: jmpq   0x7fff8a10dffc   ; cerror
   0x7fff8a10ce49: ret
   0x7fff8a10ce4a: nop

164
```
```

```
  thread #5: tid = 0x0004, 0x00007fff8a10ce42 libsystem_kernel.dylib`__semwait_signal + 10,
stop reason = signal SIGSTOP
    frame #0: 0x00007fff8a10ce42 libsystem_kernel.dylib`__semwait_signal + 10
libsystem_kernel.dylib`__semwait_signal + 10:
-> 0x7fff8a10ce42:  jae     0x7fff8a10ce49              ; __semwait_signal + 17
   0x7fff8a10ce44:  jmpq    0x7fff8a10dffc              ; cerror
   0x7fff8a10ce49:  ret
   0x7fff8a10ce4a:  nop
  thread #6: tid = 0x0005, 0x00007fff8a10ce42 libsystem_kernel.dylib`__semwait_signal + 10,
stop reason = signal SIGSTOP
    frame #0: 0x00007fff8a10ce42 libsystem_kernel.dylib`__semwait_signal + 10
libsystem_kernel.dylib`__semwait_signal + 10:
-> 0x7fff8a10ce42:  jae     0x7fff8a10ce49              ; __semwait_signal + 17
   0x7fff8a10ce44:  jmpq    0x7fff8a10dffc              ; cerror
   0x7fff8a10ce49:  ret
   0x7fff8a10ce4a:  nop
```

3.   Go to the identifed problem core thread 1 (thread #2):

```
(lldb) thread select 2
* thread #2: tid = 0x0001, 0x00000001027ec905 App6`procF + 53, stop reason = signal SIGSTOP
    frame #0: 0x00000001027ec905 App6`procF + 53
App6`procF + 53:
-> 0x1027ec905:  callq  0x1027ecc70                    ; symbol stub for: memset
   0x1027ec90a:  movl   $4294967295, -528(%rbp)
   0x1027ec914:  movl   -12(%rbp), %esi
   0x1027ec917:  addl   $1, %esi
```

```
(lldb) bt
* thread #2: tid = 0x0001, 0x00000001027ec905 App6`procF + 53, stop reason = signal SIGSTOP
    frame #0: 0x00000001027ec905 App6`procF + 53
    frame #1: 0x00000001027ec938 App6`procF + 104
    frame #2: 0x00000001027ec938 App6`procF + 104
    frame #3: 0x00000001027ec938 App6`procF + 104
    frame #4: 0x00000001027ec938 App6`procF + 104
    frame #5: 0x00000001027ec938 App6`procF + 104
    frame #6: 0x00000001027ec938 App6`procF + 104
    frame #7: 0x00000001027ec938 App6`procF + 104
    frame #8: 0x00000001027ec938 App6`procF + 104
    frame #9: 0x00000001027ec938 App6`procF + 104
    frame #10: 0x00000001027ec938 App6`procF + 104
    frame #11: 0x00000001027ec938 App6`procF + 104
    frame #12: 0x00000001027ec938 App6`procF + 104
    frame #13: 0x00000001027ec938 App6`procF + 104
    frame #14: 0x00000001027ec938 App6`procF + 104
    frame #15: 0x00000001027ec938 App6`procF + 104
    frame #16: 0x00000001027ec938 App6`procF + 104
    frame #17: 0x00000001027ec938 App6`procF + 104
    [...]
    frame #931: 0x00000001027ec938 App6`procF + 104
    frame #932: 0x00000001027ec938 App6`procF + 104
    frame #933: 0x00000001027ec938 App6`procF + 104
    frame #934: 0x00000001027ec938 App6`procF + 104
    frame #935: 0x00000001027ec938 App6`procF + 104
    frame #936: 0x00000001027ec938 App6`procF + 104
    frame #937: 0x00000001027ec938 App6`procF + 104
    frame #938: 0x00000001027ec938 App6`procF + 104
    frame #939: 0x00000001027ec938 App6`procF + 104
```

```
frame #940: 0x00000001027ec938 App6`procF + 104
frame #941: 0x00000001027ec938 App6`procF + 104
frame #942: 0x00000001027ec938 App6`procF + 104
frame #943: 0x00000001027ec938 App6`procF + 104
frame #944: 0x00000001027ec938 App6`procF + 104
frame #945: 0x00000001027ec938 App6`procF + 104
frame #946: 0x00000001027ec938 App6`procF + 104
frame #947: 0x00000001027ec938 App6`procF + 104
frame #948: 0x00000001027ec938 App6`procF + 104
frame #949: 0x00000001027ec938 App6`procF + 104
frame #950: 0x00000001027ec938 App6`procF + 104
frame #951: 0x00000001027ec938 App6`procF + 104
frame #952: 0x00000001027ec938 App6`procF + 104
frame #953: 0x00000001027ec938 App6`procF + 104
frame #954: 0x00000001027ec938 App6`procF + 104
frame #955: 0x00000001027ec938 App6`procF + 104
frame #956: 0x00000001027ec938 App6`procF + 104
frame #957: 0x00000001027ec938 App6`procF + 104
frame #958: 0x00000001027ec938 App6`procF + 104
frame #959: 0x00000001027ec938 App6`procF + 104
frame #960: 0x00000001027ec938 App6`procF + 104
frame #961: 0x00000001027ec938 App6`procF + 104
frame #962: 0x00000001027ec938 App6`procF + 104
frame #963: 0x00000001027ec938 App6`procF + 104
frame #964: 0x00000001027ec96e App6`procE + 14
frame #965: 0x00000001027ec98a App6`bar_one + 26
frame #966: 0x00000001027ec999 App6`foo_one + 9
frame #967: 0x00000001027ec9b1 App6`thread_one + 17
frame #968: 0x00007fff84db88bf libsystem_c.dylib`_pthread_start + 335
frame #969: 0x00007fff84dbbb75 libsystem_c.dylib`thread_start + 13
```

Note: In the diagnostics report the stack trace was truncated at the frame #512. The command **bt** output shows the full stack trace.

4.   Check if this is a stack overflow indeed. Stack region can be identified from the diagnostic report or vmmap_3769.log based on thread number.

```
Virtual Memory Map of process 3769 (App6)
Output report format:  2.2  -- 64-bit process

==== Non-writable regions for process 3769
__TEXT                 00000001027ec000-00000001027ed000 [    4K] r-x/rwx SM=COW  /Users/DumpAnalysis/Documents/AMCDA-
Dumps/Apps/App6/Build/Products/Release/App6
__LINKEDIT             00000001027ee000-00000001027ef000 [    4K] r--/rwx SM=COW  /Users/DumpAnalysis/Documents/AMCDA-
Dumps/Apps/App6/Build/Products/Release/App6
MALLOC metadata        00000001027ef000-00000001027f0000 [    4K] r--/rwx SM=ZER
MALLOC guard page      00000001027f1000-00000001027f2000 [    4K] ---/rwx SM=NUL
MALLOC guard page      0000000102807000-0000000102809000 [    8K] ---/rwx SM=NUL
MALLOC guard page      000000010281e000-000000010281f000 [    4K] ---/rwx SM=NUL
MALLOC metadata        000000010281f000-0000000102820000 [    4K] r--/rwx SM=PRV
STACK GUARD            0000000102820000-0000000102821000 [    4K] ---/rwx SM=NUL  stack guard for thread 1
STACK GUARD            0000000102a00000-0000000102a01000 [    4K] ---/rwx SM=NUL  stack guard for thread 2
STACK GUARD            0000000102a83000-0000000102a84000 [    4K] ---/rwx SM=NUL  stack guard for thread 3
STACK GUARD            0000000102b06000-0000000102b07000 [    4K] ---/rwx SM=NUL  stack guard for thread 4
STACK GUARD            0000000102b89000-0000000102b8a000 [    4K] ---/rwx SM=NUL  stack guard for thread 5
STACK GUARD            00007fff5e3ec000-00007fff61bec000 [ 56.0M] ---/rwx SM=NUL  stack guard for thread 0
__TEXT                 00007fff623ec000-00007fff62421000 [  212K] r-x/rwx SM=COW  /usr/lib/dyld
__LINKEDIT             00007fff6245d000-00007fff62470000 [   76K] r--/rwx SM=COW  /usr/lib/dyld
__TEXT                 00007fff849f2000-00007fff84a10000 [  120K] r-x/r-x SM=COW  /usr/lib/system/libxpc.dylib
__TEXT                 00007fff84d68000-00007fff84d6a000 [    8K] r-x/r-x SM=COW
/usr/lib/system/libsystem_blocks.dylib
__TEXT                 00007fff84d6a000-00007fff84e48000 [  888K] r-x/r-x SM=COW  /usr/lib/system/libsystem_c.dylib
__TEXT                 00007fff85022000-00007fff85031000 [   60K] r-x/r-x SM=COW  /usr/lib/system/libdispatch.dylib
__TEXT                 00007fff855f0000-00007fff855f2000 [    8K] r-x/r-x SM=COW  /usr/lib/system/libunc.dylib
__TEXT                 00007fff85ae3000-00007fff85ae5000 [    8K] r-x/r-x SM=COW  /usr/lib/system/libremovefile.dylib
```

```
__TEXT                  00007fff89114000-00007fff89119000 [   20K] r-x/r-x SM=COW
/usr/lib/system/libmathCommon.A.dylib
__TEXT                  00007fff89119000-00007fff8911e000 [   20K] r-x/r-x SM=COW  /usr/lib/system/libdyld.dylib
__TEXT                  00007fff89740000-00007fff89742000 [    8K] r-x/r-x SM=COW
/usr/lib/system/libsystem_sandbox.dylib
__TEXT                  00007fff8a0ef000-00007fff8a0f6000 [   28K] r-x/r-x SM=COW  /usr/lib/system/libmacho.dylib
__TEXT                  00007fff8a0f6000-00007fff8a117000 [  132K] r-x/r-x SM=COW
/usr/lib/system/libsystem_kernel.dylib
__TEXT                  00007fff8a2ac000-00007fff8a2b5000 [   36K] r-x/r-x SM=COW
/usr/lib/system/libsystem_dnssd.dylib
__TEXT                  00007fff8ae26000-00007fff8ae62000 [  240K] r-x/r-x SM=COW  /usr/lib/system/libsystem_info.dylib
__TEXT                  00007fff8b248000-00007fff8b24b000 [   12K] r-x/r-x SM=COW  /usr/lib/system/libquarantine.dylib
__TEXT                  00007fff8b3b4000-00007fff8b3b5000 [    4K] r-x/r-x SM=COW  /usr/lib/system/libkeymgr.dylib
__TEXT                  00007fff8b3dd000-00007fff8b3e3000 [   24K] r-x/r-x SM=COW  /usr/lib/system/libcompiler_rt.dylib
__TEXT                  00007fff8bd1a000-00007fff8bd1c000 [    8K] r-x/r-x SM=COW  /usr/lib/system/libdnsinfo.dylib
__TEXT                  00007fff8c528000-00007fff8c52e000 [   24K] r-x/r-x SM=COW
/usr/lib/system/libsystem_network.dylib
__TEXT                  00007fff8cfa3000-00007fff8cfae000 [   44K] r-x/r-x SM=COW  /usr/lib/system/liblaunch.dylib
__TEXT                  00007fff8fe02000-00007fff8fe0a000 [   32K] r-x/r-x SM=COW  /usr/lib/system/libcopyfile.dylib
__TEXT                  00007fff8fe4b000-00007fff8fe8e000 [  268K] r-x/r-x SM=COW
/usr/lib/system/libcommonCrypto.dylib
__TEXT                  00007fff90c0f000-00007fff90c19000 [   40K] r-x/r-x SM=COW
/usr/lib/system/libsystem_notify.dylib
__TEXT                  00007fff91376000-00007fff913a4000 [  184K] r-x/r-x SM=COW  /usr/lib/libSystem.B.dylib
__TEXT                  00007fff91489000-00007fff91490000 [   28K] r-x/r-x SM=COW  /usr/lib/system/libunwind.dylib
__TEXT                  00007fff91a22000-00007fff91a28000 [   24K] r-x/r-x SM=COW  /usr/lib/system/libcache.dylib
__LINKEDIT              00007fff91b86000-00007fff94b30000 [ 47.7M] r--/r-- SM=COW  /usr/lib/system/libxpc.dylib
shared memory           00007ffffe00000-00007ffffe02000 [    8K] r-x/r-x SM=SHM

==== Writable regions for process 3769
__DATA                  00000001027ed000-00000001027ee000 [    4K] rw-/rwx SM=PRV  /Users/DumpAnalysis/Documents/AMCDA-
Dumps/Apps/App6/Build/Products/Release/App6
MALLOC metadata         00000001027f0000-00000001027f1000 [    4K] rw-/rwx SM=ZER
MALLOC metadata         00000001027f2000-0000000102807000 [   84K] rw-/rwx SM=PRV
MALLOC metadata         0000000102809000-000000010281e000 [   84K] rw-/rwx SM=PRV
Stack                   0000000102821000-00000001028a3000 [  520K] rw-/rwx SM=PRV  thread 1
MALLOC_TINY             0000000102900000-0000000102a00000 [ 1024K] rw-/rwx SM=PRV  DefaultMallocZone_0x1027ef000
Stack                   0000000102a01000-0000000102a83000 [  520K] rw-/rwx SM=PRV  thread 2
Stack                   0000000102a84000-0000000102b06000 [  520K] rw-/rwx SM=PRV  thread 3
Stack                   0000000102b07000-0000000102b89000 [  520K] rw-/rwx SM=PRV  thread 4
Stack                   0000000102b8a000-0000000102c0c000 [  520K] rw-/rwx SM=PRV  thread 5
Stack                   00007fff61bec000-00007fff623eb000 [ 8188K] rw-/rwx SM=ZER  thread 0
Stack                   00007fff623eb000-00007fff623ec000 [    4K] rw-/rwx SM=COW  thread 0
__DATA                  00007fff62421000-00007fff6245d000 [  240K] rw-/rwx SM=COW  /usr/lib/dyld
__DATA                  00007fff749c0000-00007fff749c3000 [   12K] rw-/rwx SM=COW  /usr/lib/system/libxpc.dylib
__DATA                  00007fff74a60000-00007fff74a61000 [    4K] rw-/rwx SM=COW
/usr/lib/system/libsystem_blocks.dylib
__DATA                  00007fff74a61000-00007fff74a71000 [   64K] rw-/rwx SM=COW  /usr/lib/system/libsystem_c.dylib
__DATA                  00007fff74ac4000-00007fff74aca000 [   24K] rw-/rwx SM=COW  /usr/lib/system/libdispatch.dylib
__DATA                  00007fff74b90000-00007fff74b91000 [    4K] rw-/rwx SM=COW  /usr/lib/system/libunc.dylib
__DATA                  00007fff74c11000-00007fff74c12000 [    4K] rw-/rw- SM=COW  /usr/lib/system/libremovefile.dylib
__DATA                  00007fff75141000-00007fff75142000 [    4K] rw-/rwx SM=COW  /usr/lib/system/libdyld.dylib
__DATA                  00007fff751a3000-00007fff751a4000 [    4K] rw-/rwx SM=COW
/usr/lib/system/libsystem_sandbox.dylib
__DATA                  00007fff75281000-00007fff75282000 [    4K] rw-/rwx SM=COW  /usr/lib/system/libmacho.dylib
__DATA                  00007fff75282000-00007fff75285000 [   12K] rw-/rwx SM=COW
/usr/lib/system/libsystem_kernel.dylib
__DATA                  00007fff752d8000-00007fff752d9000 [    4K] rw-/rwx SM=COW
/usr/lib/system/libsystem_dnssd.dylib
__DATA                  00007fff75453000-00007fff75456000 [   12K] rw-/rwx SM=COW  /usr/lib/system/libsystem_info.dylib
__DATA                  00007fff7551f000-00007fff75520000 [    4K] rw-/rwx SM=COW  /usr/lib/system/libquarantine.dylib
__DATA                  00007fff75559000-00007fff7555a000 [    4K] rw-/rwx SM=COW  /usr/lib/system/libkeymgr.dylib
__DATA                  00007fff75563000-00007fff75564000 [    4K] rw-/rwx SM=COW  /usr/lib/system/libcompiler_rt.dylib
__DATA                  00007fff75633000-00007fff75634000 [    4K] rw-/rw- SM=COW  /usr/lib/system/libdnsinfo.dylib
__DATA                  00007fff756d6000-00007fff756d7000 [    4K] rw-/rw- SM=COW
/usr/lib/system/libsystem_network.dylib
__DATA                  00007fff75813000-00007fff75814000 [    4K] rw-/rwx SM=COW  /usr/lib/system/liblaunch.dylib
__DATA                  00007fff75e41000-00007fff75e42000 [    4K] rw-/rw- SM=COW  /usr/lib/system/libcopyfile.dylib
__DATA                  00007fff75e4a000-00007fff75e50000 [   24K] rw-/rw- SM=COW
/usr/lib/system/libcommonCrypto.dylib
__DATA                  00007fff76342000-00007fff76343000 [    4K] rw-/rw- SM=COW
/usr/lib/system/libsystem_notify.dylib
__DATA                  00007fff763fd000-00007fff763fe000 [    4K] rw-/rw- SM=COW  /usr/lib/libSystem.B.dylib
__DATA                  00007fff76401000-00007fff76402000 [    4K] rw-/rw- SM=COW  /usr/lib/system/libunwind.dylib
__DATA                  00007fff764ab000-00007fff764ac000 [    4K] rw-/rw- SM=COW  /usr/lib/system/libcache.dylib
```

```
==== Legend
SM=sharing mode:
        COW=copy_on_write PRV=private NUL=empty ALI=aliased
        SHM=shared ZER=zero_filled S/A=shared_alias

==== Summary for process 3769
ReadOnly portion of Libraries: Total=50.2M resident=50.2M(100%) swapped_out_or_unallocated=0K(0%)
Writable regions: Total=28.6M written=108K(0%) resident=20.6M(72%) swapped_out=0K(0%) unallocated=8244K(28%)

REGION TYPE                    VIRTUAL
===========                    =======
MALLOC                          1024K        see MALLOC ZONE table below
MALLOC guard page                16K
MALLOC metadata                 180K
STACK GUARD                     56.0M
Stack                           10.5M
__DATA                          464K
__LINKEDIT                      47.7M
__TEXT                          2484K
shared memory                    8K
===========                    =======
TOTAL                          118.4M

                        VIRTUAL ALLOCATION     BYTES
MALLOC ZONE                SIZE      COUNT   ALLOCATED   % FULL
===========             =======  =========  =========   ======
DefaultMallocZone_0x1027ef000   1024K        33        2240      0%
```

5.   We check that manually based on the stack pointer value:

```
(lldb) x $rsp
0x102820e40: 00 00 00 00 00 00 00 00 00 00 00 00 00 00 00 00   ................
0x102820e50: 00 00 00 00 00 00 00 00 00 00 00 00 00 00 00 00   ................
```

Note: We see that the stack pointer is in stack guard page range. We see contents because non-read attribute is applied to code execution but memory contents were saved in this core dump.

```
(lldb) f 1
frame #1: 0x00000001027ec938 App6`procF + 104
App6`procF + 104:
-> 0x1027ec938:  movq    1785(%rip), %rax          ; (void *)0x00007fff74a67f60:
__stack_chk_guard
   0x1027ec93f:  movq    (%rax), %rax
   0x1027ec942:  movq    -8(%rbp), %rdx
   0x1027ec946:  cmpq    %rdx, %rax

(lldb) re r rsp
    rsp = 0x0000000102821060

(lldb) f 2
frame #2: 0x00000001027ec938 App6`procF + 104
App6`procF + 104:
-> 0x1027ec938:  movq    1785(%rip), %rax          ; (void *)0x00007fff74a67f60:
__stack_chk_guard
   0x1027ec93f:  movq    (%rax), %rax
   0x1027ec942:  movq    -8(%rbp), %rdx
   0x1027ec946:  cmpq    %rdx, %rax

(lldb) re r rsp
    rsp = 0x0000000102821280
```

Note: We see that in all other frames the stack pointer is in the range of stack pages.

6.   Dump the bottom of the raw stack to see execution residue such as thread startup code:

```
(lldb) x/1024a 0x00000001028a3000-0x4000 --force
0x10289f000: 0x0000000000000000
0x10289f008: 0x0000000000000000
0x10289f010: 0x0000000000000000
0x10289f018: 0x0000000000000000
0x10289f020: 0x0000000000000000
0x10289f028: 0x0000000000000000
0x10289f030: 0x0000000000000000
0x10289f038: 0x0000000000000000
0x10289f040: 0x0000000000000000
0x10289f048: 0x0000000000000000
0x10289f050: 0x0000000000000000
0x10289f058: 0x0000000000000000
0x10289f060: 0x0000000000000000
0x10289f068: 0x0000000000000000
0x10289f070: 0x0000000000000000
0x10289f078: 0x0000000000000000
0x10289f080: 0x0000000000000000
0x10289f088: 0x0000000000000000
0x10289f090: 0x0000000000000000
0x10289f098: 0x0000000000000000
0x10289f0a0: 0x0000000000000000
0x10289f0a8: 0x0000000000000000
0x10289f0b0: 0x0000000000000000
0x10289f0b8: 0x0000000000000000
0x10289f0c0: 0x0000000000000000
0x10289f0c8: 0x0000000000000000
0x10289f0d0: 0x0000000000000000
0x10289f0d8: 0x0000000000000000
0x10289f0e0: 0x0000000f00000000
0x10289f0e8: 0x74e4ebf24818a8b6
0x10289f0f0: 0x000000010289f310
0x10289f0f8: 0x00000001027ec938 App6`procF + 104
0x10289f100: 0x00000000ffffffff
0x10289f108: 0x000000000000000f
0x10289f110: 0x00000000ffffffff
0x10289f118: 0x0000000000000000
0x10289f120: 0x0000000000000000
0x10289f128: 0x0000000000000000
0x10289f130: 0x0000000000000000
0x10289f138: 0x0000000000000000
0x10289f140: 0x0000000000000000
0x10289f148: 0x0000000000000000
0x10289f150: 0x0000000000000000
0x10289f158: 0x0000000000000000
0x10289f160: 0x0000000000000000
0x10289f168: 0x0000000000000000
0x10289f170: 0x0000000000000000
0x10289f178: 0x0000000000000000
0x10289f180: 0x0000000000000000
0x10289f188: 0x0000000000000000
0x10289f190: 0x0000000000000000
0x10289f198: 0x0000000000000000
0x10289f1a0: 0x0000000000000000
0x10289f1a8: 0x0000000000000000
0x10289f1b0: 0x0000000000000000
0x10289f1b8: 0x0000000000000000
0x10289f1c0: 0x0000000000000000
```

```
0x10289f1c8:  0x0000000000000000
0x10289f1d0:  0x0000000000000000
0x10289f1d8:  0x0000000000000000
0x10289f1e0:  0x0000000000000000
0x10289f1e8:  0x0000000000000000
0x10289f1f0:  0x0000000000000000
0x10289f1f8:  0x0000000000000000
0x10289f200:  0x0000000000000000
0x10289f208:  0x0000000000000000
0x10289f210:  0x0000000000000000
0x10289f218:  0x0000000000000000
0x10289f220:  0x0000000000000000
0x10289f228:  0x0000000000000000
0x10289f230:  0x0000000000000000
0x10289f238:  0x0000000000000000
0x10289f240:  0x0000000000000000
0x10289f248:  0x0000000000000000
0x10289f250:  0x0000000000000000
0x10289f258:  0x0000000000000000
0x10289f260:  0x0000000000000000
0x10289f268:  0x0000000000000000
0x10289f270:  0x0000000000000000
0x10289f278:  0x0000000000000000
0x10289f280:  0x0000000000000000
0x10289f288:  0x0000000000000000
0x10289f290:  0x0000000000000000
0x10289f298:  0x0000000000000000
0x10289f2a0:  0x0000000000000000
0x10289f2a8:  0x0000000000000000
0x10289f2b0:  0x0000000000000000
0x10289f2b8:  0x0000000000000000
0x10289f2c0:  0x0000000000000000
0x10289f2c8:  0x0000000000000000
0x10289f2d0:  0x0000000000000000
0x10289f2d8:  0x0000000000000000
0x10289f2e0:  0x0000000000000000
0x10289f2e8:  0x0000000000000000
0x10289f2f0:  0x0000000000000000
0x10289f2f8:  0x0000000000000000
0x10289f300:  0x0000000e00000000
0x10289f308:  0x74e4ebf24818a8b6
0x10289f310:  0x000000010289f530
0x10289f318:  0x00000001027ec938 App6`procF + 104
0x10289f320:  0x00000000ffffffff
0x10289f328:  0x000000000000000e
0x10289f330:  0x00000000ffffffff
0x10289f338:  0x0000000000000000
0x10289f340:  0x0000000000000000
0x10289f348:  0x0000000000000000
0x10289f350:  0x0000000000000000
0x10289f358:  0x0000000000000000
0x10289f360:  0x0000000000000000
[...]
0x1028a0a40:  0x0000000000000000
0x1028a0a48:  0x0000000000000000
0x1028a0a50:  0x0000000000000000
0x1028a0a58:  0x0000000000000000
0x1028a0a60:  0x0000000362427d80
0x1028a0a68:  0x74e4ebf24818a8b6
0x1028a0a70:  0x00000001028a0c90
```

```
0x1028a0a78:  0x00000001027ec938 App6`procF + 104
0x1028a0a80:  0x00000000ffffffff
0x1028a0a88:  0x0000000000000003
0x1028a0a90:  0x00000000ffffffff
0x1028a0a98:  0x0000000000000000
0x1028a0aa0:  0x0000000000000000
0x1028a0aa8:  0x0000000000000000
0x1028a0ab0:  0x0000000000000000
0x1028a0ab8:  0x0000000000000000
0x1028a0ac0:  0x0000000000000000
0x1028a0ac8:  0x0000000000000000
0x1028a0ad0:  0x0000000000000000
0x1028a0ad8:  0x0000000000000000
0x1028a0ae0:  0x0000000000000000
0x1028a0ae8:  0x0000000000000000
0x1028a0af0:  0x0000000000000000
0x1028a0af8:  0x0000000000000000
0x1028a0b00:  0x0000000000000000
0x1028a0b08:  0x0000000000000000
0x1028a0b10:  0x0000000000000000
0x1028a0b18:  0x0000000000000000
0x1028a0b20:  0x0000000000000000
0x1028a0b28:  0x0000000000000000
0x1028a0b30:  0x0000000000000000
0x1028a0b38:  0x0000000000000000
0x1028a0b40:  0x0000000000000000
0x1028a0b48:  0x0000000000000000
0x1028a0b50:  0x0000000000000000
0x1028a0b58:  0x0000000000000000
0x1028a0b60:  0x0000000000000000
0x1028a0b68:  0x0000000000000000
0x1028a0b70:  0x0000000000000000
0x1028a0b78:  0x0000000000000000
0x1028a0b80:  0x0000000000000000
0x1028a0b88:  0x0000000000000000
0x1028a0b90:  0x0000000000000000
0x1028a0b98:  0x0000000000000000
0x1028a0ba0:  0x0000000000000000
0x1028a0ba8:  0x0000000000000000
0x1028a0bb0:  0x0000000000000000
0x1028a0bb8:  0x0000000000000000
0x1028a0bc0:  0x0000000000000000
0x1028a0bc8:  0x0000000000000000
0x1028a0bd0:  0x0000000000000000
0x1028a0bd8:  0x0000000000000000
0x1028a0be0:  0x0000000000000000
0x1028a0be8:  0x0000000000000000
0x1028a0bf0:  0x0000000000000000
0x1028a0bf8:  0x0000000000000000
0x1028a0c00:  0x0000000000000000
0x1028a0c08:  0x0000000000000000
0x1028a0c10:  0x0000000000000000
0x1028a0c18:  0x0000000000000000
0x1028a0c20:  0x0000000000000000
0x1028a0c28:  0x0000000000000000
0x1028a0c30:  0x0000000000000000
0x1028a0c38:  0x0000000000000000
0x1028a0c40:  0x0000000000000000
0x1028a0c48:  0x0000000000000000
0x1028a0c50:  0x0000000000000000
```

```
0x1028a0c58:  0x0000000000000000
0x1028a0c60:  0x0000000000000000
0x1028a0c68:  0x0000000000000000
0x1028a0c70:  0x0000000000000000
0x1028a0c78:  0x0000000000000000
0x1028a0c80:  0x00000002028a0eb0
0x1028a0c88:  0x74e4ebf24818a8b6
0x1028a0c90:  0x00000001028a0eb0
0x1028a0c98:  0x000000001027ec938 App6`procF + 104
0x1028a0ca0:  0x00000000ffffffff
0x1028a0ca8:  0x0000000000000002
0x1028a0cb0:  0x00000000ffffffff
0x1028a0cb8:  0x0000000000000000
0x1028a0cc0:  0x0000000000000000
0x1028a0cc8:  0x0000000000000000
0x1028a0cd0:  0x0000000000000000
0x1028a0cd8:  0x0000000000000000
0x1028a0ce0:  0x0000000000000000
0x1028a0ce8:  0x0000000000000000
0x1028a0cf0:  0x0000000000000000
0x1028a0cf8:  0x0000000000000000
0x1028a0d00:  0x0000000000000000
0x1028a0d08:  0x0000000000000000
0x1028a0d10:  0x0000000000000000
0x1028a0d18:  0x0000000000000000
0x1028a0d20:  0x0000000000000000
0x1028a0d28:  0x0000000000000000
0x1028a0d30:  0x0000000000000000
0x1028a0d38:  0x0000000000000000
0x1028a0d40:  0x0000000000000000
0x1028a0d48:  0x0000000000000000
0x1028a0d50:  0x0000000000000000
0x1028a0d58:  0x0000000000000000
0x1028a0d60:  0x0000000000000000
0x1028a0d68:  0x0000000000000000
0x1028a0d70:  0x0000000000000000
0x1028a0d78:  0x0000000000000000
0x1028a0d80:  0x0000000000000000
0x1028a0d88:  0x0000000000000000
0x1028a0d90:  0x0000000000000000
0x1028a0d98:  0x0000000000000000
0x1028a0da0:  0x0000000000000000
0x1028a0da8:  0x0000000000000000
0x1028a0db0:  0x0000000000000000
0x1028a0db8:  0x0000000000000000
0x1028a0dc0:  0x0000000000000000
0x1028a0dc8:  0x0000000000000000
0x1028a0dd0:  0x0000000000000000
0x1028a0dd8:  0x0000000000000000
0x1028a0de0:  0x0000000000000000
0x1028a0de8:  0x0000000000000000
0x1028a0df0:  0x0000000000000000
0x1028a0df8:  0x0000000000000000
0x1028a0e00:  0x0000000000000000
0x1028a0e08:  0x0000000000000000
0x1028a0e10:  0x0000000000000000
0x1028a0e18:  0x0000000000000000
0x1028a0e20:  0x0000000000000000
0x1028a0e28:  0x0000000000000000
0x1028a0e30:  0x0000000000000000
```

```
0x1028a0e38: 0x0000000000000000
0x1028a0e40: 0x0000000000000000
0x1028a0e48: 0x0000000000000000
0x1028a0e50: 0x0000000000000000
0x1028a0e58: 0x0000000000000000
0x1028a0e60: 0x0000000000000000
0x1028a0e68: 0x0000000000000000
0x1028a0e70: 0x0000000000000000
0x1028a0e78: 0x0000000000000000
0x1028a0e80: 0x0000000000000000
0x1028a0e88: 0x0000000000000000
0x1028a0e90: 0x0000000000000000
0x1028a0e98: 0x0000000000000000
0x1028a0ea0: 0x0000000100000000
0x1028a0ea8: 0x74e4ebf24818a8b6
0x1028a0eb0: 0x00000001028a0ec0
0x1028a0eb8: 0x00000001027ec96e App6`procE + 14
0x1028a0ec0: 0x00000001028a0ee0
0x1028a0ec8: 0x00000001027ec98a App6`bar_one + 26
0x1028a0ed0: 0x0000000000000000
0x1028a0ed8: 0x0000000000000000
0x1028a0ee0: 0x00000001028a0ef0
0x1028a0ee8: 0x00000001027ec999 App6`foo_one + 9
0x1028a0ef0: 0x00000001028a0f10
0x1028a0ef8: 0x00000001027ec9b1 App6`thread_one + 17
0x1028a0f00: 0x0000000000000000
0x1028a0f08: 0x0000000000000000
0x1028a0f10: 0x00000001028a0f50
0x1028a0f18: 0x00007fff84db88bf libsystem_c.dylib`_pthread_start + 335
0x1028a0f20: 0x0000000000000000
0x1028a0f28: 0x0000000000000000
0x1028a0f30: 0x0000000000000000
0x1028a0f38: 0x0000000000000000
0x1028a0f40: 0x0000000000000000
0x1028a0f48: 0x0000000000000000
0x1028a0f50: 0x00000001028a0f78
0x1028a0f58: 0x00007fff84dbbb75 libsystem_c.dylib`thread_start + 13
0x1028a0f60: 0x0000000000000000
0x1028a0f68: 0x0000000000000000
0x1028a0f70: 0x0000000000000000
0x1028a0f78: 0x0000000000000000
0x1028a0f80: 0x0000000000000000
0x1028a0f88: 0x0000000000000000
0x1028a0f90: 0x0000000000000000
0x1028a0f98: 0x0000000000000000
0x1028a0fa0: 0x0000000000000000
0x1028a0fa8: 0x0000000000000000
0x1028a0fb0: 0x0000000000000000
0x1028a0fb8: 0x0000000000000000
0x1028a0fc0: 0x0000000000000000
0x1028a0fc8: 0x0000000000000000
0x1028a0fd0: 0x0000000000000000
0x1028a0fd8: 0x0000000000000000
0x1028a0fe0: 0x0000000000000000
0x1028a0fe8: 0x0000000000000000
0x1028a0ff0: 0x0000000000000000
0x1028a0ff8: 0x0000000000000000
```

Note: We see that the reconstruction of the stack trace is possible because of the standard function prologue and epilogue:

```
[...]
0x1028a0ea0: 0x0000000100000000
0x1028a0ea8: 0x74e4ebf24818a8b6
0x1028a0eb0: 0x00000001028a0ec0
0x1028a0eb8: 0x00000001027ec96e App6`procE + 14
0x1028a0ec0: 0x00000001028a0ee0
0x1028a0ec8: 0x00000001027ec98a App6`bar_one + 26
0x1028a0ed0: 0x0000000000000000
0x1028a0ed8: 0x0000000000000000
0x1028a0f10: 0x00000001028a0f50
0x1028a0f18: 0x00007fff84db88bf libsystem_c.dylib`_pthread_start + 335
[...]

(lldb) di -n procF
App6`procF:
    0x1027ec8d0:  pushq   %rbp
    0x1027ec8d1:  movq    %rsp, %rbp
    0x1027ec8d4:  subq    $528, %rsp
    0x1027ec8db:  movq    1878(%rip), %rax          ; (void *)0x00007fff74a67f60:
__stack_chk_guard
    0x1027ec8e2:  movq    (%rax), %rax
    0x1027ec8e5:  movq    %rax, -8(%rbp)
    0x1027ec8e9:  movl    $0, %esi
    0x1027ec8ee:  movabsq $512, %rdx
    0x1027ec8f8:  leaq    -528(%rbp), %rax
    0x1027ec8ff:  movl    %edi, -12(%rbp)
    0x1027ec902:  movq    %rax, %rdi
    0x1027ec905:  callq   0x1027ecc70              ; symbol stub for: memset
    0x1027ec90a:  movl    $4294967295, -528(%rbp)
    0x1027ec914:  movl    -12(%rbp), %esi
    0x1027ec917:  addl    $1, %esi
    0x1027ec91d:  movl    %esi, -520(%rbp)
    0x1027ec923:  movl    $4294967295, -512(%rbp)
    0x1027ec92d:  movl    -520(%rbp), %edi
    0x1027ec933:  callq   0x1027ec8d0              ; procF
 -> 0x1027ec938:  movq    1785(%rip), %rax          ; (void *)0x00007fff74a67f60:
__stack_chk_guard
    0x1027ec93f:  movq    (%rax), %rax
    0x1027ec942:  movq    -8(%rbp), %rdx
    0x1027ec946:  cmpq    %rdx, %rax
    0x1027ec949:  jne     0x1027ec958             ; procF + 136
    0x1027ec94f:  addq    $528, %rsp
    0x1027ec956:  popq    %rbp
    0x1027ec957:  ret
    0x1027ec958:  callq   0x1027ecc64             ; symbol stub for: __stack_chk_fail
    0x1027ec95d:  nopl    (%rax)
```

Exercise A7 (GDB)

- **Goal:** Learn how to identify active threads

- **Patterns:** Divide by Zero, Active Thread

- \AMCDA-Dumps\Exercise-A7-GDB.pdf

Exercise A7 (GDB)

Goal: Learn how to identify active threads

Patterns: Divide by Zero, Active Thread

1.   Identify the problem thread and application specific diagnostic from the diagnostic report App7_3971.crash (including non-waiting threads):

```
Process:        App7 [3971]
Path:           /Users/USER/Documents/*/App7
Identifier:     App7
Version:        ??? (???)
Code Type:      X86-64 (Native)
Parent Process: bash [1549]

Date/Time:      2012-07-25 19:25:40.165 +0100
OS Version:     Mac OS X 10.7.4 (11E53)
Report Version: 9
Sleep/Wake UUID: 4C0A9B6D-7E93-4764-8BC3-971D136863D8

Crashed Thread: 3

Exception Type:  EXC_ARITHMETIC (SIGFPE)
Exception Codes: EXC_I386_DIV (divide by zero)

Thread 0:: Dispatch queue: com.apple.main-thread
0   libsystem_kernel.dylib          0x00007fff8a10ce42 __semwait_signal + 10
1   libsystem_c.dylib               0x00007fff84d6edea nanosleep + 164
2   libsystem_c.dylib               0x00007fff84d6ec2c sleep + 61
3   libsystem_c.dylib               0x00007fff84d6ec08 sleep + 25
4   App7                            0x000000010a6dfaf3 main + 195
5   App7                            0x000000010a6df5d4 start + 52

Thread 1:
0   libsystem_c.dylib               0x00007fff84dc99f0 _simple_asl_init + 0
1   libsystem_c.dylib               0x00007fff84db7e06 pthread_once + 86
2   libsystem_c.dylib               0x00007fff84dca53d _simple_asl_log_prog + 48
3   libsystem_c.dylib               0x00007fff84da8064 __stack_chk_fail + 211
4   App7                            0x000000010a6df817 procA + 87

Thread 2:
0   libsystem_kernel.dylib          0x00007fff8a10ce42 __semwait_signal + 10
1   libsystem_c.dylib               0x00007fff84d6edea nanosleep + 164
2   libsystem_c.dylib               0x00007fff84d6ec2c sleep + 61
3   libsystem_c.dylib               0x00007fff84d6ec08 sleep + 25
4   App7                            0x000000010a6df89f bar_two + 31
5   App7                            0x000000010a6df8b9 foo_two + 9
6   App7                            0x000000010a6df8d1 thread_two + 17
7   libsystem_c.dylib               0x00007fff84db88bf _pthread_start + 335
8   libsystem_c.dylib               0x00007fff84dbbb75 thread_start + 13

Thread 3 Crashed:
0   App7                            0x000000010a6df68e procD + 14
1   App7                            0x000000010a6df6b3 procC + 19
2   App7                            0x000000010a6df90a bar_three + 26
3   App7                            0x000000010a6df929 foo_three + 9
4   App7                            0x000000010a6df941 thread_three + 17
5   libsystem_c.dylib               0x00007fff84db88bf _pthread_start + 335
6   libsystem_c.dylib               0x00007fff84dbbb75 thread_start + 13
```

```
Thread 4:
0   libsystem_kernel.dylib          0x00007fff8a10ce42 __semwait_signal + 10
1   libsystem_c.dylib               0x00007fff84d6edea nanosleep + 164
2   libsystem_c.dylib               0x00007fff84d6ec2c sleep + 61
3   libsystem_c.dylib               0x00007fff84d6ec08 sleep + 25
4   App7                            0x000000010a6df97f bar_four + 31
5   App7                            0x000000010a6df999 foo_four + 9
6   App7                            0x000000010a6df9b1 thread_four + 17
7   libsystem_c.dylib               0x00007fff84db88bf _pthread_start + 335
8   libsystem_c.dylib               0x00007fff84dbbb75 thread_start + 13

Thread 5:
0   App7                            0x000000010a6df615 procF + 53
1   App7                            0x000000010a6df648 procF + 104
2   App7                            0x000000010a6df648 procF + 104
3   App7                            0x000000010a6df67e procE + 14
4   App7                            0x000000010a6df9ea bar_five + 26
5   App7                            0x000000010a6df9f9 foo_five + 9
6   App7                            0x000000010a6dfa11 thread_five + 17
7   libsystem_c.dylib               0x00007fff84db88bf _pthread_start + 335
8   libsystem_c.dylib               0x00007fff84dbbb75 thread_start + 13

Thread 3 crashed with X86 Thread State (64-bit):
  rax: 0x0000000000000001  rbx: 0x0000000000000000  rcx: 0x00007fff8a10ce42  rdx: 0x0000000000000000
  rdi: 0x0000000000000001  rsi: 0x0000000000000000  rbp: 0x000000010aa03eb0  rsp: 0x000000010aa03eb0
   r8: 0x000000000000012c   r9: 0x0000000000000000  r10: 0x0000000000000001  r11: 0x00007fff75284228
  r12: 0x0000000000001403  r13: 0x000000010aa04000  r14: 0x0000000000000000  r15: 0x000000010a6df930
  rip: 0x000000010a6df68e  rfl: 0x0000000000010206  cr2: 0x0000000108ded000
Logical CPU: 1

Binary Images:
       0x10a6de000 -        0x10a6dffff +App7 (??? - ???) <47049673-762D-31BE-9669-4095FEF620D5>
/Users/USER/Documents/*/App7
    0x7fff6a2de000 -     0x7fff6a312baf  dyld (195.6 - ???) <0CD1B35B-A28F-32DA-B72E-452EAD609613> /usr/lib/dyld
    0x7fff849f2000 -     0x7fff84a0ffff  libxpc.dylib (77.19.0 - compatibility 1.0.0) <9F57891B-D7EF-3050-BEDD-
21E7C6668248> /usr/lib/system/libxpc.dylib
    0x7fff84d68000 -     0x7fff84d69ff7  libsystem_blocks.dylib (53.0.0 - compatibility 1.0.0) <8BCA214A-8992-34B2-
A8B9-B74DEACA1869> /usr/lib/system/libsystem_blocks.dylib
    0x7fff84d6a000 -     0x7fff84e47fef  libsystem_c.dylib (763.13.0 - compatibility 1.0.0) <41B43515-2806-3FBC-ACF1-
A16F35B7E290> /usr/lib/system/libsystem_c.dylib
    0x7fff85022000 -     0x7fff85030fff  libdispatch.dylib (187.9.0 - compatibility 1.0.0) <1D5BE322-A9B9-3BCE-8FAC-
076FB07CF54A> /usr/lib/system/libdispatch.dylib
    0x7fff855f0000 -     0x7fff855f1fff  libunc.dylib (24.0.0 - compatibility 1.0.0) <337960EE-0A85-3DD0-A760-
7134CF4C0AFF> /usr/lib/system/libunc.dylib
    0x7fff85ae3000 -     0x7fff85ae4ff7  libremovefile.dylib (21.1.0 - compatibility 1.0.0) <739E6C83-AA52-3C6C-A680-
B37FE2888A04> /usr/lib/system/libremovefile.dylib
    0x7fff89114000 -     0x7fff89118fff  libmathCommon.A.dylib (2026.0.0 - compatibility 1.0.0) <FF83AFF7-42B2-306E-
90AF-D539C51A4542> /usr/lib/system/libmathCommon.A.dylib
    0x7fff89119000 -     0x7fff8911dfff  libdyld.dylib (195.5.0 - compatibility 1.0.0) <380C3F44-0CA7-3514-8080-
46D1C9DF4FCD> /usr/lib/system/libdyld.dylib
    0x7fff89740000 -     0x7fff89741ff7  libsystem_sandbox.dylib (??? - ???) <96D38E74-F18F-3CCB-A20B-E8E3ADC4E166>
/usr/lib/system/libsystem_sandbox.dylib
    0x7fff8a0ef000 -     0x7fff8a0f5fff  libmacho.dylib (800.0.0 - compatibility 1.0.0) <165514D7-1BFA-38EF-A151-
676DCD21FB64> /usr/lib/system/libmacho.dylib
    0x7fff8a0f6000 -     0x7fff8a116fff  libsystem_kernel.dylib (1699.26.8 - compatibility 1.0.0) <1DDC0B0F-DB2A-34D6-
895D-E5B2B5618946> /usr/lib/system/libsystem_kernel.dylib
    0x7fff8a2ac000 -     0x7fff8a2b4fff  libsystem_dnssd.dylib (??? - ???) <D9BB1F87-A42B-3CBC-9DC2-FC07FCEF0016>
/usr/lib/system/libsystem_dnssd.dylib
    0x7fff8ae26000 -     0x7fff8ae61fff  libsystem_info.dylib (??? - ???) <35F90252-2AE1-32C5-8D34-782C614D9639>
/usr/lib/system/libsystem_info.dylib
    0x7fff8b248000 -     0x7fff8b24afff  libquarantine.dylib (36.6.0 - compatibility 1.0.0) <0EBF714B-4B69-3E1F-9A7D-
6BBC2AACB310> /usr/lib/system/libquarantine.dylib
    0x7fff8b3b4000 -     0x7fff8b3b4fff  libkeymgr.dylib (23.0.0 - compatibility 1.0.0) <61EFED6A-A407-301E-B454-
CD18314F0075> /usr/lib/system/libkeymgr.dylib
    0x7fff8b3dd000 -     0x7fff8b3e2fff  libcompiler_rt.dylib (6.0.0 - compatibility 1.0.0) <98ECD5F6-E85C-32A5-98CD-
8911230CB66A> /usr/lib/system/libcompiler_rt.dylib
    0x7fff8bd1a000 -     0x7fff8bd1bfff  libdnsinfo.dylib (395.11.0 - compatibility 1.0.0) <853BAAA5-270F-3FDC-B025-
D448DB72E1C3> /usr/lib/system/libdnsinfo.dylib
    0x7fff8c528000 -     0x7fff8c52dff7  libsystem_network.dylib (??? - ???) <5DE7024E-1D2D-34A2-80F4-08326331A75B>
/usr/lib/system/libsystem_network.dylib
    0x7fff8cfa3000 -     0x7fff8cfadff7  liblaunch.dylib (392.38.0 - compatibility 1.0.0) <6ECB7F19-B384-32C1-8652-
2463C1CF4815> /usr/lib/system/liblaunch.dylib
    0x7fff8fe02000 -     0x7fff8fe09fff  libcopyfile.dylib (85.1.0 - compatibility 1.0.0) <0AB51EE2-E914-358C-AC19-
47BC024BDAE7> /usr/lib/system/libcopyfile.dylib
    0x7fff8fe4b000 -     0x7fff8fe8dff7  libcommonCrypto.dylib (55010.0.0 - compatibility 1.0.0) <BB770C22-8C57-365A-
8716-4A3C36AE7BFB> /usr/lib/system/libcommonCrypto.dylib
```

```
      0x7fff90c0f000 -     0x7fff90c18ff7  libsystem_notify.dylib (80.1.0 - compatibility 1.0.0) <A4D651E3-D1C6-3934-
AD49-7A104FD14596> /usr/lib/system/libsystem_notify.dylib
      0x7fff91376000 -     0x7fff913a3fe7  libSystem.B.dylib (159.1.0 - compatibility 1.0.0) <7BEBB139-50BB-3112-947A-
F4AA168F991C> /usr/lib/libSystem.B.dylib
      0x7fff91489000 -     0x7fff9148fff7  libunwind.dylib (30.0.0 - compatibility 1.0.0) <1E9C6C8C-CBE8-3F4B-A5B5-
E03E3AB53231> /usr/lib/system/libunwind.dylib
      0x7fff91a22000 -     0x7fff91a27fff  libcache.dylib (47.0.0 - compatibility 1.0.0) <1571C3AB-BCB2-38CD-B3B2-
C5FC3F927C6A> /usr/lib/system/libcache.dylib

External Modification Summary:
  Calls made by other processes targeting this process:
    task_for_pid: 2
    thread_create: 0
    thread_set_state: 0
  Calls made by this process:
    task_for_pid: 0
    thread_create: 0
    thread_set_state: 0
  Calls made by all processes on this machine:
    task_for_pid: 6380
    thread_create: 0
    thread_set_state: 0

VM Region Summary:
ReadOnly portion of Libraries: Total=50.2M resident=50.2M(100%) swapped_out_or_unallocated=0K(0%)
Writable regions: Total=38.9M written=12.8M(33%) resident=42.6M(110%) swapped_out=0K(0%)
unallocated=16777216.0T(45221404475392%)

REGION TYPE              VIRTUAL
===========              =======
MALLOC                    1220K
Stack                     66.6M
__DATA                     464K
__LINKEDIT                47.7M
__TEXT                    2488K
shared memory               12K
===========              =======
TOTAL                    118.4M
```

2.   Load a core dump core.3971 and App7 executable:

```
$ gdb -c ~/Documents/AMCDA-Dumps/core.3971 -e ~/Documents/AMCDA-
Dumps/Apps/App7/Build/Products/Release/App7
GNU gdb 6.3.50-20050815 (Apple version gdb-1820) (Sat Jun 16 02:40:11 UTC 2012)
Copyright 2004 Free Software Foundation, Inc.
GDB is free software, covered by the GNU General Public License, and you are
welcome to change it and/or distribute copies of it under certain conditions.
Type "show copying" to see the conditions.
There is absolutely no warranty for GDB.  Type "show warranty" for details.
This GDB was configured as "x86_64-apple-darwin".
Reading symbols for shared libraries . done
Reading symbols for shared libraries ......................... done
#0  0x00007fff8a10ce42 in __semwait_signal ()
```

3.   Go to the identifed problem core thread 3 (thread #4) and identify the problem instruction:

```
(gdb) thread 4
[Switching to thread 4 (core thread 3)]
0x000000010a6df68e in procD ()
```

```
(gdb) x/i $rip
0x10a6df68e <procD+14>:    idiv    %esi

(gdb) info r rsi
rsi             0x0  0
```

4.   Check the currently executing instruction of identified non-waiting core thread 1 (thread #2) and compare stack pointer with stack region boundaries:

```
(gdb) thread 2
[Switching to thread 2 (core thread 1)]
0x00007fff84dc99f0 in _simple_asl_init ()

(gdb) x/i $rip
0x7fff84dc99f0 <_simple_asl_init>:      push    %rbp

(gdb) info r rsp
rsp             0x10a793d78 0x10a793d78

(gdb) maintenance info sections
Exec file:
    `/Users/DumpAnalysis/Documents/AMCDA-Dumps/Apps/App7/Build/Products/Release/App7', file type mach-o-le.
    0x0000000000000000->0x0000000000000000 at 0x00000000: LC_SEGMENT.__PAGEZERO ALLOC LOAD CODE HAS_CONTENTS
    0x0000000100000000->0x0000000100002000 at 0x00000000: LC_SEGMENT.__TEXT ALLOC LOAD CODE HAS_CONTENTS
    0x00000001000015a0->0x0000000100001b03 at 0x000015a0: LC_SEGMENT.__TEXT.__text ALLOC LOAD READONLY CODE
HAS_CONTENTS
    0x0000000100001b04->0x0000000100001b2e at 0x00001b04: LC_SEGMENT.__TEXT.__stubs ALLOC LOAD CODE HAS_CONTENTS
    0x0000000100001b30->0x0000000100001b86 at 0x00001b30: LC_SEGMENT.__TEXT.__stub_helper ALLOC LOAD CODE HAS_CONTENTS
    0x0000000100001b90->0x0000000100001bf4 at 0x00001b90: LC_SEGMENT.__TEXT.__const ALLOC LOAD CODE HAS_CONTENTS
    0x0000000100001bf4->0x0000000100001bfe at 0x00001bf4: LC_SEGMENT.__TEXT.__cstring ALLOC LOAD CODE HAS_CONTENTS
    0x0000000100001bfe->0x0000000100001c4e at 0x00001bfe: LC_SEGMENT.__TEXT.__unwind_info ALLOC LOAD CODE HAS_CONTENTS
    0x0000000100001c50->0x0000000100002000 at 0x00001c50: LC_SEGMENT.__TEXT.__eh_frame ALLOC LOAD CODE HAS_CONTENTS
    0x0000000100002000->0x0000000100003000 at 0x00002000: LC_SEGMENT.__DATA ALLOC LOAD CODE HAS_CONTENTS
    0x0000000100002000->0x0000000100002028 at 0x00002000: LC_SEGMENT.__DATA.__program_vars ALLOC LOAD CODE
HAS_CONTENTS
    0x0000000100002028->0x0000000100002038 at 0x00002028: LC_SEGMENT.__DATA.__nl_symbol_ptr ALLOC LOAD CODE
HAS_CONTENTS
    0x0000000100002038->0x0000000100002040 at 0x00002038: LC_SEGMENT.__DATA.__got ALLOC LOAD CODE HAS_CONTENTS
    0x0000000100002040->0x0000000100002078 at 0x00002040: LC_SEGMENT.__DATA.__la_symbol_ptr ALLOC LOAD CODE
HAS_CONTENTS
    0x0000000100002078->0x0000000100002098 at 0x00000000: LC_SEGMENT.__DATA.__common ALLOC
    0x0000000100003000->0x0000000100003584 at 0x00003000: LC_SEGMENT.__LINKEDIT ALLOC LOAD CODE HAS_CONTENTS
    0x0000000000000000->0x0000000000000260 at 0x00003140: LC_SYMTAB.stabs HAS_CONTENTS
    0x0000000000000000->0x00000000000001a0 at 0x000033e4: LC_SYMTAB.stabstr HAS_CONTENTS
    0x0000000000000000->0x0000000000000170 at 0x00003140: LC_DYSYMTAB.localstabs HAS_CONTENTS
    0x0000000000000000->0x00000000000000f0 at 0x000032b0: LC_DYSYMTAB.nonlocalstabs HAS_CONTENTS
    0x0000000000000000->0x0000000000000018 at 0x000005a0: LC_LOAD_DYLINKER HAS_CONTENTS
    0x0000000000000000->0x00000000000000a8 at 0x000005f0: LC_THREAD.x86_THREAD_STATE64.0 HAS_CONTENTS
    0x0000000000000000->0x0000000000000030 at 0x000006a0: LC_LOAD_DYLIB HAS_CONTENTS
Core file:
    `/Users/DumpAnalysis/Documents/AMCDA-Dumps/core.3971', file type mach-o-le.
    0x000000010a6de000->0x000000010a6e0000 at 0x00002000: LC_SEGMENT. ALLOC LOAD CODE HAS_CONTENTS
    0x000000010a6e0000->0x000000010a6e1000 at 0x00004000: LC_SEGMENT. ALLOC LOAD CODE HAS_CONTENTS
    0x000000010a6e1000->0x000000010a6e2000 at 0x00005000: LC_SEGMENT. ALLOC LOAD CODE HAS_CONTENTS
    0x000000010a6e2000->0x000000010a6e3000 at 0x00006000: LC_SEGMENT. ALLOC LOAD CODE HAS_CONTENTS
    0x000000010a6e3000->0x000000010a6e4000 at 0x00007000: LC_SEGMENT. ALLOC LOAD CODE HAS_CONTENTS
    0x000000010a6e4000->0x000000010a6e5000 at 0x00008000: LC_SEGMENT. ALLOC LOAD CODE HAS_CONTENTS
    0x000000010a6e5000->0x000000010a6fa000 at 0x00009000: LC_SEGMENT. ALLOC LOAD CODE HAS_CONTENTS
    0x000000010a6fa000->0x000000010a6fb000 at 0x0001e000: LC_SEGMENT. ALLOC LOAD CODE HAS_CONTENTS
    0x000000010a6fb000->0x000000010a6fc000 at 0x0001f000: LC_SEGMENT. ALLOC LOAD CODE HAS_CONTENTS
    0x000000010a6fc000->0x000000010a711000 at 0x00020000: LC_SEGMENT. ALLOC LOAD CODE HAS_CONTENTS
    0x000000010a711000->0x000000010a712000 at 0x00035000: LC_SEGMENT. ALLOC LOAD CODE HAS_CONTENTS
    0x000000010a712000->0x000000010a713000 at 0x00036000: LC_SEGMENT. ALLOC LOAD CODE HAS_CONTENTS
    0x000000010a713000->0x000000010a714000 at 0x00037000: LC_SEGMENT. ALLOC LOAD CODE HAS_CONTENTS
    0x000000010a714000->0x000000010a796000 at 0x00038000: LC_SEGMENT. ALLOC LOAD CODE HAS_CONTENTS
    0x000000010a800000->0x000000010a900000 at 0x000ba000: LC_SEGMENT. ALLOC LOAD CODE HAS_CONTENTS
    0x000000010a900000->0x000000010a901000 at 0x001ba000: LC_SEGMENT. ALLOC LOAD CODE HAS_CONTENTS
    0x000000010a901000->0x000000010a983000 at 0x001bb000: LC_SEGMENT. ALLOC LOAD CODE HAS_CONTENTS
    0x000000010a983000->0x000000010a984000 at 0x0023d000: LC_SEGMENT. ALLOC LOAD CODE HAS_CONTENTS
    0x000000010a984000->0x000000010aa06000 at 0x0023e000: LC_SEGMENT. ALLOC LOAD CODE HAS_CONTENTS
```

179

```
0x000000010aa06000->0x000000010aa07000 at 0x002c0000: LC_SEGMENT. ALLOC LOAD CODE HAS_CONTENTS
0x000000010aa07000->0x000000010aa89000 at 0x002c1000: LC_SEGMENT. ALLOC LOAD CODE HAS_CONTENTS
0x000000010aa89000->0x000000010aa8a000 at 0x00343000: LC_SEGMENT. ALLOC LOAD CODE HAS_CONTENTS
0x000000010aa8a000->0x000000010ab0c000 at 0x00344000: LC_SEGMENT. ALLOC LOAD CODE HAS_CONTENTS
0x00007fff662de000->0x00007fff69ade000 at 0x003c6000: LC_SEGMENT. ALLOC LOAD CODE HAS_CONTENTS
0x00007fff69ade000->0x00007fff6a2dd000 at 0x03bc6000: LC_SEGMENT. ALLOC LOAD CODE HAS_CONTENTS
0x00007fff6a2dd000->0x00007fff6a2de000 at 0x043c5000: LC_SEGMENT. ALLOC LOAD CODE HAS_CONTENTS
0x00007fff6a2de000->0x00007fff6a313000 at 0x043c6000: LC_SEGMENT. ALLOC LOAD CODE HAS_CONTENTS
0x00007fff6a313000->0x00007fff6a315000 at 0x043fb000: LC_SEGMENT. ALLOC LOAD CODE HAS_CONTENTS
0x00007fff6a315000->0x00007fff6a34f000 at 0x043fd000: LC_SEGMENT. ALLOC LOAD CODE HAS_CONTENTS
0x00007fff6a34f000->0x00007fff6a362000 at 0x04437000: LC_SEGMENT. ALLOC LOAD CODE HAS_CONTENTS
0x00007fff749b8000->0x00007fff74a00000 at 0x0444a000: LC_SEGMENT. ALLOC LOAD CODE HAS_CONTENTS
0x00007fff74a00000->0x00007fff74c00000 at 0x04492000: LC_SEGMENT. ALLOC LOAD CODE HAS_CONTENTS
0x00007fff74c00000->0x00007fff74e00000 at 0x04692000: LC_SEGMENT. ALLOC LOAD CODE HAS_CONTENTS
0x00007fff74e00000->0x00007fff75000000 at 0x04892000: LC_SEGMENT. ALLOC LOAD CODE HAS_CONTENTS
0x00007fff75000000->0x00007fff75200000 at 0x04a92000: LC_SEGMENT. ALLOC LOAD CODE HAS_CONTENTS
0x00007fff75200000->0x00007fff75400000 at 0x04c92000: LC_SEGMENT. ALLOC LOAD CODE HAS_CONTENTS
0x00007fff75400000->0x00007fff75600000 at 0x04e92000: LC_SEGMENT. ALLOC LOAD CODE HAS_CONTENTS
0x00007fff75600000->0x00007fff75800000 at 0x05092000: LC_SEGMENT. ALLOC LOAD CODE HAS_CONTENTS
0x00007fff75800000->0x00007fff75a00000 at 0x05292000: LC_SEGMENT. ALLOC LOAD CODE HAS_CONTENTS
0x00007fff75a00000->0x00007fff75c00000 at 0x05492000: LC_SEGMENT. ALLOC LOAD CODE HAS_CONTENTS
0x00007fff75c00000->0x00007fff75e00000 at 0x05692000: LC_SEGMENT. ALLOC LOAD CODE HAS_CONTENTS
0x00007fff75e00000->0x00007fff76200000 at 0x05892000: LC_SEGMENT. ALLOC LOAD CODE HAS_CONTENTS
0x00007fff76200000->0x00007fff76400000 at 0x05c92000: LC_SEGMENT. ALLOC LOAD CODE HAS_CONTENTS
0x00007fff76400000->0x00007fff764ac000 at 0x05e92000: LC_SEGMENT. ALLOC LOAD CODE HAS_CONTENTS
0x00007fff849b8000->0x00007fff91a28000 at 0x05f3e000: LC_SEGMENT. ALLOC LOAD CODE HAS_CONTENTS
0x00007fff91a28000->0x00007fff94b30000 at 0x12fae000: LC_SEGMENT. ALLOC LOAD CODE HAS_CONTENTS
0x00007fffffe00000->0x00007fffffe02000 at 0x160b6000: LC_SEGMENT. ALLOC LOAD CODE HAS_CONTENTS
0x0000000000000000->0x00000000000000b0 at 0x00000d68: LC_THREAD.x86_THREAD_STATE.0 HAS_CONTENTS
0x0000000000000000->0x0000000000000214 at 0x00000e20: LC_THREAD.x86_FLOAT_STATE.0 HAS_CONTENTS
0x0000000000000000->0x0000000000000018 at 0x0000103c: LC_THREAD.x86_EXCEPTION_STATE.0 HAS_CONTENTS
0x0000000000000000->0x00000000000000b0 at 0x00001064: LC_THREAD.x86_THREAD_STATE.1 HAS_CONTENTS
0x0000000000000000->0x0000000000000214 at 0x0000111c: LC_THREAD.x86_FLOAT_STATE.1 HAS_CONTENTS
0x0000000000000000->0x0000000000000018 at 0x00001338: LC_THREAD.x86_EXCEPTION_STATE.1 HAS_CONTENTS
0x0000000000000000->0x00000000000000b0 at 0x00001360: LC_THREAD.x86_THREAD_STATE.2 HAS_CONTENTS
0x0000000000000000->0x0000000000000214 at 0x00001418: LC_THREAD.x86_FLOAT_STATE.2 HAS_CONTENTS
0x0000000000000000->0x0000000000000018 at 0x00001634: LC_THREAD.x86_EXCEPTION_STATE.2 HAS_CONTENTS
0x0000000000000000->0x00000000000000b0 at 0x0000165c: LC_THREAD.x86_THREAD_STATE.3 HAS_CONTENTS
0x0000000000000000->0x0000000000000214 at 0x00001714: LC_THREAD.x86_FLOAT_STATE.3 HAS_CONTENTS
0x0000000000000000->0x0000000000000018 at 0x00001930: LC_THREAD.x86_EXCEPTION_STATE.3 HAS_CONTENTS
0x0000000000000000->0x00000000000000b0 at 0x00001958: LC_THREAD.x86_THREAD_STATE.4 HAS_CONTENTS
0x0000000000000000->0x0000000000000214 at 0x00001a10: LC_THREAD.x86_FLOAT_STATE.4 HAS_CONTENTS
0x0000000000000000->0x0000000000000018 at 0x00001c2c: LC_THREAD.x86_EXCEPTION_STATE.4 HAS_CONTENTS
0x0000000000000000->0x00000000000000b0 at 0x00001c54: LC_THREAD.x86_THREAD_STATE.5 HAS_CONTENTS
0x0000000000000000->0x0000000000000214 at 0x00001d0c: LC_THREAD.x86_FLOAT_STATE.5 HAS_CONTENTS
0x0000000000000000->0x0000000000000018 at 0x00001f28: LC_THREAD.x86_EXCEPTION_STATE.5 HAS_CONTENTS
```

5.   Check the currently executing instruction of identified non-waiting core thread 5 (thread #6) and compare stack pointer with stack region boundaries:

```
(gdb) thread 6
[Switching to thread 6 (core thread 5)]
0x000000010a6df615 in procF ()

(gdb) x/i $rip
0x10a6df615 <procF+53>:    callq  0x10a6dfb1c <dyld_stub_memset>

(gdb) x/i 0x10a6dfb1c
0x10a6dfb1c <dyld_stub_memset>: jmpq   *0x53e(%rip)        # 0x10a6e0060

(gdb) info r rsp
rsp            0x10ab06e60 0x10ab06e60
```

```
(gdb) maintenance info sections
Exec file:
    `/Users/DumpAnalysis/Documents/AMCDA-Dumps/Apps/App7/Build/Products/Release/App7', file type mach-o-le.
    0x0000000000000000->0x0000000000000000 at 0x00000000: LC_SEGMENT.__PAGEZERO ALLOC LOAD CODE HAS_CONTENTS
    0x0000000100000000->0x0000000100002000 at 0x00000000: LC_SEGMENT.__TEXT ALLOC LOAD CODE HAS_CONTENTS
    0x00000001000015a0->0x0000000100001b03 at 0x000015a0: LC_SEGMENT.__TEXT.__text ALLOC LOAD READONLY CODE
HAS_CONTENTS
    0x0000000100001b04->0x0000000100001b2e at 0x00001b04: LC_SEGMENT.__TEXT.__stubs ALLOC LOAD CODE HAS_CONTENTS
    0x0000000100001b30->0x0000000100001b86 at 0x00001b30: LC_SEGMENT.__TEXT.__stub_helper ALLOC LOAD CODE HAS_CONTENTS
    0x0000000100001b90->0x0000000100001bf4 at 0x00001b90: LC_SEGMENT.__TEXT.__const ALLOC LOAD CODE HAS_CONTENTS
    0x0000000100001bf4->0x0000000100001bfe at 0x00001bf4: LC_SEGMENT.__TEXT.__cstring ALLOC LOAD CODE HAS_CONTENTS
    0x0000000100001bfe->0x0000000100001c4e at 0x00001bfe: LC_SEGMENT.__TEXT.__unwind_info ALLOC LOAD CODE HAS_CONTENTS
    0x0000000100001c50->0x0000000100002000 at 0x00001c50: LC_SEGMENT.__TEXT.__eh_frame ALLOC LOAD CODE HAS_CONTENTS
    0x0000000100002000->0x0000000100003000 at 0x00002000: LC_SEGMENT.__DATA ALLOC LOAD CODE HAS_CONTENTS
    0x0000000100002000->0x0000000100002028 at 0x00002000: LC_SEGMENT.__DATA.__program_vars ALLOC LOAD CODE
HAS_CONTENTS
    0x0000000100002028->0x0000000100002038 at 0x00002028: LC_SEGMENT.__DATA.__nl_symbol_ptr ALLOC LOAD CODE
HAS_CONTENTS
    0x0000000100002038->0x0000000100002040 at 0x00002038: LC_SEGMENT.__DATA.__got ALLOC LOAD CODE HAS_CONTENTS
    0x0000000100002040->0x0000000100002078 at 0x00002040: LC_SEGMENT.__DATA.__la_symbol_ptr ALLOC LOAD CODE
HAS_CONTENTS
    0x0000000100002078->0x0000000100002098 at 0x00000000: LC_SEGMENT.__DATA.__common ALLOC
    0x0000000100003000->0x0000000100003584 at 0x00003000: LC_SEGMENT.__LINKEDIT ALLOC LOAD CODE HAS_CONTENTS
    0x0000000000000000->0x0000000000000260 at 0x00003140: LC_SYMTAB.stabs HAS_CONTENTS
    0x0000000000000000->0x00000000000001a0 at 0x000033e4: LC_SYMTAB.stabstr HAS_CONTENTS
    0x0000000000000000->0x0000000000000170 at 0x00003140: LC_DYSYMTAB.localstabs HAS_CONTENTS
    0x0000000000000000->0x00000000000000f0 at 0x000032b0: LC_DYSYMTAB.nonlocalstabs HAS_CONTENTS
    0x0000000000000000->0x0000000000000018 at 0x000005a0: LC_LOAD_DYLINKER HAS_CONTENTS
    0x0000000000000000->0x00000000000000a8 at 0x000005f0: LC_THREAD.x86_THREAD_STATE64.0 HAS_CONTENTS
    0x0000000000000000->0x0000000000000030 at 0x000006a0: LC_LOAD_DYLIB HAS_CONTENTS
Core file:
    `/Users/DumpAnalysis/Documents/AMCDA-Dumps/core.3971', file type mach-o-le.
    0x000000010a6de000->0x000000010a6e0000 at 0x00002000: LC_SEGMENT. ALLOC LOAD CODE HAS_CONTENTS
    0x000000010a6e0000->0x000000010a6e1000 at 0x00004000: LC_SEGMENT. ALLOC LOAD CODE HAS_CONTENTS
    0x000000010a6e1000->0x000000010a6e2000 at 0x00005000: LC_SEGMENT. ALLOC LOAD CODE HAS_CONTENTS
    0x000000010a6e2000->0x000000010a6e3000 at 0x00006000: LC_SEGMENT. ALLOC LOAD CODE HAS_CONTENTS
    0x000000010a6e3000->0x000000010a6e4000 at 0x00007000: LC_SEGMENT. ALLOC LOAD CODE HAS_CONTENTS
    0x000000010a6e4000->0x000000010a6e5000 at 0x00008000: LC_SEGMENT. ALLOC LOAD CODE HAS_CONTENTS
    0x000000010a6e5000->0x000000010a6fa000 at 0x00009000: LC_SEGMENT. ALLOC LOAD CODE HAS_CONTENTS
    0x000000010a6fa000->0x000000010a6fb000 at 0x0001e000: LC_SEGMENT. ALLOC LOAD CODE HAS_CONTENTS
    0x000000010a6fb000->0x000000010a6fc000 at 0x0001f000: LC_SEGMENT. ALLOC LOAD CODE HAS_CONTENTS
    0x000000010a6fc000->0x000000010a711000 at 0x00020000: LC_SEGMENT. ALLOC LOAD CODE HAS_CONTENTS
    0x000000010a711000->0x000000010a712000 at 0x00035000: LC_SEGMENT. ALLOC LOAD CODE HAS_CONTENTS
    0x000000010a712000->0x000000010a713000 at 0x00036000: LC_SEGMENT. ALLOC LOAD CODE HAS_CONTENTS
    0x000000010a713000->0x000000010a714000 at 0x00037000: LC_SEGMENT. ALLOC LOAD CODE HAS_CONTENTS
    0x000000010a714000->0x000000010a796000 at 0x00038000: LC_SEGMENT. ALLOC LOAD CODE HAS_CONTENTS
    0x000000010a800000->0x000000010a900000 at 0x000ba000: LC_SEGMENT. ALLOC LOAD CODE HAS_CONTENTS
    0x000000010a900000->0x000000010a901000 at 0x001ba000: LC_SEGMENT. ALLOC LOAD CODE HAS_CONTENTS
    0x000000010a901000->0x000000010a983000 at 0x001bb000: LC_SEGMENT. ALLOC LOAD CODE HAS_CONTENTS
    0x000000010a983000->0x000000010a984000 at 0x0023d000: LC_SEGMENT. ALLOC LOAD CODE HAS_CONTENTS
    0x000000010a984000->0x000000010aa06000 at 0x0023e000: LC_SEGMENT. ALLOC LOAD CODE HAS_CONTENTS
    0x000000010aa06000->0x000000010aa07000 at 0x002c0000: LC_SEGMENT. ALLOC LOAD CODE HAS_CONTENTS
    0x000000010aa07000->0x000000010aa89000 at 0x002c1000: LC_SEGMENT. ALLOC LOAD CODE HAS_CONTENTS
    0x000000010aa89000->0x000000010aa8a000 at 0x00343000: LC_SEGMENT. ALLOC LOAD CODE HAS_CONTENTS
    0x000000010aa8a000->0x000000010ab0c000 at 0x00344000: LC_SEGMENT. ALLOC LOAD CODE HAS_CONTENTS
    0x00007fff662de000->0x00007fff69ade000 at 0x003c6000: LC_SEGMENT. ALLOC LOAD CODE HAS_CONTENTS
    0x00007fff69ade000->0x00007fff6a2dd000 at 0x03bc6000: LC_SEGMENT. ALLOC LOAD CODE HAS_CONTENTS
    0x00007fff6a2dd000->0x00007fff6a2de000 at 0x043c5000: LC_SEGMENT. ALLOC LOAD CODE HAS_CONTENTS
    0x00007fff6a2de000->0x00007fff6a313000 at 0x043c6000: LC_SEGMENT. ALLOC LOAD CODE HAS_CONTENTS
    0x00007fff6a313000->0x00007fff6a315000 at 0x043fb000: LC_SEGMENT. ALLOC LOAD CODE HAS_CONTENTS
    0x00007fff6a315000->0x00007fff6a34f000 at 0x043fd000: LC_SEGMENT. ALLOC LOAD CODE HAS_CONTENTS
    0x00007fff6a34f000->0x00007fff6a362000 at 0x04437000: LC_SEGMENT. ALLOC LOAD CODE HAS_CONTENTS
    0x00007fff749b8000->0x00007fff74a00000 at 0x0444a000: LC_SEGMENT. ALLOC LOAD CODE HAS_CONTENTS
    0x00007fff74a00000->0x00007fff74c00000 at 0x04492000: LC_SEGMENT. ALLOC LOAD CODE HAS_CONTENTS
    0x00007fff74c00000->0x00007fff74e00000 at 0x04692000: LC_SEGMENT. ALLOC LOAD CODE HAS_CONTENTS
    0x00007fff74e00000->0x00007fff75000000 at 0x04892000: LC_SEGMENT. ALLOC LOAD CODE HAS_CONTENTS
    0x00007fff75000000->0x00007fff75200000 at 0x04a92000: LC_SEGMENT. ALLOC LOAD CODE HAS_CONTENTS
    0x00007fff75200000->0x00007fff75400000 at 0x04c92000: LC_SEGMENT. ALLOC LOAD CODE HAS_CONTENTS
    0x00007fff75400000->0x00007fff75600000 at 0x04e92000: LC_SEGMENT. ALLOC LOAD CODE HAS_CONTENTS
    0x00007fff75600000->0x00007fff75800000 at 0x05092000: LC_SEGMENT. ALLOC LOAD CODE HAS_CONTENTS
    0x00007fff75800000->0x00007fff75a00000 at 0x05292000: LC_SEGMENT. ALLOC LOAD CODE HAS_CONTENTS
    0x00007fff75a00000->0x00007fff75c00000 at 0x05492000: LC_SEGMENT. ALLOC LOAD CODE HAS_CONTENTS
    0x00007fff75c00000->0x00007fff75e00000 at 0x05692000: LC_SEGMENT. ALLOC LOAD CODE HAS_CONTENTS
    0x00007fff75e00000->0x00007fff76200000 at 0x05892000: LC_SEGMENT. ALLOC LOAD CODE HAS_CONTENTS
    0x00007fff76200000->0x00007fff76400000 at 0x05c92000: LC_SEGMENT. ALLOC LOAD CODE HAS_CONTENTS
    0x00007fff76400000->0x00007fff764ac000 at 0x05e92000: LC_SEGMENT. ALLOC LOAD CODE HAS_CONTENTS
```

```
0x00007fff849b8000->0x00007fff91a28000 at 0x05f3e000: LC_SEGMENT. ALLOC LOAD CODE HAS_CONTENTS
0x00007fff91a28000->0x00007fff94b30000 at 0x12fae000: LC_SEGMENT. ALLOC LOAD CODE HAS_CONTENTS
0x00007ffffffe00000->0x00007ffffffe02000 at 0x160b6000: LC_SEGMENT. ALLOC LOAD CODE HAS_CONTENTS
0x0000000000000000->0x00000000000000b0 at 0x00000d68: LC_THREAD.x86_THREAD_STATE.0 HAS_CONTENTS
0x0000000000000000->0x0000000000000214 at 0x00000e20: LC_THREAD.x86_FLOAT_STATE.0 HAS_CONTENTS
0x0000000000000000->0x0000000000000018 at 0x0000103c: LC_THREAD.x86_EXCEPTION_STATE.0 HAS_CONTENTS
0x0000000000000000->0x00000000000000b0 at 0x00001064: LC_THREAD.x86_THREAD_STATE.1 HAS_CONTENTS
0x0000000000000000->0x0000000000000214 at 0x0000111c: LC_THREAD.x86_FLOAT_STATE.1 HAS_CONTENTS
0x0000000000000000->0x0000000000000018 at 0x00001338: LC_THREAD.x86_EXCEPTION_STATE.1 HAS_CONTENTS
0x0000000000000000->0x00000000000000b0 at 0x00001360: LC_THREAD.x86_THREAD_STATE.2 HAS_CONTENTS
0x0000000000000000->0x0000000000000214 at 0x00001418: LC_THREAD.x86_FLOAT_STATE.2 HAS_CONTENTS
0x0000000000000000->0x0000000000000018 at 0x00001634: LC_THREAD.x86_EXCEPTION_STATE.2 HAS_CONTENTS
0x0000000000000000->0x00000000000000b0 at 0x0000165c: LC_THREAD.x86_THREAD_STATE.3 HAS_CONTENTS
0x0000000000000000->0x0000000000000214 at 0x00001714: LC_THREAD.x86_FLOAT_STATE.3 HAS_CONTENTS
0x0000000000000000->0x0000000000000018 at 0x00001930: LC_THREAD.x86_EXCEPTION_STATE.3 HAS_CONTENTS
0x0000000000000000->0x00000000000000b0 at 0x00001958: LC_THREAD.x86_THREAD_STATE.4 HAS_CONTENTS
0x0000000000000000->0x0000000000000214 at 0x00001a10: LC_THREAD.x86_FLOAT_STATE.4 HAS_CONTENTS
0x0000000000000000->0x0000000000000018 at 0x00001c2c: LC_THREAD.x86_EXCEPTION_STATE.4 HAS_CONTENTS
0x0000000000000000->0x00000000000000b0 at 0x00001c54: LC_THREAD.x86_THREAD_STATE.5 HAS_CONTENTS
0x0000000000000000->0x0000000000000214 at 0x00001d0c: LC_THREAD.x86_FLOAT_STATE.5 HAS_CONTENTS
0x0000000000000000->0x0000000000000018 at 0x00001f28: LC_THREAD.x86_EXCEPTION_STATE.5 HAS_CONTENTS
```

Exercise A7 (LLDB)

- **Goal:** Learn how to identify active threads

- **Patterns:** Divide by Zero, Active Thread

- \AMCDA-Dumps\Exercise-A7-LLDB.pdf

Exercise A7 (LLDB)

Goal: Learn how to identify active threads

Patterns: Divide by Zero, Active Thread

1.   Identify the problem thread and application specific diagnostic from the diagnostic report App7_3971.crash (including non-waiting threads):

```
Process:         App7 [3971]
Path:            /Users/USER/Documents/*/App7
Identifier:      App7
Version:         ??? (???)
Code Type:       X86-64 (Native)
Parent Process:  bash [1549]

Date/Time:       2012-07-25 19:25:40.165 +0100
OS Version:      Mac OS X 10.7.4 (11E53)
Report Version:  9
Sleep/Wake UUID: 4C0A9B6D-7E93-4764-8BC3-971D136863D8

Crashed Thread:  3

Exception Type:  EXC_ARITHMETIC (SIGFPE)
Exception Codes: EXC_I386_DIV (divide by zero)

Thread 0:: Dispatch queue: com.apple.main-thread
0   libsystem_kernel.dylib          0x00007fff8a10ce42 __semwait_signal + 10
1   libsystem_c.dylib               0x00007fff84d6edea nanosleep + 164
2   libsystem_c.dylib               0x00007fff84d6ec2c sleep + 61
3   libsystem_c.dylib               0x00007fff84d6ec08 sleep + 25
4   App7                            0x000000010a6dfaf3 main + 195
5   App7                            0x000000010a6df5d4 start + 52

Thread 1:
0   libsystem_c.dylib               0x00007fff84dc99f0 _simple_asl_init + 0
1   libsystem_c.dylib               0x00007fff84db7e06 pthread_once + 86
2   libsystem_c.dylib               0x00007fff84dca53d _simple_asl_log_prog + 48
3   libsystem_c.dylib               0x00007fff84da8064 __stack_chk_fail + 211
4   App7                            0x000000010a6df817 procA + 87

Thread 2:
0   libsystem_kernel.dylib          0x00007fff8a10ce42 __semwait_signal + 10
1   libsystem_c.dylib               0x00007fff84d6edea nanosleep + 164
2   libsystem_c.dylib               0x00007fff84d6ec2c sleep + 61
3   libsystem_c.dylib               0x00007fff84d6ec08 sleep + 25
4   App7                            0x000000010a6df89f bar_two + 31
5   App7                            0x000000010a6df8b9 foo_two + 9
6   App7                            0x000000010a6df8d1 thread_two + 17
7   libsystem_c.dylib               0x00007fff84db88bf _pthread_start + 335
8   libsystem_c.dylib               0x00007fff84dbbb75 thread_start + 13

Thread 3 Crashed:
0   App7                            0x000000010a6df68e procD + 14
1   App7                            0x000000010a6df6b3 procC + 19
2   App7                            0x000000010a6df90a bar_three + 26
3   App7                            0x000000010a6df929 foo_three + 9
4   App7                            0x000000010a6df941 thread_three + 17
5   libsystem_c.dylib               0x00007fff84db88bf _pthread_start + 335
6   libsystem_c.dylib               0x00007fff84dbbb75 thread_start + 13
```

```
Thread 4:
0   libsystem_kernel.dylib          0x00007fff8a10ce42 __semwait_signal + 10
1   libsystem_c.dylib               0x00007fff84d6edea nanosleep + 164
2   libsystem_c.dylib               0x00007fff84d6ec2c sleep + 61
3   libsystem_c.dylib               0x00007fff84d6ec08 sleep + 25
4   App7                            0x000000010a6df97f bar_four + 31
5   App7                            0x000000010a6df999 foo_four + 9
6   App7                            0x000000010a6df9b1 thread_four + 17
7   libsystem_c.dylib               0x00007fff84db88bf _pthread_start + 335
8   libsystem_c.dylib               0x00007fff84dbbb75 thread_start + 13

Thread 5:
0   App7                            0x000000010a6df615 procF + 53
1   App7                            0x000000010a6df648 procF + 104
2   App7                            0x000000010a6df648 procF + 104
3   App7                            0x000000010a6df67e procE + 14
4   App7                            0x000000010a6df9ea bar_five + 26
5   App7                            0x000000010a6df9f9 foo_five + 9
6   App7                            0x000000010a6dfa11 thread_five + 17
7   libsystem_c.dylib               0x00007fff84db88bf _pthread_start + 335
8   libsystem_c.dylib               0x00007fff84dbbb75 thread_start + 13

Thread 3 crashed with X86 Thread State (64-bit):
  rax: 0x0000000000000001  rbx: 0x0000000000000000  rcx: 0x00007fff8a10ce42  rdx: 0x0000000000000000
  rdi: 0x0000000000000001  rsi: 0x0000000000000000  rbp: 0x000000010aa03eb0  rsp: 0x000000010aa03eb0
   r8: 0x000000000000012c   r9: 0x0000000000000000  r10: 0x0000000000000001  r11: 0x00007fff75284228
  r12: 0x0000000000001403  r13: 0x000000010aa04000  r14: 0x0000000000000000  r15: 0x000000010a6df930
  rip: 0x000000010a6df68e  rfl: 0x0000000000010206  cr2: 0x0000000108ded000
Logical CPU: 1

Binary Images:
       0x10a6de000 -        0x10a6dffff +App7 (??? - ???) <47049673-762D-31BE-9669-4095FEF620D5>
/Users/USER/Documents/*/App7
    0x7fff6a2de000 -     0x7fff6a312baf  dyld (195.6 - ???) <0CD1B35B-A28F-32DA-B72E-452EAD609613> /usr/lib/dyld
    0x7fff849f2000 -     0x7fff84a0ffff  libxpc.dylib (77.19.0 - compatibility 1.0.0) <9F57891B-D7EF-3050-BEDD-
21E7C6668248> /usr/lib/system/libxpc.dylib
    0x7fff84d68000 -     0x7fff84d69ff7  libsystem_blocks.dylib (53.0.0 - compatibility 1.0.0) <8BCA214A-8992-34B2-
A8B9-B74DEACA1869> /usr/lib/system/libsystem_blocks.dylib
    0x7fff84d6a000 -     0x7fff84e47fef  libsystem_c.dylib (763.13.0 - compatibility 1.0.0) <41B43515-2806-3FBC-ACF1-
A16F35B7E290> /usr/lib/system/libsystem_c.dylib
    0x7fff85022000 -     0x7fff85030fff  libdispatch.dylib (187.9.0 - compatibility 1.0.0) <1D5BE322-A9B9-3BCE-8FAC-
076FB07CF54A> /usr/lib/system/libdispatch.dylib
    0x7fff855f0000 -     0x7fff855f1fff  libunc.dylib (24.0.0 - compatibility 1.0.0) <337960EE-0A85-3DD0-A760-
7134CF4C0AFF> /usr/lib/system/libunc.dylib
    0x7fff85ae3000 -     0x7fff85ae4ff7  libremovefile.dylib (21.1.0 - compatibility 1.0.0) <739E6C83-AA52-3C6C-A680-
B37FE2888A04> /usr/lib/system/libremovefile.dylib
    0x7fff89114000 -     0x7fff89118fff  libmathCommon.A.dylib (2026.0.0 - compatibility 1.0.0) <FF83AFF7-42B2-306E-
90AF-D539C51A4542> /usr/lib/system/libmathCommon.A.dylib
    0x7fff89119000 -     0x7fff8911dfff  libdyld.dylib (195.5.0 - compatibility 1.0.0) <380C3F44-0CA7-3514-8080-
46D1C9DF4FCD> /usr/lib/system/libdyld.dylib
    0x7fff89740000 -     0x7fff89741ff7  libsystem_sandbox.dylib (??? - ???) <96D38E74-F18F-3CCB-A20B-E8E3ADC4E166>
/usr/lib/system/libsystem_sandbox.dylib
    0x7fff8a0ef000 -     0x7fff8a0f5ff7  libmacho.dylib (800.0.0 - compatibility 1.0.0) <165514D7-1BFA-38EF-A151-
676DCD21FB64> /usr/lib/system/libmacho.dylib
    0x7fff8a0f6000 -     0x7fff8a116fff  libsystem_kernel.dylib (1699.26.8 - compatibility 1.0.0) <1DDC0B0F-DB2A-34D6-
895D-E5B2B5618946> /usr/lib/system/libsystem_kernel.dylib
    0x7fff8a2ac000 -     0x7fff8a2b4fff  libsystem_dnssd.dylib (??? - ???) <D9BB1F87-A42B-3CBC-9DC2-FC07FCEF0016>
/usr/lib/system/libsystem_dnssd.dylib
    0x7fff8ae26000 -     0x7fff8ae61fff  libsystem_info.dylib (??? - ???) <35F90252-2AE1-32C5-8D34-782C614D9639>
/usr/lib/system/libsystem_info.dylib
    0x7fff8b248000 -     0x7fff8b24afff  libquarantine.dylib (36.6.0 - compatibility 1.0.0) <0EBF714B-4B69-3E1F-9A7D-
6BBC2AACB310> /usr/lib/system/libquarantine.dylib
    0x7fff8b3b4000 -     0x7fff8b3b4fff  libkeymgr.dylib (23.0.0 - compatibility 1.0.0) <61EFED6A-A407-301E-B454-
CD18314F0075> /usr/lib/system/libkeymgr.dylib
    0x7fff8b3dd000 -     0x7fff8b3e2fff  libcompiler_rt.dylib (6.0.0 - compatibility 1.0.0) <98ECD5F6-E85C-32A5-98CD-
8911230CB66A> /usr/lib/system/libcompiler_rt.dylib
    0x7fff8bd1a000 -     0x7fff8bd1bfff  libdnsinfo.dylib (395.11.0 - compatibility 1.0.0) <853BAAA5-270F-3FDC-B025-
D448DB72E1C3> /usr/lib/system/libdnsinfo.dylib
    0x7fff8c528000 -     0x7fff8c52dff7  libsystem_network.dylib (??? - ???) <5DE7024E-1D2D-34A2-80F4-08326331A75B>
/usr/lib/system/libsystem_network.dylib
    0x7fff8cfa3000 -     0x7fff8cfadff7  liblaunch.dylib (392.38.0 - compatibility 1.0.0) <6ECB7F19-B384-32C1-8652-
2463C1CF4815> /usr/lib/system/liblaunch.dylib
    0x7fff8fe02000 -     0x7fff8fe09fff  libcopyfile.dylib (85.1.0 - compatibility 1.0.0) <0AB51EE2-E914-358C-AC19-
47BC024BDAE7> /usr/lib/system/libcopyfile.dylib
    0x7fff8fe4b000 -     0x7fff8fe8dff7  libcommonCrypto.dylib (55010.0.0 - compatibility 1.0.0) <BB770C22-8C57-365A-
8716-4A3C36AE7BFB> /usr/lib/system/libcommonCrypto.dylib
```

```
    0x7fff90c0f000 -     0x7fff90c18ff7  libsystem_notify.dylib (80.1.0 - compatibility 1.0.0) <A4D651E3-D1C6-3934-
AD49-7A104FD14596> /usr/lib/system/libsystem_notify.dylib
    0x7fff91376000 -     0x7fff913a3fe7  libSystem.B.dylib (159.1.0 - compatibility 1.0.0) <7BEBB139-50BB-3112-947A-
F4AA168F991C> /usr/lib/libSystem.B.dylib
    0x7fff91489000 -     0x7fff9148fff7  libunwind.dylib (30.0.0 - compatibility 1.0.0) <1E9C6C8C-CBE8-3F4B-A5B5-
E03E3AB53231> /usr/lib/system/libunwind.dylib
    0x7fff91a22000 -     0x7fff91a27fff  libcache.dylib (47.0.0 - compatibility 1.0.0) <1571C3AB-BCB2-38CD-B3B2-
C5FC3F927C6A> /usr/lib/system/libcache.dylib

External Modification Summary:
  Calls made by other processes targeting this process:
    task_for_pid: 2
    thread_create: 0
    thread_set_state: 0
  Calls made by this process:
    task_for_pid: 0
    thread_create: 0
    thread_set_state: 0
  Calls made by all processes on this machine:
    task_for_pid: 6380
    thread_create: 0
    thread_set_state: 0

VM Region Summary:
ReadOnly portion of Libraries: Total=50.2M resident=50.2M(100%) swapped_out_or_unallocated=0K(0%)
Writable regions: Total=38.9M written=12.8M(33%) resident=42.6M(110%) swapped_out=0K(0%)
unallocated=16777216.0T(45221404475392%)

REGION TYPE            VIRTUAL
===========            =======
MALLOC                   1220K
Stack                    66.6M
__DATA                    464K
__LINKEDIT               47.7M
__TEXT                   2488K
shared memory              12K
===========            =======
TOTAL                   118.4M
```

2.   Load a core dump core.3971 and App7 executable:

$ lldb -c ~/Documents/AMCDA-Dumps/core.3971 -f ~/Documents/AMCDA-Dumps/Apps/App7/Build/Products/Release/App7

error: core.3971 is a corrupt mach-o file: load command 46 LC_SEGMENT_64 has a fileoff + filesize (0x160b8000) that extends beyond the end of the file (0x160b6000), the segment will be truncated

Core file '/Users/DumpAnalysis/Documents/AMCDA-Dumps/core.3971' (x86_64) was loaded.
Process 0 stopped
* thread #1: tid = 0x0000, 0x00007fff8a10ce42 libsystem_kernel.dylib`__semwait_signal + 10, stop reason = signal SIGSTOP
    frame #0: 0x00007fff8a10ce42 libsystem_kernel.dylib`__semwait_signal + 10
libsystem_kernel.dylib`__semwait_signal + 10:
-> 0x7fff8a10ce42: jae   0x7fff8a10ce49   ; __semwait_signal + 17
   0x7fff8a10ce44: jmpq   0x7fff8a10dffc   ; cerror
   0x7fff8a10ce49: ret
   0x7fff8a10ce4a: nop

```
  thread #2: tid = 0x0001, 0x00007fff84dc99f0 libsystem_c.dylib`_simple_asl_init, stop reason =
signal SIGSTOP
    frame #0: 0x00007fff84dc99f0 libsystem_c.dylib`_simple_asl_init
libsystem_c.dylib`_simple_asl_init:
-> 0x7fff84dc99f0:  pushq  %rbp
   0x7fff84dc99f1:  movq   %rsp, %rbp
   0x7fff84dc99f4:  cmpl   $0, -271961711(%rip)       ; stack_logging_spin_lock + 3
   0x7fff84dc99fb:  jne    0x7fff84dc9a4b             ; _simple_asl_init + 91
  thread #3: tid = 0x0002, 0x00007fff8a10ce42 libsystem_kernel.dylib`__semwait_signal + 10,
stop reason = signal SIGSTOP
    frame #0: 0x00007fff8a10ce42 libsystem_kernel.dylib`__semwait_signal + 10
libsystem_kernel.dylib`__semwait_signal + 10:
-> 0x7fff8a10ce42:  jae    0x7fff8a10ce49             ; __semwait_signal + 17
   0x7fff8a10ce44:  jmpq   0x7fff8a10dffc             ; cerror
   0x7fff8a10ce49:  ret
   0x7fff8a10ce4a:  nop
  thread #4: tid = 0x0003, 0x000000010a6df68e App7`procD + 14, stop reason = signal SIGSTOP
    frame #0: 0x000000010a6df68e App7`procD + 14
App7`procD + 14:
-> 0x10a6df68e:  idivl  %esi
   0x10a6df690:  movl   %esi, -12(%rbp)
   0x10a6df693:  popq   %rbp
   0x10a6df694:  ret
  thread #5: tid = 0x0004, 0x00007fff8a10ce42 libsystem_kernel.dylib`__semwait_signal + 10,
stop reason = signal SIGSTOP
    frame #0: 0x00007fff8a10ce42 libsystem_kernel.dylib`__semwait_signal + 10
libsystem_kernel.dylib`__semwait_signal + 10:
-> 0x7fff8a10ce42:  jae    0x7fff8a10ce49             ; __semwait_signal + 17
   0x7fff8a10ce44:  jmpq   0x7fff8a10dffc             ; cerror
   0x7fff8a10ce49:  ret
   0x7fff8a10ce4a:  nop
  thread #6: tid = 0x0005, 0x000000010a6df615 App7`procF + 53, stop reason = signal SIGSTOP
    frame #0: 0x000000010a6df615 App7`procF + 53
App7`procF + 53:
-> 0x10a6df615:  callq  0x10a6dfb1c                   ; symbol stub for: memset
   0x10a6df61a:  movl   $4294967295, -4112(%rbp)
   0x10a6df624:  movl   -12(%rbp), %esi
   0x10a6df627:  addl   $1, %esi
```

3.   Go to the problem core thread 3 (thread #4) that was reported as *crashed* and identify the problem
instruction:

```
(lldb) thread select 4
* thread #4: tid = 0x0003, 0x000000010a6df68e App7`procD + 14, stop reason = signal SIGSTOP
    frame #0: 0x000000010a6df68e App7`procD + 14
App7`procD + 14:
-> 0x10a6df68e:  idivl  %esi
   0x10a6df690:  movl   %esi, -12(%rbp)
   0x10a6df693:  popq   %rbp
   0x10a6df694:  ret
```

Note: Another way is to inspect the current instruction pointer:

```
(lldb) x/i $rip
0x10a6df68e:  f7 fe  idivl  %esi
```

Note: Now check the divisor (**esi** is a 32-bit part of 64-bit **rsi** register):

```
(lldb) re r rsi
    rsi = 0x0000000000000000
```

4.   Check the currently executing instruction of identified non-waiting core thread 1 (thread #2) and compare stack pointer with stack region boundaries:

```
(lldb) thread select 2
* thread #2: tid = 0x0001, 0x00007fff84dc99f0 libsystem_c.dylib`_simple_asl_init, stop reason =
signal SIGSTOP
    frame #0: 0x00007fff84dc99f0 libsystem_c.dylib`_simple_asl_init
libsystem_c.dylib`_simple_asl_init:
-> 0x7fff84dc99f0:  pushq   %rbp
   0x7fff84dc99f1:  movq    %rsp, %rbp
   0x7fff84dc99f4:  cmpl    $0, -271961711(%rip)        ; stack_logging_spin_lock + 3
   0x7fff84dc99fb:  jne     0x7fff84dc9a4b              ; _simple_asl_init + 91
```

```
(lldb) re r rsp
    rsp = 0x000000010a793d78
```

Note: We can see stack regions in vmmap_3971.log:

```
Virtual Memory Map of process 3971 (App7)
Output report format:  2.2  -- 64-bit process

==== Non-writable regions for process 3971
__TEXT                 000000010a6de000-000000010a6e0000 [    8K] r-x/rwx SM=COW  /Users/DumpAnalysis/Documents/AMCDA-
Dumps/Apps/App7/Build/Products/Release/App7
__LINKEDIT             000000010a6e1000-000000010a6e2000 [    4K] r--/rwx SM=COW  /Users/DumpAnalysis/Documents/AMCDA-
Dumps/Apps/App7/Build/Products/Release/App7
MALLOC metadata        000000010a6e2000-000000010a6e3000 [    4K] r--/rwx SM=ZER
MALLOC guard page      000000010a6e4000-000000010a6e5000 [    4K] ---/rwx SM=NUL
MALLOC guard page      000000010a6fa000-000000010a6fc000 [    8K] ---/rwx SM=NUL
MALLOC guard page      000000010a711000-000000010a712000 [    4K] ---/rwx SM=NUL
MALLOC metadata        000000010a712000-000000010a713000 [    4K] r--/rwx SM=PRV
STACK GUARD            000000010a713000-000000010a714000 [    4K] ---/rwx SM=NUL  stack guard for thread 1
STACK GUARD            000000010a900000-000000010a901000 [    4K] ---/rwx SM=NUL  stack guard for thread 2
STACK GUARD            000000010a983000-000000010a984000 [    4K] ---/rwx SM=NUL  stack guard for thread 3
STACK GUARD            000000010aa06000-000000010aa07000 [    4K] ---/rwx SM=NUL  stack guard for thread 4
STACK GUARD            000000010aa89000-000000010aa8a000 [    4K] ---/rwx SM=NUL  stack guard for thread 5
STACK GUARD            00007fff662de000-00007fff69ade000 [  56.0M] ---/rwx SM=NUL  stack guard for thread 0
__TEXT                 00007fff6a2de000-00007fff6a313000 [  212K] r-x/rwx SM=COW  /usr/lib/dyld
__LINKEDIT             00007fff6a34f000-00007fff6a362000 [   76K] r--/rwx SM=COW  /usr/lib/dyld
__TEXT                 00007fff849f2000-00007fff84a10000 [  120K] r-x/r-x SM=COW  /usr/lib/system/libxpc.dylib
__TEXT                 00007fff84d68000-00007fff84d6a000 [    8K] r-x/r-x SM=COW
/usr/lib/system/libsystem_blocks.dylib
__TEXT                 00007fff84d6a000-00007fff84e48000 [  888K] r-x/r-x SM=COW  /usr/lib/system/libsystem_c.dylib
__TEXT                 00007fff85022000-00007fff85031000 [   60K] r-x/r-x SM=COW  /usr/lib/system/libdispatch.dylib
__TEXT                 00007fff855f0000-00007fff855f2000 [    8K] r-x/r-x SM=COW  /usr/lib/system/libunc.dylib
__TEXT                 00007fff85ae3000-00007fff85ae5000 [    8K] r-x/r-x SM=COW  /usr/lib/system/libremovefile.dylib
__TEXT                 00007fff89114000-00007fff89119000 [   20K] r-x/r-x SM=COW
/usr/lib/system/libmathCommon.A.dylib
__TEXT                 00007fff89119000-00007fff8911e000 [   20K] r-x/r-x SM=COW  /usr/lib/system/libdyld.dylib
__TEXT                 00007fff89740000-00007fff89742000 [    8K] r-x/r-x SM=COW
/usr/lib/system/libsystem_sandbox.dylib
__TEXT                 00007fff8a0ef000-00007fff8a0f6000 [   28K] r-x/r-x SM=COW  /usr/lib/system/libmacho.dylib
__TEXT                 00007fff8a0f6000-00007fff8a117000 [  132K] r-x/r-x SM=COW
/usr/lib/system/libsystem_kernel.dylib
__TEXT                 00007fff8a2ac000-00007fff8a2b5000 [   36K] r-x/r-x SM=COW
/usr/lib/system/libsystem_dnssd.dylib
__TEXT                 00007fff8ae26000-00007fff8ae62000 [  240K] r-x/r-x SM=COW  /usr/lib/system/libsystem_info.dylib
__TEXT                 00007fff8b248000-00007fff8b24b000 [   12K] r-x/r-x SM=COW  /usr/lib/system/libquarantine.dylib
__TEXT                 00007fff8b3b4000-00007fff8b3b5000 [    4K] r-x/r-x SM=COW  /usr/lib/system/libkeymgr.dylib
```

```
__TEXT              00007fff8b3dd000-00007fff8b3e3000 [   24K] r-x/r-x SM=COW  /usr/lib/system/libcompiler_rt.dylib
__TEXT              00007fff8bd1a000-00007fff8bd1c000 [    8K] r-x/r-x SM=COW  /usr/lib/system/libdnsinfo.dylib
__TEXT              00007fff8c528000-00007fff8c52e000 [   24K] r-x/r-x SM=COW
/usr/lib/system/libsystem_network.dylib
__TEXT              00007fff8cfa3000-00007fff8cfae000 [   44K] r-x/r-x SM=COW  /usr/lib/system/liblaunch.dylib
__TEXT              00007fff8fe02000-00007fff8fe0a000 [   32K] r-x/r-x SM=COW  /usr/lib/system/libcopyfile.dylib
__TEXT              00007fff8fe4b000-00007fff8fe8e000 [  268K] r-x/r-x SM=COW
/usr/lib/system/libcommonCrypto.dylib
__TEXT              00007fff90c0f000-00007fff90c19000 [   40K] r-x/r-x SM=COW
/usr/lib/system/libsystem_notify.dylib
__TEXT              00007fff91376000-00007fff913a4000 [  184K] r-x/r-x SM=COW  /usr/lib/libSystem.B.dylib
__TEXT              00007fff91489000-00007fff91490000 [   28K] r-x/r-x SM=COW  /usr/lib/system/libunwind.dylib
__TEXT              00007fff91a22000-00007fff91a28000 [   24K] r-x/r-x SM=COW  /usr/lib/system/libcache.dylib
__LINKEDIT          00007fff91b86000-00007fff94b30000 [ 47.7M] r--/r-- SM=COW  /usr/lib/system/libxpc.dylib
shared memory       00007ffffffe00000-00007ffffffe02000 [    8K] r-x/r-x SM=SHM

==== Writable regions for process 3971
__DATA              000000010a6e0000-000000010a6e1000 [    4K] rw-/rwx SM=PRV  /Users/DumpAnalysis/Documents/AMCDA-
Dumps/Apps/App7/Build/Products/Release/App7
MALLOC metadata     000000010a6e3000-000000010a6e4000 [    4K] rw-/rwx SM=ZER
MALLOC metadata     000000010a6e5000-000000010a6fa000 [   84K] rw-/rwx SM=PRV
MALLOC metadata     000000010a6fc000-000000010a711000 [   84K] rw-/rwx SM=PRV
Stack               000000010a714000-000000010a796000 [  520K] rw-/rwx SM=PRV  thread 1
MALLOC_TINY         000000010a800000-000000010a900000 [ 1024K] rw-/rwx SM=PRV  DefaultMallocZone_0x10a6e2000
Stack               000000010a901000-000000010a983000 [  520K] rw-/rwx SM=PRV  thread 2
Stack               000000010a984000-000000010aa06000 [  520K] rw-/rwx SM=PRV  thread 3
Stack               000000010aa07000-000000010aa89000 [  520K] rw-/rwx SM=PRV  thread 4
Stack               000000010aa8a000-000000010ab0c000 [  520K] rw-/rwx SM=PRV  thread 5
Stack               00007fff69ade000-00007fff6a2dd000 [ 8188K] rw-/rwx SM=ZER  thread 0
Stack               00007fff6a2dd000-00007fff6a2de000 [    4K] rw-/rwx SM=COW  thread 0
__DATA              00007fff6a313000-00007fff6a34f000 [  240K] rw-/rwx SM=COW  /usr/lib/dyld
__DATA              00007fff749c0000-00007fff749c3000 [   12K] rw-/rwx SM=COW  /usr/lib/system/libxpc.dylib
__DATA              00007fff74a60000-00007fff74a61000 [    4K] rw-/rwx SM=COW
/usr/lib/system/libsystem_blocks.dylib
__DATA              00007fff74a61000-00007fff74a71000 [   64K] rw-/rwx SM=COW  /usr/lib/system/libsystem_c.dylib
__DATA              00007fff74ac4000-00007fff74aca000 [   24K] rw-/rwx SM=COW  /usr/lib/system/libdispatch.dylib
__DATA              00007fff74b90000-00007fff74b91000 [    4K] rw-/rwx SM=COW  /usr/lib/system/libunc.dylib
__DATA              00007fff74c11000-00007fff74c12000 [    4K] rw-/rw- SM=COW  /usr/lib/system/libremovefile.dylib
__DATA              00007fff75141000-00007fff75142000 [    4K] rw-/rwx SM=COW  /usr/lib/system/libdyld.dylib
__DATA              00007fff751a3000-00007fff751a4000 [    4K] rw-/rwx SM=COW
/usr/lib/system/libsystem_sandbox.dylib
__DATA              00007fff75281000-00007fff75282000 [    4K] rw-/rwx SM=COW  /usr/lib/system/libmacho.dylib
__DATA              00007fff75282000-00007fff75285000 [   12K] rw-/rwx SM=COW
/usr/lib/system/libsystem_kernel.dylib
__DATA              00007fff752d8000-00007fff752d9000 [    4K] rw-/rwx SM=COW
/usr/lib/system/libsystem_dnssd.dylib
__DATA              00007fff75453000-00007fff75456000 [   12K] rw-/rwx SM=COW  /usr/lib/system/libsystem_info.dylib
__DATA              00007fff7551f000-00007fff75520000 [    4K] rw-/rwx SM=COW  /usr/lib/system/libquarantine.dylib
__DATA              00007fff75559000-00007fff7555a000 [    4K] rw-/rwx SM=COW  /usr/lib/system/libkeymgr.dylib
__DATA              00007fff75563000-00007fff75564000 [    4K] rw-/rwx SM=COW  /usr/lib/system/libcompiler_rt.dylib
__DATA              00007fff75633000-00007fff75634000 [    4K] rw-/rw- SM=COW  /usr/lib/system/libdnsinfo.dylib
__DATA              00007fff756d6000-00007fff756d7000 [    4K] rw-/rw- SM=COW
/usr/lib/system/libsystem_network.dylib
__DATA              00007fff75813000-00007fff75814000 [    4K] rw-/rwx SM=COW  /usr/lib/system/liblaunch.dylib
__DATA              00007fff75e41000-00007fff75e42000 [    4K] rw-/rw- SM=COW  /usr/lib/system/libcopyfile.dylib
__DATA              00007fff75e4a000-00007fff75e50000 [   24K] rw-/rw- SM=COW
/usr/lib/system/libcommonCrypto.dylib
__DATA              00007fff76342000-00007fff76343000 [    4K] rw-/rw- SM=COW
/usr/lib/system/libsystem_notify.dylib
__DATA              00007fff763fd000-00007fff763fe000 [    4K] rw-/rw- SM=COW  /usr/lib/libSystem.B.dylib
__DATA              00007fff76401000-00007fff76402000 [    4K] rw-/rw- SM=COW  /usr/lib/system/libunwind.dylib
__DATA              00007fff764ab000-00007fff764ac000 [    4K] rw-/rw- SM=COW  /usr/lib/system/libcache.dylib

==== Legend
SM=sharing mode:
        COW=copy_on_write PRV=private NUL=empty ALI=aliased
        SHM=shared ZER=zero_filled S/A=shared_alias

==== Summary for process 3971
ReadOnly portion of Libraries: Total=50.2M resident=50.2M(100%) swapped_out_or_unallocated=0K(0%)
Writable regions: Total=28.6M written=108K(0%) resident=20.6M(72%) swapped_out=0K(0%) unallocated=8244K(28%)
```

```
REGION TYPE              VIRTUAL
===========              =======
MALLOC                     1024K    see MALLOC ZONE table below
MALLOC guard page           16K
MALLOC metadata            180K
STACK GUARD                56.0M
Stack                      10.5M
__DATA                     464K
__LINKEDIT                 47.7M
__TEXT                     2488K
shared memory                8K
===========              =======
TOTAL                     118.4M

                         VIRTUAL ALLOCATION    BYTES
MALLOC ZONE                 SIZE     COUNT  ALLOCATED  % FULL
===========              =======  ========= =========  ======
DefaultMallocZone_0x10a6e2000  1024K        33       2240      0%
```

Note: We see that the value of **RSP** is inside the stack segment so **push** instruction would succeed (this is not a stack overflow case).

5.   Check the currently executing instruction of identified non-waiting core thread 5 (thread #6) and identifiy *call* target:

```
(lldb) thread select 6
* thread #6: tid = 0x0005, 0x000000010a6df615 App7`procF + 53, stop reason = signal SIGSTOP
    frame #0: 0x000000010a6df615 App7`procF + 53
App7`procF + 53:
-> 0x10a6df615:  callq  0x10a6dfb1c                 ; symbol stub for: memset
   0x10a6df61a:  movl   $4294967295, -4112(%rbp)
   0x10a6df624:  movl   -12(%rbp), %esi
   0x10a6df627:  addl   $1, %esi

(lldb) x/i 0x10a6dfb1c
0x10a6dfb1c:  ff 25 3e 05 00 00  jmpq   *1342(%rip)   ; (void *)0x00007fff84e0b5e0: memset
```

Exercise A8 (GDB)

- **Goal:** Learn how to identify runtime exceptions, past execution residue and stack traces, identify handled exceptions

- **Patterns:** C++ Exception, Execution Residue, Coincidental Symbolic Information, Handled Exception

- \AMCDA-Dumps\Exercise-A8-GDB.pdf

Exercise A8 (GDB)

Goal: Learn how to identify runtime exceptions, past execution residue and stack traces, identify handled exceptions

Patterns: C++ Exception, Execution Residue, Coincidental Symbolic Information, Handled Exception

1.   Identify the problem thread and application specific diagnostic from the diagnostic report App8_4472.crash:

```
Process:         App8 [4472]
Path:            /Users/USER/Documents/*/App8
Identifier:      App8
Version:         ??? (???)
Code Type:       X86-64 (Native)
Parent Process:  bash [1549]

Date/Time:       2012-07-25 22:34:17.717 +0100
OS Version:      Mac OS X 10.7.4 (11E53)
Report Version:  9
Sleep/Wake UUID: 4C0A9B6D-7E93-4764-8BC3-971D136863D8

Crashed Thread:  1

Exception Type:  EXC_CRASH (SIGABRT)
Exception Codes: 0x0000000000000000, 0x0000000000000000

Application Specific Information:
terminate called throwing an exception
abort() called

Thread 0:: Dispatch queue: com.apple.main-thread
0   libsystem_kernel.dylib          0x00007fff8a10ce42 __semwait_signal + 10
1   libsystem_c.dylib               0x00007fff84d6edea nanosleep + 164
2   libsystem_c.dylib               0x00007fff84d6ec2c sleep + 61
3   libsystem_c.dylib               0x00007fff84d6ec08 sleep + 25
4   App8                            0x000000010f7f66f3 main + 195
5   App8                            0x000000010f7f6134 start + 52

Thread 1 Crashed:
0   libsystem_kernel.dylib          0x00007fff8a10cce2 __pthread_kill + 10
1   libsystem_c.dylib               0x00007fff84dba7d2 pthread_kill + 95
2   libsystem_c.dylib               0x00007fff84daba7a abort + 143
3   libc++abi.dylib                 0x00007fff90aa07bc abort_message + 214
4   libc++abi.dylib                 0x00007fff90a9dfcf default_terminate() + 28
5   libc++abi.dylib                 0x00007fff90a9e001 safe_handler_caller(void (*)()) + 11
6   libc++abi.dylib                 0x00007fff90a9e05c std::terminate() + 16
7   libc++abi.dylib                 0x00007fff90a9f152 __cxa_throw + 114
8   App8                            0x000000010f7f62c8 procB() + 168
9   App8                            0x000000010f7f6389 procA() + 9
10  App8                            0x000000010f7f644a procNH() + 26
11  App8                            0x000000010f7f64a9 bar_one() + 9
12  App8                            0x000000010f7f64b9 foo_one() + 9
13  App8                            0x000000010f7f64d1 thread_one(void*) + 17
14  libsystem_c.dylib               0x00007fff84db88bf _pthread_start + 335
15  libsystem_c.dylib               0x00007fff84dbbb75 thread_start + 13

Thread 2:
0   libsystem_kernel.dylib          0x00007fff8a10ce42 __semwait_signal + 10
1   libsystem_c.dylib               0x00007fff84d6edea nanosleep + 164
2   libsystem_c.dylib               0x00007fff84d6ec2c sleep + 61
3   libsystem_c.dylib               0x00007fff84d6ec08 sleep + 25
4   App8                            0x000000010f7f648c procNE() + 60
5   App8                            0x000000010f7f64f9 bar_two() + 9
6   App8                            0x000000010f7f6509 foo_two() + 9
7   App8                            0x000000010f7f6521 thread_two(void*) + 17
8   libsystem_c.dylib               0x00007fff84db88bf _pthread_start + 335
9   libsystem_c.dylib               0x00007fff84dbbb75 thread_start + 13
```

```
Thread 3:
0    libsystem_kernel.dylib              0x00007fff8a10ce42 __semwait_signal + 10
1    libsystem_c.dylib                   0x00007fff84d6edea nanosleep + 164
2    libsystem_c.dylib                   0x00007fff84d6ec2c sleep + 61
3    libsystem_c.dylib                   0x00007fff84d6ec08 sleep + 25
4    App8                                0x000000010f7f63d7 procH() + 55
5    App8                                0x000000010f7f6549 bar_three() + 9
6    App8                                0x000000010f7f6559 foo_three() + 9
7    App8                                0x000000010f7f6571 thread_three(void*) + 17
8    libsystem_c.dylib                   0x00007fff84db88bf _pthread_start + 335
9    libsystem_c.dylib                   0x00007fff84dbbb75 thread_start + 13

Thread 4:
0    libsystem_kernel.dylib              0x00007fff8a10ce42 __semwait_signal + 10
1    libsystem_c.dylib                   0x00007fff84d6edea nanosleep + 164
2    libsystem_c.dylib                   0x00007fff84d6ec2c sleep + 61
3    libsystem_c.dylib                   0x00007fff84d6ec08 sleep + 25
4    App8                                0x000000010f7f648c procNE() + 60
5    App8                                0x000000010f7f6599 bar_four() + 9
6    App8                                0x000000010f7f65a9 foo_four() + 9
7    App8                                0x000000010f7f65c1 thread_four(void*) + 17
8    libsystem_c.dylib                   0x00007fff84db88bf _pthread_start + 335
9    libsystem_c.dylib                   0x00007fff84dbbb75 thread_start + 13

Thread 5:
0    libsystem_kernel.dylib              0x00007fff8a10ce42 __semwait_signal + 10
1    libsystem_c.dylib                   0x00007fff84d6edea nanosleep + 164
2    libsystem_c.dylib                   0x00007fff84d6ec2c sleep + 61
3    libsystem_c.dylib                   0x00007fff84d6ec08 sleep + 25
4    App8                                0x000000010f7f648c procNE() + 60
5    App8                                0x000000010f7f65e9 bar_five() + 9
6    App8                                0x000000010f7f65f9 foo_five() + 9
7    App8                                0x000000010f7f6611 thread_five(void*) + 17
8    libsystem_c.dylib                   0x00007fff84db88bf _pthread_start + 335
9    libsystem_c.dylib                   0x00007fff84dbbb75 thread_start + 13

Thread 1 crashed with X86 Thread State (64-bit):
  rax: 0x0000000000000000  rbx: 0x0000000000000006  rcx: 0x000000010f8aac58  rdx: 0x0000000000000000
  rdi: 0x0000000000001203  rsi: 0x0000000000000006  rbp: 0x000000010f8aac80  rsp: 0x000000010f8aac58
   r8: 0x00007fff74a67fb8   r9: 0x000000000000000a  r10: 0x00007fff8a10cd0a  r11: 0xffffff80002da8d0
  r12: 0x0000000000001203  r13: 0x000000010f8ab000  r14: 0x000000010f8ab000  r15: 0x000000010f8aadd0
  rip: 0x00007fff8a10cce2  rfl: 0x0000000000000246  cr2: 0x00007fff74a61a28
Logical CPU: 0

Binary Images:
       0x10f7f5000 -        0x10f7f6ff7 +App8 (??? - ???) <C689381B-7AA9-3185-B9CB-E0A9A25BEF77>
/Users/USER/Documents/*/App8
    0x7fff6f3f5000 -     0x7fff6f429baf  dyld (195.6 - ???) <0CD1B35B-A28F-32DA-B72E-452EAD609613> /usr/lib/dyld
    0x7fff849f2000 -     0x7fff84a0ffff  libxpc.dylib (77.19.0 - compatibility 1.0.0) <9F57891B-D7EF-3050-BEDD-
21E7C6668248> /usr/lib/system/libxpc.dylib
    0x7fff84d68000 -     0x7fff84d69ff7  libsystem_blocks.dylib (53.0.0 - compatibility 1.0.0) <8BCA214A-8992-34B2-
A8B9-B74DEACA1869> /usr/lib/system/libsystem_blocks.dylib
    0x7fff84d6a000 -     0x7fff84e47fef  libsystem_c.dylib (763.13.0 - compatibility 1.0.0) <41B43515-2806-3FBC-ACF1-
A16F35B7E290> /usr/lib/system/libsystem_c.dylib
    0x7fff85022000 -     0x7fff85030fff  libdispatch.dylib (187.9.0 - compatibility 1.0.0) <1D5BE322-A9B9-3BCE-8FAC-
076FB07CF54A> /usr/lib/system/libdispatch.dylib
    0x7fff855f0000 -     0x7fff855f1fff  libunc.dylib (24.0.0 - compatibility 1.0.0) <337960EE-0A85-3DD0-A760-
7134CF4C0AFF> /usr/lib/system/libunc.dylib
    0x7fff85ae3000 -     0x7fff85ae4ff7  libremovefile.dylib (21.1.0 - compatibility 1.0.0) <739E6C83-AA52-3C6C-A680-
B37FE2888A04> /usr/lib/system/libremovefile.dylib
    0x7fff89114000 -     0x7fff89118fff  libmathCommon.A.dylib (2026.0.0 - compatibility 1.0.0) <FF83AFF7-42B2-306E-
90AF-D539C51A4542> /usr/lib/system/libmathCommon.A.dylib
    0x7fff89119000 -     0x7fff8911dfff  libdyld.dylib (195.5.0 - compatibility 1.0.0) <380C3F44-0CA7-3514-8080-
46D1C9DF4FCD> /usr/lib/system/libdyld.dylib
    0x7fff89740000 -     0x7fff89741ff7  libsystem_sandbox.dylib (??? - ???) <96D38E74-F18F-3CCB-A20B-E8E3ADC4E166>
/usr/lib/system/libsystem_sandbox.dylib
    0x7fff8a0ef000 -     0x7fff8a0f5fff  libmacho.dylib (800.0.0 - compatibility 1.0.0) <165514D7-1BFA-38EF-A151-
676DCD21FB64> /usr/lib/system/libmacho.dylib
    0x7fff8a0f6000 -     0x7fff8a116fff  libsystem_kernel.dylib (1699.26.8 - compatibility 1.0.0) <1DDC0B0F-DB2A-34D6-
895D-E5B2B5618946> /usr/lib/system/libsystem_kernel.dylib
    0x7fff8a2ac000 -     0x7fff8a2b4fff  libsystem_dnssd.dylib (??? - ???) <D9BB1F87-A42B-3CBC-9DC2-FC07FCEF0016>
/usr/lib/system/libsystem_dnssd.dylib
    0x7fff8ae26000 -     0x7fff8ae61fff  libsystem_info.dylib (??? - ???) <35F90252-2AE1-32C5-8D34-782C614D9639>
/usr/lib/system/libsystem_info.dylib
    0x7fff8b248000 -     0x7fff8b24afff  libquarantine.dylib (36.6.0 - compatibility 1.0.0) <0EBF714B-4B69-3E1F-9A7D-
6BBC2AACB310> /usr/lib/system/libquarantine.dylib
```
193

```
      0x7fff8b3b4000 -    0x7fff8b3b4fff  libkeymgr.dylib (23.0.0 - compatibility 1.0.0) <61EFED6A-A407-301E-B454-
CD18314F0075> /usr/lib/system/libkeymgr.dylib
      0x7fff8b3dd000 -    0x7fff8b3e2fff  libcompiler_rt.dylib (6.0.0 - compatibility 1.0.0) <98ECD5F6-E85C-32A5-98CD-
8911230CB66A> /usr/lib/system/libcompiler_rt.dylib
      0x7fff8bd1a000 -    0x7fff8bd1bfff  libdnsinfo.dylib (395.11.0 - compatibility 1.0.0) <853BAAA5-270F-3FDC-B025-
D448DB72E1C3> /usr/lib/system/libdnsinfo.dylib
      0x7fff8c528000 -    0x7fff8c52dff7  libsystem_network.dylib (??? - ???) <5DE7024E-1D2D-34A2-80F4-08326331A75B>
/usr/lib/system/libsystem_network.dylib
      0x7fff8cfa3000 -    0x7fff8cfadff7  liblaunch.dylib (392.38.0 - compatibility 1.0.0) <6ECB7F19-B384-32C1-8652-
2463C1CF4815> /usr/lib/system/liblaunch.dylib
      0x7fff8dad3000 -    0x7fff8db46fff  libstdc++.6.dylib (52.0.0 - compatibility 7.0.0) <6BDD43E4-A4B1-379E-9ED5-
8C713653DFF2> /usr/lib/libstdc++.6.dylib
      0x7fff8fe02000 -    0x7fff8fe09fff  libcopyfile.dylib (85.1.0 - compatibility 1.0.0) <0AB51EE2-E914-358C-AC19-
47BC024BDAE7> /usr/lib/system/libcopyfile.dylib
      0x7fff8fe4b000 -    0x7fff8fe8dff7  libcommonCrypto.dylib (55010.0.0 - compatibility 1.0.0) <BB770C22-8C57-365A-
8716-4A3C36AE7BFB> /usr/lib/system/libcommonCrypto.dylib
      0x7fff90a98000 -    0x7fff90aa3ff7  libc++abi.dylib (14.0.0 - compatibility 1.0.0) <8FF3D766-D678-36F6-84AC-
423C878E6D14> /usr/lib/libc++abi.dylib
      0x7fff90c0f000 -    0x7fff90c18ff7  libsystem_notify.dylib (80.1.0 - compatibility 1.0.0) <A4D651E3-D1C6-3934-
AD49-7A104FD14596> /usr/lib/system/libsystem_notify.dylib
      0x7fff91376000 -    0x7fff913a3fe7  libSystem.B.dylib (159.1.0 - compatibility 1.0.0) <7BEBB139-50BB-3112-947A-
F4AA168F991C> /usr/lib/libSystem.B.dylib
      0x7fff91489000 -    0x7fff9148fff7  libunwind.dylib (30.0.0 - compatibility 1.0.0) <1E9C6C8C-CBE8-3F4B-A5B5-
E03E3AB53231> /usr/lib/system/libunwind.dylib
      0x7fff91a22000 -    0x7fff91a27fff  libcache.dylib (47.0.0 - compatibility 1.0.0) <1571C3AB-BCB2-38CD-B3B2-
C5FC3F927C6A> /usr/lib/system/libcache.dylib

External Modification Summary:
  Calls made by other processes targeting this process:
    task_for_pid: 2
    thread_create: 0
    thread_set_state: 0
  Calls made by this process:
    task_for_pid: 0
    thread_create: 0
    thread_set_state: 0
  Calls made by all processes on this machine:
    task_for_pid: 7055
    thread_create: 0
    thread_set_state: 0

VM Region Summary:
ReadOnly portion of Libraries: Total=50.7M resident=50.7M(100%) swapped_out_or_unallocated=0K(0%)
Writable regions: Total=38.9M written=17.9M(46%) resident=42.6M(110%) swapped_out=0K(0%)
unallocated=16777216.0T(45221404475392%)


REGION TYPE                VIRTUAL
===========                =======
MALLOC                     1220K
Stack                      66.6M
__DATA                     504K
__LINKEDIT                 47.7M
__TEXT                     3000K
shared memory              12K
===========                =======
TOTAL                      118.9M
```

2. Load a core dump core.4472 and App8 executable:

```
$ gdb -c ~/Documents/AMCDA-Dumps/core.4472 -e ~/Documents/AMCDA-
Dumps/Apps/App8/Build/Products/Release/App8
GNU gdb 6.3.50-20050815 (Apple version gdb-1820) (Sat Jun 16 02:40:11 UTC 2012)
Copyright 2004 Free Software Foundation, Inc.
GDB is free software, covered by the GNU General Public License, and you are
welcome to change it and/or distribute copies of it under certain conditions.
Type "show copying" to see the conditions.
There is absolutely no warranty for GDB.  Type "show warranty" for details.
This GDB was configured as "x86_64-apple-darwin".
Reading symbols for shared libraries . done
Reading symbols for shared libraries .......................... done
#0  0x00007fff8a10ce42 in __semwait_signal ()
```

3. Go to the core thread 2 (thread #3), identify execution residue of work functions and check their correctness:

```
(gdb) thread 3
[Switching to thread 3 (core thread 2)]
0x00007fff8a10ce42 in __semwait_signal ()

(gdb) bt
#0  0x00007fff8a10ce42 in __semwait_signal ()
#1  0x00007fff84d6edea in nanosleep ()
#2  0x00007fff84d6ec2c in sleep ()
#3  0x00007fff84d6ec08 in sleep ()
#4  0x000000010f7f648c in procNE ()
#5  0x000000010f7f64f9 in bar_two ()
#6  0x000000010f7f6509 in foo_two ()
#7  0x000000010f7f6521 in thread_two ()
#8  0x00007fff84db88bf in _pthread_start ()
#9  0x00007fff84dbbb75 in thread_start ()

(gdb) x/512a $rsp-2000
0x10fa80628: 0x0     0x0
0x10fa80638: 0x0     0x0
0x10fa80648: 0x0     0x0
0x10fa80658: 0x0     0x0
0x10fa80668: 0x0     0x0
0x10fa80678: 0x0     0x0
0x10fa80688: 0x0     0x0
0x10fa80698: 0x0     0x0
0x10fa806a8: 0x0     0x0
0x10fa806b8: 0x0     0x0
0x10fa806c8: 0x0     0x0
0x10fa806d8: 0x0     0x0
0x10fa806e8: 0x0     0x0
0x10fa806f8: 0x0     0x0
0x10fa80708: 0x0     0x0
0x10fa80718: 0x0     0x0
0x10fa80728: 0x0     0x0
0x10fa80738: 0x0     0x0
0x10fa80748: 0x0     0x0
0x10fa80758: 0x0     0x0
0x10fa80768: 0x0     0x0
0x10fa80778: 0x0     0x0
```

```
0x10fa80788: 0x0     0x0
0x10fa80798: 0x0     0x0
0x10fa807a8: 0x0     0x0
0x10fa807b8: 0x0     0x0
0x10fa807c8: 0x0     0x0
0x10fa807d8: 0x0     0x0
0x10fa807e8: 0x0     0x0
0x10fa807f8: 0x0     0x0
0x10fa80808: 0x0     0x0
0x10fa80818: 0x0     0x0
0x10fa80828: 0x0     0x0
0x10fa80838: 0x0     0x0
0x10fa80848: 0x0     0x0
0x10fa80858: 0x0     0x0
0x10fa80868: 0x0     0x0
0x10fa80878: 0x0     0x0
0x10fa80888: 0x0     0x0
0x10fa80898: 0x0     0x0
0x10fa808a8: 0x0     0x0
0x10fa808b8: 0x0     0x0
---Type <return> to continue, or q <return> to quit---
0x10fa808c8: 0x0     0x0
0x10fa808d8: 0x0     0x0
0x10fa808e8: 0x0     0x0
0x10fa808f8: 0x0     0x0
0x10fa80908: 0x0     0x0
0x10fa80918: 0x0     0x0
0x10fa80928: 0x0     0x0
0x10fa80938: 0x0     0x0
0x10fa80948: 0x0     0x0
0x10fa80958: 0x0     0x0
0x10fa80968: 0x0     0x0
0x10fa80978: 0x0     0x0
0x10fa80988: 0x0     0x0
0x10fa80998: 0x0     0x0
0x10fa809a8: 0x0     0x0
0x10fa809b8: 0x0     0x0
0x10fa809c8: 0x0     0x0
0x10fa809d8: 0x0     0x10fa809f0
0x10fa809e8: 0x10f7f6159 <_Z6work_8v+9>0x10fa80a00
0x10fa809f8: 0x10f7f6169 <_Z6work_7v+9>0x10fa80a10
0x10fa80a08: 0x10f7f6179 <_Z6work_6v+9>0x10fa80a20
0x10fa80a18: 0x10f7f6189 <_Z6work_5v+9>0x10fa80a30
0x10fa80a28: 0x10f7f6199 <_Z6work_4v+9>0x10fa80a40
0x10fa80a38: 0x10f7f61a9 <_Z6work_3v+9>0x10fa80a50
0x10fa80a48: 0x10f7f61b9 <_Z6work_2v+9>0x10fa80a60
0x10fa80a58: 0x10f7f61c9 <_Z6work_1v+9>0x10fa80e80
0x10fa80a68: 0x10f7f61ee <_Z4workv+30> 0x0
0x10fa80a78: 0x0     0x0
0x10fa80a88: 0x0     0x0
0x10fa80a98: 0x0     0x0
0x10fa80aa8: 0x0     0x0
0x10fa80ab8: 0x0     0x0
0x10fa80ac8: 0x0     0x0
0x10fa80ad8: 0x0     0x0
0x10fa80ae8: 0x0     0x0
0x10fa80af8: 0x0     0x0
0x10fa80b08: 0x0     0x0
0x10fa80b18: 0x0     0x0
0x10fa80b28: 0x0     0x0
```

```
0x10fa80b38: 0x0      0x0
0x10fa80b48: 0x0      0x0
0x10fa80b58: 0x0      0x0
---Type <return> to continue, or q <return> to quit---
0x10fa80b68: 0x0      0x0
0x10fa80b78: 0x0      0x0
0x10fa80b88: 0x0      0x0
0x10fa80b98: 0x0      0x0
0x10fa80ba8: 0x0      0x0
0x10fa80bb8: 0x0      0x0
0x10fa80bc8: 0x0      0x0
0x10fa80bd8: 0x0      0x0
0x10fa80be8: 0x0      0x0
0x10fa80bf8: 0x0      0x0
0x10fa80c08: 0x0      0x0
0x10fa80c18: 0x0      0x0
0x10fa80c28: 0x0      0x0
0x10fa80c38: 0x0      0x0
0x10fa80c48: 0x0      0x0
0x10fa80c58: 0x0      0x0
0x10fa80c68: 0x0      0x0
0x10fa80c78: 0x0      0x0
0x10fa80c88: 0x0      0x0
0x10fa80c98: 0x0      0x0
0x10fa80ca8: 0x0      0x0
0x10fa80cb8: 0x0      0x0
0x10fa80cc8: 0x0      0x0
0x10fa80cd8: 0x0      0x0
0x10fa80ce8: 0x0      0x0
0x10fa80cf8: 0x0      0x0
0x10fa80d08: 0x0      0x0
0x10fa80d18: 0x0      0x0
0x10fa80d28: 0x0      0x0
0x10fa80d38: 0x0      0x0
0x10fa80d48: 0x7fff8a10ad71 <mach_msg+73>      0x0
0x10fa80d58: 0x0      0x300000018
0x10fa80d68: 0x10fa80e00  0x1303
0x10fa80d78: 0x10fa81000  0x10fa80e48
0x10fa80d88: 0x10f7f6510 <_Z10thread_twoPv>   0x10fa80df0
0x10fa80d98: 0x7fff8a0f784f <clock_get_time+76>      0x0
0x10fa80da8: 0x2c00001200 0x160300000000
0x10fa80db8: 0x44cffffff800x100000000
0x10fa80dc8: 0x1852200000000      0x338092a6
0x10fa80dd8: 0x7fff00000008      0x10fa80e38
0x10fa80de8: 0x10fa80e48  0x10fa80e20
0x10fa80df8: 0x7fff84d6edea <nanosleep+164>   0x338092a600018522
---Type <return> to continue, or q <return> to quit---
0x10fa80e08: 0x0      0x7fffffff
0x10fa80e18: 0x0      0x10fa80e60
0x10fa80e28: 0x7fff84d6ec2c <sleep+61> 0x0
0x10fa80e38: 0x0      0x0
0x10fa80e48: 0x7fffffff   0x0
0x10fa80e58: 0xffffffff   0x10fa80ea0
0x10fa80e68: 0x7fff84d6ec08 <sleep+25> 0x0
0x10fa80e78: 0xb5a42821d4d7e840  0x10fa80e90
0x10fa80e88: 0x10f7f6379 <_Z6procNBv+9>0x10fa80ea0
0x10fa80e98: 0x0      0x10fa80ed0
0x10fa80ea8: 0x10f7f648c <_Z6procNEv+60>      0x0
0x10fa80eb8: 0x0      0x0
0x10fa80ec8: 0x0      0x10fa80ee0
```

```
0x10fa80ed8: 0x10f7f64f9 <_Z7bar_twov+9>      0x10fa80ef0
0x10fa80ee8: 0x10f7f6509 <_Z7foo_twov+9>      0x10fa80f10
0x10fa80ef8: 0x10f7f6521 <_Z10thread_twoPv+17>      0x0
0x10fa80f08: 0x0    0x10fa80f50
0x10fa80f18: 0x7fff84db88bf <_pthread_start+335>      0x0
0x10fa80f28: 0x0    0x0
0x10fa80f38: 0x0    0x0
0x10fa80f48: 0x0    0x10fa80f78
0x10fa80f58: 0x7fff84dbbb75 <thread_start+13> 0x0
0x10fa80f68: 0x0    0x0
0x10fa80f78: 0x0    0x0
0x10fa80f88: 0x0    0x0
0x10fa80f98: 0x0    0x0
0x10fa80fa8: 0x0    0x0
0x10fa80fb8: 0x0    0x0
0x10fa80fc8: 0x0    0x0
0x10fa80fd8: 0x0    0x0
0x10fa80fe8: 0x0    0x0
0x10fa80ff8: 0x0    0x54485244
0x10fa81008: 0x0    0x701010100000000
0x10fa81018: 0x1000 0xa0000001f
0x10fa81028: 0x0    0x0
0x10fa81038: 0x0    0x130300000000
0x10fa81048: 0x10f7f6510 <_Z10thread_twoPv>      0x0
0x10fa81058: 0x3    0x10fa81000
0x10fa81068: 0x0    0x0
0x10fa81078: 0x0    0x0
0x10fa81088: 0x0    0x0
0x10fa81098: 0x0    0x0
---Type <return> to continue, or q <return> to quit---
0x10fa810a8: 0x0    0x0
0x10fa810b8: 0x0    0x0
0x10fa810c8: 0x0    0x0
0x10fa810d8: 0x0    0x0
0x10fa810e8: 0x0    0x0
0x10fa810f8: 0x0    0x0
0x10fa81108: 0x0    0x0
0x10fa81118: 0x0    0x0
0x10fa81128: 0x0    0x0
0x10fa81138: 0x0    0x0
0x10fa81148: 0x0    0x0
0x10fa81158: 0x0    0x0
0x10fa81168: 0x0    0x0
0x10fa81178: 0x0    0x0
0x10fa81188: 0x0    0x0
0x10fa81198: 0x0    0x0
0x10fa811a8: 0x0    0x0
0x10fa811b8: 0x0    0x0
0x10fa811c8: 0x0    0x0
0x10fa811d8: 0x0    0x0
0x10fa811e8: 0x0    0x0
0x10fa811f8: 0x0    0x0
0x10fa81208: 0x0    0x0
0x10fa81218: 0x0    0x0
0x10fa81228: 0x0    0x0
0x10fa81238: 0x0    0x0
0x10fa81248: 0x0    0x0
0x10fa81258: 0x0    0x0
0x10fa81268: 0x0    0x0
0x10fa81278: 0x0    0x0
```

```
0x10fa81288:  0x0      0x0
0x10fa81298:  0x0      0x0
0x10fa812a8:  0x0      0x0
0x10fa812b8:  0x0      0x0
0x10fa812c8:  0x0      0x0
0x10fa812d8:  0x0      0x0
0x10fa812e8:  0x0      0x0
0x10fa812f8:  0x0      0x0
0x10fa81308:  0x0      0x0
0x10fa81318:  0x0      0x0
0x10fa81328:  0x0      0x0
0x10fa81338:  0x0      0x0
---Type <return> to continue, or q <return> to quit---
0x10fa81348:  0x0      0x0
0x10fa81358:  0x0      0x0
0x10fa81368:  0x0      0x0
0x10fa81378:  0x0      0x0
0x10fa81388:  0x0      0x0
0x10fa81398:  0x0      0x0
0x10fa813a8:  0x0      0x0
0x10fa813b8:  0x0      0x0
0x10fa813c8:  0x0      0x0
0x10fa813d8:  0x0      0x0
0x10fa813e8:  0x0      0x0
0x10fa813f8:  0x0      0x0
0x10fa81408:  0x0      0x0
0x10fa81418:  0x0      0x0
0x10fa81428:  0x0      0x0
0x10fa81438:  0x0      0x0
0x10fa81448:  0x0      0x0
0x10fa81458:  0x0      0x0
0x10fa81468:  0x0      0x0
0x10fa81478:  0x0      0x0
0x10fa81488:  0x0      0x0
0x10fa81498:  0x0      0x0
0x10fa814a8:  0x0      0x0
0x10fa814b8:  0x0      0x0
0x10fa814c8:  0x0      0x0
0x10fa814d8:  0x0      0x0
0x10fa814e8:  0x0      0x0
0x10fa814f8:  0x0      0x0
0x10fa81508:  0x0      0x0
0x10fa81518:  0x0      0x0
0x10fa81528:  0x0      0x0
0x10fa81538:  0x0      0x0
0x10fa81548:  0x0      0x0
0x10fa81558:  0x0      0x0
0x10fa81568:  0x0      0x0
0x10fa81578:  0x0      0x0
0x10fa81588:  0x0      0x0
0x10fa81598:  0x0      0x0
0x10fa815a8:  0x0      0x0
0x10fa815b8:  0x0      0x0
0x10fa815c8:  0x0      0x0
0x10fa815d8:  0x0      0x0
---Type <return> to continue, or q <return> to quit---
0x10fa815e8:  0x0      0x0
0x10fa815f8:  0x0      0x0
0x10fa81608:  0x0      0x0
0x10fa81618:  0x0      0x0
```

```
(gdb) disassemble 0x10f7f61a9
Dump of assembler code for function _Z6work_3v:
0x000000010f7f61a0 <_Z6work_3v+0>:     push   %rbp
0x000000010f7f61a1 <_Z6work_3v+1>:     mov    %rsp,%rbp
0x000000010f7f61a4 <_Z6work_3v+4>:     callq  0x10f7f6190 <_Z6work_4v>
0x000000010f7f61a9 <_Z6work_3v+9>:     pop    %rbp
0x000000010f7f61aa <_Z6work_3v+10>:    retq
0x000000010f7f61ab <_Z6work_3v+11>:    nopl   0x0(%rax,%rax,1)
End of assembler dump.
```

4.   Go to the core thread 3 (thread #4) and identify handled exception processing code:

```
(gdb) thread 4
[Switching to thread 4 (core thread 3)]
0x00007fff8a10ce42 in __semwait_signal ()

(gdb) bt
#0  0x00007fff8a10ce42 in __semwait_signal ()
#1  0x00007fff84d6edea in nanosleep ()
#2  0x00007fff84d6ec2c in sleep ()
#3  0x00007fff84d6ec08 in sleep ()
#4  0x000000010f7f63d7 in procH ()
#5  0x000000010f7f6549 in bar_three ()
#6  0x000000010f7f6559 in foo_three ()
#7  0x000000010f7f6571 in thread_three ()
#8  0x00007fff84db88bf in _pthread_start ()
#9  0x00007fff84dbbb75 in thread_start ()

(gdb) x/512a $rsp-2000
0x10fb03608: 0x10fb04000    0x0
0x10fb03618: 0x10f7f6560 <_Z12thread_threePv> 0x10f7f63b7 <_Z5procHv+23>
0x10fb03628: 0x0    0x0
0x10fb03638: 0x0    0x0
0x10fb03648: 0x7fff76401a08 <_ZL17sThisAddressSpace> 0x0
0x10fb03658: 0x0    0x0
0x10fb03668: 0x0    0x0
0x10fb03678: 0x0    0x0
0x10fb03688: 0x0    0x0
0x10fb03698: 0x0    0x0
0x10fb036a8: 0x0    0x0
0x10fb036b8: 0x0    0x0
0x10fb036c8: 0x0    0x0
0x10fb036d8: 0x0    0x0
0x10fb036e8: 0x0    0x0
0x10fb036f8: 0x0    0x0
0x10fb03708: 0x0    0x0
0x10fb03718: 0x0    0x0
0x10fb03728: 0x0    0x0
0x10fb03738: 0x0    0x0
0x10fb03748: 0x0    0x0
0x10fb03758: 0x0    0x0
0x10fb03768: 0x0    0x0
0x10fb03778: 0x0    0x0
```

```
0x10fb03788: 0x0     0x0
0x10fb03798: 0x0     0x0
0x10fb037a8: 0x0     0x0
0x10fb037b8: 0x0     0x0
0x10fb037c8: 0x0     0x0
0x10fb037d8: 0x0     0x0
0x10fb037e8: 0x0     0x0
0x10fb037f8: 0x0     0x0
0x10fb03808: 0x0     0x0
0x10fb03818: 0x0     0x0
0x10fb03828: 0x0     0x0
0x10fb03838: 0x0     0x0
0x10fb03848: 0x0     0x0
0x10fb03858: 0x0     0x0
0x10fb03868: 0x0     0x0
0x10fb03878: 0x0     0x0
0x10fb03888: 0x0     0x0
0x10fb03898: 0x0     0x0
---Type <return> to continue, or q <return> to quit---
0x10fb038a8: 0x0     0x0
0x10fb038b8: 0x0     0x0
0x10fb038c8: 0x0     0x0
0x10fb038d8: 0x0     0x0
0x10fb038e8: 0x0     0x0
0x10fb038f8: 0x0     0x0
0x10fb03908: 0x10fb03e90  0x10f7f63a0 <_Z5procHv>
0x10fb03918: 0x10f7f6430 <_Z6procNHv>  0x10f7f68fc <GCC_except_table15>
0x10fb03928: 0x7fff90a9e6f4 <__gxx_personality_v0>  0x0
0x10fb03938: 0x0     0x51000000
0x10fb03948: 0x0     0x10f7f5000
0x10fb03958: 0x7fff764010a0
<_ZTVN9libunwind12UnwindCursorINS_17LocalAddressSpaceENS_16Registers_x86_64EEE+16>
       0x10f7f63a0 <_Z5procHv>
0x10fb03968: 0x10f7f6430 <_Z6procNHv>  0x10f7f68fc <GCC_except_table15>
0x10fb03978: 0x7fff90a9e6f4 <__gxx_personality_v0>  0x0
0x10fb03988: 0x0     0x51000000
0x10fb03998: 0x0     0x10f7f5000
0x10fb039a8: 0x10f900980  0x10f900918
0x10fb039b8: 0x1503 0x0
0x10fb039c8: 0x10f7f6560 <_Z12thread_threePv> 0x10fb03df0
0x10fb039d8: 0x7fff9148e0fb <_Unwind_Resume+72>    0x10fb03e90
0x10fb039e8: 0x10f900918  0x10f900918
0x10fb039f8: 0x0     0x0
0x10fb03a08: 0x10fb039e8  0x10fb03dd8
0x10fb03a18: 0x10fb03df0  0x10fb039e0
0x10fb03a28: 0x10f7fca00  0x8
0x10fb03a38: 0x4000 0x7fff9148e0b3 <_Unwind_Resume>
0x10fb03a48: 0x1503 0x10fb04000
0x10fb03a58: 0x0     0x10f7f6560 <_Z12thread_threePv>
0x10fb03a68: 0x7fff9148e0ce <_Unwind_Resume+27>    0x0
0x10fb03a78: 0x0     0x0
0x10fb03a88: 0x0     0x0
0x10fb03a98: 0x0     0x0
```

```
0x10fb03aa8: 0x0     0x0
0x10fb03ab8: 0x0     0x0
0x10fb03ac8: 0x0     0x0
0x10fb03ad8: 0x0     0x0
0x10fb03ae8: 0x7fff6f433118     0x10fb03b40
0x10fb03af8: 0x7fff6f409b60     0x0
0x10fb03b08: 0x10fb03cc0  0x10f7f8207
0x10fb03b18: 0x10fb03cc0  0x7fff6f433118
0x10fb03b28: 0x10f7f8200  0x1
---Type <return> to continue, or q <return> to quit---
0x10fb03b38: 0x10f7f8207  0x10fb03b80
0x10fb03b48: 0x7fff6f403f50     0x10f7f8207
0x10fb03b58: 0x10fb03cc0  0x7fff6f4321e0
0x10fb03b68: 0x10f7f8200  0x1
0x10fb03b78: 0x7fff6f432330     0x10fb03bd0
0x10fb03b88: 0x7fff6f409b60     0x10fb03bd0
0x10fb03b98: 0x10fb03d50  0x10f7f81a4
0x10fb03ba8: 0x10fb03d50  0x7fff6f432330
0x10fb03bb8: 0x10f7f8100  0x1
0x10fb03bc8: 0x10f7f81a4  0x10fb03c10
0x10fb03bd8: 0x7fff6f403f50     0x10f7f81a4
0x10fb03be8: 0x10fb03d50  0x7fff6f432140
0x10fb03bf8: 0x10f7f8100  0x1
0x10fb03c08: 0x10f7f81a4  0x10fb03c50
0x10fb03c18: 0x7fff6f403f50     0x10fb03cc0
0x10fb03c28: 0x10f7f81a4  0x7fff6f42a110
0x10fb03c38: 0x7fff6f42a110     0x7fff6f430d80
0x10fb03c48: 0x10f7f8100  0x7fff6f430d80
0x10fb03c58: 0x7fff6f432330     0x10fb03ca0
0x10fb03c68: 0x7fff6f404eb9     0x7fff6f42a110
0x10fb03c78: 0x10fb03d50  0x7fff6f430d80
0x10fb03c88: 0x10f7f8100  0x1
0x10fb03c98: 0x7fff6f42a110     0x10fb03cf0
0x10fb03ca8: 0x7fff6f40c6bd     0x10fb03d50
0x10fb03cb8: 0x10f7f8268  0x10f7f81a4
0x10fb03cc8: 0x10f7f8268  0x10f7f7090
0x10fb03cd8: 0x10f7f81b8  0x10f7f81a4
0x10fb03ce8: 0x1     0x10fb03d80
0x10fb03cf8: 0x7fff6f40c9cd     0x10f7f81a4
0x10fb03d08: 0x0     0x7fff6f41c65c
0x10fb03d18: 0x7fff8911a5c0 <_Z21dyldGlobalLockReleasev>   0x7fff90a9e355 <__cxa_begin_catch>
0x10fb03d28: 0x7fff8a10ad71 <mach_msg+73>     0x101000000000000
0x10fb03d38: 0x7fff6f42a110     0x300000018
0x10fb03d48: 0x10fb03de0  0x1503
0x10fb03d58: 0x10fb04000  0x10fb03e28
0x10fb03d68: 0x10f7f6560 <_Z12thread_threePv> 0x10fb03dd0
0x10fb03d78: 0x7fff8a0f784f <clock_get_time+76>     0x100000000
0x10fb03d88: 0x2c00001200 0x1b0300000000
0x10fb03d98: 0x44c000000200x100000000
0x10fb03da8: 0x1852200000000     0x33850396
0x10fb03db8: 0x7fff00000008     0x10fb03e18
0x10fb03dc8: 0x10fb03e28  0x10fb03e00
---Type <return> to continue, or q <return> to quit---
```

```
0x10fb03dd8: 0x7fff84d6edea <nanosleep+164>   0x3385039600018522
0x10fb03de8: 0x0    0x7ffffff
0x10fb03df8: 0x0    0x10fb03e40
0x10fb03e08: 0x7fff84d6ec2c <sleep+61> 0x1503
0x10fb03e18: 0x10fb04000   0x10f900918
0x10fb03e28: 0x7ffffff    0x0
0x10fb03e38: 0xffffffff    0x10fb03e80
0x10fb03e48: 0x7fff84d6ec08 <sleep+25> 0x0
0x10fb03e58: 0x10f900918   0x10fb03e80
0x10fb03e68: 0x7fff90a9e366 <__cxa_begin_catch+17>   0x10fb03ed0
0x10fb03e78: 0x0    0x10fb03ed0
0x10fb03e88: 0x10f7f63d7 <_Z5procHv+55>0x0
0x10fb03e98: 0x0    0x0
0x10fb03ea8: 0x0    0x0
0x10fb03eb8: 0x10f900938   0x100000000
0x10fb03ec8: 0x10f900918   0x10fb03ee0
0x10fb03ed8: 0x10f7f6549 <_Z9bar_threev+9>   0x10fb03ef0
0x10fb03ee8: 0x10f7f6559 <_Z9foo_threev+9>   0x10fb03f10
0x10fb03ef8: 0x10f7f6571 <_Z12thread_threePv+17>   0x0
0x10fb03f08: 0x0    0x10fb03f50
0x10fb03f18: 0x7fff84db88bf <_pthread_start+335>   0x0
0x10fb03f28: 0x0    0x0
0x10fb03f38: 0x0    0x0
0x10fb03f48: 0x0    0x10fb03f78
0x10fb03f58: 0x7fff84dbbb75 <thread_start+13> 0x0
0x10fb03f68: 0x0    0x0
0x10fb03f78: 0x0    0x0
0x10fb03f88: 0x0    0x0
0x10fb03f98: 0x0    0x0
0x10fb03fa8: 0x0    0x0
0x10fb03fb8: 0x0    0x0
0x10fb03fc8: 0x0    0x0
0x10fb03fd8: 0x0    0x0
0x10fb03fe8: 0x0    0x0
0x10fb03ff8: 0x0    0x54485244
0x10fb04008: 0x0    0x701010100000000
0x10fb04018: 0x1000 0xa0000001f
0x10fb04028: 0x0    0x0
0x10fb04038: 0x0    0x150300000000
0x10fb04048: 0x10f7f6560 <_Z12thread_threePv> 0x0
0x10fb04058: 0x3    0x10fb04000
0x10fb04068: 0x0    0x0
---Type <return> to continue, or q <return> to quit---
0x10fb04078: 0x0    0x0
0x10fb04088: 0x0    0x0
0x10fb04098: 0x0    0x0
0x10fb040a8: 0x0    0x0
0x10fb040b8: 0x0    0x0
0x10fb040c8: 0x0    0x0
0x10fb040d8: 0x0    0x0
0x10fb040e8: 0x0    0x0
0x10fb040f8: 0x0    0x0
0x10fb04108: 0x0    0x0
```

```
0x10fb04118:  0x0      0x0
0x10fb04128:  0x0      0x0
0x10fb04138:  0x0      0x0
0x10fb04148:  0x0      0x0
0x10fb04158:  0x0      0x0
0x10fb04168:  0x0      0x0
0x10fb04178:  0x0      0x0
0x10fb04188:  0x0      0x0
0x10fb04198:  0x0      0x0
0x10fb041a8:  0x0      0x0
0x10fb041b8:  0x0      0x0
0x10fb041c8:  0x0      0x0
0x10fb041d8:  0x0      0x0
0x10fb041e8:  0x0      0x0
0x10fb041f8:  0x0      0x0
0x10fb04208:  0x0      0x0
0x10fb04218:  0x0      0x0
0x10fb04228:  0x0      0x0
0x10fb04238:  0x0      0x0
0x10fb04248:  0x0      0x0
0x10fb04258:  0x0      0x0
0x10fb04268:  0x0      0x0
0x10fb04278:  0x0      0x0
0x10fb04288:  0x0      0x0
0x10fb04298:  0x0      0x0
0x10fb042a8:  0x0      0x0
0x10fb042b8:  0x0      0x0
0x10fb042c8:  0x0      0x0
0x10fb042d8:  0x0      0x0
0x10fb042e8:  0x0      0x0
0x10fb042f8:  0x0      0x0
0x10fb04308:  0x0      0x0
---Type <return> to continue, or q <return> to quit---
0x10fb04318:  0x0      0x0
0x10fb04328:  0x0      0x0
0x10fb04338:  0x0      0x0
0x10fb04348:  0x0      0x0
0x10fb04358:  0x0      0x0
0x10fb04368:  0x0      0x0
0x10fb04378:  0x0      0x0
0x10fb04388:  0x0      0x0
0x10fb04398:  0x0      0x0
0x10fb043a8:  0x0      0x0
0x10fb043b8:  0x0      0x0
0x10fb043c8:  0x0      0x0
0x10fb043d8:  0x0      0x0
0x10fb043e8:  0x0      0x0
0x10fb043f8:  0x0      0x0
0x10fb04408:  0x0      0x0
0x10fb04418:  0x0      0x0
0x10fb04428:  0x0      0x0
0x10fb04438:  0x0      0x0
0x10fb04448:  0x0      0x0
```

```
0x10fb04458:  0x0      0x0
0x10fb04468:  0x0      0x0
0x10fb04478:  0x0      0x0
0x10fb04488:  0x0      0x0
0x10fb04498:  0x0      0x0
0x10fb044a8:  0x0      0x0
0x10fb044b8:  0x0      0x0
0x10fb044c8:  0x0      0x0
0x10fb044d8:  0x0      0x0
0x10fb044e8:  0x0      0x0
0x10fb044f8:  0x0      0x0
0x10fb04508:  0x0      0x0
0x10fb04518:  0x0      0x0
0x10fb04528:  0x0      0x0
0x10fb04538:  0x0      0x0
0x10fb04548:  0x0      0x0
0x10fb04558:  0x0      0x0
0x10fb04568:  0x0      0x0
0x10fb04578:  0x0      0x0
0x10fb04588:  0x0      0x0
0x10fb04598:  0x0      0x0
0x10fb045a8:  0x0      0x0
---Type <return> to continue, or q <return> to quit---
0x10fb045b8:  0x0      0x0
0x10fb045c8:  0x0      0x0
0x10fb045d8:  0x0      0x0
0x10fb045e8:  0x0      0x0
0x10fb045f8:  0x0      0x0
```

Exercise A8 (LLDB)

- **Goal:** Learn how to identify runtime exceptions, past execution residue and stack traces, identify handled exceptions

- **Patterns:** C++ Exception, Execution Residue, Coincidental Symbolic Information, Handled Exception

- \AMCDA-Dumps\Exercise-A8-LLDB.pdf

Exercise A8 (LLDB)

Goal: Learn how to identify runtime exceptions, past execution residue and stack traces, identify handled exceptions

Patterns: C++ Exception, Execution Residue, Coincidental Symbolic Information, Handled Exception

1.   Identify the problem thread and application specific diagnostic from the diagnostic report App8_4472.crash:

```
Process:        App8 [4472]
Path:           /Users/USER/Documents/*/App8
Identifier:     App8
Version:        ??? (???)
Code Type:      X86-64 (Native)
Parent Process: bash [1549]

Date/Time:      2012-07-25 22:34:17.717 +0100
OS Version:     Mac OS X 10.7.4 (11E53)
Report Version: 9
Sleep/Wake UUID: 4C0A9B6D-7E93-4764-8BC3-971D136863D8

Crashed Thread: 1

Exception Type:  EXC_CRASH (SIGABRT)
Exception Codes: 0x0000000000000000, 0x0000000000000000

Application Specific Information:
terminate called throwing an exception
abort() called

Thread 0:: Dispatch queue: com.apple.main-thread
0   libsystem_kernel.dylib          0x00007fff8a10ce42 __semwait_signal + 10
1   libsystem_c.dylib               0x00007fff84d6edea nanosleep + 164
2   libsystem_c.dylib               0x00007fff84d6ec2c sleep + 61
3   libsystem_c.dylib               0x00007fff84d6ec08 sleep + 25
4   App8                            0x000000010f7f66f3 main + 195
5   App8                            0x000000010f7f6134 start + 52

Thread 1 Crashed:
0   libsystem_kernel.dylib          0x00007fff8a10cce2 __pthread_kill + 10
1   libsystem_c.dylib               0x00007fff84dba7d2 pthread_kill + 95
2   libsystem_c.dylib               0x00007fff84daba7a abort + 143
3   libc++abi.dylib                 0x00007fff90aa07bc abort_message + 214
4   libc++abi.dylib                 0x00007fff90a9dfcf default_terminate() + 28
5   libc++abi.dylib                 0x00007fff90a9e001 safe_handler_caller(void (*)()) + 11
6   libc++abi.dylib                 0x00007fff90a9e05c std::terminate() + 16
7   libc++abi.dylib                 0x00007fff90a9f152 __cxa_throw + 114
8   App8                            0x000000010f7f62c8 procB() + 168
9   App8                            0x000000010f7f6389 procA() + 9
10  App8                            0x000000010f7f644a procNH() + 26
11  App8                            0x000000010f7f64a9 bar_one() + 9
12  App8                            0x000000010f7f64b9 foo_one() + 9
13  App8                            0x000000010f7f64d1 thread_one(void*) + 17
14  libsystem_c.dylib               0x00007fff84db88bf _pthread_start + 335
15  libsystem_c.dylib               0x00007fff84dbbb75 thread_start + 13

Thread 2:
0   libsystem_kernel.dylib          0x00007fff8a10ce42 __semwait_signal + 10
1   libsystem_c.dylib               0x00007fff84d6edea nanosleep + 164
2   libsystem_c.dylib               0x00007fff84d6ec2c sleep + 61
3   libsystem_c.dylib               0x00007fff84d6ec08 sleep + 25
4   App8                            0x000000010f7f648c procNE() + 60
5   App8                            0x000000010f7f64f9 bar_two() + 9
6   App8                            0x000000010f7f6509 foo_two() + 9
7   App8                            0x000000010f7f6521 thread_two(void*) + 17
8   libsystem_c.dylib               0x00007fff84db88bf _pthread_start + 335
9   libsystem_c.dylib               0x00007fff84dbbb75 thread_start + 13
```

```
Thread 3:
0   libsystem_kernel.dylib          0x00007fff8a10ce42 __semwait_signal + 10
1   libsystem_c.dylib               0x00007fff84d6edea nanosleep + 164
2   libsystem_c.dylib               0x00007fff84d6ec2c sleep + 61
3   libsystem_c.dylib               0x00007fff84d6ec08 sleep + 25
4   App8                            0x000000010f7f63d7 procH() + 55
5   App8                            0x000000010f7f6549 bar_three() + 9
6   App8                            0x000000010f7f6559 foo_three() + 9
7   App8                            0x000000010f7f6571 thread_three(void*) + 17
8   libsystem_c.dylib               0x00007fff84db88bf _pthread_start + 335
9   libsystem_c.dylib               0x00007fff84dbbb75 thread_start + 13

Thread 4:
0   libsystem_kernel.dylib          0x00007fff8a10ce42 __semwait_signal + 10
1   libsystem_c.dylib               0x00007fff84d6edea nanosleep + 164
2   libsystem_c.dylib               0x00007fff84d6ec2c sleep + 61
3   libsystem_c.dylib               0x00007fff84d6ec08 sleep + 25
4   App8                            0x000000010f7f648c procNE() + 60
5   App8                            0x000000010f7f6599 bar_four() + 9
6   App8                            0x000000010f7f65a9 foo_four() + 9
7   App8                            0x000000010f7f65c1 thread_four(void*) + 17
8   libsystem_c.dylib               0x00007fff84db88bf _pthread_start + 335
9   libsystem_c.dylib               0x00007fff84dbbb75 thread_start + 13

Thread 5:
0   libsystem_kernel.dylib          0x00007fff8a10ce42 __semwait_signal + 10
1   libsystem_c.dylib               0x00007fff84d6edea nanosleep + 164
2   libsystem_c.dylib               0x00007fff84d6ec2c sleep + 61
3   libsystem_c.dylib               0x00007fff84d6ec08 sleep + 25
4   App8                            0x000000010f7f648c procNE() + 60
5   App8                            0x000000010f7f65e9 bar_five() + 9
6   App8                            0x000000010f7f65f9 foo_five() + 9
7   App8                            0x000000010f7f6611 thread_five(void*) + 17
8   libsystem_c.dylib               0x00007fff84db88bf _pthread_start + 335
9   libsystem_c.dylib               0x00007fff84dbbb75 thread_start + 13

Thread 1 crashed with X86 Thread State (64-bit):
  rax: 0x0000000000000000  rbx: 0x0000000000000006  rcx: 0x000000010f8aac58  rdx: 0x0000000000000000
  rdi: 0x0000000000001203  rsi: 0x0000000000000006  rbp: 0x000000010f8aac80  rsp: 0x000000010f8aac58
   r8: 0x00007fff74a67fb8   r9: 0x000000000000000a  r10: 0x00007fff8a10cd0a  r11: 0xffffff80002da8d0
  r12: 0x0000000000001203  r13: 0x000000010f8ab000  r14: 0x000000010f8ab000  r15: 0x000000010f8aadd0
  rip: 0x00007fff8a10cce2  rfl: 0x0000000000000246  cr2: 0x00007fff74a61a28
Logical CPU: 0

Binary Images:
       0x10f7f5000 -        0x10f7f6ff7 +App8 (??? - ???) <C689381B-7AA9-3185-B9CB-E0A9A25BEF77>
/Users/USER/Documents/*/App8
    0x7fff6f3f5000 -     0x7fff6f429baf  dyld (195.6 - ???) <0CD1B35B-A28F-32DA-B72E-452EAD609613> /usr/lib/dyld
    0x7fff849f2000 -     0x7fff84a0ffff  libxpc.dylib (77.19.0 - compatibility 1.0.0) <9F57891B-D7EF-3050-BEDD-
21E7C6668248> /usr/lib/system/libxpc.dylib
    0x7fff84d68000 -     0x7fff84d69ff7  libsystem_blocks.dylib (53.0.0 - compatibility 1.0.0) <8BCA214A-8992-34B2-
A8B9-B74DEACA1869> /usr/lib/system/libsystem_blocks.dylib
    0x7fff84d6a000 -     0x7fff84e47fef  libsystem_c.dylib (763.13.0 - compatibility 1.0.0) <41B43515-2806-3FBC-ACF1-
A16F35B7E290> /usr/lib/system/libsystem_c.dylib
    0x7fff85022000 -     0x7fff85030fff  libdispatch.dylib (187.9.0 - compatibility 1.0.0) <1D5BE322-A9B9-3BCE-8FAC-
076FB07CF54A> /usr/lib/system/libdispatch.dylib
    0x7fff855f0000 -     0x7fff855f1fff  libunc.dylib (24.0.0 - compatibility 1.0.0) <337960EE-0A85-3DD0-A760-
7134CF4C0AFF> /usr/lib/system/libunc.dylib
    0x7fff85ae3000 -     0x7fff85ae4ff7  libremovefile.dylib (21.1.0 - compatibility 1.0.0) <739E6C83-AA52-3C6C-A680-
B37FE2888A04> /usr/lib/system/libremovefile.dylib
    0x7fff89114000 -     0x7fff89118fff  libmathCommon.A.dylib (2026.0.0 - compatibility 1.0.0) <FF83AFF7-42B2-306E-
90AF-D539C51A4542> /usr/lib/system/libmathCommon.A.dylib
    0x7fff89119000 -     0x7fff8911dfff  libdyld.dylib (195.5.0 - compatibility 1.0.0) <380C3F44-0CA7-3514-8080-
46D1C9DF4FCD> /usr/lib/system/libdyld.dylib
    0x7fff89740000 -     0x7fff89741ff7  libsystem_sandbox.dylib (??? - ???) <96D38E74-F18F-3CCB-A20B-E8E3ADC4E166>
/usr/lib/system/libsystem_sandbox.dylib
    0x7fff8a0ef000 -     0x7fff8a0f5fff  libmacho.dylib (800.0.0 - compatibility 1.0.0) <165514D7-1BFA-38EF-A151-
676DCD21FB64> /usr/lib/system/libmacho.dylib
    0x7fff8a0f6000 -     0x7fff8a116fff  libsystem_kernel.dylib (1699.26.8 - compatibility 1.0.0) <1DDC0B0F-DB2A-34D6-
895D-E5B2B5618946> /usr/lib/system/libsystem_kernel.dylib
    0x7fff8a2ac000 -     0x7fff8a2b4fff  libsystem_dnssd.dylib (??? - ???) <D9BB1F87-A42B-3CBC-9DC2-FC07FCEF0016>
/usr/lib/system/libsystem_dnssd.dylib
    0x7fff8ae26000 -     0x7fff8ae61fff  libsystem_info.dylib (??? - ???) <35F90252-2AE1-32C5-8D34-782C614D9639>
/usr/lib/system/libsystem_info.dylib
    0x7fff8b248000 -     0x7fff8b24afff  libquarantine.dylib (36.6.0 - compatibility 1.0.0) <0EBF714B-4B69-3E1F-9A7D-
6BBC2AACB310> /usr/lib/system/libquarantine.dylib
```

```
       0x7fff8b3b4000 -     0x7fff8b3b4fff  libkeymgr.dylib (23.0.0 - compatibility 1.0.0) <61EFED6A-A407-301E-B454-
CD18314F0075> /usr/lib/system/libkeymgr.dylib
       0x7fff8b3dd000 -     0x7fff8b3e2fff  libcompiler_rt.dylib (6.0.0 - compatibility 1.0.0) <98ECD5F6-E85C-32A5-98CD-
8911230CB66A> /usr/lib/system/libcompiler_rt.dylib
       0x7fff8bd1a000 -     0x7fff8bd1bfff  libdnsinfo.dylib (395.11.0 - compatibility 1.0.0) <853BAAA5-270F-3FDC-B025-
D448DB72E1C3> /usr/lib/system/libdnsinfo.dylib
       0x7fff8c528000 -     0x7fff8c52dff7  libsystem_network.dylib (??? - ???) <5DE7024E-1D2D-34A2-80F4-08326331A75B>
/usr/lib/system/libsystem_network.dylib
       0x7fff8cfa3000 -     0x7fff8cfadff7  liblaunch.dylib (392.38.0 - compatibility 1.0.0) <6ECB7F19-B384-32C1-8652-
2463C1CF4815> /usr/lib/system/liblaunch.dylib
       0x7fff8dad3000 -     0x7fff8db46fff  libstdc++.6.dylib (52.0.0 - compatibility 7.0.0) <6BDD43E4-A4B1-379E-9ED5-
8C713653DFF2> /usr/lib/libstdc++.6.dylib
       0x7fff8fe02000 -     0x7fff8fe09fff  libcopyfile.dylib (85.1.0 - compatibility 1.0.0) <0AB51EE2-E914-358C-AC19-
47BC024BDAE7> /usr/lib/system/libcopyfile.dylib
       0x7fff8fe4b000 -     0x7fff8fe8dff7  libcommonCrypto.dylib (55010.0.0 - compatibility 1.0.0) <BB770C22-8C57-365A-
8716-4A3C36AE7BFB> /usr/lib/system/libcommonCrypto.dylib
       0x7fff90a98000 -     0x7fff90aa3ff7  libc++abi.dylib (14.0.0 - compatibility 1.0.0) <8FF3D766-D678-36F6-84AC-
423C878E6D14> /usr/lib/libc++abi.dylib
       0x7fff90c0f000 -     0x7fff90c18ff7  libsystem_notify.dylib (80.1.0 - compatibility 1.0.0) <A4D651E3-D1C6-3934-
AD49-7A104FD14596> /usr/lib/system/libsystem_notify.dylib
       0x7fff91376000 -     0x7fff913a3fe7  libSystem.B.dylib (159.1.0 - compatibility 1.0.0) <7BEBB139-50BB-3112-947A-
F4AA168F991C> /usr/lib/libSystem.B.dylib
       0x7fff91489000 -     0x7fff9148fff7  libunwind.dylib (30.0.0 - compatibility 1.0.0) <1E9C6C8C-CBE8-3F4B-A5B5-
E03E3AB53231> /usr/lib/system/libunwind.dylib
       0x7fff91a22000 -     0x7fff91a27fff  libcache.dylib (47.0.0 - compatibility 1.0.0) <1571C3AB-BCB2-38CD-B3B2-
C5FC3F927C6A> /usr/lib/system/libcache.dylib

External Modification Summary:
  Calls made by other processes targeting this process:
    task_for_pid: 2
    thread_create: 0
    thread_set_state: 0
  Calls made by this process:
    task_for_pid: 0
    thread_create: 0
    thread_set_state: 0
  Calls made by all processes on this machine:
    task_for_pid: 7055
    thread_create: 0
    thread_set_state: 0

VM Region Summary:
ReadOnly portion of Libraries: Total=50.7M resident=50.7M(100%) swapped_out_or_unallocated=0K(0%)
Writable regions: Total=38.9M written=17.9M(46%) resident=42.6M(110%) swapped_out=0K(0%)
unallocated=16777216.0T(45221404475392%)

REGION TYPE              VIRTUAL
===========              =======
MALLOC                     1220K
Stack                      66.6M
__DATA                      504K
__LINKEDIT                 47.7M
__TEXT                     3000K
shared memory                12K
===========              =======
TOTAL                     118.9M
```

2.   Load a core dump core.4472 and App8 executable:

$ lldb -c ~/Documents/AMCDA-Dumps/core.4472 -f ~/Documents/AMCDA-Dumps/Apps/App8/Build/Products/Release/App8

error: core.4472 is a corrupt mach-o file: load command 46 LC_SEGMENT_64 has a fileoff +
filesize (0x160b8000) that extends beyond the end of the file (0x160b6000), the segment will be
truncated

Core file '/Users/DumpAnalysis/Documents/AMCDA-Dumps/core.4472' (x86_64) was loaded.
Process 0 stopped

```
* thread #1: tid = 0x0000, 0x00007fff8a10ce42 libsystem_kernel.dylib`__semwait_signal + 10,
stop reason = signal SIGSTOP
    frame #0: 0x00007fff8a10ce42 libsystem_kernel.dylib`__semwait_signal + 10
libsystem_kernel.dylib`__semwait_signal + 10:
-> 0x7fff8a10ce42:  jae    0x7fff8a10ce49            ; __semwait_signal + 17
   0x7fff8a10ce44:  jmpq   0x7fff8a10dffc            ; cerror
   0x7fff8a10ce49:  ret
   0x7fff8a10ce4a:  nop
  thread #2: tid = 0x0001, 0x00007fff8a10cce2 libsystem_kernel.dylib`__pthread_kill + 10, stop
reason = signal SIGSTOP
    frame #0: 0x00007fff8a10cce2 libsystem_kernel.dylib`__pthread_kill + 10
libsystem_kernel.dylib`__pthread_kill + 10:
-> 0x7fff8a10cce2:  jae    0x7fff8a10cce9            ; __pthread_kill + 17
   0x7fff8a10cce4:  jmpq   0x7fff8a10dffc            ; cerror
   0x7fff8a10cce9:  ret
   0x7fff8a10ccea:  nop
  thread #3: tid = 0x0002, 0x00007fff8a10ce42 libsystem_kernel.dylib`__semwait_signal + 10,
stop reason = signal SIGSTOP
    frame #0: 0x00007fff8a10ce42 libsystem_kernel.dylib`__semwait_signal + 10
libsystem_kernel.dylib`__semwait_signal + 10:
-> 0x7fff8a10ce42:  jae    0x7fff8a10ce49            ; __semwait_signal + 17
   0x7fff8a10ce44:  jmpq   0x7fff8a10dffc            ; cerror
   0x7fff8a10ce49:  ret
   0x7fff8a10ce4a:  nop
  thread #4: tid = 0x0003, 0x00007fff8a10ce42 libsystem_kernel.dylib`__semwait_signal + 10,
stop reason = signal SIGSTOP
    frame #0: 0x00007fff8a10ce42 libsystem_kernel.dylib`__semwait_signal + 10
libsystem_kernel.dylib`__semwait_signal + 10:
-> 0x7fff8a10ce42:  jae    0x7fff8a10ce49            ; __semwait_signal + 17
   0x7fff8a10ce44:  jmpq   0x7fff8a10dffc            ; cerror
   0x7fff8a10ce49:  ret
   0x7fff8a10ce4a:  nop
  thread #5: tid = 0x0004, 0x00007fff8a10ce42 libsystem_kernel.dylib`__semwait_signal + 10,
stop reason = signal SIGSTOP
    frame #0: 0x00007fff8a10ce42 libsystem_kernel.dylib`__semwait_signal + 10
libsystem_kernel.dylib`__semwait_signal + 10:
-> 0x7fff8a10ce42:  jae    0x7fff8a10ce49            ; __semwait_signal + 17
   0x7fff8a10ce44:  jmpq   0x7fff8a10dffc            ; cerror
   0x7fff8a10ce49:  ret
   0x7fff8a10ce4a:  nop
  thread #6: tid = 0x0005, 0x00007fff8a10ce42 libsystem_kernel.dylib`__semwait_signal + 10,
stop reason = signal SIGSTOP
    frame #0: 0x00007fff8a10ce42 libsystem_kernel.dylib`__semwait_signal + 10
libsystem_kernel.dylib`__semwait_signal + 10:
-> 0x7fff8a10ce42:  jae    0x7fff8a10ce49            ; __semwait_signal + 17
   0x7fff8a10ce44:  jmpq   0x7fff8a10dffc            ; cerror
   0x7fff8a10ce49:  ret
   0x7fff8a10ce4a:  nop
```

3.   Go to the core thread 2 (thread #3), identify execution residue of work functions and check their correctness:

```
(lldb) thread select 3
* thread #3: tid = 0x0002, 0x00007fff8a10ce42 libsystem_kernel.dylib`__semwait_signal + 10,
stop reason = signal SIGSTOP
    frame #0: 0x00007fff8a10ce42 libsystem_kernel.dylib`__semwait_signal + 10
libsystem_kernel.dylib`__semwait_signal + 10:
-> 0x7fff8a10ce42:  jae    0x7fff8a10ce49            ; __semwait_signal + 17
   0x7fff8a10ce44:  jmpq   0x7fff8a10dffc            ; cerror
   0x7fff8a10ce49:  ret
   0x7fff8a10ce4a:  nop

(lldb) bt
* thread #3: tid = 0x0002, 0x00007fff8a10ce42 libsystem_kernel.dylib`__semwait_signal + 10,
stop reason = signal SIGSTOP
    frame #0: 0x00007fff8a10ce42 libsystem_kernel.dylib`__semwait_signal + 10
    frame #1: 0x00007fff84d6edea libsystem_c.dylib`nanosleep + 164
    frame #2: 0x00007fff84d6ec2c libsystem_c.dylib`sleep + 61
    frame #3: 0x00007fff84d6ec08 libsystem_c.dylib`sleep + 25
    frame #4: 0x000000010f7f648c App8`procNE() + 60
    frame #5: 0x000000010f7f64f9 App8`bar_two() + 9
    frame #6: 0x000000010f7f6509 App8`foo_two() + 9
    frame #7: 0x000000010f7f6521 App8`thread_two(void*) + 17
    frame #8: 0x00007fff84db88bf libsystem_c.dylib`_pthread_start + 335
    frame #9: 0x00007fff84dbbb75 libsystem_c.dylib`thread_start + 13

(lldb) x/512a $rsp-2000 --force
0x10fa80628: 0x0000000000000000
0x10fa80630: 0x0000000000000000
0x10fa80638: 0x0000000000000000
0x10fa80640: 0x0000000000000000
0x10fa80648: 0x0000000000000000
[...]
0x10fa809d0: 0x0000000000000000
0x10fa809d8: 0x0000000000000000
0x10fa809e0: 0x000000010fa809f0
0x10fa809e8: 0x000000010f7f6159 App8`work_8() + 9
0x10fa809f0: 0x000000010fa80a00
0x10fa809f8: 0x000000010f7f6169 App8`work_7() + 9
0x10fa80a00: 0x000000010fa80a10
0x10fa80a08: 0x000000010f7f6179 App8`work_6() + 9
0x10fa80a10: 0x000000010fa80a20
0x10fa80a18: 0x000000010f7f6189 App8`work_5() + 9
0x10fa80a20: 0x000000010fa80a30
0x10fa80a28: 0x000000010f7f6199 App8`work_4() + 9
0x10fa80a30: 0x000000010fa80a40
0x10fa80a38: 0x000000010f7f61a9 App8`work_3() + 9
0x10fa80a40: 0x000000010fa80a50
0x10fa80a48: 0x000000010f7f61b9 App8`work_2() + 9
0x10fa80a50: 0x000000010fa80a60
0x10fa80a58: 0x000000010f7f61c9 App8`work_1() + 9
0x10fa80a60: 0x000000010fa80e80
0x10fa80a68: 0x000000010f7f61ee App8`work() + 30
0x10fa80a70: 0x0000000000000000
0x10fa80a78: 0x0000000000000000
0x10fa80a80: 0x0000000000000000
0x10fa80a88: 0x0000000000000000
[...]
0x10fa80d30: 0x0000000000000000
```

```
0x10fa80d38: 0x0000000000000000
0x10fa80d40: 0x0000000000000000
0x10fa80d48: 0x00007fff8a10ad71  libsystem_kernel.dylib`mach_msg + 73
0x10fa80d50: 0x0000000000000000
0x10fa80d58: 0x0000000000000000
0x10fa80d60: 0x0000000300000018
0x10fa80d68: 0x000000010fa80e00
0x10fa80d70: 0x0000000000001303
0x10fa80d78: 0x000000010fa81000
0x10fa80d80: 0x000000010fa80e48
0x10fa80d88: 0x000000010f7f6510  App8`thread_two(void*)
0x10fa80d90: 0x000000010fa80df0
0x10fa80d98: 0x00007fff8a0f784f  libsystem_kernel.dylib`clock_get_time + 76
0x10fa80da0: 0x0000000000000000
0x10fa80da8: 0x0000002c00001200
0x10fa80db0: 0x0000160300000000
0x10fa80db8: 0x0000044cffffff80
0x10fa80dc0: 0x0000000100000000
0x10fa80dc8: 0x0001852200000000
0x10fa80dd0: 0x00000000338092a6
0x10fa80dd8: 0x00007fff00000008
0x10fa80de0: 0x000000010fa80e38
0x10fa80de8: 0x000000010fa80e48
0x10fa80df0: 0x000000010fa80e20
0x10fa80df8: 0x00007fff84d6edea  libsystem_c.dylib`nanosleep + 164
0x10fa80e00: 0x338092a600018522
0x10fa80e08: 0x0000000000000000
0x10fa80e10: 0x000000007fffffff
0x10fa80e18: 0x0000000000000000
0x10fa80e20: 0x000000010fa80e60
0x10fa80e28: 0x00007fff84d6ec2c  libsystem_c.dylib`sleep + 61
0x10fa80e30: 0x0000000000000000
0x10fa80e38: 0x0000000000000000
0x10fa80e40: 0x0000000000000000
0x10fa80e48: 0x000000007fffffff
0x10fa80e50: 0x0000000000000000
0x10fa80e58: 0x00000000ffffffff
0x10fa80e60: 0x000000010fa80ea0
0x10fa80e68: 0x00007fff84d6ec08  libsystem_c.dylib`sleep + 25
0x10fa80e70: 0x0000000000000000
0x10fa80e78: 0xb5a42821d4d7e840
0x10fa80e80: 0x000000010fa80e90
0x10fa80e88: 0x000000010f7f6379  App8`procNB() + 9
0x10fa80e90: 0x000000010fa80ea0
0x10fa80e98: 0x0000000000000000
0x10fa80ea0: 0x000000010fa80ed0
0x10fa80ea8: 0x000000010f7f648c  App8`procNE() + 60
0x10fa80eb0: 0x0000000000000000
0x10fa80eb8: 0x0000000000000000
0x10fa80ec0: 0x0000000000000000
0x10fa80ec8: 0x0000000000000000
0x10fa80ed0: 0x000000010fa80ee0
0x10fa80ed8: 0x000000010f7f64f9  App8`bar_two() + 9
0x10fa80ee0: 0x000000010fa80ef0
0x10fa80ee8: 0x000000010f7f6509  App8`foo_two() + 9
0x10fa80ef0: 0x000000010fa80f10
0x10fa80ef8: 0x000000010f7f6521  App8`thread_two(void*) + 17
0x10fa80f00: 0x0000000000000000
0x10fa80f08: 0x0000000000000000
0x10fa80f10: 0x000000010fa80f50
```

```
0x10fa80f18: 0x00007fff84db88bf libsystem_c.dylib`_pthread_start + 335
0x10fa80f20: 0x0000000000000000
0x10fa80f28: 0x0000000000000000
0x10fa80f30: 0x0000000000000000
0x10fa80f38: 0x0000000000000000
0x10fa80f40: 0x0000000000000000
0x10fa80f48: 0x0000000000000000
0x10fa80f50: 0x000000010fa80f78
0x10fa80f58: 0x00007fff84dbbb75 libsystem_c.dylib`thread_start + 13
0x10fa80f60: 0x0000000000000000
0x10fa80f68: 0x0000000000000000
0x10fa80f70: 0x0000000000000000
0x10fa80f78: 0x0000000000000000
0x10fa80f80: 0x0000000000000000
0x10fa80f88: 0x0000000000000000
0x10fa80f90: 0x0000000000000000
0x10fa80f98: 0x0000000000000000
0x10fa80fa0: 0x0000000000000000
0x10fa80fa8: 0x0000000000000000
0x10fa80fb0: 0x0000000000000000
0x10fa80fb8: 0x0000000000000000
0x10fa80fc0: 0x0000000000000000
0x10fa80fc8: 0x0000000000000000
0x10fa80fd0: 0x0000000000000000
0x10fa80fd8: 0x0000000000000000
0x10fa80fe0: 0x0000000000000000
0x10fa80fe8: 0x0000000000000000
0x10fa80ff0: 0x0000000000000000
0x10fa80ff8: 0x0000000000000000
0x10fa81000: 0x0000000054485244
0x10fa81008: 0x0000000000000000
0x10fa81010: 0x0701010100000000
0x10fa81018: 0x0000000000001000
0x10fa81020: 0x0000000a0000001f
0x10fa81028: 0x0000000000000000
0x10fa81030: 0x0000000000000000
0x10fa81038: 0x0000000000000000
0x10fa81040: 0x0000130300000000
0x10fa81048: 0x000000010f7f6510 App8`thread_two(void*)
0x10fa81050: 0x0000000000000000
0x10fa81058: 0x0000000000000003
0x10fa81060: 0x000000010fa81000
0x10fa81068: 0x0000000000000000
[…]
0x10fa815f8: 0x0000000000000000
0x10fa81600: 0x0000000000000000
0x10fa81608: 0x0000000000000000
0x10fa81610: 0x0000000000000000
0x10fa81618: 0x0000000000000000
0x10fa81620: 0x0000000000000000

(lldb) di -a 0x000000010f7f61a9
App8`work_3():
    0x10f7f61a0:  pushq   %rbp
    0x10f7f61a1:  movq    %rsp, %rbp
    0x10f7f61a4:  callq   0x10f7f6190                   ; work_4()
    0x10f7f61a9:  popq    %rbp
    0x10f7f61aa:  ret
    0x10f7f61ab:  nopl    (%rax,%rax)
```

4.   Go to the core thread 3 (thread #4) and identify handled exception processing code:

```
(lldb) thread select 4
* thread #4: tid = 0x0003, 0x00007fff8a10ce42 libsystem_kernel.dylib`__semwait_signal + 10,
stop reason = signal SIGSTOP
    frame #0: 0x00007fff8a10ce42 libsystem_kernel.dylib`__semwait_signal + 10
libsystem_kernel.dylib`__semwait_signal + 10:
-> 0x7fff8a10ce42:  jae    0x7fff8a10ce49            ; __semwait_signal + 17
   0x7fff8a10ce44:  jmpq   0x7fff8a10dffc            ; cerror
   0x7fff8a10ce49:  ret
   0x7fff8a10ce4a:  nop

(lldb) bt
* thread #4: tid = 0x0003, 0x00007fff8a10ce42 libsystem_kernel.dylib`__semwait_signal + 10,
stop reason = signal SIGSTOP
    frame #0: 0x00007fff8a10ce42 libsystem_kernel.dylib`__semwait_signal + 10
    frame #1: 0x00007fff84d6edea libsystem_c.dylib`nanosleep + 164
    frame #2: 0x00007fff84d6ec2c libsystem_c.dylib`sleep + 61
    frame #3: 0x00007fff84d6ec08 libsystem_c.dylib`sleep + 25
    frame #4: 0x000000010f7f63d7 App8`procH() + 55
    frame #5: 0x000000010f7f6549 App8`bar_three() + 9
    frame #6: 0x000000010f7f6559 App8`foo_three() + 9
    frame #7: 0x000000010f7f6571 App8`thread_three(void*) + 17
    frame #8: 0x00007fff84db88bf libsystem_c.dylib`_pthread_start + 335
    frame #9: 0x00007fff84dbbb75 libsystem_c.dylib`thread_start + 13

(lldb) x/512a $rsp-2000 --force
0x10fb03608: 0x000000010fb04000
0x10fb03610: 0x0000000000000000
0x10fb03618: 0x000000010f7f6560 App8`thread_three(void*)
0x10fb03620: 0x000000010f7f63b7 App8`procH() + 23
0x10fb03628: 0x0000000000000000
0x10fb03630: 0x0000000000000000
0x10fb03638: 0x0000000000000000
0x10fb03640: 0x0000000000000000
0x10fb03648: 0x00007fff76401a08 libunwind.dylib`sThisAddressSpace
0x10fb03650: 0x0000000000000000
0x10fb03658: 0x0000000000000000
0x10fb03660: 0x0000000000000000
0x10fb03668: 0x0000000000000000
0x10fb03670: 0x0000000000000000
0x10fb03678: 0x0000000000000000
0x10fb03680: 0x0000000000000000
0x10fb03688: 0x0000000000000000
0x10fb03690: 0x0000000000000000
0x10fb03698: 0x0000000000000000
0x10fb036a0: 0x0000000000000000
0x10fb036a8: 0x0000000000000000
0x10fb036b0: 0x0000000000000000
0x10fb036b8: 0x0000000000000000
0x10fb036c0: 0x0000000000000000
0x10fb036c8: 0x0000000000000000
```

```
0x10fb036d0:  0x0000000000000000
0x10fb036d8:  0x0000000000000000
0x10fb036e0:  0x0000000000000000
0x10fb036e8:  0x0000000000000000
0x10fb036f0:  0x0000000000000000
0x10fb036f8:  0x0000000000000000
0x10fb03700:  0x0000000000000000
0x10fb03708:  0x0000000000000000
0x10fb03710:  0x0000000000000000
0x10fb03718:  0x0000000000000000
0x10fb03720:  0x0000000000000000
0x10fb03728:  0x0000000000000000
0x10fb03730:  0x0000000000000000
0x10fb03738:  0x0000000000000000
0x10fb03740:  0x0000000000000000
0x10fb03748:  0x0000000000000000
0x10fb03750:  0x0000000000000000
0x10fb03758:  0x0000000000000000
0x10fb03760:  0x0000000000000000
0x10fb03768:  0x0000000000000000
0x10fb03770:  0x0000000000000000
0x10fb03778:  0x0000000000000000
0x10fb03780:  0x0000000000000000
0x10fb03788:  0x0000000000000000
0x10fb03790:  0x0000000000000000
0x10fb03798:  0x0000000000000000
0x10fb037a0:  0x0000000000000000
0x10fb037a8:  0x0000000000000000
0x10fb037b0:  0x0000000000000000
0x10fb037b8:  0x0000000000000000
0x10fb037c0:  0x0000000000000000
0x10fb037c8:  0x0000000000000000
0x10fb037d0:  0x0000000000000000
0x10fb037d8:  0x0000000000000000
0x10fb037e0:  0x0000000000000000
0x10fb037e8:  0x0000000000000000
0x10fb037f0:  0x0000000000000000
0x10fb037f8:  0x0000000000000000
0x10fb03800:  0x0000000000000000
0x10fb03808:  0x0000000000000000
0x10fb03810:  0x0000000000000000
0x10fb03818:  0x0000000000000000
0x10fb03820:  0x0000000000000000
0x10fb03828:  0x0000000000000000
0x10fb03830:  0x0000000000000000
0x10fb03838:  0x0000000000000000
0x10fb03840:  0x0000000000000000
0x10fb03848:  0x0000000000000000
0x10fb03850:  0x0000000000000000
0x10fb03858:  0x0000000000000000
0x10fb03860:  0x0000000000000000
0x10fb03868:  0x0000000000000000
0x10fb03870:  0x0000000000000000
```

```
0x10fb03878: 0x0000000000000000
0x10fb03880: 0x0000000000000000
0x10fb03888: 0x0000000000000000
0x10fb03890: 0x0000000000000000
0x10fb03898: 0x0000000000000000
0x10fb038a0: 0x0000000000000000
0x10fb038a8: 0x0000000000000000
0x10fb038b0: 0x0000000000000000
0x10fb038b8: 0x0000000000000000
0x10fb038c0: 0x0000000000000000
0x10fb038c8: 0x0000000000000000
0x10fb038d0: 0x0000000000000000
0x10fb038d8: 0x0000000000000000
0x10fb038e0: 0x0000000000000000
0x10fb038e8: 0x0000000000000000
0x10fb038f0: 0x0000000000000000
0x10fb038f8: 0x0000000000000000
0x10fb03900: 0x0000000000000000
0x10fb03908: 0x000000010fb03e90
0x10fb03910: 0x000000010f7f63a0 App8`procH()
0x10fb03918: 0x000000010f7f6430 App8`procNH()
0x10fb03920: 0x000000010f7f68fc App8`GCC_except_table15
0x10fb03928: 0x00007fff90a9e6f4 libc++abi.dylib`__gxx_personality_v0
0x10fb03930: 0x0000000000000000
0x10fb03938: 0x0000000000000000
0x10fb03940: 0x0000000051000000
0x10fb03948: 0x0000000000000000
0x10fb03950: 0x000000010f7f5000
0x10fb03958: 0x00007fff764010a0 vtable for
libunwind::UnwindCursor<libunwind::LocalAddressSpace, libunwind::Registers_x86_64> + 16
0x10fb03960: 0x000000010f7f63a0 App8`procH()
0x10fb03968: 0x000000010f7f6430 App8`procNH()
0x10fb03970: 0x000000010f7f68fc App8`GCC_except_table15
0x10fb03978: 0x00007fff90a9e6f4 libc++abi.dylib`__gxx_personality_v0
0x10fb03980: 0x0000000000000000
0x10fb03988: 0x0000000000000000
0x10fb03990: 0x0000000051000000
0x10fb03998: 0x0000000000000000
0x10fb039a0: 0x000000010f7f5000
0x10fb039a8: 0x000000010f900980
0x10fb039b0: 0x000000010f900918
0x10fb039b8: 0x0000000000001503
0x10fb039c0: 0x0000000000000000
0x10fb039c8: 0x000000010f7f6560 App8`thread_three(void*)
0x10fb039d0: 0x000000010fb03df0
0x10fb039d8: 0x00007fff9148e0fb libunwind.dylib`_Unwind_Resume + 72
0x10fb039e0: 0x000000010fb03e90
0x10fb039e8: 0x000000010f900918
0x10fb039f0: 0x000000010f900918
0x10fb039f8: 0x0000000000000000
0x10fb03a00: 0x0000000000000000
0x10fb03a08: 0x000000010fb039e8
0x10fb03a10: 0x000000010fb03dd8 -> 0x00007fff84d6edea libsystem_c.dylib`nanosleep + 164
```

```
0x10fb03a18: 0x000000010fb03df0
0x10fb03a20: 0x000000010fb039e0
0x10fb03a28: 0x000000010f7fca00
0x10fb03a30: 0x0000000000000008
0x10fb03a38: 0x0000000000004000
0x10fb03a40: 0x00007fff9148e0b3 libunwind.dylib`_Unwind_Resume
0x10fb03a48: 0x0000000000001503
0x10fb03a50: 0x000000010fb04000
0x10fb03a58: 0x0000000000000000
0x10fb03a60: 0x000000010f7f6560 App8`thread_three(void*)
0x10fb03a68: 0x00007fff9148e0ce libunwind.dylib`_Unwind_Resume + 27
0x10fb03a70: 0x0000000000000000
0x10fb03a78: 0x0000000000000000
0x10fb03a80: 0x0000000000000000
0x10fb03a88: 0x0000000000000000
0x10fb03a90: 0x0000000000000000
0x10fb03a98: 0x0000000000000000
0x10fb03aa0: 0x0000000000000000
0x10fb03aa8: 0x0000000000000000
0x10fb03ab0: 0x0000000000000000
0x10fb03ab8: 0x0000000000000000
0x10fb03ac0: 0x0000000000000000
0x10fb03ac8: 0x0000000000000000
0x10fb03ad0: 0x0000000000000000
0x10fb03ad8: 0x0000000000000000
0x10fb03ae0: 0x0000000000000000
0x10fb03ae8: 0x00007fff6f433118 dyld`initialPoolContent + 11240
0x10fb03af0: 0x000000010fb03b40
0x10fb03af8: 0x00007fff6f409b60 dyld`ImageLoaderMachOCompressed::findExportedSymbol(char
const*, ImageLoader const**) const + 86
0x10fb03b00: 0x0000000000000000
0x10fb03b08: 0x000000010fb03cc0 -> 0x000000010f7f81a4
0x10fb03b10: 0x000000010f7f8207
0x10fb03b18: 0x000000010fb03cc0 -> 0x000000010f7f81a4
0x10fb03b20: 0x00007fff6f433118 dyld`initialPoolContent + 11240
0x10fb03b28: 0x000000010f7f8200
0x10fb03b30: 0x0000000000000001
0x10fb03b38: 0x000000010f7f8207
0x10fb03b40: 0x000000010fb03b80
0x10fb03b48: 0x00007fff6f403f50 dyld`ImageLoaderMachO::findExportedSymbol(char const*, bool,
ImageLoader const**) const + 48
0x10fb03b50: 0x000000010f7f8207
0x10fb03b58: 0x000000010fb03cc0 -> 0x000000010f7f81a4
0x10fb03b60: 0x00007fff6f4321e0 dyld`initialPoolContent + 7344
0x10fb03b68: 0x000000010f7f8200
0x10fb03b70: 0x0000000000000001
0x10fb03b78: 0x00007fff6f432330 dyld`initialPoolContent + 7680
0x10fb03b80: 0x000000010fb03bd0
0x10fb03b88: 0x00007fff6f409b60 dyld`ImageLoaderMachOCompressed::findExportedSymbol(char
const*, ImageLoader const**) const + 86
0x10fb03b90: 0x000000010fb03bd0
0x10fb03b98: 0x000000010fb03d50
0x10fb03ba0: 0x000000010f7f81a4
```

```
0x10fb03ba8: 0x000000010fb03d50
0x10fb03bb0: 0x00007fff6f432330 dyld`initialPoolContent + 7680
0x10fb03bb8: 0x000000010f7f8100
0x10fb03bc0: 0x0000000000000001
0x10fb03bc8: 0x000000010f7f81a4
0x10fb03bd0: 0x000000010fb03c10
0x10fb03bd8: 0x00007fff6f403f50 dyld`ImageLoaderMachO::findExportedSymbol(char const*, bool,
ImageLoader const**) const + 48
0x10fb03be0: 0x000000010f7f81a4
0x10fb03be8: 0x000000010fb03d50
0x10fb03bf0: 0x00007fff6f432140 dyld`initialPoolContent + 7184
0x10fb03bf8: 0x000000010f7f8100
0x10fb03c00: 0x0000000000000001
0x10fb03c08: 0x000000010f7f81a4
0x10fb03c10: 0x000000010fb03c50 -> 0x00007fff6f430d80 dyld`initialPoolContent + 2128
0x10fb03c18: 0x00007fff6f403f50 dyld`ImageLoaderMachO::findExportedSymbol(char const*, bool,
ImageLoader const**) const + 48
0x10fb03c20: 0x000000010fb03cc0 -> 0x000000010f7f81a4
0x10fb03c28: 0x000000010f7f81a4
0x10fb03c30: 0x00007fff6f42a110 dyld::gLinkContext
0x10fb03c38: 0x00007fff6f42a110 dyld::gLinkContext
0x10fb03c40: 0x00007fff6f430d80 dyld`initialPoolContent + 2128
0x10fb03c48: 0x000000010f7f8100
0x10fb03c50: 0x00007fff6f430d80 dyld`initialPoolContent + 2128
0x10fb03c58: 0x00007fff6f432330 dyld`initialPoolContent + 7680
0x10fb03c60: 0x000000010fb03ca0
0x10fb03c68: 0x00007fff6f404eb9 dyld`ImageLoaderMachO::getSymbolAddress(ImageLoader::Symbol
const*, ImageLoader const*, ImageLoader::LinkContext const&, bool) const + 47
0x10fb03c70: 0x00007fff6f42a110 dyld::gLinkContext
0x10fb03c78: 0x000000010fb03d50
0x10fb03c80: 0x00007fff6f430d80 dyld`initialPoolContent + 2128
0x10fb03c88: 0x000000010f7f8100
0x10fb03c90: 0x0000000000000001
0x10fb03c98: 0x00007fff6f42a110 dyld::gLinkContext
0x10fb03ca0: 0x000000010fb03cf0
0x10fb03ca8: 0x00007fff6f40c6bd
dyld`ImageLoaderMachOCompressed::resolve(ImageLoader::LinkContext const&, char const*, unsigned
char, int, ImageLoader const**, ImageLoaderMachOCompressed::LastLookup*, bool) + 329
0x10fb03cb0: 0x000000010fb03d50
0x10fb03cb8: 0x000000010f7f8268
0x10fb03cc0: 0x000000010f7f81a4
0x10fb03cc8: 0x000000010f7f8268
0x10fb03cd0: 0x000000010f7f7090 (void *)0x00007fff90a9e355: __cxa_begin_catch
0x10fb03cd8: 0x000000010f7f81b8
0x10fb03ce0: 0x000000010f7f81a4
0x10fb03ce8: 0x0000000000000001
0x10fb03cf0: 0x000000010fb03d80
0x10fb03cf8: 0x00007fff6f40c9cd dyld`ImageLoaderMachOCompressed::doBindFastLazySymbol(unsigned
int, ImageLoader::LinkContext const&, void (*)(), void (*)()) + 703
0x10fb03d00: 0x000000010f7f81a4
0x10fb03d08: 0x0000000000000000
0x10fb03d10: 0x00007fff6f41c65c "lazy "
0x10fb03d18: 0x00007fff8911a5c0 libdyld.dylib`dyldGlobalLockRelease()
```

```
0x10fb03d20: 0x00007fff90a9e355 libc++abi.dylib`__cxa_begin_catch
0x10fb03d28: 0x00007fff8a10ad71 libsystem_kernel.dylib`mach_msg + 73
0x10fb03d30: 0x0101000000000000
0x10fb03d38: 0x00007fff6f42a110 dyld::gLinkContext
0x10fb03d40: 0x0000000300000018
0x10fb03d48: 0x000000010fb03de0
0x10fb03d50: 0x0000000000001503
0x10fb03d58: 0x000000010fb04000
0x10fb03d60: 0x000000010fb03e28
0x10fb03d68: 0x000000010f7f6560 App8`thread_three(void*)
0x10fb03d70: 0x000000010fb03dd0
0x10fb03d78: 0x00007fff8a0f784f libsystem_kernel.dylib`clock_get_time + 76
0x10fb03d80: 0x0000000100000000
0x10fb03d88: 0x0000002c00001200
0x10fb03d90: 0x00001b0300000000
0x10fb03d98: 0x0000044c00000020
0x10fb03da0: 0x0000000100000000
0x10fb03da8: 0x0001852200000000
0x10fb03db0: 0x0000000033850396
0x10fb03db8: 0x00007fff00000008
0x10fb03dc0: 0x000000010fb03e18
0x10fb03dc8: 0x000000010fb03e28
0x10fb03dd0: 0x000000010fb03e00
0x10fb03dd8: 0x00007fff84d6edea libsystem_c.dylib`nanosleep + 164
0x10fb03de0: 0x3385039600018522
0x10fb03de8: 0x0000000000000000
0x10fb03df0: 0x000000007fffffff
0x10fb03df8: 0x0000000000000000
0x10fb03e00: 0x000000010fb03e40
0x10fb03e08: 0x00007fff84d6ec2c libsystem_c.dylib`sleep + 61
0x10fb03e10: 0x0000000000001503
0x10fb03e18: 0x000000010fb04000
0x10fb03e20: 0x000000010f900918
0x10fb03e28: 0x000000007fffffff
0x10fb03e30: 0x0000000000000000
0x10fb03e38: 0x00000000ffffffff
0x10fb03e40: 0x000000010fb03e80
0x10fb03e48: 0x00007fff84d6ec08 libsystem_c.dylib`sleep + 25
0x10fb03e50: 0x0000000000000000
0x10fb03e58: 0x000000010f900918
0x10fb03e60: 0x000000010fb03e80
0x10fb03e68: 0x00007fff90a9e366 libc++abi.dylib`__cxa_begin_catch + 17
0x10fb03e70: 0x000000010fb03ed0
0x10fb03e78: 0x0000000000000000
0x10fb03e80: 0x000000010fb03ed0
0x10fb03e88: 0x000000010f7f63d7 App8`procH() + 55
0x10fb03e90: 0x0000000000000000
0x10fb03e98: 0x0000000000000000
0x10fb03ea0: 0x0000000000000000
0x10fb03ea8: 0x0000000000000000
0x10fb03eb0: 0x0000000000000000
0x10fb03eb8: 0x000000010f900938
0x10fb03ec0: 0x0000000100000000
```

```
0x10fb03ec8: 0x000000010f900918
0x10fb03ed0: 0x000000010fb03ee0
0x10fb03ed8: 0x000000010f7f6549  App8`bar_three() + 9
0x10fb03ee0: 0x000000010fb03ef0
0x10fb03ee8: 0x000000010f7f6559  App8`foo_three() + 9
0x10fb03ef0: 0x000000010fb03f10
0x10fb03ef8: 0x000000010f7f6571  App8`thread_three(void*) + 17
0x10fb03f00: 0x0000000000000000
0x10fb03f08: 0x0000000000000000
0x10fb03f10: 0x000000010fb03f50
0x10fb03f18: 0x00007fff84db88bf  libsystem_c.dylib`_pthread_start + 335
0x10fb03f20: 0x0000000000000000
0x10fb03f28: 0x0000000000000000
0x10fb03f30: 0x0000000000000000
0x10fb03f38: 0x0000000000000000
0x10fb03f40: 0x0000000000000000
0x10fb03f48: 0x0000000000000000
0x10fb03f50: 0x000000010fb03f78
0x10fb03f58: 0x00007fff84dbbb75  libsystem_c.dylib`thread_start + 13
0x10fb03f60: 0x0000000000000000
0x10fb03f68: 0x0000000000000000
0x10fb03f70: 0x0000000000000000
0x10fb03f78: 0x0000000000000000
0x10fb03f80: 0x0000000000000000
0x10fb03f88: 0x0000000000000000
0x10fb03f90: 0x0000000000000000
0x10fb03f98: 0x0000000000000000
0x10fb03fa0: 0x0000000000000000
0x10fb03fa8: 0x0000000000000000
0x10fb03fb0: 0x0000000000000000
0x10fb03fb8: 0x0000000000000000
0x10fb03fc0: 0x0000000000000000
0x10fb03fc8: 0x0000000000000000
0x10fb03fd0: 0x0000000000000000
0x10fb03fd8: 0x0000000000000000
0x10fb03fe0: 0x0000000000000000
0x10fb03fe8: 0x0000000000000000
0x10fb03ff0: 0x0000000000000000
0x10fb03ff8: 0x0000000000000000
0x10fb04000: 0x0000000054485244
0x10fb04008: 0x0000000000000000
0x10fb04010: 0x0701010100000000
0x10fb04018: 0x0000000000001000
0x10fb04020: 0x0000000a0000001f
0x10fb04028: 0x0000000000000000
0x10fb04030: 0x0000000000000000
0x10fb04038: 0x0000000000000000
0x10fb04040: 0x0000150300000000
0x10fb04048: 0x000000010f7f6560  App8`thread_three(void*)
[…]
0x10fb045f8: 0x0000000000000000
0x10fb04600: 0x0000000000000000
```

Exercise A9 (GDB)

- **Goal:** Learn how to identify heap leaks

- **Patterns:** Heap Leak, Execution Residue, Module Hint

- \AMCDA-Dumps\Exercise-A9-GDB.pdf

Exercise A9 (GDB)

Goal: Learn how to identify heap leaks

Patterns: Heap Leak, Execution Residue, Module Hint

1.   Identify heap memory consumption from the diagnostic report App9_1883.crash:

```
Process:        App9 [1883]
Path:           /Users/USER/Documents/*/App9
Identifier:     App9
Version:        ??? (???)
Code Type:      X86-64 (Native)
Parent Process: bash [223]

Date/Time:      2012-07-29 15:16:39.131 +0100
OS Version:     Mac OS X 10.7.4 (11E53)
Report Version: 9

Crashed Thread: 0  Dispatch queue: com.apple.main-thread

Exception Type:  EXC_CRASH (SIGABRT)
Exception Codes: 0x0000000000000000, 0x0000000000000000

Thread 0 Crashed:: Dispatch queue: com.apple.main-thread
0   libsystem_kernel.dylib          0x00007fff8ed7de42 __semwait_signal + 10
1   libsystem_c.dylib               0x00007fff899dfdea nanosleep + 164
2   libsystem_c.dylib               0x00007fff899dfc2c sleep + 61
3   libsystem_c.dylib               0x00007fff899dfc08 sleep + 25
4   App9                            0x000000010cdb8bc3 main + 195
5   App9                            0x000000010cdb87c4 start + 52

Thread 1:
0   libsystem_kernel.dylib          0x00007fff8ed7de42 __semwait_signal + 10
1   libsystem_c.dylib               0x00007fff899dfdea nanosleep + 164
2   libsystem_c.dylib               0x00007fff899dfc2c sleep + 61
3   libsystem_c.dylib               0x00007fff899dfc08 sleep + 25
4   App9                            0x000000010cdb8942 bar_one + 18
5   App9                            0x000000010cdb8959 foo_one + 9
6   App9                            0x000000010cdb8971 thread_one + 17
7   libsystem_c.dylib               0x00007fff89a298bf _pthread_start + 335
8   libsystem_c.dylib               0x00007fff89a2cb75 thread_start + 13

Thread 2:
0   libsystem_kernel.dylib          0x00007fff8ed7de42 __semwait_signal + 10
1   libsystem_c.dylib               0x00007fff899dfdea nanosleep + 164
2   libsystem_c.dylib               0x00007fff899dfc2c sleep + 61
3   libsystem_c.dylib               0x00007fff899dfc08 sleep + 25
4   App9                            0x000000010cdb88f3 procB + 51
5   App9                            0x000000010cdb8924 procA + 36
6   App9                            0x000000010cdb8999 bar_two + 9
7   App9                            0x000000010cdb89a9 foo_two + 9
8   App9                            0x000000010cdb89c1 thread_two + 17
9   libsystem_c.dylib               0x00007fff89a298bf _pthread_start + 335
10  libsystem_c.dylib               0x00007fff89a2cb75 thread_start + 13

Thread 3:
0   libsystem_kernel.dylib          0x00007fff8ed7de42 __semwait_signal + 10
1   libsystem_c.dylib               0x00007fff899dfdea nanosleep + 164
2   libsystem_c.dylib               0x00007fff899dfc2c sleep + 61
3   libsystem_c.dylib               0x00007fff899dfc08 sleep + 25
4   App9                            0x000000010cdb89f2 bar_three + 18
5   App9                            0x000000010cdb8a09 foo_three + 9
6   App9                            0x000000010cdb8a21 thread_three + 17
7   libsystem_c.dylib               0x00007fff89a298bf _pthread_start + 335
8   libsystem_c.dylib               0x00007fff89a2cb75 thread_start + 13

Thread 4:
```

```
0    libsystem_kernel.dylib          0x00007fff8ed7de42 __semwait_signal + 10
1    libsystem_c.dylib               0x00007fff899dfdea nanosleep + 164
2    libsystem_c.dylib               0x00007fff899dfc2c sleep + 61
3    libsystem_c.dylib               0x00007fff899dfc08 sleep + 25
4    App9                            0x000000010cdb8a52 bar_four + 18
5    App9                            0x000000010cdb8a69 foo_four + 9
6    App9                            0x000000010cdb8a81 thread_four + 17
7    libsystem_c.dylib               0x00007fff89a298bf _pthread_start + 335
8    libsystem_c.dylib               0x00007fff89a2cb75 thread_start + 13

Thread 5:
0    libsystem_kernel.dylib          0x00007fff8ed7de42 __semwait_signal + 10
1    libsystem_c.dylib               0x00007fff899dfdea nanosleep + 164
2    libsystem_c.dylib               0x00007fff899dfc2c sleep + 61
3    libsystem_c.dylib               0x00007fff899dfc08 sleep + 25
4    App9                            0x000000010cdb8ab2 bar_five + 18
5    App9                            0x000000010cdb8ac9 foo_five + 9
6    App9                            0x000000010cdb8ae1 thread_five + 17
7    libsystem_c.dylib               0x00007fff89a298bf _pthread_start + 335
8    libsystem_c.dylib               0x00007fff89a2cb75 thread_start + 13

Thread 0 crashed with X86 Thread State (64-bit):
  rax: 0x0000000000000004  rbx: 0x00007fff6c9b7a28  rcx: 0x00007fff6c9b79e8  rdx: 0x0000000000000001
  rdi: 0x0000000000000c03  rsi: 0x0000000000000000  rbp: 0x00007fff6c9b7a10  rsp: 0x00007fff6c9b79e8
   r8: 0x000000007fffffff   r9: 0x0000000000000000  r10: 0x0000000000000001  r11: 0xffffff80002da8d0
  r12: 0x0000000000000000  r13: 0x0000000000000000  r14: 0x00007fff6c9b7a38  r15: 0x0000000000000000
  rip: 0x00007fff8ed7de42  rfl: 0x0000000000000247  cr2: 0x000000010d18e880
Logical CPU: 0

Binary Images:
       0x10cdb8000 -        0x10cdb8ff7 +App9 (??? - ???) <BC6060DB-9637-3D3B-A78C-3A46AD6DC83C>
/Users/USER/Documents/*/App9
    0x7fff6c9b8000 -     0x7fff6c9ecbaf  dyld (195.6 - ???) <0CD1B35B-A28F-32DA-B72E-452EAD609613> /usr/lib/dyld
    0x7fff89663000 -     0x7fff89680fff  libxpc.dylib (77.19.0 - compatibility 1.0.0) <9F57891B-D7EF-3050-BEDD-
21E7C6668248> /usr/lib/system/libxpc.dylib
    0x7fff899d9000 -     0x7fff899daff7  libsystem_blocks.dylib (53.0.0 - compatibility 1.0.0) <8BCA214A-8992-34B2-
A8B9-B74DEACA1869> /usr/lib/system/libsystem_blocks.dylib
    0x7fff899db000 -     0x7fff89ab8fef  libsystem_c.dylib (763.13.0 - compatibility 1.0.0) <41B43515-2806-3FBC-ACF1-
A16F35B7E290> /usr/lib/system/libsystem_c.dylib
    0x7fff89c93000 -     0x7fff89ca1fff  libdispatch.dylib (187.9.0 - compatibility 1.0.0) <1D5BE322-A9B9-3BCE-8FAC-
076FB07CF54A> /usr/lib/system/libdispatch.dylib
    0x7fff8a261000 -     0x7fff8a262fff  libunc.dylib (24.0.0 - compatibility 1.0.0) <337960EE-0A85-3DD0-A760-
7134CF4C0AFF> /usr/lib/system/libunc.dylib
    0x7fff8a754000 -     0x7fff8a755ff7  libremovefile.dylib (21.1.0 - compatibility 1.0.0) <739E6C83-AA52-3C6C-A680-
B37FE2888A04> /usr/lib/system/libremovefile.dylib
    0x7fff8dd85000 -     0x7fff8dd89fff  libmathCommon.A.dylib (2026.0.0 - compatibility 1.0.0) <FF83AFF7-42B2-306E-
90AF-D539C51A4542> /usr/lib/system/libmathCommon.A.dylib
    0x7fff8dd8a000 -     0x7fff8dd8efff  libdyld.dylib (195.5.0 - compatibility 1.0.0) <380C3F44-0CA7-3514-8080-
46D1C9DF4FCD> /usr/lib/system/libdyld.dylib
    0x7fff8e3b1000 -     0x7fff8e3b2ff7  libsystem_sandbox.dylib (??? - ???) <96D38E74-F18F-3CCB-A20B-E8E3ADC4E166>
/usr/lib/system/libsystem_sandbox.dylib
    0x7fff8ed60000 -     0x7fff8ed66fff  libmacho.dylib (800.0.0 - compatibility 1.0.0) <165514D7-1BFA-38EF-A151-
676DCD21FB64> /usr/lib/system/libmacho.dylib
    0x7fff8ed67000 -     0x7fff8ed87fff  libsystem_kernel.dylib (1699.26.8 - compatibility 1.0.0) <1DDC0B0F-DB2A-34D6-
895D-E5B2B5618946> /usr/lib/system/libsystem_kernel.dylib
    0x7fff8ef1d000 -     0x7fff8ef25fff  libsystem_dnssd.dylib (??? - ???) <D9BB1F87-A42B-3CBC-9DC2-FC07FCEF0016>
/usr/lib/system/libsystem_dnssd.dylib
    0x7fff8fa97000 -     0x7fff8fad2fff  libsystem_info.dylib (??? - ???) <35F90252-2AE1-32C5-8D34-782C614D9639>
/usr/lib/system/libsystem_info.dylib
    0x7fff8feb9000 -     0x7fff8febbfff  libquarantine.dylib (36.6.0 - compatibility 1.0.0) <0EBF714B-4B69-3E1F-9A7D-
6BBC2AACB310> /usr/lib/system/libquarantine.dylib
    0x7fff90025000 -     0x7fff90025fff  libkeymgr.dylib (23.0.0 - compatibility 1.0.0) <61EFED6A-A407-301E-B454-
CD18314F0075> /usr/lib/system/libkeymgr.dylib
    0x7fff9004e000 -     0x7fff90053fff  libcompiler_rt.dylib (6.0.0 - compatibility 1.0.0) <98ECD5F6-E85C-32A5-98CD-
8911230CB66A> /usr/lib/system/libcompiler_rt.dylib
    0x7fff9098b000 -     0x7fff9098cfff  libdnsinfo.dylib (395.11.0 - compatibility 1.0.0) <853BAAA5-270F-3FDC-B025-
D448DB72E1C3> /usr/lib/system/libdnsinfo.dylib
    0x7fff91199000 -     0x7fff9119eff7  libsystem_network.dylib (??? - ???) <5DE7024E-1D2D-34A2-80F4-08326331A75B>
/usr/lib/system/libsystem_network.dylib
    0x7fff91c14000 -     0x7fff91c1eff7  liblaunch.dylib (392.38.0 - compatibility 1.0.0) <6ECB7F19-B384-32C1-8652-
2463C1CF4815> /usr/lib/system/liblaunch.dylib
    0x7fff94a73000 -     0x7fff94a7dfff  libcopyfile.dylib (85.1.0 - compatibility 1.0.0) <0AB51EE2-E914-358C-AC19-
47BC024BDAE7> /usr/lib/system/libcopyfile.dylib
    0x7fff94abc000 -     0x7fff94afeff7  libcommonCrypto.dylib (55010.0.0 - compatibility 1.0.0) <BB770C22-8C57-365A-
8716-4A3C36AE7BFB> /usr/lib/system/libcommonCrypto.dylib
```

```
    0x7fff95880000 -     0x7fff95889ff7  libsystem_notify.dylib (80.1.0 - compatibility 1.0.0) <A4D651E3-D1C6-3934-
AD49-7A104FD14596> /usr/lib/system/libsystem_notify.dylib
    0x7fff95fe7000 -     0x7fff96014fe7  libSystem.B.dylib (159.1.0 - compatibility 1.0.0) <7BEBB139-50BB-3112-947A-
F4AA168F991C> /usr/lib/libSystem.B.dylib
    0x7fff960fa000 -     0x7fff96100ff7  libunwind.dylib (30.0.0 - compatibility 1.0.0) <1E9C6C8C-CBE8-3F4B-A5B5-
E03E3AB53231> /usr/lib/system/libunwind.dylib
    0x7fff96693000 -     0x7fff96698fff  libcache.dylib (47.0.0 - compatibility 1.0.0) <1571C3AB-BCB2-38CD-B3B2-
C5FC3F927C6A> /usr/lib/system/libcache.dylib

External Modification Summary:
  Calls made by other processes targeting this process:
    task_for_pid: 4
    thread_create: 0
    thread_set_state: 0
  Calls made by this process:
    task_for_pid: 0
    thread_create: 0
    thread_set_state: 0
  Calls made by all processes on this machine:
    task_for_pid: 3111
    thread_create: 0
    thread_set_state: 0

VM Region Summary:
ReadOnly portion of Libraries: Total=50.2M resident=50.2M(100%) swapped_out_or_unallocated=0K(0%)
Writable regions: Total=1.3G written=9348K(1%) resident=724.9M(57%) swapped_out=557.4M(44%) unallocated=556.0M(43%)

REGION TYPE                    VIRTUAL
===========                    =======
MALLOC                            1.2G
Stack                            66.6M
__DATA                            464K
__LINKEDIT                       47.7M
__TEXT                           2484K
shared memory                      12K
===========                    =======
TOTAL                             1.3G
```

2.   Load a core dump core.1883 and App9 executable:

$ gdb -c ~/Documents/AMCDA-Dumps/core.1883 -e ~/Documents/AMCDA-Dumps/Apps/App9/Build/Products/Release/App9
```
GNU gdb 6.3.50-20050815 (Apple version gdb-1820) (Sat Jun 16 02:40:11 UTC 2012)
Copyright 2004 Free Software Foundation, Inc.
GDB is free software, covered by the GNU General Public License, and you are
welcome to change it and/or distribute copies of it under certain conditions.
Type "show copying" to see the conditions.
There is absolutely no warranty for GDB.  Type "show warranty" for details.
This GDB was configured as "x86_64-apple-darwin".Reading symbols for shared libraries .. done

Reading symbols for shared libraries . done
Reading symbols for shared libraries ........................ done
#0  0x00007fff8ed7de42 in __semwait_signal ()
```

3.   Identify "segment stream":

```
(gdb) maintenance info sections
Exec file:
    `/Users/DumpAnalysis/Documents/AMCDA-Dumps/Apps/App9/Build/Products/Release/App9', file type mach-o-le.
    0x0000000000000000->0x0000000000000000 at 0x00000000: LC_SEGMENT.__PAGEZERO ALLOC LOAD CODE HAS_CONTENTS
    0x0000000100000000->0x0000000100001000 at 0x00000000: LC_SEGMENT.__TEXT ALLOC LOAD CODE HAS_CONTENTS
    0x0000000100000790->0x0000000100000bd3 at 0x00000790: LC_SEGMENT.__TEXT.__text ALLOC LOAD READONLY CODE HAS_CONTENTS
    0x0000000100000bd4->0x0000000100000bf2 at 0x00000bd4: LC_SEGMENT.__TEXT.__stubs ALLOC LOAD CODE HAS_CONTENTS
    0x0000000100000bf4->0x0000000100000c36 at 0x00000bf4: LC_SEGMENT.__TEXT.__stub_helper ALLOC LOAD CODE HAS_CONTENTS
    0x0000000100000c36->0x0000000100000c47 at 0x00000c36: LC_SEGMENT.__TEXT.__cstring ALLOC LOAD CODE HAS_CONTENTS
    0x0000000100000c47->0x0000000100000c97 at 0x00000c47: LC_SEGMENT.__TEXT.__unwind_info ALLOC LOAD CODE HAS_CONTENTS
    0x0000000100000c98->0x0000000100000ff8 at 0x00000c98: LC_SEGMENT.__TEXT.__eh_frame ALLOC LOAD CODE HAS_CONTENTS
    0x0000000100001000->0x0000000100002000 at 0x00001000: LC_SEGMENT.__DATA ALLOC LOAD CODE HAS_CONTENTS
    0x0000000100001000->0x0000000100001028 at 0x00001000: LC_SEGMENT.__DATA.__program_vars ALLOC LOAD CODE HAS_CONTENTS
    0x0000000100001028->0x0000000100001038 at 0x00001028: LC_SEGMENT.__DATA.__nl_symbol_ptr ALLOC LOAD CODE HAS_CONTENTS
    0x0000000100001038->0x0000000100001060 at 0x00001038: LC_SEGMENT.__DATA.__la_symbol_ptr ALLOC LOAD CODE HAS_CONTENTS
    0x0000000100001060->0x0000000100001080 at 0x00000000: LC_SEGMENT.__DATA.__common ALLOC
    0x0000000100002000->0x00000001000024a8 at 0x00002000: LC_SEGMENT.__LINKEDIT ALLOC LOAD CODE HAS_CONTENTS
    0x0000000000000000->0x0000000000000210 at 0x00002100: LC_SYMTAB.stabs HAS_CONTENTS
    0x0000000000000000->0x0000000000000168 at 0x00002340: LC_SYMTAB.stabstr HAS_CONTENTS
    0x0000000000000000->0x0000000000000150 at 0x00002100: LC_DYSYMTAB.localstabs HAS_CONTENTS
    0x0000000000000000->0x00000000000000c0 at 0x00002250: LC_DYSYMTAB.nonlocalstabs HAS_CONTENTS
    0x0000000000000000->0x0000000000000018 at 0x00000500: LC_LOAD_DYLINKER HAS_CONTENTS
    0x0000000000000000->0x00000000000000a8 at 0x00000550: LC_THREAD.x86_THREAD_STATE64.0 HAS_CONTENTS
    0x0000000000000000->0x0000000000000030 at 0x00000600: LC_LOAD_DYLIB HAS_CONTENTS
Core file:
    `/Users/DumpAnalysis/Documents/AMCDA-Dumps/core.1883', file type mach-o-le.
    0x000000010cdb8000->0x000000010cdb9000 at 0x00018000: LC_SEGMENT. ALLOC LOAD CODE HAS_CONTENTS
    0x000000010cdb9000->0x000000010cdba000 at 0x00019000: LC_SEGMENT. ALLOC LOAD CODE HAS_CONTENTS
    0x000000010cdba000->0x000000010cdbb000 at 0x0001a000: LC_SEGMENT. ALLOC LOAD CODE HAS_CONTENTS
    0x000000010cdbb000->0x000000010cdbc000 at 0x0001b000: LC_SEGMENT. ALLOC LOAD CODE HAS_CONTENTS
    0x000000010cdbc000->0x000000010cdbd000 at 0x0001c000: LC_SEGMENT. ALLOC LOAD CODE HAS_CONTENTS
    0x000000010cdbd000->0x000000010cdbe000 at 0x0001d000: LC_SEGMENT. ALLOC LOAD CODE HAS_CONTENTS
    0x000000010cdbe000->0x000000010cdd3000 at 0x0001e000: LC_SEGMENT. ALLOC LOAD CODE HAS_CONTENTS
    0x000000010cdd3000->0x000000010cdd4000 at 0x00033000: LC_SEGMENT. ALLOC LOAD CODE HAS_CONTENTS
    0x000000010cdd4000->0x000000010cdd5000 at 0x00034000: LC_SEGMENT. ALLOC LOAD CODE HAS_CONTENTS
    0x000000010cdd5000->0x000000010cdea000 at 0x00035000: LC_SEGMENT. ALLOC LOAD CODE HAS_CONTENTS
    0x000000010cdea000->0x000000010cdeb000 at 0x0004a000: LC_SEGMENT. ALLOC LOAD CODE HAS_CONTENTS
    0x000000010cdeb000->0x000000010cdec000 at 0x0004b000: LC_SEGMENT. ALLOC LOAD CODE HAS_CONTENTS
    0x000000010cdec000->0x000000010cdf5000 at 0x0004c000: LC_SEGMENT. ALLOC LOAD CODE HAS_CONTENTS
    0x000000010cdf5000->0x000000010cdfd000 at 0x00055000: LC_SEGMENT. ALLOC LOAD CODE HAS_CONTENTS
    0x000000010ce00000->0x000000010cf00000 at 0x0005d000: LC_SEGMENT. ALLOC LOAD CODE HAS_CONTENTS
---Type <return> to continue, or q <return> to quit---
    0x000000010cf00000->0x000000010cf01000 at 0x0015d000: LC_SEGMENT. ALLOC LOAD CODE HAS_CONTENTS
    0x000000010cf01000->0x000000010cf83000 at 0x0015e000: LC_SEGMENT. ALLOC LOAD CODE HAS_CONTENTS
    0x000000010cf83000->0x000000010cf84000 at 0x001e0000: LC_SEGMENT. ALLOC LOAD CODE HAS_CONTENTS
    0x000000010cf84000->0x000000010d006000 at 0x001e1000: LC_SEGMENT. ALLOC LOAD CODE HAS_CONTENTS
    0x000000010d006000->0x000000010d007000 at 0x00263000: LC_SEGMENT. ALLOC LOAD CODE HAS_CONTENTS
    0x000000010d007000->0x000000010d089000 at 0x00264000: LC_SEGMENT. ALLOC LOAD CODE HAS_CONTENTS
    0x000000010d089000->0x000000010d08a000 at 0x002e6000: LC_SEGMENT. ALLOC LOAD CODE HAS_CONTENTS
    0x000000010d08a000->0x000000010d10c000 at 0x002e7000: LC_SEGMENT. ALLOC LOAD CODE HAS_CONTENTS
    0x000000010d10c000->0x000000010d10d000 at 0x00369000: LC_SEGMENT. ALLOC LOAD CODE HAS_CONTENTS
    0x000000010d10d000->0x000000010d18f000 at 0x0036a000: LC_SEGMENT. ALLOC LOAD CODE HAS_CONTENTS
    0x00007fa0db400000->0x00007fa0db500000 at 0x003ec000: LC_SEGMENT. ALLOC LOAD CODE HAS_CONTENTS
    0x00007fa0db500000->0x00007fa0db600000 at 0x004ec000: LC_SEGMENT. ALLOC LOAD CODE HAS_CONTENTS
    0x00007fa0db600000->0x00007fa0db700000 at 0x005ec000: LC_SEGMENT. ALLOC LOAD CODE HAS_CONTENTS
    0x00007fa0db700000->0x00007fa0db800000 at 0x006ec000: LC_SEGMENT. ALLOC LOAD CODE HAS_CONTENTS
    0x00007fa0db800000->0x00007fa0db900000 at 0x007ec000: LC_SEGMENT. ALLOC LOAD CODE HAS_CONTENTS
    0x00007fa0db900000->0x00007fa0dba00000 at 0x008ec000: LC_SEGMENT. ALLOC LOAD CODE HAS_CONTENTS
    0x00007fa0dba00000->0x00007fa0dbb00000 at 0x009ec000: LC_SEGMENT. ALLOC LOAD CODE HAS_CONTENTS
    0x00007fa0dbb00000->0x00007fa0dbc00000 at 0x00aec000: LC_SEGMENT. ALLOC LOAD CODE HAS_CONTENTS
    0x00007fa0dbc00000->0x00007fa0dbd00000 at 0x00bec000: LC_SEGMENT. ALLOC LOAD CODE HAS_CONTENTS
    0x00007fa0dbd00000->0x00007fa0dbe00000 at 0x00cec000: LC_SEGMENT. ALLOC LOAD CODE HAS_CONTENTS
    0x00007fa0dbe00000->0x00007fa0dbf00000 at 0x00dec000: LC_SEGMENT. ALLOC LOAD CODE HAS_CONTENTS
    0x00007fa0dbf00000->0x00007fa0dc000000 at 0x00eec000: LC_SEGMENT. ALLOC LOAD CODE HAS_CONTENTS
    0x00007fa0dc000000->0x00007fa0dc100000 at 0x00fec000: LC_SEGMENT. ALLOC LOAD CODE HAS_CONTENTS
    0x00007fa0dc100000->0x00007fa0dc200000 at 0x010ec000: LC_SEGMENT. ALLOC LOAD CODE HAS_CONTENTS
    0x00007fa0dc200000->0x00007fa0dc300000 at 0x011ec000: LC_SEGMENT. ALLOC LOAD CODE HAS_CONTENTS
    0x00007fa0dc300000->0x00007fa0dc400000 at 0x012ec000: LC_SEGMENT. ALLOC LOAD CODE HAS_CONTENTS
    0x00007fa0dc400000->0x00007fa0dc500000 at 0x013ec000: LC_SEGMENT. ALLOC LOAD CODE HAS_CONTENTS
    0x00007fa0dc500000->0x00007fa0dc600000 at 0x014ec000: LC_SEGMENT. ALLOC LOAD CODE HAS_CONTENTS
    0x00007fa0dc600000->0x00007fa0dc700000 at 0x015ec000: LC_SEGMENT. ALLOC LOAD CODE HAS_CONTENTS
    0x00007fa0dc700000->0x00007fa0dc800000 at 0x016ec000: LC_SEGMENT. ALLOC LOAD CODE HAS_CONTENTS
    0x00007fa0dc800000->0x00007fa0dc900000 at 0x017ec000: LC_SEGMENT. ALLOC LOAD CODE HAS_CONTENTS
    0x00007fa0dc900000->0x00007fa0dca00000 at 0x018ec000: LC_SEGMENT. ALLOC LOAD CODE HAS_CONTENTS
    0x00007fa0dca00000->0x00007fa0dcb00000 at 0x019ec000: LC_SEGMENT. ALLOC LOAD CODE HAS_CONTENTS
    0x00007fa0dcb00000->0x00007fa0dcc00000 at 0x01aec000: LC_SEGMENT. ALLOC LOAD CODE HAS_CONTENTS
    0x00007fa0dcc00000->0x00007fa0dcd00000 at 0x01bec000: LC_SEGMENT. ALLOC LOAD CODE HAS_CONTENTS
    0x00007fa0dcd00000->0x00007fa0dce00000 at 0x01cec000: LC_SEGMENT. ALLOC LOAD CODE HAS_CONTENTS
    0x00007fa0dce00000->0x00007fa0dcf00000 at 0x01dec000: LC_SEGMENT. ALLOC LOAD CODE HAS_CONTENTS
    0x00007fa0dcf00000->0x00007fa0dd000000 at 0x01eec000: LC_SEGMENT. ALLOC LOAD CODE HAS_CONTENTS
    0x00007fa0dd000000->0x00007fa0dd100000 at 0x01fec000: LC_SEGMENT. ALLOC LOAD CODE HAS_CONTENTS
    0x00007fa0dd100000->0x00007fa0dd200000 at 0x020ec000: LC_SEGMENT. ALLOC LOAD CODE HAS_CONTENTS
```

---Type <return> to continue, or q <return> to quit---
```
    0x00007fa0dd200000->0x00007fa0dd300000 at 0x021ec000: LC_SEGMENT. ALLOC LOAD CODE HAS_CONTENTS
    0x00007fa0dd300000->0x00007fa0dd400000 at 0x022ec000: LC_SEGMENT. ALLOC LOAD CODE HAS_CONTENTS
    0x00007fa0dd400000->0x00007fa0dd500000 at 0x023ec000: LC_SEGMENT. ALLOC LOAD CODE HAS_CONTENTS
    0x00007fa0dd500000->0x00007fa0dd600000 at 0x024ec000: LC_SEGMENT. ALLOC LOAD CODE HAS_CONTENTS
    0x00007fa0dd600000->0x00007fa0dd700000 at 0x025ec000: LC_SEGMENT. ALLOC LOAD CODE HAS_CONTENTS
    0x00007fa0dd700000->0x00007fa0dd800000 at 0x026ec000: LC_SEGMENT. ALLOC LOAD CODE HAS_CONTENTS
    0x00007fa0dd800000->0x00007fa0dd900000 at 0x027ec000: LC_SEGMENT. ALLOC LOAD CODE HAS_CONTENTS
    0x00007fa0dd900000->0x00007fa0dda00000 at 0x028ec000: LC_SEGMENT. ALLOC LOAD CODE HAS_CONTENTS
    0x00007fa0dda00000->0x00007fa0ddb00000 at 0x029ec000: LC_SEGMENT. ALLOC LOAD CODE HAS_CONTENTS
    0x00007fa0ddb00000->0x00007fa0ddc00000 at 0x02aec000: LC_SEGMENT. ALLOC LOAD CODE HAS_CONTENTS
    0x00007fa0ddc00000->0x00007fa0ddd00000 at 0x02bec000: LC_SEGMENT. ALLOC LOAD CODE HAS_CONTENTS
    0x00007fa0ddd00000->0x00007fa0dde00000 at 0x02cec000: LC_SEGMENT. ALLOC LOAD CODE HAS_CONTENTS
    0x00007fa0dde00000->0x00007fa0ddf00000 at 0x02dec000: LC_SEGMENT. ALLOC LOAD CODE HAS_CONTENTS
    0x00007fa0ddf00000->0x00007fa0de000000 at 0x02eec000: LC_SEGMENT. ALLOC LOAD CODE HAS_CONTENTS
    0x00007fa0de000000->0x00007fa0de100000 at 0x02fec000: LC_SEGMENT. ALLOC LOAD CODE HAS_CONTENTS
    0x00007fa0de100000->0x00007fa0de200000 at 0x030ec000: LC_SEGMENT. ALLOC LOAD CODE HAS_CONTENTS
    0x00007fa0de200000->0x00007fa0de300000 at 0x031ec000: LC_SEGMENT. ALLOC LOAD CODE HAS_CONTENTS
    0x00007fa0de300000->0x00007fa0de400000 at 0x032ec000: LC_SEGMENT. ALLOC LOAD CODE HAS_CONTENTS
    0x00007fa0de400000->0x00007fa0de500000 at 0x033ec000: LC_SEGMENT. ALLOC LOAD CODE HAS_CONTENTS
    0x00007fa0de500000->0x00007fa0de600000 at 0x034ec000: LC_SEGMENT. ALLOC LOAD CODE HAS_CONTENTS
    0x00007fa0de600000->0x00007fa0de700000 at 0x035ec000: LC_SEGMENT. ALLOC LOAD CODE HAS_CONTENTS
    0x00007fa0de700000->0x00007fa0de800000 at 0x036ec000: LC_SEGMENT. ALLOC LOAD CODE HAS_CONTENTS
    0x00007fa0de800000->0x00007fa0de900000 at 0x037ec000: LC_SEGMENT. ALLOC LOAD CODE HAS_CONTENTS
    0x00007fa0de900000->0x00007fa0dea00000 at 0x038ec000: LC_SEGMENT. ALLOC LOAD CODE HAS_CONTENTS
    0x00007fa0dea00000->0x00007fa0deb00000 at 0x039ec000: LC_SEGMENT. ALLOC LOAD CODE HAS_CONTENTS
    0x00007fa0deb00000->0x00007fa0dec00000 at 0x03aec000: LC_SEGMENT. ALLOC LOAD CODE HAS_CONTENTS
    0x00007fa0dec00000->0x00007fa0ded00000 at 0x03bec000: LC_SEGMENT. ALLOC LOAD CODE HAS_CONTENTS
    0x00007fa0ded00000->0x00007fa0dee00000 at 0x03cec000: LC_SEGMENT. ALLOC LOAD CODE HAS_CONTENTS
    0x00007fa0dee00000->0x00007fa0def00000 at 0x03dec000: LC_SEGMENT. ALLOC LOAD CODE HAS_CONTENTS
    0x00007fa0def00000->0x00007fa0df000000 at 0x03eec000: LC_SEGMENT. ALLOC LOAD CODE HAS_CONTENTS
    0x00007fa0df000000->0x00007fa0df100000 at 0x03fec000: LC_SEGMENT. ALLOC LOAD CODE HAS_CONTENTS
    0x00007fa0df100000->0x00007fa0df200000 at 0x040ec000: LC_SEGMENT. ALLOC LOAD CODE HAS_CONTENTS
    0x00007fa0df200000->0x00007fa0df300000 at 0x041ec000: LC_SEGMENT. ALLOC LOAD CODE HAS_CONTENTS
    0x00007fa0df300000->0x00007fa0df400000 at 0x042ec000: LC_SEGMENT. ALLOC LOAD CODE HAS_CONTENTS
    0x00007fa0df400000->0x00007fa0df500000 at 0x043ec000: LC_SEGMENT. ALLOC LOAD CODE HAS_CONTENTS
    0x00007fa0df500000->0x00007fa0df600000 at 0x044ec000: LC_SEGMENT. ALLOC LOAD CODE HAS_CONTENTS
    0x00007fa0df600000->0x00007fa0df700000 at 0x045ec000: LC_SEGMENT. ALLOC LOAD CODE HAS_CONTENTS
    0x00007fa0df700000->0x00007fa0df800000 at 0x046ec000: LC_SEGMENT. ALLOC LOAD CODE HAS_CONTENTS
    0x00007fa0df800000->0x00007fa0df900000 at 0x047ec000: LC_SEGMENT. ALLOC LOAD CODE HAS_CONTENTS
    0x00007fa0df900000->0x00007fa0dfa00000 at 0x048ec000: LC_SEGMENT. ALLOC LOAD CODE HAS_CONTENTS
```
---Type <return> to continue, or q <return> to quit---
```
    0x00007fa0dfa00000->0x00007fa0dfb00000 at 0x049ec000: LC_SEGMENT. ALLOC LOAD CODE HAS_CONTENTS
    0x00007fa0dfb00000->0x00007fa0dfc00000 at 0x04aec000: LC_SEGMENT. ALLOC LOAD CODE HAS_CONTENTS
    0x00007fa0dfc00000->0x00007fa0dfd00000 at 0x04bec000: LC_SEGMENT. ALLOC LOAD CODE HAS_CONTENTS
    0x00007fa0dfd00000->0x00007fa0dfe00000 at 0x04cec000: LC_SEGMENT. ALLOC LOAD CODE HAS_CONTENTS
    0x00007fa0dfe00000->0x00007fa0dff00000 at 0x04dec000: LC_SEGMENT. ALLOC LOAD CODE HAS_CONTENTS
    0x00007fa0dff00000->0x00007fa0e0000000 at 0x04eec000: LC_SEGMENT. ALLOC LOAD CODE HAS_CONTENTS
    0x00007fa0e0000000->0x00007fa0e0100000 at 0x04fec000: LC_SEGMENT. ALLOC LOAD CODE HAS_CONTENTS
    0x00007fa0e0100000->0x00007fa0e0200000 at 0x050ec000: LC_SEGMENT. ALLOC LOAD CODE HAS_CONTENTS
    0x00007fa0e0200000->0x00007fa0e0300000 at 0x051ec000: LC_SEGMENT. ALLOC LOAD CODE HAS_CONTENTS
    0x00007fa0e0300000->0x00007fa0e0400000 at 0x052ec000: LC_SEGMENT. ALLOC LOAD CODE HAS_CONTENTS
    0x00007fa0e0400000->0x00007fa0e0500000 at 0x053ec000: LC_SEGMENT. ALLOC LOAD CODE HAS_CONTENTS
    0x00007fa0e0500000->0x00007fa0e0600000 at 0x054ec000: LC_SEGMENT. ALLOC LOAD CODE HAS_CONTENTS
    0x00007fa0e0600000->0x00007fa0e0700000 at 0x055ec000: LC_SEGMENT. ALLOC LOAD CODE HAS_CONTENTS
    0x00007fa0e0700000->0x00007fa0e0800000 at 0x056ec000: LC_SEGMENT. ALLOC LOAD CODE HAS_CONTENTS
    0x00007fa0e0800000->0x00007fa0e0900000 at 0x057ec000: LC_SEGMENT. ALLOC LOAD CODE HAS_CONTENTS
    0x00007fa0e0900000->0x00007fa0e0a00000 at 0x058ec000: LC_SEGMENT. ALLOC LOAD CODE HAS_CONTENTS
    0x00007fa0e0a00000->0x00007fa0e0b00000 at 0x059ec000: LC_SEGMENT. ALLOC LOAD CODE HAS_CONTENTS
    0x00007fa0e0b00000->0x00007fa0e0c00000 at 0x05aec000: LC_SEGMENT. ALLOC LOAD CODE HAS_CONTENTS
    0x00007fa0e0c00000->0x00007fa0e0d00000 at 0x05bec000: LC_SEGMENT. ALLOC LOAD CODE HAS_CONTENTS
    0x00007fa0e0d00000->0x00007fa0e0e00000 at 0x05cec000: LC_SEGMENT. ALLOC LOAD CODE HAS_CONTENTS
    0x00007fa0e0e00000->0x00007fa0e0f00000 at 0x05dec000: LC_SEGMENT. ALLOC LOAD CODE HAS_CONTENTS
    0x00007fa0e0f00000->0x00007fa0e1000000 at 0x05eec000: LC_SEGMENT. ALLOC LOAD CODE HAS_CONTENTS
    0x00007fa0e1000000->0x00007fa0e1100000 at 0x05fec000: LC_SEGMENT. ALLOC LOAD CODE HAS_CONTENTS
    0x00007fa0e1100000->0x00007fa0e1200000 at 0x060ec000: LC_SEGMENT. ALLOC LOAD CODE HAS_CONTENTS
    0x00007fa0e1200000->0x00007fa0e1300000 at 0x061ec000: LC_SEGMENT. ALLOC LOAD CODE HAS_CONTENTS
    0x00007fa0e1300000->0x00007fa0e1400000 at 0x062ec000: LC_SEGMENT. ALLOC LOAD CODE HAS_CONTENTS
    0x00007fa0e1400000->0x00007fa0e1500000 at 0x063ec000: LC_SEGMENT. ALLOC LOAD CODE HAS_CONTENTS
    0x00007fa0e1500000->0x00007fa0e1600000 at 0x064ec000: LC_SEGMENT. ALLOC LOAD CODE HAS_CONTENTS
    0x00007fa0e1600000->0x00007fa0e1700000 at 0x065ec000: LC_SEGMENT. ALLOC LOAD CODE HAS_CONTENTS
    0x00007fa0e1700000->0x00007fa0e1800000 at 0x066ec000: LC_SEGMENT. ALLOC LOAD CODE HAS_CONTENTS
    0x00007fa0e1800000->0x00007fa0e1900000 at 0x067ec000: LC_SEGMENT. ALLOC LOAD CODE HAS_CONTENTS
    0x00007fa0e1900000->0x00007fa0e1a00000 at 0x068ec000: LC_SEGMENT. ALLOC LOAD CODE HAS_CONTENTS
    0x00007fa0e1a00000->0x00007fa0e1b00000 at 0x069ec000: LC_SEGMENT. ALLOC LOAD CODE HAS_CONTENTS
    0x00007fa0e1b00000->0x00007fa0e1c00000 at 0x06aec000: LC_SEGMENT. ALLOC LOAD CODE HAS_CONTENTS
    0x00007fa0e1c00000->0x00007fa0e1d00000 at 0x06bec000: LC_SEGMENT. ALLOC LOAD CODE HAS_CONTENTS
    0x00007fa0e1d00000->0x00007fa0e1e00000 at 0x06cec000: LC_SEGMENT. ALLOC LOAD CODE HAS_CONTENTS
    0x00007fa0e1e00000->0x00007fa0e1f00000 at 0x06dec000: LC_SEGMENT. ALLOC LOAD CODE HAS_CONTENTS
    0x00007fa0e1f00000->0x00007fa0e2000000 at 0x06eec000: LC_SEGMENT. ALLOC LOAD CODE HAS_CONTENTS
    0x00007fa0e2000000->0x00007fa0e2100000 at 0x06fec000: LC_SEGMENT. ALLOC LOAD CODE HAS_CONTENTS
    0x00007fa0e2100000->0x00007fa0e2200000 at 0x070ec000: LC_SEGMENT. ALLOC LOAD CODE HAS_CONTENTS
```
---Type <return> to continue, or q <return> to quit---
```
    0x00007fa0e2200000->0x00007fa0e2300000 at 0x071ec000: LC_SEGMENT. ALLOC LOAD CODE HAS_CONTENTS
    0x00007fa0e2300000->0x00007fa0e2400000 at 0x072ec000: LC_SEGMENT. ALLOC LOAD CODE HAS_CONTENTS
    0x00007fa0e2400000->0x00007fa0e2500000 at 0x073ec000: LC_SEGMENT. ALLOC LOAD CODE HAS_CONTENTS
```

```
0x00007fa0e2500000->0x00007fa0e2600000 at 0x074ec000: LC_SEGMENT. ALLOC LOAD CODE HAS_CONTENTS
0x00007fa0e2600000->0x00007fa0e2700000 at 0x075ec000: LC_SEGMENT. ALLOC LOAD CODE HAS_CONTENTS
0x00007fa0e2700000->0x00007fa0e2800000 at 0x076ec000: LC_SEGMENT. ALLOC LOAD CODE HAS_CONTENTS
0x00007fa0e2800000->0x00007fa0e2900000 at 0x077ec000: LC_SEGMENT. ALLOC LOAD CODE HAS_CONTENTS
0x00007fa0e2900000->0x00007fa0e2a00000 at 0x078ec000: LC_SEGMENT. ALLOC LOAD CODE HAS_CONTENTS
0x00007fa0e2a00000->0x00007fa0e2b00000 at 0x079ec000: LC_SEGMENT. ALLOC LOAD CODE HAS_CONTENTS
0x00007fa0e2b00000->0x00007fa0e2c00000 at 0x07aec000: LC_SEGMENT. ALLOC LOAD CODE HAS_CONTENTS
0x00007fa0e2c00000->0x00007fa0e2d00000 at 0x07bec000: LC_SEGMENT. ALLOC LOAD CODE HAS_CONTENTS
0x00007fa0e2d00000->0x00007fa0e2e00000 at 0x07cec000: LC_SEGMENT. ALLOC LOAD CODE HAS_CONTENTS
0x00007fa0e2e00000->0x00007fa0e2f00000 at 0x07dec000: LC_SEGMENT. ALLOC LOAD CODE HAS_CONTENTS
0x00007fa0e2f00000->0x00007fa0e3000000 at 0x07eec000: LC_SEGMENT. ALLOC LOAD CODE HAS_CONTENTS
0x00007fa0e3000000->0x00007fa0e3100000 at 0x07fec000: LC_SEGMENT. ALLOC LOAD CODE HAS_CONTENTS
0x00007fa0e3100000->0x00007fa0e3200000 at 0x080ec000: LC_SEGMENT. ALLOC LOAD CODE HAS_CONTENTS
0x00007fa0e3200000->0x00007fa0e3300000 at 0x081ec000: LC_SEGMENT. ALLOC LOAD CODE HAS_CONTENTS
0x00007fa0e3300000->0x00007fa0e3400000 at 0x082ec000: LC_SEGMENT. ALLOC LOAD CODE HAS_CONTENTS
0x00007fa0e3400000->0x00007fa0e3500000 at 0x083ec000: LC_SEGMENT. ALLOC LOAD CODE HAS_CONTENTS
0x00007fa0e3500000->0x00007fa0e3600000 at 0x084ec000: LC_SEGMENT. ALLOC LOAD CODE HAS_CONTENTS
0x00007fa0e3600000->0x00007fa0e3700000 at 0x085ec000: LC_SEGMENT. ALLOC LOAD CODE HAS_CONTENTS
0x00007fa0e3700000->0x00007fa0e3800000 at 0x086ec000: LC_SEGMENT. ALLOC LOAD CODE HAS_CONTENTS
0x00007fa0e3800000->0x00007fa0e3900000 at 0x087ec000: LC_SEGMENT. ALLOC LOAD CODE HAS_CONTENTS
0x00007fa0e3900000->0x00007fa0e3a00000 at 0x088ec000: LC_SEGMENT. ALLOC LOAD CODE HAS_CONTENTS
0x00007fa0e3a00000->0x00007fa0e3b00000 at 0x089ec000: LC_SEGMENT. ALLOC LOAD CODE HAS_CONTENTS
0x00007fa0e3b00000->0x00007fa0e3c00000 at 0x08aec000: LC_SEGMENT. ALLOC LOAD CODE HAS_CONTENTS
0x00007fa0e3c00000->0x00007fa0e3d00000 at 0x08bec000: LC_SEGMENT. ALLOC LOAD CODE HAS_CONTENTS
0x00007fa0e3d00000->0x00007fa0e3e00000 at 0x08cec000: LC_SEGMENT. ALLOC LOAD CODE HAS_CONTENTS
0x00007fa0e3e00000->0x00007fa0e3f00000 at 0x08dec000: LC_SEGMENT. ALLOC LOAD CODE HAS_CONTENTS
0x00007fa0e3f00000->0x00007fa0e4000000 at 0x08eec000: LC_SEGMENT. ALLOC LOAD CODE HAS_CONTENTS
0x00007fa0e4000000->0x00007fa0e4100000 at 0x08fec000: LC_SEGMENT. ALLOC LOAD CODE HAS_CONTENTS
0x00007fa0e4100000->0x00007fa0e4200000 at 0x090ec000: LC_SEGMENT. ALLOC LOAD CODE HAS_CONTENTS
0x00007fa0e4200000->0x00007fa0e4300000 at 0x091ec000: LC_SEGMENT. ALLOC LOAD CODE HAS_CONTENTS
0x00007fa0e4300000->0x00007fa0e4400000 at 0x092ec000: LC_SEGMENT. ALLOC LOAD CODE HAS_CONTENTS
0x00007fa0e4400000->0x00007fa0e4500000 at 0x093ec000: LC_SEGMENT. ALLOC LOAD CODE HAS_CONTENTS
0x00007fa0e4500000->0x00007fa0e4600000 at 0x094ec000: LC_SEGMENT. ALLOC LOAD CODE HAS_CONTENTS
0x00007fa0e4600000->0x00007fa0e4700000 at 0x095ec000: LC_SEGMENT. ALLOC LOAD CODE HAS_CONTENTS
0x00007fa0e4700000->0x00007fa0e4800000 at 0x096ec000: LC_SEGMENT. ALLOC LOAD CODE HAS_CONTENTS
0x00007fa0e4800000->0x00007fa0e4900000 at 0x097ec000: LC_SEGMENT. ALLOC LOAD CODE HAS_CONTENTS
0x00007fa0e4900000->0x00007fa0e4a00000 at 0x098ec000: LC_SEGMENT. ALLOC LOAD CODE HAS_CONTENTS
---Type <return> to continue, or q <return> to quit---
0x00007fa0e4a00000->0x00007fa0e4b00000 at 0x099ec000: LC_SEGMENT. ALLOC LOAD CODE HAS_CONTENTS
0x00007fa0e4b00000->0x00007fa0e4c00000 at 0x09aec000: LC_SEGMENT. ALLOC LOAD CODE HAS_CONTENTS
0x00007fa0e4c00000->0x00007fa0e4d00000 at 0x09bec000: LC_SEGMENT. ALLOC LOAD CODE HAS_CONTENTS
0x00007fa0e4d00000->0x00007fa0e4e00000 at 0x09cec000: LC_SEGMENT. ALLOC LOAD CODE HAS_CONTENTS
0x00007fa0e4e00000->0x00007fa0e4f00000 at 0x09dec000: LC_SEGMENT. ALLOC LOAD CODE HAS_CONTENTS
0x00007fa0e4f00000->0x00007fa0e5000000 at 0x09eec000: LC_SEGMENT. ALLOC LOAD CODE HAS_CONTENTS
0x00007fa0e5000000->0x00007fa0e5100000 at 0x09fec000: LC_SEGMENT. ALLOC LOAD CODE HAS_CONTENTS
0x00007fa0e5100000->0x00007fa0e5200000 at 0x0a0ec000: LC_SEGMENT. ALLOC LOAD CODE HAS_CONTENTS
0x00007fa0e5200000->0x00007fa0e5300000 at 0x0a1ec000: LC_SEGMENT. ALLOC LOAD CODE HAS_CONTENTS
0x00007fa0e5300000->0x00007fa0e5400000 at 0x0a2ec000: LC_SEGMENT. ALLOC LOAD CODE HAS_CONTENTS
0x00007fa0e5400000->0x00007fa0e5500000 at 0x0a3ec000: LC_SEGMENT. ALLOC LOAD CODE HAS_CONTENTS
0x00007fa0e5500000->0x00007fa0e5600000 at 0x0a4ec000: LC_SEGMENT. ALLOC LOAD CODE HAS_CONTENTS
0x00007fa0e5600000->0x00007fa0e5700000 at 0x0a5ec000: LC_SEGMENT. ALLOC LOAD CODE HAS_CONTENTS
0x00007fa0e5700000->0x00007fa0e5800000 at 0x0a6ec000: LC_SEGMENT. ALLOC LOAD CODE HAS_CONTENTS
0x00007fa0e5800000->0x00007fa0e5900000 at 0x0a7ec000: LC_SEGMENT. ALLOC LOAD CODE HAS_CONTENTS
0x00007fa0e5900000->0x00007fa0e5a00000 at 0x0a8ec000: LC_SEGMENT. ALLOC LOAD CODE HAS_CONTENTS
0x00007fa0e5a00000->0x00007fa0e5b00000 at 0x0a9ec000: LC_SEGMENT. ALLOC LOAD CODE HAS_CONTENTS
0x00007fa0e5b00000->0x00007fa0e5c00000 at 0x0aaec000: LC_SEGMENT. ALLOC LOAD CODE HAS_CONTENTS
0x00007fa0e5c00000->0x00007fa0e5d00000 at 0x0abec000: LC_SEGMENT. ALLOC LOAD CODE HAS_CONTENTS
0x00007fa0e5d00000->0x00007fa0e5e00000 at 0x0acec000: LC_SEGMENT. ALLOC LOAD CODE HAS_CONTENTS
0x00007fa0e5e00000->0x00007fa0e5f00000 at 0x0adec000: LC_SEGMENT. ALLOC LOAD CODE HAS_CONTENTS
0x00007fa0e5f00000->0x00007fa0e6000000 at 0x0aeec000: LC_SEGMENT. ALLOC LOAD CODE HAS_CONTENTS
0x00007fa0e6000000->0x00007fa0e6100000 at 0x0afec000: LC_SEGMENT. ALLOC LOAD CODE HAS_CONTENTS
0x00007fa0e6100000->0x00007fa0e6200000 at 0x0b0ec000: LC_SEGMENT. ALLOC LOAD CODE HAS_CONTENTS
0x00007fa0e6200000->0x00007fa0e6300000 at 0x0b1ec000: LC_SEGMENT. ALLOC LOAD CODE HAS_CONTENTS
0x00007fa0e6300000->0x00007fa0e6400000 at 0x0b2ec000: LC_SEGMENT. ALLOC LOAD CODE HAS_CONTENTS
0x00007fa0e6400000->0x00007fa0e6500000 at 0x0b3ec000: LC_SEGMENT. ALLOC LOAD CODE HAS_CONTENTS
0x00007fa0e6500000->0x00007fa0e6600000 at 0x0b4ec000: LC_SEGMENT. ALLOC LOAD CODE HAS_CONTENTS
0x00007fa0e6600000->0x00007fa0e6700000 at 0x0b5ec000: LC_SEGMENT. ALLOC LOAD CODE HAS_CONTENTS
0x00007fa0e6700000->0x00007fa0e6800000 at 0x0b6ec000: LC_SEGMENT. ALLOC LOAD CODE HAS_CONTENTS
0x00007fa0e6800000->0x00007fa0e6900000 at 0x0b7ec000: LC_SEGMENT. ALLOC LOAD CODE HAS_CONTENTS
0x00007fa0e6900000->0x00007fa0e6a00000 at 0x0b8ec000: LC_SEGMENT. ALLOC LOAD CODE HAS_CONTENTS
0x00007fa0e6a00000->0x00007fa0e6b00000 at 0x0b9ec000: LC_SEGMENT. ALLOC LOAD CODE HAS_CONTENTS
0x00007fa0e6b00000->0x00007fa0e6c00000 at 0x0baec000: LC_SEGMENT. ALLOC LOAD CODE HAS_CONTENTS
0x00007fa0e6c00000->0x00007fa0e6d00000 at 0x0bbec000: LC_SEGMENT. ALLOC LOAD CODE HAS_CONTENTS
0x00007fa0e6d00000->0x00007fa0e6e00000 at 0x0bcec000: LC_SEGMENT. ALLOC LOAD CODE HAS_CONTENTS
0x00007fa0e6e00000->0x00007fa0e6f00000 at 0x0bdec000: LC_SEGMENT. ALLOC LOAD CODE HAS_CONTENTS
0x00007fa0e6f00000->0x00007fa0e7000000 at 0x0beec000: LC_SEGMENT. ALLOC LOAD CODE HAS_CONTENTS
0x00007fa0e7000000->0x00007fa0e7100000 at 0x0bfec000: LC_SEGMENT. ALLOC LOAD CODE HAS_CONTENTS
0x00007fa0e7100000->0x00007fa0e7200000 at 0x0c0ec000: LC_SEGMENT. ALLOC LOAD CODE HAS_CONTENTS
---Type <return> to continue, or q <return> to quit---
0x00007fa0e7200000->0x00007fa0e7300000 at 0x0c1ec000: LC_SEGMENT. ALLOC LOAD CODE HAS_CONTENTS
0x00007fa0e7300000->0x00007fa0e7400000 at 0x0c2ec000: LC_SEGMENT. ALLOC LOAD CODE HAS_CONTENTS
0x00007fa0e7400000->0x00007fa0e7500000 at 0x0c3ec000: LC_SEGMENT. ALLOC LOAD CODE HAS_CONTENTS
0x00007fa0e7500000->0x00007fa0e7600000 at 0x0c4ec000: LC_SEGMENT. ALLOC LOAD CODE HAS_CONTENTS
0x00007fa0e7600000->0x00007fa0e7700000 at 0x0c5ec000: LC_SEGMENT. ALLOC LOAD CODE HAS_CONTENTS
0x00007fa0e7700000->0x00007fa0e7800000 at 0x0c6ec000: LC_SEGMENT. ALLOC LOAD CODE HAS_CONTENTS
0x00007fa0e7800000->0x00007fa0e7900000 at 0x0c7ec000: LC_SEGMENT. ALLOC LOAD CODE HAS_CONTENTS
```

```
0x00007fa0e7900000->0x00007fa0e7a00000 at 0x0c8ec000: LC_SEGMENT. ALLOC LOAD CODE HAS_CONTENTS
0x00007fa0e7a00000->0x00007fa0e7b00000 at 0x0c9ec000: LC_SEGMENT. ALLOC LOAD CODE HAS_CONTENTS
0x00007fa0e7b00000->0x00007fa0e7c00000 at 0x0caec000: LC_SEGMENT. ALLOC LOAD CODE HAS_CONTENTS
0x00007fa0e7c00000->0x00007fa0e7d00000 at 0x0cbec000: LC_SEGMENT. ALLOC LOAD CODE HAS_CONTENTS
0x00007fa0e7d00000->0x00007fa0e7e00000 at 0x0ccec000: LC_SEGMENT. ALLOC LOAD CODE HAS_CONTENTS
0x00007fa0e7e00000->0x00007fa0e7f00000 at 0x0cdec000: LC_SEGMENT. ALLOC LOAD CODE HAS_CONTENTS
0x00007fa0e7f00000->0x00007fa0e8000000 at 0x0ceec000: LC_SEGMENT. ALLOC LOAD CODE HAS_CONTENTS
0x00007fa0e8000000->0x00007fa0e8100000 at 0x0cfec000: LC_SEGMENT. ALLOC LOAD CODE HAS_CONTENTS
0x00007fa0e8100000->0x00007fa0e8200000 at 0x0d0ec000: LC_SEGMENT. ALLOC LOAD CODE HAS_CONTENTS
0x00007fa0e8200000->0x00007fa0e8300000 at 0x0d1ec000: LC_SEGMENT. ALLOC LOAD CODE HAS_CONTENTS
0x00007fa0e8300000->0x00007fa0e8400000 at 0x0d2ec000: LC_SEGMENT. ALLOC LOAD CODE HAS_CONTENTS
0x00007fa0e8400000->0x00007fa0e8500000 at 0x0d3ec000: LC_SEGMENT. ALLOC LOAD CODE HAS_CONTENTS
0x00007fa0e8500000->0x00007fa0e8600000 at 0x0d4ec000: LC_SEGMENT. ALLOC LOAD CODE HAS_CONTENTS
0x00007fa0e8600000->0x00007fa0e8700000 at 0x0d5ec000: LC_SEGMENT. ALLOC LOAD CODE HAS_CONTENTS
0x00007fa0e8700000->0x00007fa0e8800000 at 0x0d6ec000: LC_SEGMENT. ALLOC LOAD CODE HAS_CONTENTS
0x00007fa0e8800000->0x00007fa0e8900000 at 0x0d7ec000: LC_SEGMENT. ALLOC LOAD CODE HAS_CONTENTS
0x00007fa0e8900000->0x00007fa0e8a00000 at 0x0d8ec000: LC_SEGMENT. ALLOC LOAD CODE HAS_CONTENTS
0x00007fa0e8a00000->0x00007fa0e8b00000 at 0x0d9ec000: LC_SEGMENT. ALLOC LOAD CODE HAS_CONTENTS
0x00007fa0e8b00000->0x00007fa0e8c00000 at 0x0daec000: LC_SEGMENT. ALLOC LOAD CODE HAS_CONTENTS
0x00007fa0e8c00000->0x00007fa0e8d00000 at 0x0dbec000: LC_SEGMENT. ALLOC LOAD CODE HAS_CONTENTS
0x00007fa0e8d00000->0x00007fa0e8e00000 at 0x0dcec000: LC_SEGMENT. ALLOC LOAD CODE HAS_CONTENTS
0x00007fa0e8e00000->0x00007fa0e8f00000 at 0x0ddec000: LC_SEGMENT. ALLOC LOAD CODE HAS_CONTENTS
0x00007fa0e8f00000->0x00007fa0e9000000 at 0x0deec000: LC_SEGMENT. ALLOC LOAD CODE HAS_CONTENTS
0x00007fa0e9000000->0x00007fa0e9100000 at 0x0dfec000: LC_SEGMENT. ALLOC LOAD CODE HAS_CONTENTS
0x00007fa0eb400000->0x00007fa0eb500000 at 0x0e0ec000: LC_SEGMENT. ALLOC LOAD CODE HAS_CONTENTS
0x00007fa0eb500000->0x00007fa0eb600000 at 0x0e1ec000: LC_SEGMENT. ALLOC LOAD CODE HAS_CONTENTS
0x00007fa0eb600000->0x00007fa0eb700000 at 0x0e2ec000: LC_SEGMENT. ALLOC LOAD CODE HAS_CONTENTS
0x00007fa0eb700000->0x00007fa0eb800000 at 0x0e3ec000: LC_SEGMENT. ALLOC LOAD CODE HAS_CONTENTS
0x00007fa0eb800000->0x00007fa0eb900000 at 0x0e4ec000: LC_SEGMENT. ALLOC LOAD CODE HAS_CONTENTS
0x00007fa0eb900000->0x00007fa0eba00000 at 0x0e5ec000: LC_SEGMENT. ALLOC LOAD CODE HAS_CONTENTS
0x00007fa0eba00000->0x00007fa0ebb00000 at 0x0e6ec000: LC_SEGMENT. ALLOC LOAD CODE HAS_CONTENTS
0x00007fa0ebb00000->0x00007fa0ebc00000 at 0x0e7ec000: LC_SEGMENT. ALLOC LOAD CODE HAS_CONTENTS
0x00007fa0ebc00000->0x00007fa0ebd00000 at 0x0e8ec000: LC_SEGMENT. ALLOC LOAD CODE HAS_CONTENTS
---Type <return> to continue, or q <return> to quit---
0x00007fa0ebd00000->0x00007fa0ebe00000 at 0x0e9ec000: LC_SEGMENT. ALLOC LOAD CODE HAS_CONTENTS
0x00007fa0ebe00000->0x00007fa0ebf00000 at 0x0eaec000: LC_SEGMENT. ALLOC LOAD CODE HAS_CONTENTS
0x00007fa0ebf00000->0x00007fa0ec000000 at 0x0ebec000: LC_SEGMENT. ALLOC LOAD CODE HAS_CONTENTS
0x00007fa0ec000000->0x00007fa0ec100000 at 0x0ecec000: LC_SEGMENT. ALLOC LOAD CODE HAS_CONTENTS
0x00007fa0ec100000->0x00007fa0ec200000 at 0x0edec000: LC_SEGMENT. ALLOC LOAD CODE HAS_CONTENTS
0x00007fa0ec200000->0x00007fa0ec300000 at 0x0eeec000: LC_SEGMENT. ALLOC LOAD CODE HAS_CONTENTS
0x00007fa0ec300000->0x00007fa0ec400000 at 0x0efec000: LC_SEGMENT. ALLOC LOAD CODE HAS_CONTENTS
0x00007fa0ec400000->0x00007fa0ec500000 at 0x0f0ec000: LC_SEGMENT. ALLOC LOAD CODE HAS_CONTENTS
0x00007fa0ec500000->0x00007fa0ec600000 at 0x0f1ec000: LC_SEGMENT. ALLOC LOAD CODE HAS_CONTENTS
0x00007fa0ec600000->0x00007fa0ec700000 at 0x0f2ec000: LC_SEGMENT. ALLOC LOAD CODE HAS_CONTENTS
0x00007fa0ec700000->0x00007fa0ec800000 at 0x0f3ec000: LC_SEGMENT. ALLOC LOAD CODE HAS_CONTENTS
0x00007fa0ec800000->0x00007fa0ec900000 at 0x0f4ec000: LC_SEGMENT. ALLOC LOAD CODE HAS_CONTENTS
0x00007fa0ec900000->0x00007fa0eca00000 at 0x0f5ec000: LC_SEGMENT. ALLOC LOAD CODE HAS_CONTENTS
0x00007fa0eca00000->0x00007fa0ecb00000 at 0x0f6ec000: LC_SEGMENT. ALLOC LOAD CODE HAS_CONTENTS
0x00007fa0ecb00000->0x00007fa0ecc00000 at 0x0f7ec000: LC_SEGMENT. ALLOC LOAD CODE HAS_CONTENTS
0x00007fa0ecc00000->0x00007fa0ecd00000 at 0x0f8ec000: LC_SEGMENT. ALLOC LOAD CODE HAS_CONTENTS
0x00007fa0ecd00000->0x00007fa0ece00000 at 0x0f9ec000: LC_SEGMENT. ALLOC LOAD CODE HAS_CONTENTS
0x00007fa0ece00000->0x00007fa0ecf00000 at 0x0faec000: LC_SEGMENT. ALLOC LOAD CODE HAS_CONTENTS
0x00007fa0ecf00000->0x00007fa0ed000000 at 0x0fbec000: LC_SEGMENT. ALLOC LOAD CODE HAS_CONTENTS
0x00007fa0ed000000->0x00007fa0ed100000 at 0x0fcec000: LC_SEGMENT. ALLOC LOAD CODE HAS_CONTENTS
0x00007fa0ed100000->0x00007fa0ed200000 at 0x0fdec000: LC_SEGMENT. ALLOC LOAD CODE HAS_CONTENTS
0x00007fa0ed200000->0x00007fa0ed300000 at 0x0feec000: LC_SEGMENT. ALLOC LOAD CODE HAS_CONTENTS
0x00007fa0ed300000->0x00007fa0ed400000 at 0x0ffec000: LC_SEGMENT. ALLOC LOAD CODE HAS_CONTENTS
0x00007fa0ed400000->0x00007fa0ed500000 at 0x100ec000: LC_SEGMENT. ALLOC LOAD CODE HAS_CONTENTS
0x00007fa0ed500000->0x00007fa0ed600000 at 0x101ec000: LC_SEGMENT. ALLOC LOAD CODE HAS_CONTENTS
0x00007fa0ed600000->0x00007fa0ed700000 at 0x102ec000: LC_SEGMENT. ALLOC LOAD CODE HAS_CONTENTS
0x00007fa0ed700000->0x00007fa0ed800000 at 0x103ec000: LC_SEGMENT. ALLOC LOAD CODE HAS_CONTENTS
0x00007fa0ed800000->0x00007fa0ed900000 at 0x104ec000: LC_SEGMENT. ALLOC LOAD CODE HAS_CONTENTS
0x00007fa0ed900000->0x00007fa0eda00000 at 0x105ec000: LC_SEGMENT. ALLOC LOAD CODE HAS_CONTENTS
0x00007fa0eda00000->0x00007fa0edb00000 at 0x106ec000: LC_SEGMENT. ALLOC LOAD CODE HAS_CONTENTS
0x00007fa0edb00000->0x00007fa0edc00000 at 0x107ec000: LC_SEGMENT. ALLOC LOAD CODE HAS_CONTENTS
0x00007fa0edc00000->0x00007fa0edd00000 at 0x108ec000: LC_SEGMENT. ALLOC LOAD CODE HAS_CONTENTS
0x00007fa0edd00000->0x00007fa0ede00000 at 0x109ec000: LC_SEGMENT. ALLOC LOAD CODE HAS_CONTENTS
0x00007fa0ede00000->0x00007fa0edf00000 at 0x10aec000: LC_SEGMENT. ALLOC LOAD CODE HAS_CONTENTS
0x00007fa0edf00000->0x00007fa0ee000000 at 0x10bec000: LC_SEGMENT. ALLOC LOAD CODE HAS_CONTENTS
0x00007fa0ee000000->0x00007fa0ee100000 at 0x10cec000: LC_SEGMENT. ALLOC LOAD CODE HAS_CONTENTS
0x00007fa0ee100000->0x00007fa0ee200000 at 0x10dec000: LC_SEGMENT. ALLOC LOAD CODE HAS_CONTENTS
0x00007fa0ee200000->0x00007fa0ee300000 at 0x10eec000: LC_SEGMENT. ALLOC LOAD CODE HAS_CONTENTS
0x00007fa0ee300000->0x00007fa0ee400000 at 0x10fec000: LC_SEGMENT. ALLOC LOAD CODE HAS_CONTENTS
0x00007fa0ee400000->0x00007fa0ee500000 at 0x110ec000: LC_SEGMENT. ALLOC LOAD CODE HAS_CONTENTS
---Type <return> to continue, or q <return> to quit---
0x00007fa0ee500000->0x00007fa0ee600000 at 0x111ec000: LC_SEGMENT. ALLOC LOAD CODE HAS_CONTENTS
0x00007fa0ee600000->0x00007fa0ee700000 at 0x112ec000: LC_SEGMENT. ALLOC LOAD CODE HAS_CONTENTS
0x00007fa0ee700000->0x00007fa0ee800000 at 0x113ec000: LC_SEGMENT. ALLOC LOAD CODE HAS_CONTENTS
0x00007fa0ee800000->0x00007fa0ee900000 at 0x114ec000: LC_SEGMENT. ALLOC LOAD CODE HAS_CONTENTS
0x00007fa0ee900000->0x00007fa0eea00000 at 0x115ec000: LC_SEGMENT. ALLOC LOAD CODE HAS_CONTENTS
0x00007fa0eea00000->0x00007fa0eeb00000 at 0x116ec000: LC_SEGMENT. ALLOC LOAD CODE HAS_CONTENTS
0x00007fa0eeb00000->0x00007fa0eec00000 at 0x117ec000: LC_SEGMENT. ALLOC LOAD CODE HAS_CONTENTS
0x00007fa0eec00000->0x00007fa0eed00000 at 0x118ec000: LC_SEGMENT. ALLOC LOAD CODE HAS_CONTENTS
0x00007fa0eed00000->0x00007fa0eee00000 at 0x119ec000: LC_SEGMENT. ALLOC LOAD CODE HAS_CONTENTS
0x00007fa0eee00000->0x00007fa0eef00000 at 0x11aec000: LC_SEGMENT. ALLOC LOAD CODE HAS_CONTENTS
0x00007fa0eef00000->0x00007fa0ef000000 at 0x11bec000: LC_SEGMENT. ALLOC LOAD CODE HAS_CONTENTS
```

```
0x00007fa0ef000000->0x00007fa0ef100000 at 0x11cec000: LC_SEGMENT. ALLOC LOAD CODE HAS_CONTENTS
0x00007fa0ef100000->0x00007fa0ef200000 at 0x11dec000: LC_SEGMENT. ALLOC LOAD CODE HAS_CONTENTS
0x00007fa0ef200000->0x00007fa0ef300000 at 0x11eec000: LC_SEGMENT. ALLOC LOAD CODE HAS_CONTENTS
0x00007fa0ef300000->0x00007fa0ef400000 at 0x11fec000: LC_SEGMENT. ALLOC LOAD CODE HAS_CONTENTS
0x00007fa0ef400000->0x00007fa0ef500000 at 0x120ec000: LC_SEGMENT. ALLOC LOAD CODE HAS_CONTENTS
0x00007fa0ef500000->0x00007fa0ef600000 at 0x121ec000: LC_SEGMENT. ALLOC LOAD CODE HAS_CONTENTS
0x00007fa0ef600000->0x00007fa0ef700000 at 0x122ec000: LC_SEGMENT. ALLOC LOAD CODE HAS_CONTENTS
0x00007fa0ef700000->0x00007fa0ef800000 at 0x123ec000: LC_SEGMENT. ALLOC LOAD CODE HAS_CONTENTS
0x00007fa0ef800000->0x00007fa0ef900000 at 0x124ec000: LC_SEGMENT. ALLOC LOAD CODE HAS_CONTENTS
0x00007fa0ef900000->0x00007fa0efa00000 at 0x125ec000: LC_SEGMENT. ALLOC LOAD CODE HAS_CONTENTS
0x00007fa0efa00000->0x00007fa0efb00000 at 0x126ec000: LC_SEGMENT. ALLOC LOAD CODE HAS_CONTENTS
0x00007fa0efb00000->0x00007fa0efc00000 at 0x127ec000: LC_SEGMENT. ALLOC LOAD CODE HAS_CONTENTS
0x00007fa0efc00000->0x00007fa0efd00000 at 0x128ec000: LC_SEGMENT. ALLOC LOAD CODE HAS_CONTENTS
0x00007fa0efd00000->0x00007fa0efe00000 at 0x129ec000: LC_SEGMENT. ALLOC LOAD CODE HAS_CONTENTS
0x00007fa0efe00000->0x00007fa0eff00000 at 0x12aec000: LC_SEGMENT. ALLOC LOAD CODE HAS_CONTENTS
0x00007fa0eff00000->0x00007fa0f0000000 at 0x12bec000: LC_SEGMENT. ALLOC LOAD CODE HAS_CONTENTS
0x00007fa0f0000000->0x00007fa0f0100000 at 0x12cec000: LC_SEGMENT. ALLOC LOAD CODE HAS_CONTENTS
0x00007fa0f0100000->0x00007fa0f0200000 at 0x12dec000: LC_SEGMENT. ALLOC LOAD CODE HAS_CONTENTS
0x00007fa0f0200000->0x00007fa0f0300000 at 0x12eec000: LC_SEGMENT. ALLOC LOAD CODE HAS_CONTENTS
0x00007fa0f0300000->0x00007fa0f0400000 at 0x12fec000: LC_SEGMENT. ALLOC LOAD CODE HAS_CONTENTS
0x00007fa0f0400000->0x00007fa0f0500000 at 0x130ec000: LC_SEGMENT. ALLOC LOAD CODE HAS_CONTENTS
0x00007fa0f0500000->0x00007fa0f0600000 at 0x131ec000: LC_SEGMENT. ALLOC LOAD CODE HAS_CONTENTS
0x00007fa0f0600000->0x00007fa0f0700000 at 0x132ec000: LC_SEGMENT. ALLOC LOAD CODE HAS_CONTENTS
0x00007fa0f0700000->0x00007fa0f0800000 at 0x133ec000: LC_SEGMENT. ALLOC LOAD CODE HAS_CONTENTS
0x00007fa0f0800000->0x00007fa0f0900000 at 0x134ec000: LC_SEGMENT. ALLOC LOAD CODE HAS_CONTENTS
0x00007fa0f0900000->0x00007fa0f0a00000 at 0x135ec000: LC_SEGMENT. ALLOC LOAD CODE HAS_CONTENTS
0x00007fa0f0a00000->0x00007fa0f0b00000 at 0x136ec000: LC_SEGMENT. ALLOC LOAD CODE HAS_CONTENTS
0x00007fa0f0b00000->0x00007fa0f0c00000 at 0x137ec000: LC_SEGMENT. ALLOC LOAD CODE HAS_CONTENTS
0x00007fa0f0c00000->0x00007fa0f0d00000 at 0x138ec000: LC_SEGMENT. ALLOC LOAD CODE HAS_CONTENTS
---Type <return> to continue, or q <return> to quit---
0x00007fa0f0d00000->0x00007fa0f0e00000 at 0x139ec000: LC_SEGMENT. ALLOC LOAD CODE HAS_CONTENTS
0x00007fa0f0e00000->0x00007fa0f0f00000 at 0x13aec000: LC_SEGMENT. ALLOC LOAD CODE HAS_CONTENTS
0x00007fa0f0f00000->0x00007fa0f1000000 at 0x13bec000: LC_SEGMENT. ALLOC LOAD CODE HAS_CONTENTS
0x00007fa0f1000000->0x00007fa0f1100000 at 0x13cec000: LC_SEGMENT. ALLOC LOAD CODE HAS_CONTENTS
0x00007fa0f1100000->0x00007fa0f1200000 at 0x13dec000: LC_SEGMENT. ALLOC LOAD CODE HAS_CONTENTS
0x00007fa0f1200000->0x00007fa0f1300000 at 0x13eec000: LC_SEGMENT. ALLOC LOAD CODE HAS_CONTENTS
0x00007fa0f1300000->0x00007fa0f1400000 at 0x13fec000: LC_SEGMENT. ALLOC LOAD CODE HAS_CONTENTS
0x00007fa0f1400000->0x00007fa0f1500000 at 0x140ec000: LC_SEGMENT. ALLOC LOAD CODE HAS_CONTENTS
0x00007fa0f1500000->0x00007fa0f1600000 at 0x141ec000: LC_SEGMENT. ALLOC LOAD CODE HAS_CONTENTS
0x00007fa0f1600000->0x00007fa0f1700000 at 0x142ec000: LC_SEGMENT. ALLOC LOAD CODE HAS_CONTENTS
0x00007fa0f1700000->0x00007fa0f1800000 at 0x143ec000: LC_SEGMENT. ALLOC LOAD CODE HAS_CONTENTS
0x00007fa0f1800000->0x00007fa0f1900000 at 0x144ec000: LC_SEGMENT. ALLOC LOAD CODE HAS_CONTENTS
0x00007fa0f1900000->0x00007fa0f1a00000 at 0x145ec000: LC_SEGMENT. ALLOC LOAD CODE HAS_CONTENTS
0x00007fa0f1a00000->0x00007fa0f1b00000 at 0x146ec000: LC_SEGMENT. ALLOC LOAD CODE HAS_CONTENTS
0x00007fa0f1b00000->0x00007fa0f1c00000 at 0x147ec000: LC_SEGMENT. ALLOC LOAD CODE HAS_CONTENTS
0x00007fa0f1c00000->0x00007fa0f1d00000 at 0x148ec000: LC_SEGMENT. ALLOC LOAD CODE HAS_CONTENTS
0x00007fa0f1d00000->0x00007fa0f1e00000 at 0x149ec000: LC_SEGMENT. ALLOC LOAD CODE HAS_CONTENTS
0x00007fa0f1e00000->0x00007fa0f1f00000 at 0x14aec000: LC_SEGMENT. ALLOC LOAD CODE HAS_CONTENTS
0x00007fa0f1f00000->0x00007fa0f2000000 at 0x14bec000: LC_SEGMENT. ALLOC LOAD CODE HAS_CONTENTS
0x00007fa0f2000000->0x00007fa0f2100000 at 0x14cec000: LC_SEGMENT. ALLOC LOAD CODE HAS_CONTENTS
0x00007fa0f2100000->0x00007fa0f2200000 at 0x14dec000: LC_SEGMENT. ALLOC LOAD CODE HAS_CONTENTS
0x00007fa0f2200000->0x00007fa0f2300000 at 0x14eec000: LC_SEGMENT. ALLOC LOAD CODE HAS_CONTENTS
0x00007fa0f2300000->0x00007fa0f2400000 at 0x14fec000: LC_SEGMENT. ALLOC LOAD CODE HAS_CONTENTS
0x00007fa0f2400000->0x00007fa0f2500000 at 0x150ec000: LC_SEGMENT. ALLOC LOAD CODE HAS_CONTENTS
0x00007fa0f2500000->0x00007fa0f2600000 at 0x151ec000: LC_SEGMENT. ALLOC LOAD CODE HAS_CONTENTS
0x00007fa0f2600000->0x00007fa0f2700000 at 0x152ec000: LC_SEGMENT. ALLOC LOAD CODE HAS_CONTENTS
0x00007fa0f2700000->0x00007fa0f2800000 at 0x153ec000: LC_SEGMENT. ALLOC LOAD CODE HAS_CONTENTS
0x00007fa0f2800000->0x00007fa0f2900000 at 0x154ec000: LC_SEGMENT. ALLOC LOAD CODE HAS_CONTENTS
0x00007fa0f2900000->0x00007fa0f2a00000 at 0x155ec000: LC_SEGMENT. ALLOC LOAD CODE HAS_CONTENTS
0x00007fa0f2a00000->0x00007fa0f2b00000 at 0x156ec000: LC_SEGMENT. ALLOC LOAD CODE HAS_CONTENTS
0x00007fa0f2b00000->0x00007fa0f2c00000 at 0x157ec000: LC_SEGMENT. ALLOC LOAD CODE HAS_CONTENTS
0x00007fa0f2c00000->0x00007fa0f2d00000 at 0x158ec000: LC_SEGMENT. ALLOC LOAD CODE HAS_CONTENTS
0x00007fa0f2d00000->0x00007fa0f2e00000 at 0x159ec000: LC_SEGMENT. ALLOC LOAD CODE HAS_CONTENTS
0x00007fa0f2e00000->0x00007fa0f2f00000 at 0x15aec000: LC_SEGMENT. ALLOC LOAD CODE HAS_CONTENTS
0x00007fa0f2f00000->0x00007fa0f3000000 at 0x15bec000: LC_SEGMENT. ALLOC LOAD CODE HAS_CONTENTS
0x00007fa0f3000000->0x00007fa0f3100000 at 0x15cec000: LC_SEGMENT. ALLOC LOAD CODE HAS_CONTENTS
0x00007fa0f3100000->0x00007fa0f3200000 at 0x15dec000: LC_SEGMENT. ALLOC LOAD CODE HAS_CONTENTS
0x00007fa0f3200000->0x00007fa0f3300000 at 0x15eec000: LC_SEGMENT. ALLOC LOAD CODE HAS_CONTENTS
0x00007fa0f3300000->0x00007fa0f3400000 at 0x15fec000: LC_SEGMENT. ALLOC LOAD CODE HAS_CONTENTS
0x00007fa0f3400000->0x00007fa0f3500000 at 0x160ec000: LC_SEGMENT. ALLOC LOAD CODE HAS_CONTENTS
---Type <return> to continue, or q <return> to quit---
0x00007fa0f3500000->0x00007fa0f3600000 at 0x161ec000: LC_SEGMENT. ALLOC LOAD CODE HAS_CONTENTS
0x00007fa0f3600000->0x00007fa0f3700000 at 0x162ec000: LC_SEGMENT. ALLOC LOAD CODE HAS_CONTENTS
0x00007fa0f3700000->0x00007fa0f3800000 at 0x163ec000: LC_SEGMENT. ALLOC LOAD CODE HAS_CONTENTS
0x00007fa0f3800000->0x00007fa0f3900000 at 0x164ec000: LC_SEGMENT. ALLOC LOAD CODE HAS_CONTENTS
0x00007fa0f3900000->0x00007fa0f3a00000 at 0x165ec000: LC_SEGMENT. ALLOC LOAD CODE HAS_CONTENTS
0x00007fa0f3a00000->0x00007fa0f3b00000 at 0x166ec000: LC_SEGMENT. ALLOC LOAD CODE HAS_CONTENTS
0x00007fa0f3b00000->0x00007fa0f3c00000 at 0x167ec000: LC_SEGMENT. ALLOC LOAD CODE HAS_CONTENTS
0x00007fa0f3c00000->0x00007fa0f3d00000 at 0x168ec000: LC_SEGMENT. ALLOC LOAD CODE HAS_CONTENTS
0x00007fa0f3d00000->0x00007fa0f3e00000 at 0x169ec000: LC_SEGMENT. ALLOC LOAD CODE HAS_CONTENTS
0x00007fa0f3e00000->0x00007fa0f3f00000 at 0x16aec000: LC_SEGMENT. ALLOC LOAD CODE HAS_CONTENTS
0x00007fa0f3f00000->0x00007fa0f4000000 at 0x16bec000: LC_SEGMENT. ALLOC LOAD CODE HAS_CONTENTS
0x00007fa0f4000000->0x00007fa0f4100000 at 0x16cec000: LC_SEGMENT. ALLOC LOAD CODE HAS_CONTENTS
0x00007fa0f4100000->0x00007fa0f4200000 at 0x16dec000: LC_SEGMENT. ALLOC LOAD CODE HAS_CONTENTS
0x00007fa0f4200000->0x00007fa0f4300000 at 0x16eec000: LC_SEGMENT. ALLOC LOAD CODE HAS_CONTENTS
0x00007fa0f4300000->0x00007fa0f4400000 at 0x16fec000: LC_SEGMENT. ALLOC LOAD CODE HAS_CONTENTS
```

```
0x00007fa0f4400000->0x00007fa0f4500000 at 0x170ec000: LC_SEGMENT. ALLOC LOAD CODE HAS_CONTENTS
0x00007fa0f4500000->0x00007fa0f4600000 at 0x171ec000: LC_SEGMENT. ALLOC LOAD CODE HAS_CONTENTS
0x00007fa0f4600000->0x00007fa0f4700000 at 0x172ec000: LC_SEGMENT. ALLOC LOAD CODE HAS_CONTENTS
0x00007fa0f4700000->0x00007fa0f4800000 at 0x173ec000: LC_SEGMENT. ALLOC LOAD CODE HAS_CONTENTS
0x00007fa0f4800000->0x00007fa0f4900000 at 0x174ec000: LC_SEGMENT. ALLOC LOAD CODE HAS_CONTENTS
0x00007fa0f4900000->0x00007fa0f4a00000 at 0x175ec000: LC_SEGMENT. ALLOC LOAD CODE HAS_CONTENTS
0x00007fa0f4a00000->0x00007fa0f4b00000 at 0x176ec000: LC_SEGMENT. ALLOC LOAD CODE HAS_CONTENTS
0x00007fa0f4b00000->0x00007fa0f4c00000 at 0x177ec000: LC_SEGMENT. ALLOC LOAD CODE HAS_CONTENTS
0x00007fa0f4c00000->0x00007fa0f4d00000 at 0x178ec000: LC_SEGMENT. ALLOC LOAD CODE HAS_CONTENTS
0x00007fa0f4d00000->0x00007fa0f4e00000 at 0x179ec000: LC_SEGMENT. ALLOC LOAD CODE HAS_CONTENTS
0x00007fa0f4e00000->0x00007fa0f4f00000 at 0x17aec000: LC_SEGMENT. ALLOC LOAD CODE HAS_CONTENTS
0x00007fa0f4f00000->0x00007fa0f5000000 at 0x17bec000: LC_SEGMENT. ALLOC LOAD CODE HAS_CONTENTS
0x00007fa0f5000000->0x00007fa0f5100000 at 0x17cec000: LC_SEGMENT. ALLOC LOAD CODE HAS_CONTENTS
0x00007fa0f5100000->0x00007fa0f5200000 at 0x17dec000: LC_SEGMENT. ALLOC LOAD CODE HAS_CONTENTS
0x00007fa0f5200000->0x00007fa0f5300000 at 0x17eec000: LC_SEGMENT. ALLOC LOAD CODE HAS_CONTENTS
0x00007fa0f5300000->0x00007fa0f5400000 at 0x17fec000: LC_SEGMENT. ALLOC LOAD CODE HAS_CONTENTS
0x00007fa0f5400000->0x00007fa0f5500000 at 0x180ec000: LC_SEGMENT. ALLOC LOAD CODE HAS_CONTENTS
0x00007fa0f5500000->0x00007fa0f5600000 at 0x181ec000: LC_SEGMENT. ALLOC LOAD CODE HAS_CONTENTS
0x00007fa0f5600000->0x00007fa0f5700000 at 0x182ec000: LC_SEGMENT. ALLOC LOAD CODE HAS_CONTENTS
0x00007fa0f5700000->0x00007fa0f5800000 at 0x183ec000: LC_SEGMENT. ALLOC LOAD CODE HAS_CONTENTS
0x00007fa0f5800000->0x00007fa0f5900000 at 0x184ec000: LC_SEGMENT. ALLOC LOAD CODE HAS_CONTENTS
0x00007fa0f5900000->0x00007fa0f5a00000 at 0x185cc000: LC_SEGMENT. ALLOC LOAD CODE IIA5_CONTENTS
0x00007fa0f5a00000->0x00007fa0f5b00000 at 0x186ec000: LC_SEGMENT. ALLOC LOAD CODE HAS_CONTENTS
0x00007fa0f5b00000->0x00007fa0f5c00000 at 0x187ec000: LC_SEGMENT. ALLOC LOAD CODE HAS_CONTENTS
0x00007fa0f5c00000->0x00007fa0f5d00000 at 0x188ec000: LC_SEGMENT. ALLOC LOAD CODE HAS_CONTENTS
---Type <return> to continue, or q <return> to quit---
0x00007fa0f5d00000->0x00007fa0f5e00000 at 0x189ec000: LC_SEGMENT. ALLOC LOAD CODE HAS_CONTENTS
0x00007fa0f5e00000->0x00007fa0f5f00000 at 0x18aec000: LC_SEGMENT. ALLOC LOAD CODE HAS_CONTENTS
0x00007fa0f5f00000->0x00007fa0f6000000 at 0x18bec000: LC_SEGMENT. ALLOC LOAD CODE HAS_CONTENTS
0x00007fa0f6000000->0x00007fa0f6100000 at 0x18cec000: LC_SEGMENT. ALLOC LOAD CODE HAS_CONTENTS
0x00007fa0f6100000->0x00007fa0f6200000 at 0x18dec000: LC_SEGMENT. ALLOC LOAD CODE HAS_CONTENTS
0x00007fa0f6200000->0x00007fa0f6300000 at 0x18eec000: LC_SEGMENT. ALLOC LOAD CODE HAS_CONTENTS
0x00007fa0f6300000->0x00007fa0f6400000 at 0x18fec000: LC_SEGMENT. ALLOC LOAD CODE HAS_CONTENTS
0x00007fa0f6400000->0x00007fa0f6500000 at 0x190ec000: LC_SEGMENT. ALLOC LOAD CODE HAS_CONTENTS
0x00007fa0f6500000->0x00007fa0f6600000 at 0x191ec000: LC_SEGMENT. ALLOC LOAD CODE HAS_CONTENTS
0x00007fa0f6600000->0x00007fa0f6700000 at 0x192ec000: LC_SEGMENT. ALLOC LOAD CODE HAS_CONTENTS
0x00007fa0f6700000->0x00007fa0f6800000 at 0x193ec000: LC_SEGMENT. ALLOC LOAD CODE HAS_CONTENTS
0x00007fa0f6800000->0x00007fa0f6900000 at 0x194ec000: LC_SEGMENT. ALLOC LOAD CODE HAS_CONTENTS
0x00007fa0f6900000->0x00007fa0f6a00000 at 0x195ec000: LC_SEGMENT. ALLOC LOAD CODE HAS_CONTENTS
0x00007fa0f6a00000->0x00007fa0f6b00000 at 0x196ec000: LC_SEGMENT. ALLOC LOAD CODE HAS_CONTENTS
0x00007fa0f6b00000->0x00007fa0f6c00000 at 0x197ec000: LC_SEGMENT. ALLOC LOAD CODE HAS_CONTENTS
0x00007fa0f6c00000->0x00007fa0f6d00000 at 0x198ec000: LC_SEGMENT. ALLOC LOAD CODE HAS_CONTENTS
0x00007fa0f6d00000->0x00007fa0f6e00000 at 0x199ec000: LC_SEGMENT. ALLOC LOAD CODE HAS_CONTENTS
0x00007fa0f6e00000->0x00007fa0f6f00000 at 0x19aec000: LC_SEGMENT. ALLOC LOAD CODE HAS_CONTENTS
0x00007fa0f6f00000->0x00007fa0f7000000 at 0x19bec000: LC_SEGMENT. ALLOC LOAD CODE HAS_CONTENTS
0x00007fa0f7000000->0x00007fa0f7100000 at 0x19cec000: LC_SEGMENT. ALLOC LOAD CODE HAS_CONTENTS
0x00007fa0f7100000->0x00007fa0f7200000 at 0x19dec000: LC_SEGMENT. ALLOC LOAD CODE HAS_CONTENTS
0x00007fa0f7200000->0x00007fa0f7300000 at 0x19eec000: LC_SEGMENT. ALLOC LOAD CODE HAS_CONTENTS
0x00007fa0f7300000->0x00007fa0f7400000 at 0x19fec000: LC_SEGMENT. ALLOC LOAD CODE HAS_CONTENTS
0x00007fa0f7400000->0x00007fa0f7500000 at 0x1a0ec000: LC_SEGMENT. ALLOC LOAD CODE HAS_CONTENTS
0x00007fa0f7500000->0x00007fa0f7600000 at 0x1a1ec000: LC_SEGMENT. ALLOC LOAD CODE HAS_CONTENTS
0x00007fa0f7600000->0x00007fa0f7700000 at 0x1a2ec000: LC_SEGMENT. ALLOC LOAD CODE HAS_CONTENTS
0x00007fa0f7700000->0x00007fa0f7800000 at 0x1a3ec000: LC_SEGMENT. ALLOC LOAD CODE HAS_CONTENTS
0x00007fa0f7800000->0x00007fa0f7900000 at 0x1a4ec000: LC_SEGMENT. ALLOC LOAD CODE HAS_CONTENTS
0x00007fa0f7900000->0x00007fa0f7a00000 at 0x1a5ec000: LC_SEGMENT. ALLOC LOAD CODE HAS_CONTENTS
0x00007fa0f7a00000->0x00007fa0f7b00000 at 0x1a6ec000: LC_SEGMENT. ALLOC LOAD CODE HAS_CONTENTS
0x00007fa0f7b00000->0x00007fa0f7c00000 at 0x1a7ec000: LC_SEGMENT. ALLOC LOAD CODE HAS_CONTENTS
0x00007fa0f7c00000->0x00007fa0f7d00000 at 0x1a8ec000: LC_SEGMENT. ALLOC LOAD CODE HAS_CONTENTS
0x00007fa0f7d00000->0x00007fa0f7e00000 at 0x1a9ec000: LC_SEGMENT. ALLOC LOAD CODE HAS_CONTENTS
0x00007fa0f7e00000->0x00007fa0f7f00000 at 0x1aaec000: LC_SEGMENT. ALLOC LOAD CODE HAS_CONTENTS
0x00007fa0f7f00000->0x00007fa0f8000000 at 0x1abec000: LC_SEGMENT. ALLOC LOAD CODE HAS_CONTENTS
0x00007fa0f8000000->0x00007fa0f8100000 at 0x1acec000: LC_SEGMENT. ALLOC LOAD CODE HAS_CONTENTS
0x00007fa0f8100000->0x00007fa0f8200000 at 0x1adec000: LC_SEGMENT. ALLOC LOAD CODE HAS_CONTENTS
0x00007fa0f8200000->0x00007fa0f8300000 at 0x1aeec000: LC_SEGMENT. ALLOC LOAD CODE HAS_CONTENTS
0x00007fa0f8300000->0x00007fa0f8400000 at 0x1afec000: LC_SEGMENT. ALLOC LOAD CODE HAS_CONTENTS
0x00007fa0f8400000->0x00007fa0f8500000 at 0x1b0ec000: LC_SEGMENT. ALLOC LOAD CODE HAS_CONTENTS
---Type <return> to continue, or q <return> to quit---
0x00007fa0f8500000->0x00007fa0f8600000 at 0x1b1ec000: LC_SEGMENT. ALLOC LOAD CODE HAS_CONTENTS
0x00007fa0f8600000->0x00007fa0f8700000 at 0x1b2ec000: LC_SEGMENT. ALLOC LOAD CODE HAS_CONTENTS
0x00007fa0f8700000->0x00007fa0f8800000 at 0x1b3ec000: LC_SEGMENT. ALLOC LOAD CODE HAS_CONTENTS
0x00007fa0f8800000->0x00007fa0f8900000 at 0x1b4ec000: LC_SEGMENT. ALLOC LOAD CODE HAS_CONTENTS
0x00007fa0f8900000->0x00007fa0f8a00000 at 0x1b5ec000: LC_SEGMENT. ALLOC LOAD CODE HAS_CONTENTS
0x00007fa0f8a00000->0x00007fa0f8b00000 at 0x1b6ec000: LC_SEGMENT. ALLOC LOAD CODE HAS_CONTENTS
0x00007fa0f8b00000->0x00007fa0f8c00000 at 0x1b7ec000: LC_SEGMENT. ALLOC LOAD CODE HAS_CONTENTS
0x00007fa0f8c00000->0x00007fa0f8d00000 at 0x1b8ec000: LC_SEGMENT. ALLOC LOAD CODE HAS_CONTENTS
0x00007fa0f8d00000->0x00007fa0f8e00000 at 0x1b9ec000: LC_SEGMENT. ALLOC LOAD CODE HAS_CONTENTS
0x00007fa0f8e00000->0x00007fa0f8f00000 at 0x1baec000: LC_SEGMENT. ALLOC LOAD CODE HAS_CONTENTS
0x00007fa0f8f00000->0x00007fa0f9000000 at 0x1bbec000: LC_SEGMENT. ALLOC LOAD CODE HAS_CONTENTS
0x00007fa0f9000000->0x00007fa0f9100000 at 0x1bcec000: LC_SEGMENT. ALLOC LOAD CODE HAS_CONTENTS
0x00007fa0f9100000->0x00007fa0f9200000 at 0x1bdec000: LC_SEGMENT. ALLOC LOAD CODE HAS_CONTENTS
0x00007fa0f9200000->0x00007fa0f9300000 at 0x1beec000: LC_SEGMENT. ALLOC LOAD CODE HAS_CONTENTS
0x00007fa0f9300000->0x00007fa0f9400000 at 0x1bfec000: LC_SEGMENT. ALLOC LOAD CODE HAS_CONTENTS
0x00007fa0f9400000->0x00007fa0f9500000 at 0x1c0ec000: LC_SEGMENT. ALLOC LOAD CODE HAS_CONTENTS
0x00007fa0f9500000->0x00007fa0f9600000 at 0x1c1ec000: LC_SEGMENT. ALLOC LOAD CODE HAS_CONTENTS
0x00007fa0f9600000->0x00007fa0f9700000 at 0x1c2ec000: LC_SEGMENT. ALLOC LOAD CODE HAS_CONTENTS
0x00007fa0f9700000->0x00007fa0f9800000 at 0x1c3ec000: LC_SEGMENT. ALLOC LOAD CODE HAS_CONTENTS
```

```
0x00007fa0f9800000->0x00007fa0f9900000 at 0x1c4ec000: LC_SEGMENT. ALLOC LOAD CODE HAS_CONTENTS
0x00007fa0f9900000->0x00007fa0f9a00000 at 0x1c5ec000: LC_SEGMENT. ALLOC LOAD CODE HAS_CONTENTS
0x00007fa0f9a00000->0x00007fa0f9b00000 at 0x1c6ec000: LC_SEGMENT. ALLOC LOAD CODE HAS_CONTENTS
0x00007fa0f9b00000->0x00007fa0f9c00000 at 0x1c7ec000: LC_SEGMENT. ALLOC LOAD CODE HAS_CONTENTS
0x00007fa0f9c00000->0x00007fa0f9d00000 at 0x1c8ec000: LC_SEGMENT. ALLOC LOAD CODE HAS_CONTENTS
0x00007fa0f9d00000->0x00007fa0f9e00000 at 0x1c9ec000: LC_SEGMENT. ALLOC LOAD CODE HAS_CONTENTS
0x00007fa0f9e00000->0x00007fa0f9f00000 at 0x1caec000: LC_SEGMENT. ALLOC LOAD CODE HAS_CONTENTS
0x00007fa0f9f00000->0x00007fa0fa000000 at 0x1cbec000: LC_SEGMENT. ALLOC LOAD CODE HAS_CONTENTS
0x00007fa0fa000000->0x00007fa0fa100000 at 0x1ccec000: LC_SEGMENT. ALLOC LOAD CODE HAS_CONTENTS
0x00007fa0fa100000->0x00007fa0fa200000 at 0x1cdec000: LC_SEGMENT. ALLOC LOAD CODE HAS_CONTENTS
0x00007fa0fa200000->0x00007fa0fa300000 at 0x1ceec000: LC_SEGMENT. ALLOC LOAD CODE HAS_CONTENTS
0x00007fa0fa300000->0x00007fa0fa400000 at 0x1cfec000: LC_SEGMENT. ALLOC LOAD CODE HAS_CONTENTS
0x00007fa0fa400000->0x00007fa0fa500000 at 0x1d0ec000: LC_SEGMENT. ALLOC LOAD CODE HAS_CONTENTS
0x00007fa0fa500000->0x00007fa0fa600000 at 0x1d1ec000: LC_SEGMENT. ALLOC LOAD CODE HAS_CONTENTS
0x00007fa0fa600000->0x00007fa0fa700000 at 0x1d2ec000: LC_SEGMENT. ALLOC LOAD CODE HAS_CONTENTS
0x00007fa0fa700000->0x00007fa0fa800000 at 0x1d3ec000: LC_SEGMENT. ALLOC LOAD CODE HAS_CONTENTS
0x00007fa0fa800000->0x00007fa0fa900000 at 0x1d4ec000: LC_SEGMENT. ALLOC LOAD CODE HAS_CONTENTS
0x00007fa0fa900000->0x00007fa0faa00000 at 0x1d5ec000: LC_SEGMENT. ALLOC LOAD CODE HAS_CONTENTS
0x00007fa0faa00000->0x00007fa0fab00000 at 0x1d6ec000: LC_SEGMENT. ALLOC LOAD CODE HAS_CONTENTS
0x00007fa0fab00000->0x00007fa0fac00000 at 0x1d7ec000: LC_SEGMENT. ALLOC LOAD CODE HAS_CONTENTS
0x00007fa0fac00000->0x00007fa0fad00000 at 0x1d8ec000: LC_SEGMENT. ALLOC LOAD CODE HAS_CONTENTS
---Type <return> to continue, or q <return> to quit---
0x00007fa0fad00000->0x00007fa0fae00000 at 0x1d9ec000: LC_SEGMENT. ALLOC LOAD CODE HAS_CONTENTS
0x00007fa0fae00000->0x00007fa0faf00000 at 0x1daec000: LC_SEGMENT. ALLOC LOAD CODE HAS_CONTENTS
0x00007fa0faf00000->0x00007fa0fb000000 at 0x1dbec000: LC_SEGMENT. ALLOC LOAD CODE HAS_CONTENTS
0x00007fa0fb000000->0x00007fa0fb100000 at 0x1dcec000: LC_SEGMENT. ALLOC LOAD CODE HAS_CONTENTS
0x00007fa0fb100000->0x00007fa0fb200000 at 0x1ddec000: LC_SEGMENT. ALLOC LOAD CODE HAS_CONTENTS
0x00007fa0fb200000->0x00007fa0fb300000 at 0x1deec000: LC_SEGMENT. ALLOC LOAD CODE HAS_CONTENTS
0x00007fa0fb400000->0x00007fa0fb500000 at 0x1dfec000: LC_SEGMENT. ALLOC LOAD CODE HAS_CONTENTS
0x00007fa0fb500000->0x00007fa0fb600000 at 0x1e0ec000: LC_SEGMENT. ALLOC LOAD CODE HAS_CONTENTS
0x00007fa0fb600000->0x00007fa0fb700000 at 0x1e1ec000: LC_SEGMENT. ALLOC LOAD CODE HAS_CONTENTS
0x00007fa0fb700000->0x00007fa0fb800000 at 0x1e2ec000: LC_SEGMENT. ALLOC LOAD CODE HAS_CONTENTS
0x00007fa0fb800000->0x00007fa0fb900000 at 0x1e3ec000: LC_SEGMENT. ALLOC LOAD CODE HAS_CONTENTS
0x00007fa0fb900000->0x00007fa0fba00000 at 0x1e4ec000: LC_SEGMENT. ALLOC LOAD CODE HAS_CONTENTS
0x00007fa0fba00000->0x00007fa0fbb00000 at 0x1e5ec000: LC_SEGMENT. ALLOC LOAD CODE HAS_CONTENTS
0x00007fa0fbb00000->0x00007fa0fbc00000 at 0x1e6ec000: LC_SEGMENT. ALLOC LOAD CODE HAS_CONTENTS
0x00007fa0fbc00000->0x00007fa0fbd00000 at 0x1e7ec000: LC_SEGMENT. ALLOC LOAD CODE HAS_CONTENTS
0x00007fa0fbd00000->0x00007fa0fbe00000 at 0x1e8ec000: LC_SEGMENT. ALLOC LOAD CODE HAS_CONTENTS
0x00007fa0fbe00000->0x00007fa0fbf00000 at 0x1e9ec000: LC_SEGMENT. ALLOC LOAD CODE HAS_CONTENTS
0x00007fa0fbf00000->0x00007fa0fc000000 at 0x1eaec000: LC_SEGMENT. ALLOC LOAD CODE HAS_CONTENTS
0x00007fa0fc000000->0x00007fa0fc100000 at 0x1ebec000: LC_SEGMENT. ALLOC LOAD CODE HAS_CONTENTS
0x00007fa0fc100000->0x00007fa0fc200000 at 0x1ecec000: LC_SEGMENT. ALLOC LOAD CODE HAS_CONTENTS
0x00007fa0fc200000->0x00007fa0fc300000 at 0x1edec000: LC_SEGMENT. ALLOC LOAD CODE HAS_CONTENTS
0x00007fa0fc300000->0x00007fa0fc400000 at 0x1eeec000: LC_SEGMENT. ALLOC LOAD CODE HAS_CONTENTS
0x00007fa0fc400000->0x00007fa0fc500000 at 0x1efec000: LC_SEGMENT. ALLOC LOAD CODE HAS_CONTENTS
0x00007fa0fc500000->0x00007fa0fc600000 at 0x1f0ec000: LC_SEGMENT. ALLOC LOAD CODE HAS_CONTENTS
0x00007fa0fc600000->0x00007fa0fc700000 at 0x1f1ec000: LC_SEGMENT. ALLOC LOAD CODE HAS_CONTENTS
0x00007fa0fc700000->0x00007fa0fc800000 at 0x1f2ec000: LC_SEGMENT. ALLOC LOAD CODE HAS_CONTENTS
0x00007fa0fc800000->0x00007fa0fc900000 at 0x1f3ec000: LC_SEGMENT. ALLOC LOAD CODE HAS_CONTENTS
0x00007fa0fc900000->0x00007fa0fca00000 at 0x1f4ec000: LC_SEGMENT. ALLOC LOAD CODE HAS_CONTENTS
0x00007fa0fca00000->0x00007fa0fcb00000 at 0x1f5ec000: LC_SEGMENT. ALLOC LOAD CODE HAS_CONTENTS
0x00007fa0fcb00000->0x00007fa0fcc00000 at 0x1f6ec000: LC_SEGMENT. ALLOC LOAD CODE HAS_CONTENTS
0x00007fa0fcc00000->0x00007fa0fcd00000 at 0x1f7ec000: LC_SEGMENT. ALLOC LOAD CODE HAS_CONTENTS
0x00007fa0fcd00000->0x00007fa0fce00000 at 0x1f8ec000: LC_SEGMENT. ALLOC LOAD CODE HAS_CONTENTS
0x00007fa0fce00000->0x00007fa0fcf00000 at 0x1f9ec000: LC_SEGMENT. ALLOC LOAD CODE HAS_CONTENTS
0x00007fa0fcf00000->0x00007fa0fd000000 at 0x1faec000: LC_SEGMENT. ALLOC LOAD CODE HAS_CONTENTS
0x00007fa0fd000000->0x00007fa0fd100000 at 0x1fbec000: LC_SEGMENT. ALLOC LOAD CODE HAS_CONTENTS
0x00007fa0fd100000->0x00007fa0fd200000 at 0x1fcec000: LC_SEGMENT. ALLOC LOAD CODE HAS_CONTENTS
0x00007fa0fd200000->0x00007fa0fd300000 at 0x1fdec000: LC_SEGMENT. ALLOC LOAD CODE HAS_CONTENTS
0x00007fa0fd300000->0x00007fa0fd400000 at 0x1feec000: LC_SEGMENT. ALLOC LOAD CODE HAS_CONTENTS
0x00007fa0fd400000->0x00007fa0fd500000 at 0x1ffec000: LC_SEGMENT. ALLOC LOAD CODE HAS_CONTENTS
0x00007fa0fd500000->0x00007fa0fd600000 at 0x200ec000: LC_SEGMENT. ALLOC LOAD CODE HAS_CONTENTS
---Type <return> to continue, or q <return> to quit---
0x00007fa0fd600000->0x00007fa0fd700000 at 0x201ec000: LC_SEGMENT. ALLOC LOAD CODE HAS_CONTENTS
0x00007fa0fd700000->0x00007fa0fd800000 at 0x202ec000: LC_SEGMENT. ALLOC LOAD CODE HAS_CONTENTS
0x00007fa0fd800000->0x00007fa0fd900000 at 0x203ec000: LC_SEGMENT. ALLOC LOAD CODE HAS_CONTENTS
0x00007fa0fd900000->0x00007fa0fda00000 at 0x204ec000: LC_SEGMENT. ALLOC LOAD CODE HAS_CONTENTS
0x00007fa0fda00000->0x00007fa0fdb00000 at 0x205ec000: LC_SEGMENT. ALLOC LOAD CODE HAS_CONTENTS
0x00007fa0fdb00000->0x00007fa0fdc00000 at 0x206ec000: LC_SEGMENT. ALLOC LOAD CODE HAS_CONTENTS
0x00007fa0fdc00000->0x00007fa0fdd00000 at 0x207ec000: LC_SEGMENT. ALLOC LOAD CODE HAS_CONTENTS
0x00007fa0fdd00000->0x00007fa0fde00000 at 0x208ec000: LC_SEGMENT. ALLOC LOAD CODE HAS_CONTENTS
0x00007fa0fde00000->0x00007fa0fdf00000 at 0x209ec000: LC_SEGMENT. ALLOC LOAD CODE HAS_CONTENTS
0x00007fa0fdf00000->0x00007fa0fe000000 at 0x20aec000: LC_SEGMENT. ALLOC LOAD CODE HAS_CONTENTS
0x00007fa0fe000000->0x00007fa0fe100000 at 0x20bec000: LC_SEGMENT. ALLOC LOAD CODE HAS_CONTENTS
0x00007fa0fe100000->0x00007fa0fe200000 at 0x20cec000: LC_SEGMENT. ALLOC LOAD CODE HAS_CONTENTS
0x00007fa0fe200000->0x00007fa0fe300000 at 0x20dec000: LC_SEGMENT. ALLOC LOAD CODE HAS_CONTENTS
0x00007fa0fe300000->0x00007fa0fe400000 at 0x20eec000: LC_SEGMENT. ALLOC LOAD CODE HAS_CONTENTS
0x00007fa0fe400000->0x00007fa0fe500000 at 0x20fec000: LC_SEGMENT. ALLOC LOAD CODE HAS_CONTENTS
0x00007fa0fe500000->0x00007fa0fe600000 at 0x210ec000: LC_SEGMENT. ALLOC LOAD CODE HAS_CONTENTS
0x00007fa0fe600000->0x00007fa0fe700000 at 0x211ec000: LC_SEGMENT. ALLOC LOAD CODE HAS_CONTENTS
0x00007fa0fe700000->0x00007fa0fe800000 at 0x212ec000: LC_SEGMENT. ALLOC LOAD CODE HAS_CONTENTS
0x00007fa0fe800000->0x00007fa0fe900000 at 0x213ec000: LC_SEGMENT. ALLOC LOAD CODE HAS_CONTENTS
0x00007fa0fe900000->0x00007fa0fea00000 at 0x214ec000: LC_SEGMENT. ALLOC LOAD CODE HAS_CONTENTS
0x00007fa0fea00000->0x00007fa0feb00000 at 0x215ec000: LC_SEGMENT. ALLOC LOAD CODE HAS_CONTENTS
0x00007fa0feb00000->0x00007fa0fec00000 at 0x216ec000: LC_SEGMENT. ALLOC LOAD CODE HAS_CONTENTS
0x00007fa0fec00000->0x00007fa0fed00000 at 0x217ec000: LC_SEGMENT. ALLOC LOAD CODE HAS_CONTENTS
```

```
0x00007fa0fed00000->0x00007fa0fee00000 at 0x218ec000: LC_SEGMENT. ALLOC LOAD CODE HAS_CONTENTS
0x00007fa0fee00000->0x00007fa0fef00000 at 0x219ec000: LC_SEGMENT. ALLOC LOAD CODE HAS_CONTENTS
0x00007fa0fef00000->0x00007fa0ff000000 at 0x21aec000: LC_SEGMENT. ALLOC LOAD CODE HAS_CONTENTS
0x00007fa0ff000000->0x00007fa0ff100000 at 0x21bec000: LC_SEGMENT. ALLOC LOAD CODE HAS_CONTENTS
0x00007fa0ff100000->0x00007fa0ff200000 at 0x21cec000: LC_SEGMENT. ALLOC LOAD CODE HAS_CONTENTS
0x00007fa0ff200000->0x00007fa0ff300000 at 0x21dec000: LC_SEGMENT. ALLOC LOAD CODE HAS_CONTENTS
0x00007fa0ff300000->0x00007fa0ff400000 at 0x21eec000: LC_SEGMENT. ALLOC LOAD CODE HAS_CONTENTS
0x00007fa0ff400000->0x00007fa0ff500000 at 0x21fec000: LC_SEGMENT. ALLOC LOAD CODE HAS_CONTENTS
0x00007fa0ff500000->0x00007fa0ff600000 at 0x220ec000: LC_SEGMENT. ALLOC LOAD CODE HAS_CONTENTS
0x00007fa0ff600000->0x00007fa0ff700000 at 0x221ec000: LC_SEGMENT. ALLOC LOAD CODE HAS_CONTENTS
0x00007fa0ff700000->0x00007fa0ff800000 at 0x222ec000: LC_SEGMENT. ALLOC LOAD CODE HAS_CONTENTS
0x00007fa0ff800000->0x00007fa0ff900000 at 0x223ec000: LC_SEGMENT. ALLOC LOAD CODE HAS_CONTENTS
0x00007fa0ff900000->0x00007fa0ffa00000 at 0x224ec000: LC_SEGMENT. ALLOC LOAD CODE HAS_CONTENTS
0x00007fa0ffa00000->0x00007fa0ffb00000 at 0x225ec000: LC_SEGMENT. ALLOC LOAD CODE HAS_CONTENTS
0x00007fa0ffb00000->0x00007fa0ffc00000 at 0x226ec000: LC_SEGMENT. ALLOC LOAD CODE HAS_CONTENTS
0x00007fa0ffc00000->0x00007fa0ffd00000 at 0x227ec000: LC_SEGMENT. ALLOC LOAD CODE HAS_CONTENTS
0x00007fa0ffd00000->0x00007fa0ffe00000 at 0x228ec000: LC_SEGMENT. ALLOC LOAD CODE HAS_CONTENTS
---Type <return> to continue, or q <return> to quit---
0x00007fa0ffe00000->0x00007fa0fff00000 at 0x229ec000: LC_SEGMENT. ALLOC LOAD CODE HAS_CONTENTS
0x00007fa0fff00000->0x00007fa100000000 at 0x22aec000: LC_SEGMENT. ALLOC LOAD CODE HAS_CONTENTS
0x00007fa100000000->0x00007fa100100000 at 0x22bec000: LC_SEGMENT. ALLOC LOAD CODE HAS_CONTENTS
0x00007fa100100000->0x00007fa100200000 at 0x22cec000: LC_SEGMENT. ALLOC LOAD CODE HAS_CONTENTS
0x00007fa100200000->0x00007fa100300000 at 0x22dec000: LC_SEGMENT. ALLOC LOAD CODE HAS_CONTENTS
0x00007fa100300000->0x00007fa100400000 at 0x22eec000: LC_SEGMENT. ALLOC LOAD CODE HAS_CONTENTS
0x00007fa100400000->0x00007fa100500000 at 0x22fec000: LC_SEGMENT. ALLOC LOAD CODE HAS_CONTENTS
0x00007fa100500000->0x00007fa100600000 at 0x230ec000: LC_SEGMENT. ALLOC LOAD CODE HAS_CONTENTS
0x00007fa100600000->0x00007fa100700000 at 0x231ec000: LC_SEGMENT. ALLOC LOAD CODE HAS_CONTENTS
0x00007fa100700000->0x00007fa100800000 at 0x232ec000: LC_SEGMENT. ALLOC LOAD CODE HAS_CONTENTS
0x00007fa100800000->0x00007fa100900000 at 0x233ec000: LC_SEGMENT. ALLOC LOAD CODE HAS_CONTENTS
0x00007fa100900000->0x00007fa100a00000 at 0x234ec000: LC_SEGMENT. ALLOC LOAD CODE HAS_CONTENTS
0x00007fa100a00000->0x00007fa100b00000 at 0x235ec000: LC_SEGMENT. ALLOC LOAD CODE HAS_CONTENTS
0x00007fa100b00000->0x00007fa100c00000 at 0x236ec000: LC_SEGMENT. ALLOC LOAD CODE HAS_CONTENTS
0x00007fa100c00000->0x00007fa100d00000 at 0x237ec000: LC_SEGMENT. ALLOC LOAD CODE HAS_CONTENTS
0x00007fa100d00000->0x00007fa100e00000 at 0x238ec000: LC_SEGMENT. ALLOC LOAD CODE HAS_CONTENTS
0x00007fa100e00000->0x00007fa100f00000 at 0x239ec000: LC_SEGMENT. ALLOC LOAD CODE HAS_CONTENTS
0x00007fa100f00000->0x00007fa101000000 at 0x23aec000: LC_SEGMENT. ALLOC LOAD CODE HAS_CONTENTS
0x00007fa101000000->0x00007fa101100000 at 0x23bec000: LC_SEGMENT. ALLOC LOAD CODE HAS_CONTENTS
0x00007fa101100000->0x00007fa101200000 at 0x23cec000: LC_SEGMENT. ALLOC LOAD CODE HAS_CONTENTS
0x00007fa101200000->0x00007fa101300000 at 0x23dec000: LC_SEGMENT. ALLOC LOAD CODE HAS_CONTENTS
0x00007fa101300000->0x00007fa101400000 at 0x23eec000: LC_SEGMENT. ALLOC LOAD CODE HAS_CONTENTS
0x00007fa101400000->0x00007fa101500000 at 0x23fec000: LC_SEGMENT. ALLOC LOAD CODE HAS_CONTENTS
0x00007fa101500000->0x00007fa101600000 at 0x240ec000: LC_SEGMENT. ALLOC LOAD CODE HAS_CONTENTS
0x00007fa101600000->0x00007fa101700000 at 0x241ec000: LC_SEGMENT. ALLOC LOAD CODE HAS_CONTENTS
0x00007fa101700000->0x00007fa101800000 at 0x242ec000: LC_SEGMENT. ALLOC LOAD CODE HAS_CONTENTS
0x00007fa101800000->0x00007fa101900000 at 0x243ec000: LC_SEGMENT. ALLOC LOAD CODE HAS_CONTENTS
0x00007fa101900000->0x00007fa101a00000 at 0x244ec000: LC_SEGMENT. ALLOC LOAD CODE HAS_CONTENTS
0x00007fa101a00000->0x00007fa101b00000 at 0x245ec000: LC_SEGMENT. ALLOC LOAD CODE HAS_CONTENTS
0x00007fa101b00000->0x00007fa101c00000 at 0x246ec000: LC_SEGMENT. ALLOC LOAD CODE HAS_CONTENTS
0x00007fa101c00000->0x00007fa101d00000 at 0x247ec000: LC_SEGMENT. ALLOC LOAD CODE HAS_CONTENTS
0x00007fa101d00000->0x00007fa101e00000 at 0x248ec000: LC_SEGMENT. ALLOC LOAD CODE HAS_CONTENTS
0x00007fa101e00000->0x00007fa101f00000 at 0x249ec000: LC_SEGMENT. ALLOC LOAD CODE HAS_CONTENTS
0x00007fa101f00000->0x00007fa102000000 at 0x24aec000: LC_SEGMENT. ALLOC LOAD CODE HAS_CONTENTS
0x00007fa102000000->0x00007fa102100000 at 0x24bec000: LC_SEGMENT. ALLOC LOAD CODE HAS_CONTENTS
0x00007fa102100000->0x00007fa102200000 at 0x24cec000: LC_SEGMENT. ALLOC LOAD CODE HAS_CONTENTS
0x00007fa102200000->0x00007fa102300000 at 0x24dec000: LC_SEGMENT. ALLOC LOAD CODE HAS_CONTENTS
0x00007fa102300000->0x00007fa102400000 at 0x24eec000: LC_SEGMENT. ALLOC LOAD CODE HAS_CONTENTS
0x00007fa102400000->0x00007fa102500000 at 0x24fec000: LC_SEGMENT. ALLOC LOAD CODE HAS_CONTENTS
0x00007fa102500000->0x00007fa102600000 at 0x250ec000: LC_SEGMENT. ALLOC LOAD CODE HAS_CONTENTS
---Type <return> to continue, or q <return> to quit---
0x00007fa102600000->0x00007fa102700000 at 0x251ec000: LC_SEGMENT. ALLOC LOAD CODE HAS_CONTENTS
0x00007fa102700000->0x00007fa102800000 at 0x252ec000: LC_SEGMENT. ALLOC LOAD CODE HAS_CONTENTS
0x00007fa102800000->0x00007fa102900000 at 0x253ec000: LC_SEGMENT. ALLOC LOAD CODE HAS_CONTENTS
0x00007fa102900000->0x00007fa102a00000 at 0x254ec000: LC_SEGMENT. ALLOC LOAD CODE HAS_CONTENTS
0x00007fa102a00000->0x00007fa102b00000 at 0x255ec000: LC_SEGMENT. ALLOC LOAD CODE HAS_CONTENTS
0x00007fa102b00000->0x00007fa102c00000 at 0x256ec000: LC_SEGMENT. ALLOC LOAD CODE HAS_CONTENTS
0x00007fa102c00000->0x00007fa102d00000 at 0x257ec000: LC_SEGMENT. ALLOC LOAD CODE HAS_CONTENTS
0x00007fa102d00000->0x00007fa102e00000 at 0x258ec000: LC_SEGMENT. ALLOC LOAD CODE HAS_CONTENTS
0x00007fa102e00000->0x00007fa102f00000 at 0x259ec000: LC_SEGMENT. ALLOC LOAD CODE HAS_CONTENTS
0x00007fa102f00000->0x00007fa103000000 at 0x25aec000: LC_SEGMENT. ALLOC LOAD CODE HAS_CONTENTS
0x00007fa103000000->0x00007fa103100000 at 0x25bec000: LC_SEGMENT. ALLOC LOAD CODE HAS_CONTENTS
0x00007fa103100000->0x00007fa103200000 at 0x25cec000: LC_SEGMENT. ALLOC LOAD CODE HAS_CONTENTS
0x00007fa103200000->0x00007fa103300000 at 0x25dec000: LC_SEGMENT. ALLOC LOAD CODE HAS_CONTENTS
0x00007fa103300000->0x00007fa103400000 at 0x25eec000: LC_SEGMENT. ALLOC LOAD CODE HAS_CONTENTS
0x00007fa103400000->0x00007fa103500000 at 0x25fec000: LC_SEGMENT. ALLOC LOAD CODE HAS_CONTENTS
0x00007fa103500000->0x00007fa103600000 at 0x260ec000: LC_SEGMENT. ALLOC LOAD CODE HAS_CONTENTS
0x00007fa103600000->0x00007fa103700000 at 0x261ec000: LC_SEGMENT. ALLOC LOAD CODE HAS_CONTENTS
0x00007fa103700000->0x00007fa103800000 at 0x262ec000: LC_SEGMENT. ALLOC LOAD CODE HAS_CONTENTS
0x00007fa103800000->0x00007fa103900000 at 0x263ec000: LC_SEGMENT. ALLOC LOAD CODE HAS_CONTENTS
0x00007fa103900000->0x00007fa103a00000 at 0x264ec000: LC_SEGMENT. ALLOC LOAD CODE HAS_CONTENTS
0x00007fa103a00000->0x00007fa103b00000 at 0x265ec000: LC_SEGMENT. ALLOC LOAD CODE HAS_CONTENTS
0x00007fa103b00000->0x00007fa103c00000 at 0x266ec000: LC_SEGMENT. ALLOC LOAD CODE HAS_CONTENTS
0x00007fa103c00000->0x00007fa103d00000 at 0x267ec000: LC_SEGMENT. ALLOC LOAD CODE HAS_CONTENTS
0x00007fa103d00000->0x00007fa103e00000 at 0x268ec000: LC_SEGMENT. ALLOC LOAD CODE HAS_CONTENTS
0x00007fa103e00000->0x00007fa103f00000 at 0x269ec000: LC_SEGMENT. ALLOC LOAD CODE HAS_CONTENTS
0x00007fa103f00000->0x00007fa104000000 at 0x26aec000: LC_SEGMENT. ALLOC LOAD CODE HAS_CONTENTS
0x00007fa104000000->0x00007fa104100000 at 0x26bec000: LC_SEGMENT. ALLOC LOAD CODE HAS_CONTENTS
```

```
0x00007fa104100000->0x00007fa104200000 at 0x26cec000: LC_SEGMENT. ALLOC LOAD CODE HAS_CONTENTS
0x00007fa104200000->0x00007fa104300000 at 0x26dec000: LC_SEGMENT. ALLOC LOAD CODE HAS_CONTENTS
0x00007fa104300000->0x00007fa104400000 at 0x26eec000: LC_SEGMENT. ALLOC LOAD CODE HAS_CONTENTS
0x00007fa104400000->0x00007fa104500000 at 0x26fec000: LC_SEGMENT. ALLOC LOAD CODE HAS_CONTENTS
0x00007fa104500000->0x00007fa104600000 at 0x270ec000: LC_SEGMENT. ALLOC LOAD CODE HAS_CONTENTS
0x00007fa104600000->0x00007fa104700000 at 0x271ec000: LC_SEGMENT. ALLOC LOAD CODE HAS_CONTENTS
0x00007fa104700000->0x00007fa104800000 at 0x272ec000: LC_SEGMENT. ALLOC LOAD CODE HAS_CONTENTS
0x00007fa104800000->0x00007fa104900000 at 0x273ec000: LC_SEGMENT. ALLOC LOAD CODE HAS_CONTENTS
0x00007fa104900000->0x00007fa104a00000 at 0x274ec000: LC_SEGMENT. ALLOC LOAD CODE HAS_CONTENTS
0x00007fa104a00000->0x00007fa104b00000 at 0x275ec000: LC_SEGMENT. ALLOC LOAD CODE HAS_CONTENTS
0x00007fa104b00000->0x00007fa104c00000 at 0x276ec000: LC_SEGMENT. ALLOC LOAD CODE HAS_CONTENTS
0x00007fa104c00000->0x00007fa104d00000 at 0x277ec000: LC_SEGMENT. ALLOC LOAD CODE HAS_CONTENTS
0x00007fa104d00000->0x00007fa104e00000 at 0x278ec000: LC_SEGMENT. ALLOC LOAD CODE HAS_CONTENTS
---Type <return> to continue, or q <return> to quit---
0x00007fa104e00000->0x00007fa104f00000 at 0x279ec000: LC_SEGMENT. ALLOC LOAD CODE HAS_CONTENTS
0x00007fa104f00000->0x00007fa105000000 at 0x27aec000: LC_SEGMENT. ALLOC LOAD CODE HAS_CONTENTS
0x00007fa105000000->0x00007fa105100000 at 0x27bec000: LC_SEGMENT. ALLOC LOAD CODE HAS_CONTENTS
0x00007fa105100000->0x00007fa105200000 at 0x27cec000: LC_SEGMENT. ALLOC LOAD CODE HAS_CONTENTS
0x00007fa105200000->0x00007fa105300000 at 0x27dec000: LC_SEGMENT. ALLOC LOAD CODE HAS_CONTENTS
0x00007fa105300000->0x00007fa105400000 at 0x27eec000: LC_SEGMENT. ALLOC LOAD CODE HAS_CONTENTS
0x00007fa105400000->0x00007fa105500000 at 0x27fec000: LC_SEGMENT. ALLOC LOAD CODE HAS_CONTENTS
0x00007fa105500000->0x00007fa105600000 at 0x280ec000: LC_SEGMENT. ALLOC LOAD CODE HAS_CONTENTS
0x00007fa105600000->0x00007fa105700000 at 0x281ec000: LC_SEGMENT. ALLOC LOAD CODE HAS_CONTENTS
0x00007fa105700000->0x00007fa105800000 at 0x282ec000: LC_SEGMENT. ALLOC LOAD CODE HAS_CONTENTS
0x00007fa105800000->0x00007fa105900000 at 0x283ec000: LC_SEGMENT. ALLOC LOAD CODE HAS_CONTENTS
0x00007fa105900000->0x00007fa105a00000 at 0x284ec000: LC_SEGMENT. ALLOC LOAD CODE HAS_CONTENTS
0x00007fa105a00000->0x00007fa105b00000 at 0x285ec000: LC_SEGMENT. ALLOC LOAD CODE HAS_CONTENTS
0x00007fa105b00000->0x00007fa105c00000 at 0x286ec000: LC_SEGMENT. ALLOC LOAD CODE HAS_CONTENTS
0x00007fa105c00000->0x00007fa105d00000 at 0x287ec000: LC_SEGMENT. ALLOC LOAD CODE HAS_CONTENTS
0x00007fa105d00000->0x00007fa105e00000 at 0x288ec000: LC_SEGMENT. ALLOC LOAD CODE HAS_CONTENTS
0x00007fa105e00000->0x00007fa105f00000 at 0x289ec000: LC_SEGMENT. ALLOC LOAD CODE HAS_CONTENTS
0x00007fa105f00000->0x00007fa106000000 at 0x28aec000: LC_SEGMENT. ALLOC LOAD CODE HAS_CONTENTS
0x00007fa106000000->0x00007fa106100000 at 0x28bec000: LC_SEGMENT. ALLOC LOAD CODE HAS_CONTENTS
0x00007fa106100000->0x00007fa106200000 at 0x28cec000: LC_SEGMENT. ALLOC LOAD CODE HAS_CONTENTS
0x00007fa106200000->0x00007fa106300000 at 0x28dec000: LC_SEGMENT. ALLOC LOAD CODE HAS_CONTENTS
0x00007fa106300000->0x00007fa106400000 at 0x28eec000: LC_SEGMENT. ALLOC LOAD CODE HAS_CONTENTS
0x00007fa106400000->0x00007fa106500000 at 0x28fec000: LC_SEGMENT. ALLOC LOAD CODE HAS_CONTENTS
0x00007fa106500000->0x00007fa106600000 at 0x290ec000: LC_SEGMENT. ALLOC LOAD CODE HAS_CONTENTS
0x00007fa106600000->0x00007fa106700000 at 0x291ec000: LC_SEGMENT. ALLOC LOAD CODE HAS_CONTENTS
0x00007fa106700000->0x00007fa106800000 at 0x292ec000: LC_SEGMENT. ALLOC LOAD CODE HAS_CONTENTS
0x00007fa106800000->0x00007fa106900000 at 0x293ec000: LC_SEGMENT. ALLOC LOAD CODE HAS_CONTENTS
0x00007fa106900000->0x00007fa106a00000 at 0x294ec000: LC_SEGMENT. ALLOC LOAD CODE HAS_CONTENTS
0x00007fa106a00000->0x00007fa106b00000 at 0x295ec000: LC_SEGMENT. ALLOC LOAD CODE HAS_CONTENTS
0x00007fa106b00000->0x00007fa106c00000 at 0x296ec000: LC_SEGMENT. ALLOC LOAD CODE HAS_CONTENTS
0x00007fa106c00000->0x00007fa106d00000 at 0x297ec000: LC_SEGMENT. ALLOC LOAD CODE HAS_CONTENTS
0x00007fa106d00000->0x00007fa106e00000 at 0x298ec000: LC_SEGMENT. ALLOC LOAD CODE HAS_CONTENTS
0x00007fa106e00000->0x00007fa106f00000 at 0x299ec000: LC_SEGMENT. ALLOC LOAD CODE HAS_CONTENTS
0x00007fa106f00000->0x00007fa107000000 at 0x29aec000: LC_SEGMENT. ALLOC LOAD CODE HAS_CONTENTS
0x00007fa107000000->0x00007fa107100000 at 0x29bec000: LC_SEGMENT. ALLOC LOAD CODE HAS_CONTENTS
0x00007fa107100000->0x00007fa107200000 at 0x29cec000: LC_SEGMENT. ALLOC LOAD CODE HAS_CONTENTS
0x00007fa107200000->0x00007fa107300000 at 0x29dec000: LC_SEGMENT. ALLOC LOAD CODE HAS_CONTENTS
0x00007fa107300000->0x00007fa107400000 at 0x29eec000: LC_SEGMENT. ALLOC LOAD CODE HAS_CONTENTS
0x00007fa107400000->0x00007fa107500000 at 0x29fec000: LC_SEGMENT. ALLOC LOAD CODE HAS_CONTENTS
0x00007fa107500000->0x00007fa107600000 at 0x2a0ec000: LC_SEGMENT. ALLOC LOAD CODE HAS_CONTENTS
---Type <return> to continue, or q <return> to quit---
0x00007fa107600000->0x00007fa107700000 at 0x2a1ec000: LC_SEGMENT. ALLOC LOAD CODE HAS_CONTENTS
0x00007fa107700000->0x00007fa107800000 at 0x2a2ec000: LC_SEGMENT. ALLOC LOAD CODE HAS_CONTENTS
0x00007fa107800000->0x00007fa107900000 at 0x2a3ec000: LC_SEGMENT. ALLOC LOAD CODE HAS_CONTENTS
0x00007fa107900000->0x00007fa107a00000 at 0x2a4ec000: LC_SEGMENT. ALLOC LOAD CODE HAS_CONTENTS
0x00007fa107a00000->0x00007fa107b00000 at 0x2a5ec000: LC_SEGMENT. ALLOC LOAD CODE HAS_CONTENTS
0x00007fa107b00000->0x00007fa107c00000 at 0x2a6ec000: LC_SEGMENT. ALLOC LOAD CODE HAS_CONTENTS
0x00007fa107c00000->0x00007fa107d00000 at 0x2a7ec000: LC_SEGMENT. ALLOC LOAD CODE HAS_CONTENTS
0x00007fa107d00000->0x00007fa107e00000 at 0x2a8ec000: LC_SEGMENT. ALLOC LOAD CODE HAS_CONTENTS
0x00007fa107e00000->0x00007fa107f00000 at 0x2a9ec000: LC_SEGMENT. ALLOC LOAD CODE HAS_CONTENTS
0x00007fa107f00000->0x00007fa108000000 at 0x2aaec000: LC_SEGMENT. ALLOC LOAD CODE HAS_CONTENTS
0x00007fa108000000->0x00007fa108100000 at 0x2abec000: LC_SEGMENT. ALLOC LOAD CODE HAS_CONTENTS
0x00007fa108100000->0x00007fa108200000 at 0x2acec000: LC_SEGMENT. ALLOC LOAD CODE HAS_CONTENTS
0x00007fa108200000->0x00007fa108300000 at 0x2adec000: LC_SEGMENT. ALLOC LOAD CODE HAS_CONTENTS
0x00007fa108300000->0x00007fa108400000 at 0x2aeec000: LC_SEGMENT. ALLOC LOAD CODE HAS_CONTENTS
0x00007fa108400000->0x00007fa108500000 at 0x2afec000: LC_SEGMENT. ALLOC LOAD CODE HAS_CONTENTS
0x00007fa108500000->0x00007fa108600000 at 0x2b0ec000: LC_SEGMENT. ALLOC LOAD CODE HAS_CONTENTS
0x00007fa108600000->0x00007fa108700000 at 0x2b1ec000: LC_SEGMENT. ALLOC LOAD CODE HAS_CONTENTS
0x00007fa108700000->0x00007fa108800000 at 0x2b2ec000: LC_SEGMENT. ALLOC LOAD CODE HAS_CONTENTS
0x00007fa108800000->0x00007fa108900000 at 0x2b3ec000: LC_SEGMENT. ALLOC LOAD CODE HAS_CONTENTS
0x00007fa108900000->0x00007fa108a00000 at 0x2b4ec000: LC_SEGMENT. ALLOC LOAD CODE HAS_CONTENTS
0x00007fa108a00000->0x00007fa108b00000 at 0x2b5ec000: LC_SEGMENT. ALLOC LOAD CODE HAS_CONTENTS
0x00007fa108b00000->0x00007fa108c00000 at 0x2b6ec000: LC_SEGMENT. ALLOC LOAD CODE HAS_CONTENTS
0x00007fa108c00000->0x00007fa108d00000 at 0x2b7ec000: LC_SEGMENT. ALLOC LOAD CODE HAS_CONTENTS
0x00007fa108d00000->0x00007fa108e00000 at 0x2b8ec000: LC_SEGMENT. ALLOC LOAD CODE HAS_CONTENTS
0x00007fa108e00000->0x00007fa108f00000 at 0x2b9ec000: LC_SEGMENT. ALLOC LOAD CODE HAS_CONTENTS
0x00007fa108f00000->0x00007fa109000000 at 0x2baec000: LC_SEGMENT. ALLOC LOAD CODE HAS_CONTENTS
0x00007fa109000000->0x00007fa109100000 at 0x2bbec000: LC_SEGMENT. ALLOC LOAD CODE HAS_CONTENTS
0x00007fa109100000->0x00007fa109200000 at 0x2bcec000: LC_SEGMENT. ALLOC LOAD CODE HAS_CONTENTS
0x00007fa109200000->0x00007fa109300000 at 0x2bdec000: LC_SEGMENT. ALLOC LOAD CODE HAS_CONTENTS
0x00007fa109300000->0x00007fa109400000 at 0x2beec000: LC_SEGMENT. ALLOC LOAD CODE HAS_CONTENTS
0x00007fa109400000->0x00007fa109500000 at 0x2bfec000: LC_SEGMENT. ALLOC LOAD CODE HAS_CONTENTS
```

```
      0x00007fa109500000->0x00007fa109600000 at 0x2c0ec000: LC_SEGMENT. ALLOC LOAD CODE HAS_CONTENTS
      0x00007fa109600000->0x00007fa109700000 at 0x2c1ec000: LC_SEGMENT. ALLOC LOAD CODE HAS_CONTENTS
      0x00007fa109700000->0x00007fa109800000 at 0x2c2ec000: LC_SEGMENT. ALLOC LOAD CODE HAS_CONTENTS
      0x00007fa109800000->0x00007fa109900000 at 0x2c3ec000: LC_SEGMENT. ALLOC LOAD CODE HAS_CONTENTS
      0x00007fa109900000->0x00007fa109a00000 at 0x2c4ec000: LC_SEGMENT. ALLOC LOAD CODE HAS_CONTENTS
      0x00007fa109a00000->0x00007fa109b00000 at 0x2c5ec000: LC_SEGMENT. ALLOC LOAD CODE HAS_CONTENTS
      0x00007fa109b00000->0x00007fa109c00000 at 0x2c6ec000: LC_SEGMENT. ALLOC LOAD CODE HAS_CONTENTS
      0x00007fa109c00000->0x00007fa109d00000 at 0x2c7ec000: LC_SEGMENT. ALLOC LOAD CODE HAS_CONTENTS
      0x00007fa109d00000->0x00007fa109e00000 at 0x2c8ec000: LC_SEGMENT. ALLOC LOAD CODE HAS_CONTENTS
---Type <return> to continue, or q <return> to quit---
      0x00007fa109e00000->0x00007fa109f00000 at 0x2c9ec000: LC_SEGMENT. ALLOC LOAD CODE HAS_CONTENTS
      0x00007fa109f00000->0x00007fa10a000000 at 0x2caec000: LC_SEGMENT. ALLOC LOAD CODE HAS_CONTENTS
      0x00007fa10a000000->0x00007fa10a100000 at 0x2cbec000: LC_SEGMENT. ALLOC LOAD CODE HAS_CONTENTS
      0x00007fa10a100000->0x00007fa10a200000 at 0x2ccec000: LC_SEGMENT. ALLOC LOAD CODE HAS_CONTENTS
      0x00007fa10a200000->0x00007fa10a300000 at 0x2cdec000: LC_SEGMENT. ALLOC LOAD CODE HAS_CONTENTS
      0x00007fa10a300000->0x00007fa10a400000 at 0x2ceec000: LC_SEGMENT. ALLOC LOAD CODE HAS_CONTENTS
      0x00007fa10a400000->0x00007fa10a500000 at 0x2cfec000: LC_SEGMENT. ALLOC LOAD CODE HAS_CONTENTS
      0x00007fa10a500000->0x00007fa10a600000 at 0x2d0ec000: LC_SEGMENT. ALLOC LOAD CODE HAS_CONTENTS
      0x00007fa10a600000->0x00007fa10a700000 at 0x2d1ec000: LC_SEGMENT. ALLOC LOAD CODE HAS_CONTENTS
      0x00007fa10a700000->0x00007fa10a800000 at 0x2d2ec000: LC_SEGMENT. ALLOC LOAD CODE HAS_CONTENTS
      0x00007fa10a800000->0x00007fa10a900000 at 0x2d3ec000: LC_SEGMENT. ALLOC LOAD CODE HAS_CONTENTS
      0x00007fa10a900000->0x00007fa10aa00000 at 0x2d4ec000: LC_SEGMENT. ALLOC LOAD CODE HAS_CONTENTS
      0x00007fa10aa00000->0x00007fa10ab00000 at 0x2d5ec000: LC_SEGMENT. ALLOC LOAD CODE HAS_CONTENTS
      0x00007fa10ab00000->0x00007fa10ac00000 at 0x2d6ec000: LC_SEGMENT. ALLOC LOAD CODE HAS_CONTENTS
      0x00007fa10ac00000->0x00007fa10ad00000 at 0x2d7ec000: LC_SEGMENT. ALLOC LOAD CODE HAS_CONTENTS
      0x00007fa10ad00000->0x00007fa10ae00000 at 0x2d8ec000: LC_SEGMENT. ALLOC LOAD CODE HAS_CONTENTS
      0x00007fa10ae00000->0x00007fa10af00000 at 0x2d9ec000: LC_SEGMENT. ALLOC LOAD CODE HAS_CONTENTS
      0x00007fa10af00000->0x00007fa10b000000 at 0x2daec000: LC_SEGMENT. ALLOC LOAD CODE HAS_CONTENTS
      0x00007fa10b000000->0x00007fa10b100000 at 0x2dbec000: LC_SEGMENT. ALLOC LOAD CODE HAS_CONTENTS
      0x00007fa10b100000->0x00007fa10b200000 at 0x2dcec000: LC_SEGMENT. ALLOC LOAD CODE HAS_CONTENTS
      0x00007fa10b200000->0x00007fa10b300000 at 0x2ddec000: LC_SEGMENT. ALLOC LOAD CODE HAS_CONTENTS
      0x00007fa10b400000->0x00007fa10b500000 at 0x2deec000: LC_SEGMENT. ALLOC LOAD CODE HAS_CONTENTS
      0x00007fa10b500000->0x00007fa10b600000 at 0x2dfec000: LC_SEGMENT. ALLOC LOAD CODE HAS_CONTENTS
      0x00007fa10b600000->0x00007fa10b700000 at 0x2e0ec000: LC_SEGMENT. ALLOC LOAD CODE HAS_CONTENTS
      0x00007fa10b700000->0x00007fa10b800000 at 0x2e1ec000: LC_SEGMENT. ALLOC LOAD CODE HAS_CONTENTS
      0x00007fa10b800000->0x00007fa10b900000 at 0x2e2ec000: LC_SEGMENT. ALLOC LOAD CODE HAS_CONTENTS
      0x00007fa10b900000->0x00007fa10ba00000 at 0x2e3ec000: LC_SEGMENT. ALLOC LOAD CODE HAS_CONTENTS
      0x00007fa10ba00000->0x00007fa10bb00000 at 0x2e4ec000: LC_SEGMENT. ALLOC LOAD CODE HAS_CONTENTS
      0x00007fa10bb00000->0x00007fa10bc00000 at 0x2e5ec000: LC_SEGMENT. ALLOC LOAD CODE HAS_CONTENTS
      0x00007fa10bc00000->0x00007fa10bd00000 at 0x2e6ec000: LC_SEGMENT. ALLOC LOAD CODE HAS_CONTENTS
      0x00007fa10bd00000->0x00007fa10be00000 at 0x2e7ec000: LC_SEGMENT. ALLOC LOAD CODE HAS_CONTENTS
      0x00007fa10be00000->0x00007fa10bf00000 at 0x2e8ec000: LC_SEGMENT. ALLOC LOAD CODE HAS_CONTENTS
      0x00007fa10bf00000->0x00007fa10c000000 at 0x2e9ec000: LC_SEGMENT. ALLOC LOAD CODE HAS_CONTENTS
      0x00007fa10c000000->0x00007fa10c100000 at 0x2eaec000: LC_SEGMENT. ALLOC LOAD CODE HAS_CONTENTS
      0x00007fa10c100000->0x00007fa10c200000 at 0x2ebec000: LC_SEGMENT. ALLOC LOAD CODE HAS_CONTENTS
      0x00007fa10c200000->0x00007fa10c300000 at 0x2ecec000: LC_SEGMENT. ALLOC LOAD CODE HAS_CONTENTS
      0x00007fa10c300000->0x00007fa10c400000 at 0x2edec000: LC_SEGMENT. ALLOC LOAD CODE HAS_CONTENTS
      0x00007fa10c400000->0x00007fa10c500000 at 0x2eeec000: LC_SEGMENT. ALLOC LOAD CODE HAS_CONTENTS
      0x00007fa10c500000->0x00007fa10c600000 at 0x2efec000: LC_SEGMENT. ALLOC LOAD CODE HAS_CONTENTS
      0x00007fa10c600000->0x00007fa10c700000 at 0x2f0ec000: LC_SEGMENT. ALLOC LOAD CODE HAS_CONTENTS
---Type <return> to continue, or q <return> to quit---
      0x00007fa10c700000->0x00007fa10c800000 at 0x2f1ec000: LC_SEGMENT. ALLOC LOAD CODE HAS_CONTENTS
      0x00007fa10c800000->0x00007fa10c900000 at 0x2f2ec000: LC_SEGMENT. ALLOC LOAD CODE HAS_CONTENTS
      0x00007fa10c900000->0x00007fa10ca00000 at 0x2f3ec000: LC_SEGMENT. ALLOC LOAD CODE HAS_CONTENTS
      0x00007fa10ca00000->0x00007fa10cb00000 at 0x2f4ec000: LC_SEGMENT. ALLOC LOAD CODE HAS_CONTENTS
      0x00007fa10cb00000->0x00007fa10cc00000 at 0x2f5ec000: LC_SEGMENT. ALLOC LOAD CODE HAS_CONTENTS
      0x00007fa10cc00000->0x00007fa10cd00000 at 0x2f6ec000: LC_SEGMENT. ALLOC LOAD CODE HAS_CONTENTS
      0x00007fa10cd00000->0x00007fa10ce00000 at 0x2f7ec000: LC_SEGMENT. ALLOC LOAD CODE HAS_CONTENTS
      0x00007fa10ce00000->0x00007fa10cf00000 at 0x2f8ec000: LC_SEGMENT. ALLOC LOAD CODE HAS_CONTENTS
      0x00007fa10cf00000->0x00007fa10d000000 at 0x2f9ec000: LC_SEGMENT. ALLOC LOAD CODE HAS_CONTENTS
      0x00007fa10d000000->0x00007fa10d100000 at 0x2faec000: LC_SEGMENT. ALLOC LOAD CODE HAS_CONTENTS
      0x00007fa10d100000->0x00007fa10d200000 at 0x2fbec000: LC_SEGMENT. ALLOC LOAD CODE HAS_CONTENTS
      0x00007fa10d200000->0x00007fa10d300000 at 0x2fcec000: LC_SEGMENT. ALLOC LOAD CODE HAS_CONTENTS
      0x00007fa10d300000->0x00007fa10d400000 at 0x2fdec000: LC_SEGMENT. ALLOC LOAD CODE HAS_CONTENTS
      0x00007fa10d400000->0x00007fa10d500000 at 0x2feec000: LC_SEGMENT. ALLOC LOAD CODE HAS_CONTENTS
      0x00007fa10d500000->0x00007fa10d600000 at 0x2ffec000: LC_SEGMENT. ALLOC LOAD CODE HAS_CONTENTS
      0x00007fa10d600000->0x00007fa10d700000 at 0x300ec000: LC_SEGMENT. ALLOC LOAD CODE HAS_CONTENTS
      0x00007fa10d700000->0x00007fa10d800000 at 0x301ec000: LC_SEGMENT. ALLOC LOAD CODE HAS_CONTENTS
      0x00007fa10d800000->0x00007fa10d900000 at 0x302ec000: LC_SEGMENT. ALLOC LOAD CODE HAS_CONTENTS
      0x00007fa10d900000->0x00007fa10da00000 at 0x303ec000: LC_SEGMENT. ALLOC LOAD CODE HAS_CONTENTS
      0x00007fa10da00000->0x00007fa10db00000 at 0x304ec000: LC_SEGMENT. ALLOC LOAD CODE HAS_CONTENTS
      0x00007fa10db00000->0x00007fa10dc00000 at 0x305ec000: LC_SEGMENT. ALLOC LOAD CODE HAS_CONTENTS
      0x00007fa10dc00000->0x00007fa10dd00000 at 0x306ec000: LC_SEGMENT. ALLOC LOAD CODE HAS_CONTENTS
      0x00007fa10dd00000->0x00007fa10de00000 at 0x307ec000: LC_SEGMENT. ALLOC LOAD CODE HAS_CONTENTS
      0x00007fa10de00000->0x00007fa10df00000 at 0x308ec000: LC_SEGMENT. ALLOC LOAD CODE HAS_CONTENTS
      0x00007fa10df00000->0x00007fa10e000000 at 0x309ec000: LC_SEGMENT. ALLOC LOAD CODE HAS_CONTENTS
      0x00007fa10e000000->0x00007fa10e100000 at 0x30aec000: LC_SEGMENT. ALLOC LOAD CODE HAS_CONTENTS
      0x00007fa10e100000->0x00007fa10e200000 at 0x30bec000: LC_SEGMENT. ALLOC LOAD CODE HAS_CONTENTS
      0x00007fa10e200000->0x00007fa10e300000 at 0x30cec000: LC_SEGMENT. ALLOC LOAD CODE HAS_CONTENTS
      0x00007fa10e300000->0x00007fa10e400000 at 0x30dec000: LC_SEGMENT. ALLOC LOAD CODE HAS_CONTENTS
      0x00007fa10e400000->0x00007fa10e500000 at 0x30eec000: LC_SEGMENT. ALLOC LOAD CODE HAS_CONTENTS
      0x00007fa10e500000->0x00007fa10e600000 at 0x30fec000: LC_SEGMENT. ALLOC LOAD CODE HAS_CONTENTS
      0x00007fa10e600000->0x00007fa10e700000 at 0x310ec000: LC_SEGMENT. ALLOC LOAD CODE HAS_CONTENTS
      0x00007fa10e700000->0x00007fa10e800000 at 0x311ec000: LC_SEGMENT. ALLOC LOAD CODE HAS_CONTENTS
      0x00007fa10e800000->0x00007fa10e900000 at 0x312ec000: LC_SEGMENT. ALLOC LOAD CODE HAS_CONTENTS
      0x00007fa10e900000->0x00007fa10ea00000 at 0x313ec000: LC_SEGMENT. ALLOC LOAD CODE HAS_CONTENTS
```

```
0x00007fa10ea00000->0x00007fa10eb00000 at 0x314ec000: LC_SEGMENT. ALLOC LOAD CODE HAS_CONTENTS
0x00007fa10eb00000->0x00007fa10ec00000 at 0x315ec000: LC_SEGMENT. ALLOC LOAD CODE HAS_CONTENTS
0x00007fa10ec00000->0x00007fa10ed00000 at 0x316ec000: LC_SEGMENT. ALLOC LOAD CODE HAS_CONTENTS
0x00007fa10ed00000->0x00007fa10ee00000 at 0x317ec000: LC_SEGMENT. ALLOC LOAD CODE HAS_CONTENTS
0x00007fa10ee00000->0x00007fa10ef00000 at 0x318ec000: LC_SEGMENT. ALLOC LOAD CODE HAS_CONTENTS
---Type <return> to continue, or q <return> to quit---
0x00007fa10ef00000->0x00007fa10f000000 at 0x319ec000: LC_SEGMENT. ALLOC LOAD CODE HAS_CONTENTS
0x00007fa10f000000->0x00007fa10f100000 at 0x31aec000: LC_SEGMENT. ALLOC LOAD CODE HAS_CONTENTS
0x00007fa10f100000->0x00007fa10f200000 at 0x31bec000: LC_SEGMENT. ALLOC LOAD CODE HAS_CONTENTS
0x00007fa10f200000->0x00007fa10f300000 at 0x31cec000: LC_SEGMENT. ALLOC LOAD CODE HAS_CONTENTS
0x00007fa10f300000->0x00007fa10f400000 at 0x31dec000: LC_SEGMENT. ALLOC LOAD CODE HAS_CONTENTS
0x00007fa10f400000->0x00007fa10f500000 at 0x31eec000: LC_SEGMENT. ALLOC LOAD CODE HAS_CONTENTS
0x00007fa10f500000->0x00007fa10f600000 at 0x31fec000: LC_SEGMENT. ALLOC LOAD CODE HAS_CONTENTS
0x00007fa10f600000->0x00007fa10f700000 at 0x320ec000: LC_SEGMENT. ALLOC LOAD CODE HAS_CONTENTS
0x00007fa10f700000->0x00007fa10f800000 at 0x321ec000: LC_SEGMENT. ALLOC LOAD CODE HAS_CONTENTS
0x00007fa10f800000->0x00007fa10f900000 at 0x322ec000: LC_SEGMENT. ALLOC LOAD CODE HAS_CONTENTS
0x00007fa10f900000->0x00007fa10fa00000 at 0x323ec000: LC_SEGMENT. ALLOC LOAD CODE HAS_CONTENTS
0x00007fa10fa00000->0x00007fa10fb00000 at 0x324ec000: LC_SEGMENT. ALLOC LOAD CODE HAS_CONTENTS
0x00007fa10fb00000->0x00007fa10fc00000 at 0x325ec000: LC_SEGMENT. ALLOC LOAD CODE HAS_CONTENTS
0x00007fa10fc00000->0x00007fa10fd00000 at 0x326ec000: LC_SEGMENT. ALLOC LOAD CODE HAS_CONTENTS
0x00007fa10fd00000->0x00007fa10fe00000 at 0x327ec000: LC_SEGMENT. ALLOC LOAD CODE HAS_CONTENTS
0x00007fa10fe00000->0x00007fa10ff00000 at 0x328ec000: LC_SEGMENT. ALLOC LOAD CODE HAS_CONTENTS
0x00007fa10ff00000->0x00007fa110000000 at 0x329ec000: LC_SEGMENT. ALLOC LOAD CODE HAS_CONTENTS
0x00007fa110000000->0x00007fa110100000 at 0x32aec000: LC_SEGMENT. ALLOC LOAD CODE HAS_CONTENTS
0x00007fa110100000->0x00007fa110200000 at 0x32bec000: LC_SEGMENT. ALLOC LOAD CODE HAS_CONTENTS
0x00007fa110200000->0x00007fa110300000 at 0x32cec000: LC_SEGMENT. ALLOC LOAD CODE HAS_CONTENTS
0x00007fa110300000->0x00007fa110400000 at 0x32dec000: LC_SEGMENT. ALLOC LOAD CODE HAS_CONTENTS
0x00007fa110400000->0x00007fa110500000 at 0x32eec000: LC_SEGMENT. ALLOC LOAD CODE HAS_CONTENTS
0x00007fa110500000->0x00007fa110600000 at 0x32fec000: LC_SEGMENT. ALLOC LOAD CODE HAS_CONTENTS
0x00007fa110600000->0x00007fa110700000 at 0x330ec000: LC_SEGMENT. ALLOC LOAD CODE HAS_CONTENTS
0x00007fa110700000->0x00007fa110800000 at 0x331ec000: LC_SEGMENT. ALLOC LOAD CODE HAS_CONTENTS
0x00007fa110800000->0x00007fa110900000 at 0x332ec000: LC_SEGMENT. ALLOC LOAD CODE HAS_CONTENTS
0x00007fa110900000->0x00007fa110a00000 at 0x333ec000: LC_SEGMENT. ALLOC LOAD CODE HAS_CONTENTS
0x00007fa110a00000->0x00007fa110b00000 at 0x334ec000: LC_SEGMENT. ALLOC LOAD CODE HAS_CONTENTS
0x00007fa110b00000->0x00007fa110c00000 at 0x335ec000: LC_SEGMENT. ALLOC LOAD CODE HAS_CONTENTS
0x00007fa110c00000->0x00007fa110d00000 at 0x336ec000: LC_SEGMENT. ALLOC LOAD CODE HAS_CONTENTS
0x00007fa110d00000->0x00007fa110e00000 at 0x337ec000: LC_SEGMENT. ALLOC LOAD CODE HAS_CONTENTS
0x00007fa110e00000->0x00007fa110f00000 at 0x338ec000: LC_SEGMENT. ALLOC LOAD CODE HAS_CONTENTS
0x00007fa110f00000->0x00007fa111000000 at 0x339ec000: LC_SEGMENT. ALLOC LOAD CODE HAS_CONTENTS
0x00007fa111000000->0x00007fa111100000 at 0x33aec000: LC_SEGMENT. ALLOC LOAD CODE HAS_CONTENTS
0x00007fa111100000->0x00007fa111200000 at 0x33bec000: LC_SEGMENT. ALLOC LOAD CODE HAS_CONTENTS
0x00007fa111200000->0x00007fa111300000 at 0x33cec000: LC_SEGMENT. ALLOC LOAD CODE HAS_CONTENTS
0x00007fa111300000->0x00007fa111400000 at 0x33dec000: LC_SEGMENT. ALLOC LOAD CODE HAS_CONTENTS
0x00007fa111400000->0x00007fa111500000 at 0x33eec000: LC_SEGMENT. ALLOC LOAD CODE HAS_CONTENTS
0x00007fa111500000->0x00007fa111600000 at 0x33fec000: LC_SEGMENT. ALLOC LOAD CODE HAS_CONTENTS
0x00007fa111600000->0x00007fa111700000 at 0x340ec000: LC_SEGMENT. ALLOC LOAD CODE HAS_CONTENTS
---Type <return> to continue, or q <return> to quit---
0x00007fa111700000->0x00007fa111800000 at 0x341ec000: LC_SEGMENT. ALLOC LOAD CODE HAS_CONTENTS
0x00007fa111800000->0x00007fa111900000 at 0x342ec000: LC_SEGMENT. ALLOC LOAD CODE HAS_CONTENTS
0x00007fa111900000->0x00007fa111a00000 at 0x343ec000: LC_SEGMENT. ALLOC LOAD CODE HAS_CONTENTS
0x00007fa111a00000->0x00007fa111b00000 at 0x344ec000: LC_SEGMENT. ALLOC LOAD CODE HAS_CONTENTS
0x00007fa111b00000->0x00007fa111c00000 at 0x345ec000: LC_SEGMENT. ALLOC LOAD CODE HAS_CONTENTS
0x00007fa111c00000->0x00007fa111d00000 at 0x346ec000: LC_SEGMENT. ALLOC LOAD CODE HAS_CONTENTS
0x00007fa111d00000->0x00007fa111e00000 at 0x347ec000: LC_SEGMENT. ALLOC LOAD CODE HAS_CONTENTS
0x00007fa111e00000->0x00007fa111f00000 at 0x348ec000: LC_SEGMENT. ALLOC LOAD CODE HAS_CONTENTS
0x00007fa111f00000->0x00007fa112000000 at 0x349ec000: LC_SEGMENT. ALLOC LOAD CODE HAS_CONTENTS
0x00007fa112000000->0x00007fa112100000 at 0x34aec000: LC_SEGMENT. ALLOC LOAD CODE HAS_CONTENTS
0x00007fa112100000->0x00007fa112200000 at 0x34bec000: LC_SEGMENT. ALLOC LOAD CODE HAS_CONTENTS
0x00007fa112200000->0x00007fa112300000 at 0x34cec000: LC_SEGMENT. ALLOC LOAD CODE HAS_CONTENTS
0x00007fa112300000->0x00007fa112400000 at 0x34dec000: LC_SEGMENT. ALLOC LOAD CODE HAS_CONTENTS
0x00007fa112400000->0x00007fa112500000 at 0x34eec000: LC_SEGMENT. ALLOC LOAD CODE HAS_CONTENTS
0x00007fa112500000->0x00007fa112600000 at 0x34fec000: LC_SEGMENT. ALLOC LOAD CODE HAS_CONTENTS
0x00007fa112600000->0x00007fa112700000 at 0x350ec000: LC_SEGMENT. ALLOC LOAD CODE HAS_CONTENTS
0x00007fa112700000->0x00007fa112800000 at 0x351ec000: LC_SEGMENT. ALLOC LOAD CODE HAS_CONTENTS
0x00007fa112800000->0x00007fa112900000 at 0x352ec000: LC_SEGMENT. ALLOC LOAD CODE HAS_CONTENTS
0x00007fa112900000->0x00007fa112a00000 at 0x353ec000: LC_SEGMENT. ALLOC LOAD CODE HAS_CONTENTS
0x00007fa112a00000->0x00007fa112b00000 at 0x354ec000: LC_SEGMENT. ALLOC LOAD CODE HAS_CONTENTS
0x00007fa112b00000->0x00007fa112c00000 at 0x355ec000: LC_SEGMENT. ALLOC LOAD CODE HAS_CONTENTS
0x00007fa112c00000->0x00007fa112d00000 at 0x356ec000: LC_SEGMENT. ALLOC LOAD CODE HAS_CONTENTS
0x00007fa112d00000->0x00007fa112e00000 at 0x357ec000: LC_SEGMENT. ALLOC LOAD CODE HAS_CONTENTS
0x00007fa112e00000->0x00007fa112f00000 at 0x358ec000: LC_SEGMENT. ALLOC LOAD CODE HAS_CONTENTS
0x00007fa112f00000->0x00007fa113000000 at 0x359ec000: LC_SEGMENT. ALLOC LOAD CODE HAS_CONTENTS
0x00007fa113000000->0x00007fa113100000 at 0x35aec000: LC_SEGMENT. ALLOC LOAD CODE HAS_CONTENTS
0x00007fa113100000->0x00007fa113200000 at 0x35bec000: LC_SEGMENT. ALLOC LOAD CODE HAS_CONTENTS
0x00007fa113200000->0x00007fa113300000 at 0x35cec000: LC_SEGMENT. ALLOC LOAD CODE HAS_CONTENTS
0x00007fa113300000->0x00007fa113400000 at 0x35dec000: LC_SEGMENT. ALLOC LOAD CODE HAS_CONTENTS
0x00007fa113400000->0x00007fa113500000 at 0x35eec000: LC_SEGMENT. ALLOC LOAD CODE HAS_CONTENTS
0x00007fa113500000->0x00007fa113600000 at 0x35fec000: LC_SEGMENT. ALLOC LOAD CODE HAS_CONTENTS
0x00007fa113600000->0x00007fa113700000 at 0x360ec000: LC_SEGMENT. ALLOC LOAD CODE HAS_CONTENTS
0x00007fa113700000->0x00007fa113800000 at 0x361ec000: LC_SEGMENT. ALLOC LOAD CODE HAS_CONTENTS
0x00007fa113800000->0x00007fa113900000 at 0x362ec000: LC_SEGMENT. ALLOC LOAD CODE HAS_CONTENTS
0x00007fa113900000->0x00007fa113a00000 at 0x363ec000: LC_SEGMENT. ALLOC LOAD CODE HAS_CONTENTS
0x00007fa113a00000->0x00007fa113b00000 at 0x364ec000: LC_SEGMENT. ALLOC LOAD CODE HAS_CONTENTS
0x00007fa113b00000->0x00007fa113c00000 at 0x365ec000: LC_SEGMENT. ALLOC LOAD CODE HAS_CONTENTS
0x00007fa113c00000->0x00007fa113d00000 at 0x366ec000: LC_SEGMENT. ALLOC LOAD CODE HAS_CONTENTS
0x00007fa113d00000->0x00007fa113e00000 at 0x367ec000: LC_SEGMENT. ALLOC LOAD CODE HAS_CONTENTS
```

```
        0x00007fa113e00000->0x00007fa113f00000 at 0x368ec000: LC_SEGMENT. ALLOC LOAD CODE HAS_CONTENTS
---Type <return> to continue, or q <return> to quit---
        0x00007fa113f00000->0x00007fa114000000 at 0x369ec000: LC_SEGMENT. ALLOC LOAD CODE HAS_CONTENTS
        0x00007fa114000000->0x00007fa114100000 at 0x36aec000: LC_SEGMENT. ALLOC LOAD CODE HAS_CONTENTS
        0x00007fa114100000->0x00007fa114200000 at 0x36bec000: LC_SEGMENT. ALLOC LOAD CODE HAS_CONTENTS
        0x00007fa114200000->0x00007fa114300000 at 0x36cec000: LC_SEGMENT. ALLOC LOAD CODE HAS_CONTENTS
        0x00007fa114300000->0x00007fa114400000 at 0x36dec000: LC_SEGMENT. ALLOC LOAD CODE HAS_CONTENTS
        0x00007fa114400000->0x00007fa114500000 at 0x36eec000: LC_SEGMENT. ALLOC LOAD CODE HAS_CONTENTS
        0x00007fa114500000->0x00007fa114600000 at 0x36fec000: LC_SEGMENT. ALLOC LOAD CODE HAS_CONTENTS
        0x00007fa114600000->0x00007fa114700000 at 0x370ec000: LC_SEGMENT. ALLOC LOAD CODE HAS_CONTENTS
        0x00007fa114700000->0x00007fa114800000 at 0x371ec000: LC_SEGMENT. ALLOC LOAD CODE HAS_CONTENTS
        0x00007fa114800000->0x00007fa114900000 at 0x372ec000: LC_SEGMENT. ALLOC LOAD CODE HAS_CONTENTS
        0x00007fa114900000->0x00007fa114a00000 at 0x373ec000: LC_SEGMENT. ALLOC LOAD CODE HAS_CONTENTS
        0x00007fa114a00000->0x00007fa114b00000 at 0x374ec000: LC_SEGMENT. ALLOC LOAD CODE HAS_CONTENTS
        0x00007fa114b00000->0x00007fa114c00000 at 0x375ec000: LC_SEGMENT. ALLOC LOAD CODE HAS_CONTENTS
        0x00007fa114c00000->0x00007fa114d00000 at 0x376ec000: LC_SEGMENT. ALLOC LOAD CODE HAS_CONTENTS
        0x00007fa114d00000->0x00007fa114e00000 at 0x377ec000: LC_SEGMENT. ALLOC LOAD CODE HAS_CONTENTS
        0x00007fa114e00000->0x00007fa114f00000 at 0x378ec000: LC_SEGMENT. ALLOC LOAD CODE HAS_CONTENTS
        0x00007fa114f00000->0x00007fa115000000 at 0x379ec000: LC_SEGMENT. ALLOC LOAD CODE HAS_CONTENTS
        0x00007fa115000000->0x00007fa115100000 at 0x37aec000: LC_SEGMENT. ALLOC LOAD CODE HAS_CONTENTS
        0x00007fa115100000->0x00007fa115200000 at 0x37bec000: LC_SEGMENT. ALLOC LOAD CODE HAS_CONTENTS
        0x00007fa115200000->0x00007fa115300000 at 0x37cec000: LC_SEGMENT. ALLOC LOAD CODE HAS_CONTENTS
        0x00007fa115300000->0x00007fa115400000 at 0x37dec000: LC_SEGMENT. ALLOC LOAD CODE HAS_CONTENTS
        0x00007fa115400000->0x00007fa115500000 at 0x37eec000: LC_SEGMENT. ALLOC LOAD CODE HAS_CONTENTS
        0x00007fa115500000->0x00007fa115600000 at 0x37fec000: LC_SEGMENT. ALLOC LOAD CODE HAS_CONTENTS
        0x00007fa115600000->0x00007fa115700000 at 0x380ec000: LC_SEGMENT. ALLOC LOAD CODE HAS_CONTENTS
        0x00007fa115700000->0x00007fa115800000 at 0x381ec000: LC_SEGMENT. ALLOC LOAD CODE HAS_CONTENTS
        0x00007fa115800000->0x00007fa115900000 at 0x382ec000: LC_SEGMENT. ALLOC LOAD CODE HAS_CONTENTS
        0x00007fa115900000->0x00007fa115a00000 at 0x383ec000: LC_SEGMENT. ALLOC LOAD CODE HAS_CONTENTS
        0x00007fa115a00000->0x00007fa115b00000 at 0x384ec000: LC_SEGMENT. ALLOC LOAD CODE HAS_CONTENTS
        0x00007fa115b00000->0x00007fa115c00000 at 0x385ec000: LC_SEGMENT. ALLOC LOAD CODE HAS_CONTENTS
        0x00007fa115c00000->0x00007fa115d00000 at 0x386ec000: LC_SEGMENT. ALLOC LOAD CODE HAS_CONTENTS
        0x00007fa115d00000->0x00007fa115e00000 at 0x387ec000: LC_SEGMENT. ALLOC LOAD CODE HAS_CONTENTS
        0x00007fa115e00000->0x00007fa115f00000 at 0x388ec000: LC_SEGMENT. ALLOC LOAD CODE HAS_CONTENTS
        0x00007fa115f00000->0x00007fa116000000 at 0x389ec000: LC_SEGMENT. ALLOC LOAD CODE HAS_CONTENTS
        0x00007fa116000000->0x00007fa116100000 at 0x38aec000: LC_SEGMENT. ALLOC LOAD CODE HAS_CONTENTS
        0x00007fa116100000->0x00007fa116200000 at 0x38bec000: LC_SEGMENT. ALLOC LOAD CODE HAS_CONTENTS
        0x00007fa116200000->0x00007fa116300000 at 0x38cec000: LC_SEGMENT. ALLOC LOAD CODE HAS_CONTENTS
        0x00007fa116300000->0x00007fa116400000 at 0x38dec000: LC_SEGMENT. ALLOC LOAD CODE HAS_CONTENTS
        0x00007fa116400000->0x00007fa116500000 at 0x38eec000: LC_SEGMENT. ALLOC LOAD CODE HAS_CONTENTS
        0x00007fa116500000->0x00007fa116600000 at 0x38fec000: LC_SEGMENT. ALLOC LOAD CODE HAS_CONTENTS
        0x00007fa116600000->0x00007fa116700000 at 0x390ec000: LC_SEGMENT. ALLOC LOAD CODE HAS_CONTENTS
---Type <return> to continue, or q <return> to quit---
        0x00007fa116700000->0x00007fa116800000 at 0x391ec000: LC_SEGMENT. ALLOC LOAD CODE HAS_CONTENTS
        0x00007fa116800000->0x00007fa116900000 at 0x392ec000: LC_SEGMENT. ALLOC LOAD CODE HAS_CONTENTS
        0x00007fa116900000->0x00007fa116a00000 at 0x393ec000: LC_SEGMENT. ALLOC LOAD CODE HAS_CONTENTS
        0x00007fa116a00000->0x00007fa116b00000 at 0x394ec000: LC_SEGMENT. ALLOC LOAD CODE HAS_CONTENTS
        0x00007fa116b00000->0x00007fa116c00000 at 0x395ec000: LC_SEGMENT. ALLOC LOAD CODE HAS_CONTENTS
        0x00007fa116c00000->0x00007fa116d00000 at 0x396ec000: LC_SEGMENT. ALLOC LOAD CODE HAS_CONTENTS
        0x00007fa116d00000->0x00007fa116e00000 at 0x397ec000: LC_SEGMENT. ALLOC LOAD CODE HAS_CONTENTS
        0x00007fa116e00000->0x00007fa116f00000 at 0x398ec000: LC_SEGMENT. ALLOC LOAD CODE HAS_CONTENTS
        0x00007fa116f00000->0x00007fa117000000 at 0x399ec000: LC_SEGMENT. ALLOC LOAD CODE HAS_CONTENTS
        0x00007fa117000000->0x00007fa117100000 at 0x39aec000: LC_SEGMENT. ALLOC LOAD CODE HAS_CONTENTS
        0x00007fa117100000->0x00007fa117200000 at 0x39bec000: LC_SEGMENT. ALLOC LOAD CODE HAS_CONTENTS
        0x00007fa117200000->0x00007fa117300000 at 0x39cec000: LC_SEGMENT. ALLOC LOAD CODE HAS_CONTENTS
        0x00007fa117300000->0x00007fa117400000 at 0x39dec000: LC_SEGMENT. ALLOC LOAD CODE HAS_CONTENTS
        0x00007fa117400000->0x00007fa117500000 at 0x39eec000: LC_SEGMENT. ALLOC LOAD CODE HAS_CONTENTS
        0x00007fa117500000->0x00007fa117600000 at 0x39fec000: LC_SEGMENT. ALLOC LOAD CODE HAS_CONTENTS
        0x00007fa117600000->0x00007fa117700000 at 0x3a0ec000: LC_SEGMENT. ALLOC LOAD CODE HAS_CONTENTS
        0x00007fa117700000->0x00007fa117800000 at 0x3a1ec000: LC_SEGMENT. ALLOC LOAD CODE HAS_CONTENTS
        0x00007fa117800000->0x00007fa117900000 at 0x3a2ec000: LC_SEGMENT. ALLOC LOAD CODE HAS_CONTENTS
        0x00007fa117900000->0x00007fa117a00000 at 0x3a3ec000: LC_SEGMENT. ALLOC LOAD CODE HAS_CONTENTS
        0x00007fa117a00000->0x00007fa117b00000 at 0x3a4ec000: LC_SEGMENT. ALLOC LOAD CODE HAS_CONTENTS
        0x00007fa117b00000->0x00007fa117c00000 at 0x3a5ec000: LC_SEGMENT. ALLOC LOAD CODE HAS_CONTENTS
        0x00007fa117c00000->0x00007fa117d00000 at 0x3a6ec000: LC_SEGMENT. ALLOC LOAD CODE HAS_CONTENTS
        0x00007fa117d00000->0x00007fa117e00000 at 0x3a7ec000: LC_SEGMENT. ALLOC LOAD CODE HAS_CONTENTS
        0x00007fa117e00000->0x00007fa117f00000 at 0x3a8ec000: LC_SEGMENT. ALLOC LOAD CODE HAS_CONTENTS
        0x00007fa117f00000->0x00007fa118000000 at 0x3a9ec000: LC_SEGMENT. ALLOC LOAD CODE HAS_CONTENTS
        0x00007fa118000000->0x00007fa118100000 at 0x3aaec000: LC_SEGMENT. ALLOC LOAD CODE HAS_CONTENTS
        0x00007fa118100000->0x00007fa118200000 at 0x3abec000: LC_SEGMENT. ALLOC LOAD CODE HAS_CONTENTS
        0x00007fa118200000->0x00007fa118300000 at 0x3acec000: LC_SEGMENT. ALLOC LOAD CODE HAS_CONTENTS
        0x00007fa118300000->0x00007fa118400000 at 0x3adec000: LC_SEGMENT. ALLOC LOAD CODE HAS_CONTENTS
        0x00007fa118400000->0x00007fa118500000 at 0x3aeec000: LC_SEGMENT. ALLOC LOAD CODE HAS_CONTENTS
        0x00007fa118500000->0x00007fa118600000 at 0x3afec000: LC_SEGMENT. ALLOC LOAD CODE HAS_CONTENTS
        0x00007fa118600000->0x00007fa118700000 at 0x3b0ec000: LC_SEGMENT. ALLOC LOAD CODE HAS_CONTENTS
        0x00007fa118700000->0x00007fa118800000 at 0x3b1ec000: LC_SEGMENT. ALLOC LOAD CODE HAS_CONTENTS
        0x00007fa118800000->0x00007fa118900000 at 0x3b2ec000: LC_SEGMENT. ALLOC LOAD CODE HAS_CONTENTS
        0x00007fa118900000->0x00007fa118a00000 at 0x3b3ec000: LC_SEGMENT. ALLOC LOAD CODE HAS_CONTENTS
        0x00007fa118a00000->0x00007fa118b00000 at 0x3b4ec000: LC_SEGMENT. ALLOC LOAD CODE HAS_CONTENTS
        0x00007fa118b00000->0x00007fa118c00000 at 0x3b5ec000: LC_SEGMENT. ALLOC LOAD CODE HAS_CONTENTS
        0x00007fa118c00000->0x00007fa118d00000 at 0x3b6ec000: LC_SEGMENT. ALLOC LOAD CODE HAS_CONTENTS
        0x00007fa118d00000->0x00007fa118e00000 at 0x3b7ec000: LC_SEGMENT. ALLOC LOAD CODE HAS_CONTENTS
        0x00007fa118e00000->0x00007fa118f00000 at 0x3b8ec000: LC_SEGMENT. ALLOC LOAD CODE HAS_CONTENTS
---Type <return> to continue, or q <return> to quit---
        0x00007fa118f00000->0x00007fa119000000 at 0x3b9ec000: LC_SEGMENT. ALLOC LOAD CODE HAS_CONTENTS
        0x00007fa119000000->0x00007fa119100000 at 0x3baec000: LC_SEGMENT. ALLOC LOAD CODE HAS_CONTENTS
```

```
0x00007fa119100000->0x00007fa119200000 at 0x3bbec000: LC_SEGMENT. ALLOC LOAD CODE HAS_CONTENTS
0x00007fa119200000->0x00007fa119300000 at 0x3bcec000: LC_SEGMENT. ALLOC LOAD CODE HAS_CONTENTS
0x00007fa119300000->0x00007fa119400000 at 0x3bdec000: LC_SEGMENT. ALLOC LOAD CODE HAS_CONTENTS
0x00007fa119400000->0x00007fa119500000 at 0x3beec000: LC_SEGMENT. ALLOC LOAD CODE HAS_CONTENTS
0x00007fa119500000->0x00007fa119600000 at 0x3bfec000: LC_SEGMENT. ALLOC LOAD CODE HAS_CONTENTS
0x00007fa119600000->0x00007fa119700000 at 0x3c0ec000: LC_SEGMENT. ALLOC LOAD CODE HAS_CONTENTS
0x00007fa119700000->0x00007fa119800000 at 0x3c1ec000: LC_SEGMENT. ALLOC LOAD CODE HAS_CONTENTS
0x00007fa119800000->0x00007fa119900000 at 0x3c2ec000: LC_SEGMENT. ALLOC LOAD CODE HAS_CONTENTS
0x00007fa119900000->0x00007fa119a00000 at 0x3c3ec000: LC_SEGMENT. ALLOC LOAD CODE HAS_CONTENTS
0x00007fa119a00000->0x00007fa119b00000 at 0x3c4ec000: LC_SEGMENT. ALLOC LOAD CODE HAS_CONTENTS
0x00007fa119b00000->0x00007fa119c00000 at 0x3c5ec000: LC_SEGMENT. ALLOC LOAD CODE HAS_CONTENTS
0x00007fa119c00000->0x00007fa119d00000 at 0x3c6ec000: LC_SEGMENT. ALLOC LOAD CODE HAS_CONTENTS
0x00007fa119d00000->0x00007fa119e00000 at 0x3c7ec000: LC_SEGMENT. ALLOC LOAD CODE HAS_CONTENTS
0x00007fa119e00000->0x00007fa119f00000 at 0x3c8ec000: LC_SEGMENT. ALLOC LOAD CODE HAS_CONTENTS
0x00007fa119f00000->0x00007fa11a000000 at 0x3c9ec000: LC_SEGMENT. ALLOC LOAD CODE HAS_CONTENTS
0x00007fa11a000000->0x00007fa11a100000 at 0x3caec000: LC_SEGMENT. ALLOC LOAD CODE HAS_CONTENTS
0x00007fa11a100000->0x00007fa11a200000 at 0x3cbec000: LC_SEGMENT. ALLOC LOAD CODE HAS_CONTENTS
0x00007fa11a200000->0x00007fa11a300000 at 0x3ccec000: LC_SEGMENT. ALLOC LOAD CODE HAS_CONTENTS
0x00007fa11a300000->0x00007fa11a400000 at 0x3cdec000: LC_SEGMENT. ALLOC LOAD CODE HAS_CONTENTS
0x00007fa11a400000->0x00007fa11a500000 at 0x3ceec000: LC_SEGMENT. ALLOC LOAD CODE HAS_CONTENTS
0x00007fa11a500000->0x00007fa11a600000 at 0x3cfec000: LC_SEGMENT. ALLOC LOAD CODE HAS_CONTENTS
0x00007fa11a600000->0x00007fa11a700000 at 0x3d0ec000: LC_SEGMENT. ALLOC LOAD CODE HAS_CONTENTS
0x00007fa11a700000->0x00007fa11a800000 at 0x3d1ec000: LC_SEGMENT. ALLOC LOAD CODE HAS_CONTENTS
0x00007fa11a800000->0x00007fa11a900000 at 0x3d2ec000: LC_SEGMENT. ALLOC LOAD CODE HAS_CONTENTS
0x00007fa11a900000->0x00007fa11aa00000 at 0x3d3ec000: LC_SEGMENT. ALLOC LOAD CODE HAS_CONTENTS
0x00007fa11aa00000->0x00007fa11ab00000 at 0x3d4ec000: LC_SEGMENT. ALLOC LOAD CODE HAS_CONTENTS
0x00007fa11ab00000->0x00007fa11ac00000 at 0x3d5ec000: LC_SEGMENT. ALLOC LOAD CODE HAS_CONTENTS
0x00007fa11ac00000->0x00007fa11ad00000 at 0x3d6ec000: LC_SEGMENT. ALLOC LOAD CODE HAS_CONTENTS
0x00007fa11ad00000->0x00007fa11ae00000 at 0x3d7ec000: LC_SEGMENT. ALLOC LOAD CODE HAS_CONTENTS
0x00007fa11ae00000->0x00007fa11af00000 at 0x3d8ec000: LC_SEGMENT. ALLOC LOAD CODE HAS_CONTENTS
0x00007fa11af00000->0x00007fa11b000000 at 0x3d9ec000: LC_SEGMENT. ALLOC LOAD CODE HAS_CONTENTS
0x00007fa11b000000->0x00007fa11b100000 at 0x3daec000: LC_SEGMENT. ALLOC LOAD CODE HAS_CONTENTS
0x00007fa11b100000->0x00007fa11b200000 at 0x3dbec000: LC_SEGMENT. ALLOC LOAD CODE HAS_CONTENTS
0x00007fa11b200000->0x00007fa11b300000 at 0x3dcec000: LC_SEGMENT. ALLOC LOAD CODE HAS_CONTENTS
0x00007fa11b300000->0x00007fa11b400000 at 0x3ddec000: LC_SEGMENT. ALLOC LOAD CODE HAS_CONTENTS
0x00007fa11b400000->0x00007fa11b500000 at 0x3deec000: LC_SEGMENT. ALLOC LOAD CODE HAS_CONTENTS
0x00007fa11b500000->0x00007fa11b600000 at 0x3dfec000: LC_SEGMENT. ALLOC LOAD CODE HAS_CONTENTS
0x00007fa11b600000->0x00007fa11b700000 at 0x3e0ec000: LC_SEGMENT. ALLOC LOAD CODE HAS_CONTENTS
---Type <return> to continue, or q <return> to quit---
0x00007fa11b700000->0x00007fa11b800000 at 0x3e1ec000: LC_SEGMENT. ALLOC LOAD CODE HAS_CONTENTS
0x00007fa11b800000->0x00007fa11b900000 at 0x3e2ec000: LC_SEGMENT. ALLOC LOAD CODE HAS_CONTENTS
0x00007fa11b900000->0x00007fa11ba00000 at 0x3e3ec000: LC_SEGMENT. ALLOC LOAD CODE HAS_CONTENTS
0x00007fa11ba00000->0x00007fa11bb00000 at 0x3e4ec000: LC_SEGMENT. ALLOC LOAD CODE HAS_CONTENTS
0x00007fa11bb00000->0x00007fa11bc00000 at 0x3e5ec000: LC_SEGMENT. ALLOC LOAD CODE HAS_CONTENTS
0x00007fa11bc00000->0x00007fa11bd00000 at 0x3e6ec000: LC_SEGMENT. ALLOC LOAD CODE HAS_CONTENTS
0x00007fa11bd00000->0x00007fa11be00000 at 0x3e7ec000: LC_SEGMENT. ALLOC LOAD CODE HAS_CONTENTS
0x00007fa11be00000->0x00007fa11bf00000 at 0x3e8ec000: LC_SEGMENT. ALLOC LOAD CODE HAS_CONTENTS
0x00007fa11bf00000->0x00007fa11c000000 at 0x3e9ec000: LC_SEGMENT. ALLOC LOAD CODE HAS_CONTENTS
0x00007fa11c000000->0x00007fa11c100000 at 0x3eaec000: LC_SEGMENT. ALLOC LOAD CODE HAS_CONTENTS
0x00007fa11c100000->0x00007fa11c200000 at 0x3ebec000: LC_SEGMENT. ALLOC LOAD CODE HAS_CONTENTS
0x00007fa11c200000->0x00007fa11c300000 at 0x3ecec000: LC_SEGMENT. ALLOC LOAD CODE HAS_CONTENTS
0x00007fa11c300000->0x00007fa11c400000 at 0x3edec000: LC_SEGMENT. ALLOC LOAD CODE HAS_CONTENTS
0x00007fa11c400000->0x00007fa11c500000 at 0x3eeec000: LC_SEGMENT. ALLOC LOAD CODE HAS_CONTENTS
0x00007fa11c500000->0x00007fa11c600000 at 0x3efec000: LC_SEGMENT. ALLOC LOAD CODE HAS_CONTENTS
0x00007fa11c600000->0x00007fa11c700000 at 0x3f0ec000: LC_SEGMENT. ALLOC LOAD CODE HAS_CONTENTS
0x00007fa11c700000->0x00007fa11c800000 at 0x3f1ec000: LC_SEGMENT. ALLOC LOAD CODE HAS_CONTENTS
0x00007fa11c800000->0x00007fa11c900000 at 0x3f2ec000: LC_SEGMENT. ALLOC LOAD CODE HAS_CONTENTS
0x00007fa11c900000->0x00007fa11ca00000 at 0x3f3ec000: LC_SEGMENT. ALLOC LOAD CODE HAS_CONTENTS
0x00007fa11ca00000->0x00007fa11cb00000 at 0x3f4ec000: LC_SEGMENT. ALLOC LOAD CODE HAS_CONTENTS
0x00007fa11cb00000->0x00007fa11cc00000 at 0x3f5ec000: LC_SEGMENT. ALLOC LOAD CODE HAS_CONTENTS
0x00007fa11cc00000->0x00007fa11cd00000 at 0x3f6ec000: LC_SEGMENT. ALLOC LOAD CODE HAS_CONTENTS
0x00007fa11cd00000->0x00007fa11ce00000 at 0x3f7ec000: LC_SEGMENT. ALLOC LOAD CODE HAS_CONTENTS
0x00007fa11ce00000->0x00007fa11cf00000 at 0x3f8ec000: LC_SEGMENT. ALLOC LOAD CODE HAS_CONTENTS
0x00007fa11cf00000->0x00007fa11d000000 at 0x3f9ec000: LC_SEGMENT. ALLOC LOAD CODE HAS_CONTENTS
0x00007fa11d000000->0x00007fa11d100000 at 0x3faec000: LC_SEGMENT. ALLOC LOAD CODE HAS_CONTENTS
0x00007fa11d100000->0x00007fa11d200000 at 0x3fbec000: LC_SEGMENT. ALLOC LOAD CODE HAS_CONTENTS
0x00007fa11d200000->0x00007fa11d300000 at 0x3fcec000: LC_SEGMENT. ALLOC LOAD CODE HAS_CONTENTS
0x00007fa11d300000->0x00007fa11d400000 at 0x3fdec000: LC_SEGMENT. ALLOC LOAD CODE HAS_CONTENTS
0x00007fa11d400000->0x00007fa11d500000 at 0x3feec000: LC_SEGMENT. ALLOC LOAD CODE HAS_CONTENTS
0x00007fa11d500000->0x00007fa11d600000 at 0x3ffec000: LC_SEGMENT. ALLOC LOAD CODE HAS_CONTENTS
0x00007fa11d600000->0x00007fa11d700000 at 0x400ec000: LC_SEGMENT. ALLOC LOAD CODE HAS_CONTENTS
0x00007fa11d700000->0x00007fa11d800000 at 0x401ec000: LC_SEGMENT. ALLOC LOAD CODE HAS_CONTENTS
0x00007fa11d800000->0x00007fa11d900000 at 0x402ec000: LC_SEGMENT. ALLOC LOAD CODE HAS_CONTENTS
0x00007fa11d900000->0x00007fa11da00000 at 0x403ec000: LC_SEGMENT. ALLOC LOAD CODE HAS_CONTENTS
0x00007fa11da00000->0x00007fa11db00000 at 0x404ec000: LC_SEGMENT. ALLOC LOAD CODE HAS_CONTENTS
0x00007fa11db00000->0x00007fa11dc00000 at 0x405ec000: LC_SEGMENT. ALLOC LOAD CODE HAS_CONTENTS
0x00007fa11dc00000->0x00007fa11dd00000 at 0x406ec000: LC_SEGMENT. ALLOC LOAD CODE HAS_CONTENTS
0x00007fa11dd00000->0x00007fa11de00000 at 0x407ec000: LC_SEGMENT. ALLOC LOAD CODE HAS_CONTENTS
0x00007fa11de00000->0x00007fa11df00000 at 0x408ec000: LC_SEGMENT. ALLOC LOAD CODE HAS_CONTENTS
---Type <return> to continue, or q <return> to quit---
0x00007fa11df00000->0x00007fa11e000000 at 0x409ec000: LC_SEGMENT. ALLOC LOAD CODE HAS_CONTENTS
0x00007fa11e000000->0x00007fa11e100000 at 0x40aec000: LC_SEGMENT. ALLOC LOAD CODE HAS_CONTENTS
0x00007fa11e100000->0x00007fa11e200000 at 0x40bec000: LC_SEGMENT. ALLOC LOAD CODE HAS_CONTENTS
0x00007fa11e200000->0x00007fa11e300000 at 0x40cec000: LC_SEGMENT. ALLOC LOAD CODE HAS_CONTENTS
0x00007fa11e300000->0x00007fa11e400000 at 0x40dec000: LC_SEGMENT. ALLOC LOAD CODE HAS_CONTENTS
0x00007fa11e400000->0x00007fa11e500000 at 0x40eec000: LC_SEGMENT. ALLOC LOAD CODE HAS_CONTENTS
```

```
0x00007fa11e500000->0x00007fa11e600000 at 0x40fec000: LC_SEGMENT. ALLOC LOAD CODE HAS_CONTENTS
0x00007fa11e600000->0x00007fa11e700000 at 0x410ec000: LC_SEGMENT. ALLOC LOAD CODE HAS_CONTENTS
0x00007fa11e700000->0x00007fa11e800000 at 0x411ec000: LC_SEGMENT. ALLOC LOAD CODE HAS_CONTENTS
0x00007fa11e800000->0x00007fa11e900000 at 0x412ec000: LC_SEGMENT. ALLOC LOAD CODE HAS_CONTENTS
0x00007fa11e900000->0x00007fa11ea00000 at 0x413ec000: LC_SEGMENT. ALLOC LOAD CODE HAS_CONTENTS
0x00007fa11ea00000->0x00007fa11eb00000 at 0x414ec000: LC_SEGMENT. ALLOC LOAD CODE HAS_CONTENTS
0x00007fa11eb00000->0x00007fa11ec00000 at 0x415ec000: LC_SEGMENT. ALLOC LOAD CODE HAS_CONTENTS
0x00007fa11ec00000->0x00007fa11ed00000 at 0x416ec000: LC_SEGMENT. ALLOC LOAD CODE HAS_CONTENTS
0x00007fa11ed00000->0x00007fa11ee00000 at 0x417ec000: LC_SEGMENT. ALLOC LOAD CODE HAS_CONTENTS
0x00007fa11ee00000->0x00007fa11ef00000 at 0x418ec000: LC_SEGMENT. ALLOC LOAD CODE HAS_CONTENTS
0x00007fa11ef00000->0x00007fa11f000000 at 0x419ec000: LC_SEGMENT. ALLOC LOAD CODE HAS_CONTENTS
0x00007fa11f000000->0x00007fa11f100000 at 0x41aec000: LC_SEGMENT. ALLOC LOAD CODE HAS_CONTENTS
0x00007fa11f100000->0x00007fa11f200000 at 0x41bec000: LC_SEGMENT. ALLOC LOAD CODE HAS_CONTENTS
0x00007fa11f200000->0x00007fa11f300000 at 0x41cec000: LC_SEGMENT. ALLOC LOAD CODE HAS_CONTENTS
0x00007fa11f300000->0x00007fa11f400000 at 0x41dec000: LC_SEGMENT. ALLOC LOAD CODE HAS_CONTENTS
0x00007fa11f400000->0x00007fa11f500000 at 0x41eec000: LC_SEGMENT. ALLOC LOAD CODE HAS_CONTENTS
0x00007fa11f500000->0x00007fa11f600000 at 0x41fec000: LC_SEGMENT. ALLOC LOAD CODE HAS_CONTENTS
0x00007fa11f600000->0x00007fa11f700000 at 0x420ec000: LC_SEGMENT. ALLOC LOAD CODE HAS_CONTENTS
0x00007fa11f700000->0x00007fa11f800000 at 0x421ec000: LC_SEGMENT. ALLOC LOAD CODE HAS_CONTENTS
0x00007fa11f800000->0x00007fa11f900000 at 0x422ec000: LC_SEGMENT. ALLOC LOAD CODE HAS_CONTENTS
0x00007fa11f900000->0x00007fa11fa00000 at 0x423ec000: LC_SEGMENT. ALLOC LOAD CODE HAS_CONTENTS
0x00007fa11fa00000->0x00007fa11fb00000 at 0x424ec000: LC_SEGMENT. ALLOC LOAD CODE HAS_CONTENTS
0x00007fa11fb00000->0x00007fa11fc00000 at 0x425ec000: LC_SEGMENT. ALLOC LOAD CODE HAS_CONTENTS
0x00007fa11fc00000->0x00007fa11fd00000 at 0x426ec000: LC_SEGMENT. ALLOC LOAD CODE HAS_CONTENTS
0x00007fa11fd00000->0x00007fa11fe00000 at 0x427ec000: LC_SEGMENT. ALLOC LOAD CODE HAS_CONTENTS
0x00007fa11fe00000->0x00007fa11ff00000 at 0x428ec000: LC_SEGMENT. ALLOC LOAD CODE HAS_CONTENTS
0x00007fa11ff00000->0x00007fa120000000 at 0x429ec000: LC_SEGMENT. ALLOC LOAD CODE HAS_CONTENTS
0x00007fa120000000->0x00007fa120100000 at 0x42aec000: LC_SEGMENT. ALLOC LOAD CODE HAS_CONTENTS
0x00007fa120100000->0x00007fa120200000 at 0x42bec000: LC_SEGMENT. ALLOC LOAD CODE HAS_CONTENTS
0x00007fa120200000->0x00007fa120300000 at 0x42cec000: LC_SEGMENT. ALLOC LOAD CODE HAS_CONTENTS
0x00007fa120300000->0x00007fa120400000 at 0x42dec000: LC_SEGMENT. ALLOC LOAD CODE HAS_CONTENTS
0x00007fa120400000->0x00007fa120500000 at 0x42eec000: LC_SEGMENT. ALLOC LOAD CODE HAS_CONTENTS
0x00007fa120500000->0x00007fa120600000 at 0x42fec000: LC_SEGMENT. ALLOC LOAD CODE HAS_CONTENTS
0x00007fa120600000->0x00007fa120700000 at 0x430ec000: LC_SEGMENT. ALLOC LOAD CODE HAS_CONTENTS
---Type <return> to continue, or q <return> to quit---
0x00007fa120700000->0x00007fa120800000 at 0x431ec000: LC_SEGMENT. ALLOC LOAD CODE HAS_CONTENTS
0x00007fa120800000->0x00007fa120900000 at 0x432ec000: LC_SEGMENT. ALLOC LOAD CODE HAS_CONTENTS
0x00007fa120900000->0x00007fa120a00000 at 0x433ec000: LC_SEGMENT. ALLOC LOAD CODE HAS_CONTENTS
0x00007fa120a00000->0x00007fa120b00000 at 0x434ec000: LC_SEGMENT. ALLOC LOAD CODE HAS_CONTENTS
0x00007fa120b00000->0x00007fa120c00000 at 0x435ec000: LC_SEGMENT. ALLOC LOAD CODE HAS_CONTENTS
0x00007fa120c00000->0x00007fa120d00000 at 0x436ec000: LC_SEGMENT. ALLOC LOAD CODE HAS_CONTENTS
0x00007fa120d00000->0x00007fa120e00000 at 0x437ec000: LC_SEGMENT. ALLOC LOAD CODE HAS_CONTENTS
0x00007fa120e00000->0x00007fa120f00000 at 0x438ec000: LC_SEGMENT. ALLOC LOAD CODE HAS_CONTENTS
0x00007fa120f00000->0x00007fa121000000 at 0x439ec000: LC_SEGMENT. ALLOC LOAD CODE HAS_CONTENTS
0x00007fa121000000->0x00007fa121100000 at 0x43aec000: LC_SEGMENT. ALLOC LOAD CODE HAS_CONTENTS
0x00007fa121100000->0x00007fa121200000 at 0x43bec000: LC_SEGMENT. ALLOC LOAD CODE HAS_CONTENTS
0x00007fa121200000->0x00007fa121300000 at 0x43cec000: LC_SEGMENT. ALLOC LOAD CODE HAS_CONTENTS
0x00007fa121300000->0x00007fa121400000 at 0x43dec000: LC_SEGMENT. ALLOC LOAD CODE HAS_CONTENTS
0x00007fa121400000->0x00007fa121500000 at 0x43eec000: LC_SEGMENT. ALLOC LOAD CODE HAS_CONTENTS
0x00007fa121500000->0x00007fa121600000 at 0x43fec000: LC_SEGMENT. ALLOC LOAD CODE HAS_CONTENTS
0x00007fa121600000->0x00007fa121700000 at 0x440ec000: LC_SEGMENT. ALLOC LOAD CODE HAS_CONTENTS
0x00007fa121700000->0x00007fa121800000 at 0x441ec000: LC_SEGMENT. ALLOC LOAD CODE HAS_CONTENTS
0x00007fa121800000->0x00007fa121900000 at 0x442ec000: LC_SEGMENT. ALLOC LOAD CODE HAS_CONTENTS
0x00007fa121900000->0x00007fa121a00000 at 0x443ec000: LC_SEGMENT. ALLOC LOAD CODE HAS_CONTENTS
0x00007fa121a00000->0x00007fa121b00000 at 0x444ec000: LC_SEGMENT. ALLOC LOAD CODE HAS_CONTENTS
0x00007fa121b00000->0x00007fa121c00000 at 0x445ec000: LC_SEGMENT. ALLOC LOAD CODE HAS_CONTENTS
0x00007fa121c00000->0x00007fa121d00000 at 0x446ec000: LC_SEGMENT. ALLOC LOAD CODE HAS_CONTENTS
0x00007fa121d00000->0x00007fa121e00000 at 0x447ec000: LC_SEGMENT. ALLOC LOAD CODE HAS_CONTENTS
0x00007fa121e00000->0x00007fa121f00000 at 0x448ec000: LC_SEGMENT. ALLOC LOAD CODE HAS_CONTENTS
0x00007fa121f00000->0x00007fa122000000 at 0x449ec000: LC_SEGMENT. ALLOC LOAD CODE HAS_CONTENTS
0x00007fa122000000->0x00007fa122100000 at 0x44aec000: LC_SEGMENT. ALLOC LOAD CODE HAS_CONTENTS
0x00007fa122100000->0x00007fa122200000 at 0x44bec000: LC_SEGMENT. ALLOC LOAD CODE HAS_CONTENTS
0x00007fa122200000->0x00007fa122300000 at 0x44cec000: LC_SEGMENT. ALLOC LOAD CODE HAS_CONTENTS
0x00007fa122300000->0x00007fa122400000 at 0x44dec000: LC_SEGMENT. ALLOC LOAD CODE HAS_CONTENTS
0x00007fa122400000->0x00007fa122500000 at 0x44eec000: LC_SEGMENT. ALLOC LOAD CODE HAS_CONTENTS
0x00007fa122500000->0x00007fa122600000 at 0x44fec000: LC_SEGMENT. ALLOC LOAD CODE HAS_CONTENTS
0x00007fa122600000->0x00007fa122700000 at 0x450ec000: LC_SEGMENT. ALLOC LOAD CODE HAS_CONTENTS
0x00007fa122700000->0x00007fa122800000 at 0x451ec000: LC_SEGMENT. ALLOC LOAD CODE HAS_CONTENTS
0x00007fa122800000->0x00007fa122900000 at 0x452ec000: LC_SEGMENT. ALLOC LOAD CODE HAS_CONTENTS
0x00007fa122900000->0x00007fa122a00000 at 0x453ec000: LC_SEGMENT. ALLOC LOAD CODE HAS_CONTENTS
0x00007fa122a00000->0x00007fa122b00000 at 0x454ec000: LC_SEGMENT. ALLOC LOAD CODE HAS_CONTENTS
0x00007fa122b00000->0x00007fa122c00000 at 0x455ec000: LC_SEGMENT. ALLOC LOAD CODE HAS_CONTENTS
0x00007fa122c00000->0x00007fa122d00000 at 0x456ec000: LC_SEGMENT. ALLOC LOAD CODE HAS_CONTENTS
0x00007fa122d00000->0x00007fa122e00000 at 0x457ec000: LC_SEGMENT. ALLOC LOAD CODE HAS_CONTENTS
0x00007fa122e00000->0x00007fa122f00000 at 0x458ec000: LC_SEGMENT. ALLOC LOAD CODE HAS_CONTENTS
---Type <return> to continue, or q <return> to quit---
0x00007fa122f00000->0x00007fa123000000 at 0x459ec000: LC_SEGMENT. ALLOC LOAD CODE HAS_CONTENTS
0x00007fa123000000->0x00007fa123100000 at 0x45aec000: LC_SEGMENT. ALLOC LOAD CODE HAS_CONTENTS
0x00007fa123100000->0x00007fa123200000 at 0x45bec000: LC_SEGMENT. ALLOC LOAD CODE HAS_CONTENTS
0x00007fa123200000->0x00007fa123300000 at 0x45cec000: LC_SEGMENT. ALLOC LOAD CODE HAS_CONTENTS
0x00007fa123300000->0x00007fa123400000 at 0x45dec000: LC_SEGMENT. ALLOC LOAD CODE HAS_CONTENTS
0x00007fa123400000->0x00007fa123500000 at 0x45eec000: LC_SEGMENT. ALLOC LOAD CODE HAS_CONTENTS
0x00007fa123500000->0x00007fa123600000 at 0x45fec000: LC_SEGMENT. ALLOC LOAD CODE HAS_CONTENTS
0x00007fa123600000->0x00007fa123700000 at 0x460ec000: LC_SEGMENT. ALLOC LOAD CODE HAS_CONTENTS
0x00007fa123700000->0x00007fa123800000 at 0x461ec000: LC_SEGMENT. ALLOC LOAD CODE HAS_CONTENTS
0x00007fa123800000->0x00007fa123900000 at 0x462ec000: LC_SEGMENT. ALLOC LOAD CODE HAS_CONTENTS
```

```
0x00007fa123900000->0x00007fa123a00000 at 0x463ec000: LC_SEGMENT. ALLOC LOAD CODE HAS_CONTENTS
0x00007fa123a00000->0x00007fa123b00000 at 0x464ec000: LC_SEGMENT. ALLOC LOAD CODE HAS_CONTENTS
0x00007fa123b00000->0x00007fa123c00000 at 0x465ec000: LC_SEGMENT. ALLOC LOAD CODE HAS_CONTENTS
0x00007fa123c00000->0x00007fa123d00000 at 0x466ec000: LC_SEGMENT. ALLOC LOAD CODE HAS_CONTENTS
0x00007fa123d00000->0x00007fa123e00000 at 0x467ec000: LC_SEGMENT. ALLOC LOAD CODE HAS_CONTENTS
0x00007fa123e00000->0x00007fa123f00000 at 0x468ec000: LC_SEGMENT. ALLOC LOAD CODE HAS_CONTENTS
0x00007fa123f00000->0x00007fa124000000 at 0x469ec000: LC_SEGMENT. ALLOC LOAD CODE HAS_CONTENTS
0x00007fa124000000->0x00007fa124100000 at 0x46aec000: LC_SEGMENT. ALLOC LOAD CODE HAS_CONTENTS
0x00007fa124100000->0x00007fa124200000 at 0x46bec000: LC_SEGMENT. ALLOC LOAD CODE HAS_CONTENTS
0x00007fa124200000->0x00007fa124300000 at 0x46cec000: LC_SEGMENT. ALLOC LOAD CODE HAS_CONTENTS
0x00007fa124300000->0x00007fa124400000 at 0x46dec000: LC_SEGMENT. ALLOC LOAD CODE HAS_CONTENTS
0x00007fa124400000->0x00007fa124500000 at 0x46eec000: LC_SEGMENT. ALLOC LOAD CODE HAS_CONTENTS
0x00007fa124500000->0x00007fa124600000 at 0x46fec000: LC_SEGMENT. ALLOC LOAD CODE HAS_CONTENTS
0x00007fa124600000->0x00007fa124700000 at 0x470ec000: LC_SEGMENT. ALLOC LOAD CODE HAS_CONTENTS
0x00007fa124700000->0x00007fa124800000 at 0x471ec000: LC_SEGMENT. ALLOC LOAD CODE HAS_CONTENTS
0x00007fa124800000->0x00007fa124900000 at 0x472ec000: LC_SEGMENT. ALLOC LOAD CODE HAS_CONTENTS
0x00007fa124900000->0x00007fa124a00000 at 0x473ec000: LC_SEGMENT. ALLOC LOAD CODE HAS_CONTENTS
0x00007fa124a00000->0x00007fa124b00000 at 0x474ec000: LC_SEGMENT. ALLOC LOAD CODE HAS_CONTENTS
0x00007fa124b00000->0x00007fa124c00000 at 0x475ec000: LC_SEGMENT. ALLOC LOAD CODE HAS_CONTENTS
0x00007fa124c00000->0x00007fa124d00000 at 0x476ec000: LC_SEGMENT. ALLOC LOAD CODE HAS_CONTENTS
0x00007fa124d00000->0x00007fa124e00000 at 0x477ec000: LC_SEGMENT. ALLOC LOAD CODE HAS_CONTENTS
0x00007fa124e00000->0x00007fa124f00000 at 0x478ec000: LC_SEGMENT. ALLOC LOAD CODE HAS_CONTENTS
0x00007fa124f00000->0x00007fa125000000 at 0x479ec000: LC_SEGMENT. ALLOC LOAD CODE HAS_CONTENTS
0x00007fa125000000->0x00007fa125100000 at 0x47aec000: LC_SEGMENT. ALLOC LOAD CODE HAS_CONTENTS
0x00007fa125100000->0x00007fa125200000 at 0x47bec000: LC_SEGMENT. ALLOC LOAD CODE HAS_CONTENTS
0x00007fa125200000->0x00007fa125300000 at 0x47cec000: LC_SEGMENT. ALLOC LOAD CODE HAS_CONTENTS
0x00007fa125300000->0x00007fa125400000 at 0x47dec000: LC_SEGMENT. ALLOC LOAD CODE HAS_CONTENTS
0x00007fa125400000->0x00007fa125500000 at 0x47eec000: LC_SEGMENT. ALLOC LOAD CODE HAS_CONTENTS
0x00007fa125500000->0x00007fa125600000 at 0x47fec000: LC_SEGMENT. ALLOC LOAD CODE HAS_CONTENTS
0x00007fa125600000->0x00007fa125700000 at 0x480ec000: LC_SEGMENT. ALLOC LOAD CODE HAS_CONTENTS
---Type <return> to continue, or q <return> to quit---
0x00007fa125700000->0x00007fa125800000 at 0x481ec000: LC_SEGMENT. ALLOC LOAD CODE HAS_CONTENTS
0x00007fa125800000->0x00007fa125900000 at 0x482ec000: LC_SEGMENT. ALLOC LOAD CODE HAS_CONTENTS
0x00007fa125900000->0x00007fa125a00000 at 0x483ec000: LC_SEGMENT. ALLOC LOAD CODE HAS_CONTENTS
0x00007fa125a00000->0x00007fa125b00000 at 0x484ec000: LC_SEGMENT. ALLOC LOAD CODE HAS_CONTENTS
0x00007fa125b00000->0x00007fa125c00000 at 0x485ec000: LC_SEGMENT. ALLOC LOAD CODE HAS_CONTENTS
0x00007fa125c00000->0x00007fa125d00000 at 0x486ec000: LC_SEGMENT. ALLOC LOAD CODE HAS_CONTENTS
0x00007fa125d00000->0x00007fa125e00000 at 0x487ec000: LC_SEGMENT. ALLOC LOAD CODE HAS_CONTENTS
0x00007fa125e00000->0x00007fa125f00000 at 0x488ec000: LC_SEGMENT. ALLOC LOAD CODE HAS_CONTENTS
0x00007fa125f00000->0x00007fa126000000 at 0x489ec000: LC_SEGMENT. ALLOC LOAD CODE HAS_CONTENTS
0x00007fa126000000->0x00007fa126100000 at 0x48aec000: LC_SEGMENT. ALLOC LOAD CODE HAS_CONTENTS
0x00007fa126100000->0x00007fa126200000 at 0x48bec000: LC_SEGMENT. ALLOC LOAD CODE HAS_CONTENTS
0x00007fa126200000->0x00007fa126300000 at 0x48cec000: LC_SEGMENT. ALLOC LOAD CODE HAS_CONTENTS
0x00007fa126300000->0x00007fa126400000 at 0x48dec000: LC_SEGMENT. ALLOC LOAD CODE HAS_CONTENTS
0x00007fa126400000->0x00007fa126500000 at 0x48eec000: LC_SEGMENT. ALLOC LOAD CODE HAS_CONTENTS
0x00007fa126500000->0x00007fa126600000 at 0x48fec000: LC_SEGMENT. ALLOC LOAD CODE HAS_CONTENTS
0x00007fa126600000->0x00007fa126700000 at 0x490ec000: LC_SEGMENT. ALLOC LOAD CODE HAS_CONTENTS
0x00007fa126700000->0x00007fa126800000 at 0x491ec000: LC_SEGMENT. ALLOC LOAD CODE HAS_CONTENTS
0x00007fa126800000->0x00007fa126900000 at 0x492ec000: LC_SEGMENT. ALLOC LOAD CODE HAS_CONTENTS
0x00007fa126900000->0x00007fa126a00000 at 0x493ec000: LC_SEGMENT. ALLOC LOAD CODE HAS_CONTENTS
0x00007fa126a00000->0x00007fa126b00000 at 0x494ec000: LC_SEGMENT. ALLOC LOAD CODE HAS_CONTENTS
0x00007fa126b00000->0x00007fa126c00000 at 0x495ec000: LC_SEGMENT. ALLOC LOAD CODE HAS_CONTENTS
0x00007fa126c00000->0x00007fa126d00000 at 0x496ec000: LC_SEGMENT. ALLOC LOAD CODE HAS_CONTENTS
0x00007fa126d00000->0x00007fa126e00000 at 0x497ec000: LC_SEGMENT. ALLOC LOAD CODE HAS_CONTENTS
0x00007fa126e00000->0x00007fa126f00000 at 0x498ec000: LC_SEGMENT. ALLOC LOAD CODE HAS_CONTENTS
0x00007fa126f00000->0x00007fa127000000 at 0x499ec000: LC_SEGMENT. ALLOC LOAD CODE HAS_CONTENTS
0x00007fa127000000->0x00007fa127100000 at 0x49aec000: LC_SEGMENT. ALLOC LOAD CODE HAS_CONTENTS
0x00007fa127100000->0x00007fa127200000 at 0x49bec000: LC_SEGMENT. ALLOC LOAD CODE HAS_CONTENTS
0x00007fa127200000->0x00007fa127300000 at 0x49cec000: LC_SEGMENT. ALLOC LOAD CODE HAS_CONTENTS
0x00007fa127300000->0x00007fa127400000 at 0x49dec000: LC_SEGMENT. ALLOC LOAD CODE HAS_CONTENTS
0x00007fa127400000->0x00007fa127500000 at 0x49eec000: LC_SEGMENT. ALLOC LOAD CODE HAS_CONTENTS
0x00007fa127500000->0x00007fa127600000 at 0x49fec000: LC_SEGMENT. ALLOC LOAD CODE HAS_CONTENTS
0x00007fa127600000->0x00007fa127700000 at 0x4a0ec000: LC_SEGMENT. ALLOC LOAD CODE HAS_CONTENTS
0x00007fa127700000->0x00007fa127800000 at 0x4a1ec000: LC_SEGMENT. ALLOC LOAD CODE HAS_CONTENTS
0x00007fa127800000->0x00007fa127900000 at 0x4a2ec000: LC_SEGMENT. ALLOC LOAD CODE HAS_CONTENTS
0x00007fa127900000->0x00007fa127a00000 at 0x4a3ec000: LC_SEGMENT. ALLOC LOAD CODE HAS_CONTENTS
0x00007fa127a00000->0x00007fa127b00000 at 0x4a4ec000: LC_SEGMENT. ALLOC LOAD CODE HAS_CONTENTS
0x00007fa127b00000->0x00007fa127c00000 at 0x4a5ec000: LC_SEGMENT. ALLOC LOAD CODE HAS_CONTENTS
0x00007fa127c00000->0x00007fa127d00000 at 0x4a6ec000: LC_SEGMENT. ALLOC LOAD CODE HAS_CONTENTS
0x00007fa127d00000->0x00007fa127e00000 at 0x4a7ec000: LC_SEGMENT. ALLOC LOAD CODE HAS_CONTENTS
0x00007fa127e00000->0x00007fa127f00000 at 0x4a8ec000: LC_SEGMENT. ALLOC LOAD CODE HAS_CONTENTS
---Type <return> to continue, or q <return> to quit---
0x00007fa127f00000->0x00007fa128000000 at 0x4a9ec000: LC_SEGMENT. ALLOC LOAD CODE HAS_CONTENTS
0x00007fa128000000->0x00007fa128100000 at 0x4aaec000: LC_SEGMENT. ALLOC LOAD CODE HAS_CONTENTS
0x00007fa128100000->0x00007fa128200000 at 0x4abec000: LC_SEGMENT. ALLOC LOAD CODE HAS_CONTENTS
0x00007fa128200000->0x00007fa128300000 at 0x4acec000: LC_SEGMENT. ALLOC LOAD CODE HAS_CONTENTS
0x00007fa128300000->0x00007fa128400000 at 0x4adec000: LC_SEGMENT. ALLOC LOAD CODE HAS_CONTENTS
0x00007fa128400000->0x00007fa128500000 at 0x4aeec000: LC_SEGMENT. ALLOC LOAD CODE HAS_CONTENTS
0x00007fa128500000->0x00007fa128600000 at 0x4afec000: LC_SEGMENT. ALLOC LOAD CODE HAS_CONTENTS
0x00007fa128600000->0x00007fa128700000 at 0x4b0ec000: LC_SEGMENT. ALLOC LOAD CODE HAS_CONTENTS
0x00007fa128700000->0x00007fa128800000 at 0x4b1ec000: LC_SEGMENT. ALLOC LOAD CODE HAS_CONTENTS
0x00007fa128800000->0x00007fa128900000 at 0x4b2ec000: LC_SEGMENT. ALLOC LOAD CODE HAS_CONTENTS
0x00007fa128900000->0x00007fa128a00000 at 0x4b3ec000: LC_SEGMENT. ALLOC LOAD CODE HAS_CONTENTS
0x00007fa128a00000->0x00007fa128b00000 at 0x4b4ec000: LC_SEGMENT. ALLOC LOAD CODE HAS_CONTENTS
0x00007fa128b00000->0x00007fa128c00000 at 0x4b5ec000: LC_SEGMENT. ALLOC LOAD CODE HAS_CONTENTS
0x00007fa128c00000->0x00007fa128d00000 at 0x4b6ec000: LC_SEGMENT. ALLOC LOAD CODE HAS_CONTENTS
```

```
0x00007fa128d00000->0x00007fa128e00000 at 0x4b7ec000: LC_SEGMENT. ALLOC LOAD CODE HAS_CONTENTS
0x00007fa128e00000->0x00007fa128f00000 at 0x4b8ec000: LC_SEGMENT. ALLOC LOAD CODE HAS_CONTENTS
0x00007fa128f00000->0x00007fa129000000 at 0x4b9ec000: LC_SEGMENT. ALLOC LOAD CODE HAS_CONTENTS
0x00007fa129000000->0x00007fa129100000 at 0x4baec000: LC_SEGMENT. ALLOC LOAD CODE HAS_CONTENTS
0x00007fa129100000->0x00007fa129200000 at 0x4bbec000: LC_SEGMENT. ALLOC LOAD CODE HAS_CONTENTS
0x00007fa129200000->0x00007fa129300000 at 0x4bcec000: LC_SEGMENT. ALLOC LOAD CODE HAS_CONTENTS
0x00007fa129300000->0x00007fa129400000 at 0x4bdec000: LC_SEGMENT. ALLOC LOAD CODE HAS_CONTENTS
0x00007fa129400000->0x00007fa129500000 at 0x4beec000: LC_SEGMENT. ALLOC LOAD CODE HAS_CONTENTS
0x00007fa129500000->0x00007fa129600000 at 0x4bfec000: LC_SEGMENT. ALLOC LOAD CODE HAS_CONTENTS
0x00007fa129600000->0x00007fa129700000 at 0x4c0ec000: LC_SEGMENT. ALLOC LOAD CODE HAS_CONTENTS
0x00007fa129700000->0x00007fa129800000 at 0x4c1ec000: LC_SEGMENT. ALLOC LOAD CODE HAS_CONTENTS
0x00007fa129800000->0x00007fa129900000 at 0x4c2ec000: LC_SEGMENT. ALLOC LOAD CODE HAS_CONTENTS
0x00007fa129900000->0x00007fa129a00000 at 0x4c3ec000: LC_SEGMENT. ALLOC LOAD CODE HAS_CONTENTS
0x00007fa129a00000->0x00007fa129b00000 at 0x4c4ec000: LC_SEGMENT. ALLOC LOAD CODE HAS_CONTENTS
0x00007fa129b00000->0x00007fa129c00000 at 0x4c5ec000: LC_SEGMENT. ALLOC LOAD CODE HAS_CONTENTS
0x00007fa129c00000->0x00007fa129d00000 at 0x4c6ec000: LC_SEGMENT. ALLOC LOAD CODE HAS_CONTENTS
0x00007fa129d00000->0x00007fa129e00000 at 0x4c7ec000: LC_SEGMENT. ALLOC LOAD CODE HAS_CONTENTS
0x00007fa129e00000->0x00007fa129f00000 at 0x4c8ec000: LC_SEGMENT. ALLOC LOAD CODE HAS_CONTENTS
0x00007fa129f00000->0x00007fa12a000000 at 0x4c9ec000: LC_SEGMENT. ALLOC LOAD CODE HAS_CONTENTS
0x00007fa12a000000->0x00007fa12a100000 at 0x4caec000: LC_SEGMENT. ALLOC LOAD CODE HAS_CONTENTS
0x00007fa12a100000->0x00007fa12a200000 at 0x4cbec000: LC_SEGMENT. ALLOC LOAD CODE HAS_CONTENTS
0x00007fa12a200000->0x00007fa12a300000 at 0x4ccec000: LC_SEGMENT. ALLOC LOAD CODE HAS_CONTENTS
0x00007fa12a300000->0x00007fa12a400000 at 0x4cdec000: LC_SEGMENT. ALLOC LOAD CODE HAS_CONTENTS
0x00007fa12a400000->0x00007fa12a500000 at 0x4ceec000: LC_SEGMENT. ALLOC LOAD CODE HAS_CONTENTS
0x00007fa12a500000->0x00007fa12a600000 at 0x4cfec000: LC_SEGMENT. ALLOC LOAD CODE HAS_CONTENTS
0x00007fa12a600000->0x00007fa12a700000 at 0x4d0ec000: LC_SEGMENT. ALLOC LOAD CODE HAS_CONTENTS
---Type <return> to continue, or q <return> to quit---
0x00007fa12a700000->0x00007fa12a800000 at 0x4d1ec000: LC_SEGMENT. ALLOC LOAD CODE HAS_CONTENTS
0x00007fa12a800000->0x00007fa12a900000 at 0x4d2ec000: LC_SEGMENT. ALLOC LOAD CODE HAS_CONTENTS
0x00007fa12a900000->0x00007fa12aa00000 at 0x4d3ec000: LC_SEGMENT. ALLOC LOAD CODE HAS_CONTENTS
0x00007fa12aa00000->0x00007fa12ab00000 at 0x4d4ec000: LC_SEGMENT. ALLOC LOAD CODE HAS_CONTENTS
0x00007fa12ab00000->0x00007fa12ac00000 at 0x4d5ec000: LC_SEGMENT. ALLOC LOAD CODE HAS_CONTENTS
0x00007fa12ac00000->0x00007fa12ad00000 at 0x4d6ec000: LC_SEGMENT. ALLOC LOAD CODE HAS_CONTENTS
0x00007fa12ad00000->0x00007fa12ae00000 at 0x4d7ec000: LC_SEGMENT. ALLOC LOAD CODE HAS_CONTENTS
0x00007fa12ae00000->0x00007fa12af00000 at 0x4d8ec000: LC_SEGMENT. ALLOC LOAD CODE HAS_CONTENTS
0x00007fa12af00000->0x00007fa12b000000 at 0x4d9ec000: LC_SEGMENT. ALLOC LOAD CODE HAS_CONTENTS
0x00007fa12b000000->0x00007fa12b100000 at 0x4daec000: LC_SEGMENT. ALLOC LOAD CODE HAS_CONTENTS
0x00007fa12b100000->0x00007fa12b200000 at 0x4dbec000: LC_SEGMENT. ALLOC LOAD CODE HAS_CONTENTS
0x00007fa12b200000->0x00007fa12b300000 at 0x4dcec000: LC_SEGMENT. ALLOC LOAD CODE HAS_CONTENTS
0x00007fff689b8000->0x00007fff6c1b8000 at 0x4ddec000: LC_SEGMENT. ALLOC LOAD CODE HAS_CONTENTS
0x00007fff6c1b8000->0x00007fff6c9b7000 at 0x515ec000: LC_SEGMENT. ALLOC LOAD CODE HAS_CONTENTS
0x00007fff6c9b7000->0x00007fff6c9b8000 at 0x51deb000: LC_SEGMENT. ALLOC LOAD CODE HAS_CONTENTS
0x00007fff6c9b8000->0x00007fff6c9ed000 at 0x51dec000: LC_SEGMENT. ALLOC LOAD CODE HAS_CONTENTS
0x00007fff6c9ed000->0x00007fff6c9ef000 at 0x51e21000: LC_SEGMENT. ALLOC LOAD CODE HAS_CONTENTS
0x00007fff6c9ef000->0x00007fff6ca29000 at 0x51e23000: LC_SEGMENT. ALLOC LOAD CODE HAS_CONTENTS
0x00007fff6ca29000->0x00007fff6ca3c000 at 0x51e5d000: LC_SEGMENT. ALLOC LOAD CODE HAS_CONTENTS
0x00007fff79629000->0x00007fff79800000 at 0x51e70000: LC_SEGMENT. ALLOC LOAD CODE HAS_CONTENTS
0x00007fff79800000->0x00007fff79a00000 at 0x52047000: LC_SEGMENT. ALLOC LOAD CODE HAS_CONTENTS
0x00007fff79a00000->0x00007fff79c00000 at 0x52247000: LC_SEGMENT. ALLOC LOAD CODE HAS_CONTENTS
0x00007fff79c00000->0x00007fff79e00000 at 0x52447000: LC_SEGMENT. ALLOC LOAD CODE HAS_CONTENTS
0x00007fff79e00000->0x00007fff7a000000 at 0x52647000: LC_SEGMENT. ALLOC LOAD CODE HAS_CONTENTS
0x00007fff7a000000->0x00007fff7a200000 at 0x52847000: LC_SEGMENT. ALLOC LOAD CODE HAS_CONTENTS
0x00007fff7a200000->0x00007fff7a400000 at 0x52a47000: LC_SEGMENT. ALLOC LOAD CODE HAS_CONTENTS
0x00007fff7a400000->0x00007fff7a600000 at 0x52c47000: LC_SEGMENT. ALLOC LOAD CODE HAS_CONTENTS
0x00007fff7a600000->0x00007fff7a800000 at 0x52e47000: LC_SEGMENT. ALLOC LOAD CODE HAS_CONTENTS
0x00007fff7a800000->0x00007fff7aa00000 at 0x53047000: LC_SEGMENT. ALLOC LOAD CODE HAS_CONTENTS
0x00007fff7aa00000->0x00007fff7ae00000 at 0x53247000: LC_SEGMENT. ALLOC LOAD CODE HAS_CONTENTS
0x00007fff7ae00000->0x00007fff7b000000 at 0x53647000: LC_SEGMENT. ALLOC LOAD CODE HAS_CONTENTS
0x00007fff7b000000->0x00007fff7b11d000 at 0x53847000: LC_SEGMENT. ALLOC LOAD CODE HAS_CONTENTS
0x00007fff89629000->0x00007fff96699000 at 0x53964000: LC_SEGMENT. ALLOC LOAD CODE HAS_CONTENTS
0x00007fff96699000->0x00007fff997a1000 at 0x609d4000: LC_SEGMENT. ALLOC LOAD CODE HAS_CONTENTS
0x00007ffffffe00000->0x00007fffffffe02000 at 0x63adc000: LC_SEGMENT. ALLOC LOAD CODE HAS_CONTENTS
0x0000000000000000->0x00000000000000b0 at 0x00016b00: LC_THREAD.x86_THREAD_STATE.0 HAS_CONTENTS
0x0000000000000000->0x0000000000000214 at 0x00016bb8: LC_THREAD.x86_FLOAT_STATE.0 HAS_CONTENTS
0x0000000000000000->0x0000000000000018 at 0x00016dd4: LC_THREAD.x86_EXCEPTION_STATE.0 HAS_CONTENTS
0x0000000000000000->0x00000000000000b0 at 0x00016dfc: LC_THREAD.x86_THREAD_STATE.1 HAS_CONTENTS
0x0000000000000000->0x0000000000000214 at 0x00016eb4: LC_THREAD.x86_FLOAT_STATE.1 HAS_CONTENTS
---Type <return> to continue, or q <return> to quit---
0x0000000000000000->0x0000000000000018 at 0x000170d0: LC_THREAD.x86_EXCEPTION_STATE.1 HAS_CONTENTS
0x0000000000000000->0x00000000000000b0 at 0x000170f8: LC_THREAD.x86_THREAD_STATE.2 HAS_CONTENTS
0x0000000000000000->0x0000000000000214 at 0x000171b0: LC_THREAD.x86_FLOAT_STATE.2 HAS_CONTENTS
0x0000000000000000->0x0000000000000018 at 0x000173cc: LC_THREAD.x86_EXCEPTION_STATE.2 HAS_CONTENTS
0x0000000000000000->0x00000000000000b0 at 0x000173f4: LC_THREAD.x86_THREAD_STATE.3 HAS_CONTENTS
0x0000000000000000->0x0000000000000214 at 0x000174ac: LC_THREAD.x86_FLOAT_STATE.3 HAS_CONTENTS
0x0000000000000000->0x0000000000000018 at 0x000176c8: LC_THREAD.x86_EXCEPTION_STATE.3 HAS_CONTENTS
0x0000000000000000->0x00000000000000b0 at 0x000176f0: LC_THREAD.x86_THREAD_STATE.4 HAS_CONTENTS
0x0000000000000000->0x0000000000000214 at 0x000177a8: LC_THREAD.x86_FLOAT_STATE.4 HAS_CONTENTS
0x0000000000000000->0x0000000000000018 at 0x000179c4: LC_THREAD.x86_EXCEPTION_STATE.4 HAS_CONTENTS
0x0000000000000000->0x00000000000000b0 at 0x000179ec: LC_THREAD.x86_THREAD_STATE.5 HAS_CONTENTS
0x0000000000000000->0x0000000000000214 at 0x00017aa4: LC_THREAD.x86_FLOAT_STATE.5 HAS_CONTENTS
0x0000000000000000->0x0000000000000018 at 0x00017cc0: LC_THREAD.x86_EXCEPTION_STATE.5 HAS_CONTENTS
```

4.   Calculate the size of the segment 0x00007fa0e2b00000->0x00007fa0e2c00000 in pointers:

```
(gdb) print (0x00007fa0e2c00000 - 0x00007fa0e2b00000)/8
$1 = 131072
```

5.   Examine the segment contents for any execution residue and hints:

```
(gdb) x/131072a 0x00007fa0e2b00000
0x7fa0e2b00000:     0x657461636f6c6c61   0x79726f6d656d2064
0x7fa0e2b00010:     0x0    0x0
0x7fa0e2b00020:     0x10cdb87d0 <procD> 0x0
0x7fa0e2b00030:     0x0    0x0
0x7fa0e2b00040:     0x0    0x0
0x7fa0e2b00050:     0x0    0x0
0x7fa0e2b00060:     0x0    0x0
0x7fa0e2b00070:     0x0    0x0
0x7fa0e2b00080:     0x0    0x0
0x7fa0e2b00090:     0x0    0x0
0x7fa0e2b000a0:     0x0    0x0
0x7fa0e2b000b0:     0x0    0x0
0x7fa0e2b000c0:     0x0    0x0
0x7fa0e2b000d0:     0x0    0x0
0x7fa0e2b000e0:     0x0    0x0
0x7fa0e2b000f0:     0x0    0x0
0x7fa0e2b00100:     0x657461636f6c6c61   0x79726f6d656d2064
0x7fa0e2b00110:     0x0    0x0
0x7fa0e2b00120:     0x10cdb87d0 <procD> 0x0
0x7fa0e2b00130:     0x0    0x0
0x7fa0e2b00140:     0x0    0x0
0x7fa0e2b00150:     0x0    0x0
0x7fa0e2b00160:     0x0    0x0
0x7fa0e2b00170:     0x0    0x0
0x7fa0e2b00180:     0x0    0x0
0x7fa0e2b00190:     0x0    0x0
0x7fa0e2b001a0:     0x0    0x0
0x7fa0e2b001b0:     0x0    0x0
0x7fa0e2b001c0:     0x0    0x0
0x7fa0e2b001d0:     0x0    0x0
0x7fa0e2b001e0:     0x0    0x0
0x7fa0e2b001f0:     0x0    0x0
0x7fa0e2b00200:     0x657461636f6c6c61   0x79726f6d656d2064
0x7fa0e2b00210:     0x0    0x0
0x7fa0e2b00220:     0x10cdb87d0 <procD> 0x0
0x7fa0e2b00230:     0x0    0x0
0x7fa0e2b00240:     0x0    0x0
0x7fa0e2b00250:     0x0    0x0
0x7fa0e2b00260:     0x0    0x0
0x7fa0e2b00270:     0x0    0x0
---Type <return> to continue, or q <return> to quit---
0x7fa0e2b00280:     0x0    0x0
0x7fa0e2b00290:     0x0    0x0
0x7fa0e2b002a0:     0x0    0x0
0x7fa0e2b002b0:     0x0    0x0
0x7fa0e2b002c0:     0x0    0x0
0x7fa0e2b002d0:     0x0    0x0
0x7fa0e2b002e0:     0x0    0x0
0x7fa0e2b002f0:     0x0    0x0
0x7fa0e2b00300:     0x657461636f6c6c61   0x79726f6d656d2064
0x7fa0e2b00310:     0x0    0x0
```

```
0x7fa0e2b00320:     0x10cdb87d0 <procD> 0x0
0x7fa0e2b00330:     0x0      0x0
0x7fa0e2b00340:     0x0      0x0
0x7fa0e2b00350:     0x0      0x0
0x7fa0e2b00360:     0x0      0x0
0x7fa0e2b00370:     0x0      0x0
0x7fa0e2b00380:     0x0      0x0
0x7fa0e2b00390:     0x0      0x0
0x7fa0e2b003a0:     0x0      0x0
0x7fa0e2b003b0:     0x0      0x0
0x7fa0e2b003c0:     0x0      0x0
0x7fa0e2b003d0:     0x0      0x0
0x7fa0e2b003e0:     0x0      0x0
0x7fa0e2b003f0:     0x0      0x0
0x7fa0e2b00400:     0x657461636f6c6c61  0x79726f6d656d2064
0x7fa0e2b00410:     0x0      0x0
0x7fa0e2b00420:     0x10cdb87d0 <procD> 0x0
0x7fa0e2b00430:     0x0      0x0
0x7fa0e2b00440:     0x0      0x0
0x7fa0e2b00450:     0x0      0x0
0x7fa0e2b00460:     0x0      0x0
0x7fa0e2b00470:     0x0      0x0
0x7fa0e2b00480:     0x0      0x0
0x7fa0e2b00490:     0x0      0x0
0x7fa0e2b004a0:     0x0      0x0
0x7fa0e2b004b0:     0x0      0x0
0x7fa0e2b004c0:     0x0      0x0
0x7fa0e2b004d0:     0x0      0x0
0x7fa0e2b004e0:     0x0      0x0
0x7fa0e2b004f0:     0x0      0x0
---Type <return> to continue, or q <return> to quit---
0x7fa0e2b00500:     0x657461636f6c6c61  0x79726f6d656d2064
0x7fa0e2b00510:     0x0      0x0
0x7fa0e2b00520:     0x10cdb87d0 <procD> 0x0
0x7fa0e2b00530:     0x0      0x0
0x7fa0e2b00540:     0x0      0x0
0x7fa0e2b00550:     0x0      0x0
0x7fa0e2b00560:     0x0      0x0
0x7fa0e2b00570:     0x0      0x0
0x7fa0e2b00580:     0x0      0x0
0x7fa0e2b00590:     0x0      0x0
0x7fa0e2b005a0:     0x0      0x0
0x7fa0e2b005b0:     0x0      0x0
0x7fa0e2b005c0:     0x0      0x0
0x7fa0e2b005d0:     0x0      0x0
0x7fa0e2b005e0:     0x0      0x0
0x7fa0e2b005f0:     0x0      0x0
0x7fa0e2b00600:     0x657461636f6c6c61  0x79726f6d656d2064
0x7fa0e2b00610:     0x0      0x0
0x7fa0e2b00620:     0x10cdb87d0 <procD> 0x0
0x7fa0e2b00630:     0x0      0x0
0x7fa0e2b00640:     0x0      0x0
0x7fa0e2b00650:     0x0      0x0
0x7fa0e2b00660:     0x0      0x0
0x7fa0e2b00670:     0x0      0x0
0x7fa0e2b00680:     0x0      0x0
0x7fa0e2b00690:     0x0      0x0
0x7fa0e2b006a0:     0x0      0x0
0x7fa0e2b006b0:     0x0      0x0
0x7fa0e2b006c0:     0x0      0x0
```

```
0x7fa0e2b006d0:     0x0     0x0
0x7fa0e2b006e0:     0x0     0x0
0x7fa0e2b006f0:     0x0     0x0
0x7fa0e2b00700:     0x657461636f6c6c61  0x79726f6d656d2064
0x7fa0e2b00710:     0x0     0x0
0x7fa0e2b00720:     0x10cdb87d0 <procD> 0x0
0x7fa0e2b00730:     0x0     0x0
0x7fa0e2b00740:     0x0     0x0
0x7fa0e2b00750:     0x0     0x0
0x7fa0e2b00760:     0x0     0x0
0x7fa0e2b00770:     0x0     0x0
---Type <return> to continue, or q <return> to quit---q
Quit


(gdb) x/s 0x7fa0e2b00700
0x7fa0e2b00700:     "allocated memory"
```

6.   Compare the consequent vmmap logs vmmap_1883_1.log, vmmap_1883_2.log and vmmap_1883_3.log saved at different times:

```
Virtual Memory Map of process 1883 (App9)
Output report format:  2.2  -- 64-bit process

==== Non-writable regions for process 1883
__TEXT              000000010cdb8000-000000010cdb9000 [    4K] r-x/rwx SM=COW  /Users/DumpAnalysis/Documents/AMCDA-
Dumps/Apps/App9/Build/Products/Release/App9
__LINKEDIT          000000010cdba000-000000010cdbb000 [    4K] r--/rwx SM=COW  /Users/DumpAnalysis/Documents/AMCDA-
Dumps/Apps/App9/Build/Products/Release/App9
MALLOC metadata     000000010cdbb000-000000010cdbc000 [    4K] r--/rwx SM=ZER
MALLOC guard page   000000010cdbd000-000000010cdbe000 [    4K] ---/rwx SM=NUL
MALLOC guard page   000000010cdd3000-000000010cdd5000 [    8K] ---/rwx SM=NUL
MALLOC guard page   000000010cdea000-000000010cdeb000 [    4K] ---/rwx SM=NUL
MALLOC metadata     000000010cdeb000-000000010cdec000 [    4K] r--/rwx SM=PRV
STACK GUARD         000000010cf00000-000000010cf01000 [    4K] ---/rwx SM=NUL  stack guard for thread 1
STACK GUARD         000000010cf83000-000000010cf84000 [    4K] ---/rwx SM=NUL  stack guard for thread 2
STACK GUARD         000000010d006000-000000010d007000 [    4K] ---/rwx SM=NUL  stack guard for thread 3
STACK GUARD         000000010d089000-000000010d08a000 [    4K] ---/rwx SM=NUL  stack guard for thread 4
STACK GUARD         000000010d10c000-000000010d10d000 [    4K] ---/rwx SM=NUL  stack guard for thread 5
STACK GUARD         00007fff689b8000-00007fff6c1b8000 [ 56.0M] ---/rwx SM=NUL  stack guard for thread 0
__TEXT              00007fff6c9b8000-00007fff6c9ed000 [  212K] r-x/rwx SM=COW  /usr/lib/dyld
__LINKEDIT          00007fff6ca29000-00007fff6ca3c000 [   76K] r--/rwx SM=COW  /usr/lib/dyld
__TEXT              00007fff89663000-00007fff89681000 [  120K] r-x/r-x SM=COW  /usr/lib/system/libxpc.dylib
__TEXT              00007fff899d9000-00007fff899db000 [    8K] r-x/r-x SM=COW  /usr/lib/system/libsystem_blocks.dylib
__TEXT              00007fff899db000-00007fff89ab9000 [  888K] r-x/r-x SM=COW  /usr/lib/system/libsystem_c.dylib
__TEXT              00007fff89c93000-00007fff89ca2000 [   60K] r-x/r-x SM=COW  /usr/lib/system/libdispatch.dylib
__TEXT              00007fff8a261000-00007fff8a263000 [    8K] r-x/r-x SM=COW  /usr/lib/system/libunc.dylib
__TEXT              00007fff8a754000-00007fff8a756000 [    8K] r-x/r-x SM=COW  /usr/lib/system/libremovefile.dylib
__TEXT              00007fff8dd85000-00007fff8dd8a000 [   20K] r-x/r-x SM=COW  /usr/lib/system/libmathCommon.A.dylib
__TEXT              00007fff8dd8a000-00007fff8dd8f000 [   20K] r-x/r-x SM=COW  /usr/lib/system/libdyld.dylib
__TEXT              00007fff8e3b1000-00007fff8e3b3000 [    8K] r-x/r-x SM=COW  /usr/lib/system/libsystem_sandbox.dylib
__TEXT              00007fff8ed60000-00007fff8ed67000 [   28K] r-x/r-x SM=COW  /usr/lib/system/libmacho.dylib
__TEXT              00007fff8ed67000-00007fff8ed88000 [  132K] r-x/r-x SM=COW  /usr/lib/system/libsystem_kernel.dylib
__TEXT              00007fff8ef1d000-00007fff8ef26000 [   36K] r-x/r-x SM=COW  /usr/lib/system/libsystem_dnssd.dylib
__TEXT              00007fff8fa97000-00007fff8fad3000 [  240K] r-x/r-x SM=COW  /usr/lib/system/libsystem_info.dylib
__TEXT              00007fff8feb9000-00007fff8febc000 [   12K] r-x/r-x SM=COW  /usr/lib/system/libquarantine.dylib
__TEXT              00007fff90025000-00007fff90026000 [    4K] r-x/r-x SM=COW  /usr/lib/system/libkeymgr.dylib
__TEXT              00007fff9004e000-00007fff90054000 [   24K] r-x/r-x SM=COW  /usr/lib/system/libcompiler_rt.dylib
__TEXT              00007fff9098b000-00007fff9098d000 [    8K] r-x/r-x SM=COW  /usr/lib/system/libdnsinfo.dylib
__TEXT              00007fff91199000-00007fff9119f000 [   24K] r-x/r-x SM=COW  /usr/lib/system/libsystem_network.dylib
__TEXT              00007fff91c14000-00007fff91c1f000 [   44K] r-x/r-x SM=COW  /usr/lib/system/liblaunch.dylib
__TEXT              00007fff94a73000-00007fff94a7b000 [   32K] r-x/r-x SM=COW  /usr/lib/system/libcopyfile.dylib
__TEXT              00007fff94abc000-00007fff94aff000 [  268K] r-x/r-x SM=COW  /usr/lib/system/libcommonCrypto.dylib
__TEXT              00007fff95880000-00007fff9588a000 [   40K] r-x/r-x SM=COW  /usr/lib/system/libsystem_notify.dylib
__TEXT              00007fff95fe7000-00007fff96015000 [  184K] r-x/r-x SM=COW  /usr/lib/libSystem.B.dylib
__TEXT              00007fff960fa000-00007fff96101000 [   28K] r-x/r-x SM=COW  /usr/lib/system/libunwind.dylib
__TEXT              00007fff96693000-00007fff96699000 [   24K] r-x/r-x SM=COW  /usr/lib/system/libcache.dylib
__LINKEDIT          00007fff967f7000-00007fff997a1000 [ 47.7M] r--/r-- SM=COW  /usr/lib/system/libxpc.dylib
shared memory       00007ffffe00000-00007ffffe02000 [    8K] r-x/r-x SM=SHM
```

```
==== Writable regions for process 1883
__DATA       000000010cdb9000-000000010cdba000 [    4K] rw-/rwx SM=PRV  /Users/DumpAnalysis/Documents/AMCDA-
Dumps/Apps/App9/Build/Products/Release/App9
MALLOC metadata  000000010cdbc000-000000010cdbd000 [    4K] rw-/rwx SM=ZER
MALLOC metadata  000000010cdbe000-000000010cdd3000 [   84K] rw-/rwx SM=PRV
MALLOC metadata  000000010cdd5000-000000010cdea000 [   84K] rw-/rwx SM=PRV
MALLOC_TINY      000000010ce00000-000000010cf00000 [ 1024K] rw-/rwx SM=PRV  DefaultMallocZone_0x10cdbb000
Stack            000000010cf01000-000000010cf83000 [  520K] rw-/rwx SM=PRV  thread 1
Stack            000000010cf84000-000000010d006000 [  520K] rw-/rwx SM=PRV  thread 2
Stack            000000010d007000-000000010d089000 [  520K] rw-/rwx SM=PRV  thread 3
Stack            000000010d08a000-000000010d10c000 [  520K] rw-/rwx SM=PRV  thread 4
Stack            000000010d10d000-000000010d18f000 [  520K] rw-/rwx SM=PRV  thread 5
MALLOC_TINY      00007fa10b400000-00007fa10b600000 [ 2048K] rw-/rwx SM=PRV  DefaultMallocZone_0x10cdbb000
Stack            00007fff6c1b8000-00007fff6c9b7000 [ 8188K] rw-/rwx SM=ZER  thread 0
Stack            00007fff6c9b7000-00007fff6c9b8000 [    4K] rw-/rwx SM=COW  thread 0
__DATA           00007fff6c9ed000-00007fff6ca29000 [  240K] rw-/rwx SM=COW  /usr/lib/dyld
__DATA           00007fff79631000-00007fff79634000 [   12K] rw-/rwx SM=COW  /usr/lib/system/libxpc.dylib
__DATA           00007fff796d1000-00007fff796d2000 [    4K] rw-/rwx SM=COW  /usr/lib/system/libsystem_blocks.dylib
__DATA           00007fff796d2000-00007fff796e2000 [   64K] rw-/rwx SM=COW  /usr/lib/system/libsystem_c.dylib
__DATA           00007fff79735000-00007fff7973b000 [   24K] rw-/rwx SM=COW  /usr/lib/system/libdispatch.dylib
__DATA           00007fff79801000-00007fff79802000 [    4K] rw-/rwx SM=COW  /usr/lib/system/libunc.dylib
__DATA           00007fff79882000-00007fff79883000 [    4K] rw-/rw- SM=COW  /usr/lib/system/libremovefile.dylib
__DATA           00007fff79db2000-00007fff79db3000 [    4K] rw-/rwx SM=COW  /usr/lib/system/libdyld.dylib
__DATA           00007fff79e14000-00007fff79e15000 [    4K] rw-/rwx SM=COW  /usr/lib/system/libsystem_sandbox.dylib
__DATA           00007fff79ef2000-00007fff79ef3000 [    4K] rw-/rwx SM=COW  /usr/lib/system/libmacho.dylib
__DATA           00007fff79ef3000-00007fff79ef6000 [   12K] rw-/rwx SM=COW  /usr/lib/system/libsystem_kernel.dylib
__DATA           00007fff79f49000-00007fff79f4a000 [    4K] rw-/rwx SM=COW  /usr/lib/system/libsystem_dnssd.dylib
__DATA           00007fff7a0c4000-00007fff7a0c7000 [   12K] rw-/rwx SM=COW  /usr/lib/system/libsystem_info.dylib
__DATA           00007fff7a190000-00007fff7a191000 [    4K] rw-/rwx SM=COW  /usr/lib/system/libquarantine.dylib
__DATA           00007fff7a1ca000-00007fff7a1cb000 [    4K] rw-/rwx SM=COW  /usr/lib/system/libkeymgr.dylib
__DATA           00007fff7a1d4000-00007fff7a1d5000 [    4K] rw-/rwx SM=COW  /usr/lib/system/libcompiler_rt.dylib
__DATA           00007fff7a2a4000-00007fff7a2a5000 [    4K] rw-/rw- SM=COW  /usr/lib/system/libdnsinfo.dylib
__DATA           00007fff7a347000-00007fff7a348000 [    4K] rw-/rw- SM=COW  /usr/lib/system/libsystem_network.dylib
__DATA           00007fff7a484000-00007fff7a485000 [    4K] rw-/rw- SM=COW  /usr/lib/system/liblaunch.dylib
__DATA           00007fff7aab2000-00007fff7aab3000 [    4K] rw-/rw- SM=COW  /usr/lib/system/libcopyfile.dylib
__DATA           00007fff7aabb000-00007fff7aac1000 [   24K] rw-/rw- SM=COW  /usr/lib/system/libcommonCrypto.dylib
__DATA           00007fff7afb3000-00007fff7afb4000 [    4K] rw-/rw- SM=COW  /usr/lib/system/libsystem_notify.dylib
__DATA           00007fff7b06e000-00007fff7b06f000 [    4K] rw-/rw- SM=COW  /usr/lib/libSystem.B.dylib
__DATA           00007fff7b072000-00007fff7b073000 [    4K] rw-/rw- SM=COW  /usr/lib/system/libunwind.dylib
__DATA           00007fff7b11c000-00007fff7b11d000 [    4K] rw-/rw- SM=COW  /usr/lib/system/libcache.dylib

==== Legend
SM=sharing mode:
        COW=copy_on_write PRV=private NUL=empty ALI=aliased
        SHM=shared ZER=zero_filled S/A=shared_alias

==== Summary for process 1883
ReadOnly portion of Libraries: Total=50.2M resident=14.3M(28%) swapped_out_or_unallocated=35.9M(72%)
Writable regions: Total=31.1M written=1388K(4%) resident=10.2M(33%) swapped_out=11.6M(37%) unallocated=20.9M(67%)

REGION TYPE                 VIRTUAL
===========                 =======
MALLOC                        3072K      see MALLOC ZONE table below
MALLOC guard page               16K
MALLOC metadata                180K
STACK GUARD                   56.0M
Stack                         10.5M
__DATA                         464K
__LINKEDIT                    47.7M
__TEXT                        2484K
shared memory                    8K
===========                 =======
TOTAL                        120.4M

                       VIRTUAL  ALLOCATION     BYTES
MALLOC ZONE               SIZE       COUNT  ALLOCATED  % FULL
===========            =======  ==========  =========  ======
DefaultMallocZone_0x10cdbb000   3072K   5033   1252K   40%
```

```
Virtual Memory Map of process 1883 (App9)
Output report format:  2.2  -- 64-bit process

==== Non-writable regions for process 1883
__TEXT                 000000010cdb8000-000000010cdb9000 [    4K] r-x/rwx SM=COW  /Users/DumpAnalysis/Documents/AMCDA-
Dumps/Apps/App9/Build/Products/Release/App9
__LINKEDIT             000000010cdba000-000000010cdbb000 [    4K] r--/rwx SM=COW  /Users/DumpAnalysis/Documents/AMCDA-
Dumps/Apps/App9/Build/Products/Release/App9
MALLOC metadata        000000010cdbb000-000000010cdbc000 [    4K] r--/rwx SM=COW
MALLOC guard page      000000010cdbd000-000000010cdbe000 [    4K] ---/rwx SM=NUL
MALLOC guard page      000000010cdd3000-000000010cdd5000 [    8K] ---/rwx SM=NUL
MALLOC guard page      000000010cdea000-000000010cdeb000 [    4K] ---/rwx SM=NUL
MALLOC metadata        000000010cdeb000-000000010cdec000 [    4K] r--/rwx SM=COW
STACK GUARD            000000010cf00000-000000010cf01000 [    4K] ---/rwx SM=NUL  stack guard for thread 1
STACK GUARD            000000010cf83000-000000010cf84000 [    4K] ---/rwx SM=NUL  stack guard for thread 2
STACK GUARD            000000010d006000-000000010d007000 [    4K] ---/rwx SM=NUL  stack guard for thread 3
STACK GUARD            000000010d089000-000000010d08a000 [    4K] ---/rwx SM=NUL  stack guard for thread 4
STACK GUARD            000000010d10c000-000000010d10d000 [    4K] ---/rwx SM=NUL  stack guard for thread 5
STACK GUARD            00007fff689b8000-00007fff6c1b8000 [ 56.0M] ---/rwx SM=NUL  stack guard for thread 0
__TEXT                 00007fff6c9b8000-00007fff6c9ed000 [  212K] r-x/rwx SM=COW  /usr/lib/dyld
__LINKEDIT             00007fff6ca29000-00007fff6ca3c000 [   76K] r--/rwx SM=COW  /usr/lib/dyld
__TEXT                 00007fff89663000-00007fff89681000 [  120K] r-x/r-x SM=COW  /usr/lib/system/libxpc.dylib
__TEXT                 00007fff899d9000-00007fff899db000 [    8K] r-x/r-x SM=COW  /usr/lib/system/libsystem_blocks.dylib
__TEXT                 00007fff899db000-00007fff89ab9000 [  888K] r-x/r-x SM=COW  /usr/lib/system/libsystem_c.dylib
__TEXT                 00007fff89c93000-00007fff89ca2000 [   60K] r-x/r-x SM=COW  /usr/lib/system/libdispatch.dylib
__TEXT                 00007fff8a261000-00007fff8a263000 [    8K] r-x/r-x SM=COW  /usr/lib/system/libunc.dylib
__TEXT                 00007fff8a754000-00007fff8a756000 [    8K] r-x/r-x SM=COW  /usr/lib/system/libremovefile.dylib
__TEXT                 00007fff8dd85000-00007fff8dd8a000 [   20K] r-x/r-x SM=COW  /usr/lib/system/libmathCommon.A.dylib
__TEXT                 00007fff8dd8a000-00007fff8dd8f000 [   20K] r-x/r-x SM=COW  /usr/lib/system/libdyld.dylib
__TEXT                 00007fff8e3b1000-00007fff8e3b3000 [    8K] r-x/r-x SM=COW  /usr/lib/system/libsystem_sandbox.dylib
__TEXT                 00007fff8ed60000-00007fff8ed67000 [   28K] r-x/r-x SM=COW  /usr/lib/system/libmacho.dylib
__TEXT                 00007fff8ed67000-00007fff8ed88000 [  132K] r-x/r-x SM=COW  /usr/lib/system/libsystem_kernel.dylib
__TEXT                 00007fff8ef1d000-00007fff8ef26000 [   36K] r-x/r-x SM=COW  /usr/lib/system/libsystem_dnssd.dylib
__TEXT                 00007fff8fa97000-00007fff8fad3000 [  240K] r-x/r-x SM=COW  /usr/lib/system/libsystem_info.dylib
__TEXT                 00007fff8feb9000-00007fff8febc000 [   12K] r-x/r-x SM=COW  /usr/lib/system/libquarantine.dylib
__TEXT                 00007fff90025000-00007fff90026000 [    4K] r-x/r-x SM=COW  /usr/lib/system/libkeymgr.dylib
__TEXT                 00007fff9004e000-00007fff90054000 [   24K] r-x/r-x SM=COW  /usr/lib/system/libcompiler_rt.dylib
__TEXT                 00007fff9098b000-00007fff9098d000 [    8K] r-x/r-x SM=COW  /usr/lib/system/libdnsinfo.dylib
__TEXT                 00007fff91199000-00007fff9119f000 [   24K] r-x/r-x SM=COW  /usr/lib/system/libsystem_network.dylib
__TEXT                 00007fff91c14000-00007fff91c1f000 [   44K] r-x/r-x SM=COW  /usr/lib/system/liblaunch.dylib
__TEXT                 00007fff94a73000-00007fff94a7b000 [   32K] r-x/r-x SM=COW  /usr/lib/system/libcopyfile.dylib
__TEXT                 00007fff94abc000-00007fff94aff000 [  268K] r-x/r-x SM=COW  /usr/lib/system/libcommonCrypto.dylib
__TEXT                 00007fff95880000-00007fff95888000 [   40K] r-x/r-x SM=COW  /usr/lib/system/libsystem_notify.dylib
__TEXT                 00007fff95fe7000-00007fff96015000 [  184K] r-x/r-x SM=COW  /usr/lib/libSystem.B.dylib
__TEXT                 00007fff960fa000-00007fff96101000 [   28K] r-x/r-x SM=COW  /usr/lib/system/libunwind.dylib
__TEXT                 00007fff96693000-00007fff96699000 [   24K] r-x/r-x SM=COW  /usr/lib/system/libcache.dylib
__LINKEDIT             00007fff967f7000-00007fff997a1000 [ 47.7M] r--/r-- SM=COW  /usr/lib/system/libxpc.dylib
shared memory          00007ffffe00000-00007ffffe02000 [    8K] r-x/r-x SM=SHM

==== Writable regions for process 1883
__DATA                 000000010cdb9000-000000010cdba000 [    4K] rw-/rwx SM=PRV  /Users/DumpAnalysis/Documents/AMCDA-
Dumps/Apps/App9/Build/Products/Release/App9
MALLOC metadata        000000010cdbc000-000000010cdbd000 [    4K] rw-/rwx SM=PRV
MALLOC metadata        000000010cdbe000-000000010cdd3000 [   84K] rw-/rwx SM=PRV
MALLOC metadata        000000010cdd5000-000000010cdea000 [   84K] rw-/rwx SM=COW
MALLOC metadata        000000010cdec000-000000010cdf5000 [   36K] rw-/rwx SM=PRV
MALLOC_TINY            000000010ce00000-000000010cf00000 [ 1024K] rw-/rwx SM=PRV  DefaultMallocZone_0x10cdbb000
Stack                  000000010cf01000-000000010cf83000 [  520K] rw-/rwx SM=PRV  thread 1
Stack                  000000010cf84000-000000010d006000 [  520K] rw-/rwx SM=PRV  thread 2
Stack                  000000010d007000-000000010d089000 [  520K] rw-/rwx SM=PRV  thread 3
Stack                  000000010d08a000-000000010d10c000 [  520K] rw-/rwx SM=PRV  thread 4
Stack                  000000010d10d000-000000010d18f000 [  520K] rw-/rwx SM=PRV  thread 5
MALLOC_TINY            00007fa0fb400000-00007fa102400000 [112.0M] rw-/rwx SM=PRV  DefaultMallocZone_0x10cdbb000
MALLOC_TINY            00007fa10b400000-00007fa12b300000 [511.0M] rw-/rwx SM=PRV  DefaultMallocZone_0x10cdbb000
Stack                  00007fff6c1b8000-00007fff6c9b7000 [ 8188K] rw-/rwx SM=ZER  thread 0
Stack                  00007fff6c9b7000-00007fff6c9b8000 [    4K] rw-/rwx SM=COW  thread 0
__DATA                 00007fff6c9ed000-00007fff6ca29000 [  240K] rw-/rwx SM=COW  /usr/lib/dyld
__DATA                 00007fff79631000-00007fff79634000 [   12K] rw-/rwx SM=COW  /usr/lib/system/libxpc.dylib
__DATA                 00007fff796d1000-00007fff796d2000 [    4K] rw-/rwx SM=COW  /usr/lib/system/libsystem_blocks.dylib
__DATA                 00007fff796d2000-00007fff796e2000 [   64K] rw-/rwx SM=COW  /usr/lib/system/libsystem_c.dylib
__DATA                 00007fff79735000-00007fff7973b000 [   24K] rw-/rwx SM=COW  /usr/lib/system/libdispatch.dylib
__DATA                 00007fff79801000-00007fff79802000 [    4K] rw-/rw- SM=COW  /usr/lib/system/libunc.dylib
__DATA                 00007fff79882000-00007fff79883000 [    4K] rw-/rw- SM=COW  /usr/lib/system/libremovefile.dylib
__DATA                 00007fff79db2000-00007fff79db3000 [    4K] rw-/rwx SM=COW  /usr/lib/system/libdyld.dylib
__DATA                 00007fff79e14000-00007fff79e15000 [    4K] rw-/rwx SM=COW  /usr/lib/system/libsystem_sandbox.dylib
__DATA                 00007fff79ef2000-00007fff79ef3000 [    4K] rw-/rwx SM=COW  /usr/lib/system/libmacho.dylib
__DATA                 00007fff79ef3000-00007fff79ef6000 [   12K] rw-/rwx SM=COW  /usr/lib/system/libsystem_kernel.dylib
__DATA                 00007fff79f49000-00007fff79f4a000 [    4K] rw-/rwx SM=COW  /usr/lib/system/libsystem_dnssd.dylib
__DATA                 00007fff7a0c4000-00007fff7a0c7000 [   12K] rw-/rwx SM=COW  /usr/lib/system/libsystem_info.dylib
__DATA                 00007fff7a190000-00007fff7a191000 [    4K] rw-/rwx SM=COW  /usr/lib/system/libquarantine.dylib
__DATA                 00007fff7a1ca000-00007fff7a1cb000 [    4K] rw-/rwx SM=COW  /usr/lib/system/libkeymgr.dylib
__DATA                 00007fff7a1d4000-00007fff7a1d5000 [    4K] rw-/rwx SM=COW  /usr/lib/system/libcompiler_rt.dylib
__DATA                 00007fff7a2a4000-00007fff7a2a5000 [    4K] rw-/rw- SM=COW  /usr/lib/system/libdnsinfo.dylib
__DATA                 00007fff7a347000-00007fff7a348000 [    4K] rw-/rw- SM=COW  /usr/lib/system/libsystem_network.dylib
__DATA                 00007fff7a484000-00007fff7a485000 [    4K] rw-/rwx SM=COW  /usr/lib/system/liblaunch.dylib
__DATA                 00007fff7aab2000-00007fff7aab3000 [    4K] rw-/rw- SM=COW  /usr/lib/system/libcopyfile.dylib
```

```
__DATA                  00007fff7aabb000-00007fff7aac1000 [    24K] rw-/rw- SM=COW  /usr/lib/system/libcommonCrypto.dylib
__DATA                  00007fff7afb3000-00007fff7afb4000 [     4K] rw-/rw- SM=COW  /usr/lib/system/libsystem_notify.dylib
__DATA                  00007fff7b06e000-00007fff7b06f000 [     4K] rw-/rw- SM=COW  /usr/lib/libSystem.B.dylib
__DATA                  00007fff7b072000-00007fff7b073000 [     4K] rw-/rw- SM=COW  /usr/lib/system/libunwind.dylib
__DATA                  00007fff7b11c000-00007fff7b11d000 [     4K] rw-/rw- SM=COW  /usr/lib/system/libcache.dylib

==== Legend
SM=sharing mode:
        COW=copy_on_write PRV=private NUL=empty ALI=aliased
        SHM=shared ZER=zero_filled S/A=shared_alias

==== Summary for process 1883
ReadOnly portion of Libraries: Total=50.2M resident=12.5M(25%) swapped_out_or_unallocated=37.6M(75%)
Writable regions: Total=652.1M written=621.4M(95%) resident=487.1M(75%) swapped_out=154.8M(24%) unallocated=164.9M(25%)

REGION TYPE                     VIRTUAL
===========                     =======
MALLOC                           624.0M         see MALLOC ZONE table below
MALLOC guard page                  16K
MALLOC metadata                   216K
STACK GUARD                       56.0M
Stack                             10.5M
__DATA                            464K
__LINKEDIT                        47.7M
__TEXT                            2484K
shared memory                       8K
===========                     =======
TOTAL                            741.4M

                        VIRTUAL ALLOCATION      BYTES
MALLOC ZONE                SIZE      COUNT  ALLOCATED  % FULL
===========             =======  =========  =========  ======
DefaultMallocZone_0x10cdbb000   624.0M   2505033     611.6M     98%
```

Virtual Memory Map of process 1883 (App9)
Output report format: 2.2 -- 64-bit process

```
==== Non-writable regions for process 1883
__TEXT                  000000010cdb8000-000000010cdb9000 [     4K] r-x/rwx SM=COW  /Users/DumpAnalysis/Documents/AMCDA-
Dumps/Apps/App9/Build/Products/Release/App9
__LINKEDIT              000000010cdba000-000000010cdbb000 [     4K] r--/rwx SM=COW  /Users/DumpAnalysis/Documents/AMCDA-
Dumps/Apps/App9/Build/Products/Release/App9
MALLOC metadata         000000010cdbb000-000000010cdbc000 [     4K] r--/rwx SM=COW
MALLOC guard page       000000010cdbd000-000000010cdbe000 [     4K] ---/rwx SM=NUL
MALLOC guard page       000000010cdd3000-000000010cdd5000 [     8K] ---/rwx SM=NUL
MALLOC guard page       000000010cdea000-000000010cdeb000 [     4K] ---/rwx SM=NUL
MALLOC metadata         000000010cdeb000-000000010cdec000 [     4K] r--/rwx SM=COW
STACK GUARD             000000010cf00000-000000010cf01000 [     4K] ---/rwx SM=NUL  stack guard for thread 1
STACK GUARD             000000010cf83000-000000010cf84000 [     4K] ---/rwx SM=NUL  stack guard for thread 2
STACK GUARD             000000010d006000-000000010d007000 [     4K] ---/rwx SM=NUL  stack guard for thread 3
STACK GUARD             000000010d089000-000000010d08a000 [     4K] ---/rwx SM=NUL  stack guard for thread 4
STACK GUARD             000000010d10c000-000000010d10d000 [     4K] ---/rwx SM=NUL  stack guard for thread 5
STACK GUARD             00007fff689b8000-00007fff6c1b8000 [  56.0M] ---/rwx SM=NUL  stack guard for thread 0
__TEXT                  00007fff6c9b8000-00007fff6c9ed000 [   212K] r-x/rwx SM=COW  /usr/lib/dyld
__LINKEDIT              00007fff6ca29000-00007fff6ca3c000 [    76K] r--/rwx SM=COW  /usr/lib/dyld
__TEXT                  00007fff89663000-00007fff89681000 [   120K] r-x/r-x SM=COW  /usr/lib/system/libxpc.dylib
__TEXT                  00007fff899d9000-00007fff899db000 [     8K] r-x/r-x SM=COW  /usr/lib/system/libsystem_blocks.dylib
__TEXT                  00007fff899db000-00007fff89ab9000 [   888K] r-x/r-x SM=COW  /usr/lib/system/libsystem_c.dylib
__TEXT                  00007fff89c93000-00007fff89ca2000 [    60K] r-x/r-x SM=COW  /usr/lib/system/libdispatch.dylib
__TEXT                  00007fff8a261000-00007fff8a263000 [     8K] r-x/r-x SM=COW  /usr/lib/system/libunc.dylib
__TEXT                  00007fff8a754000-00007fff8a756000 [     8K] r-x/r-x SM=COW  /usr/lib/system/libremovefile.dylib
__TEXT                  00007fff8dd85000-00007fff8dd8a000 [    20K] r-x/r-x SM=COW  /usr/lib/system/libmathCommon.A.dylib
__TEXT                  00007fff8dd8a000-00007fff8dd8f000 [    20K] r-x/r-x SM=COW  /usr/lib/system/libdyld.dylib
__TEXT                  00007fff8e3b1000-00007fff8e3b3000 [     8K] r-x/r-x SM=COW  /usr/lib/system/libsystem_sandbox.dylib
__TEXT                  00007fff8ed60000-00007fff8ed67000 [    28K] r-x/r-x SM=COW  /usr/lib/system/libmacho.dylib
__TEXT                  00007fff8ed67000-00007fff8ed88000 [   132K] r-x/r-x SM=COW  /usr/lib/system/libsystem_kernel.dylib
__TEXT                  00007fff8ef1d000-00007fff8ef26000 [    36K] r-x/r-x SM=COW  /usr/lib/system/libsystem_dnssd.dylib
__TEXT                  00007fff8fa97000-00007fff8fad3000 [   240K] r-x/r-x SM=COW  /usr/lib/system/libsystem_info.dylib
__TEXT                  00007fff8feb9000-00007fff8febc000 [    12K] r-x/r-x SM=COW  /usr/lib/system/libquarantine.dylib
__TEXT                  00007fff90025000-00007fff90026000 [     4K] r-x/r-x SM=COW  /usr/lib/system/libkeymgr.dylib
__TEXT                  00007fff9004e000-00007fff90054000 [    24K] r-x/r-x SM=COW  /usr/lib/system/libcompiler_rt.dylib
__TEXT                  00007fff9098b000-00007fff9098d000 [     8K] r-x/r-x SM=COW  /usr/lib/system/libdnsinfo.dylib
__TEXT                  00007fff91199000-00007fff9119f000 [    24K] r-x/r-x SM=COW  /usr/lib/system/libsystem_network.dylib
__TEXT                  00007fff91c14000-00007fff91c1f000 [    44K] r-x/r-x SM=COW  /usr/lib/system/liblaunch.dylib
__TEXT                  00007fff94a73000-00007fff94a7b000 [    32K] r-x/r-x SM=COW  /usr/lib/system/libcopyfile.dylib
__TEXT                  00007fff94abc000-00007fff94aff000 [   268K] r-x/r-x SM=COW  /usr/lib/system/libcommonCrypto.dylib
__TEXT                  00007fff95880000-00007fff9588a000 [    40K] r-x/r-x SM=COW  /usr/lib/system/libsystem_notify.dylib
__TEXT                  00007fff95fe7000-00007fff96015000 [   184K] r-x/r-x SM=COW  /usr/lib/libSystem.B.dylib
__TEXT                  00007fff960fa000-00007fff96101000 [    28K] r-x/r-x SM=COW  /usr/lib/system/libunwind.dylib
__TEXT                  00007fff96693000-00007fff96699000 [    24K] r-x/r-x SM=COW  /usr/lib/system/libcache.dylib
__LINKEDIT              00007fff967f7000-00007fff997a1000 [  47.7M] r--/r-- SM=COW  /usr/lib/system/libxpc.dylib
shared memory           00007ffffffe00000-00007ffffffe02000 [     8K] r-x/r-x SM=SHM
```

```
==== Writable regions for process 1883
__DATA               000000010cdb9000-000000010cdba000 [    4K] rw-/rwx SM=PRV  /Users/DumpAnalysis/Documents/AMCDA-
Dumps/Apps/App9/Build/Products/Release/App9
MALLOC metadata      000000010cdbc000-000000010cdbd000 [    4K] rw-/rwx SM=PRV
MALLOC metadata      000000010cdbe000-000000010cdd3000 [   84K] rw-/rwx SM=PRV
MALLOC metadata      000000010cdd5000-000000010cdea000 [   84K] rw-/rwx SM=COW
MALLOC metadata      000000010cdec000-000000010cdfd000 [   68K] rw-/rwx SM=PRV
MALLOC_TINY          000000010ce00000-000000010cf00000 [ 1024K] rw-/rwx SM=COW  DefaultMallocZone_0x10cdbb000
Stack                000000010cf01000-000000010cf83000 [  520K] rw-/rwx SM=PRV  thread 1
Stack                000000010cf84000-000000010d006000 [  520K] rw-/rwx SM=PRV  thread 2
Stack                000000010d007000-000000010d089000 [  520K] rw-/rwx SM=PRV  thread 3
Stack                000000010d08a000-000000010d10c000 [  520K] rw-/rwx SM=PRV  thread 4
Stack                000000010d10d000-000000010d18f000 [  520K] rw-/rwx SM=PRV  thread 5
MALLOC_TINY          00007fa0db400000-00007fa0e9100000 [221.0M] rw-/rwx SM=PRV  DefaultMallocZone_0x10cdbb000
MALLOC_TINY          00007fa0eb400000-00007fa0fb300000 [255.0M] rw-/rwx SM=PRV  DefaultMallocZone_0x10cdbb000
MALLOC_TINY          00007fa0fb400000-00007fa100800000 [ 84.0M] rw-/rwx SM=COW  DefaultMallocZone_0x10cdbb000
MALLOC_TINY          00007fa100800000-00007fa100a00000 [ 2048K] rw-/rwx SM=PRV  DefaultMallocZone_0x10cdbb000
MALLOC_TINY          00007fa100a00000-00007fa101400000 [ 10.0M] rw-/rwx SM=COW  DefaultMallocZone_0x10cdbb000
MALLOC_TINY          00007fa101400000-00007fa101500000 [ 1024K] rw-/rwx SM=PRV  DefaultMallocZone_0x10cdbb000
MALLOC_TINY          00007fa101500000-00007fa101e00000 [ 9216K] rw-/rwx SM=COW  DefaultMallocZone_0x10cdbb000
MALLOC_TINY          00007fa101e00000-00007fa102100000 [ 3072K] rw-/rwx SM=PRV  DefaultMallocZone_0x10cdbb000
MALLOC_TINY          00007fa102100000-00007fa102200000 [ 1024K] rw-/rwx SM=COW  DefaultMallocZone_0x10cdbb000
MALLOC_TINY          00007fa102200000-00007fa10b300000 [145.0M] rw-/rwx SM=PRV  DefaultMallocZone_0x10cdbb000
MALLOC_TINY          00007fa10b400000-00007fa12b300000 [511.0M] rw-/rwx SM=COW  DefaultMallocZone_0x10cdbb000
Stack                00007fff6c1b8000-00007fff6c9b7000 [ 8188K] rw-/rwx SM=ZER  thread 0
Stack                00007fff6c9b7000-00007fff6c9b8000 [    4K] rw-/rwx SM=COW  thread 0
__DATA               00007fff6c9ed000-00007fff6ca29000 [  240K] rw-/rwx SM=COW  /usr/lib/dyld
__DATA               00007fff79631000-00007fff79634000 [   12K] rw-/rwx SM=COW  /usr/lib/system/libxpc.dylib
__DATA               00007fff796d1000-00007fff796d2000 [    4K] rw-/rwx SM=COW  /usr/lib/system/libsystem_blocks.dylib
__DATA               00007fff796d2000-00007fff796e2000 [   64K] rw-/rwx SM=COW  /usr/lib/system/libsystem_c.dylib
__DATA               00007fff79735000-00007fff7973b000 [   24K] rw-/rwx SM=COW  /usr/lib/system/libdispatch.dylib
__DATA               00007fff79801000-00007fff79802000 [    4K] rw-/rw- SM=COW  /usr/lib/system/libunc.dylib
__DATA               00007fff79882000-00007fff79883000 [    4K] rw-/rw- SM=COW  /usr/lib/system/libremovefile.dylib
__DATA               00007fff79db2000-00007fff79db3000 [    4K] rw-/rwx SM=COW  /usr/lib/system/libdyld.dylib
__DATA               00007fff79e14000-00007fff79e15000 [    4K] rw-/rwx SM=COW  /usr/lib/system/libsystem_sandbox.dylib
__DATA               00007fff79ef2000-00007fff79ef3000 [    4K] rw-/rwx SM=COW  /usr/lib/system/libmacho.dylib
__DATA               00007fff79ef3000-00007fff79ef6000 [   12K] rw-/rwx SM=COW  /usr/lib/system/libsystem_kernel.dylib
__DATA               00007fff79f49000-00007fff79f4a000 [    4K] rw-/rwx SM=COW  /usr/lib/system/libsystem_dnssd.dylib
__DATA               00007fff7a0c4000-00007fff7a0c7000 [   12K] rw-/rwx SM=COW  /usr/lib/system/libsystem_info.dylib
__DATA               00007fff7a190000-00007fff7a191000 [    4K] rw-/rwx SM=COW  /usr/lib/system/libquarantine.dylib
__DATA               00007fff7a1ca000-00007fff7a1cb000 [    4K] rw-/rwx SM=COW  /usr/lib/system/libkeymgr.dylib
__DATA               00007fff7a1d4000-00007fff7a1d5000 [    4K] rw-/rwx SM=COW  /usr/lib/system/libcompiler_rt.dylib
__DATA               00007fff7a2a4000-00007fff7a2a5000 [    4K] rw-/rw- SM=COW  /usr/lib/system/libdnsinfo.dylib
__DATA               00007fff7a347000-00007fff7a348000 [    4K] rw-/rw- SM=COW  /usr/lib/system/libsystem_network.dylib
__DATA               00007fff7a484000-00007fff7a485000 [    4K] rw-/rwx SM=COW  /usr/lib/system/liblaunch.dylib
__DATA               00007fff7aab2000-00007fff7aab3000 [    4K] rw-/rw- SM=COW  /usr/lib/system/libcopyfile.dylib
__DATA               00007fff7aabb000-00007fff7aac1000 [   24K] rw-/rw- SM=COW  /usr/lib/system/libcommonCrypto.dylib
__DATA               00007fff7afb3000-00007fff7afb4000 [    4K] rw-/rw- SM=COW  /usr/lib/system/libsystem_notify.dylib
__DATA               00007fff7b06e000-00007fff7b06f000 [    4K] rw-/rw- SM=COW  /usr/lib/libSystem.B.dylib
__DATA               00007fff7b072000-00007fff7b073000 [    4K] rw-/rw- SM=COW  /usr/lib/system/libunwind.dylib
__DATA               00007fff7b11c000-00007fff7b11d000 [    4K] rw-/rw- SM=COW  /usr/lib/system/libcache.dylib

==== Legend
SM=sharing mode:
        COW=copy_on_write PRV=private NUL=empty ALI=aliased
        SHM=shared ZER=zero_filled S/A=shared_alias

==== Summary for process 1883
ReadOnly portion of Libraries: Total=50.2M resident=12.5M(25%) swapped_out_or_unallocated=37.6M(75%)
Writable regions: Total=1.2G written=625.5M(49%) resident=450.2M(35%) swapped_out=811.8M(64%) unallocated=820.7M(65%)


REGION TYPE                      VIRTUAL
===========                      =======
MALLOC                           1.2G        see MALLOC ZONE table below
MALLOC guard page                16K
MALLOC metadata                  248K
STACK GUARD                      56.0M
Stack                            10.5M
__DATA                           464K
__LINKEDIT                       47.7M
__TEXT                           2484K
shared memory                    8K
===========                      =======
TOTAL                            1.3G


                               VIRTUAL ALLOCATION    BYTES
MALLOC ZONE                      SIZE    COUNT   ALLOCATED  % FULL
===========                      =======  =========  =========  ======
DefaultMallocZone_0x10cdbb000    1.2G     5005033    1.2G       98%
```

247

Exercise A9 (LLDB)

- **Goal:** Learn how to identify heap leaks

- **Patterns:** Heap Leak, Execution Residue, Module Hint

- \AMCDA-Dumps\Exercise-A9-LLDB.pdf

Goal: Learn how to identify heap leaks

Patterns: Heap Leak, Execution Residue, Module Hint

1.   Identify heap memory consumption from the diagnostic report App9_1883.crash:

```
Process:        App9 [1883]
Path:           /Users/USER/Documents/*/App9
Identifier:     App9
Version:        ??? (???)
Code Type:      X86-64 (Native)
Parent Process: bash [223]

Date/Time:      2012-07-29 15:16:39.131 +0100
OS Version:     Mac OS X 10.7.4 (11E53)
Report Version: 9


Crashed Thread: 0  Dispatch queue: com.apple.main-thread


Exception Type:  EXC_CRASH (SIGABRT)
Exception Codes: 0x0000000000000000, 0x0000000000000000

Thread 0 Crashed:: Dispatch queue: com.apple.main-thread
0   libsystem_kernel.dylib          0x00007fff8ed7de42 __semwait_signal + 10
1   libsystem_c.dylib               0x00007fff899dfdea nanosleep + 164
2   libsystem_c.dylib               0x00007fff899dfc2c sleep + 61
3   libsystem_c.dylib               0x00007fff899dfc08 sleep + 25
4   App9                            0x000000010cdb8bc3 main + 195
5   App9                            0x000000010cdb87c4 start + 52

Thread 1:
0   libsystem_kernel.dylib          0x00007fff8ed7de42 __semwait_signal + 10
1   libsystem_c.dylib               0x00007fff899dfdea nanosleep + 164
2   libsystem_c.dylib               0x00007fff899dfc2c sleep + 61
3   libsystem_c.dylib               0x00007fff899dfc08 sleep + 25
4   App9                            0x000000010cdb8942 bar_one + 18
5   App9                            0x000000010cdb8959 foo_one + 9
6   App9                            0x000000010cdb8971 thread_one + 17
7   libsystem_c.dylib               0x00007fff89a298bf _pthread_start + 335
8   libsystem_c.dylib               0x00007fff89a2cb75 thread_start + 13

Thread 2:
0   libsystem_kernel.dylib          0x00007fff8ed7de42 __semwait_signal + 10
1   libsystem_c.dylib               0x00007fff899dfdea nanosleep + 164
2   libsystem_c.dylib               0x00007fff899dfc2c sleep + 61
3   libsystem_c.dylib               0x00007fff899dfc08 sleep + 25
4   App9                            0x000000010cdb88f3 procB + 51
5   App9                            0x000000010cdb8924 procA + 36
6   App9                            0x000000010cdb8999 bar_two + 9
7   App9                            0x000000010cdb89a9 foo_two + 9
8   App9                            0x000000010cdb89c1 thread_two + 17
9   libsystem_c.dylib               0x00007fff89a298bf _pthread_start + 335
10  libsystem_c.dylib               0x00007fff89a2cb75 thread_start + 13

Thread 3:
0   libsystem_kernel.dylib          0x00007fff8ed7de42 __semwait_signal + 10
1   libsystem_c.dylib               0x00007fff899dfdea nanosleep + 164
2   libsystem_c.dylib               0x00007fff899dfc2c sleep + 61
3   libsystem_c.dylib               0x00007fff899dfc08 sleep + 25
4   App9                            0x000000010cdb89f2 bar_three + 18
5   App9                            0x000000010cdb8a09 foo_three + 9
6   App9                            0x000000010cdb8a21 thread_three + 17
7   libsystem_c.dylib               0x00007fff89a298bf _pthread_start + 335
8   libsystem_c.dylib               0x00007fff89a2cb75 thread_start + 13
```

```
Thread 4:
0   libsystem_kernel.dylib          0x00007fff8ed7de42 __semwait_signal + 10
1   libsystem_c.dylib               0x00007fff899dfdea nanosleep + 164
2   libsystem_c.dylib               0x00007fff899dfc2c sleep + 61
3   libsystem_c.dylib               0x00007fff899dfc08 sleep + 25
4   App9                            0x000000010cdb8a52 bar_four + 18
5   App9                            0x000000010cdb8a69 foo_four + 9
6   App9                            0x000000010cdb8a81 thread_four + 17
7   libsystem_c.dylib               0x00007fff89a298bf _pthread_start + 335
8   libsystem_c.dylib               0x00007fff89a2cb75 thread_start + 13

Thread 5:
0   libsystem_kernel.dylib          0x00007fff8ed7de42 __semwait_signal + 10
1   libsystem_c.dylib               0x00007fff899dfdea nanosleep + 164
2   libsystem_c.dylib               0x00007fff899dfc2c sleep + 61
3   libsystem_c.dylib               0x00007fff899dfc08 sleep + 25
4   App9                            0x000000010cdb8ab2 bar_five + 18
5   App9                            0x000000010cdb8ac9 foo_five + 9
6   App9                            0x000000010cdb8ae1 thread_five + 17
7   libsystem_c.dylib               0x00007fff89a298bf _pthread_start + 335
8   libsystem_c.dylib               0x00007fff89a2cb75 thread_start + 13

Thread 0 crashed with X86 Thread State (64-bit):
   rax: 0x0000000000000004  rbx: 0x00007fff6c9b7a28  rcx: 0x00007fff6c9b79e8  rdx: 0x0000000000000001
   rdi: 0x0000000000000c03  rsi: 0x0000000000000000  rbp: 0x00007fff6c9b7a10  rsp: 0x00007fff6c9b79e8
    r8: 0x000000007fffffff   r9: 0x0000000000000000  r10: 0x0000000000000001  r11: 0xffffff80002da8d0
   r12: 0x0000000000000000  r13: 0x0000000000000000  r14: 0x00007fff6c9b7a38  r15: 0x0000000000000000
   rip: 0x00007fff8ed7de42  rfl: 0x0000000000000247  cr2: 0x000000010d18e880
Logical CPU: 0

Binary Images:
       0x10cdb8000 -        0x10cdb8ff7 +App9 (??? - ???) <BC6060DB-9637-3D3B-A78C-3A46AD6DC83C>
/Users/USER/Documents/*/App9
    0x7fff6c9b8000 -        0x7fff6c9ecbaf  dyld (195.6 - ???) <0CD1B35B-A28F-32DA-B72E-452EAD609613> /usr/lib/dyld
    0x7fff89663000 -        0x7fff89680fff  libxpc.dylib (77.19.0 - compatibility 1.0.0) <9F57891B-D7EF-3050-BEDD-
21E7C6668248> /usr/lib/system/libxpc.dylib
    0x7fff899d9000 -        0x7fff899daff7  libsystem_blocks.dylib (53.0.0 - compatibility 1.0.0) <8BCA214A-8992-34B2-
A8B9-B74DEACA1869> /usr/lib/system/libsystem_blocks.dylib
    0x7fff899db000 -        0x7fff89ab8fef  libsystem_c.dylib (763.13.0 - compatibility 1.0.0) <41B43515-2806-3FBC-ACF1-
A16F35B7E290> /usr/lib/system/libsystem_c.dylib
    0x7fff89c93000 -        0x7fff89ca1fff  libdispatch.dylib (187.9.0 - compatibility 1.0.0) <1D5BE322-A9B9-3BCE-8FAC-
076FB07CF54A> /usr/lib/system/libdispatch.dylib
    0x7fff8a261000 -        0x7fff8a262fff  libunc.dylib (24.0.0 - compatibility 1.0.0) <337960EE-0A85-3DD0-A760-
7134CF4C0AFF> /usr/lib/system/libunc.dylib
    0x7fff8a754000 -        0x7fff8a755ff7  libremovefile.dylib (21.1.0 - compatibility 1.0.0) <739E6C83-AA52-3C6C-A680-
B37FE2888A04> /usr/lib/system/libremovefile.dylib
    0x7fff8dd85000 -        0x7fff8dd89fff  libmathCommon.A.dylib (2026.0.0 - compatibility 1.0.0) <FF83AFF7-42B2-306E-
90AF-D539C51A4542> /usr/lib/system/libmathCommon.A.dylib
    0x7fff8dd8a000 -        0x7fff8dd8efff  libdyld.dylib (195.5.0 - compatibility 1.0.0) <380C3F44-0CA7-3514-8080-
46D1C9DF4FCD> /usr/lib/system/libdyld.dylib
    0x7fff8e3b1000 -        0x7fff8e3b2ff7  libsystem_sandbox.dylib (??? - ???) <96D38E74-F18F-3CCB-A20B-E8E3ADC4E166>
/usr/lib/system/libsystem_sandbox.dylib
    0x7fff8ed60000 -        0x7fff8ed66fff  libmacho.dylib (800.0.0 - compatibility 1.0.0) <165514D7-1BFA-38EF-A151-
676DCD21FB64> /usr/lib/system/libmacho.dylib
    0x7fff8ed67000 -        0x7fff8ed87fff  libsystem_kernel.dylib (1699.26.8 - compatibility 1.0.0) <1DDC0B0F-DB2A-34D6-
895D-E5B2B5618946> /usr/lib/system/libsystem_kernel.dylib
    0x7fff8ef1d000 -        0x7fff8ef25fff  libsystem_dnssd.dylib (??? - ???) <D9BB1F87-A42B-3CBC-9DC2-FC07FCEF0016>
/usr/lib/system/libsystem_dnssd.dylib
    0x7fff8fa97000 -        0x7fff8fad2fff  libsystem_info.dylib (??? - ???) <35F90252-2AE1-32C5-8D34-782C614D9639>
/usr/lib/system/libsystem_info.dylib
    0x7fff8feb9000 -        0x7fff8febbfff  libquarantine.dylib (36.6.0 - compatibility 1.0.0) <0EBF714B-4B69-3E1F-9A7D-
6BBC2AACB310> /usr/lib/system/libquarantine.dylib
    0x7fff90025000 -        0x7fff90025fff  libkeymgr.dylib (23.0.0 - compatibility 1.0.0) <61EFED6A-A407-301E-B454-
CD18314F0075> /usr/lib/system/libkeymgr.dylib
    0x7fff9004e000 -        0x7fff90053fff  libcompiler_rt.dylib (6.0.0 - compatibility 1.0.0) <98ECD5F6-E85C-32A5-98CD-
8911230CB66A> /usr/lib/system/libcompiler_rt.dylib
    0x7fff9098b000 -        0x7fff9098cfff  libdnsinfo.dylib (395.11.0 - compatibility 1.0.0) <853BAAA5-270F-3FDC-B025-
D448DB72E1C3> /usr/lib/system/libdnsinfo.dylib
    0x7fff91199000 -        0x7fff9119eff7  libsystem_network.dylib (??? - ???) <5DE7024E-1D2D-34A2-80F4-08326331A75B>
/usr/lib/system/libsystem_network.dylib
    0x7fff91c14000 -        0x7fff91c1eff7  liblaunch.dylib (392.38.0 - compatibility 1.0.0) <6ECB7F19-B384-32C1-8652-
2463C1CF4815> /usr/lib/system/liblaunch.dylib
    0x7fff94a73000 -        0x7fff94a7afff  libcopyfile.dylib (85.1.0 - compatibility 1.0.0) <0AB51EE2-E914-358C-AC19-
47BC024BDAE7> /usr/lib/system/libcopyfile.dylib
    0x7fff94abc000 -        0x7fff94afeff7  libcommonCrypto.dylib (55010.0.0 - compatibility 1.0.0) <BB770C22-8C57-365A-
8716-4A3C36AE7BFB> /usr/lib/system/libcommonCrypto.dylib
```

```
    0x7fff95880000 -     0x7fff95889ff7  libsystem_notify.dylib (80.1.0 - compatibility 1.0.0) <A4D651E3-D1C6-3934-
AD49-7A104FD14596> /usr/lib/system/libsystem_notify.dylib
    0x7fff95fe7000 -     0x7fff96014fe7  libSystem.B.dylib (159.1.0 - compatibility 1.0.0) <7BEBB139-50BB-3112-947A-
F4AA168F991C> /usr/lib/libSystem.B.dylib
    0x7fff960fa000 -     0x7fff96100ff7  libunwind.dylib (30.0.0 - compatibility 1.0.0) <1E9C6C8C-CBE8-3F4B-A5B5-
E03E3AB53231> /usr/lib/system/libunwind.dylib
    0x7fff96693000 -     0x7fff96698fff  libcache.dylib (47.0.0 - compatibility 1.0.0) <1571C3AB-BCB2-38CD-B3B2-
C5FC3F927C6A> /usr/lib/system/libcache.dylib

External Modification Summary:
  Calls made by other processes targeting this process:
    task_for_pid: 4
    thread_create: 0
    thread_set_state: 0
  Calls made by this process:
    task_for_pid: 0
    thread_create: 0
    thread_set_state: 0
  Calls made by all processes on this machine:
    task_for_pid: 3111
    thread_create: 0
    thread_set_state: 0

VM Region Summary:
ReadOnly portion of Libraries: Total=50.2M resident=50.2M(100%) swapped_out_or_unallocated=0K(0%)
Writable regions: Total=1.3G written=9348K(1%) resident=724.9M(57%) swapped_out=557.4M(44%) unallocated=556.0M(43%)

REGION TYPE                 VIRTUAL
===========                 =======
MALLOC                         1.2G
Stack                         66.6M
__DATA                         464K
__LINKEDIT                    47.7M
__TEXT                        2484K
shared memory                   12K
===========                 =======
TOTAL                          1.3G
```

2.   Load a core dump core.1883 and App9 executable:

$ lldb -c ~/Documents/AMCDA-Dumps/core.1883 -f ~/Documents/AMCDA-Dumps/Apps/App9/Build/Products/Release/App9

```
error: core.1883 is a corrupt mach-o file: load command 1289 LC_SEGMENT_64 has a fileoff +
filesize (0x63ade000) that extends beyond the end of the file (0x63adc000), the segment will be
truncated
Core file '/Users/DumpAnalysis/Documents/AMCDA-Dumps/core.1883' (x86_64) was loaded.
Process 0 stopped
* thread #1: tid = 0x0000, 0x00007fff8ed7de42 libsystem_kernel.dylib`__semwait_signal + 10,
stop reason = signal SIGSTOP
    frame #0: 0x00007fff8ed7de42 libsystem_kernel.dylib`__semwait_signal + 10
libsystem_kernel.dylib`__semwait_signal + 10:
-> 0x7fff8ed7de42:  jae     0x7fff8ed7de49            ; __semwait_signal + 17
   0x7fff8ed7de44:  jmpq    0x7fff8ed7effc            ; cerror
   0x7fff8ed7de49:  ret
   0x7fff8ed7de4a:  nop
  thread #2: tid = 0x0001, 0x00007fff8ed7de42 libsystem_kernel.dylib`__semwait_signal + 10,
stop reason = signal SIGSTOP
    frame #0: 0x00007fff8ed7de42 libsystem_kernel.dylib`__semwait_signal + 10
libsystem_kernel.dylib`__semwait_signal + 10:
-> 0x7fff8ed7de42:  jae     0x7fff8ed7de49            ; __semwait_signal + 17
   0x7fff8ed7de44:  jmpq    0x7fff8ed7effc            ; cerror
   0x7fff8ed7de49:  ret
```

```
0x7fff8ed7de4a:   nop
  thread #3: tid = 0x0002, 0x00007fff8ed7de42 libsystem_kernel.dylib`__semwait_signal + 10,
stop reason = signal SIGSTOP
    frame #0: 0x00007fff8ed7de42 libsystem_kernel.dylib`__semwait_signal + 10
libsystem_kernel.dylib`__semwait_signal + 10:
-> 0x7fff8ed7de42:   jae    0x7fff8ed7de49            ; __semwait_signal + 17
   0x7fff8ed7de44:   jmpq   0x7fff8ed7effc            ; cerror
   0x7fff8ed7de49:   ret
   0x7fff8ed7de4a:   nop
  thread #4: tid = 0x0003, 0x00007fff8ed7de42 libsystem_kernel.dylib`__semwait_signal + 10,
stop reason = signal SIGSTOP
    frame #0: 0x00007fff8ed7de42 libsystem_kernel.dylib`__semwait_signal + 10
libsystem_kernel.dylib`__semwait_signal + 10:
-> 0x7fff8ed7de42:   jae    0x7fff8ed7de49            ; __semwait_signal + 17
   0x7fff8ed7de44:   jmpq   0x7fff8ed7effc            ; cerror
   0x7fff8ed7de49:   ret
   0x7fff8ed7de4a:   nop
  thread #5: tid = 0x0004, 0x00007fff8ed7de42 libsystem_kernel.dylib`__semwait_signal + 10,
stop reason = signal SIGSTOP
    frame #0: 0x00007fff8ed7de42 libsystem_kernel.dylib`__semwait_signal + 10
libsystem_kernel.dylib`__semwait_signal + 10:
-> 0x7fff8ed7de42:   jae    0x7fff8ed7de49            ; __semwait_signal + 17
   0x7fff8ed7de44:   jmpq   0x7fff8ed7effc            ; cerror
   0x7fff8ed7de49:   ret
   0x7fff8ed7de4a:   nop
  thread #6: tid = 0x0005, 0x00007fff8ed7de42 libsystem_kernel.dylib`__semwait_signal + 10,
stop reason = signal SIGSTOP
    frame #0: 0x00007fff8ed7de42 libsystem_kernel.dylib`__semwait_signal + 10
libsystem_kernel.dylib`__semwait_signal + 10:
-> 0x7fff8ed7de42:   jae    0x7fff8ed7de49            ; __semwait_signal + 17
   0x7fff8ed7de44:   jmpq   0x7fff8ed7effc            ; cerror
   0x7fff8ed7de49:   ret
   0x7fff8ed7de4a:   nop
```

3.   Identify "section stream":

```
(lldb) image dump sections core.1883
Sections for '/Users/DumpAnalysis/Documents/AMCDA-Dumps/core.1883' (x86_64):
  SectID    Type            Load Address                                      File Off.  File Size  Flags       Section Name
  --------- --------------- ------------------------------------------------- ---------- ---------- ---------- ----------------------------
  0x00000100 container       [0x000000010cdb8000-0x000000010cdb9000)*  0x00018000 0x00001000 0x0000ed81 core.1883.
  0x00000200 container       [0x000000010cdb9000-0x000000010cdba000)*  0x00019000 0x00001000 0x00000000 core.1883.
  0x00000300 container       [0x000000010cdba000-0x000000010cdbb000)*  0x0001a000 0x00001000 0x00000000 core.1883.
  0x00000400 container       [0x000000010cdbb000-0x000000010cdbc000)*  0x0001b000 0x00001000 0x72006100 core.1883.
  0x00000500 container       [0x000000010cdbc000-0x000000010cdbd000)*  0x0001c000 0x00001000 0x00000000 core.1883.
  0x00000600 container       [0x000000010cdbd000-0x000000010cdbe000)*  0x0001d000 0x00001000 0x00000000 core.1883.
  0x00000700 container       [0x000000010cdbe000-0x000000010cdd3000)*  0x0001e000 0x00015000 0x00000000 core.1883.
  0x00000800 container       [0x000000010cdd3000-0x000000010cdd4000)*  0x00033000 0x00001000 0x00008600 core.1883.
  0x00000900 container       [0x000000010cdd4000-0x000000010cdd5000)*  0x00034000 0x00001000 0x00000000 core.1883.
  0x00000a00 container       [0x000000010cdd5000-0x000000010cdea000)*  0x00035000 0x00015000 0x00000000 core.1883.
  0x00000b00 container       [0x000000010cdea000-0x000000010cdeb000)*  0x0004a000 0x00001000 0x00000000 core.1883.
  0x00000c00 container       [0x000000010cdeb000-0x000000010cdec000)*  0x0004b000 0x00001000 0x00000000 core.1883.
  0x00000d00 container       [0x000000010cdec000-0x000000010cdf5000)*  0x0004c000 0x00009000 0x77000000 core.1883.
  0x00000e00 container       [0x000000010cdf5000-0x000000010cdfd000)*  0x00055000 0x00008000 0x00000000 core.1883.
  0x00000f00 container       [0x000000010ce00000-0x000000010cf00000)*  0x0005d000 0x00100000 0x00000000 core.1883.
  0x00001000 container       [0x000000010cf00000-0x000000010cf01000)*  0x0015d000 0x00001000 0x00000000 core.1883.
  0x00001100 container       [0x000000010cf01000-0x000000010cf83000)*  0x0015e000 0x00082000 0x094d0900 core.1883.
  0x00001200 container       [0x000000010cf83000-0x000000010cf84000)*  0x001e0000 0x00001000 0x00000000 core.1883.
  0x00001300 container       [0x000000010cf84000-0x000000010d006000)*  0x001e1000 0x00082000 0x00000000 core.1883.
  0x00001400 container       [0x000000010d006000-0x000000010d007000)*  0x00263000 0x00001000 0x00000000 core.1883.
  0x00001500 container       [0x000000010d007000-0x000000010d089000)*  0x00264000 0x00082000 0xaef039cc core.1883.
  0x00001600 container       [0x000000010d089000-0x000000010d08a000)*  0x002e6000 0x00001000 0x00000000 core.1883.
```

252

```
0x00001700 container    [0x000000010d08a000-0x000000010d10c000)* 0x002e7000 0x00082000 0x00000000 core.1883.
0x00001800 container    [0x000000010d10c000-0x000000010d10d000)* 0x00369000 0x00001000 0x00000000 core.1883.
0x00001900 container    [0x000000010d10d000-0x000000010d18f000)* 0x0036a000 0x00082000 0x0000414e core.1883.
0x00001a00 container    [0x00007fa0db400000-0x00007fa0db500000)* 0x003ec000 0x00100000 0x00000000 core.1883.
0x00001b00 container    [0x00007fa0db500000-0x00007fa0db600000)* 0x004ec000 0x00100000 0x00000000 core.1883.
0x00001c00 container    [0x00007fa0db600000-0x00007fa0db700000)* 0x005ec000 0x00100000 0x00000000 core.1883.
0x00001d00 container    [0x00007fa0db700000-0x00007fa0db800000)* 0x006ec000 0x00100000 0x00000000 core.1883.
0x00001e00 container    [0x00007fa0db800000-0x00007fa0db900000)* 0x007ec000 0x00100000 0x00000000 core.1883.
0x00001f00 container    [0x00007fa0db900000-0x00007fa0dba00000)* 0x008ec000 0x00100000 0x03000000 core.1883.
0x00002000 container    [0x00007fa0dba00000-0x00007fa0dbb00000)* 0x009ec000 0x00100000 0x0600a000 core.1883.
0x00002100 container    [0x00007fa0dbb00000-0x00007fa0dbc00000)* 0x00aec000 0x00100000 0x00000000 core.1883.
0x00002200 container    [0x00007fa0dbc00000-0x00007fa0dbd00000)* 0x00bec000 0x00100000 0x00000000 core.1883.
0x00002300 container    [0x00007fa0dbd00000-0x00007fa0dbe00000)* 0x00cec000 0x00100000 0x00000000 core.1883.
0x00002400 container    [0x00007fa0dbe00000-0x00007fa0dbf00000)* 0x00dec000 0x00100000 0x73007500 core.1883.
0x00002500 container    [0x00007fa0dbf00000-0x00007fa0dc000000)* 0x00eec000 0x00100000 0x9d3bb9ca core.1883.
0x00002600 container    [0x00007fa0dc000000-0x00007fa0dc100000)* 0x00fec000 0x00100000 0x0000a200 core.1883.
0x00002700 container    [0x00007fa0dc100000-0x00007fa0dc200000)* 0x010ec000 0x00100000 0xf2c6418f core.1883.
0x00002800 container    [0x00007fa0dc200000-0x00007fa0dc300000)* 0x011ec000 0x00100000 0x00000000 core.1883.
0x00002900 container    [0x00007fa0dc300000-0x00007fa0dc400000)* 0x012ec000 0x00100000 0x00000000 core.1883.
0x00002a00 container    [0x00007fa0dc400000-0x00007fa0dc500000)* 0x013ec000 0x00100000 0x00000000 core.1883.
0x00002b00 container    [0x00007fa0dc500000-0x00007fa0dc600000)* 0x014ec000 0x00100000 0x00000000 core.1883.
0x00002c00 container    [0x00007fa0dc600000-0x00007fa0dc700000)* 0x015ec000 0x00100000 0x65006300 core.1883.
0x00002d00 container    [0x00007fa0dc700000-0x00007fa0dc800000)* 0x016ec000 0x00100000 0x934e0000 core.1883.
0x00002e00 container    [0x00007fa0dc800000-0x00007fa0dc900000)* 0x017ec000 0x00100000 0xa6f102ca core.1883.
0x00002f00 container    [0x00007fa0dc900000-0x00007fa0dca00000)* 0x018ec000 0x00100000 0x00000000 core.1883.
0x00003000 container    [0x00007fa0dca00000-0x00007fa0dcb00000)* 0x019ec000 0x00100000 0x00000000 core.1883.
0x00003100 container    [0x00007fa0dcb00000-0x00007fa0dcc00000)* 0x01aec000 0x00100000 0x00000000 core.1883.
0x00003200 container    [0x00007fa0dcc00000-0x00007fa0dcd00000)* 0x01bec000 0x00100000 0x78007800 core.1883.
0x00003300 container    [0x00007fa0dcd00000-0x00007fa0dce00000)* 0x01cec000 0x00100000 0x0d8b934e core.1883.
0x00003400 container    [0x00007fa0dce00000-0x00007fa0dcf00000)* 0x01dec000 0x00100000 0x00000000 core.1883.
0x00003500 container    [0x00007fa0dcf00000-0x00007fa0dd000000)* 0x01eec000 0x00100000 0x00000000 core.1883.
0x00003600 container    [0x00007fa0dd000000-0x00007fa0dd100000)* 0x01fec000 0x00100000 0x78007800 core.1883.
0x00003700 container    [0x00007fa0dd100000-0x00007fa0dd200000)* 0x020ec000 0x00100000 0x6a006f00 core.1883.
0x00003800 container    [0x00007fa0dd200000-0x00007fa0dd300000)* 0x021ec000 0x00100000 0x0d8b934e core.1883.
0x00003900 container    [0x00007fa0dd300000-0x00007fa0dd400000)* 0x022ec000 0x00100000 0x6e004900 core.1883.
0x00003a00 container    [0x00007fa0dd400000-0x00007fa0dd500000)* 0x023ec000 0x00100000 0x00000000 core.1883.
0x00003b00 container    [0x00007fa0dd500000-0x00007fa0dd600000)* 0x024ec000 0x00100000 0x00000100 core.1883.
0x00003c00 container    [0x00007fa0dd600000-0x00007fa0dd700000)* 0x025ec000 0x00100000 0x00000000 core.1883.
0x00003d00 container    [0x00007fa0dd700000-0x00007fa0dd800000)* 0x026ec000 0x00100000 0x03000000 core.1883.
0x00003e00 container    [0x00007fa0dd800000-0x00007fa0dd900000)* 0x027ec000 0x00100000 0x00000000 core.1883.
0x00003f00 container    [0x00007fa0dd900000-0x00007fa0dda00000)* 0x028ec000 0x00100000 0xe4140216 core.1883.
0x00004000 container    [0x00007fa0dda00000-0x00007fa0ddb00000)* 0x029ec000 0x00100000 0x70007600 core.1883.
0x00004100 container    [0x00007fa0ddb00000-0x00007fa0ddc00000)* 0x02aec000 0x00100000 0x38cc3938 core.1883.
0x00004200 container    [0x00007fa0ddc00000-0x00007fa0ddd00000)* 0x02bec000 0x00100000 0xf61c0500 core.1883.
0x00004300 container    [0x00007fa0ddd00000-0x00007fa0dde00000)* 0x02cec000 0x00100000 0x07000000 core.1883.
0x00004400 container    [0x00007fa0dde00000-0x00007fa0ddf00000)* 0x02dec000 0x00100000 0x00000000 core.1883.
0x00004500 container    [0x00007fa0ddf00000-0x00007fa0de000000)* 0x02eec000 0x00100000 0x36003000 core.1883.
0x00004600 container    [0x00007fa0de000000-0x00007fa0de100000)* 0x02fec000 0x00100000 0x234f0000 core.1883.
0x00004700 container    [0x00007fa0de100000-0x00007fa0de200000)* 0x030ec000 0x00100000 0x74003000 core.1883.
0x00004800 container    [0x00007fa0de200000-0x00007fa0de300000)* 0x031ec000 0x00100000 0x00000000 core.1883.
0x00004900 container    [0x00007fa0de300000-0x00007fa0de400000)* 0x032ec000 0x00100000 0x6e005f00 core.1883.
0x00004a00 container    [0x00007fa0de400000-0x00007fa0de500000)* 0x033ec000 0x00100000 0x0000ed41 core.1883.
0x00004b00 container    [0x00007fa0de500000-0x00007fa0de600000)* 0x034ec000 0x00100000 0x73006300 core.1883.
0x00004c00 container    [0x00007fa0de600000-0x00007fa0de700000)* 0x035ec000 0x00100000 0x00000000 core.1883.
0x00004d00 container    [0x00007fa0de700000-0x00007fa0de800000)* 0x036ec000 0x00100000 0x70007600 core.1883.
0x00004e00 container    [0x00007fa0de800000-0x00007fa0de900000)* 0x037ec000 0x00100000 0xdbcbb7cb core.1883.
0x00004f00 container    [0x00007fa0de900000-0x00007fa0dea00000)* 0x038ec000 0x00100000 0xf71c0500 core.1883.
0x00005000 container    [0x00007fa0dea00000-0x00007fa0deb00000)* 0x039ec000 0x00100000 0x30003000 core.1883.
0x00005100 container    [0x00007fa0deb00000-0x00007fa0dec00000)* 0x03aec000 0x00100000 0x00000000 core.1883.
0x00005200 container    [0x00007fa0dec00000-0x00007fa0ded00000)* 0x03bec000 0x00100000 0x00000000 core.1883.
0x00005300 container    [0x00007fa0ded00000-0x00007fa0dee00000)* 0x03cec000 0x00100000 0x19000000 core.1883.
0x00005400 container    [0x00007fa0dee00000-0x00007fa0def00000)* 0x03dec000 0x00100000 0x00000000 core.1883.
0x00005500 container    [0x00007fa0def00000-0x00007fa0df000000)* 0x03eec000 0x00100000 0x75004200 core.1883.
0x00005600 container    [0x00007fa0df000000-0x00007fa0df100000)* 0x03fec000 0x00100000 0x00000000 core.1883.
0x00005700 container    [0x00007fa0df100000-0x00007fa0df200000)* 0x040ec000 0x00100000 0x00000000 core.1883.
0x00005800 container    [0x00007fa0df200000-0x00007fa0df300000)* 0x041ec000 0x00100000 0x00000000 core.1883.
0x00005900 container    [0x00007fa0df300000-0x00007fa0df400000)* 0x042ec000 0x00100000 0x69007300 core.1883.
0x00005a00 container    [0x00007fa0df400000-0x00007fa0df500000)* 0x043ec000 0x00100000 0x5d9264cb core.1883.
0x00005b00 container    [0x00007fa0df500000-0x00007fa0df600000)* 0x044ec000 0x00100000 0x00000000 core.1883.
0x00005c00 container    [0x00007fa0df600000-0x00007fa0df700000)* 0x045ec000 0x00100000 0x00000000 core.1883.
0x00005d00 container    [0x00007fa0df700000-0x00007fa0df800000)* 0x046ec000 0x00100000 0x00000000 core.1883.
0x00005e00 container    [0x00007fa0df800000-0x00007fa0df900000)* 0x047ec000 0x00100000 0x33003500 core.1883.
0x00005f00 container    [0x00007fa0df900000-0x00007fa0dfa00000)* 0x048ec000 0x00100000 0xe44f0000 core.1883.
0x00006000 container    [0x00007fa0dfa00000-0x00007fa0dfb00000)* 0x049ec000 0x00100000 0x00000000 core.1883.
0x00006100 container    [0x00007fa0dfb00000-0x00007fa0dfc00000)* 0x04aec000 0x00100000 0x00000000 core.1883.
0x00006200 container    [0x00007fa0dfc00000-0x00007fa0dfd00000)* 0x04bec000 0x00100000 0x63006e00 core.1883.
0x00006300 container    [0x00007fa0dfd00000-0x00007fa0dfe00000)* 0x04cec000 0x00100000 0x3d3838cc core.1883.
0x00006400 container    [0x00007fa0dfe00000-0x00007fa0dff00000)* 0x04dec000 0x00100000 0x00000000 core.1883.
0x00006500 container    [0x00007fa0dff00000-0x00007fa0e0000000)* 0x04eec000 0x00100000 0x00000000 core.1883.
0x00006600 container    [0x00007fa0e0000000-0x00007fa0e0100000)* 0x04fec000 0x00100000 0x00000000 core.1883.
0x00006700 container    [0x00007fa0e0100000-0x00007fa0e0200000)* 0x050ec000 0x00100000 0x65007400 core.1883.
0x00006800 container    [0x00007fa0e0200000-0x00007fa0e0300000)* 0x051ec000 0x00100000 0x00000000 core.1883.
0x00006900 container    [0x00007fa0e0300000-0x00007fa0e0400000)* 0x052ec000 0x00100000 0x65006700 core.1883.
0x00006a00 container    [0x00007fa0e0400000-0x00007fa0e0500000)* 0x053ec000 0x00100000 0x00000000 core.1883.
0x00006b00 container    [0x00007fa0e0500000-0x00007fa0e0600000)* 0x054ec000 0x00100000 0x00000000 core.1883.
0x00006c00 container    [0x00007fa0e0600000-0x00007fa0e0700000)* 0x055ec000 0x00100000 0x00000000 core.1883.
```

```
0x00006d00 container    [0x00007fa0e0700000-0x00007fa0e0800000)* 0x056ec000 0x00100000 0x70006100 core.1883.
0x00006e00 container    [0x00007fa0e0800000-0x00007fa0e0900000)* 0x057ec000 0x00100000 0x00000000 core.1883.
0x00006f00 container    [0x00007fa0e0900000-0x00007fa0e0a00000)* 0x058ec000 0x00100000 0x40000200 core.1883.
0x00007000 container    [0x00007fa0e0a00000-0x00007fa0e0b00000)* 0x059ec000 0x00100000 0x00000000 core.1883.
0x00007100 container    [0x00007fa0e0b00000-0x00007fa0e0c00000)* 0x05aec000 0x00100000 0x26000000 core.1883.
0x00007200 container    [0x00007fa0e0c00000-0x00007fa0e0d00000)* 0x05bec000 0x00100000 0x00000000 core.1883.
0x00007300 container    [0x00007fa0e0d00000-0x00007fa0e0e00000)* 0x05cec000 0x00100000 0x25002400 core.1883.
0x00007400 container    [0x00007fa0e0e00000-0x00007fa0e0f00000)* 0x05dec000 0x00100000 0x00000000 core.1883.
0x00007500 container    [0x00007fa0e0f00000-0x00007fa0e1000000)* 0x05eec000 0x00100000 0x06000000 core.1883.
0x00007600 container    [0x00007fa0e1000000-0x00007fa0e1100000)* 0x05fec000 0x00100000 0x6e006f00 core.1883.
0x00007700 container    [0x00007fa0e1100000-0x00007fa0e1200000)* 0x060ec000 0x00100000 0x0000051d core.1883.
0x00007800 container    [0x00007fa0e1200000-0x00007fa0e1300000)* 0x061ec000 0x00100000 0x6f006300 core.1883.
0x00007900 container    [0x00007fa0e1300000-0x00007fa0e1400000)* 0x062ec000 0x00100000 0x05000600 core.1883.
0x00007a00 container    [0x00007fa0e1400000-0x00007fa0e1500000)* 0x063ec000 0x00100000 0x72007400 core.1883.
0x00007b00 container    [0x00007fa0e1500000-0x00007fa0e1600000)* 0x064ec000 0x00100000 0x6c006900 core.1883.
0x00007c00 container    [0x00007fa0e1600000-0x00007fa0e1700000)* 0x065ec000 0x00100000 0x2e007400 core.1883.
0x00007d00 container    [0x00007fa0e1700000-0x00007fa0e1800000)* 0x066ec000 0x00100000 0x75006300 core.1883.
0x00007e00 container    [0x00007fa0e1800000-0x00007fa0e1900000)* 0x067ec000 0x00100000 0x01000000 core.1883.
0x00007f00 container    [0x00007fa0e1900000-0x00007fa0e1a00000)* 0x068ec000 0x00100000 0x00000000 core.1883.
0x00008000 container    [0x00007fa0e1a00000-0x00007fa0e1b00000)* 0x069ec000 0x00100000 0x00000000 core.1883.
0x00008100 container    [0x00007fa0e1b00000-0x00007fa0e1c00000)* 0x06aec000 0x00100000 0x9a000000 core.1883.
0x00008200 container    [0x00007fa0e1c00000-0x00007fa0e1d00000)* 0x06bec000 0x00100000 0x6c006900 core.1883.
0x00008300 container    [0x00007fa0e1d00000-0x00007fa0e1e00000)* 0x06cec000 0x00100000 0x69006600 core.1883.
0x00008400 container    [0x00007fa0e1e00000-0x00007fa0e1f00000)* 0x06dec000 0x00100000 0x00000400 core.1883.
0x00008500 container    [0x00007fa0e1f00000-0x00007fa0e2000000)* 0x06eec000 0x00100000 0x6c006f00 core.1883.
0x00008600 container    [0x00007fa0e2000000-0x00007fa0e2100000)* 0x06fec000 0x00100000 0x06007200 core.1883.
0x00008700 container    [0x00007fa0e2100000-0x00007fa0e2200000)* 0x070ec000 0x00100000 0x73006b00 core.1883.
0x00008800 container    [0x00007fa0e2200000-0x00007fa0e2300000)* 0x071ec000 0x00100000 0x2e006500 core.1883.
0x00008900 container    [0x00007fa0e2300000-0x00007fa0e2400000)* 0x072ec000 0x00100000 0xc9410000 core.1883.
0x00008a00 container    [0x00007fa0e2400000-0x00007fa0e2500000)* 0x073ec000 0x00100000 0x49007900 core.1883.
0x00008b00 container    [0x00007fa0e2500000-0x00007fa0e2600000)* 0x074ec000 0x00100000 0x00000000 core.1883.
0x00008c00 container    [0x00007fa0e2600000-0x00007fa0e2700000)* 0x075ec000 0x00100000 0x00000400 core.1883.
0x00008d00 container    [0x00007fa0e2700000-0x00007fa0e2800000)* 0x076ec000 0x00100000 0x0000391d core.1883.
0x00008e00 container    [0x00007fa0e2800000-0x00007fa0e2900000)* 0x077ec000 0x00100000 0x6c007000 core.1883.
0x00008f00 container    [0x00007fa0e2900000-0x00007fa0e2a00000)* 0x078ec000 0x00100000 0x00007300 core.1883.
0x00009000 container    [0x00007fa0e2a00000-0x00007fa0e2b00000)* 0x079ec000 0x00100000 0x00000000 core.1883.
0x00009100 container    [0x00007fa0e2b00000-0x00007fa0e2c00000)* 0x07aec000 0x00100000 0x00000000 core.1883.
0x00009200 container    [0x00007fa0e2c00000-0x00007fa0e2d00000)* 0x07bec000 0x00100000 0x00000000 core.1883.
0x00009300 container    [0x00007fa0e2d00000-0x00007fa0e2e00000)* 0x07cec000 0x00100000 0x00000000 core.1883.
0x00009400 container    [0x00007fa0e2e00000-0x00007fa0e2f00000)* 0x07dec000 0x00100000 0x00000000 core.1883.
0x00009500 container    [0x00007fa0e2f00000-0x00007fa0e3000000)* 0x07eec000 0x00100000 0x00000000 core.1883.
0x00009600 container    [0x00007fa0e3000000-0x00007fa0e3100000)* 0x07fec000 0x00100000 0x00000000 core.1883.
0x00009700 container    [0x00007fa0e3100000-0x00007fa0e3200000)* 0x080ec000 0x00100000 0x00000000 core.1883.
0x00009800 container    [0x00007fa0e3200000-0x00007fa0e3300000)* 0x081ec000 0x00100000 0x00000000 core.1883.
0x00009900 container    [0x00007fa0e3300000-0x00007fa0e3400000)* 0x082ec000 0x00100000 0x00000000 core.1883.
0x00009a00 container    [0x00007fa0e3400000-0x00007fa0e3500000)* 0x083ec000 0x00100000 0x00000000 core.1883.
0x00009b00 container    [0x00007fa0e3500000-0x00007fa0e3600000)* 0x084ec000 0x00100000 0x00000000 core.1883.
0x00009c00 container    [0x00007fa0e3600000-0x00007fa0e3700000)* 0x085ec000 0x00100000 0x00000000 core.1883.
0x00009d00 container    [0x00007fa0e3700000-0x00007fa0e3800000)* 0x086ec000 0x00100000 0x00000000 core.1883.
0x00009e00 container    [0x00007fa0e3800000-0x00007fa0e3900000)* 0x087ec000 0x00100000 0x00000000 core.1883.
0x00009f00 container    [0x00007fa0e3900000-0x00007fa0e3a00000)* 0x088ec000 0x00100000 0x00000000 core.1883.
0x0000a000 container    [0x00007fa0e3a00000-0x00007fa0e3b00000)* 0x089ec000 0x00100000 0x00000000 core.1883.
0x0000a100 container    [0x00007fa0e3b00000-0x00007fa0e3c00000)* 0x08aec000 0x00100000 0x00000000 core.1883.
0x0000a200 container    [0x00007fa0e3c00000-0x00007fa0e3d00000)* 0x08bec000 0x00100000 0x00000000 core.1883.
0x0000a300 container    [0x00007fa0e3d00000-0x00007fa0e3e00000)* 0x08cec000 0x00100000 0x00000000 core.1883.
0x0000a400 container    [0x00007fa0e3e00000-0x00007fa0e3f00000)* 0x08dec000 0x00100000 0x00000000 core.1883.
0x0000a500 container    [0x00007fa0e3f00000-0x00007fa0e4000000)* 0x08eec000 0x00100000 0x00000000 core.1883.
0x0000a600 container    [0x00007fa0e4000000-0x00007fa0e4100000)* 0x08fec000 0x00100000 0x00000000 core.1883.
0x0000a700 container    [0x00007fa0e4100000-0x00007fa0e4200000)* 0x090ec000 0x00100000 0x00000000 core.1883.
0x0000a800 container    [0x00007fa0e4200000-0x00007fa0e4300000)* 0x091ec000 0x00100000 0x00000000 core.1883.
0x0000a900 container    [0x00007fa0e4300000-0x00007fa0e4400000)* 0x092ec000 0x00100000 0x00000000 core.1883.
0x0000aa00 container    [0x00007fa0e4400000-0x00007fa0e4500000)* 0x093ec000 0x00100000 0x00000000 core.1883.
0x0000ab00 container    [0x00007fa0e4500000-0x00007fa0e4600000)* 0x094ec000 0x00100000 0x00000000 core.1883.
0x0000ac00 container    [0x00007fa0e4600000-0x00007fa0e4700000)* 0x095ec000 0x00100000 0x00000000 core.1883.
0x0000ad00 container    [0x00007fa0e4700000-0x00007fa0e4800000)* 0x096ec000 0x00100000 0x00000000 core.1883.
0x0000ae00 container    [0x00007fa0e4800000-0x00007fa0e4900000)* 0x097ec000 0x00100000 0x00000000 core.1883.
0x0000af00 container    [0x00007fa0e4900000-0x00007fa0e4a00000)* 0x098ec000 0x00100000 0x176817a2 core.1883.
0x0000b000 container    [0x00007fa0e4a00000-0x00007fa0e4b00000)* 0x099ec000 0x00100000 0x176e1826 core.1883.
0x0000b100 container    [0x00007fa0e4b00000-0x00007fa0e4c00000)* 0x09aec000 0x00100000 0xda051407 core.1883.
0x0000b200 container    [0x00007fa0e4c00000-0x00007fa0e4d00000)* 0x09bec000 0x00100000 0x01007300 core.1883.
0x0000b300 container    [0x00007fa0e4d00000-0x00007fa0e4e00000)* 0x09cec000 0x00100000 0x00000d8b core.1883.
0x0000b400 container    [0x00007fa0e4e00000-0x00007fa0e4f00000)* 0x09dec000 0x00100000 0x923638cc core.1883.
0x0000b500 container    [0x00007fa0e4f00000-0x00007fa0e5000000)* 0x09eec000 0x00100000 0x0e002d00 core.1883.
0x0000b600 container    [0x00007fa0e5000000-0x00007fa0e5100000)* 0x09fec000 0x00100000 0xed410000 core.1883.
0x0000b700 container    [0x00007fa0e5100000-0x00007fa0e5200000)* 0x0a0ec000 0x00100000 0x75004200 core.1883.
0x0000b800 container    [0x00007fa0e5200000-0x00007fa0e5300000)* 0x0a1ec000 0x00100000 0x00000000 core.1883.
0x0000b900 container    [0x00007fa0e5300000-0x00007fa0e5400000)* 0x0a2ec000 0x00100000 0x67ca7990 core.1883.
0x0000ba00 container    [0x00007fa0e5400000-0x00007fa0e5500000)* 0x0a3ec000 0x00100000 0x00000000 core.1883.
0x0000bb00 container    [0x00007fa0e5500000-0x00007fa0e5600000)* 0x0a4ec000 0x00100000 0x0000ed41 core.1883.
0x0000bc00 container    [0x00007fa0e5600000-0x00007fa0e5700000)* 0x0a5ec000 0x00100000 0x70006900 core.1883.
0x0000bd00 container    [0x00007fa0e5700000-0x00007fa0e5800000)* 0x0a6ec000 0x00100000 0x00000000 core.1883.
0x0000be00 container    [0x00007fa0e5800000-0x00007fa0e5900000)* 0x0a7ec000 0x00100000 0xb9ca84c2 core.1883.
0x0000bf00 container    [0x00007fa0e5900000-0x00007fa0e5a00000)* 0x0a8ec000 0x00100000 0x20000000 core.1883.
0x0000c000 container    [0x00007fa0e5a00000-0x00007fa0e5b00000)* 0x0a9ec000 0x00100000 0x00000000 core.1883.
0x0000c100 container    [0x00007fa0e5b00000-0x00007fa0e5c00000)* 0x0aaec000 0x00100000 0x01004c00 core.1883.
0x0000c200 container    [0x00007fa0e5c00000-0x00007fa0e5d00000)* 0x0abec000 0x00100000 0x0000128b core.1883.
```

```
0x0000c300 container    [0x00007fa0e5d00000-0x00007fa0e5e00000)*  0x0acec000 0x00100000 0x02ca0ff0 core.1883.
0x0000c400 container    [0x00007fa0e5e00000-0x00007fa0e5f00000)*  0x0adec000 0x00100000 0x00000000 core.1883.
0x0000c500 container    [0x00007fa0e5f00000-0x00007fa0e6000000)*  0x0aeec000 0x00100000 0x00000000 core.1883.
0x0000c600 container    [0x00007fa0e6000000-0x00007fa0e6100000)*  0x0afec000 0x00100000 0x72006500 core.1883.
0x0000c700 container    [0x00007fa0e6100000-0x00007fa0e6200000)*  0x0b0ec000 0x00100000 0x4a8b934e core.1883.
0x0000c800 container    [0x00007fa0e6200000-0x00007fa0e6300000)*  0x0b1ec000 0x00100000 0xb9ca5ffa core.1883.
0x0000c900 container    [0x00007fa0e6300000-0x00007fa0e6400000)*  0x0b2ec000 0x00100000 0x16000000 core.1883.
0x0000ca00 container    [0x00007fa0e6400000-0x00007fa0e6500000)*  0x0b3ec000 0x00100000 0x00000100 core.1883.
0x0000cb00 container    [0x00007fa0e6500000-0x00007fa0e6600000)*  0x0b4ec000 0x00100000 0x77006500 core.1883.
0x0000cc00 container    [0x00007fa0e6600000-0x00007fa0e6700000)*  0x0b5ec000 0x00100000 0x00000000 core.1883.
0x0000cd00 container    [0x00007fa0e6700000-0x00007fa0e6800000)*  0x0b6ec000 0x00100000 0x09ccfceb core.1883.
0x0000ce00 container    [0x00007fa0e6800000-0x00007fa0e6900000)*  0x0b7ec000 0x00100000 0x2d000000 core.1883.
0x0000cf00 container    [0x00007fa0e6900000-0x00007fa0e6a00000)*  0x0b8ec000 0x00100000 0x00000000 core.1883.
0x0000d000 container    [0x00007fa0e6a00000-0x00007fa0e6b00000)*  0x0b9ec000 0x00100000 0x01006100 core.1883.
0x0000d100 container    [0x00007fa0e6b00000-0x00007fa0e6c00000)*  0x0baec000 0x00100000 0x00004e8b core.1883.
0x0000d200 container    [0x00007fa0e6c00000-0x00007fa0e6d00000)*  0x0bbec000 0x00100000 0x00000000 core.1883.
0x0000d300 container    [0x00007fa0e6d00000-0x00007fa0e6e00000)*  0x0bcec000 0x00100000 0x6e006500 core.1883.
0x0000d400 container    [0x00007fa0e6e00000-0x00007fa0e6f00000)*  0x0bdec000 0x00100000 0x00000000 core.1883.
0x0000d500 container    [0x00007fa0e6f00000-0x00007fa0e7000000)*  0x0beec000 0x00100000 0x00000200 core.1883.
0x0000d600 container    [0x00007fa0e7000000-0x00007fa0e7100000)*  0x0bfec000 0x00100000 0x00000000 core.1883.
0x0000d700 container    [0x00007fa0e7100000-0x00007fa0e7200000)*  0x0c0ec000 0x00100000 0xb9cad33b core.1883.
0x0000d800 container    [0x00007fa0e7200000-0x00007fa0e7300000)*  0x0c1ec000 0x00100000 0x2d000000 core.1883.
0x0000d900 container    [0x00007fa0e7300000-0x00007fa0e7400000)*  0x0c2ec000 0x00100000 0x000075cd core.1883.
0x0000da00 container    [0x00007fa0e7400000-0x00007fa0e7500000)*  0x0c3ec000 0x00100000 0x63006500 core.1883.
0x0000db00 container    [0x00007fa0e7500000-0x00007fa0e7600000)*  0x0c4ec000 0x00100000 0x00000000 core.1883.
0x0000dc00 container    [0x00007fa0e7600000-0x00007fa0e7700000)*  0x0c5ec000 0x00100000 0x4b848cca core.1883.
0x0000dd00 container    [0x00007fa0e7700000-0x00007fa0e7800000)*  0x0c6ec000 0x00100000 0x00000000 core.1883.
0x0000de00 container    [0x00007fa0e7800000-0x00007fa0e7900000)*  0x0c7ec000 0x00100000 0x01000000 core.1883.
0x0000df00 container    [0x00007fa0e7900000-0x00007fa0e7a00000)*  0x0c8ec000 0x00100000 0x5dd10000 core.1883.
0x0000e000 container    [0x00007fa0e7a00000-0x00007fa0e7b00000)*  0x0c9ec000 0x00100000 0x00000000 core.1883.
0x0000e100 container    [0x00007fa0e7b00000-0x00007fa0e7c00000)*  0x0caec000 0x00100000 0x01000000 core.1883.
0x0000e200 container    [0x00007fa0e7c00000-0x00007fa0e7d00000)*  0x0cbec000 0x00100000 0x02000000 core.1883.
0x0000e300 container    [0x00007fa0e7d00000-0x00007fa0e7e00000)*  0x0ccec000 0x00100000 0x00000000 core.1883.
0x0000e400 container    [0x00007fa0e7e00000-0x00007fa0e7f00000)*  0x0cdec000 0x00100000 0x00000000 core.1883.
0x0000e500 container    [0x00007fa0e7f00000-0x00007fa0e8000000)*  0x0ceec000 0x00100000 0x46006400 core.1883.
0x0000e600 container    [0x00007fa0e8000000-0x00007fa0e8100000)*  0x0cfec000 0x00100000 0x00000000 core.1883.
0x0000e700 container    [0x00007fa0e8100000-0x00007fa0e8200000)*  0x0d0ec000 0x00100000 0x00008000 core.1883.
0x0000e800 container    [0x00007fa0e8200000-0x00007fa0e8300000)*  0x0d1ec000 0x00100000 0x00000000 core.1883.
0x0000e900 container    [0x00007fa0e8300000-0x00007fa0e8400000)*  0x0d2ec000 0x00100000 0x00009236 core.1883.
0x0000ea00 container    [0x00007fa0e8400000-0x00007fa0e8500000)*  0x0d3ec000 0x00100000 0x73007900 core.1883.
0x0000eb00 container    [0x00007fa0e8500000-0x00007fa0e8600000)*  0x0d4ec000 0x00100000 0x00000000 core.1883.
0x0000ec00 container    [0x00007fa0e8600000-0x00007fa0e8700000)*  0x0d5ec000 0x00100000 0x72005000 core.1883.
0x0000ed00 container    [0x00007fa0e8700000-0x00007fa0e8800000)*  0x0d6ec000 0x00100000 0x00000000 core.1883.
0x0000ee00 container    [0x00007fa0e8800000-0x00007fa0e8900000)*  0x0d7ec000 0x00100000 0x000076cd core.1883.
0x0000ef00 container    [0x00007fa0e8900000-0x00007fa0e8a00000)*  0x0d8ec000 0x00100000 0x78006500 core.1883.
0x0000f000 container    [0x00007fa0e8a00000-0x00007fa0e8b00000)*  0x0d9ec000 0x00100000 0x00000000 core.1883.
0x0000f100 container    [0x00007fa0e8b00000-0x00007fa0e8c00000)*  0x0daec000 0x00100000 0x01006500 core.1883.
0x0000f200 container    [0x00007fa0e8c00000-0x00007fa0e8d00000)*  0x0dbec000 0x00100000 0x00000f8b core.1883.
0x0000f300 container    [0x00007fa0e8d00000-0x00007fa0e8e00000)*  0x0dcec000 0x00100000 0x64cb0b0f core.1883.
0x0000f400 container    [0x00007fa0e8e00000-0x00007fa0e8f00000)*  0x0ddec000 0x00100000 0x10000000 core.1883.
0x0000f500 container    [0x00007fa0e8f00000-0x00007fa0e9000000)*  0x0deec000 0x00100000 0x00000000 core.1883.
0x0000f600 container    [0x00007fa0e9000000-0x00007fa0e9100000)*  0x0dfec000 0x00100000 0x01007300 core.1883.
0x0000f700 container    [0x00007fa0eb400000-0x00007fa0eb500000)*  0x0e0ec000 0x00100000 0x0000558b core.1883.
0x0000f800 container    [0x00007fa0eb500000-0x00007fa0eb600000)*  0x0e1ec000 0x00100000 0xbaac39cc core.1883.
0x0000f900 container    [0x00007fa0eb600000-0x00007fa0eb700000)*  0x0e2ec000 0x00100000 0x00000300 core.1883.
0x0000fa00 container    [0x00007fa0eb700000-0x00007fa0eb800000)*  0x0e3ec000 0x00100000 0x65007600 core.1883.
0x0000fb00 container    [0x00007fa0eb800000-0x00007fa0eb900000)*  0x0e4ec000 0x00100000 0x00000000 core.1883.
0x0000fc00 container    [0x00007fa0eb900000-0x00007fa0eba00000)*  0x0e5ec000 0x00100000 0x70006100 core.1883.
0x0000fd00 container    [0x00007fa0eba00000-0x00007fa0ebb00000)*  0x0e6ec000 0x00100000 0x934e0000 core.1883.
0x0000fe00 container    [0x00007fa0ebb00000-0x00007fa0ebc00000)*  0x0e7ec000 0x00100000 0x339264cb core.1883.
0x0000ff00 container    [0x00007fa0ebc00000-0x00007fa0ebd00000)*  0x0e8ec000 0x00100000 0x00002a00 core.1883.
0x00010000 container    [0x00007fa0ebd00000-0x00007fa0ebe00000)*  0x0e9ec000 0x00100000 0x00000000 core.1883.
0x00010100 container    [0x00007fa0ebe00000-0x00007fa0ebf00000)*  0x0eaec000 0x00100000 0x65007200 core.1883.
0x00010200 container    [0x00007fa0ebf00000-0x00007fa0ec000000)*  0x0ebec000 0x00100000 0x00000000 core.1883.
0x00010300 container    [0x00007fa0ec000000-0x00007fa0ec100000)*  0x0ecec000 0x00100000 0x00000100 core.1883.
0x00010400 container    [0x00007fa0ec100000-0x00007fa0ec200000)*  0x0edec000 0x00100000 0x00000000 core.1883.
0x00010500 container    [0x00007fa0ec200000-0x00007fa0ec300000)*  0x0eeec000 0x00100000 0x00000000 core.1883.
0x00010600 container    [0x00007fa0ec300000-0x00007fa0ec400000)*  0x0efec000 0x00100000 0x73007300 core.1883.
0x00010700 container    [0x00007fa0ec400000-0x00007fa0ec500000)*  0x0f0ec000 0x00100000 0x00000100 core.1883.
0x00010800 container    [0x00007fa0ec500000-0x00007fa0ec600000)*  0x0f1ec000 0x00100000 0x02000100 core.1883.
0x00010900 container    [0x00007fa0ec600000-0x00007fa0ec700000)*  0x0f2ec000 0x00100000 0x00000000 core.1883.
0x00010a00 container    [0x00007fa0ec700000-0x00007fa0ec800000)*  0x0f3ec000 0x00100000 0x00000000 core.1883.
0x00010b00 container    [0x00007fa0ec800000-0x00007fa0ec900000)*  0x0f4ec000 0x00100000 0x61002e00 core.1883.
0x00010c00 container    [0x00007fa0ec900000-0x00007fa0eca00000)*  0x0f5ec000 0x00100000 0x00000000 core.1883.
0x00010d00 container    [0x00007fa0eca00000-0x00007fa0ecb00000)*  0x0f6ec000 0x00100000 0xc4dc5cca core.1883.
0x00010e00 container    [0x00007fa0ecb00000-0x00007fa0ecc00000)*  0x0f7ec000 0x00100000 0x00000000 core.1883.
0x00010f00 container    [0x00007fa0ecc00000-0x00007fa0ecd00000)*  0x0f8ec000 0x00100000 0x00000000 core.1883.
0x00011000 container    [0x00007fa0ecd00000-0x00007fa0ece00000)*  0x0f9ec000 0x00100000 0x02000000 core.1883.
0x00011100 container    [0x00007fa0ece00000-0x00007fa0ecf00000)*  0x0faec000 0x00100000 0x00000100 core.1883.
0x00011200 container    [0x00007fa0ecf00000-0x00007fa0ed000000)*  0x0fbec000 0x00100000 0x01000000 core.1883.
0x00011300 container    [0x00007fa0ed000000-0x00007fa0ed100000)*  0x0fcec000 0x00100000 0x00000000 core.1883.
0x00011400 container    [0x00007fa0ed100000-0x00007fa0ed200000)*  0x0fdec000 0x00100000 0x00000100 core.1883.
0x00011500 container    [0x00007fa0ed200000-0x00007fa0ed300000)*  0x0feec000 0x00100000 0xa0000000 core.1883.
0x00011600 container    [0x00007fa0ed300000-0x00007fa0ed400000)*  0x0ffec000 0x00100000 0x00000000 core.1883.
0x00011700 container    [0x00007fa0ed400000-0x00007fa0ed500000)*  0x100ec000 0x00100000 0x00000100 core.1883.
0x00011800 container    [0x00007fa0ed500000-0x00007fa0ed600000)*  0x101ec000 0x00100000 0x09cc53ec core.1883.
```

```
0x00011900 container    [0x00007fa0ed600000-0x00007fa0ed700000)* 0x102ec000 0x00100000 0x10000000 core.1883.
0x00011a00 container    [0x00007fa0ed700000-0x00007fa0ed800000)* 0x103ec000 0x00100000 0x00000000 core.1883.
0x00011b00 container    [0x00007fa0ed800000-0x00007fa0ed900000)* 0x104ec000 0x00100000 0x570d0000 core.1883.
0x00011c00 container    [0x00007fa0ed900000-0x00007fa0eda00000)* 0x105ec000 0x00100000 0x00000000 core.1883.
0x00011d00 container    [0x00007fa0eda00000-0x00007fa0edb00000)* 0x106ec000 0x00100000 0x00000000 core.1883.
0x00011e00 container    [0x00007fa0edb00000-0x00007fa0edc00000)* 0x107ec000 0x00100000 0x00000000 core.1883.
0x00011f00 container    [0x00007fa0edc00000-0x00007fa0edd00000)* 0x108ec000 0x00100000 0x00000000 core.1883.
0x00012000 container    [0x00007fa0edd00000-0x00007fa0ede00000)* 0x109ec000 0x00100000 0x00000000 core.1883.
0x00012100 container    [0x00007fa0ede00000-0x00007fa0edf00000)* 0x10aec000 0x00100000 0x00000000 core.1883.
0x00012200 container    [0x00007fa0edf00000-0x00007fa0ee000000)* 0x10bec000 0x00100000 0xbe122813 core.1883.
0x00012300 container    [0x00007fa0ee000000-0x00007fa0ee100000)* 0x10cec000 0x00100000 0xfa017202 core.1883.
0x00012400 container    [0x00007fa0ee100000-0x00007fa0ee200000)* 0x10dec000 0x00100000 0x00000000 core.1883.
0x00012500 container    [0x00007fa0ee200000-0x00007fa0ee300000)* 0x10eec000 0x00100000 0x6f007300 core.1883.
0x00012600 container    [0x00007fa0ee300000-0x00007fa0ee400000)* 0x10fec000 0x00100000 0x00000000 core.1883.
0x00012700 container    [0x00007fa0ee400000-0x00007fa0ee500000)* 0x110ec000 0x00100000 0xaa450000 core.1883.
0x00012800 container    [0x00007fa0ee500000-0x00007fa0ee600000)* 0x111ec000 0x00100000 0x00000000 core.1883.
0x00012900 container    [0x00007fa0ee600000-0x00007fa0ee700000)* 0x112ec000 0x00100000 0x00000000 core.1883.
0x00012a00 container    [0x00007fa0ee700000-0x00007fa0ee800000)* 0x113ec000 0x00100000 0x00000000 core.1883.
0x00012b00 container    [0x00007fa0ee800000-0x00007fa0ee900000)* 0x114ec000 0x00100000 0x6e006900 core.1883.
0x00012c00 container    [0x00007fa0ee900000-0x00007fa0eea00000)* 0x115ec000 0x00100000 0x00000000 core.1883.
0x00012d00 container    [0x00007fa0eea00000-0x00007fa0eeb00000)* 0x116ec000 0x00100000 0x00000000 core.1883.
0x00012e00 container    [0x00007fa0eeb00000-0x00007fa0eec00000)* 0x117ec000 0x00100000 0x00000000 core.1883.
0x00012f00 container    [0x00007fa0eec00000-0x00007fa0eed00000)* 0x118ec000 0x00100000 0x50006800 core.1883.
0x00013000 container    [0x00007fa0eed00000-0x00007fa0eee00000)* 0x119ec000 0x00100000 0x69006c00 core.1883.
0x00013100 container    [0x00007fa0eee00000-0x00007fa0eef00000)* 0x11aec000 0x00100000 0x00000000 core.1883.
0x00013200 container    [0x00007fa0eef00000-0x00007fa0ef000000)* 0x11bec000 0x00100000 0x72007000 core.1883.
0x00013300 container    [0x00007fa0ef000000-0x00007fa0ef100000)* 0x11cec000 0x00100000 0x49cb9e3b core.1883.
0x00013400 container    [0x00007fa0ef100000-0x00007fa0ef200000)* 0x11dec000 0x00100000 0x00002a00 core.1883.
0x00013500 container    [0x00007fa0ef200000-0x00007fa0ef300000)* 0x11eec000 0x00100000 0x00000000 core.1883.
0x00013600 container    [0x00007fa0ef300000-0x00007fa0ef400000)* 0x11fec000 0x00100000 0x00000000 core.1883.
0x00013700 container    [0x00007fa0ef400000-0x00007fa0ef500000)* 0x120ec000 0x00100000 0x13000000 core.1883.
0x00013800 container    [0x00007fa0ef500000-0x00007fa0ef600000)* 0x121ec000 0x00100000 0x00000000 core.1883.
0x00013900 container    [0x00007fa0ef600000-0x00007fa0ef700000)* 0x122ec000 0x00100000 0x00000000 core.1883.
0x00013a00 container    [0x00007fa0ef700000-0x00007fa0ef800000)* 0x123ec000 0x00100000 0x00000000 core.1883.
0x00013b00 container    [0x00007fa0ef800000-0x00007fa0ef900000)* 0x124ec000 0x00100000 0x78006500 core.1883.
0x00013c00 container    [0x00007fa0ef900000-0x00007fa0efa00000)* 0x125ec000 0x00100000 0x0000ed41 core.1883.
0x00013d00 container    [0x00007fa0efa00000-0x00007fa0efb00000)* 0x126ec000 0x00100000 0x6e006500 core.1883.
0x00013e00 container    [0x00007fa0efb00000-0x00007fa0efc00000)* 0x127ec000 0x00100000 0x00000000 core.1883.
0x00013f00 container    [0x00007fa0efc00000-0x00007fa0efd00000)* 0x128ec000 0x00100000 0x6f006600 core.1883.
0x00014000 container    [0x00007fa0efd00000-0x00007fa0efe00000)* 0x129ec000 0x00100000 0x00000000 core.1883.
0x00014100 container    [0x00007fa0efe00000-0x00007fa0eff00000)* 0x12aec000 0x00100000 0x00000000 core.1883.
0x00014200 container    [0x00007fa0eff00000-0x00007fa0f0000000)* 0x12bec000 0x00100000 0x00000000 core.1883.
0x00014300 container    [0x00007fa0f0000000-0x00007fa0f0100000)* 0x12cec000 0x00100000 0x00000100 core.1883.
0x00014400 container    [0x00007fa0f0100000-0x00007fa0f0200000)* 0x12dec000 0x00100000 0x00000000 core.1883.
0x00014500 container    [0x00007fa0f0200000-0x00007fa0f0300000)* 0x12eec000 0x00100000 0x00000000 core.1883.
0x00014600 container    [0x00007fa0f0300000-0x00007fa0f0400000)* 0x12fec000 0x00100000 0x01000000 core.1883.
0x00014700 container    [0x00007fa0f0400000-0x00007fa0f0500000)* 0x130ec000 0x00100000 0x00000000 core.1883.
0x00014800 container    [0x00007fa0f0500000-0x00007fa0f0600000)* 0x131ec000 0x00100000 0x00000000 core.1883.
0x00014900 container    [0x00007fa0f0600000-0x00007fa0f0700000)* 0x132ec000 0x00100000 0x4f100000 core.1883.
0x00014a00 container    [0x00007fa0f0700000-0x00007fa0f0800000)* 0x133ec000 0x00100000 0x00000000 core.1883.
0x00014b00 container    [0x00007fa0f0800000-0x00007fa0f0900000)* 0x134ec000 0x00100000 0x00000000 core.1883.
0x00014c00 container    [0x00007fa0f0900000-0x00007fa0f0a00000)* 0x135ec000 0x00100000 0x00000000 core.1883.
0x00014d00 container    [0x00007fa0f0a00000-0x00007fa0f0b00000)* 0x136ec000 0x00100000 0x03000000 core.1883.
0x00014e00 container    [0x00007fa0f0b00000-0x00007fa0f0c00000)* 0x137ec000 0x00100000 0x02007900 core.1883.
0x00014f00 container    [0x00007fa0f0c00000-0x00007fa0f0d00000)* 0x138ec000 0x00100000 0x00001e8b core.1883.
0x00015000 container    [0x00007fa0f0d00000-0x00007fa0f0e00000)* 0x139ec000 0x00100000 0x00000000 core.1883.
0x00015100 container    [0x00007fa0f0e00000-0x00007fa0f0f00000)* 0x13aec000 0x00100000 0x00000000 core.1883.
0x00015200 container    [0x00007fa0f0f00000-0x00007fa0f1000000)* 0x13bec000 0x00100000 0x02007300 core.1883.
0x00015300 container    [0x00007fa0f1000000-0x00007fa0f1100000)* 0x13cec000 0x00100000 0x00001e8b core.1883.
0x00015400 container    [0x00007fa0f1100000-0x00007fa0f1200000)* 0x13dec000 0x00100000 0x00000000 core.1883.
0x00015500 container    [0x00007fa0f1200000-0x00007fa0f1300000)* 0x13eec000 0x00100000 0x00000000 core.1883.
0x00015600 container    [0x00007fa0f1300000-0x00007fa0f1400000)* 0x13fec000 0x00100000 0x00000000 core.1883.
0x00015700 container    [0x00007fa0f1400000-0x00007fa0f1500000)* 0x140ec000 0x00100000 0x00000000 core.1883.
0x00015800 container    [0x00007fa0f1500000-0x00007fa0f1600000)* 0x141ec000 0x00100000 0x00000000 core.1883.
0x00015900 container    [0x00007fa0f1600000-0x00007fa0f1700000)* 0x142ec000 0x00100000 0x00000000 core.1883.
0x00015a00 container    [0x00007fa0f1700000-0x00007fa0f1800000)* 0x143ec000 0x00100000 0x67cad245 core.1883.
0x00015b00 container    [0x00007fa0f1800000-0x00007fa0f1900000)* 0x144ec000 0x00100000 0x00000000 core.1883.
0x00015c00 container    [0x00007fa0f1900000-0x00007fa0f1a00000)* 0x145ec000 0x00100000 0x00000000 core.1883.
0x00015d00 container    [0x00007fa0f1a00000-0x00007fa0f1b00000)* 0x146ec000 0x00100000 0x00000000 core.1883.
0x00015e00 container    [0x00007fa0f1b00000-0x00007fa0f1c00000)* 0x147ec000 0x00100000 0x16007400 core.1883.
0x00015f00 container    [0x00007fa0f1c00000-0x00007fa0f1d00000)* 0x148ec000 0x00100000 0x00000100 core.1883.
0x00016000 container    [0x00007fa0f1d00000-0x00007fa0f1e00000)* 0x149ec000 0x00100000 0x73007400 core.1883.
0x00016100 container    [0x00007fa0f1e00000-0x00007fa0f1f00000)* 0x14aec000 0x00100000 0x00000000 core.1883.
0x00016200 container    [0x00007fa0f1f00000-0x00007fa0f2000000)* 0x14bec000 0x00100000 0x70002e00 core.1883.
0x00016300 container    [0x00007fa0f2000000-0x00007fa0f2100000)* 0x14cec000 0x00100000 0x00000000 core.1883.
0x00016400 container    [0x00007fa0f2100000-0x00007fa0f2200000)* 0x14dec000 0x00100000 0x00000000 core.1883.
0x00016500 container    [0x00007fa0f2200000-0x00007fa0f2300000)* 0x14eec000 0x00100000 0x00000000 core.1883.
0x00016600 container    [0x00007fa0f2300000-0x00007fa0f2400000)* 0x14fec000 0x00100000 0x67ca5910 core.1883.
0x00016700 container    [0x00007fa0f2400000-0x00007fa0f2500000)* 0x150ec000 0x00100000 0x00000000 core.1883.
0x00016800 container    [0x00007fa0f2500000-0x00007fa0f2600000)* 0x151ec000 0x00100000 0x01000000 core.1883.
0x00016900 container    [0x00007fa0f2600000-0x00007fa0f2700000)* 0x152ec000 0x00100000 0x73006900 core.1883.
0x00016a00 container    [0x00007fa0f2700000-0x00007fa0f2800000)* 0x153ec000 0x00100000 0xe44f0000 core.1883.
0x00016b00 container    [0x00007fa0f2800000-0x00007fa0f2900000)* 0x154ec000 0x00100000 0x00000000 core.1883.
0x00016c00 container    [0x00007fa0f2900000-0x00007fa0f2a00000)* 0x155ec000 0x00100000 0x00000000 core.1883.
0x00016d00 container    [0x00007fa0f2a00000-0x00007fa0f2b00000)* 0x156ec000 0x00100000 0x53100000 core.1883.
0x00016e00 container    [0x00007fa0f2b00000-0x00007fa0f2c00000)* 0x157ec000 0x00100000 0x8f3bb9ca core.1883.
```

```
0x00016f00 container    [0x00007fa0f2c00000-0x00007fa0f2d00000)* 0x158ec000 0x00100000 0x16005310 core.1883.
0x00017000 container    [0x00007fa0f2d00000-0x00007fa0f2e00000)* 0x159ec000 0x00100000 0x695138cc core.1883.
0x00017100 container    [0x00007fa0f2e00000-0x00007fa0f2f00000)* 0x15aec000 0x00100000 0x00000300 core.1883.
0x00017200 container    [0x00007fa0f2f00000-0x00007fa0f3000000)* 0x15bec000 0x00100000 0x6e006500 core.1883.
0x00017300 container    [0x00007fa0f3000000-0x00007fa0f3100000)* 0x15cec000 0x00100000 0x00000000 core.1883.
0x00017400 container    [0x00007fa0f3100000-0x00007fa0f3200000)* 0x15dec000 0x00100000 0x65006400 core.1883.
0x00017500 container    [0x00007fa0f3200000-0x00007fa0f3300000)* 0x15eec000 0x00100000 0x00000000 core.1883.
0x00017600 container    [0x00007fa0f3300000-0x00007fa0f3400000)* 0x15fec000 0x00100000 0x13000000 core.1883.
0x00017700 container    [0x00007fa0f3400000-0x00007fa0f3500000)* 0x160ec000 0x00100000 0x00000000 core.1883.
0x00017800 container    [0x00007fa0f3500000-0x00007fa0f3600000)* 0x161ec000 0x00100000 0x00000000 core.1883.
0x00017900 container    [0x00007fa0f3600000-0x00007fa0f3700000)* 0x162ec000 0x00100000 0x00000000 core.1883.
0x00017a00 container    [0x00007fa0f3700000-0x00007fa0f3800000)* 0x163ec000 0x00100000 0x00000000 core.1883.
0x00017b00 container    [0x00007fa0f3800000-0x00007fa0f3900000)* 0x164ec000 0x00100000 0x73007200 core.1883.
0x00017c00 container    [0x00007fa0f3900000-0x00007fa0f3a00000)* 0x165ec000 0x00100000 0x00000000 core.1883.
0x00017d00 container    [0x00007fa0f3a00000-0x00007fa0f3b00000)* 0x166ec000 0x00100000 0x00000000 core.1883.
0x00017e00 container    [0x00007fa0f3b00000-0x00007fa0f3c00000)* 0x167ec000 0x00100000 0x00000000 core.1883.
0x00017f00 container    [0x00007fa0f3c00000-0x00007fa0f3d00000)* 0x168ec000 0x00100000 0x61004d00 core.1883.
0x00018000 container    [0x00007fa0f3d00000-0x00007fa0f3e00000)* 0x169ec000 0x00100000 0x07cc0bb6 core.1883.
0x00018100 container    [0x00007fa0f3e00000-0x00007fa0f3f00000)* 0x16aec000 0x00100000 0x05000000 core.1883.
0x00018200 container    [0x00007fa0f3f00000-0x00007fa0f4000000)* 0x16bec000 0x00100000 0x00000000 core.1883.
0x00018300 container    [0x00007fa0f4000000-0x00007fa0f4100000)* 0x16cec000 0x00100000 0x00000000 core.1883.
0x00018400 container    [0x00007fa0f4100000-0x00007fa0f4200000)* 0x16dec000 0x00100000 0x65006400 core.1883.
0x00018500 container    [0x00007fa0f4200000-0x00007fa0f4300000)* 0x16eec000 0x00100000 0x00000000 core.1883.
0x00018600 container    [0x00007fa0f4300000-0x00007fa0f4400000)* 0x16fec000 0x00100000 0x00000000 core.1883.
0x00018700 container    [0x00007fa0f4400000-0x00007fa0f4500000)* 0x170ec000 0x00100000 0x00000000 core.1883.
0x00018800 container    [0x00007fa0f4500000-0x00007fa0f4600000)* 0x171ec000 0x00100000 0x71006500 core.1883.
0x00018900 container    [0x00007fa0f4600000-0x00007fa0f4700000)* 0x172ec000 0x00100000 0x00000000 core.1883.
0x00018a00 container    [0x00007fa0f4700000-0x00007fa0f4800000)* 0x173ec000 0x00100000 0x00000000 core.1883.
0x00018b00 container    [0x00007fa0f4800000-0x00007fa0f4900000)* 0x174ec000 0x00100000 0x00000000 core.1883.
0x00018c00 container    [0x00007fa0f4900000-0x00007fa0f4a00000)* 0x175ec000 0x00100000 0x00000000 core.1883.
0x00018d00 container    [0x00007fa0f4a00000-0x00007fa0f4b00000)* 0x176ec000 0x00100000 0x00000000 core.1883.
0x00018e00 container    [0x00007fa0f4b00000-0x00007fa0f4c00000)* 0x177ec000 0x00100000 0x00000000 core.1883.
0x00018f00 container    [0x00007fa0f4c00000-0x00007fa0f4d00000)* 0x178ec000 0x00100000 0x00000000 core.1883.
0x00019000 container    [0x00007fa0f4d00000-0x00007fa0f4e00000)* 0x179ec000 0x00100000 0x00000000 core.1883.
0x00019100 container    [0x00007fa0f4e00000-0x00007fa0f4f00000)* 0x17aec000 0x00100000 0x00000000 core.1883.
0x00019200 container    [0x00007fa0f4f00000-0x00007fa0f5000000)* 0x17bec000 0x00100000 0x00000000 core.1883.
0x00019300 container    [0x00007fa0f5000000-0x00007fa0f5100000)* 0x17cec000 0x00100000 0x1ce81d0c core.1883.
0x00019400 container    [0x00007fa0f5100000-0x00007fa0f5200000)* 0x17dec000 0x00100000 0xb0121a13 core.1883.
0x00019500 container    [0x00007fa0f5200000-0x00007fa0f5300000)* 0x17eec000 0x00100000 0xac450000 core.1883.
0x00019600 container    [0x00007fa0f5300000-0x00007fa0f5400000)* 0x17fec000 0x00100000 0x32003200 core.1883.
0x00019700 container    [0x00007fa0f5400000-0x00007fa0f5500000)* 0x180ec000 0x00100000 0x223e844f core.1883.
0x00019800 container    [0x00007fa0f5500000-0x00007fa0f5600000)* 0x181ec000 0x00100000 0x00000000 core.1883.
0x00019900 container    [0x00007fa0f5600000-0x00007fa0f5700000)* 0x182ec000 0x00100000 0x00000000 core.1883.
0x00019a00 container    [0x00007fa0f5700000-0x00007fa0f5800000)* 0x183ec000 0x00100000 0x32002e00 core.1883.
0x00019b00 container    [0x00007fa0f5800000-0x00007fa0f5900000)* 0x184ec000 0x00100000 0x00002081 core.1883.
0x00019c00 container    [0x00007fa0f5900000-0x00007fa0f5a00000)* 0x185ec000 0x00100000 0x00000000 core.1883.
0x00019d00 container    [0x00007fa0f5a00000-0x00007fa0f5b00000)* 0x186ec000 0x00100000 0x00000000 core.1883.
0x00019e00 container    [0x00007fa0f5b00000-0x00007fa0f5c00000)* 0x187ec000 0x00100000 0x31003000 core.1883.
0x00019f00 container    [0x00007fa0f5c00000-0x00007fa0f5d00000)* 0x188ec000 0x00100000 0x1af0a9cb core.1883.
0x0001a000 container    [0x00007fa0f5d00000-0x00007fa0f5e00000)* 0x189ec000 0x00100000 0x00000000 core.1883.
0x0001a100 container    [0x00007fa0f5e00000-0x00007fa0f5f00000)* 0x18aec000 0x00100000 0x00000000 core.1883.
0x0001a200 container    [0x00007fa0f5f00000-0x00007fa0f6000000)* 0x18bec000 0x00100000 0x00000000 core.1883.
0x0001a300 container    [0x00007fa0f6000000-0x00007fa0f6100000)* 0x18cec000 0x00100000 0x76006f00 core.1883.
0x0001a400 container    [0x00007fa0f6100000-0x00007fa0f6200000)* 0x18dec000 0x00100000 0x00000000 core.1883.
0x0001a500 container    [0x00007fa0f6200000-0x00007fa0f6300000)* 0x18eec000 0x00100000 0x00000000 core.1883.
0x0001a600 container    [0x00007fa0f6300000-0x00007fa0f6400000)* 0x18fec000 0x00100000 0x00000000 core.1883.
0x0001a700 container    [0x00007fa0f6400000-0x00007fa0f6500000)* 0x190ec000 0x00100000 0x33003800 core.1883.
0x0001a800 container    [0x00007fa0f6500000-0x00007fa0f6600000)* 0x191ec000 0x00100000 0x00000000 core.1883.
0x0001a900 container    [0x00007fa0f6600000-0x00007fa0f6700000)* 0x192ec000 0x00100000 0x01000000 core.1883.
0x0001aa00 container    [0x00007fa0f6700000-0x00007fa0f6800000)* 0x193ec000 0x00100000 0x00000000 core.1883.
0x0001ab00 container    [0x00007fa0f6800000-0x00007fa0f6900000)* 0x194ec000 0x00100000 0x1d009423 core.1883.
0x0001ac00 container    [0x00007fa0f6900000-0x00007fa0f6a00000)* 0x195ec000 0x00100000 0xdbcb3fbd core.1883.
0x0001ad00 container    [0x00007fa0f6a00000-0x00007fa0f6b00000)* 0x196ec000 0x00100000 0x00000000 core.1883.
0x0001ae00 container    [0x00007fa0f6b00000-0x00007fa0f6c00000)* 0x197ec000 0x00100000 0x00000000 core.1883.
0x0001af00 container    [0x00007fa0f6c00000-0x00007fa0f6d00000)* 0x198ec000 0x00100000 0x00000000 core.1883.
0x0001b000 container    [0x00007fa0f6d00000-0x00007fa0f6e00000)* 0x199ec000 0x00100000 0x65007200 core.1883.
0x0001b100 container    [0x00007fa0f6e00000-0x00007fa0f6f00000)* 0x19aec000 0x00100000 0x00000000 core.1883.
0x0001b200 container    [0x00007fa0f6f00000-0x00007fa0f7000000)* 0x19bec000 0x00100000 0x00000000 core.1883.
0x0001b300 container    [0x00007fa0f7000000-0x00007fa0f7100000)* 0x19cec000 0x00100000 0x00000000 core.1883.
0x0001b400 container    [0x00007fa0f7100000-0x00007fa0f7200000)* 0x19dec000 0x00100000 0x39003000 core.1883.
0x0001b500 container    [0x00007fa0f7200000-0x00007fa0f7300000)* 0x19eec000 0x00100000 0x00000000 core.1883.
0x0001b600 container    [0x00007fa0f7300000-0x00007fa0f7400000)* 0x19fec000 0x00100000 0x3e000100 core.1883.
0x0001b700 container    [0x00007fa0f7400000-0x00007fa0f7500000)* 0x1a0ec000 0x00100000 0x00000000 core.1883.
0x0001b800 container    [0x00007fa0f7500000-0x00007fa0f7600000)* 0x1a1ec000 0x00100000 0x40000000 core.1883.
0x0001b900 container    [0x00007fa0f7600000-0x00007fa0f7700000)* 0x1a2ec000 0x00100000 0x00000000 core.1883.
0x0001ba00 container    [0x00007fa0f7700000-0x00007fa0f7800000)* 0x1a3ec000 0x00100000 0x00000000 core.1883.
0x0001bb00 container    [0x00007fa0f7800000-0x00007fa0f7900000)* 0x1a4ec000 0x00100000 0x00000000 core.1883.
0x0001bc00 container    [0x00007fa0f7900000-0x00007fa0f7a00000)* 0x1a5ec000 0x00100000 0x00000000 core.1883.
0x0001bd00 container    [0x00007fa0f7a00000-0x00007fa0f7b00000)* 0x1a6ec000 0x00100000 0x30003200 core.1883.
0x0001be00 container    [0x00007fa0f7b00000-0x00007fa0f7c00000)* 0x1a7ec000 0x00100000 0x00000000 core.1883.
0x0001bf00 container    [0x00007fa0f7c00000-0x00007fa0f7d00000)* 0x1a8ec000 0x00100000 0x00000000 core.1883.
0x0001c000 container    [0x00007fa0f7d00000-0x00007fa0f7e00000)* 0x1a9ec000 0x00100000 0x00000000 core.1883.
0x0001c100 container    [0x00007fa0f7e00000-0x00007fa0f7f00000)* 0x1aaec000 0x00100000 0x31003500 core.1883.
0x0001c200 container    [0x00007fa0f7f00000-0x00007fa0f8000000)* 0x1abec000 0x00100000 0xa7cadbcb core.1883.
0x0001c300 container    [0x00007fa0f8000000-0x00007fa0f8100000)* 0x1acec000 0x00100000 0x00000000 core.1883.
0x0001c400 container    [0x00007fa0f8100000-0x00007fa0f8200000)* 0x1adec000 0x00100000 0x00000000 core.1883.
```

```
0x0001c500 container    [0x00007fa0f8200000-0x00007fa0f8300000)* 0x1aeec000 0x00100000 0x00000000 core.1883.
0x0001c600 container    [0x00007fa0f8300000-0x00007fa0f8400000)* 0x1afec000 0x00100000 0x02007900 core.1883.
0x0001c700 container    [0x00007fa0f8400000-0x00007fa0f8500000)* 0x1b0ec000 0x00100000 0x0000b4d7 core.1883.
0x0001c800 container    [0x00007fa0f8500000-0x00007fa0f8600000)* 0x1b1ec000 0x00100000 0x00000000 core.1883.
0x0001c900 container    [0x00007fa0f8600000-0x00007fa0f8700000)* 0x1b2ec000 0x00100000 0x00000000 core.1883.
0x0001ca00 container    [0x00007fa0f8700000-0x00007fa0f8800000)* 0x1b3ec000 0x00100000 0x72006300 core.1883.
0x0001cb00 container    [0x00007fa0f8800000-0x00007fa0f8900000)* 0x1b4ec000 0x00100000 0x01000000 core.1883.
0x0001cc00 container    [0x00007fa0f8900000-0x00007fa0f8a00000)* 0x1b5ec000 0x00100000 0x03000000 core.1883.
0x0001cd00 container    [0x00007fa0f8a00000-0x00007fa0f8b00000)* 0x1b6ec000 0x00100000 0x00000000 core.1883.
0x0001ce00 container    [0x00007fa0f8b00000-0x00007fa0f8c00000)* 0x1b7ec000 0x00100000 0x32003100 core.1883.
0x0001cf00 container    [0x00007fa0f8c00000-0x00007fa0f8d00000)* 0x1b8ec000 0x00100000 0xedcb8014 core.1883.
0x0001d000 container    [0x00007fa0f8d00000-0x00007fa0f8e00000)* 0x1b9ec000 0x00100000 0x00000000 core.1883.
0x0001d100 container    [0x00007fa0f8e00000-0x00007fa0f8f00000)* 0x1baec000 0x00100000 0x00000000 core.1883.
0x0001d200 container    [0x00007fa0f8f00000-0x00007fa0f9000000)* 0x1bbec000 0x00100000 0x00000000 core.1883.
0x0001d300 container    [0x00007fa0f9000000-0x00007fa0f9100000)* 0x1bcec000 0x00100000 0x65007600 core.1883.
0x0001d400 container    [0x00007fa0f9100000-0x00007fa0f9200000)* 0x1bdec000 0x00100000 0x00000000 core.1883.
0x0001d500 container    [0x00007fa0f9200000-0x00007fa0f9300000)* 0x1beec000 0x00100000 0x00000000 core.1883.
0x0001d600 container    [0x00007fa0f9300000-0x00007fa0f9400000)* 0x1bfec000 0x00100000 0x00000000 core.1883.
0x0001d700 container    [0x00007fa0f9400000-0x00007fa0f9500000)* 0x1c0ec000 0x00100000 0x37003200 core.1883.
0x0001d800 container    [0x00007fa0f9500000-0x00007fa0f9600000)* 0x1c1ec000 0x00100000 0x00000000 core.1883.
0x0001d900 container    [0x00007fa0f9600000-0x00007fa0f9700000)* 0x1c2ec000 0x00100000 0x3e000100 core.1883.
0x0001da00 container    [0x00007fa0f9700000-0x00007fa0f9800000)* 0x1c3ec000 0x00100000 0x00000000 core.1883.
0x0001db00 container    [0x00007fa0f9800000-0x00007fa0f9900000)* 0x1c4ec000 0x00100000 0x32001d00 core.1883.
0x0001dc00 container    [0x00007fa0f9900000-0x00007fa0f9a00000)* 0x1c5ec000 0x00100000 0x6bec09cc core.1883.
0x0001dd00 container    [0x00007fa0f9a00000-0x00007fa0f9b00000)* 0x1c6ec000 0x00100000 0x00000000 core.1883.
0x0001de00 container    [0x00007fa0f9b00000-0x00007fa0f9c00000)* 0x1c7ec000 0x00100000 0x00000000 core.1883.
0x0001df00 container    [0x00007fa0f9c00000-0x00007fa0f9d00000)* 0x1c8ec000 0x00100000 0x00000000 core.1883.
0x0001e000 container    [0x00007fa0f9d00000-0x00007fa0f9e00000)* 0x1c9ec000 0x00100000 0x31003600 core.1883.
0x0001e100 container    [0x00007fa0f9e00000-0x00007fa0f9f00000)* 0x1caec000 0x00100000 0x00000000 core.1883.
0x0001e200 container    [0x00007fa0f9f00000-0x00007fa0fa000000)* 0x1cbec000 0x00100000 0x0000760d core.1883.
0x0001e300 container    [0x00007fa0fa000000-0x00007fa0fa100000)* 0x1ccec000 0x00100000 0x00000000 core.1883.
0x0001e400 container    [0x00007fa0fa100000-0x00007fa0fa200000)* 0x1cdec000 0x00100000 0x31003200 core.1883.
0x0001e500 container    [0x00007fa0fa200000-0x00007fa0fa300000)* 0x1ceec000 0x00100000 0x00000000 core.1883.
0x0001e600 container    [0x00007fa0fa300000-0x00007fa0fa400000)* 0x1cfec000 0x00100000 0x6d5d3400 core.1883.
0x0001e700 container    [0x00007fa0fa400000-0x00007fa0fa500000)* 0x1d0ec000 0x00100000 0x00000000 core.1883.
0x0001e800 container    [0x00007fa0fa500000-0x00007fa0fa600000)* 0x1d1ec000 0x00100000 0x00004000 core.1883.
0x0001e900 container    [0x00007fa0fa600000-0x00007fa0fa700000)* 0x1d2ec000 0x00100000 0x15000000 core.1883.
0x0001ea00 container    [0x00007fa0fa700000-0x00007fa0fa800000)* 0x1d3ec000 0x00100000 0x00000000 core.1883.
0x0001eb00 container    [0x00007fa0fa800000-0x00007fa0fa900000)* 0x1d4ec000 0x00100000 0x4a000100 core.1883.
0x0001ec00 container    [0x00007fa0fa900000-0x00007fa0faa00000)* 0x1d5ec000 0x00100000 0x00000000 core.1883.
0x0001ed00 container    [0x00007fa0faa00000-0x00007fa0fab00000)* 0x1d6ec000 0x00100000 0x37003000 core.1883.
0x0001ee00 container    [0x00007fa0fab00000-0x00007fa0fac00000)* 0x1d7ec000 0x00100000 0x00000000 core.1883.
0x0001ef00 container    [0x00007fa0fac00000-0x00007fa0fad00000)* 0x1d8ec000 0x00100000 0x09000000 core.1883.
0x0001f000 container    [0x00007fa0fad00000-0x00007fa0fae00000)* 0x1d9ec000 0x00100000 0x00000000 core.1883.
0x0001f100 container    [0x00007fa0fae00000-0x00007fa0faf00000)* 0x1daec000 0x00100000 0x33003200 core.1883.
0x0001f200 container    [0x00007fa0faf00000-0x00007fa0fb000000)* 0x1dbec000 0x00100000 0x00009744 core.1883.
0x0001f300 container    [0x00007fa0fb000000-0x00007fa0fb100000)* 0x1dcec000 0x00100000 0x00000000 core.1883.
0x0001f400 container    [0x00007fa0fb100000-0x00007fa0fb200000)* 0x1ddec000 0x00100000 0x00000000 core.1883.
0x0001f500 container    [0x00007fa0fb200000-0x00007fa0fb300000)* 0x1deec000 0x00100000 0x00000000 core.1883.
0x0001f600 container    [0x00007fa0fb400000-0x00007fa0fb500000)* 0x1dfec000 0x00100000 0x82000200 core.1883.
0x0001f700 container    [0x00007fa0fb500000-0x00007fa0fb600000)* 0x1e0ec000 0x00100000 0x00000000 core.1883.
0x0001f800 container    [0x00007fa0fb600000-0x00007fa0fb700000)* 0x1e1ec000 0x00100000 0x00000000 core.1883.
0x0001f900 container    [0x00007fa0fb700000-0x00007fa0fb800000)* 0x1e2ec000 0x00100000 0x00000000 core.1883.
0x0001fa00 container    [0x00007fa0fb800000-0x00007fa0fb900000)* 0x1e3ec000 0x00100000 0x38cc3438 core.1883.
0x0001fb00 container    [0x00007fa0fb900000-0x00007fa0fba00000)* 0x1e4ec000 0x00100000 0x00000000 core.1883.
0x0001fc00 container    [0x00007fa0fba00000-0x00007fa0fbb00000)* 0x1e5ec000 0x00100000 0x00000000 core.1883.
0x0001fd00 container    [0x00007fa0fbb00000-0x00007fa0fbc00000)* 0x1e6ec000 0x00100000 0x00000000 core.1883.
0x0001fe00 container    [0x00007fa0fbc00000-0x00007fa0fbd00000)* 0x1e7ec000 0x00100000 0x00000000 core.1883.
0x0001ff00 container    [0x00007fa0fbd00000-0x00007fa0fbe00000)* 0x1e8ec000 0x00100000 0x00000000 core.1883.
0x00020000 container    [0x00007fa0fbe00000-0x00007fa0fbf00000)* 0x1e9ec000 0x00100000 0x00000000 core.1883.
0x00020100 container    [0x00007fa0fbf00000-0x00007fa0fc000000)* 0x1eaec000 0x00100000 0x00000000 core.1883.
0x00020200 container    [0x00007fa0fc000000-0x00007fa0fc100000)* 0x1ebec000 0x00100000 0x00000000 core.1883.
0x00020300 container    [0x00007fa0fc100000-0x00007fa0fc200000)* 0x1ecec000 0x00100000 0x00000000 core.1883.
0x00020400 container    [0x00007fa0fc200000-0x00007fa0fc300000)* 0x1edec000 0x00100000 0x00000000 core.1883.
0x00020500 container    [0x00007fa0fc300000-0x00007fa0fc400000)* 0x1eeec000 0x00100000 0x00000000 core.1883.
0x00020600 container    [0x00007fa0fc400000-0x00007fa0fc500000)* 0x1efec000 0x00100000 0x521d1e8c core.1883.
0x00020700 container    [0x00007fa0fc500000-0x00007fa0fc600000)* 0x1f0ec000 0x00100000 0x00000000 core.1883.
0x00020800 container    [0x00007fa0fc600000-0x00007fa0fc700000)* 0x1f1ec000 0x00100000 0x00000000 core.1883.
0x00020900 container    [0x00007fa0fc700000-0x00007fa0fc800000)* 0x1f2ec000 0x00100000 0x00000000 core.1883.
0x00020a00 container    [0x00007fa0fc800000-0x00007fa0fc900000)* 0x1f3ec000 0x00100000 0x00000000 core.1883.
0x00020b00 container    [0x00007fa0fc900000-0x00007fa0fca00000)* 0x1f4ec000 0x00100000 0x00000000 core.1883.
0x00020c00 container    [0x00007fa0fca00000-0x00007fa0fcb00000)* 0x1f5ec000 0x00100000 0x00000000 core.1883.
0x00020d00 container    [0x00007fa0fcb00000-0x00007fa0fcc00000)* 0x1f6ec000 0x00100000 0x00000000 core.1883.
0x00020e00 container    [0x00007fa0fcc00000-0x00007fa0fcd00000)* 0x1f7ec000 0x00100000 0x00000000 core.1883.
0x00020f00 container    [0x00007fa0fcd00000-0x00007fa0fce00000)* 0x1f8ec000 0x00100000 0x00000000 core.1883.
0x00021000 container    [0x00007fa0fce00000-0x00007fa0fcf00000)* 0x1f9ec000 0x00100000 0x00000000 core.1883.
0x00021100 container    [0x00007fa0fcf00000-0x00007fa0fd000000)* 0x1faec000 0x00100000 0x00000000 core.1883.
0x00021200 container    [0x00007fa0fd000000-0x00007fa0fd100000)* 0x1fbec000 0x00100000 0x00000000 core.1883.
0x00021300 container    [0x00007fa0fd100000-0x00007fa0fd200000)* 0x1fcec000 0x00100000 0x00000000 core.1883.
0x00021400 container    [0x00007fa0fd200000-0x00007fa0fd300000)* 0x1fdec000 0x00100000 0x00000000 core.1883.
0x00021500 container    [0x00007fa0fd300000-0x00007fa0fd400000)* 0x1feec000 0x00100000 0x00000000 core.1883.
0x00021600 container    [0x00007fa0fd400000-0x00007fa0fd500000)* 0x1ffec000 0x00100000 0x00000000 core.1883.
0x00021700 container    [0x00007fa0fd500000-0x00007fa0fd600000)* 0x200ec000 0x00100000 0x00000000 core.1883.
0x00021800 container    [0x00007fa0fd600000-0x00007fa0fd700000)* 0x201ec000 0x00100000 0x00000000 core.1883.
0x00021900 container    [0x00007fa0fd700000-0x00007fa0fd800000)* 0x202ec000 0x00100000 0x00000000 core.1883.
0x00021a00 container    [0x00007fa0fd800000-0x00007fa0fd900000)* 0x203ec000 0x00100000 0x00000000 core.1883.
```

```
0x00021b00 container    [0x00007fa0fd900000-0x00007fa0fda00000)* 0x204ec000 0x00100000 0x00000000 core.1883.
0x00021c00 container    [0x00007fa0fda00000-0x00007fa0fdb00000)* 0x205ec000 0x00100000 0x00000000 core.1883.
0x00021d00 container    [0x00007fa0fdb00000-0x00007fa0fdc00000)* 0x206ec000 0x00100000 0x00000000 core.1883.
0x00021e00 container    [0x00007fa0fdc00000-0x00007fa0fdd00000)* 0x207ec000 0x00100000 0x00000000 core.1883.
0x00021f00 container    [0x00007fa0fdd00000-0x00007fa0fde00000)* 0x208ec000 0x00100000 0x00000000 core.1883.
0x00022000 container    [0x00007fa0fde00000-0x00007fa0fdf00000)* 0x209ec000 0x00100000 0x00000000 core.1883.
0x00022100 container    [0x00007fa0fdf00000-0x00007fa0fe000000)* 0x20aec000 0x00100000 0x00000000 core.1883.
0x00022200 container    [0x00007fa0fe000000-0x00007fa0fe100000)* 0x20bec000 0x00100000 0x00000000 core.1883.
0x00022300 container    [0x00007fa0fe100000-0x00007fa0fe200000)* 0x20cec000 0x00100000 0x00000000 core.1883.
0x00022400 container    [0x00007fa0fe200000-0x00007fa0fe300000)* 0x20dec000 0x00100000 0x00000000 core.1883.
0x00022500 container    [0x00007fa0fe300000-0x00007fa0fe400000)* 0x20eec000 0x00100000 0x00000000 core.1883.
0x00022600 container    [0x00007fa0fe400000-0x00007fa0fe500000)* 0x20fec000 0x00100000 0x00000000 core.1883.
0x00022700 container    [0x00007fa0fe500000-0x00007fa0fe600000)* 0x210ec000 0x00100000 0x00000000 core.1883.
0x00022800 container    [0x00007fa0fe600000-0x00007fa0fe700000)* 0x211ec000 0x00100000 0x00000000 core.1883.
0x00022900 container    [0x00007fa0fe700000-0x00007fa0fe800000)* 0x212ec000 0x00100000 0x00000000 core.1883.
0x00022a00 container    [0x00007fa0fe800000-0x00007fa0fe900000)* 0x213ec000 0x00100000 0x00000000 core.1883.
0x00022b00 container    [0x00007fa0fe900000-0x00007fa0fea00000)* 0x214ec000 0x00100000 0x00000000 core.1883.
0x00022c00 container    [0x00007fa0fea00000-0x00007fa0feb00000)* 0x215ec000 0x00100000 0x00000000 core.1883.
0x00022d00 container    [0x00007fa0feb00000-0x00007fa0fec00000)* 0x216ec000 0x00100000 0x00000000 core.1883.
0x00022e00 container    [0x00007fa0fec00000-0x00007fa0fed00000)* 0x217ec000 0x00100000 0x00000000 core.1883.
0x00022f00 container    [0x00007fa0fed00000-0x00007fa0fee00000)* 0x218ec000 0x00100000 0x00000000 core.1883.
0x00023000 container    [0x00007fa0fee00000-0x00007fa0fef00000)* 0x219ec000 0x00100000 0x00000000 core.1883.
0x00023100 container    [0x00007fa0fef00000-0x00007fa0ff000000)* 0x21aec000 0x00100000 0x00000000 core.1883.
0x00023200 container    [0x00007fa0ff000000-0x00007fa0ff100000)* 0x21bec000 0x00100000 0x00000000 core.1883.
0x00023300 container    [0x00007fa0ff100000-0x00007fa0ff200000)* 0x21cec000 0x00100000 0x00000000 core.1883.
0x00023400 container    [0x00007fa0ff200000-0x00007fa0ff300000)* 0x21dec000 0x00100000 0x00000000 core.1883.
0x00023500 container    [0x00007fa0ff300000-0x00007fa0ff400000)* 0x21eec000 0x00100000 0x00000000 core.1883.
0x00023600 container    [0x00007fa0ff400000-0x00007fa0ff500000)* 0x21fec000 0x00100000 0x00000000 core.1883.
0x00023700 container    [0x00007fa0ff500000-0x00007fa0ff600000)* 0x220ec000 0x00100000 0x00000000 core.1883.
0x00023800 container    [0x00007fa0ff600000-0x00007fa0ff700000)* 0x221ec000 0x00100000 0x00000000 core.1883.
0x00023900 container    [0x00007fa0ff700000-0x00007fa0ff800000)* 0x222ec000 0x00100000 0x00000a03 core.1883.
0x00023a00 container    [0x00007fa0ff800000-0x00007fa0ff900000)* 0x223ec000 0x00100000 0x00000000 core.1883.
0x00023b00 container    [0x00007fa0ff900000-0x00007fa0ffa00000)* 0x224ec000 0x00100000 0x00000000 core.1883.
0x00023c00 container    [0x00007fa0ffa00000-0x00007fa0ffb00000)* 0x225ec000 0x00100000 0x00000000 core.1883.
0x00023d00 container    [0x00007fa0ffb00000-0x00007fa0ffc00000)* 0x226ec000 0x00100000 0x00000000 core.1883.
0x00023e00 container    [0x00007fa0ffc00000-0x00007fa0ffd00000)* 0x227ec000 0x00100000 0x00000000 core.1883.
0x00023f00 container    [0x00007fa0ffd00000-0x00007fa0ffe00000)* 0x228ec000 0x00100000 0x00000000 core.1883.
0x00024000 container    [0x00007fa0ffe00000-0x00007fa0fff00000)* 0x229ec000 0x00100000 0x00000000 core.1883.
0x00024100 container    [0x00007fa0fff00000-0x00007fa100000000)* 0x22aec000 0x00100000 0x00000000 core.1883.
0x00024200 container    [0x00007fa100000000-0x00007fa100100000)* 0x22bec000 0x00100000 0x00000000 core.1883.
0x00024300 container    [0x00007fa100100000-0x00007fa100200000)* 0x22cec000 0x00100000 0x00000000 core.1883.
0x00024400 container    [0x00007fa100200000-0x00007fa100300000)* 0x22dec000 0x00100000 0x00000000 core.1883.
0x00024500 container    [0x00007fa100300000-0x00007fa100400000)* 0x22eec000 0x00100000 0x00000000 core.1883.
0x00024600 container    [0x00007fa100400000-0x00007fa100500000)* 0x22fec000 0x00100000 0x00000000 core.1883.
0x00024700 container    [0x00007fa100500000-0x00007fa100600000)* 0x230ec000 0x00100000 0x00000000 core.1883.
0x00024800 container    [0x00007fa100600000-0x00007fa100700000)* 0x231ec000 0x00100000 0x00000000 core.1883.
0x00024900 container    [0x00007fa100700000-0x00007fa100800000)* 0x232ec000 0x00100000 0x00000000 core.1883.
0x00024a00 container    [0x00007fa100800000-0x00007fa100900000)* 0x233ec000 0x00100000 0x00000000 core.1883.
0x00024b00 container    [0x00007fa100900000-0x00007fa100a00000)* 0x234ec000 0x00100000 0x00000000 core.1883.
0x00024c00 container    [0x00007fa100a00000-0x00007fa100b00000)* 0x235ec000 0x00100000 0x00000000 core.1883.
0x00024d00 container    [0x00007fa100b00000-0x00007fa100c00000)* 0x236ec000 0x00100000 0x00000000 core.1883.
0x00024e00 container    [0x00007fa100c00000-0x00007fa100d00000)* 0x237ec000 0x00100000 0x00000000 core.1883.
0x00024f00 container    [0x00007fa100d00000-0x00007fa100e00000)* 0x238ec000 0x00100000 0x00000000 core.1883.
0x00025000 container    [0x00007fa100e00000-0x00007fa100f00000)* 0x239ec000 0x00100000 0x00000000 core.1883.
0x00025100 container    [0x00007fa100f00000-0x00007fa101000000)* 0x23aec000 0x00100000 0x00000000 core.1883.
0x00025200 container    [0x00007fa101000000-0x00007fa101100000)* 0x23bec000 0x00100000 0x00000000 core.1883.
0x00025300 container    [0x00007fa101100000-0x00007fa101200000)* 0x23cec000 0x00100000 0x00000000 core.1883.
0x00025400 container    [0x00007fa101200000-0x00007fa101300000)* 0x23dec000 0x00100000 0x00000000 core.1883.
0x00025500 container    [0x00007fa101300000-0x00007fa101400000)* 0x23eec000 0x00100000 0x00000000 core.1883.
0x00025600 container    [0x00007fa101400000-0x00007fa101500000)* 0x23fec000 0x00100000 0x00000000 core.1883.
0x00025700 container    [0x00007fa101500000-0x00007fa101600000)* 0x240ec000 0x00100000 0x00000000 core.1883.
0x00025800 container    [0x00007fa101600000-0x00007fa101700000)* 0x241ec000 0x00100000 0x00000000 core.1883.
0x00025900 container    [0x00007fa101700000-0x00007fa101800000)* 0x242ec000 0x00100000 0x00000000 core.1883.
0x00025a00 container    [0x00007fa101800000-0x00007fa101900000)* 0x243ec000 0x00100000 0x00000000 core.1883.
0x00025b00 container    [0x00007fa101900000-0x00007fa101a00000)* 0x244ec000 0x00100000 0x00000000 core.1883.
0x00025c00 container    [0x00007fa101a00000-0x00007fa101b00000)* 0x245ec000 0x00100000 0x00000000 core.1883.
0x00025d00 container    [0x00007fa101b00000-0x00007fa101c00000)* 0x246ec000 0x00100000 0x00000000 core.1883.
0x00025e00 container    [0x00007fa101c00000-0x00007fa101d00000)* 0x247ec000 0x00100000 0x00000000 core.1883.
0x00025f00 container    [0x00007fa101d00000-0x00007fa101e00000)* 0x248ec000 0x00100000 0x00000000 core.1883.
0x00026000 container    [0x00007fa101e00000-0x00007fa101f00000)* 0x249ec000 0x00100000 0x00000000 core.1883.
0x00026100 container    [0x00007fa101f00000-0x00007fa102000000)* 0x24aec000 0x00100000 0x00000000 core.1883.
0x00026200 container    [0x00007fa102000000-0x00007fa102100000)* 0x24bec000 0x00100000 0x00000000 core.1883.
0x00026300 container    [0x00007fa102100000-0x00007fa102200000)* 0x24cec000 0x00100000 0x00000000 core.1883.
0x00026400 container    [0x00007fa102200000-0x00007fa102300000)* 0x24dec000 0x00100000 0x00000000 core.1883.
0x00026500 container    [0x00007fa102300000-0x00007fa102400000)* 0x24eec000 0x00100000 0x00000000 core.1883.
0x00026600 container    [0x00007fa102400000-0x00007fa102500000)* 0x24fec000 0x00100000 0x00000000 core.1883.
0x00026700 container    [0x00007fa102500000-0x00007fa102600000)* 0x250ec000 0x00100000 0x00000000 core.1883.
0x00026800 container    [0x00007fa102600000-0x00007fa102700000)* 0x251ec000 0x00100000 0x00000000 core.1883.
0x00026900 container    [0x00007fa102700000-0x00007fa102800000)* 0x252ec000 0x00100000 0x00000000 core.1883.
0x00026a00 container    [0x00007fa102800000-0x00007fa102900000)* 0x253ec000 0x00100000 0x00000000 core.1883.
0x00026b00 container    [0x00007fa102900000-0x00007fa102a00000)* 0x254ec000 0x00100000 0x00000000 core.1883.
0x00026c00 container    [0x00007fa102a00000-0x00007fa102b00000)* 0x255ec000 0x00100000 0x00000000 core.1883.
0x00026d00 container    [0x00007fa102b00000-0x00007fa102c00000)* 0x256ec000 0x00100000 0x00000000 core.1883.
0x00026e00 container    [0x00007fa102c00000-0x00007fa102d00000)* 0x257ec000 0x00100000 0x00000000 core.1883.
0x00026f00 container    [0x00007fa102d00000-0x00007fa102e00000)* 0x258ec000 0x00100000 0x00000000 core.1883.
0x00027000 container    [0x00007fa102e00000-0x00007fa102f00000)* 0x259ec000 0x00100000 0x00000000 core.1883.
```

```
0x00027100 container    [0x00007fa102f00000-0x00007fa103000000)* 0x25aec000 0x00100000 0x00000000 core.1883.
0x00027200 container    [0x00007fa103000000-0x00007fa103100000)* 0x25bec000 0x00100000 0x00000000 core.1883.
0x00027300 container    [0x00007fa103100000-0x00007fa103200000)* 0x25cec000 0x00100000 0x00000000 core.1883.
0x00027400 container    [0x00007fa103200000-0x00007fa103300000)* 0x25dec000 0x00100000 0x00000000 core.1883.
0x00027500 container    [0x00007fa103300000-0x00007fa103400000)* 0x25eec000 0x00100000 0x00000000 core.1883.
0x00027600 container    [0x00007fa103400000-0x00007fa103500000)* 0x25fec000 0x00100000 0x00000000 core.1883.
0x00027700 container    [0x00007fa103500000-0x00007fa103600000)* 0x260ec000 0x00100000 0x00000000 core.1883.
0x00027800 container    [0x00007fa103600000-0x00007fa103700000)* 0x261ec000 0x00100000 0x00000000 core.1883.
0x00027900 container    [0x00007fa103700000-0x00007fa103800000)* 0x262ec000 0x00100000 0x00000000 core.1883.
0x00027a00 container    [0x00007fa103800000-0x00007fa103900000)* 0x263ec000 0x00100000 0x00000000 core.1883.
0x00027b00 container    [0x00007fa103900000-0x00007fa103a00000)* 0x264ec000 0x00100000 0x00000000 core.1883.
0x00027c00 container    [0x00007fa103a00000-0x00007fa103b00000)* 0x265ec000 0x00100000 0x00000000 core.1883.
0x00027d00 container    [0x00007fa103b00000-0x00007fa103c00000)* 0x266ec000 0x00100000 0x00000000 core.1883.
0x00027e00 container    [0x00007fa103c00000-0x00007fa103d00000)* 0x267ec000 0x00100000 0x00000000 core.1883.
0x00027f00 container    [0x00007fa103d00000-0x00007fa103e00000)* 0x268ec000 0x00100000 0x00000000 core.1883.
0x00028000 container    [0x00007fa103e00000-0x00007fa103f00000)* 0x269ec000 0x00100000 0x00000000 core.1883.
0x00028100 container    [0x00007fa103f00000-0x00007fa104000000)* 0x26aec000 0x00100000 0x00000000 core.1883.
0x00028200 container    [0x00007fa104000000-0x00007fa104100000)* 0x26bec000 0x00100000 0x00000000 core.1883.
0x00028300 container    [0x00007fa104100000-0x00007fa104200000)* 0x26cec000 0x00100000 0x00000000 core.1883.
0x00028400 container    [0x00007fa104200000-0x00007fa104300000)* 0x26dec000 0x00100000 0x00000000 core.1883.
0x00028500 container    [0x00007fa104300000-0x00007fa104400000)* 0x26eec000 0x00100000 0x00000000 core.1883.
0x00028600 container    [0x00007fa104400000-0x00007fa104500000)* 0x26fec000 0x00100000 0x00000000 core.1883.
0x00028700 container    [0x00007fa104500000-0x00007fa104600000)* 0x270ec000 0x00100000 0x00000000 core.1883.
0x00028800 container    [0x00007fa104600000-0x00007fa104700000)* 0x271ec000 0x00100000 0x00000000 core.1883.
0x00028900 container    [0x00007fa104700000-0x00007fa104800000)* 0x272ec000 0x00100000 0x00000000 core.1883.
0x00028a00 container    [0x00007fa104800000-0x00007fa104900000)* 0x273ec000 0x00100000 0x00000000 core.1883.
0x00028b00 container    [0x00007fa104900000-0x00007fa104a00000)* 0x274ec000 0x00100000 0x00000000 core.1883.
0x00028c00 container    [0x00007fa104a00000-0x00007fa104b00000)* 0x275ec000 0x00100000 0x00000000 core.1883.
0x00028d00 container    [0x00007fa104b00000-0x00007fa104c00000)* 0x276ec000 0x00100000 0x00000000 core.1883.
0x00028e00 container    [0x00007fa104c00000-0x00007fa104d00000)* 0x277ec000 0x00100000 0x00000000 core.1883.
0x00028f00 container    [0x00007fa104d00000-0x00007fa104e00000)* 0x278ec000 0x00100000 0x00000000 core.1883.
0x00029000 container    [0x00007fa104e00000-0x00007fa104f00000)* 0x279ec000 0x00100000 0x00000000 core.1883.
0x00029100 container    [0x00007fa104f00000-0x00007fa105000000)* 0x27aec000 0x00100000 0x00000000 core.1883.
0x00029200 container    [0x00007fa105000000-0x00007fa105100000)* 0x27bec000 0x00100000 0x00000000 core.1883.
0x00029300 container    [0x00007fa105100000-0x00007fa105200000)* 0x27cec000 0x00100000 0x00000000 core.1883.
0x00029400 container    [0x00007fa105200000-0x00007fa105300000)* 0x27dec000 0x00100000 0x00000000 core.1883.
0x00029500 container    [0x00007fa105300000-0x00007fa105400000)* 0x27eec000 0x00100000 0x00000000 core.1883.
0x00029600 container    [0x00007fa105400000-0x00007fa105500000)* 0x27fec000 0x00100000 0x00000000 core.1883.
0x00029700 container    [0x00007fa105500000-0x00007fa105600000)* 0x280ec000 0x00100000 0x00000000 core.1883.
0x00029800 container    [0x00007fa105600000-0x00007fa105700000)* 0x281ec000 0x00100000 0x00000000 core.1883.
0x00029900 container    [0x00007fa105700000-0x00007fa105800000)* 0x282ec000 0x00100000 0x00000000 core.1883.
0x00029a00 container    [0x00007fa105800000-0x00007fa105900000)* 0x283ec000 0x00100000 0x00000000 core.1883.
0x00029b00 container    [0x00007fa105900000-0x00007fa105a00000)* 0x284ec000 0x00100000 0x00000000 core.1883.
0x00029c00 container    [0x00007fa105a00000-0x00007fa105b00000)* 0x285ec000 0x00100000 0x00000000 core.1883.
0x00029d00 container    [0x00007fa105b00000-0x00007fa105c00000)* 0x286ec000 0x00100000 0x00000000 core.1883.
0x00029e00 container    [0x00007fa105c00000-0x00007fa105d00000)* 0x287ec000 0x00100000 0x00000000 core.1883.
0x00029f00 container    [0x00007fa105d00000-0x00007fa105e00000)* 0x288ec000 0x00100000 0x00000000 core.1883.
0x0002a000 container    [0x00007fa105e00000-0x00007fa105f00000)* 0x289ec000 0x00100000 0x00000000 core.1883.
0x0002a100 container    [0x00007fa105f00000-0x00007fa106000000)* 0x28aec000 0x00100000 0x00000000 core.1883.
0x0002a200 container    [0x00007fa106000000-0x00007fa106100000)* 0x28bec000 0x00100000 0x00000000 core.1883.
0x0002a300 container    [0x00007fa106100000-0x00007fa106200000)* 0x28cec000 0x00100000 0x00000000 core.1883.
0x0002a400 container    [0x00007fa106200000-0x00007fa106300000)* 0x28dec000 0x00100000 0x00000000 core.1883.
0x0002a500 container    [0x00007fa106300000-0x00007fa106400000)* 0x28eec000 0x00100000 0x00000000 core.1883.
0x0002a600 container    [0x00007fa106400000-0x00007fa106500000)* 0x28fec000 0x00100000 0x00000000 core.1883.
0x0002a700 container    [0x00007fa106500000-0x00007fa106600000)* 0x290ec000 0x00100000 0x00000000 core.1883.
0x0002a800 container    [0x00007fa106600000-0x00007fa106700000)* 0x291ec000 0x00100000 0x00000000 core.1883.
0x0002a900 container    [0x00007fa106700000-0x00007fa106800000)* 0x292ec000 0x00100000 0x00000000 core.1883.
0x0002aa00 container    [0x00007fa106800000-0x00007fa106900000)* 0x293ec000 0x00100000 0x00000000 core.1883.
0x0002ab00 container    [0x00007fa106900000-0x00007fa106a00000)* 0x294ec000 0x00100000 0x00000e03 core.1883.
0x0002ac00 container    [0x00007fa106a00000-0x00007fa106b00000)* 0x295ec000 0x00100000 0x00000000 core.1883.
0x0002ad00 container    [0x00007fa106b00000-0x00007fa106c00000)* 0x296ec000 0x00100000 0x00000000 core.1883.
0x0002ae00 container    [0x00007fa106c00000-0x00007fa106d00000)* 0x297ec000 0x00100000 0x00000000 core.1883.
0x0002af00 container    [0x00007fa106d00000-0x00007fa106e00000)* 0x298ec000 0x00100000 0x00000000 core.1883.
0x0002b000 container    [0x00007fa106e00000-0x00007fa106f00000)* 0x299ec000 0x00100000 0x00000000 core.1883.
0x0002b100 container    [0x00007fa106f00000-0x00007fa107000000)* 0x29aec000 0x00100000 0x00000000 core.1883.
0x0002b200 container    [0x00007fa107000000-0x00007fa107100000)* 0x29bec000 0x00100000 0x00000000 core.1883.
0x0002b300 container    [0x00007fa107100000-0x00007fa107200000)* 0x29cec000 0x00100000 0x00000000 core.1883.
0x0002b400 container    [0x00007fa107200000-0x00007fa107300000)* 0x29dec000 0x00100000 0x00000000 core.1883.
0x0002b500 container    [0x00007fa107300000-0x00007fa107400000)* 0x29eec000 0x00100000 0x00000000 core.1883.
0x0002b600 container    [0x00007fa107400000-0x00007fa107500000)* 0x29fec000 0x00100000 0x00000000 core.1883.
0x0002b700 container    [0x00007fa107500000-0x00007fa107600000)* 0x2a0ec000 0x00100000 0x00000000 core.1883.
0x0002b800 container    [0x00007fa107600000-0x00007fa107700000)* 0x2a1ec000 0x00100000 0x00000000 core.1883.
0x0002b900 container    [0x00007fa107700000-0x00007fa107800000)* 0x2a2ec000 0x00100000 0x00000000 core.1883.
0x0002ba00 container    [0x00007fa107800000-0x00007fa107900000)* 0x2a3ec000 0x00100000 0x00000000 core.1883.
0x0002bb00 container    [0x00007fa107900000-0x00007fa107a00000)* 0x2a4ec000 0x00100000 0x00000000 core.1883.
0x0002bc00 container    [0x00007fa107a00000-0x00007fa107b00000)* 0x2a5ec000 0x00100000 0x00000000 core.1883.
0x0002bd00 container    [0x00007fa107b00000-0x00007fa107c00000)* 0x2a6ec000 0x00100000 0x00000000 core.1883.
0x0002be00 container    [0x00007fa107c00000-0x00007fa107d00000)* 0x2a7ec000 0x00100000 0x00000000 core.1883.
0x0002bf00 container    [0x00007fa107d00000-0x00007fa107e00000)* 0x2a8ec000 0x00100000 0x00000000 core.1883.
0x0002c000 container    [0x00007fa107e00000-0x00007fa107f00000)* 0x2a9ec000 0x00100000 0x00000000 core.1883.
0x0002c100 container    [0x00007fa107f00000-0x00007fa108000000)* 0x2aaec000 0x00100000 0x00000000 core.1883.
0x0002c200 container    [0x00007fa108000000-0x00007fa108100000)* 0x2abec000 0x00100000 0x00000000 core.1883.
0x0002c300 container    [0x00007fa108100000-0x00007fa108200000)* 0x2acec000 0x00100000 0x00000000 core.1883.
0x0002c400 container    [0x00007fa108200000-0x00007fa108300000)* 0x2adec000 0x00100000 0x00000000 core.1883.
0x0002c500 container    [0x00007fa108300000-0x00007fa108400000)* 0x2aeec000 0x00100000 0x00000000 core.1883.
0x0002c600 container    [0x00007fa108400000-0x00007fa108500000)* 0x2afec000 0x00100000 0x00000000 core.1883.
```

```
0x0002c700 container      [0x00007fa108500000-0x00007fa108600000)* 0x2b0ec000 0x00100000 0x00000000 core.1883.
0x0002c800 container      [0x00007fa108600000-0x00007fa108700000)* 0x2b1ec000 0x00100000 0x00000000 core.1883.
0x0002c900 container      [0x00007fa108700000-0x00007fa108800000)* 0x2b2ec000 0x00100000 0x00000000 core.1883.
0x0002ca00 container      [0x00007fa108800000-0x00007fa108900000)* 0x2b3ec000 0x00100000 0x00000000 core.1883.
0x0002cb00 container      [0x00007fa108900000-0x00007fa108a00000)* 0x2b4ec000 0x00100000 0x00000000 core.1883.
0x0002cc00 container      [0x00007fa108a00000-0x00007fa108b00000)* 0x2b5ec000 0x00100000 0x00000000 core.1883.
0x0002cd00 container      [0x00007fa108b00000-0x00007fa108c00000)* 0x2b6ec000 0x00100000 0x00000000 core.1883.
0x0002ce00 container      [0x00007fa108c00000-0x00007fa108d00000)* 0x2b7ec000 0x00100000 0x00000000 core.1883.
0x0002cf00 container      [0x00007fa108d00000-0x00007fa108e00000)* 0x2b8ec000 0x00100000 0x00000000 core.1883.
0x0002d000 container      [0x00007fa108e00000-0x00007fa108f00000)* 0x2b9ec000 0x00100000 0x00000000 core.1883.
0x0002d100 container      [0x00007fa108f00000-0x00007fa109000000)* 0x2baec000 0x00100000 0x00000000 core.1883.
0x0002d200 container      [0x00007fa109000000-0x00007fa109100000)* 0x2bbec000 0x00100000 0x00000000 core.1883.
0x0002d300 container      [0x00007fa109100000-0x00007fa109200000)* 0x2bcec000 0x00100000 0x00000000 core.1883.
0x0002d400 container      [0x00007fa109200000-0x00007fa109300000)* 0x2bdec000 0x00100000 0x00000000 core.1883.
0x0002d500 container      [0x00007fa109300000-0x00007fa109400000)* 0x2beec000 0x00100000 0x00000000 core.1883.
0x0002d600 container      [0x00007fa109400000-0x00007fa109500000)* 0x2bfec000 0x00100000 0x00000000 core.1883.
0x0002d700 container      [0x00007fa109500000-0x00007fa109600000)* 0x2c0ec000 0x00100000 0x00000000 core.1883.
0x0002d800 container      [0x00007fa109600000-0x00007fa109700000)* 0x2c1ec000 0x00100000 0x00000000 core.1883.
0x0002d900 container      [0x00007fa109700000-0x00007fa109800000)* 0x2c2ec000 0x00100000 0x00000000 core.1883.
0x0002da00 container      [0x00007fa109800000-0x00007fa109900000)* 0x2c3ec000 0x00100000 0x00000000 core.1883.
0x0002db00 container      [0x00007fa109900000-0x00007fa109a00000)* 0x2c4ec000 0x00100000 0x00000000 core.1883.
0x0002dc00 container      [0x00007fa109a00000-0x00007fa109b00000)* 0x2c5ec000 0x00100000 0x00000000 core.1883.
0x0002dd00 container      [0x00007fa109b00000-0x00007fa109c00000)* 0x2c6ec000 0x00100000 0x00000000 core.1883.
0x0002de00 container      [0x00007fa109c00000-0x00007fa109d00000)* 0x2c7ec000 0x00100000 0x00000000 core.1883.
0x0002df00 container      [0x00007fa109d00000-0x00007fa109e00000)* 0x2c8ec000 0x00100000 0x00000000 core.1883.
0x0002e000 container      [0x00007fa109e00000-0x00007fa109f00000)* 0x2c9ec000 0x00100000 0x00000000 core.1883.
0x0002e100 container      [0x00007fa109f00000-0x00007fa10a000000)* 0x2caec000 0x00100000 0x00000000 core.1883.
0x0002e200 container      [0x00007fa10a000000-0x00007fa10a100000)* 0x2cbec000 0x00100000 0x00000000 core.1883.
0x0002e300 container      [0x00007fa10a100000-0x00007fa10a200000)* 0x2ccec000 0x00100000 0x00000000 core.1883.
0x0002e400 container      [0x00007fa10a200000-0x00007fa10a300000)* 0x2cdec000 0x00100000 0x00010000 core.1883.
0x0002e500 container      [0x00007fa10a300000-0x00007fa10a400000)* 0x2ceec000 0x00100000 0x00000000 core.1883.
0x0002e600 container      [0x00007fa10a400000-0x00007fa10a500000)* 0x2cfec000 0x00100000 0x00000000 core.1883.
0x0002e700 container      [0x00007fa10a500000-0x00007fa10a600000)* 0x2d0ec000 0x00100000 0x00000000 core.1883.
0x0002e800 container      [0x00007fa10a600000-0x00007fa10a700000)* 0x2d1ec000 0x00100000 0x00000000 core.1883.
0x0002e900 container      [0x00007fa10a700000-0x00007fa10a800000)* 0x2d2ec000 0x00100000 0x00000000 core.1883.
0x0002ea00 container      [0x00007fa10a800000-0x00007fa10a900000)* 0x2d3ec000 0x00100000 0x00000000 core.1883.
0x0002eb00 container      [0x00007fa10a900000-0x00007fa10aa00000)* 0x2d4ec000 0x00100000 0x00000000 core.1883.
0x0002ec00 container      [0x00007fa10aa00000-0x00007fa10ab00000)* 0x2d5ec000 0x00100000 0x00000000 core.1883.
0x0002ed00 container      [0x00007fa10ab00000-0x00007fa10ac00000)* 0x2d6ec000 0x00100000 0x00000000 core.1883.
0x0002ee00 container      [0x00007fa10ac00000-0x00007fa10ad00000)* 0x2d7ec000 0x00100000 0x00000000 core.1883.
0x0002ef00 container      [0x00007fa10ad00000-0x00007fa10ae00000)* 0x2d8ec000 0x00100000 0x00000000 core.1883.
0x0002f000 container      [0x00007fa10ae00000-0x00007fa10af00000)* 0x2d9ec000 0x00100000 0x00000000 core.1883.
0x0002f100 container      [0x00007fa10af00000-0x00007fa10b000000)* 0x2daec000 0x00100000 0x00000000 core.1883.
0x0002f200 container      [0x00007fa10b000000-0x00007fa10b100000)* 0x2dbec000 0x00100000 0x00000000 core.1883.
0x0002f300 container      [0x00007fa10b100000-0x00007fa10b200000)* 0x2dcec000 0x00100000 0x00000000 core.1883.
0x0002f400 container      [0x00007fa10b200000-0x00007fa10b300000)* 0x2ddec000 0x00100000 0x00000000 core.1883.
0x0002f500 container      [0x00007fa10b400000-0x00007fa10b500000)* 0x2deec000 0x00100000 0x00000000 core.1883.
0x0002f600 container      [0x00007fa10b500000-0x00007fa10b600000)* 0x2dfec000 0x00100000 0x00000000 core.1883.
0x0002f700 container      [0x00007fa10b600000-0x00007fa10b700000)* 0x2e0ec000 0x00100000 0x00000000 core.1883.
0x0002f800 container      [0x00007fa10b700000-0x00007fa10b800000)* 0x2e1ec000 0x00100000 0x00000000 core.1883.
0x0002f900 container      [0x00007fa10b800000-0x00007fa10b900000)* 0x2e2ec000 0x00100000 0x00000000 core.1883.
0x0002fa00 container      [0x00007fa10b900000-0x00007fa10ba00000)* 0x2e3ec000 0x00100000 0x00000000 core.1883.
0x0002fb00 container      [0x00007fa10ba00000-0x00007fa10bb00000)* 0x2e4ec000 0x00100000 0x00000000 core.1883.
0x0002fc00 container      [0x00007fa10bb00000-0x00007fa10bc00000)* 0x2e5ec000 0x00100000 0x00000000 core.1883.
0x0002fd00 container      [0x00007fa10bc00000-0x00007fa10bd00000)* 0x2e6ec000 0x00100000 0x00000000 core.1883.
0x0002fe00 container      [0x00007fa10bd00000-0x00007fa10be00000)* 0x2e7ec000 0x00100000 0x00000000 core.1883.
0x0002ff00 container      [0x00007fa10be00000-0x00007fa10bf00000)* 0x2e8ec000 0x00100000 0x00000000 core.1883.
0x00030000 container      [0x00007fa10bf00000-0x00007fa10c000000)* 0x2e9ec000 0x00100000 0x00000000 core.1883.
0x00030100 container      [0x00007fa10c000000-0x00007fa10c100000)* 0x2eaec000 0x00100000 0x00000000 core.1883.
0x00030200 container      [0x00007fa10c100000-0x00007fa10c200000)* 0x2ebec000 0x00100000 0x00000000 core.1883.
0x00030300 container      [0x00007fa10c200000-0x00007fa10c300000)* 0x2ecec000 0x00100000 0x00000000 core.1883.
0x00030400 container      [0x00007fa10c300000-0x00007fa10c400000)* 0x2edec000 0x00100000 0x00000000 core.1883.
0x00030500 container      [0x00007fa10c400000-0x00007fa10c500000)* 0x2eeec000 0x00100000 0x00000000 core.1883.
0x00030600 container      [0x00007fa10c500000-0x00007fa10c600000)* 0x2efec000 0x00100000 0x00000000 core.1883.
0x00030700 container      [0x00007fa10c600000-0x00007fa10c700000)* 0x2f0ec000 0x00100000 0x00000000 core.1883.
0x00030800 container      [0x00007fa10c700000-0x00007fa10c800000)* 0x2f1ec000 0x00100000 0x00000000 core.1883.
0x00030900 container      [0x00007fa10c800000-0x00007fa10c900000)* 0x2f2ec000 0x00100000 0x00000000 core.1883.
0x00030a00 container      [0x00007fa10c900000-0x00007fa10ca00000)* 0x2f3ec000 0x00100000 0x00000000 core.1883.
0x00030b00 container      [0x00007fa10ca00000-0x00007fa10cb00000)* 0x2f4ec000 0x00100000 0x00000000 core.1883.
0x00030c00 container      [0x00007fa10cb00000-0x00007fa10cc00000)* 0x2f5ec000 0x00100000 0x00000000 core.1883.
0x00030d00 container      [0x00007fa10cc00000-0x00007fa10cd00000)* 0x2f6ec000 0x00100000 0x00000000 core.1883.
0x00030e00 container      [0x00007fa10cd00000-0x00007fa10ce00000)* 0x2f7ec000 0x00100000 0x00000000 core.1883.
0x00030f00 container      [0x00007fa10ce00000-0x00007fa10cf00000)* 0x2f8ec000 0x00100000 0x00000000 core.1883.
0x00031000 container      [0x00007fa10cf00000-0x00007fa10d000000)* 0x2f9ec000 0x00100000 0x00000000 core.1883.
0x00031100 container      [0x00007fa10d000000-0x00007fa10d100000)* 0x2faec000 0x00100000 0x00000000 core.1883.
0x00031200 container      [0x00007fa10d100000-0x00007fa10d200000)* 0x2fbec000 0x00100000 0x00000000 core.1883.
0x00031300 container      [0x00007fa10d200000-0x00007fa10d300000)* 0x2fcec000 0x00100000 0x00000000 core.1883.
0x00031400 container      [0x00007fa10d300000-0x00007fa10d400000)* 0x2fdec000 0x00100000 0x00000000 core.1883.
0x00031500 container      [0x00007fa10d400000-0x00007fa10d500000)* 0x2feec000 0x00100000 0x00000000 core.1883.
0x00031600 container      [0x00007fa10d500000-0x00007fa10d600000)* 0x2ffec000 0x00100000 0x00000000 core.1883.
0x00031700 container      [0x00007fa10d600000-0x00007fa10d700000)* 0x300ec000 0x00100000 0x00000000 core.1883.
0x00031800 container      [0x00007fa10d700000-0x00007fa10d800000)* 0x301ec000 0x00100000 0x00000000 core.1883.
0x00031900 container      [0x00007fa10d800000-0x00007fa10d900000)* 0x302ec000 0x00100000 0x00000000 core.1883.
0x00031a00 container      [0x00007fa10d900000-0x00007fa10da00000)* 0x303ec000 0x00100000 0x00000000 core.1883.
0x00031b00 container      [0x00007fa10da00000-0x00007fa10db00000)* 0x304ec000 0x00100000 0x00000000 core.1883.
0x00031c00 container      [0x00007fa10db00000-0x00007fa10dc00000)* 0x305ec000 0x00100000 0x00000000 core.1883.
```

```
0x00031d00 container    [0x00007fa10dc00000-0x00007fa10dd00000)* 0x306ec000 0x00100000 0x00010000 core.1883.
0x00031e00 container    [0x00007fa10dd00000-0x00007fa10de00000)* 0x307ec000 0x00100000 0x00000000 core.1883.
0x00031f00 container    [0x00007fa10de00000-0x00007fa10df00000)* 0x308ec000 0x00100000 0x00000000 core.1883.
0x00032000 container    [0x00007fa10df00000-0x00007fa10e000000)* 0x309ec000 0x00100000 0x00000000 core.1883.
0x00032100 container    [0x00007fa10e000000-0x00007fa10e100000)* 0x30aec000 0x00100000 0x00000000 core.1883.
0x00032200 container    [0x00007fa10e100000-0x00007fa10e200000)* 0x30bec000 0x00100000 0x00000000 core.1883.
0x00032300 container    [0x00007fa10e200000-0x00007fa10e300000)* 0x30cec000 0x00100000 0x00000000 core.1883.
0x00032400 container    [0x00007fa10e300000-0x00007fa10e400000)* 0x30dec000 0x00100000 0x00000000 core.1883.
0x00032500 container    [0x00007fa10e400000-0x00007fa10e500000)* 0x30eec000 0x00100000 0x00000000 core.1883.
0x00032600 container    [0x00007fa10e500000-0x00007fa10e600000)* 0x30fec000 0x00100000 0x00000000 core.1883.
0x00032700 container    [0x00007fa10e600000-0x00007fa10e700000)* 0x310ec000 0x00100000 0x00000000 core.1883.
0x00032800 container    [0x00007fa10e700000-0x00007fa10e800000)* 0x311ec000 0x00100000 0x00000000 core.1883.
0x00032900 container    [0x00007fa10e800000-0x00007fa10e900000)* 0x312ec000 0x00100000 0x00000000 core.1883.
0x00032a00 container    [0x00007fa10e900000-0x00007fa10ea00000)* 0x313ec000 0x00100000 0x00000000 core.1883.
0x00032b00 container    [0x00007fa10ea00000-0x00007fa10eb00000)* 0x314ec000 0x00100000 0x00000000 core.1883.
0x00032c00 container    [0x00007fa10eb00000-0x00007fa10ec00000)* 0x315ec000 0x00100000 0x00000000 core.1883.
0x00032d00 container    [0x00007fa10ec00000-0x00007fa10ed00000)* 0x316ec000 0x00100000 0x00000000 core.1883.
0x00032e00 container    [0x00007fa10ed00000-0x00007fa10ee00000)* 0x317ec000 0x00100000 0x00000000 core.1883.
0x00032f00 container    [0x00007fa10ee00000-0x00007fa10ef00000)* 0x318ec000 0x00100000 0x00000000 core.1883.
0x00033000 container    [0x00007fa10ef00000-0x00007fa10f000000)* 0x319ec000 0x00100000 0x00000000 core.1883.
0x00033100 container    [0x00007fa10f000000-0x00007fa10f100000)* 0x31aec000 0x00100000 0x00000000 core.1883.
0x00033200 container    [0x00007fa10f100000-0x00007fa10f200000)* 0x31bec000 0x00100000 0x00000000 core.1883.
0x00033300 container    [0x00007fa10f200000-0x00007fa10f300000)* 0x31cec000 0x00100000 0x00000000 core.1883.
0x00033400 container    [0x00007fa10f300000-0x00007fa10f400000)* 0x31dec000 0x00100000 0x00000000 core.1883.
0x00033500 container    [0x00007fa10f400000-0x00007fa10f500000)* 0x31eec000 0x00100000 0x00000000 core.1883.
0x00033600 container    [0x00007fa10f500000-0x00007fa10f600000)* 0x31fec000 0x00100000 0x00000000 core.1883.
0x00033700 container    [0x00007fa10f600000-0x00007fa10f700000)* 0x320ec000 0x00100000 0x00000000 core.1883.
0x00033800 container    [0x00007fa10f700000-0x00007fa10f800000)* 0x321ec000 0x00100000 0x00000000 core.1883.
0x00033900 container    [0x00007fa10f800000-0x00007fa10f900000)* 0x322ec000 0x00100000 0x00000000 core.1883.
0x00033a00 container    [0x00007fa10f900000-0x00007fa10fa00000)* 0x323ec000 0x00100000 0x00000000 core.1883.
0x00033b00 container    [0x00007fa10fa00000-0x00007fa10fb00000)* 0x324ec000 0x00100000 0x00000000 core.1883.
0x00033c00 container    [0x00007fa10fb00000-0x00007fa10fc00000)* 0x325ec000 0x00100000 0x00000000 core.1883.
0x00033d00 container    [0x00007fa10fc00000-0x00007fa10fd00000)* 0x326ec000 0x00100000 0x00000000 core.1883.
0x00033e00 container    [0x00007fa10fd00000-0x00007fa10fe00000)* 0x327ec000 0x00100000 0x00000000 core.1883.
0x00033f00 container    [0x00007fa10fe00000-0x00007fa10ff00000)* 0x328ec000 0x00100000 0x00000000 core.1883.
0x00034000 container    [0x00007fa10ff00000-0x00007fa110000000)* 0x329ec000 0x00100000 0x00000000 core.1883.
0x00034100 container    [0x00007fa110000000-0x00007fa110100000)* 0x32aec000 0x00100000 0x00000000 core.1883.
0x00034200 container    [0x00007fa110100000-0x00007fa110200000)* 0x32bec000 0x00100000 0x00000000 core.1883.
0x00034300 container    [0x00007fa110200000-0x00007fa110300000)* 0x32cec000 0x00100000 0x00000000 core.1883.
0x00034400 container    [0x00007fa110300000-0x00007fa110400000)* 0x32dec000 0x00100000 0x00000000 core.1883.
0x00034500 container    [0x00007fa110400000-0x00007fa110500000)* 0x32eec000 0x00100000 0x00000000 core.1883.
0x00034600 container    [0x00007fa110500000-0x00007fa110600000)* 0x32fec000 0x00100000 0x00000000 core.1883.
0x00034700 container    [0x00007fa110600000-0x00007fa110700000)* 0x330ec000 0x00100000 0x00000000 core.1883.
0x00034800 container    [0x00007fa110700000-0x00007fa110800000)* 0x331ec000 0x00100000 0x00000000 core.1883.
0x00034900 container    [0x00007fa110800000-0x00007fa110900000)* 0x332ec000 0x00100000 0x00000000 core.1883.
0x00034a00 container    [0x00007fa110900000-0x00007fa110a00000)* 0x333ec000 0x00100000 0x00000000 core.1883.
0x00034b00 container    [0x00007fa110a00000-0x00007fa110b00000)* 0x334ec000 0x00100000 0x00000000 core.1883.
0x00034c00 container    [0x00007fa110b00000-0x00007fa110c00000)* 0x335ec000 0x00100000 0x00000000 core.1883.
0x00034d00 container    [0x00007fa110c00000-0x00007fa110d00000)* 0x336ec000 0x00100000 0x00000000 core.1883.
0x00034e00 container    [0x00007fa110d00000-0x00007fa110e00000)* 0x337ec000 0x00100000 0x00000000 core.1883.
0x00034f00 container    [0x00007fa110e00000-0x00007fa110f00000)* 0x338ec000 0x00100000 0x00000000 core.1883.
0x00035000 container    [0x00007fa110f00000-0x00007fa111000000)* 0x339ec000 0x00100000 0x00000000 core.1883.
0x00035100 container    [0x00007fa111000000-0x00007fa111100000)* 0x33aec000 0x00100000 0x00000000 core.1883.
0x00035200 container    [0x00007fa111100000-0x00007fa111200000)* 0x33bec000 0x00100000 0x00000000 core.1883.
0x00035300 container    [0x00007fa111200000-0x00007fa111300000)* 0x33cec000 0x00100000 0x00000000 core.1883.
0x00035400 container    [0x00007fa111300000-0x00007fa111400000)* 0x33dec000 0x00100000 0x00000000 core.1883.
0x00035500 container    [0x00007fa111400000-0x00007fa111500000)* 0x33eec000 0x00100000 0x00020000 core.1883.
0x00035600 container    [0x00007fa111500000-0x00007fa111600000)* 0x33fec000 0x00100000 0x00010000 core.1883.
0x00035700 container    [0x00007fa111600000-0x00007fa111700000)* 0x340ec000 0x00100000 0xe0010000 core.1883.
0x00035800 container    [0x00007fa111700000-0x00007fa111800000)* 0x341ec000 0x00100000 0x00000000 core.1883.
0x00035900 container    [0x00007fa111800000-0x00007fa111900000)* 0x342ec000 0x00100000 0x00000000 core.1883.
0x00035a00 container    [0x00007fa111900000-0x00007fa111a00000)* 0x343ec000 0x00100000 0x00000000 core.1883.
0x00035b00 container    [0x00007fa111a00000-0x00007fa111b00000)* 0x344ec000 0x00100000 0x00000000 core.1883.
0x00035c00 container    [0x00007fa111b00000-0x00007fa111c00000)* 0x345ec000 0x00100000 0x00000000 core.1883.
0x00035d00 container    [0x00007fa111c00000-0x00007fa111d00000)* 0x346ec000 0x00100000 0x00000000 core.1883.
0x00035e00 container    [0x00007fa111d00000-0x00007fa111e00000)* 0x347ec000 0x00100000 0x00000000 core.1883.
0x00035f00 container    [0x00007fa111e00000-0x00007fa111f00000)* 0x348ec000 0x00100000 0x00000000 core.1883.
0x00036000 container    [0x00007fa111f00000-0x00007fa112000000)* 0x349ec000 0x00100000 0x00000000 core.1883.
0x00036100 container    [0x00007fa112000000-0x00007fa112100000)* 0x34aec000 0x00100000 0x00000000 core.1883.
0x00036200 container    [0x00007fa112100000-0x00007fa112200000)* 0x34bec000 0x00100000 0x00000000 core.1883.
0x00036300 container    [0x00007fa112200000-0x00007fa112300000)* 0x34cec000 0x00100000 0x00000000 core.1883.
0x00036400 container    [0x00007fa112300000-0x00007fa112400000)* 0x34dec000 0x00100000 0x00000000 core.1883.
0x00036500 container    [0x00007fa112400000-0x00007fa112500000)* 0x34eec000 0x00100000 0x00000000 core.1883.
0x00036600 container    [0x00007fa112500000-0x00007fa112600000)* 0x34fec000 0x00100000 0x00000000 core.1883.
0x00036700 container    [0x00007fa112600000-0x00007fa112700000)* 0x350ec000 0x00100000 0x00000000 core.1883.
0x00036800 container    [0x00007fa112700000-0x00007fa112800000)* 0x351ec000 0x00100000 0x00000000 core.1883.
0x00036900 container    [0x00007fa112800000-0x00007fa112900000)* 0x352ec000 0x00100000 0x00000000 core.1883.
0x00036a00 container    [0x00007fa112900000-0x00007fa112a00000)* 0x353ec000 0x00100000 0x00000000 core.1883.
0x00036b00 container    [0x00007fa112a00000-0x00007fa112b00000)* 0x354ec000 0x00100000 0x00000000 core.1883.
0x00036c00 container    [0x00007fa112b00000-0x00007fa112c00000)* 0x355ec000 0x00100000 0x00000000 core.1883.
0x00036d00 container    [0x00007fa112c00000-0x00007fa112d00000)* 0x356ec000 0x00100000 0x00000000 core.1883.
0x00036e00 container    [0x00007fa112d00000-0x00007fa112e00000)* 0x357ec000 0x00100000 0x00000000 core.1883.
0x00036f00 container    [0x00007fa112e00000-0x00007fa112f00000)* 0x358ec000 0x00100000 0x00000000 core.1883.
0x00037000 container    [0x00007fa112f00000-0x00007fa113000000)* 0x359ec000 0x00100000 0x00000000 core.1883.
0x00037100 container    [0x00007fa113000000-0x00007fa113100000)* 0x35aec000 0x00100000 0x00000000 core.1883.
0x00037200 container    [0x00007fa113100000-0x00007fa113200000)* 0x35bec000 0x00100000 0x00000000 core.1883.
```

```
0x00037300 container      [0x00007fa113200000-0x00007fa113300000)* 0x35cec000 0x00100000 0x00000000 core.1883.
0x00037400 container      [0x00007fa113300000-0x00007fa113400000)* 0x35dec000 0x00100000 0x00000000 core.1883.
0x00037500 container      [0x00007fa113400000-0x00007fa113500000)* 0x35eec000 0x00100000 0x00000000 core.1883.
0x00037600 container      [0x00007fa113500000-0x00007fa113600000)* 0x35fec000 0x00100000 0x00000000 core.1883.
0x00037700 container      [0x00007fa113600000-0x00007fa113700000)* 0x360ec000 0x00100000 0x00000000 core.1883.
0x00037800 container      [0x00007fa113700000-0x00007fa113800000)* 0x361ec000 0x00100000 0x00000000 core.1883.
0x00037900 container      [0x00007fa113800000-0x00007fa113900000)* 0x362ec000 0x00100000 0x00000000 core.1883.
0x00037a00 container      [0x00007fa113900000-0x00007fa113a00000)* 0x363ec000 0x00100000 0x00000000 core.1883.
0x00037b00 container      [0x00007fa113a00000-0x00007fa113b00000)* 0x364ec000 0x00100000 0x00000000 core.1883.
0x00037c00 container      [0x00007fa113b00000-0x00007fa113c00000)* 0x365ec000 0x00100000 0x00000000 core.1883.
0x00037d00 container      [0x00007fa113c00000-0x00007fa113d00000)* 0x366ec000 0x00100000 0x00000000 core.1883.
0x00037e00 container      [0x00007fa113d00000-0x00007fa113e00000)* 0x367ec000 0x00100000 0x00000000 core.1883.
0x00037f00 container      [0x00007fa113e00000-0x00007fa113f00000)* 0x368ec000 0x00100000 0x00000000 core.1883.
0x00038000 container      [0x00007fa113f00000-0x00007fa114000000)* 0x369ec000 0x00100000 0x00000000 core.1883.
0x00038100 container      [0x00007fa114000000-0x00007fa114100000)* 0x36aec000 0x00100000 0x00000000 core.1883.
0x00038200 container      [0x00007fa114100000-0x00007fa114200000)* 0x36bec000 0x00100000 0x00000000 core.1883.
0x00038300 container      [0x00007fa114200000-0x00007fa114300000)* 0x36cec000 0x00100000 0x00000000 core.1883.
0x00038400 container      [0x00007fa114300000-0x00007fa114400000)* 0x36dec000 0x00100000 0x00000000 core.1883.
0x00038500 container      [0x00007fa114400000-0x00007fa114500000)* 0x36eec000 0x00100000 0x00000000 core.1883.
0x00038600 container      [0x00007fa114500000-0x00007fa114600000)* 0x36fec000 0x00100000 0x00000000 core.1883.
0x00038700 container      [0x00007fa114600000-0x00007fa114700000)* 0x370ec000 0x00100000 0x00000000 core.1883.
0x00038800 container      [0x00007fa114700000-0x00007fa114800000)* 0x371ec000 0x00100000 0x00000000 core.1883.
0x00038900 container      [0x00007fa114800000-0x00007fa114900000)* 0x372ec000 0x00100000 0x00000000 core.1883.
0x00038a00 container      [0x00007fa114900000-0x00007fa114a00000)* 0x373ec000 0x00100000 0x00000000 core.1883.
0x00038b00 container      [0x00007fa114a00000-0x00007fa114b00000)* 0x374ec000 0x00100000 0x00000000 core.1883.
0x00038c00 container      [0x00007fa114b00000-0x00007fa114c00000)* 0x375ec000 0x00100000 0x00000000 core.1883.
0x00038d00 container      [0x00007fa114c00000-0x00007fa114d00000)* 0x376ec000 0x00100000 0x00000000 core.1883.
0x00038e00 container      [0x00007fa114d00000-0x00007fa114e00000)* 0x377ec000 0x00100000 0x00000407 core.1883.
0x00038f00 container      [0x00007fa114e00000-0x00007fa114f00000)* 0x378ec000 0x00100000 0x00001603 core.1883.
0x00039000 container      [0x00007fa114f00000-0x00007fa115000000)* 0x379ec000 0x00100000 0x00002b07 core.1883.
0x00039100 container      [0x00007fa115000000-0x00007fa115100000)* 0x37aec000 0x00100000 0x00000000 core.1883.
0x00039200 container      [0x00007fa115100000-0x00007fa115200000)* 0x37bec000 0x00100000 0x00000000 core.1883.
0x00039300 container      [0x00007fa115200000-0x00007fa115300000)* 0x37cec000 0x00100000 0x00000000 core.1883.
0x00039400 container      [0x00007fa115300000-0x00007fa115400000)* 0x37dec000 0x00100000 0x00000000 core.1883.
0x00039500 container      [0x00007fa115400000-0x00007fa115500000)* 0x37eec000 0x00100000 0x00000000 core.1883.
0x00039600 container      [0x00007fa115500000-0x00007fa115600000)* 0x37fec000 0x00100000 0x00000000 core.1883.
0x00039700 container      [0x00007fa115600000-0x00007fa115700000)* 0x380ec000 0x00100000 0x00000000 core.1883.
0x00039800 container      [0x00007fa115700000-0x00007fa115800000)* 0x381ec000 0x00100000 0x00000000 core.1883.
0x00039900 container      [0x00007fa115800000-0x00007fa115900000)* 0x382ec000 0x00100000 0x00000000 core.1883.
0x00039a00 container      [0x00007fa115900000-0x00007fa115a00000)* 0x383ec000 0x00100000 0x00000000 core.1883.
0x00039b00 container      [0x00007fa115a00000-0x00007fa115b00000)* 0x384ec000 0x00100000 0x00000000 core.1883.
0x00039c00 container      [0x00007fa115b00000-0x00007fa115c00000)* 0x385ec000 0x00100000 0x00000000 core.1883.
0x00039d00 container      [0x00007fa115c00000-0x00007fa115d00000)* 0x386ec000 0x00100000 0x00000000 core.1883.
0x00039e00 container      [0x00007fa115d00000-0x00007fa115e00000)* 0x387ec000 0x00100000 0x00000000 core.1883.
0x00039f00 container      [0x00007fa115e00000-0x00007fa115f00000)* 0x388ec000 0x00100000 0x00000000 core.1883.
0x0003a000 container      [0x00007fa115f00000-0x00007fa116000000)* 0x389ec000 0x00100000 0x00000000 core.1883.
0x0003a100 container      [0x00007fa116000000-0x00007fa116100000)* 0x38aec000 0x00100000 0x00000000 core.1883.
0x0003a200 container      [0x00007fa116100000-0x00007fa116200000)* 0x38bec000 0x00100000 0x00000000 core.1883.
0x0003a300 container      [0x00007fa116200000-0x00007fa116300000)* 0x38cec000 0x00100000 0x00000000 core.1883.
0x0003a400 container      [0x00007fa116300000-0x00007fa116400000)* 0x38dec000 0x00100000 0x00000000 core.1883.
0x0003a500 container      [0x00007fa116400000-0x00007fa116500000)* 0x38eec000 0x00100000 0x00000000 core.1883.
0x0003a600 container      [0x00007fa116500000-0x00007fa116600000)* 0x38fec000 0x00100000 0x00000000 core.1883.
0x0003a700 container      [0x00007fa116600000-0x00007fa116700000)* 0x390ec000 0x00100000 0x00000000 core.1883.
0x0003a800 container      [0x00007fa116700000-0x00007fa116800000)* 0x391ec000 0x00100000 0x00000000 core.1883.
0x0003a900 container      [0x00007fa116800000-0x00007fa116900000)* 0x392ec000 0x00100000 0x00000000 core.1883.
0x0003aa00 container      [0x00007fa116900000-0x00007fa116a00000)* 0x393ec000 0x00100000 0x00000000 core.1883.
0x0003ab00 container      [0x00007fa116a00000-0x00007fa116b00000)* 0x394ec000 0x00100000 0x00000000 core.1883.
0x0003ac00 container      [0x00007fa116b00000-0x00007fa116c00000)* 0x395ec000 0x00100000 0x00000000 core.1883.
0x0003ad00 container      [0x00007fa116c00000-0x00007fa116d00000)* 0x396ec000 0x00100000 0x00000000 core.1883.
0x0003ae00 container      [0x00007fa116d00000-0x00007fa116e00000)* 0x397ec000 0x00100000 0x00000000 core.1883.
0x0003af00 container      [0x00007fa116e00000-0x00007fa116f00000)* 0x398ec000 0x00100000 0x00000000 core.1883.
0x0003b000 container      [0x00007fa116f00000-0x00007fa117000000)* 0x399ec000 0x00100000 0x00000000 core.1883.
0x0003b100 container      [0x00007fa117000000-0x00007fa117100000)* 0x39aec000 0x00100000 0x00000000 core.1883.
0x0003b200 container      [0x00007fa117100000-0x00007fa117200000)* 0x39bec000 0x00100000 0x00000000 core.1883.
0x0003b300 container      [0x00007fa117200000-0x00007fa117300000)* 0x39cec000 0x00100000 0x00000000 core.1883.
0x0003b400 container      [0x00007fa117300000-0x00007fa117400000)* 0x39dec000 0x00100000 0x00000000 core.1883.
0x0003b500 container      [0x00007fa117400000-0x00007fa117500000)* 0x39eec000 0x00100000 0x00000000 core.1883.
0x0003b600 container      [0x00007fa117500000-0x00007fa117600000)* 0x39fec000 0x00100000 0x00000000 core.1883.
0x0003b700 container      [0x00007fa117600000-0x00007fa117700000)* 0x3a0ec000 0x00100000 0x00000000 core.1883.
0x0003b800 container      [0x00007fa117700000-0x00007fa117800000)* 0x3a1ec000 0x00100000 0x00000000 core.1883.
0x0003b900 container      [0x00007fa117800000-0x00007fa117900000)* 0x3a2ec000 0x00100000 0x00000000 core.1883.
0x0003ba00 container      [0x00007fa117900000-0x00007fa117a00000)* 0x3a3ec000 0x00100000 0x00000000 core.1883.
0x0003bb00 container      [0x00007fa117a00000-0x00007fa117b00000)* 0x3a4ec000 0x00100000 0x00000000 core.1883.
0x0003bc00 container      [0x00007fa117b00000-0x00007fa117c00000)* 0x3a5ec000 0x00100000 0x00000000 core.1883.
0x0003bd00 container      [0x00007fa117c00000-0x00007fa117d00000)* 0x3a6ec000 0x00100000 0x00000000 core.1883.
0x0003be00 container      [0x00007fa117d00000-0x00007fa117e00000)* 0x3a7ec000 0x00100000 0x00000000 core.1883.
0x0003bf00 container      [0x00007fa117e00000-0x00007fa117f00000)* 0x3a8ec000 0x00100000 0x00000000 core.1883.
0x0003c000 container      [0x00007fa117f00000-0x00007fa118000000)* 0x3a9ec000 0x00100000 0x00000000 core.1883.
0x0003c100 container      [0x00007fa118000000-0x00007fa118100000)* 0x3aaec000 0x00100000 0x00000000 core.1883.
0x0003c200 container      [0x00007fa118100000-0x00007fa118200000)* 0x3abec000 0x00100000 0x00000000 core.1883.
0x0003c300 container      [0x00007fa118200000-0x00007fa118300000)* 0x3acec000 0x00100000 0x00000000 core.1883.
0x0003c400 container      [0x00007fa118300000-0x00007fa118400000)* 0x3adec000 0x00100000 0x00000000 core.1883.
0x0003c500 container      [0x00007fa118400000-0x00007fa118500000)* 0x3aeec000 0x00100000 0x00000000 core.1883.
0x0003c600 container      [0x00007fa118500000-0x00007fa118600000)* 0x3afec000 0x00100000 0x00000000 core.1883.
0x0003c700 container      [0x00007fa118600000-0x00007fa118700000)* 0x3b0ec000 0x00100000 0x00000000 core.1883.
0x0003c800 container      [0x00007fa118700000-0x00007fa118800000)* 0x3b1ec000 0x00100000 0x00000000 core.1883.
```

```
0x0003c900 container    [0x00007fa118800000-0x00007fa118900000)* 0x3b2ec000 0x00100000 0x00000000 core.1883.
0x0003ca00 container    [0x00007fa118900000-0x00007fa118a00000)* 0x3b3ec000 0x00100000 0x00000000 core.1883.
0x0003cb00 container    [0x00007fa118a00000-0x00007fa118b00000)* 0x3b4ec000 0x00100000 0x00000000 core.1883.
0x0003cc00 container    [0x00007fa118b00000-0x00007fa118c00000)* 0x3b5ec000 0x00100000 0x00000000 core.1883.
0x0003cd00 container    [0x00007fa118c00000-0x00007fa118d00000)* 0x3b6ec000 0x00100000 0x00000000 core.1883.
0x0003ce00 container    [0x00007fa118d00000-0x00007fa118e00000)* 0x3b7ec000 0x00100000 0x00000000 core.1883.
0x0003cf00 container    [0x00007fa118e00000-0x00007fa118f00000)* 0x3b8ec000 0x00100000 0x00000000 core.1883.
0x0003d000 container    [0x00007fa118f00000-0x00007fa119000000)* 0x3b9ec000 0x00100000 0x00000000 core.1883.
0x0003d100 container    [0x00007fa119000000-0x00007fa119100000)* 0x3baec000 0x00100000 0x00000000 core.1883.
0x0003d200 container    [0x00007fa119100000-0x00007fa119200000)* 0x3bbec000 0x00100000 0x00000000 core.1883.
0x0003d300 container    [0x00007fa119200000-0x00007fa119300000)* 0x3bcec000 0x00100000 0x00000000 core.1883.
0x0003d400 container    [0x00007fa119300000-0x00007fa119400000)* 0x3bdec000 0x00100000 0x00000000 core.1883.
0x0003d500 container    [0x00007fa119400000-0x00007fa119500000)* 0x3beec000 0x00100000 0x00000000 core.1883.
0x0003d600 container    [0x00007fa119500000-0x00007fa119600000)* 0x3bfec000 0x00100000 0x00000000 core.1883.
0x0003d700 container    [0x00007fa119600000-0x00007fa119700000)* 0x3c0ec000 0x00100000 0x00000000 core.1883.
0x0003d800 container    [0x00007fa119700000-0x00007fa119800000)* 0x3c1ec000 0x00100000 0x00000000 core.1883.
0x0003d900 container    [0x00007fa119800000-0x00007fa119900000)* 0x3c2ec000 0x00100000 0x00000000 core.1883.
0x0003da00 container    [0x00007fa119900000-0x00007fa119a00000)* 0x3c3ec000 0x00100000 0x00000000 core.1883.
0x0003db00 container    [0x00007fa119a00000-0x00007fa119b00000)* 0x3c4ec000 0x00100000 0x00000000 core.1883.
0x0003dc00 container    [0x00007fa119b00000-0x00007fa119c00000)* 0x3c5ec000 0x00100000 0x00000000 core.1883.
0x0003dd00 container    [0x00007fa119c00000-0x00007fa119d00000)* 0x3c6ec000 0x00100000 0x00000000 core.1883.
0x0003de00 container    [0x00007fa119d00000-0x00007fa119e00000)* 0x3c7ec000 0x00100000 0x00000000 core.1883.
0x0003df00 container    [0x00007fa119e00000-0x00007fa119f00000)* 0x3c8ec000 0x00100000 0x00000000 core.1883.
0x0003e000 container    [0x00007fa119f00000-0x00007fa11a000000)* 0x3c9ec000 0x00100000 0x0000000b core.1883.
0x0003e100 container    [0x00007fa11a000000-0x00007fa11a100000)* 0x3caec000 0x00100000 0x00000000 core.1883.
0x0003e200 container    [0x00007fa11a100000-0x00007fa11a200000)* 0x3cbec000 0x00100000 0x00000000 core.1883.
0x0003e300 container    [0x00007fa11a200000-0x00007fa11a300000)* 0x3ccec000 0x00100000 0x00000000 core.1883.
0x0003e400 container    [0x00007fa11a300000-0x00007fa11a400000)* 0x3cdec000 0x00100000 0x00000000 core.1883.
0x0003e500 container    [0x00007fa11a400000-0x00007fa11a500000)* 0x3ceec000 0x00100000 0x00000000 core.1883.
0x0003e600 container    [0x00007fa11a500000-0x00007fa11a600000)* 0x3cfec000 0x00100000 0x00000000 core.1883.
0x0003e700 container    [0x00007fa11a600000-0x00007fa11a700000)* 0x3d0ec000 0x00100000 0x00000000 core.1883.
0x0003e800 container    [0x00007fa11a700000-0x00007fa11a800000)* 0x3d1ec000 0x00100000 0x00000000 core.1883.
0x0003e900 container    [0x00007fa11a800000-0x00007fa11a900000)* 0x3d2ec000 0x00100000 0x00000000 core.1883.
0x0003ea00 container    [0x00007fa11a900000-0x00007fa11aa00000)* 0x3d3ec000 0x00100000 0x00000000 core.1883.
0x0003eb00 container    [0x00007fa11aa00000-0x00007fa11ab00000)* 0x3d4ec000 0x00100000 0x00000000 core.1883.
0x0003ec00 container    [0x00007fa11ab00000-0x00007fa11ac00000)* 0x3d5ec000 0x00100000 0x00000000 core.1883.
0x0003ed00 container    [0x00007fa11ac00000-0x00007fa11ad00000)* 0x3d6ec000 0x00100000 0x00000000 core.1883.
0x0003ee00 container    [0x00007fa11ad00000-0x00007fa11ae00000)* 0x3d7ec000 0x00100000 0x00000000 core.1883.
0x0003ef00 container    [0x00007fa11ae00000-0x00007fa11af00000)* 0x3d8ec000 0x00100000 0x00000000 core.1883.
0x0003f000 container    [0x00007fa11af00000-0x00007fa11b000000)* 0x3d9ec000 0x00100000 0x00000000 core.1883.
0x0003f100 container    [0x00007fa11b000000-0x00007fa11b100000)* 0x3daec000 0x00100000 0x00000000 core.1883.
0x0003f200 container    [0x00007fa11b100000-0x00007fa11b200000)* 0x3dbec000 0x00100000 0x00000000 core.1883.
0x0003f300 container    [0x00007fa11b200000-0x00007fa11b300000)* 0x3dcec000 0x00100000 0x00000000 core.1883.
0x0003f400 container    [0x00007fa11b300000-0x00007fa11b400000)* 0x3ddec000 0x00100000 0x00000000 core.1883.
0x0003f500 container    [0x00007fa11b400000-0x00007fa11b500000)* 0x3deec000 0x00100000 0x00000000 core.1883.
0x0003f600 container    [0x00007fa11b500000-0x00007fa11b600000)* 0x3dfec000 0x00100000 0x00000000 core.1883.
0x0003f700 container    [0x00007fa11b600000-0x00007fa11b700000)* 0x3e0ec000 0x00100000 0x00000000 core.1883.
0x0003f800 container    [0x00007fa11b700000-0x00007fa11b800000)* 0x3e1ec000 0x00100000 0x00000000 core.1883.
0x0003f900 container    [0x00007fa11b800000-0x00007fa11b900000)* 0x3e2ec000 0x00100000 0x00000000 core.1883.
0x0003fa00 container    [0x00007fa11b900000-0x00007fa11ba00000)* 0x3e3ec000 0x00100000 0x00000000 core.1883.
0x0003fb00 container    [0x00007fa11ba00000-0x00007fa11bb00000)* 0x3e4ec000 0x00100000 0x00000000 core.1883.
0x0003fc00 container    [0x00007fa11bb00000-0x00007fa11bc00000)* 0x3e5ec000 0x00100000 0x00000000 core.1883.
0x0003fd00 container    [0x00007fa11bc00000-0x00007fa11bd00000)* 0x3e6ec000 0x00100000 0x00000000 core.1883.
0x0003fe00 container    [0x00007fa11bd00000-0x00007fa11be00000)* 0x3e7ec000 0x00100000 0x00000000 core.1883.
0x0003ff00 container    [0x00007fa11be00000-0x00007fa11bf00000)* 0x3e8ec000 0x00100000 0x00000000 core.1883.
0x00040000 container    [0x00007fa11bf00000-0x00007fa11c000000)* 0x3e9ec000 0x00100000 0x0000080b core.1883.
0x00040100 container    [0x00007fa11c000000-0x00007fa11c100000)* 0x3eaec000 0x00100000 0x00001a03 core.1883.
0x00040200 container    [0x00007fa11c100000-0x00007fa11c200000)* 0x3ebec000 0x00100000 0x00000000 core.1883.
0x00040300 container    [0x00007fa11c200000-0x00007fa11c300000)* 0x3ecec000 0x00100000 0x00000000 core.1883.
0x00040400 container    [0x00007fa11c300000-0x00007fa11c400000)* 0x3edec000 0x00100000 0x00000000 core.1883.
0x00040500 container    [0x00007fa11c400000-0x00007fa11c500000)* 0x3eeec000 0x00100000 0x00000000 core.1883.
0x00040600 container    [0x00007fa11c500000-0x00007fa11c600000)* 0x3efec000 0x00100000 0x00000000 core.1883.
0x00040700 container    [0x00007fa11c600000-0x00007fa11c700000)* 0x3f0ec000 0x00100000 0x00000000 core.1883.
0x00040800 container    [0x00007fa11c700000-0x00007fa11c800000)* 0x3f1ec000 0x00100000 0x00000000 core.1883.
0x00040900 container    [0x00007fa11c800000-0x00007fa11c900000)* 0x3f2ec000 0x00100000 0x00000000 core.1883.
0x00040a00 container    [0x00007fa11c900000-0x00007fa11ca00000)* 0x3f3ec000 0x00100000 0x00000000 core.1883.
0x00040b00 container    [0x00007fa11ca00000-0x00007fa11cb00000)* 0x3f4ec000 0x00100000 0x00000000 core.1883.
0x00040c00 container    [0x00007fa11cb00000-0x00007fa11cc00000)* 0x3f5ec000 0x00100000 0x00000000 core.1883.
0x00040d00 container    [0x00007fa11cc00000-0x00007fa11cd00000)* 0x3f6ec000 0x00100000 0x00000000 core.1883.
0x00040e00 container    [0x00007fa11cd00000-0x00007fa11ce00000)* 0x3f7ec000 0x00100000 0x00000000 core.1883.
0x00040f00 container    [0x00007fa11ce00000-0x00007fa11cf00000)* 0x3f8ec000 0x00100000 0x00000000 core.1883.
0x00041000 container    [0x00007fa11cf00000-0x00007fa11d000000)* 0x3f9ec000 0x00100000 0x00000000 core.1883.
0x00041100 container    [0x00007fa11d000000-0x00007fa11d100000)* 0x3faec000 0x00100000 0x00000000 core.1883.
0x00041200 container    [0x00007fa11d100000-0x00007fa11d200000)* 0x3fbec000 0x00100000 0x00000000 core.1883.
0x00041300 container    [0x00007fa11d200000-0x00007fa11d300000)* 0x3fcec000 0x00100000 0x00000000 core.1883.
0x00041400 container    [0x00007fa11d300000-0x00007fa11d400000)* 0x3fdec000 0x00100000 0x00000000 core.1883.
0x00041500 container    [0x00007fa11d400000-0x00007fa11d500000)* 0x3feec000 0x00100000 0x00000000 core.1883.
0x00041600 container    [0x00007fa11d500000-0x00007fa11d600000)* 0x3ffec000 0x00100000 0x00000000 core.1883.
0x00041700 container    [0x00007fa11d600000-0x00007fa11d700000)* 0x400ec000 0x00100000 0x00000000 core.1883.
0x00041800 container    [0x00007fa11d700000-0x00007fa11d800000)* 0x401ec000 0x00100000 0x00000000 core.1883.
0x00041900 container    [0x00007fa11d800000-0x00007fa11d900000)* 0x402ec000 0x00100000 0x00000000 core.1883.
0x00041a00 container    [0x00007fa11d900000-0x00007fa11da00000)* 0x403ec000 0x00100000 0x00000000 core.1883.
0x00041b00 container    [0x00007fa11da00000-0x00007fa11db00000)* 0x404ec000 0x00100000 0x00000000 core.1883.
0x00041c00 container    [0x00007fa11db00000-0x00007fa11dc00000)* 0x405ec000 0x00100000 0x00000000 core.1883.
0x00041d00 container    [0x00007fa11dc00000-0x00007fa11dd00000)* 0x406ec000 0x00100000 0x00000000 core.1883.
0x00041e00 container    [0x00007fa11dd00000-0x00007fa11de00000)* 0x407ec000 0x00100000 0x00000000 core.1883.
```

```
0x00041f00 container    [0x00007fa11de000-0x00007fa11df00000)* 0x408ec000 0x00100000 0x00000000 core.1883.
0x00042000 container    [0x00007fa11df000-0x00007fa11e00000)* 0x409ec000 0x00100000 0x00000000 core.1883.
0x00042100 container    [0x00007fa11e0000-0x00007fa11e10000)* 0x40aec000 0x00100000 0x00000000 core.1883.
0x00042200 container    [0x00007fa11e1000-0x00007fa11e20000)* 0x40bec000 0x00100000 0x00000000 core.1883.
0x00042300 container    [0x00007fa11e2000-0x00007fa11e30000)* 0x40cec000 0x00100000 0x00000000 core.1883.
0x00042400 container    [0x00007fa11e3000-0x00007fa11e40000)* 0x40dec000 0x00100000 0x00000000 core.1883.
0x00042500 container    [0x00007fa11e4000-0x00007fa11e50000)* 0x40eec000 0x00100000 0x00000000 core.1883.
0x00042600 container    [0x00007fa11e5000-0x00007fa11e60000)* 0x40fec000 0x00100000 0x00000000 core.1883.
0x00042700 container    [0x00007fa11e6000-0x00007fa11e70000)* 0x410ec000 0x00100000 0x00000000 core.1883.
0x00042800 container    [0x00007fa11e7000-0x00007fa11e80000)* 0x411ec000 0x00100000 0x00000000 core.1883.
0x00042900 container    [0x00007fa11e8000-0x00007fa11e90000)* 0x412ec000 0x00100000 0x00000000 core.1883.
0x00042a00 container    [0x00007fa11e9000-0x00007fa11ea00000)* 0x413ec000 0x00100000 0x00000000 core.1883.
0x00042b00 container    [0x00007fa11ea000-0x00007fa11eb00000)* 0x414ec000 0x00100000 0x00000000 core.1883.
0x00042c00 container    [0x00007fa11eb000-0x00007fa11ec00000)* 0x415ec000 0x00100000 0x00000000 core.1883.
0x00042d00 container    [0x00007fa11ec000-0x00007fa11ed00000)* 0x416ec000 0x00100000 0x00000000 core.1883.
0x00042e00 container    [0x00007fa11ed000-0x00007fa11ee00000)* 0x417ec000 0x00100000 0x00000000 core.1883.
0x00042f00 container    [0x00007fa11ee000-0x00007fa11ef00000)* 0x418ec000 0x00100000 0x00000000 core.1883.
0x00043000 container    [0x00007fa11ef000-0x00007fa11f000000)* 0x419ec000 0x00100000 0x00000000 core.1883.
0x00043100 container    [0x00007fa11f0000-0x00007fa11f10000)* 0x41aec000 0x00100000 0x00000000 core.1883.
0x00043200 container    [0x00007fa11f1000-0x00007fa11f20000)* 0x41bec000 0x00100000 0x00000000 core.1883.
0x00043300 container    [0x00007fa11f2000-0x00007fa11f30000)* 0x41cec000 0x00100000 0x00000000 core.1883.
0x00043400 container    [0x00007fa11f3000-0x00007fa11f40000)* 0x41dec000 0x00100000 0x00000000 core.1883.
0x00043500 container    [0x00007fa11f4000-0x00007fa11f50000)* 0x41eec000 0x00100000 0x00000000 core.1883.
0x00043600 container    [0x00007fa11f5000-0x00007fa11f60000)* 0x41fec000 0x00100000 0x00000000 core.1883.
0x00043700 container    [0x00007fa11f6000-0x00007fa11f70000)* 0x420ec000 0x00100000 0x00000000 core.1883.
0x00043800 container    [0x00007fa11f7000-0x00007fa11f80000)* 0x421ec000 0x00100000 0x00000000 core.1883.
0x00043900 container    [0x00007fa11f8000-0x00007fa11f90000)* 0x422ec000 0x00100000 0x00010000 core.1883.
0x00043a00 container    [0x00007fa11f9000-0x00007fa11fa00000)* 0x423ec000 0x00100000 0x00010000 core.1883.
0x00043b00 container    [0x00007fa11fa000-0x00007fa11fb00000)* 0x424ec000 0x00100000 0x00000000 core.1883.
0x00043c00 container    [0x00007fa11fb000-0x00007fa11fc00000)* 0x425ec000 0x00100000 0x00000000 core.1883.
0x00043d00 container    [0x00007fa11fc000-0x00007fa11fd00000)* 0x426ec000 0x00100000 0x00000000 core.1883.
0x00043e00 container    [0x00007fa11fd000-0x00007fa11fe00000)* 0x427ec000 0x00100000 0x00000000 core.1883.
0x00043f00 container    [0x00007fa11fe000-0x00007fa11ff00000)* 0x428ec000 0x00100000 0x00000000 core.1883.
0x00044000 container    [0x00007fa11ff000-0x00007fa120000000)* 0x429ec000 0x00100000 0x00000000 core.1883.
0x00044100 container    [0x00007fa1200000-0x00007fa120100000)* 0x42aec000 0x00100000 0x00000000 core.1883.
0x00044200 container    [0x00007fa1201000-0x00007fa120200000)* 0x42bec000 0x00100000 0x00000000 core.1883.
0x00044300 container    [0x00007fa1202000-0x00007fa120300000)* 0x42cec000 0x00100000 0x00000000 core.1883.
0x00044400 container    [0x00007fa1203000-0x00007fa120400000)* 0x42dec000 0x00100000 0x00000000 core.1883.
0x00044500 container    [0x00007fa1204000-0x00007fa120500000)* 0x42eec000 0x00100000 0x00000000 core.1883.
0x00044600 container    [0x00007fa1205000-0x00007fa120600000)* 0x42fec000 0x00100000 0x00000000 core.1883.
0x00044700 container    [0x00007fa1206000-0x00007fa120700000)* 0x430ec000 0x00100000 0x00000000 core.1883.
0x00044800 container    [0x00007fa1207000-0x00007fa120800000)* 0x431ec000 0x00100000 0x00000000 core.1883.
0x00044900 container    [0x00007fa1208000-0x00007fa120900000)* 0x432ec000 0x00100000 0x00000000 core.1883.
0x00044a00 container    [0x00007fa1209000-0x00007fa120a00000)* 0x433ec000 0x00100000 0x00000000 core.1883.
0x00044b00 container    [0x00007fa120a000-0x00007fa120b00000)* 0x434ec000 0x00100000 0x00000000 core.1883.
0x00044c00 container    [0x00007fa120b000-0x00007fa120c00000)* 0x435ec000 0x00100000 0x00000000 core.1883.
0x00044d00 container    [0x00007fa120c000-0x00007fa120d00000)* 0x436ec000 0x00100000 0x00000000 core.1883.
0x00044e00 container    [0x00007fa120d000-0x00007fa120e00000)* 0x437ec000 0x00100000 0x00000000 core.1883.
0x00044f00 container    [0x00007fa120e000-0x00007fa120f00000)* 0x438ec000 0x00100000 0x00000000 core.1883.
0x00045000 container    [0x00007fa120f000-0x00007fa121000000)* 0x439ec000 0x00100000 0x00000000 core.1883.
0x00045100 container    [0x00007fa1210000-0x00007fa121100000)* 0x43aec000 0x00100000 0x00000000 core.1883.
0x00045200 container    [0x00007fa1211000-0x00007fa121200000)* 0x43bec000 0x00100000 0x00000000 core.1883.
0x00045300 container    [0x00007fa1212000-0x00007fa121300000)* 0x43cec000 0x00100000 0x00000000 core.1883.
0x00045400 container    [0x00007fa1213000-0x00007fa121400000)* 0x43dec000 0x00100000 0x00000000 core.1883.
0x00045500 container    [0x00007fa1214000-0x00007fa121500000)* 0x43eec000 0x00100000 0x00000000 core.1883.
0x00045600 container    [0x00007fa1215000-0x00007fa121600000)* 0x43fec000 0x00100000 0x00000000 core.1883.
0x00045700 container    [0x00007fa1216000-0x00007fa121700000)* 0x440ec000 0x00100000 0x00000000 core.1883.
0x00045800 container    [0x00007fa1217000-0x00007fa121800000)* 0x441ec000 0x00100000 0x00000000 core.1883.
0x00045900 container    [0x00007fa1218000-0x00007fa121900000)* 0x442ec000 0x00100000 0x00000000 core.1883.
0x00045a00 container    [0x00007fa1219000-0x00007fa121a00000)* 0x443ec000 0x00100000 0x00000000 core.1883.
0x00045b00 container    [0x00007fa121a000-0x00007fa121b00000)* 0x444ec000 0x00100000 0x00000000 core.1883.
0x00045c00 container    [0x00007fa121b000-0x00007fa121c00000)* 0x445ec000 0x00100000 0x00000000 core.1883.
0x00045d00 container    [0x00007fa121c000-0x00007fa121d00000)* 0x446ec000 0x00100000 0x00000000 core.1883.
0x00045e00 container    [0x00007fa121d000-0x00007fa121e00000)* 0x447ec000 0x00100000 0x00000000 core.1883.
0x00045f00 container    [0x00007fa121e000-0x00007fa121f00000)* 0x448ec000 0x00100000 0x00000000 core.1883.
0x00046000 container    [0x00007fa121f000-0x00007fa122000000)* 0x449ec000 0x00100000 0x00000000 core.1883.
0x00046100 container    [0x00007fa1220000-0x00007fa122100000)* 0x44aec000 0x00100000 0x00000000 core.1883.
0x00046200 container    [0x00007fa1221000-0x00007fa122200000)* 0x44bec000 0x00100000 0x00000000 core.1883.
0x00046300 container    [0x00007fa1222000-0x00007fa122300000)* 0x44cec000 0x00100000 0x00000000 core.1883.
0x00046400 container    [0x00007fa1223000-0x00007fa122400000)* 0x44dec000 0x00100000 0x00000000 core.1883.
0x00046500 container    [0x00007fa1224000-0x00007fa122500000)* 0x44eec000 0x00100000 0x00000000 core.1883.
0x00046600 container    [0x00007fa1225000-0x00007fa122600000)* 0x44fec000 0x00100000 0x00000000 core.1883.
0x00046700 container    [0x00007fa1226000-0x00007fa122700000)* 0x450ec000 0x00100000 0x00000000 core.1883.
0x00046800 container    [0x00007fa1227000-0x00007fa122800000)* 0x451ec000 0x00100000 0x00000000 core.1883.
0x00046900 container    [0x00007fa1228000-0x00007fa122900000)* 0x452ec000 0x00100000 0x00000000 core.1883.
0x00046a00 container    [0x00007fa1229000-0x00007fa122a00000)* 0x453ec000 0x00100000 0x00000000 core.1883.
0x00046b00 container    [0x00007fa122a000-0x00007fa122b00000)* 0x454ec000 0x00100000 0x00000000 core.1883.
0x00046c00 container    [0x00007fa122b000-0x00007fa122c00000)* 0x455ec000 0x00100000 0x00000000 core.1883.
0x00046d00 container    [0x00007fa122c000-0x00007fa122d00000)* 0x456ec000 0x00100000 0x00000000 core.1883.
0x00046e00 container    [0x00007fa122d000-0x00007fa122e00000)* 0x457ec000 0x00100000 0x00000000 core.1883.
0x00046f00 container    [0x00007fa122e000-0x00007fa122f00000)* 0x458ec000 0x00100000 0x00000000 core.1883.
0x00047000 container    [0x00007fa122f000-0x00007fa123000000)* 0x459ec000 0x00100000 0x00000000 core.1883.
0x00047100 container    [0x00007fa1230000-0x00007fa123100000)* 0x45aec000 0x00100000 0x00000000 core.1883.
0x00047200 container    [0x00007fa1231000-0x00007fa123200000)* 0x45bec000 0x00100000 0x00020000 core.1883.
0x00047300 container    [0x00007fa1232000-0x00007fa123300000)* 0x45cec000 0x00100000 0x00000000 core.1883.
0x00047400 container    [0x00007fa1233000-0x00007fa123400000)* 0x45dec000 0x00100000 0x00000000 core.1883.
```

```
0x00047500 container    [0x00007fa123400000-0x00007fa123500000)* 0x45eec000 0x00100000 0x00000000 core.1883.
0x00047600 container    [0x00007fa123500000-0x00007fa123600000)* 0x45fec000 0x00100000 0x00000000 core.1883.
0x00047700 container    [0x00007fa123600000-0x00007fa123700000)* 0x460ec000 0x00100000 0x00000000 core.1883.
0x00047800 container    [0x00007fa123700000-0x00007fa123800000)* 0x461ec000 0x00100000 0x00000000 core.1883.
0x00047900 container    [0x00007fa123800000-0x00007fa123900000)* 0x462ec000 0x00100000 0x00000000 core.1883.
0x00047a00 container    [0x00007fa123900000-0x00007fa123a00000)* 0x463ec000 0x00100000 0x00000000 core.1883.
0x00047b00 container    [0x00007fa123a00000-0x00007fa123b00000)* 0x464ec000 0x00100000 0x00000000 core.1883.
0x00047c00 container    [0x00007fa123b00000-0x00007fa123c00000)* 0x465ec000 0x00100000 0x00000000 core.1883.
0x00047d00 container    [0x00007fa123c00000-0x00007fa123d00000)* 0x466ec000 0x00100000 0x00000000 core.1883.
0x00047e00 container    [0x00007fa123d00000-0x00007fa123e00000)* 0x467ec000 0x00100000 0x00000000 core.1883.
0x00047f00 container    [0x00007fa123e00000-0x00007fa123f00000)* 0x468ec000 0x00100000 0x00000000 core.1883.
0x00048000 container    [0x00007fa123f00000-0x00007fa124000000)* 0x469ec000 0x00100000 0x00000000 core.1883.
0x00048100 container    [0x00007fa124000000-0x00007fa124100000)* 0x46aec000 0x00100000 0x00000000 core.1883.
0x00048200 container    [0x00007fa124100000-0x00007fa124200000)* 0x46bec000 0x00100000 0x00000000 core.1883.
0x00048300 container    [0x00007fa124200000-0x00007fa124300000)* 0x46cec000 0x00100000 0x00000000 core.1883.
0x00048400 container    [0x00007fa124300000-0x00007fa124400000)* 0x46dec000 0x00100000 0x00000000 core.1883.
0x00048500 container    [0x00007fa124400000-0x00007fa124500000)* 0x46eec000 0x00100000 0x00000000 core.1883.
0x00048600 container    [0x00007fa124500000-0x00007fa124600000)* 0x46fec000 0x00100000 0x00000000 core.1883.
0x00048700 container    [0x00007fa124600000-0x00007fa124700000)* 0x470ec000 0x00100000 0x00000000 core.1883.
0x00048800 container    [0x00007fa124700000-0x00007fa124800000)* 0x471ec000 0x00100000 0x00000000 core.1883.
0x00048900 container    [0x00007fa124800000-0x00007fa124900000)* 0x472ec000 0x00100000 0x00000000 core.1883.
0x00048a00 container    [0x00007fa124900000-0x00007fa124a00000)* 0x473ec000 0x00100000 0x00000000 core.1883.
0x00048b00 container    [0x00007fa124a00000-0x00007fa124b00000)* 0x474ec000 0x00100000 0x00000000 core.1883.
0x00048c00 container    [0x00007fa124b00000-0x00007fa124c00000)* 0x475ec000 0x00100000 0x00000000 core.1883.
0x00048d00 container    [0x00007fa124c00000-0x00007fa124d00000)* 0x476ec000 0x00100000 0x00000000 core.1883.
0x00048e00 container    [0x00007fa124d00000-0x00007fa124e00000)* 0x477ec000 0x00100000 0x00000000 core.1883.
0x00048f00 container    [0x00007fa124e00000-0x00007fa124f00000)* 0x478ec000 0x00100000 0x00000000 core.1883.
0x00049000 container    [0x00007fa124f00000-0x00007fa125000000)* 0x479ec000 0x00100000 0x00000000 core.1883.
0x00049100 container    [0x00007fa125000000-0x00007fa125100000)* 0x47aec000 0x00100000 0x00000000 core.1883.
0x00049200 container    [0x00007fa125100000-0x00007fa125200000)* 0x47bec000 0x00100000 0x00000000 core.1883.
0x00049300 container    [0x00007fa125200000-0x00007fa125300000)* 0x47cec000 0x00100000 0x00000000 core.1883.
0x00049400 container    [0x00007fa125300000-0x00007fa125400000)* 0x47dec000 0x00100000 0x00000000 core.1883.
0x00049500 container    [0x00007fa125400000-0x00007fa125500000)* 0x47eec000 0x00100000 0x00000000 core.1883.
0x00049600 container    [0x00007fa125500000-0x00007fa125600000)* 0x47fec000 0x00100000 0x00000000 core.1883.
0x00049700 container    [0x00007fa125600000-0x00007fa125700000)* 0x480ec000 0x00100000 0x00000000 core.1883.
0x00049800 container    [0x00007fa125700000-0x00007fa125800000)* 0x481ec000 0x00100000 0x00000000 core.1883.
0x00049900 container    [0x00007fa125800000-0x00007fa125900000)* 0x482ec000 0x00100000 0x00000000 core.1883.
0x00049a00 container    [0x00007fa125900000-0x00007fa125a00000)* 0x483ec000 0x00100000 0x00000000 core.1883.
0x00049b00 container    [0x00007fa125a00000-0x00007fa125b00000)* 0x484ec000 0x00100000 0x00000000 core.1883.
0x00049c00 container    [0x00007fa125b00000-0x00007fa125c00000)* 0x485ec000 0x00100000 0x00000000 core.1883.
0x00049d00 container    [0x00007fa125c00000-0x00007fa125d00000)* 0x486ec000 0x00100000 0x00000000 core.1883.
0x00049e00 container    [0x00007fa125d00000-0x00007fa125e00000)* 0x487ec000 0x00100000 0x00000000 core.1883.
0x00049f00 container    [0x00007fa125e00000-0x00007fa125f00000)* 0x488ec000 0x00100000 0x00000000 core.1883.
0x0004a000 container    [0x00007fa125f00000-0x00007fa126000000)* 0x489ec000 0x00100000 0x00000000 core.1883.
0x0004a100 container    [0x00007fa126000000-0x00007fa126100000)* 0x48aec000 0x00100000 0x00000000 core.1883.
0x0004a200 container    [0x00007fa126100000-0x00007fa126200000)* 0x48bec000 0x00100000 0x00000000 core.1883.
0x0004a300 container    [0x00007fa126200000-0x00007fa126300000)* 0x48cec000 0x00100000 0x00000000 core.1883.
0x0004a400 container    [0x00007fa126300000-0x00007fa126400000)* 0x48dec000 0x00100000 0x00000000 core.1883.
0x0004a500 container    [0x00007fa126400000-0x00007fa126500000)* 0x48eec000 0x00100000 0x00000000 core.1883.
0x0004a600 container    [0x00007fa126500000-0x00007fa126600000)* 0x48fec000 0x00100000 0x00000000 core.1883.
0x0004a700 container    [0x00007fa126600000-0x00007fa126700000)* 0x490ec000 0x00100000 0x00000000 core.1883.
0x0004a800 container    [0x00007fa126700000-0x00007fa126800000)* 0x491ec000 0x00100000 0x00000000 core.1883.
0x0004a900 container    [0x00007fa126800000-0x00007fa126900000)* 0x492ec000 0x00100000 0x00000000 core.1883.
0x0004aa00 container    [0x00007fa126900000-0x00007fa126a00000)* 0x493ec000 0x00100000 0x00000000 core.1883.
0x0004ab00 container    [0x00007fa126a00000-0x00007fa126b00000)* 0x494ec000 0x00100000 0x00020000 core.1883.
0x0004ac00 container    [0x00007fa126b00000-0x00007fa126c00000)* 0x495ec000 0x00100000 0x00010000 core.1883.
0x0004ad00 container    [0x00007fa126c00000-0x00007fa126d00000)* 0x496ec000 0x00100000 0x00020000 core.1883.
0x0004ae00 container    [0x00007fa126d00000-0x00007fa126e00000)* 0x497ec000 0x00100000 0x00010000 core.1883.
0x0004af00 container    [0x00007fa126e00000-0x00007fa126f00000)* 0x498ec000 0x00100000 0x00010000 core.1883.
0x0004b000 container    [0x00007fa126f00000-0x00007fa127000000)* 0x499ec000 0x00100000 0x00000000 core.1883.
0x0004b100 container    [0x00007fa127000000-0x00007fa127100000)* 0x49aec000 0x00100000 0x00000000 core.1883.
0x0004b200 container    [0x00007fa127100000-0x00007fa127200000)* 0x49bec000 0x00100000 0x00000000 core.1883.
0x0004b300 container    [0x00007fa127200000-0x00007fa127300000)* 0x49cec000 0x00100000 0x00000000 core.1883.
0x0004b400 container    [0x00007fa127300000-0x00007fa127400000)* 0x49dec000 0x00100000 0x00000000 core.1883.
0x0004b500 container    [0x00007fa127400000-0x00007fa127500000)* 0x49eec000 0x00100000 0x00000000 core.1883.
0x0004b600 container    [0x00007fa127500000-0x00007fa127600000)* 0x49fec000 0x00100000 0x00000000 core.1883.
0x0004b700 container    [0x00007fa127600000-0x00007fa127700000)* 0x4a0ec000 0x00100000 0x00000000 core.1883.
0x0004b800 container    [0x00007fa127700000-0x00007fa127800000)* 0x4a1ec000 0x00100000 0x00000000 core.1883.
0x0004b900 container    [0x00007fa127800000-0x00007fa127900000)* 0x4a2ec000 0x00100000 0x00000000 core.1883.
0x0004ba00 container    [0x00007fa127900000-0x00007fa127a00000)* 0x4a3ec000 0x00100000 0x00000000 core.1883.
0x0004bb00 container    [0x00007fa127a00000-0x00007fa127b00000)* 0x4a4ec000 0x00100000 0x00000000 core.1883.
0x0004bc00 container    [0x00007fa127b00000-0x00007fa127c00000)* 0x4a5ec000 0x00100000 0x00000000 core.1883.
0x0004bd00 container    [0x00007fa127c00000-0x00007fa127d00000)* 0x4a6ec000 0x00100000 0x00000000 core.1883.
0x0004be00 container    [0x00007fa127d00000-0x00007fa127e00000)* 0x4a7ec000 0x00100000 0x00000000 core.1883.
0x0004bf00 container    [0x00007fa127e00000-0x00007fa127f00000)* 0x4a8ec000 0x00100000 0x00000000 core.1883.
0x0004c000 container    [0x00007fa127f00000-0x00007fa128000000)* 0x4a9ec000 0x00100000 0x00000000 core.1883.
0x0004c100 container    [0x00007fa128000000-0x00007fa128100000)* 0x4aaec000 0x00100000 0x00000000 core.1883.
0x0004c200 container    [0x00007fa128100000-0x00007fa128200000)* 0x4abec000 0x00100000 0x00000000 core.1883.
0x0004c300 container    [0x00007fa128200000-0x00007fa128300000)* 0x4acec000 0x00100000 0x00000000 core.1883.
0x0004c400 container    [0x00007fa128300000-0x00007fa128400000)* 0x4adec000 0x00100000 0x00000000 core.1883.
0x0004c500 container    [0x00007fa128400000-0x00007fa128500000)* 0x4aeec000 0x00100000 0x00000000 core.1883.
0x0004c600 container    [0x00007fa128500000-0x00007fa128600000)* 0x4afec000 0x00100000 0x00000000 core.1883.
0x0004c700 container    [0x00007fa128600000-0x00007fa128700000)* 0x4b0ec000 0x00100000 0x00000000 core.1883.
0x0004c800 container    [0x00007fa128700000-0x00007fa128800000)* 0x4b1ec000 0x00100000 0x00000000 core.1883.
0x0004c900 container    [0x00007fa128800000-0x00007fa128900000)* 0x4b2ec000 0x00100000 0x00000000 core.1883.
0x0004ca00 container    [0x00007fa128900000-0x00007fa128a00000)* 0x4b3ec000 0x00100000 0x00000000 core.1883.
```

```
0x0004cb00 container         [0x00007fa128a00000-0x00007fa128b00000)* 0x4b4ec000 0x00100000 0x00000000 core.1883.
0x0004cc00 container         [0x00007fa128b00000-0x00007fa128c00000)* 0x4b5ec000 0x00100000 0x00000000 core.1883.
0x0004cd00 container         [0x00007fa128c00000-0x00007fa128d00000)* 0x4b6ec000 0x00100000 0x00000000 core.1883.
0x0004ce00 container         [0x00007fa128d00000-0x00007fa128e00000)* 0x4b7ec000 0x00100000 0x00000000 core.1883.
0x0004cf00 container         [0x00007fa128e00000-0x00007fa128f00000)* 0x4b8ec000 0x00100000 0x00000000 core.1883.
0x0004d000 container         [0x00007fa128f00000-0x00007fa129000000)* 0x4b9ec000 0x00100000 0x00000000 core.1883.
0x0004d100 container         [0x00007fa129000000-0x00007fa129100000)* 0x4baec000 0x00100000 0x00000000 core.1883.
0x0004d200 container         [0x00007fa129100000-0x00007fa129200000)* 0x4bbec000 0x00100000 0x00000000 core.1883.
0x0004d300 container         [0x00007fa129200000-0x00007fa129300000)* 0x4bcec000 0x00100000 0x00000000 core.1883.
0x0004d400 container         [0x00007fa129300000-0x00007fa129400000)* 0x4bdec000 0x00100000 0x00000000 core.1883.
0x0004d500 container         [0x00007fa129400000-0x00007fa129500000)* 0x4beec000 0x00100000 0x00000000 core.1883.
0x0004d600 container         [0x00007fa129500000-0x00007fa129600000)* 0x4bfec000 0x00100000 0x00000000 core.1883.
0x0004d700 container         [0x00007fa129600000-0x00007fa129700000)* 0x4c0ec000 0x00100000 0x00000000 core.1883.
0x0004d800 container         [0x00007fa129700000-0x00007fa129800000)* 0x4c1ec000 0x00100000 0x00000000 core.1883.
0x0004d900 container         [0x00007fa129800000-0x00007fa129900000)* 0x4c2ec000 0x00100000 0x00000000 core.1883.
0x0004da00 container         [0x00007fa129900000-0x00007fa129a00000)* 0x4c3ec000 0x00100000 0x00000000 core.1883.
0x0004db00 container         [0x00007fa129a00000-0x00007fa129b00000)* 0x4c4ec000 0x00100000 0x00000000 core.1883.
0x0004dc00 container         [0x00007fa129b00000-0x00007fa129c00000)* 0x4c5ec000 0x00100000 0x00000000 core.1883.
0x0004dd00 container         [0x00007fa129c00000-0x00007fa129d00000)* 0x4c6ec000 0x00100000 0x00000000 core.1883.
0x0004de00 container         [0x00007fa129d00000-0x00007fa129e00000)* 0x4c7ec000 0x00100000 0x00000000 core.1883.
0x0004df00 container         [0x00007fa129e00000-0x00007fa129f00000)* 0x4c8ec000 0x00100000 0x00000000 core.1883.
0x0004e000 container         [0x00007fa129f00000-0x00007fa12a000000)* 0x4c9ec000 0x00100000 0x00000000 core.1883.
0x0004e100 container         [0x00007fa12a000000-0x00007fa12a100000)* 0x4caec000 0x00100000 0x00000000 core.1883.
0x0004e200 container         [0x00007fa12a100000-0x00007fa12a200000)* 0x4cbec000 0x00100000 0x00000000 core.1883.
0x0004e300 container         [0x00007fa12a200000-0x00007fa12a300000)* 0x4ccec000 0x00100000 0x00000000 core.1883.
0x0004e400 container         [0x00007fa12a300000-0x00007fa12a400000)* 0x4cdec000 0x00100000 0x00001003 core.1883.
0x0004e500 container         [0x00007fa12a400000-0x00007fa12a500000)* 0x4ceec000 0x00100000 0x00002303 core.1883.
0x0004e600 container         [0x00007fa12a500000-0x00007fa12a600000)* 0x4cfec000 0x00100000 0x00003607 core.1883.
0x0004e700 container         [0x00007fa12a600000-0x00007fa12a700000)* 0x4d0ec000 0x00100000 0x00004e83 core.1883.
0x0004e800 container         [0x00007fa12a700000-0x00007fa12a800000)* 0x4d1ec000 0x00100000 0x00007453 core.1883.
0x0004e900 container         [0x00007fa12a800000-0x00007fa12a900000)* 0x4d2ec000 0x00100000 0x00000000 core.1883.
0x0004ea00 container         [0x00007fa12a900000-0x00007fa12aa00000)* 0x4d3ec000 0x00100000 0x00000000 core.1883.
0x0004eb00 container         [0x00007fa12aa00000-0x00007fa12ab00000)* 0x4d4ec000 0x00100000 0x00000000 core.1883.
0x0004ec00 container         [0x00007fa12ab00000-0x00007fa12ac00000)* 0x4d5ec000 0x00100000 0x00000000 core.1883.
0x0004ed00 container         [0x00007fa12ac00000-0x00007fa12ad00000)* 0x4d6ec000 0x00100000 0x00000000 core.1883.
0x0004ee00 container         [0x00007fa12ad00000-0x00007fa12ae00000)* 0x4d7ec000 0x00100000 0x00000000 core.1883.
0x0004ef00 container         [0x00007fa12ae00000-0x00007fa12af00000)* 0x4d8ec000 0x00100000 0x00000000 core.1883.
0x0004f000 container         [0x00007fa12af00000-0x00007fa12b000000)* 0x4d9ec000 0x00100000 0x00000000 core.1883.
0x0004f100 container         [0x00007fa12b000000-0x00007fa12b100000)* 0x4daec000 0x00100000 0x00000000 core.1883.
0x0004f200 container         [0x00007fa12b100000-0x00007fa12b200000)* 0x4dbec000 0x00100000 0x00000000 core.1883.
0x0004f300 container         [0x00007fa12b200000-0x00007fa12b300000)* 0x4dcec000 0x00100000 0x00000000 core.1883.
0x0004f400 container         [0x00007fff689b8000-0x00007fff6c1b8000)* 0x4ddec000 0x03800000 0x00000000 core.1883.
0x0004f500 container         [0x00007fff6c1b8000-0x00007fff6c9b7000)* 0x515ec000 0x007ff000 0x00000000 core.1883.
0x0004f600 container         [0x00007fff6c9b7000-0x00007fff6c9b8000)* 0x51deb000 0x00001000 0x00000000 core.1883.
0x0004f700 container         [0x00007fff6c9b8000-0x00007fff6c9ed000)* 0x51dec000 0x00035000 0x00000000 core.1883.
0x0004f800 container         [0x00007fff6c9ed000-0x00007fff6c9ef000)* 0x51e21000 0x00002000 0x00000000 core.1883.
0x0004f900 container         [0x00007fff6c9ef000-0x00007fff6ca29000)* 0x51e23000 0x0003a000 0x00000000 core.1883.
0x0004fa00 container         [0x00007fff6ca29000-0x00007fff6ca3c000)* 0x51e5d000 0x00013000 0x00000000 core.1883.
0x0004fb00 container         [0x00007fff79629000-0x00007fff79800000)* 0x51e70000 0x001d7000 0x00000000 core.1883.
0x0004fc00 container         [0x00007fff79800000-0x00007fff79a00000)* 0x52047000 0x00200000 0x00000000 core.1883.
0x0004fd00 container         [0x00007fff79a00000-0x00007fff79c00000)* 0x52247000 0x00200000 0x00000000 core.1883.
0x0004fe00 container         [0x00007fff79c00000-0x00007fff79e00000)* 0x52447000 0x00200000 0x00000000 core.1883.
0x0004ff00 container         [0x00007fff79e00000-0x00007fff7a000000)* 0x52647000 0x00200000 0x00000000 core.1883.
0x00050000 container         [0x00007fff7a000000-0x00007fff7a200000)* 0x52847000 0x00200000 0x00000000 core.1883.
0x00050100 container         [0x00007fff7a200000-0x00007fff7a400000)* 0x52a47000 0x00200000 0x00000000 core.1883.
0x00050200 container         [0x00007fff7a400000-0x00007fff7a600000)* 0x52c47000 0x00200000 0x00000000 core.1883.
0x00050300 container         [0x00007fff7a600000-0x00007fff7a800000)* 0x52e47000 0x00200000 0x00000000 core.1883.
0x00050400 container         [0x00007fff7a800000-0x00007fff7aa00000)* 0x53047000 0x00200000 0x00000000 core.1883.
0x00050500 container         [0x00007fff7aa00000-0x00007fff7ae00000)* 0x53247000 0x00400000 0x00000000 core.1883.
0x00050600 container         [0x00007fff7ae00000-0x00007fff7b000000)* 0x53647000 0x00200000 0x00000000 core.1883.
0x00050700 container         [0x00007fff7b000000-0x00007fff7b11d000)* 0x53847000 0x0011d000 0x00000000 core.1883.
0x00050800 container         [0x00007fff89629000-0x00007fff96699000)* 0x53964000 0x0d070000 0x00000000 core.1883.
0x00050900 container         [0x00007fff96699000-0x00007fff997a1000)* 0x609d4000 0x03108000 0x00000000 core.1883.
0x00050a00 container         [0x00007fffffe00000-0x00007fffffe02000)* 0x63adc000 0x00000000 0x00000000 core.1883.
```

4.   Calculate the size of the segment 0x00007fa0e2b00000 - 0x00007fa0e2c00000 in pointers:

```
(lldb) print (0x00007fa0e2c00000 - 0x00007fa0e2b00000)/8
(long) $0 = 131072
```

5.   Examine the segment contents for any execution residue and hints:

```
(lldb) x/131072a 0x00007fa0e2b00000 --force
0x7fa0e2b00000: 0x657461636f6c6c61
0x7fa0e2b00008: 0x79726f6d656d2064
0x7fa0e2b00010: 0x0000000000000000
0x7fa0e2b00018: 0x0000000000000000
0x7fa0e2b00020: 0x000000010cdb87d0 App9`procD
```

```
0x7fa0e2b00028:   0x0000000000000000
0x7fa0e2b00030:   0x0000000000000000
0x7fa0e2b00038:   0x0000000000000000
0x7fa0e2b00040:   0x0000000000000000
0x7fa0e2b00048:   0x0000000000000000
0x7fa0e2b00050:   0x0000000000000000
0x7fa0e2b00058:   0x0000000000000000
0x7fa0e2b00060:   0x0000000000000000
0x7fa0e2b00068:   0x0000000000000000
0x7fa0e2b00070:   0x0000000000000000
0x7fa0e2b00078:   0x0000000000000000
0x7fa0e2b00080:   0x0000000000000000
0x7fa0e2b00088:   0x0000000000000000
0x7fa0e2b00090:   0x0000000000000000
0x7fa0e2b00098:   0x0000000000000000
0x7fa0e2b000a0:   0x0000000000000000
0x7fa0e2b000a8:   0x0000000000000000
0x7fa0e2b000b0:   0x0000000000000000
0x7fa0e2b000b8:   0x0000000000000000
0x7fa0e2b000c0:   0x0000000000000000
0x7fa0e2b000c8:   0x0000000000000000
0x7fa0e2b000d0:   0x0000000000000000
0x7fa0e2b000d8:   0x0000000000000000
0x7fa0e2b000e0:   0x0000000000000000
0x7fa0e2b000e8:   0x0000000000000000
0x7fa0e2b000f0:   0x0000000000000000
0x7fa0e2b000f8:   0x0000000000000000
0x7fa0e2b00100:   0x657461636f6c6c61
0x7fa0e2b00108:   0x79726f6d656d2064
0x7fa0e2b00110:   0x0000000000000000
0x7fa0e2b00118:   0x0000000000000000
0x7fa0e2b00120:   0x000000010cdb87d0   App9`procD
0x7fa0e2b00128:   0x0000000000000000
0x7fa0e2b00130:   0x0000000000000000
0x7fa0e2b00138:   0x0000000000000000
0x7fa0e2b00140:   0x0000000000000000
0x7fa0e2b00148:   0x0000000000000000
0x7fa0e2b00150:   0x0000000000000000
0x7fa0e2b00158:   0x0000000000000000
0x7fa0e2b00160:   0x0000000000000000
0x7fa0e2b00168:   0x0000000000000000
0x7fa0e2b00170:   0x0000000000000000
0x7fa0e2b00178:   0x0000000000000000
0x7fa0e2b00180:   0x0000000000000000
0x7fa0e2b00188:   0x0000000000000000
0x7fa0e2b00190:   0x0000000000000000
0x7fa0e2b00198:   0x0000000000000000
0x7fa0e2b001a0:   0x0000000000000000
0x7fa0e2b001a8:   0x0000000000000000
0x7fa0e2b001b0:   0x0000000000000000
0x7fa0e2b001b8:   0x0000000000000000
0x7fa0e2b001c0:   0x0000000000000000
0x7fa0e2b001c8:   0x0000000000000000
0x7fa0e2b001d0:   0x0000000000000000
0x7fa0e2b001d8:   0x0000000000000000
0x7fa0e2b001e0:   0x0000000000000000
0x7fa0e2b001e8:   0x0000000000000000
0x7fa0e2b001f0:   0x0000000000000000
0x7fa0e2b001f8:   0x0000000000000000
0x7fa0e2b00200:   0x657461636f6c6c61
```

```
0x7fa0e2b00208:  0x79726f6d656d2064
0x7fa0e2b00210:  0x0000000000000000
0x7fa0e2b00218:  0x0000000000000000
0x7fa0e2b00220:  0x000000010cdb87d0  App9`procD
0x7fa0e2b00228:  0x0000000000000000
0x7fa0e2b00230:  0x0000000000000000
0x7fa0e2b00238:  0x0000000000000000
0x7fa0e2b00240:  0x0000000000000000
0x7fa0e2b00248:  0x0000000000000000
0x7fa0e2b00250:  0x0000000000000000
0x7fa0e2b00258:  0x0000000000000000
0x7fa0e2b00260:  0x0000000000000000
0x7fa0e2b00268:  0x0000000000000000
0x7fa0e2b00270:  0x0000000000000000
0x7fa0e2b00278:  0x0000000000000000
0x7fa0e2b00280:  0x0000000000000000
0x7fa0e2b00288:  0x0000000000000000
0x7fa0e2b00290:  0x0000000000000000
0x7fa0e2b00298:  0x0000000000000000
0x7fa0e2b002a0:  0x0000000000000000
0x7fa0e2b002a8:  0x0000000000000000
0x7fa0e2b002b0:  0x0000000000000000
0x7fa0e2b002b8:  0x0000000000000000
0x7fa0e2b002c0:  0x0000000000000000
0x7fa0e2b002c8:  0x0000000000000000
0x7fa0e2b002d0:  0x0000000000000000
0x7fa0e2b002d8:  0x0000000000000000
0x7fa0e2b002e0:  0x0000000000000000
0x7fa0e2b002e8:  0x0000000000000000
0x7fa0e2b002f0:  0x0000000000000000
0x7fa0e2b002f8:  0x0000000000000000
0x7fa0e2b00300:  0x657461636f6c6c61
0x7fa0e2b00308:  0x79726f6d656d2064
0x7fa0e2b00310:  0x0000000000000000
0x7fa0e2b00318:  0x0000000000000000
0x7fa0e2b00320:  0x000000010cdb87d0  App9`procD
0x7fa0e2b00328:  0x0000000000000000
0x7fa0e2b00330:  0x0000000000000000
0x7fa0e2b00338:  0x0000000000000000
0x7fa0e2b00340:  0x0000000000000000
0x7fa0e2b00348:  0x0000000000000000
0x7fa0e2b00350:  0x0000000000000000
0x7fa0e2b00358:  0x0000000000000000
0x7fa0e2b00360:  0x0000000000000000
0x7fa0e2b00368:  0x0000000000000000
0x7fa0e2b00370:  0x0000000000000000
0x7fa0e2b00378:  0x0000000000000000
0x7fa0e2b00380:  0x0000000000000000
0x7fa0e2b00388:  0x0000000000000000
0x7fa0e2b00390:  0x0000000000000000
0x7fa0e2b00398:  0x0000000000000000
0x7fa0e2b003a0:  0x0000000000000000
0x7fa0e2b003a8:  0x0000000000000000
0x7fa0e2b003b0:  0x0000000000000000
0x7fa0e2b003b8:  0x0000000000000000
0x7fa0e2b003c0:  0x0000000000000000
0x7fa0e2b003c8:  0x0000000000000000
0x7fa0e2b003d0:  0x0000000000000000
0x7fa0e2b003d8:  0x0000000000000000
0x7fa0e2b003e0:  0x0000000000000000
```

```
0x7fa0e2b003e8: 0x0000000000000000
0x7fa0e2b003f0: 0x0000000000000000
0x7fa0e2b003f8: 0x0000000000000000
0x7fa0e2b00400: 0x657461636f6c6c61
0x7fa0e2b00408: 0x79726f6d656d2064
0x7fa0e2b00410: 0x0000000000000000
0x7fa0e2b00418: 0x0000000000000000
0x7fa0e2b00420: 0x000000010cdb87d0  App9`procD
0x7fa0e2b00428: 0x0000000000000000
0x7fa0e2b00430: 0x0000000000000000
0x7fa0e2b00438: 0x0000000000000000
0x7fa0e2b00440: 0x0000000000000000
0x7fa0e2b00448: 0x0000000000000000
0x7fa0e2b00450: 0x0000000000000000
0x7fa0e2b00458: 0x0000000000000000
0x7fa0e2b00460: 0x0000000000000000
0x7fa0e2b00468: 0x0000000000000000
0x7fa0e2b00470: 0x0000000000000000
0x7fa0e2b00478: 0x0000000000000000
0x7fa0e2b00480: 0x0000000000000000
0x7fa0e2b00488: 0x0000000000000000
0x7fa0e2b00490: 0x0000000000000000
0x7fa0e2b00498: 0x0000000000000000
0x7fa0e2b004a0: 0x0000000000000000
0x7fa0e2b004a8: 0x0000000000000000
0x7fa0e2b004b0: 0x0000000000000000
0x7fa0e2b004b8: 0x0000000000000000
0x7fa0e2b004c0: 0x0000000000000000
0x7fa0e2b004c8: 0x0000000000000000
0x7fa0e2b004d0: 0x0000000000000000
0x7fa0e2b004d8: 0x0000000000000000
0x7fa0e2b004e0: 0x0000000000000000
0x7fa0e2b004e8: 0x0000000000000000
0x7fa0e2b004f0: 0x0000000000000000
0x7fa0e2b004f8: 0x0000000000000000
0x7fa0e2b00500: 0x657461636f6c6c61
0x7fa0e2b00508: 0x79726f6d656d2064
0x7fa0e2b00510: 0x0000000000000000
0x7fa0e2b00518: 0x0000000000000000
0x7fa0e2b00520: 0x000000010cdb87d0  App9`procD
0x7fa0e2b00528: 0x0000000000000000
0x7fa0e2b00530: 0x0000000000000000
0x7fa0e2b00538: 0x0000000000000000
0x7fa0e2b00540: 0x0000000000000000
0x7fa0e2b00548: 0x0000000000000000
0x7fa0e2b00550: 0x0000000000000000
0x7fa0e2b00558: 0x0000000000000000
0x7fa0e2b00560: 0x0000000000000000
0x7fa0e2b00568: 0x0000000000000000
0x7fa0e2b00570: 0x0000000000000000
0x7fa0e2b00578: 0x0000000000000000
[...]

(lldb) x/s 0x7fa0e2b00500
0x7fa0e2b00500:      "allocated memory"
```

6.   Compare the consequent vmmap logs vmmap_1883_1.log, vmmap_1883_2.log and vmmap_1883_3.log taking at different time:

```
Virtual Memory Map of process 1883 (App9)
Output report format:  2.2  -- 64-bit process

==== Non-writable regions for process 1883
__TEXT               000000010cdb8000-000000010cdb9000 [    4K] r-x/rwx SM=COW  /Users/DumpAnalysis/Documents/AMCDA-
Dumps/Apps/App9/Build/Products/Release/App9
__LINKEDIT           000000010cdba000-000000010cdbb000 [    4K] r--/rwx SM=COW  /Users/DumpAnalysis/Documents/AMCDA-
Dumps/Apps/App9/Build/Products/Release/App9
MALLOC metadata      000000010cdbb000-000000010cdbc000 [    4K] r--/rwx SM=ZER
MALLOC guard page    000000010cdbd000-000000010cdbe000 [    4K] ---/rwx SM=NUL
MALLOC guard page    000000010cdd3000-000000010cdd5000 [    8K] ---/rwx SM=NUL
MALLOC guard page    000000010cdea000-000000010cdeb000 [    4K] ---/rwx SM=NUL
MALLOC metadata      000000010cdeb000-000000010cdec000 [    4K] r--/rwx SM=PRV
STACK GUARD          000000010cf00000-000000010cf01000 [    4K] ---/rwx SM=NUL  stack guard for thread 1
STACK GUARD          000000010cf83000-000000010cf84000 [    4K] ---/rwx SM=NUL  stack guard for thread 2
STACK GUARD          000000010d006000-000000010d007000 [    4K] ---/rwx SM=NUL  stack guard for thread 3
STACK GUARD          000000010d089000-000000010d08a000 [    4K] ---/rwx SM=NUL  stack guard for thread 4
STACK GUARD          000000010d10c000-000000010d10d000 [    4K] ---/rwx SM=NUL  stack guard for thread 5
STACK GUARD          00007fff689b8000-00007fff6c1b8000 [ 56.0M] ---/rwx SM=NUL  stack guard for thread 0
__TEXT               00007fff6c9b8000-00007fff6c9ed000 [  212K] r-x/rwx SM=COW  /usr/lib/dyld
__LINKEDIT           00007fff6ca29000-00007fff6ca3c000 [   76K] r--/rwx SM=COW  /usr/lib/dyld
__TEXT               00007fff89663000-00007fff89681000 [  120K] r-x/r-x SM=COW  /usr/lib/system/libxpc.dylib
__TEXT               00007fff899d9000-00007fff899db000 [    8K] r-x/r-x SM=COW  /usr/lib/system/libsystem_blocks.dylib
__TEXT               00007fff899db000-00007fff89ab9000 [  888K] r-x/r-x SM=COW  /usr/lib/system/libsystem_c.dylib
__TEXT               00007fff89c93000-00007fff89ca2000 [   60K] r-x/r-x SM=COW  /usr/lib/system/libdispatch.dylib
__TEXT               00007fff8a261000-00007fff8a263000 [    8K] r-x/r-x SM=COW  /usr/lib/system/libunc.dylib
__TEXT               00007fff8a754000-00007fff8a756000 [    8K] r-x/r-x SM=COW  /usr/lib/system/libremovefile.dylib
__TEXT               00007fff8dd85000-00007fff8dd8a000 [   20K] r-x/r-x SM=COW  /usr/lib/system/libmathCommon.A.dylib
__TEXT               00007fff8dd8a000-00007fff8dd8f000 [   20K] r-x/r-x SM=COW  /usr/lib/system/libdyld.dylib
__TEXT               00007fff8e3b1000-00007fff8e3b3000 [    8K] r-x/r-x SM=COW  /usr/lib/system/libsystem_sandbox.dylib
__TEXT               00007fff8ed60000-00007fff8ed67000 [   28K] r-x/r-x SM=COW  /usr/lib/system/libmacho.dylib
__TEXT               00007fff8ed67000-00007fff8ed88000 [  132K] r-x/r-x SM=COW  /usr/lib/system/libsystem_kernel.dylib
__TEXT               00007fff8ef1d000-00007fff8ef26000 [   36K] r-x/r-x SM=COW  /usr/lib/system/libsystem_dnssd.dylib
__TEXT               00007fff8fa97000-00007fff8fad3000 [  240K] r-x/r-x SM=COW  /usr/lib/system/libsystem_info.dylib
__TEXT               00007fff8feb9000-00007fff8febc000 [   12K] r-x/r-x SM=COW  /usr/lib/system/libquarantine.dylib
__TEXT               00007fff90025000-00007fff90026000 [    4K] r-x/r-x SM=COW  /usr/lib/system/libkeymgr.dylib
__TEXT               00007fff9004e000-00007fff90054000 [   24K] r-x/r-x SM=COW  /usr/lib/system/libcompiler_rt.dylib
__TEXT               00007fff9098b000-00007fff9098d000 [    8K] r-x/r-x SM=COW  /usr/lib/system/libdnsinfo.dylib
__TEXT               00007fff91199000-00007fff9119f000 [   24K] r-x/r-x SM=COW  /usr/lib/system/libsystem_network.dylib
__TEXT               00007fff91c14000-00007fff91c1f000 [   44K] r-x/r-x SM=COW  /usr/lib/system/liblaunch.dylib
__TEXT               00007fff94a73000-00007fff94a7b000 [   32K] r-x/r-x SM=COW  /usr/lib/system/libcopyfile.dylib
__TEXT               00007fff94abc000-00007fff94aff000 [  268K] r-x/r-x SM=COW  /usr/lib/system/libcommonCrypto.dylib
__TEXT               00007fff95880000-00007fff9588a000 [   40K] r-x/r-x SM=COW  /usr/lib/system/libsystem_notify.dylib
__TEXT               00007fff95fe7000-00007fff96015000 [  184K] r-x/r-x SM=COW  /usr/lib/libSystem.B.dylib
__TEXT               00007fff960fa000-00007fff96101000 [   28K] r-x/r-x SM=COW  /usr/lib/system/libunwind.dylib
__TEXT               00007fff96693000-00007fff96699000 [   24K] r-x/r-x SM=COW  /usr/lib/system/libcache.dylib
__LINKEDIT           00007fff967f7000-00007fff997a1000 [ 47.7M] r--/r-- SM=COW  /usr/lib/system/libxpc.dylib
shared memory        00007ffffe00000-00007ffffe02000 [    8K] r-x/r-x SM=SHM

==== Writable regions for process 1883
__DATA               000000010cdb9000-000000010cdba000 [    4K] rw-/rwx SM=PRV  /Users/DumpAnalysis/Documents/AMCDA-
Dumps/Apps/App9/Build/Products/Release/App9
MALLOC metadata      000000010cdbc000-000000010cdbd000 [    4K] rw-/rwx SM=ZER
MALLOC metadata      000000010cdbe000-000000010cdd3000 [   84K] rw-/rwx SM=PRV
MALLOC metadata      000000010cdd5000-000000010cdea000 [   84K] rw-/rwx SM=PRV
MALLOC_TINY          000000010ce00000-000000010cf00000 [ 1024K] rw-/rwx SM=PRV  DefaultMallocZone_0x10cdbb000
Stack                000000010cf01000-000000010cf83000 [  520K] rw-/rwx SM=PRV  thread 1
Stack                000000010cf84000-000000010d006000 [  520K] rw-/rwx SM=PRV  thread 2
Stack                000000010d007000-000000010d089000 [  520K] rw-/rwx SM=PRV  thread 3
Stack                000000010d08a000-000000010d10c000 [  520K] rw-/rwx SM=PRV  thread 4
Stack                000000010d10d000-000000010d18f000 [  520K] rw-/rwx SM=PRV  thread 5
MALLOC_TINY          00007fa10b400000-00007fa10b600000 [ 2048K] rw-/rwx SM=PRV  DefaultMallocZone_0x10cdbb000
Stack                00007fff6c1b8000-00007fff6c9b7000 [ 8188K] rw-/rwx SM=ZER  thread 0
Stack                00007fff6c9b7000-00007fff6c9b8000 [    4K] rw-/rwx SM=COW  thread 0
__DATA               00007fff6c9ed000-00007fff6ca29000 [  240K] rw-/rwx SM=COW  /usr/lib/dyld
__DATA               00007fff79631000-00007fff79634000 [   12K] rw-/rwx SM=COW  /usr/lib/system/libxpc.dylib
__DATA               00007fff796d1000-00007fff796d2000 [    4K] rw-/rwx SM=COW  /usr/lib/system/libsystem_blocks.dylib
__DATA               00007fff796d2000-00007fff796e2000 [   64K] rw-/rwx SM=COW  /usr/lib/system/libsystem_c.dylib
__DATA               00007fff79735000-00007fff7973b000 [   24K] rw-/rwx SM=COW  /usr/lib/system/libdispatch.dylib
__DATA               00007fff79801000-00007fff79802000 [    4K] rw-/rw- SM=COW  /usr/lib/system/libunc.dylib
__DATA               00007fff79882000-00007fff79883000 [    4K] rw-/rw- SM=COW  /usr/lib/system/libremovefile.dylib
__DATA               00007fff79db2000-00007fff79db3000 [    4K] rw-/rwx SM=COW  /usr/lib/system/libdyld.dylib
__DATA               00007fff79e14000-00007fff79e15000 [    4K] rw-/rwx SM=COW  /usr/lib/system/libsystem_sandbox.dylib
__DATA               00007fff79ef2000-00007fff79ef3000 [    4K] rw-/rwx SM=COW  /usr/lib/system/libmacho.dylib
__DATA               00007fff79ef3000-00007fff79ef6000 [   12K] rw-/rwx SM=COW  /usr/lib/system/libsystem_kernel.dylib
__DATA               00007fff79f49000-00007fff79f4a000 [    4K] rw-/rwx SM=COW  /usr/lib/system/libsystem_dnssd.dylib
__DATA               00007fff7a0c4000-00007fff7a0c7000 [   12K] rw-/rwx SM=COW  /usr/lib/system/libsystem_info.dylib
__DATA               00007fff7a190000-00007fff7a191000 [    4K] rw-/rwx SM=COW  /usr/lib/system/libquarantine.dylib
__DATA               00007fff7a1ca000-00007fff7a1cb000 [    4K] rw-/rwx SM=COW  /usr/lib/system/libkeymgr.dylib
__DATA               00007fff7a1d4000-00007fff7a1d5000 [    4K] rw-/rwx SM=COW  /usr/lib/system/libcompiler_rt.dylib
__DATA               00007fff7a2a4000-00007fff7a2a5000 [    4K] rw-/rw- SM=COW  /usr/lib/system/libdnsinfo.dylib
```

```
__DATA          00007fff7a347000-00007fff7a348000 [    4K] rw-/rw- SM=COW  /usr/lib/system/libsystem_network.dylib
__DATA          00007fff7a484000-00007fff7a485000 [    4K] rw-/rwx SM=COW  /usr/lib/system/liblaunch.dylib
__DATA          00007fff7aab2000-00007fff7aab3000 [    4K] rw-/rw- SM=COW  /usr/lib/system/libcopyfile.dylib
__DATA          00007fff7aabb000-00007fff7aac1000 [   24K] rw-/rw- SM=COW  /usr/lib/system/libcommonCrypto.dylib
__DATA          00007fff7afb3000-00007fff7afb4000 [    4K] rw-/rw- SM=COW  /usr/lib/system/libsystem_notify.dylib
__DATA          00007fff7b06e000-00007fff7b06f000 [    4K] rw-/rw- SM=COW  /usr/lib/libSystem.B.dylib
__DATA          00007fff7b072000-00007fff7b073000 [    4K] rw-/rw- SM=COW  /usr/lib/system/libunwind.dylib
__DATA          00007fff7b11c000-00007fff7b11d000 [    4K] rw-/rw- SM=COW  /usr/lib/system/libcache.dylib

==== Legend
SM=sharing mode:
        COW=copy_on_write PRV=private NUL=empty ALI=aliased
        SHM=shared ZER=zero_filled S/A=shared_alias

==== Summary for process 1883
ReadOnly portion of Libraries: Total=50.2M resident=14.3M(28%) swapped_out_or_unallocated=35.9M(72%)
Writable regions: Total=31.1M written=1388K(4%) resident=10.2M(33%) swapped_out=11.6M(37%) unallocated=20.9M(67%)

REGION TYPE                     VIRTUAL
===========                     =======
MALLOC                          3072K       see MALLOC ZONE table below
MALLOC guard page                16K
MALLOC metadata                 180K
STACK GUARD                     56.0M
Stack                           10.5M
__DATA                          464K
__LINKEDIT                      47.7M
__TEXT                          2484K
shared memory                    8K
===========                     =======
TOTAL                           120.4M


                        VIRTUAL ALLOCATION     BYTES
MALLOC ZONE                SIZE     COUNT   ALLOCATED  % FULL
===========             =======  =========  =========  ======
DefaultMallocZone_0x10cdbb000  3072K    5033       1252K     40%



Virtual Memory Map of process 1883 (App9)
Output report format:  2.2  -- 64-bit process


==== Non-writable regions for process 1883
__TEXT          000000010cdb8000-000000010cdb9000 [    4K] r-x/rwx SM=COW  /Users/DumpAnalysis/Documents/AMCDA-
Dumps/Apps/App9/Build/Products/Release/App9
__LINKEDIT      000000010cdba000-000000010cdbb000 [    4K] r--/rwx SM=COW  /Users/DumpAnalysis/Documents/AMCDA-
Dumps/Apps/App9/Build/Products/Release/App9
MALLOC metadata 000000010cdbb000-000000010cdbc000 [    4K] r--/rwx SM=COW
MALLOC guard page 000000010cdbd000-000000010cdbe000 [    4K] ---/rwx SM=NUL
MALLOC guard page 000000010cdd3000-000000010cdd5000 [    8K] ---/rwx SM=NUL
MALLOC guard page 000000010cdea000-000000010cdeb000 [    4K] ---/rwx SM=NUL
MALLOC metadata 000000010cdeb000-000000010cdec000 [    4K] r--/rwx SM=COW
STACK GUARD     000000010cf00000-000000010cf01000 [    4K] ---/rwx SM=NUL  stack guard for thread 1
STACK GUARD     000000010cf83000-000000010cf84000 [    4K] ---/rwx SM=NUL  stack guard for thread 2
STACK GUARD     000000010d006000-000000010d007000 [    4K] ---/rwx SM=NUL  stack guard for thread 3
STACK GUARD     000000010d089000-000000010d08a000 [    4K] ---/rwx SM=NUL  stack guard for thread 4
STACK GUARD     000000010d10c000-000000010d10d000 [    4K] ---/rwx SM=NUL  stack guard for thread 5
STACK GUARD     00007fff689b8000-00007fff6c1b8000 [ 56.0M] ---/rwx SM=NUL  stack guard for thread 0
__TEXT          00007fff6c9b8000-00007fff6c9ed000 [  212K] r-x/rwx SM=COW  /usr/lib/dyld
__LINKEDIT      00007fff6ca29000-00007fff6ca3c000 [   76K] r--/rwx SM=COW  /usr/lib/dyld
__TEXT          00007fff89663000-00007fff89681000 [  120K] r-x/r-x SM=COW  /usr/lib/system/libxpc.dylib
__TEXT          00007fff899d9000-00007fff899db000 [    8K] r-x/r-x SM=COW  /usr/lib/system/libsystem_blocks.dylib
__TEXT          00007fff899db000-00007fff89ab9000 [  888K] r-x/r-x SM=COW  /usr/lib/system/libsystem_c.dylib
__TEXT          00007fff89c93000-00007fff89ca2000 [   60K] r-x/r-x SM=COW  /usr/lib/system/libdispatch.dylib
__TEXT          00007fff8a261000-00007fff8a263000 [    8K] r-x/r-x SM=COW  /usr/lib/system/libunc.dylib
__TEXT          00007fff8a754000-00007fff8a756000 [    8K] r-x/r-x SM=COW  /usr/lib/system/libremovefile.dylib
__TEXT          00007fff8dd85000-00007fff8dd8a000 [   20K] r-x/r-x SM=COW  /usr/lib/system/libmathCommon.A.dylib
__TEXT          00007fff8dd8a000-00007fff8dd8f000 [   20K] r-x/r-x SM=COW  /usr/lib/system/libdyld.dylib
__TEXT          00007fff8e3b1000-00007fff8e3b3000 [    8K] r-x/r-x SM=COW  /usr/lib/system/libsystem_sandbox.dylib
__TEXT          00007fff8ed60000-00007fff8ed67000 [   28K] r-x/r-x SM=COW  /usr/lib/system/libmacho.dylib
__TEXT          00007fff8ed67000-00007fff8ed88000 [  132K] r-x/r-x SM=COW  /usr/lib/system/libsystem_kernel.dylib
__TEXT          00007fff8ef1d000-00007fff8ef26000 [   36K] r-x/r-x SM=COW  /usr/lib/system/libsystem_dnssd.dylib
__TEXT          00007fff8fa97000-00007fff8fad3000 [  240K] r-x/r-x SM=COW  /usr/lib/system/libsystem_info.dylib
__TEXT          00007fff8feb9000-00007fff8febc000 [   12K] r-x/r-x SM=COW  /usr/lib/system/libquarantine.dylib
__TEXT          00007fff90025000-00007fff90026000 [    4K] r-x/r-x SM=COW  /usr/lib/system/libkeymgr.dylib
__TEXT          00007fff9004e000-00007fff90054000 [   24K] r-x/r-x SM=COW  /usr/lib/system/libcompiler_rt.dylib
__TEXT          00007fff9098b000-00007fff9098d000 [    8K] r-x/r-x SM=COW  /usr/lib/system/libdnsinfo.dylib
__TEXT          00007fff91199000-00007fff9119f000 [   24K] r-x/r-x SM=COW  /usr/lib/system/libsystem_network.dylib
__TEXT          00007fff91c14000-00007fff91c1f000 [   44K] r-x/r-x SM=COW  /usr/lib/system/liblaunch.dylib
__TEXT          00007fff94a73000-00007fff94a7b000 [   32K] r-x/r-x SM=COW  /usr/lib/system/libcopyfile.dylib
__TEXT          00007fff94abc000-00007fff94aff000 [  268K] r-x/r-x SM=COW  /usr/lib/system/libcommonCrypto.dylib
__TEXT          00007fff95880000-00007fff9588a000 [   40K] r-x/r-x SM=COW  /usr/lib/system/libsystem_notify.dylib
__TEXT          00007fff95fe7000-00007fff96015000 [  184K] r-x/r-x SM=COW  /usr/lib/libSystem.B.dylib
__TEXT          00007fff960fa000-00007fff96101000 [   28K] r-x/r-x SM=COW  /usr/lib/system/libunwind.dylib
__TEXT          00007fff96693000-00007fff96699000 [   24K] r-x/r-x SM=COW  /usr/lib/system/libcache.dylib
__LINKEDIT      00007fff967f7000-00007fff997a1000 [ 47.7M] r--/r-- SM=COW  /usr/lib/system/libxpc.dylib
```

```
shared memory          00007fffffe00000-00007fffffe02000 [    8K] r-x/r-x SM=SHM

==== Writable regions for process 1883
__DATA                 000000010cdb9000-000000010cdba000 [    4K] rw-/rwx SM=PRV  /Users/DumpAnalysis/Documents/AMCDA-
Dumps/Apps/App9/Build/Products/Release/App9
MALLOC metadata        000000010cdbc000-000000010cdbd000 [    4K] rw-/rwx SM=PRV
MALLOC metadata        000000010cdbe000-000000010cdd3000 [   84K] rw-/rwx SM=PRV
MALLOC metadata        000000010cdd5000-000000010cdea000 [   84K] rw-/rwx SM=COW
MALLOC metadata        000000010cdec000-000000010cdf5000 [   36K] rw-/rwx SM=PRV
MALLOC_TINY            000000010ce00000-000000010cf00000 [ 1024K] rw-/rwx SM=PRV  DefaultMallocZone_0x10cdbb000
Stack                  000000010cf01000-000000010cf83000 [  520K] rw-/rwx SM=PRV  thread 1
Stack                  000000010cf84000-000000010d006000 [  520K] rw-/rwx SM=PRV  thread 2
Stack                  000000010d007000-000000010d089000 [  520K] rw-/rwx SM=PRV  thread 3
Stack                  000000010d08a000-000000010d10c000 [  520K] rw-/rwx SM=PRV  thread 4
Stack                  000000010d10d000-000000010d18f000 [  520K] rw-/rwx SM=PRV  thread 5
MALLOC_TINY            00007fa0fb400000-00007fa102400000 [  112.0M] rw-/rwx SM=PRV  DefaultMallocZone_0x10cdbb000
MALLOC_TINY            00007fa10b400000-00007fa12b300000 [511.0M] rw-/rwx SM=PRV  DefaultMallocZone_0x10cdbb000
Stack                  00007fff6c1b8000-00007fff6c9b7000 [ 8188K] rw-/rwx SM=ZER  thread 0
Stack                  00007fff6c9b7000-00007fff6c9b8000 [    4K] rw-/rwx SM=COW  thread 0
__DATA                 00007fff6c9ed000-00007fff6ca29000 [  240K] rw-/rwx SM=COW  /usr/lib/dyld
__DATA                 00007fff79631000-00007fff79634000 [   12K] rw-/rwx SM=COW  /usr/lib/system/libxpc.dylib
__DATA                 00007fff796d1000-00007fff796d2000 [    4K] rw-/rwx SM=COW  /usr/lib/system/libsystem_blocks.dylib
__DATA                 00007fff796d2000-00007fff796e2000 [   64K] rw-/rwx SM=COW  /usr/lib/system/libsystem_c.dylib
__DATA                 00007fff79735000-00007fff7973b000 [   24K] rw-/rwx SM=COW  /usr/lib/system/libdispatch.dylib
__DATA                 00007fff79801000-00007fff79802000 [    4K] rw-/rw- SM=COW  /usr/lib/system/libunc.dylib
__DATA                 00007fff79882000-00007fff79883000 [    4K] rw-/rw- SM=COW  /usr/lib/system/libremovefile.dylib
__DATA                 00007fff79db2000-00007fff79db3000 [    4K] rw-/rwx SM=COW  /usr/lib/system/libdyld.dylib
__DATA                 00007fff79e14000-00007fff79e15000 [    4K] rw-/rwx SM=COW  /usr/lib/system/libsystem_sandbox.dylib
__DATA                 00007fff79ef2000-00007fff79ef3000 [    4K] rw-/rwx SM=COW  /usr/lib/system/libmacho.dylib
__DATA                 00007fff79ef3000-00007fff79ef6000 [   12K] rw-/rwx SM=COW  /usr/lib/system/libsystem_kernel.dylib
__DATA                 00007fff79f49000-00007fff79f4a000 [    4K] rw-/rwx SM=COW  /usr/lib/system/libsystem_dnssd.dylib
__DATA                 00007fff7a0c4000-00007fff7a0c7000 [   12K] rw-/rwx SM=COW  /usr/lib/system/libsystem_info.dylib
__DATA                 00007fff7a190000-00007fff7a191000 [    4K] rw-/rwx SM=COW  /usr/lib/system/libquarantine.dylib
__DATA                 00007fff7a1ca000-00007fff7a1cb000 [    4K] rw-/rwx SM=COW  /usr/lib/system/libkeymgr.dylib
__DATA                 00007fff7a1d4000-00007fff7a1d5000 [    4K] rw-/rwx SM=COW  /usr/lib/system/libcompiler_rt.dylib
__DATA                 00007fff7a2a4000-00007fff7a2a5000 [    4K] rw-/rw- SM=COW  /usr/lib/system/libdnsinfo.dylib
__DATA                 00007fff7a347000-00007fff7a348000 [    4K] rw-/rw- SM=COW  /usr/lib/system/libsystem_network.dylib
__DATA                 00007fff7a484000-00007fff7a485000 [    4K] rw-/rwx SM=COW  /usr/lib/system/liblaunch.dylib
__DATA                 00007fff7aab2000-00007fff7aab3000 [    4K] rw-/rw- SM=COW  /usr/lib/system/libcopyfile.dylib
__DATA                 00007fff7aabb000-00007fff7aac1000 [   24K] rw-/rw- SM=COW  /usr/lib/system/libcommonCrypto.dylib
__DATA                 00007fff7afb3000-00007fff7afb4000 [    4K] rw-/rw- SM=COW  /usr/lib/system/libsystem_notify.dylib
__DATA                 00007fff7b06e000-00007fff7b06f000 [    4K] rw-/rw- SM=COW  /usr/lib/libSystem.B.dylib
__DATA                 00007fff7b072000-00007fff7b073000 [    4K] rw-/rw- SM=COW  /usr/lib/system/libunwind.dylib
__DATA                 00007fff7b11c000-00007fff7b11d000 [    4K] rw-/rw- SM=COW  /usr/lib/system/libcache.dylib

==== Legend
SM=sharing mode:
        COW=copy_on_write PRV=private NUL=empty ALI=aliased
        SHM=shared ZER=zero_filled S/A=shared_alias

==== Summary for process 1883
ReadOnly portion of Libraries: Total=50.2M resident=12.5M(25%) swapped_out_or_unallocated=37.6M(75%)
Writable regions: Total=652.1M written=621.4M(95%) resident=487.1M(75%) swapped_out=154.8M(24%) unallocated=164.9M(25%)


REGION TYPE                    VIRTUAL
===========                    =======
MALLOC                          624.0M        see MALLOC ZONE table below
MALLOC guard page                16K
MALLOC metadata                 216K
STACK GUARD                     56.0M
Stack                           10.5M
__DATA                          464K
__LINKEDIT                      47.7M
__TEXT                         2484K
shared memory                     8K
===========                    =======
TOTAL                          741.4M


                               VIRTUAL  ALLOCATION     BYTES
MALLOC ZONE                       SIZE       COUNT  ALLOCATED  % FULL
===========                    =======  ==========  =========  ======
DefaultMallocZone_0x10cdbb000   624.0M     2505033     611.6M     98%



Virtual Memory Map of process 1883 (App9)
Output report format:  2.2  -- 64-bit process


==== Non-writable regions for process 1883
__TEXT                 000000010cdb8000-000000010cdb9000 [    4K] r-x/rwx SM=COW  /Users/DumpAnalysis/Documents/AMCDA-
Dumps/Apps/App9/Build/Products/Release/App9
__LINKEDIT             000000010cdba000-000000010cdbb000 [    4K] r--/rwx SM=COW  /Users/DumpAnalysis/Documents/AMCDA-
Dumps/Apps/App9/Build/Products/Release/App9
MALLOC metadata        000000010cdbb000-000000010cdbc000 [    4K] r--/rwx SM=COW
MALLOC guard page      000000010cdbd000-000000010cdbe000 [    4K] ---/rwx SM=NUL
MALLOC guard page      000000010cdd3000-000000010cdd5000 [    8K] ---/rwx SM=NUL
```

273

```
MALLOC guard page     000000010cdea000-000000010cdeb000 [    4K] ---/rwx SM=NUL
MALLOC metadata       000000010cdeb000-000000010cdec000 [    4K] r--/rwx SM=COW
STACK GUARD           000000010cf00000-000000010cf01000 [    4K] ---/rwx SM=NUL   stack guard for thread 1
STACK GUARD           000000010cf83000-000000010cf84000 [    4K] ---/rwx SM=NUL   stack guard for thread 2
STACK GUARD           000000010d006000-000000010d007000 [    4K] ---/rwx SM=NUL   stack guard for thread 3
STACK GUARD           000000010d089000-000000010d08a000 [    4K] ---/rwx SM=NUL   stack guard for thread 4
STACK GUARD           000000010d10c000-000000010d10d000 [    4K] ---/rwx SM=NUL   stack guard for thread 5
STACK GUARD           00007fff689b8000-00007fff6c1b8000 [ 56.0M] ---/rwx SM=NUL   stack guard for thread 0
__TEXT                00007fff6c9b8000-00007fff6c9ed000 [  212K] r-x/rwx SM=COW   /usr/lib/dyld
__LINKEDIT            00007fff6ca29000-00007fff6ca3c000 [   76K] r--/rwx SM=COW   /usr/lib/dyld
__TEXT                00007fff89663000-00007fff89681000 [  120K] r-x/r-x SM=COW   /usr/lib/system/libxpc.dylib
__TEXT                00007fff899d9000-00007fff899db000 [    8K] r-x/r-x SM=COW   /usr/lib/system/libsystem_blocks.dylib
__TEXT                00007fff899db000-00007fff89ab9000 [  888K] r-x/r-x SM=COW   /usr/lib/system/libsystem_c.dylib
__TEXT                00007fff89c93000-00007fff89ca2000 [   60K] r-x/r-x SM=COW   /usr/lib/system/libdispatch.dylib
__TEXT                00007fff8a261000-00007fff8a263000 [    8K] r-x/r-x SM=COW   /usr/lib/system/libunc.dylib
__TEXT                00007fff8a754000-00007fff8a756000 [    8K] r-x/r-x SM=COW   /usr/lib/system/libremovefile.dylib
__TEXT                00007fff8dd85000-00007fff8dd8a000 [   20K] r-x/r-x SM=COW   /usr/lib/system/libmathCommon.A.dylib
__TEXT                00007fff8dd8a000-00007fff8dd8f000 [   20K] r-x/r-x SM=COW   /usr/lib/system/libdyld.dylib
__TEXT                00007fff8e3b1000-00007fff8e3b3000 [    8K] r-x/r-x SM=COW   /usr/lib/system/libsystem_sandbox.dylib
__TEXT                00007fff8ed60000-00007fff8ed67000 [   28K] r-x/r-x SM=COW   /usr/lib/system/libmacho.dylib
__TEXT                00007fff8ed67000-00007fff8ed88000 [  132K] r-x/r-x SM=COW   /usr/lib/system/libsystem_kernel.dylib
__TEXT                00007fff8ef1d000-00007fff8ef26000 [   36K] r-x/r-x SM=COW   /usr/lib/system/libsystem_dnssd.dylib
__TEXT                00007fff8fa97000-00007fff8fad3000 [  240K] r-x/r-x SM=COW   /usr/lib/system/libsystem_info.dylib
__TEXT                00007fff8feb9000-00007fff8febc000 [   12K] r-x/r-x SM=COW   /usr/lib/system/libquarantine.dylib
__TEXT                00007fff90025000-00007fff90026000 [    4K] r-x/r-x SM=COW   /usr/lib/system/libkeymgr.dylib
__TEXT                00007fff9004e000-00007fff90054000 [   24K] r-x/r-x SM=COW   /usr/lib/system/libcompiler_rt.dylib
__TEXT                00007fff9098b000-00007fff9098d000 [    8K] r-x/r-x SM=COW   /usr/lib/system/libdnsinfo.dylib
__TEXT                00007fff91199000-00007fff9119f000 [   24K] r-x/r-x SM=COW   /usr/lib/system/libsystem_network.dylib
__TEXT                00007fff91c14000-00007fff91c1f000 [   44K] r-x/r-x SM=COW   /usr/lib/system/liblaunch.dylib
__TEXT                00007fff94a73000-00007fff94a7b000 [   32K] r-x/r-x SM=COW   /usr/lib/system/libcopyfile.dylib
__TEXT                00007fff94abc000-00007fff94aff000 [  268K] r-x/r-x SM=COW   /usr/lib/system/libcommonCrypto.dylib
__TEXT                00007fff95880000-00007fff9588a000 [   40K] r-x/r-x SM=COW   /usr/lib/system/libsystem_notify.dylib
__TEXT                00007fff95fe7000-00007fff96015000 [  184K] r-x/r-x SM=COW   /usr/lib/libSystem.B.dylib
__TEXT                00007fff960fa000-00007fff96101000 [   28K] r-x/r-x SM=COW   /usr/lib/system/libunwind.dylib
__TEXT                00007fff96693000-00007fff96699000 [   24K] r-x/r-x SM=COW   /usr/lib/system/libcache.dylib
__LINKEDIT            00007fff967f7000-00007fff997a1000 [ 47.7M] r--/r-- SM=COW   /usr/lib/system/libxpc.dylib
shared memory         00007fffffe00000-00007fffffe02000 [    8K] r-x/r-x SM=SHM


==== Writable regions for process 1883
__DATA                000000010cdb9000-000000010cdba000 [    4K] rw-/rwx SM=PRV   /Users/DumpAnalysis/Documents/AMCDA-
Dumps/Apps/App9/Build/Products/Release/App9
MALLOC metadata       000000010cdbc000-000000010cdbd000 [    4K] rw-/rwx SM=PRV
MALLOC metadata       000000010cdbe000-000000010cdd3000 [   84K] rw-/rwx SM=PRV
MALLOC metadata       000000010cdd5000-000000010cdea000 [   84K] rw-/rwx SM=COW
MALLOC metadata       000000010cdec000-000000010cdfd000 [   68K] rw-/rwx SM=PRV
MALLOC_TINY           000000010ce00000-000000010cf00000 [ 1024K] rw-/rwx SM=COW   DefaultMallocZone_0x10cdbb000
Stack                 000000010cf01000-000000010cf83000 [  520K] rw-/rwx SM=PRV   thread 1
Stack                 000000010cf84000-000000010d006000 [  520K] rw-/rwx SM=PRV   thread 2
Stack                 000000010d007000-000000010d089000 [  520K] rw-/rwx SM=PRV   thread 3
Stack                 000000010d08a000-000000010d10c000 [  520K] rw-/rwx SM=PRV   thread 4
Stack                 000000010d10d000-000000010d18f000 [  520K] rw-/rwx SM=PRV   thread 5
MALLOC_TINY           00007fa0db400000-00007fa0e9100000 [221.0M] rw-/rwx SM=PRV   DefaultMallocZone_0x10cdbb000
MALLOC_TINY           00007fa0eb400000-00007fa0fb300000 [255.0M] rw-/rwx SM=PRV   DefaultMallocZone_0x10cdbb000
MALLOC_TINY           00007fa0fb400000-00007fa100800000 [ 84.0M] rw-/rwx SM=COW   DefaultMallocZone_0x10cdbb000
MALLOC_TINY           00007fa100800000-00007fa100a00000 [ 2048K] rw-/rwx SM=PRV   DefaultMallocZone_0x10cdbb000
MALLOC_TINY           00007fa100a00000-00007fa101400000 [ 10.0M] rw-/rwx SM=COW   DefaultMallocZone_0x10cdbb000
MALLOC_TINY           00007fa101400000-00007fa101500000 [ 1024K] rw-/rwx SM=PRV   DefaultMallocZone_0x10cdbb000
MALLOC_TINY           00007fa101500000-00007fa101e00000 [ 9216K] rw-/rwx SM=COW   DefaultMallocZone_0x10cdbb000
MALLOC_TINY           00007fa101e00000-00007fa102100000 [ 3072K] rw-/rwx SM=PRV   DefaultMallocZone_0x10cdbb000
MALLOC_TINY           00007fa102100000-00007fa102200000 [ 1024K] rw-/rwx SM=PRV   DefaultMallocZone_0x10cdbb000
MALLOC_TINY           00007fa102200000-00007fa10b300000 [145.0M] rw-/rwx SM=PRV   DefaultMallocZone_0x10cdbb000
MALLOC_TINY           00007fa10b400000-00007fa12b300000 [511.0M] rw-/rwx SM=PRV   DefaultMallocZone_0x10cdbb000
Stack                 00007fff6c1b8000-00007fff6c9b7000 [ 8188K] rw-/rwx SM=ZER   thread 0
Stack                 00007fff6c9b7000-00007fff6c9b8000 [    4K] rw-/rwx SM=PRV   thread 0
__DATA                00007fff6c9ed000-00007fff6ca29000 [  240K] rw-/rwx SM=COW   /usr/lib/dyld
__DATA                00007fff79631000-00007fff79634000 [   12K] rw-/rwx SM=COW   /usr/lib/system/libxpc.dylib
__DATA                00007fff796d1000-00007fff796d2000 [    4K] rw-/rwx SM=COW   /usr/lib/system/libsystem_blocks.dylib
__DATA                00007fff796d2000-00007fff796e2000 [   64K] rw-/rwx SM=COW   /usr/lib/system/libsystem_c.dylib
__DATA                00007fff79735000-00007fff7973b000 [   24K] rw-/rwx SM=COW   /usr/lib/system/libdispatch.dylib
__DATA                00007fff79801000-00007fff79802000 [    4K] rw-/rw- SM=COW   /usr/lib/system/libunc.dylib
__DATA                00007fff79882000-00007fff79883000 [    4K] rw-/rw- SM=COW   /usr/lib/system/libremovefile.dylib
__DATA                00007fff79db2000-00007fff79db3000 [    4K] rw-/rwx SM=COW   /usr/lib/system/libdyld.dylib
__DATA                00007fff79e14000-00007fff79e15000 [    4K] rw-/rwx SM=COW   /usr/lib/system/libsystem_sandbox.dylib
__DATA                00007fff79ef2000-00007fff79ef3000 [    4K] rw-/rwx SM=COW   /usr/lib/system/libmacho.dylib
__DATA                00007fff79ef3000-00007fff79ef6000 [   12K] rw-/rwx SM=COW   /usr/lib/system/libsystem_kernel.dylib
__DATA                00007fff79f49000-00007fff79f4a000 [    4K] rw-/rwx SM=COW   /usr/lib/system/libsystem_dnssd.dylib
__DATA                00007fff7a0c4000-00007fff7a0c7000 [   12K] rw-/rwx SM=COW   /usr/lib/system/libsystem_info.dylib
__DATA                00007fff7a190000-00007fff7a191000 [    4K] rw-/rwx SM=COW   /usr/lib/system/libquarantine.dylib
__DATA                00007fff7a1ca000-00007fff7a1cb000 [    4K] rw-/rwx SM=COW   /usr/lib/system/libkeymgr.dylib
__DATA                00007fff7a1d4000-00007fff7a1d5000 [    4K] rw-/rwx SM=COW   /usr/lib/system/libcompiler_rt.dylib
__DATA                00007fff7a2a4000-00007fff7a2a5000 [    4K] rw-/rw- SM=COW   /usr/lib/system/libdnsinfo.dylib
__DATA                00007fff7a347000-00007fff7a348000 [    4K] rw-/rw- SM=COW   /usr/lib/system/libsystem_network.dylib
__DATA                00007fff7a484000-00007fff7a485000 [    4K] rw-/rwx SM=COW   /usr/lib/system/liblaunch.dylib
__DATA                00007fff7aab2000-00007fff7aab3000 [    4K] rw-/rw- SM=COW   /usr/lib/system/libcopyfile.dylib
__DATA                00007fff7aabb000-00007fff7aac1000 [   24K] rw-/rw- SM=COW   /usr/lib/system/libcommonCrypto.dylib
__DATA                00007fff7afb3000-00007fff7afb4000 [    4K] rw-/rw- SM=COW   /usr/lib/system/libsystem_notify.dylib
```

```
__DATA           00007fff7b06e000-00007fff7b06f000 [    4K] rw-/rw- SM=COW  /usr/lib/libSystem.B.dylib
__DATA           00007fff7b072000-00007fff7b073000 [    4K] rw-/rw- SM=COW  /usr/lib/system/libunwind.dylib
__DATA           00007fff7b11c000-00007fff7b11d000 [    4K] rw-/rw- SM=COW  /usr/lib/system/libcache.dylib

==== Legend
SM=sharing mode:
        COW=copy_on_write PRV=private NUL=empty ALI=aliased
        SHM=shared ZER=zero_filled S/A=shared_alias

==== Summary for process 1883
ReadOnly portion of Libraries: Total=50.2M resident=12.5M(25%) swapped_out_or_unallocated=37.6M(75%)
Writable regions: Total=1.2G written=625.5M(49%) resident=450.2M(35%) swapped_out=811.8M(64%) unallocated=820.7M(65%)

REGION TYPE                VIRTUAL
===========                =======
MALLOC                        1.2G        see MALLOC ZONE table below
MALLOC guard page              16K
MALLOC metadata               248K
STACK GUARD                  56.0M
Stack                        10.5M
__DATA                        464K
__LINKEDIT                   47.7M
__TEXT                       2484K
shared memory                   8K
===========                =======
TOTAL                         1.3G

                           VIRTUAL ALLOCATION      BYTES
MALLOC ZONE                   SIZE      COUNT  ALLOCATED  % FULL
===========                ======= ==========  =========  ======
DefaultMallocZone_0x10cdbb000  1.2G    5005033       1.2G     98%
```

275

Exercise A10 (GDB)

- **Goal:** Learn how to identify heap contention wait chains, synchronization issues, advanced disassembly, dump arrays

- **Patterns:** Double Free, Heap Contention, Wait Chain, Critical Region, Self-Diagnosis

- \AMCDA-Dumps\Exercise-A10-GDB.pdf

Exercise A10 (GDB)

Goal: Learn how to identify heap contention wait chains, synchronization issues, advanced disassembly, dump arrays

Patterns: Heap Corruption, Heap Contention, Wait Chain, Critical Region, Self-Diagnostics

1.   Identify heap memory corruption and contention from the diagnostic report App10_2057.crash:

```
Process:          App10 [2057]
Path:             /Users/USER/Documents/*/App10
Identifier:       App10
Version:          ??? (???)
Code Type:        X86-64 (Native)
Parent Process:   bash [223]

Date/Time:        2012-07-29 16:50:17.472 +0100
OS Version:       Mac OS X 10.7.4 (11E53)
Report Version:   9


Crashed Thread:   3

Exception Type:   EXC_CRASH (SIGABRT)
Exception Codes:  0x0000000000000000, 0x0000000000000000

Application Specific Information:
*** error for object 0x7ff01c8ae600: double free


Thread 0:: Dispatch queue: com.apple.main-thread
0   libsystem_kernel.dylib          0x00007fff8ed7de42 __semwait_signal + 10
1   libsystem_c.dylib               0x00007fff899dfdea nanosleep + 164
2   libsystem_c.dylib               0x00007fff899dfc2c sleep + 61
3   libsystem_c.dylib               0x00007fff899dfc08 sleep + 25
4   App10                           0x0000000102e6fc63 main + 195
5   App10                           0x0000000102e6f924 start + 52

Thread 1:
0   App10                           0x0000000102e6f9b2 proc + 130
1   App10                           0x0000000102e6fa19 bar_one + 9
2   App10                           0x0000000102e6fa29 foo_one + 9
3   App10                           0x0000000102e6fa41 thread_one + 17
4   libsystem_c.dylib               0x00007fff89a298bf _pthread_start + 335
5   libsystem_c.dylib               0x00007fff89a2cb75 thread_start + 13

Thread 2:
0   libsystem_c.dylib               0x00007fff89a7d385 _spin_lock$VARIANT$mp + 53
1   libsystem_c.dylib               0x00007fff89a28dd1 pthread_once + 33
2   libsystem_c.dylib               0x00007fff89a3b53d _simple_asl_log_prog + 48
3   libsystem_c.dylib               0x00007fff89a7aaa4 _malloc_vprintf + 363
4   libsystem_c.dylib               0x00007fff89a7ab47 malloc_printf + 141
5   libsystem_c.dylib               0x00007fff89a3e3ed szone_error + 268
6   libsystem_c.dylib               0x00007fff89a3fe2a free_tiny_botch + 93
7   libsystem_c.dylib               0x00007fff89a7b789 free + 194
8   App10                           0x0000000102e6f9d2 proc + 162
9   App10                           0x0000000102e6fa69 bar_two + 9
10  App10                           0x0000000102e6fa79 foo_two + 9
11  App10                           0x0000000102e6fa91 thread_two + 17
12  libsystem_c.dylib               0x00007fff89a298bf _pthread_start + 335
13  libsystem_c.dylib               0x00007fff89a2cb75 thread_start + 13
```

```
Thread 3 Crashed:
0   libsystem_kernel.dylib          0x00007fff8ed7dce2 __pthread_kill + 10
1   libsystem_c.dylib               0x00007fff89a2b7d2 pthread_kill + 95
2   libsystem_c.dylib               0x00007fff89a1ca7a abort + 143
3   libsystem_c.dylib               0x00007fff89a3e4ac szone_error + 459
4   libsystem_c.dylib               0x00007fff89a3fe8c free_small_botch + 93
5   libsystem_c.dylib               0x00007fff89a7b789 free + 194
6   App10                           0x0000000102e6f9d2 proc + 162
7   App10                           0x0000000102e6fab9 bar_three + 9
8   App10                           0x0000000102e6fac9 foo_three + 9
9   App10                           0x0000000102e6fae1 thread_three + 17
10  libsystem_c.dylib               0x00007fff89a298bf _pthread_start + 335
11  libsystem_c.dylib               0x00007fff89a2cb75 thread_start + 13

Thread 4:
0   libsystem_c.dylib               0x00007fff89a7d385 _spin_lock$VARIANT$mp + 53
1   libsystem_c.dylib               0x00007fff89a28dd1 pthread_once + 33
2   libsystem_c.dylib               0x00007fff89a3b53d _simple_asl_log_prog + 48
3   libsystem_c.dylib               0x00007fff89a7aaa4 _malloc_vprintf + 363
4   libsystem_c.dylib               0x00007fff89a7ab47 malloc_printf + 141
5   libsystem_c.dylib               0x00007fff89a3e3ed szone_error + 268
6   libsystem_c.dylib               0x00007fff89a3fe8c free_small_botch + 93
7   libsystem_c.dylib               0x00007fff89a7b789 free + 194
8   App10                           0x0000000102e6f9d2 proc + 162
9   App10                           0x0000000102e6fb09 bar_four + 9
10  App10                           0x0000000102e6fb19 foo_four + 9
11  App10                           0x0000000102e6fb31 thread_four + 17
12  libsystem_c.dylib               0x00007fff89a298bf _pthread_start + 335
13  libsystem_c.dylib               0x00007fff89a2cb75 thread_start + 13

Thread 5:
0   libsystem_c.dylib               0x00007fff89a7d385 _spin_lock$VARIANT$mp + 53
1   libsystem_c.dylib               0x00007fff89a28dd1 pthread_once + 33
2   libsystem_c.dylib               0x00007fff89a3b53d _simple_asl_log_prog + 48
3   libsystem_c.dylib               0x00007fff89a7aaa4 _malloc_vprintf + 363
4   libsystem_c.dylib               0x00007fff89a7ab47 malloc_printf + 141
5   libsystem_c.dylib               0x00007fff89a7b800 free + 313
6   App10                           0x0000000102e6f9d2 proc + 162
7   App10                           0x0000000102e6fb59 bar_five + 9
8   App10                           0x0000000102e6fb69 foo_five + 9
9   App10                           0x0000000102e6fb81 thread_five + 17
10  libsystem_c.dylib               0x00007fff89a298bf _pthread_start + 335
11  libsystem_c.dylib               0x00007fff89a2cb75 thread_start + 13

Thread 3 crashed with X86 Thread State (64-bit):
  rax: 0x0000000000000000  rbx: 0x0000000000000006  rcx: 0x0000000103186cc8  rdx: 0x0000000000000000
  rdi: 0x0000000000001403  rsi: 0x0000000000000006  rbp: 0x0000000103186cf0  rsp: 0x0000000103186cc8
   r8: 0x00007fff796d8fb8   r9: 0x0000000000000000  r10: 0x00007fff8ed7dd0a  r11: 0xffffff80002da8d0
  r12: 0x0000000102e85000  r13: 0x0000000102eb6000  r14: 0x0000000103187000  r15: 0x0000000102eb60c0
  rip: 0x00007fff8ed7dce2  rfl: 0x0000000000000246  cr2: 0x0000000102ebe000
Logical CPU: 0

Binary Images:
      0x102e6f000 -        0x102e6fff7 +App10 (??? - ???) <607A175D-7333-377A-9259-9821C980C49E>
/Users/USER/Documents/*/App10
    0x7fff62a6f000 -    0x7fff62aa3baf  dyld (195.6 - ???) <0CD1B35B-A28F-32DA-B72E-452EAD609613> /usr/lib/dyld
    0x7fff89663000 -    0x7fff89680fff  libxpc.dylib (77.19.0 - compatibility 1.0.0) <9F57891B-D7EF-3050-BEDD-
21E7C6668248> /usr/lib/system/libxpc.dylib
    0x7fff899d9000 -    0x7fff899daff7  libsystem_blocks.dylib (53.0.0 - compatibility 1.0.0) <8BCA214A-8992-34B2-
A8B9-B74DEACA1869> /usr/lib/system/libsystem_blocks.dylib
    0x7fff899db000 -    0x7fff89ab8fef  libsystem_c.dylib (763.13.0 - compatibility 1.0.0) <41B43515-2806-3FBC-ACF1-
A16F35B7E290> /usr/lib/system/libsystem_c.dylib
    0x7fff89c93000 -    0x7fff89ca1fff  libdispatch.dylib (187.9.0 - compatibility 1.0.0) <1D5BE322-A9B9-3BCE-8FAC-
076FB07CF54A> /usr/lib/system/libdispatch.dylib
    0x7fff8a261000 -    0x7fff8a262fff  libunc.dylib (24.0.0 - compatibility 1.0.0) <337960EE-0A85-3DD0-A760-
7134CF4C0AFF> /usr/lib/system/libunc.dylib
    0x7fff8a754000 -    0x7fff8a755ff7  libremovefile.dylib (21.1.0 - compatibility 1.0.0) <739E6C83-AA52-3C6C-A680-
B37FE2888A04> /usr/lib/system/libremovefile.dylib
    0x7fff8dd85000 -    0x7fff8dd89fff  libmathCommon.A.dylib (2026.0.0 - compatibility 1.0.0) <FF83AFF7-42B2-306E-
90AF-D539C51A4542> /usr/lib/system/libmathCommon.A.dylib
    0x7fff8dd8a000 -    0x7fff8dd8efff  libdyld.dylib (195.5.0 - compatibility 1.0.0) <380C3F44-0CA7-3514-8080-
46D1C9DF4FCD> /usr/lib/system/libdyld.dylib
    0x7fff8e3b1000 -    0x7fff8e3b2ff7  libsystem_sandbox.dylib (??? - ???) <96D38E74-F18F-3CCB-A20B-E8E3ADC4E166>
/usr/lib/system/libsystem_sandbox.dylib
    0x7fff8ed60000 -    0x7fff8ed66fff  libmacho.dylib (800.0.0 - compatibility 1.0.0) <165514D7-1BFA-38EF-A151-
676DCD21FB64> /usr/lib/system/libmacho.dylib
```

```
      0x7fff8ed67000 -        0x7fff8ed87fff  libsystem_kernel.dylib (1699.26.8 - compatibility 1.0.0) <1DDC0B0F-DB2A-34D6-
895D-E5B2B5618946> /usr/lib/system/libsystem_kernel.dylib
      0x7fff8ef1d000 -        0x7fff8ef25fff  libsystem_dnssd.dylib (??? - ???) <D9BB1F87-A42B-3CBC-9DC2-FC07FCEF0016>
/usr/lib/system/libsystem_dnssd.dylib
      0x7fff8fa97000 -        0x7fff8fad2fff  libsystem_info.dylib (??? - ???) <35F90252-2AE1-32C5-8D34-782C614D9639>
/usr/lib/system/libsystem_info.dylib
      0x7fff8feb9000 -        0x7fff8febbfff  libquarantine.dylib (36.6.0 - compatibility 1.0.0) <0EBF714B-4B69-3E1F-9A7D-
6BBC2AACB310> /usr/lib/system/libquarantine.dylib
      0x7fff90025000 -        0x7fff90025fff  libkeymgr.dylib (23.0.0 - compatibility 1.0.0) <61EFED6A-A407-301E-B454-
CD18314F0075> /usr/lib/system/libkeymgr.dylib
      0x7fff9004e000 -        0x7fff90053fff  libcompiler_rt.dylib (6.0.0 - compatibility 1.0.0) <98ECD5F6-E85C-32A5-98CD-
8911230CB66A> /usr/lib/system/libcompiler_rt.dylib
      0x7fff9098b000 -        0x7fff9098cfff  libdnsinfo.dylib (395.11.0 - compatibility 1.0.0) <853BAAA5-270F-3FDC-B025-
D448DB72E1C3> /usr/lib/system/libdnsinfo.dylib
      0x7fff91199000 -        0x7fff9119eff7  libsystem_network.dylib (??? - ???) <5DE7024E-1D2D-34A2-80F4-08326331A75B>
/usr/lib/system/libsystem_network.dylib
      0x7fff91c14000 -        0x7fff91c1eff7  liblaunch.dylib (392.38.0 - compatibility 1.0.0) <6ECB7F19-B384-32C1-8652-
2463C1CF4815> /usr/lib/system/liblaunch.dylib
      0x7fff94a73000 -        0x7fff94a7afff  libcopyfile.dylib (85.1.0 - compatibility 1.0.0) <0AB51EE2-E914-358C-AC19-
47BC024BDAE7> /usr/lib/system/libcopyfile.dylib
      0x7fff94abc000 -        0x7fff94afeff7  libcommonCrypto.dylib (55010.0.0 - compatibility 1.0.0) <BB770C22-8C57-365A-
8716-4A3C36AE7BFB> /usr/lib/system/libcommonCrypto.dylib
      0x7fff95880000 -        0x7fff95889ff7  libsystem_notify.dylib (80.1.0 - compatibility 1.0.0) <A4D651E3-D1C6-3934-
AD49-7A104FD14596> /usr/lib/system/libsystem_notify.dylib
      0x7fff95fe7000 -        0x7fff96014fe7  libSystem.B.dylib (159.1.0 - compatibility 1.0.0) <7BEBB139-50BB-3112-947A-
F4AA168F991C> /usr/lib/libSystem.B.dylib
      0x7fff960fa000 -        0x7fff96100ff7  libunwind.dylib (30.0.0 - compatibility 1.0.0) <1E9C6C8C-CBE8-3F4B-A5B5-
E03E3AB53231> /usr/lib/system/libunwind.dylib
      0x7fff96693000 -        0x7fff96698fff  libcache.dylib (47.0.0 - compatibility 1.0.0) <1571C3AB-BCB2-38CD-B3B2-
C5FC3F927C6A> /usr/lib/system/libcache.dylib

External Modification Summary:
  Calls made by other processes targeting this process:
    task_for_pid: 0
    thread_create: 0
    thread_set_state: 0
  Calls made by this process:
    task_for_pid: 0
    thread_create: 0
    thread_set_state: 0
  Calls made by all processes on this machine:
    task_for_pid: 3467
    thread_create: 0
    thread_set_state: 0

VM Region Summary:
ReadOnly portion of Libraries: Total=50.2M resident=50.2M(100%) swapped_out_or_unallocated=0K(0%)
Writable regions: Total=65.0M written=47.9M(74%) resident=68.3M(105%) swapped_out=0K(0%)
unallocated=16777216.0T(27064902090752%)

REGION TYPE              VIRTUAL
===========              =======
MALLOC                     27.2M
Stack                      66.6M
__DATA                      540K
__LINKEDIT                 47.7M
__TEXT                     2484K
shared memory                36K
===========              =======
TOTAL                     144.5M
```

2.   Load a core dump core.2057 and App10 executable:


```
$ gdb -c ~/Documents/AMCDA-Dumps/core.2057 -e ~/Documents/AMCDA-
Dumps/Apps/App10/Build/Products/Release/App10
GNU gdb 6.3.50-20050815 (Apple version gdb-1820) (Sat Jun 16 02:40:11 UTC 2012)
Copyright 2004 Free Software Foundation, Inc.
GDB is free software, covered by the GNU General Public License, and you are
welcome to change it and/or distribute copies of it under certain conditions.
Type "show copying" to see the conditions.
There is absolutely no warranty for GDB.  Type "show warranty" for details.
This GDB was configured as "x86_64-apple-darwin".Reading symbols for shared libraries .. done

Reading symbols for shared libraries . done
Reading symbols for shared libraries ........................ done
#0  0x00007fff8ed7de42 in __semwait_signal ()
```


3.   Check all threads and identify problem top frames:

```
(gdb) info threads
  6 0x00007fff89a7d385 in spin_lock$VARIANT$mp ()
  5 0x00007fff89a7d385 in spin_lock$VARIANT$mp ()
  4 0x00007fff8ed7dce2 in __pthread_kill ()
  3 0x00007fff89a7d385 in spin_lock$VARIANT$mp ()
  2 0x0000000102e6f9b2 in proc ()
* 1 0x00007fff8ed7de42 in __semwait_signal ()
```


4.   Check thread 2 and find where it was being executed:

```
(gdb) thread 2
[Switching to thread 2 (core thread 1)]
0x0000000102e6f9b2 in proc ()

(gdb) x/i $rip
0x102e6f9b2 <proc+130>:    mov     %esi,-0x14(%rbp)

(gdb) x/xw $rbp-0x14
0x103080ebc: 0x00002710

(gdb) disassemble proc
Dump of assembler code for function proc:
0x0000000102e6f930 <proc+0>:    push    %rbp
0x0000000102e6f931 <proc+1>:    mov     %rsp,%rbp
0x0000000102e6f934 <proc+4>:    sub     $0x20,%rsp
0x0000000102e6f938 <proc+8>:    lea     0x751(%rip),%rax      # 0x102e70090 <pAllocBuf>
0x0000000102e6f93f <proc+15>:   mov     %rax,-0x10(%rbp)
0x0000000102e6f943 <proc+19>:   callq   0x102e6fc8c <dyld_stub_rand>
0x0000000102e6f948 <proc+24>:   movslq  %eax,%rcx
0x0000000102e6f94b <proc+27>:   imul    $0x68db8bad,%rcx,%rcx
0x0000000102e6f952 <proc+34>:   mov     %rcx,%rdx
0x0000000102e6f955 <proc+37>:   shr     $0x3f,%rdx
0x0000000102e6f959 <proc+41>:   mov     %edx,%esi
0x0000000102e6f95b <proc+43>:   sar     $0x2c,%rcx
0x0000000102e6f95f <proc+47>:   mov     %ecx,%edi
0x0000000102e6f961 <proc+49>:   lea     (%rdi,%rsi,1),%esi
0x0000000102e6f964 <proc+52>:   imul    $0x2710,%esi,%esi
```

```
0x0000000102e6f96a <proc+58>:    sub     %esi,%eax
0x0000000102e6f96c <proc+60>:    mov     %eax,-0x4(%rbp)
0x0000000102e6f96f <proc+63>:    callq   0x102e6fc8c <dyld_stub_rand>
0x0000000102e6f974 <proc+68>:    movslq  %eax,%rcx
0x0000000102e6f977 <proc+71>:    imul    $0x68db8bad,%rcx,%rcx
0x0000000102e6f97e <proc+78>:    mov     %rcx,%rdx
0x0000000102e6f981 <proc+81>:    shr     $0x3f,%rdx
0x0000000102e6f985 <proc+85>:    mov     %edx,%esi
0x0000000102e6f987 <proc+87>:    sar     $0x2c,%rcx
0x0000000102e6f98b <proc+91>:    mov     %ecx,%edi
0x0000000102e6f98d <proc+93>:    lea     (%rdi,%rsi,1),%esi
0x0000000102e6f990 <proc+96>:    imul    $0x2710,%esi,%esi
0x0000000102e6f996 <proc+102>:   mov     %eax,%edi
0x0000000102e6f998 <proc+104>:   sub     %esi,%edi
0x0000000102e6f99a <proc+106>:   mov     $0x2710,%esi
0x0000000102e6f99f <proc+111>:   mov     %edi,-0x8(%rbp)
0x0000000102e6f9a2 <proc+114>:   movslq  -0x4(%rbp),%rcx
0x0000000102e6f9a6 <proc+118>:   mov     -0x10(%rbp),%rdx
0x0000000102e6f9aa <proc+122>:   cmpq    $0x0,(%rdx,%rcx,8)
0x0000000102e6f9b2 <proc+130>:   mov     %esi,-0x14(%rbp)
0x0000000102e6f9b5 <proc+133>:   mov     %eax,-0x18(%rbp)
0x0000000102e6f9b8 <proc+136>:   je      0x102e6f9e5 <proc+181>
0x0000000102e6f9be <proc+142>:   lea     0x6cb(%rip),%rax        # 0x102e70090 <pAllocBuf>
0x0000000102e6f9c5 <proc+149>:   movslq  -0x4(%rbp),%rcx
---Type <return> to continue, or q <return> to quit---
0x0000000102e6f9c9 <proc+153>:   mov     (%rax,%rcx,8),%rdi
0x0000000102e6f9cd <proc+157>:   callq   0x102e6fc7a <dyld_stub_free>
0x0000000102e6f9d2 <proc+162>:   lea     0x6b7(%rip),%rax        # 0x102e70090 <pAllocBuf>
0x0000000102e6f9d9 <proc+169>:   movslq  -0x4(%rbp),%rcx
0x0000000102e6f9dd <proc+173>:   movq    $0x0,(%rax,%rcx,8)
0x0000000102e6f9e5 <proc+181>:   movslq  -0x8(%rbp),%rdi
0x0000000102e6f9e9 <proc+185>:   callq   0x102e6fc80 <dyld_stub_malloc>
0x0000000102e6f9ee <proc+190>:   lea     0x69b(%rip),%rdi        # 0x102e70090 <pAllocBuf>
0x0000000102e6f9f5 <proc+197>:   movslq  -0x4(%rbp),%rcx
0x0000000102e6f9f9 <proc+201>:   mov     %rax,(%rdi,%rcx,8)
0x0000000102e6f9fd <proc+205>:   jmpq    0x102e6f938 <proc+8>
0x0000000102e6fa02 <proc+210>:   nopw    %cs:0x0(%rax,%rax,1)
End of assembler dump.
```

5.   Check thread 4 and find where it was being executed:

```
(gdb) thread 4
[Switching to thread 4 (core thread 3)]
0x00007fff8ed7dce2 in __pthread_kill ()

(gdb) bt
#0   0x00007fff8ed7dce2 in __pthread_kill ()
#1   0x00007fff89a2b7d2 in pthread_kill ()
#2   0x00007fff89a1ca7a in abort ()
#3   0x00007fff89a3e4ac in szone_error ()
#4   0x00007fff89a3fe8c in free_small_botch ()
#5   0x00007fff89a7b789 in free ()
#6   0x0000000102e6f9d2 in proc ()
#7   0x0000000102e6fab9 in bar_three ()
#8   0x0000000102e6fac9 in foo_three ()
#9   0x0000000102e6fae1 in thread_three ()
#10  0x00007fff89a298bf in _pthread_start ()
#11  0x00007fff89a2cb75 in thread_start ()
```

```
(gdb) disassemble proc
Dump of assembler code for function proc:
0x0000000102e6f930 <proc+0>:     push   %rbp
0x0000000102e6f931 <proc+1>:     mov    %rsp,%rbp
0x0000000102e6f934 <proc+4>:     sub    $0x20,%rsp
0x0000000102e6f938 <proc+8>:     lea    0x751(%rip),%rax      # 0x102e70090 <pAllocBuf>
0x0000000102e6f93f <proc+15>:    mov    %rax,-0x10(%rbp)
0x0000000102e6f943 <proc+19>:    callq  0x102e6fc8c <dyld_stub_rand>
0x0000000102e6f948 <proc+24>:    movslq %eax,%rcx
0x0000000102e6f94b <proc+27>:    imul   $0x68db8bad,%rcx,%rcx
0x0000000102e6f952 <proc+34>:    mov    %rcx,%rdx
0x0000000102e6f955 <proc+37>:    shr    $0x3f,%rdx
0x0000000102e6f959 <proc+41>:    mov    %edx,%esi
0x0000000102e6f95b <proc+43>:    sar    $0x2c,%rcx
0x0000000102e6f95f <proc+47>:    mov    %ecx,%edi
0x0000000102e6f961 <proc+49>:    lea    (%rdi,%rsi,1),%esi
0x0000000102e6f964 <proc+52>:    imul   $0x2710,%esi,%esi
0x0000000102e6f96a <proc+58>:    sub    %esi,%eax
0x0000000102e6f96c <proc+60>:    mov    %eax,-0x4(%rbp)
0x0000000102e6f96f <proc+63>:    callq  0x102e6fc8c <dyld_stub_rand>
0x0000000102e6f974 <proc+68>:    movslq %eax,%rcx
0x0000000102e6f977 <proc+71>:    imul   $0x68db8bad,%rcx,%rcx
0x0000000102e6f97e <proc+78>:    mov    %rcx,%rdx
0x0000000102e6f981 <proc+81>:    shr    $0x3f,%rdx
0x0000000102e6f985 <proc+85>:    mov    %edx,%esi
0x0000000102e6f987 <proc+87>:    sar    $0x2c,%rcx
0x0000000102e6f98b <proc+91>:    mov    %ecx,%edi
0x0000000102e6f98d <proc+93>:    lea    (%rdi,%rsi,1),%esi
0x0000000102e6f990 <proc+96>:    imul   $0x2710,%esi,%esi
0x0000000102e6f996 <proc+102>:   mov    %eax,%edi
0x0000000102e6f998 <proc+104>:   sub    %esi,%edi
0x0000000102e6f99a <proc+106>:   mov    $0x2710,%esi
0x0000000102e6f99f <proc+111>:   mov    %edi,-0x8(%rbp)
0x0000000102e6f9a2 <proc+114>:   movslq -0x4(%rbp),%rcx
0x0000000102e6f9a6 <proc+118>:   mov    -0x10(%rbp),%rdx
0x0000000102e6f9aa <proc+122>:   cmpq   $0x0,(%rdx,%rcx,8)
0x0000000102e6f9b2 <proc+130>:   mov    %esi,-0x14(%rbp)
0x0000000102e6f9b5 <proc+133>:   mov    %eax,-0x18(%rbp)
0x0000000102e6f9b8 <proc+136>:   je     0x102e6f9e5 <proc+181>
0x0000000102e6f9be <proc+142>:   lea    0x6cb(%rip),%rax      # 0x102e70090 <pAllocBuf>
0x0000000102e6f9c5 <proc+149>:   movslq -0x4(%rbp),%rcx
---Type <return> to continue, or q <return> to quit---
0x0000000102e6f9c9 <proc+153>:   mov    (%rax,%rcx,8),%rdi
0x0000000102e6f9cd <proc+157>:   callq  0x102e6fc7a <dyld_stub_free>
0x0000000102e6f9d2 <proc+162>:   lea    0x6b7(%rip),%rax      # 0x102e70090 <pAllocBuf>
0x0000000102e6f9d9 <proc+169>:   movslq -0x4(%rbp),%rcx
0x0000000102e6f9dd <proc+173>:   movq   $0x0,(%rax,%rcx,8)
0x0000000102e6f9e5 <proc+181>:   movslq -0x8(%rbp),%rdi
0x0000000102e6f9e9 <proc+185>:   callq  0x102e6fc80 <dyld_stub_malloc>
0x0000000102e6f9ee <proc+190>:   lea    0x69b(%rip),%rdi      # 0x102e70090 <pAllocBuf>
0x0000000102e6f9f5 <proc+197>:   movslq -0x4(%rbp),%rcx
0x0000000102e6f9f9 <proc+201>:   mov    %rax,(%rdi,%rcx,8)
0x0000000102e6f9fd <proc+205>:   jmpq   0x102e6f938 <proc+8>
0x0000000102e6fa02 <proc+210>:   nopw   %cs:0x0(%rax,%rax,1)
End of assembler dump.
```

6.   Check threads waiting for spin lock synchronization and identify a diagnostic message:

```
(gdb) info threads
   6 0x00007fff89a7d385 in spin_lock$VARIANT$mp ()
   5 0x00007fff89a7d385 in spin_lock$VARIANT$mp ()
 * 4 0x00007fff8ed7dce2 in __pthread_kill ()
   3 0x00007fff89a7d385 in spin_lock$VARIANT$mp ()
   2 0x0000000102e6f9b2 in proc ()
   1 0x00007fff8ed7de42 in __semwait_signal ()

(gdb) thread 6
[Switching to thread 6 (core thread 5)]
0x00007fff89a7d385 in spin_lock$VARIANT$mp ()

(gdb) bt
#0  0x00007fff89a7d385 in spin_lock$VARIANT$mp ()
#1  0x00007fff89a28dd1 in pthread_once ()
#2  0x00007fff89a3b53d in _simple_asl_log_prog ()
#3  0x00007fff89a7aaa4 in _malloc_vprintf ()
#4  0x00007fff89a7ab47 in malloc_printf ()
#5  0x00007fff89a7b800 in free ()
#6  0x0000000102e6f9d2 in proc ()
#7  0x0000000102e6fb59 in bar_five ()
#8  0x0000000102e6fb69 in foo_five ()
#9  0x0000000102e6fb81 in thread_five ()
#10 0x00007fff89a298bf in _pthread_start ()
#11 0x00007fff89a2cb75 in thread_start ()

(gdb) disassemble free
Dump of assembler code for function free:
0x00007fff89a7b6c7 <free+0>:    push   %rbp
0x00007fff89a7b6c8 <free+1>:    mov    %rsp,%rbp
0x00007fff89a7b6cb <free+4>:    push   %r15
0x00007fff89a7b6cd <free+6>:    push   %r14
0x00007fff89a7b6cf <free+8>:    push   %r13
0x00007fff89a7b6d1 <free+10>:   push   %r12
0x00007fff89a7b6d3 <free+12>:   push   %rbx
0x00007fff89a7b6d4 <free+13>:   sub    $0x18,%rsp
0x00007fff89a7b6d8 <free+17>:   mov    %rdi,%rbx
0x00007fff89a7b6db <free+20>:   test   %rbx,%rbx
0x00007fff89a7b6de <free+23>:   je     0x7fff89a7b857 <free+400>
0x00007fff89a7b6e4 <free+29>:   cmpl   $0x0,-0x103a252b(%rip)        # 0x7fff796d91c0 <malloc_num_zones>
0x00007fff89a7b6eb <free+36>:   jne    0x7fff89a7b6fa <free+51>
0x00007fff89a7b6ed <free+38>:   movq   $0x0,-0x30(%rbp)
0x00007fff89a7b6f5 <free+46>:   jmpq   0x7fff89a7b7ef <free+296>
0x00007fff89a7b6fa <free+51>:   mov    -0x103a2549(%rip),%rax       # 0x7fff796d91b8 <malloc_zones>
0x00007fff89a7b701 <free+58>:   mov    (%rax),%r14
0x00007fff89a7b704 <free+61>:   mov    %r14,%rdi
0x00007fff89a7b707 <free+64>:   mov    %rbx,%rsi
0x00007fff89a7b70a <free+67>:   callq  *0x10(%r14)
0x00007fff89a7b70e <free+71>:   test   %rax,%rax
0x00007fff89a7b711 <free+74>:   je     0x7fff89a7b78e <free+199>
0x00007fff89a7b713 <free+76>:   mov    %rax,-0x30(%rbp)
0x00007fff89a7b717 <free+80>:   mov    %rax,%r15
0x00007fff89a7b71a <free+83>:   test   %r14,%r14
0x00007fff89a7b71d <free+86>:   je     0x7fff89a7b7ef <free+296>
0x00007fff89a7b723 <free+92>:   cmpl   $0x6,0x68(%r14)
0x00007fff89a7b728 <free+97>:   jb     0x7fff89a7b84c <free+389>
0x00007fff89a7b72e <free+103>:  cmpq   $0x0,0x78(%r14)
0x00007fff89a7b733 <free+108>:  je     0x7fff89a7b84c <free+389>
0x00007fff89a7b739 <free+114>:  mov    -0x103a2570(%rip),%rax       # 0x7fff796d91d0 <malloc_logger>
0x00007fff89a7b740 <free+121>:  test   %rax,%rax
0x00007fff89a7b743 <free+124>:  je     0x7fff89a7b75a <free+147>
0x00007fff89a7b745 <free+126>:  mov    $0xc,%edi
0x00007fff89a7b74a <free+131>:  xor    %ecx,%ecx
0x00007fff89a7b74c <free+133>:  xor    %r9d,%r9d
0x00007fff89a7b74f <free+136>:  mov    %r14,%rsi
0x00007fff89a7b752 <free+139>:  mov    %rbx,%rdx
```

```
0x00007fff89a7b755 <free+142>:    xor     %r8d,%r8d
---Type <return> to continue, or q <return> to quit---
0x00007fff89a7b758 <free+145>:    callq   *%rax
0x00007fff89a7b75a <free+147>:    mov     -0x103a2594(%rip),%eax          # 0x7fff796d91cc <malloc_check_start>
0x00007fff89a7b760 <free+153>:    test    %eax,%eax
0x00007fff89a7b762 <free+155>:    je      0x7fff89a7b77c <free+181>
0x00007fff89a7b764 <free+157>:    mov     -0x103a25a2(%rip),%ecx          # 0x7fff796d91c8 <malloc_check_counter>
0x00007fff89a7b76a <free+163>:    lea     0x1(%rcx),%edx
0x00007fff89a7b76d <free+166>:    mov     %edx,-0x103a25ab(%rip)          # 0x7fff796d91c8 <malloc_check_counter>
0x00007fff89a7b773 <free+172>:    cmp     %eax,%ecx
0x00007fff89a7b775 <free+174>:    jb      0x7fff89a7b77c <free+181>
0x00007fff89a7b777 <free+176>:    callq   0x7fff89a7ace4 <internal_check>
0x00007fff89a7b77c <free+181>:    mov     %r14,%rdi
0x00007fff89a7b77f <free+184>:    mov     %rbx,%rsi
0x00007fff89a7b782 <free+187>:    mov     %r15,%rdx
0x00007fff89a7b785 <free+190>:    callq   *0x78(%r14)
0x00007fff89a7b789 <free+194>:    jmpq    0x7fff89a7b857 <free+400>
0x00007fff89a7b78e <free+199>:    mov     -0x103a6ccd(%rip),%r14          # 0x7fff796d4ac8 <pFRZCounterLive>
0x00007fff89a7b795 <free+206>:    mov     %r14,-0x38(%rbp)
0x00007fff89a7b799 <free+210>:    lock incl (%r14)
0x00007fff89a7b79d <free+214>:    mov     $0x1,%r15d
0x00007fff89a7b7a3 <free+220>:    mov     -0x103a25f2(%rip),%r12          # 0x7fff796d91b8 <malloc_zones>
0x00007fff89a7b7aa <free+227>:    mov     -0x103a25f1(%rip),%r13d         # 0x7fff796d91c0 <malloc_num_zones>
0x00007fff89a7b7b1 <free+234>:    jmp     0x7fff89a7b7da <free+275>
0x00007fff89a7b7b3 <free+236>:    mov     %rax,-0x30(%rbp)
0x00007fff89a7b7b7 <free+240>:    mov     -0x38(%rbp),%r15
0x00007fff89a7b7bb <free+244>:    lock decl (%r15)
0x00007fff89a7b7bf <free+248>:    jmpq    0x7fff89a7b717 <free+80>
0x00007fff89a7b7c4 <free+253>:    mov     (%r12,%r15,8),%r14
0x00007fff89a7b7c8 <free+257>:    mov     %r14,%rdi
0x00007fff89a7b7cb <free+260>:    mov     %rbx,%rsi
0x00007fff89a7b7ce <free+263>:    callq   *0x10(%r14)
0x00007fff89a7b7d2 <free+267>:    test    %rax,%rax
0x00007fff89a7b7d5 <free+270>:    jne     0x7fff89a7b7b3 <free+236>
0x00007fff89a7b7d7 <free+272>:    inc     %r15
0x00007fff89a7b7da <free+275>:    cmp     %r13d,%r15d
0x00007fff89a7b7dd <free+278>:    jb      0x7fff89a7b7c4 <free+253>
0x00007fff89a7b7df <free+280>:    movq    $0x0,-0x30(%rbp)
0x00007fff89a7b7e7 <free+288>:    mov     -0x38(%rbp),%r14
0x00007fff89a7b7eb <free+292>:    lock decl (%r14)
0x00007fff89a7b7ef <free+296>:    lea     0x173c6(%rip),%rdi              # 0x7fff89a92bbc <Malloc_Facility+3228>
0x00007fff89a7b7f6 <free+303>:    xor     %al,%al
---Type <return> to continue, or q <return> to quit---
0x00007fff89a7b7f8 <free+305>:    mov     %rbx,%rsi
0x00007fff89a7b7fb <free+308>:    callq   0x7fff89a825da <dyld_stub_malloc_printf>
0x00007fff89a7b800 <free+313>:    callq   0x7fff89a7b6bc <malloc_error_break>
0x00007fff89a7b805 <free+318>:    testb   $0x50,-0x103a2634(%rip)         # 0x7fff796d91d8 <malloc_debug_flags>
0x00007fff89a7b80c <free+325>:    je      0x7fff89a7b857 <free+400>
0x00007fff89a7b80e <free+327>:    callq   0x7fff89a3a872 <_simple_salloc>
0x00007fff89a7b813 <free+332>:    test    %rax,%rax
0x00007fff89a7b816 <free+335>:    jne     0x7fff89a7b821 <free+346>
0x00007fff89a7b818 <free+337>:    lea     0x17451(%rip),%rax             # 0x7fff89a92c70 <Malloc_Facility+3408>
0x00007fff89a7b81f <free+344>:    jmp     0x7fff89a7b840 <free+377>
0x00007fff89a7b821 <free+346>:    mov     %rax,%r14
0x00007fff89a7b824 <free+349>:    lea     0x17405(%rip),%rsi             # 0x7fff89a92c30 <Malloc_Facility+3344>
0x00007fff89a7b82b <free+356>:    xor     %al,%al
0x00007fff89a7b82d <free+358>:    mov     %r14,%rdi
0x00007fff89a7b830 <free+361>:    mov     %rbx,%rdx
0x00007fff89a7b833 <free+364>:    callq   0x7fff89a3b481 <_simple_sprintf>
0x00007fff89a7b838 <free+369>:    mov     %r14,%rdi
0x00007fff89a7b83b <free+372>:    callq   0x7fff89a3a052 <_simple_string>
0x00007fff89a7b840 <free+377>:    mov     %rax,-0x103a8e1f(%rip)         # 0x7fff796d2a28 <gCRAnnotations+8>
0x00007fff89a7b847 <free+384>:    callq   0x7fff89a1c9eb <abort>
0x00007fff89a7b84c <free+389>:    mov     %r14,%rdi
0x00007fff89a7b84f <free+392>:    mov     %rbx,%rsi
0x00007fff89a7b852 <free+395>:    callq   0x7fff89a825ec <dyld_stub_malloc_zone_free>
0x00007fff89a7b857 <free+400>:    add     $0x18,%rsp
0x00007fff89a7b85b <free+404>:    pop     %rbx
0x00007fff89a7b85c <free+405>:    pop     %r12
0x00007fff89a7b85e <free+407>:    pop     %r13
0x00007fff89a7b860 <free+409>:    pop     %r14
0x00007fff89a7b862 <free+411>:    pop     %r15
0x00007fff89a7b864 <free+413>:    pop     %rbp
0x00007fff89a7b865 <free+414>:    retq
End of assembler dump.
```

```
(gdb) x/s 0x7fff89a92bbc
0x7fff89a92bbc <Malloc_Facility+3228>:   "*** error for object %p: pointer being freed was not
allocated\n*** set a breakpoint in malloc_error_break to debug\n"
```

7.   Check the address of being freed:

```
(gdb) bt
#0   0x00007fff89a7d385 in spin_lock$VARIANT$mp ()
#1   0x00007fff89a28dd1 in pthread_once ()
#2   0x00007fff89a3b53d in _simple_asl_log_prog ()
#3   0x00007fff89a7aaa4 in _malloc_vprintf ()
#4   0x00007fff89a7ab47 in malloc_printf ()
#5   0x00007fff89a7b800 in free ()
#6   0x0000000102e6f9d2 in proc ()
#7   0x0000000102e6fb59 in bar_five ()
#8   0x0000000102e6fb69 in foo_five ()
#9   0x0000000102e6fb81 in thread_five ()
#10  0x00007fff89a298bf in _pthread_start ()
#11  0x00007fff89a2cb75 in thread_start ()
```

```
(gdb) disassemble proc
Dump of assembler code for function proc:
0x0000000102e6f930 <proc+0>:     push   %rbp
0x0000000102e6f931 <proc+1>:     mov    %rsp,%rbp
0x0000000102e6f934 <proc+4>:     sub    $0x20,%rsp
0x0000000102e6f938 <proc+8>:     lea    0x751(%rip),%rax        # 0x102e70090 <pAllocBuf>
0x0000000102e6f93f <proc+15>:    mov    %rax,-0x10(%rbp)
0x0000000102e6f943 <proc+19>:    callq  0x102e6fc8c <dyld_stub_rand>
0x0000000102e6f948 <proc+24>:    movslq %eax,%rcx
0x0000000102e6f94b <proc+27>:    imul   $0x68db8bad,%rcx,%rcx
0x0000000102e6f952 <proc+34>:    mov    %rcx,%rdx
0x0000000102e6f955 <proc+37>:    shr    $0x3f,%rdx
0x0000000102e6f959 <proc+41>:    mov    %edx,%esi
0x0000000102e6f95b <proc+43>:    sar    $0x2c,%rcx
0x0000000102e6f95f <proc+47>:    mov    %ecx,%edi
0x0000000102e6f961 <proc+49>:    lea    (%rdi,%rsi,1),%esi
0x0000000102e6f964 <proc+52>:    imul   $0x2710,%esi,%esi
0x0000000102e6f96a <proc+58>:    sub    %esi,%eax
0x0000000102e6f96c <proc+60>:    mov    %eax,-0x4(%rbp)
0x0000000102e6f96f <proc+63>:    callq  0x102e6fc8c <dyld_stub_rand>
0x0000000102e6f974 <proc+68>:    movslq %eax,%rcx
0x0000000102e6f977 <proc+71>:    imul   $0x68db8bad,%rcx,%rcx
0x0000000102e6f97e <proc+78>:    mov    %rcx,%rdx
0x0000000102e6f981 <proc+81>:    shr    $0x3f,%rdx
0x0000000102e6f985 <proc+85>:    mov    %edx,%esi
0x0000000102e6f987 <proc+87>:    sar    $0x2c,%rcx
0x0000000102e6f98b <proc+91>:    mov    %ecx,%edi
0x0000000102e6f98d <proc+93>:    lea    (%rdi,%rsi,1),%esi
0x0000000102e6f990 <proc+96>:    imul   $0x2710,%esi,%esi
0x0000000102e6f996 <proc+102>:   mov    %eax,%edi
0x0000000102e6f998 <proc+104>:   sub    %esi,%edi
0x0000000102e6f99a <proc+106>:   mov    $0x2710,%esi
0x0000000102e6f99f <proc+111>:   mov    %edi,-0x8(%rbp)
0x0000000102e6f9a2 <proc+114>:   movslq -0x4(%rbp),%rcx
0x0000000102e6f9a6 <proc+118>:   mov    -0x10(%rbp),%rdx
0x0000000102e6f9aa <proc+122>:   cmpq   $0x0,(%rdx,%rcx,8)
0x0000000102e6f9b2 <proc+130>:   mov    %esi,-0x14(%rbp)
0x0000000102e6f9b5 <proc+133>:   mov    %eax,-0x18(%rbp)
0x0000000102e6f9b8 <proc+136>:   je     0x102e6f9e5 <proc+181>
0x0000000102e6f9be <proc+142>:   lea    0x6cb(%rip),%rax        # 0x102e70090 <pAllocBuf>
```

```
0x0000000102e6f9c5 <proc+149>:   movslq  -0x4(%rbp),%rcx
---Type <return> to continue, or q <return> to quit---
0x0000000102e6f9c9 <proc+153>:   mov     (%rax,%rcx,8),%rdi
0x0000000102e6f9cd <proc+157>:   callq   0x102e6fc7a <dyld_stub_free>
0x0000000102e6f9d2 <proc+162>:   lea     0x6b7(%rip),%rax      # 0x102e70090 <pAllocBuf>
0x0000000102e6f9d9 <proc+169>:   movslq  -0x4(%rbp),%rcx
0x0000000102e6f9dd <proc+173>:   movq    $0x0,(%rax,%rcx,8)
0x0000000102e6f9e5 <proc+181>:   movslq  -0x8(%rbp),%rdi
0x0000000102e6f9e9 <proc+185>:   callq   0x102e6fc80 <dyld_stub_malloc>
0x0000000102e6f9ee <proc+190>:   lea     0x69b(%rip),%rdi      # 0x102e70090 <pAllocBuf>
0x0000000102e6f9f5 <proc+197>:   movslq  -0x4(%rbp),%rcx
0x0000000102e6f9f9 <proc+201>:   mov     %rax,(%rdi,%rcx,8)
0x0000000102e6f9fd <proc+205>:   jmpq    0x102e6f938 <proc+8>
0x0000000102e6fa02 <proc+210>:   nopw    %cs:0x0(%rax,%rax,1)
End of assembler dump.


(gdb) frame 6
#6  0x0000000102e6f9d2 in proc ()

(gdb) x/dw $rbp-4
0x10328cecc: 2574


(gdb) x/xg 0x102e70090+2574*8
0x102e75100 <pAllocBuf+20592>:   0x00007ff01c9edc00

(gdb) x/xg 0x00007ff01c9edc00
0x7ff01c9edc00:       0x4000000000000000
```

8.   Check that the identified address 0x00007ff01c9edc00 and the problem address from the crash report 0x7ff01c8ae600 belong to the same section:


```
(gdb) maintenance info section
Exec file:
    `/Users/DumpAnalysis/Documents/AMCDA-Dumps/Apps/App10/Build/Products/Release/App10', file type mach-o-le.
    0x0000000000000000->0x0000000000000000 at 0x00000000: LC_SEGMENT.__PAGEZERO ALLOC LOAD CODE HAS_CONTENTS
    0x0000000100000000->0x0000000100001000 at 0x00000000: LC_SEGMENT.__TEXT ALLOC LOAD CODE HAS_CONTENTS
    0x00000001000008f0->0x0000000100000c73 at 0x000008f0: LC_SEGMENT.__TEXT.__text ALLOC LOAD READONLY CODE HAS_CONTENTS
    0x0000000100000c74->0x0000000100000c98 at 0x00000c74: LC_SEGMENT.__TEXT.__stubs ALLOC LOAD CODE HAS_CONTENTS
    0x0000000100000c98->0x0000000100000ce4 at 0x00000c98: LC_SEGMENT.__TEXT.__stub_helper ALLOC LOAD CODE HAS_CONTENTS
    0x0000000100000ce4->0x0000000100000d34 at 0x00000ce4: LC_SEGMENT.__TEXT.__unwind_info ALLOC LOAD CODE HAS_CONTENTS
    0x0000000100000d38->0x0000000100000ff8 at 0x00000d38: LC_SEGMENT.__TEXT.__eh_frame ALLOC LOAD CODE HAS_CONTENTS
    0x0000000100001000->0x0000000100002000 at 0x00001000: LC_SEGMENT.__DATA ALLOC LOAD CODE HAS_CONTENTS
    0x0000000100001000->0x0000000100001028 at 0x00001000: LC_SEGMENT.__DATA.__program_vars ALLOC LOAD CODE HAS_CONTENTS
    0x0000000100001028->0x0000000100001038 at 0x00001028: LC_SEGMENT.__DATA.__nl_symbol_ptr ALLOC LOAD CODE HAS_CONTENTS
    0x0000000100001038->0x0000000100001068 at 0x00001038: LC_SEGMENT.__DATA.__la_symbol_ptr ALLOC LOAD CODE HAS_CONTENTS
    0x0000000100001070->0x0000000100014910 at 0x00000000: LC_SEGMENT.__DATA.__common ALLOC
    0x0000000100015000->0x0000000100015468 at 0x00002000: LC_SEGMENT.__LINKEDIT ALLOC LOAD CODE HAS_CONTENTS
    0x0000000000000000->0x00000000000001f0 at 0x000020f8: LC_SYMTAB.stabs HAS_CONTENTS
    0x0000000000000000->0x0000000000000148 at 0x00002320: LC_SYMTAB.stabstr HAS_CONTENTS
    0x0000000000000000->0x0000000000000120 at 0x000020f8: LC_DYSYMTAB.localstabs HAS_CONTENTS
    0x0000000000000000->0x00000000000000d0 at 0x00002218: LC_DYSYMTAB.nonlocalstabs HAS_CONTENTS
    0x0000000000000000->0x0000000000000018 at 0x000004b0: LC_LOAD_DYLINKER HAS_CONTENTS
    0x0000000000000000->0x0000000000000a8 at 0x00000500: LC_THREAD.x86_THREAD_STATE64.0 HAS_CONTENTS
    0x0000000000000000->0x0000000000000030 at 0x000005b0: LC_LOAD_DYLIB HAS_CONTENTS
Core file:
    `/Users/DumpAnalysis/Documents/AMCDA-Dumps/core.2057', file type mach-o-le.
    0x0000000102e6f000->0x0000000102e70000 at 0x00003000: LC_SEGMENT. ALLOC LOAD CODE HAS_CONTENTS
    0x0000000102e70000->0x0000000102e71000 at 0x00004000: LC_SEGMENT. ALLOC LOAD CODE HAS_CONTENTS
    0x0000000102e71000->0x0000000102e84000 at 0x00005000: LC_SEGMENT. ALLOC LOAD CODE HAS_CONTENTS
    0x0000000102e84000->0x0000000102e85000 at 0x00018000: LC_SEGMENT. ALLOC LOAD CODE HAS_CONTENTS
    0x0000000102e85000->0x0000000102e86000 at 0x00019000: LC_SEGMENT. ALLOC LOAD CODE HAS_CONTENTS
    0x0000000102e86000->0x0000000102e87000 at 0x0001a000: LC_SEGMENT. ALLOC LOAD CODE HAS_CONTENTS
    0x0000000102e87000->0x0000000102e88000 at 0x0001b000: LC_SEGMENT. ALLOC LOAD CODE HAS_CONTENTS
    0x0000000102e88000->0x0000000102e9d000 at 0x0001c000: LC_SEGMENT. ALLOC LOAD CODE HAS_CONTENTS
    0x0000000102e9d000->0x0000000102e9e000 at 0x00031000: LC_SEGMENT. ALLOC LOAD CODE HAS_CONTENTS
    0x0000000102e9e000->0x0000000102e9f000 at 0x00032000: LC_SEGMENT. ALLOC LOAD CODE HAS_CONTENTS
    0x0000000102e9f000->0x0000000102eb4000 at 0x00033000: LC_SEGMENT. ALLOC LOAD CODE HAS_CONTENTS
    0x0000000102eb4000->0x0000000102eb5000 at 0x00048000: LC_SEGMENT. ALLOC LOAD CODE HAS_CONTENTS
    0x0000000102eb5000->0x0000000102eb6000 at 0x00049000: LC_SEGMENT. ALLOC LOAD CODE HAS_CONTENTS
    0x0000000102eb6000->0x0000000102eb7000 at 0x0004a000: LC_SEGMENT. ALLOC LOAD CODE HAS_CONTENTS
    0x0000000102eb8000->0x0000000102ebd000 at 0x0004b000: LC_SEGMENT. ALLOC LOAD CODE HAS_CONTENTS
```

```
      0x0000000102f00000->0x0000000103000000 at 0x00050000: LC_SEGMENT. ALLOC LOAD CODE HAS_CONTENTS
---Type <return> to continue, or q <return> to quit---
      0x0000000103000000->0x0000000103001000 at 0x00150000: LC_SEGMENT. ALLOC LOAD CODE HAS_CONTENTS
      0x0000000103001000->0x0000000103083000 at 0x00151000: LC_SEGMENT. ALLOC LOAD CODE HAS_CONTENTS
      0x0000000103083000->0x0000000103084000 at 0x001d3000: LC_SEGMENT. ALLOC LOAD CODE HAS_CONTENTS
      0x0000000103084000->0x0000000103106000 at 0x001d4000: LC_SEGMENT. ALLOC LOAD CODE HAS_CONTENTS
      0x0000000103106000->0x0000000103107000 at 0x00256000: LC_SEGMENT. ALLOC LOAD CODE HAS_CONTENTS
      0x0000000103107000->0x0000000103189000 at 0x00257000: LC_SEGMENT. ALLOC LOAD CODE HAS_CONTENTS
      0x0000000103189000->0x000000010318a000 at 0x002d9000: LC_SEGMENT. ALLOC LOAD CODE HAS_CONTENTS
      0x000000010318a000->0x000000010320c000 at 0x002da000: LC_SEGMENT. ALLOC LOAD CODE HAS_CONTENTS
      0x000000010320c000->0x000000010320d000 at 0x0035c000: LC_SEGMENT. ALLOC LOAD CODE HAS_CONTENTS
      0x000000010320d000->0x000000010328f000 at 0x0035d000: LC_SEGMENT. ALLOC LOAD CODE HAS_CONTENTS
      0x00007ff01b400000->0x00007ff01b500000 at 0x003df000: LC_SEGMENT. ALLOC LOAD CODE HAS_CONTENTS
      0x00007ff01b500000->0x00007ff01b600000 at 0x004df000: LC_SEGMENT. ALLOC LOAD CODE HAS_CONTENTS
      0x00007ff01b800000->0x00007ff01c000000 at 0x005df000: LC_SEGMENT. ALLOC LOAD CODE HAS_CONTENTS
      0x00007ff01c800000->0x00007ff01d000000 at 0x00ddf000: LC_SEGMENT. ALLOC LOAD CODE HAS_CONTENTS
      0x00007ff01d000000->0x00007ff01d800000 at 0x015df000: LC_SEGMENT. ALLOC LOAD CODE HAS_CONTENTS
      0x00007fff5ea6f000->0x00007fff6226f000 at 0x01ddf000: LC_SEGMENT. ALLOC LOAD CODE HAS_CONTENTS
      0x00007fff6226f000->0x00007fff62a6f000 at 0x055df000: LC_SEGMENT. ALLOC LOAD CODE HAS_CONTENTS
      0x00007fff62a6f000->0x00007fff62aa4000 at 0x05ddf000: LC_SEGMENT. ALLOC LOAD CODE HAS_CONTENTS
      0x00007fff62aa4000->0x00007fff62aa6000 at 0x05e14000: LC_SEGMENT. ALLOC LOAD CODE HAS_CONTENTS
      0x00007fff62aa6000->0x00007fff62ae0000 at 0x05e16000: LC_SEGMENT. ALLOC LOAD CODE HAS_CONTENTS
      0x00007fff62ae0000->0x00007fff62af3000 at 0x05e50000: LC_SEGMENT. ALLOC LOAD CODE HAS_CONTENTS
      0x00007fff79629000->0x00007fff79800000 at 0x05e63000: LC_SEGMENT. ALLOC LOAD CODE HAS_CONTENTS
      0x00007fff79800000->0x00007fff79a00000 at 0x0603a000: LC_SEGMENT. ALLOC LOAD CODE HAS_CONTENTS
      0x00007fff79a00000->0x00007fff79c00000 at 0x0623a000: LC_SEGMENT. ALLOC LOAD CODE HAS_CONTENTS
      0x00007fff79c00000->0x00007fff79e00000 at 0x0643a000: LC_SEGMENT. ALLOC LOAD CODE HAS_CONTENTS
      0x00007fff79e00000->0x00007fff7a000000 at 0x0663a000: LC_SEGMENT. ALLOC LOAD CODE HAS_CONTENTS
      0x00007fff7a000000->0x00007fff7a200000 at 0x0683a000: LC_SEGMENT. ALLOC LOAD CODE HAS_CONTENTS
      0x00007fff7a200000->0x00007fff7a400000 at 0x06a3a000: LC_SEGMENT. ALLOC LOAD CODE HAS_CONTENTS
      0x00007fff7a400000->0x00007fff7a600000 at 0x06c3a000: LC_SEGMENT. ALLOC LOAD CODE HAS_CONTENTS
      0x00007fff7a600000->0x00007fff7a800000 at 0x06e3a000: LC_SEGMENT. ALLOC LOAD CODE HAS_CONTENTS
      0x00007fff7a800000->0x00007fff7aa00000 at 0x0703a000: LC_SEGMENT. ALLOC LOAD CODE HAS_CONTENTS
      0x00007fff7aa00000->0x00007fff7ae00000 at 0x0723a000: LC_SEGMENT. ALLOC LOAD CODE HAS_CONTENTS
      0x00007fff7ae00000->0x00007fff7b000000 at 0x0763a000: LC_SEGMENT. ALLOC LOAD CODE HAS_CONTENTS
      0x00007fff7b000000->0x00007fff7b11d000 at 0x0783a000: LC_SEGMENT. ALLOC LOAD CODE HAS_CONTENTS
      0x00007fff89629000->0x00007fff96699000 at 0x07957000: LC_SEGMENT. ALLOC LOAD CODE HAS_CONTENTS
      0x00007fff96699000->0x00007fff997a1000 at 0x149c7000: LC_SEGMENT. ALLOC LOAD CODE HAS_CONTENTS
      0x00007ffffffe00000->0x00007ffffffe02000 at 0x17acf000: LC_SEGMENT. ALLOC LOAD CODE HAS_CONTENTS
      0x0000000000000000->0x00000000000000b0 at 0x00000f18: LC_THREAD.x86_THREAD_STATE.0 HAS_CONTENTS
      0x0000000000000000->0x0000000000000214 at 0x00000fd0: LC_THREAD.x86_FLOAT_STATE.0 HAS_CONTENTS
      0x0000000000000000->0x0000000000000018 at 0x000011ec: LC_THREAD.x86_EXCEPTION_STATE.0 HAS_CONTENTS
---Type <return> to continue, or q <return> to quit---
      0x0000000000000000->0x00000000000000b0 at 0x00001214: LC_THREAD.x86_THREAD_STATE.1 HAS_CONTENTS
      0x0000000000000000->0x0000000000000214 at 0x000012cc: LC_THREAD.x86_FLOAT_STATE.1 HAS_CONTENTS
      0x0000000000000000->0x0000000000000018 at 0x000014e8: LC_THREAD.x86_EXCEPTION_STATE.1 HAS_CONTENTS
      0x0000000000000000->0x00000000000000b0 at 0x00001510: LC_THREAD.x86_THREAD_STATE.2 HAS_CONTENTS
      0x0000000000000000->0x0000000000000214 at 0x000015c8: LC_THREAD.x86_FLOAT_STATE.2 HAS_CONTENTS
      0x0000000000000000->0x0000000000000018 at 0x000017e4: LC_THREAD.x86_EXCEPTION_STATE.2 HAS_CONTENTS
      0x0000000000000000->0x00000000000000b0 at 0x0000180c: LC_THREAD.x86_THREAD_STATE.3 HAS_CONTENTS
      0x0000000000000000->0x0000000000000214 at 0x000018c4: LC_THREAD.x86_FLOAT_STATE.3 HAS_CONTENTS
      0x0000000000000000->0x0000000000000018 at 0x00001ae0: LC_THREAD.x86_EXCEPTION_STATE.3 HAS_CONTENTS
      0x0000000000000000->0x00000000000000b0 at 0x00001b08: LC_THREAD.x86_THREAD_STATE.4 HAS_CONTENTS
      0x0000000000000000->0x0000000000000214 at 0x00001bc0: LC_THREAD.x86_FLOAT_STATE.4 HAS_CONTENTS
      0x0000000000000000->0x0000000000000018 at 0x00001ddc: LC_THREAD.x86_EXCEPTION_STATE.4 HAS_CONTENTS
      0x0000000000000000->0x00000000000000b0 at 0x00001e04: LC_THREAD.x86_THREAD_STATE.5 HAS_CONTENTS
      0x0000000000000000->0x0000000000000214 at 0x00001ebc: LC_THREAD.x86_FLOAT_STATE.5 HAS_CONTENTS
      0x0000000000000000->0x0000000000000018 at 0x000020d8: LC_THREAD.x86_EXCEPTION_STATE.5 HAS_CONTENTS
```

9.   Dump the first 1000 elements of array pAllocBuf (0x102e70090) found in the *proc* function disassembly and identify a few addresses at the beginning:

```
(gdb) print/x *0x102e70090@1000
$2 = {0x0 <repeats 36 times>, 0x1cb9d400, 0x7ff0, 0x0 <repeats 42 times>, 0x1cb99000, 0x7ff0,
0x0 <repeats 14 times>, 0x1b92d600,
  0x7ff0, 0x0, 0x0, 0x1b40ab80, 0x7ff0, 0x0, 0x0, 0x0, 0x0, 0x1b86f600, 0x7ff0, 0x0, 0x0,
0x1cae4400, 0x7ff0, 0x0, 0x0, 0x0, 0x0,
  0x0, 0x0, 0x1ca72000, 0x7ff0, 0x0 <repeats 16 times>, 0x1cb3de00, 0x7ff0, 0x0, 0x0, 0x0, 0x0,
0x0, 0x0, 0x0, 0x0, 0x1c800000,
  0x7ff0, 0x0 <repeats 38 times>, 0x1c914200, 0x7ff0, 0x1b84ee00, 0x7ff0, 0x0, 0x0, 0x0, 0x0,
0x0, 0x0, 0x0, 0x0, 0x0, 0x0,
  0x1c9a2600, 0x7ff0, 0x0, 0x0, 0x0, 0x0, 0x0, 0x0, 0x0, 0x0, 0x1b4007b0, 0x7ff0, 0x0, 0x0,
0x0, 0x0, 0x0, 0x0, 0x0, 0x0,
  0x1d056a00, 0x7ff0, 0x0, 0x0, 0x0, 0x0, 0x0, 0x0, 0x1b882000, 0x7ff0, 0x0, 0x0, 0x0, 0x0,
0x1c9dba00, 0x7ff0, 0x1caf9000, 0x7ff0,
  0x0, 0x0, 0x0, 0x0, 0x0, 0x0, 0x0, 0x0, 0x0, 0x0, 0x1b89a600, 0x7ff0, 0x1d0e9a00, 0x7ff0, 0x0
<repeats 48 times>, 0x2f03b60, 0x1,
  0x0 <repeats 32 times>, 0x1b8c3e00, 0x7ff0, 0x0 <repeats 14 times>, 0x1cb61200, 0x7ff0, 0x0,
0x0, 0x1cbc8e00, 0x7ff0,
  0x0 <repeats 26 times>...}
```

Exercise A10 (LLDB)

- **Goal:** Learn how to identify heap contention wait chains, synchronization issues, advanced disassembly, dump arrays

- **Patterns:** Double Free, Heap Contention, Wait Chain, Critical Region, Self-Diagnosis

- \AMCDA-Dumps\Exercise-A10-LLDB.pdf

Exercise A10 (LLDB)

Goal: Learn how to identify heap contention wait chains, synchronization issues, advanced disassembly, dump arrays

Patterns: Heap Corruption, Heap Contention, Wait Chain, Critical Region, Self-Diagnostics

1.   Identify heap memory corruption and contention from the diagnostic report App10_2057.crash:

```
Process:        App10 [2057]
Path:           /Users/USER/Documents/*/App10
Identifier:     App10
Version:        ??? (???)
Code Type:      X86-64 (Native)
Parent Process: bash [223]

Date/Time:      2012-07-29 16:50:17.472 +0100
OS Version:     Mac OS X 10.7.4 (11E53)
Report Version: 9

Crashed Thread: 3

Exception Type:  EXC_CRASH (SIGABRT)
Exception Codes: 0x0000000000000000, 0x0000000000000000

Application Specific Information:
*** error for object 0x7ff01c8ae600: double free


Thread 0:: Dispatch queue: com.apple.main-thread
0   libsystem_kernel.dylib          0x00007fff8ed7de42 __semwait_signal + 10
1   libsystem_c.dylib               0x00007fff899dfdea nanosleep + 164
2   libsystem_c.dylib               0x00007fff899dfc2c sleep + 61
3   libsystem_c.dylib               0x00007fff899dfc08 sleep + 25
4   App10                           0x0000000102e6fc63 main + 195
5   App10                           0x0000000102e6f924 start + 52

Thread 1:
0   App10                           0x0000000102e6f9b2 proc + 130
1   App10                           0x0000000102e6fa19 bar_one + 9
2   App10                           0x0000000102e6fa29 foo_one + 9
3   App10                           0x0000000102e6fa41 thread_one + 17
4   libsystem_c.dylib               0x00007fff89a298bf _pthread_start + 335
5   libsystem_c.dylib               0x00007fff89a2cb75 thread_start + 13

Thread 2:
0   libsystem_c.dylib               0x00007fff89a7d385 _spin_lock$VARIANT$mp + 53
1   libsystem_c.dylib               0x00007fff89a28dd1 pthread_once + 33
2   libsystem_c.dylib               0x00007fff89a3b53d _simple_asl_log_prog + 48
3   libsystem_c.dylib               0x00007fff89a7aaa4 _malloc_vprintf + 363
4   libsystem_c.dylib               0x00007fff89a7ab47 malloc_printf + 141
5   libsystem_c.dylib               0x00007fff89a3e3ed szone_error + 268
6   libsystem_c.dylib               0x00007fff89a3fe2a free_tiny_botch + 93
7   libsystem_c.dylib               0x00007fff89a7b789 free + 194
8   App10                           0x0000000102e6f9d2 proc + 162
9   App10                           0x0000000102e6fa69 bar_two + 9
10  App10                           0x0000000102e6fa79 foo_two + 9
11  App10                           0x0000000102e6fa91 thread_two + 17
12  libsystem_c.dylib               0x00007fff89a298bf _pthread_start + 335
13  libsystem_c.dylib               0x00007fff89a2cb75 thread_start + 13
```

```
Thread 3 Crashed:
0   libsystem_kernel.dylib          0x00007fff8ed7dce2 __pthread_kill + 10
1   libsystem_c.dylib               0x00007fff89a2b7d2 pthread_kill + 95
2   libsystem_c.dylib               0x00007fff89a1ca7a abort + 143
3   libsystem_c.dylib               0x00007fff89a3e4ac szone_error + 459
4   libsystem_c.dylib               0x00007fff89a3fe8c free_small_botch + 93
5   libsystem_c.dylib               0x00007fff89a7b789 free + 194
6   App10                           0x0000000102e6f9d2 proc + 162
7   App10                           0x0000000102e6fab9 bar_three + 9
8   App10                           0x0000000102e6fac9 foo_three + 9
9   App10                           0x0000000102e6fae1 thread_three + 17
10  libsystem_c.dylib               0x00007fff89a298bf _pthread_start + 335
11  libsystem_c.dylib               0x00007fff89a2cb75 thread_start + 13

Thread 4:
0   libsystem_c.dylib               0x00007fff89a7d385 _spin_lock$VARIANT$mp + 53
1   libsystem_c.dylib               0x00007fff89a28dd1 pthread_once + 33
2   libsystem_c.dylib               0x00007fff89a3b53d _simple_asl_log_prog + 48
3   libsystem_c.dylib               0x00007fff89a7aaa4 _malloc_vprintf + 363
4   libsystem_c.dylib               0x00007fff89a7ab47 malloc_printf + 141
5   libsystem_c.dylib               0x00007fff89a3e3ed szone_error + 268
6   libsystem_c.dylib               0x00007fff89a3fe8c free_small_botch + 93
7   libsystem_c.dylib               0x00007fff89a7b789 free + 194
8   App10                           0x0000000102e6f9d2 proc + 162
9   App10                           0x0000000102e6fb09 bar_four + 9
10  App10                           0x0000000102e6fb19 foo_four + 9
11  App10                           0x0000000102e6fb31 thread_four + 17
12  libsystem_c.dylib               0x00007fff89a298bf _pthread_start + 335
13  libsystem_c.dylib               0x00007fff89a2cb75 thread_start + 13

Thread 5:
0   libsystem_c.dylib               0x00007fff89a7d385 _spin_lock$VARIANT$mp + 53
1   libsystem_c.dylib               0x00007fff89a28dd1 pthread_once + 33
2   libsystem_c.dylib               0x00007fff89a3b53d _simple_asl_log_prog + 48
3   libsystem_c.dylib               0x00007fff89a7aaa4 _malloc_vprintf + 363
4   libsystem_c.dylib               0x00007fff89a7ab47 malloc_printf + 141
5   libsystem_c.dylib               0x00007fff89a7b800 free + 313
6   App10                           0x0000000102e6f9d2 proc + 162
7   App10                           0x0000000102e6fb59 bar_five + 9
8   App10                           0x0000000102e6fb69 foo_five + 9
9   App10                           0x0000000102e6fb81 thread_five + 17
10  libsystem_c.dylib               0x00007fff89a298bf _pthread_start + 335
11  libsystem_c.dylib               0x00007fff89a2cb75 thread_start + 13

Thread 3 crashed with X86 Thread State (64-bit):
  rax: 0x0000000000000000  rbx: 0x0000000000000006  rcx: 0x0000000103186cc8  rdx: 0x0000000000000000
  rdi: 0x0000000000001403  rsi: 0x0000000000000006  rbp: 0x0000000103186cf0  rsp: 0x0000000103186cc8
   r8: 0x00007fff796d8fb8   r9: 0x0000000000000000  r10: 0x00007fff8ed7dd0a  r11: 0xffffff80002da8d0
  r12: 0x0000000102e85000  r13: 0x0000000102eb6000  r14: 0x0000000103187000  r15: 0x0000000102eb60c0
  rip: 0x00007fff8ed7dce2  rfl: 0x0000000000000246  cr2: 0x0000000102ebe000
Logical CPU: 0

Binary Images:
       0x102e6f000 -        0x102e6fff7 +App10 (??? - ???) <607A175D-7333-377A-9259-9821C980C49E>
/Users/USER/Documents/*/App10
    0x7fff62a6f000 -     0x7fff62aa3baf  dyld (195.6 - ???) <0CD1B35B-A28F-32DA-B72E-452EAD609613> /usr/lib/dyld
    0x7fff89663000 -     0x7fff89680fff  libxpc.dylib (77.19.0 - compatibility 1.0.0) <9F57891B-D7EF-3050-BEDD-
21E7C6668248> /usr/lib/system/libxpc.dylib
    0x7fff899d9000 -     0x7fff899daff7  libsystem_blocks.dylib (53.0.0 - compatibility 1.0.0) <8BCA214A-8992-34B2-
A8B9-B74DEACA1869> /usr/lib/system/libsystem_blocks.dylib
    0x7fff899db000 -     0x7fff89ab8fef  libsystem_c.dylib (763.13.0 - compatibility 1.0.0) <41B43515-2806-3FBC-ACF1-
A16F35B7E290> /usr/lib/system/libsystem_c.dylib
    0x7fff89c93000 -     0x7fff89ca1fff  libdispatch.dylib (187.9.0 - compatibility 1.0.0) <1D5BE322-A9B9-3BCE-8FAC-
076FB07CF54A> /usr/lib/system/libdispatch.dylib
    0x7fff8a261000 -     0x7fff8a262fff  libunc.dylib (24.0.0 - compatibility 1.0.0) <337960EE-0A85-3DD0-A760-
7134CF4C0AFF> /usr/lib/system/libunc.dylib
    0x7fff8a754000 -     0x7fff8a755ff7  libremovefile.dylib (21.1.0 - compatibility 1.0.0) <739E6C83-AA52-3C6C-A680-
B37FE2888A04> /usr/lib/system/libremovefile.dylib
    0x7fff8dd85000 -     0x7fff8dd89fff  libmathCommon.A.dylib (2026.0.0 - compatibility 1.0.0) <FF83AFF7-42B2-306E-
90AF-D539C51A4542> /usr/lib/system/libmathCommon.A.dylib
    0x7fff8dd8a000 -     0x7fff8dd8efff  libdyld.dylib (195.5.0 - compatibility 1.0.0) <380C3F44-0CA7-3514-8080-
46D1C9DF4FCD> /usr/lib/system/libdyld.dylib
    0x7fff8e3b1000 -     0x7fff8e3b2ff7  libsystem_sandbox.dylib (??? - ???) <96D38E74-F18F-3CCB-A20B-E8E3ADC4E166>
/usr/lib/system/libsystem_sandbox.dylib
    0x7fff8ed60000 -     0x7fff8ed66fff  libmacho.dylib (800.0.0 - compatibility 1.0.0) <165514D7-1BFA-38EF-A151-
676DCD21FB64> /usr/lib/system/libmacho.dylib
```

291

```
     0x7fff8ed67000 -       0x7fff8ed87fff  libsystem_kernel.dylib (1699.26.8 - compatibility 1.0.0) <1DDC0B0F-DB2A-34D6-
895D-E5B2B5618946> /usr/lib/system/libsystem_kernel.dylib
     0x7fff8ef1d000 -       0x7fff8ef25fff  libsystem_dnssd.dylib (??? - ???) <D9BB1F87-A42B-3CBC-9DC2-FC07FCEF0016>
/usr/lib/system/libsystem_dnssd.dylib
     0x7fff8fa97000 -       0x7fff8fad2fff  libsystem_info.dylib (??? - ???) <35F90252-2AE1-32C5-8D34-782C614D9639>
/usr/lib/system/libsystem_info.dylib
     0x7fff8feb9000 -       0x7fff8febbfff  libquarantine.dylib (36.6.0 - compatibility 1.0.0) <0EBF714B-4B69-3E1F-9A7D-
6BBC2AACB310> /usr/lib/system/libquarantine.dylib
     0x7fff90025000 -       0x7fff90025fff  libkeymgr.dylib (23.0.0 - compatibility 1.0.0) <61EFED6A-A407-301E-B454-
CD18314F0075> /usr/lib/system/libkeymgr.dylib
     0x7fff9004e000 -       0x7fff90053fff  libcompiler_rt.dylib (6.0.0 - compatibility 1.0.0) <98ECD5F6-E85C-32A5-98CD-
8911230CB66A> /usr/lib/system/libcompiler_rt.dylib
     0x7fff9098b000 -       0x7fff9098cfff  libdnsinfo.dylib (395.11.0 - compatibility 1.0.0) <853BAAA5-270F-3FDC-B025-
D448DB72E1C3> /usr/lib/system/libdnsinfo.dylib
     0x7fff91199000 -       0x7fff9119eff7  libsystem_network.dylib (??? - ???) <5DE7024E-1D2D-34A2-80F4-08326331A75B>
/usr/lib/system/libsystem_network.dylib
     0x7fff91c14000 -       0x7fff91c1eff7  liblaunch.dylib (392.38.0 - compatibility 1.0.0) <6ECB7F19-B384-32C1-8652-
2463C1CF4815> /usr/lib/system/liblaunch.dylib
     0x7fff94a73000 -       0x7fff94a7afff  libcopyfile.dylib (85.1.0 - compatibility 1.0.0) <0AB51EE2-E914-358C-AC19-
47BC024BDAE7> /usr/lib/system/libcopyfile.dylib
     0x7fff94abc000 -       0x7fff94afeff7  libcommonCrypto.dylib (55010.0.0 - compatibility 1.0.0) <BB770C22-8C57-365A-
8716-4A3C36AE7BFB> /usr/lib/system/libcommonCrypto.dylib
     0x7fff95880000 -       0x7fff95889ff7  libsystem_notify.dylib (80.1.0 - compatibility 1.0.0) <A4D651E3-D1C6-3934-
AD49-7A104FD14596> /usr/lib/system/libsystem_notify.dylib
     0x7fff95fe7000 -       0x7fff96014fe7  libSystem.B.dylib (159.1.0 - compatibility 1.0.0) <7BEBB139-50BB-3112-947A-
F4AA168F991C> /usr/lib/libSystem.B.dylib
     0x7fff960fa000 -       0x7fff96100ff7  libunwind.dylib (30.0.0 - compatibility 1.0.0) <1E9C6C8C-CBE8-3F4B-A5B5-
E03E3AB53231> /usr/lib/system/libunwind.dylib
     0x7fff96693000 -       0x7fff96698fff  libcache.dylib (47.0.0 - compatibility 1.0.0) <1571C3AB-BCB2-38CD-B3B2-
C5FC3F927C6A> /usr/lib/system/libcache.dylib

External Modification Summary:
  Calls made by other processes targeting this process:
    task_for_pid: 0
    thread_create: 0
    thread_set_state: 0
  Calls made by this process:
    task_for_pid: 0
    thread_create: 0
    thread_set_state: 0
  Calls made by all processes on this machine:
    task_for_pid: 3467
    thread_create: 0
    thread_set_state: 0

VM Region Summary:
ReadOnly portion of Libraries: Total=50.2M resident=50.2M(100%) swapped_out_or_unallocated=0K(0%)
Writable regions: Total=65.0M written=47.9M(74%) resident=68.3M(105%) swapped_out=0K(0%)
unallocated=16777216.0T(27064902090752%)

REGION TYPE                 VIRTUAL
===========                 =======
MALLOC                       27.2M
Stack                        66.6M
__DATA                        540K
__LINKEDIT                   47.7M
__TEXT                       2484K
shared memory                  36K
===========                 =======
TOTAL                       144.5M
```

Note: We see that core thread #1 is running and not waiting, core thread #2 is blocked in a spinlock, core thread #3 crashed when freeing memory, core threads #4 and #5 are blocked in a spinlock.

2.   Load a core dump core.2057 and App10 executable:

$ lldb -c ~/Documents/AMCDA-Dumps/core.2057 -f ~/Documents/AMCDA-Dumps/Apps/App10/Build/Products/Release/App10

```
error: core.2057 is a corrupt mach-o file: load command 52 LC_SEGMENT_64 has a fileoff +
filesize (0x17ad1000) that extends beyond the end of the file (0x17acf000), the segment will be
truncated
Core file '/Users/DumpAnalysis/Documents/AMCDA-Dumps/core.2057' (x86_64) was loaded.
Process 0 stopped
* thread #1: tid = 0x0000, 0x00007fff8ed7de42 libsystem_kernel.dylib`__semwait_signal + 10,
stop reason = signal SIGSTOP
    frame #0: 0x00007fff8ed7de42 libsystem_kernel.dylib`__semwait_signal + 10
libsystem_kernel.dylib`__semwait_signal + 10:
-> 0x7fff8ed7de42:  jae    0x7fff8ed7de49               ; __semwait_signal + 17
   0x7fff8ed7de44:  jmpq   0x7fff8ed7effc               ; cerror
   0x7fff8ed7de49:  ret
   0x7fff8ed7de4a:  nop
  thread #2: tid = 0x0001, 0x0000000102e6f9b2 App10`proc + 130, stop reason = signal SIGSTOP
    frame #0: 0x0000000102e6f9b2 App10`proc + 130
App10`proc + 130:
-> 0x102e6f9b2:  movl   %esi, -20(%rbp)
   0x102e6f9b5:  movl   %eax, -24(%rbp)
   0x102e6f9b8:  je     0x102e6f9e5               ; proc + 181
   0x102e6f9be:  leaq   1739(%rip), %rax
  thread #3: tid = 0x0002, 0x00007fff89a7d385 libsystem_c.dylib`OSSpinLockLock$VARIANT$mp + 53,
stop reason = signal SIGSTOP
    frame #0: 0x00007fff89a7d385 libsystem_c.dylib`OSSpinLockLock$VARIANT$mp + 53
libsystem_c.dylib`OSSpinLockLock$VARIANT$mp + 53:
-> 0x7fff89a7d385:  jmp    0x7fff89a7d353               ; OSSpinLockLock$VARIANT$mp + 3
   0x7fff89a7d387:  nop

libsystem_c.dylib`OSSpinLockUnlock:
   0x7fff89a7d388:  movl   $0, (%rdi)

libsystem_c.dylib`spin_unlock + 6:
   0x7fff89a7d38e:  ret
  thread #4: tid = 0x0003, 0x00007fff8ed7dce2 libsystem_kernel.dylib`__pthread_kill + 10, stop
reason = signal SIGSTOP
    frame #0: 0x00007fff8ed7dce2 libsystem_kernel.dylib`__pthread_kill + 10
libsystem_kernel.dylib`__pthread_kill + 10:
-> 0x7fff8ed7dce2:  jae    0x7fff8ed7dce9               ; __pthread_kill + 17
   0x7fff8ed7dce4:  jmpq   0x7fff8ed7effc               ; cerror
   0x7fff8ed7dce9:  ret
   0x7fff8ed7dcea:  nop
```

```
  thread #5: tid = 0x0004, 0x00007fff89a7d385 libsystem_c.dylib`OSSpinLockLock$VARIANT$mp + 53,
stop reason = signal SIGSTOP
    frame #0: 0x00007fff89a7d385 libsystem_c.dylib`OSSpinLockLock$VARIANT$mp + 53
libsystem_c.dylib`OSSpinLockLock$VARIANT$mp + 53:
-> 0x7fff89a7d385:  jmp    0x7fff89a7d353            ; OSSpinLockLock$VARIANT$mp + 3
   0x7fff89a7d387:  nop


libsystem_c.dylib`OSSpinLockUnlock:
   0x7fff89a7d388:  movl   $0, (%rdi)


libsystem_c.dylib`spin_unlock + 6:
   0x7fff89a7d38e:  ret
  thread #6: tid = 0x0005, 0x00007fff89a7d385 libsystem_c.dylib`OSSpinLockLock$VARIANT$mp + 53,
stop reason = signal SIGSTOP
    frame #0: 0x00007fff89a7d385 libsystem_c.dylib`OSSpinLockLock$VARIANT$mp + 53
libsystem_c.dylib`OSSpinLockLock$VARIANT$mp + 53:
-> 0x7fff89a7d385:  jmp    0x7fff89a7d353            ; OSSpinLockLock$VARIANT$mp + 3
   0x7fff89a7d387:  nop


libsystem_c.dylib`OSSpinLockUnlock:
   0x7fff89a7d388:  movl   $0, (%rdi)


libsystem_c.dylib`spin_unlock + 6:
   0x7fff89a7d38e:  ret
```

3.   Check thread 2 (core thread #1) and find where it was being executed:

```
(lldb) thread select 2
[* thread #2: tid = 0x0001, 0x0000000102e6f9b2 App10`proc + 130, stop reason = signal SIGSTOP
    frame #0: 0x0000000102e6f9b2 App10`proc + 130
App10`proc + 130:
-> 0x102e6f9b2:  movl   %esi, -20(%rbp)
   0x102e6f9b5:  movl   %eax, -24(%rbp)
   0x102e6f9b8:  je     0x102e6f9e5               ; proc + 181
   0x102e6f9be:  leaq   1739(%rip), %rax

(lldb) x/i $rip
0x102e6f9b2:  89 75 ec  movl   %esi, -20(%rbp)

(lldb) x/xw $rbp-0x14
0x103080ebc: 0x00002710
```

```
(lldb) di -n proc
App10`proc:
    0x102e6f930:  pushq   %rbp
    0x102e6f931:  movq    %rsp, %rbp
    0x102e6f934:  subq    $32, %rsp
    0x102e6f938:  leaq    1873(%rip), %rax
    0x102e6f93f:  movq    %rax, -16(%rbp)
    0x102e6f943:  callq   0x102e6fc8c              ; symbol stub for: rand
    0x102e6f948:  movslq  %eax, %rcx
    0x102e6f94b:  imulq   $1759218605, %rcx, %rcx
    0x102e6f952:  movq    %rcx, %rdx
    0x102e6f955:  shrq    $63, %rdx
    0x102e6f959:  movl    %edx, %esi
    0x102e6f95b:  sarq    $44, %rcx
    0x102e6f95f:  movl    %ecx, %edi
    0x102e6f961:  leal    (%rdi,%rsi), %esi
    0x102e6f964:  imull   $10000, %esi, %esi
    0x102e6f96a:  subl    %esi, %eax
    0x102e6f96c:  movl    %eax, -4(%rbp)
    0x102e6f96f:  callq   0x102e6fc8c              ; symbol stub for: rand
    0x102e6f974:  movslq  %eax, %rcx
    0x102e6f977:  imulq   $1759218605, %rcx, %rcx
    0x102e6f97e:  movq    %rcx, %rdx
    0x102e6f981:  shrq    $63, %rdx
    0x102e6f985:  movl    %edx, %esi
    0x102e6f987:  sarq    $44, %rcx
    0x102e6f98b:  movl    %ecx, %edi
    0x102e6f98d:  leal    (%rdi,%rsi), %esi
    0x102e6f990:  imull   $10000, %esi, %esi
    0x102e6f996:  movl    %eax, %edi
    0x102e6f998:  subl    %esi, %edi
    0x102e6f99a:  movl    $10000, %esi
    0x102e6f99f:  movl    %edi, -8(%rbp)
    0x102e6f9a2:  movslq  -4(%rbp), %rcx
    0x102e6f9a6:  movq    -16(%rbp), %rdx
    0x102e6f9aa:  cmpq    $0, (%rdx,%rcx,8)
->  0x102e6f9b2:  movl    %esi, -20(%rbp)
    0x102e6f9b5:  movl    %eax, -24(%rbp)
    0x102e6f9b8:  je      0x102e6f9e5             ; proc + 181
    0x102e6f9be:  leaq    1739(%rip), %rax
    0x102e6f9c5:  movslq  -4(%rbp), %rcx
    0x102e6f9c9:  movq    (%rax,%rcx,8), %rdi
    0x102e6f9cd:  callq   0x102e6fc7a             ; symbol stub for: free
    0x102e6f9d2:  leaq    1719(%rip), %rax
    0x102e6f9d9:  movslq  -4(%rbp), %rcx
    0x102e6f9dd:  movq    $0, (%rax,%rcx,8)
    0x102e6f9e5:  movslq  -8(%rbp), %rdi
    0x102e6f9e9:  callq   0x102e6fc80             ; symbol stub for: malloc
    0x102e6f9ee:  leaq    1691(%rip), %rdi
    0x102e6f9f5:  movslq  -4(%rbp), %rcx
    0x102e6f9f9:  movq    %rax, (%rdi,%rcx,8)
    0x102e6f9fd:  jmpq    0x102e6f938             ; proc + 8
    0x102e6fa02:  nopw    %cs:(%rax,%rax)
```

Note: we see indeed that the dump was saved in the middle of *proc* function execution.

4.   Check thread 4 (core thread #3) and find where it was being executed:

```
(lldb) thread select 4
* thread #4: tid = 0x0003, 0x00007fff8ed7dce2 libsystem_kernel.dylib`__pthread_kill + 10, stop
reason = signal SIGSTOP
    frame #0: 0x00007fff8ed7dce2 libsystem_kernel.dylib`__pthread_kill + 10
libsystem_kernel.dylib`__pthread_kill + 10:
-> 0x7fff8ed7dce2:  jae    0x7fff8ed7dce9            ; __pthread_kill + 17
   0x7fff8ed7dce4:  jmpq   0x7fff8ed7effc            ; cerror
   0x7fff8ed7dce9:  ret
   0x7fff8ed7dcea:  nop

(lldb) bt
* thread #4: tid = 0x0003, 0x00007fff8ed7dce2 libsystem_kernel.dylib`__pthread_kill + 10, stop
reason = signal SIGSTOP
    frame #0: 0x00007fff8ed7dce2 libsystem_kernel.dylib`__pthread_kill + 10
    frame #1: 0x00007fff89a2b7d2 libsystem_c.dylib`pthread_kill + 95
    frame #2: 0x00007fff89a1ca7a libsystem_c.dylib`abort + 143
    frame #3: 0x00007fff89a3e4ac libsystem_c.dylib`szone_error + 459
    frame #4: 0x00007fff89a3fe8c libsystem_c.dylib`free_small_botch + 93
    frame #5: 0x00007fff89a7b789 libsystem_c.dylib`free + 194
    frame #6: 0x0000000102e6f9d2 App10`proc + 162
    frame #7: 0x0000000102e6fab9 App10`bar_three + 9
    frame #8: 0x0000000102e6fac9 App10`foo_three + 9
    frame #9: 0x0000000102e6fae1 App10`thread_three + 17
    frame #10: 0x00007fff89a298bf libsystem_c.dylib`_pthread_start + 335
    frame #11: 0x00007fff89a2cb75 libsystem_c.dylib`thread_start + 13

(lldb) di -n proc
App10`proc:
   0x102e6f930:  pushq  %rbp
   0x102e6f931:  movq   %rsp, %rbp
   0x102e6f934:  subq   $32, %rsp
   0x102e6f938:  leaq   1873(%rip), %rax
   0x102e6f93f:  movq   %rax, -16(%rbp)
   0x102e6f943:  callq  0x102e6fc8c               ; symbol stub for: rand
   0x102e6f948:  movslq %eax, %rcx
   0x102e6f94b:  imulq  $1759218605, %rcx, %rcx
   0x102e6f952:  movq   %rcx, %rdx
   0x102e6f955:  shrq   $63, %rdx
   0x102e6f959:  movl   %edx, %esi
   0x102e6f95b:  sarq   $44, %rcx
   0x102e6f95f:  movl   %ecx, %edi
   0x102e6f961:  leal   (%rdi,%rsi), %esi
   0x102e6f964:  imull  $10000, %esi, %esi
   0x102e6f96a:  subl   %esi, %eax
   0x102e6f96c:  movl   %eax, -4(%rbp)
   0x102e6f96f:  callq  0x102e6fc8c               ; symbol stub for: rand
   0x102e6f974:  movslq %eax, %rcx
   0x102e6f977:  imulq  $1759218605, %rcx, %rcx
   0x102e6f97e:  movq   %rcx, %rdx
   0x102e6f981:  shrq   $63, %rdx
   0x102e6f985:  movl   %edx, %esi
   0x102e6f987:  sarq   $44, %rcx
   0x102e6f98b:  movl   %ecx, %edi
   0x102e6f98d:  leal   (%rdi,%rsi), %esi
```

```
0x102e6f990:  imull  $10000, %esi, %esi
0x102e6f996:  movl   %eax, %edi
0x102e6f998:  subl   %esi, %edi
0x102e6f99a:  movl   $10000, %esi
0x102e6f99f:  movl   %edi, -8(%rbp)
0x102e6f9a2:  movslq -4(%rbp), %rcx
0x102e6f9a6:  movq   -16(%rbp), %rdx
0x102e6f9aa:  cmpq   $0, (%rdx,%rcx,8)
0x102e6f9b2:  movl   %esi, -20(%rbp)
0x102e6f9b5:  movl   %eax, -24(%rbp)
0x102e6f9b8:  je     0x102e6f9e5            ; proc + 181
0x102e6f9be:  leaq   1739(%rip), %rax
0x102e6f9c5:  movslq -4(%rbp), %rcx
0x102e6f9c9:  movq   (%rax,%rcx,8), %rdi
0x102e6f9cd:  callq  0x102e6fc7a            ; symbol stub for: free
0x102e6f9d2:  leaq   1719(%rip), %rax
0x102e6f9d9:  movslq -4(%rbp), %rcx
0x102e6f9dd:  movq   $0, (%rax,%rcx,8)
0x102e6f9e5:  movslq -8(%rbp), %rdi
0x102e6f9e9:  callq  0x102e6fc80            ; symbol stub for: malloc
0x102e6f9ee:  leaq   1691(%rip), %rdi
0x102e6f9f5:  movslq -4(%rbp), %rcx
0x102e6f9f9:  movq   %rax, (%rdi,%rcx,8)
0x102e6f9fd:  jmpq   0x102e6f938            ; proc + 8
0x102e6fa02:  nopw   %cs:(%rax,%rax)
```

5.   Check threads waiting for spin lock synchronization and identify a diagnostic message:

```
(lldb) thread list
Process 0 stopped
  thread #1: tid = 0x0000, 0x00007fff8ed7de42 libsystem_kernel.dylib`__semwait_signal + 10, stop reason = signal
SIGSTOP
  thread #2: tid = 0x0001, 0x0000000102e6f9b2 App10`proc + 130, stop reason = signal SIGSTOP
  thread #3: tid = 0x0002, 0x00007fff89a7d385 libsystem_c.dylib`OSSpinLockLock$VARIANT$mp + 53, stop reason = signal
SIGSTOP
* thread #4: tid = 0x0003, 0x00007fff8ed7dce2 libsystem_kernel.dylib`__pthread_kill + 10, stop reason = signal SIGSTOP
  thread #5: tid = 0x0004, 0x00007fff89a7d385 libsystem_c.dylib`OSSpinLockLock$VARIANT$mp + 53, stop reason = signal
SIGSTOP
  thread #6: tid = 0x0005, 0x00007fff89a7d385 libsystem_c.dylib`OSSpinLockLock$VARIANT$mp + 53, stop reason = signal
SIGSTOP

(lldb) thread select 6
* thread #6: tid = 0x0005, 0x00007fff89a7d385 libsystem_c.dylib`OSSpinLockLock$VARIANT$mp + 53,
stop reason = signal SIGSTOP
    frame #0: 0x00007fff89a7d385 libsystem_c.dylib`OSSpinLockLock$VARIANT$mp + 53
libsystem_c.dylib`OSSpinLockLock$VARIANT$mp + 53:
-> 0x7fff89a7d385:  jmp    0x7fff89a7d353            ; OSSpinLockLock$VARIANT$mp + 3
   0x7fff89a7d387:  nop

libsystem_c.dylib`OSSpinLockUnlock:
   0x7fff89a7d388:  movl   $0, (%rdi)

libsystem_c.dylib`spin_unlock + 6:
   0x7fff89a7d38e:  ret
```

```
(lldb) bt
* thread #6: tid = 0x0005, 0x00007fff89a7d385 libsystem_c.dylib`OSSpinLockLock$VARIANT$mp + 53,
stop reason = signal SIGSTOP
    frame #0: 0x00007fff89a7d385 libsystem_c.dylib`OSSpinLockLock$VARIANT$mp + 53
    frame #1: 0x00007fff89a28dd1 libsystem_c.dylib`pthread_once + 33
    frame #2: 0x00007fff89a3b53d libsystem_c.dylib`_simple_asl_log_prog + 48
    frame #3: 0x00007fff89a7aaa4 libsystem_c.dylib`_malloc_vprintf + 363
    frame #4: 0x00007fff89a7ab47 libsystem_c.dylib`malloc_printf + 141
    frame #5: 0x00007fff89a7b800 libsystem_c.dylib`free + 313
    frame #6: 0x0000000102e6f9d2 App10`proc + 162
    frame #7: 0x0000000102e6fb59 App10`bar_five + 9
    frame #8: 0x0000000102e6fb69 App10`foo_five + 9
    frame #9: 0x0000000102e6fb81 App10`thread_five + 17
    frame #10: 0x00007fff89a298bf libsystem_c.dylib`_pthread_start + 335
    frame #11: 0x00007fff89a2cb75 libsystem_c.dylib`thread_start + 13

(lldb) di -n free
libsystem_c.dylib`free:
   0x7fff89a7b6c7:  pushq   %rbp
   0x7fff89a7b6c8:  movq    %rsp, %rbp
   0x7fff89a7b6cb:  pushq   %r15
   0x7fff89a7b6cd:  pushq   %r14
   0x7fff89a7b6cf:  pushq   %r13
   0x7fff89a7b6d1:  pushq   %r12
   0x7fff89a7b6d3:  pushq   %rbx
   0x7fff89a7b6d4:  subq    $24, %rsp
   0x7fff89a7b6d8:  movq    %rdi, %rbx
   0x7fff89a7b6db:  testq   %rbx, %rbx
   0x7fff89a7b6de:  je      0x7fff89a7b857       ; free + 400
   0x7fff89a7b6e4:  cmpl    $0, -272246059(%rip) ; malloc_zones + 7
   0x7fff89a7b6eb:  jne     0x7fff89a7b6fa       ; free + 51
   0x7fff89a7b6ed:  movq    $0, -48(%rbp)
   0x7fff89a7b6f5:  jmpq    0x7fff89a7b7ef       ; free + 296
   0x7fff89a7b6fa:  movq    -272246089(%rip), %rax ; malloc_zones
   0x7fff89a7b701:  movq    (%rax), %r14
   0x7fff89a7b704:  movq    %r14, %rdi
   0x7fff89a7b707:  movq    %rbx, %rsi
   0x7fff89a7b70a:  callq   *16(%r14)
   0x7fff89a7b70e:  testq   %rax, %rax
   0x7fff89a7b711:  je      0x7fff89a7b78e       ; free + 199
   0x7fff89a7b713:  movq    %rax, -48(%rbp)
   0x7fff89a7b717:  movq    %rax, %r15
   0x7fff89a7b71a:  testq   %r14, %r14
   0x7fff89a7b71d:  je      0x7fff89a7b7ef       ; free + 296
   0x7fff89a7b723:  cmpl    $6, 104(%r14)
   0x7fff89a7b728:  jb      0x7fff89a7b84c       ; free + 389
   0x7fff89a7b72e:  cmpq    $0, 120(%r14)
   0x7fff89a7b733:  je      0x7fff89a7b84c       ; free + 389
   0x7fff89a7b739:  movq    -272246128(%rip), %rax ; malloc_logger
   0x7fff89a7b740:  testq   %rax, %rax
   0x7fff89a7b743:  je      0x7fff89a7b75a       ; free + 147
   0x7fff89a7b745:  movl    $12, %edi
   0x7fff89a7b74a:  xorl    %ecx, %ecx
   0x7fff89a7b74c:  xorl    %r9d, %r9d
   0x7fff89a7b74f:  movq    %r14, %rsi
   0x7fff89a7b752:  movq    %rbx, %rdx
   0x7fff89a7b755:  xorl    %r8d, %r8d
   0x7fff89a7b758:  callq   *%rax
   0x7fff89a7b75a:  movl    -272246164(%rip), %eax ; malloc_check_start
   0x7fff89a7b760:  testl   %eax, %eax
   0x7fff89a7b762:  je      0x7fff89a7b77c       ; free + 181
   0x7fff89a7b764:  movl    -272246178(%rip), %ecx ; malloc_check_counter
   0x7fff89a7b76a:  leal    1(%rcx), %edx
   0x7fff89a7b76d:  movl    %edx, -272246187(%rip) ; malloc_check_counter
   0x7fff89a7b773:  cmpl    %eax, %ecx
   0x7fff89a7b775:  jb      0x7fff89a7b77c       ; free + 181
   0x7fff89a7b777:  callq   0x7fff89a7ace4       ; internal_check
   0x7fff89a7b77c:  movq    %r14, %rdi
   0x7fff89a7b77f:  movq    %rbx, %rsi
   0x7fff89a7b782:  movq    %r15, %rdx
   0x7fff89a7b785:  callq   *120(%r14)
   0x7fff89a7b789:  jmpq    0x7fff89a7b857       ; free + 400
```

```
0x7fff89a7b78e:   movq   -272264397(%rip), %r14     ; pFRZCounterLive
0x7fff89a7b795:   movq   %r14, -56(%rbp)
0x7fff89a7b799:   lock
0x7fff89a7b79a:   incl   (%r14)
0x7fff89a7b79d:   movl   $1, %r15d
0x7fff89a7b7a3:   movq   -272246258(%rip), %r12     ; malloc_zones
0x7fff89a7b7aa:   movl   -272246257(%rip), %r13d    ; malloc_num_zones
0x7fff89a7b7b1:   jmp    0x7fff89a7b7da             ; free + 275
0x7fff89a7b7b3:   movq   %rax, -48(%rbp)
0x7fff89a7b7b7:   movq   -56(%rbp), %r15
0x7fff89a7b7bb:   lock
0x7fff89a7b7bc:   decl   (%r15)
0x7fff89a7b7bf:   jmpq   0x7fff89a7b717             ; free + 80
0x7fff89a7b7c4:   movq   (%r12,%r15,8), %r14
0x7fff89a7b7c8:   movq   %r14, %rdi
0x7fff89a7b7cb:   movq   %rbx, %rsi
0x7fff89a7b7ce:   callq  *16(%r14)
0x7fff89a7b7d2:   testq  %rax, %rax
0x7fff89a7b7d5:   jne    0x7fff89a7b7b3             ; free + 236
0x7fff89a7b7d7:   incq   %r15
0x7fff89a7b7da:   cmpl   %r13d, %r15d
0x7fff89a7b7dd:   jb     0x7fff89a7b7c4             ; free + 253
0x7fff89a7b7df:   movq   $0, -48(%rbp)
0x7fff89a7b7e7:   movq   -56(%rbp), %r14
0x7fff89a7b7eb:   lock
0x7fff89a7b7ec:   decl   (%r14)
0x7fff89a7b7ef:   leaq   95174(%rip), %rdi          ; "*** error for object %p: pointer being freed was not
allocated\n*** set a breakpoint in malloc_error_break to debug\n"
0x7fff89a7b7f6:   xorb   %al, %al
0x7fff89a7b7f8:   movq   %rbx, %rsi
0x7fff89a7b7fb:   callq  0x7fff89a825da             ; symbol stub for: malloc_printf
0x7fff89a7b800:   callq  0x7fff89a7b6bc             ; malloc_error_break
0x7fff89a7b805:   testb  $80, -272246324(%rip)      ; malloc_logger + 7
0x7fff89a7b80c:   je     0x7fff89a7b857             ; free + 400
0x7fff89a7b80e:   callq  0x7fff89a3a872             ; _simple_salloc
0x7fff89a7b813:   testq  %rax, %rax
0x7fff89a7b816:   jne    0x7fff89a7b821             ; free + 346
0x7fff89a7b818:   leaq   95313(%rip), %rax          ; "*** error: pointer being freed was not allocated\n"
0x7fff89a7b81f:   jmp    0x7fff89a7b840             ; free + 377
0x7fff89a7b821:   movq   %rax, %r14
0x7fff89a7b824:   leaq   95237(%rip), %rsi          ; "*** error for object %p: pointer being freed was not
allocated\n"
0x7fff89a7b82b:   xorb   %al, %al
0x7fff89a7b82d:   movq   %r14, %rdi
0x7fff89a7b830:   movq   %rbx, %rdx
0x7fff89a7b833:   callq  0x7fff89a3b481             ; _simple_sprintf
0x7fff89a7b838:   movq   %r14, %rdi
0x7fff89a7b83b:   callq  0x7fff89a3a052             ; _simple_string
0x7fff89a7b840:   movq   %rax, -272272927(%rip)     ; gCRAnnotations + 8
0x7fff89a7b847:   callq  0x7fff89a1c9eb             ; abort
0x7fff89a7b84c:   movq   %r14, %rdi
0x7fff89a7b84f:   movq   %rbx, %rsi
0x7fff89a7b852:   callq  0x7fff89a825ec             ; symbol stub for: malloc_zone_free
0x7fff89a7b857:   addq   $24, %rsp
0x7fff89a7b85b:   popq   %rbx
0x7fff89a7b85c:   popq   %r12
0x7fff89a7b85e:   popq   %r13
0x7fff89a7b860:   popq   %r14
0x7fff89a7b862:   popq   %r15
0x7fff89a7b864:   popq   %rbp
0x7fff89a7b865:   ret

dyld`free:
0x7fff62a80d07:   pushq  %rbp
0x7fff62a80d08:   movq   %rsp, %rbp
0x7fff62a80d0b:   leaq   144654(%rip), %rax          ; dyld::gLibSystemHelpers
0x7fff62a80d12:   movq   (%rax), %rax
0x7fff62a80d15:   testq  %rax, %rax
0x7fff62a80d18:   je     0x7fff62a80d53             ; free + 76
0x7fff62a80d1a:   cmpq   144111(%rip), %rdi          ; (void *)0x00007fff62a6f000
0x7fff62a80d21:   jb     0x7fff62a80d2f             ; free + 40
0x7fff62a80d23:   leaq   374790(%rip), %rcx          ;
ImageLoaderMachOClassic::bindIndirectSymbolPointers(ImageLoader::LinkContext const&, bool, bool)::alreadyWarned (.b)
0x7fff62a80d2a:   cmpq   %rcx, %rdi
0x7fff62a80d2d:   jb     0x7fff62a80d53             ; free + 76
0x7fff62a80d2f:   leaq   144314(%rip), %rcx          ; initialPool
```

```
0x7fff62a80d36:  jmp    0x7fff62a80d47           ; free + 64
0x7fff62a80d38:  leaq   24(%rcx), %rdx
0x7fff62a80d3c:  cmpq   %rdi, %rdx
0x7fff62a80d3f:  jae    0x7fff62a80d47           ; free + 64
0x7fff62a80d41:  cmpq   %rdi, 16(%rcx)
0x7fff62a80d45:  ja     0x7fff62a80d53           ; free + 76
0x7fff62a80d47:  movq   (%rcx), %rcx
0x7fff62a80d4a:  testq  %rcx, %rcx
0x7fff62a80d4d:  jne    0x7fff62a80d38           ; free + 49
0x7fff62a80d4f:  popq   %rbp
0x7fff62a80d50:  jmpq   *40(%rax)
0x7fff62a80d53:  popq   %rbp
0x7fff62a80d54:  ret
```

(lldb) **x/s 0x7fff89a92bbc**
```
0x7fff89a92bbc <Malloc_Facility+3228>:   "*** error for object %p: pointer being freed was not
allocated\n*** set a breakpoint in malloc_error_break to debug\n"
```

6.   Check the address of being freed:

(lldb) **bt**
```
* thread #6: tid = 0x0005, 0x00007fff89a7d385 libsystem_c.dylib`OSSpinLockLock$VARIANT$mp + 53,
stop reason = signal SIGSTOP
    frame #0: 0x00007fff89a7d385 libsystem_c.dylib`OSSpinLockLock$VARIANT$mp + 53
    frame #1: 0x00007fff89a28dd1 libsystem_c.dylib`pthread_once + 33
    frame #2: 0x00007fff89a3b53d libsystem_c.dylib`_simple_asl_log_prog + 48
    frame #3: 0x00007fff89a7aaa4 libsystem_c.dylib`_malloc_vprintf + 363
    frame #4: 0x00007fff89a7ab47 libsystem_c.dylib`malloc_printf + 141
    frame #5: 0x00007fff89a7b800 libsystem_c.dylib`free + 313
    frame #6: 0x0000000102e6f9d2 App10`proc + 162
    frame #7: 0x0000000102e6fb59 App10`bar_five + 9
    frame #8: 0x0000000102e6fb69 App10`foo_five + 9
    frame #9: 0x0000000102e6fb81 App10`thread_five + 17
    frame #10: 0x00007fff89a298bf libsystem_c.dylib`_pthread_start + 335
    frame #11: 0x00007fff89a2cb75 libsystem_c.dylib`thread_start + 13
```

(lldb) **di -n proc**
```
App10`proc:
   0x102e6f930:  pushq  %rbp
   0x102e6f931:  movq   %rsp, %rbp
   0x102e6f934:  subq   $32, %rsp
   0x102e6f938:  leaq   1873(%rip), %rax
   0x102e6f93f:  movq   %rax, -16(%rbp)
   0x102e6f943:  callq  0x102e6fc8c              ; symbol stub for: rand
   0x102e6f948:  movslq %eax, %rcx
   0x102e6f94b:  imulq  $1759218605, %rcx, %rcx
   0x102e6f952:  movq   %rcx, %rdx
   0x102e6f955:  shrq   $63, %rdx
   0x102e6f959:  movl   %edx, %esi
   0x102e6f95b:  sarq   $44, %rcx
   0x102e6f95f:  movl   %ecx, %edi
   0x102e6f961:  leal   (%rdi,%rsi), %esi
   0x102e6f964:  imull  $10000, %esi, %esi
   0x102e6f96a:  subl   %esi, %eax
   0x102e6f96c:  movl   %eax, -4(%rbp)
   0x102e6f96f:  callq  0x102e6fc8c              ; symbol stub for: rand
   0x102e6f974:  movslq %eax, %rcx
   0x102e6f977:  imulq  $1759218605, %rcx, %rcx
   0x102e6f97e:  movq   %rcx, %rdx
   0x102e6f981:  shrq   $63, %rdx
   0x102e6f985:  movl   %edx, %esi
   0x102e6f987:  sarq   $44, %rcx
   0x102e6f98b:  movl   %ecx, %edi
```

```
0x102e6f98d:  leal    (%rdi,%rsi), %esi
0x102e6f990:  imull   $10000, %esi, %esi
0x102e6f996:  movl    %eax, %edi
0x102e6f998:  subl    %esi, %edi
0x102e6f99a:  movl    $10000, %esi
0x102e6f99f:  movl    %edi, -8(%rbp)
0x102e6f9a2:  movslq  -4(%rbp), %rcx
0x102e6f9a6:  movq    -16(%rbp), %rdx
0x102e6f9aa:  cmpq    $0, (%rdx,%rcx,8)
0x102e6f9b2:  movl    %esi, -20(%rbp)
0x102e6f9b5:  movl    %eax, -24(%rbp)
0x102e6f9b8:  je      0x102e6f9e5             ; proc + 181
0x102e6f9be:  leaq    1739(%rip), %rax
0x102e6f9c5:  movslq  -4(%rbp), %rcx
0x102e6f9c9:  movq    (%rax,%rcx,8), %rdi
0x102e6f9cd:  callq   0x102e6fc7a            ; symbol stub for: free
0x102e6f9d2:  leaq    1719(%rip), %rax
0x102e6f9d9:  movslq  -4(%rbp), %rcx
0x102e6f9dd:  movq    $0, (%rax,%rcx,8)
0x102e6f9e5:  movslq  -8(%rbp), %rdi
0x102e6f9e9:  callq   0x102e6fc80            ; symbol stub for: malloc
0x102e6f9ee:  leaq    1691(%rip), %rdi
0x102e6f9f5:  movslq  -4(%rbp), %rcx
0x102e6f9f9:  movq    %rax, (%rdi,%rcx,8)
0x102e6f9fd:  jmpq    0x102e6f938            ; proc + 8
0x102e6fa02:  nopw    %cs:(%rax,%rax)
```

Note: There were some calculations going on before *free* call. The parameter passed was in RDI and the calculation of that value involved RAX, RCX and 8. The latter value looks like the size of a pointer value; RCX is probably used as an index into the base address from RAX. Let's examine these registers.

```
(lldb) frame 6
frame #6: 0x0000000102e6f9d2 App10`proc + 162
App10`proc + 162:
-> 0x102e6f9d2:  leaq    1719(%rip), %rax
   0x102e6f9d9:  movslq  -4(%rbp), %rcx
   0x102e6f9dd:  movq    $0, (%rax,%rcx,8)
   0x102e6f9e5:  movslq  -8(%rbp), %rdi

(lldb) re r rbp
     rbp = 0x000000010328ced0

(lldb) x/dw 0x000000010328ced0-4
0x10328cecc: 2574

(lldb) print/x 0x102e6f9d9+1719
(long) $6 = 0x0000000102e70090

(lldb) x/xg 0x102e70090+2574*8
0x102e75100 0x00007ff01c9edc00

(lldb) x/xg 0x00007ff01c9edc00
0x7ff01c9edc00:     0x4000000000000000
```

7.   Check that the identified address 0x00007ff01c9edc00 and the problem address from the crash report 0x7ff01c8ae600 belong to the same section:

301

```
(lldb) image dump sections core.2057
Sections for '/Users/DumpAnalysis/Documents/AMCDA-Dumps/core.2057' (x86_64):
  SectID     Type             Load Address                                       File Off.  File Size  Flags      Section Name
  ---------- ---------------- -------------------------------------------------- ---------- ---------- ---------- ----------------------------
  0x00000100 container        [0x0000000102e6f000-0x0000000102e70000)*           0x00003000 0x00001000 0x00000000 core.2057.
  0x00000200 container        [0x0000000102e70000-0x0000000102e71000)*           0x00004000 0x00001000 0x00000000 core.2057.
  0x00000300 container        [0x0000000102e71000-0x0000000102e84000)*           0x00005000 0x00013000 0x00000000 core.2057.
  0x00000400 container        [0x0000000102e84000-0x0000000102e85000)*           0x00018000 0x00001000 0x00000000 core.2057.
  0x00000500 container        [0x0000000102e85000-0x0000000102e86000)*           0x00019000 0x00001000 0x00000000 core.2057.
  0x00000600 container        [0x0000000102e86000-0x0000000102e87000)*           0x0001a000 0x00001000 0x00000000 core.2057.
  0x00000700 container        [0x0000000102e87000-0x0000000102e88000)*           0x0001b000 0x00001000 0x00000000 core.2057.
  0x00000800 container        [0x0000000102e88000-0x0000000102e9d000)*           0x0001c000 0x00015000 0x00000000 core.2057.
  0x00000900 container        [0x0000000102e9d000-0x0000000102e9e000)*           0x00031000 0x00001000 0x00000000 core.2057.
  0x00000a00 container        [0x0000000102e9e000-0x0000000102e9f000)*           0x00032000 0x00001000 0x00000000 core.2057.
  0x00000b00 container        [0x0000000102e9f000-0x0000000102eb4000)*           0x00033000 0x00015000 0x00000000 core.2057.
  0x00000c00 container        [0x0000000102eb4000-0x0000000102eb5000)*           0x00048000 0x00001000 0x00000000 core.2057.
  0x00000d00 container        [0x0000000102eb5000-0x0000000102eb6000)*           0x00049000 0x00001000 0x00000000 core.2057.
  0x00000e00 container        [0x0000000102eb6000-0x0000000102eb7000)*           0x0004a000 0x00001000 0x00000000 core.2057.
  0x00000f00 container        [0x0000000102eb8000-0x0000000102ebd000)*           0x0004b000 0x00005000 0x00000000 core.2057.
  0x00001000 container        [0x0000000102f00000-0x0000000103000000)*           0x00050000 0x00100000 0x00000000 core.2057.
  0x00001100 container        [0x0000000103000000-0x0000000103001000)*           0x00150000 0x00001000 0x00000000 core.2057.
  0x00001200 container        [0x0000000103001000-0x0000000103083000)*           0x00151000 0x00082000 0x00000000 core.2057.
  0x00001300 container        [0x0000000103083000-0x0000000103084000)*           0x001d3000 0x00001000 0x00000000 core.2057.
  0x00001400 container        [0x0000000103084000-0x0000000103106000)*           0x001d4000 0x00082000 0x00000000 core.2057.
  0x00001500 container        [0x0000000103106000-0x0000000103107000)*           0x00256000 0x00001000 0x00000000 core.2057.
  0x00001600 container        [0x0000000103107000-0x0000000103189000)*           0x00257000 0x00082000 0x00000000 core.2057.
  0x00001700 container        [0x0000000103189000-0x000000010318a000)*           0x002d9000 0x00001000 0x00000000 core.2057.
  0x00001800 container        [0x000000010318a000-0x000000010320c000)*           0x002da000 0x00082000 0x00000000 core.2057.
  0x00001900 container        [0x000000010320c000-0x000000010320d000)*           0x0035c000 0x00001000 0x00000000 core.2057.
  0x00001a00 container        [0x000000010320d000-0x000000010328f000)*           0x0035d000 0x00082000 0x00000000 core.2057.
  0x00001b00 container        [0x00007ff01b400000-0x00007ff01b500000)*           0x003df000 0x00100000 0x00000000 core.2057.
  0x00001c00 container        [0x00007ff01b500000-0x00007ff01b600000)*           0x004df000 0x00100000 0x00000000 core.2057.
  0x00001d00 container        [0x00007ff01b800000-0x00007ff01c000000)*           0x005df000 0x00800000 0x00000000 core.2057.
  0x00001e00 container        [0x00007ff01c800000-0x00007ff01d000000)*           0x00ddf000 0x00800000 0x00000000 core.2057.
  0x00001f00 container        [0x00007ff01d000000-0x00007ff01d800000)*           0x015df000 0x00800000 0x00000000 core.2057.
  0x00002000 container        [0x00007fff5ea6f000-0x00007fff6226f000)*           0x01ddf000 0x03800000 0x00000000 core.2057.
  0x00002100 container        [0x00007fff6226f000-0x00007fff62a6f000)*           0x055df000 0x00800000 0x00000000 core.2057.
  0x00002200 container        [0x00007fff62a6f000-0x00007fff62aa4000)*           0x05ddf000 0x00035000 0x00000000 core.2057.
  0x00002300 container        [0x00007fff62aa4000-0x00007fff62aa6000)*           0x05e14000 0x00002000 0x00000000 core.2057.
  0x00002400 container        [0x00007fff62aa6000-0x00007fff62ae0000)*           0x05e16000 0x0003a000 0x00000000 core.2057.
  0x00002500 container        [0x00007fff62ae0000-0x00007fff62af3000)*           0x05e50000 0x00013000 0x00000000 core.2057.
  0x00002600 container        [0x00007fff79629000-0x00007fff79800000)*           0x05e63000 0x001d7000 0x00000000 core.2057.
  0x00002700 container        [0x00007fff79800000-0x00007fff79a00000)*           0x0603a000 0x00200000 0x00000000 core.2057.
  0x00002800 container        [0x00007fff79a00000-0x00007fff79c00000)*           0x0623a000 0x00200000 0x00000000 core.2057.
  0x00002900 container        [0x00007fff79c00000-0x00007fff79e00000)*           0x0643a000 0x00200000 0x00000000 core.2057.
  0x00002a00 container        [0x00007fff79e00000-0x00007fff7a000000)*           0x0663a000 0x00200000 0x00000000 core.2057.
  0x00002b00 container        [0x00007fff7a000000-0x00007fff7a200000)*           0x0683a000 0x00200000 0x00000000 core.2057.
  0x00002c00 container        [0x00007fff7a200000-0x00007fff7a400000)*           0x06a3a000 0x00200000 0x00000000 core.2057.
  0x00002d00 container        [0x00007fff7a400000-0x00007fff7a600000)*           0x06c3a000 0x00200000 0x00000000 core.2057.
  0x00002e00 container        [0x00007fff7a600000-0x00007fff7a800000)*           0x06e3a000 0x00200000 0x00000000 core.2057.
  0x00002f00 container        [0x00007fff7a800000-0x00007fff7aa00000)*           0x0703a000 0x00200000 0x00000000 core.2057.
  0x00003000 container        [0x00007fff7aa00000-0x00007fff7ae00000)*           0x0723a000 0x00400000 0x00000000 core.2057.
  0x00003100 container        [0x00007fff7ae00000-0x00007fff7b000000)*           0x0763a000 0x00200000 0x00000000 core.2057.
  0x00003200 container        [0x00007fff7b000000-0x00007fff7b11d000)*           0x0783a000 0x0011d000 0x00000000 core.2057.
  0x00003300 container        [0x00007fff89629000-0x00007fff96699000)*           0x07957000 0x0d070000 0x00000000 core.2057.
  0x00003400 container        [0x00007fff96699000-0x00007fff997a1000)*           0x149c7000 0x03108000 0x00000000 core.2057.
  0x00003500 container        [0x00007ffffe00000-0x00007ffffe02000)*            0x17acf000 0x00000000 0x00000000 core.2057.
```

8.   Dump the first 1000 elements of array (0x102e70090) found in the *proc* function disassembly and identify a few addresses at the beginning:

```
(lldb)  x/1000xg 0x102e70090 --force
0x102e70090:  0x0000000000000000 0x0000000000000000
0x102e700a0:  0x0000000000000000 0x0000000000000000
0x102e700b0:  0x0000000000000000 0x0000000000000000
0x102e700c0:  0x0000000000000000 0x0000000000000000
0x102e700d0:  0x0000000000000000 0x0000000000000000
0x102e700e0:  0x0000000000000000 0x0000000000000000
0x102e700f0:  0x0000000000000000 0x0000000000000000
0x102e70100:  0x0000000000000000 0x0000000000000000
0x102e70110:  0x0000000000000000 0x0000000000000000
0x102e70120:  0x00007ff01cb9d400 0x0000000000000000
0x102e70130:  0x0000000000000000 0x0000000000000000
0x102e70140:  0x0000000000000000 0x0000000000000000
0x102e70150:  0x0000000000000000 0x0000000000000000
0x102e70160:  0x0000000000000000 0x0000000000000000
0x102e70170:  0x0000000000000000 0x0000000000000000
```

```
0x102e70180:  0x0000000000000000  0x0000000000000000
0x102e70190:  0x0000000000000000  0x0000000000000000
0x102e701a0:  0x0000000000000000  0x0000000000000000
0x102e701b0:  0x0000000000000000  0x0000000000000000
0x102e701c0:  0x0000000000000000  0x0000000000000000
0x102e701d0:  0x00007ff01cb99000  0x0000000000000000
0x102e701e0:  0x0000000000000000  0x0000000000000000
0x102e701f0:  0x0000000000000000  0x0000000000000000
0x102e70200:  0x0000000000000000  0x0000000000000000
0x102e70210:  0x00007ff01b92d600  0x0000000000000000
0x102e70220:  0x00007ff01b40ab80  0x0000000000000000
0x102e70230:  0x0000000000000000  0x00007ff01b86f600
0x102e70240:  0x0000000000000000  0x00007ff01cae4400
0x102e70250:  0x0000000000000000  0x0000000000000000
[...]
```

Exercise A11 (GDB)

- **Goal:** Learn how to identify synchronization wait chains, deadlocks, hidden and handled exceptions

- **Patterns:** Wait Chains, Deadlock, Execution Residue, Handled Exception

- \AMCDA-Dumps\Exercise-A11-GDB.pdf

Exercise A11 (GDB)

Goal: Learn how to identify synchronization wait chains, deadlocks, hidden and handled exceptions

Patterns: Wait Chains, Deadlock, Execution Residue, Handled Exception

1.   Identify possible wait chain and deadlock in the diagnostic report App11_2281.crash:

```
Process:         App11 [2281]
Path:            /Users/USER/Documents/*/App11
Identifier:      App11
Version:         ??? (???)
Code Type:       X86-64 (Native)
Parent Process:  bash [223]

Date/Time:       2012-07-29 18:58:31.916 +0100
OS Version:      Mac OS X 10.7.4 (11E53)
Report Version:  9


Crashed Thread:  0  Dispatch queue: com.apple.main-thread


Exception Type:  EXC_CRASH (SIGABRT)
Exception Codes: 0x0000000000000000, 0x0000000000000000


Thread 0 Crashed:: Dispatch queue: com.apple.main-thread
0   libsystem_kernel.dylib         0x00007fff8ed7de42 __semwait_signal + 10
1   libsystem_c.dylib              0x00007fff899dfdea nanosleep + 164
2   libsystem_c.dylib              0x00007fff899dfc2c sleep + 61
3   libsystem_c.dylib              0x00007fff899dfc08 sleep + 25
4   App11                          0x0000000105051b75 main + 261
5   App11                          0x0000000105051774 start + 52


Thread 1:
0   libsystem_kernel.dylib         0x00007fff8ed7de42 __semwait_signal + 10
1   libsystem_c.dylib              0x00007fff899dfdea nanosleep + 164
2   libsystem_c.dylib              0x00007fff899dfc2c sleep + 61
3   libsystem_c.dylib              0x00007fff899dfc08 sleep + 25
4   App11                          0x00000001050518c2 bar_one() + 18
5   App11                          0x00000001050518d9 foo_one() + 9
6   App11                          0x00000001050518f1 thread_one(void*) + 17
7   libsystem_c.dylib              0x00007fff89a298bf _pthread_start + 335
8   libsystem_c.dylib              0x00007fff89a2cb75 thread_start + 13


Thread 2:
0   libsystem_kernel.dylib         0x00007fff8ed7dbf2 __psynch_mutexwait + 10
1   libsystem_c.dylib              0x00007fff89a281a1 pthread_mutex_lock + 545
2   App11                          0x0000000105051833 procA() + 115
3   App11                          0x0000000105051919 bar_two() + 9
4   App11                          0x0000000105051929 foo_two() + 9
5   App11                          0x0000000105051941 thread_two(void*) + 17
6   libsystem_c.dylib              0x00007fff89a298bf _pthread_start + 335
7   libsystem_c.dylib              0x00007fff89a2cb75 thread_start + 13


Thread 3:
0   libsystem_kernel.dylib         0x00007fff8ed7de42 __semwait_signal + 10
1   libsystem_c.dylib              0x00007fff899dfdea nanosleep + 164
2   libsystem_c.dylib              0x00007fff899dfc2c sleep + 61
3   libsystem_c.dylib              0x00007fff899dfc08 sleep + 25
4   App11                          0x0000000105051972 bar_three() + 18
5   App11                          0x0000000105051989 foo_three() + 9
6   App11                          0x00000001050519a1 thread_three(void*) + 17
7   libsystem_c.dylib              0x00007fff89a298bf _pthread_start + 335
8   libsystem_c.dylib              0x00007fff89a2cb75 thread_start + 13
```

```
Thread 4:
0   libsystem_kernel.dylib          0x00007fff8ed7dbf2 __psynch_mutexwait + 10
1   libsystem_c.dylib               0x00007fff89a281a1 pthread_mutex_lock + 545
2   App11                           0x0000000105051873 procB() + 35
3   App11                           0x00000001050519c9 bar_four() + 9
4   App11                           0x00000001050519d9 foo_four() + 9
5   App11                           0x00000001050519f1 thread_four(void*) + 17
6   libsystem_c.dylib               0x00007fff89a298bf _pthread_start + 335
7   libsystem_c.dylib               0x00007fff89a2cb75 thread_start + 13

Thread 5:
0   libsystem_kernel.dylib          0x00007fff8ed7de42 __semwait_signal + 10
1   libsystem_c.dylib               0x00007fff899dfdea nanosleep + 164
2   libsystem_c.dylib               0x00007fff899dfc2c sleep + 61
3   libsystem_c.dylib               0x00007fff899dfc08 sleep + 25
4   App11                           0x0000000105051a22 bar_five() + 18
5   App11                           0x0000000105051a39 foo_five() + 9
6   App11                           0x0000000105051a51 thread_five(void*) + 17
7   libsystem_c.dylib               0x00007fff89a298bf _pthread_start + 335
8   libsystem_c.dylib               0x00007fff89a2cb75 thread_start + 13

Thread 0 crashed with X86 Thread State (64-bit):
  rax: 0x0000000000000004  rbx: 0x00007fff64c50a08  rcx: 0x00007fff64c509c8  rdx: 0x0000000000000001
  rdi: 0x0000000000000c03  rsi: 0x0000000000000000  rbp: 0x00007fff64c509f0  rsp: 0x00007fff64c509c8
   r8: 0x000000007fffffff   r9: 0x0000000000000000  r10: 0x0000000000000001  r11: 0xffffff80002da8d0
  r12: 0x0000000000000000  r13: 0x0000000000000000  r14: 0x00007fff64c50a18  r15: 0x0000000000000000
  rip: 0x00007fff8ed7de42  rfl: 0x0000000000000247  cr2: 0x000000010548e880
Logical CPU: 0

Binary Images:
       0x105051000 -        0x105051fff +App11 (??? - ???) <A6D8D8F4-D61C-3295-A579-D55006FBA826>
/Users/USER/Documents/*/App11
    0x7fff64c51000 -        0x7fff64c85baf  dyld (195.6 - ???) <0CD1B35B-A28F-32DA-B72E-452EAD609613> /usr/lib/dyld
    0x7fff89663000 -        0x7fff89680fff  libxpc.dylib (77.19.0 - compatibility 1.0.0) <9F57891B-D7EF-3050-BEDD-
21E7C6668248> /usr/lib/system/libxpc.dylib
    0x7fff899d9000 -        0x7fff899daff7  libsystem_blocks.dylib (53.0.0 - compatibility 1.0.0) <8BCA214A-8992-34B2-
A8B9-B74DEACA1869> /usr/lib/system/libsystem_blocks.dylib
    0x7fff899db000 -        0x7fff89ab8fef  libsystem_c.dylib (763.13.0 - compatibility 1.0.0) <41B43515-2806-3FBC-ACF1-
A16F35B7E290> /usr/lib/system/libsystem_c.dylib
    0x7fff89c93000 -        0x7fff89ca1fff  libdispatch.dylib (187.9.0 - compatibility 1.0.0) <1D5BE322-A9B9-3BCE-8FAC-
076FB07CF54A> /usr/lib/system/libdispatch.dylib
    0x7fff8a261000 -        0x7fff8a262fff  libunc.dylib (24.0.0 - compatibility 1.0.0) <337960EE-0A85-3DD0-A760-
7134CF4C0AFF> /usr/lib/system/libunc.dylib
    0x7fff8a754000 -        0x7fff8a755ff7  libremovefile.dylib (21.1.0 - compatibility 1.0.0) <739E6C83-AA52-3C6C-A680-
B37FE2888A04> /usr/lib/system/libremovefile.dylib
    0x7fff8dd85000 -        0x7fff8dd89fff  libmathCommon.A.dylib (2026.0.0 - compatibility 1.0.0) <FF83AFF7-42B2-306E-
90AF-D539C51A4542> /usr/lib/system/libmathCommon.A.dylib
    0x7fff8dd8a000 -        0x7fff8dd8efff  libdyld.dylib (195.5.0 - compatibility 1.0.0) <380C3F44-0CA7-3514-8080-
46D1C9DF4FCD> /usr/lib/system/libdyld.dylib
    0x7fff8e3b1000 -        0x7fff8e3b2ff7  libsystem_sandbox.dylib (??? - ???) <96D38E74-F18F-3CCB-A20B-E8E3ADC4E166>
/usr/lib/system/libsystem_sandbox.dylib
    0x7fff8ed60000 -        0x7fff8ed66fff  libmacho.dylib (800.0.0 - compatibility 1.0.0) <165514D7-1BFA-38EF-A151-
676DCD21FB64> /usr/lib/system/libmacho.dylib
    0x7fff8ed67000 -        0x7fff8ed87fff  libsystem_kernel.dylib (1699.26.8 - compatibility 1.0.0) <1DDC0B0F-DB2A-34D6-
895D-E5B2B5618946> /usr/lib/system/libsystem_kernel.dylib
    0x7fff8ef1d000 -        0x7fff8ef25fff  libsystem_dnssd.dylib (??? - ???) <D9BB1F87-A42B-3CBC-9DC2-FC07FCEF0016>
/usr/lib/system/libsystem_dnssd.dylib
    0x7fff8fa97000 -        0x7fff8fad2fff  libsystem_info.dylib (??? - ???) <35F90252-2AE1-32C5-8D34-782C614D9639>
/usr/lib/system/libsystem_info.dylib
    0x7fff8feb9000 -        0x7fff8febbfff  libquarantine.dylib (36.6.0 - compatibility 1.0.0) <0EBF714B-4B69-3E1F-9A7D-
6BBC2AACB310> /usr/lib/system/libquarantine.dylib
    0x7fff90025000 -        0x7fff90025fff  libkeymgr.dylib (23.0.0 - compatibility 1.0.0) <61EFED6A-A407-301E-B454-
CD18314F0075> /usr/lib/system/libkeymgr.dylib
    0x7fff9004e000 -        0x7fff90053fff  libcompiler_rt.dylib (6.0.0 - compatibility 1.0.0) <98ECD5F6-E85C-32A5-98CD-
8911230CB66A> /usr/lib/system/libcompiler_rt.dylib
    0x7fff9098b000 -        0x7fff9098cfff  libdnsinfo.dylib (395.11.0 - compatibility 1.0.0) <853BAAA5-270F-3FDC-B025-
D448DB72E1C3> /usr/lib/system/libdnsinfo.dylib
    0x7fff91199000 -        0x7fff9119eff7  libsystem_network.dylib (??? - ???) <5DE7024E-1D2D-34A2-80F4-08326331A75B>
/usr/lib/system/libsystem_network.dylib
    0x7fff91c14000 -        0x7fff91c1eff7  liblaunch.dylib (392.38.0 - compatibility 1.0.0) <6ECB7F19-B384-32C1-8652-
2463C1CF4815> /usr/lib/system/liblaunch.dylib
    0x7fff92744000 -        0x7fff927b7fff  libstdc++.6.dylib (52.0.0 - compatibility 7.0.0) <6BDD43E4-A4B1-379E-9ED5-
8C713653DFF2> /usr/lib/libstdc++.6.dylib
    0x7fff94a73000 -        0x7fff94a7afff  libcopyfile.dylib (85.1.0 - compatibility 1.0.0) <0AB51EE2-E914-358C-AC19-
47BC024BDAE7> /usr/lib/system/libcopyfile.dylib
```

```
  0x7fff94abc000 -     0x7fff94afeff7  libcommonCrypto.dylib (55010.0.0 - compatibility 1.0.0) <BB770C22-8C57-365A-
8716-4A3C36AE7BFB> /usr/lib/system/libcommonCrypto.dylib
  0x7fff95709000 -     0x7fff95714ff7  libc++abi.dylib (14.0.0 - compatibility 1.0.0) <8FF3D766-D678-36F6-84AC-
423C878E6D14> /usr/lib/libc++abi.dylib
  0x7fff95880000 -     0x7fff95889ff7  libsystem_notify.dylib (80.1.0 - compatibility 1.0.0) <A4D651E3-D1C6-3934-
AD49-7A104FD14596> /usr/lib/system/libsystem_notify.dylib
  0x7fff95fe7000 -     0x7fff96014fe7  libSystem.B.dylib (159.1.0 - compatibility 1.0.0) <7BEBB139-50BB-3112-947A-
F4AA168F991C> /usr/lib/libSystem.B.dylib
  0x7fff960fa000 -     0x7fff96100ff7  libunwind.dylib (30.0.0 - compatibility 1.0.0) <1E9C6C8C-CBE8-3F4B-A5B5-
E03E3AB53231> /usr/lib/system/libunwind.dylib
  0x7fff96693000 -     0x7fff96698fff  libcache.dylib (47.0.0 - compatibility 1.0.0) <1571C3AB-BCB2-38CD-B3B2-
C5FC3F927C6A> /usr/lib/system/libcache.dylib

External Modification Summary:
  Calls made by other processes targeting this process:
    task_for_pid: 0
    thread_create: 0
    thread_set_state: 0
  Calls made by this process:
    task_for_pid: 0
    thread_create: 0
    thread_set_state: 0
  Calls made by all processes on this machine:
    task_for_pid: 3722
    thread_create: 0
    thread_set_state: 0

VM Region Summary:
ReadOnly portion of Libraries: Total=50.7M resident=50.7M(100%) swapped_out_or_unallocated=0K(0%)
Writable regions: Total=39.9M written=26.8M(67%) resident=43.2M(108%) swapped_out=0K(0%)
unallocated=16777216.0T(44088103534592%)

REGION TYPE                   VIRTUAL
===========                   =======
MALLOC                          2244K
Stack                           66.6M
__DATA                           504K
__LINKEDIT                      47.7M
__TEXT                          2996K
shared memory                     12K
===========                   =======
TOTAL                          119.9M
```

2.   Load a core dump core.2281, App11 executable and list all threads:

$ gdb -c ~/Documents/AMCDA-Dumps/core.2281 -e ~/Documents/AMCDA-Dumps/Apps/App11/Build/Products/Release/App11

```
GNU gdb 6.3.50-20050815 (Apple version gdb-1820) (Sat Jun 16 02:40:11 UTC 2012)
Copyright 2004 Free Software Foundation, Inc.
GDB is free software, covered by the GNU General Public License, and you are
welcome to change it and/or distribute copies of it under certain conditions.
Type "show copying" to see the conditions.
There is absolutely no warranty for GDB.  Type "show warranty" for details.
This GDB was configured as "x86_64-apple-darwin".Reading symbols for shared libraries ... done

Reading symbols for shared libraries . done
Reading symbols for shared libraries .......................... done
#0  0x00007fff8ed7de42 in __semwait_signal ()
```

```
(gdb) info threads
   6 0x00007fff8ed7de42 in __semwait_signal ()
   5 0x00007fff8ed7dbf2 in __psynch_mutexwait ()
   4 0x00007fff8ed7de42 in __semwait_signal ()
   3 0x00007fff8ed7dbf2 in __psynch_mutexwait ()
   2 0x00007fff8ed7de42 in __semwait_signal ()
 * 1 0x00007fff8ed7de42 in __semwait_signal ()
```

3.   Check thread 5 and its waiting code:

```
(gdb) thread 5
[Switching to thread 5 (core thread 4)]
0x00007fff8ed7dbf2 in __psynch_mutexwait ()

(gdb) bt
#0  0x00007fff8ed7dbf2 in __psynch_mutexwait ()
#1  0x00007fff89a281a1 in pthread_mutex_lock ()
#2  0x0000000105051873 in procB ()
#3  0x00000001050519c9 in bar_four ()
#4  0x00000001050519d9 in foo_four ()
#5  0x00000001050519f1 in thread_four ()
#6  0x00007fff89a298bf in _pthread_start ()
#7  0x00007fff89a2cb75 in thread_start ()

(gdb) disassemble procB
Dump of assembler code for function _Z5procBv:
0x0000000105051850 <_Z5procBv+0>:    push   %rbp
0x0000000105051851 <_Z5procBv+1>:    mov    %rsp,%rbp
0x0000000105051854 <_Z5procBv+4>:    sub    $0x20,%rsp
0x0000000105051858 <_Z5procBv+8>:    lea    0x899(%rip),%rdi      # 0x1050520f8 <mutexB>
0x000000010505185f <_Z5procBv+15>:   callq  0x105051bb0 <dyld_stub_pthread_mutex_lock>
0x0000000105051864 <_Z5procBv+20>:   lea    0x84d(%rip),%rdi      # 0x1050520b8 <mutexA>
0x000000010505186b <_Z5procBv+27>:   mov    %eax,-0x4(%rbp)
0x000000010505186e <_Z5procBv+30>:   callq  0x105051bb0 <dyld_stub_pthread_mutex_lock>
0x0000000105051873 <_Z5procBv+35>:   mov    $0x1e,%edi
0x0000000105051878 <_Z5procBv+40>:   mov    %eax,-0x8(%rbp)
0x000000010505187b <_Z5procBv+43>:   callq  0x105051bbc <dyld_stub_sleep>
0x0000000105051880 <_Z5procBv+48>:   lea    0x831(%rip),%rdi      # 0x1050520b8 <mutexA>
0x0000000105051887 <_Z5procBv+55>:   mov    %eax,-0xc(%rbp)
0x000000010505188a <_Z5procBv+58>:   callq  0x105051bb0 <dyld_stub_pthread_mutex_lock>
0x000000010505188f <_Z5procBv+63>:   lea    0x862(%rip),%rdi      # 0x1050520f8 <mutexB>
0x0000000105051896 <_Z5procBv+70>:   mov    %eax,-0x10(%rbp)
0x0000000105051899 <_Z5procBv+73>:   callq  0x105051bb0 <dyld_stub_pthread_mutex_lock>
0x000000010505189e <_Z5procBv+78>:   mov    %eax,-0x14(%rbp)
0x00000001050518a1 <_Z5procBv+81>:   add    $0x20,%rsp
0x00000001050518a5 <_Z5procBv+85>:   pop    %rbp
0x00000001050518a6 <_Z5procBv+86>:   retq
0x00000001050518a7 <_Z5procBv+87>:   nopw   0x0(%rax,%rax,1)
End of assembler dump.
```

Note: we see the thread owns mutexB but is waiting for mutexA.

4.   Check thread 3 and its waiting code:

```
(gdb) thread 3
[Switching to thread 3 (core thread 2)]
0x00007fff8ed7dbf2 in __psynch_mutexwait ()

 (gdb) bt
#0  0x00007fff8ed7dbf2 in __psynch_mutexwait ()
#1  0x00007fff89a281a1 in pthread_mutex_lock ()
#2  0x0000000105051833 in procA ()
#3  0x0000000105051919 in bar_two ()
#4  0x0000000105051929 in foo_two ()
#5  0x0000000105051941 in thread_two ()
#6  0x00007fff89a298bf in _pthread_start ()
#7  0x00007fff89a2cb75 in thread_start ()

(gdb) disassemble procA
Dump of assembler code for function _Z5procAv:
0x00000001050517c0 <_Z5procAv+0>:    push   %rbp
0x00000001050517c1 <_Z5procAv+1>:    mov    %rsp,%rbp
0x00000001050517c4 <_Z5procAv+4>:    sub    $0x30,%rsp
0x00000001050517c8 <_Z5procAv+8>:    lea    0x8e9(%rip),%rdi        # 0x1050520b8 <mutexA>
0x00000001050517cf <_Z5procAv+15>:   callq  0x105051bb0 <dyld_stub_pthread_mutex_lock>
0x00000001050517d4 <_Z5procAv+20>:   mov    %eax,-0x10(%rbp)
0x00000001050517d7 <_Z5procAv+23>:   jmpq   0x1050517dc <_Z5procAv+28>
0x00000001050517dc <_Z5procAv+28>:   callq  0x105051780 <_Z5procCv>
0x00000001050517e1 <_Z5procAv+33>:   jmpq   0x1050517e6 <_Z5procAv+38>
0x00000001050517e6 <_Z5procAv+38>:   lea    0x8cb(%rip),%rdi        # 0x1050520b8 <mutexA>
0x00000001050517ed <_Z5procAv+45>:   callq  0x105051bb6 <dyld_stub_pthread_mutex_unlock>
0x00000001050517f2 <_Z5procAv+50>:   mov    %eax,-0x14(%rbp)
0x00000001050517f5 <_Z5procAv+53>:   jmpq   0x1050517fa <_Z5procAv+58>
0x00000001050517fa <_Z5procAv+58>:   jmpq   0x10505181a <_Z5procAv+90>
0x00000001050517ff <_Z5procAv+63>:   mov    %edx,%ecx
0x0000000105051801 <_Z5procAv+65>:   mov    %rax,-0x8(%rbp)
0x0000000105051805 <_Z5procAv+69>:   mov    %ecx,-0xc(%rbp)
0x0000000105051808 <_Z5procAv+72>:   mov    -0x8(%rbp),%rdi
0x000000010505180c <_Z5procAv+76>:   callq  0x105051b8c <dyld_stub___cxa_begin_catch>
0x0000000105051811 <_Z5procAv+81>:   mov    %rax,-0x20(%rbp)
0x0000000105051815 <_Z5procAv+85>:   callq  0x105051b92 <dyld_stub___cxa_end_catch>
0x000000010505181a <_Z5procAv+90>:   mov    $0x14,%edi
0x000000010505181f <_Z5procAv+95>:   callq  0x105051bbc <dyld_stub_sleep>
0x0000000105051824 <_Z5procAv+100>:  lea    0x8cd(%rip),%rdi        # 0x1050520f8 <mutexB>
0x000000010505182b <_Z5procAv+107>:  mov    %eax,-0x24(%rbp)
0x000000010505182e <_Z5procAv+110>:  callq  0x105051bb0 <dyld_stub_pthread_mutex_lock>
0x0000000105051833 <_Z5procAv+115>:  lea    0x8be(%rip),%rdi        # 0x1050520f8 <mutexB>
0x000000010505183a <_Z5procAv+122>:  mov    %eax,-0x28(%rbp)
0x000000010505183d <_Z5procAv+125>:  callq  0x105051bb6 <dyld_stub_pthread_mutex_unlock>
0x0000000105051842 <_Z5procAv+130>:  mov    %eax,-0x2c(%rbp)
0x0000000105051845 <_Z5procAv+133>:  add    $0x30,%rsp
0x0000000105051849 <_Z5procAv+137>:  pop    %rbp
0x000000010505184a <_Z5procAv+138>:  retq
0x000000010505184b <_Z5procAv+139>:  nopl   0x0(%rax,%rax,1)
End of assembler dump.
```

Note: we see that the thread is waiting for mutexB and possibly owns mutexA.

5. We notice catch function calls and check if they were called:

```
(gdb) x/50a $rsp-400
0x105303cb8: 0x7fff64c686bd        0x105303d60
0x105303cc8: 0x105304000  0x10505308d
0x105303cd8: 0x105053138  0x105052058
0x105303ce8: 0x10505309f  0x10505308d
0x105303cf8: 0x1    0x105303d90
0x105303d08: 0x7fff64c689cd        0x10505308d
0x105303d18: 0x0    0x7fff64c7865c
0x105303d28: 0x7fff8dd8b5c0 <_Z21dyldGlobalLockReleasev>   0x7fff9570f3d6 <__cxa_end_catch>
0x105303d38: 0x10505308d  0x1017fff64c80001
0x105303d48: 0x7fff64c86110        0x7fff64c8cd80
0x105303d58: 0x105053138  0x7fff64c8e330
0x105303d68: 0x39   0x1303
0x105303d78: 0x7fff8ed7bd71 <mach_msg+73>      0x0
0x105303d88: 0x105051930 <_Z10thread_twoPv>    0x300000018
0x105303d98: 0x105303e30  0x1303
0x105303da8: 0x105304000  0x105303e78
0x105303db8: 0x105051930 <_Z10thread_twoPv>    0x105303e20
0x105303dc8: 0x7fff8ed6884f <clock_get_time+76>       0x7ff500000000
0x105303dd8: 0x2c00001200 0x105303e00
0x105303de8: 0x7fff899e11ed <cthread_set_errno_self+14>    0x105303e68
0x105303df8: 0x105303e78  0x105303e50
0x105303e08: 0x7fff8ed7f01d <cerror+33>0x105303e28
0x105303e18: 0x105303e78  0x105303e50
0x105303e28: 0x1050520f8 <mutexB>        0x105052110 <mutexB+24>
0x105303e38: 0x105051930 <_Z10thread_twoPv>    0x105303e90
```

Exercise A11 (LLDB)

- **Goal:** Learn how to identify synchronization wait chains, deadlocks, hidden and handled exceptions

- **Patterns:** Wait Chains, Deadlock, Execution Residue, Handled Exception

- \AMCDA-Dumps\Exercise-A11-LLDB.pdf

Exercise A11 (LLDB)

Goal: Learn how to identify synchronization wait chains, deadlocks, hidden and handled exceptions

Patterns: Wait Chains, Deadlock, Execution Residue, Handled Exception

1.   Identify possible wait chain and deadlock in the diagnostic report App11_2281.crash:

```
Process:        App11 [2281]
Path:           /Users/USER/Documents/*/App11
Identifier:     App11
Version:        ??? (???)                    .
Code Type:      X86-64 (Native)
Parent Process: bash [223]

Date/Time:      2012-07-29 18:58:31.916 +0100
OS Version:     Mac OS X 10.7.4 (11E53)
Report Version: 9

Crashed Thread: 0  Dispatch queue: com.apple.main-thread

Exception Type:  EXC_CRASH (SIGABRT)
Exception Codes: 0x0000000000000000, 0x0000000000000000

Thread 0 Crashed:: Dispatch queue: com.apple.main-thread
0   libsystem_kernel.dylib          0x00007fff8ed7de42 __semwait_signal + 10
1   libsystem_c.dylib               0x00007fff899dfdea nanosleep + 164
2   libsystem_c.dylib               0x00007fff899dfc2c sleep + 61
3   libsystem_c.dylib               0x00007fff899dfc08 sleep + 25
4   App11                           0x0000000105051b75 main + 261
5   App11                           0x0000000105051774 start + 52

Thread 1:
0   libsystem_kernel.dylib          0x00007fff8ed7de42 __semwait_signal + 10
1   libsystem_c.dylib               0x00007fff899dfdea nanosleep + 164
2   libsystem_c.dylib               0x00007fff899dfc2c sleep + 61
3   libsystem_c.dylib               0x00007fff899dfc08 sleep + 25
4   App11                           0x00000001050518c2 bar_one() + 18
5   App11                           0x00000001050518d9 foo_one() + 9
6   App11                           0x00000001050518f1 thread_one(void*) + 17
7   libsystem_c.dylib               0x00007fff89a298bf _pthread_start + 335
8   libsystem_c.dylib               0x00007fff89a2cb75 thread_start + 13

Thread 2:
0   libsystem_kernel.dylib          0x00007fff8ed7dbf2 __psynch_mutexwait + 10
1   libsystem_c.dylib               0x00007fff89a281a1 pthread_mutex_lock + 545
2   App11                           0x0000000105051833 procA() + 115
3   App11                           0x0000000105051919 bar_two() + 9
4   App11                           0x0000000105051929 foo_two() + 9
5   App11                           0x0000000105051941 thread_two(void*) + 17
6   libsystem_c.dylib               0x00007fff89a298bf _pthread_start + 335
7   libsystem_c.dylib               0x00007fff89a2cb75 thread_start + 13

Thread 3:
0   libsystem_kernel.dylib          0x00007fff8ed7de42 __semwait_signal + 10
1   libsystem_c.dylib               0x00007fff899dfdea nanosleep + 164
2   libsystem_c.dylib               0x00007fff899dfc2c sleep + 61
3   libsystem_c.dylib               0x00007fff899dfc08 sleep + 25
4   App11                           0x0000000105051972 bar_three() + 18
5   App11                           0x0000000105051989 foo_three() + 9
6   App11                           0x00000001050519a1 thread_three(void*) + 17
7   libsystem_c.dylib               0x00007fff89a298bf _pthread_start + 335
8   libsystem_c.dylib               0x00007fff89a2cb75 thread_start + 13
```

```
Thread 4:
0   libsystem_kernel.dylib              0x00007fff8ed7dbf2 __psynch_mutexwait + 10
1   libsystem_c.dylib                   0x00007fff89a281a1 pthread_mutex_lock + 545
2   App11                               0x0000000105051873 procB() + 35
3   App11                               0x00000001050519c9 bar_four() + 9
4   App11                               0x00000001050519d9 foo_four() + 9
5   App11                               0x00000001050519f1 thread_four(void*) + 17
6   libsystem_c.dylib                   0x00007fff89a298bf _pthread_start + 335
7   libsystem_c.dylib                   0x00007fff89a2cb75 thread_start + 13

Thread 5:
0   libsystem_kernel.dylib              0x00007fff8ed7de42 __semwait_signal + 10
1   libsystem_c.dylib                   0x00007fff899dfdea nanosleep + 164
2   libsystem_c.dylib                   0x00007fff899dfc2c sleep + 61
3   libsystem_c.dylib                   0x00007fff899dfc08 sleep + 25
4   App11                               0x0000000105051a22 bar_five() + 18
5   App11                               0x0000000105051a39 foo_five() + 9
6   App11                               0x0000000105051a51 thread_five(void*) + 17
7   libsystem_c.dylib                   0x00007fff89a298bf _pthread_start + 335
8   libsystem_c.dylib                   0x00007fff89a2cb75 thread_start + 13

Thread 0 crashed with X86 Thread State (64-bit):
  rax: 0x0000000000000004  rbx: 0x00007fff64c50a08  rcx: 0x00007fff64c509c8  rdx: 0x0000000000000001
  rdi: 0x0000000000000c03  rsi: 0x0000000000000000  rbp: 0x00007fff64c509f0  rsp: 0x00007fff64c509c8
   r8: 0x000000007ffffffff   r9: 0x0000000000000000  r10: 0x0000000000000001  r11: 0xffffff80002da8d0
  r12: 0x0000000000000000  r13: 0x0000000000000000  r14: 0x00007fff64c50a18  r15: 0x0000000000000000
  rip: 0x00007fff8ed7de42  rfl: 0x0000000000000247  cr2: 0x000000010548e880
Logical CPU: 0

Binary Images:
       0x105051000 -        0x105051fff +App11 (??? - ???) <A6D8D8F4-D61C-3295-A579-D55006FBA826>
/Users/USER/Documents/*/App11
    0x7fff64c51000 -     0x7fff64c85baf  dyld (195.6 - ???) <0CD1B35B-A28F-32DA-B72E-452EAD609613> /usr/lib/dyld
    0x7fff89663000 -     0x7fff89680fff  libxpc.dylib (77.19.0 - compatibility 1.0.0) <9F57891B-D7EF-3050-BEDD-
21E7C6668248> /usr/lib/system/libxpc.dylib
    0x7fff899d9000 -     0x7fff899daff7  libsystem_blocks.dylib (53.0.0 - compatibility 1.0.0) <8BCA214A-8992-34B2-
A8B9-B74DEACA1869> /usr/lib/system/libsystem_blocks.dylib
    0x7fff899db000 -     0x7fff89ab8fef  libsystem_c.dylib (763.13.0 - compatibility 1.0.0) <41B43515-2806-3FBC-ACF1-
A16F35B7E290> /usr/lib/system/libsystem_c.dylib
    0x7fff89c93000 -     0x7fff89ca1fff  libdispatch.dylib (187.9.0 - compatibility 1.0.0) <1D5BE322-A9B9-3BCE-8FAC-
076FB07CF54A> /usr/lib/system/libdispatch.dylib
    0x7fff8a261000 -     0x7fff8a262fff  libunc.dylib (24.0.0 - compatibility 1.0.0) <337960EE-0A85-3DD0-A760-
7134CF4C0AFF> /usr/lib/system/libunc.dylib
    0x7fff8a754000 -     0x7fff8a755ff7  libremovefile.dylib (21.1.0 - compatibility 1.0.0) <739E6C83-AA52-3C6C-A680-
B37FE2888A04> /usr/lib/system/libremovefile.dylib
    0x7fff8dd85000 -     0x7fff8dd89fff  libmathCommon.A.dylib (2026.0.0 - compatibility 1.0.0) <FF83AFF7-42B2-306E-
90AF-D539C51A4542> /usr/lib/system/libmathCommon.A.dylib
    0x7fff8dd8a000 -     0x7fff8dd8efff  libdyld.dylib (195.5.0 - compatibility 1.0.0) <380C3F44-0CA7-3514-8080-
46D1C9DF4FCD> /usr/lib/system/libdyld.dylib
    0x7fff8e3b1000 -     0x7fff8e3b2ff7  libsystem_sandbox.dylib (??? - ???) <96D38E74-F18F-3CCB-A20B-E8E3ADC4E166>
/usr/lib/system/libsystem_sandbox.dylib
    0x7fff8ed60000 -     0x7fff8ed66fff  libmacho.dylib (800.0.0 - compatibility 1.0.0) <165514D7-1BFA-38EF-A151-
676DCD21FB64> /usr/lib/system/libmacho.dylib
    0x7fff8ed67000 -     0x7fff8ed87fff  libsystem_kernel.dylib (1699.26.8 - compatibility 1.0.0) <1DDC0B0F-DB2A-34D6-
895D-E5B2B5618946> /usr/lib/system/libsystem_kernel.dylib
    0x7fff8ef1d000 -     0x7fff8ef25fff  libsystem_dnssd.dylib (??? - ???) <D9BB1F87-A42B-3CBC-9DC2-FC07FCEF0016>
/usr/lib/system/libsystem_dnssd.dylib
    0x7fff8fa97000 -     0x7fff8fad2fff  libsystem_info.dylib (??? - ???) <35F90252-2AE1-32C5-8D34-782C614D9639>
/usr/lib/system/libsystem_info.dylib
    0x7fff8feb9000 -     0x7fff8febbfff  libquarantine.dylib (36.6.0 - compatibility 1.0.0) <0EBF714B-4B69-3E1F-9A7D-
6BBC2AACB310> /usr/lib/system/libquarantine.dylib
    0x7fff90025000 -     0x7fff90025fff  libkeymgr.dylib (23.0.0 - compatibility 1.0.0) <61EFED6A-A407-301E-B454-
CD18314F0075> /usr/lib/system/libkeymgr.dylib
    0x7fff9004e000 -     0x7fff90053fff  libcompiler_rt.dylib (6.0.0 - compatibility 1.0.0) <98ECD5F6-E85C-32A5-98CD-
8911230CB66A> /usr/lib/system/libcompiler_rt.dylib
    0x7fff9098b000 -     0x7fff9098cfff  libdnsinfo.dylib (395.11.0 - compatibility 1.0.0) <853BAAA5-270F-3FDC-B025-
D448DB72E1C3> /usr/lib/system/libdnsinfo.dylib
    0x7fff91199000 -     0x7fff9119eff7  libsystem_network.dylib (??? - ???) <5DE7024E-1D2D-34A2-80F4-08326331A75B>
/usr/lib/system/libsystem_network.dylib
    0x7fff91c14000 -     0x7fff91c1eff7  liblaunch.dylib (392.38.0 - compatibility 1.0.0) <6ECB7F19-B384-32C1-8652-
2463C1CF4815> /usr/lib/system/liblaunch.dylib
    0x7fff92744000 -     0x7fff927b7fff  libstdc++.6.dylib (52.0.0 - compatibility 7.0.0) <6BDD43E4-A4B1-379E-9ED5-
8C713653DFF2> /usr/lib/libstdc++.6.dylib
    0x7fff94a73000 -     0x7fff94a7afff  libcopyfile.dylib (85.1.0 - compatibility 1.0.0) <0AB51EE2-E914-358C-AC19-
47BC024BDAE7> /usr/lib/system/libcopyfile.dylib
```

```
       0x7fff94abc000 -     0x7fff94afeff7  libcommonCrypto.dylib (55010.0.0 - compatibility 1.0.0) <BB770C22-8C57-365A-
8716-4A3C36AE7BFB> /usr/lib/system/libcommonCrypto.dylib
       0x7fff95709000 -     0x7fff95714ff7  libc++abi.dylib (14.0.0 - compatibility 1.0.0) <8FF3D766-D678-36F6-84AC-
423C878E6D14> /usr/lib/libc++abi.dylib
       0x7fff95880000 -     0x7fff95889ff7  libsystem_notify.dylib (80.1.0 - compatibility 1.0.0) <A4D651E3-D1C6-3934-
AD49-7A104FD14596> /usr/lib/system/libsystem_notify.dylib
       0x7fff95fe7000 -     0x7fff96014fe7  libSystem.B.dylib (159.1.0 - compatibility 1.0.0) <7BEBB139-50BB-3112-947A-
F4AA168F991C> /usr/lib/libSystem.B.dylib
       0x7fff960fa000 -     0x7fff96100ff7  libunwind.dylib (30.0.0 - compatibility 1.0.0) <1E9C6C8C-CBE8-3F4B-A5B5-
E03E3AB53231> /usr/lib/system/libunwind.dylib
       0x7fff96693000 -     0x7fff96698fff  libcache.dylib (47.0.0 - compatibility 1.0.0) <1571C3AB-BCB2-38CD-B3B2-
C5FC3F927C6A> /usr/lib/system/libcache.dylib

External Modification Summary:
  Calls made by other processes targeting this process:
    task_for_pid: 0
    thread_create: 0
    thread_set_state: 0
  Calls made by this process:
    task_for_pid: 0
    thread_create: 0
    thread_set_state: 0
  Calls made by all processes on this machine:
    task_for_pid: 3722
    thread_create: 0
    thread_set_state: 0

VM Region Summary:
ReadOnly portion of Libraries: Total=50.7M resident=50.7M(100%) swapped_out_or_unallocated=0K(0%)
Writable regions: Total=39.9M written=26.8M(67%) resident=43.2M(108%) swapped_out=0K(0%)
unallocated=16777216.0T(44088103534592%)

REGION TYPE              VIRTUAL
===========              =======
MALLOC                    2244K
Stack                     66.6M
__DATA                     504K
__LINKEDIT                47.7M
__TEXT                    2996K
shared memory               12K
===========              =======
TOTAL                    119.9M
```

Note: We see core threads #2 and #4 blocked waiting for a mutex lock.

2.   Load a core dump core.2281, App11 executable and list all threads:

$ lldb -c ~/Documents/AMCDA-Dumps/core.2281 -f ~/Documents/AMCDA-Dumps/Apps/App11/Build/Products/Release/App11

error: core.2281 is a corrupt mach-o file: load command 45 LC_SEGMENT_64 has a fileoff +
filesize (0x161b7000) that extends beyond the end of the file (0x161b5000), the segment will be
truncated
Core file '/Users/DumpAnalysis/Documents/AMCDA-Dumps/core.2281' (x86_64) was loaded.
Process 0 stopped
* thread #1: tid = 0x0000, 0x00007fff8ed7de42 libsystem_kernel.dylib`__semwait_signal + 10,
stop reason = signal SIGSTOP
    frame #0: 0x00007fff8ed7de42 libsystem_kernel.dylib`__semwait_signal + 10
libsystem_kernel.dylib`__semwait_signal + 10:
-> 0x7fff8ed7de42: jae   0x7fff8ed7de49   ; __semwait_signal + 17
   0x7fff8ed7de44: jmpq   0x7fff8ed7effc   ; cerror
   0x7fff8ed7de49: ret
   0x7fff8ed7de4a: nop

```
    thread #2: tid = 0x0001, 0x00007fff8ed7de42 libsystem_kernel.dylib`__semwait_signal + 10,
stop reason = signal SIGSTOP
        frame #0: 0x00007fff8ed7de42 libsystem_kernel.dylib`__semwait_signal + 10
libsystem_kernel.dylib`__semwait_signal + 10:
-> 0x7fff8ed7de42:  jae     0x7fff8ed7de49              ; __semwait_signal + 17
   0x7fff8ed7de44:  jmpq    0x7fff8ed7effc              ; cerror
   0x7fff8ed7de49:  ret
   0x7fff8ed7de4a:  nop
    thread #3: tid = 0x0002, 0x00007fff8ed7dbf2 libsystem_kernel.dylib`__psynch_mutexwait + 10,
stop reason = signal SIGSTOP
        frame #0: 0x00007fff8ed7dbf2 libsystem_kernel.dylib`__psynch_mutexwait + 10
libsystem_kernel.dylib`__psynch_mutexwait + 10:
-> 0x7fff8ed7dbf2:  jae     0x7fff8ed7dbf9              ; __psynch_mutexwait + 17
   0x7fff8ed7dbf4:  jmpq    0x7fff8ed7effc              ; cerror
   0x7fff8ed7dbf9:  ret
   0x7fff8ed7dbfa:  nop
    thread #4: tid = 0x0003, 0x00007fff8ed7de42 libsystem_kernel.dylib`__semwait_signal + 10,
stop reason = signal SIGSTOP
        frame #0: 0x00007fff8ed7de42 libsystem_kernel.dylib`__semwait_signal + 10
libsystem_kernel.dylib`__semwait_signal + 10:
-> 0x7fff8ed7de42:  jae     0x7fff8ed7de49              ; __semwait_signal + 17
   0x7fff8ed7de44:  jmpq    0x7fff8ed7effc              ; cerror
   0x7fff8ed7de49:  ret
   0x7fff8ed7de4a:  nop
    thread #5: tid = 0x0004, 0x00007fff8ed7dbf2 libsystem_kernel.dylib`__psynch_mutexwait + 10,
stop reason = signal SIGSTOP
        frame #0: 0x00007fff8ed7dbf2 libsystem_kernel.dylib`__psynch_mutexwait + 10
libsystem_kernel.dylib`__psynch_mutexwait + 10:
-> 0x7fff8ed7dbf2:  jae     0x7fff8ed7dbf9              ; __psynch_mutexwait + 17
   0x7fff8ed7dbf4:  jmpq    0x7fff8ed7effc              ; cerror
   0x7fff8ed7dbf9:  ret
   0x7fff8ed7dbfa:  nop
    thread #6: tid = 0x0005, 0x00007fff8ed7de42 libsystem_kernel.dylib`__semwait_signal + 10,
stop reason = signal SIGSTOP
        frame #0: 0x00007fff8ed7de42 libsystem_kernel.dylib`__semwait_signal + 10
libsystem_kernel.dylib`__semwait_signal + 10:
-> 0x7fff8ed7de42:  jae     0x7fff8ed7de49              ; __semwait_signal + 17
   0x7fff8ed7de44:  jmpq    0x7fff8ed7effc              ; cerror
   0x7fff8ed7de49:  ret
   0x7fff8ed7de4a:  nop
```

2.   Check thread 5 (core thread #4) and its waiting code:

```
(lldb) thread select 5
* thread #5: tid = 0x0004, 0x00007fff8ed7dbf2 libsystem_kernel.dylib`__psynch_mutexwait + 10,
stop reason = signal SIGSTOP
        frame #0: 0x00007fff8ed7dbf2 libsystem_kernel.dylib`__psynch_mutexwait + 10
libsystem_kernel.dylib`__psynch_mutexwait + 10:
-> 0x7fff8ed7dbf2:  jae     0x7fff8ed7dbf9              ; __psynch_mutexwait + 17
   0x7fff8ed7dbf4:  jmpq    0x7fff8ed7effc              ; cerror
   0x7fff8ed7dbf9:  ret
```

```
        0x7fff8ed7dbfa:  nop

(lldb) bt
* thread #5: tid = 0x0004, 0x00007fff8ed7dbf2 libsystem_kernel.dylib`__psynch_mutexwait + 10,
stop reason = signal SIGSTOP
    frame #0: 0x00007fff8ed7dbf2 libsystem_kernel.dylib`__psynch_mutexwait + 10
    frame #1: 0x00007fff89a281a1 libsystem_c.dylib`pthread_mutex_lock + 545
    frame #2: 0x0000000105051873 App11`procB() + 35
    frame #3: 0x00000001050519c9 App11`bar_four() + 9
    frame #4: 0x00000001050519d9 App11`foo_four() + 9
    frame #5: 0x00000001050519f1 App11`thread_four(void*) + 17
    frame #6: 0x00007fff89a298bf libsystem_c.dylib`_pthread_start + 335
    frame #7: 0x00007fff89a2cb75 libsystem_c.dylib`thread_start + 13


(lldb) di -n procB
App11`procB():
    0x105051850:  pushq   %rbp
    0x105051851:  movq    %rsp, %rbp
    0x105051854:  subq    $32, %rsp
    0x105051858:  leaq    2201(%rip), %rdi
    0x10505185f:  callq   0x105051bb0             ; symbol stub for: pthread_mutex_lock
    0x105051864:  leaq    2125(%rip), %rdi        ; mutexA
    0x10505186b:  movl    %eax, -4(%rbp)
    0x10505186e:  callq   0x105051bb0             ; symbol stub for: pthread_mutex_lock
    0x105051873:  movl    $30, %edi
    0x105051878:  movl    %eax, -8(%rbp)
    0x10505187b:  callq   0x105051bbc             ; symbol stub for: sleep
    0x105051880:  leaq    2097(%rip), %rdi        ; mutexA
    0x105051887:  movl    %eax, -12(%rbp)
    0x10505188a:  callq   0x105051bb0             ; symbol stub for: pthread_mutex_lock
    0x10505188f:  leaq    2146(%rip), %rdi
    0x105051896:  movl    %eax, -16(%rbp)
    0x105051899:  callq   0x105051bb0             ; symbol stub for: pthread_mutex_lock
    0x10505189e:  movl    %eax, -20(%rbp)
    0x1050518a1:  addq    $32, %rsp
    0x1050518a5:  popq    %rbp
    0x1050518a6:  ret
    0x1050518a7:  nopw    (%rax,%rax)
```

Note: We see that mutexA was passed to the second mutex lock call but we don't see in annotated disassembly what mutex was passed to the first call. We see the thread owns mutex ??? but is waiting for mutexA. Let's find out the mutex address

```
(lldb)  print/x 0x10505185f+2201
(long) $0 = 0x00000001050520f8
```

3.   Check thread 3 and its waiting code:

```
(lldb) thread select 3
* thread #3: tid = 0x0002, 0x00007fff8ed7dbf2 libsystem_kernel.dylib`__psynch_mutexwait + 10,
stop reason = signal SIGSTOP
    frame #0: 0x00007fff8ed7dbf2 libsystem_kernel.dylib`__psynch_mutexwait + 10
libsystem_kernel.dylib`__psynch_mutexwait + 10:
-> 0x7fff8ed7dbf2:  jae    0x7fff8ed7dbf9          ; __psynch_mutexwait + 17
   0x7fff8ed7dbf4:  jmpq   0x7fff8ed7effc          ; cerror
   0x7fff8ed7dbf9:  ret
   0x7fff8ed7dbfa:  nop
```

```
(lldb) bt
* thread #3: tid = 0x0002, 0x00007fff8ed7dbf2 libsystem_kernel.dylib`__psynch_mutexwait + 10,
stop reason = signal SIGSTOP
    frame #0: 0x00007fff8ed7dbf2 libsystem_kernel.dylib`__psynch_mutexwait + 10
    frame #1: 0x00007fff89a281a1 libsystem_c.dylib`pthread_mutex_lock + 545
    frame #2: 0x0000000105051833 App11`procA() + 115
    frame #3: 0x0000000105051919 App11`bar_two() + 9
    frame #4: 0x0000000105051929 App11`foo_two() + 9
    frame #5: 0x0000000105051941 App11`thread_two(void*) + 17
    frame #6: 0x00007fff89a298bf libsystem_c.dylib`_pthread_start + 335
    frame #7: 0x00007fff89a2cb75 libsystem_c.dylib`thread_start + 13
```

```
(lldb) di -n procA
App11`procA():
   0x1050517c0:  pushq  %rbp
   0x1050517c1:  movq   %rsp, %rbp
   0x1050517c4:  subq   $48, %rsp
   0x1050517c8:  leaq   2281(%rip), %rdi         ; mutexA
   0x1050517cf:  callq  0x105051bb0              ; symbol stub for: pthread_mutex_lock
   0x1050517d4:  movl   %eax, -16(%rbp)
   0x1050517d7:  jmpq   0x1050517dc              ; procA() + 28
   0x1050517dc:  callq  0x105051780              ; procC()
   0x1050517e1:  jmpq   0x1050517e6              ; procA() + 38
   0x1050517e6:  leaq   2251(%rip), %rdi         ; mutexA
   0x1050517ed:  callq  0x105051bb6              ; symbol stub for: pthread_mutex_unlock
   0x1050517f2:  movl   %eax, -20(%rbp)
   0x1050517f5:  jmpq   0x1050517fa              ; procA() + 58
   0x1050517fa:  jmpq   0x10505181a              ; procA() + 90
   0x1050517ff:  movl   %edx, %ecx
   0x105051801:  movq   %rax, -8(%rbp)
   0x105051805:  movl   %ecx, -12(%rbp)
   0x105051808:  movq   -8(%rbp), %rdi
   0x10505180c:  callq  0x105051b8c              ; symbol stub for: __cxa_begin_catch
   0x105051811:  movq   %rax, -32(%rbp)
   0x105051815:  callq  0x105051b92              ; symbol stub for: __cxa_end_catch
   0x10505181a:  movl   $20, %edi
   0x10505181f:  callq  0x105051bbc              ; symbol stub for: sleep
   0x105051824:  leaq   2253(%rip), %rdi
   0x10505182b:  movl   %eax, -36(%rbp)
   0x10505182e:  callq  0x105051bb0              ; symbol stub for: pthread_mutex_lock
   0x105051833:  leaq   2238(%rip), %rdi
   0x10505183a:  movl   %eax, -40(%rbp)
   0x10505183d:  callq  0x105051bb6              ; symbol stub for: pthread_mutex_unlock
   0x105051842:  movl   %eax, -44(%rbp)
   0x105051845:  addq   $48, %rsp
   0x105051849:  popq   %rbp
   0x10505184a:  ret
   0x10505184b:  nopl   (%rax,%rax)
```

Note: We see that the thread is waiting for mutex **???** and possibly owns mutexA. Let's now check if both **???** mutexes reeferenced in procA and procB.

```
(lldb) print/x 0x10505182b+2253
(long) $1 = 0x00000001050520f8
```

Note: We see that both refernces to **???** mutexes have the same address 0x00000001050520f8. Let's name it mutexB. One thread running through procB owns mutexB and is waiting for mutexA. The other thread running through procA owns mutexA (not released because of some exception) and is waiting for mutexB. We have an example of a deadlock here.

4.   We notice catch function calls and check if they were called (execution residue):

```
(lldb) x/50a $rsp-400
0x105303cb8: 0x00007fff64c686bd
dyld`ImageLoaderMachOCompressed::resolve(ImageLoader::LinkContext const&, char const*, unsigned
char, int, ImageLoader const**, ImageLoaderMachOCompressed::LastLookup*, bool) + 329
0x105303cc0: 0x0000000105303d60 -> 0x00007fff64c8e330 dyld`initialPoolContent + 7680
0x105303cc8: 0x0000000105304000
0x105303cd0: 0x000000010505308d
0x105303cd8: 0x0000000105053138
0x105303ce0: 0x0000000105052058  (void *)0x00007fff9570f3d6: __cxa_end_catch
0x105303ce8: 0x000000010505309f
0x105303cf0: 0x000000010505308d
0x105303cf8: 0x0000000000000001
0x105303d00: 0x0000000105303d90
0x105303d08: 0x00007fff64c689cd dyld`ImageLoaderMachOCompressed::doBindFastLazySymbol(unsigned
int, ImageLoader::LinkContext const&, void (*)(), void (*)()) + 703
0x105303d10: 0x000000010505308d
0x105303d18: 0x0000000000000000
0x105303d20: 0x00007fff64c7865c "lazy "
0x105303d28: 0x00007fff8dd8b5c0 libdyld.dylib`dyldGlobalLockRelease()
0x105303d30: 0x00007fff9570f3d6 libc++abi.dylib`__cxa_end_catch
0x105303d38: 0x000000010505308d
0x105303d40: 0x01017fff64c80001
0x105303d48: 0x00007fff64c86110 dyld::gLinkContext
0x105303d50: 0x00007fff64c8cd80 dyld`initialPoolContent + 2128
0x105303d58: 0x0000000105053138
0x105303d60: 0x00007fff64c8e330 dyld`initialPoolContent + 7680
0x105303d68: 0x0000000000000039
0x105303d70: 0x0000000000001303
0x105303d78: 0x00007fff8ed7bd71 libsystem_kernel.dylib`mach_msg + 73
0x105303d80: 0x0000000000000000
0x105303d88: 0x0000000105051930 App11`thread_two(void*)
0x105303d90: 0x0000000300000018
0x105303d98: 0x0000000105303e30 -> 0x0000000105052110
0x105303da0: 0x0000000000001303
0x105303da8: 0x0000000105304000
0x105303db0: 0x0000000105303e78
0x105303db8: 0x0000000105051930 App11`thread_two(void*)
0x105303dc0: 0x0000000105303e20
0x105303dc8: 0x00007fff8ed6884f libsystem_kernel.dylib`clock_get_time + 76
0x105303dd0: 0x00007ff500000000
0x105303dd8: 0x0000002c00001200
0x105303de0: 0x0000000105303e00
0x105303de8: 0x00007fff899e11ed libsystem_c.dylib`cthread_set_errno_self + 14
0x105303df0: 0x0000000105303e68
0x105303df8: 0x0000000105303e78
```

```
0x105303e00: 0x0000000105303e50
0x105303e08: 0x00007fff8ed7f01d libsystem_kernel.dylib`cerror + 33
0x105303e10: 0x0000000105303e28 -> 0x00000001050520f8
0x105303e18: 0x0000000105303e78
0x105303e20: 0x0000000105303e50
0x105303e28: 0x00000001050520f8
0x105303e30: 0x0000000105052110
0x105303e38: 0x0000000105051930 App11`thread_two(void*)
0x105303e40: 0x0000000105303e90
```

Exercise A12 (GDB)

- **Goal:** Learn how to dump memory for post-processing, get the list of functions and module variables, load symbols, inspect arguments and local variables

- **Patterns:** Module Variable

- \AMCDA-Dumps\Exercise-A12-GDB.pdf

Exercise A12 (GDB)

Goal: Learn how to dump memory for post-processing, get the list of functions and module variables, load symbols, inspect arguments and local variables

Patterns: Module Variable

1.   Load a core dump core.2281 and App11 executable:

```
$ gdb -c ~/Documents/AMCDA-Dumps/core.2281 -e ~/Documents/AMCDA-
Dumps/Apps/App11/Build/Products/Release/App11
GNU gdb 6.3.50-20050815 (Apple version gdb-1820) (Sat Jun 16 02:40:11 UTC 2012)
Copyright 2004 Free Software Foundation, Inc.
GDB is free software, covered by the GNU General Public License, and you are
welcome to change it and/or distribute copies of it under certain conditions.
Type "show copying" to see the conditions.
There is absolutely no warranty for GDB.  Type "show warranty" for details.
This GDB was configured as "x86_64-apple-darwin".Reading symbols for shared libraries ... done

Reading symbols for shared libraries . done
Reading symbols for shared libraries ......................... done
#0  0x00007fff8ed7de42 in __semwait_signal ()
```

2.   Check the current thread stack trace:

```
(gdb) bt
#0  0x00007fff8ed7de42 in __semwait_signal ()
#1  0x00007fff899dfdea in nanosleep ()
#2  0x00007fff899dfc2c in sleep ()
#3  0x00007fff899dfc08 in sleep ()
#4  0x0000000105051b75 in main ()
```

3.   Disable automatic symbol location:

```
(gdb) show locate-dsym
Locate dSYM files using the DebugSymbols framework is on.

(gdb) set locate-dsym 0

(gdb) show locate-dsym
Locate dSYM files using the DebugSymbols framework is off.
```

4.   Open Symbols.zip in Finder (it should automatically unzip itself) and then check stack trace again:

```
(gdb) bt
#0  0x00007fff8ed7de42 in __semwait_signal ()
#1  0x00007fff899dfdea in nanosleep ()
#2  0x00007fff899dfc2c in sleep ()
#3  0x00007fff899dfc08 in sleep ()
#4  0x0000000105051b75 in main ()
```

5.   Find the code section for main:

```
(gdb) maintenance info sections
Exec file:
    `/Users/DumpAnalysis/Documents/AMCDA-Dumps/Apps/App11/Build/Products/Release/App11', file type mach-o-le.
    0x0000000000000000->0x0000000000000000 at 0x00000000: LC_SEGMENT.__PAGEZERO ALLOC LOAD CODE HAS_CONTENTS
    0x0000000100000000->0x0000000100001000 at 0x00000000: LC_SEGMENT.__TEXT ALLOC LOAD CODE HAS_CONTENTS
    0x0000000100000740->0x0000000100000b85 at 0x00000740: LC_SEGMENT.__TEXT.__text ALLOC LOAD READONLY CODE HAS_CONTENTS
    0x0000000100000b86->0x0000000100000bc2 at 0x00000b86: LC_SEGMENT.__TEXT.__stubs ALLOC LOAD CODE HAS_CONTENTS
    0x0000000100000bc4->0x0000000100000c38 at 0x00000bc4: LC_SEGMENT.__TEXT.__stub_helper ALLOC LOAD CODE HAS_CONTENTS
    0x0000000100000c38->0x0000000100000c60 at 0x00000c38: LC_SEGMENT.__TEXT.__gcc_except_tab ALLOC LOAD CODE HAS_CONTENTS
    0x0000000100000c60->0x0000000100000cc8 at 0x00000c60: LC_SEGMENT.__TEXT.__unwind_info ALLOC LOAD CODE HAS_CONTENTS
    0x0000000100000cc8->0x0000000100001000 at 0x00000cc8: LC_SEGMENT.__TEXT.__eh_frame ALLOC LOAD CODE HAS_CONTENTS
    0x0000000100001000->0x0000000100002000 at 0x00001000: LC_SEGMENT.__DATA ALLOC LOAD CODE HAS_CONTENTS
    0x0000000100001000->0x0000000100001028 at 0x00001000: LC_SEGMENT.__DATA.__program_vars ALLOC LOAD CODE HAS_CONTENTS
    0x0000000100001028->0x0000000100001038 at 0x00001028: LC_SEGMENT.__DATA.__nl_symbol_ptr ALLOC LOAD CODE HAS_CONTENTS
    0x0000000100001038->0x0000000100001048 at 0x00001038: LC_SEGMENT.__DATA.__got ALLOC LOAD CODE HAS_CONTENTS
    0x0000000100001048->0x0000000100001098 at 0x00001048: LC_SEGMENT.__DATA.__la_symbol_ptr ALLOC LOAD CODE HAS_CONTENTS
    0x0000000100001098->0x0000000100001138 at 0x00001098: LC_SEGMENT.__DATA.__common ALLOC
    0x0000000100002000->0x00000001000026f8 at 0x00002000: LC_SEGMENT.__LINKEDIT ALLOC LOAD CODE HAS_CONTENTS
    0x0000000000000000->0x0000000000000290 at 0x000021b8: LC_SYMTAB.stabs HAS_CONTENTS
    0x0000000000000000->0x0000000000000250 at 0x000024a8: LC_SYMTAB.stabstr HAS_CONTENTS
    0x0000000000000000->0x0000000000000160 at 0x000021b8: LC_DYSYMTAB.localstabs HAS_CONTENTS
    0x0000000000000000->0x0000000000000130 at 0x00002318: LC_DYSYMTAB.nonlocalstabs HAS_CONTENTS
    0x0000000000000000->0x0000000000000018 at 0x00000550: LC_LOAD_DYLINKER HAS_CONTENTS
    0x0000000000000000->0x00000000000000a8 at 0x000005a0: LC_THREAD.x86_THREAD_STATE64.0 HAS_CONTENTS
    0x0000000000000000->0x0000000000000030 at 0x00000650: LC_LOAD_DYLIB HAS_CONTENTS
    0x0000000000000000->0x0000000000000030 at 0x00000688: LC_LOAD_DYLIB HAS_CONTENTS
Core file:
    `/Users/DumpAnalysis/Documents/AMCDA-Dumps/core.2281', file type mach-o-le.
    0x0000000105051000->0x0000000105052000 at 0x00002000: LC_SEGMENT. ALLOC LOAD CODE HAS_CONTENTS
    0x0000000105052000->0x0000000105053000 at 0x00003000: LC_SEGMENT. ALLOC LOAD CODE HAS_CONTENTS
    0x0000000105053000->0x0000000105054000 at 0x00004000: LC_SEGMENT. ALLOC LOAD CODE HAS_CONTENTS
    0x0000000105054000->0x0000000105055000 at 0x00005000: LC_SEGMENT. ALLOC LOAD CODE HAS_CONTENTS
    0x0000000105055000->0x0000000105056000 at 0x00006000: LC_SEGMENT. ALLOC LOAD CODE HAS_CONTENTS
    0x0000000105056000->0x0000000105057000 at 0x00007000: LC_SEGMENT. ALLOC LOAD CODE HAS_CONTENTS
    0x0000000105057000->0x000000010506c000 at 0x00008000: LC_SEGMENT. ALLOC LOAD CODE HAS_CONTENTS
    0x000000010506c000->0x000000010506d000 at 0x0001d000: LC_SEGMENT. ALLOC LOAD CODE HAS_CONTENTS
    0x000000010506d000->0x000000010506e000 at 0x0001e000: LC_SEGMENT. ALLOC LOAD CODE HAS_CONTENTS
    0x000000010506e000->0x0000000105083000 at 0x0001f000: LC_SEGMENT. ALLOC LOAD CODE HAS_CONTENTS
    0x0000000105083000->0x0000000105084000 at 0x00034000: LC_SEGMENT. ALLOC LOAD CODE HAS_CONTENTS
    0x0000000105084000->0x0000000105085000 at 0x00035000: LC_SEGMENT. ALLOC LOAD CODE HAS_CONTENTS
    0x0000000105100000->0x0000000105200000 at 0x00036000: LC_SEGMENT. ALLOC LOAD CODE HAS_CONTENTS
---Type <return> to continue, or q <return> to quit---
    0x0000000105200000->0x0000000105201000 at 0x00136000: LC_SEGMENT. ALLOC LOAD CODE HAS_CONTENTS
    0x0000000105201000->0x0000000105283000 at 0x00137000: LC_SEGMENT. ALLOC LOAD CODE HAS_CONTENTS
    0x0000000105283000->0x0000000105284000 at 0x001b9000: LC_SEGMENT. ALLOC LOAD CODE HAS_CONTENTS
    0x0000000105284000->0x0000000105306000 at 0x001ba000: LC_SEGMENT. ALLOC LOAD CODE HAS_CONTENTS
    0x0000000105306000->0x0000000105307000 at 0x0023c000: LC_SEGMENT. ALLOC LOAD CODE HAS_CONTENTS
    0x0000000105307000->0x0000000105389000 at 0x0023d000: LC_SEGMENT. ALLOC LOAD CODE HAS_CONTENTS
    0x0000000105389000->0x000000010538a000 at 0x002bf000: LC_SEGMENT. ALLOC LOAD CODE HAS_CONTENTS
    0x000000010538a000->0x000000010540c000 at 0x002c0000: LC_SEGMENT. ALLOC LOAD CODE HAS_CONTENTS
    0x000000010540c000->0x000000010540d000 at 0x00342000: LC_SEGMENT. ALLOC LOAD CODE HAS_CONTENTS
    0x000000010540d000->0x000000010548f000 at 0x00343000: LC_SEGMENT. ALLOC LOAD CODE HAS_CONTENTS
    0x00007ff538c00000->0x00007ff538d00000 at 0x003c5000: LC_SEGMENT. ALLOC LOAD CODE HAS_CONTENTS
    0x00007fff60c51000->0x00007fff64451000 at 0x004c5000: LC_SEGMENT. ALLOC LOAD CODE HAS_CONTENTS
    0x00007fff64451000->0x00007fff64c51000 at 0x03cc5000: LC_SEGMENT. ALLOC LOAD CODE HAS_CONTENTS
    0x00007fff64c51000->0x00007fff64c86000 at 0x044c5000: LC_SEGMENT. ALLOC LOAD CODE HAS_CONTENTS
    0x00007fff64c86000->0x00007fff64c88000 at 0x044fa000: LC_SEGMENT. ALLOC LOAD CODE HAS_CONTENTS
    0x00007fff64c88000->0x00007fff64cc2000 at 0x044fc000: LC_SEGMENT. ALLOC LOAD CODE HAS_CONTENTS
    0x00007fff64cc2000->0x00007fff64cd5000 at 0x04536000: LC_SEGMENT. ALLOC LOAD CODE HAS_CONTENTS
    0x00007fff79629000->0x00007fff79800000 at 0x04549000: LC_SEGMENT. ALLOC LOAD CODE HAS_CONTENTS
    0x00007fff79800000->0x00007fff79a00000 at 0x04720000: LC_SEGMENT. ALLOC LOAD CODE HAS_CONTENTS
    0x00007fff79a00000->0x00007fff79c00000 at 0x04920000: LC_SEGMENT. ALLOC LOAD CODE HAS_CONTENTS
    0x00007fff79c00000->0x00007fff79e00000 at 0x04b20000: LC_SEGMENT. ALLOC LOAD CODE HAS_CONTENTS
    0x00007fff79e00000->0x00007fff7a000000 at 0x04d20000: LC_SEGMENT. ALLOC LOAD CODE HAS_CONTENTS
    0x00007fff7a000000->0x00007fff7a200000 at 0x04f20000: LC_SEGMENT. ALLOC LOAD CODE HAS_CONTENTS
    0x00007fff7a200000->0x00007fff7a400000 at 0x05120000: LC_SEGMENT. ALLOC LOAD CODE HAS_CONTENTS
    0x00007fff7a400000->0x00007fff7a600000 at 0x05320000: LC_SEGMENT. ALLOC LOAD CODE HAS_CONTENTS
    0x00007fff7a600000->0x00007fff7a800000 at 0x05520000: LC_SEGMENT. ALLOC LOAD CODE HAS_CONTENTS
```

```
    0x00007fff7a800000->0x00007fff7aa00000 at 0x05720000: LC_SEGMENT. ALLOC LOAD CODE HAS_CONTENTS
    0x00007fff7aa00000->0x00007fff7ae00000 at 0x05920000: LC_SEGMENT. ALLOC LOAD CODE HAS_CONTENTS
    0x00007fff7ae00000->0x00007fff7b000000 at 0x05d20000: LC_SEGMENT. ALLOC LOAD CODE HAS_CONTENTS
    0x00007fff7b000000->0x00007fff7b11d000 at 0x05f20000: LC_SEGMENT. ALLOC LOAD CODE HAS_CONTENTS
    0x00007fff89629000->0x00007fff96699000 at 0x0603d000: LC_SEGMENT. ALLOC LOAD CODE HAS_CONTENTS
    0x00007fff96699000->0x00007fff997a1000 at 0x130ad000: LC_SEGMENT. ALLOC LOAD CODE HAS_CONTENTS
    0x00007ffffffffe00000->0x00007ffffffffe02000 at 0x161b5000: LC_SEGMENT. ALLOC LOAD CODE HAS_CONTENTS
    0x0000000000000000->0x00000000000000b0 at 0x00000d20: LC_THREAD.x86_THREAD_STATE.0 HAS_CONTENTS
    0x0000000000000000->0x0000000000000214 at 0x00000dd8: LC_THREAD.x86_FLOAT_STATE.0 HAS_CONTENTS
    0x0000000000000000->0x0000000000000018 at 0x00000ff4: LC_THREAD.x86_EXCEPTION_STATE.0 HAS_CONTENTS
    0x0000000000000000->0x00000000000000b0 at 0x0000101c: LC_THREAD.x86_THREAD_STATE.1 HAS_CONTENTS
    0x0000000000000000->0x0000000000000214 at 0x000010d4: LC_THREAD.x86_FLOAT_STATE.1 HAS_CONTENTS
    0x0000000000000000->0x0000000000000018 at 0x000012f0: LC_THREAD.x86_EXCEPTION_STATE.1 HAS_CONTENTS
    0x0000000000000000->0x00000000000000b0 at 0x00001318: LC_THREAD.x86_THREAD_STATE.2 HAS_CONTENTS
---Type <return> to continue, or q <return> to quit---
    0x0000000000000000->0x0000000000000214 at 0x000013d0: LC_THREAD.x86_FLOAT_STATE.2 HAS_CONTENTS
    0x0000000000000000->0x0000000000000018 at 0x000015ec: LC_THREAD.x86_EXCEPTION_STATE.2 HAS_CONTENTS
    0x0000000000000000->0x00000000000000b0 at 0x00001614: LC_THREAD.x86_THREAD_STATE.3 HAS_CONTENTS
    0x0000000000000000->0x0000000000000214 at 0x000016cc: LC_THREAD.x86_FLOAT_STATE.3 HAS_CONTENTS
    0x0000000000000000->0x0000000000000018 at 0x000018e8: LC_THREAD.x86_EXCEPTION_STATE.3 HAS_CONTENTS
    0x0000000000000000->0x00000000000000b0 at 0x00001910: LC_THREAD.x86_THREAD_STATE.4 HAS_CONTENTS
    0x0000000000000000->0x0000000000000214 at 0x000019c8: LC_THREAD.x86_FLOAT_STATE.4 HAS_CONTENTS
    0x0000000000000000->0x0000000000000018 at 0x00001be4: LC_THREAD.x86_EXCEPTION_STATE.4 HAS_CONTENTS
    0x0000000000000000->0x00000000000000b0 at 0x00001c0c: LC_THREAD.x86_THREAD_STATE.5 HAS_CONTENTS
    0x0000000000000000->0x0000000000000214 at 0x00001cc4: LC_THREAD.x86_FLOAT_STATE.5 HAS_CONTENTS
    0x0000000000000000->0x0000000000000018 at 0x00001ee0: LC_THREAD.x86_EXCEPTION_STATE.5 HAS_CONTENTS
```

6.   Load a symbol file ~/Documents/AMCDA-Dumps/Symbols/App11.dSYM/Contents/Resources/DWARF/App11 (choose **y** when asked)

```
(gdb) add-symbol-file ~/Documents/AMCDA-Dumps/Symbols/App11.dSYM/Contents/Resources/DWARF/App11
0x0000000105051000
warning: add-symbol-file doesn't work on dSYM files, use "add-dsym" instead.
add symbol table from file "/Users/DumpAnalysis/Documents/AMCDA-
Dumps/Symbols/App11.dSYM/Contents/Resources/DWARF/App11" at
      LC_SEGMENT.__TEXT = 0x105051000
(y or n) y
Reading symbols from /Users/DumpAnalysis/Documents/AMCDA-
Dumps/Symbols/App11.dSYM/Contents/Resources/DWARF/App11...done.
```

7.   The preceding command is useful when you need to force symbols on a particular section. If we just have the corresponding dSYM file we can use this command:

```
(gdb) add-dsym ~/Documents/AMCDA-Dumps/Symbols/App11.dSYM
Added dsym "/Users/DumpAnalysis/Documents/AMCDA-Dumps/Symbols/App11.dSYM" to "[memory object
"/Users/DumpAnalysis/Documents/AMCDA-Dumps/Apps/App11/Build/Products/Release/App11"
at 0x105051000]".
```

8.   List all thread stack traces:

```
(gdb) thread apply all bt

Thread 6 (core thread 5):
#0  0x00007fff8ed7de42 in __semwait_signal ()
#1  0x00007fff899dfdea in nanosleep ()
#2  0x00007fff899dfc2c in sleep ()
#3  0x00007fff899dfc08 in sleep ()
#4  0x0000000105051a22 in bar_five () at /Users/DumpAnalysis/Documents/AMCDA-Dumps/Apps/App11/App11/main.cpp:70
#5  0x0000000105051a39 in foo_five () at /Users/DumpAnalysis/Documents/AMCDA-Dumps/Apps/App11/App11/main.cpp:70
#6  0x0000000105051a51 in thread_five (arg=0x0) at /Users/DumpAnalysis/Documents/AMCDA-
Dumps/Apps/App11/App11/main.cpp:70
#7  0x00007fff89a298bf in _pthread_start ()
#8  0x00007fff89a2cb75 in thread_start ()
```

```
Thread 5 (core thread 4):
#0  0x00007fff8ed7dbf2 in __psynch_mutexwait ()
#1  0x00007fff89a281a1 in pthread_mutex_lock ()
#2  0x0000000105051873 in procB () at /Users/DumpAnalysis/Documents/AMCDA-Dumps/Apps/App11/App11/main.cpp:43
#3  0x00000001050519c9 in bar_four () at /Users/DumpAnalysis/Documents/AMCDA-Dumps/Apps/App11/App11/main.cpp:69
#4  0x00000001050519d9 in foo_four () at /Users/DumpAnalysis/Documents/AMCDA-Dumps/Apps/App11/App11/main.cpp:69
#5  0x00000001050519f1 in thread_four (arg=0x0) at /Users/DumpAnalysis/Documents/AMCDA-
Dumps/Apps/App11/App11/main.cpp:69
#6  0x00007fff89a298bf in _pthread_start ()
#7  0x00007fff89a2cb75 in thread_start ()

Thread 4 (core thread 3):
#0  0x00007fff8ed7de42 in __semwait_signal ()
#1  0x00007fff899dfdea in nanosleep ()
#2  0x00007fff899dfc2c in sleep ()
#3  0x00007fff899dfc08 in sleep ()
#4  0x0000000105051972 in bar_three () at /Users/DumpAnalysis/Documents/AMCDA-Dumps/Apps/App11/App11/main.cpp:68
#5  0x0000000105051989 in foo_three () at /Users/DumpAnalysis/Documents/AMCDA-Dumps/Apps/App11/App11/main.cpp:68
#6  0x00000001050519a1 in thread three (arg=0x0) at /Users/DumpAnalysis/Documents/AMCDA-
Dumps/Apps/App11/App11/main.cpp:68
#7  0x00007fff89a298bf in _pthread_start ()
#8  0x00007fff89a2cb75 in thread_start ()

Thread 3 (core thread 2):
#0  0x00007fff8ed7dbf2 in __psynch_mutexwait ()
#1  0x00007fff89a281a1 in pthread_mutex_lock ()
#2  0x0000000105051833 in procA () at /Users/DumpAnalysis/Documents/AMCDA-Dumps/Apps/App11/App11/main.cpp:36
#3  0x0000000105051919 in bar_two () at /Users/DumpAnalysis/Documents/AMCDA-Dumps/Apps/App11/App11/main.cpp:67
#4  0x0000000105051929 in foo_two () at /Users/DumpAnalysis/Documents/AMCDA-Dumps/Apps/App11/App11/main.cpp:67
#5  0x0000000105051941 in thread_two (arg=0x0) at /Users/DumpAnalysis/Documents/AMCDA-
Dumps/Apps/App11/App11/main.cpp:67
---Type <return> to continue, or q <return> to quit---
#6  0x00007fff89a298bf in _pthread_start ()
#7  0x00007fff89a2cb75 in thread_start ()

Thread 2 (core thread 1):
#0  0x00007fff8ed7de42 in __semwait_signal ()
#1  0x00007fff899dfdea in nanosleep ()
#2  0x00007fff899dfc2c in sleep ()
#3  0x00007fff899dfc08 in sleep ()
#4  0x00000001050518c2 in bar_one () at /Users/DumpAnalysis/Documents/AMCDA-Dumps/Apps/App11/App11/main.cpp:66
#5  0x00000001050518d9 in foo_one () at /Users/DumpAnalysis/Documents/AMCDA-Dumps/Apps/App11/App11/main.cpp:66
#6  0x00000001050518f1 in thread_one (arg=0x0) at /Users/DumpAnalysis/Documents/AMCDA-
Dumps/Apps/App11/App11/main.cpp:66
#7  0x00007fff89a298bf in _pthread_start ()
#8  0x00007fff89a2cb75 in thread_start ()

Thread 1 (core thread 0):
#0  0x00007fff8ed7de42 in __semwait_signal ()
#1  0x00007fff899dfdea in nanosleep ()
#2  0x00007fff899dfc2c in sleep ()
#3  0x00007fff899dfc08 in sleep ()
#4  0x0000000105051b75 in main (argc=1, argv=0x7fff64c50b08)
    at /Users/DumpAnalysis/Documents/AMCDA-Dumps/Apps/App11/App11/main.cpp:86
```

9.   Switch to frame 4 of the current thread and list arguments and locals:

```
(gdb) bt
#0  0x00007fff8ed7de42 in __semwait_signal ()
#1  0x00007fff899dfdea in nanosleep ()
#2  0x00007fff899dfc2c in sleep ()
#3  0x00007fff899dfc08 in sleep ()
#4  0x0000000105051b75 in main (argc=1, argv=0x7fff64c50b08)
    at /Users/DumpAnalysis/Documents/AMCDA-Dumps/Apps/App11/App11/main.cpp:86
```

```
(gdb) frame 4
#4  0x0000000105051b75 in main (argc=1, argv=0x7fff64c50b08)
    at /Users/DumpAnalysis/Documents/AMCDA-Dumps/Apps/App11/App11/main.cpp:86
86          sleep(-1);

(gdb) info args
argc = 1
argv = (const char **) 0x7fff64c50b08

(gdb) info locals
No locals.
```

10.   Examine argv array:

```
(gdb) print argv[0]
$2 = 0x7fff64c50c40 "/Users/DumpAnalysis/Documents/AMCDA-
Dumps/Apps/App11/Build/Products/Release/App11"

(gdb) print *argv@10
$5 = {0x7fff64c50c40 "/Users/DumpAnalysis/Documents/AMCDA-
Dumps/Apps/App11/Build/Products/Release/App11", 0x0,
  0x7fff64c50c92 "TERM_PROGRAM=Apple_Terminal", 0x7fff64c50cae "TERM=xterm-256color",
0x7fff64c50cc2 "SHELL=/bin/bash",
  0x7fff64c50cd2 "TMPDIR=/var/folders/ww/rmtqfhl93yj4213dnl2rqy6w0000gn/T/",
  0x7fff64c50d0b "Apple_PubSub_Socket_Render=/tmp/launch-rYkVmo/Render", 0x7fff64c50d40
"TERM_PROGRAM_VERSION=303.2",
  0x7fff64c50d5b "TERM_SESSION_ID=DF914445-7472-4D90-B23F-C3FE6BF95B89", 0x7fff64c50d90
"USER=DumpAnalysis"}
```

11.   Dump region 0x00007fff64c51000 - 0x00007fff64c86000 to a binary file:

```
(gdb) dump memory ~/Documents/AMCDA-Dumps/mem.raw 0x00007fff64c51000 0x00007fff64c86000
```

12.   Check in Finder and use your favorite application to open it. I use Photoshop to interpret it as a picture:

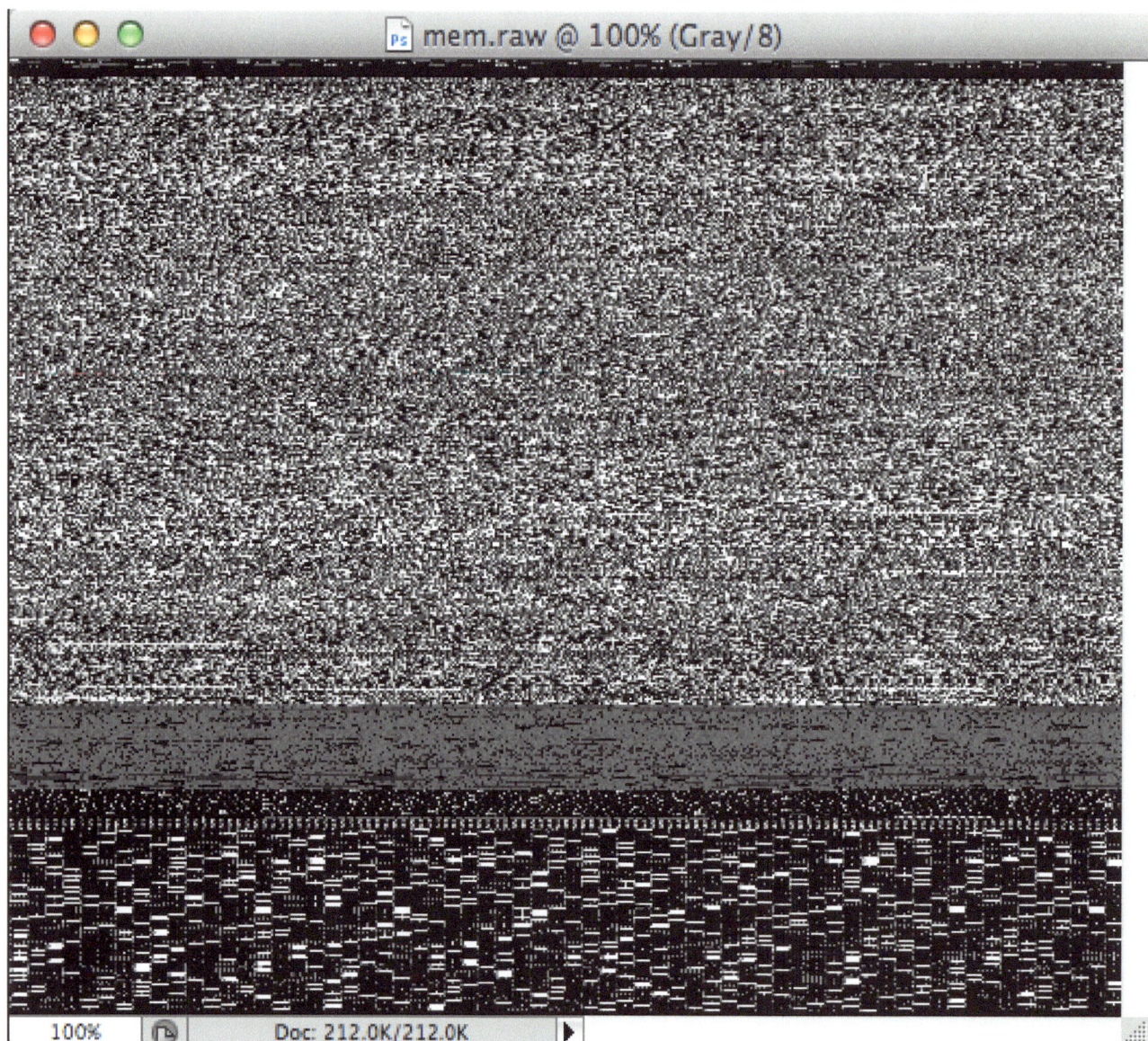

13.   List all functions:

```
(gdb) info functions
All defined functions:

File /Users/DumpAnalysis/Documents/AMCDA-Dumps/Apps/App11/App11/main.cpp:
void bar_five();
void bar_four();
void bar_one();
void bar_three();
void bar_two();
void foo_five();
void foo_four();
void foo_one();
void foo_three();
void foo_two();
int main(int, const char **);
void procA();
void procB();
void procC();
void *thread_five(void*);
void *thread_four(void*);
void *thread_one(void*);
void *thread_three(void*);
void *thread_two(void*);


Non-debugging symbols:
0x00007fff5fc01000  __dyld_stub_binding_helper
0x00007fff5fc01008  __dyld_dyld_func_lookup
0x00007fff5fc01010  __dyld_offset_to_dyld_all_image_infos
0x00007fff5fc01028  __dyld__dyld_start
0x00007fff5fc0106c  __dyld_dyld_fatal_error
0x00007fff5fc0106e  __dyld_ZN13dyldbootstrap5startEPK12macho_headeriPPKclS2_
0x00007fff5fc01354  __dyld_Z30coresymbolication_unload_imageP25CSCppDyldSharedMemoryPagePK11ImageLoader
0x00007fff5fc01412  __dyld_ZN4dyld15findMappedRangeEm
0x00007fff5fc01461  __dyld_ZN4dyldL17setNewProgramVarsERK11ProgramVars
0x00007fff5fc014d8  __dyld_ZN4dyld17getExecutablePathEv
0x00007fff5fc014e5  __dyld_ZN4dyld22mainExecutablePreboundEv
0x00007fff5fc01505  __dyld_ZN4dyld14mainExecutableEv
0x00007fff5fc01512  __dyld_ZN4dyld21findImageByMachHeaderEPK11mach_header
0x00007fff5fc0151c  __dyld_ZN4dyld26findImageContainingAddressEPKv
0x00007fff5fc01526  __dyld_ZN4dyld17clearErrorMessageEv
0x00007fff5fc01533  __dyld_ZN4dyld15getErrorMessageEv
---Type <return> to continue, or q <return> to quit---
0x00007fff5fc01540  __dyld_ZN4dyldL15setErrorStringsEjPKcS1_S1_
0x00007fff5fc01568  __dyld_ZN4dyld24registerUndefinedHandlerEPFvPKcE
0x00007fff5fc01575  __dyld_ZN4dyldL16undefinedHandlerEPKc
0x00007fff5fc0158a  __dyld_ZN4dyldL10setContextEPK12macho_headeriPPKcS5_S5_
0x00007fff5fc01750  __dyld_ZN4dyldL14libraryLocatorEPKcbS1_PKN11ImageLoader10RPathChainE
0x00007fff5fc01793  __dyld_ZN4dyldL19terminationRecorderEP11ImageLoader
0x00007fff5fc017b5  __dyld_ZN4dyld22flatFindExportedSymbolEPKcPPKN11ImageLoader6SymbolEPPKS2_
0x00007fff5fc017cb  __dyld_ZN4dyld27findCoalescedExportedSymbolEPKcPPKN11ImageLoader6SymbolEPPKS2_
0x00007fff5fc017e4  __dyld_ZN4dyld18getCoalescedImagesEPP11ImageLoader
0x00007fff5fc01844  __dyld_ZN4dyldL16getMappedRegionsEPN11ImageLoader12MappedRegionE
0x00007fff5fc01891  __dyld_ZN4dyldL12notifySingleE17dyld_image_statesPK11ImageLoader
0x00007fff5fc01a57  __dyld_ZN4dyldL11notifyBatchE17dyld_image_states
0x00007fff5fc01a65  __dyld_ZN4dyld11removeImageEP11ImageLoader
0x00007fff5fc01d33  __dyld_ZN4dyldL12registerDOFsERKSt6vectorIN11ImageLoader7DOFInfoESaIS2_EE
0x00007fff5fc01f12  __dyld_ZN4dyldL14clearAllDepthsEv
0x00007fff5fc01f37  __dyld_ZN4dyldL10imageCountEv
0x00007fff5fc01f4f  __dyld_ZN4dyld13inSharedCacheEPKc
0x00007fff5fc01f73  __dyld_ZN4dyld13getImageCountEv
0x00007fff5fc01f8b  __dyld_ZN4dyld14forEachImageDoEPFvP11ImageLoaderPvES2_
0x00007fff5fc01fe2  __dyld_ZN4dyld15getIndexedImageEj
0x00007fff5fc0200c  __dyld_ZN4dyld10validImageEPK11ImageLoader
0x00007fff5fc02041  __dyld_ZN4dyld25findImageContainingSymbolEPKv
0x00007fff5fc0208b  __dyld___tcf_0
0x00007fff5fc020a6  __dyld___tcf_1
0x00007fff5fc020c1  __dyld___tcf_2
0x00007fff5fc020dc  __dyld___tcf_3
0x00007fff5fc020f7  __dyld___tcf_4
0x00007fff5fc02112  __dyld___tcf_5
0x00007fff5fc0212d  __dyld___tcf_6
0x00007fff5fc02160  __dyld___tcf_7
0x00007fff5fc02193  __dyld___tcf_8
```

```
0x00007fff5fc021ae    __dyld__ZN4dyldL23_shared_region_check_npEPy
0x00007fff5fc021d3    __dyld__ZN4dyldL20removePathWithPrefixEPPKcS1_
0x00007fff5fc0225a    __dyld__ZN4dyldL18paths_expand_rootsEPPKcS1_S1_
0x00007fff5fc022f5    __dyld__ZN4dyld15setErrorMessageEPKc
0x00007fff5fc0230e    __dyld__ZN4dyldL14parseColonListEPKcS1_
0x00007fff5fc02635    __dyld__ZN4dyldL21appendParsedColonListEPKcS1_PPKS1_
0x00007fff5fc026fd    __dyld__ZN4dyldL11fatFindBestEPK10fat_headerPyS3_
0x00007fff5fc02750    __dyld__ZN4dyld19openSharedCacheFileEv
0x00007fff5fc02801    __dyld__ZN4dyldL29getDylibVersionAndInstallnameEPKcPjPc
---Type <return> to continue, or q <return> to quit---q
Quit
```

14.   List all variables:

```
(gdb) info variables
All defined variables:

File /Users/DumpAnalysis/Documents/AMCDA-Dumps/Apps/App11/App11/main.cpp:
pthread_mutex_t mutexA;
pthread_mutex_t mutexB;

Non-debugging symbols:
0x00007fff5fc35060    __dyld_sDyldInfo.0
0x00007fff5fc35068    __dyld_sDyldInfo.1
0x00007fff5fc35070    __dyld_sDyldInfo.2
0x00007fff5fc35078    __dyld_sDyldInfo.3
0x00007fff5fc35080    __dyld_sDyldInfo.4
0x00007fff5fc35088    __dyld_sDyldTextEnd
0x00007fff5fc35090    __dyld__task_reply_port
0x00007fff5fc35094    __dyld_mach_task_self_
0x00007fff5fc35098    __dyld___stack_chk_guard
0x00007fff5fc350a0    __dyld__ZN4dyldL23sFrameworkFallbackPathsE
0x00007fff5fc350d0    __dyld__ZN4dyldL21sLibraryFallbackPathsE
0x00007fff5fc350f0    __dyld__ZL11initialPool
0x00007fff5fc35110    __dyld__ZN4dyld12gLinkContextE
0x00007fff5fc35220    __dyld__ZN4dyld17gLibSystemHelpersE
0x00007fff5fc35230    __dyld__ZN4dyldL17sSharedCacheSlideE
0x00007fff5fc35240    __dyld_dyld_shared_cache_ranges
0x00007fff5fc35290    __dyld__ZN11ImageLoader27fgImagesUsedFromSharedCacheE
0x00007fff5fc352a0    __dyld__ZN11ImageLoader19fgInterposingTuplesE
0x00007fff5fc352b8    __dyld__ZN11ImageLoader24fgTotalLoadLibrariesTimeE
0x00007fff5fc352c0    __dyld__ZN11ImageLoader17fgTotalRebaseTimeE
0x00007fff5fc352c8    __dyld__ZN11ImageLoader15fgTotalBindTimeE
0x00007fff5fc352d0    __dyld__ZN11ImageLoader19fgTotalWeakBindTimeE
0x00007fff5fc352d8    __dyld__ZN11ImageLoader10fgTotalDOFE
0x00007fff5fc352e0    __dyld__ZN11ImageLoader15fgTotalInitTimeE
0x00007fff5fc352e8    __dyld__ZN11ImageLoader22fgTotalBytesPreFetchedE
0x00007fff5fc352f0    __dyld__ZN11ImageLoader18fgTotalBytesMappedE
0x00007fff5fc352f8    __dyld__ZN11ImageLoader21fgTotalSegmentsMappedE
0x00007fff5fc352fc    __dyld__ZN11ImageLoader19fgTotalRebaseFixupsE
0x00007fff5fc35300    __dyld__ZN11ImageLoader17fgTotalBindFixupsE
0x00007fff5fc35304    __dyld__ZN11ImageLoader26fgTotalBindSymbolsResolvedE
0x00007fff5fc35308    __dyld__ZN11ImageLoader24fgTotalBindImageSearchesE
0x00007fff5fc3530c    __dyld__ZN11ImageLoader29fgTotalPossibleLazyBindFixupsE
0x00007fff5fc35310    __dyld__ZN11ImageLoader21fgTotalLazyBindFixupsE
---Type <return> to continue, or q <return> to quit---
0x00007fff5fc35314    __dyld__ZN11ImageLoader27fgImagesRequiringCoalescingE
0x00007fff5fc35318    __dyld__ZN11ImageLoader21fgNextPIEDylibAddressE
0x00007fff5fc35320    __dyld__ZN11ImageLoader26fgImagesWithUsedPrebindingE
0x00007fff5fc35324    __dyld__ZN11ImageLoader26fgImagesHasWeakDefinitionsE
0x00007fff5fc35328    __dyld__ZN16ImageLoaderMachO26fgSymbolTableBinarySearchsE
0x00007fff5fc3532c    __dyld__ZN16ImageLoaderMachO19fgSymbolTrieSearchsE
0x00007fff5fc35334    __dyld__ZN11ImageLoader13fgLoadOrdinalE
0x00007fff5fc35348    __dyld__ZN4dyldL9sExecPathE
0x00007fff5fc35358    __dyld__ZN4dyldL25sMainExecutableMachHeaderE
0x00007fff5fc35360    __dyld__ZN4dyldL12sSharedCacheE
0x00007fff5fc35368    __dyld__ZN4dyldL17sUndefinedHandlerE
0x00007fff5fc35370    __dyld__ZN4dyldL10sAllImagesE
0x00007fff5fc35390    __dyld__ZN4dyldL18sAddImageCallbacksE
0x00007fff5fc353b0    __dyld__ZN4dyldL11sImageRootsE
0x00007fff5fc353d0    __dyld__ZN4dyldL29sImageFilesNeedingTerminationE
0x00007fff5fc353f0    __dyld__ZN4dyldL35sImageFilesNeedingDOFUnregistrationE
```

328

```
0x00007fff5fc35410   __dyld__ZN4dyldL21sRemoveImageCallbacksE
0x00007fff5fc35430   __dyld__ZN4dyldL15sSingleHandlersE
0x00007fff5fc354e0   __dyld__ZN4dyldL14sBatchHandlersE
0x00007fff5fc35590   __dyld__ZN4dyldL15sMainExecutableE
0x00007fff5fc355a0   __dyld__ZN4dyldL4sEnvE
0x00007fff5fc355f0   __dyld__ZL11sImageInfos
0x00007fff5fc35610   __dyld__ZL11sImageUUIDs
0x00007fff5fc35630   __dyld__ZL17sObjectFileImages
0x00007fff5fc35650   __dyld__ZN11ImageLoader23fgDynamicImageReExportsE
0x00007fff5fc35670   __dyld__ZN4dyldL15sDylibOverridesE
0x00007fff5fc35698   __dyld__ZN4dyldL19sInsertedDylibCountE
0x00007fff5fc356a8   __dyld__ZN4dyldL20sProcessIsRestrictedE
0x00007fff5fc356b0   __dyld__dyld_start_static
0x00007fff5fc356c0   __dyld__ZN4dyldL15sSharedCacheDirE
0x00007fff5fc356d0   __dyld___cxa_terminate_handler
0x00007fff5fc356d8   __dyld___cxa_unexpected_handler
0x00007fff5fc356e0   __dyld__ZL11currentPool
0x00007fff5fc356f0   __dyld__rp_alist
0x00007fff5fc35708   __dyld_rs.2
0x00007fff5fc35810   ::__dyld(long long)
0x00007fff5fc35820   __dyld___pthread_tsd_first
0x00007fff5fc35824   __dyld___pthread_tsd_start
0x00007fff5fc35828   __dyld___pthread_tsd_max
0x00007fff5fc35830   __dyld___pthread_head
---Type <return> to continue, or q <return> to quit---q
Quit
```

15.   List segment info:


```
(gdb) info target
Symbols from "[memory object "/Users/DumpAnalysis/Documents/AMCDA-Dumps/Apps/App11/Build/Products/Release/App11" at
0x105051000]".
Mach-O core dump file:
        /Users/DumpAnalysis/Documents/AMCDA-Dumps/core.2281, file type mach-o-le.
        0x0000000105051000 - 0x0000000105052000 is LC_SEGMENT.
        0x0000000105052000 - 0x0000000105053000 is LC_SEGMENT.
        0x0000000105053000 - 0x0000000105054000 is LC_SEGMENT.
        0x0000000105054000 - 0x0000000105055000 is LC_SEGMENT.
        0x0000000105055000 - 0x0000000105056000 is LC_SEGMENT.
        0x0000000105056000 - 0x0000000105057000 is LC_SEGMENT.
        0x0000000105057000 - 0x000000010506c000 is LC_SEGMENT.
        0x000000010506c000 - 0x000000010506d000 is LC_SEGMENT.
        0x000000010506d000 - 0x000000010506e000 is LC_SEGMENT.
        0x000000010506e000 - 0x0000000105083000 is LC_SEGMENT.
        0x0000000105083000 - 0x0000000105084000 is LC_SEGMENT.
        0x0000000105084000 - 0x0000000105085000 is LC_SEGMENT.
        0x0000000105100000 - 0x0000000105200000 is LC_SEGMENT.
        0x0000000105200000 - 0x0000000105201000 is LC_SEGMENT.
        0x0000000105201000 - 0x0000000105283000 is LC_SEGMENT.
        0x0000000105283000 - 0x0000000105284000 is LC_SEGMENT.
        0x0000000105284000 - 0x0000000105306000 is LC_SEGMENT.
        0x0000000105306000 - 0x0000000105307000 is LC_SEGMENT.
        0x0000000105307000 - 0x0000000105389000 is LC_SEGMENT.
        0x0000000105389000 - 0x000000010538a000 is LC_SEGMENT.
        0x000000010538a000 - 0x000000010540c000 is LC_SEGMENT.
        0x000000010540c000 - 0x000000010540d000 is LC_SEGMENT.
        0x000000010540d000 - 0x000000010548f000 is LC_SEGMENT.
        0x00007ff538c00000 - 0x00007ff538d00000 is LC_SEGMENT.
        0x00007fff60c51000 - 0x00007fff64451000 is LC_SEGMENT.
        0x00007fff64451000 - 0x00007fff64c51000 is LC_SEGMENT.
        0x00007fff64c51000 - 0x00007fff64c86000 is LC_SEGMENT.
        0x00007fff64c86000 - 0x00007fff64c88000 is LC_SEGMENT.
        0x00007fff64c88000 - 0x00007fff64cc2000 is LC_SEGMENT.
        0x00007fff64cc2000 - 0x00007fff64cd5000 is LC_SEGMENT.
        0x00007fff79629000 - 0x00007fff79800000 is LC_SEGMENT.
        0x00007fff79800000 - 0x00007fff79a00000 is LC_SEGMENT.
        0x00007fff79a00000 - 0x00007fff79c00000 is LC_SEGMENT.
        0x00007fff79c00000 - 0x00007fff79e00000 is LC_SEGMENT.
        0x00007fff79e00000 - 0x00007fff7a000000 is LC_SEGMENT.
        0x00007fff7a000000 - 0x00007fff7a200000 is LC_SEGMENT.
        0x00007fff7a200000 - 0x00007fff7a400000 is LC_SEGMENT.
        0x00007fff7a400000 - 0x00007fff7a600000 is LC_SEGMENT.
        0x00007fff7a600000 - 0x00007fff7a800000 is LC_SEGMENT.
```

---Type <return> to continue, or q <return> to quit---
```
        0x00007fff7a800000 - 0x00007fff7aa00000 is LC_SEGMENT.
        0x00007fff7aa00000 - 0x00007fff7ae00000 is LC_SEGMENT.
        0x00007fff7ae00000 - 0x00007fff7b000000 is LC_SEGMENT.
        0x00007fff7b000000 - 0x00007fff7b11d000 is LC_SEGMENT.
        0x00007fff89629000 - 0x00007fff96699000 is LC_SEGMENT.
        0x00007fff96699000 - 0x00007fff997a1000 is LC_SEGMENT.
        0x00007ffffffe00000 - 0x00007ffffffe02000 is LC_SEGMENT.
Mac OS X executable:
        /Users/DumpAnalysis/Documents/AMCDA-Dumps/Apps/App11/Build/Products/Release/App11, file type mach-o-le.
        Entry point: 0x0000000100000740
        0x0000000105051000 - 0x0000000105052000 is LC_SEGMENT.__TEXT in [memory object
"/Users/DumpAnalysis/Documents/AMCDA-Dumps/Apps/App11/Build/Products/Release/App11" at 0x105051000]
        0x0000000105051740 - 0x0000000105051b85 is LC_SEGMENT.__TEXT.__text in [memory object
"/Users/DumpAnalysis/Documents/AMCDA-Dumps/Apps/App11/Build/Products/Release/App11" at 0x105051000]
        0x0000000105051b86 - 0x0000000105051bc2 is LC_SEGMENT.__TEXT.__stubs in [memory object
"/Users/DumpAnalysis/Documents/AMCDA-Dumps/Apps/App11/Build/Products/Release/App11" at 0x105051000]
        0x0000000105051bc4 - 0x0000000105051c38 is LC_SEGMENT.__TEXT.__stub_helper in [memory object
"/Users/DumpAnalysis/Documents/AMCDA-Dumps/Apps/App11/Build/Products/Release/App11" at 0x105051000]
        0x0000000105051c38 - 0x0000000105051c60 is LC_SEGMENT.__TEXT.__gcc_except_tab in [memory object
"/Users/DumpAnalysis/Documents/AMCDA-Dumps/Apps/App11/Build/Products/Release/App11" at 0x105051000]
        0x0000000105051c60 - 0x0000000105051cc8 is LC_SEGMENT.__TEXT.__unwind_info in [memory object
"/Users/DumpAnalysis/Documents/AMCDA-Dumps/Apps/App11/Build/Products/Release/App11" at 0x105051000]
        0x0000000105051cc8 - 0x0000000105052000 is LC_SEGMENT.__TEXT.__eh_frame in [memory object
"/Users/DumpAnalysis/Documents/AMCDA-Dumps/Apps/App11/Build/Products/Release/App11" at 0x105051000]
        0x0000000105052000 - 0x0000000105053000 is LC_SEGMENT.__DATA in [memory object
"/Users/DumpAnalysis/Documents/AMCDA-Dumps/Apps/App11/Build/Products/Release/App11" at 0x105051000]
        0x0000000105052000 - 0x0000000105052028 is LC_SEGMENT.__DATA.__program_vars in [memory object
"/Users/DumpAnalysis/Documents/AMCDA-Dumps/Apps/App11/Build/Products/Release/App11" at 0x105051000]
        0x0000000105052028 - 0x0000000105052038 is LC_SEGMENT.__DATA.__nl_symbol_ptr in [memory object
"/Users/DumpAnalysis/Documents/AMCDA-Dumps/Apps/App11/Build/Products/Release/App11" at 0x105051000]
        0x0000000105052038 - 0x0000000105052048 is LC_SEGMENT.__DATA.__got in [memory object
"/Users/DumpAnalysis/Documents/AMCDA-Dumps/Apps/App11/Build/Products/Release/App11" at 0x105051000]
        0x0000000105052048 - 0x0000000105052098 is LC_SEGMENT.__DATA.__la_symbol_ptr in [memory object
"/Users/DumpAnalysis/Documents/AMCDA-Dumps/Apps/App11/Build/Products/Release/App11" at 0x105051000]
        0x0000000105052098 - 0x0000000105052138 is LC_SEGMENT.__DATA.__common in [memory object
"/Users/DumpAnalysis/Documents/AMCDA-Dumps/Apps/App11/Build/Products/Release/App11" at 0x105051000]
        0x0000000105053000 - 0x00000001050536f8 is LC_SEGMENT.__LINKEDIT in [memory object
"/Users/DumpAnalysis/Documents/AMCDA-Dumps/Apps/App11/Build/Products/Release/App11" at 0x105051000]
        0x00007fff5fc00000 - 0x00007fff5fc35000 is LC_SEGMENT.__TEXT in [memory object "/usr/lib/dyld" at
0x7fff64c51000]
        0x00007fff5fc01000 - 0x00007fff5fc23c9d is LC_SEGMENT.__TEXT.__text in [memory object "/usr/lib/dyld" at
0x7fff64c51000]
        0x00007fff5fc23ca0 - 0x00007fff5fc2877f is LC_SEGMENT.__TEXT.__cstring in [memory object "/usr/lib/dyld" at
0x7fff64c51000]
```
---Type <return> to continue, or q <return> to quit---
```
        0x00007fff5fc28780 - 0x00007fff5fc29d68 is LC_SEGMENT.__TEXT.__gcc_except_tab in [memory object
"/usr/lib/dyld" at 0x7fff64c51000]
        0x00007fff5fc29d68 - 0x00007fff5fc29d80 is LC_SEGMENT.__TEXT.__const in [memory object "/usr/lib/dyld" at
0x7fff64c51000]
        0x00007fff5fc29d80 - 0x00007fff5fc2a144 is LC_SEGMENT.__TEXT.__dof_plockstat in [memory object "/usr/lib/dyld"
at 0x7fff64c51000]
        0x00007fff5fc2a144 - 0x00007fff5fc2aa98 is LC_SEGMENT.__TEXT.__unwind_info in [memory object "/usr/lib/dyld"
at 0x7fff64c51000]
        0x00007fff5fc2aa98 - 0x00007fff5fc34bb0 is LC_SEGMENT.__TEXT.__eh_frame in [memory object "/usr/lib/dyld" at
0x7fff64c51000]
        0x00007fff5fc35000 - 0x00007fff5fc37000 is LC_SEGMENT.__DATA in [memory object "/usr/lib/dyld" at
0x7fff64c51000]
        0x00007fff5fc35000 - 0x00007fff5fc35020 is LC_SEGMENT.__DATA.__got in [memory object "/usr/lib/dyld" at
0x7fff64c51000]
        0x00007fff5fc35020 - 0x00007fff5fc35048 is LC_SEGMENT.__DATA.__mod_init_func in [memory object "/usr/lib/dyld"
at 0x7fff64c51000]
        0x00007fff5fc35060 - 0x00007fff5fc358e8 is LC_SEGMENT.__DATA.__data in [memory object "/usr/lib/dyld" at
0x7fff64c51000]
        0x00007fff5fc35900 - 0x00007fff5fc36d10 is LC_SEGMENT.__DATA.__const in [memory object "/usr/lib/dyld" at
0x7fff64c51000]
        0x00007fff5fc36d10 - 0x00007fff5fc36db0 is LC_SEGMENT.__DATA.__all_image_info in [memory object
"/usr/lib/dyld" at 0x7fff64c51000]
        0x00007fff5fc36db0 - 0x00007fff5fc36de8 is LC_SEGMENT.__DATA.__crash_info in [memory object "/usr/lib/dyld" at
0x7fff64c51000]
        0x00007fff5fc36df0 - 0x00007fff5fc3723c is LC_SEGMENT.__DATA.__common in [memory object "/usr/lib/dyld" at
0x7fff64c51000]
        0x00007fff5fc37240 - 0x00007fff5fc70641 is LC_SEGMENT.__DATA.__bss in [memory object "/usr/lib/dyld" at
0x7fff64c51000]
        0x00007fff5fc71000 - 0x00007fff5fc83e70 is LC_SEGMENT.__LINKEDIT in [memory object "/usr/lib/dyld" at
0x7fff64c51000]
```

```
        0x00007fff92744000 - 0x00007fff927b8000 is LC_SEGMENT.__TEXT in [memory object
"/usr/lib/libstdc++.6.0.9.dylib" at 0x7fff92744000]
        0x00007fff9274511c - 0x00007fff92783910 is LC_SEGMENT.__TEXT.__text in [memory object
"/usr/lib/libstdc++.6.0.9.dylib" at 0x7fff92744000]
        0x00007fff92783910 - 0x00007fff92783ab1 is LC_SEGMENT.__TEXT.__const_coal in [memory object
"/usr/lib/libstdc++.6.0.9.dylib" at 0x7fff92744000]
        0x00007fff92783ab2 - 0x00007fff92783cd4 is LC_SEGMENT.__TEXT.__stubs in [memory object
"/usr/lib/libstdc++.6.0.9.dylib" at 0x7fff92744000]
        0x00007fff92783cd4 - 0x00007fff9278404c is LC_SEGMENT.__TEXT.__stub_helper in [memory object
"/usr/lib/libstdc++.6.0.9.dylib" at 0x7fff92744000]
        0x00007fff9278404c - 0x00007fff9278fcd4 is LC_SEGMENT.__TEXT.__gcc_except_tab in [memory object
"/usr/lib/libstdc++.6.0.9.dylib" at 0x7fff92744000]
        0x00007fff9278fce0 - 0x00007fff92792237 is LC_SEGMENT.__TEXT.__cstring in [memory object
"/usr/lib/libstdc++.6.0.9.dylib" at 0x7fff92744000]
        0x00007fff92792240 - 0x00007fff92792e69 is LC_SEGMENT.__TEXT.__const in [memory object
"/usr/lib/libstdc++.6.0.9.dylib" at 0x7fff92744000]
        0x00007fff92792e69 - 0x00007fff92795639 is LC_SEGMENT.__TEXT.__unwind_info in [memory object
"/usr/lib/libstdc++.6.0.9.dylib" at 0x7fff92744000]
        0x00007fff92795640 - 0x00007fff927b8000 is LC_SEGMENT.__TEXT.__eh_frame in [memory object
"/usr/lib/libstdc++.6.0.9.dylib" at---Type <return> to continue, or q <return> to quit---
 0x7fff92744000]
        0x00007fff7a69a000 - 0x00007fff7a69f000 is LC_SEGMENT.__DATA in [memory object
"/usr/lib/libstdc++.6.0.9.dylib" at 0x7fff92744000]
        0x00007fff7a69a000 - 0x00007fff7a69a3e0 is LC_SEGMENT.__DATA.__got in [memory object
"/usr/lib/libstdc++.6.0.9.dylib" at 0x7fff92744000]
        0x00007fff7a69a3e0 - 0x00007fff7a69a3f0 is LC_SEGMENT.__DATA.__nl_symbol_ptr in [memory object
"/usr/lib/libstdc++.6.0.9.dylib" at 0x7fff92744000]
        0x00007fff7a69a3f0 - 0x00007fff7a69a6c8 is LC_SEGMENT.__DATA.__la_symbol_ptr in [memory object
"/usr/lib/libstdc++.6.0.9.dylib" at 0x7fff92744000]
        0x00007fff7a69a6c8 - 0x00007fff7a69a700 is LC_SEGMENT.__DATA.__mod_init_func in [memory object
"/usr/lib/libstdc++.6.0.9.dylib" at 0x7fff92744000]
        0x00007fff7a69a700 - 0x00007fff7a69d448 is LC_SEGMENT.__DATA.__data in [memory object
"/usr/lib/libstdc++.6.0.9.dylib" at 0x7fff92744000]
        0x00007fff7a69d450 - 0x00007fff7a69ec70 is LC_SEGMENT.__DATA.__const in [memory object
"/usr/lib/libstdc++.6.0.9.dylib" at 0x7fff92744000]
        0x00007fff7a69ec70 - 0x00007fff7a6a0960 is LC_SEGMENT.__DATA.__common in [memory object
"/usr/lib/libstdc++.6.0.9.dylib" at 0x7fff92744000]
        0x00007fff7a6a0960 - 0x00007fff7a6a1e70 is LC_SEGMENT.__DATA.__bss in [memory object
"/usr/lib/libstdc++.6.0.9.dylib" at 0x7fff92744000]
        0x00007fff967f7000 - 0x00007fff99ebc000 is LC_SEGMENT.__LINKEDIT in [memory object
"/usr/lib/libstdc++.6.0.9.dylib" at 0x7fff92744000]
        0x00007fff95fe7000 - 0x00007fff96015000 is LC_SEGMENT.__TEXT in [memory object "/usr/lib/libSystem.B.dylib" at
0x7fff95fe7000]
        0x00007fff95fe7da0 - 0x00007fff95ffb31c is LC_SEGMENT.__TEXT.__text in [memory object
"/usr/lib/libSystem.B.dylib" at 0x7fff95fe7000]
        0x00007fff95ffb31c - 0x00007fff95ffb436 is LC_SEGMENT.__TEXT.__stubs in [memory object
"/usr/lib/libSystem.B.dylib" at 0x7fff95fe7000]
        0x00007fff95ffb438 - 0x00007fff95ffb620 is LC_SEGMENT.__TEXT.__stub_helper in [memory object
"/usr/lib/libSystem.B.dylib" at 0x7fff95fe7000]
        0x00007fff95ffb620 - 0x00007fff95ffb6bc is LC_SEGMENT.__TEXT.__cstring in [memory object
"/usr/lib/libSystem.B.dylib" at 0x7fff95fe7000]
        0x00007fff95ffb6c0 - 0x00007fff96012cc0 is LC_SEGMENT.__TEXT.__const in [memory object
"/usr/lib/libSystem.B.dylib" at 0x7fff95fe7000]
        0x00007fff96012cc0 - 0x00007fff960130c8 is LC_SEGMENT.__TEXT.__unwind_info in [memory object
"/usr/lib/libSystem.B.dylib" at 0x7fff95fe7000]
        0x00007fff960130c8 - 0x00007fff96014fe8 is LC_SEGMENT.__TEXT.__eh_frame in [memory object
"/usr/lib/libSystem.B.dylib" at 0x7fff95fe7000]
        0x00007fff7b06e000 - 0x00007fff7b06f000 is LC_SEGMENT.__DATA in [memory object "/usr/lib/libSystem.B.dylib" at
0x7fff95fe7000]
        0x00007fff7b06e000 - 0x00007fff7b06e028 is LC_SEGMENT.__DATA.__got in [memory object
"/usr/lib/libSystem.B.dylib" at 0x7fff95---Type <return> to continue, or q <return> to quit---
fe7000]
        0x00007fff7b06e028 - 0x00007fff7b06e038 is LC_SEGMENT.__DATA.__nl_symbol_ptr in [memory object
"/usr/lib/libSystem.B.dylib" at 0x7fff95fe7000]
        0x00007fff7b06e038 - 0x00007fff7b06e1b0 is LC_SEGMENT.__DATA.__la_symbol_ptr in [memory object
"/usr/lib/libSystem.B.dylib" at 0x7fff95fe7000]
        0x00007fff7b06e1b0 - 0x00007fff7b06e1b8 is LC_SEGMENT.__DATA.__mod_init_func in [memory object
"/usr/lib/libSystem.B.dylib" at 0x7fff95fe7000]
        0x00007fff7b06e1b8 - 0x00007fff7b06e200 is LC_SEGMENT.__DATA.__data in [memory object
"/usr/lib/libSystem.B.dylib" at 0x7fff95fe7000]
        0x00007fff7b06e200 - 0x00007fff7b06e20c is LC_SEGMENT.__DATA.__common in [memory object
"/usr/lib/libSystem.B.dylib" at 0x7fff95fe7000]
        0x00007fff967f7000 - 0x00007fff99ebc000 is LC_SEGMENT.__LINKEDIT in [memory object
"/usr/lib/libSystem.B.dylib" at 0x7fff95fe7000]
        0x00007fff95709000 - 0x00007fff95715000 is LC_SEGMENT.__TEXT in [memory object "/usr/lib/libc++abi.dylib" at
0x7fff95709000]
```

331

```
        0x00007fff9570a2b4 - 0x00007fff957117bc is LC_SEGMENT.__TEXT.__text in [memory object
"/usr/lib/libc++abi.dylib" at 0x7fff95709000]
        0x00007fff957117bc - 0x00007fff95711882 is LC_SEGMENT.__TEXT.__stubs in [memory object
"/usr/lib/libc++abi.dylib" at 0x7fff95709000]
        0x00007fff95711884 - 0x00007fff957119e0 is LC_SEGMENT.__TEXT.__stub_helper in [memory object
"/usr/lib/libc++abi.dylib" at 0x7fff95709000]
        0x00007fff957119e0 - 0x00007fff9571256a is LC_SEGMENT.__TEXT.__cstring in [memory object
"/usr/lib/libc++abi.dylib" at 0x7fff95709000]
        0x00007fff9571256c - 0x00007fff95712e24 is LC_SEGMENT.__TEXT.__gcc_except_tab in [memory object
"/usr/lib/libc++abi.dylib" at 0x7fff95709000]
        0x00007fff95712e28 - 0x00007fff95712e30 is LC_SEGMENT.__TEXT.__const in [memory object
"/usr/lib/libc++abi.dylib" at 0x7fff95709000]
        0x00007fff95712e30 - 0x00007fff95713138 is LC_SEGMENT.__TEXT.__unwind_info in [memory object
"/usr/lib/libc++abi.dylib" at 0x7fff95709000]
        0x00007fff95713138 - 0x00007fff95714ff8 is LC_SEGMENT.__TEXT.__eh_frame in [memory object
"/usr/lib/libc++abi.dylib" at 0x7fff95709000]
        0x00007fff7af9b000 - 0x00007fff7af9d000 is LC_SEGMENT.__DATA in [memory object "/usr/lib/libc++abi.dylib" at
0x7fff95709000]
        0x00007fff7af9b000 - 0x00007fff7af9b028 is LC_SEGMENT.__DATA.__got in [memory object
"/usr/lib/libc++abi.dylib" at 0x7fff95709000]
        0x00007fff7af9b028 - 0x00007fff7af9b038 is LC_SEGMENT.__DATA.__nl_symbol_ptr in [memory object
"/usr/lib/libc++abi.dylib" at 0x7fff95709000]
        0x00007fff7af9b038 - 0x00007fff7af9b140 is LC_SEGMENT.__DATA.__la_symbol_ptr in [memory object
"/usr/lib/libc++abi.dylib" at 0x7fff95709000]
        0x00007fff7af9b140 - 0x00007fff7af9c678 is LC_SEGMENT.__DATA.__const in [memory object
"/usr/lib/libc++abi.dylib" at 0x7fff95709000]
        0x00007fff7af9c680 - 0x00007fff7af9c6f0 is LC_SEGMENT.__DATA.__data in [memory object
"/usr/lib/libc++abi.dylib" at 0x7fff957---Type <return> to continue, or q <return> to quit---
09000]
        0x00007fff7af9c6f0 - 0x00007fff7af9c728 is LC_SEGMENT.__DATA.__crash_info in [memory object
"/usr/lib/libc++abi.dylib" at 0x7fff95709000]
        0x00007fff7af9c730 - 0x00007fff7af9c998 is LC_SEGMENT.__DATA.__bss in [memory object
"/usr/lib/libc++abi.dylib" at 0x7fff95709000]
        0x00007fff7af9c998 - 0x00007fff7af9c9a0 is LC_SEGMENT.__DATA.__common in [memory object
"/usr/lib/libc++abi.dylib" at 0x7fff95709000]
        0x00007fff967f7000 - 0x00007fff99ebc000 is LC_SEGMENT.__LINKEDIT in [memory object "/usr/lib/libc++abi.dylib"
at 0x7fff95709000]
        0x00007fff96693000 - 0x00007fff96699000 is LC_SEGMENT.__TEXT in [memory object
"/usr/lib/system/libcache.dylib" at 0x7fff96693000]
        0x00007fff96694174 - 0x00007fff96696afe is LC_SEGMENT.__TEXT.__text in [memory object
"/usr/lib/system/libcache.dylib" at 0x7fff96693000]
        0x00007fff96696afe - 0x00007fff96696b88 is LC_SEGMENT.__TEXT.__stubs in [memory object
"/usr/lib/system/libcache.dylib" at 0x7fff96693000]
        0x00007fff96696b88 - 0x00007fff96696c80 is LC_SEGMENT.__TEXT.__stub_helper in [memory object
"/usr/lib/system/libcache.dylib" at 0x7fff96693000]
        0x00007fff96696c80 - 0x00007fff96696df9 is LC_SEGMENT.__TEXT.__cstring in [memory object
"/usr/lib/system/libcache.dylib" at 0x7fff96693000]
        0x00007fff96696df9 - 0x00007fff96698474 is LC_SEGMENT.__TEXT.__dof_cache in [memory object
"/usr/lib/system/libcache.dylib" at 0x7fff96693000]
        0x00007fff96698474 - 0x00007fff96698544 is LC_SEGMENT.__TEXT.__unwind_info in [memory object
"/usr/lib/system/libcache.dylib" at 0x7fff96693000]
        0x00007fff96698548 - 0x00007fff96699000 is LC_SEGMENT.__TEXT.__eh_frame in [memory object
"/usr/lib/system/libcache.dylib" at 0x7fff96693000]
        0x00007fff7b11c000 - 0x00007fff7b11d000 is LC_SEGMENT.__DATA in [memory object
"/usr/lib/system/libcache.dylib" at 0x7fff96693000]
        0x00007fff7b11c000 - 0x00007fff7b11c010 is LC_SEGMENT.__DATA.__nl_symbol_ptr in [memory object
"/usr/lib/system/libcache.dylib" at 0x7fff96693000]
        0x00007fff7b11c010 - 0x00007fff7b11c028 is LC_SEGMENT.__DATA.__got in [memory object
"/usr/lib/system/libcache.dylib" at 0x7fff96693000]
        0x00007fff7b11c028 - 0x00007fff7b11c0e0 is LC_SEGMENT.__DATA.__la_symbol_ptr in [memory object
"/usr/lib/system/libcache.dylib" at 0x7fff96693000]
        0x00007fff7b11c0e0 - 0x00007fff7b11c130 is LC_SEGMENT.__DATA.__data in [memory object
"/usr/lib/system/libcache.dylib" at 0x7fff96693000]
        0x00007fff7b11c130 - 0x00007fff7b11c170 is LC_SEGMENT.__DATA.__const in [memory object
"/usr/lib/system/libcache.dylib" at 0x7fff96693000]
        0x00007fff7b11c170 - 0x00007fff7b11c1c0 is LC_SEGMENT.__DATA.__common in [memory object
"/usr/lib/system/libcache.dylib" at 0x7fff96693000]
        0x00007fff967f7000 - 0x00007fff99ebc000 is LC_SEGMENT.__LINKEDIT in [memory object
"/usr/lib/system/libcache.dylib" at 0x7fff---Type <return> to continue, or q <return> to quit---
96693000]
        0x00007fff94abc000 - 0x00007fff94aff000 is LC_SEGMENT.__TEXT in [memory object
"/usr/lib/system/libcommonCrypto.dylib" at 0x7fff94abc000]
        0x00007fff94abd2a0 - 0x00007fff94ae81c3 is LC_SEGMENT.__TEXT.__text in [memory object
"/usr/lib/system/libcommonCrypto.dylib" at 0x7fff94abc000]
        0x00007fff94ae81c4 - 0x00007fff94ae8242 is LC_SEGMENT.__TEXT.__stubs in [memory object
"/usr/lib/system/libcommonCrypto.dylib" at 0x7fff94abc000]
```

```
        0x00007fff94ae8244 - 0x00007fff94ae8328 is LC_SEGMENT.__TEXT.__stub_helper in [memory object
"/usr/lib/system/libcommonCrypto.dylib" at 0x7fff94abc000]
        0x00007fff94ae8330 - 0x00007fff94af94a8 is LC_SEGMENT.__TEXT.__const in [memory object
"/usr/lib/system/libcommonCrypto.dylib" at 0x7fff94abc000]
        0x00007fff94af94b0 - 0x00007fff94afac86 is LC_SEGMENT.__TEXT.__cstring in [memory object
"/usr/lib/system/libcommonCrypto.dylib" at 0x7fff94abc000]
        0x00007fff94afac86 - 0x00007fff94afaf96 is LC_SEGMENT.__TEXT.__unwind_info in [memory object
"/usr/lib/system/libcommonCrypto.dylib" at 0x7fff94abc000]
        0x00007fff94afaf98 - 0x00007fff94afeff8 is LC_SEGMENT.__TEXT.__eh_frame in [memory object
"/usr/lib/system/libcommonCrypto.dylib" at 0x7fff94abc000]
        0x00007fff7aabb000 - 0x00007fff7aabd000 is LC_SEGMENT.__DATA in [memory object
"/usr/lib/system/libcommonCrypto.dylib" at 0x7fff94abc000]
        0x00007fff7aabb000 - 0x00007fff7aabb038 is LC_SEGMENT.__DATA.__got in [memory object
"/usr/lib/system/libcommonCrypto.dylib" at 0x7fff94abc000]
        0x00007fff7aabb038 - 0x00007fff7aabb048 is LC_SEGMENT.__DATA.__nl_symbol_ptr in [memory object
"/usr/lib/system/libcommonCrypto.dylib" at 0x7fff94abc000]
        0x00007fff7aabb048 - 0x00007fff7aabb0f0 is LC_SEGMENT.__DATA.__la_symbol_ptr in [memory object
"/usr/lib/system/libcommonCrypto.dylib" at 0x7fff94abc000]
        0x00007fff7aabb0f0 - 0x00007fff7aabb2b0 is LC_SEGMENT.__DATA.__data in [memory object
"/usr/lib/system/libcommonCrypto.dylib" at 0x7fff94abc000]
        0x00007fff7aabb2b0 - 0x00007fff7aabcfc8 is LC_SEGMENT.__DATA.__const in [memory object
"/usr/lib/system/libcommonCrypto.dylib" at 0x7fff94abc000]
        0x00007fff7aabcfd0 - 0x00007fff7aac01d8 is LC_SEGMENT.__DATA.__common in [memory object
"/usr/lib/system/libcommonCrypto.dylib" at 0x7fff94abc000]
        0x00007fff7aac01d8 - 0x00007fff7aac01f0 is LC_SEGMENT.__DATA.__bss in [memory object
"/usr/lib/system/libcommonCrypto.dylib" at 0x7fff94abc000]
        0x00007fff967f7000 - 0x00007fff99ebc000 is LC_SEGMENT.__LINKEDIT in [memory object
"/usr/lib/system/libcommonCrypto.dylib" at 0x7fff94abc000]
        0x00007fff9004e000 - 0x00007fff90054000 is LC_SEGMENT.__TEXT in [memory object
"/usr/lib/system/libcompiler_rt.dylib" at 0x7fff9004e000]
        0x00007fff9004ede0 - 0x00007fff90052626 is LC_SEGMENT.__TEXT.__text in [memory object
"/usr/lib/system/libcompiler_rt.dylib" at 0x7fff9004e000]
        0x00007fff90052626 - 0x00007fff90052686 is LC_SEGMENT.__TEXT.__stubs in [memory object
"/usr/lib/system/libcompiler_rt.dylib"---Type <return> to continue, or q <return> to quit---
 at 0x7fff9004e000]
        0x00007fff90052688 - 0x00007fff90052738 is LC_SEGMENT.__TEXT.__stub_helper in [memory object
"/usr/lib/system/libcompiler_rt.dylib" at 0x7fff9004e000]
        0x00007fff90052740 - 0x00007fff90052756 is LC_SEGMENT.__TEXT.__cstring in [memory object
"/usr/lib/system/libcompiler_rt.dylib" at 0x7fff9004e000]
        0x00007fff90052760 - 0x00007fff90052940 is LC_SEGMENT.__TEXT.__const in [memory object
"/usr/lib/system/libcompiler_rt.dylib" at 0x7fff9004e000]
        0x00007fff90052940 - 0x00007fff90052a4c is LC_SEGMENT.__TEXT.__unwind_info in [memory object
"/usr/lib/system/libcompiler_rt.dylib" at 0x7fff9004e000]
        0x00007fff90052a50 - 0x00007fff90054000 is LC_SEGMENT.__TEXT.__eh_frame in [memory object
"/usr/lib/system/libcompiler_rt.dylib" at 0x7fff9004e000]
        0x00007fff7a1d4000 - 0x00007fff7a1d5000 is LC_SEGMENT.__DATA in [memory object
"/usr/lib/system/libcompiler_rt.dylib" at 0x7fff9004e000]
        0x00007fff7a1d4000 - 0x00007fff7a1d4010 is LC_SEGMENT.__DATA.__nl_symbol_ptr in [memory object
"/usr/lib/system/libcompiler_rt.dylib" at 0x7fff9004e000]
        0x00007fff7a1d4010 - 0x00007fff7a1d4090 is LC_SEGMENT.__DATA.__la_symbol_ptr in [memory object
"/usr/lib/system/libcompiler_rt.dylib" at 0x7fff9004e000]
        0x00007fff967f7000 - 0x00007fff99ebc000 is LC_SEGMENT.__LINKEDIT in [memory object
"/usr/lib/system/libcompiler_rt.dylib" at 0x7fff9004e000]
        0x00007fff94a73000 - 0x00007fff94a7b000 is LC_SEGMENT.__TEXT in [memory object
"/usr/lib/system/libcopyfile.dylib" at 0x7fff94a73000]
        0x00007fff94a73e48 - 0x00007fff94a7958c is LC_SEGMENT.__TEXT.__text in [memory object
"/usr/lib/system/libcopyfile.dylib" at 0x7fff94a73000]
        0x00007fff94a7958c - 0x00007fff94a797d2 is LC_SEGMENT.__TEXT.__stubs in [memory object
"/usr/lib/system/libcopyfile.dylib" at 0x7fff94a73000]
        0x00007fff94a797d4 - 0x00007fff94a79bb0 is LC_SEGMENT.__TEXT.__stub_helper in [memory object
"/usr/lib/system/libcopyfile.dylib" at 0x7fff94a73000]
        0x00007fff94a79bb0 - 0x00007fff94a7aafc is LC_SEGMENT.__TEXT.__cstring in [memory object
"/usr/lib/system/libcopyfile.dylib" at 0x7fff94a73000]
        0x00007fff94a7ab00 - 0x00007fff94a7ac3e is LC_SEGMENT.__TEXT.__const in [memory object
"/usr/lib/system/libcopyfile.dylib" at 0x7fff94a73000]
        0x00007fff94a7ac3e - 0x00007fff94a7acb6 is LC_SEGMENT.__TEXT.__unwind_info in [memory object
"/usr/lib/system/libcopyfile.dylib" at 0x7fff94a73000]
        0x00007fff94a7acb8 - 0x00007fff94a7b000 is LC_SEGMENT.__TEXT.__eh_frame in [memory object
"/usr/lib/system/libcopyfile.dylib" at 0x7fff94a73000]
        0x00007fff7aab2000 - 0x00007fff7aab3000 is LC_SEGMENT.__DATA in [memory object
"/usr/lib/system/libcopyfile.dylib" at 0x7fff94a73000]
        0x00007fff7aab2000 - 0x00007fff7aab2010 is LC_SEGMENT.__DATA.__nl_symbol_ptr in [memory object
"/usr/lib/system/libcopyfile.dylib" at 0x7fff94a73000]
        0x00007fff7aab2010 - 0x00007fff7aab2040 is LC_SEGMENT.__DATA.__got in [memory object
"/usr/lib/system/libcopyfile.dylib" at 0---Type <return> to continue, or q <return> to quit---
x7fff94a73000]
```

```
        0x00007fff7aab2040 - 0x00007fff7aab2348 is LC_SEGMENT.__DATA.__la_symbol_ptr in [memory object
"/usr/lib/system/libcopyfile.dylib" at 0x7fff94a73000]
        0x00007fff7aab2350 - 0x00007fff7aab2370 is LC_SEGMENT.__DATA.__data in [memory object
"/usr/lib/system/libcopyfile.dylib" at 0x7fff94a73000]
        0x00007fff7aab2370 - 0x00007fff7aab2390 is LC_SEGMENT.__DATA.__const in [memory object
"/usr/lib/system/libcopyfile.dylib" at 0x7fff94a73000]
        0x00007fff967f7000 - 0x00007fff99ebc000 is LC_SEGMENT.__LINKEDIT in [memory object
"/usr/lib/system/libcopyfile.dylib" at 0x7fff94a73000]
        0x00007fff89c93000 - 0x00007fff89ca2000 is LC_SEGMENT.__TEXT in [memory object
"/usr/lib/system/libdispatch.dylib" at 0x7fff89c93000]
        0x00007fff89c94458 - 0x00007fff89ca08cd is LC_SEGMENT.__TEXT.__text in [memory object
"/usr/lib/system/libdispatch.dylib" at 0x7fff89c93000]
        0x00007fff89ca08ce - 0x00007fff89ca0b0e is LC_SEGMENT.__TEXT.__stubs in [memory object
"/usr/lib/system/libdispatch.dylib" at 0x7fff89c93000]
        0x00007fff89ca0b10 - 0x00007fff89ca0ee0 is LC_SEGMENT.__TEXT.__stub_helper in [memory object
"/usr/lib/system/libdispatch.dylib" at 0x7fff89c93000]
        0x00007fff89ca0ee0 - 0x00007fff89ca1d94 is LC_SEGMENT.__TEXT.__cstring in [memory object
"/usr/lib/system/libdispatch.dylib" at 0x7fff89c93000]
        0x00007fff89ca1da0 - 0x00007fff89ca1fb8 is LC_SEGMENT.__TEXT.__const in [memory object
"/usr/lib/system/libdispatch.dylib" at 0x7fff89c93000]
        0x00007fff89ca1fb8 - 0x00007fff89ca2000 is LC_SEGMENT.__TEXT.__unwind_info in [memory object
"/usr/lib/system/libdispatch.dylib" at 0x7fff89c93000]
        0x00007fff79735000 - 0x00007fff79738000 is LC_SEGMENT.__DATA in [memory object
"/usr/lib/system/libdispatch.dylib" at 0x7fff89c93000]
        0x00007fff79735000 - 0x00007fff79735048 is LC_SEGMENT.__DATA.__got in [memory object
"/usr/lib/system/libdispatch.dylib" at 0x7fff89c93000]
        0x00007fff79735048 - 0x00007fff79735058 is LC_SEGMENT.__DATA.__nl_symbol_ptr in [memory object
"/usr/lib/system/libdispatch.dylib" at 0x7fff89c93000]
        0x00007fff79735058 - 0x00007fff79735358 is LC_SEGMENT.__DATA.__la_symbol_ptr in [memory object
"/usr/lib/system/libdispatch.dylib" at 0x7fff89c93000]
        0x00007fff79735360 - 0x00007fff79735920 is LC_SEGMENT.__DATA.__const in [memory object
"/usr/lib/system/libdispatch.dylib" at 0x7fff89c93000]
        0x00007fff79735940 - 0x00007fff797370c0 is LC_SEGMENT.__DATA.__data in [memory object
"/usr/lib/system/libdispatch.dylib" at 0x7fff89c93000]
        0x00007fff797370c0 - 0x00007fff797370f8 is LC_SEGMENT.__DATA.__crash_info in [memory object
"/usr/lib/system/libdispatch.dylib" at 0x7fff89c93000]
        0x00007fff79737100 - 0x00007fff7973a360 is LC_SEGMENT.__DATA.__bss in [memory object
"/usr/lib/system/libdispatch.dylib" at 0x7fff89c93000]
        0x00007fff7973a360 - 0x00007fff7973a37c is LC_SEGMENT.__DATA.__common in [memory object
"/usr/lib/system/libdispatch.dylib" a---Type <return> to continue, or q <return> to quit---
t 0x7fff89c93000]
        0x00007fff967f7000 - 0x00007fff99ebc000 is LC_SEGMENT.__LINKEDIT in [memory object
"/usr/lib/system/libdispatch.dylib" at 0x7fff89c93000]
        0x00007fff9098b000 - 0x00007fff9098d000 is LC_SEGMENT.__TEXT in [memory object
"/usr/lib/system/libdnsinfo.dylib" at 0x7fff9098b000]
        0x00007fff9098c4a0 - 0x00007fff9098cb60 is LC_SEGMENT.__TEXT.__text in [memory object
"/usr/lib/system/libdnsinfo.dylib" at 0x7fff9098b000]
        0x00007fff9098cb60 - 0x00007fff9098cbd8 is LC_SEGMENT.__TEXT.__stubs in [memory object
"/usr/lib/system/libdnsinfo.dylib" at 0x7fff9098b000]
        0x00007fff9098cbd8 - 0x00007fff9098ccb0 is LC_SEGMENT.__TEXT.__stub_helper in [memory object
"/usr/lib/system/libdnsinfo.dylib" at 0x7fff9098b000]
        0x00007fff9098ccb0 - 0x00007fff9098cdc0 is LC_SEGMENT.__TEXT.__cstring in [memory object
"/usr/lib/system/libdnsinfo.dylib" at 0x7fff9098b000]
        0x00007fff9098cdc0 - 0x00007fff9098cdc8 is LC_SEGMENT.__TEXT.__const in [memory object
"/usr/lib/system/libdnsinfo.dylib" at 0x7fff9098b000]
        0x00007fff9098cdc8 - 0x00007fff9098ce24 is LC_SEGMENT.__TEXT.__unwind_info in [memory object
"/usr/lib/system/libdnsinfo.dylib" at 0x7fff9098b000]
        0x00007fff9098ce28 - 0x00007fff9098d000 is LC_SEGMENT.__TEXT.__eh_frame in [memory object
"/usr/lib/system/libdnsinfo.dylib" at 0x7fff9098b000]
        0x00007fff7a2a4000 - 0x00007fff7a2a5000 is LC_SEGMENT.__DATA in [memory object
"/usr/lib/system/libdnsinfo.dylib" at 0x7fff9098b000]
        0x00007fff7a2a4000 - 0x00007fff7a2a4010 is LC_SEGMENT.__DATA.__nl_symbol_ptr in [memory object
"/usr/lib/system/libdnsinfo.dylib" at 0x7fff9098b000]
        0x00007fff7a2a4010 - 0x00007fff7a2a4030 is LC_SEGMENT.__DATA.__got in [memory object
"/usr/lib/system/libdnsinfo.dylib" at 0x7fff9098b000]
        0x00007fff7a2a4030 - 0x00007fff7a2a40d0 is LC_SEGMENT.__DATA.__la_symbol_ptr in [memory object
"/usr/lib/system/libdnsinfo.dylib" at 0x7fff9098b000]
        0x00007fff7a2a40d0 - 0x00007fff7a2a4120 is LC_SEGMENT.__DATA.__data in [memory object
"/usr/lib/system/libdnsinfo.dylib" at 0x7fff9098b000]
        0x00007fff7a2a4120 - 0x00007fff7a2a4124 is LC_SEGMENT.__DATA.__bss in [memory object
"/usr/lib/system/libdnsinfo.dylib" at 0x7fff9098b000]
        0x00007fff967f7000 - 0x00007fff99ebc000 is LC_SEGMENT.__LINKEDIT in [memory object
"/usr/lib/system/libdnsinfo.dylib" at 0x7fff9098b000]
        0x00007fff8dd8a000 - 0x00007fff8dd8f000 is LC_SEGMENT.__TEXT in [memory object "/usr/lib/system/libdyld.dylib"
at 0x7fff8dd8a000]
```

334

```
        0x00007fff8dd8b5c0 - 0x00007fff8dd8d57c is LC_SEGMENT.__TEXT.__text in [memory object
"/usr/lib/system/libdyld.dylib" at 0x7fff8dd8a000]
        0x00007fff8dd8d57c - 0x00007fff8dd8d5fa is LC_SEGMENT.__TEXT.__stubs in [memory object
"/usr/lib/system/libdyld.dylib" at 0x7fff8dd8a000]
        0x00007fff8dd8d5fc - 0x00007fff8dd8d6e0 is LC_SEGMENT.__TEXT.__stub_helper in [memory object
"/usr/lib/system/libdyld.dylib" ---Type <return> to continue, or q <return> to quit---
at 0x7fff8dd8a000]
        0x00007fff8dd8d6e0 - 0x00007fff8dd8ddb6 is LC_SEGMENT.__TEXT.__cstring in [memory object
"/usr/lib/system/libdyld.dylib" at 0x7fff8dd8a000]
        0x00007fff8dd8ddb8 - 0x00007fff8dd8ddc0 is LC_SEGMENT.__TEXT.__const in [memory object
"/usr/lib/system/libdyld.dylib" at 0x7fff8dd8a000]
        0x00007fff8dd8ddc0 - 0x00007fff8dd8deec is LC_SEGMENT.__TEXT.__unwind_info in [memory object
"/usr/lib/system/libdyld.dylib" at 0x7fff8dd8a000]
        0x00007fff8dd8def0 - 0x00007fff8dd8f000 is LC_SEGMENT.__TEXT.__eh_frame in [memory object
"/usr/lib/system/libdyld.dylib" at 0x7fff8dd8a000]
        0x00007fff79db2000 - 0x00007fff79db3000 is LC_SEGMENT.__DATA in [memory object "/usr/lib/system/libdyld.dylib"
at 0x7fff8dd8a000]
        0x00007fff79db2000 - 0x00007fff79db2010 is LC_SEGMENT.__DATA.__dyld in [memory object
"/usr/lib/system/libdyld.dylib" at 0x7fff8dd8a000]
        0x00007fff79db2010 - 0x00007fff79db2020 is LC_SEGMENT.__DATA.__nl_symbol_ptr in [memory object
"/usr/lib/system/libdyld.dylib" at 0x7fff8dd8a000]
        0x00007fff79db2020 - 0x00007fff79db2030 is LC_SEGMENT.__DATA.__got in [memory object
"/usr/lib/system/libdyld.dylib" at 0x7fff8dd8a000]
        0x00007fff79db2030 - 0x00007fff79db20d8 is LC_SEGMENT.__DATA.__la_symbol_ptr in [memory object
"/usr/lib/system/libdyld.dylib" at 0x7fff8dd8a000]
        0x00007fff79db20e0 - 0x00007fff79db21b0 is LC_SEGMENT.__DATA.__data in [memory object
"/usr/lib/system/libdyld.dylib" at 0x7fff8dd8a000]
        0x00007fff79db21b0 - 0x00007fff79db23f0 is LC_SEGMENT.__DATA.__bss in [memory object
"/usr/lib/system/libdyld.dylib" at 0x7fff8dd8a000]
        0x00007fff79db23f0 - 0x00007fff79db23f4 is LC_SEGMENT.__DATA.__common in [memory object
"/usr/lib/system/libdyld.dylib" at 0x7fff8dd8a000]
        0x00007fff967f7000 - 0x00007fff99ebc000 is LC_SEGMENT.__LINKEDIT in [memory object
"/usr/lib/system/libdyld.dylib" at 0x7fff8dd8a000]
        0x00007fff90025000 - 0x00007fff90026000 is LC_SEGMENT.__TEXT in [memory object
"/usr/lib/system/libkeymgr.dylib" at 0x7fff90025000]
        0x00007fff900258ec - 0x00007fff90025c4e is LC_SEGMENT.__TEXT.__text in [memory object
"/usr/lib/system/libkeymgr.dylib" at 0x7fff90025000]
        0x00007fff90025c4e - 0x00007fff90025c90 is LC_SEGMENT.__TEXT.__stubs in [memory object
"/usr/lib/system/libkeymgr.dylib" at 0x7fff90025000]
        0x00007fff90025c90 - 0x00007fff90025d10 is LC_SEGMENT.__TEXT.__stub_helper in [memory object
"/usr/lib/system/libkeymgr.dylib" at 0x7fff90025000]
        0x00007fff90025d10 - 0x00007fff90025d20 is LC_SEGMENT.__TEXT.__const in [memory object
"/usr/lib/system/libkeymgr.dylib" at 0x7fff90025000]
        0x00007fff90025d20 - 0x00007fff90025d47 is LC_SEGMENT.__TEXT.__cstring in [memory object
"/usr/lib/system/libkeymgr.dylib" at 0x7fff90025000]
        0x00007fff90025d47 - 0x00007fff90025dbb is LC_SEGMENT.__TEXT.__unwind_info in [memory object
"/usr/lib/system/libkeymgr.dylib---Type <return> to continue, or q <return> to quit---
" at 0x7fff90025000]
        0x00007fff90025dc0 - 0x00007fff90026000 is LC_SEGMENT.__TEXT.__eh_frame in [memory object
"/usr/lib/system/libkeymgr.dylib" at 0x7fff90025000]
        0x00007fff7a1ca000 - 0x00007fff7a1cb000 is LC_SEGMENT.__DATA in [memory object
"/usr/lib/system/libkeymgr.dylib" at 0x7fff90025000]
        0x00007fff7a1ca000 - 0x00007fff7a1ca010 is LC_SEGMENT.__DATA.__nl_symbol_ptr in [memory object
"/usr/lib/system/libkeymgr.dylib" at 0x7fff90025000]
        0x00007fff7a1ca010 - 0x00007fff7a1ca068 is LC_SEGMENT.__DATA.__la_symbol_ptr in [memory object
"/usr/lib/system/libkeymgr.dylib" at 0x7fff90025000]
        0x00007fff7a1ca080 - 0x00007fff7a1ca0a0 is LC_SEGMENT.__DATA.__data in [memory object
"/usr/lib/system/libkeymgr.dylib" at 0x7fff90025000]
        0x00007fff7a1ca0a0 - 0x00007fff7a1ca0c0 is LC_SEGMENT.__DATA.__bss in [memory object
"/usr/lib/system/libkeymgr.dylib" at 0x7fff90025000]
        0x00007fff967f7000 - 0x00007fff99ebc000 is LC_SEGMENT.__LINKEDIT in [memory object
"/usr/lib/system/libkeymgr.dylib" at 0x7fff90025000]
        0x00007fff91c14000 - 0x00007fff91c1f000 is LC_SEGMENT.__TEXT in [memory object
"/usr/lib/system/liblaunch.dylib" at 0x7fff91c14000]
        0x00007fff91c15428 - 0x00007fff91c1c4a7 is LC_SEGMENT.__TEXT.__text in [memory object
"/usr/lib/system/liblaunch.dylib" at 0x7fff91c14000]
        0x00007fff91c1c4a8 - 0x00007fff91c1c634 is LC_SEGMENT.__TEXT.__stubs in [memory object
"/usr/lib/system/liblaunch.dylib" at 0x7fff91c14000]
        0x00007fff91c1c634 - 0x00007fff91c1c8d8 is LC_SEGMENT.__TEXT.__stub_helper in [memory object
"/usr/lib/system/liblaunch.dylib" at 0x7fff91c14000]
        0x00007fff91c1c8d8 - 0x00007fff91c1c8f0 is LC_SEGMENT.__TEXT.__const in [memory object
"/usr/lib/system/liblaunch.dylib" at 0x7fff91c14000]
        0x00007fff91c1c8f0 - 0x00007fff91c1cdac is LC_SEGMENT.__TEXT.__cstring in [memory object
"/usr/lib/system/liblaunch.dylib" at 0x7fff91c14000]
        0x00007fff91c1cdac - 0x00007fff91c1cf7c is LC_SEGMENT.__TEXT.__unwind_info in [memory object
"/usr/lib/system/liblaunch.dylib" at 0x7fff91c14000]
```

```
        0x00007fff91c1cf80 - 0x00007fff91c1eff8 is LC_SEGMENT.__TEXT.__eh_frame in [memory object
"/usr/lib/system/liblaunch.dylib" at 0x7fff91c14000]
        0x00007fff7a484000 - 0x00007fff7a485000 is LC_SEGMENT.__DATA in [memory object
"/usr/lib/system/liblaunch.dylib" at 0x7fff91c14000]
        0x00007fff7a484000 - 0x00007fff7a484018 is LC_SEGMENT.__DATA.__got in [memory object
"/usr/lib/system/liblaunch.dylib" at 0x7fff91c14000]
        0x00007fff7a484018 - 0x00007fff7a484028 is LC_SEGMENT.__DATA.__nl_symbol_ptr in [memory object
"/usr/lib/system/liblaunch.dylib" at 0x7fff91c14000]
        0x00007fff7a484028 - 0x00007fff7a484238 is LC_SEGMENT.__DATA.__la_symbol_ptr in [memory object
"/usr/lib/system/liblaunch.dylib" at 0x7fff91c14000]
        0x00007fff7a484240 - 0x00007fff7a484280 is LC_SEGMENT.__DATA.__data in [memory object
"/usr/lib/system/liblaunch.dylib" at 0x---Type <return> to continue, or q <return> to quit---
7fff91c14000]
        0x00007fff7a484280 - 0x00007fff7a4842f0 is LC_SEGMENT.__DATA.__const in [memory object
"/usr/lib/system/liblaunch.dylib" at 0x7fff91c14000]
        0x00007fff7a4842f0 - 0x00007fff7a484328 is LC_SEGMENT.__DATA.__crash_info in [memory object
"/usr/lib/system/liblaunch.dylib" at 0x7fff91c14000]
        0x00007fff7a484328 - 0x00007fff7a484330 is LC_SEGMENT.__DATA.__common in [memory object
"/usr/lib/system/liblaunch.dylib" at 0x7fff91c14000]
        0x00007fff7a484330 - 0x00007fff7a484368 is LC_SEGMENT.__DATA.__bss in [memory object
"/usr/lib/system/liblaunch.dylib" at 0x7fff91c14000]
        0x00007fff967f7000 - 0x00007fff99ebc000 is LC_SEGMENT.__LINKEDIT in [memory object
"/usr/lib/system/liblaunch.dylib" at 0x7fff91c14000]
        0x00007fff8ed60000 - 0x00007fff8ed67000 is LC_SEGMENT.__TEXT in [memory object
"/usr/lib/system/libmacho.dylib" at 0x7fff8ed60000]
        0x00007fff8ed61008 - 0x00007fff8ed65924 is LC_SEGMENT.__TEXT.__text in [memory object
"/usr/lib/system/libmacho.dylib" at 0x7fff8ed60000]
        0x00007fff8ed65924 - 0x00007fff8ed65972 is LC_SEGMENT.__TEXT.__stubs in [memory object
"/usr/lib/system/libmacho.dylib" at 0x7fff8ed60000]
        0x00007fff8ed65974 - 0x00007fff8ed65a08 is LC_SEGMENT.__TEXT.__stub_helper in [memory object
"/usr/lib/system/libmacho.dylib" at 0x7fff8ed60000]
        0x00007fff8ed65a08 - 0x00007fff8ed65df2 is LC_SEGMENT.__TEXT.__cstring in [memory object
"/usr/lib/system/libmacho.dylib" at 0x7fff8ed60000]
        0x00007fff8ed65df8 - 0x00007fff8ed65e08 is LC_SEGMENT.__TEXT.__const in [memory object
"/usr/lib/system/libmacho.dylib" at 0x7fff8ed60000]
        0x00007fff8ed65e08 - 0x00007fff8ed65e94 is LC_SEGMENT.__TEXT.__unwind_info in [memory object
"/usr/lib/system/libmacho.dylib" at 0x7fff8ed60000]
        0x00007fff8ed65e98 - 0x00007fff8ed67000 is LC_SEGMENT.__TEXT.__eh_frame in [memory object
"/usr/lib/system/libmacho.dylib" at 0x7fff8ed60000]
        0x00007fff79ef2000 - 0x00007fff79ef3000 is LC_SEGMENT.__DATA in [memory object
"/usr/lib/system/libmacho.dylib" at 0x7fff8ed60000]
        0x00007fff79ef2000 - 0x00007fff79ef2008 is LC_SEGMENT.__DATA.__got in [memory object
"/usr/lib/system/libmacho.dylib" at 0x7fff8ed60000]
        0x00007fff79ef2008 - 0x00007fff79ef2018 is LC_SEGMENT.__DATA.__nl_symbol_ptr in [memory object
"/usr/lib/system/libmacho.dylib" at 0x7fff8ed60000]
        0x00007fff79ef2018 - 0x00007fff79ef2080 is LC_SEGMENT.__DATA.__la_symbol_ptr in [memory object
"/usr/lib/system/libmacho.dylib" at 0x7fff8ed60000]
        0x00007fff79ef2080 - 0x00007fff79ef2620 is LC_SEGMENT.__DATA.__const in [memory object
"/usr/lib/system/libmacho.dylib" at 0x7fff8ed60000]
        0x00007fff79ef2620 - 0x00007fff79ef2628 is LC_SEGMENT.__DATA.__data in [memory object
"/usr/lib/system/libmacho.dylib" at 0x7fff8ed60000]
        0x00007fff79ef2628 - 0x00007fff79ef2640 is LC_SEGMENT.__DATA.__bss in [memory object
"/usr/lib/system/libmacho.dylib" at 0x7f---Type <return> to continue, or q <return> to quit---
ff8ed60000]
        0x00007fff967f7000 - 0x00007fff99ebc000 is LC_SEGMENT.__LINKEDIT in [memory object
"/usr/lib/system/libmacho.dylib" at 0x7fff8ed60000]
        0x00007fff8dd85000 - 0x00007fff8dd8a000 is LC_SEGMENT.__TEXT in [memory object
"/usr/lib/system/libmathCommon.A.dylib" at 0x7fff8dd85000]
        0x00007fff8dd86310 - 0x00007fff8dd86dda is LC_SEGMENT.__TEXT.__text in [memory object
"/usr/lib/system/libmathCommon.A.dylib" at 0x7fff8dd85000]
        0x00007fff8dd86de0 - 0x00007fff8dd89c40 is LC_SEGMENT.__TEXT.__const in [memory object
"/usr/lib/system/libmathCommon.A.dylib" at 0x7fff8dd85000]
        0x00007fff8dd89c40 - 0x00007fff8dd89ca0 is LC_SEGMENT.__TEXT.__unwind_info in [memory object
"/usr/lib/system/libmathCommon.A.dylib" at 0x7fff8dd85000]
        0x00007fff8dd89ca0 - 0x00007fff8dd8a000 is LC_SEGMENT.__TEXT.__eh_frame in [memory object
"/usr/lib/system/libmathCommon.A.dylib" at 0x7fff8dd85000]
        0x00007fff967f7000 - 0x00007fff99ebc000 is LC_SEGMENT.__LINKEDIT in [memory object
"/usr/lib/system/libmathCommon.A.dylib" at 0x7fff8dd85000]
        0x00007fff8feb9000 - 0x00007fff8febc000 is LC_SEGMENT.__TEXT in [memory object
"/usr/lib/system/libquarantine.dylib" at 0x7fff8feb9000]
        0x00007fff8feb9f4e - 0x00007fff8febb210 is LC_SEGMENT.__TEXT.__text in [memory object
"/usr/lib/system/libquarantine.dylib" at 0x7fff8feb9000]
        0x00007fff8febb210 - 0x00007fff8febb288 is LC_SEGMENT.__TEXT.__stubs in [memory object
"/usr/lib/system/libquarantine.dylib" at 0x7fff8feb9000]
        0x00007fff8febb288 - 0x00007fff8febb360 is LC_SEGMENT.__TEXT.__stub_helper in [memory object
"/usr/lib/system/libquarantine.dylib" at 0x7fff8feb9000]
```

```
        0x00007fff8febb360 - 0x00007fff8febb4a4 is LC_SEGMENT.__TEXT.__cstring in [memory object
"/usr/lib/system/libquarantine.dylib" at 0x7fff8feb9000]
        0x00007fff8febb4a8 - 0x00007fff8febb4b0 is LC_SEGMENT.__TEXT.__const in [memory object
"/usr/lib/system/libquarantine.dylib" at 0x7fff8feb9000]
        0x00007fff8febb4b0 - 0x00007fff8febb58c is LC_SEGMENT.__TEXT.__unwind_info in [memory object
"/usr/lib/system/libquarantine.dylib" at 0x7fff8feb9000]
        0x00007fff8febb590 - 0x00007fff8febc000 is LC_SEGMENT.__TEXT.__eh_frame in [memory object
"/usr/lib/system/libquarantine.dylib" at 0x7fff8feb9000]
        0x00007fff7a190000 - 0x00007fff7a191000 is LC_SEGMENT.__DATA in [memory object
"/usr/lib/system/libquarantine.dylib" at 0x7fff8feb9000]
        0x00007fff7a190000 - 0x00007fff7a190010 is LC_SEGMENT.__DATA.__nl_symbol_ptr in [memory object
"/usr/lib/system/libquarantine.dylib" at 0x7fff8feb9000]
        0x00007fff7a190010 - 0x00007fff7a190020 is LC_SEGMENT.__DATA.__got in [memory object
"/usr/lib/system/libquarantine.dylib" at 0x7fff8feb9000]
        0x00007fff7a190020 - 0x00007fff7a1900c0 is LC_SEGMENT.__DATA.__la_symbol_ptr in [memory object
"/usr/lib/system/libquarantine.dylib" at 0x7fff8feb9000]
        0x00007fff7a1900c0 - 0x00007fff7a1900e0 is LC_SEGMENT.__DATA.__const in [memory object
"/usr/lib/system/libquarantine.dylib" ---Type <return> to continue, or q <return> to quit---
at 0x7fff8feb9000]
        0x00007fff967f7000 - 0x00007fff99ebc000 is LC_SEGMENT.__LINKEDIT in [memory object
"/usr/lib/system/libquarantine.dylib" at 0x7fff8feb9000]
        0x00007fff8a754000 - 0x00007fff8a756000 is LC_SEGMENT.__TEXT in [memory object
"/usr/lib/system/libremovefile.dylib" at 0x7fff8a754000]
        0x00007fff8a754600 - 0x00007fff8a75586c is LC_SEGMENT.__TEXT.__text in [memory object
"/usr/lib/system/libremovefile.dylib" at 0x7fff8a754000]
        0x00007fff8a75586c - 0x00007fff8a755962 is LC_SEGMENT.__TEXT.__stubs in [memory object
"/usr/lib/system/libremovefile.dylib" at 0x7fff8a754000]
        0x00007fff8a755964 - 0x00007fff8a755b10 is LC_SEGMENT.__TEXT.__stub_helper in [memory object
"/usr/lib/system/libremovefile.dylib" at 0x7fff8a754000]
        0x00007fff8a755b10 - 0x00007fff8a755b6d is LC_SEGMENT.__TEXT.__cstring in [memory object
"/usr/lib/system/libremovefile.dylib" at 0x7fff8a754000]
        0x00007fff8a755b6d - 0x00007fff8a755bf9 is LC_SEGMENT.__TEXT.__unwind_info in [memory object
"/usr/lib/system/libremovefile.dylib" at 0x7fff8a754000]
        0x00007fff8a755c00 - 0x00007fff8a755ff8 is LC_SEGMENT.__TEXT.__eh_frame in [memory object
"/usr/lib/system/libremovefile.dylib" at 0x7fff8a754000]
        0x00007fff79882000 - 0x00007fff79883000 is LC_SEGMENT.__DATA in [memory object
"/usr/lib/system/libremovefile.dylib" at 0x7fff8a754000]
        0x00007fff79882000 - 0x00007fff79882010 is LC_SEGMENT.__DATA.__nl_symbol_ptr in [memory object
"/usr/lib/system/libremovefile.dylib" at 0x7fff8a754000]
        0x00007fff79882010 - 0x00007fff79882020 is LC_SEGMENT.__DATA.__got in [memory object
"/usr/lib/system/libremovefile.dylib" at 0x7fff8a754000]
        0x00007fff79882020 - 0x00007fff79882168 is LC_SEGMENT.__DATA.__la_symbol_ptr in [memory object
"/usr/lib/system/libremovefile.dylib" at 0x7fff8a754000]
        0x00007fff967f7000 - 0x00007fff99ebc000 is LC_SEGMENT.__LINKEDIT in [memory object
"/usr/lib/system/libremovefile.dylib" at 0x7fff8a754000]
        0x00007fff899d9000 - 0x00007fff899db000 is LC_SEGMENT.__TEXT in [memory object
"/usr/lib/system/libsystem_blocks.dylib" at 0x7fff899d9000]
        0x00007fff899d9885 - 0x00007fff899da57e is LC_SEGMENT.__TEXT.__text in [memory object
"/usr/lib/system/libsystem_blocks.dylib" at 0x7fff899d9000]
        0x00007fff899da57e - 0x00007fff899da5a8 is LC_SEGMENT.__TEXT.__stubs in [memory object
"/usr/lib/system/libsystem_blocks.dylib" at 0x7fff899d9000]
        0x00007fff899da5a8 - 0x00007fff899da600 is LC_SEGMENT.__TEXT.__stub_helper in [memory object
"/usr/lib/system/libsystem_blocks.dylib" at 0x7fff899d9000]
        0x00007fff899da600 - 0x00007fff899da8ce is LC_SEGMENT.__TEXT.__cstring in [memory object
"/usr/lib/system/libsystem_blocks.dylib" at 0x7fff899d9000]
        0x00007fff899da8d0 - 0x00007fff899da8d8 is LC_SEGMENT.__TEXT.__const in [memory object
"/usr/lib/system/libsystem_blocks.dylib" at 0x7fff899d9000]
        0x00007fff899da8d8 - 0x00007fff899da958 is LC_SEGMENT.__TEXT.__unwind_info in [memory object
"/usr/lib/system/libsystem_block---Type <return> to continue, or q <return> to quit---
s.dylib" at 0x7fff899d9000]
        0x00007fff899da958 - 0x00007fff899daff8 is LC_SEGMENT.__TEXT.__eh_frame in [memory object
"/usr/lib/system/libsystem_blocks.dylib" at 0x7fff899d9000]
        0x00007fff796d1000 - 0x00007fff796d2000 is LC_SEGMENT.__DATA in [memory object
"/usr/lib/system/libsystem_blocks.dylib" at 0x7fff899d9000]
        0x00007fff796d1000 - 0x00007fff796d1028 is LC_SEGMENT.__DATA.__got in [memory object
"/usr/lib/system/libsystem_blocks.dylib" at 0x7fff899d9000]
        0x00007fff796d1028 - 0x00007fff796d1038 is LC_SEGMENT.__DATA.__nl_symbol_ptr in [memory object
"/usr/lib/system/libsystem_blocks.dylib" at 0x7fff899d9000]
        0x00007fff796d1038 - 0x00007fff796d1070 is LC_SEGMENT.__DATA.__la_symbol_ptr in [memory object
"/usr/lib/system/libsystem_blocks.dylib" at 0x7fff899d9000]
        0x00007fff796d1070 - 0x00007fff796d10b8 is LC_SEGMENT.__DATA.__data in [memory object
"/usr/lib/system/libsystem_blocks.dylib" at 0x7fff899d9000]
        0x00007fff796d10c0 - 0x00007fff796d13d0 is LC_SEGMENT.__DATA.__bss in [memory object
"/usr/lib/system/libsystem_blocks.dylib" at 0x7fff899d9000]
        0x00007fff796d13d0 - 0x00007fff796d19d0 is LC_SEGMENT.__DATA.__common in [memory object
"/usr/lib/system/libsystem_blocks.dylib" at 0x7fff899d9000]
```

```
        0x00007fff967f7000 - 0x00007fff99ebc000 is LC_SEGMENT.__LINKEDIT in [memory object
"/usr/lib/system/libsystem_blocks.dylib" at 0x7fff899d9000]
        0x00007fff899db000 - 0x00007fff89ab9000 is LC_SEGMENT.__TEXT in [memory object
"/usr/lib/system/libsystem_c.dylib" at 0x7fff899db000]
        0x00007fff899dbcc0 - 0x00007fff89a820f4 is LC_SEGMENT.__TEXT.__text in [memory object
"/usr/lib/system/libsystem_c.dylib" at 0x7fff899db000]
        0x00007fff89a820f4 - 0x00007fff89a8283e is LC_SEGMENT.__TEXT.__stubs in [memory object
"/usr/lib/system/libsystem_c.dylib" at 0x7fff899db000]
        0x00007fff89a82840 - 0x00007fff89a8386c is LC_SEGMENT.__TEXT.__stub_helper in [memory object
"/usr/lib/system/libsystem_c.dylib" at 0x7fff899db000]
        0x00007fff89a83870 - 0x00007fff89a930f0 is LC_SEGMENT.__TEXT.__cstring in [memory object
"/usr/lib/system/libsystem_c.dylib" at 0x7fff899db000]
        0x00007fff89a93100 - 0x00007fff89a94f58 is LC_SEGMENT.__TEXT.__const in [memory object
"/usr/lib/system/libsystem_c.dylib" at 0x7fff899db000]
        0x00007fff89a94f58 - 0x00007fff89a95686 is LC_SEGMENT.__TEXT.__dof_magmalloc in [memory object
"/usr/lib/system/libsystem_c.dylib" at 0x7fff899db000]
        0x00007fff89a95686 - 0x00007fff89a96261 is LC_SEGMENT.__TEXT.__dof_plockstat in [memory object
"/usr/lib/system/libsystem_c.dylib" at 0x7fff899db000]
        0x00007fff89a96261 - 0x00007fff89a97921 is LC_SEGMENT.__TEXT.__unwind_info in [memory object
"/usr/lib/system/libsystem_c.dylib" at 0x7fff899db000]
        0x00007fff89a97928 - 0x00007fff89ab8ff0 is LC_SEGMENT.__TEXT.__eh_frame in [memory object
"/usr/lib/system/libsystem_c.dylib" at 0x7fff899db000]
        0x00007fff796d2000 - 0x00007fff796d9000 is LC_SEGMENT.__DATA in [memory object
"/usr/lib/system/libsystem_c.dylib" at 0x7fff8---Type <return> to continue, or q <return> to quit---
99db000]
        0x00007fff796d2000 - 0x00007fff796d2058 is LC_SEGMENT.__DATA.__got in [memory object
"/usr/lib/system/libsystem_c.dylib" at 0x7fff899db000]
        0x00007fff796d2058 - 0x00007fff796d2068 is LC_SEGMENT.__DATA.__nl_symbol_ptr in [memory object
"/usr/lib/system/libsystem_c.dylib" at 0x7fff899db000]
        0x00007fff796d2068 - 0x00007fff796d2a20 is LC_SEGMENT.__DATA.__la_symbol_ptr in [memory object
"/usr/lib/system/libsystem_c.dylib" at 0x7fff899db000]
        0x00007fff796d2a20 - 0x00007fff796d2a58 is LC_SEGMENT.__DATA.__crash_info in [memory object
"/usr/lib/system/libsystem_c.dylib" at 0x7fff899db000]
        0x00007fff796d2a60 - 0x00007fff796d4cc8 is LC_SEGMENT.__DATA.__data in [memory object
"/usr/lib/system/libsystem_c.dylib" at 0x7fff899db000]
        0x00007fff796d4cd0 - 0x00007fff796d73b0 is LC_SEGMENT.__DATA.__const in [memory object
"/usr/lib/system/libsystem_c.dylib" at 0x7fff899db000]
        0x00007fff796d73b0 - 0x00007fff796d8d30 is LC_SEGMENT.__DATA.__constrw in [memory object
"/usr/lib/system/libsystem_c.dylib" at 0x7fff899db000]
        0x00007fff796d8d30 - 0x00007fff796d9214 is LC_SEGMENT.__DATA.__common in [memory object
"/usr/lib/system/libsystem_c.dylib" at 0x7fff899db000]
        0x00007fff796d9220 - 0x00007fff796e1788 is LC_SEGMENT.__DATA.__bss in [memory object
"/usr/lib/system/libsystem_c.dylib" at 0x7fff899db000]
        0x00007fff967f7000 - 0x00007fff99ebc000 is LC_SEGMENT.__LINKEDIT in [memory object
"/usr/lib/system/libsystem_c.dylib" at 0x7fff899db000]
        0x00007fff8ef1d000 - 0x00007fff8ef26000 is LC_SEGMENT.__TEXT in [memory object
"/usr/lib/system/libsystem_dnssd.dylib" at 0x7fff8ef1d000]
        0x00007fff8ef1e2d8 - 0x00007fff8ef23500 is LC_SEGMENT.__TEXT.__text in [memory object
"/usr/lib/system/libsystem_dnssd.dylib" at 0x7fff8ef1d000]
        0x00007fff8ef23500 - 0x00007fff8ef2362c is LC_SEGMENT.__TEXT.__stubs in [memory object
"/usr/lib/system/libsystem_dnssd.dylib" at 0x7fff8ef1d000]
        0x00007fff8ef2362c - 0x00007fff8ef23830 is LC_SEGMENT.__TEXT.__stub_helper in [memory object
"/usr/lib/system/libsystem_dnssd.dylib" at 0x7fff8ef1d000]
        0x00007fff8ef23830 - 0x00007fff8ef24be4 is LC_SEGMENT.__TEXT.__cstring in [memory object
"/usr/lib/system/libsystem_dnssd.dylib" at 0x7fff8ef1d000]
        0x00007fff8ef24be4 - 0x00007fff8ef24c26 is LC_SEGMENT.__TEXT.__const in [memory object
"/usr/lib/system/libsystem_dnssd.dylib" at 0x7fff8ef1d000]
        0x00007fff8ef24c26 - 0x00007fff8ef24d4a is LC_SEGMENT.__TEXT.__unwind_info in [memory object
"/usr/lib/system/libsystem_dnssd.dylib" at 0x7fff8ef1d000]
        0x00007fff8ef24d50 - 0x00007fff8ef26000 is LC_SEGMENT.__TEXT.__eh_frame in [memory object
"/usr/lib/system/libsystem_dnssd.dylib" at 0x7fff8ef1d000]
        0x00007fff79f49000 - 0x00007fff79f4a000 is LC_SEGMENT.__DATA in [memory object
"/usr/lib/system/libsystem_dnssd.dylib" at 0x7fff8ef1d000]
        0x00007fff79f49000 - 0x00007fff79f49030 is LC_SEGMENT.__DATA.__got in [memory object
"/usr/lib/system/libsystem_dnssd.dylib" ---Type <return> to continue, or q <return> to quit---
at 0x7fff8ef1d000]
        0x00007fff79f49030 - 0x00007fff79f49040 is LC_SEGMENT.__DATA.__nl_symbol_ptr in [memory object
"/usr/lib/system/libsystem_dnssd.dylib" at 0x7fff8ef1d000]
        0x00007fff79f49040 - 0x00007fff79f491d0 is LC_SEGMENT.__DATA.__la_symbol_ptr in [memory object
"/usr/lib/system/libsystem_dnssd.dylib" at 0x7fff8ef1d000]
        0x00007fff79f491d0 - 0x00007fff79f49250 is LC_SEGMENT.__DATA.__data in [memory object
"/usr/lib/system/libsystem_dnssd.dylib" at 0x7fff8ef1d000]
        0x00007fff79f49250 - 0x00007fff79f49310 is LC_SEGMENT.__DATA.__const in [memory object
"/usr/lib/system/libsystem_dnssd.dylib" at 0x7fff8ef1d000]
        0x00007fff79f49310 - 0x00007fff79f49324 is LC_SEGMENT.__DATA.__bss in [memory object
"/usr/lib/system/libsystem_dnssd.dylib" at 0x7fff8ef1d000]
```

```
        0x00007fff967f7000 - 0x00007fff99ebc000 is LC_SEGMENT.__LINKEDIT in [memory object
"/usr/lib/system/libsystem_dnssd.dylib" at 0x7fff8ef1d000]
        0x00007fff8fa97000 - 0x00007fff8fad3000 is LC_SEGMENT.__TEXT in [memory object
"/usr/lib/system/libsystem_info.dylib" at 0x7fff8fa97000]
        0x00007fff8fa97bc0 - 0x00007fff8fac237e is LC_SEGMENT.__TEXT.__text in [memory object
"/usr/lib/system/libsystem_info.dylib" at 0x7fff8fa97000]
        0x00007fff8fac237e - 0x00007fff8fac27aa is LC_SEGMENT.__TEXT.__stubs in [memory object
"/usr/lib/system/libsystem_info.dylib" at 0x7fff8fa97000]
        0x00007fff8fac27ac - 0x00007fff8fac2eb0 is LC_SEGMENT.__TEXT.__stub_helper in [memory object
"/usr/lib/system/libsystem_info.dylib" at 0x7fff8fa97000]
        0x00007fff8fac2eb0 - 0x00007fff8fac5429 is LC_SEGMENT.__TEXT.__cstring in [memory object
"/usr/lib/system/libsystem_info.dylib" at 0x7fff8fa97000]
        0x00007fff8fac5430 - 0x00007fff8fac5580 is LC_SEGMENT.__TEXT.__const in [memory object
"/usr/lib/system/libsystem_info.dylib" at 0x7fff8fa97000]
        0x00007fff8fac5580 - 0x00007fff8fac5ce4 is LC_SEGMENT.__TEXT.__unwind_info in [memory object
"/usr/lib/system/libsystem_info.dylib" at 0x7fff8fa97000]
        0x00007fff8fac5ce8 - 0x00007fff8fad3000 is LC_SEGMENT.__TEXT.__eh_frame in [memory object
"/usr/lib/system/libsystem_info.dylib" at 0x7fff8fa97000]
        0x00007fff7a0c4000 - 0x00007fff7a0c6000 is LC_SEGMENT.__DATA in [memory object
"/usr/lib/system/libsystem_info.dylib" at 0x7fff8fa97000]
        0x00007fff7a0c4000 - 0x00007fff7a0c4058 is LC_SEGMENT.__DATA.__got in [memory object
"/usr/lib/system/libsystem_info.dylib" at 0x7fff8fa97000]
        0x00007fff7a0c4058 - 0x00007fff7a0c4068 is LC_SEGMENT.__DATA.__nl_symbol_ptr in [memory object
"/usr/lib/system/libsystem_info.dylib" at 0x7fff8fa97000]
        0x00007fff7a0c4068 - 0x00007fff7a0c45f8 is LC_SEGMENT.__DATA.__la_symbol_ptr in [memory object
"/usr/lib/system/libsystem_info.dylib" at 0x7fff8fa97000]
        0x00007fff7a0c4600 - 0x00007fff7a0c4de4 is LC_SEGMENT.__DATA.__data in [memory object
"/usr/lib/system/libsystem_info.dylib" at 0x7fff8fa97000]
        0x00007fff7a0c4df0 - 0x00007fff7a0c58e8 is LC_SEGMENT.__DATA.__const in [memory object
"/usr/lib/system/libsystem_info.dylib"---Type <return> to continue, or q <return> to quit---
 at 0x7fff8fa97000]
        0x00007fff7a0c58f0 - 0x00007fff7a0c5d80 is LC_SEGMENT.__DATA.__bss in [memory object
"/usr/lib/system/libsystem_info.dylib" at 0x7fff8fa97000]
        0x00007fff7a0c5d80 - 0x00007fff7a0c61b8 is LC_SEGMENT.__DATA.__common in [memory object
"/usr/lib/system/libsystem_info.dylib" at 0x7fff8fa97000]
        0x00007fff967f7000 - 0x00007fff99ebc000 is LC_SEGMENT.__LINKEDIT in [memory object
"/usr/lib/system/libsystem_info.dylib" at 0x7fff8fa97000]
        0x00007fff8ed67000 - 0x00007fff8ed88000 is LC_SEGMENT.__TEXT in [memory object
"/usr/lib/system/libsystem_kernel.dylib" at 0x7fff8ed67000]
        0x00007fff8ed6835c - 0x00007fff8ed7f04f is LC_SEGMENT.__TEXT.__text in [memory object
"/usr/lib/system/libsystem_kernel.dylib" at 0x7fff8ed67000]
        0x00007fff8ed7f050 - 0x00007fff8ed83a92 is LC_SEGMENT.__TEXT.__cstring in [memory object
"/usr/lib/system/libsystem_kernel.dylib" at 0x7fff8ed67000]
        0x00007fff8ed83aa0 - 0x00007fff8ed83b58 is LC_SEGMENT.__TEXT.__const in [memory object
"/usr/lib/system/libsystem_kernel.dylib" at 0x7fff8ed67000]
        0x00007fff8ed83b58 - 0x00007fff8ed83e1c is LC_SEGMENT.__TEXT.__unwind_info in [memory object
"/usr/lib/system/libsystem_kernel.dylib" at 0x7fff8ed67000]
        0x00007fff8ed83e20 - 0x00007fff8ed88000 is LC_SEGMENT.__TEXT.__eh_frame in [memory object
"/usr/lib/system/libsystem_kernel.dylib" at 0x7fff8ed67000]
        0x00007fff79ef3000 - 0x00007fff79ef6000 is LC_SEGMENT.__DATA in [memory object
"/usr/lib/system/libsystem_kernel.dylib" at 0x7fff8ed67000]
        0x00007fff79ef3000 - 0x00007fff79ef51d0 is LC_SEGMENT.__DATA.__const in [memory object
"/usr/lib/system/libsystem_kernel.dylib" at 0x7fff8ed67000]
        0x00007fff79ef51d0 - 0x00007fff79ef520c is LC_SEGMENT.__DATA.__data in [memory object
"/usr/lib/system/libsystem_kernel.dylib" at 0x7fff8ed67000]
        0x00007fff79ef5210 - 0x00007fff79ef5250 is LC_SEGMENT.__DATA.__common in [memory object
"/usr/lib/system/libsystem_kernel.dylib" at 0x7fff8ed67000]
        0x00007fff79ef5250 - 0x00007fff79ef5278 is LC_SEGMENT.__DATA.__bss in [memory object
"/usr/lib/system/libsystem_kernel.dylib" at 0x7fff8ed67000]
        0x00007fff967f7000 - 0x00007fff99ebc000 is LC_SEGMENT.__LINKEDIT in [memory object
"/usr/lib/system/libsystem_kernel.dylib" at 0x7fff8ed67000]
        0x00007fff91199000 - 0x00007fff9119f000 is LC_SEGMENT.__TEXT in [memory object
"/usr/lib/system/libsystem_network.dylib" at 0x7fff91199000]
        0x00007fff9119a719 - 0x00007fff9119daa0 is LC_SEGMENT.__TEXT.__text in [memory object
"/usr/lib/system/libsystem_network.dylib" at 0x7fff91199000]
        0x00007fff9119daa0 - 0x00007fff9119dc20 is LC_SEGMENT.__TEXT.__stubs in [memory object
"/usr/lib/system/libsystem_network.dylib" at 0x7fff91199000]
        0x00007fff9119dc20 - 0x00007fff9119deb0 is LC_SEGMENT.__TEXT.__stub_helper in [memory object
"/usr/lib/system/libsystem_network.dylib" at 0x7fff91199000]
        0x00007fff9119deb0 - 0x00007fff9119dfa5 is LC_SEGMENT.__TEXT.__cstring in [memory object
"/usr/lib/system/libsystem_network.d---Type <return> to continue, or q <return> to quit---
ylib" at 0x7fff91199000]
        0x00007fff9119dfa8 - 0x00007fff9119dfb0 is LC_SEGMENT.__TEXT.__const in [memory object
"/usr/lib/system/libsystem_network.dylib" at 0x7fff91199000]
        0x00007fff9119dfb0 - 0x00007fff9119e0d4 is LC_SEGMENT.__TEXT.__unwind_info in [memory object
"/usr/lib/system/libsystem_network.dylib" at 0x7fff91199000]
```

339

```
        0x00007fff9119e0d8 - 0x00007fff9119eff8 is LC_SEGMENT.__TEXT.__eh_frame in [memory object
"/usr/lib/system/libsystem_network.dylib" at 0x7fff91199000]
        0x00007fff7a347000 - 0x00007fff7a348000 is LC_SEGMENT.__DATA in [memory object
"/usr/lib/system/libsystem_network.dylib" at 0x7fff91199000]
        0x00007fff7a347000 - 0x00007fff7a347010 is LC_SEGMENT.__DATA.__nl_symbol_ptr in [memory object
"/usr/lib/system/libsystem_network.dylib" at 0x7fff91199000]
        0x00007fff7a347010 - 0x00007fff7a347038 is LC_SEGMENT.__DATA.__got in [memory object
"/usr/lib/system/libsystem_network.dylib" at 0x7fff91199000]
        0x00007fff7a347038 - 0x00007fff7a347238 is LC_SEGMENT.__DATA.__la_symbol_ptr in [memory object
"/usr/lib/system/libsystem_network.dylib" at 0x7fff91199000]
        0x00007fff7a347240 - 0x00007fff7a3475b4 is LC_SEGMENT.__DATA.__data in [memory object
"/usr/lib/system/libsystem_network.dylib" at 0x7fff91199000]
        0x00007fff7a3475c0 - 0x00007fff7a347618 is LC_SEGMENT.__DATA.__bss in [memory object
"/usr/lib/system/libsystem_network.dylib" at 0x7fff91199000]
        0x00007fff967f7000 - 0x00007fff99ebc000 is LC_SEGMENT.__LINKEDIT in [memory object
"/usr/lib/system/libsystem_network.dylib" at 0x7fff91199000]
        0x00007fff95880000 - 0x00007fff9588a000 is LC_SEGMENT.__TEXT in [memory object
"/usr/lib/system/libsystem_notify.dylib" at 0x7fff95880000]
        0x00007fff95881511 - 0x00007fff95887e1e is LC_SEGMENT.__TEXT.__text in [memory object
"/usr/lib/system/libsystem_notify.dylib" at 0x7fff95880000]
        0x00007fff95887e1e - 0x00007fff95887f38 is LC_SEGMENT.__TEXT.__stubs in [memory object
"/usr/lib/system/libsystem_notify.dylib" at 0x7fff95880000]
        0x00007fff95887f38 - 0x00007fff95888120 is LC_SEGMENT.__TEXT.__stub_helper in [memory object
"/usr/lib/system/libsystem_notify.dylib" at 0x7fff95880000]
        0x00007fff95888120 - 0x00007fff958881d6 is LC_SEGMENT.__TEXT.__cstring in [memory object
"/usr/lib/system/libsystem_notify.dylib" at 0x7fff95880000]
        0x00007fff958881d8 - 0x00007fff958881e0 is LC_SEGMENT.__TEXT.__const in [memory object
"/usr/lib/system/libsystem_notify.dylib" at 0x7fff95880000]
        0x00007fff958881e0 - 0x00007fff95888364 is LC_SEGMENT.__TEXT.__unwind_info in [memory object
"/usr/lib/system/libsystem_notify.dylib" at 0x7fff95880000]
        0x00007fff95888368 - 0x00007fff95889ff8 is LC_SEGMENT.__TEXT.__eh_frame in [memory object
"/usr/lib/system/libsystem_notify.dylib" at 0x7fff95880000]
        0x00007fff7afb3000 - 0x00007fff7afb4000 is LC_SEGMENT.__DATA in [memory object
"/usr/lib/system/libsystem_notify.dylib" at 0x7fff95880000]
        0x00007fff7afb3000 - 0x00007fff7afb3030 is LC_SEGMENT.__DATA.__got in [memory object
"/usr/lib/system/libsystem_notify.dylib"---Type <return> to continue, or q <return> to quit---
 at 0x7fff95880000]
        0x00007fff7afb3030 - 0x00007fff7afb3040 is LC_SEGMENT.__DATA.__nl_symbol_ptr in [memory object
"/usr/lib/system/libsystem_notify.dylib" at 0x7fff95880000]
        0x00007fff7afb3040 - 0x00007fff7afb31b8 is LC_SEGMENT.__DATA.__la_symbol_ptr in [memory object
"/usr/lib/system/libsystem_notify.dylib" at 0x7fff95880000]
        0x00007fff7afb31c0 - 0x00007fff7afb32f0 is LC_SEGMENT.__DATA.__data in [memory object
"/usr/lib/system/libsystem_notify.dylib" at 0x7fff95880000]
        0x00007fff7afb32f0 - 0x00007fff7afb3350 is LC_SEGMENT.__DATA.__const in [memory object
"/usr/lib/system/libsystem_notify.dylib" at 0x7fff95880000]
        0x00007fff7afb3350 - 0x00007fff7afb33e0 is LC_SEGMENT.__DATA.__bss in [memory object
"/usr/lib/system/libsystem_notify.dylib" at 0x7fff95880000]
        0x00007fff7afb33e0 - 0x00007fff7afb33e4 is LC_SEGMENT.__DATA.__common in [memory object
"/usr/lib/system/libsystem_notify.dylib" at 0x7fff95880000]
        0x00007fff967f7000 - 0x00007fff99ebc000 is LC_SEGMENT.__LINKEDIT in [memory object
"/usr/lib/system/libsystem_notify.dylib" at 0x7fff95880000]
        0x00007fff8e3b1000 - 0x00007fff8e3b3000 is LC_SEGMENT.__TEXT in [memory object
"/usr/lib/system/libsystem_sandbox.dylib" at 0x7fff8e3b1000]
        0x00007fff8e3b1958 - 0x00007fff8e3b258d is LC_SEGMENT.__TEXT.__text in [memory object
"/usr/lib/system/libsystem_sandbox.dylib" at 0x7fff8e3b1000]
        0x00007fff8e3b258e - 0x00007fff8e3b25f4 is LC_SEGMENT.__TEXT.__stubs in [memory object
"/usr/lib/system/libsystem_sandbox.dylib" at 0x7fff8e3b1000]
        0x00007fff8e3b25f4 - 0x00007fff8e3b26b0 is LC_SEGMENT.__TEXT.__stub_helper in [memory object
"/usr/lib/system/libsystem_sandbox.dylib" at 0x7fff8e3b1000]
        0x00007fff8e3b26b0 - 0x00007fff8e3b2956 is LC_SEGMENT.__TEXT.__cstring in [memory object
"/usr/lib/system/libsystem_sandbox.dylib" at 0x7fff8e3b1000]
        0x00007fff8e3b2958 - 0x00007fff8e3b2970 is LC_SEGMENT.__TEXT.__const in [memory object
"/usr/lib/system/libsystem_sandbox.dylib" at 0x7fff8e3b1000]
        0x00007fff8e3b2970 - 0x00007fff8e3b29fc is LC_SEGMENT.__TEXT.__unwind_info in [memory object
"/usr/lib/system/libsystem_sandbox.dylib" at 0x7fff8e3b1000]
        0x00007fff8e3b2a00 - 0x00007fff8e3b2ff8 is LC_SEGMENT.__TEXT.__eh_frame in [memory object
"/usr/lib/system/libsystem_sandbox.dylib" at 0x7fff8e3b1000]
        0x00007fff79e14000 - 0x00007fff79e15000 is LC_SEGMENT.__DATA in [memory object
"/usr/lib/system/libsystem_sandbox.dylib" at 0x7fff8e3b1000]
        0x00007fff79e14000 - 0x00007fff79e14010 is LC_SEGMENT.__DATA.__got in [memory object
"/usr/lib/system/libsystem_sandbox.dylib" at 0x7fff8e3b1000]
        0x00007fff79e14010 - 0x00007fff79e14020 is LC_SEGMENT.__DATA.__nl_symbol_ptr in [memory object
"/usr/lib/system/libsystem_sandbox.dylib" at 0x7fff8e3b1000]
        0x00007fff79e14020 - 0x00007fff79e140a8 is LC_SEGMENT.__DATA.__la_symbol_ptr in [memory object
"/usr/lib/system/libsystem_sandbox.dylib" at 0x7fff8e3b1000]
```

        0x00007fff79e140b0 - 0x00007fff79e140c3 is LC_SEGMENT.__DATA.__data in [memory object
"/usr/lib/system/libsystem_sandbox.dyli---Type <return> to continue, or q <return> to quit---
b" at 0x7fff8e3b1000]
        0x00007fff79e140d0 - 0x00007fff79e14110 is LC_SEGMENT.__DATA.__const in [memory object
"/usr/lib/system/libsystem_sandbox.dylib" at 0x7fff8e3b1000]
        0x00007fff79e14110 - 0x00007fff79e14128 is LC_SEGMENT.__DATA.__bss in [memory object
"/usr/lib/system/libsystem_sandbox.dylib" at 0x7fff8e3b1000]
        0x00007fff967f7000 - 0x00007fff99ebc000 is LC_SEGMENT.__LINKEDIT in [memory object
"/usr/lib/system/libsystem_sandbox.dylib" at 0x7fff8e3b1000]
        0x00007fff8a261000 - 0x00007fff8a263000 is LC_SEGMENT.__TEXT in [memory object "/usr/lib/system/libunc.dylib"
at 0x7fff8a261000]
        0x00007fff8a2616ad - 0x00007fff8a2628f0 is LC_SEGMENT.__TEXT.__text in [memory object
"/usr/lib/system/libunc.dylib" at 0x7fff8a261000]
        0x00007fff8a2628f0 - 0x00007fff8a262968 is LC_SEGMENT.__TEXT.__stubs in [memory object
"/usr/lib/system/libunc.dylib" at 0x7fff8a261000]
        0x00007fff8a262968 - 0x00007fff8a262a40 is LC_SEGMENT.__TEXT.__stub_helper in [memory object
"/usr/lib/system/libunc.dylib" at 0x7fff8a261000]
        0x00007fff8a262a40 - 0x00007fff8a262a50 is LC_SEGMENT.__TEXT.__const in [memory object
"/usr/lib/system/libunc.dylib" at 0x7fff8a261000]
        0x00007fff8a262a50 - 0x00007fff8a262cf9 is LC_SEGMENT.__TEXT.__cstring in [memory object
"/usr/lib/system/libunc.dylib" at 0x7fff8a261000]
        0x00007fff8a262cf9 - 0x00007fff8a262d6d is LC_SEGMENT.__TEXT.__unwind_info in [memory object
"/usr/lib/system/libunc.dylib" at 0x7fff8a261000]
        0x00007fff8a262d70 - 0x00007fff8a263000 is LC_SEGMENT.__TEXT.__eh_frame in [memory object
"/usr/lib/system/libunc.dylib" at 0x7fff8a261000]
        0x00007fff79801000 - 0x00007fff79802000 is LC_SEGMENT.__DATA in [memory object "/usr/lib/system/libunc.dylib"
at 0x7fff8a261000]
        0x00007fff79801000 - 0x00007fff79801010 is LC_SEGMENT.__DATA.__nl_symbol_ptr in [memory object
"/usr/lib/system/libunc.dylib" at 0x7fff8a261000]
        0x00007fff79801010 - 0x00007fff79801020 is LC_SEGMENT.__DATA.__got in [memory object
"/usr/lib/system/libunc.dylib" at 0x7fff8a261000]
        0x00007fff79801020 - 0x00007fff798010c0 is LC_SEGMENT.__DATA.__la_symbol_ptr in [memory object
"/usr/lib/system/libunc.dylib" at 0x7fff8a261000]
        0x00007fff798010c0 - 0x00007fff798010c2 is LC_SEGMENT.__DATA.__bss in [memory object
"/usr/lib/system/libunc.dylib" at 0x7fff8a261000]
        0x00007fff967f7000 - 0x00007fff99ebc000 is LC_SEGMENT.__LINKEDIT in [memory object
"/usr/lib/system/libunc.dylib" at 0x7fff8a261000]
        0x00007fff960fa000 - 0x00007fff96101000 is LC_SEGMENT.__TEXT in [memory object
"/usr/lib/system/libunwind.dylib" at 0x7fff960fa000]
        0x00007fff960fa894 - 0x00007fff960ff36c is LC_SEGMENT.__TEXT.__text in [memory object
"/usr/lib/system/libunwind.dylib" at 0x7fff960fa000]
        0x00007fff960ff36c - 0x00007fff960ff3c6 is LC_SEGMENT.__TEXT.__stubs in [memory object
"/usr/lib/system/libunwind.dylib" at 0---Type <return> to continue, or q <return> to quit---
x7fff960fa000]
        0x00007fff960ff3c8 - 0x00007fff960ff470 is LC_SEGMENT.__TEXT.__stub_helper in [memory object
"/usr/lib/system/libunwind.dylib" at 0x7fff960fa000]
        0x00007fff960ff470 - 0x00007fff960ffead is LC_SEGMENT.__TEXT.__cstring in [memory object
"/usr/lib/system/libunwind.dylib" at 0x7fff960fa000]
        0x00007fff960ffeb0 - 0x00007fff960ffef8 is LC_SEGMENT.__TEXT.__const in [memory object
"/usr/lib/system/libunwind.dylib" at 0x7fff960fa000]
        0x00007fff960ffef8 - 0x00007fff96100000 is LC_SEGMENT.__TEXT.__unwind_info in [memory object
"/usr/lib/system/libunwind.dylib" at 0x7fff960fa000]
        0x00007fff96100000 - 0x00007fff96100ff8 is LC_SEGMENT.__TEXT.__eh_frame in [memory object
"/usr/lib/system/libunwind.dylib" at 0x7fff960fa000]
        0x00007fff7b072000 - 0x00007fff7b073000 is LC_SEGMENT.__DATA in [memory object
"/usr/lib/system/libunwind.dylib" at 0x7fff960fa000]
        0x00007fff7b072000 - 0x00007fff7b072010 is LC_SEGMENT.__DATA.__nl_symbol_ptr in [memory object
"/usr/lib/system/libunwind.dylib" at 0x7fff960fa000]
        0x00007fff7b072010 - 0x00007fff7b072018 is LC_SEGMENT.__DATA.__got in [memory object
"/usr/lib/system/libunwind.dylib" at 0x7fff960fa000]
        0x00007fff7b072018 - 0x00007fff7b072090 is LC_SEGMENT.__DATA.__la_symbol_ptr in [memory object
"/usr/lib/system/libunwind.dylib" at 0x7fff960fa000]
        0x00007fff7b072090 - 0x00007fff7b072a01 is LC_SEGMENT.__DATA.__data in [memory object
"/usr/lib/system/libunwind.dylib" at 0x7fff960fa000]
        0x00007fff7b072a08 - 0x00007fff7b072a09 is LC_SEGMENT.__DATA.__bss in [memory object
"/usr/lib/system/libunwind.dylib" at 0x7fff960fa000]
        0x00007fff967f7000 - 0x00007fff99ebc000 is LC_SEGMENT.__LINKEDIT in [memory object
"/usr/lib/system/libunwind.dylib" at 0x7fff960fa000]
        0x00007fff89663000 - 0x00007fff89681000 is LC_SEGMENT.__TEXT in [memory object "/usr/lib/system/libxpc.dylib"
at 0x7fff89663000]
        0x00007fff89663f04 - 0x00007fff89674a40 is LC_SEGMENT.__TEXT.__text in [memory object
"/usr/lib/system/libxpc.dylib" at 0x7fff89663000]
        0x00007fff89674a40 - 0x00007fff89674e78 is LC_SEGMENT.__TEXT.__stubs in [memory object
"/usr/lib/system/libxpc.dylib" at 0x7fff89663000]
        0x00007fff89674e78 - 0x00007fff89675590 is LC_SEGMENT.__TEXT.__stub_helper in [memory object
"/usr/lib/system/libxpc.dylib" at 0x7fff89663000]

341

```
       0x00007fff89675590 - 0x00007fff89675820 is LC_SEGMENT.__TEXT.__const in [memory object
"/usr/lib/system/libxpc.dylib" at 0x7fff89663000]
       0x00007fff89675820 - 0x00007fff89678ba7 is LC_SEGMENT.__TEXT.__cstring in [memory object
"/usr/lib/system/libxpc.dylib" at 0x7fff89663000]
       0x00007fff89678ba7 - 0x00007fff8967913f is LC_SEGMENT.__TEXT.__unwind_info in [memory object
"/usr/lib/system/libxpc.dylib" at 0x7fff89663000]
       0x00007fff89679140 - 0x00007fff89681000 is LC_SEGMENT.__TEXT.__eh_frame in [memory object
"/usr/lib/system/libxpc.dylib" at 0---Type <return> to continue, or q <return> to quit---
x7fff89663000]
       0x00007fff79631000 - 0x00007fff79634000 is LC_SEGMENT.__DATA in [memory object "/usr/lib/system/libxpc.dylib"
at 0x7fff89663000]
       0x00007fff79631000 - 0x00007fff79631128 is LC_SEGMENT.__DATA.__got in [memory object
"/usr/lib/system/libxpc.dylib" at 0x7fff89663000]
       0x00007fff79631128 - 0x00007fff79631138 is LC_SEGMENT.__DATA.__nl_symbol_ptr in [memory object
"/usr/lib/system/libxpc.dylib" at 0x7fff89663000]
       0x00007fff79631138 - 0x00007fff796316d8 is LC_SEGMENT.__DATA.__la_symbol_ptr in [memory object
"/usr/lib/system/libxpc.dylib" at 0x7fff89663000]
       0x00007fff796316e0 - 0x00007fff796322d8 is LC_SEGMENT.__DATA.__const in [memory object
"/usr/lib/system/libxpc.dylib" at 0x7fff89663000]
       0x00007fff796322e0 - 0x00007fff796334b0 is LC_SEGMENT.__DATA.__data in [memory object
"/usr/lib/system/libxpc.dylib" at 0x7fff89663000]
       0x00007fff796334b0 - 0x00007fff796334e8 is LC_SEGMENT.__DATA.__crash_info in [memory object
"/usr/lib/system/libxpc.dylib" at 0x7fff89663000]
       0x00007fff796334e8 - 0x00007fff7963351d is LC_SEGMENT.__DATA.__common in [memory object
"/usr/lib/system/libxpc.dylib" at 0x7fff89663000]
       0x00007fff79633520 - 0x00007fff796335b0 is LC_SEGMENT.__DATA.__bss in [memory object
"/usr/lib/system/libxpc.dylib" at 0x7fff89663000]
       0x00007fff967f7000 - 0x00007fff99ebc000 is LC_SEGMENT.__LINKEDIT in [memory object
"/usr/lib/system/libxpc.dylib" at 0x7fff89663000]
```

Exercise A12 (LLDB)

- **Goal:** Learn how to dump memory for post-processing, get the list of functions and module variables, load symbols, inspect arguments and local variables

- **Patterns:** Module Variable

- \AMCDA-Dumps\Exercise-A12-LLDB.pdf

Exercise A12 (LLDB)

Goal: Learn how to dump memory for post-processing, get the list of functions and module variables, load symbols, inspect arguments and local variables

Patterns: Module Variable

1.   Load a core dump core.2281 and App11 executable:

```
$ lldb -c ~/Documents/AMCDA-Dumps/core.2281 -f ~/Documents/AMCDA-
Dumps/Apps/App11/Build/Products/Release/App11
error: core.2281 is a corrupt mach-o file: load command 45 LC_SEGMENT_64 has a fileoff +
filesize (0x161b7000) that extends beyond the end of the file (0x161b5000), the segment will be
truncated
Core file '/Users/DumpAnalysis/Documents/AMCDA-Dumps/core.2281' (x86_64) was loaded.
Process 0 stopped
* thread #1: tid = 0x0000, 0x00007fff8ed7de42 libsystem_kernel.dylib`__semwait_signal + 10,
stop reason = signal SIGSTOP
    frame #0: 0x00007fff8ed7de42 libsystem_kernel.dylib`__semwait_signal + 10
libsystem_kernel.dylib`__semwait_signal + 10:
-> 0x7fff8ed7de42:  jae    0x7fff8ed7de49            ; __semwait_signal + 17
   0x7fff8ed7de44:  jmpq   0x7fff8ed7effc            ; cerror
   0x7fff8ed7de49:  ret
   0x7fff8ed7de4a:  nop
  thread #2: tid = 0x0001, 0x00007fff8ed7de42 libsystem_kernel.dylib`__semwait_signal + 10,
stop reason = signal SIGSTOP
    frame #0: 0x00007fff8ed7de42 libsystem_kernel.dylib`__semwait_signal + 10
libsystem_kernel.dylib`__semwait_signal + 10:
-> 0x7fff8ed7de42:  jae    0x7fff8ed7de49            ; __semwait_signal + 17
   0x7fff8ed7de44:  jmpq   0x7fff8ed7effc            ; cerror
   0x7fff8ed7de49:  ret
   0x7fff8ed7de4a:  nop
  thread #3: tid = 0x0002, 0x00007fff8ed7dbf2 libsystem_kernel.dylib`__psynch_mutexwait + 10,
stop reason = signal SIGSTOP
    frame #0: 0x00007fff8ed7dbf2 libsystem_kernel.dylib`__psynch_mutexwait + 10
libsystem_kernel.dylib`__psynch_mutexwait + 10:
-> 0x7fff8ed7dbf2:  jae    0x7fff8ed7dbf9            ; __psynch_mutexwait + 17
   0x7fff8ed7dbf4:  jmpq   0x7fff8ed7effc            ; cerror
   0x7fff8ed7dbf9:  ret
   0x7fff8ed7dbfa:  nop
  thread #4: tid = 0x0003, 0x00007fff8ed7de42 libsystem_kernel.dylib`__semwait_signal + 10,
stop reason = signal SIGSTOP
    frame #0: 0x00007fff8ed7de42 libsystem_kernel.dylib`__semwait_signal + 10
libsystem_kernel.dylib`__semwait_signal + 10:
-> 0x7fff8ed7de42:  jae    0x7fff8ed7de49            ; __semwait_signal + 17
   0x7fff8ed7de44:  jmpq   0x7fff8ed7effc            ; cerror
   0x7fff8ed7de49:  ret
   0x7fff8ed7de4a:  nop
```

```
    thread #5: tid = 0x0004, 0x00007fff8ed7dbf2 libsystem_kernel.dylib`__psynch_mutexwait + 10,
stop reason = signal SIGSTOP
      frame #0: 0x00007fff8ed7dbf2 libsystem_kernel.dylib`__psynch_mutexwait + 10
libsystem_kernel.dylib`__psynch_mutexwait + 10:
-> 0x7fff8ed7dbf2:  jae      0x7fff8ed7dbf9              ; __psynch_mutexwait + 17
   0x7fff8ed7dbf4:  jmpq     0x7fff8ed7effc              ; cerror
   0x7fff8ed7dbf9:  ret
   0x7fff8ed7dbfa:  nop
  thread #6: tid = 0x0005, 0x00007fff8ed7de42 libsystem_kernel.dylib`__semwait_signal + 10,
stop reason = signal SIGSTOP
      frame #0: 0x00007fff8ed7de42 libsystem_kernel.dylib`__semwait_signal + 10
libsystem_kernel.dylib`__semwait_signal + 10:
-> 0x7fff8ed7de42:  jae      0x7fff8ed7de49              ; __semwait_signal + 17
   0x7fff8ed7de44:  jmpq     0x7fff8ed7effc              ; cerror
   0x7fff8ed7de49:  ret
   0x7fff8ed7de4a:  nop
```

2.   Check the current thread stack trace:

```
(lldb) bt
* thread #1: tid = 0x0000, 0x00007fff8ed7de42 libsystem_kernel.dylib`__semwait_signal + 10,
stop reason = signal SIGSTOP
    frame #0: 0x00007fff8ed7de42 libsystem_kernel.dylib`__semwait_signal + 10
    frame #1: 0x00007fff899dfdea libsystem_c.dylib`nanosleep + 164
    frame #2: 0x00007fff899dfc2c libsystem_c.dylib`sleep + 61
    frame #3: 0x00007fff899dfc08 libsystem_c.dylib`sleep + 25
    frame #4: 0x0000000105051b75 App11`main + 261
    frame #5: 0x0000000105051774 App11`start + 52
```

3.   Open Symbols.zip in Finder (it should automatically unzip itself) and then load a symbol file for App11:

```
(lldb) target symbol add ~/Documents/AMCDA-
Dumps/Symbols/App11.dSYM/Contents/Resources/DWARF/App11
symbol file '/Users/DumpAnalysis/Documents/AMCDA-
Dumps/Symbols/App11.dSYM/Contents/Resources/DWARF/App11' has been added to
'/Users/DumpAnalysis/Documents/AMCDA-Dumps/Apps/App11/Build/Products/Release/App11'
```

4.   List all thread stack traces:

```
(lldb) thread backtrace all
* thread #1: tid = 0x0000, 0x00007fff8ed7de42 libsystem_kernel.dylib`__semwait_signal + 10, stop reason = signal
SIGSTOP
    frame #0: 0x00007fff8ed7de42 libsystem_kernel.dylib`__semwait_signal + 10
    frame #1: 0x00007fff899dfdea libsystem_c.dylib`nanosleep + 164
    frame #2: 0x00007fff899dfc2c libsystem_c.dylib`sleep + 61
    frame #3: 0x00007fff899dfc08 libsystem_c.dylib`sleep + 25
    frame #4: 0x0000000105051b75 App11`main(argc=1, argv=0x00007fff64c50b08) + 261 at main.cpp:86
    frame #5: 0x0000000105051774 App11`start + 52

  thread #2: tid = 0x0001, 0x00007fff8ed7de42 libsystem_kernel.dylib`__semwait_signal + 10, stop reason = signal
SIGSTOP
    frame #0: 0x00007fff8ed7de42 libsystem_kernel.dylib`__semwait_signal + 10
    frame #1: 0x00007fff899dfdea libsystem_c.dylib`nanosleep + 164
    frame #2: 0x00007fff899dfc2c libsystem_c.dylib`sleep + 61
    frame #3: 0x00007fff899dfc08 libsystem_c.dylib`sleep + 25
    frame #4: 0x00000001050518c2 App11`bar_one() + 18 at main.cpp:66
    frame #5: 0x00000001050518d9 App11`foo_one() + 9 at main.cpp:66
    frame #6: 0x00000001050518f1 App11`thread_one(arg=0x0000000000000000) + 17 at main.cpp:66
    frame #7: 0x00007fff89a298bf libsystem_c.dylib`_pthread_start + 335
```

```
      frame #8: 0x00007fff89a2cb75 libsystem_c.dylib`thread_start + 13

   thread #3: tid = 0x0002, 0x00007fff8ed7dbf2 libsystem_kernel.dylib`__psynch_mutexwait + 10, stop reason = signal
SIGSTOP
      frame #0: 0x00007fff8ed7dbf2 libsystem_kernel.dylib`__psynch_mutexwait + 10
      frame #1: 0x00007fff89a281a1 libsystem_c.dylib`pthread_mutex_lock + 545
      frame #2: 0x0000000105051833 App11`procA() + 115 at main.cpp:36
      frame #3: 0x0000000105051919 App11`bar_two() + 9 at main.cpp:67
      frame #4: 0x0000000105051929 App11`foo_two() + 9 at main.cpp:67
      frame #5: 0x0000000105051941 App11`thread_two(arg=0x0000000000000000) + 17 at main.cpp:67
      frame #6: 0x00007fff89a298bf libsystem_c.dylib`_pthread_start + 335
      frame #7: 0x00007fff89a2cb75 libsystem_c.dylib`thread_start + 13

   thread #4: tid = 0x0003, 0x00007fff8ed7de42 libsystem_kernel.dylib`__semwait_signal + 10, stop reason = signal
SIGSTOP
      frame #0: 0x00007fff8ed7de42 libsystem_kernel.dylib`__semwait_signal + 10
      frame #1: 0x00007fff899dfdea libsystem_c.dylib`nanosleep + 164
      frame #2: 0x00007fff899dfc2c libsystem_c.dylib`sleep + 61
      frame #3: 0x00007fff899dfc08 libsystem_c.dylib`sleep + 25
      frame #4: 0x0000000105051972 App11`bar_three() + 18 at main.cpp:68
      frame #5: 0x0000000105051989 App11`foo_three() + 9 at main.cpp:68
      frame #6: 0x00000001050519a1 App11`thread_three(arg=0x0000000000000000) + 17 at main.cpp:68
      frame #7: 0x00007fff89a298bf libsystem_c.dylib`_pthread_start + 335
      frame #8: 0x00007fff89a2cb75 libsystem_c.dylib`thread_start + 13

   thread #5: tid = 0x0004, 0x00007fff8ed7dbf2 libsystem_kernel.dylib`__psynch_mutexwait + 10, stop reason = signal
SIGSTOP
      frame #0: 0x00007fff8ed7dbf2 libsystem_kernel.dylib`__psynch_mutexwait + 10
      frame #1: 0x00007fff89a281a1 libsystem_c.dylib`pthread_mutex_lock + 545
      frame #2: 0x0000000105051873 App11`procB() + 35 at main.cpp:43
      frame #3: 0x00000001050519c9 App11`bar_four() + 9 at main.cpp:69
      frame #4: 0x00000001050519d9 App11`foo_four() + 9 at main.cpp:69
      frame #5: 0x00000001050519f1 App11`thread_four(arg=0x0000000000000000) + 17 at main.cpp:69
      frame #6: 0x00007fff89a298bf libsystem_c.dylib`_pthread_start + 335
      frame #7: 0x00007fff89a2cb75 libsystem_c.dylib`thread_start + 13

   thread #6: tid = 0x0005, 0x00007fff8ed7de42 libsystem_kernel.dylib`__semwait_signal + 10, stop reason = signal
SIGSTOP
      frame #0: 0x00007fff8ed7de42 libsystem_kernel.dylib`__semwait_signal + 10
      frame #1: 0x00007fff899dfdea libsystem_c.dylib`nanosleep + 164
      frame #2: 0x00007fff899dfc2c libsystem_c.dylib`sleep + 61
      frame #3: 0x00007fff899dfc08 libsystem_c.dylib`sleep + 25
      frame #4: 0x0000000105051a22 App11`bar_five() + 18 at main.cpp:70
      frame #5: 0x0000000105051a39 App11`foo_five() + 9 at main.cpp:70
      frame #6: 0x0000000105051a51 App11`thread_five(arg=0x0000000000000000) + 17 at main.cpp:70
      frame #7: 0x00007fff89a298bf libsystem_c.dylib`_pthread_start + 335
      frame #8: 0x00007fff89a2cb75 libsystem_c.dylib`thread_start + 13
```

5.   Switch to frame 4 of the current thread and list arguments and locals:

```
(lldb) f 4
frame #4: 0x0000000105051b75 App11`main(argc=1, argv=0x00007fff64c50b08) + 261 at main.cpp:86
   83              THREAD_CREATE(four)
   84              THREAD_CREATE(five)
   85
-> 86              sleep(-1);
   87              return 0;
   88          }


(lldb) frame variable --no-locals
(int) argc = 1
(const char **) argv = 0x00007fff64c50b08

(lldb) print argv[0]
(const char *) $0 = 0x00007fff64c50c40 "/Users/DumpAnalysis/Documents/AMCDA-
Dumps/Apps/App11/Build/Products/Release/App11"

(lldb) frame variable --no-args
```

6.   Dump region 0x00007fff64c51000 - 0x00007fff64c86000 to a binary file:

```
(lldb) me r -o ~/Documents/AMCDA-Dumps/mem.raw -b 0x00007fff64c51000 0x00007fff64c86000 –force
```

7.   Check in Finder and use your favourite application to open it. I use Photoshop to interpret it as a picture:

8.   List *bar* functions:

```
(lldb) image lookup -r -s bar_
5 symbols match the regular expression 'bar_' in /Users/DumpAnalysis/Documents/AMCDA-
Dumps/Apps/App11/Build/Products/Release/App11:
        Address: App11[0x00000001000008b0] (App11.__TEXT.__text + 368)
        Summary: App11`bar_one() at main.cpp:66        Address: App11[0x0000000100000910] (App11.__TEXT.__text + 464)
        Summary: App11`bar_two() at main.cpp:67        Address: App11[0x0000000100000960] (App11.__TEXT.__text + 544)
        Summary: App11`bar_three() at main.cpp:68       Address: App11[0x00000001000009c0] (App11.__TEXT.__text +
640)
        Summary: App11`bar_four() at main.cpp:69       Address: App11[0x0000000100000a10] (App11.__TEXT.__text + 720)
        Summary: App11`bar_five() at main.cpp:70
```

347

9.   List mutexA and mutexB variables:

```
(lldb) image lookup -r -s mutex[A|B]
2 symbols match the regular expression 'mutex[A|B]' in /Users/DumpAnalysis/Documents/AMCDA-
Dumps/Apps/App11/Build/Products/Release/App11:
        Address: App11[0x00000001000010b8] (App11.__DATA.__common + 32)
        Summary: App11`mutexA        Address: App11[0x00000001000010f8] (App11.__DATA.__common + 96)
        Summary:
```

10.   List modules:

```
(lldb) image list
[  0] A6D8D8F4-D61C-3295-A579-D55006FBA826 0x0000000105051000 /Users/DumpAnalysis/Documents/AMCDA-
Dumps/Apps/App11/Build/Products/Release/App11
        /Users/DumpAnalysis/Documents/AMCDA-Dumps/Symbols/App11.dSYM/Contents/Resources/DWARF/App11
[  1] 6BDD43E4-A4B1-379E-9ED5-8C713653DFF2 0x00007fff92744000 /usr/lib/libstdc++.6.dylib (0x00007fff92744000)
[  2] 7BEBB139-50BB-3112-947A-F4AA168F991C 0x00007fff95fe7000 /usr/lib/libSystem.B.dylib (0x00007fff95fe7000)
[  3] 8FF3D766-D678-36F6-84AC-423C878E6D14 0x00007fff95709000 /usr/lib/libc++abi.dylib (0x00007fff95709000)
[  4] 1571C3AB-BCB2-38CD-B3B2-C5FC3F927C6A 0x00007fff96693000 /usr/lib/system/libcache.dylib (0x00007fff96693000)
[  5] BB770C22-8C57-365A-8716-4A3C36AE7BFB 0x00007fff94abc000 /usr/lib/system/libcommonCrypto.dylib
(0x00007fff94abc000)
[  6] 98ECD5F6-E85C-32A5-98CD-8911230CB66A 0x00007fff9004e000 /usr/lib/system/libcompiler_rt.dylib
(0x00007fff9004e000)
[  7] 0AB51EE2-E914-358C-AC19-47BC024BDAE7 0x00007fff94a73000 /usr/lib/system/libcopyfile.dylib (0x00007fff94a73000)
[  8] 1D5BE322-A9B9-3BCE-8FAC-076FB07CF54A 0x00007fff89c93000 /usr/lib/system/libdispatch.dylib (0x00007fff89c93000)
[  9] 853BAAA5-270F-3FDC-B025-D448DB72E1C3 0x00007fff9098b000 /usr/lib/system/libdnsinfo.dylib (0x00007fff9098b000)
[ 10] 380C3F44-0CA7-3514-8080-46D1C9DF4FCD 0x00007fff8dd8a000 /usr/lib/system/libdyld.dylib (0x00007fff8dd8a000)
[ 11] 61EFED6A-A407-301E-B454-CD18314F0075 0x00007fff90025000 /usr/lib/system/libkeymgr.dylib (0x00007fff90025000)
[ 12] 6ECB7F19-B384-32C1-8652-2463C1CF4815 0x00007fff91c14000 /usr/lib/system/liblaunch.dylib (0x00007fff91c14000)
[ 13] 165514D7-1BFA-38EF-A151-676DCD21FB64 0x00007fff8ed60000 /usr/lib/system/libmacho.dylib (0x00007fff8ed60000)
[ 14] FF83AFF7-42B2-306E-90AF-D539C51A4542 0x00007fff8dd85000 /usr/lib/system/libmathCommon.A.dylib
(0x00007fff8dd85000)
[ 15] 0EBF714B-4B69-3E1F-9A7D-6BBC2AACB310 0x00007fff8feb9000 /usr/lib/system/libquarantine.dylib (0x00007fff8feb9000)
[ 16] 739E6C83-AA52-3C6C-A680-B37FE2888A04 0x00007fff8a754000 /usr/lib/system/libremovefile.dylib (0x00007fff8a754000)
[ 17] 8BCA214A-8992-34B2-A8B9-B74DEACA1869 0x00007fff899d9000 /usr/lib/system/libsystem_blocks.dylib
(0x00007fff899d9000)
[ 18] 41B43515-2806-3FBC-ACF1-A16F35B7E290 0x00007fff899db000 /usr/lib/system/libsystem_c.dylib (0x00007fff899db000)
[ 19] D9BB1F87-A42B-3CBC-9DC2-FC07FCEF0016 0x00007fff8ef1d000 /usr/lib/system/libsystem_dnssd.dylib
(0x00007fff8ef1d000)
[ 20] 35F90252-2AE1-32C5-8D34-782C614D9639 0x00007fff8fa97000 /usr/lib/system/libsystem_info.dylib
(0x00007fff8fa97000)
[ 21] 1DDC0B0F-DB2A-34D6-895D-E5B2B5618946 0x00007fff8ed67000 /usr/lib/system/libsystem_kernel.dylib
(0x00007fff8ed67000)
[ 22] 5DE7024E-1D2D-34A2-80F4-08326331A75B 0x00007fff91199000 /usr/lib/system/libsystem_network.dylib
(0x00007fff91199000)
[ 23] A4D651E3-D1C6-3934-AD49-7A104FD14596 0x00007fff95880000 /usr/lib/system/libsystem_notify.dylib
(0x00007fff95880000)
[ 24] 96D38E74-F18F-3CCB-A20B-E8E3ADC4E166 0x00007fff8e3b1000 /usr/lib/system/libsystem_sandbox.dylib
(0x00007fff8e3b1000)
[ 25] 337960EE-0A85-3DD0-A760-7134CF4C0AFF 0x00007fff8a261000 /usr/lib/system/libunc.dylib (0x00007fff8a261000)
[ 26] 1E9C6C8C-CBE8-3F4B-A5B5-E03E3AB53231 0x00007fff960fa000 /usr/lib/system/libunwind.dylib (0x00007fff960fa000)
[ 27] 9F57891B-D7EF-3050-BEDD-21E7C6668248 0x00007fff89663000 /usr/lib/system/libxpc.dylib (0x00007fff89663000)
[ 28] 0CD1B35B-A28F-32DA-B72E-452EAD609613 0x00007fff64c51000 /usr/lib/dyld (0x00007fff64c51000)
```

11.   List memory regions for App11 module:

```
(lldb) image dump sections App11
Sections for '/Users/DumpAnalysis/Documents/AMCDA-Dumps/Apps/App11/Build/Products/Release/App11' (x86_64):
  SectID     Type            Load Address                              File Off.  File Size  Flags      Section Name
  ---------- --------------- ----------------------------------------  ---------- ---------- ---------- ----------------------------
  0x00000100 container       [0x0000000000000000-0x0000000100000000)*  0x00000000 0x00000000 0x00000000 App11.__PAGEZERO
  0x00000200 container       [0x0000000105051000-0x0000000105052000)   0x00000000 0x00001000 0x00000000 App11.__TEXT
  0x00000001 code            [0x0000000105051740-0x0000000105051b85)   0x00000740 0x00000445 0x80000400 App11.__TEXT.__text
  0x00000002 code            [0x0000000105051b86-0x0000000105051bc2)   0x00000b86 0x0000003c 0x80000408 App11.__TEXT.__stubs
  0x00000003 code            [0x0000000105051bc4-0x0000000105051c38)   0x00000bc4 0x00000074 0x80000400 App11.__TEXT.__stub_helper
  0x00000004 code            [0x0000000105051c38-0x0000000105051c60)   0x00000c38 0x00000028 0x00000000 App11.__TEXT.__gcc_except_tab
  0x00000005 code            [0x0000000105051c60-0x0000000105051cc8)   0x00000c60 0x00000068 0x00000000 App11.__TEXT.__unwind_info
  0x00000006 eh-frame        [0x0000000105051cc8-0x0000000105052000)   0x00000cc8 0x00000338 0x00000000 App11.__TEXT.__eh_frame
  0x00000300 container       [0x0000000105052000-0x0000000105053000)   0x00001000 0x00001000 0x00000000 App11.__DATA
  0x00000007 data            [0x0000000105052000-0x0000000105052028)   0x00001000 0x00000028 0x00000000 App11.__DATA.__program_vars
  0x00000008 data-ptrs       [0x0000000105052028-0x0000000105052038)   0x00001028 0x00000010 0x00000006 App11.__DATA.__nl_symbol_ptr
  0x00000009 data-ptrs       [0x0000000105052038-0x0000000105052048)   0x00001038 0x00000010 0x00000006 App11.__DATA.__got
  0x0000000a data-ptrs       [0x0000000105052048-0x0000000105052098)   0x00001048 0x00000050 0x00000007 App11.__DATA.__la_symbol_ptr
  0x0000000b zero-fill       [0x0000000105052098-0x0000000105052138)   0x00000000 0x00000000 0x00000001 App11.__DATA.__common
  0x00000400 container       [0x0000000105053000-0x00000001050536f8)   0x00002000 0x000006f8 0x00000000 App11.__LINKEDIT
```

348

```
0x00000200 container          [0x0000000100003000-0x0000000100005000)* 0x00002000 0x00001746 0x00000000 App11.__DWARF
0x00000001 dwarf-abbrev        [0x0000000100003000-0x000000010000314f)* 0x00002000 0x0000014f 0x00000000 App11.__DWARF.__debug_abbrev
0x00000002 dwarf-aranges       [0x000000010000314f-0x000000010000329f)* 0x0000214f 0x00000150 0x00000000 App11.__DWARF.__debug_aranges
0x00000003 dwarf-info          [0x000000010000329f-0x00000001000037dc)* 0x0000229f 0x0000053d 0x00000000 App11.__DWARF.__debug_info
0x00000004 dwarf-line          [0x00000001000037dc-0x0000000100003aba)* 0x000027dc 0x000002de 0x00000000 App11.__DWARF.__debug_line
0x00000005 dwarf-pubnames      [0x0000000100003aba-0x0000000100003d17)* 0x00002aba 0x0000025d 0x00000000 App11.__DWARF.__debug_pubnames
0x00000006 dwarf-pubtypes      [0x0000000100003d17-0x0000000100003df0)* 0x00002d17 0x000000d9 0x00000000 App11.__DWARF.__debug_pubtypes
0x00000007 dwarf-str           [0x0000000100003df0-0x000000010000418c)* 0x00002df0 0x0000039c 0x00000000 App11.__DWARF.__debug_str
0x00000008 apple-names         [0x000000010000418c-0x00000001000045a0)* 0x0000318c 0x00000414 0x00000000 App11.__DWARF.__apple_names
0x00000009 apple-types         [0x00000001000045a0-0x00000001000046fe)* 0x000035a0 0x0000015e 0x00000000 App11.__DWARF.__apple_types
0x0000000a apple-namespaces [0x00000001000046fe-0x0000000100004722)* 0x000036fe 0x00000024 0x00000000 App11.__DWARF.__apple_namespac
0x0000000b apple-objc          [0x0000000100004722-0x0000000100004746)* 0x00003722 0x00000024 0x00000000 App11.__DWARF.__apple_objc
```

Pattern Links

Active Thread	Annotated Disassembly
C++ Exception	Coincidental Symbolic Information
Critical Region	Deadlock
Divide by Zero	Double Free
Environment Hint	Execution Residue
Incorrect Stack Trace	Handled Exception
Heap Contention	Heap Corruption
Heap Leak	Local Buffer Overflow
Manual Dump	Module Hint
Module Variable	Multiple Exceptions
Not My Version	NULL Pointer (data)
NULL Pointer (code)	Paratext
Self-Diagnosis	Spiking Thread
Stack Overflow	Stack Trace
Stack Trace Collection	Wait Chain

Here are links to pattern descriptions and additional examples:

http://www.dumpanalysis.org/blog/index.php/category/core-dump-analysis/

Selected pattern descriptions are provided at the end of this book.

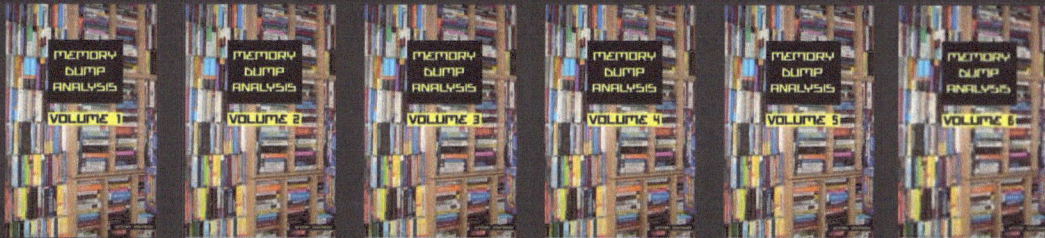

Software Diagnostics Institute:

http://www.dumpanalysis.org/

Pattern-Driven Software Diagnostics:

http://www.patterndiagnostics.com/Introduction-Software-Diagnostics-materials

Pattern-Based Software Diagnostics:

http://www.patterndiagnostics.com/pattern-based-diagnostics-materials

Debugging TV:

http://www.debugging.tv/

Rosetta Stone for Debuggers:

http://www.dumpanalysis.org/rosetta-stone-debuggers

GDB -> LLDB Map:

http://developer.apple.com/library/mac/documentation/IDEs/Conceptual/gdb_to_lldb_transition_guide/document/lldb-command-examples.html

App Source Code

```c
//
//  main.c
//  App0 - Exercise 0 - Testing Xcode GDB
//
//  Created by Dmitry Vostokov on 22/07/2012.
//  Copyright (c) 2012 Memory Dump Analysis Services. All rights reserved.
//

#include <stdlib.h>

void bar()
{
    abort();
}

void foo()
{
    bar();
}

int main(int argc, const char * argv[])
{
    foo();
    return 0;
}
```

App1

```c
//
//  main.c
//  App1 - Normal application with multiple threads
//
//  Created by Dmitry Vostokov on 23/07/2012.
//  Copyright (c) 2012 Memory Dump Analysis Services. All rights reserved.
//

#include <stdio.h>
#include <pthread.h>
#include <unistd.h>
#include <string.h>
#include <stdlib.h>

#define THREAD_DECLARE(num) void bar_##num()\
{\
    sleep(-1);\
}\
\
void foo_##num()\
{\
    bar_##num();\
}\
\
void * thread_##num (void *arg)\
{\
    foo_##num();\
\
    return 0;\
}

THREAD_DECLARE(one)
THREAD_DECLARE(two)
THREAD_DECLARE(three)
THREAD_DECLARE(four)
THREAD_DECLARE(five)

#define THREAD_CREATE(num) {pthread_t threadID_##num; pthread_create (&threadID_##num, NULL, thread_##num, NULL);}

int main(int argc, const char * argv[])
{
    THREAD_CREATE(one)
    THREAD_CREATE(two)
    THREAD_CREATE(three)
    THREAD_CREATE(four)
    THREAD_CREATE(five)

    sleep(-1);
    return 0;
}
```

App2

```c
//
//  main.c
//  App2 - Shows multiple exceptions: NULL data and NULL code pointers
//
//  Created by Dmitry Vostokov on 24/07/2012.
//  Copyright (c) 2012 Memory Dump Analysis Services. All rights reserved.
//

#include <stdio.h>
#include <pthread.h>
#include <unistd.h>
#include <string.h>
#include <stdlib.h>

void procA()
{
    int *p = NULL;
    *p = 1;
}

void procB()
{
    void (*pf)() = NULL;

    pf();
}

#define THREAD_DECLARE(num,func) void bar_##num()\
{\
func;\
}\
\
void foo_##num()\
{\
bar_##num();\
}\
\
void * thread_##num (void *arg)\
{\
foo_##num();\
\
return 0;\
}

THREAD_DECLARE(one,sleep(-1))
THREAD_DECLARE(two,procA())
THREAD_DECLARE(three,sleep(-1))
THREAD_DECLARE(four,procB())
THREAD_DECLARE(five,sleep(-1))

#define THREAD_CREATE(num) {pthread_t threadID_##num; pthread_create (&threadID_##num, NULL,
thread_##num, NULL);}
```

```
int main(int argc, const char * argv[])
{
    THREAD_CREATE(one)
    THREAD_CREATE(two)
    THREAD_CREATE(three)
    THREAD_CREATE(four)
    THREAD_CREATE(five)

    sleep(3);
    return 0;
}
```

App3

```c
//
//  main.c
//  App3 - Spiking Thread pattern
//
//  Created by Dmitry Vostokov on 24/07/2012.
//  Copyright (c) 2012 Memory Dump Analysis Services. All rights reserved.
//

#include <stdio.h>
#include <pthread.h>
#include <unistd.h>
#include <string.h>
#include <stdlib.h>
#include <math.h>

void procA()
{
    while (1)
    {
        sleep(1);
    }
}

void procB()
{
    double d = 1.0/3.0;
    while (1)
    {
        d = sqrt(d);
    }
}

#define THREAD_DECLARE(num,func) void bar_##num()\
{\
func;\
}\
\
void foo_##num()\
{\
bar_##num();\
}\
\
void * thread_##num (void *arg)\
{\
foo_##num();\
\
return 0;\
}

THREAD_DECLARE(one,sleep(-1))
THREAD_DECLARE(two,sleep(-1))
THREAD_DECLARE(three,procA())
THREAD_DECLARE(four,sleep(-1))
THREAD_DECLARE(five,procB())

#define THREAD_CREATE(num) {pthread_t threadID_##num; pthread_create (&threadID_##num, NULL,
thread_##num, NULL);}
```

```
int main(int argc, const char * argv[])
{
    THREAD_CREATE(one)
    THREAD_CREATE(two)
    THREAD_CREATE(three)
    THREAD_CREATE(four)
    THREAD_CREATE(five)

    sleep(-1);
    return 0;
}
```

App4

```
//
//  main.c
//  App4 - Heap Corruption pattern
//
//  Created by Dmitry Vostokov on 24/07/2012.
//  Copyright (c) 2012 Memory Dump Analysis Services. All rights reserved.
//

#include <stdio.h>
#include <pthread.h>
#include <unistd.h>
#include <string.h>
#include <stdlib.h>

void proc()
{
    char *p1 = (char *) malloc (1024);
    char *p2 = (char *) malloc (1024);
    char *p3 = (char *) malloc (1024);
    char *p4 = (char *) malloc (1024);
    char *p5 = (char *) malloc (1024);
    char *p6 = (char *) malloc (1024);
    char *p7 = (char *) malloc (1024);

    free(p6);
    free(p4);
    free(p2);

    strcpy(p2, "Hello Crash!");
    strcpy(p4, "Hello Crash!");
    strcpy(p6, "Hello Crash!");

    p2 = (char *) malloc (512);
    p4 = (char *) malloc (1024);
    p6 = (char *) malloc (512);

    sleep(300);

    free (p7);
    free (p6);
    free (p5);
    free (p4);
    free (p3);
    free (p2);
    free (p1);

    sleep(-1);
}
```

```c
#define THREAD_DECLARE(num,func) void bar_##num()\
{\
func;\
}\
\
void foo_##num()\
{\
bar_##num();\
}\
\
void * thread_##num (void *arg)\
{\
foo_##num();\
\
return 0;\
}

THREAD_DECLARE(one,sleep(-1))
THREAD_DECLARE(two,sleep(-1))
THREAD_DECLARE(three,proc())
THREAD_DECLARE(four,sleep(-1))
THREAD_DECLARE(five,sleep(-1))

#define THREAD_CREATE(num) {pthread_t threadID_##num; pthread_create (&threadID_##num, NULL,
thread_##num, NULL);}

int main(int argc, const char * argv[])
{
    THREAD_CREATE(one)
    THREAD_CREATE(two)
    THREAD_CREATE(three)
    THREAD_CREATE(four)
    THREAD_CREATE(five)

    sleep(-1);
    return 0;
}
```

```c
//
//  main.c
//  App5 - Local Buffer Overflow
//
//  Created by Dmitry Vostokov on 25/07/2012.
//  Copyright (c) 2012 Memory Dump Analysis Services. All rights reserved.
//

#include <stdio.h>
#include <pthread.h>
#include <unistd.h>
#include <string.h>
#include <stdlib.h>

void procB(char *buffer)
{
    char data[100] = "My New Bigger Buffer";
    memcpy (buffer, data, sizeof(data));
}

void procA()
{
    char data[10] = "My Buffer";
    procB(data);
}

#define THREAD_DECLARE(num,func) void bar_##num()\
{\
func;\
}\
\
void foo_##num()\
{\
bar_##num();\
}\
\
void * thread_##num (void *arg)\
{\
foo_##num();\
\
return 0;\
}

THREAD_DECLARE(one,procA())
THREAD_DECLARE(two,sleep(-1))
THREAD_DECLARE(three,sleep(-1))
THREAD_DECLARE(four,sleep(-1))
THREAD_DECLARE(five,sleep(-1))

#define THREAD_CREATE(num) {pthread_t threadID_##num; pthread_create (&threadID_##num, NULL,
thread_##num, NULL);}
```

```
int main(int argc, const char * argv[])
{
    THREAD_CREATE(one)
    THREAD_CREATE(two)
    THREAD_CREATE(three)
    THREAD_CREATE(four)
    THREAD_CREATE(five)

    sleep(-1);
    return 0;
}
```

```c
//
//  main.c
//  App6 - Stack Overflow
//
//  Created by Dmitry Vostokov on 25/07/2012.
//  Copyright (c) 2012 Memory Dump Analysis Services. All rights reserved.
//

#include <stdio.h>
#include <pthread.h>
#include <unistd.h>
#include <string.h>
#include <stdlib.h>

void procF(int i)
{
    int buffer[128] = {-1, 0, i+1, 0, -1};

    procF(buffer[2]);
}

void procE()
{
    procF(1);
}

#define THREAD_DECLARE(num,func) void bar_##num()\
{\
sleep(300);\
func;\
}\
\
void foo_##num()\
{\
bar_##num();\
}\
\
void * thread_##num (void *arg)\
{\
foo_##num();\
\
return 0;\
}

THREAD_DECLARE(one,procE())
THREAD_DECLARE(two,sleep(-1))
THREAD_DECLARE(three,sleep(-1))
THREAD_DECLARE(four,sleep(-1))
THREAD_DECLARE(five,sleep(-1))

#define THREAD_CREATE(num) {pthread_t threadID_##num; pthread_create (&threadID_##num, NULL,
thread_##num, NULL);}
```

```
int main(int argc, const char * argv[])
{
    THREAD_CREATE(one)
    THREAD_CREATE(two)
    THREAD_CREATE(three)
    THREAD_CREATE(four)
    THREAD_CREATE(five)

    sleep(-1);
    return 0;
}
```

```c
//
//  main.c
//  App7 - Divide by Zero and Active Threads
//
//  Created by Dmitry Vostokov on 25/07/2012.
//  Copyright (c) 2012 Memory Dump Analysis Services. All rights reserved.
//

#include <stdio.h>
#include <pthread.h>
#include <unistd.h>
#include <string.h>
#include <stdlib.h>

void procF(int i)
{
    int buffer[1024] = {-1, 0, i+1, 0, -1};

    procF(buffer[2]);
}

void procE()
{
    procF(1);
}

int procD(int a, int b)
{
    return a/b;
}

int procC()
{
    return procD(1,0);
}

void procB(char *buffer)
{
    char data[100] = "My New Bigger Buffer";
    memcpy (buffer, data, sizeof(data));
}

void procA()
{
    char data[10] = "My Buffer";
    procB(data);
}
```

```c
#define THREAD_DECLARE(num,func) void bar_##num()\
{\
sleep(300);\
func;\
}\
\
void foo_##num()\
{\
bar_##num();\
}\
\
void * thread_##num (void *arg)\
{\
foo_##num();\
\
return 0;\
}

THREAD_DECLARE(one,procA())
THREAD_DECLARE(two,sleep(-1))
THREAD_DECLARE(three,procC())
THREAD_DECLARE(four,sleep(-1))
THREAD_DECLARE(five,procE())

#define THREAD_CREATE(num) {pthread_t threadID_##num; pthread_create (&threadID_##num, NULL,
thread_##num, NULL);}

int main(int argc, const char * argv[])
{
    THREAD_CREATE(one)
    THREAD_CREATE(two)
    THREAD_CREATE(three)
    THREAD_CREATE(four)
    THREAD_CREATE(five)

    sleep(-1);
    return 0;
}
```

```cpp
//
//  main.cpp
//  App8 - C++ Exception, Execution Residue, Handled Exception
//
//  Created by Dmitry Vostokov on 25/07/2012.
//  Copyright (c) 2012 Memory Dump Analysis Services. All rights reserved.
//

#include <string>

#define def_call(name,x,y) void name##_##x() { name##_##y(); }
#define def_final(name,x) void name##_##x() { }
#define def_init(name,y,size) void name() { int arr[size]; name##_##y(); *arr=0; }

def_final(work,9)
def_call(work,8,9)
def_call(work,7,8)
def_call(work,6,7)
def_call(work,5,6)
def_call(work,4,5)
def_call(work,3,4)
def_call(work,2,3)
def_call(work,1,2)
def_init(work,1,256)

class Exception
{
    int code;
    std::string description;

public:
    Exception(int _code, std::string _desc) : code(_code), description(_desc) {}
};

void procB()
{
    throw new Exception(5, "Access Denied");
}

void procNB()
{
    work();
}

void procA()
{
    procB();
}

void procNA()
{
    procNB();
}
```

```
void procH()
{
    try {
        procA();
    } catch (...) {
        sleep(-1);
    }
}

void procNH()
{
    sleep(300);
    procA();
}

void procNE()
{
    try {
        procNA();
    }
    catch (...)
    {
    }
    sleep(-1);
}

#define THREAD_DECLARE(num,func) void bar_##num()\
{\
func;\
}\
\
void foo_##num()\
{\
bar_##num();\
}\
\
void * thread_##num (void *arg)\
{\
foo_##num();\
\
return 0;\
}

THREAD_DECLARE(one,procNH())
THREAD_DECLARE(two,procNE())
THREAD_DECLARE(three,procH())
THREAD_DECLARE(four,procNE())
THREAD_DECLARE(five,procNE())

#define THREAD_CREATE(num) {pthread_t threadID_##num; pthread_create (&threadID_##num, NULL,
thread_##num, NULL);}

int main(int argc, const char * argv[])
{
    THREAD_CREATE(one)
    THREAD_CREATE(two)
    THREAD_CREATE(three)
    THREAD_CREATE(four)
    THREAD_CREATE(five)

    sleep(-1);
    return 0;
}
```

```c
//
//  main.c
//  App9 - Heap Leak pattern
//
//  Created by Dmitry Vostokov on 28/07/2012.
//  Copyright (c) 2012 Memory Dump Analysis Services. All rights reserved.
//

#include <stdio.h>
#include <pthread.h>
#include <unistd.h>
#include <string.h>
#include <stdlib.h>

void procD()
{
}

typedef void (**PFUNC)();

void procC(int iter)
{
    for (int i = 0; i < iter; ++i)
    {
        char *p = malloc(256);
        strcpy(p, "allocated memory");

        *(PFUNC)(p + 32) = &procD;
    }
}

void procB()
{
    procC(2500000);
    sleep(300);
    procC(2500000);
    sleep(-1);
}

void procA()
{
    procC(5000);
    sleep(300);
    procB();
}
```

```
#define THREAD_DECLARE(num,func) void bar_##num()\
{\
func;\
}\
\
void foo_##num()\
{\
bar_##num();\
}\
\
void * thread_##num (void *arg)\
{\
foo_##num();\
\
return 0;\
}

THREAD_DECLARE(one,sleep(-1))
THREAD_DECLARE(two,procA())
THREAD_DECLARE(three,sleep(-1))
THREAD_DECLARE(four,sleep(-1))
THREAD_DECLARE(five,sleep(-1))

#define THREAD_CREATE(num) {pthread_t threadID_##num; pthread_create (&threadID_##num, NULL,
thread_##num, NULL);}

int main(int argc, const char * argv[])
{
    THREAD_CREATE(one)
    THREAD_CREATE(two)
    THREAD_CREATE(three)
    THREAD_CREATE(four)
    THREAD_CREATE(five)

    sleep(-1);
    return 0;
}
```

```
//
//  main.c
//  App10 - Heap Corruption, Heap Contention, Critical Region, Wait Chains, Self-Diagnostics
patterns
//
//  Created by Dmitry Vostokov on 28/07/2012.
//  Copyright (c) 2012 Memory Dump Analysis Services. All rights reserved.
//

#include <stdio.h>
#include <pthread.h>
#include <unistd.h>
#include <string.h>
#include <stdlib.h>

#define ARR_SIZE 10000

char *pAllocBuf [ARR_SIZE] = {0};

void proc()
{
    while (1)
    {
        int idx = rand()%ARR_SIZE;
        int malloc_size = rand()%ARR_SIZE;

        if (pAllocBuf[idx])
        {
            free(pAllocBuf[idx]);
            pAllocBuf[idx] = 0;
        }

        pAllocBuf[idx] = malloc(malloc_size);
    }
}

#define THREAD_DECLARE(num,func) void bar_##num()\
{\
func;\
}\
\
void foo_##num()\
{\
bar_##num();\
}\
\
void * thread_##num (void *arg)\
{\
foo_##num();\
\
return 0;\
}

THREAD_DECLARE(one,proc())
THREAD_DECLARE(two,proc())
THREAD_DECLARE(three,proc())
THREAD_DECLARE(four,proc())
THREAD_DECLARE(five,proc())
```

```c
#define THREAD_CREATE(num) {pthread_t threadID_##num; pthread_create (&threadID_##num, NULL,
thread_##num, NULL);}

int main(int argc, const char * argv[])
{
    THREAD_CREATE(one)
    THREAD_CREATE(two)
    THREAD_CREATE(three)
    THREAD_CREATE(four)
    THREAD_CREATE(five)

    sleep(-1);
    return 0;
}
```

App11

```c
//
//  main.c
//  App11 - Wait Chains, Deadlock, Handled Exception patterns
//
//  Created by Dmitry Vostokov on 28/07/2012.
//  Copyright (c) 2012 Memory Dump Analysis Services. All rights reserved.
//

#include <stdio.h>
#include <pthread.h>
#include <unistd.h>
#include <string.h>
#include <stdlib.h>

pthread_mutex_t mutexA, mutexB;

void procC()
{
    throw 0;
}

void procA()
{
    try
    {
        pthread_mutex_lock(&mutexA);
        procC();
        pthread_mutex_unlock(&mutexA);
    }
    catch(...)
    {

    }

    sleep(20);
    pthread_mutex_lock(&mutexB);
    pthread_mutex_unlock(&mutexB);
}

void procB()
{
    pthread_mutex_lock(&mutexB);
    pthread_mutex_lock(&mutexA);
    sleep(30);
    pthread_mutex_lock(&mutexA);
    pthread_mutex_lock(&mutexB);
}
```

```c
#define THREAD_DECLARE(num,func) void bar_##num()\
{\
func;\
}\
\
void foo_##num()\
{\
bar_##num();\
}\
\
void * thread_##num (void *arg)\
{\
foo_##num();\
\
return 0;\
}

THREAD_DECLARE(one,sleep(-1))
THREAD_DECLARE(two,procA())
THREAD_DECLARE(three,sleep(-1))
THREAD_DECLARE(four,procB())
THREAD_DECLARE(five,sleep(-1))

#define THREAD_CREATE(num) {pthread_t threadID_##num; pthread_create (&threadID_##num, NULL,
thread_##num, NULL);}

int main(int argc, const char * argv[])
{
    pthread_mutex_init(&mutexA, NULL);
    pthread_mutex_init(&mutexB, NULL);

    THREAD_CREATE(one)
    THREAD_CREATE(two)
    sleep(10);
    THREAD_CREATE(three)
    THREAD_CREATE(four)
    THREAD_CREATE(five)

    sleep(-1);
    return 0;
}
```

Selected Patterns

(edited articles from Software Diagnostics Institute, www.DumpAnalysis.org)

NULL Pointer (data)

This is a Mac OS X / GDB counterpart to NULL Pointer (data) pattern[1] previously described for Windows platforms:

```
(gdb) bt
#0  0×000000010d3b0e90 in bar () at main.c:15
#1  0×000000010d3b0ea9 in foo () at main.c:20
#2  0×000000010d3b0ec4 in main (argc=1, argv=0×7fff6cfafbf8) at main.c:25


(gdb) disassemble
Dump of assembler code for function bar:
0x000000010d3b0e80 <bar+0>:      push %rbp
0x000000010d3b0e81 <bar+1>:      mov %rsp,%rbp
0x000000010d3b0e84 <bar+4>:      movq $0×0,-0×8(%rbp)
0x000000010d3b0e8c <bar+12>:     mov -0×8(%rbp),%rax
0×000000010d3b0e90 <bar+16>:     movl $0×1,(%rax)
0×000000010d3b0e96 <bar+22>:     pop %bp
0×000000010d3b0e97 <bar+23>:     retq
End of assembler dump.


(gdb) p/x $rax
$1 = 0×0
```

---

[1] http://www.dumpanalysis.org/blog/index.php/2009/04/14/crash-dump-analysis-patterns-part-6b/

Users of WinDbg debugger accustomed to full thread stack traces will wonder whether a thread starts from *main*:

```
(gdb) where
#0 0x000000010d3b0e90 in bar () at main.c:15
#1 0x000000010d3b0ea9 in foo () at main.c:20
#2 0x000000010d3b0ec4 in main (argc=1, argv=0x7fff6cfafbf8) at main.c:25
```

Of course, not and by default a stack trace is shown starting from *main* function. You can change this behavior by using the following command:

```
(gdb) set backtrace past-main
```

Now we see an additional frame:

```
(gdb) where
#0 0x000000010d3b0e90 in bar () at main.c:15
#1 0x000000010d3b0ea9 in foo () at main.c:20
#2 0x000000010d3b0ec4 in main (argc=1, argv=0x7fff6cfafbf8) at main.c:25
#3 0x000000010d3b0e74 in start ()
```

Stack Trace

This is a Mac OS X / GDB counterpart to Stack Trace pattern[2] previously described for Windows platforms. Here we show a stack trace when symbols are not available and also how to apply symbols:

```
(gdb) bt
#0  0x000000010d3b0e90 in ?? ()
#1  0x000000010d3b0ea9 in ?? ()
#2  0x000000010d3b0ec4 in ?? ()
#3  0x000000010d3b0e74 in ?? ()

(gdb) maintenance info sections
Exec file:
[...]
Core file:
`/cores/core.262', file type mach-o-le.
0x000000010d3b0000->0x000000010d3b1000 at 0x00001000: LC_SEGMENT. ALLOC LOAD CODE HAS_CONTENTS
0x000000010d3b1000->0x000000010d3b2000 at 0x00002000: LC_SEGMENT. ALLOC LOAD CODE HAS_CONTENTS
0x000000010d3b2000->0x000000010d3b3000 at 0x00003000: LC_SEGMENT. ALLOC LOAD CODE HAS_CONTENTS
0x000000010d3b3000->0x000000010d3b4000 at 0x00004000: LC_SEGMENT. ALLOC LOAD CODE HAS_CONTENTS
0x000000010d3b4000->0x000000010d3b5000 at 0x00005000: LC_SEGMENT. ALLOC LOAD CODE HAS_CONTENTS
0x000000010d3b5000->0x000000010d3b6000 at 0x00006000: LC_SEGMENT. ALLOC LOAD CODE HAS_CONTENTS
0x000000010d3b6000->0x000000010d3cb000 at 0x00007000: LC_SEGMENT. ALLOC LOAD CODE HAS_CONTENTS
0x000000010d3cb000->0x000000010d3cc000 at 0x0001c000: LC_SEGMENT. ALLOC LOAD CODE HAS_CONTENTS
0x000000010d3cc000->0x000000010d3cd000 at 0x0001d000: LC_SEGMENT. ALLOC LOAD CODE HAS_CONTENTS
0x000000010d3cd000->0x000000010d3e2000 at 0x0001e000: LC_SEGMENT. ALLOC LOAD CODE HAS_CONTENTS
0x000000010d3e2000->0x000000010d3e3000 at 0x00033000: LC_SEGMENT. ALLOC LOAD CODE HAS_CONTENTS
0x000000010d3e3000->0x000000010d3e4000 at 0x00034000: LC_SEGMENT. ALLOC LOAD CODE HAS_CONTENTS
0x000000010d400000->0x000000010d500000 at 0x00035000: LC_SEGMENT. ALLOC LOAD CODE HAS_CONTENTS
[...]

(gdb) add-symbol-file ~/Documents/Work/Test.sym 0x000000010d3b0000
add symbol table from file "/Users/DumpAnalysis/Documents/Work/Test.sym" at
       LC_SEGMENT.__TEXT = 0x10d3b0000
(y or n) y
Reading symbols from /Users/DumpAnalysis/Documents/Work/Test.sym...done.

(gdb) bt
#0  0x000000010d3b0e90 in bar () at main.c:15
#1  0x000000010d3b0ea9 in foo () at main.c:20
#2  0x000000010d3b0ec4 in main (argc=1, argv=0x7fff6cfafbf8) at main.c:25
```

---

[2] http://www.dumpanalysis.org/blog/index.php/2007/09/10/crash-dump-analysis-patterns-part-25/

The first Windows pattern called Multiple Exceptions[3] in user mode now has Mac OS X equivalent. In the example below there are 3 threads and two of them experienced NULL Pointer (data) access violation exception:

```
(gdb) thread apply all bt full

Thread 3 (core thread 2):
#0 0x00000001062ffe4e in thread_two (arg=0x0) at main.c:24
        p = (int *) 0x0
#1 0x00007fff8abf58bf in _pthread_start ()
No symbol table info available.
#2 0x00007fff8abf8b75 in thread_start ()
No symbol table info available.

Thread 2 (core thread 1):
#0 0x00000001062ffe1e in thread_one (arg=0x0) at main.c:16
        p = (int *) 0x0
#1 0x00007fff8abf58bf in _pthread_start ()
No symbol table info available.
#2 0x00007fff8abf8b75 in thread_start ()
No symbol table info available.

Thread 1 (core thread 0):
#0 0x00007fff854e0e42 in __semwait_signal ()
No symbol table info available.
#1 0x00007fff8ababdea in nanosleep ()
No symbol table info available.
#2 0x00007fff8ababc2c in sleep ()
No symbol table info available.
#3 0x00000001062ffec3 in main (argc=1, argv=0x7fff65efeab8) at main.c:36
        threadID_one = (pthread_t) 0x1063b4000
        threadID_two = (pthread_t) 0x106581000

(gdb) thread 2
[Switching to thread 2 (core thread 1)]
0x00000001062ffe1e in thread_one (arg=0x0) at main.c:16
16      *p = 1;

(gdb) p/x p
$1 = 0x0
(gdb) thread 3
[Switching to thread 3 (core thread 2)]
0x00000001062ffe4e in thread_two (arg=0x0) at main.c:24
24      *p = 2;

(gdb) p/x p
$2 = 0x0
```

---

[3] http://www.dumpanalysis.org/blog/index.php/2006/10/30/crash-dump-analysis-patterns-part-1/

Shared Buffer Overwrite

This is a provisional Mac OS X example of Shared Buffer Overwrite pattern[4]. Originally we wanted to construct a default C runtime heap corruption example using malloc / free functions. Unfortunately we couldn't get heap corrupted easily as was possible in Windows Visual C++ environment by writing before or after allocated block. We printed pointers to allocated memory and they all pointed to memory blocks laid out one after another without any headers in between. Therefore, any subsequent reallocation didn't cause corruption either. So all this naturally fits into shared buffer overwrites or underwrites where corruption is only detectable when the overwritten data is used, for example, in a pointer dereference.

```c
int main(int argc, const char * argv[])
{
    char *p1 = (char *) malloc (1024);
    strcpy(p1, "Hello World!");
    printf("p1 = %p\n", p1);
    printf("*p1 = %s\n", p1);
    char *p2 = (char *) malloc (1024);
    strcpy(p2, "Hello World!");
    printf("p2 = %p\n", p2);
    printf("*p2 = %s\n", p2);
    char *p3 = (char *) malloc (1024);
    strcpy(p3, "Hello World!");
    printf("p3 = %p\n", p3);
    printf("*p3 = %s\n", p3);
    strcpy(p2-sizeof(p2), "Hello Crash!");
    strcpy(p3-sizeof(p3), "Hello Crash!");
    p2 = (char *)realloc(p2, 2048);
    printf("p2 = %p\n", p2);
    printf("*p2 = %s\n", p2);
    char *p4 = (char *) malloc (1024);
    strcpy(p4-sizeof(p4), "Hello Crash!");
    printf("p4 = %p\n", p4);
    printf("*p4 = %s\n", p4);
    p3 = (char *)realloc(p3, 2048);
    printf("p3 = %p\n", p3);
    printf("*p3 = %s\n", p3);
    char *p5 = NULL; // to force a core dump
    *p5 = 0;
    free (p4);
    free (p3);
    free (p2);
    free (p1);
    return 0;
}
```

---

[4] http://www.dumpanalysis.org/blog/index.php/2010/10/18/crash-dump-analysis-patterns-part-110/

When we run the program above we get this output:

```
p1 = 0x7fc6d9000000
*p1 = Hello World!
p2 = 0×7fc6d9001400
*p2 = Hello World!
p3 = 0×7fc6d9001800
*p3 = Hello World!
p2 = 0×7fc6d9001c00
*p2 = ash!
p4 = 0×7fc6d9001400
*p4 = ash!
p3 = 0×7fc6d9002400
*p3 = ash!
Segmentation fault: 11 (core dumped)
```

Now is GDB output:

```
(gdb) x/1024bc p1
0x7fc6d9000000: 72 'H' 101 'e' 108 'l' 108 'l' 111 'o' 32 ' ' 87 'W' 111 'o'
0×7fc6d9000008: 114 'r' 108 'l' 100 'd' 33 '!' 0 '\0' 0 '\0' 0 '\0' 0 '\0'
0×7fc6d9000010: 0 '\0' 0 '\0' 0 '\0' 0 '\0' 0 '\0' 0 '\0' 0 '\0' 0 '\0'
[…]
0×7fc6d90003e8: 0 '\0' 0 '\0' 0 '\0' 0 '\0' 0 '\0' 0 '\0' 0 '\0' 0 '\0'
0×7fc6d90003f0: 0 '\0' 0 '\0' 0 '\0' 0 '\0' 0 '\0' 0 '\0' 0 '\0' 0 '\0'
0×7fc6d90003f8: 0 '\0' 0 '\0' 0 '\0' 0 '\0' 0 '\0' 0 '\0' 0 '\0' 0 '\0'

(gdb) x/32bc p1+1024-sizeof(p1)
0×7fc6d90003f8: 0 '\0' 0 '\0' 0 '\0' 0 '\0' 0 '\0' 0 '\0' 0 '\0' 0 '\0'
0×7fc6d9000400: 42 '*' 112 'p' 51 '3' 32 ' ' 61 '=' 32 ' ' 97 'a' 115 's'
0×7fc6d9000408: 104 'h' 33 '!' 10 '\n' 100 'd' 57 '9' 48 '0' 48 '0' 50 '2'
0×7fc6d9000410: 52 '4' 48 '0' 48 '0' 10 '\n' 0 '\0' 0 '\0' 0 '\0' 0 '\0'

(gdb) x/2048bc p2
0×7fc6d9001c00: 97 'a' 115 's' 104 'h' 33 '!' 0 '\0' 32 ' ' 87 'W' 111 'o'
0×7fc6d9001c08: 114 'r' 108 'l' 100 'd' 33 '!' 0 '\0' 0 '\0' 0 '\0' 0 '\0'
0×7fc6d9001c10: 0 '\0' 0 '\0' 0 '\0' 0 '\0' 0 '\0' 0 '\0' 0 '\0' 0 '\0'
[…]
0×7fc6d9001fe8: 0 '\0' 0 '\0' 0 '\0' 0 '\0' 0 '\0' 0 '\0' 0 '\0' 0 '\0'
0×7fc6d9001ff0: 0 '\0' 0 '\0' 0 '\0' 0 '\0' 0 '\0' 0 '\0' 0 '\0' 0 '\0'
0×7fc6d9001ff8: 72 'H' 101 'e' 108 'l' 108 'l' 111 'o' 32 ' ' 67 'C' 114 'r'
0×7fc6d9002000: 0 '\0' 0 '\0' 0 '\0' 0 '\0' 0 '\0' 0 '\0' 0 '\0' 0 '\0'
0×7fc6d9002008: 0 '\0' 0 '\0' 0 '\0' 0 '\0' 0 '\0' 0 '\0' 0 '\0' 0 '\0'
[…]
0×7fc6d90023e8: 0 '\0' 0 '\0' 0 '\0' 0 '\0' 0 '\0' 0 '\0' 0 '\0' 0 '\0'
0×7fc6d90023f0: 0 '\0' 0 '\0' 0 '\0' 0 '\0' 0 '\0' 0 '\0' 0 '\0' 0 '\0'
0×7fc6d90023f8: 0 '\0' 0 '\0' 0 '\0' 0 '\0' 0 '\0' 0 '\0' 0 '\0' 0 '\0'

(gdb) x/64bc p2-sizeof(p2)
0×7fc6d9001bf8: 0 '\0' 0 '\0' 0 '\0' 0 '\0' 0 '\0' 0 '\0' 0 '\0' 0 '\0'
0×7fc6d9001c00: 97 'a' 115 's' 104 'h' 33 '!' 0 '\0' 32 ' ' 87 'W' 111 'o'
0×7fc6d9001c08: 114 'r' 108 'l' 100 'd' 33 '!' 0 '\0' 0 '\0' 0 '\0' 0 '\0'
0×7fc6d9001c10: 0 '\0' 0 '\0' 0 '\0' 0 '\0' 0 '\0' 0 '\0' 0 '\0' 0 '\0'
0×7fc6d9001c18: 0 '\0' 0 '\0' 0 '\0' 0 '\0' 0 '\0' 0 '\0' 0 '\0' 0 '\0'
0×7fc6d9001c20: 0 '\0' 0 '\0' 0 '\0' 0 '\0' 0 '\0' 0 '\0' 0 '\0' 0 '\0'
0×7fc6d9001c28: 0 '\0' 0 '\0' 0 '\0' 0 '\0' 0 '\0' 0 '\0' 0 '\0' 0 '\0'
0×7fc6d9001c30: 0 '\0' 0 '\0' 0 '\0' 0 '\0' 0 '\0' 0 '\0' 0 '\0' 0 '\0'
```

```
(gdb) x/64bc p2+2048-sizeof(p2)
0×7fc6d90023f8: 0 '\0' 0 '\0' 0 '\0' 0 '\0' 0 '\0' 0 '\0' 0 '\0' 0 '\0'
0×7fc6d9002400: 97 'a' 115 's' 104 'h' 33 '!' 0 '\0' 32 ' ' 87 'W' 111 'o'
0×7fc6d9002408: 114 'r' 108 'l' 100 'd' 33 '!' 0 '\0' 0 '\0' 0 '\0' 0 '\0'
0×7fc6d9002410: 0 '\0' 0 '\0' 0 '\0' 0 '\0' 0 '\0' 0 '\0' 0 '\0' 0 '\0'
0×7fc6d9002418: 0 '\0' 0 '\0' 0 '\0' 0 '\0' 0 '\0' 0 '\0' 0 '\0' 0 '\0'
0×7fc6d9002420: 0 '\0' 0 '\0' 0 '\0' 0 '\0' 0 '\0' 0 '\0' 0 '\0' 0 '\0'
0×7fc6d9002428: 0 '\0' 0 '\0' 0 '\0' 0 '\0' 0 '\0' 0 '\0' 0 '\0' 0 '\0'
0×7fc6d9002430: 0 '\0' 0 '\0' 0 '\0' 0 '\0' 0 '\0' 0 '\0' 0 '\0' 0 '\0'

(gdb) x/1024bc p3
0×7fc6d9002400: 97 'a' 115 's' 104 'h' 33 '!' 0 '\0' 32 ' ' 87 'W' 111 'o'
0×7fc6d9002408: 114 'r' 108 'l' 100 'd' 33 '!' 0 '\0' 0 '\0' 0 '\0' 0 '\0'
0×7fc6d9002410: 0 '\0' 0 '\0' 0 '\0' 0 '\0' 0 '\0' 0 '\0' 0 '\0' 0 '\0'
[…]
0×7fc6d90027e8: 0 '\0' 0 '\0' 0 '\0' 0 '\0' 0 '\0' 0 '\0' 0 '\0' 0 '\0'
0×7fc6d90027f0: 0 '\0' 0 '\0' 0 '\0' 0 '\0' 0 '\0' 0 '\0' 0 '\0' 0 '\0'
0×7fc6d90027f8: 0 '\0' 0 '\0' 0 '\0' 0 '\0' 0 '\0' 0 '\0' 0 '\0' 0 '\0'

(gdb) x/64bc p3-sizeof(p3)
0×7fc6d90023f8: 0 '\0' 0 '\0' 0 '\0' 0 '\0' 0 '\0' 0 '\0' 0 '\0' 0 '\0'
0×7fc6d9002400: 97 'a' 115 's' 104 'h' 33 '!' 0 '\0' 32 ' ' 87 'W' 111 'o'
0×7fc6d9002408: 114 'r' 108 'l' 100 'd' 33 '!' 0 '\0' 0 '\0' 0 '\0' 0 '\0'
0×7fc6d9002410: 0 '\0' 0 '\0' 0 '\0' 0 '\0' 0 '\0' 0 '\0' 0 '\0' 0 '\0'
0×7fc6d9002418: 0 '\0' 0 '\0' 0 '\0' 0 '\0' 0 '\0' 0 '\0' 0 '\0' 0 '\0'
0×7fc6d9002420: 0 '\0' 0 '\0' 0 '\0' 0 '\0' 0 '\0' 0 '\0' 0 '\0' 0 '\0'
0×7fc6d9002428: 0 '\0' 0 '\0' 0 '\0' 0 '\0' 0 '\0' 0 '\0' 0 '\0' 0 '\0'
0×7fc6d9002430: 0 '\0' 0 '\0' 0 '\0' 0 '\0' 0 '\0' 0 '\0' 0 '\0' 0 '\0'

(gdb) x/64bc p3+1024-sizeof(p3)
0×7fc6d90027f8: 0 '\0' 0 '\0' 0 '\0' 0 '\0' 0 '\0' 0 '\0' 0 '\0' 0 '\0'
0×7fc6d9002800: 0 '\0' 0 '\0' 0 '\0' 0 '\0' 0 '\0' 0 '\0' 0 '\0' 0 '\0'
0×7fc6d9002808: 0 '\0' 0 '\0' 0 '\0' 0 '\0' 0 '\0' 0 '\0' 0 '\0' 0 '\0'
0×7fc6d9002810: 0 '\0' 0 '\0' 0 '\0' 0 '\0' 0 '\0' 0 '\0' 0 '\0' 0 '\0'
0×7fc6d9002818: 0 '\0' 0 '\0' 0 '\0' 0 '\0' 0 '\0' 0 '\0' 0 '\0' 0 '\0'
0×7fc6d9002820: 0 '\0' 0 '\0' 0 '\0' 0 '\0' 0 '\0' 0 '\0' 0 '\0' 0 '\0'
0×7fc6d9002828: 0 '\0' 0 '\0' 0 '\0' 0 '\0' 0 '\0' 0 '\0' 0 '\0' 0 '\0'
0×7fc6d9002830: 0 '\0' 0 '\0' 0 '\0' 0 '\0' 0 '\0' 0 '\0' 0 '\0' 0 '\0'

(gdb) x/1024bc p4
0×7fc6d9001400: 97 'a' 115 's' 104 'h' 33 '!' 0 '\0' 32 ' ' 87 'W' 111 'o'
0×7fc6d9001408: 114 'r' 108 'l' 100 'd' 33 '!' 0 '\0' 0 '\0' 0 '\0' 0 '\0'
0×7fc6d9001410: 0 '\0' 0 '\0' 0 '\0' 0 '\0' 0 '\0' 0 '\0' 0 '\0' 0 '\0'
[…]
0×7fc6d90017e8: 0 '\0' 0 '\0' 0 '\0' 0 '\0' 0 '\0' 0 '\0' 0 '\0' 0 '\0'
0×7fc6d90017f0: 0 '\0' 0 '\0' 0 '\0' 0 '\0' 0 '\0' 0 '\0' 0 '\0' 0 '\0'
0×7fc6d90017f8: 72 'H' 101 'e' 108 'l' 108 'l' 111 'o' 32 ' ' 67 'C' 114 'r'

(gdb) x/64bc p4-sizeof(p4)
0×7fc6d90013f8: 72 'H' 101 'e' 108 'l' 108 'l' 111 'o' 32 ' ' 67 'C' 114 'r'
0×7fc6d9001400: 97 'a' 115 's' 104 'h' 33 '!' 0 '\0' 32 ' ' 87 'W' 111 'o'
0×7fc6d9001408: 114 'r' 108 'l' 100 'd' 33 '!' 0 '\0' 0 '\0' 0 '\0' 0 '\0'
0×7fc6d9001410: 0 '\0' 0 '\0' 0 '\0' 0 '\0' 0 '\0' 0 '\0' 0 '\0' 0 '\0'
0×7fc6d9001418: 0 '\0' 0 '\0' 0 '\0' 0 '\0' 0 '\0' 0 '\0' 0 '\0' 0 '\0'
0×7fc6d9001420: 0 '\0' 0 '\0' 0 '\0' 0 '\0' 0 '\0' 0 '\0' 0 '\0' 0 '\0'
0×7fc6d9001428: 0 '\0' 0 '\0' 0 '\0' 0 '\0' 0 '\0' 0 '\0' 0 '\0' 0 '\0'
0×7fc6d9001430: 0 '\0' 0 '\0' 0 '\0' 0 '\0' 0 '\0' 0 '\0' 0 '\0' 0 '\0'
```

```
(gdb) x/64bc p4+1024-sizeof(p4)
0×7fc6d90017f8: 72 'H' 101 'e' 108 'l' 108 'l' 111 'o' 32 ' ' 67 'C' 114 'r'
0×7fc6d9001800: 97 'a' 115 's' 104 'h' 33 '!' 0 '\0' 32 ' ' 87 'W' 111 'o'
0×7fc6d9001808: 114 'r' 108 'l' 100 'd' 33 '!' 0 '\0' 0 '\0' 0 '\0' 0 '\0'
0×7fc6d9001810: 0 '\0' 0 '\0' 0 '\0' 0 '\0' 0 '\0' 0 '\0' 0 '\0' 0 '\0'
0×7fc6d9001818: 0 '\0' 0 '\0' 0 '\0' 0 '\0' 0 '\0' 0 '\0' 0 '\0' 0 '\0'
0×7fc6d9001820: 0 '\0' 0 '\0' 0 '\0' 0 '\0' 0 '\0' 0 '\0' 0 '\0' 0 '\0'
0×7fc6d9001828: 0 '\0' 0 '\0' 0 '\0' 0 '\0' 0 '\0' 0 '\0' 0 '\0' 0 '\0'
0×7fc6d9001830: 0 '\0' 0 '\0' 0 '\0' 0 '\0' 0 '\0' 0 '\0' 0 '\0' 0 '\0'
```

Incorrect Stack Trace

Sometimes we need to check the correctness of a stack trace (backtrace) by disassembling a return address. In Debugging Tools for Windows there is **ub** WinDbg command. Here we provide such an equivalent for GDB:

```
(gdb) bt
[...]
#1 0×000000010e8cce73 in bar (ps=0×7fff6e4cbac0)
[…]

(gdb) disas 0×000000010e8cce73-10 0×000000010e8cce73
Dump of assembler code from 0×10e8cce69 to 0×10e8cce73:
0×000000010e8cce69 : mov %edi,-0×8(%rbp)
0×000000010e8cce6c : mov -0×8(%rbp),%rdi
0×000000010e8cce70 : callq *0×8(%rdi)
End of assembler dump.
```

Please note that the beginning of assembly will be dependent on how good we guessed the offset:

```
(gdb) disas 0x000000010e8cce73-0×10 0×000000010e8cce73
Dump of assembler code from 0×10e8cce63 to 0×10e8cce73:
0×000000010e8cce63 : in $0×48,%eax
0×000000010e8cce65 : sub $0×10,%esp
0×000000010e8cce68 : mov %rdi,-0×8(%rbp)
0×000000010e8cce6c : mov -0×8(%rbp),%rdi
0×000000010e8cce70 : callq *0×8(%rdi)
End of assembler dump.

(gdb) disas 0x000000010e8cce73-0×13 0×000000010e8cce73
Dump of assembler code from 0×10e8cce60 to 0×10e8cce73:
0×000000010e8cce60 : push %rbp
0×000000010e8cce61 : mov %rsp,%rbp
0×000000010e8cce64 : sub $0×10,%rsp
0×000000010e8cce68 : mov %rdi,-0×8(%rbp)
0×000000010e8cce6c : mov -0×8(%rbp),%rdi
0×000000010e8cce70 : callq *0×8(%rdi)
End of assembler dump.
```

However, we can ignore that because our goal is to check whether a CPU instruction before a return address is a *call*.

NULL Pointer (code)

This is a Mac OS X / GDB counterpart to NULL Pointer (code) pattern[5] previously described for Windows platforms:

```
(gdb) bt
#0 0x0000000000000000 in ?? ()
#1 0x000000010e8cce73 in bar (ps=0x7fff6e4cbac0)
#2 0x000000010e8cce95 in foo (ps=0x7fff6e4cbac0)
#3 0x000000010e8cced5 in main (argc=1, argv=0x7fff6e4cbb08)

(gdb) disass 0x000000010e8cce73-3 0x000000010e8cce73
Dump of assembler code from 0x10e8cce70 to 0x10e8cce73:
0x000000010e8cce70 : callq *0x8(%rdi)
End of assembler dump.

(gdb) info r rdi
rdi 0x7fff6e4cbac0 140735043910336

(gdb) x/2 0x7fff6e4cbac0
0x7fff6e4cbac0: 0x0000000a 0x00000000

(gdb) p/x *($rdi+8)
$7 = 0x0

(gdb) bt
#0 0x0000000000000000 in ?? ()
#1 0x000000010e8cce73 in bar (ps=0x7fff6e4cbac0)
#2 0x000000010e8cce95 in foo (ps=0x7fff6e4cbac0)
#3 0x000000010e8cced5 in main (argc=1, argv=0x7fff6e4cbb08)

(gdb) ptype MYSTRUCT
type = struct _MyStruct_tag {
int data;
PFUNC pfunc;
}

(gdb) print {MYSTRUCT}0x7fff6e4cbac0
$2 = {data = 10, pfunc = 0}
```

Here's the source code of the modeling application:

```
typedef void (*PFUNC)(void);

typedef struct _MyStruct_tag
{
        int data;
        PFUNC pfunc;
} MYSTRUCT;

void bar(MYSTRUCT *ps)
{
        ps->pfunc();
}
```

---

[5] http://www.dumpanalysis.org/blog/index.php/2008/04/28/crash-dump-analysis-patterns-part-6a/

```
void foo(MYSTRUCT *ps)
{
        bar(ps);
}

int main(int argc, const char * argv[])
{
        MYSTRUCT pstruct = {10, NULL};
        foo(&pstruct);
        return 0;
}
```

Spiking Thread

This is a Mac OS X / GDB counterpart to Spiking Thread pattern[6] previously described for Windows platforms:

```
(gdb) info threads
4 0x00007fff85b542df in sqrt$fenv_access_off ()
3 0x00007fff8616ee42 in __semwait_signal ()
2 0x00007fff8616ee42 in __semwait_signal ()
* 1 0x00007fff8616ee42 in __semwait_signal ()
```

We notice a non-waiting thread and switch to it:

```
(gdb) thread 4
[Switching to thread 4 (core thread 3)]
0x00007fff85b542df in sqrt$fenv_access_off ()

(gdb) bt
#0 0x00007fff85b542df in sqrt$fenv_access_off ()
#1 0x000000010cc85dc9 in thread_three (arg=0x7fff6c884ac0)
#2 0x00007fff8fac68bf in _pthread_start ()
#3 0x00007fff8fac9b75 in thread_start ()
```

If we disassemble the return address for *thread_three* function to come back from *sqrt* call we see an infinite loop:

```
(gdb) disass 0x000000010cc85dc9
Dump of assembler code for function thread_three:
0x000000010cc85db0 <thread_three+0>:    push %rbp
0x000000010cc85db1 <thread_three+1>:    mov %rsp,%rbp
0x000000010cc85db4 <thread_three+4>:    sub $0x10,%rsp
0x000000010cc85db8 <thread_three+8>:    mov %rdi,-0x10(%rbp)
0x000000010cc85dbc <thread_three+12>:   mov -0x10(%rbp),%ax
0x000000010cc85dc0 <thread_three+16>:   movsd (%rax),%xmm0
0x000000010cc85dc4 <thread_three+20>:   callq 0x10cc85eac <dyld_stub_sqrt>
0x000000010cc85dc9 <thread_three+25>:   mov -0x10(%rbp),%rax
0x000000010cc85dcd <thread_three+29>:   movsd %xmm0,(%rax)
0x000000010cc85dd1 <thread_three+33>:   jmpq 0x10cc85dbc <thread_three+12>
End of assembler dump.
```

Here's the source code of the modeling application:

```
void * thread_one (void *arg)
{
    while (1)
    {
        sleep (1);
    }
    return 0;
}
```

---

[6] http://www.dumpanalysis.org/blog/index.php/2007/05/11/crash-dump-analysis-patterns-part-14/

```c
void * thread_two (void *arg)
{
    while (1)
    {
        sleep (2);
    }
    return 0;
}

void * thread_three (void *arg)
{
    while (1)
    {
        *(double*)arg=sqrt(*(double *)arg);
    }
    return 0;
}

int main(int argc, const char * argv[])
{
    pthread_t threadID_one, threadID_two, threadID_three;
    double result = 0xffffffff;
    pthread_create (&threadID_one, NULL, thread_one, NULL);
    pthread_create (&threadID_two, NULL, thread_two, NULL);
    pthread_create (&threadID_three, NULL, thread_three, &result);
    pthread_join(threadID_three, NULL);
    return 0;
}
```

Dynamic Memory Corruption (process heap)

This is a Mac OS X / GDB counterpart to Dynamic Memory Corruption (process heap) pattern[7] previously described for Windows platforms:

```
(gdb) bt
#0 0x00007fff8479582a in __kill ()
#1 0x00007fff8e0e0a9c in abort ()
#2 0x00007fff8e1024ac in szone_error ()
#3 0x00007fff8e1024e8 in free_list_checksum_botch ()
#4 0x00007fff8e102a7b in small_free_list_remove_ptr ()
#5 0x00007fff8e106bf7 in szone_free_definite_size ()
#6 0x00007fff8e13f789 in free ()
#7 0x000000010afafe23 in main (argc=1, argv=0x7fff6abaeb08)
```

Here's the source code of the modeling application:

```c
int main(int argc, const char * argv[])
{
        char *p1 = (char *) malloc (1024);
        printf("p1 = %p\n", p1);
        char *p2 = (char *) malloc (1024);
        printf("p2 = %p\n", p2);
        char *p3 = (char *) malloc (1024);
        printf("p3 = %p\n", p3);
        char *p4 = (char *) malloc (1024);
        printf("p4 = %p\n", p4);
        char *p5 = (char *) malloc (1024);
        printf("p5 = %p\n", p5);
        char *p6 = (char *) malloc (1024);
        printf("p6 = %p\n", p6);
        char *p7 = (char *) malloc (1024);
        printf("p7 = %p\n", p7);
        free(p6);
        free(p4);
        free(p2);
        printf("Hello Crash!\n");
        strcpy(p2, "Hello Crash!");
        strcpy(p4, "Hello Crash!");
        strcpy(p6, "Hello Crash!");
        p2 = (char *) malloc (512);
        printf("p2 = %p\n", p2);
        p4 = (char *) malloc (1024);
        printf("p4 = %p\n", p4);
        p6 = (char *) malloc (512);
        printf("p6 = %p\n", p6);
        free (p7);
        free (p6);
        free (p5);
        free (p4);
        free (p3);
        free (p2);
        free (p1);
        return 0;
}
```

---

[7] http://www.dumpanalysis.org/blog/index.php/2006/10/31/crash-dump-analysis-patterns-part-2/

Double Free (process heap)

This is a Mac OS X / GDB counterpart to Double Free (process heap) pattern[8] previously described for Windows platforms:

```
(gdb) bt
#0 0x00007fff8479582a in __kill ()
#1 0x00007fff8e0e0a9c in abort ()
#2 0x00007fff8e13f84c in free ()
#3 0x00000001035a8ef4 in main (argc=1, argv=0x7fff631a7b20)

(gdb) x/2i 0x00000001035a8ef4-8
0x1035a8eec : mov -0x20(%rbp),%edi
0x1035a8eef : callq 0x1035a8f06

(gdb) frame 3
#3 0x00000001035a8ef4 in main (argc=1, argv=0x7fff631a7b20)
at .../DoubleFree/main.c:23
23 free(p2);
Current language: auto; currently minimal

(gdb) x/g $rbp-0x20
0x7fff631a7ae0: 0x00007fe6a8801400

(gdb) x/2w 0x00007fe6a8801400
0x7fe6a8801400: 0x00000000 0xb0000000
```

Here's the source code of the modeling application:

```c
int main(int argc, const char * argv[])
{
    char *p1 = (char *) malloc (1024);
    printf("p1 = %p\n", p1);
    char *p2 = (char *) malloc (1024);
    printf("p2 = %p\n", p2);
    free(p2);
    free(p1);
    free(p2);
    return 0;
}
```

---

[8] http://www.dumpanalysis.org/blog/index.php/2007/08/19/crash-dump-analysis-patterns-part-23a/

Execution Residue

This is a Mac OS X / GDB counterpart to Execution Residue pattern[9] previously described for Windows platforms:

```
(gdb) bt
#0  0x00007fff8616e82a in __kill ()
#1  0x00007fff8fab9a9c in abort ()
#2  0x000000010269dc29 in bar_5 ()
#3  0x000000010269dc39 in bar_4 ()
#4  0x000000010269dc49 in bar_3 ()
#5  0x000000010269dc59 in bar_2 ()
#6  0x000000010269dc69 in bar_1 ()
#7  0x000000010269dc79 in bar ()
#8  0x000000010269dca0 in main (argc=1, argv=0x7fff6229cb00)


(gdb) x $rsp
0x7fff6229ca38: 0x8fab9a9c
(gdb) x/1000a 0x7fff6229c000
0x7fff6229c000: 0x7fff8947b000 0x7fff8947b570
0x7fff6229c010: 0x4f3ee10c 0x7fff90cb0000
0x7fff6229c020: 0x7fff90cb04d0 0x4e938b16
[…]
0x7fff6229c5f0: 0x7fff622d8d80 0x10269d640
0x7fff6229c600: 0x7fff6229cad0 0x7fff622a460b
0x7fff6229c610: 0x100000000 0x269d000
0x7fff6229c620: 0x7fff6229c630 0x10269db59 <foo_8+9>
0x7fff6229c630: 0x7fff6229c640 0x10269db69 <foo_7+9>
0x7fff6229c640: 0x7fff6229c650 0x10269db79 <foo_6+9>
0x7fff6229c650: 0x7fff6229c660 0x10269db89 <foo_5+9>
0x7fff6229c660: 0x7fff6229c670 0x10269db99 <foo_4+9>
0x7fff6229c670: 0x7fff6229c680 0x10269dba9 <foo_3+9>
0x7fff6229c680: 0x7fff6229c690 0x10269dbb9 <foo_2+9>
0x7fff6229c690: 0x7fff6229c6a0 0x10269dbc9 <foo_1+9>
0x7fff6229c6a0: 0x7fff6229cac0 0x10269dbee <foo+30>
0x7fff6229c6b0: 0x0 0x0
0x7fff6229c6c0: 0x0 0x0
0x7fff6229c6d0: 0x0 0x0
0x7fff6229c6e0: 0x0 0x0
[…]
0x7fff6229c8d0: 0x7fff6229c960 0x7fff622b49cd
0x7fff6229c8e0: 0x10269f05c 0x0
0x7fff6229c8f0: 0x7fff622c465c 0x7fff8a31e5c0 <_Z21dyldGlobalLockReleasev>
0x7fff6229c900: 0x7fff8fab99eb <abort> 0x10269f05c
0x7fff6229c910: 0x101000000000000 0x7fff622d2110
0x7fff6229c920: 0x7fff622d8d80 0x10269f078
0x7fff6229c930: 0x7fff622daac8 0x18
0x7fff6229c940: 0x0 0x0
0x7fff6229c950: 0x10269e030 0x0
0x7fff6229c960: 0x7fff6229c980 0x7fff622a1922
0x7fff6229c970: 0x0 0x0
0x7fff6229c980: 0x7fff6229ca50 0x7fff8a31e716 <dyld_stub_binder_+13>
0x7fff6229c990: 0x1 0x7fff6229cb00
0x7fff6229c9a0: 0x7fff6229cb10 0xe223ea612ddc10b7
0x7fff6229c9b0: 0x8 0x0
0x7fff6229c9c0: 0xe223ea612ddc10b7 0x0
0x7fff6229c9d0: 0x0 0x0
```

---

[9] http://www.dumpanalysis.org/blog/index.php/2008/04/29/crash-dump-analysis-patterns-part-60/

```
0x7fff6229c9e0:  0x585f5f00474e414c 0x20435058005f4350
0x7fff6229c9f0:  0x0 0x0
0x7fff6229ca00:  0x0 0x0
0x7fff6229ca10:  0x0 0x0
0x7fff6229ca20:  0x0 0x0
0x7fff6229ca30:  0x7fff6229ca60 0x7fff8fab9a9c <abort+177>
0x7fff6229ca40:  0x0 0x0
0x7fff6229ca50:  0x7fffffffffffdf 0x0
0x7fff6229ca60:  0x7fff6229ca70 0x10269dc29 <bar_5+9>
0x7fff6229ca70:  0x7fff6229ca80 0x10269dc39 <bar_4+9>
0x7fff6229ca80:  0x7fff6229ca90 0x10269dc49 <bar_3+9>
0x7fff6229ca90:  0x7fff6229caa0 0x10269dc59 <bar_2+9>
0x7fff6229caa0:  0x7fff6229cab0 0x10269dc69 <bar_1+9>
0x7fff6229cab0:  0x7fff6229cac0 0x10269dc79 <bar+9>
0x7fff6229cac0:  0x7fff6229cae0 0x10269dca0 <main+32>
0x7fff6229cad0:  0x7fff6229cb00 0x1
0x7fff6229cae0:  0x7fff6229caf0 0x10269db34 <start+52>
0x7fff6229caf0:  0x0 0x1
0x7fff6229cb00:  0x7fff6229cc48 0x0
0x7fff6229cb10:  0x7fff6229ccae 0x7fff6229ccca
[...]
```

Here's the source code of the modeling application:

```
#define def_call(name,x,y) void name##_##x() { name##_##y(); }
#define def_final(name,x) void name##_##x() { }
#define def_final_abort(name,x) void name##_##x() { abort(); }
#define def_init(name,y) void name() { name##_##y(); }
#define def_init_alloc(name,y,size) void name() { int arr[size]; name##_##y(); *arr=0; }
def_final(foo,9)
def_call(foo,8,9)
def_call(foo,7,8)
def_call(foo,6,7)
def_call(foo,5,6)
def_call(foo,4,5)
def_call(foo,3,4)
def_call(foo,2,3)
def_call(foo,1,2)
def_init_alloc(foo,1,256)
def_final_abort(bar,5)
def_call(bar,4,5)
def_call(bar,3,4)
def_call(bar,2,3)
def_call(bar,1,2)
def_init(bar,1)

int main(int argc, const char * argv[])
{
      foo();
      bar();
}
```

Coincidental Symbolic Information

This is a Mac OS X / GDB counterpart to Coincidental Symbolic Information pattern[10] previously described for Windows platforms. The idea is the same: to disassemble the address to see if the preceding instruction is a call. If it is indeed then most likely the symbolic address is a return address from past Execution Residue:

```
(gdb) x $rsp
0x7fff6a162a38: 0x8fab9a9c

(gdb) x/1000a 0x7fff6a162000
[...]
0x7fff6a162960: 0x7fff6a162980 0x7fff6a167922
0x7fff6a162970: 0x0 0x0
0x7fff6a162980: 0x7fff6a162a50 0x7fff8a31e716 <dyld_stub_binder_+13>
0x7fff6a162990: 0x1 0x7fff6a162b00
0x7fff6a1629a0: 0x7fff6a162b10 0x7fff6a162bc0
0x7fff6a1629b0: 0x8 0x0
[...]
0x7fff6a162a00: 0x0 0x0
0x7fff6a162a10: 0x0 0x0
0x7fff6a162a20: 0x0 0x0
0x7fff6a162a30: 0x7fff6a162a60 0x7fff8fab9a9c <abort+177>
0x7fff6a162a40: 0x0 0x0
0x7fff6a162a50: 0x7fffffffffdf 0x0
[...]
0x7fff6a163040: 0x35000 0x0
0x7fff6a163050: 0x35000 0x500000007
0x7fff6a163060: 0x7 0x747865745f5f
0x7fff6a163070: 0x0 0x545845545f5f
0x7fff6a163080: 0x0 0x7fff5fc01000 <__dyld_stub_binding_helper>
0x7fff6a163090: 0x22c9d 0xc00001000
0x7fff6a1630a0: 0x0 0x80000400
[...]

(gdb) disass 0x7fff8a31e716
Dump of assembler code for function dyld_stub_binder_:
0x00007fff8a31e709 <dyld_stub_binder_+0>: mov 0x8(%rbp),%rdi
0x00007fff8a31e70d <dyld_stub_binder_+4>: mov 0x10(%rbp),%rsi
0x00007fff8a31e711 <dyld_stub_binder_+8>: callq 0x7fff8a31e86d <_Z21_dyld_fast_stub_entryPvl>
0x00007fff8a31e716 <dyld_stub_binder_+13>: mov %rax,%r11
0x00007fff8a31e719 <dyld_stub_binder_+16>: movdqa 0x40(%rsp),%xmm0
0x00007fff8a31e71f <dyld_stub_binder_+22>: movdqa 0x50(%rsp),%xmm1
0x00007fff8a31e725 <dyld_stub_binder_+28>: movdqa 0x60(%rsp),%xmm2
0x00007fff8a31e72b <dyld_stub_binder_+34>: movdqa 0x70(%rsp),%xmm3
0x00007fff8a31e731 <dyld_stub_binder_+40>: movdqa 0x80(%rsp),%xmm4
0x00007fff8a31e73a <dyld_stub_binder_+49>: movdqa 0x90(%rsp),%xmm5
0x00007fff8a31e743 <dyld_stub_binder_+58>: movdqa 0xa0(%rsp),%xmm6
0x00007fff8a31e74c <dyld_stub_binder_+67>: movdqa 0xb0(%rsp),%xmm7
0x00007fff8a31e755 <dyld_stub_binder_+76>: mov (%rsp),%rdi
0x00007fff8a31e759 <dyld_stub_binder_+80>: mov 0x8(%rsp),%rsi
0x00007fff8a31e75e <dyld_stub_binder_+85>: mov 0x10(%rsp),%rdx
0x00007fff8a31e763 <dyld_stub_binder_+90>: mov 0x18(%rsp),%rcx
0x00007fff8a31e768 <dyld_stub_binder_+95>: mov 0x20(%rsp),%r8
0x00007fff8a31e76d <dyld_stub_binder_+100>: mov 0x28(%rsp),%r9
0x00007fff8a31e772 <dyld_stub_binder_+105>: mov 0x30(%rsp),%rax
0x00007fff8a31e777 <dyld_stub_binder_+110>: add $0xc0,%rsp
```

---

[10] http://www.dumpanalysis.org/blog/index.php/2007/08/30/crash-dump-analysis-patterns-part-24/

```
0x00007fff8a31e77e <dyld_stub_binder_+117>: pop %rbp
0x00007fff8a31e77f <dyld_stub_binder_+118>: add $0x10,%rsp
0x00007fff8a31e783 <dyld_stub_binder_+122>: jmpq *%r11


(gdb) x/2i 0x7fff8fab9a9c
0x7fff8fab9a9c <abort+177>: mov $0x2710,%edi
0x7fff8fab9aa1 <abort+182>: callq 0x7fff8fab9c43 <usleep$nocancel>


(gdb) disass 0x7fff8fab9a9c-5 0x7fff8fab9a9c
Dump of assembler code from 0x7fff8fab9a97 to 0x7fff8fab9a9c:
0x00007fff8fab9a97 <abort+172>: callq 0x7fff8fb1f54a <dyld_stub_kill>
End of assembler dump.


(gdb) disass 0x7fff5fc01000
Dump of assembler code for function __dyld_stub_binding_helper:
0x00007fff5fc01000 <__dyld_stub_binding_helper+0>: add %al,(%rax)
0x00007fff5fc01002 <__dyld_stub_binding_helper+2>: add %al,(%rax)
0x00007fff5fc01004 <__dyld_stub_binding_helper+4>: add %al,(%rax)
0x00007fff5fc01006 <__dyld_stub_binding_helper+6>: add %al,(%rax)
End of assembler dump.


(gdb) x/10 0x7fff5fc01000-0x10
0x7fff5fc00ff0: 0x00000000 0x00000000 0x00000000 0x00000000
0x7fff5fc01000 <__dyld_stub_binding_helper>: 0x00000000 0x00000000 0x00000000 0x00000000
0x7fff5fc01010 <__dyld_offset_to_dyld_all_image_infos>: 0x00000000 0x00000000
```

Stack Overflow (user mode)

This is a Mac OS X / GDB counterpart to Stack Overflow (user mode) pattern[11] previously described for Windows platforms:

```
(gdb) bt 10
#0 0x0000000105dafea8 in bar (i=0)
#1 0x0000000105dafeb9 in bar (i=262102)
#2 0x0000000105dafeb9 in bar (i=262101)
#3 0x0000000105dafeb9 in bar (i=262100)
#4 0x0000000105dafeb9 in bar (i=262099)
#5 0x0000000105dafeb9 in bar (i=262098)
#6 0x0000000105dafeb9 in bar (i=262097)
#7 0x0000000105dafeb9 in bar (i=262096)
#8 0x0000000105dafeb9 in bar (i=262095)
#9 0x0000000105dafeb9 in bar (i=262094)
(More stack frames follow...)
```

There are at least 262,102 frames so we don't attempt to list them all. What we'd like to do is to get stack trace boundaries from the list of sections based on the current stack pointer address and dump the upper part of it (the stack grows from higher addresses to the lower ones) to get bottom initial stack traces:

```
(gdb) x $rsp
0x7fff651aeff0: 0x00000000
```

Because this is a stack overflow we expect the lowest stack region address to be 0x7fff651af000.

```
(gdb) maint info sections
[...]
Core file:
`/cores/core.2763', file type mach-o-le.
[...]
0x0000000105e00000->0x0000000105f00000 at 0x00035000: LC_SEGMENT. ALLOC LOAD CODE HAS_CONTENTS
0x00007fff619af000->0x00007fff651af000 at 0x00135000: LC_SEGMENT. ALLOC LOAD CODE HAS_CONTENTS
0x00007fff651af000->0x00007fff659af000 at 0x03935000: LC_SEGMENT. ALLOC LOAD CODE HAS_CONTENTS
0x00007fff659af000->0x00007fff659e4000 at 0x04135000: LC_SEGMENT. ALLOC LOAD CODE HAS_CONTENTS
0x00007fff659e4000->0x00007fff659e6000 at 0x0416a000: LC_SEGMENT. ALLOC LOAD CODE HAS_CONTENTS
[...]
```

```
(gdb) x/250a 0x00007fff659af000-2000
0x7fff659ae830: 0x0 0x1500000000
0x7fff659ae840: 0x7fff659ae860 0x105dafeb9 <bar+25>
0x7fff659ae850: 0x0 0x1400000000
0x7fff659ae860: 0x7fff659ae880 0x105dafeb9 <bar+25>
0x7fff659ae870: 0x0 0x1300000000
0x7fff659ae880: 0x7fff659ae8a0 0x105dafeb9 <bar+25>
0x7fff659ae890: 0x0 0x1200000000
0x7fff659ae8a0: 0x7fff659ae8c0 0x105dafeb9 <bar+25>
0x7fff659ae8b0: 0x0 0x1100000000
0x7fff659ae8c0: 0x7fff659ae8e0 0x105dafeb9 <bar+25>
0x7fff659ae8d0: 0x0 0x1000000000
0x7fff659ae8e0: 0x7fff659ae900 0x105dafeb9 <bar+25>
0x7fff659ae8f0: 0x0 0xf00000000
0x7fff659ae900: 0x7fff659ae920 0x105dafeb9 <bar+25>
0x7fff659ae910: 0x0 0xe00000000
```

---

[11] http://www.dumpanalysis.org/blog/index.php/2008/06/10/crash-dump-analysis-patterns-part-16b/

```
0x7fff659ae920: 0x7fff659ae940 0x105dafeb9 <bar+25>
0x7fff659ae930: 0x0 0xd00000000
0x7fff659ae940: 0x7fff659ae960 0x105dafeb9 <bar+25>
0x7fff659ae950: 0x0 0xc00000000
0x7fff659ae960: 0x7fff659ae980 0x105dafeb9 <bar+25>
0x7fff659ae970: 0x0 0xb00000000
0x7fff659ae980: 0x7fff659ae9a0 0x105dafeb9 <bar+25>
0x7fff659ae990: 0x0 0xa00000000
0x7fff659ae9a0: 0x7fff659ae9c0 0x105dafeb9 <bar+25>
0x7fff659ae9b0: 0x0 0x900000000
0x7fff659ae9c0: 0x7fff659ae9e0 0x105dafeb9 <bar+25>
0x7fff659ae9d0: 0x0 0x800000000
0x7fff659ae9e0: 0x7fff659aea00 0x105dafeb9 <bar+25>
0x7fff659ae9f0: 0x0 0x700000000
0x7fff659aea00: 0x7fff659aea20 0x105dafeb9 <bar+25>
0x7fff659aea10: 0x0 0x600000000
0x7fff659aea20: 0x7fff659aea40 0x105dafeb9 <bar+25>
0x7fff659aea30: 0x0 0x5659b9fe0
0x7fff659aea40: 0x7fff659aea60 0x105dafeb9 <bar+25
0x7fff659aea50: 0x7fff659aea70 0x4659bd31f
0x7fff659aea60: 0x7fff659aea80 0x105dafeb9 <bar+25>
0x7fff659aea70: 0x7fff659aeaf0 0x3659b031a
0x7fff659aea80: 0x7fff659aeaa0 0x105dafeb9 <bar+25>
0x7fff659aea90: 0x7fff659af5c0 0x200000000
0x7fff659aeaa0: 0x7fff659aeac0 0x105dafeb9 <bar+25>
0x7fff659aeab0: 0x100000000 0x1659aeb18
0x7fff659aeac0: 0x7fff659aead0 0x105dafece <foo+14>
0x7fff659aead0: 0x7fff659aeaf0 0x105dafeeb <main+27>
0x7fff659aeae0: 0x7fff659aeb18 0x1
—Type to continue, or q to quit—
0x7fff659aeaf0: 0x7fff659aeb08 0x105dafe94 <start+52>
0x7fff659aeb00: 0x0 0x0
[…]
0x7fff659aeff0: 0x3139336561303363 0x316235
```

Interesting that if we set the lowest frame down and try to get register info GDB crashes with a core dump:

```
(gdb) frame 262102
#262102 0x0000000105dafeb9 in bar (i=1)
13 bar(i+1);

(gdb) info r
Segmentation fault: 11 (core dumped)
```

Looking at the core dump shows that it also experienced stack overflow:

```
(gdb) bt
#0  0x00007fff8c1bacf0 in __sfvwrite ()
#1  0x00007fff8c189947 in __vfprintf ()
#2  0x00007fff8c184edb in vsnprintf_l ()
#3  0x00007fff8c1566be in __sprintf_chk ()
#4  0x000000010bd14d15 in print_displacement ()
#5  0x000000010bd10ddf in OP_E ()
#6  0x000000010bd13f9b in print_insn ()
#7  0x000000010bc164ce in length_of_this_instruction ()
#8  0x000000010bc9e296 in x86_analyze_prologue ()
#9  0x000000010bc9f1f3 in x86_frame_prev_register ()
#10 0x000000010bc91d70 in frame_register_unwind ()
#11 0x000000010bc92015 in frame_unwind_register ()
#12 0x000000010bc91d70 in frame_register_unwind ()
```

```
#13 0x000000010bc92015 in frame_unwind_register ()
#14 0x000000010bc91d70 in frame_register_unwind ()
#15 0x000000010bc92015 in frame_unwind_register ()
#16 0x000000010bc91d70 in frame_register_unwind ()
#17 0x000000010bc92015 in frame_unwind_register ()
#18 0x000000010bc91d70 in frame_register_unwind ()
#19 0x000000010bc92015 in frame_unwind_register ()
#20 0x000000010bc91d70 in frame_register_unwind ()
#21 0x000000010bc92015 in frame_unwind_register ()
#22 0x000000010bc91d70 in frame_register_unwind ()
#23 0x000000010bc92015 in frame_unwind_register ()
#24 0x000000010bc91d70 in frame_register_unwind ()
#25 0x000000010bc92015 in frame_unwind_register ()
#26 0x000000010bc91d70 in frame_register_unwind ()
#27 0x000000010bc92015 in frame_unwind_register ()
#28 0x000000010bc91d70 in frame_register_unwind ()
#29 0x000000010bc92015 in frame_unwind_register ()
#30 0x000000010bc91d70 in frame_register_unwind ()
#31 0x000000010bc92015 in frame_unwind_register ()
#32 0x000000010bc91d70 in frame_register_unwind ()
#33 0x000000010bc92015 in frame_unwind_register ()
#34 0x000000010bc91d70 in frame_register_unwind ()
#35 0x000000010bc92015 in frame_unwind_register ()
#36 0x000000010bc91d70 in frame_register_unwind ()
#37 0x000000010bc92015 in frame_unwind_register ()
#38 0x000000010bc91d70 in frame_register_unwind ()
#39 0x000000010bc92015 in frame_unwind_register ()
#40 0x000000010bc91d70 in frame_register_unwind ()
#41 0x000000010bc92015 in frame_unwind_register ()
#42 0x000000010bc91d70 in frame_register_unwind ()
#43 0x000000010bc92015 in frame_unwind_register ()
```

The source code of our modeling application:

```
void bar(int i)
{
	bar(i+1);
}

void foo()
{
	bar(1);
}

int main(int argc, const char * argv[])
{
	foo();
	return 0;
}
```

Divide by Zero (user mode)

This is a Mac OS X / GDB counterpart to Divide by Zero (user mode) pattern[12] previously described for Windows platforms:

```
(gdb) bt
#0  0x000000010d3ebe9e in bar (a=1, b=0)
#1  0x000000010d3ebec3 in foo ()
#2  0x000000010d3ebeeb in main (argc=1, argv=0x7fff6cfeab18)

(gdb) x/i 0x000000010d3ebe9e
0x10d3ebe9e : idiv %esi

(gdb) info r rsi
rsi 0x0 0
```

The modeling application source code:

```
int bar(int a, int b)
{
        return a/b;
}

int foo()
{
        return bar(1,0);
}

int main(int argc, const char * argv[])
{
        return foo();
}
```

Local Buffer Overflow

This is a Mac OS X / GDB counterpart to Local Buffer Overflow pattern[13] previously described for Windows platforms. Most of the time simple mistakes in using memory and string manipulation functions are easily detected by runtime:

```
(gdb) bt
#0 0x00007fff885e982a in __kill ()
#1 0x00007fff83288b6c in __abort ()
#2 0×00007fff8325a89f in __chk_fail ()
#3 0x00007fff8325a83e in __memcpy_chk ()
#4 0×000000010914edf3 in bar ()
#5 0×000000010914ee5e in foo ()
#6 0×000000010914ee9b in main (argc=1, argv=0×7fff68d4daf0)
```

This detection happens in a default optimized release version as well:

```
(gdb) bt
#0 0x00007fff885e982a in __kill ()
#1 0x00007fff83288b6c in __abort ()
#2 0×00007fff8325a89f in __chk_fail ()
#3 0×00007fff8325a83e in __memcpy_chk ()
#4 0×000000010f59cea8 in bar [inlined] ()
#5 0×000000010f59cea8 in foo [inlined] ()
#6 0×000000010f59cea8 in main (argc=, argv=)
```

The more sophisticated example that overwrites stack trace without being detected involves overwriting indirectly via a pointer to a local buffer passed to the called function. In such cases we might see incorrect and truncated stack traces:

```
(gdb) bt
#0 0x00007fff885e982a in __kill ()
#1 0x00007fff83288b6c in __abort ()
#2 0×00007fff83285070 in __stack_chk_fail ()
#3 0×000000010524de77 in foo ()
#4 0xca4000007fff64e5 in ?? ()
```

```
(gdb) bt
#0 0x00007fff885e982a in __kill ()
#1 0x00007fff83288b6c in __abort ()
#2 0×00007fff83285070 in __stack_chk_fail ()
#3 0×0000000105ad8df7 in foo ()
```

Inspection of the raw stack shows ASCII-like memory values around *foo* symbolic reference instead of expected *main* and *start* functions:

```
(gdb) info r rsp
rsp 0x7fff656d79d8 0x7fff656d79d8
```

---

[13] http://www.dumpanalysis.org/blog/index.php/2007/11/14/crash-dump-analysis-patterns-part-36/

```
(gdb) x/100a 0x7fff656d79d8
0x7fff656d79d8: 0x7fff83288b6c <__abort+193> 0x0
0x7fff656d79e8: 0x0 0xffffffdf
0x7fff656d79f8: 0x7fff656d7a40 0x7fff656d7a80
0x7fff656d7a08: 0x7fff83285070 <__guard_setup> 0x6675426c61636f4c
0x7fff656d7a18: 0x7265764f726566 0x0
0x7fff656d7a28: 0x0 0x0
0x7fff656d7a38: 0x0 0x73205d343336325b
0x7fff656d7a48: 0x65766f206b636174 0x776f6c6672
0x7fff656d7a58: 0x0 0x0
0x7fff656d7a68: 0x0 0x343336326d7ab0
0x7fff656d7a78: 0x0 0x7fff656d7ab0
0x7fff656d7a88: 0x105ad8df7 0xb1887b8452358ac4
0x7fff656d7a98: 0x794d000000000000 0x6769422077654e20
0x7fff656d7aa8: 0x6666754220726567 0x7265
0x7fff656d7ab8: 0x0 0x0
0x7fff656d7ac8: 0x0 0x0
0x7fff656d7ad8: 0x0 0x0
0x7fff656d7ae8: 0x0 0x0
[…]
```

The modeling application source code:

```
void bar(char *buffer)
{
        char data[100] = "My New Bigger Buffer";
        memcpy (buffer, data, sizeof(data));
}

void foo()
{
        char data[10] = "My Buffer";
        bar(data);
}

int main(int argc, const char * argv[])
{
        foo();
        return 0;
}
```

C++ Exception

This is a Mac OS X / GDB counterpart to C++ Exception pattern[14] previously described for Windows platforms:

```
(gdb) bt
#0 0x00007fff88bd582a in __kill ()
#1 0x00007fff8c184a9c in abort ()
#2 0x00007fff852f57bc in abort_message ()
#3 0x00007fff852f2fcf in default_terminate ()
#4 0x00007fff852f3001 in safe_handler_caller ()
#5 0x00007fff852f305c in std::terminate ()
#6 0x00007fff852f4152 in __cxa_throw ()
#7 0x000000010e402be8 in bar ()
#8 0x000000010e402c99 in foo ()
#9 0x000000010e402cbb in main (argc=1, argv=0x7fff6e001b18)
```

The modeling application source code:

```cpp
class Exception
{
        int code;
        std::string description;
        public:
        Exception(int _code, std::string _desc) : code(_code), description(_desc) {}
};

void bar()
{
        throw new Exception(5, "Access Denied");
}

void foo()
{
        bar();
}

int main(int argc, const char * argv[])
{
        foo();
        return 0;
}
```

---

[14] http://www.dumpanalysis.org/blog/index.php/2008/10/21/crash-dump-analysis-patterns-part-77/

This is a Mac OS X / GDB counterpart to Truncated Dump pattern[15] previously described for Windows platforms:

```
(gdb) info threads
Cannot access memory at address 0x7fff885e9e42
4 0x00007fff885e9e42 in ?? ()
3 0x00007fff885e9e42 in ?? ()
2 0x00007fff885e9e42 in ?? ()
* 1 0x00007fff885e9e42 in ?? ()
warning: Couldn't restore frame in current thread, at frame 0
0x00007fff885e9e42 in ?? ()

(gdb) disass 0x00007fff885e9e42
No function contains specified address.

(gdb) info r rsp
rsp 0x7fff67fe8a18 0x7fff67fe8a18

(gdb) x/100a 0x7fff67fe8a18
0x7fff67fe8a18: Cannot access memory at address 0x7fff67fe8a18
```

This often happens if there is no space to save a full core dump.

---

15 http://www.dumpanalysis.org/blog/index.php/2007/07/20/crash-dump-analysis-patterns-part-18/

This is the first pattern that emerged after applying the same pattern-driven software diagnostics methodology to Mac OS X. We had problems using GDB which is so portable that hardly has operating system support like WinDbg has. Fortunately, we found a workaround by complementing core dumps with logs and reports from OS such as crash reports and vmmap data. We call this pattern **Paratext** which we borrowed from the concept of an extended software trace[16] and software narratology[17] where it borrowed the same concept from literary interpretation (paratext[18]). Typical examples of such pattern usage can be the list of modules with version and path info, application crash specific information, memory region names with attribution and boundaries:

```
// from .crash reports
```

```
0x108f99000 - 0x109044ff7 com.apple.FontBook (198.4 - 198) <7244D36E-4563-3E42-BA46-1F279D30A6CE> /Applications/Font
Book.app/Contents/MacOS/Font Book
```

```
Exception Type: EXC_BAD_INSTRUCTION (SIGILL)
Exception Codes: 0x0000000000000001, 0x0000000000000000
```

```
Application Specific Information:
objc[195]: garbage collection is OFF
*** error for object 0x7fd7fb818e08: incorrect checksum for freed object - object was probably modified after being
freed.
```

```
// from vmmap logs
```

```
[...]
==== Writable regions for process 966
[...]
Stack                 0000000101f71000-0000000101ff3000 [ 520K] rw-/rwx SM=PRV thread 1
MALLOC_LARGE          0000000103998000-00000001039b8000 [ 128K] rw-/rwx SM=PRV DefaultMallocZone_0x101e6e000
MALLOC_SMALL (freed)  00000001039b9000-00000001039bb000 [  8K] rw-/rwx SM=PRV
mapped file           0000000103a05000-0000000103f32000 [5300K] rw-/rwx SM=COW
...box.framework/Versions/A/Resources/Extras2.rsrc
mapped file           0000000104409000-00000001046d2000 [2852K] rw-/rwx SM=COW /System/Library/Fonts/Helvetica.dfont
MALLOC_LARGE          0000000104f6e000-0000000104f8e000 [ 128K] rw-/rwx SM=PRV DefaultMallocZone_0x101e6e000
MALLOC_LARGE (freed)  0000000108413000-0000000108540000 [1204K] rw-/rwx SM=COW
MALLOC_LARGE (freed)  0000000108540000-0000000108541000 [  4K] rw-/rwx SM=PRV
MALLOC_TINY           00007fefe0c00000-00007fefe0d00000 [1024K] rw-/rwx SM=COW DefaultMallocZone_0x101e6e000
MALLOC_TINY           00007fefe0d00000-00007fefe0e00000 [1024K] rw-/rwx SM=PRV DispatchContinuations_0x101f38000
MALLOC_TINY           00007fefe0e00000-00007fefe0f00000 [1024K] rw-/rwx SM=COW DefaultMallocZone_0x101e6e000
MALLOC_SMALL          00007fefe1000000-00007fefe107b000 [ 492K] rw-/rwx SM=ZER DefaultMallocZone_0x101e6e000
MALLOC_SMALL          00007fefe107b000-00007fefe1083000 [ 32K] rw-/rwx SM=PRV DefaultMallocZone_0x101e6e000
MALLOC_SMALL          00007fefe1083000-00007fefe1149000 [ 792K] rw-/rwx SM=ZER DefaultMallocZone_0x101e6e000
MALLOC_SMALL (freed)  00007fefe1149000-00007fefe1166000 [ 116K] rw-/rwx SM=PRV DefaultMallocZone_0x101e6e000
MALLOC_SMALL (freed)  00007fefe1166000-00007fefe1800000 [6760K] rw-/rwx SM=ZER DefaultMallocZone_0x101e6e000
MALLOC_SMALL          00007fefe1800000-00007fefe18ff000 [1020K] rw-/rwx SM=ZER DefaultMallocZone_0x101e6e000
MALLOC_SMALL (freed)  00007fefe18ff000-00007fefe1901000 [  8K] rw-/rwx SM=PRV DefaultMallocZone_0x101e6e000
MALLOC_SMALL          00007fefe1901000-00007fefe2000000 [7164K] rw-/rwx SM=ZER DefaultMallocZone_0x101e6e000
MALLOC_TINY (freed)   00007fefe2000000-00007fefe2100000 [1024K] rw-/rwx SM=PRV DispatchContinuations_0x101f38000
MALLOC_TINY           00007fefe2100000-00007fefe2200000 [1024K] rw-/rwx SM=PRV DefaultMallocZone_0x101e6e000
Stack                 00007fff61186000-00007fff61985000 [8188K] rw-/rwx SM=ZER thread 0
Stack                 00007fff61985000-00007fff61986000 [  4K] rw-/rwx SM=COW
[...]
```

---

[16] http://www.dumpanalysis.org/blog/index.php/2010/06/13/the-extended-software-trace/

[17] http://www.dumpanalysis.com/Introduction-Software-Narratology-materials

[18] http://en.wikipedia.org/wiki/Paratext